Annual Review of
Entomology

Production Editor: Cleo X. Ray
Bibliographic Quality Control: Mary A. Glass
Electronic Content Coordinator: Suzanne K. Moses
Illustration Editor: Douglas Beckner

Annual Review of Entomology

Volume 57, 2012

May R. Berenbaum, *Editor*
University of Illinois, Urbana-Champaign

Ring T. Cardé, *Associate Editor*
University of California, Riverside

Gene E. Robinson, *Associate Editor*
University of Illinois, Urbana-Champaign

www.annualreviews.org • science@annualreviews.org • 650-493-4400

Annual Reviews
4139 El Camino Way • P.O. Box 10139 • Palo Alto, California 94303-0139

Annual Reviews
Palo Alto, California, USA

International Standard Serial Number: 0066-4170
International Standard Book Number: 978-0-8243-0157-6
Library of Congress Catalog Card Number: A56-5750

♾ The paper used in this publication meets the minimum requirements of American National Standards for Information Sciences—Permanence of Paper for Printed Library Materials, ANSI Z39.48-1992.

TYPESET BY APTARA
PRINTED AND BOUND BY FRIESENS CORPORATION, ALTONA, MANITOBA, CANADA

Preface

Keeping up with the advances in entomological science has never been more challenging. More than 5,000 articles are published yearly in those 83 journals classified as "Entomology" by the Institute of Scientific Information, with perhaps an equal, or greater, number of papers on insects and closely allied groups published in journals devoted to related disciplinary areas. Granted, search engines such as the Web of Science and Google Scholar now enable us to troll the literature efficiently, searching for articles relevant to our own research interests. But discovering, tracking, and integrating findings in areas beyond our own specialty topics remain a huge challenge. What can be missed is the linkage of your area with discoveries in related fields.

The *Annual Review of Entomology* (*ARE*) aims to keep us abreast of the latest findings across our discipline by providing authoritative syntheses of topics from acarines to zorapterans. This has been a 66-year-long tradition of *ARE*. In 1956 the inaugural issue of ARE stated in its preface that its "primary objective is to publish authoritative and concise treatments of definitive subjects of current interest." That goal is unchanged, but the burgeoning literature and the complexity of many areas of research have dictated that our reviews on average have become narrower in scope. It becomes evermore unlikely that one review can fairly document an entire area. Moreover, as research topics become increasingly integrated across the various biological disciplines, the proportion of multiauthor entries continues to rise. In Volume 1, 15 of the reviews were authored by a single author and 6 others had two authors. The current issue contains 22 reviews; only 5 were single-authored and the remainder averaged 2.7 authors. This is not to be lamented, as it largely reflects the increasingly collaborative and interdisciplinary nature of entomological pursuits. The continuing value of these reviews to scientists, teachers, and students is reflected in part by *ARE*'s ranking as the most highly cited journal in entomology. We rely on *ARE* for definitive reviews authored by noted experts.

How are the topics selected? Twenty-five years ago nearly all topics and author invitations were generated from suggestions from the Editorial Committee, sifted from 150 or more possibilities considered over a day-long meeting. The Editorial Committee identified topics in need of review, and we assumed that the selected authors would agree to prepare the review. It was rare for unsolicited topics (those coming in "over the transom") to be selected. Now our selections come from a mix of proposals submitted by unsolicited authors and by colleagues solicited by the Editorial Committee. We evaluate a proposed topic on the strength of its prospectus (Why this topic? Why now? Why this author?) and how well it fits into a formula that ensures that all areas of entomology receive appropriate coverage.

The origin and continued relevance of entomology as a distinct, taxon-based discipline is rooted in its complementary objectives: documenting the importance and diversity of insects and their biology and devising methods to mitigate the effects of pests on the environment, agriculture, and the health of humans and other animals. The melding of basic and applied objectives in our discipline has some distinct advantages. Often the model insect species selected for explorations of fundamental questions in insect physiology and molecular studies, for example, are insects of economic or health importance. This duality provides an added benefit: The information generated can be useful in the management of these pests. Conversely, the need to devise new management techniques provides resources that can be marshaled to aid basic studies. *ARE* continues to embrace this duality. Our discipline also has been quick to embrace new techniques and opportunities, such as cladistics, 40 years ago. Today, the deciphering of insect genomes and the quest to understand gene functionality and how and why genomes differ among individuals, species, and lineages is becoming an integral component of nearly every facet of entomology.

This is my thirteenth year as an Associate Editor of the *Annual Review of Entomology* and my eighteenth year on its Editorial Committee. This service has been one of the most rewarding activities of my career (which dates to my beginning graduate school in entomology 46 years ago). Selecting which subjects to review connects the Editorial Committee with the sweep of our discipline and generates a lively but collegial debate on which topics would best serve our discipline.

We hope that you find as much stimulation in the current volume as we had in its conception. Our Production Editor, Cleo X. Ray, deserves much credit for the quality of *ARE*, while the scientific excellence of the articles of course is due to the authors themselves.

Ring T. Cardé
For the Editorial Committee

Annual Review of Entomology

Volume 57, 2012

Contents

Indexes

Errata

An online log of corrections to *Annual Review of Entomology* articles may be found at http://ento.annualreviews.org/errata.shtml

Related Articles

From the ***Annual Review of Ecology, Evolution, and Systematics***, Volume 42 (2011)

Native Pollinators in Anthropogenic Habitats
Rachael Winfree, Ignasi Bartomeus, and Daniel P. Cariveau

Ehrlich and Raven Revisited: Mechanisms Underlying Codiversification of Plants and Enemies
Niklas Janz

An Evolutionary Perspective on Self-Organized Division of Labor in Social Insects
Ana Duarte, Franz J. Weissing, Ido Pen, and Laurent Keller

Evolution of *Anopheles gambiae* in Relation to Humans and Malaria
Bradley J. White, Frank H. Collins, and Nora J. Besansky

Long-Term Ecological Records and Their Relevance to Climate Change Predictions for a Warmer World
K.J. Willis and G.M. MacDonald

On the Use of Stable Isotopes in Trophic Ecology
William J. Boecklen, Christopher T. Yarnes, Bethany A. Cook, and Avis C. James

Phylogenetic Methods in Biogeography
Fredrik Ronquist and Isabel Sanmartín

From the ***Annual Review of Genetics***, Volume 45 (2011)

The Genetics of Hybrid Incompatibilities
Shamoni Maheshwari and Daniel A. Barbash

From the ***Annual Review of Microbiology***, Volume 65 (2011)

Gene Regulation in *Borrelia burgdorferi*
D. Scott Samuels

Metabolic Pathways Required for the Intracellular Survival of *Leishmania*
Malcolm J. McConville and Thomas Naderer

From the ***Annual Review of Phytopathology***, Volume 49 (2011)

Application of High-Throughput DNA Sequencing in Phytopathology
David J. Studholme, Rachel H. Glover, and Neil Boonham

Aspergillus flavus
Saori Amaike and Nancy P. Keller

Diverse Targets of Phytoplasma Effectors: From Plant Development to Defense Against Insects
Akiko Sugio, Allyson M. MacLean, Heather N. Kingdom, Victoria M. Grieve, R. Manimekalai, and Saskia A. Hogenhout

Emerging Virus Diseases Transmitted by Whiteflies
Jesús Navas-Castillo, Elvira Fiallo-Olive, and Sonia Sánchez-Campos

Hormone Crosstalk in Plant Disease and Defense: More Than Just JASMONATE-SALICYLATE Antagonism
Alexandre Robert-Seilaniantz, Murray Grant, and Jonathan D.G. Jones

Plant-Parasite Coevolution: Bridging the Gap Between Genetics and Ecology
James K.M. Brown and Aurélien Tellier

Insect Responses to Major Landscape-Level Disturbance

T.D. Schowalter

Entomology Department, Louisiana State University Agricultural Center, Baton Rouge, Louisiana 70803; email: tschowalter@agcenter.lsu.edu

Annu. Rev. Entomol. 2012. 57:1–20

First published online as a Review in Advance on August 29, 2011

The *Annual Review of Entomology* is online at ento.annualreviews.org

This article's doi:
10.1146/annurev-ento-120710-100610

0066-4170/12/0107-0001$20.00

Keywords

tolerance, dispersal, succession, local extinction, outbreak, population dynamics

Abstract

Disturbances are abrupt events that dramatically alter habitat conditions and resource distribution for populations and communities. Terrestrial landscapes are subject to various disturbance events that create a matrix of patches with different histories of disturbance and recovery. Species tolerances to extreme conditions during disturbance or to altered habitat or resource conditions following disturbances determine responses to disturbance. Intolerant populations may become locally extinct, whereas other species respond positively to the creation of new habitat or resource conditions. Local extinction represents a challenge for conservation biologists. On the other hand, outbreaks of herbivorous species often are triggered by abundant or stressed hosts and relaxation of predation following disturbances. These insect responses can cause further changes in ecosystem conditions and predispose communities to future disturbances. Improved understanding of insect responses to disturbance will improve prediction of population and community dynamics, as well as ecosystem and global changes.

INTRODUCTION

Disturbances are relatively abrupt events in time and space that substantially alter habitat conditions and resource distribution across landscapes (130, 133, 142). The extreme change in conditions created by disturbances is among the most significant factors affecting populations and communities, leading to local extinction of susceptible species and elevated populations of others that can exploit postdisturbance resources or predator-free space.

Insects are affected directly and indirectly by conditions produced during and after disturbances, and some show life-history strategies that likely reflect adaptations to disturbances (e.g., 110). Insect responses affect their interactions with other species and the resulting pathways and rates of energy and nutrient fluxes (102). Furthermore, insect responses to natural disturbances determine their responses to anthropogenic changes, often with serious consequences for ecosystem services on which humans depend (103). In particular, outbreaks of herbivores and disease vectors often are triggered by management practices (particularly harvest, species replacement, and change in fire frequency or intensity) that create favorable resource or habitat conditions similar to those resulting from natural disturbances (103, 129, 144). Local extinction of susceptible species potentially threatens others that depend on them for food, pollination, or seed dispersal (120). In some cases, insect responses alter community and ecosystem conditions in ways that increase the likelihood of subsequent disturbances (e.g., 12, 90, 119).

This review emphasizes insect responses to landscape-level disturbances. Topics include disturbance characteristics and their direct and indirect effects on abiotic conditions and postdisturbance conditions that affect insect populations in disturbed landscapes. Given the breadth of this topic, some aspects cannot be addressed adequately. Responses of aquatic insects to aquatic disturbances are not addressed in this review, and effects of anthropogenic pollutants and climate change are addressed only to the extent that they relate to insect ability to tolerate toxic materials produced during disturbances. Insect responses to natural disturbances largely determine their responses to anthropogenic disturbances that may imitate natural disturbances to varying degrees. Finally, this review addresses consequences of disturbance-induced changes in insect abundances for community interactions, ecosystem processes, and ecosystem services.

Adaptation: increased tolerance to disturbance, or other environmental changes, as a result of shifts in gene frequencies in response to intense selection during or after a disturbance

Disturbance event: the occurrence of an abrupt and extreme departure from the normal range of variation in abiotic conditions, within a relatively short time period, sufficient to cause measurable change in abundance or distribution of resources, populations, and communities

Disturbance type: categorized by the physical variables that depart from normal ranges

Disturbance magnitude: the extent of departure from normal ranges in abiotic conditions (intensity) and in population and community structure (severity)

Disturbance frequency: the number of events per unit time or the average return time between events

Disturbance extent: the area affected by a disturbance

DISTURBANCE CHARACTERISTICS

Each disturbance event is characterized by a unique combination of type, magnitude, frequency, and extent that determines its effect on various organisms (130, 133). Superimposing a sequence of events on the landscape creates a mosaic of patches that differ in their disturbance histories (**Figure 1**). For example, over a 20-year period a rain forest in Puerto Rico experienced two major hurricanes (Hugo in 1989 and Georges in 1998) that broke or toppled trees on the windward sides of slopes over large areas and caused numerous landslides, several moderate hurricanes (Luis and Marilyn 1995, Bertha and Hortense in 1996, Erika in 1997, Jose in 1999, and Jeanne in 2004) that caused substantial defoliation and flooding, a number of minor hurricanes and tropical storms, a major drought (1994–1995, during which precipitation was only 41% of the annual mean), and several minor droughts (1991, 1996, 2001, and 2003), as well as an overall drying trend of 2 mm year^{-1} since 1988 (51). The particular sequence of disturbances affects insect species responses (7, 23, 109). A species adapted to poststorm conditions, but eliminated by a previous fire, would not be represented in the poststorm community. Responses of litter arthropod and canopy Lepidoptera to canopy-opening disturbances can reflect filtering of species composition by previous harvests as early as 60 years earlier (109, 118).

Figure 1

Examples of disturbances to illustrate variation in type, magnitude, extent, and contrast between disturbed and surrounding landscape patches. (*a*) Fire in oak savanna (note sites of high and low flame height and intensity). (*b*) Hurricane effect on coastal deciduous forest. (*c*) Landslide resulting from heavy rainfall. (*d*) Volcanic eruption (note fresh lava flow on left and zones of burning and exposure to fumes in vegetation fragment).

Type

Disturbance types vary in the conditions they impose on organisms, including insects. Severe storms, especially tropical cyclones, dislodge or injure insects and initiate landslides and flooding that redistribute sediments and bury organisms. Fires and volcanic eruptions impose extreme high temperatures, whereas ice storms impose extreme low temperatures. Fires and volcanic eruptions also fill the air with ash and caustic gases, and lava or ash deposition burns and buries organisms. The eruption of Mount St. Helens in 1980, for example, deposited up to 30 kg ash m^{-2} at depths of 1 to 8 cm over an area of 54,000 km^2 (27).

Insect outbreaks often are considered to be disturbances because they kill plants and alter distribution of biomass over large areas (16, 17, 73, 77). Outbreaks also can predispose ecosystems to subsequent abiotic or biotic disturbances (e.g., 90, 119). Although consideration of outbreaks as disturbances, rather than disturbance-induced changes in trophic interactions, remains a matter of perspective (100, 106), the significant interactions between insect outbreaks and abiotic disturbances require consideration in management of ecosystem resources and services (see below).

Magnitude

Disturbances vary in intensity and severity. Intensity often may be difficult to measure, e.g., actual temperature during a fire or velocity of wind gusts during a storm. Magnitude is measured more often by the severity of effects on species and ecosystems. A low-intensity ground fire affects primarily surface-dwelling organisms, many of which may be adapted to this level of disturbance, whereas the intense heat of a fire storm (created by convection during catastrophic wildfire) penetrates more deeply into soil and wood and kills a larger proportion of the community (124, 139). A minor flood slowly filling a floodplain for a few days affects fewer insects than does a major flood that scours and inundates the landscape for weeks (e.g., 132). Dead vegetation deprives many insects of food resources and alters microclimatic conditions that affect habitat quality (69, 141). However, some species thrive under the altered conditions (105, 125).

Frequency

Disturbances vary in their return interval. Fire intense enough to kill most vegetation occurred, on average, every 200 years since 1633 in a montane forest landscape in western North America (128), whereas hurricanes of this magnitude recur every 10 to 60 years at sites in the Caribbean region (51). Frequency, with respect to generation times, of a particular disturbance type affects the rate of selection for adaptive traits that confer tolerance (resistance) to disturbance. Infrequently disturbed ecosystems, such as tropical forests, may be affected most by disturbances because dominant species in these ecosystems experience too few disturbances to drive selection for tolerance. Long-lived organisms, especially perennial plants, are more likely to experience disturbances consistently among generations, leading to stronger selection for adaptive traits.

Insects with short life spans relative to disturbance return intervals experience less selective pressure for adaptation to disturbance than do longer-lived species. Nevertheless, some insect species show apparent adaptations to disturbance. Some wood-boring insects, which have life spans of 2 to 10 years, are attracted to sources of heat or smoke, indicative of dead wood resources in fire-killed trees (33, 110). Several ant species characteristic of floodplain habitats have adapted to periodic flooding by forming floating mats of ants and larvae that may be dispersed downstream (148). Avoidance of dense overstory and accumulated litter by ground-pupating larvae of the pandora moth, *Coloradia pandora* Blake (Saturniidae), may reflect adaptation to minimize mortality during fire, which occurs every five years, on average, compared to a two-year life cycle for this moth (85). Dispersal ability is an important adaptation for species exploiting temporary, unstable conditions (60). Many species (especially Lepidoptera and Coleoptera) that characterize infrequently disturbed forests are flightless, or at least weak dispersers, whereas species that characterize temporary, frequently disturbed habitats (such as many aphids) produce large numbers of strong dispersers.

Disturbances of greater severity typically occur at lower frequency. Increasing disturbance magnitude or frequency generally reduces species diversity (7, 44, 84), because fewer species are able to tolerate more extreme changes in habitat or resource conditions. Hanula & Wade (49) reported that most forest floor species decreased in abundance, but some species increased, with increasing fire frequency. De Mazancourt et al. (29) suggested that high biodiversity increases the likelihood that some species have genotypes that are adapted to altered conditions. Arrival of adapted colonists of various species from other areas augments community recovery (see below).

Timing of disturbances, relative to insect developmental stage, also affects insect responses. Winged adults may be able to escape as conditions become intolerable, whereas exposed pupae would be most vulnerable to disturbance. On the other hand, Martin-R. et al. (79) reported that experimental fires set during different developmental stages of spittlebug, *Aeneolamia albofasciata* (Lallemand) (Cercopidae), in buffelgrass, *Cenchrus ciliaris* L., grassland in Sonora, Mexico, eliminated spittlebugs for at least four years after burning, regardless of developmental stage at the time of burning.

Source-sink relationship: colonization of disturbed sites (sink) through dispersal of individuals from population centers (source) in other parts of the landscape

Tolerance range: the range of values between lethal maxima and minima, for any environmental variable (or combination of variables), under which exposed organisms can survive

Extent

Disturbances range in extent from a few hectares to continental, but the magnitude of particular disturbances varies across landscapes due to variation in topography, substrate condition, or vegetation, e.g., intervening hills, bedrock outcrops, bodies of water, or patches of vegetation that are resistant to particular disturbances. Veblen et al. (128) reported that fire has affected 59% and snow avalanches 9% of a montane forest landscape in western North America since 1633, compared to 39% by outbreaks of spruce beetle, *Dendroctonus rufipennis* (Kirby) (Curculionidae). The 1998 flood in Bangladesh inundated nearly 70% (about 100,000 km^2) of the country (72), leaving few refuges for insects intolerant of immersion. Heavy rains producing such floods typically saturate soils over a much larger area. Lava and ash from volcanic eruptions can cover thousands of square kilometers (27), but volcanic gases can affect atmospheric chemistry and climate globally (81). El Niño events in the southern Pacific Ocean also affect climate and insects globally (114, 125, 147). Insect outbreaks themselves are capable of consuming or killing most host plants over thousands of square kilometers (e.g., 91, 102, 104).

The extent of disturbed area affects insect responses. Populations restricted to areas smaller than the disturbed area are likely to disappear. This threat creates a challenge for conservation biologists, who must work to conserve large enough areas, or sufficient distribution of increasingly isolated refuges, to maintain adequate population sizes of target species vulnerable to large-scale disturbance (48). Colonization typically progresses inward from the edges of disturbed areas, as dispersing individuals from population sources find such "sinks," so smaller areas can be colonized more quickly than larger areas (6, 112). Insects with limited mobility may require considerable time to colonize large areas (66). More extensive disturbances, or disturbances that result in greater contrast between disturbed and undisturbed patches (e.g., **Figure 1*d***), create steeper gradients in postdisturbance temperature and relative humidity between disturbed and undisturbed patches, with sharper boundaries relative to insect tolerance ranges (112). However, edges of disturbed areas may provide unique resources for insects, e.g., species that exploit forest plants that are stressed by exposure or are favored by higher light available at the edge of a disturbed area (66, 97).

INSECT RESPONSES

Individual insects have specific tolerance ranges to abiotic conditions that dictate their ability to survive exposure to extreme temperatures, water availability, chemical concentrations, or other factors during and after a disturbance. Variable ecosystem conditions typically select for wider tolerance ranges than do more stable conditions. Although changes in abiotic conditions during disturbances can affect insects directly (e.g., burning, drowning, particle blocking of spiracles), disturbances also affect insects indirectly through changes in resource quality and availability and in exposure to predation or parasitism (e.g., 3, 59, 80, 85, 97, 113, 125). Population size and degree of genetic heterogeneity affect survival during disturbance (7). As habitat conditions change, intolerant individuals or species disappear, but tolerant species may be favored by reduced predation or improved resource conditions following disturbance (97, 101, 105). Because survival and reproduction of individual insects determine population size, distribution, and subsequent effects on community and ecosystem recovery, this section focuses on factors that affect insect responses directly and indirectly.

Direct Effects of Abiotic Changes

Disturbances alter abiotic conditions to varying degrees depending on disturbance type and severity. Insects are particularly vulnerable to changes in temperature, water availability, and air or water chemistry because of their relatively large surface area/volume ratio and limited homeostatic ability. Although some habitats may protect insects from disturbances, and some insects may be able to escape as conditions approach tolerance limits (62, 143), survival of many depends on physiological tolerance ranges relative to environmental extremes.

Temperature extremes. Fires and volcanic eruptions, in particular, create lethal temperatures for insects unable to escape. Disturbances that reduce vegetation cover subsequently expose surviving or colonizing insects to elevated surface temperatures. Ulyshen et al. (124) found that fire reduced abundances, but not species representation, of wood-boring beetles in coarse woody debris. Beetles were relatively protected in larger-diameter logs. Bark beetles (Curculionidae) in subcortical tissues, however, are vulnerable to heat mortality (139). Small, flightless litter species only need to move a few millimeters vertically within the soil profile to avoid lethal temperatures and desiccation during fire or canopy-opening disturbances (111). Nevertheless, Hanula & Wade (49) found that abundances of most forest floor species (especially predators) were reduced by prescribed burning and were reduced more by annual than by biennial or quadrennial burning, but a few species (especially detritivores) increased in abundance with more frequent burning.

Survival at high temperatures requires high body water content or access to water, because desiccation at low relative humidity causes death (45). Disturbances that reduce riparian canopy cover significantly increase water temperature, and reduce oxygen levels, of aquatic patches especially in the summer (64, 98). A distinct riparian fauna may be vulnerable to canopy-opening disturbance within 30 m of streams (98). However, stream grazers may respond positively to increased primary production resulting from higher light level when riparian canopies are opened (64).

Conversely, unseasonable ice storms or extreme cold periods also kill exposed insects. Ability to survive depends on prior preconditioning to sublethal temperatures (65) or physiological mechanisms, such as production of cryoprotectants to prevent intracellular ice formation and voiding the gut to prevent food particles from serving as nuclei for ice formation (45).

Precipitation extremes. Water availability becomes particularly limited during drought or excessive during floods, but high temperatures during fire or volcanic eruption may severely reduce relative humidity. Maintenance of water balance becomes a challenge for small organisms such as insects, but some insects are capable of minimizing water loss or tolerating dehydration (41). The exoskeleton is an important mechanism for control of water exchange. Larger, more heavily sclerotized arthropods are less susceptible to desiccation or waterlogging than are smaller, more delicate species (3, 63).

Extreme dehydration may trigger the onset of anhydrobiosis, a physiological state characterized by an absence of free water and of measurable metabolism (45, 137). Survival during anhydrobiosis requires stabilization of membranes and enzymes by compounds other than water, e.g., glycerol and trehalose, whose synthesis is stimulated by dehydration (45). Among insects only some larval Diptera and adult Collembola undergo anhydrobiosis (45). Hinton (54, 55) reported that the chironomid fly *Polypedilum vanderplanki* Hint., found in temporary pools in central Africa, withstands repeated dehydration to 8% of body water content. At 3% body water content, this midge is capable of surviving temperatures from −270°C to 100°C.

On the other hand, insects subjected to flooding must contend with excess water. Subterranean termites can survive short periods of inundation by entering a quiescent state; relative abilities of species to withstand periods of flooding correspond to their utilization of aboveground or belowground wood resources (35). Litter-dwelling ants are vulnerable to seasonal flooding in Amazonian forests (84). Specialist predators were virtually eliminated by flooding; one *Hypoponera* species (Formicidae) was adapted to a high degree of flooding, increasing in abundance with the frequency and duration of flooding. Webb & Pullin (132) found that pupae of the wetland butterfly *Lycaena dispar batavus* Oberthur (Lycaenidae) could tolerate 28 days of submergence, but survival was negatively correlated with duration of submergence between 28 and 84 days. However, inundation affects oxygen availability (see below), as well as water balance.

Wind speed and water flow. High wind speeds and water flow during storms dislodge and displace exposed insects, as well as sediment and organic debris, crushing or injuring many individuals. Some may survive and be able to move around and colonize new habitats to which they are relocated, but immature and sedentary insects most likely perish. Torres (122) documented several insect species, including a swarm of desert locusts, *Schistocerca gregaria* Forsskål (Acrididae), that were blown across the Atlantic Ocean from North Africa to Puerto Rico by hurricane winds. Although most species did not survive, such transport provides an opportunity to colonize habitats across major barriers and may explain the relative homogeneity of biotas among Caribbean islands (122).

Air and water quality. Some disturbances alter atmospheric and water quality. Fire and volcanic eruptions, in particular, release toxic abiotic and biotic gases and particulate materials, but high winds during storms and high river levels during flooding also increase the amount of dissolved and suspended materials that may affect exposed insects.

Oxygen supply is especially critical to survival but may become limiting during or after some disturbances, such as soil saturation during flooding or burial by sedimentation or ash fall. Many insects can tolerate short periods of anoxia, but prolonged periods result in reduced survival and developmental abnormalities (57). Adult alder leaf beetles, *Agelastica alni* (L.) (Chrysomelidae), which overwinter in frequently waterlogged or flooded riparian soil, showed a reduction in metabolic activity after 3 days to 2% of normal metabolic activity (68). Larval tiger beetles, *Phaeoxantha klugii* Chaudroir (Carabidae), found in central Amazonian floodplains tolerate anoxic conditions in flooded soils for up to 3.5 months at 29°C (146). This exceptional degree of anoxia tolerance appeared to require several days of induction as water levels rose, suggesting vulnerability to more rapid inundation. Brust & Hoback (18) found that tolerance to hypoxia among several tiger beetles (*Cicindela* spp.) was not related to likelihood of immersion.

Increased concentrations of atmospheric CO_2 that result from fire, volcanic eruption, or other causes appear to have little direct effect on insects or other arthropods. Fluorides, sulfur compounds, nitrogen oxides, ozone, and other toxic fumes affect many insect species directly, although the physiological mechanisms of toxicity are not well known (3, 52, 53). Disruption of epicuticular or spiracular tissues by these reactive chemicals may be involved.

Soil and water pH affects a variety of chemical reactions, including enzymatic activity. Changes in pH resulting from deposition of ash and release of caustic gases from fire or volcanic eruptions affect osmotic exchange, gill or spiracular surfaces, and digestive processes. Changes in pH often are correlated with other chemical changes, such as increased concentrations of nitrogen or sulfur compounds, and effects of pH change may be difficult to separate from other factors. Van Straalen & Verhoef (126) found that several species of soil collembolans and oribatid mites varied in their responses to acidic or alkaline soil conditions.

Dust and ash from volcanic eruptions or fires kill many insects, apparently because they absorb and abrade the thin epicuticular wax-lipid film that is the principal barrier to water loss, causing death by desiccation (3, 27, 78). Insects exposed to volcanic debris also can suffer gut epithelial stress from accumulation of heavy metals (96). Ash accumulation and retention by aquatic insects following the eruption of Mount St. Helens were affected by exoskeletal sculpturing, armature, and pubescence (40). Substantial accumulation was noted on respiratory structures, potentially interfering with respiration. Ash-covered insects showed increased activity and orientation upstream, which successfully washed off ash within 24 h. However, ash coating over cobbles, pebbles, and sand significantly inhibited colonization of these substrates (20).

Indirect Effects of Postdisturbance Changes

Insects that survive the direct effects of disturbance must contend with altered habitat conditions and resource availability. Disturbances destroy some habitats and resources and alter distribution or quality of others for a period, during which community and ecosystem conditions recover to a semblance of predisturbance conditions (ecological succession). Some insect species respond positively, others negatively, to these changes in community and ecosystem conditions owing to adaptive characteristics and trophic interactions (21, 26, 32, 36, 49, 56, 84, 88, 89, 105, 140). Species that increase in abundance following disturbance typically are favored by exposed conditions, stressed or rapidly growing plants, or detrital resources. In addition, some may be promoted by decoupling of predator-prey relationships in patches of enemy-free space.

Exposure. Disturbances that remove vegetation cover or litter expose insects to a wider range of ambient temperature and relative humidity (24, 98) and predators (14). Arboreal beetle responses to typhoon disturbance in tropical rain forest in Australia reflected species' adaptations to moisture, with more xerophilic species increasing in abundance and mesophilic species decreasing in abundance following canopy opening and general drying of the forest (42). Furthermore, reproduction, especially egg hatch, may be reduced at high temperature and low relative humidity (121).

Some ant species, e.g., *Solenopsis invicta* Buren and *Atta laevigata* F. Smith (Formicidae), preferentially colonize bare soil habitats to soil covered by vegetation or litter (117, 127). However, other species may be unable to survive the extreme temperatures of exposed sites. Meisel (83) reported that the army ant, *Eciton burchellii* Westwood (Formicidae), is restricted to forest fragments in Costa Rica, because workers survived less than 3 min at 51°C (the midday temperature of surrounding pastures) and only 18 min at 43°C.

Resource abundance and quality. Insects dependent on lost resources may disappear, but some insects flourish on surviving hosts that are stressed and less capable of defense or on new hosts that exploit reduced competition or predation. Sap-sucking hemipterans are favored by rapid growth of early-successional plants (101, 104, 108). Other species also respond to rapid growth of early-successional plants (13, 123). Carabid beetle abundance and species richness increased in riparian forests subject to periodic flooding, compared to nonflooded sites, indicating that flooding contributed to habitat suitability for these beetles (22, 74).

Disturbances that create large amounts of coarse woody debris (fires and storms) or stressed trees (droughts and storms) are typical triggers for bark beetle and wood borer outbreaks (16, 36, 80, 93). Acoustic cues from cavitating cell walls may attract bark beetles to water-stressed trees (80). Many wood-boring insects, such as wood wasps (Siricidae) and beetles (especially Buprestidae), are attracted to sources of smoke, infrared radiation, or volatile tree chemicals emitted from burned or injured trees over distances of up to 50 km (33, 39, 86, 94, 110, 138). These cues signal the availability of dead trees, typically rare in undisturbed forests, that are suitable sites for reproduction.

Plants stressed by disturbance, especially drought, frequently trigger outbreaks of some herbivorous insect species (80, 105, 125, 134–136). Defoliator outbreaks commonly reflect abundant water-stressed plants (102, 105, 125), perhaps reflecting changes in plant defensive chemistry, but this is not always the case (46). Interestingly, locust outbreaks appear to be triggered by either drought or flooding disturbances. A 1000-year record of locust outbreaks in China indicated that outbreaks typically originated in floodplain refuges, which are characterized by adequate vegetation and suitable oviposition sites, during drought years and years after flooding (116). Droughts increase the availability of suitable oviposition sites, as well as stressed vegetation, as water recedes, whereas similar conditions occur in formerly flooded areas in the year after flooding.

On the other hand, many herbivorous insects become less abundant on stressed host plants (92, 105, 131). A major drought in Pacific northwestern North America virtually eliminated the dominant folivore, a bud moth, *Zeiraphera hesperiana* Mutuura & Freeman (Tortricidae), and favored its replacement by the western spruce budworm, *Choristoneura occidentalis* Freeman (Tortricidae), and the balsam fir sawfly, *Neodiprion abietis* (Harris) (Diprionidae). Following the drought, *Z. hesperiana* recovered its dominance, and *C. occidentalis* and *N. abietis* disappeared (**Figure 2**) (101, 102). Schowalter et al. (105) reported that some herbivorous species increased, whereas others decreased, in abundance on creosote bushes, *Larrea tridentata* (DC) Coville, subjected to an experimental moisture gradient. Obviously, response to plant water status varies widely among herbivorous insects (71).

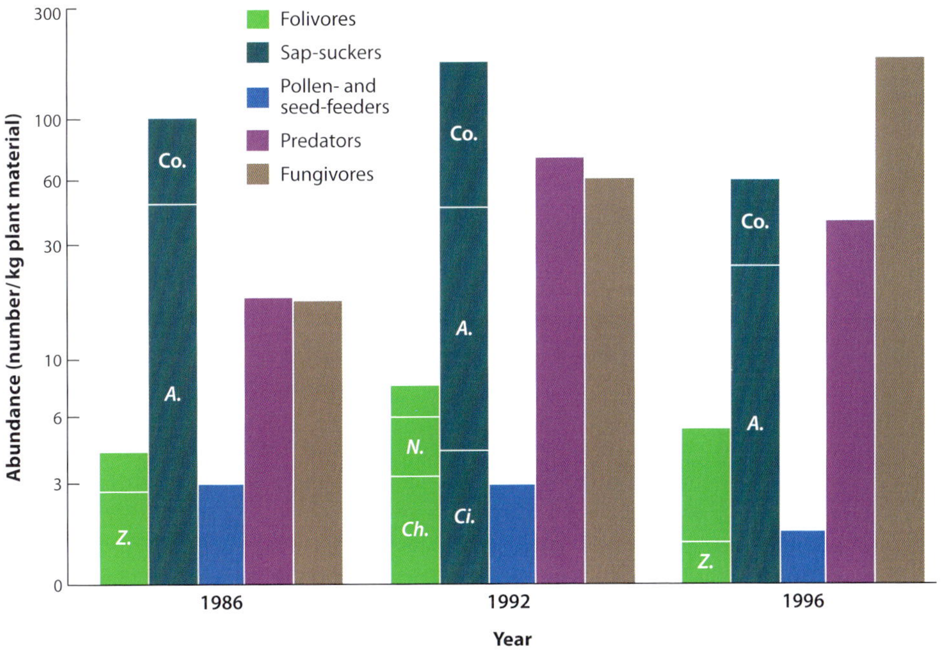

Figure 2

Drought-induced change in forest canopy insect species composition, followed by recovery in western Oregon. 1986 and 1996 were relatively normal wet years; 1992 was near the end of a drought period (1987–1993). Abbreviations: *Z.*, *Zeiraphera hesperiana*; *Ch.*, *Choristoneura occidentalis*; *N.*, *Neodiprion abietis*; *Ci.*, *Cinara* spp.; *A.*, *Adelges cooleyi*; Co., Coccoidea (four species). Note the log scale of abundance. From Reference 102 with permission from Elsevier.

Variation in response to plant stress is not clearly associated with changes in plant defensive chemistry. Hale et al. (46) reported that drought-stressed black poplar, *Populus nigra* L., increased phenolic glycoside concentrations, with differing effects on gypsy moth, *Lymantria dispar* (L.) (Lymantriidae), and whitemarked tussock moth, *Orgyia leucostigma* (J.E. Smith) (Lymantriidae). Forest canopy-opening disturbances often result in increased production of phenolics by early-successional plants growing under conditions of higher light availability (59, 113). However, despite higher foliar phenolic concentrations, many herbivores increased in abundance following Hurricane Opal in southeastern North America (59).

Even within families and genera, individual species respond quite differently to disturbances. Among Hemiptera, some scale insect species increased in abundance, and others decreased, during forest canopy recovery from hurricanes in Puerto Rico (104). Root bark beetles [e.g., *Hylastes nigrinus* (Mannerheim) (Curculionidae)] are attracted to chemicals emanating from exposed stump surfaces that advertise suitable conditions for brood development, and become more abundant following forest thinning (144), whereas stem-feeding bark beetles [e.g., *Dendroctonus* spp. (Curculionidae)] are sensitive to tree spacing and become less abundant in thinned forests (4, 99, 107).

Responses also vary among disturbance types. Paquin & Coderre (89) compared forest floor arthropod responses to forest clearing versus fire. Decomposers were less abundant, whereas predators were more abundant, in cleared plots than in undisturbed plots. Arthropod abundance overall was reduced 96% following experimental fire, but some organisms survived due to their occurrence in deeper soil levels or to the patchy effect of fire. Abundances of some species differed between cleared and burned plots.

Following disturbance, populations and ecosystems may recover to their predisturbance condition at rates that reflect the extent of change and the size of the disturbed area. Recovery can be as quick as a few months for rapidly reproducing species or assemblages, such as many insects, or for patches in landscape matrices that facilitate dispersal (36, 50). In contrast, recovery can be long, taking years to centuries for long-lived, slowly reproducing species or assemblages. Factors that delay recovery of plant communities also influence recovery of habitat conditions and rates of insect recovery. Insects often influence rates of community recovery. Herbivorous species can accelerate replacement of earlier successional host plant species by later successional nonhost plant species (28, 123). If the disturbance-free interval is shorter than the time needed for recovery, then earlier-successional communities may persist.

Predator/parasite abundance and foraging activity. Disturbances affect abundances and foraging activity of predators and their prey differently, creating areas of concentrated predation or of predator-free space (47, 75, 120). Insects at higher trophic levels appear to be particularly susceptible to disturbances (37, 47, 89, 104, 120), although some carabid beetle species increase in abundance in burned sites (37). Parasitoids commonly have a lower temperature tolerance than their hosts, and different thermal tolerances affect the temporal synchronization of parasitoid and host during the season (47). Beuzelin et al. (11) reported a threefold reduction in red imported fire ant (*S. invicta*) in areas inundated by storm surge during Hurricane Rita. Entomopathogen abundance may be reduced in disturbed areas by exposure to UV radiation (97). Reduced predation or parasitism in disturbed areas may permit prey species to increase in abundance.

RESPONSES TO ANTHROPOGENIC DISTURBANCES

Anthropogenic disturbances, including harvest, altered fire regimes, road construction, and release of toxic materials, such as oil spills and industrial effluents, have become a pervasive environmental factor. Insect responses to such disturbances reflect the degree to which direct and indirect effects resemble those of natural disturbances, e.g., forest harvest may elicit responses similar to other canopy-opening disturbances (21, 89). Gandhi et al. (38) compared forest floor beetle assemblages in remnant forest patches within harvested landscapes and burned landscapes and found that, whereas assemblages in remnant patches within harvested landscapes resembled those of uncut forest, they differed significantly from assemblages in remnant patches within burned forest, indicating that fire creates unique habitats within the landscape. Anthropogenic disturbances also introduce novel conditions, e.g., large numbers of cut stumps with exposed fresh surfaces and inground root systems that provide unique habitats for root-feeding insects (144) and sharp boundaries that alter the steepness of environmental gradients between disturbed and undisturbed patches and restrict dispersal of species intolerant of exposed conditions (24, 50). Catastrophic wildfires in western North America that have resulted from fuel accumulation during a century of fire suppression also may create conditions different from those of low-intensity ground fires to which species have adapted (2, 25).

Landscape matrix or mosaic: the patchwork of distinct communities on the landscape that represent different combinations and histories of disturbances and colonization

Anthropogenic disturbances differ from natural disturbances in their frequency, duration, and scale. Whereas the return frequency of stand-replacing fire in coniferous forests of the Pacific Northwest was about 500 years, harvest practices now restart forest recovery every 70 to 100 years (25). Ecosystem fragmentation and conversion to agricultural or urban uses have dramatic effects on survival and movement of various insects. Braschler et al. (15) found that many orthopterans avoided the mown matrix in a fragmented grassland, likely because of the lack of shelter. As a consequence, small populations became increasingly isolated in diminishing remnant patches of grassland, increasing their vulnerability to local extinction if large areas are mown simultaneously. Stream channelization and levee construction may threaten floodplain insects that depend on periodic flooding (22, 74). Extended periods of submersion resulting from dam operation may exceed the ability of many floodplain species to tolerate hypoxic conditions (19).

Anthropogenic changes also may exacerbate the effect of natural disturbances. Clearing land and impounding reservoirs have occurred simultaneously over large areas of the globe. These practices alter surface albedo in ways that increase regional warming, storm intensity (34, 58), runoff, and stream discharge. As a result, the average return time for floods of 100-year severity is likely to shrink to 30 years (72). Vegetation removal and smoke from fires that accompany forest conversion to agricultural or urban land use reduce cloud cover (from 38% in clean air to 0% in heavy smoke) and increase the altitude at which water condenses, leading to more violent thunderstorms and hail rather than warm rain (1, 5, 70). The increased frequency of extreme disturbances will affect insects and other organisms in ways that are difficult to predict (43).

CONSEQUENCES OF POPULATION CHANGES

Disturbance-induced changes in insect populations affect subsequent community and ecosystem processes. In some cases, insects respond in ways that substantially alter community recovery or predispose ecosystems to subsequent disturbances (28).

Community Recovery

Elderd (30) and Elderd & Doak (31) used manipulative experiments to demonstrate that increased herbivory by grasshoppers following flood events significantly reduced survival of a common riparian plant, *Mimulus guttatus* DC, that otherwise is favored by flooding. Bishop (13) found that several herbivorous insect species suppressed populations of lupine, *Lupinus lepidus* Douglas ex Lindl., an important early-successional, nitrogen-fixing plant, following the eruption of Mount

St. Helens, thereby affecting the rate of nutrient recovery and vegetative succession. Bark beetle populations increasing in injured or stressed conifers can reach sizes capable of killing surrounding uninjured trees over large areas (107).

Although outbreaks have been targets of pest management, they may alleviate stressful conditions and facilitate community and ecosystem development, at least in some cases. Drought-stressed plants may show higher survival when defoliated than when nondefoliated (67, 115). Canopy openings resulting from spruce budworm, *Choristoneura fumiferana* (Clemens) (Tortricidae), outbreaks had a greater diversity of saplings and trees and larger perimeter/area ratios than did canopy openings resulting from harvest practices, suggesting that stand recovery and contributions by the surrounding forest should be greater in budworm-generated openings than in harvest-generated openings (9). Alteration of vegetation composition by insects may tailor overall biotic demand for water and nutrients to prevailing conditions at a site, e.g., replacement of N-rich species by low-N species (10, 67, 95). Succession from pioneer pine forest to late-successional fir forest in western North America can be retarded or advanced by insects, depending primarily on moisture availability and the condition of the dominant vegetation (103). When moisture is adequate (e.g., in riparian corridors and at high elevations), mountain pine beetle, *Dendroctonus ponderosae* Hopkins (Curculionidae), advances succession by facilitating the replacement of host pines by more shade-tolerant, fire-intolerant understory firs. However, limited moisture and short fire return intervals at lower elevations favor pine dominance. In the absence of fire during drought periods, *C. occidentalis*, Douglas-fir tussock moth, *Orgyia pseudotsugata* (McDunnough) (Lymantriidae), and fir engraver beetle, *Scolytus ventralis* LeConte (Curculionidae), concentrate on the understory firs, truncating (or reversing) succession.

Some disturbance-induced changes in insect abundance and distribution increase the transmission rate of human and animal diseases (114, 129, 147). Flooding or canopy opening or both increase habitat for mosquitoes and other insect vectors. Vittor et al. (129) found that increased abundance and biting rate of the mosquito *Anopheles darlingi* Root (Culicidae), which is responsible for transmission of malaria to humans, in Peru were related to deforestation and road development. Stapp et al. (114) and Zhou et al. (147) reported increased incidence of human and wildlife diseases associated with El Niño–induced increases in abundances of insect vectors.

Promotion of Future Disturbances

Insect outbreaks can predispose ecosystems to subsequent disturbances. Severe defoliation can increase plant vulnerability to other mortality agents, e.g., bark beetles (145). Outbreaks also affect the probability or severity of abiotic disturbances, especially fire or storms (76).

Increased fuel accumulation generally has been considered to increase the likelihood and severity of fire (82), but this is not necessarily the case. Bebi et al. (8) concluded that mortality of spruce, *Picea engelmannii* Parry ex. Engelm., to the spruce beetle, *Dendroctonus rufipennis* (Kirby) (Curculionidae), did not increase the occurrence of subsequent fires. The probability of fire resulting from outbreaks depends on the amount and decomposition rate of increased litter. Grasshopper outbreaks that reduce grass biomass should reduce the severity of subsequent grassland fire. Outbreaks that increase only fine litter material (e.g., foliage fragments) increase the probability but reduce the intensity of fire, whereas outbreaks that increase coarse woody debris (especially of standing boles that increase the abundance of ladder fuels) are more likely to increase the risk of catastrophic fire (61).

Insect outbreaks that open the canopy increase penetration of high wind speeds but also reduce wind resistance of defoliated trees. Pruning at least 80% of the canopy can reduce wind stress significantly (87). Wind-related tree mortality following spruce budworm defoliation in eastern

Canada was related to outbreak severity and peaked 11 to 15 years after the outbreak, due to greater exposure of surviving trees to wind (119).

CONCLUSIONS

Insect responses to major landscape-level disturbance are dictated by disturbance characteristics, insect exposure to disturbance effects, and tolerance to altered conditions during and after the disturbance. Disturbances can eliminate populations of exposed or poorly adapted insects, but tolerant insects may survive or colonize the altered ecosystem. Postdisturbance responses include outbreaks of species that exploit abundant, stressed, or detrital resources.

Relatively few studies have documented insect responses to natural disturbances, compared to anthropogenic disturbances, largely because of unpredictability and statistical problems in comparing unreplicated disturbed and undisturbed patches. Some studies have fortuitously experienced superimposed disturbances that permitted comparison of pre- and postdisturbance abundances or activity. Other studies have employed experimental fire or canopy-opening manipulations to evaluate the effects of designed treatments on insects, but such manipulations may not reflect all conditions created by natural disturbances. Nevertheless, such experiments have provided the most useful data on insect responses to disturbances. Clearly, more research is needed on insect responses to natural disturbances and combinations of disturbances in order to improve prediction of responses that affect resource management goals and ecosystem services.

SUMMARY POINTS

1. Disturbances are relatively abrupt changes in environmental conditions that kill susceptible organisms and significantly alter the abundance and distribution of resources for surviving organisms.
2. Because of their small size and limited homeostatic ability, exposed insects are particularly sensitive to extreme temperatures and other variables that occur during or after disturbances.
3. Some species experience local extinction if habitat conditions exceed their tolerance ranges or if their resources disappear.
4. Disturbances often trigger outbreaks of herbivorous species favored by stressed or abundant hosts following disturbance.
5. Responses to anthropogenic disturbances depend on similarity between conditions created by anthropogenic disturbances and conditions created by natural disturbances that have shaped insect life-history adaptations.
6. Insect responses affect the rate or direction of community recovery from disturbance, affect the epidemiology of human or animal diseases, and may increase the likelihood of subsequent disturbances.
7. Additional studies on insect responses to multiple natural and anthropogenic changes are needed to improve prediction and management of outbreaks or endangered species.

DISCLOSURE STATEMENT

The author is not aware of any affiliations, memberships, funding, or financial holdings that might be perceived as affecting the objectivity of this review.

ACKNOWLEDGMENTS

B. Elderd, S. Heuberger, and J. Trumble provided helpful comments on the draft manuscript. This paper is published with the approval of the Director of the Louisiana Agricultural Experiment Station, as manuscript number 2011-234-5569.

LITERATURE CITED

1. Ackerman AS, Toon OB, Stevens DE, Heymsfield AJ, Ramanathan V, Welton EJ. 2000. Reduction of tropical cloudiness by soot. *Science* 288:1042–47
2. Agee JK. 1993. *Fire Ecology of Pacific Northwest Forests*. Washington, DC: Island
3. Alstad DN, Edmunds GF Jr, Weinstein LH. 1982. Effects of air pollutants on insect populations. *Annu. Rev. Entomol.* 27:369–84
4. Amman GD, McGregor MD, Schmitz RF, Oakes RD. 1988. Susceptibility of lodgepole pine to infestation by mountain pine beetles following partial cutting of stands. *Can. J. For. Res.* 18:688–95
5. Andreae MO, Rosenfeld D, Artaxo P, Costa AA, Frank GP, et al. 2004. Smoking rain clouds over the Amazon. *Science* 303:1337–42
6. Antunes SC, Curado N, Castro BB, Gonçalves F. 2009. Short-term recovery of soil functional parameters and edaphic macro-arthropod community after a forest fire. *J. Soils Sediments* 9:267–78
7. Ballinger A, Lake PS, MacNally RM. 2007. Do terrestrial invertebrates experience floodplains as landscape mosaics? Immediate and longer-term effects of flooding on ant assemblages in a floodplain forest. *Oecologia* 152:227–38
8. Bebi P, Kilakowski D, Veblen TT. 2003. Interactions between fire and spruce beetles in a subalpine Rocky Mountain forest landscape. *Ecology* 84:362–71
9. Belle-Isle J, Kneeshaw D. 2007. A stand and landscape comparison of the effects of a spruce budworm (*Choristoneura fumiferana* (Clem.)) outbreak to the combined effects of harvesting and thinning on forest structure. *For. Ecol. Manag.* 246:163–74
10. Belovsky GE, Slade JB. 2000. Insect herbivory accelerates nutrient cycling and increases plant production. *Proc. Natl. Acad. Sci. USA* 97:14412–17
11. Beuzelin JM, Reagan TE, Akbar W, Courmier HJ, Flanagan JW, Blouin DC. 2009. Impact of Hurricane Rita storm surge on sugarcane borer (Lepidoptera: Crambidae) management in Louisiana. *J. Econ. Entomol.* 102:1054–61
12. Bigler C, Kulakowski D, Veblen TT. 2005. Multiple disturbance interactions and drought influence fire severity in Rocky Mountain subalpine forests. *Ecology* 86:3018–29
13. Bishop JG. 2002. Early primary succession on Mount St. Helens: impact of insect herbivores on colonizing lupines. *Ecology* 83:191–202
14. Björklund N, Nordlander G, Bylund H. 2003. Host-plant acceptance on mineral soil and humus by the pine weevil, *Hylobius abietis* (L.). *Agric. For. Entomol.* 5:61–65
15. Braschler B, Marini L, Thommen GH, Baur B. 2009. Effects of small-scale grassland fragmentation and frequent mowing on population density and species diversity of orthopterans: a long-term study. *Ecol. Entomol.* 34:321–29
16. Breshears DD, Cobb NS, Rich PM, Price KP, Allen CD, et al. 2005. Regional vegetation die-off in response to global-change-type drought. *Proc. Natl. Acad. Sci. USA* 102:15144–48
17. Brown M, Black TA, Nesic Z, Foord VN, Spittlehouse DL, et al. 2010. Impact of mountain pine beetle on the net ecosystem production of lodgepole pine stands in British Columbia. *Agric. For. Meteorol.* 150:254–64
18. Brust ML, Hoback WW. 2009. Hypoxia tolerance in adult and larval *Cicindela* tiger beetles varies by life history but not habitat association. *Ann. Entomol. Soc. Am.* 102:462–66
19. Brust ML, Hoback WW, Skinner KF, Knisley CB. 2005. Differential immersion survival by populations of *Cicindela hirticollis* (Coleoptera: Cicindelidae). *Ann. Entomol. Soc. Am.* 98:973–79
20. Brusven MA, Hornig CE. 1984. Effects of suspended and deposited volcanic ash on survival and behavior of stream insects. *J. Kans. Entomol. Soc.* 57:55–62

21. Buddle CM, Langor DW, Pohl GR, Spence JR. 2006. Arthropod responses to harvesting and wildfire: implications for emulation of natural disturbance in forest management. *Biol. Conserv.* 128:346–57
22. Cartron JLE, Molles MC Jr, Schuetz JF, Crawford CS, Dahm CN. 2003. Ground arthropods as potential indicators of flooding regime in the riparian forest of the middle Rio Grande, New Mexico. *Environ. Entomol.* 32:1075–84
23. Chase JM. 2007. Drought mediates the importance of stochastic community assembly. *Proc. Natl. Acad. Sci. USA* 104:17430–34
24. Chen J, Franklin JF, Spies TA. 1995. Growing-season microclimatic gradients from clearcut edges into old-growth Douglas-fir forests. *Ecol. Appl.* 5:74–86
25. Christensen NL Jr, Gregory SV, Hagenstein PR, Heberlein TA, Hendee JC, et al. 2000. *Environmental Issues in Pacific Northwest Forest Management*. Washington, DC: Natl. Acad. Press
26. Cleary DFR, Grill A. 2004. Butterfly response to severe ENSO-induced forest fires in Borneo. *Ecol. Entomol.* 29:666–76
27. Cook RJ, Barron JC, Papendick RI, Williams GJ III. 1981. Impact on agriculture of the Mount St. Helens eruptions. *Science* 211:16–22
28. Davidson DW. 1993. The effects of herbivory and granivory on terrestrial plant succession. *Oikos* 68:23–35
29. de Mazancourt C, Johnson E, Barradough TG. 2008. Biodiversity inhibits species' evolutionary responses to changing environments. *Ecol. Lett.* 11:380–88
30. Elderd BD. 2006. Disturbance-mediated trophic interactions and plant performance. *Oecologia* 147:261–71
31. Elderd BD, Doak DF. 2006. Comparing the direct and community-mediated effects of disturbance on plant population dynamics: flooding, herbivory and *Mimulus guttatus*. *J. Ecol.* 94:656–69
32. Evans EW. 1988. Community dynamics of prairie grasshoppers subjected to periodic fire: predictable trajectories or random walks in time? *Oikos* 52:283–92
33. Evans WG. 1966. Perception of infrared radiation from forest fires by *Melanophila acuminata* de Geer (Buprestidae, Coleoptera). *Ecology* 47:1061–65
34. Foley JA, Costa MH, Delire C, Ramankutty N, Snyder P. 2003. Green surprise? How terrestrial ecosystems could affect Earth's climate. *Front. Ecol. Environ.* 1:38–44
35. Forschler BT, Henderson G. 1995. Subterranenan termite behavioral reaction to water and survival of inundation: implications for field populations. *Environ. Entomol.* 24:1592–97
36. Gandhi KJK, Gilmore DW, Katovich SA, Mattson WJ, Spence SR, Seybold SJ. 2007. Physical effects of weather events on the abundance and diversity of insects in North American forests. *Environ. Rev.* 15:113–52
37. Gandhi KJK, Gilmore DW, Katovich SA, Mattson WJ, Zasada JC, Seybold SJ. 2008. Catastrophic windstorm and fuel-reduction treatments alter ground beetle (Coleoptera: Carabidae) assemblages in a North American sub-boreal forest. *For. Ecol. Manag.* 256:1104–23
38. Gandhi KJK, Spence JR, Langor DW, Morgantini LE, Cryer KJ. 2004. Harvest retention patches are insufficient as stand analogues of fire residuals for litter-dwelling beetles in northern coniferous forests. *Can. J. For. Res.* 34:1319–31
39. Gara RI, Geiszler DR, Littke WR. 1984. Primary attraction of the mountain pine beetle to lodgepole pine in Oregon. *Ann. Entomol. Soc. Am.* 77:333–34
40. Gersich FM, Brusven MA. 1982. Volcanic ash accumulation and ash-voiding mechanisms of aquatic insects. *J. Kans. Entomol. Soc.* 55:290–96
41. Gibbs AG, Matzkin LM. 2001. Evolution of water balance in the genus *Drosophila*. *J. Exp. Biol.* 204:2331–38
42. Grimbacher PS, Stork NE. 2009. How do beetle assemblages respond to cyclonic disturbance of a fragmented tropical rainforest landscape? *Oecologia* 161:591–99
43. Gutschick VP, BassiriRad H. 2010. Biological extreme events: a research framework. *Eos Trans. Am. Geophys. Union* 91:85–86
44. Haddad NM, Holyoak M, Mata TM, Davies KF, Melbourne BA, Preston K. 2008. Species' traits predict the effects of disturbance and productivity on diversity. *Ecol. Lett.* 11:348–56

45. Hadley NF. 1994. *Water Relations of Terrestrial Arthropods*. San Diego, CA: Academic
46. Hale BK, Herms DA, Hansen RC, Clausen TP, Arnold D. 2005. Effects of drought stress and nutrient availability on dry matter allocation, phenolic glycosides, and rapid induced resistance of poplar to two lymantriid defoliators. *J. Chem. Ecol.* 31:2601–20
47. Hance T, van Baaren J, Vernon P, Boivin B. 2007. Impact of extreme temperatures on parasitoids in a climate change perspective. *Annu. Rev. Entomol.* 52:107–26
48. Hanski I, Simberloff D. 1997. The metapopulation approach, its history, conceptual domain, and application to conservation. In *Metapopulation Biology: Ecology, Genetics and Evolution*, ed. IA Hanski, ME Gilpin, pp. 5–26. San Diego, CA: Academic
49. Hanula JL, Wade DD. 2003. Influence of long-term dormant-season burning and fire exclusion on ground-dwelling arthropod populations in longleaf pine flatwoods ecosystems. *For. Ecol. Manag.* 175:163–84
50. Haynes KJ, Cronin JT. 2003. Matrix composition affects the spatial ecology of a prairie planthopper. *Ecology* 84:2856–66
51. Heartsill-Scalley T, Scatena FN, Estrada C, McDowell WH, Lugo AE. 2007. Disturbance and long-term patterns of rainfall and throughfall nutrient fluxes in a subtropical wet forest in Puerto Rico. *J. Hydrol.* 333:472–85
52. Heliövaara K, Väisänen R. 1986. Industrial air pollution and the pine bark bug, *Aradus cinnamomeus* Panz. (Het., Aradidae). *Z. Angew Entomol.* 101:469–78
53. Heliövaara K, Väisänen R. 1993. *Insects and Pollution*. Boca Raton, FL: CRC Press
54. Hinton HE 1960. A fly larva that tolerates dehydration and temperatures of −270° to +102°C. *Nature* 188:336–37
55. Hinton HE. 1960. Cryptobiosis in the larva of *Polypedilum vanderplanki* Hint. (Chironomidae). *J. Insect Physiol.* 5:286–315
56. Hirao T, Murakami M, Iwamoto J, Takafumi H, Oguma H. 2008. Scale-dependent effects of windthrow disturbance on forest arthropod communities. *Ecol. Res.* 23:189–96
57. Hoback WW, Stanley DW. 2001. Insects in hypoxia. *J. Insect Physiol.* 47:533–42
58. Hossain F, Jeyachandran I, Pielke R. 2009. Have large dams altered extreme precipitation patterns? *Eos Trans. Am. Geophys. Union* 90:453–54
59. Hunter MD, Forkner RE. 1999. Hurricane damage influences foliar polyphenolics and subsequent herbivory on surviving trees. *Ecology* 80:2676–82
60. Janzen DH. 1977. What are dandelions and aphids? *Am. Nat.* 111:586–89
61. Jenkins MJ, Herbertson E, Page W, Jorgensen CA. 2008. Bark beetles, fuels, fires and implications for forest management in the Intermountain West. *For. Ecol. Manag.* 254:16–34
62. Johnson DM. 2004. Life history and demography of *Cephaloleia fenestrata* (Hispinae: Chrysomelidae: Coleoptera). *Biotropica* 36:352–61
63. Kharboutli MS, Mack TP. 1993. Tolerance of the striped earwig (Dermaptera: Labiduridae) to hot and dry conditions. *Environ. Entomol.* 22:663–68
64. Kiffney PM, Richardson JS, Bull JP. 2003. Responses of periphyton and insects to experimental manipulation of riparian buffer width along forest streams. *J. Appl. Ecol.* 40:1060–76
65. Kim Y, Kim N. 1997. Cold hardiness in *Spodoptera exigua* (Lepidoptera: Noctuidae). *Environ. Entomol.* 26:1117–23
66. Knight TM, Holt RD. 2005. Fire generates spatial gradients in herbivory: an example from a Florida sandhill ecosystem. *Ecology* 86:587–93
67. Kolb TE, Dodds KA, Clancy KM. 1999. Effect of western spruce budworm defoliation on the physiology and growth of potted Douglas-fir seedlings. *For. Sci.* 45:280–91
68. Kölsch G, Jakobi K, Wegener G, Braune HJ. 2002. Energy metabolism and metabolic rate of the alder leaf beetle, *Agelastica alni* (L.) (Coleoptera: Chrysomelidae) under aerobic and anaerobic conditions: a microcalorimetric study. *J. Insect Physiol.* 48:143–51
69. Koptur S, Rodriguez MC, Oberbauer SF, Weekley C, Herndon A. 2002. Herbivore-free time? Damage to new leaves of woody plants after Hurricane Andrew. *Biotropica* 34:547–54
70. Koren I, Kaufman YJ, Remer LA, Martins JV. 2004. Measurement of the effect of Amazon smoke on inhibition of cloud formation. *Science* 303:1342–45

71. Koricheva J, Larsson S, Haukioja E. 1998. Insect performance on experimentally stressed woody plants: a meta-analysis. *Annu. Rev. Entomol.* 43:195–216
72. Kundzewicz ZW, Hirabayashi Y, Kanae S. 1998. River floods in the changing climate—observations and projections. *Water Resour. Manag.* 24:2633–46
73. Kurz WA, Dymond CC, Stinson G, Rampley GJ, Neilson ET, et al. 2008. Mountain pine beetle and forest carbon feedback to climate change. *Nature* 452:987–90
74. Lambeets K, Vendegehuchte ML, Maelfait JP, Bonte D. 2008. Understanding the impact of flooding on trait-displacements and shifts in assemblage structure of predatory arthropods on river banks. *J. Anim. Ecol.* 77:1162–74
75. Lancaster J. 1996. Scaling the effects of predation and disturbance in a patchy environment. *Oecologia* 107:321–31
76. Lynch HJ, Renkin RA, Crabtree RL, Moorcroft PR. 2006. The influence of previous mountain pine beetle (*Dendroctonus ponderosae*) activity on the 1988 Yellowstone fires. *Ecosystems* 9:1318–27
77. MacLean DA. 2004. Predicting forest insect disturbance regimes for use in emulating natural disturbance. In *Emulating Natural Forest Landscape Disturbances: Concepts and Applications*, ed. AH Perera, LJ Buse, MG Weber, pp. 69–82. New York: Columbia Univ. Press
78. Marske KA, Ivie MA, Hilton GM. 2007. Effects of volcanic ash on the forest canopy insects of Montserrat, West Indies. *Environ. Entomol.* 36:817–25
79. Martin-R M, Cox JR, Ibarra-F F, Alston DG, Banner RE, Malechek JC. 1999. Spittlebug and buffelgrass responses to summer fires in Mexico. *J. Range Manag.* 52:621–25
80. Mattson WJ, Haack RA. 1987. The role of drought in outbreaks of plant-eating insects. *BioScience* 37:110–18
81. McCormick MP, Thomason LW, Trepte CR. 1995. Atmospheric effects of the Mt. Pinatubo eruption. *Nature* 373:399–404
82. McCullough DG, Werner RA, Neumann D. 1998. Fire and insects in northern and boreal forest ecosystems of North America. *Annu. Rev. Entomol.* 43:107–27
83. Meisel JE. 2006. Thermal ecology of the Neotropical army ant, *Eciton burchellii. Ecol. Appl.* 16:913–22
84. Mertl AL, Wilkie KTR, Traniello JFA. 2009. Impact of flooding on the species richness, density and composition of Amazonian litter-nesting ants. *Biotropica* 41:633–41
85. Miller KK, Wagner MR. 1984. Factors influencing pupal distribution of the pandora moth (Lepidoptera: Saturniidae) and their relationship to prescribed burning. *Environ. Entomol.* 13:430–31
86. Mitchell RG, Martin RE. 1980. Fire and insects in pine culture of the Pacific Northwest. *Proc. Conf. Fire For. Meteorol.* 6:182–90
87. Moore JR, Maguire DA. 2005. Natural sway frequencies and damping ratios of trees: influence of crown structure. *Trees* 19:363–73
88. Moretti M, Legg C. 2009. Combining plant and animal traits to assess community functional responses to disturbance. *Ecography* 32:299–309
89. Paquin P, Coderre D. 1997. Deforestation and fire impact on edaphic insect larvae and other macroarthropods. *Environ. Entomol.* 26:21–30
90. Parker TJ, Clancy KM, Mathiasen RL. 2006. Interactions among fire, insects and pathogens in coniferous forests of the interior western United States and Canada. *Agric. For. Entomol.* 8:167–89
91. Pfadt RE, Hardy DM. 1987. A historical look at rangeland grasshoppers and the value of grasshopper control programs. In *Integrated Pest Management on Rangeland*, ed. JL Capinera, pp. 183–95. Boulder, CO: Westview
92. Price PW. 1991. The plant vigor hypothesis and herbivore attack. *Oikos* 62:244–51
93. Raffa KF, Aukema BH, Bentz BJ, Carroll AL, Hicke JA, Turner MG, Romme WH. 2008. Cross-scale drivers of natural disturbances prone to anthropogenic amplification: the dynamics of bark beetle eruptions. *BioScience* 58:501–17
94. Raffa KF, Phillips TW, Salom SM. 1993. Strategies and mechanisms of host colonization by bark beetles. In *Beetle-Pathogen Interactions in Conifer Forests*, ed. TD Schowalter, GM Filip, pp. 103–28. London: Academic
95. Ritchie ME, Tilman D, Knops JMH. 1998. Herbivore effects on plant and nitrogen dynamics in oak savanna. *Ecology* 79:165–77

96. Rodrigues A, Cunha L, Amaral A, Medeiros J, Garcia P. 2008. Bioavailability of heavy metals and their effects on the midgut cells of a phytophagous insect inhabiting volcanic environments. *Sci. Total Environ.* 406:116–22
97. Roland J, Kaupp WJ. 1995. Reduced transmission of forest tent caterpillar (Lepidoptera: Lasiocampidae) nuclear polyhedrosis virus at the forest edge. *Environ. Entomol.* 24:1175–78
98. Rykken JJ, Moldenke AR, Olson DH. 2007. Headwater riparian forest-floor invertebrate communities associated with alternative forest management practices. *Ecol. Appl.* 17:1168–83
99. Sartwell C, Stevens RE. 1975. Mountain pine beetle in ponderosa pine: prospects for silvicultural control in second-growth stands. *J. For.* 73:136–40
100. Schowalter TD. 1985. Adaptations of insects to disturbance. In *The Ecology of Natural Disturbance and Patch Dynamics*, ed. STA Pickett, PS White, pp. 235–52. Orlando, FL: Academic
101. Schowalter TD. 1995. Canopy arthropod communities in relation to forest age and alternative harvest practices in western Oregon. *For. Ecol. Manag.* 78:115–25
102. Schowalter TD. 2011. *Insect Ecology: An Ecosystem Approach*. San Diego, CA: Elsevier/Academic. 3rd ed.
103. Schowalter TD. 2008. Insect herbivore responses to management practices in conifer forests in North America. *J. Sustain. For.* 26:204–22
104. Schowalter TD, Ganio LM. 2003. Diel, seasonal and disturbance-induced variation in invertebrate assemblages. In *Arthropods of Tropical Forests*, ed. Y Basset, V Novotny, SE Miller, RL Kitching, pp. 315–28. Cambridge, UK: Cambridge Univ. Press
105. Schowalter TD, Lightfoot DC, Whitford WG. 1999. Diversity of arthropod responses to host-plant water stress in a desert ecosystem in southern New Mexico. *Am. Midl. Nat.* 142:281–90
106. Schowalter TD, Lowman MD. 1999. Forest herbivory by insects. In *Ecosystems of the World: Ecosystems of Disturbed Ground*, ed. LR Walker, pp. 269–85. Amsterdam: Elsevier
107. Schowalter TD, Turchin P. 1993. Southern pine beetle infestation development: interaction between pine and hardwood basal areas. *For. Sci.* 39:201–10
108. Schowalter TD, Webb JW, Crossley DA Jr. 1981. Community structure and nutrient content of canopy arthropods in clearcut and uncut forest ecosystems. *Ecology* 62:1010–19
109. Schowalter TD, Zhang YL, Rykken JJ. 2003. Litter invertebrate responses to variable density thinning in western Washington forest. *Ecol. Appl.* 13:1204–11
110. Schütz S, Weissbecker B, Hummel HE, Apel KH, Schmitz H, Bleckmann H. 1999. Insect antenna as a smoke detector. *Nature* 398:298–99
111. Seastedt TR, Crossley DA Jr. 1981. Microarthropod response following cable logging and clear-cutting in the southern Appalachians. *Ecology* 62:126–35
112. Shure DJ, Phillips DL. 1991. Patch size of forest openings and arthropod populations. *Oecologia* 86: 325–34
113. Shure DJ, Wilson LA. 1993. Patch-size effects on plant phenolics in successional openings of the southern Appalachians. *Ecology* 74:55–67
114. Stapp P, Antolin MF, Ball M. 2004. Patterns of extinction in prairie dog metapopulations: plague outbreaks follow El Niño events. *Front. Ecol. Environ.* 2:235–40
115. Sthultz CM, Gehring CA, Whitham TG. 2009. Deadly combination of genes and drought: increased mortality of herbivore-resistant trees in a foundation species. *Glob. Chang. Biol.* 15:1949–61
116. Stige LC, Chan KS, Zhang Z, Frank D, Stenseth NC. 2007. Thousand-year-long Chinese time series reveals climatic forcing of decadal locust dynamics. *Proc. Natl. Acad. Sci. USA* 104:16188–93
117. Stiles JH, Jones RH. 1998. Distribution of the red imported fire ant, *Solenopsis invicta*, in road and powerline habitats. *Landsc. Ecol.* 13:335–46
118. Summerville KS, Courard-Houri D, Dupont MM. 2009. The legacy of timber harvest: Do patterns of species dominance suggest recovery of lepidopteran communities in managed hardwood stands? *For. Ecol. Manag.* 259:8–13
119. Taylor SL, MacLean DA. 2009. Legacy of insect defoliators: increased wind-related mortality two decades after a spruce budworm outbreak. *For. Sci.* 55:256–67
120. Thies C, Steffan-Dewenter I, Tscharntke T. 2003. Effects of landscape context on herbivory and parasitism at different spatial scales. *Oikos* 101:18–25

121. Tisdale RA, Wagner MR. 1990. Effects of photoperiod, temperature, and humidity on oviposition and egg development of *Neodiprion fulviceps* (Hymenoptera: Diprionidae) on cut branches of ponderosa pine. *Environ. Entomol.* 19:456–58
122. Torres JA. 1988. Tropical cyclone effects on insect colonization and abundance in Puerto Rico. *Acta Cient.* 2:40–44
123. Torres JA. 1992. Lepidoptera outbreaks in response to successional changes after the passage of Hurricane Hugo in Puerto Rico. *J. Trop. Ecol.* 8:285–98
124. Ulyshen MD, Horn S, Barnes B, Gandhi KJK. 2010. Impacts of prescribed fire on saproxylic beetles in loblolly pine logs. *Insect Conserv. Divers.* 3:247–51
125. Van Bael SA, Aiello A, Valderrama A, Medianero E, Samaniego M, Wright SJ. 2004. General herbivore outbreak following an El Niño-related drought in a lowland Panamanian forest. *J. Trop. Ecol.* 20:625–33
126. Van Straalen NM, Verhoef HA. 1997. The development of a bioindicator system for soil acidity based on arthropod pH preferences. *J. Appl. Ecol.* 34:217–32
127. Vasconcelos HL, Vieira-Neto EHM, Mundim FM. 2006. Roads alter the colonization dynamics of a keystone herbivore in Neotropical savannas. *Biotropica* 38:661–65
128. Veblen TT, Hadley KS, Nel EM, Kitzberger T, Reid M, Villalba R. 1994. Disturbance regime and disturbance interactions in a Rocky Mountain subalpine forest. *J. Ecol.* 82:125–35
129. Vittor AY, Gilman RH, Tielsch J, Glass G, Shields T, et al. 2006. The effect of deforestation on the human-biting rate of *Anopheles darlingi*, the primary vector of falciparum malaria in the Peruvian Amazon. *Am. J. Trop. Med. Hyg.* 74:3–11
130. Walker LR, Willig MR. 1999. An introduction to terrestrial disturbances. In *Ecosystems of the World: Ecosystems of Disturbed Ground*, ed. LR Walker, pp. 1–16. Amsterdam:Elsevier
131. Waring GL, Price PW. 1990. Plant water stress and gall formation (Cecidomyiidae: *Asphondylia* spp.) on creosote bush (*Larrea tridentata*). *Ecol. Entomol.* 15:87–95
132. Webb MR, Pullin AS. 1998. Effects of submergence by winter floods on diapausing caterpillars of a wetland butterfly, *Lycaena dispar batavus*. *Ecol. Entomol.* 23:96–99
133. White PS, Pickett STA. 1985. Natural disturbance and patch dynamics: an introduction. In *The Ecology of Natural Disturbance and Patch Dynamics*, ed. STA Pickett, PS White, pp. 3–13. Orlando, FL: Academic
134. White TCR. 1969. An index to measure weather-induced stress of trees associated with outbreaks of psyllids in Australia. *Ecology* 50:905–9
135. White TCR. 1976. Weather, food and plagues of locusts. *Oecologia* 22:119–34
136. White TCR. 1984. The abundance of invertebrate herbivores in relation to the availability of nitrogen in stressed food plants. *Oecologia* 63:90–105
137. Whitford WG. 1992. Effects of climate change on soil biotic communities and soil processes. In *Global Warming and Biological Diversity*, ed. RL Peters, TE Lovejoy, pp. 124–36. New Haven, CT: Yale Univ. Press
138. Wickman BE. 1964. Attack habits of *Melanophila consputa* on fire-killed pines. *Pan-Pac. Entomol.* 40:183–86
139. Wikars LO. 2002. Dependence on fire in wood-living insects: an experiment with burned and unburned spruce and birch logs. *J. Insect Conserv.* 6:1–12
140. Wikars LO, Schimmel J. 2001. Immediate effects of fire-severity on soil invertebrates in cut and uncut pine forests. *For. Ecol. Manag.* 141:189–200
141. Willig MR, Camilo GR. 1991. The effect of Hurricane Hugo on six invertebrate species in the Luquillo Experimental Forest of Puerto Rico. *Biotropica* 23:455–61
142. Willig MR, Walker LR. 1999. Disturbance in terrestrial ecosystems: salient themes, synthesis, and future directions. In *Ecosystems of the World: Ecosystems of Disturbed Ground*, ed. LR Walker, pp. 747–67. Amsterdam: Elsevier
143. Wilson EO. 1986. The organization of flood evacuation in the ant genus *Pheidole* (Hymenoptera: Formicidae). *Insectes Soc.* 33:458–69
144. Witcosky JJ, Schowalter TD, Hansen EM. 1986. The influence of time of precommercial thinning on the colonization of Douglas-fir by three species of root-colonizing insects. *Can. J. For. Res.* 16:745–49

145. Wright LC, Berryman AA, Wickman BE. 1986. Abundance of the fir engraver, *Scolytus ventralis*, and the Douglas-fir beetle, *Dendroctonus pseudotsugae*, following tree defoliation by the Douglas-fir tussock moth, *Orgyia pseudotsugata*. *Can. Entomol.* 116:293–305
146. Zerm M, Adis J. 2003. Exceptional anoxia resistance in larval tiger beetle, *Phaeoxantha klugii* (Coleoptera: Cicindelidae). *Physiol. Entomol.* 28:150–53
147. Zhou J, Lau WKM, Masuoka PM, Andre RG, Chamberlin J, et al. 2002. El Niño helps spread bartonellosis epidemics in Peru. *Eos Trans. Am. Geophys. Union* 83:157, 160–61
148. Anderson C, Theraulaz G, Deneubourg J-L. 2002. Self-assemblages in insect societies. *Insectes Soc.* 49:99–110

Sound Strategies: The 65-Million-Year-Old Battle Between Bats and Insects

William E. Conner* and Aaron J. Corcoran

Department of Biology, Wake Forest University, Winston-Salem, North Carolina 27106; email: conner@wfu.edu

Annu. Rev. Entomol. 2012. 57:21–39

First published online as a Review in Advance on August 29, 2011

The *Annual Review of Entomology* is online at ento.annualreviews.org

This article's doi: 10.1146/annurev-ento-121510-133537

0066-4170/12/0107-0021$20.00

*Corresponding author

Keywords

acoustic aposematism, arms race, coevolution, echolocation, mimicry, predator-prey interaction, sonar jamming

Abstract

The intimate details regarding the coevolution of bats and moths have been elucidated over the past 50 years. The bat-moth story began with the evolution of bat sonar, an exquisite ultrasonic system for tracking prey through the night sky. Moths countered with ears tuned to the high frequencies of bat echolocation and with evasive action through directed turns, loops, spirals, drops, and power dives. Some bat species responded by moving the frequency and intensity of their echolocation cries away from the peak sensitivity of moth ears, and the arms race was on. Tiger moths countered by producing anti-bat sounds. Do the sounds advertise moth toxicity, similar to the bright coloration of butterflies; do they startle the bat, giving the moth a momentary advantage in their aerobatic battle; or do they jam the sonar of the bat? The answer is yes. They do all and more in different situations and in different species. Any insect that flies at night must deal with bat predation. Beetles, mantids, true crickets, mole crickets, katydids, green lacewings, and locusts have anti-bat strategies, and we have just scratched the surface. In an exciting new twist, researchers are taking the technologies developed in the laboratory back into the field, where they are poised to appreciate the full richness of this remarkable predator-prey interaction.

INTRODUCTION

Tymbal organ: the sound-producing structure in arctiine moths

An ancient battle rages high above our heads in the night sky. Bats, the consummate nocturnal predators, hunt their insect prey using ultrasonic sonar. Insects counter with myriad behaviors including aerobatic evasions, stealthy adaptations, and anti-bat sounds. The bat-moth story is one of the pillars of neuroethology—predator and prey interactions at their most sophisticated. It rests squarely on the shoulders of two research giants. Donald Griffin laid out the basics of bat echolocation in his classic text *Listening in the Dark* (54), and Kenneth Roeder illuminated insects' counteradaptions in *Nerve Cells and Insect Behavior* (97). In one of his last scientific papers in 2001, Griffin referred to the bat-moth story as a magic well that continues to provide scientists with refreshing insights (55). Here we share what we and researchers in other laboratories have learned from these charismatic animals and their duels in the dark. For treatments from additional perspectives, see Fullard (40), Miller & Surlykke (84), Waters (120), and Ratcliffe (93).

BAT ECHOLOCATION

One of the most important factors in the successful adaptive radiation of bats is their effective echolocation system. All but some Old World fruit bats use echolocation as a means of spatial orientation in the dark, and a large number actively pursue prey either partially or completely guided by sonar (32, 69, 89, 102, 103). Laryngeal echolocation appears to have evolved once in an ancestor of extant species, followed by a rich radiation of echolocation strategies with considerable convergence on successful paradigms (68, 69). Echolocating bats emit ultrasonic pulses and listen for the presence, delay, and harmonic structure of the echoes reflected from objects in the environment. The frequency of the echolocation calls varies from 8 to 215 kHz depending on the bat species. The pulse repetition rate of the calls can vary from roughly 3 to approximately 200 pulses s^{-1} (103, 105). The echolocation prowess of bats has reached its highest expression in the aerial insect-eating bats, which use echolocation to detect, locate, identify, and track prey in flight (**Figure 1**). The echolocation sequence of hunting insectivorous bats involves three main phases: search, approach, and terminal (buzz) (56, 105). During the search phase the bat's flight is relatively straight and the bat produces echolocation calls with a low repetition rate (3–15 Hz) and relatively long duration (5–30 ms). The approach phase begins when a bat first responds to a target by turning toward it and increasing the pulse repetition rate. During the terminal (buzz) phase the bat emits a group of short pulses (0.5–1.0 ms) at a high rate (100–200 Hz) as it closes on its airborne target (71, 72, 103, 105, 110). Echolocating bats vary the intensity, pulse repetition rate, frequency-time structure, directionality, and harmonic components of their echolocation calls according to the situation (50, 51, 108). This plasticity allows them to avoid obstacles and locate objects in different habitats. Bats typically have wing morphologies and echolocation repertoires specialized for the habitat in which they forage (92), and they impose a strong selective pressure for defensive counteradaptations by insects (40, 84). It is appropriate to consider the implications of this predation pressure on the defenses of insects.

MOTH HEARING

Tympanic organs (ears) sensitive to ultrasound have evolved multiple times in nocturnal Lepidoptera and exist in nearly half of extant species (93, 98, 104). High-frequency ears arose from vibration-sensitive proprioreceptors in the thorax (e.g., Noctuoidea), abdomen (e.g., Pyralidae and Geometridae), and mouthparts (e.g., some Sphingidae). These sensors preadapted moths for the detection of airborne sound and the echolocation emissions of bats (49, 123). In the noctuid

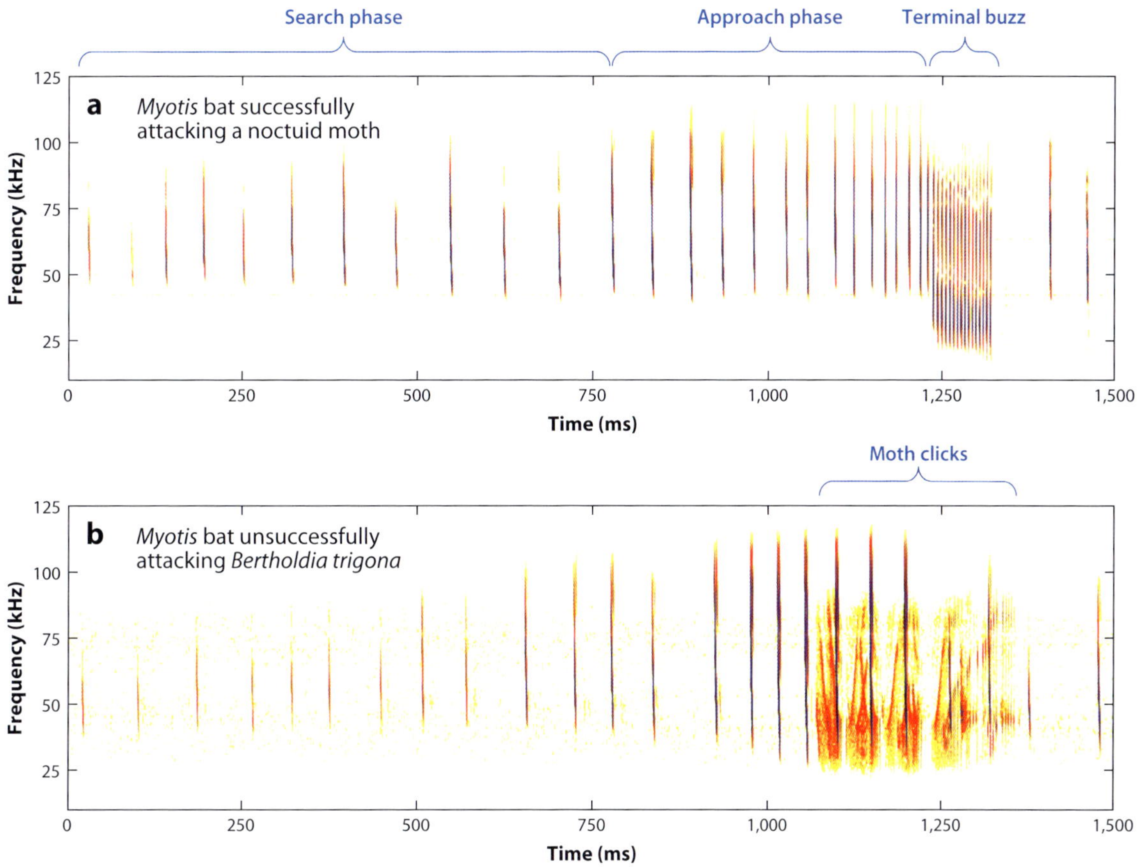

Figure 1

Echolocation sequences of a *Myotis* sp. bat (*a*) successfully attacking a tethered noctuid moth and (*b*) unsuccessfully attacking a tethered sonar-jamming *Bertholdia trigona*. Recordings were made in the field in southeastern Arizona with moths tethered to a 10-m pole and a miniature microphone placed 30 cm above each moth target. See text for a description of echolocation phases.

subfamily Arctiinae, the tiger moths that are the focus of our laboratory, the tympanic membranes are located on the thorax and are typically most sensitive to frequencies between 30 and 50 kHz (38). They are directed to the side, below, and to the rear of the moth (22, 84), optimal for detecting pursuing bats. The tuning of the ears of individual species is often matched to the specific acoustic characteristics of the sympatric bat communities with which they have evolved (33, 38, 39, 41, 43, 107, 111). Moth ears are simple in neurophysiological design, with from one to four sound-sensitive cells, yet they provide their bearers with critical information about their acoustic surroundings (84). They are sufficiently sensitive to detect the echolocation cries of most bats before the bats can register their echo (52, 97). Moth species capable of detecting bats have a clear survival advantage (up to 40%) over species that lack ears (1, 2, 24, 97, 98). It is customary to divide prey defenses into two categories: Primary defenses prevent detection by the predator and secondary defenses enhance survival after detection (27, 93). Moth ears can mediate both types of defenses. If the moth hears the bat first and turns away, avoiding detection, the response would be considered a primary defense. If the moth responds after detection by the bat with more complex aerobatic maneuvers or sound production, the responses would be secondary defenses.

ANSWERING BATS

In addition to hearing ultrasound, many arctiines are also capable of producing ultrasound in the form of short, repetitive clicks in response to tactile stimulation and the ultrasonic signals of echolocating bats (4, 8, 9, 21, 23, 25, 34, 37, 44, 82). The sound-producing organs of arctiines are tymbals, modified cuticular plates (episternites) on either side of the third segment of the thorax. Located ventrolaterally, just above the third pair of legs, each tymbal is clearly visible as a translucent bubble often free of scales. Modified steering muscles beneath the cuticle move the tymbals. As the muscles contract and relax, the cuticle flexes in and out, producing clicks (46). The anterior edge of the tymbal of many species is adorned with small ridges called microtymbals. During the flexion and relaxation cycle the microtymbals produce microclicks, which add complexity to the sounds produced (**Figure 2**). The resulting sounds register their peak intensity in the ultrasonic frequencies ranging from 30 to 75 kHz (4, 21, 44) and have sound pressure levels as high as 119 dB measured at 2 cm (101). Sound production originated in arctiids as a survival

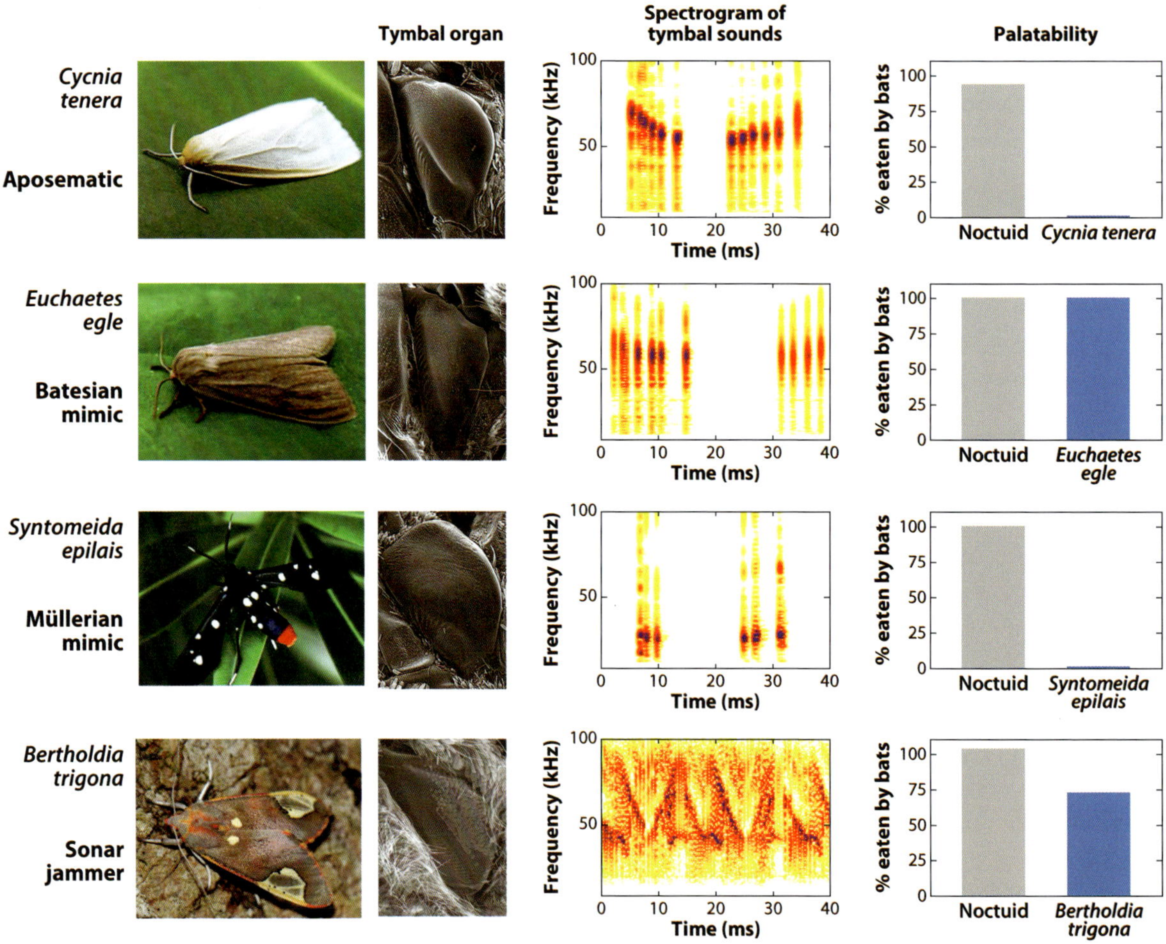

Figure 2

Tiger moth acoustic defense strategies. Column 1: Species name, image, and defensive strategy. Column 2: Scanning electron micrographs of the tymbal organs of each species. Column 3: Spectrogram of tymbal sounds. Column 4: Palatability of species compared to noctuid controls. Data from References 3, 4, 19, 65, and 66.

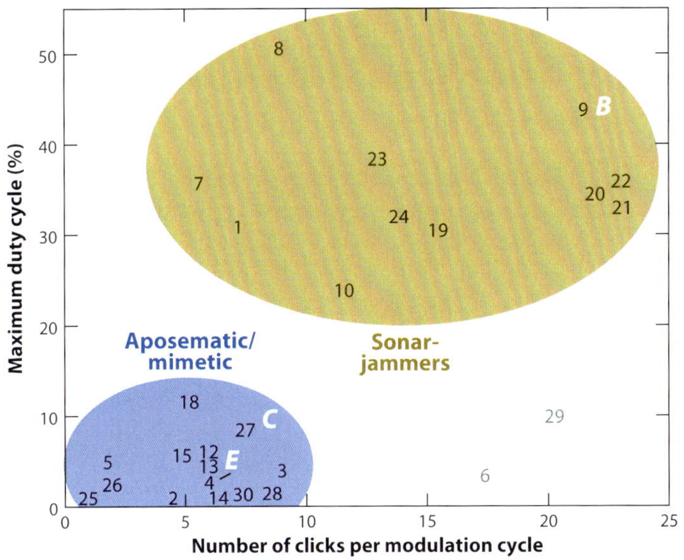

Figure 3

Classification of anti-bat moth sounds plotted in acoustic space along maximum duty cycle (percent of time occupied by sound) and modulation cycle complexity (number of clicks per modulation cycle) axes. Each number represents a species. The sonar-jammers cluster contains *Bertholdia trigona* (*B*) and the aposematic/mimetic cluster contains *Cycnia tenera* (*C*) and *Euchaetes egle* (*E*). Colored areas show proposed acoustic strategies.

tactic against echolocating bats (40) but has been secondarily co-opted for sexual communication (16). It is important to note that ultrasound communication in nonarctiid lepidopteran lineages has evolved by different evolutionary paths (88, 106).

Blest (8) was the first to attempt a serious study of the diversity of tiger moth sounds. On Barro Colorado Island in the Canal Zone, at Volcán and Santa Clara near the Panamá-Costa Rica border, and in Arima Valley of Trinidad, he monitored the sound production of some 180 species without the aid of sophisticated recording equipment. Fullard & Fenton (44) added 24 North American species to the list with detailed sound analysis, and Barber & Conner (4) recorded 84 species on the western slopes of the Andes in Ecuador. In 2010, Corcoran et al. (21) described the diversity of tiger moth sounds in multidimensional acoustic space using a principal component analysis that arrayed the variation in the characteristics of anti-bat sounds along multiple axes. They found that the sounds are not homogeneous but instead vary along a frequency axis, along a duty cycle (percent of time occupied by clicks)/frequency modulation axis, and along a modulation cycle complexity axis (number of clicks produced during flexion and relaxation of the tymbal). Tiger moth species fell into two distinct clusters based on the characteristics of their sounds. One cluster comprised species that produced sound with low duty cycles (<20%) and with relatively few clicks per tymbal activation. The second cluster comprised species with high duty cycles (>20%) and many clicks per tymbal activation (**Figure 3**). This finding is a clue that anti-bat tiger moth sounds can function in fundamentally different ways.

Duty cycle: the percentage of time occupied by sound

Modulation cycle: sound produced by one flexion and relaxation of a tymbal organ

CHEMICAL DEFENSES

Tiger moths are well known for the defensive chemicals that they produce de novo or sequester from their host plants (90, 121). Their chemical repertoire includes biogenic amines, lichen phenolics, azoxyglycosides, and iridoid glycosides (11). The pyrrolizidine alkaloids (PAs) and the cardiac glycosides (CGs) are prominent in both their potency and in the number of species that sequester or produce them (57). PAs have a variety of effects on vertebrates, ranging from bitter taste in low concentrations to tissue damage and death in high concentrations (58, 77). In the context of conditioned avoidance by predators, however, the most important factor for the defensive properties of PAs is their bitter taste. PAs are also effective feeding deterrents for invertebrate and vertebrate predators such as spiders, sucking bugs, birds, and bats (28, 29, 65). Arctiids acquire and sequester PAs in two ways: as larvae while feeding on their PA-laden host plants (57, 119) and as adults imbibing PAs from the surface of withered PA-containing plants (10, 18, 53). The pharmacological effects of cardenolides (cardiac glycosides) stem from their inhibition of the Na^+/K^+ ATPases and the activation of emesis (12). Arctiid larvae obtain CGs from their food plants (usually Asclepiadaceae or Apocynaceae), sequester them in body tissues, and then transfer them to the adult stage through metamorphosis (7, 118). The toxins can be stored in the integument and hemolymph of larvae and adults and are sometimes exuded via secretions from the adults' cervical glands. Both PAs and CGs are effective in deterring bat predation (65, 94).

CG: cardiac glycoside

PA: pyrrolizidine alkaloid

Acoustic aposematism: a prey strategy in which sound warns the predator of the noxious characteristics of the prey

THE BAT-MOTH STORY

The bat-moth story is one of the most sophisticated predator-prey interactions known. The elegant system of acoustic orientation and prey detection of bats renders them extremely capable predators. Arctiid moths have evolved ears, sound-producing structures, and chemical defenses that protect them. Most researchers agree that arctiids generate ultrasonic clicks as a defensive strategy against echolocating bats (95). Several general (and not mutually exclusive) hypotheses concerning the bat-moth acoustic interaction have been proposed (21, 94). The startle hypothesis argues that the sounds elicit the mammalian startle reflex (6, 27, 67, 83). The jamming hypothesis maintains that the sounds confuse the bat by interfering with its echolocation system (45, 48, 83, 85, 94, 109). The aposematism hypothesis claims that the sounds warn the bat of the moth's distastefulness (1, 2, 24, 25, 109). Simply put, these defense mechanisms either orient the bat by providing it with information that it uses to make an attack decision (aposematism) or disorient the bat by interrupting the normal flow of echo information required to complete a successful capture (jamming and startle) (21).

It is clear that all three hypotheses—jamming, startle, and acoustic aposematism—might function in any given interaction. However, it seems highly unlikely that the three hypotheses have the same selective value in nature. Rather, one has provided the main selective advantage driving the evolution of the tymbal and sound production in the Arctiinae. See Ratcliffe & Fullard (94) for a more synthetic view.

STARTLE

Proponents of the startle hypothesis suggest that tiger moths produce a deimatic display that exploits the mammalian startle reflex and gain a momentary advantage that may allow them to escape (27, 60, 63). However, although free-flying bats were initially startled by the low-duty-cycle moth clicks of *Cycnia tenera*, they quickly habituated to them (from one to three presentations in a single night) (6), suggesting that the startle effect is ephemeral and unlikely to be effective under natural conditions for long periods. A more recent study with the high-duty-cycle moth *Bertholdia trigona* found startle-like effects that last for longer periods (up to 40 presentations over two nights) and has resurrected the possibility that they play an important role at least for naive bats (20).

ACOUSTIC APOSEMATISM

The aposematism hypothesis suggests that bats learn to associate moth clicks with the chemical defenses typical of many arctiids. Dunning (23) was the first to find evidence for acoustic aposematism. She presented two groups of moths to caged bats: live unpalatable arctiids capable of producing sound and a control group composed of silent palatable nonarctiid species. The bats avoided clicking arctiids more often than nonclicking species. In a similar study, using caged bats Eckrich & Boppré (26) found evidence for the importance of moth defensive chemistry on the efficacy of sound. Dunning and colleagues later presented arctiids with their tymbals destroyed to free-foraging bats and observed that, on average, bats captured more muted arctiids than sound-producing arctiids. After capture the bats rejected a large proportion of the muted arctiids relative to control nontoxic and nonacoustic moths (23, 24). If jamming or startle alone accounted for the interaction, the researchers should not have observed the dependence of the results on the defensive chemistry of the moths.

C+S+: unpalatable moth that produces sound

C+S−: unpalatable moth that does not produce sound

C−S+: palatable moth that produces sound

C−S−: palatable moth that does not produce sound

Batesian mimicry: a prey strategy in which a palatable individual, the mimic, resembles an unpalatable or otherwise noxious individual and benefits from the resemblance vis-à-vis predators

Müllerian mimicry: a prey strategy in which unpalatable or otherwise noxious species resemble each other, gaining an advantage by sharing the burden of educating predators

Stronger evidence for acoustic aposematism was obtained with a learning approach (66). It is based on the idea that the pattern of a naive (i.e., have never been exposed to moth sounds) bat's success in capturing clicking moths over successive foraging nights should vary for each of the three proposed moth click functions (startle, jamming, and aposematism) and depend on whether the moth is chemically protected (C+) or not (C−) (**Figure 4*a***). Acoustic aposematism would be an effective defense only for C+ moths. Naive bats must learn to associate clicks with distastefulness, so they should initially catch, taste, and drop sound-producing (S+) and distasteful (C+) moths, and then learn to avoid them. The startle response would have the opposite pattern: Bats would at first be startled but then habituate to the clicks; this response should be the same for C+ and C− moths. Jamming would be effective immediately and would remain an effective deterrent for both C+ and C− moths. Common to all the hypotheses is the assumption that bats catch silent S−C+ and S−C− moths as well as controls. The strength of this approach is in its ability to disentangle the defensive effects of clicking and chemistry and its use of naive individuals to obtain results untainted by previous experience.

By choosing moth species that naturally vary in chemistry and sound production ability, or by experimentally manipulating an individual species to vary in these properties, Hristov & Conner (66) could present all possibilities: C+S+, C+S−, C−S+, and C−S− to naive big brown bats. Moths from each of the four groups were presented on a tether to a different group of bats flying individually in a flight room. The changes in the proportions of moths caught and eaten over time were recorded in the form of learning curves (**Figure 4*b***). The results were consistent only with the acoustic aposematism hypothesis—moth clicks were effective at deterring bats only when they were paired with defensive chemistry, and the bats first had to learn this association before the defense became effective. The same results were obtained using multiple moth species (**Figure 4*b***) and by experimentally manipulating an individual arctiid species to fit the four defensive categories (66).

ACOUSTIC MIMICRY

The results described above strongly support the acoustic aposematism hypothesis. Given the evidence for acoustic aposematism, one would expect at least some arctiids to exploit the system through mimicry. Some palatable species should produce sounds but not back them up with defensive chemistry (Batesian mimicry), whereas some unpalatable species should benefit from bearing an acoustic resemblance to other more common unpalatable species (Müllerian mimicry). The latter species would benefit by spreading the costs of educating predators across more individuals.

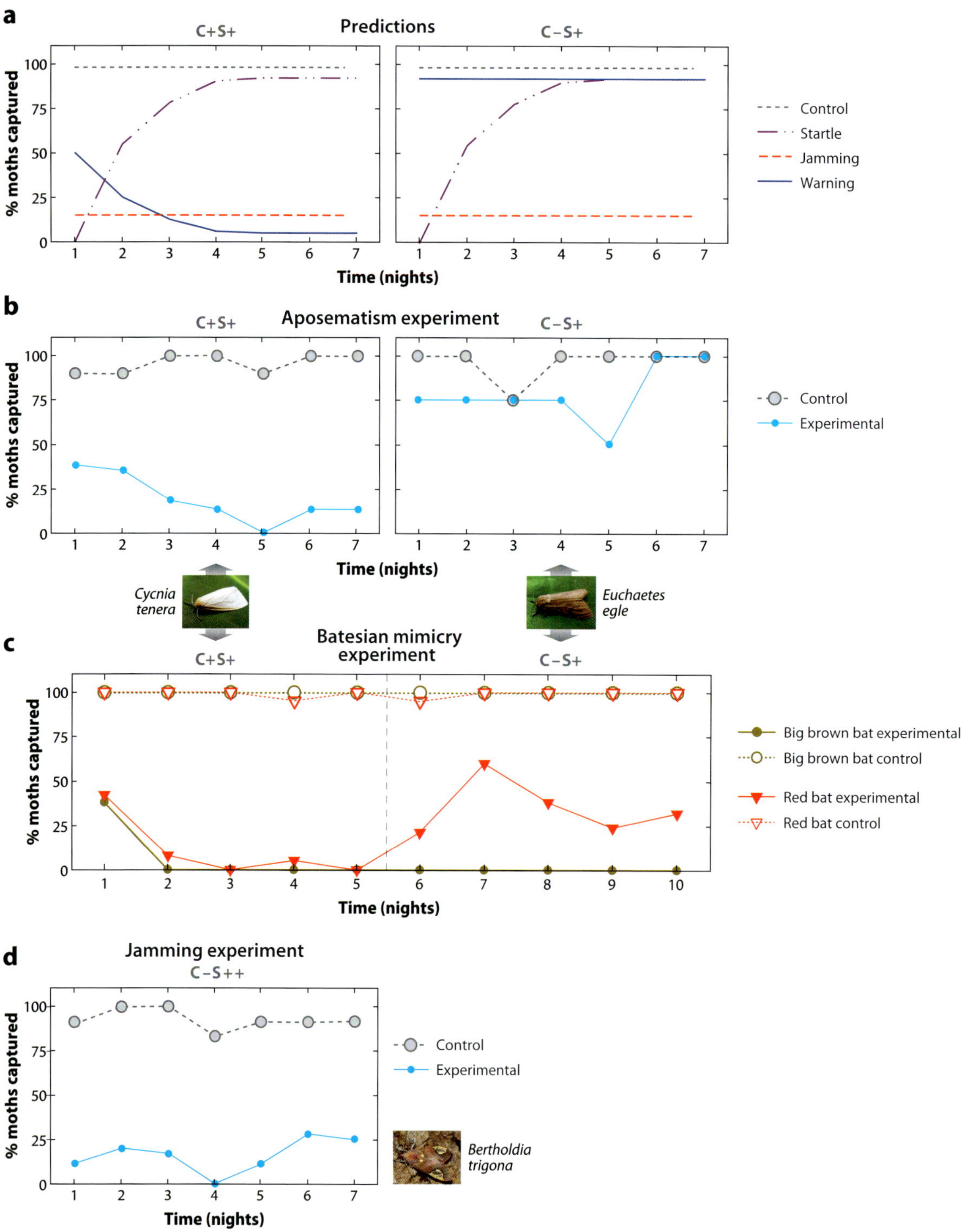
a
Predictions
C+S+
C−S+
% moths captured
100
75
50
25
0
1 2 3 4 5 6 7
Time (nights)
Control
Startle
Jamming
Warning
b
Aposematism experiment
C+S+
C−S+
Control
Experimental
Cycnia tenera
Euchaetes egle
c
Batesian mimicry experiment
C+S+
C−S+
1 2 3 4 5 6 7 8 9 10
Big brown bat experimental
Big brown bat control
Red bat experimental
Red bat control
d
Jamming experiment
C−S++
Control
Experimental
Bertholdia trigona

The learning paradigm gave a unique opportunity to explore these relationships and see whether they function in nature as predicted (5).

Certain moth species (e.g., *Euchaetes egle*) produce sound but have no defensive compounds when raised on their natural host plants. Because sounds alone appear ineffective at jamming or startling bats, it was suggested that these species are acoustic mimics (66). Interestingly, the seasonal phenology of *E. egle* overlaps with *Cycnia tenera*—a common unpalatable species with a similar acoustic signature—which also suggests that *E. egle* may be an acoustic mimic. Dunning found a similar situation for the palatable arctiid *Pyrrharctia isabella* (23) but was unable to confirm her contention under natural conditions. The learning approach allowed for a test of the efficacy of mimicry in a more natural setting.

Sonar jamming: a prey strategy in which the prey sounds render bat sonar less effective

Barber & Conner (5) first presented the toxic and sound-producing model moth *C. tenera* to naive big brown (*Eptesicus fuscus*) or red bats (*Lasiuris borealis*) for five nights (**Figure 4*c***). The bats quickly learned to associate the clicking moths with bad taste and stopped catching them, again illustrating acoustic aposematism. On nights 6 through 10 they presented a second clicking species. This was the critical test of mimicry. They found that the experienced bats generalized clicking species and treated the mimic much like the model, i.e., they did not attempt to catch them (**Figure 4*c***) (3, 5). On the final night of the experiment they disabled the tymbals of the mimics. The bats immediately began to catch the mimics. This clearly illustrated that the tymbal sound (and not any other sensory modality) was the cue that the bats were using to discern the relationship between the first and second moth species. The results showed that *Euchaetes egle* is a Batesian mimic of *C. tenera* (**Figure 4*c***) and that *Syntomeida epilais* is an effective Müllerian mimic of *C. tenera* and vice versa. Acoustic mimics were most effective against big brown bats (beetle specialists that occasionally include moths in their diet) but were still significantly effective against many red bats (moth specialists) (5).

Later work (3) based on the three-dimensional reconstruction of bat flight tracks as they approached model and mimic suggested that the bats can actually distinguish between moths on the basis of their sounds but choose to generalize the warning signal and avoid both model and mimic. Perhaps this is because of the severity of the punishment associated with mistakenly tasting a model.

SONAR JAMMING

Sonar jamming has been a popular hypothesis for anti-bat moth sounds for many years (45, 48), and until recently no hard evidence for it existed in natural bat-moth interactions. Field studies in the cloud forests of western Ecuador identified moth species that have acoustic signals one order of magnitude more complex than those previously described (4). Members of the genus *Bertholdia* stood out because they produce acoustic signals in response to bat cries that are far more complex than would appear to be necessary to advertise distastefulness (**Figure 2**). They have a very high

Figure 4

Predicted and observed success of naive bats attacking arctiid and control moths over successive nights. (*a*) The success of bats attacking chemically defended (C+S+) and palatable (C−S+) clicking moths should vary according to three proposed moth click functions. (*b*) Acoustic aposematism experiment. Naive big brown bat success attacking toxic, clicking *Cycnia tenera* and palatable, clicking *Euchaetes egle* matches predictions of the aposematism hypothesis. (*c*) Batesian mimicry experiment. Red bats (*Lasiuris borealis*) and big brown bats (*Eptesicus fuscus*) learned to avoid *C. tenera* but then avoid subsequently presented *E. egle* due to Batesian mimicry. Intermediate red bat success on days 6–10 reflect three bats that discovered the mimics and four bats that were fooled. (*d*) Jamming experiment. Big brown bats attacking the abundantly clicking and palatable *Bertholdia trigona* demonstrate a response consistent only with the sonar-jamming hypothesis. Adapted from References 3, 4, 19, and 66.

duty cycle, a high degree of frequency modulation, and larger numbers of clicks per tymbal activation cycle, and the clicks are produced during the final moments of a bat's attack—just when jamming should be most effective. These characteristics suggest that they may have evolved to jam the echolocation system of a bat. Feeding experiments showed that *Bertholdia trigona* is palatable to big brown bats; this provided the opportunity to experimentally separate warning sound from jamming again using the learning approach (19). The *Bertholdia* clicks were extremely effective at deterring attacking bats right away (as opposed to the aposematic moths, which require an initial learning period to be effective), and the effect persisted over seven foraging nights. This was the response predicted to be the hallmark of sonar jamming (**Figure 4*d***). Furthermore, bioacoustics analysis of sonar cries during bat attacks on *Bertholdia* revealed changes in echolocation behavior consistent with the jamming hypothesis (19, 20). This was the first conclusive evidence that moth clicks, or any other defensive animal sounds, jam the echolocation system of a predator.

JAMMING MECHANISM

Three mechanisms have been proposed to explain how moth clicks might jam bat sonar. Fullard and colleagues (45, 48) suggested that because some moth clicks and echolocation calls have similar temporal and spectral properties, bats could mistake clicks for echoes returning from nonexistent objects and become thoroughly confused. This hypothesis, the phantom echo hypothesis, has received little empirical support (20, 21, 83, 109, 114, 115). A second possibility, the ranging hypothesis, raised by Miller (83), is that the clicks disrupt the neural mechanism that encodes the time of arrival of the moth's echo and thus gives the bat the distance (or range) of the moth. Miller (83) found that moth clicks can degrade bats' ranging ability by up to 400%, but only when clicks occur in a narrow 2-ms time window preceding the arrival of echoes. Tougaard et al. (114, 115) demonstrated that moth clicks interfere with the neural responses of single units in the lateral lemniscus of big brown bats—a nucleus implicated in target ranging—but again only when they fall within a 2-ms window preceding the test signal (or simulated echo). They concluded that because moths cannot time their clicks to precede echoes, only moth clicks produced at a very high rate, or duty cycle, would effectively interfere with bat sonar. Finally, it is conceivable that moths clicks mask the presence of echoes, much like white noise would, rendering the moth invisible (85, 117).

Distinguishing among the hypotheses for how moth clicks jam bat sonar is not an easy proposition. But the phantom echo hypothesis, the ranging interference hypothesis, and the masking hypothesis should leave telltale clues in the flight tracks and acoustic emissions of bats as they approach a jamming moth. Corcoran et al. (20) again took advantage of *B. trigona* and the way in which naive big brown bats approach them. They found that bats approach control noctuid moths directly. Bats gradually increase their echolocation rate, refreshing their "sonar screens" more rapidly as they approach the target. In the last moments before contact they produce a terminal buzz to get an accurate fix of the exact location of the moth and then cup the moth in their tail membrane for capture. This stereotyped choreography takes place in less than 600 ms. How they approach a clicking *Bertholdia* is another matter. If the moth clicks function as phantom targets, the bats would be expected to veer toward the phantoms to pursue them or perhaps perceive them as clutter (like the echoes from the twigs of a bush) and move quickly away. If the moth clicks interfere with the ability of the bat to determine the exact range of the target, the bats might be expected to miss their target by an amount characteristic of the degree of range interference and to make repeated capture attempts. And last, if the clicks are masking the echo, you might expect the bats to lose the ability to track their target completely. When the experiment was carried out, the bats were first startled by the avid sound producer. After a period of habituation, the bats continued pursuing the moths as they clicked but narrowly missed by a distance predicted by the ranging interference hypothesis. The bats did not make capture attempts either on the moths or on the locations of phantom targets. These results are most consistent with the hypothesis that clicks interfere with the bats' ranging program. *Bertholdia* appears to be able to confuse the bat about its exact location (20).

TAKING THE BAT-MOTH STORY BACK TO THE FIELD

Much of the research described above was done in dark, sound-attenuated rooms viewed with infrared-sensitive video cameras and monitored using one or an array of high-frequency microphones. Although this has allowed researchers to gather evidence for acoustic aposematism, mimicry, and sonar jamming, it falls short of the ultimate goal to decipher what bats and moths actually do in the night sky. The methods and equipment can be made field portable (59, 64), allowing researchers to return to the field. Throughout the world, unfettered bats and moths are battling under the watchful eyes of modern technology. It is here that new strategies and counterstrategies of the bat-moth arms race will be revealed.

A DIVERSITY OF EARS AND ANTI-BAT STRATEGIES

Moths are not the only insects to evolve bat detectors (84). Insect ears have evolved in at least 7 of 27 insect orders (62). The proprioreceptor precursors are found throughout the bodies of insects and so too are ears (62, 122).

Beetles

Tiger beetles (Cicindelidae) possess ultrasound-sensitive ears (107, 125, 129, 130). Their ears are tucked neatly away under the fore of their elytra; thus they only hear when they are in flight, when their elytra are elevated. Hearing appears to be a shared primitive trait in the family. Many tiger beetles respond to bat sonar with head roles, elytra swings, and changes in wingbeat frequency that should result in altered flight trajectories and render them a more difficult target for bats. Much like tiger moths, several North American genera answer the sonar signals of feeding bats with trains of ultrasonic clicks. The sounds are produced by swinging the elytra down into the path of the flapping hindwings. The function of the tiger moth clicks, whether warning, startle, mimicry, or jamming, are not yet known.

Some night-flying dynastine scarab beetles (Scarabaeidae) also have ultrasound-sensitive ears (34, 36). They are located on the cervical membranes and represent an independent evolution of auditory organs in the Coleoptera. In response to simulated bat cries (20–80 kHz) beetles executed a head role characteristic of in-flight turning and dropped to the ground, classic anti-bat maneuvers (35). Because some bat species are beetle specialists (14), it seems likely that many more beetles will prove sensitive to ultrasound and display anti-bat behaviors.

Mantids

Yager & Hoy (126) discovered a median cyclopean ear in praying mantids (Mantodea). Although the ear is composed of two tympanic membranes on the ventral midline of the thorax, it functions as a single unit, hence the term cyclopean. Sixty-five percent of all mantids have them and they are generally sensitive to sounds between 25 and 50 kHz (124). In *Parasphendale agrionina* (Mantidae), the ears mediate a suite of defensive behaviors that include extension of the forelegs, rolling the head to the side, changes in wingbeat and excursion, and curling of the abdomen upward (127). The behaviors result in clear evasive maneuvers—dives, turns, and spirals—that thwart capture by echolocating bats (128).

Lacewings

One of the most interesting insect bat detectors is the ear found on the wings of green lacewings (Chrysopidae). The ear is a swelling located on the radial vein of the forewings (80). When a green lacewing detects the sonar signals of a bat, it folds its wings and drops rapidly. To render its trajectory less predictable, it extends its wings, i.e., puts on its air breaks, at random intervals (81). Interestingly, bats may counter dropping strategies by approaching targets from underneath (see Bat Countermeasures to Insect Defenses: The Arms Race, below).

Crickets

Female true crickets (Gryllidae) including Australian oceanic field crickets, *Teleogryllus oceanicus*, use their ears to localize the low-frequency calling song of potential mates. A second high-frequency peak in the sensitivity of their hearing (86) allows them to detect and steer away from bats while searching for mates (78, 79, 86, 91). Similar responses have been noted in members of the genus *Gryllus* (30, 63). Cricket ears are located just below the "knee" (tibia-femur joint) on the forelegs in the location of the proprioreceptive subgenal organ in other insects.

Mole Crickets

As their name implies, male mole crickets (Gryllotalpidae) dig burrows. They position themselves in a trumpet-shaped burrow and project their mating call with great intensity. Females fly to the males guided by the calling song. Like true crickets, gryllotalpids define their acoustic world by frequency. Low-carrier frequencies define mates and high-carrier frequencies define predators, bats (76).

Katydids

Recent studies indicate that some katydids (Tettigoniidae) can detect the bat sonar signal of gleaning bats (31, 113). In response to the echolocation calls of sympatric bats, they shut down their own acoustic courtship displays to avoid passive detection by gleaners. Flying *Neoconocephalus ensiger* shows classic bat avoidance in the presence of bat-like ultrasound. Within 50 ms of receiving a sound pulse, they close all four wings and begin a free fall (75).

Locusts

Adult migratory locusts (*Locusta migratoria*: Acrididae) speed up their flight and turn away from ultrasonic pulses that mimic bat echolocation calls. This response is mediated by paired abdominal tympana (96) and is considered an early warning system for bats. Interestingly, African tribes take advantage of the high-frequency hearing of locusts by rapping a metallic pot to deflect medium-sized swarms of locusts from their property (96).

Earless Insects

Insects without ears are not totally at the mercy of echolocating predators. Nocturnal moths that lack bat-detecting ears should fly particularly fast or fly erratically (74). Another option is to fly close to vegetation in what bioacousticians refer to as the clutter zone, an area in which the echoes of the prey are lost in the myriad echoes from nearby vegetation (73). Lekking ghost moths (*Hepialus humuli*) appear to use this strategy. They carry out their sexual flight displays within 0.5 m of the surrounding vegetation and gain protection by exploiting the clutter zone (99). Water striders may employ a similar strategy against gleaning bats by staying near the edges of water during times of peak bat activity (112). Earless moths have also been shown to avoid the peak foraging times of bats (47, 74), to decrease the total time in flight, or both (13, 87). Taking this to the extreme, some groups (including eared species) have become increasingly diurnal and thus avoid bat predation to a great extent (40, 43).

Clutter zone: a zone near vegetation or other substrates in which prey echoes blend in with the echoes of the background and make prey detection more difficult

Allotonic frequency hypothesis: the idea that over evolutionary time bat species shift the frequency of their echolocation signals away from the frequencies to which moths are most sensitive

BAT COUNTERMEASURES TO INSECT DEFENSES: THE ARMS RACE

For the predator-prey interactions described above to be called an arms race, the two players must be locked in an evolutionary struggle with sequential adaptations and counteradaptions (100). The current frequency sensitivity of moth ears is clearly the result of the selective pressures of bats. The question is, Have bats countered? Fullard was the first to address this issue with the allotonic frequency hypothesis. He argued that some bats have lowered the frequency of their echolocation sonar, rendering them difficult for the moths to detect (40). Other bat species may have countered by moving to ultrahigh frequencies above the frequency sensitivity of their moth targets. Although both patterns have been seen in various bat species, each can be argued to have additional advantages such as high resolution at high frequencies and greater echolocation range at lower frequency (100), making counteradaption less clear.

The recent discovery of stealth echolocation has provided the strongest evidence for a counteradaption on the part of a bat (52). *Barbastella barbastellus*, a vespertilionid bat that specializes on eared moth prey, has countered moth hearing by producing echolocation calls 10 to 100 times lower in intensity than related aerial hawking bats (also see 42). This decreases the distance at which the moth can detect the bat by one order of magnitude and gives the bat a distinct advantage when approaching eared prey. Stealth echolocation does come at a cost. The maximum distance at which the bat detects the moth decreases three- to fourfold. This suggests that the adaptation is solely a counteradaptation to moth hearing and bears no further advantage in echolocation strategy.

The nervous systems of insects key not only on the frequency of bat calls but also on the timing of the calls that clue the insect of an impending attack. One example is the call repetition rate of approach-phase echolocation. It has been suggested that big brown bats can omit the critical timing parameters as they approach a target, depriving the insect of the information that it needs to trigger evasive action. This may also be construed as a counteradaptation (116).

Researchers are becoming more sophisticated in their study and understanding of pursuit strategies in bats (50, 51). It appears that specific maneuvers employed by red bats, such as approaching prey from below and using their tail membranes to anticipate and thwart dropping behavior, may represent counteradaptions to predictable prey evasion tactics. Additional research is needed here.

THE FUTURE

As efficient nocturnal predators, bats have been shown to limit arthropod abundance in some habitats (70). New molecular methods applied to bat guano provide a summary of the insects eaten by bats (14, 15) and point out how little we know about the details of this important predator-prey interaction. Following in the footsteps of Roeder, most researchers have concentrated on bat-moth interactions, but there is much more to learn. Countless species of insects representing at least nine orders are known to be active at night and are eaten by bats. We know about the workings of only a handful of insect ears and even fewer animals that answer echolocation. Like the deepest ocean trench or the most isolated rainforest valley, the night sky remains largely unexplored. Using the beautiful analogy of Donald Griffin (55): The magic well remains full.

SUMMARY POINTS

1. Echolocating bats have been a major selective force on nocturnal insects, resulting in an escalating arms race of bat sonar adaptations and insect anti-bat counteradaptations.
2. Some insects produce anti-bat sounds when they detect the sonar signals of attacking bats.
3. Anti-bat sounds function in acoustic aposematism, startle, Batesian mimicry, Müllerian mimicry, and sonar jamming.
4. Sonar jamming appears to function by interfering with the target-ranging program of bats.
5. Moths, beetles, mantids, lacewings, crickets, mole crickets, katydids, and locusts can detect the sonar emissions of bats and exhibit various forms of anti-bat behavior.
6. Researchers are beginning to use sophisticated high-speed infrared videography and high-frequency microphone arrays to study bat-insect interactions under natural conditions.
7. The nocturnal sky remains a largely unexplored habitat that will yield a multitude of exciting predator-prey interactions in the future.

DISCLOSURE STATEMENT

The authors are not aware of any affiliations, memberships, funding, or financial holdings that might be perceived as affecting the objectivity of this review.

ACKNOWLEDGMENTS

This review is dedicated to the memory of Professor Thomas Eisner of Cornell University. Tom relished the defensive strategies of insects and was an inspiration to us all. We thank Jesse Barber, Nickolay Hristov, and Mark Sanderford for comments on an early version of the manuscript and for providing photographs.

LITERATURE CITED

1. Acharya L, Fenton MB. 1992. Echolocation behavior of vespertilionid bats (*Lasiurus cinereus* and *Lasiurus borealis*) attacking airborne targets including arctiid moths. *Can. J. Zool.* 70:1292–98
2. Acharya L, Fenton MB. 1999. Bat attacks and moth defensive behaviour around street lights. *Can. J. Zool.* 77:27–33
3. Barber JR, Chadwell B, Garrett N, French B, Conner WE. 2009. Naïve bats discriminate arctiid moth warning sounds but generalize their aposematic meaning. *J. Exp. Biol.* 212:2141–48

4. Barber JR, Conner WE. 2006. Tiger moth responses to simulated bat attack: duty cycle and timing. *J. Exp. Biol.* 209:2637–50
5. Barber JR, Conner WE. 2007. Acoustic mimicry in a predator-prey interaction. *Proc. Natl. Acad. Sci. USA* 104:9331–34
6. Bates DL, Fenton MN. 1990. Aposematism or startle? Predators learn their responses to the defense of prey. *Can. J. Zool.* 68:49–52
7. Black DW. 1976. *Studies on cardiac glycoside storage in moths.* PhD diss. Univ. Miami. 87 pp.
8. Blest AD. 1964. Protective display and sound production in some New World arctiid and ctenuchid moths. *Zoologica* 49:161–81
9. Blest AD, Collett TS, Pye JD. 1963. The generation of ultrasonic signals by a New World arctiid moth. *Proc. R. Soc. Lond. Sci. Ser. B* 158:196–207
10. Boppré M. 1990. Lepidoptera and pyrrolizidine alkaloids, exemplification of complexity in chemical ecology. *J. Chem. Ecol.* 16:165–85
11. Bowers MD. 2009. Chemical defenses in woolly bears: sequestration and efficacy against predators and parasitoids. See Ref. 17, pp. 83–101
12. Brower LP. 1984. Chemical defenses in butterflies. In *The Biology of Butterflies*, ed. RI Vane-Wright, PR Ackery, pp. 109–34. London: Academic
13. Cardone B, Fullard JH. 1988. Auditory characteristics and sexual dimorphism is the gypsy moth. *Physiol. Entomol.* 13:9–14
14. Clare EL, Barber BR, Sweeney BW, Herbert PD, Fenton MB. 2011. Eating local: influences of habitat on the diet of little brown bats (*Myotis lucifugus*). *Mol. Ecol.* 20:1772–80
15. Clare EL, Fraser EE, Braid HE, Fenton MB, Hebert DN. 2009. Species on the menu of a generalist predator, the Easter red bat (*Lasiurus borealis*): using a molecular approach to detect arthropod prey. *Mol. Ecol.* 18(11):2532–42
16. Conner WE. 1999. *Un chant d'appel amoureux*: acoustic communication in moths. *J. Exp. Biol.* 202:1711–23
17. Conner WE, ed. 2009. *Tiger Moths and Woolly Bears: Behavior, Ecology, and Evolution of the Arctiidae.* New York: Oxford Univ. Press
18. Conner WE, Jordan AT. 2009. From armaments to ornaments: the relationship between chemical defense and sex in tiger moths. See Ref. 17, pp. 155–72
19. Corcoran AJ, Barber JR, Conner WE. 2009. Tiger moth jams bat sonar. *Science* 325:325–27
20. Corcoran AJ, Barber JR, Hristov NI, Conner WE. 2011. How do tiger moths jam bat sonar? *J. Exp. Biol.* 214:2416–25
21. Corcoran AJ, Conner WE, Barber JR. 2010. Anti-bat tiger moth sounds: form and function. *Curr. Zool.* 56(3):358–69
22. Coro F, Mojena O, Alonso N, Castellanos O. 1986. Direcionalidad horizontal del órgano timpánico en dos especies de lepidópteros. *Cien. Biol.* 36:31–38
23. Dunning DC. 1968. Warning sounds of moths. *Z. Tierpsychol.* 25:129–38
24. Dunning DC, Acharya L, Merriman CB, Ferro LD. 1992. Interactions between bats and arctiid moths. *Can. J. Zool.* 70:2218–23
25. Dunning DC, Roeder KD. 1965. Moth sounds and the insect-catching behavior of bats. *Science* 147:173–74
26. Eckrich M, Boppré M. 1990. Chemical versus acoustic cues in the defense of arctiid moths (Lepidoptera) against small mammals. *Verh. Dtsch. Zool. Ges.* 83:632
27. Edmunds M. 1974. *Defence in Animals: A Survey of Anti-Predator Defences.* Essex, UK: Longman
28. Eisner T, Eisner M. 1991. Unpalatability of the pyrrolizidine alkaloid-containing moth *Utetheisa ornatrix*, and its larva, to wolf spiders. *Psyche* 98:111–18
29. Eisner T, Meinwald J. 2003. Alkaloid-derived pheromones and sexual selection in Lepidoptera. In *Insect Pheromone Biochemistry and Molecular Biology*, ed. GJ Blomquist, RG Vogt, pp. 341–68. Orlando, FL: Academic
30. Farris HE, Forrest TG, Hoy RR. 1998. The effect of ultrasound on the attractiveness of acoustic mating signals. *Physiol. Entomol.* 23:322–28

5. Conducts first test of acoustic mimicry in a predator-prey system.

15. Applies modern molecular methods to determine insects eaten by bats.

19. Provides first definitive proof of sonar jamming in a predator-prey system.

31. Faure PA, Hoy RR. 2000. The sounds of silence: cessation of singing and song pausing are ultrasound-induced acoustic startle behaviors in the katydid *Neoconocephalus ensiger* (Orthoptera; Tettigoniidae). *J. Comp. Physiol. A* 186:129–42
32. Fenton MB. 1990. The foraging behavior and ecology of animal eating bats. *Can. J. Zool.* 68:411–22
33. Fenton MB, Fullard JH. 1981. Moth hearing and the feeding strategies of bats. *Am. Sci.* 69:266–74
34. Fenton MB, Roeder KD. 1974. The microtymbals of some Arctiidae. *J. Lepidopt. Soc.* 28:205–11
35. Forrest TG, Farris HE, Hoy RR. 1995. Ultrasound acoustic startle response in scarab beetles. *J. Exp. Biol.* 198:2593–98
36. Forrest TG, Read MP, Farris HE, Hoy RR. 1997. A tympanal hearing organ in scarab beetles. *J. Exp. Biol.* 200:601–6
37. Fullard JH. 1979. Behavioral analyses of auditory sensitivity in *Cycnia tenera* H. (Lepidoptera: Arctiidae). *J. Comp. Physiol.* 129:79–83
38. Fullard JH. 1988. The tuning of moth ears. *Experientia* 44:423–28
39. Fullard JH. 1994. Auditory changes in noctuid moths endemic to a bat-free habitat. *J. Evol. Biol.* 7:435–45
40. Fullard JH. 1998. The sensory coevolution of moths and bats. In *Comparative Hearing: Insects*, ed. RR Hoy, AN Popper, RR Fay, pp. 279–326. New York: Springer
41. Fullard JH, Barclay RMR. 1980. Audition in spring species of arctiid moths as a possible response to differential levels of insectivorous bat predation. *Can. J. Zool.* 58:1745–50
42. Fullard JH, Dawson JW. 1997. The echolocation calls of the spotted bat *Euderma maculatum* are relatively inaudible to moths. *J. Exp. Biol.* 200:129–37
43. Fullard JH, Dawson JW, Otero LD, Surlykke A. 1997. Bat-deafness in day-flying moths (Lepidoptera, Notodontidae, Dioptinae). *J. Comp. Physiol.* 181:477–83
44. Fullard JH, Fenton MB. 1977. Acoustic and behavioral analyses of the sounds produced by some species of Nearctic Arctiidae (Lepidoptera). *Can. J. Zool.* 55:1213–24
45. **Fullard JH, Fenton MB, Simmons JA. 1979. Jamming bat echolocation: the clicks of arctiid moths. *Can. J. Zool.* 57:647–49**
46. Fullard JH, Heller B. 1990. Functional organization of the arctiid moth tymbal (Insecta, Lepidoptera). *J. Morphol.* 204:57–65
47. Fullard JH, Otero LD, Orellana A, Surlykke A. 1993. Auditory sensitivity and diel flight activity in Neotropical Lepidoptera. *Ann. Entomol. Soc. Am.* 93:956–65
48. Fullard JH, Simmons JA, Saillant PA. 1994. Jamming bat echolocation: The dogbane tiger moth *Cycnia tenera* times its clicks to the terminal attack calls of the big brown bat *Eptesicus fuscus*. *J. Exp. Biol.* 194:285–98
49. Fullard JH, Yack JE. 1993. The evolutionary biology of insect hearing. *Trends Ecol. Evol.* 8:248–52
50. **Ghose K, Moss CF. 2003. The sonar beam pattern of a flying bat as it tracks tethered insects. *J. Acoust. Soc. Am.* 114:1120–31**
51. Ghose K, Moss CF. 2006. Steering and hearing: A bat's acoustic gaze is linked to its flight motor output by a delayed adaptive linear law. *J. Neurosci.* 26(6):1704–10
52. **Goerlitz HR, ter Hofstede HM, Zeale MRK, Jones G, Holderied MW. 2010. An aerial-hawking bat uses stealth echolocation to counter moth hearing. *Curr. Biol.* 20:1568–72**
53. Goss GJ. 1979. The interaction between moths and plants containing pyrrolizidine alkaloids. *Environ. Entomol.* 8:487–93
54. Griffin DR. 1958. *Listening in the Dark*. New Haven, CT: Yale Univ. Press
55. Griffin DR. 2001. Return to the magic well: echolocation behavior of bats and responses of insect prey. *Bioscience* 51(7):555–56
56. Griffin DR, Webster FA, Michael CR. 1960. The echolocation of flying insects by bats. *Anim. Behav.* 8:55–61
57. Hartmann T. 2009. Pyrrolizidine alkaloids: the successful adoption of a plant chemical defense. See Ref. 17, pp. 55–81
58. Hartmann T, Witte L. 1995. Chemistry, biology, and chemoecology of the pyrrolizidine alkaloids. In *Alkaloids: Chemical and Biological Perspectives*, ed. SW Pelletier, 9:155–233. Oxford: Pergamon
59. Holderied MW, Baker CJ, Vespe M, Jones G. 2008. Understanding signal design during the pursuit of aerial insects by echolocating bats: tools and applications. *Integr. Comp. Biol.* 48:74–84

45. Suggests that moths might jam bat sonar.

50. Uses state-of-the-art technology in visualization of bat echolocation and insect-tracking strategies in time and space.

52. Provides the first definitive proof that the bat-moth interaction is truly an arms race.

60. Hoy RR. 1989. Startle, categorical response, and attention in acoustic behavior of insects. *Annu. Rev. Neurosci.* 12:355–75
61. Hoy RR. 1992. The evolution of hearing in insects as an adaptation to predation from bats. In *The Evolutionary Biology of Hearing*, ed. DB Webster, RR Fay, AN Popper, pp. 115–30. New York: Springer
62. Hoy RR. 1998. Acute as a bug's ear: an informal discussion of hearing in insects. In *Comparative Hearing: Insects*, ed. RR Hoy, AN Popper, RR Fay, pp. 1–17. New York: Springer
63. Hoy RR, Nolen T, Brodfuehrer P. 1989. The neuroethology of acoustic startle and escape in flying insects. *J. Exp. Biol.* 146:287–306
64. Hristov NI, Betke M, Kunz TH. 2008. Applications of thermal infrared imaging for research in aeroecology. *Integr. Comp. Physiol.* 48:50–59
65. Hristov NI, Conner WE. 2005. Predator-prey interactions: effectiveness of tiger moth chemical defenses against insectivorous bats. *Chemoecology* 15:105–13
66. Hristov NI, Conner WE. 2005. Sound strategy: acoustic aposematism in the bat-tiger moth arms race. *Naturwissenschaften* 92:164–69
67. Humphries DA, Driver PM. 1970. Protean defense by prey animals. *Oecologia* 5:285–302
68. **Jones G, Holderied MW. 2006. Bat echolocation calls: adaptation and convergent evolution. *Proc. R. Soc. Lond. Sci. Ser. B* 274:905–12**

68. Summarizes the evolution of the echolocation strategies of bats.

69. Jones G, Teeling EC. 2006. The evolution of echolocation in bats. *Trends Ecol. Evol.* 21:149–56
70. **Kalka MB, Smith AR, Kalko EKV. 2008. Bats limit arthropods and herbivory in a tropical forest. *Science* 320:71**

70. Provides definitive evidence that bats limit arthropod abundance in tropical forests.

71. Kalko EKV. 1995. Foraging behavior, capture techniques, and echolocation in European pipistrelle bats. *Anim. Behav.* 50:861–80
72. Kalko EKV, Schnitzler H-U. 1989. The echolocation and hunting behavior of Daubenton's bat, *Myotis daubentoni*. *Behav. Ecol. Sociobiol.* 24:225–38
73. Kalko EKV, Schnitzler H-U. 1993. Plasticity in echolocation signals of European pipistrelle bats in search flight: implication for habitat use and prey detection. *Behav. Ecol. Sociobiol.* 33:415–28
74. Lewis FP, Fullard JH, Morrill SB. 1993. Auditory influences on the flight behaviour of moths in a Nearctic site. II. Flight times, heights, and erraticism. *Can. J. Zool.* 71:1562–68
75. Libersat F, Hoy RR. 1991. Ultrasonic startle behaviour in bush crickets (Orthoptera: Tettigoniidae). *J. Comp. Physiol. A* 169:507–14
76. Mason AC, Forrest TG, Hoy RR. 1998. Hearing in mole crickets (Orthoptera: Gryllotalpidae) at sonic and ultrasonic frequencies. *J. Exp. Biol.* 201:1967–79
77. Mattocks AR. 1968. *Chemistry and Toxicology of Pyrrolizidine Alkaloids*. London: Academic
78. May ML, Brodfuehrer PD, Hoy RR. 1988. Kinematic and aerodynamic aspects of ultrasound-induced negative phonotaxis in flying Australian field crickets (*Teleogryllus oceanicus*). *J. Comp. Physiol.* 164:243–49
79. May ML, Hoy RR. 1990. Ultrasound induced yaw movements in the flying Australian field cricket (*Teleogryllus oceanicus*). *J. Exp. Biol.* 149:177–89
80. Miller LA. 1970. Structure of the green lacewing tympanal organ (*Chrysopa carnea*, Neuroptera). *J. Morphol.* 131:359–82
81. Miller LA. 1975. The behavior of green lacewings, *Chrysopa carnea*, in the presence of ultrasound. *J. Insect Physiol.* 21:205–19
82. Miller LA. 1983. How insects detect and avoid bats. In *Neuroethology and Behavioral Physiology*, ed. F Huber, H Markl, pp. 251–66. Berlin: Springer
83. Miller LA. 1991. Arctiid moth clicks can degrade the accuracy of range difference discrimination in echolocating big brown bats *Eptesicus fuscus*. *J. Comp. Physiol. A* 168:571–79
84. Miller LA, Surlykke A. 2001. How some insects detect and avoid being eaten by bats: tactics and countertactics of prey and predator. *BioScience* 51(7):570–81
85. Møhl B, Surlykke A. 1989. Detection of sonar signals in the presence of pulses of masking noise by the echolocating bat *Eptesicus fuscus*. *J. Comp. Physiol. A* 165:119–24
86. Moiseff A, Pollack GS, Hoy RR. 1978. Steering responses of flying crickets to sound and ultrasound: mate attraction and predator avoidance. *Proc. Natl. Acad. Sci. USA* 75(8):4052–56
87. Morrill SB, Fullard JH. 1992. Auditory influences on the flight behavior of moths in a Nearctic site. I. Flight tendency. *Can. J. Zool.* 70:1097–101

88. Nakano R, Ishikawa Y, Tatsuki S, Skals N, Surlykke A, Takanahi T. 2009. Private ultrasonic whispering in moths. *Commun. Integr. Biol.* 2(2):123–26
89. Neuweiler G. 1989. Foraging ecology and audition in echolocating bats. *Trends Ecol. Evol.* 6:160–66
90. Nishida R. 2002. Sequestration of defensive substances from plants by Lepidoptera. *Annu. Rev. Entomol.* 47:57–92
91. Nolan TG, Hoy RR. 1986. Phonotaxis in flying crickets. I. Attraction to the calling song and avoidance of bat-like ultrasound are discrete behaviors. *J. Comp. Physiol.* 159:423–39
92. Norberg UM, Raynor JMV. 1987. Ecological morphology and flight in bats (Mammalia; Chiroptera): wing adaptations, flight performance, foraging strategy and echolocation. *Philos. Trans. R. Soc. Lond. B* 316:335–427
93. Ratcliffe JM. 2010. Predator-prey interaction in an auditory world. In *Cognitive Ecology II*, ed. R Dukas, JM Ratcliffe, pp. 201–28. Chicago: Univ. Chicago Press
94. Ratcliffe JM, Fullard JH. 2005. The adaptive function of tiger moth clicks against echolocating bats: an experimental and synthetic approach. *J. Exp. Biol.* 208:4689–98
95. Ratcliffe JM, Nydam ML. 2008. Multimodal warning signals for a multiple predator world. *Nature* 455:96–99

95. First to use a community-level molecular phylogeny to dissect the role of acoustic and visual signals in moths.

96. Robert D. 1989. The auditory behaviour of flying locusts. *J. Exp. Biol.* 147:279–301
97. Roeder KD. 1967. *Nerve Cells and Insect Behavior*. Cambridge, MA: Harvard Univ. Press. 2nd ed.
98. Roeder KD, Treat AE. 1957. Ultrasonic reception by the tympanic organ of noctuid moths. *J. Exp. Zool.* 134:127–58
99. Rydell J. 1998. Bat defense in lekking ghost swifts (*Hepialus humuli*), a moth without ultrasonic hearing. *Proc. R. Soc. Lond. Sci. Ser. B* 265:1373–76
100. Rydell J, Jones G, Waters D. 1995. Echolocating bats and hearing moths: Who are the winners? *Oikos* 73:419–24
101. Sanderford MV, Conner WE. 1990. Courtship sounds of the polka-dot wasp moth, *Syntomeida epilais* Wlk. *Naturwissenschaften* 77:345–47
102. Schnitzler H-U, Henson OW. 1980. Performance of airborne animal sonar systems: I. Microchiroptera. In *Animal Sonar Systems*, ed. RG Busnel, JF Fish, pp. 109–81. New York: Plenum
103. Schnitzler H-U, Kalko EKV. 2001. Echolocation by insect eating bats. *Bioscience* 51(7):557–69
104. Scoble MJ. 1995. *The Lepidoptera: Form, Function, and Diversity*. London: Natural History Museum and Oxford Univ. Press
105. Simmons JA, Fenton MB, O'Farrell MJ. 1979. Echolocation and pursuit of prey by bats. *Science* 203:16–21
106. Spangler HG. 1988. Moth hearing, defense, and communication. *Annu. Rev. Entomol.* 33:59–81
107. Surlykke A. 1986. Moth hearing on the Faeroe Islands, an area without bats. *Physiol. Entomol.* 11:221–25
108. Surlykke A, Ghose K, Moss CF. 2009. Acoustic scanning of natural scenes by echolocation in the big brown bat, *Eptesicus fuscus*. *J. Exp. Biol.* 212:1011–20
109. Surlykke A, Miller LA. 1985. The influence of arctiid moth clicks on bat echolocation: jamming or warning? *J. Comp. Physiol. A* 156:831–43
110. Surlykke A, Moss CF. 2000. Echolocation behavior of big brown bats, *Eptesicus fuscus*, in the field and the laboratory. *J. Acoust. Soc. Am.* 108(5):2419–29
111. Surlykke A, Skals N, Rydell J, Svensson M. 1998. Sonic hearing in a diurnal geometrid moth, *Archiearis parthenias*, temporally isolated from bats. *Naturwissenschaften* 85:36–37
112. Svensson AM, Danielsson I, Rydell J. 2002. Avoidance of bats by water striders (*Aquarius najas*, Hemiptera). *Hydrobiologia* 489:83–90
113. ter Hofstede HM, Kalko EKV, Fullard JH. 2010. Auditory-based defense against gleaning bats in Neotropical katydids (Orthoptera: Tettigoniidae). *J. Comp. Physiol. A* 196(5):349–58
114. Tougaard J, Casseday JH, Covey E. 1998. Arctiid moths and bat echolocation: Broad band clicks interfere with neural responses to auditory stimuli in the nuclei of the lateral lemniscus of the big brown bat. *J. Comp. Physiol. A* 182:203–15
115. Tougaard J, Miller LA, Simmons JA. 2004. The role of arctiid moths in defense against echolocating bats: interference with temporal processing. In *Advances in the Study of Echolocation in Bats and Dolphins*, ed. JA Thomas, CF Moss, M Vater, pp. 365–71. Chicago: Univ. Chicago Press

116. Triblehorn JD, Ghose K, Bohn K, Moss CF, Yager DD. 2008. Free-flight encounters between praying mantids (*Parasphendale agrionina*) and bats (*Eptesicus fuscus*). *J. Exp. Biol.* 211:555–62
117. Troest N, Møhl B. 1986. The detection of phantom targets in noise by serotine bats: negative evidence for the coherent receiver. *J. Comp Physiol. A* 159:559–67
118. von Nickisch-Rosenegk E, Detzel A, Wink M. 1990. Carrier-mediated uptake of digitoxin by larvae of the cardenolide sequestering moth, *Syntomeida epilais*. *Naturwissenschaften* 77:336–38
119. von Nickisch-Rosenegk E, Schneider D, Wink M. 1990. Time course of pyrrolizidine alkaloid processing in the alkaloid exploiting arctiid moth, *Creatonotus transiens*. *Z. Naturforsch. C* 45:881–94
120. Waters DA. 2003. Bats and moths: What is there left to learn? *Physiol. Entomol.* 28:237–50
121. Weller SJ, Jacobson NL, Conner WE. 1999. The evolution of chemical defenses and mating systems in tiger moths (Lepidoptera: Arctiidae). *Biol. J. Linn. Soc.* 68:557–78
122. Yack J, Fullard JH. 1990. The mechanoreceptive origin of insect tympanal organs: a comparative study of similar nerves in tympanate and atympanate moths. *J. Comp. Neurol.* 300:523–34
123. Yack J, Scudder GGE, Fullard JH. 1999. Evolution of the metathoracic tympanal ear and its mesothoracic homologue in the Macrolepidoptera (Insecta). *Zoomorphology* 119:93–103
124. Yager DD. 1999. Hearing. In *The Praying Mantids*, ed. FR Prete, H Wells, PH Wells, LE Hurd, pp. 93–116. Baltimore, MD: Johns Hopkins Univ. Press
125. Yager DD, Cook AP, Pearson DL, Spangler HG. 2000. A comparative study of ultrasound-triggered behavior in tiger beetles (Cicindelidae). *J. Zool. Lond.* 251:355–68
126. Yager DD, Hoy RR. 1986. The cyclopean ear: a new sense for the praying mantis. *Science* 231:727–29
127. Yager DD, May ML. 1990. Ultrasound-triggered, flight-gated evasive maneuvers in the praying mantis, *Parasphendale agrionina* (Gerst.). II: tethered flight. *J. Exp. Biol.* 152:41–58
128. Yager DD, May ML, Fenton MB. 1990. Ultrasound-triggered, flight-gated evasive maneuvers in the praying mantis, *Parasphendale agrionina* (Gerst.). I: free-flight. *J. Exp. Biol.* 152:17–39
129. Yager DD, Spangler HG. 1995. Characterization of auditory afferents in the tiger beetle, *Cicindela marutha* Dow. *J. Comp. Physiol. A* 176:587–600
130. Yager DD, Spangler HG. 1997. Behavioral response to ultrasound by the tiger beetle, *Cicindela marutha* Dow combines aerodynamic changes and sound production. *J. Exp. Biol.* 200:649–59

Approaches and Incentives to Implement Integrated Pest Management that Addresses Regional and Environmental Issues

Michael J. Brewer[1,*] and Peter B. Goodell[2]

[1]Texas AgriLife Research & Department of Entomology, Texas AgriLife Research and Extension Center Corpus Christi, Texas A&M University, Corpus Christi, Texas 78406; email: mjbrewer@ag.tamu.edu

[2]Statewide Integrated Pest Management Program, Cooperative Extension, Kearney Agricultural Center, University of California, Parlier, California 93648; email: ipmpbg@uckac.edu

Annu. Rev. Entomol. 2012. 57:41–59

First published online as a Review in Advance on August 29, 2011

The *Annual Review of Entomology* is online at ento.annualreviews.org

This article's doi: 10.1146/annurev-ento-120709-144748

0066-4170/12/0107-0041$20.00

*Corresponding author

Keywords

IPM, areawide pest management, landscape scale, multifunctional solutions, resource conservation, agri-environment schemes

Abstract

Agricultural, environmental, and social and policy interests have influenced integrated pest management (IPM) from its inception. The first 50 years of IPM paid special attention to field-based management and market-driven decision making. Concurrently, IPM strategies became available that were best applied both within and beyond the bounds of individual fields and that also provided environmental benefits. This generated an incentives dilemma for farmers: selecting IPM activities for individual fields on the basis of market-based economics versus selecting IPM activities best applied regionally that have longer-term benefits, including environmental benefits, that accrue to the broader community as well as the farmer. Over the past several decades, public-supported incentives, such as financial incentives available to farmers from conservation programs for farms, have begun to be employed to encourage use of conservation techniques, including strategies with IPM relevance. Combining private investments with public support may effectively address the incentives dilemma when advanced IPM strategies are used regionally and provide public goods such as those benefiting resource conservation. This review focuses on adaptation of IPM to these broader issues, on transitions of IPM from primarily individual field-based decision making to coordinated community decision making, and on the form of partnerships needed to gain long-lasting regional and environmental benefits.

INTRODUCTION

There is nothing new to the statement that implementing integrated pest management (IPM) is challenging (22, 23, 108). Excellent presentations of the mechanics of IPM and recommendations to evaluate and accelerate IPM implementation are available in Volume 43 of the *Annual Review of Entomology* (71) and in IPM texts (73, 84, 86, 91). The first 50 years of IPM have paid special attention to the application of IPM to individual fields to increase economic competitiveness while minimizing adverse environmental effects. Concurrently, IPM strategies became available that are best applied with consideration of information and management actions beyond the bounds of individual fields. Theory and supporting empirical research show the potential for pest management enhancement when areawide application of appropriate IPM technologies are deployed (3, 5, 47, 72). Over the past several decades, new forms of public-supported incentives have begun to be employed to encourage the use of conservation techniques, including strategies with IPM relevance, with the intent of relieving environmental risks on agricultural lands and surrounding areas (21, 27).

This review provides background on 50 years of development and implementation of IPM on (*a*) the transition from classic field-based management to a broader management perspective to gain regional benefits. We then focus on advancements during the past several decades in considering (*b*) the broader landscape in implementing IPM and steps used to address the incentives dilemma when advanced IPM strategies are used to provide public goods such as those benefitting resource conservation, and (*c*) the expansion of public-supported conservation-based financial incentives as a specific example to enable farmer participation in conservation efforts that conceptually join conservation and agriculture interests, including IPM. Last, we propose refinements and partnerships of existing agricultural, environmental, and social and policy processes needed to encourage implementation of IPM needed to obtain lasting regional and environmental benefits.

FROM FIELD-BASED MANAGEMENT TO A BROADER PERSPECTIVE

IPM approaches and supporting decision-making tools have evolved since the initial focus of IPM on remedial measures, typically in the form of pesticides, to suppress pests below a level to prevent loss that exceeds the cost of controlling the pest. The economic injury level concept and an outline for its application (the economic threshold) to trigger insecticide use were formally presented by Stern et al. in 1959 (106). Thereafter, IPM approaches and supporting tools were refined for direct application to cropping systems, as presented in many *Annual Review of Entomology* reviews spanning the 1960s through the 1990s (71, 94, 110). In addition, a wealth of IPM strategies and supporting decision-making tools for specific pest-crop cases have been published in the scientific literature, as summarized in reviews in the *Annual Review of Entomology* (e.g., 81, 98) and in IPM texts (36, 73, 84, 86, 91).

A Focus on Field-Based Decision Making and Market-Based Incentives

Implicit in the conceptual development of IPM and explicit in most applications was the emphasis on timing of insecticides, used as a remedial measure to manage a pest expected to cause unacceptable damage, based on market standards and applied to an individual cropping field (22, 36, 106). A mathematical approach was introduced to calculate an estimate of insect activity or, less commonly, plant injury, termed the economic threshold, that when exceeded justified use of an insecticide to manage the pest. Economic thresholds are based on economic costs and values associated with applying pesticides, marketing the crop, and anticipating damage from understanding pest density–crop damage relationships. Pest sampling methods and objective decision-making criteria were developed for cropping system applications to compare measurements taken in an individual field with economic thresholds expressed in the same unit of measure (94). A significant body of research on specific pest-crop cases occurred during the 1960s through the 1990s, and applications were summarized (36, 55, 92).

This approach was an excellent fit for private management entities such as individually or family-owned farms where owners, farm managers, and pest management consultants are responsible for individual fields or small clusters of fields. The incentive structure for implementing IPM centered on market-based costs and values. Agricultural management decisions occurred at the level of individual fields or clusters of fields on a farm, and near-term financial risks were carried by the farm management entity (93, 94, 108, 122). The following exceptions occurred that in good part reinforced the field- and market-based management orientation. Public-supported ministries, agencies, and agricultural research and extension arms of public universities implemented regulations of farm activities, such as pesticide use restrictions, and provided regional pest and environmental risk information and guidance that affected IPM within the field-based decision-making framework (71, 91). Advancements in host plant resistance, crop biotechnology, and pesticide technology related to pest management shifted some decision making before planting but still maintained the field-based focus (74, 104). Collective farming, either imposed or encouraged by governments or special communities, also affected IPM decision making in many parts of the world. Here some early and impressive strides in regional pest management occurred owing to indigenous knowledge or government-directed actions (3, 4, 23, 77, 82). But in large part specific actions to manage pests relied on field-based decision making to trigger pesticide use, especially in countries where much of the development of IPM occurred and where international markets and government relationships were dominant (9, 23).

This framework was applicable to predominant economic, technological, and social conditions of modern agriculture. It was arguably effective in encouraging IPM adoption, improving pest management, and minimizing adverse environmental effects associated with pesticide use. Reductions in pesticide use and associated reductions in human health risks and pollutants were seen when economic thresholds and supporting pest sampling were adopted in field, vegetable, and fruit cropping systems (52, 105). Significant use of IPM in high-value cropping systems measured by the same indicators was reported (103), especially when guided by independent pest management consultants (12, 13). Other policy-manifested actions were mandatory environmental and worker safety regulations tied to pesticide availability and use (9, 88, 100). These were preset conditions in which field-based management occurred. The strides in environmental protection when IPM was employed were arguably impressive, although counter-explanations associated with technology advancement and economic considerations have been offered (122). Regardless of the degree of success, IPM was advocated by agricultural, governmental, agribusiness, and environmental entities in many parts of the world (50, 82). The irony was that pesticide use, and possibly associated environmental risk, increased concurrently as agriculture expanded and intensified (23, 96).

Transitions to Broader Scales and the Incentives Dilemma

Others concluded that IPM adoption by these, in good part, pesticide-related measures was inconsistent with the evolving perspective of IPM to embrace multiple and more sustainable strategies that are well suited to manage pest complexes and maintain a healthy environment (4, 29, 122). This argument centered on ecological aspects of sustainability and environmental considerations of IPM. It recognized that advanced and more sustainable IPM strategies such as biological control and habitat manipulation had not been as readily applied in modern agriculture as pest sampling and economic thresholds to support more judicious use of pesticides. Yet the ecological potential to enhance pest management and to be proactive in addressing environmental concerns was sound (3, 5, 47, 71). Therefore, other social and policy actions were desirable to aid farmers in their management choices affecting pesticide use and environmental protection, including different kinds of incentives and other policy instruments to address an incentives dilemma for farmers. Farmers largely carry the burden of selecting IPM activities for individual fields on the basis of market-driven economics versus selecting IPM activities best applied regionally that have longer-term benefits, including environmental benefits, that accrue to the broader community as well as the farmer. Regional IPM strategies also associated with public goods such as resource conservation were typically more costly in coordination, materials and technology, and deployment (9, 33, 102). One could arguably conclude that future advancement in IPM implementation at broader scales associated with public goods is bleak (29, 122).

Yet for IPM, the steps of transition to address regional and environmental issues began early in its development. Early IPM concepts recognized the importance of considering natural controls and adverse effects of pesticides on them (106). Inroads were made to include biological control and pesticide effects on environmental quality in the IPM decision-making process. The contribution to pest mortality through the action of biological control agents was estimated and used to modify economic thresholds for fruitworms in tomatoes (59), spider mites in almonds (120), caterpillars in alfalfa (49), and aphids in walnuts (109). Also, the potential adverse effects of selected pesticides were used to refine economic thresholds (56). These modifications focused on field-based management, in keeping with IPM decision making of the time.

A holistic perspective came from the framework of IPM as a hierarchy of approaches, scales of implementation, and types of incentives to achieve adoption. Kogan (71) provided an excellent review and synthesis, beginning with the use of economic thresholds and pest sampling that were oriented toward individual field application primarily by market-driven factors within a regulatory framework. The more advanced levels of IPM were based on using multiple strategies and monitoring activities that provided benefits across pest complexes, environmental quality concerns, and farm and regional scales. This advanced level of IPM required a greater knowledge base of agroecology, expanded community involvement, and new forms of incentives (71, 108). Other complementary views focused on lowering risks and raising sustainability by using multifunctional strategies, implementing nonconflicting agricultural and environmental policies, and engaging community networks of knowledge and leadership (9, 27, 63). Advancing IPM and addressing risk elements of pest management technologies through transitional phases were elements of these viewpoints (9, 71).

The foresight to ask "who pays?" was clear: Environmental and other societal and policy interests and market implications of the modifications were discussed and debated (33, 93). Unfortunately, the special needs for different kinds of incentives during much of the development of more advanced IPM strategies were limited largely to public-supported research, education, demonstrations, and special cases of public support for eradication and prevention efforts (9, 30, 62, 71). It was also argued that mandatory pesticide regulations were limited in scope in regard to environmental protection in many parts of the world, that government-sponsored market-support programs were offsetting costs of pesticides, and that indirect environmental and economic costs of pesticide use were not considered in policy and field-level decision making (9, 23, 93, 96).

A reasonable synthesis of the state of the science and practice of IPM during its first 50 years of modern development is that IPM adoption occurred most readily at the scale of the individual field. IPM adoption centered on pest sampling and economic thresholds for pesticide decision making, driven primarily by market factors within a pesticide regulatory framework. Implementation of more advanced approaches that utilize information and actions at broader scales is more challenging. It requires additional societal acceptance, community cooperation, and different forms of incentives to encourage implementation (71). The pace of transition and the incentives dilemma for advanced IPM strategies that provide public goods are of special relevance, given the environmental impact of agricultural intensification including pesticide effects on nontarget organisms, loss of biodiversity, and degradation of soil, water, and air resources (39, 96). Yet the stage was set for consideration of broader ecological, economic, and social views to develop and support IPM that addresses regional and environmental issues.

CONSIDERATION OF THE BROADER LANDSCAPE AND GAINING ENVIRONMENTAL BENEFITS

Over the past few decades a detailed development of IPM approaches has occurred with a more regional orientation to enhance pest management and gain additional environmental benefits. However, as noted in the previous section, the vast majority of IPM strategies implemented successfully occurred at the local field level. At best, multiple organisms might have been considered in developing a solution, for example, choosing compatible target-specific pesticides, pheromone technology, or specific crop varieties that have multiple traits resistant to several pests (74, 101, 104, 113). More commonly, farmer-adopted IPM strategies responded to single-pest outbreaks within a narrow framework of time and space using pesticides and underutilized nonpesticide alternatives (29). Several concerns with this approach from a landscape perspective were notable. Local, individual pest management decisions did not necessarily affect the wider landscape, but accumulated outcomes from multiple field pesticide applications could cause regional adverse environmental harm to water and air quality and biodiversity (96, 101). Also, IPM actions applied with regional coordination could enhance pest management areawide and for longer periods than when applied in an uncoordinated field-by-field basis (72, 122).

Environmental Health Considerations and Mitigation

Perhaps the best documented examples of adverse regional environmental impacts when using pesticides over the past two decades are for surface water and groundwater. Between 1992 and 2001, pesticides were detected in nearly 90% of the streams and rivers surveyed in the United States (39). Pesticides in water and riparian sediment presented risk to aquatic invertebrates, fish, and humans (38). The primary routes of entry from agriculture were pesticide-laden water due to runoff caused by storm events and excessive irrigation, or due to drift from field to surface water. Groundwater was another resource affected by external farm inputs, both pesticides and nutrients. Pesticides were detected but did not exceed human risk benchmarks in 61% of samples from shallow groundwater used for drinking water and in 33% of samples from deeper aquifers (38). The broad detection of herbicides throughout the Midwest provided an excellent example of almost-uniform individual economic-driven decision making across a large agricultural region that resulted in regional resource degradation of the Mississippi River and Delta system (39).

In addition to pest management impact on water quality, IPM decisions involving pesticides applied in field-based management contributed to impaired air quality in limited areas. Six air basins in California were declared nonattainment areas for meeting national clean air quality standards, including the major agricultural regions of the San Joaquin and Sacramento Valleys (41). Additives present in selected fumigant and nonfumigant pesticides contributed volatile organic compounds (VOCs), which led to the formation of ozone. Adverse effects on biodiversity due to agricultural intensification were also well known, as exemplified in the major reductions of plants and animals occurring in the European countryside. Adverse regional effects were related to both forms of intensification of agriculture: high chemical inputs including pesticide use and high concentration of land area devoted to a limited number of crops (6, 7, 65, 115).

A number of strategies with combined IPM and environmental value were available to mitigate these risks. Cultural practices such as winter sanitation in almond orchards reduced the need for midseason treatments of naval orangeworm (*Amyelois transitella*) (121), vegetative ground cover limited runoff of pesticides (61), and use of polyacrylamide, sediment traps, and vegetative ditch banks reduced the amount of contaminated sediment leaving a field (79). Improved application technology reduced pesticide drift (14, 70), and a shift to alternative pesticide products reduced risk to the environment (31, 44, 80) and human health (46). In Europe, strategies related to IPM were implemented with varying success in reducing risk to farmland birds and biodiversity. For example, field margins left unmowed served as habitat for native plants, birds, and insects including pollinators and biological control agents. They also served as filters for nutrients and pesticide runoff (25, 32, 64).

Areawide Pest Management and Decision Making

Areawide pest management was viewed by some investigators as a branch of IPM that stimulated detailed consideration of the broader agricultural landscape, whereas others emphasized its distinctiveness. It differed from IPM centered on application of individual on-farm actions by applying IPM strategies regionally in a coordinated manner to maintain the pest below economic-damaging levels for longer periods across broader areas (30, 122). Transitioning the individual nature of field-based decision making to the community nature of regional decision-making approaches began with an emphasis on areawide management of key pests on major crops that had special interest to groups of farmers, and had complementary private and public support (72). Areawide pest management programs varied greatly in the level of regional pest threat, technologies deployed, types of agreements, and level of private and public investment in the program.

Most successes of areawide management were aimed at a single key pest in a region, where the benefits and justification of the areawide actions were primarily pest driven, with secondary environmental benefits obtained if pesticide risk was reduced (30). This typically involved entering into voluntary or farmer-supported mandated agreements. In some cases, the goal was eradication, such as the boll weevil (*Anthonomus grandis grandis*) in cotton (2), or prevention of a new pest from invading a region, such as the potential introduction of pink bollworm (*Pectinophora gossypiella*) into San Joaquin Valley cotton (California) (53). These programs were structured around farmer-supported mandates. Others attempted voluntary measures to regulate the population of a key pest across an area to reduce the threat to any individual farmer. For example, mating disruption of the codling moth (*Cydia pomonella*) in pears (67) and vine moths in grapes (60) was adopted by a sufficient number of farmers to have the desired regional pest management effect. An arguably effective and simple case of an areawide approach was exemplified by the case of the silverleaf whitefly (*Bemisia argentifolii*) in Arizona. An agreement within a farmer community defined by the cropping system and insecticide use patterns specified voluntary adherence to guidelines for use of key active ingredients of insecticides in order to sustain crop protection (89). There are fewer examples that embrace management of multiple pests or across multiple crops, including an insect pest complex of tomato (113) and citrus insect pests (45, 122). Last, the development of more localized pest control districts functioned for decades as areawide biological control zones (45) (see sidebar Fillmore Citrus Protective District, 1922–2004). These programs benefitted from a combination of technology advancement, grower collectives and agreements, and partially public-supported services.

FILLMORE CITRUS PROTECTIVE DISTRICT, 1922–2004

In 1922, a group of local citrus growers in the Fillmore citrus district (California) formed a pest management protective district. Threatened by invasive citrus pests, growers realized that only by banding together to share the risk could they individually survive. Giving up their individual rights for IPM decision making, they turned the decisions for pest management over to the District, allowing the District to place resources where they would do the most good for the community. Membership was strictly voluntary and services were paid through self-assessment of members. The spread of California red scale infestations was greatly limited within the District from 1922 to 1928. In 1926, a new pest arrived that was not effectively controlled with fumigation, and a District-financed insectary was built to provide a supply of natural enemies. Over the years, the Fillmore Insectary provided natural enemies for scale pests, moving away from reliance on pesticides to more biological control. Unfortunately, the citrus economic conditions in 2003 required a shift to fruit and vegetable crops, the common interests of the local citrus community dissolved, and the District and Insectary closed (45).

Above we focused on the agricultural pest threat and the regional process for areawide pest management decision making. An agroecological key to program success was considering the landscape in which the cropping system and pests coexist, as demonstrated by empirical evidence (6, 10, 114) and supported by metapopulation dynamics and landscape ecology theory (30, 78). The agroecological goal was to favor crop production at the expense of the pest with least interference to the ecosystem in which it is embedded, an approach also consistent with the concept of ecological engineering for pest management (47). The dispersal characteristics of the pest (17), the strength of individual plants to act as sources or sinks (19) and the potential for biological control (48, 114) needed to be understood to optimize cropping system planning. Planning included a combination of in-field local action to consistently manage pests in crops and noncultivated fields, regional action in shifting cropping patterns to those less favorable to pests, and both local and regional action in increasing the planting of food and shelter habitat for natural enemies and native pollinators (48, 72, 95). Cropping systems varied in these areawide programs: Crop mosaics shifted in time and space, continually changing advantage among various pests, their crop hosts, and the surrounding environment. The surrounding environment also varied in biodiversity and vegetation complexity, thus having an effect on biological control agents (10, 114).

Overall, the driving force of areawide pest management programs was the recognition that economical pest management was dependent on everyone working together. Success of such programs depended on this recognition regionally, adequate agricultural and ecological knowledge, availability of appropriate IPM technologies, social aspects of local leadership and community structure, and effective social and policy tools such as formal agreements and public support (30, 62, 99, 101).

Approaches to Address the Incentives Dilemma

Coordinated regional effort to obtain durable pest management effects was challenging. The desire for community cooperation and relinquishing control of some field-based management decisions must be greater than the desire to control individual fields and farms. Combined with strong agreements and common goals as presented above, various forms of incentives may assist in moving to this tipping point for community decision making (8, 11, 93).

The manner in which this incentives dilemma had been addressed in areawide programs varied from no public support beyond technical guidance from extension and research services, to substantial public investment because of the severity of the pest situation or because of proactive actions to gain additional environmental benefits. First, consider the case of the areawide eradication effort for the boll weevil in the cotton belt of the United States, which was implemented at a subcontinental scale progressively over 30 years and continues today. Based on regional insect pest suppression (68), this program benefitted from supporting incentives in the form of joined public and private financing and technical support, and farmer- and legislative-approved regulations. Pairing governmental and farmer-supported actions led to significant achievements, albeit not without ecological and economic controversy. The boll weevil now remains only in southern Texas (2, 108).

Conservation programs for farms: public-supported voluntary incentives programs, known as agri-environment schemes in Europe and conservation programs for working lands in the United States

Second, consider the case of regional decision making facilitated by the size of the management entity. In this case, a single farming operation was of such a large scale that uniform crop and noncrop management actions could be taken across a broad area to influence the movement of the western tarnished plant bug (*Lygus hesperus*). The impact on susceptible cotton was minimized by placing sources (seed alfalfa and safflower) on the downwind margins of large cotton fields (42). Field sources of the *L. hesperus* were managed by timing insecticide application on safflower to suppress the population before they became winged adults (85). Alfalfa, a preferred host and sink, was introduced, and movement was mitigated by leaving strips of uncut alfalfa as preferred habitat (111). Finally, sources of the *L. hesperus* were concentrated to create the smallest perimeter-to-area ratio to minimize the border between cotton and safflower (43). Combined, all these steps resulted in minimal pesticide intervention for this key pest of cotton.

Third, consider the case of addressing pest complexes regionally with largely private investments coming from multiple management entities. The example of the Fillmore Citrus Protective District (45) (see sidebar Fillmore Citrus Protective District, 1922–2004) is an example of the rare creation of a voluntary district that had longevity, utilized private investments obtained from farmer self-assessments to run the program, and emphasized use of advanced IPM strategies with environmental benefits. Public support was limited to traditional extension and research of government agencies and affiliated universities. Last, the reader is referred to the following section for examples of utilizing public-supported incentives of conservation programs for farms to encourage farmer adoption of IPM-related techniques that provide additional environmental benefits.

Developing regional goals of agricultural benefits (less risk to income, production with reduced external inputs) and additional benefits contributing to the public good (improved environmental quality and countryside aesthetics) requires consideration of the landscape, regional decision making, and addressing the incentives dilemma. Single-entity management of large farms, farming community investment in local management districts, and public support have been used to overcome the incentives dilemma. Public support may come in the form of traditional technical assistance of public research and extension that provides the knowledge base needed for implementation, and financial incentives to offset costs associated with actions to gain regional and environmental benefits.

CONNECTIONS TO PUBLIC-SUPPORTED CONSERVATION FOR FARMS

As discussed above, IPM strategies with regional pest management value and expanded environmental benefits have presented the challenges of broadening the scale of entomological and environmental information gathered, incorporating it into a joint field and regional decision-making structure, and supporting it with broader-based incentives. In this section, major conservation programs for farms are introduced that may complement IPM and partly satisfy these challenges.

Conservation Programs for Farms

In review of the published literature, the major conservation programs devoted to agricultural lands were found principally in developed countries, especially in the United States and Canada (27, 88), the European Union and nonmember countries of Europe (27, 64, 66), and selected other countries (119). Set-aside programs sponsor taking agricultural lands out of production, which affects insect conservation and pest management (35, 54, 117). Here, we focused on programs for lands in agricultural production where public-supported financial incentives were offered to farmers to adopt conservation techniques that addressed resources in a state of current or potential degradation related to agricultural activities (27, 64, 66, 88). IPM complements this approach: Advanced IPM strategies provide various environmental benefits when properly implemented (8, 11). Moving resource conservation onto agricultural lands, especially in developed countries where intensive agriculture occurs, was encouraged in the ecological restoration literature. Ecologically, this was justified by the substantial portion of the land mass devoted to agriculture; recognition of declines in biodiversity and quality of soil, water, and air resources associated with agricultural intensification; and the need for connectivity of resources across natural and agricultural landscapes (6, 24, 87, 119). Economic support for this effort, in the form of conservation-based financial incentives to farmers, obtained wider policy support over the past two decades, as this form of agricultural financial assistance fits into the green box exception of World Trade Organization rules (27).

Conservation techniques: known as options or prescriptions (Europe) and practices (United States); incentives are provided to farmers to encourage their use

Green box exception: agricultural subsidies supporting environmental protection with no trade-distorting effects, mostly implemented in the United States and European Union

Resources of conservation concern: natural resources in a current or potential state of degradation, as targeted by conservation programs for farms

In Europe, a large group of conservation programs for farms became available as financially supported in good part by the Common Agricultural Policy of the European Union and by other public support mechanisms of nonmember countries such as Switzerland (27, 66). The primary conservation goals and the resources of conservation concern varied across countries, with a strong history and emphasis on farmland bird conservation in the United Kingdom; bird and other biodiversity interests in the Netherlands, Switzerland, Spain, Ireland, and other countries; and agricultural pollutant issues in Germany, Sweden, Denmark, and other countries. A common theme was that agricultural intensification adversely affected the quality of the countryside, and conservation efforts on agricultural lands could reverse this trend if properly applied (6, 16, 64, 66). In the United States, conservation programs for farms were also available, with the largest programs offered by the U.S. Department of Agriculture Natural Resources Conservation Service (USDA NRCS). The USDA NRCS conservation programs were initiated to address soil loss from agricultural lands, and a significant expansion occurred to address a broad array of agriculture-related resources of conservation concern beginning in the 1990s. Soil loss and sediment loading of waterways, nutrient and pesticide loading of groundwater and surface water, and air pollutants from agricultural operations were major thrusts of the programs (88). Some state-level support was available in the form of technical assistance, regulations, and, in rare cases, special taxation zones (41, 76).

Key Issues Facing Conservation Programs and Relationship to IPM

The strong species degradation orientation of programs in Europe and the pollutant orientation of programs in the United States affected the connectivity of the programs to entomology and IPM. These contrasts in emphases resulted in some differences in the listings of techniques available to farmers in the programs. Program evaluations reported that some techniques addressed multiple resources of conservation concerns, whereas others were designed more with ecological considerations of targeted resources of special conservation concern, such as uncommon species and pollutants in a selected region where degradation of the resource was high (32, 58, 66). For example, natural vegetation field margins left unmowed served as filters for nutrients and pesticide runoff as well as habitat for native plants, birds, insects, and other species contributing to ecosystem health (25, 32, 58). In contrast, midfield refuges of perennial grasses placed in strips through cereal fields (beetle banks) provided stronger ecological benefits for targeted breeding bird species of interest (107) but had less utility as a filtering system. Entomology components of studies focused on insects as food to species of conservation concern, as indicators of environmental quality, occasionally as resources of conservation concern themselves, and uncommonly as pests (see sidebar Conservation of Farmland Birds and Links to Insects and references therein). In the United States, entomology interactions with the conservation programs were limited largely to expert opinion on the benefits of pesticide application technologies and advanced IPM strategies to address pesticide-related resource concerns of water and air quality (11, 57, 58) and to evaluation of farmer selection of conservation program techniques that had effects on insect management (41, 58).

The risk of degradation of the resources of conservation concern provided an informative contrast of likely factors associated with program progress and impediments and how the programs related to entomology and IPM. Conservation programs that achieved the greatest success in decreasing the threat to resources of conservation concern were those that made available to farmers well-designed techniques and typically involved resources under a high threat of degradation in specific regions where the threat occurred. The programs themselves may have addressed a broader array of resources of conservation concern but had targeted subprograms or flexibility to focus on local resources of special concern (32, 76, 90). Programs focused on broader resources of conservation concern commonly had greater variability of success in reducing threats to the resources across regions where the program was implemented (64, 66, 107).

Other ecological and agricultural issues associated with program structure affected program progress. Evaluation studies showed that technique effectiveness may vary across selected species of interest (34, 69, 107), in scale of implementation (83, 107), and in locality of implementation as affected by landscape diversity and farm management intensity and interests (115). For example, regional biodiversity benefits were greater in diverse landscapes than in landscapes that were relatively simple (115). See the sidebar Conservation of Farmland Birds and Links to Insects as an instructive example.

Social and policy viewpoints were also important in assessing the potential for IPM involvement in conservation programs for farms (9, 11, 18). When operational considerations were similar, farmers tended to select techniques with higher payments, which did not necessarily reflect greater environmental benefits in the Midwest. IPM techniques available to address farm pollutant concerns had low incentive payments and low farmer selection. In the United Kingdom,

CONSERVATION OF FARMLAND BIRDS AND LINKS TO INSECTS

Conservation programs for farms in the United Kingdom and elsewhere in Europe have focused on farmland birds. Known habitat requirements and other ecological factors associated with species health were used to assess risk of farm activities and to design techniques to reverse species decline. Program efforts benefitted species of special concern such as the gray partridge (*Perdix perdix*) and cirl bunting (*Emberiza cirlus*) for which techniques were especially designed, had variable effects on other farmland birds, and had mixed to limited benefits to biodiversity (7, 16, 32, 64, 90, 107). Insects were found valuable as a food resource for species of special conservation concern (64, 118), as indicators of broader biodiversity health (7, 15, 34, 64–66, 69, 107), and as taxa of additional resource concern such as butterflies and pollinators (1, 28, 64, 83, 97). Explicit studies on pest management implications were more limited but impressive in detail. For example, conservation headlands and beetle bank techniques included pesticide use restrictions and partial reliance on biological controls to control pests in cereal fields (32, 107).

some techniques such as beetle banks were less selected by farmers when technique choices were available, because of the perceived technical difficulties and higher costs to implement beetle banks within the crop (107). In contrast, agricultural participation in program delineation of techniques and payment levels and local flexibility to provide reasonable accommodations to local farmer interests were valuable in encouraging use of IPM strategies to gain conservation benefits (8, 57, 58). Understanding goals and attributes of conservation programs for farms and their challenges was important in establishing positive interactions between the IPM community and conservation programs (11).

Overall, multiple viewpoints are valuable in assessing conservation program progress and impediments and opportunities to integrate IPM into the programs: a conservation view such as resources of conservation concern and the techniques available to address the concerns, an agricultural view such as farmer levels of participation and agricultural community involvement in decision making within the program, and a policy view such as complementary support from cooperating ministries, agencies, and private concerns (18, 21, 27). Issues identified in conservation program evaluations are in many instances similar to those facing IPM as it transitions to more use of IPM strategies with regional pest management value and expanded environmental benefits (see first two sections of this review). The value of IPM to the goals of public-supported conservation programs and their shared challenges in attaining regional goals and broad benefits becomes clear from this multifunctional perspective.

NEXT STEPS TO IMPLEMENTING IPM THAT ADDRESSES REGIONAL AND ENVIRONMENTAL ISSUES

Incentivizing people to implement IPM with regional pest management and environmental value reflects the age-old incentives dilemma as applied to agriculture. How do members of a community relinquish their near-term self-interests stemming from a market-based agricultural system to a less tangible and future good that has broad public benefits?

The Nature of the Problem

The examples reviewed demonstrate the challenge for individuals to transition from their market-based interests to broader interests that require community involvement and areawide decision making. This problem of individual freedom to access common resources (i.e., the natural resource base on which agriculture depends) is well described as the tragedy of the commons (51). In the example provided in Hardin's essay (51), a community of herdsman utilize the same common grazing area. The system of sharing the resource without overexploitation works at lower herd population levels but breaks down when individuals begin to increase production capacity. Individuals attempt to gain the productive advantage over neighbors by exploiting commonly held resources.

Although Hardin's argument (51) is aimed mostly at the need to feed an exploding human population, the dilemma remains the same for addressing regional and environmental issues as related to agriculture, including IPM (99). Individual actions to increase production and profit do not in themselves lead to wider environmental degradation; after all, the common resources of a healthy agroecosystem are resilient (3, 6). However, many individuals all acting in an arguably reasonable way in a market-driven system have adversely affected air and water quality and biodiversity, reducing the resiliency of the common natural resources system needed for individual success (38, 87).

Enabling Farmers Through Partnerships

This review has examined the literature for examples of communities working together in reducing agricultural and environmental risks through application of IPM strategies. This approach is consistent with conservation ecology interests of contributing to the resiliency of healthy agroecosystems (112) and with agroecology interests of implementing advanced levels of IPM (3, 29, 71). It places IPM as a supporter of landscapes with healthy ecosystem services, including provisioning (food, fiber, fuel, fresh water), which requires the supporting services (nutrient cycling, soil formation, natural enemies, pollinators) as well as the regulating (climate, flood, water quality) and even cultural (aesthetic, spiritual, educational, recreational) services (24).

A functional model to implement IPM strategies with regional and environmental value must be respectful of agricultural, environmental, and social and policy interests and in our view benefits from and requires partnerships. It must include social and policy aspects (both community leadership and individual motivation for addressing such issues) and economic and agricultural aspects (sharing near-term farm risks and long-term rewards of public goods through both market-driven and public-supported incentives) (21, 26, 40, 75). At some point, farmers must be enabled to move beyond their reactive posture of responding to individual problems and to begin to develop a process to address multiple issues. But they live in a largely market-driven and regulatory system with variable external support that is just beginning as of the past few decades to move from production-based incentives to conservation-based incentives. Are there transitional steps that lead to regional, multifunctional, nonconflicting efforts of farmers, public programs, and private organizations?

Depending on the number of issues confronting an individual farmer, diverse public agencies and private entities may require planning to address specific concerns related to agriculture and IPM. The planning process may target compliance of environmental regulations (88, 100), criteria to access public financial support related to conservation (11, 27, 66), and participation in performance-based assessments required in contracts with food and fiber processors (20). The plans may be simple best management practices adapted from technical support provided by extension and research services of ministries, agencies, and universities and may involve detailed third-party certification such as eco-labeling (37).

IPM can play a central role in addressing multiple environmental and human safety issues and in achieving its pest management goals through such planning processes. Ideally, these processes are linked to a combination of private and public-supported incentives (50). For example, in the United States, USDA NRCS and local extension and research services of public land-grant universities have created ad hoc partnerships to improve communication, establish pest management standards in conservation programs, and improve IPM skill sets through training of USDA NRCS staff and private contracted providers (11). In special initiatives, conservation planning and IPM planning are linked, and detailed farm plans are developed on the basis of best management practices including IPM (11, 57, 116). The purpose of such planning activities is to provide a reflective process for the farmer. The farmer, pest management consultant, and conservationist review IPM strategies currently utilized and their potential effects on soil, water, and air. They set farm goals to increase use of IPM strategies that reduce the risk to resources of conservation concern while meeting market-driven standards. In parts of the United States, this process is a prerequisite to obtain financial incentives from conservation programs for farms. In selected cases, the planning process itself is financially supported. However, these initiatives suffer from the ad hoc nature of the partnerships (11). In contrast, as presented in this review, partnerships are commonly solidified by strong agreements in successful cases of areawide pest management (72). We recommend solidifying the agriculture and conservation connections through formal agreements to ensure establishment of durable interaction and shared responsibility to attain agricultural and conservation goals. This is especially crucial when public funds are involved.

Regionalizing effort to attain long-lasting multiple benefits is a related challenge. Current efforts have had variable success by combining regulatory mandates with a voluntary system of technical assistance and financial incentives to encourage regional community action. Success has been most apparent when risks are high, resources and regions of interest are well defined, technologies for reducing the risks are well known, and financial support is available (30, 32). Said with some reservation and sadness, society may have now transitioned to the point that broader-based risks such as biodiversity loss and region-wide detection of water and air pollutants are of sufficient community concern to stimulate more regional activities, especially in areas of intense agricultural production. The growing suite of conservation programs for farms in partnership with agricultural interests such as IPM has a role to play in encouraging regional activities with environmental benefits (9, 11, 64, 66).

In this case as well as other partnerships, we encourage equal consideration of agricultural, environmental, and social and policy interests to ensure strong effort to attain unified goals when addressing regional and environmental issues. These partnerships should sponsor community-based decision-making processes and invite the coordination of technical and financial incentives from private and public entities. Specific to IPM, we envision joining interests and sharing risks and resources to enable farmers to implement more advanced IPM strategies at participation levels needed to attain long-lasting regional pest management and conservation benefits. This partnership requires farmers, environmentalists, public agencies, and private entities to think beyond their short-term objectives, establish effective agreements and common goals, and reconcile and join market-based and public-based incentives to attain multiple short-term and long-term benefits to agriculture and the environment.

SUMMARY POINTS

1. During its first 50 years of modern development, IPM adoption occurred readily at the scale of the individual field and farm, with the most common application centered on pest sampling and economic thresholds for pesticide decision making driven primarily by market factors within a pesticide regulatory framework.
2. As advanced IPM strategies became available for areawide application, farmers have been challenged to reconcile the additional costs and risks with benefits that are longer term and accrue to the broader community as well as the farmer, resulting in an incentives dilemma for farmers when IPM strategies are chosen. Implementation of these advanced IPM strategies has been slow compared with those associated with individual field-based market-driven management.
3. Single-entity management of large farms, farming community investment in local management districts, and public support have been used to overcome the incentives dilemma. Public support may come in the form of traditional technical assistance of public research and extension and financial incentives to offset costs and reduce individual risk.
4. Addressing the incentives dilemma for advanced IPM strategies that provide environmental benefits is of special relevance, given the impact of agricultural intensification including pesticide effects on nontarget organisms, loss of biodiversity, and degradation of soil, water, and air resources.

5. In the past several decades, public-supported, conservation-based financial incentives provided to farmers obtained wider public policy support consistent with international trade agreements. The major conservation programs providing these financial incentives were found principally in developed countries, especially in the United States and European Union.
6. The strong species degradation orientation of European programs and the pollutant orientation of U.S. programs affected their connectivity to IPM. Successful linkage to IPM has been most apparent when risks are high, relevant IPM technologies are available, and financial incentives are flexible and reasonable to address locally relevant issues that resonate with farmers.
7. We encourage private and public partnerships that give equal consideration to agricultural, environmental, and social/policy interests to enable farmers to address regional and environmental issues within a market-based and regulatory framework. Such a partnership requires thinking beyond short-term objectives, effective agreements and common goals, and reconciliation and joining of market-based and public-based incentives to attain multifunctional benefits to agriculture and the environment.

DISCLOSURE STATEMENT

The authors are not aware of any affiliations, memberships, funding, or financial holdings that might be perceived as affecting the objectivity of this review.

ACKNOWLEDGMENTS

The authors thank Lois Strole and Stephanie Klock for securing references and formatting this review. We thank the many participants of professional society symposia, agency planning sessions, and public meetings whose public comments have assisted us in consolidating our approach to this topic. We also thank the anonymous reviewers for their comments and insights. We thank Texas AgriLife Research and the U.C. Statewide IPM Program for supporting our work on this review.

LITERATURE CITED

1. Albrecht M, Duelli P, Muller C, Kleijn D, Schmid B. 2007. The Swiss agri-environment scheme enhances pollinator diversity and plant reproductive success in nearby intensively managed farmland. *J. Appl. Ecol.* 44:813–22
2. Allen CT. 2008. Boll weevil eradication: an areawide pest management effort. In *Areawide Pest Management*, ed. O Koul, G Cuperus, N Elliott, pp. 467–559. Wallingford, UK: CAB International
3. Altieri MA. 1994. *Biodiversity and Pest Management in Agroecosystems*. New York: Food Products Press. 185 pp.
4. Altieri MA, Letourneau DK, Davis JR. 1983. Developing sustainable agroecosystems. *BioScience* 33:45–49
5. Barbosa P, ed. 1998. *Conservation Biological Control*. San Diego, CA: Academic. 396 pp.
6. Benton TG, Vickery JA, Wilson JD. 2003. Farmland biodiversity: Is habitat heterogeneity the key? *Trends Ecol. Evol.* 18:182–88
7. Berendse F, Chamberlain D, Kleijn D, Schekkerman H. 2004. Declining biodiversity in agricultural landscapes and the effectiveness of agri-environment schemes. *Ambio* 33:499–502
8. Brewer MJ, Hoard RJ, Landis JN, Elworth LE. 2004. The case and opportunity for public-supported financial incentives to implement integrated pest management. *J. Econ. Entomol.* 97:1782–89

9. Brewer MJ, Ishii-Eiteman M. 2009. Integrated pest management, with special focus on sustainability and risk: principles, policy and practice. In *Critical Food Issues: Problems and State-of-the-Art Solutions Worldwide*, ed. LE Phoenix, pp. 33–52. Santa Barbara, CA: Praeger
10. Brewer MJ, Noma T, Elliott NC. 2008. A landscape perspective in managing vegetation for beneficial plant-pest-natural enemy interactions: a foundation for areawide pest management. In *Areawide Pest Management: Theory and Implementation*, ed. O Koul, G Cuperus, N Elliott, pp. 81–96. Wallingford, UK: CAB International
11. **Brewer MJ, Rajotte EG, Kaplan JR, Goodell PB, Biddinger DJ, et al. 2009. Opportunities, experiences, and strategies to connect integrated pest management to US Department of Agriculture conservation programs. *Am. Entomol.* 55:140–46**

11. Reviews challenges and strategies of IPM community engagement in USDA conservation programs for farms.

12. Brodt S, Goodell PB, Krebill-Prather RL, Vargas RN. 2007. California cotton growers utilize integrated pest management. *Calif. Agric.* 61:24–30
13. Brodt S, Zalom FG, Krebill-Prather R, Bentley W, Pickel C, et al. 2005. Almond growers rely on pest control advisors for integrated pest management. *Calif. Agric.* 59:242–48
14. Brown DL, Giles D, Oliver M, Klassen P. 2008. Targeted spray technology to reduce pesticide in runoff from dormant orchards. *Crop Prot.* 27:545–52
15. Butler S, Brooks D, Feber R, Storkey J, Vickery J, Norris K. 2009. A cross-taxonomic index for quantifying the health of farmland biodiversity. *J. Appl. Ecol.* 46:1154–62
16. Butler SJ, Boccaccio L, Gregory RD, Vorisek P, Norris K. 2010. Quantifying the impact of land-use change to European farmland bird populations. *Agric. Ecosyst. Environ.* 137:348–57
17. Byrne DN. 2008. Dispersal and migration of insects and their importance in pest management. See Ref. 72, pp. 60–80
18. Carey PD, Short C, Morris C, Hunt J, Priscott A, et al. 2009. The multi-disciplinary evaluation of a national agri-environment scheme. *J. Environ. Manage.* 69:71–91
19. Carrière Y, Ellsworth P, Dutilleul P, Kirk C, Barkley V, Antilla L. 2006. A GIS-based approach for areawide pest management: the scales of *Lygus hesperus* movements to cotton from alfalfa, weeds, and cotton. *Entomol. Exp. Appl.* 118:203–10
20. Casey F, Boody G. 2007. *An Assessment of Performance-Based Indicators and Payments for Resource Conservation on Agricultural Lands, Conservation Economics White Paper 8.* Minneapolis: Defenders of Wildlife. 28 pp.
21. **Casey F, Schmitz A, Swinton S, Zilberman D, eds. 1999. *Flexible Incentives for the Adoption of Environmental Technologies in Agriculture.* Norwell, MA: Kluwer Acad. 384 pp.**

21. Presents theory and application of incentives to encourage farmer adoption of technologies such as IPM.

22. Castle SJ, Goodell PB, Palumbo JC. 2009. Implementing principles of the integrated control concept 50 years later—current challenges in IPM for arthropod pests. *Pest Manage. Sci.* 65:1263–64
23. Corbet PS. 1981. Non-entomological impediments to the adoption of integrated pest management. *Prot. Ecol.* 3:183–202
24. Corvalan C, Hales S, McMichael A, Butler C, McMichael AJ. 2005. *Ecosystems and Human Well-Being, Health Synthesis: A Report of the Millennium Ecosystem Assessment.* Geneva: WHO Press. 53 pp.
25. Critchley CNR, Allen DS, Fowbert JA, Mole AC, Gundrey AL. 2004. Habitat establishment on arable land: assessment of an agri-environment scheme in England, UK. *Biol. Conserv.* 119:429–42
26. Dale VH, Polasky S. 2007. Measures of the effects of agricultural practices on ecosystem services. *Ecol. Econ.* 64:286–96
27. **Dobbs TL, Pretty JN. 2004. Agri-environmental stewardship schemes and "multifunctionality." *Rev. Agric. Econ.* 26:220–37**

27. In reviewing European conservation programs, multifunctionality is presented as a key to success.

28. Dover JW. 1997. Conservation headlands: effects on butterfly distribution and behaviour. *Agric. Ecosyst. Environ.* 63:31–49
29. Ehler LE. 2006. Integrated pest management (IPM): definition, historical development and implementation, and the other IPM. *Pest Manage. Sci.* 62:787–89
30. Elliott NC, Onstad DW, Brewer MJ. 2008. History and ecological basis for areawide pest management. See Ref. 72, pp. 15–33
31. Epstein L, Bassein S, Zalom F. 2000. Almond and stone fruit growers reduce OP, increase pyrethroid use in dormant sprays. *Calif. Agric.* 54:14–19

32. Ewald JA, Aebischer NJ, Richardson SM, Grice PV, Cooke AI. 2010. The effect of agri-environment schemes on grey partridges at the farm level in England. *Agric. Ecosyst. Environ.* 138:55–63
33. Falconer K. 2002. Pesticide environmental indicators and environmental policy. *J. Environ. Manage.* 65:285–300
34. Feehan J, Gillmor DA, Culleton N. 2005. Effects of an agri-environment scheme on farmland biodiversity in Ireland. *Agric. Ecosyst. Environ.* 107:275–86
35. Firbank LG, Smart SM, Crabb J, Critchley CNR, Fowbert JW, et al. 2003. Agronomic and ecological costs and benefits of set-aside in England. *Agric. Ecosyst. Environ.* 95:73–85
36. Frisbie RE, Adkisson PL, eds. 1986. *Integrated Pest Management on Major Agricultural Systems.* College Station: Texas Agric. Exp. Stn., MP-1616. 743 pp.
37. Galarraga Gallastegui I. 2002. The use of eco-labels: a review of the literature. *Eur. Environ.* 12:316–31
38. Gilliom RJ. 2007. Pesticides in US streams and groundwater. *Environ. Sci. Technol.* 41:3408–14
39. Gilliom RJ, Barbash JE, Crawford CG, Hamilton PA, Martin JD, et al. 2006. The quality of our nation's water—pesticides in the nation's streams and ground water, 1992–2001. Circular 1291. US Geol. Surv., Reston, VA.
40. Goldman RL, Thompson BH, Daily GC. 2007. Institutional incentives for managing the landscape: inducing cooperation for the production of ecosystem services. *Ecol. Econ.* 64:333–43
41. Goodell P, Fossen M, Hartley C. 2011. Volatile organic compounds, pesticides and IPM: dealing with air quality standards in pest management in California, US. *Outlooks Pest Manage.* 22:10–13
42. Goodell P, Lynn-Patterson K. 2010. Integrated pest management at the landscape scale: tracing the tale of cotton IPM in the San Joaquin Valley of Central California. In *Landscape Management for Functional Biodiversity*, 56:55–61. Cambridge, UK: Int. Org. Biol. Control – WPRS Working Group
43. Goodell PB. 2010. Managing the ecosystem for IPM: effect of reduced irrigation allotments. In *Proceedings of California Plant and Soil Conference*, pp. 26–31. Visalia: Calif. Chapter Am. Soc. Agron.
44. Goodell PB, Montez G, Wilhoit L. 2006. Shifting patterns in insecticide use on cotton in California: 1993 to 2004. In *Proceedings of Beltwide Cotton Production Research Conferences*, pp. 1367–73. San Antonio, TX: Natl. Cotton Counc.
45. Graebner L, Moreno DS, Baritelle JL. 1984. The Fillmore Citrus Protective District: a success story in integrated pest management. *Bull. Entomol. Soc. Am.* 30:27–33
46. Grafton-Cardwell EE, Godfrey LD, Chaney WE, Bentley WJ. 2005. Various novel insecticides are less toxic to humans, more specific to key pests. *Calif. Agric.* 59:29–34
47. Gurr G, Scarratt S, Wratten S, Brendt L, Irvin N. 2004. Ecological engineering, habitat manipulation and pest management. See Ref. 48, pp. 1–12
48. Gurr GM, Wratten SD, Altieri MA, eds. 2004. *Ecological Engineering for Pest Management: Advances in Habitat Manipulation for Arthropods.* Collingwood, Aust.: CSIRO Publishing. 225 pp.
49. Hagen KS, van den Bosch R, Dahlsten DL. 1971. The importance of naturally-occurring biological control in the western United States. In *Biological Control*, ed. CB Huffacker, pp. 253–93. New York: Plenum
50. Hamerschlag K, Kaplan J. 2007. *More Integrated Pest Management Please. How USDA Could Deliver Greater Environmental Benefits from Farm Bill Conservation Programs.* New York: Nat. Resour. Defense Counc. 29 pp.
51. **Hardin G. 1968. The tragedy of the commons. *Science* 162:1243–48**
52. Harris MK. 2001. IPM, what has it delivered? A Texas case history emphasizing cotton, sorghum, and pecan. *Plant Dis.* 85:112–21
53. Henneberry T, Naranjo S. 1998. Integrated management approaches for pink bollworm in the southwestern United States. *Integr. Pest Manage. Rev.* 3:31–52
54. Herkert JR. 2009. Response of bird populations to farmland set-aside programs. *Conserv. Biol.* 23:1036–40
55. Higley LG, Pedigo LP, eds. 1996. *Economic Thresholds for Integrated Pest Management.* Lincoln: Univ. Neb. Press. 327 pp.
56. Higley LG, Wintersteen WK. 1992. A novel approach to environmental risk assessment of pesticides as a basis for incorporating environmental costs into economic injury levels. *Am. Entomol.* 38:34–39
57. Hirsch RM, Miller MM. 2008. Progressive planning to address multiple resource concerns: integrated pest management in Wisconsin orchards. *J. Soil Water Conserv.* 63:40A–43A

51. Provides an agricultural perspective in setting aside individual needs and working toward the greater good.

58. Hoard RJ, Brewer MJ. 2006. Adoption of pest, nutrient, and conservation vegetation management using financial incentives provided by a US Department of Agriculture conservation program. *HortTechnology* 16:306–11
59. Hoffmann MP, Wilson LT, Zalom FG, Hilton RJ. 1991. Dynamic sequential sampling plan for *Helicoverpa zea* (Lepidoptera: Noctuidae) eggs in processing tomatoes: parasitism and temporal patterns. *Environ. Entomol.* 20:1005–12
60. Ioriatti O. 2008. Grape areawide pest management in Italy. See Ref. 72, pp. 208–25
61. Joyce BA, Wallender WW, Angermann T, Wilson BW, Werner I, et al. 2004. Using infiltration enhancement and soil water management to reduce diazinon in runoff. *J. Am. Water Resour. Assoc.* 40:1063–70
62. Keenan SP, Burgener PA. 2008. Social and economic aspects of areawide pest management. In *Areawide Pest Management: Theory and Implementation*, ed. O Koul, G Cuperus, N Elliott, pp. 97–116. Wallingford, UK: CAB International
63. Khanna M, Millock K, Zilberman D. 1999. Sustainability, technology and incentives. See Ref. 21, pp. 97–118
64. **Kleijn D, Baquero RA, Clough Y, Diaz M, De Esteban J, et al. 2006. Mixed biodiversity benefits of agri-environment schemes in five European countries. *Ecol. Lett.* 9:243–54**
65. Kleijn D, Kohler F, Baldi A, Batary P, Concepcion ED, et al. 2009. On the relationship between farmland biodiversity and land-use intensity in Europe. *Proc. R. Soc. B Biol. Sci.* 276:903–9
66. Kleijn D, Sutherland WJ. 2003. How effective are European agri-environment schemes in conserving and promoting biodiversity? *J. Appl. Ecol.* 40:947–69
67. Knight A. 2008. Codling moth areawide pest management. See Ref. 72, pp. 159–90
68. Knipling EF. 1979. *The Basic Principles of Insect Pest Population Suppression and Management*. Washington, DC: USDA, Agric. Handb. 512. 659 pp.
69. Knop E, Kleijn D, Herzog F, Schmid B. 2006. Effectiveness of the Swiss agri-environment scheme in promoting biodiversity. *J. Appl. Ecol.* 43:120–27
70. Koch H, Weisser P. 2000. Sensor equipped orchard spraying—efficacy, savings and drift reduction. *Asp. Appl. Biol.* 57:357–62
71. **Kogan M. 1998. Integrated pest management: historical perspectives and contemporary developments. *Annu. Rev. Entomol.* 43:243–70**
72. **Koul O, Cuperus G, Elliott N, eds. 2008. *Areawide Pest Management, Theory and Implementation*. Wallingford, UK: CAB International. 590 pp.**
73. Koul O, Dhaliwal GS, Curperus GW, eds. 2004. *Integrated Pest Management: Potential, Constraints and Challenges*. Wallingford, UK: CABI Publishing. 336 pp.
74. Koziel MG, Carozzi NB, Warren GW. 1998. Transgenic plants for control of insect pests. In *Agricultural Biotechnology*, ed. A Altman, pp. 283–94. New York: Marcel Dekker
75. Kroeger T, Casey F. 2007. An assessment of market-based approaches to providing ecosystem services on agricultural lands. *Ecol. Econ.* 64:321–32
76. Lee DJ, Milon JW. 1999. Flexible incentives and water quality control technologies for the Everglades agricultural area. See Ref. 21, pp. 211–27
77. Letourneau DK. 1994. Bean fly, management practices, and biological control in Malawian subsistence agriculture. *Agric. Ecosyst. Environ.* 50:103–11
78. Levins R. 1969. Some demographic and genetic consequences of environmental heterogeneity for biological control. *Bull. Entomol. Soc. Am.* 15:237–40
79. Long RF, Hanson BR, Fulton AE, Weston DP. 2010. Mitigation techniques reduce sediment in runoff from furrow-irrigated cropland. *Calif. Agric.* 64:135–40
80. Long RF, Nett M, Putnam DH, Shan G, Schmierer J, Reed B. 2002. Insecticide choice for alfalfa may protect water quality. *Calif. Agric.* 56:163–69
81. Madsen HF, Morgan CVG. 1970. Pome fruit pests and their control. *Annu. Rev. Entomol.* 15:295–320
82. Mareida KM, Dakouo D, Mota-Sanchez D, eds. 2003. *Integrated Pest Management in the Global Arena*. Wallingford, UK: CABI Publ. 512 pp.
83. Merckx T, Feber RE, Riordan P, Townsend MC, Bourn NAD, et al. 2009. Optimizing the biodiversity gain from agri-environment schemes. *Agric. Ecosyst. Environ.* 130:177–82

64. Provides an in-depth review and ecological evaluation of European conservation programs for farms.

71. Presents a contemporary view of simple and advanced levels of IPM.

72. Reviews theory and provides multiple applications of areawide pest management.

84. Metcalf RL, Luckmann WH. 1982. *Introduction to Insect Pest Management*. New York: Wiley. 577 pp.
85. Mueller AJ, Stern VM. 1974. Timing of pesticide treatments on safflower to prevent *Lygus* from dispersing to cotton. *J. Econ. Entomol.* 67:77–80
86. Norris RF, Caswell-Chen EP, Kogan M. 2003. *Concepts in Integrated Pest Management*. Upper Saddle River, NJ: Prentice Hall. 586 pp.
87. Novacek MJ, Cleland EE. 2001. The current biodiversity extinction event: scenarios for mitigation and recovery. *Proc. Natl. Acad. Sci. USA* 98:5466–70
88. Ogg ACW. 1999. Evaluation of EPA programs and policies that impact agriculture. See Ref. 21, pp. 27–42
89. Palumbo J, Horowitz A, Prabhaker N. 2001. Insecticidal control and resistance management for *Bemisia tabaci*. *Crop Prot.* 20:739–65
90. Peach WJ, Lovett LJ, Wotton SR, Jeffs C. 2001. Countryside stewardship delivers cirl buntings (*Emberiza cirlus*) in Devon, UK. *Biol. Conserv.* 101:361–73
91. Pedigo LP. 1999. *Entomology and Pest Management*. Upper Saddle River, NJ: Prentice Hall. 691 pp. 3rd ed.
92. Pedigo LP, Buntin GD, eds. 1993. *Handbook of Sampling Methods for Arthropods in Agriculture*. Boca Raton, FL: CRC Press. 714 pp.
93. Pedigo LP, Higley LG. 1992. The economic injury level concept and environmental quality: a new perspective. *Am. Entomol.* 38:12–21
94. Pedigo LP, Hutchins SH, Higley LG. 1986. Economic injury levels in theory and practice. *Annu. Rev. Entomol.* 31:341–68
95. Pfiffner L, Wyss E. 2004. Use of sown wildflower strips to enhance natural enemies of agricultural pests. In *Ecological Engineering for Pest Management: Advances in Habitat Manipulation for Arthropods*, ed. G Gurr, S Wratten, M Altieri, pp. 165–86. Collingwood, Aust.: CSIRO Publishing
96. Pimentel D, Acquay H, Biltonen M, Rice P, Silva M, et al. 1992. Environmental and economic costs of pesticide use. *BioScience* 42:750–60

96. Reviews the shortfalls of IPM and argues it still is the solution even if adding to environmental concern.

97. Pywell RF, Warman EA, Hulmes L, Hulmes S, Nuttall P, et al. 2006. Effectiveness of new agri-environment schemes in providing foraging resources for bumblebees in intensively farmed landscapes. *Biol. Conserv.* 129:192–206
98. Ragsdale DW, Landis DA, Brodeur J, Heimpel GE, Desneux N. 2011. Ecology and management of the soybean aphid in North America. *Annu. Rev. Entomol.* 56:375–99
99. Randall A. 1999. Providing for the common good in an era of resurgent individualism. See Ref. 21, pp. 324–37
100. Ribaudo M, Caswell MF. 1999. Environmental regulation in agriculture and the adoption of environmental technology. See Ref. 21, pp. 7–25
101. Schellhorn NA, Macfadyen SA, Bianchi FJJA, Williams DG, Zalucki MP. 2008. Managing ecosystem services in broadacre landscapes: What are the appropriate spatial scales? *Aust. J. Exp. Agric.* 48:1549–59
102. Segerson K. 1999. Flexible incentives: a unifying framework for policy analysis. See Ref. 21, pp. 79–95
103. Shennan C, Cecchettini CL, Goldman GB, Zalom FG. 2001. Profiles of California farmers by degree of IPM use as indicated by self-descriptions in a phone survey. *Agric. Ecosyst. Environ.* 84:267–75
104. Smith CM. 2004. Plant resistance against pests: issues and strategies. See Ref. 73, pp. 147–68
105. Smith DT, Harris MK, Liu T-X. 2002. Adoption of pest management practices by vegetable growers: a case study. *Am. Entomol.* 48:236–42
106. Stern V, Smith R, van den Bosch R, Hagen K. 1959. The integration of chemical and biological control of the spotted alfalfa aphid: the integrated control concept. *Hilgardia* 29:81–101

106. Outlines the fundamental concepts of IPM, which are still relevant 50 years later.

107. Stevens DK, Bradbury RB. 2006. Effects of the Arable Stewardship Pilot Scheme on breeding birds at field and farm-scales. *Agric. Ecosyst. Environ.* 112:283–90
108. Stoner KA, Sawyer AJ, Shelton AM. 1986. Constraints to the implementation of IPM programs in the USA: a course outline. *Agric. Ecosyst. Environ.* 17:253–68
109. Strand L. 2003. Insects and mites. In *Integrated Pest Management in Walnuts*, ed. M Flint, pp. 35–74. Berkeley: Univ. Calif., Agric. Nat. Resour.
110. Strickland AH. 1961. Sampling crop pests and their hosts. *Annu. Rev. Entomol.* 6:201–20

111. Summers C, Goodell P, Mueller S. 2004. Lygus bug management by alfalfa harvest manipulation. In *Encyclopedia of Pest Management*, ed. D Pimentel, pp. 322–25. Boca Raton, FL: CRC Press
112. Tilman D, Cassman K, Matson P, Naylor R, Polasky S. 2002. Agricultural sustainability and the costs and benefits of intensive production practices. *Nature* 418:671–77
113. Trumble JT, Alvarado-Rodriguez B. 1993. Development and economic evaluation of an IPM program for fresh market tomato production in Mexico. *Agric. Ecosyst. Environ.* 43:267–84
114. Tscharntke T, Bommarco R, Clough Y, Crist TO, Kleijn D, et al. 2007. Conservation biological control and enemy diversity on a landscape scale. *Biol. Control* 43:294–309
115. Tscharntke T, Klein AM, Kruess A, Steffan-Dewenter I, Thies C. 2005. Landscape perspectives on agricultural intensification and biodiversity—ecosystem service management. *Ecol. Lett.* 8:857–74
116. University of California Statewide IPM Program. 2011. UC IPM pest management guidelines. In *Series 3430 to 3473*, ed. T Martin, B Ohlendorf. Davis: Univ. Calif., Agric. Nat. Resour.
117. Van Buskirk J, Willi Y. 2004. Enhancement of farmland biodiversity within set-aside land. *Conserv. Biol.* 18:987–94
118. Vickery J, Carter N, Fuller RJ. 2002. The potential value of managed cereal field margins as foraging habitats for farmland birds in the UK. *Agric. Ecosyst. Environ.* 89:41–52
119. Wade MR, Gurr GM, Wratten SD. 2008. Ecological restoration of farmland: progress and prospects. *Philos. Trans. R. Soc. B Biol. Sci.* 363:831–47
120. Zalom FG, Hoy MA, Wilson LT, Barnett WW. 1984. Sampling mites in almonds II. Presence-absence sequential sampling for *Tetranychus* mites species. *Hilgardia* 52:14–24
121. Zalom FG, Weakley C, Hendricks LC, Bentley WJ, Barnett WW, Connell JH. 1984. Cultural management of the navel orangeworm by winter sanitation. *Calif. Agric.* 38:28
122. Zalucki MP, Adamson D, Furlong MJ. 2009. The future of IPM: whither or wither? *Aust. J. Entomol.* 48:85–96

Transmission of Flea-Borne Zoonotic Agents*

Rebecca J. Eisen** and Kenneth L. Gage

Division of Vector-Borne Diseases, Centers for Disease Control and Prevention, Fort Collins, Colorado 30333; email: dyn2@cdc.gov

Annu. Rev. Entomol. 2012. 57:61–82

First published online as a Review in Advance on August 29, 2011

The *Annual Review of Entomology* is online at ento.annualreviews.org

This article's doi:
10.1146/annurev-ento-120710-100717

0066-4170/12/0107-0061$20.00

**Corresponding author

Keywords

flea, vector-borne disease, plague, murine typhus, *Rickettsia felis*, *Bartonella*

Abstract

Flea-borne zoonoses such as plague (*Yersinia pestis*) and murine typhus (*Rickettsia typhi*) caused significant numbers of human cases in the past and remain a public health concern. Other flea-borne human pathogens have emerged recently (e.g., *Bartonella henselae*, *Rickettsia felis*), and their mechanisms of transmission and impact on human health are not fully understood. Our review focuses on the ecology and epidemiology of the flea-borne bacterial zoonoses mentioned above with an emphasis on recent advancements in our understanding of how these organisms are transmitted by fleas, maintained in zoonotic cycles, and transmitted to humans. Emphasis is given to plague because of the considerable number of studies generated during the first decade of the twenty-first century that arose, in part, because of renewed interest in potential agents of bioterrorism, including *Y. pestis*.

INTRODUCTION

Throughout the world, vector-borne diseases cause significant morbidity and mortality. The majority of recent research and reviews of vector-borne zoonoses focuses on tick- and mosquito-borne illnesses, such as Lyme disease and West Nile virus disease (15, 60, 98, 104). By contrast, relatively little attention has been paid to flea-borne zoonoses such as plague (*Yersinia pestis*) and murine typhus (*Rickettsia typhi*), which historically have caused significant numbers of human cases. Although the incidence of plague has declined considerably, it still causes regional outbreaks with many fatalities. Murine typhus also remains common in many areas, and neither disease has been eliminated or greatly reduced in its range. Other flea-borne human pathogens also have emerged recently (e.g., *Bartonella henselae*, *Rickettsia felis*), suggesting that much remains to be learned about the potential role of fleas as disease vectors. Our review focuses on the ecology and epidemiology of the flea-borne bacterial zoonoses mentioned above with an emphasis on recent advancements in our understanding of how these organisms are transmitted by fleas, maintained in zoonotic cycles, and transmitted to humans. Emphasis is given to plague because of the considerable number of studies generated during the first decade of the twenty-first century that arose, in part, because of renewed interest in potential agents of bioterrorism, including *Y. pestis*. The role of fleas in the transmission of myxoma virus, a disease of rabbits, and as intermediate hosts for tapeworms is beyond the scope of this review.

PLAGUE (*YERSINIA PESTIS*)

Overview of Plague Epidemiology

Plague, caused by the gram-negative bacterium *Y. pestis*, is a severe, primarily flea-borne, rodent-associated zoonosis characterized by natural cycles with quiescent periods that are punctuated by rapidly spreading epizootics (10). The majority of human infections are believed to occur during epizootic periods when susceptible rodent hosts perish in large numbers, thus increasing the likelihood of human encounters with infectious animals, animal carcasses, or fleas that abandon their dead or dying *Y. pestis*–infected hosts (56).

In humans, plague most commonly presents in the bubonic form of the disease, which is often associated with the bite of an infectious flea or direct contact between infectious host body fluids and open skin lesions or abrasions on human skin. Bubonic plague is characterized by sudden onset of fever, chills, headache, malaise, and regional lymphadenopathy (30). Primary septicemic plague, which is often attributed to cutaneous exposure to *Y. pestis*, is less common and is characterized by fever and sepsis without regional lymphadenopathy (30). Septicemic plague also can occur secondarily to bubonic plague. Finally, among the three most common plague presentations, the primary pneumonic form of the disease, which is acquired through inhalation of plague bacteria contained in respiratory droplets or other materials, is the least common, but the most severe and rapidly progressing, form. Pneumonic plague also can occur through hematogenous spread of *Y. pestis* to the lungs (30). Although human plague cases are rare in modern times, fatality rates range from 50% to 60% for the bubonic form of the disease to nearly 100% for pneumonic infections (80, 99). However, outcome of infection is substantially improved by early diagnosis followed by appropriate antimicrobial therapy (25). The low fatality rates reported frequently from some countries probably represent considerable levels of misdiagnosis (100).

Historically, *Y. pestis* has caused at least three pandemics. The first pandemic, known as Justinian's plague, occurred in the sixth century. It is believed to have begun in Central Asia, then it dispersed and caused epidemics that infected nearly 100,000,000 persons in Asia, Africa, and

Europe (114). The second pandemic, now referred to as the "Black Death," occurred in the fourteenth century and caused approximately 50,000,000 fatalities worldwide, with half the victims in Asia and Africa and the other half in Europe. That pandemic is notable for killing nearly one-quarter of Europe's population. The third pandemic, known as the "Modern Pandemic," originated in China's Yunnan Province in the 1850s and rapidly spread along the tin and opium routes to port cities in southeast China. Although India was the country most severely affected by this pandemic and most regions experienced case loads numbering only in the hundreds to thousands, the pandemic left a long-standing mark on other regions of the world, as ships carrying plague-infected rats and their fleas introduced *Y. pestis* into port cities around the world and established new plague foci in North America, parts of Africa, Madagascar, and southern Asia (31, 36, 56, 63, 81, 100). With improvements in sanitation, vector control, and availability of effective antibiotics, there has been a sharp decline in epidemicity of plague throughout the world (114). For example, from 1954 to 1997, the World Health Organization was notified of 80,613 human plague cases from 38 countries. During this 44-year period, the largest proportion of cases (58.4%) were reported from Asia (114). By contrast, in recent decades, most human plague cases have been reported from eastern Africa and Madagascar (91, 114, 126).

Overview of Plague Ecology

The distribution of *Y. pestis* is heterogeneous at global, regional, and local spatial scales. Despite global introductions of the pathogen, *Y. pestis* has become established only in localities with landscapes and climatic conditions that are suitable for maintaining rodent and flea populations at sufficiently high levels to support enzootic or epizootic transmission. For example, in the early 1900s, *Y. pestis* was introduced via rat-infested ships into the ports of New Orleans, Louisiana, and Galveston, Texas. Despite brief commensal rat-associated epidemics in both of these cities, the disease was eliminated through improvements in sanitation, such as reduction of food or harborage for rats, and through the improved wharf systems that included inspection and quarantine of ships (82). In contrast, following its introduction into the Port of San Francisco, California, *Y. pestis* spread from urban rats to sylvatic rodent hosts. Although improved sanitation reduced the number of human plague cases, *Y. pestis* became established in California and spread east until reaching its current extent, approximately along the 100th meridian, in the 1940s (3, 50, 82, 89). Within the western states where plague is established in enzootic cycles, its distribution is heterogeneous.

Recent studies have sought to identify landscape, vegetation, and meteorological variables that define the ecological niche of plague and identify areas of elevated risk for human exposure to plague bacteria within plague-endemic regions (24, 28, 41, 43, 44, 90, 93, 130). The majority of these studies have focused on Africa and North America. For example, at a continental scale, African plague foci were defined by positive associations with elevation, potential evapotranspiration, mean diurnal temperature range, annual rainfall, and December-normalized difference vegetation index; on the basis of these variables, much of sub-Saharan Africa was considered suitable for *Y. pestis* transmission (93). Studies that focused on more-local spatial scales determined that elevation and vegetation were key predictors of risk in Uganda and Tanzania. Specifically, in eastern Tanzania, plague was focused at higher elevations (1,200–2,000 m) and in areas with seasonal vegetation changes, suggesting that risk was lower in forested areas relative to surrounding areas (92). Similarly, in northwestern Uganda, plague risk was more elevated in sites situated above 1,300 m than in those below as well as in areas that were wetter with less vegetative growth and had more bare soil during the dry season when agricultural plots were typically fallow. These variables are suggestive of a positive association between elevated plague risk and cultivation of annual agricultural crops (44, 130). Indeed, a subsequent study that evaluated residential risk

ADVANCES IN SPATIAL RISK MODELING

Recent advances in the integration of geographic information systems and statistical analyses have allowed researchers to identify environmental risk factors for many vector-borne diseases. The resulting statistical models can be displayed in map format allowing for the visualization of disease risk probabilities across areas where surveillance may not have been performed. The use of such models and their integration into decision support systems for the prediction, prevention, and control of vector-borne diseases was reviewed recently (37).

factors for plague showed that homesteads situated in areas classified as elevated risk for plague on the basis of these remotely sensed variables were more likely to grow or dry corn within 30 m of the residence when compared with areas classified as low risk (84) (see sidebar, Advances in Spatial Risk Modeling).

Within the epidemiological focus in the southwestern United States, human risk of exposure to plague bacteria was determined to be highest around 2,300 m, in vegetation types defined as piñon-juniper or Ponderosa pine and in wetter areas (41, 43, 46). In California, the distribution of plague-infected California ground-squirrel populations was characterized on the basis of precipitation in the wettest quarter of the year and the warmest temperature in the warmest month of the year (65).

Spatial and temporal distributions of plague are often associated with temperature and rainfall patterns. Worldwide, more than 95% of plague cases are reported from areas with average temperatures that exceed 13°C, with most outbreaks occurring in regions where these temperatures vary from 24°C to 27°C; epidemic activity typically subsides when temperatures exceed 27°C (18, 19, 26). Within plague foci, epizootics occur sporadically. Although the drivers of plague epizootics are not well defined, their timing is often associated with temperature and rainfall patterns (42, 55, 56). Several quantitative models have revealed that, within the relatively arid plague-enzootic regions such as those in the western United States and Kazakhstan, increased moisture levels prior to a transmission season are typically favorable for epizootic activity, whereas elevated temperatures during the transmission season are often unfavorable (11, 16, 23, 49, 95, 109, 110, 112). Based on these observations, a trophic cascade hypothesis was proposed in which elevated precipitation is presumed to increase primary vegetative production, which enhances the supply of potential food sources and harborage for small mammals (49, 95). As small-mammal populations increase, flea-infestation rates may also increase. In addition, the added soil moisture may increase daily survival rates of fleas, which increases the probability that the contact rates between infectious fleas and susceptible hosts will increase, thus increasing the probability of an epizootic (38, 83).

Several studies from North America and Central Asia lend credence to the trophic cascade hypothesis. For example, in the western United States, interannual variation in reported human plague cases was positively associated with the Pacific Decadal Oscillation value for March and a negative association with the mean number of days above 37°C. In this region, a positive Pacific Decadal Oscillation value is typically associated with milder and wetter conditions, which may be conducive for local transmission of *Y. pestis*: Fewer hot days and increased moisture may have relatively low impact on flea mortality, and vegetative cover would be expected to increase under these conditions (11). Within epidemiological foci in the southwestern United States, human and pet cases of plague occurred more frequently following periods with above-average precipitation (16, 49, 95), and case counts were negatively affected by elevated temperatures during the observation year (16, 49). Similarly, plague epizootics in prairie dog colonies in Montana were positively associated with time-lagged precipitation and number of warm days, but they were negatively associated with the number of hot days (23). Likewise, in north-central Colorado, plague-related die-offs of prairie dogs frequently followed El Niño events (110). In Central Asia, continued persistence and spread of plague in great gerbils (*Rhombomys opimus*) in Kazakhstan is dependent on threshold population sizes of this important host species (27, 29). Furthermore, plague among great gerbils is positively correlated with wetter summers and warmer springs (112).

Pathogen Development within the Vertebrate Host

Owing to the small amount of blood that a flea consumes per blood meal (0.1–0.3 μl) (61, 94), for transmission from vertebrate host to vector to occur reliably, bacteremia must be at least 10^6 cfu ml^{-1} of blood (48, 83). In laboratory animals, bacterial concentrations usually reach 10^8 to 10^9 cfu ml^{-1} of blood (17, 32, 106). Achieving such high bacterial concentrations virtually guarantees that hosts will die of sequelae associated with late-stage *Y. pestis* infections. However, this apparent cost to *Y. pestis* of killing its host appears to be balanced by the benefit of increased probabilities that at least some fleas will complete feeding prior to the host's death and, thus, acquire sufficient numbers of bacteria to become infectious to other animals during subsequent blood feedings (56). In addition, plague-induced host mortality increases the likelihood of transmission to another host of the same or different species either through transmission by direct contact with the infectious carcass or by forcing newly infected fleas to seek alternative hosts (42, 61).

Y. pestis has adapted several strategies for attaining such high bacterial concentrations in its host. After plague bacteria are introduced into a susceptible vertebrate host through the bite of an infectious flea, several bacterial genes are upregulated that allow the bacteria to evade the immune system and disseminate to the lymphatic system. Although recent work has cast doubt on its role (59, 122), Pla, a surface protease encoded on the pPla plasmid, is typically believed to be required for dissemination from the intradermal bite site (78). Shortly after infection, *Y. pestis* infects macrophages that serve as transport for the bacteria to regional lymph nodes. Within the lymph nodes, they multiply, express F1 antigen (caf1) and pH6 antigen, and ultimately give rise to the characteristic buboes (highly swollen lymph nodes that are heavily infected with *Y. pestis)* that are associated with bubonic plague (115). Upon leaving the macrophage, *Y. pestis* bears F1 capsular antigen and expresses pH6 antigen (PsaA), both of these aid in resistance to further phagocytosis (34), thus enabling the bacteria to circulate freely in the bloodstream and multiply rapidly to reach quickly densities ($>10^6$ bacteria/ml blood) that are sufficient to infect feeding fleas (48, 106).

Mechanisms of Flea-Borne Transmission

Since it was first described by Bacot & Martin in 1914, the blocked flea model has endured as the dominant mechanism of flea-borne transmission of *Y. pestis*. Under this paradigm, fleas become infected with plague bacteria by consuming blood harboring high concentrations of *Y. pestis* (typically $\geq 10^6$ cfu ml^{-1}) (48, 83). Initially, bacteria colonize and multiply within the midgut and proventriculus, which is a globular structure situated between the esophagus and midgut and which is lined interiorly with a series of spines that prevent ingested blood from back-flowing to the mouthparts. Over a period of 2 to 3 weeks postinfection (p.i.), but as early as 5 days p.i., multiplication of bacteria within the proventriculus can cause an occlusion or blockage that prevents newly ingested blood from reaching the midgut. Recent studies have demonstrated that a group of chromosomal genes called the hemin storage locus is required for colonization of the proventriculus and production of the biofilm that is responsible for blockage formation (62). The blockage serves two functions that are likely to increase the probability of transmission. First, it prevents newly ingested blood from reaching the midgut, which causes the flea to starve. As a result, the infected flea increases the number of blood meals it consumes per day, which is likely to result in higher vectorial capacity (47, 83). In addition, the increased feeding causes vigorous movements of blood in the foregut, which may cause cleavage of the *Y. pestis*–rich blockage that can be regurgitated during current or subsequent blood meals. Second, the blockage disrupts the normal function of the proventriculus and allows infected blood to reflux from the midgut to the mouthparts.

Vectorial capacity: a measure of the average number of infectious bites by all vectors feeding on a host in a single day

Extrinsic incubation period: the time elapsed from when a vector becomes infected until it is able to transmit the acquired pathogen

Early-phase transmission: a mechanism of *Y. pestis* transmission by unblocked fleas occurring prior to when a blockage would be expected to develop

Although Bacot & Martin noted that partially blocked fleas may be more efficient vectors than fully blocked fleas (9), the classical blocked flea paradigm that is based on the fully blocked flea model dominated the plague literature for nearly a century and presented this model as the primary and only significant mode of flea-borne transmission. Indeed, vector efficiency has often been equated with a flea's ability to form a proventricular blockage (50, 61, 63, 77, 79, 83, 100). However, most infected fleas do not form blockages, and among those that do, the time elapsed from becoming infected to forming the blockage is ordinarily at least 2 to 3 weeks (**Table 1**). Among *Xenopsylla cheopis* that form a blockage, laboratory-based studies have consistently demonstrated that vectorial capacity is quite low (**Table 1**). Given the absence of blockages in many flea species that are presumed to be important vectors (17, 40, 42, 50, 56) as well as the long extrinsic incubation period and low transmission efficiency associated with blocked flea transmission, recent studies have questioned whether this transmission mechanism is sufficient to explain the rapid rates of spread within susceptible host populations that typify plague epizootics (38, 120).

Alternative sources of infection that do not involve fleas (e.g., direct contact with infected hosts or carcasses and persistence of *Y. pestis* in soil) have been proposed as drivers of plague epizootics (33, 42, 120). However, empirical evidence demonstrates that ridding hosts of their fleas effectively halts pathogen transmission, thus the role of fleas in epizootic transmission cannot be eliminated (39, 58, 66, 100, 108). Although the blocked flea paradigm has been acknowledged as important during interepizootic transmission, some have suggested that mechanical transmission by unblocked fleas is significant during epizootics (17, 72, 73, 102). True mechanical transmission, which would occur as a result of contamination of the flea's mouthparts by viable *Y. pestis*, would render fleas infectious immediately after exposure to plague bacteria and would explain the observed rapid rates of transmission. However, this mechanism has been discounted by some because of their belief that plague bacteria survive on the mouth parts for fewer than 3 h (12).

Recently, an alternative flea-borne mode of transmission, termed early-phase transmission, was described (38). The early-phase model refers to transmission by unblocked fleas during the time period prior to the earliest time point during which a complete blockage is able to form. This mode of transmission is characterized by a short extrinsic incubation period (e.g., as early as 3 h p.i.) (38) and, in some cases, transmission efficiencies that rival those observed for blocked *X. cheopis* (38, 47, 127, 128). To date, early-phase vector efficiency has been tested for six North American flea species (38, 39, 45, 47, 127, 128); although each species was capable of early-phase transmission, efficiency was highly variable. These results were consistent with earlier studies that reported transmission by unblocked fleas 1 to 4 days p.i. (9, 17, 48, 64, 86, 100, 117, 125). In these instances, the results were often viewed as anomalous or attributed to occurring by mass action (i.e., unnaturally high flea loads) and were largely ignored. However, these findings suggest that numerous flea species are capable of early-phase transmission.

The biological mechanism of early-phase transmission has not been elucidated, but in contrast to the blocked flea model of transmission, biofilm is not required for early-phase transmission (118). Regardless of the biological mechanism of early-phase transmission, which may involve a combination of mechanical transmission and regurgitation of midgut or esophageal contents containing *Y. pestis*, several studies have demonstrated the significance of this mode of transmission at the population level. For example, simple vectorial capacity modeling concludes that, on the

Table 1 Experimentally confirmed flea vectors of *Yersinia pestis* in North America[a]

Flea species	Natural hosts in North America	Pathogen-acquisition efficiency	Vector efficiency (number of fleas used)	Mean number of days for EIP (range)	Likelihood of infected fleas blocking (mean days to block)	Reference
Aetheca wagneri	Various mice	≥30%	6% (18)	49 (49)	5% (ND)	71
		79%	1% (185)	3 (3)	0% (ND)	45
Ctenocephalides felis	Domestic cats	≥85%	0% (14)[b]	ND	ND	125
		93%	0.6% (174)	2 (2)	0% (ND)	39
Echidnophaga gallinaceus	Poultry	80%	23% (48)[c]	ND	23% ND	17
Epitedia wenmanni	Deer mice	≥36%	12% (48)	30 (15–61)	18% (ND)	71
Eumolpianus eumolpi	Chipmunks	26%	6% (31)	78 (78)	ND	50
Hoplopsyllus anomalus	Ground squirrels	23%	20% (5)	35 (35)	ND	50
Hystrichopsylla linsdalei	Voles, mice	≥57%	4% (84)	ND	20% (ND)	72
Malaraeus telchinum	Mice, jumping mice, voles	≥17%	4% (115)[c]	23 (4–38)	0% (ND)	17
Megabothris abantis	Mice, jumping mice, voles	≥40%	3% (75)	24 (22–26)	12% (17)[c]	17
		≥75%	12% (8)	28 (9–47)	37% (ND)	71
Nosopsyllus fasciatus	Domestic mice and rats	≥42%	13% (47)[c]	20 (11–29)	23% (16)[c]	17
		26%	20% (51)	41 (41)	ND	50
Opisodasys nesiotis	Deer mice	≥54%	4% (46)[c]	14 (5–19)	22% (8)[c]	17
Orchopeas sexdentatus	Wood rats	≥70%	9% (53)[c]	11 (6–15)	28% (7)[c]	17
		28%	6% (81)	38 (38)	ND	50
Oropsylla bruneri	Ground squirrels	61%	50% (8)	30 (21–34)	ND	101
Oropsylla hirsuta	Prairie dogs	28%	4% (70)	102 (102)	ND	50
		100%	5.2% (~270)	1 (1)	0% (ND)	127
Oropsylla idahoensis	Various rodents	≥7%	0% (61)[b]	ND	0% (ND)	17
Oropsylla labis	Ground squirrels, prairie dogs	24%	8% (178)	35(35)	ND	50
		24%	10% (~60)	ND	ND	69
Oropsylla montana	Ground squirrels	≥25%	1.5% (66)[c]	4 (4)	3% (8)[c]	17
		≥73%	2% (446)[c]	ND	ND	64
		≥35%	4% (65)	ND	13% ND	71
		84%	48% (67)	10 (3–27)	ND	125
		20%	11% (19)	53 (53)	ND	50
		≥51%	2% (196)[c]	23 (4–37)	ND	48
		85%	52% (41)	ND	ND	123
		20%	11% (~20)	ND	ND	69
		96%	ND	10 (4–20)	ND	32
		100%	>10% (317)	<1 (<1)	0% (ND)	38
		100%	>11% (48)	1 (1)	0% (ND)	39
		100%	10% (69)	1 (1)	0% (ND)	45
Oropsylla rupestris	Ground squirrels	42%	67% (3)	28 (28)	ND	50
Oropsylla tuberculata	Ground squirrels, prairie dogs	33%	10% (10)	32 (32)	ND	50
Oropsylla tuberculata cynomuris	Ground squirrels, prairie dogs	>88%	17% (~256)	1 (1)	0% (ND)	128

(Continued)

Table 1 (*Continued*)

Flea species	Natural hosts in North America	Pathogen-acquisition efficiency	Vector efficiency (number of fleas used)	Mean number of days for EIP (range)	Likelihood of infected fleas blocking (mean days to block)	Reference
Pleochaetis exilis	Grasshopper mice	≥42%	25% (8)	12.5 (12–13)	25% (ND)	71
Polygenis gwyni	Cotton rats	≥83%	27% (88)[c]	ND (2–23)	67% (ND)	64
Pulex irritans	Various mammals	≥31%	0% (57)[b,c]	ND	2% (11)[c]	17
Thrassis acamantis	Marmots	29%	13% (8)	7 (7)	ND	50
Thrassis arizonensis	Ground squirrels	44%	5% (58)	41 (41)	ND	50
Thrassis bacchi	Ground squirrels	≥53%	33% (18)	25 (8–46)	33% (ND)	71
		24%	40% (10)	28 (23–32)	ND	101
Thrassis fotus	Ground squirrels	≥47%	20% (10)	22 (15–28)	30% (ND)	71
Thrassis francisi	Ground squirrels	14%	19% (21)	27 (27)	ND	50
Thrassis pandorae	Ground squirrels	18%	10% (58)	45 (45)	ND	50
		18%	10% (~20)	ND	ND	69
Xenopsylla cheopis	Domestic rats	72%	38% (53)	12 (5–18)	58% (12)	17
		>70%	13% (95)	16 (6–32)	2% (19)	48
		100%	6.4% (103)	1 (1)	0% (ND)	47
		38%	20% (140)	21 (21)	ND	50
		54%	33% (27)	21 (21)	60% (10–40)	72
		97%	72% (29)	ND	77% (ND)	73
		96%	30% (47)	16 (6–33)	ND	125
		77%	48% (79)	22 (11–49)	70% (ND)	71
		96%	69% (29)	ND	79% (5–30)	74
		~75%	45% (31)	14 (7–28)	38% (14)	83
		63%	38% (34)	<14	ND	64
		96%	ND	16 (6–34)	ND	32
		98%	29% (49)	ND	ND	123

[a]Including data on pathogen-acquisition efficiency (percentage of fleas infected after feeding on an infected host), vector efficiency (percentage of infected fleas that transmit *Y. pestis*), time elapsed between *Y. pestis* acquisition and transmission [i.e., extrinsic incubation period (EIP)], and likelihood and timing of infected fleas becoming blocked. Previously published in the *Journal of Medical Entomology* (40).

[b]Transmission demonstrated only in mass-feeding experiments.

[c]Assuming that all fleas were infected.

ND, not determined.

basis of flea-infestation rates observed in the field, this mode of transmission could be sufficient to explain epizootic transmission for some flea species (38, 47, 127, 128).

Summary of Key Vertebrate Species Involved in Transmission Cycles

Although plague is primarily a disease of rodents, nearly all mammals can become infected with *Y. pestis*, but the response to infection differs between species or within populations of the same species (10, 56). As reviewed recently (42, 56), there are several theories to explain how *Y. pestis* is maintained during epizootic and interepizootic periods. Some have proposed that plague bacteria are maintained in enzootic cycles by host species that display a heterogeneous response to infection. Within a population of "maintenance" or enzootic hosts, some individuals are highly susceptible to infection and harbor the very high concentrations of bacteria required for flea-borne transmission prior to perishing from the infection. As a result, fleas infesting these hosts acquire infection, and host death forces them to seek new hosts, thus perpetuating the transmission cycle. Other individuals in the same population may be capable of mounting a sufficient immune response to survive the infection. These immune hosts serve to slow the rate of transmission within the host population. Epizootics, or periods of rapid spread, are believed to occur when infectious fleas spill over from enzootic cycles into populations of highly susceptible epizootic or "amplifying" host populations. In contrast, others have proposed that plague could be maintained within epizootic host populations (not requiring multiple-species involvement) if the spatial structure of populations is sufficient. For example, a metapopulation structure that consists of several local populations connected via host or flea movement may allow for long-term persistence of plague bacteria through a series of local extinctions followed by recolonization. Across plague foci, host-flea complexes involved in *Y. pestis* transmission vary. A summary of such complexes was presented by Gratz (58) and is summarized in **Table 2**.

Summary of Key Flea Species Involved in Pathogen Transmission

Naturally acquired *Y. pestis* infections have been reported from approximately 250 flea species (40, 100, 111). However, only a small fraction of these are considered to be efficient vectors—that is, they (*a*) become infected after feeding on a bacteremic host, (*b*) live long enough for the bacteria to multiply to sufficient numbers to ensure transmission, and (*c*) are able to transfer *Y. pestis* to a susceptible host at concentrations adequate to cause infection (40, 58). In addition to possessing the ability to acquire, maintain, and transmit plague bacteria, the probability of a flea playing a key role in maintaining enzootic transmission cycles or serving as a bridging vector either between rodent species or from zoonotic hosts to humans is dependent on (*a*) how efficiently the infected flea is able to transfer bacteria to the host, (*b*) host preferences, (*c*) infestation rates, (*d*) the length of the extrinsic incubation period (i.e., the time period from when a flea becomes infected to when it is able to transmit), (*e*) the length of time an infected flea remains infectious in the presence or absence of subsequent blood meals, and (*f*) the flea's daily biting rate (40). For example, *X. cheopis* is considered a highly efficient vector, as it is capable of transmission by early-phase and classical mechanisms (17, 32, 47, 48, 50, 64, 71–74, 83, 123, 125). Thus, fairly low numbers of these rat fleas per host are required to maintain transmission cycles. Although they feed primarily on commensal rats, they also infest sylvatic rodents; thus, this flea has been implicated in enzootic transmission and as a bridging vector between rodent host species. In addition, the flea is common in human dwellings, readily bites humans, and has been implicated as a bridging vector to humans from zoonotic cycles (4, 50, 58, 63, 100). By contrast, cat fleas (*Ctenocephalides felis*) are commonly encountered in human dwellings within some plague foci, but they are inefficient vectors of *Y. pestis* and are rarely collected from commensal or sylvatic rodent hosts. Thus, they are unlikely to serve as bridging vectors or play a major role in plague epidemics or epizootics (4, 58)

A recent review of vector competency and efficiency studies for North American fleas revealed that among the approximately 230 species described in the western United States, only approximately 28 have been laboratory-confirmed vectors of *Y. pestis* (40) (for a summary of those studies, see **Table 2**). Most of these studies focused on flea species that were abundant on hosts affected by plague as the pathogen spread eastward in the United States during the first half of the twentieth century. It is quite likely that many more species are capable of serving as vectors of *Y. pestis*, but their competency to do so has not been evaluated in the laboratory. Furthermore, among the

Table 2 Primary rodent hosts and flea vectors of *Yersinia pestis* within established plague foci[a]

Plague focus (countries)	Rodent hosts	Flea vectors
Southern Africa (South Africa, Lesotho, Namibia, Zimbabwe)	*Tatera afra* *Tatera brantsi* *Tatera leucogaster* *Otomys irroratus* *Mastomys coucha* *Mastomys natalensis* *Rattus rattus* *Rhabdomys pumilio*	*Dinopsyllus ellobius* *Xenopsylla brasiliensis* *Xenopsylla cheopis* *Xenopsylla philoxera*
East Africa (Kenya, Tanzania, Uganda, Mozambique, Madagascar)	*Arvicanthis abyssinicus* *Arvicanthis niloticus* *Cricetomys gambianus* *Grammomys dloichurus* *Lemniscomys striatus* *Lophuromys flavopunctatus* *Lophuromys sikapusi* *Mastomys natalensis* *Otomys angoniensis* *Otomys denti* *Pelomys fallax* *Petrodromus tetradactylus* *Rattus rattus* *Rhabdomys pumilio* *Tatera robusta*	*Ctenophthalmus bacopus* *Ctenophthalmus cabirus* *Dinopsyllus lypusus* *Pulex irritans* *Xenopsylla brasiliensis* *Xenopsylla cheopis*
Central Africa (Democratic Republic of Congo)	*Arvicanthis abyssinicus* *Lemniscomys striatus* *Mastomys natalensis* *Rattus rattus*	*Ctenophthalmus cabirus* *Ctenophthalmus phyris* *Dinopsyllus lypusus* *Xenopsylla brasiliensis*
Northwest Africa (Mauritania)	*Gerbillus gerbillus* *Gerbillus nanus* *Jaculus jaculus* *Psammomys obesus*	*Synosternus cleopatrae* *Xenopsylla cheopis* *Xenopsylla ramesis* *Xenopsylla nubica*
North Africa (Libya)	*Gerbillus gerbillus* *Meriones shawi*	*Nosopsylla henleyi* *Xenopsylla cheopis* *Xenopsylla ramesis* *Xenopsylla taractes*
Arabian Peninsula (Yemen)	*Meriones rex* *Rattus rattus*	–
Southwestern Asia (Iran)	*Meriones tristrami* *Meriones vinogradovi* *Tatera indica*	*Stenoponia tripectinata* *Xenopsylla buxtoni*
Russian Federation and former Soviet Republics (northwest Caspian focus, focus between the Volga River and the Ural Mountains, focus on the left bank of the Ural River, focus in the Transcaucasia, central Asian desert focus, Tian-Shan focus, Pamir-Alai focus, Transbaikalian focus, High Altai and Tuva Autonomous Region focus)	*Citellus dauricus* *Citellus pygmaeus* *Citellus undulatus* *Marmota babacina* *Marmota caudata* *Marmota sibirica* *Meriones libycus erythrourus* *Meriones meridianus*	*Ceratophyllus caspius* *Ceratophyllus laeviceps* *Ceratophyllus lebedwi* *Ceratophyllus tesquorum* *Ctenophthalmus teres* *Ctenophthalmus wladimiri* *Frontopsylla luculenta* *Neopsylla setosa*

(*Continued*)

Table 2 (*Continued*)

Plague focus (countries)	Rodent hosts	Flea vectors
	Meriones tamariscinus *Microtus arvalis* *Putorius eversmanni* *Rhombomys opimus*	*Oropsylla silantiewi* *Rhadinopsylla cedestis* *Rhadinopsylla ventricosa* *Xenopsylla conformis* *Xenopsylla gerbilli* *Xenopsylla hirtipes* *Xenopsylla nuttalli* *Xenopsylla skrjabini*
Southeast Asia and the Western Pacific (India, Nepal, Myanmar, Indonesia, Vietnam, China)	*Apodemus chevrieri* *Apodemus speciosus* *Bandicota bengalensis* *Eothenomys miletus* *Marmota bobac* *Marmota baibacina* *Marmota caudata* *Marmota himalayana* *Meriones unguiculatus* *Microtus brandti* *Rattus exulans* *Rattus flavipectus* *Rattus nitidus* *Rattus norvegicus* *Rattus rattus* *Spermophilus alaschanicus* *Spermophilus dauricus* *Spermophilus undulatus* *Suncus murinus* *Tatera indica*	*Amphipsylla primaries* *Callopsylla dolabris* *Citellophilus tesquorum* *Citellophilus sungaris* *Ctenophthalmus quadrates* *Frontopsylla luculenta* *Neopsylla pleskei* *Neopsylla specialis* *Nosopsyllus fasciatus* *Nosopsyllus laeviceps* *Oropsylla silantiewi* *Rhadinopsylla li* *Pulex irritans* *Xenopsylla astia* *Xenopsylla brasiliensis* *Xenopsylla cheopis* *Xenopsylla conformis*
North America (United States)	*Cynomys gunnisoni* *Cynomys ludovicianus* *Cynomys leucurus* *Cynomys parvidens* *Eutamias* spp. *Neotoma* spp. *Spermophilus beecheyi* *Spermophilus variegatus*	*Hoplopsyllus anomalous* *Orchopeas sexdentatus* *Oropsylla montana* *Oropsylla hirsuta* *Oropsylla tuberculata*
South America (Bolivia, Brazil, Ecuador, Peru)	*Akodon mollis* *Galea musteloides* *Graomys griseoflavus* *Oryzomys andinus* *Oryzomys xanthaeolus* *Rattus rattus* *Sciurus stramineus* *Zygodontomys lasiurus pixuna*	*Polygenis litargus* *Xenopsylla cheopis*

[a]Data were tabulated using primary references cited in Reference 58.

species that have been examined, many of these studies focused on transmission via the classical blockage mechanism, and early-phase time points were often not evaluated. In short, it is quite likely that the list of plague vectors is considerably longer than what has been described to date, and when early-phase time points are considered, transmission efficiency for some flea species may be higher than initially realized.

MURINE TYPHUS (*RICKETTSIA TYPHI*)

Overview of Murine Typhus Epidemiology and Ecology

Murine typhus, also called flea-borne or endemic typhus, is a rickettsial illness caused by infection with the typhus group rickettsia, *Rickettsia typhi* (formerly *Rickettsia mooseri*) (5). The disease is widespread and occurs in many, if not most, areas where commensal rats (*Rattus rattus* and closely allied species as well as *Rattus norvegicus*) and the Oriental rat flea (*X. cheopis*) are found. In the past, thousands of cases occurred in the warmer southern regions of the United States, but this number has decreased to only a few hundred in recent decades, most of which occur in Texas, California, and Hawaii (2, 22, 85). Similar reductions in the incidence of this disease appear to have occurred in other developed countries in temperate zones. Although associated primarily with commensal rats and rat fleas (5, 116), *R. typhi* also is reported to occur in extramurine maintenance cycles involving such hosts and vectors as opossums (*Didelphis virginiana*) and cat fleas (*Ctenocephalides felis*), respectively (129). Murine typhus in humans is often relatively mild compared with louse-borne typhus, a disease caused by another related rickettsiae (*Rickettsia prowazekii*) (35). Typically, cases can be treated successfully with antibiotics, although fatalities occasionally occur, most often among elderly patients (5). Common signs and symptoms include a characteristic rickettsial rash (macular in appearance), fever, headache, chills, achiness, and prostration. Respiratory and gastrointestinal symptoms are not uncommon and multiorgan involvement is often indicated by abnormal laboratory findings in hematologic, respiratory, hepatic, and renal system tests. In addition to flea-bite exposures, humans reportedly have become infected through airborne exposures, presumably as a result of inhaling infectious flea fecal material in dust (116).

Pathogen Development within the Vertebrate Host

Upon invading the vertebrate host, *R. typhi* invades the endothelial cells lining the blood vessels of its host (119). Once inside these host cells, murine typhus rickettsia, which are obligate intracellular bacteria, multiply until they cause their host cells to burst, releasing large numbers of rickettsiae into the bloodstream where they can infect other endothelial cells or be picked up by a feeding flea vector. As more endothelial cells within capillary vessels are destroyed, blood cells leak from the vessels, resulting in the typical macular rash of murine typhus and causing pathological complications including detectable hemorrhaging, hypotension, and renal dysfunction in severe cases.

Mechanisms of Flea-Borne Transmission

Unlike many vector-borne disease agents, *R. typhi* can gain entry to its vertebrate hosts through contamination with infectious flea feces at the location of flea feeding, a process that can be aided by host rubbing or scratching of the bite site or transferring infectious rickettsia on contaminated fingers or other objects to mucus membranes or conjunctiva (5). Some have reported that infection also can occur directly from flea bites, although the importance of this route remains uncertain (8, 51). When a competent reservoir host becomes infected, the rickettsiae multiply in the endothelial cells of the host's vasculature, resulting in the eventual destruction of infected cells and the release of large numbers of *R. typhi* into the host's bloodstream. Upon ingestion by a blood-feeding flea, the rickettsiae pass to the flea's midgut where they invade and multiply within epithelial cells. As occurs in the vertebrate host endothelial cells, proliferation of *R. typhi* in midgut epithelium cells eventually results in the destruction of these cells and release of hundreds of rickettsiae into the midgut lumen for each cell destroyed. Midgut infections typically begin at a particular focal point, and they eventually spread until most midgut epithelial cells are infected. Despite the large proportion of midgut epithelial cells infected, *R. typhi* seems to cause little damage to its flea vector, as indicated by the fact that fleas become infected for life and yet do not appear to suffer significant decreases in longevity or reproductive output (5). Presumably this is in part due to the fact that the epithelial layer in the flea's midgut is replaced at a sufficiently rapid rate to overcome any pathogenic effects of *R. typhi* infection. Once *R. typhi* burst from infected epithelial cells into the lumen of the midgut, a process that usually takes 3 to 4 days to become detectable, they can be incorporated into and shed with the flea's feces, which are infectious for mammalian hosts and the source of infection for most cases of murine typhus. Typically, fleas can become infectious approximately 10 days after acquiring infection and can remain infectious throughout the remainder of their adult lives. Although maintenance of *R. typhi* is thought to occur primarily through flea to vertebrate host to flea transmission, this rickettsia has been reported to invade the ovary tissues of female fleas, reportedly resulting in transovarial transmission (52).

Summary of Key Vertebrate Species Involved in Transmission Cycles

In most instances, commensal rats are the primary vertebrate species involved in local transmission cycles of *R. typhi*. These rats serve not only as blood meal sources for fleas, but also as amplifying hosts for infecting fleas with *R. typhi*. Although evidence of *R. typhi* infection in nonmurine vertebrate hosts has been reported, the importance of extramurine cycles of *R. typhi* remains unclear (5, 116). Infection of opossums (*Didelphis virginiana*) has been reported in the United States, and these animals appear to be epidemiologically important in Texas and California and serve as primary vertebrate hosts for extramurine transmission cycles in these areas. In California, cats frequently have been found to have *R. typhi* antibodies and may be important hosts in this state as well as other areas (22). Elsewhere in the world, murine rodents other than *Rattus* spp., including the African giant pouched rat (*Cricetomys gambiae*), have been suggested to play roles in local *R. typhi* cycles (5, 7, 116).

Summary of Key Flea Species Involved in Pathogen Transmission

X. cheopis is the primary vector of *R. typhi* in most locations around the world. Other flea species, however, have been demonstrated to transmit *R. typhi* under experimental conditions or have been found infected under natural conditions (5, 116) and may be locally important vectors. Among the ten flea species identified by Azad (5) as potential vectors, eight frequently occur on rats. In addition to *X. cheopis*, two other *Xenopsylla* species (*X. astia* and *X. brasiliensis*) appear to be effective vectors. The northern rat flea (*Nosopsyllus fasciatus*), which is common on commensal rats in temperate latitudes, becomes infected with *R. typhi* and could transmit this rickettsia among rats, but most epidemiological evidence suggest this flea plays little role in the transmission of murine typhus to humans. The widespread flea *Leptopsylla segnis*, which occurs on house mice and rats, has been found infected with *R. typhi* and can support multiplication of this rickettsia in its midgut. Another flea species, *Pulex irritans*, which is often called the human flea, is rarely found on rats and occurs most commonly on larger animals, such as carnivores, pigs and certain other ungulates, as well as opossums. This species is an efficient vector for *R. typhi* under laboratory conditions, but its lack of association with rats under natural conditions makes it unlikely to be an important vector in most locations. It should be noted, however, that *P. irritans* is found fairly often on opossums, and as previously stated, these animals have been implicated as natural hosts in Texas and California. Probably the best evidence that a nonmurine-infesting flea can serve as a significant vector of *R. typhi* is provided by studies done in Texas and California on extramurine cycles involving opossums and cat fleas (*Ctenocephalides felis*) (6, 22). In addition to being found frequently infected with *R. typhi* in nature, this flea is also a competent vector of *R. typhi* under laboratory conditions (52).

RICKETTSIA FELIS

R. felis is a relatively recently identified rickettsial species that was initially referred to as the ELB agent (so termed for the EL Laboratory in Soquel, California) following its identification in a cat flea colony (1). First believed to be a typhus or spotted fever group rickettsia, more recent phylogenetic analyses have placed *R. felis* in a genetically distinct "transitional group" of rickettsiae (57). Further studies have found this rickettsial species to be nearly worldwide in its distribution, an observation attributed by some to its association with the similarly cosmopolitan cat flea (103). Although genetically distinct from *R. typhi*, *R. felis* has been identified in patients suffering murine typhus-like illnesses, frequently accompanied by an eruption or eschar (96, 97, 105), suggesting that the pathology of *R. felis* infections may be similar to that of other rickettsial infections and primarily related to the destruction of endothelial cells lining the host's blood vessels. A serosurvey of humans in Spain indicated that 7.1% of humans tested in the study area were seropositive for *R. felis* antibodies, suggesting human infection with this rickettsia is common but under-recognized (103).

At present, relatively little is known about the ecology and epidemiology of *R. felis* and *R. felis*–related illness. Presumably, humans acquire infection following exposure to infectious cat fleas or perhaps other infected flea species, including *Ctenocephalides canis*, that at least occasionally feed on humans. Despite its widespread association with cat fleas, *R. felis* has been identified in a variety of other flea species, including those that normally feed on domestic animals, rodents, insectivores and marsupials (97, 103). These other fleas include widespread species with low host specificity such as *C. canis*, *P. irritans*, *Echidnophaga gallinacea*, and *Tunga penetrans*, as well as rat fleas (*X. cheopis* and *X. brasiliensis*) and other fleas of rodents or insectivores (*Archaeopsylla erinacei*, *Anomiopsyllus nudata*, *Polygenis atopus*, *Ctenophthalmus* sp., and other unidentified rodent fleas). Although the distribution of *R. felis* is commonly assumed to coincide closely with that of the cat flea, other flea species have been found infected in sites that have few, if any, cat fleas (113), suggesting that *R. felis* is either more widespread than currently believed or perhaps consists of multiple genotypes, including some that are not closely associated with cat fleas. Ticks also have been reported to be naturally infected, but the significance of these reports remains to be demonstrated (103). Although laboratory transmission by cat fleas or other potential vectors through exposure of vertebrate hosts to infectious flea bites or flea feces, and subsequent recovery of viable *R. felis* from these hosts, has yet to be demonstrated, it is inferred on the basis of the identification of wild-caught mammals that are seropositive for *R. felis* antibodies and experiments demonstrating the appearance of *R. felis* antibodies and polymerase chain reaction (PCR)-positive blood samples from cats that had been fed upon by *R. felis*–infected cat fleas (103). Among the mammalian species found to be seropositive or PCR positive in nature are the Virginia opossum, cats, and dogs (103). Other mammalian species harboring *R. felis*–infested fleas also may become infected, but this has yet to be demonstrated. In addition to any flea to mammal to flea transmission that may occur, *R. felis* also can be transmitted transovarially for at least 12 generations without feeding on infectious, rickettsemic hosts, suggesting such transmission is important for the maintenance of this rickettsia in nature (121). No evidence for sexual transmission between male and female fleas was observed in these studies. Experiments to test whether *R. felis* could be transmitted from flea to flea through feeding of flea larvae on infectious flea feces also failed to yield positive results (103). Within the flea, *R. felis* has been identified in cells of the midgut epithelium, muscles, fat bodies, ovaries, tracheal matrix, epithelial sheath of the testes, and salivary glands (103). Identification of *R. felis* in salivary gland tissue suggests that secretion of infectious saliva during feeding is a possible mode of transmission to mammalian hosts, but this awaits confirmation. Another potential mode of horizontal transmission may be infectious cofeeding involving infected and uninfected fleas feeding in close proximity to each other, a process that has been reported for tick-borne viruses and *Borrelia burgdorferi* (103).

BARTONELLOSIS

Bartonella is a gram-negative bacteria that infects primarily red blood cells but can also be found associated with host endothelial, dendritic, and CD34+ cells, which include lymphopoietic stem and progenitor cells, small-vessel endothelial cells, and embryonic fibroblasts (13). Of the more than 20 species described, more than half infect either healthy or immune-compromised humans (88). Among the most important of these are the causative agents of three well-characterized illnesses: Oroya fever (*Bartonella bacilliformis*), trench fever (*Bartonella quintana*) and cat scratch disease (*B. henselae*). Among these three diseases, only the last is believed to be transmitted by fleas, although *B. henselae* can also be spread by the bites or scratches of infected cats (87). Typical symptoms of cat scratch infection include an erythema or pustule at the site of inoculation, fever, mild headache, and regional lymphadenopathy that can persist for several months. Occasionally (5–15% of cases), cases experience more severe complications, including encephalitis, retinitis, and endocarditis (87). Other *Bartonella* species, including those associated with rodents, rabbits, and dogs or cats also have been implicated as likely sources of human illness owing to their association with cases of endocarditis, retinitis, septicemia, myocarditis, and illnesses that appear very similar to cat scratch disease (13, 88). In addition, newly recognized species continue to be implicated as human pathogens, as demonstrated by the recent isolation and characterization of *Bartonella tamiae* from human patients in Thailand (76).

An even greater array of new genospecies continues to be described from a wide variety of mammal species, including various rodents, bats, insectivores, wild and domestic ungulates, and carnivores (13, 20, 75). Even nonmammalian species, such as loggerhead sea turtles, reportedly are infected with species of *Bartonella* (13), suggesting that these microbes are among the most widely distributed blood-associated bacteria in the world. What is less certain, however, is the medical and ecological significance of this wide diversity of species. Although some are pathogenic, others are collected from apparently healthy hosts who appear to be suffering few, if any, ill effects as a result of their infections. As noted for *R. felis*, much remains to be learned about how these bacteria are transmitted and maintained in nature. Although arthropod vectors have been implicated as sources of transmission for a few species, this is not true for most. The relative importance of vector-borne and other modes of transmission, such as scratching or biting by the host, also has yet to be determined for many species, including *B. henselae*, which apparently can spread through flea bites, cat bites, and cat scratches.

The list of flea species found naturally infected with various species of *Bartonella* continues to grow, but as noted by Billeter et al. (13), who reviewed this evidence, it is difficult to evaluate the significance of many of these reports because blood-feeding arthropods, including fleas, would be expected to ingest large numbers of *Bartonella* as a result of this bacteria's utilization of erythrocytes as their primary host cells. Nevertheless, there is an emerging body of experimental evidence indicating that fleas are vectors of some species of *Bartonella* (13). *Bartonella* sp. also appear to be important members of the microbial communities naturally found infecting fleas (70), although their effects on these fleas remain unknown. When cat fleas collected from bacteremic, commercially reared cats were placed on kittens demonstrated to be free of detectable *B. henselae* infections, the kittens became bacteremic (21). Unfortunately, a similar group of control kittens were not maintained in the absence of fleas to ensure that they were free of *B. henselae* infection prior to the experiment. Despite this problem, it seems likely that *C. felis* did transmit *B. henselae* to the susceptible kittens. In another experiment, *B. henselae* was transmitted to cats through inoculation of infectious fleas feces, suggesting this species can be transmitted in a manner similar to that observed for the murine typhus rickettsia (54). These results also suggest that humans could become infected with *B. henselae* as a result of being scratched by a cat that had claws contaminated by *B. henselae*–containing flea feces (53). In another study, wild-caught rodent fleas (*Ctenophthalmus nobilis nobilis*) removed from wild bank voles were later able to transmit both *Bartonella grahamii* and *Bartonella taylorii* to laboratory-reared bank voles over a period of four weeks, as indicated by the fact that 21 of 28 voles developed PCR-detectable *Bartonella* bacteremias involving one or both of these bacteria (14).

TULAREMIA (*FRANCISELLA TULARENSIS*)

Tularemia is a bacterial zoonosis of rodents and lagomorphs caused by infection with *Francisella tularensis*. Cases in humans can be serious, although fatality rates are typically less than 5%. Common symptoms include fever, swollen and painful lymph glands, and skin ulcers that are often located at the site of an arthropod bite. The disease can be transmitted not only through arthropod bites, but also by direct contact with body fluids of infected animals, ingestion of contaminated food or water, or, rarely, by inhalation of infectious materials. The most important vectors are ticks and deer flies. Fleas appear to play little role in transmitting tularemia under natural conditions. However, fleas have been reported to be capable of transmitting *F. tularensis* infrequently under some circumstances (67), presumably through mechanical transmission, as demonstrated by one study that reported positive results in only 6 of 116 experiments performed with fleas and another study where transmission occurred only within the first five days after fleas had taken an infectious blood meal (68).

SUMMARY POINTS

1. In the past decade, associations between plague risk and environmental variables have been quantified within a statistical framework and used to generate predictive risk models.
2. For nearly a century, the dominant theory in the medical entomology literature for transmission of *Y. pestis* was based on the blocked flea model. Recently, studies have demonstrated that blockage is not required for efficient transmission and that the extrinsic incubation period is shorter than previously assumed. This mode of transmission, termed early-phase transmission, provides an explanation for how plague spreads so rapidly during epizootic periods. The exact mechanism by which early-phase transmission occurs has not yet been defined.

3. *R. felis* is a recently identified rickettsial species that has a worldwide distribution. Serosurveys suggest that human infections with this agent are common but under-recognized. Laboratory-based transmission studies have not yet conclusively demonstrated vector competence of cat fleas or other vector species. Furthermore, it is largely unknown how *R. felis* is maintained in enzootic cycles.
4. Among the numerous *Bartonella* species described to date, only a few have been implicated as disease agents in humans, and only one of these, *B. henselae*, is believed to be flea borne. *Bartonella* species may be the most widely distributed blood-associated bacteria in the world, but their medical and ecological significance is uncertain.

DISCLOSURE STATEMENT

The authors are not aware of any affiliations, memberships, funding, or financial holdings that might be perceived as affecting the objectivity of this review.

LITERATURE CITED

1. Adams JR, Schmidtmann ET, Azad AF. 1990. Infection of colonized cat fleas, *Ctenocephalides felis* (Bouche), with a rickettsia-like microorganism. *Am. J. Trop. Med. Hyg.* 43:400–9
2. Adjemian J, Parks S, McElroy K, Campbell J, Eremeeva ME, et al. 2010. Murine Typhus in Austin, Texas, USA, 2008. *Emerg. Infect. Dis.* 16:412–17
3. Adjemian JZ, Foley P, Gage KL, Foley JE. 2007. Initiation and spread of traveling waves of plague, *Yersinia pestis*, in the western United States. *Am. J. Trop. Med. Hyg.* 76:365–75
4. Amatre G, Babi N, Enscore RE, Ogen-Odoi A, Atiku LA, et al. 2009. Flea diversity and infestation prevalence on rodents in a plague-endemic region of Uganda. *Am. J. Trop. Med. Hyg.* 81:718–24
5. Azad AF. 1990. Epidemiology of murine typhus. *Annu. Rev. Entomol.* 35:553–69
6. Azad AF, Beard CB. 1998. Rickettsial pathogens and their arthropod vectors. *Emerg. Infect. Dis.* 4:179–86
7. **Azad AF, Radulovic S, Higgins JA, Noden BH, Troyer JM. 1997. Flea-borne rickettsioses: ecologic considerations. *Emerg. Infect. Dis.* 3:319–27**
8. Azad AF, Traub R. 1989. Experimental transmission of murine typhus by *Xenopsylla cheopis* flea bites. *Med. Vet. Entomol.* 3:429–33
9. Bacot AW, Martin CJ. 1914. Observations on the mechanism of the transmission of plague by fleas. *J. Hyg.* 13(Plague Suppl. III):423–39
10. Barnes AM. 1982. Surveillance and control of bubonic plague in the United States. *Symp. Zool. Soc. Lond.* 50:237–70
11. Ben Ari T, Gershunov A, Gage KL, Snall T, Ettestad P, et al. 2008. Human plague in the USA: the importance of regional and local climate. *Biol. Lett.* 4:737–40
12. Bibikova VA. 1977. Contemporary views on the interrelationships between fleas and the pathogens of human and animal diseases. *Annu. Rev. Entomol.* 22:23–32
13. **Billeter SA, Levy MG, Chomel BB, Breitschwerdt EB. 2008. Vector transmission of *Bartonella* species with emphasis on the potential for tick transmission. *Med. Vet. Entomol.* 22:1–15**
14. Bown KJ, Bennett M, Begon M. 2004. Flea-borne *Bartonella grahamii* and *Bartonella taylorii* in bank voles. *Emerg. Infect. Dis.* 10:684–87
15. Brault AC. 2009. Changing patterns of West Nile virus transmission: altered vector competence and host susceptibility. *Vet. Res.* 40:43
16. Brown HE, Ettestad P, Reynolds PJ, Brown TL, Hatton ES, et al. 2010. Climatic predictors of the intra- and inter-annual distributions of plague cases in New Mexico based on 29 years of animal-based surveillance data. *Am. J. Trop. Med. Hyg.* 82:95–102

7. Reviews the ecology and transmission of *R. typhi* and provides early observations on *R. felis* and its ecology and potential role in human disease.

13. Summarizes the limited amount of information known about the transmission of *Bartonella* by fleas and other arthropods.

17. Burroughs AL. 1947. Sylvatic plague studies: the vector efficiency of nine species of fleas compared with *Xenopsylla cheopis*. *J. Hyg.* 43:371–96
18. Cavanaugh DC, Marshall JD. 1972. The influence of climate on the seasonal prevalence of plague in the Republic of Vietnam. *J. Wildl. Dis.* 8:85–93
19. Cavanaugh DC, Williams JE. 1980. Plague: some ecological interrelationships. In *Fleas*, ed. R Traub, H Starcke, pp. 245–56. Rotterdam: AA Balkema
20. Chomel BB, Kasten RW. 2010. Bartonellosis, an increasingly recognized zoonosis. *J. Appl. Microbiol.* 109:743–50
21. Chomel BB, Kasten RW, Floyd-Hawkins K, Chi B, Yamamoto K, et al. 1996. Experimental transmission of *Bartonella henselae* by the cat flea. *J. Clin. Microbiol.* 34:1952–56
22. Civen R, Ngo V. 2008. Murine typhus: an unrecognized suburban vectorborne disease. *Clin. Infect. Dis.* 46:913–18
23. Collinge SK, Johnson WC, Ray C, Matchett R, Grensten J, et al. 2005. Testing the generality of the trophic-cascade model for plague. *Ecohealth* 2:102–12
24. Collinge SK, Johnson WC, Ray C, Matchett R, Grensten J, et al. 2005. Landscape structure and plague occurrence in black-tailed prairie dogs on grasslands of the western USA. *Landsc. Ecol.* 20:941–55
25. Crook LD, Tempest B. 1992. Plague. A clinical review of 27 cases. *Arch. Intern. Med.* 152:1253–56
26. Davis DHS. 1953. Plague in Africa from 1935 to 1949: a survey of wild rodents in African territories. *Bull. WHO* 9:655–700
27. Davis S, Begon M, De Bruyn L, Ageyev VS, Klassovskiy NL, et al. 2004. Predictive thresholds for plague in Kazakhstan. *Science* 304:736–38
28. Davis S, Klassovskiy N, Ageyev V, Suleimenov B, Atshabar B, et al. 2007. Plague metapopulation dynamics in a natural reservoir: the burrow system as the unit of study. *Epidemiol. Infect.* 135:740–48
29. Davis S, Trapman P, Leirs H, Begon M, Heesterbeek JA. 2008. The abundance threshold for plague as a critical percolation phenomenon. *Nature* 454:634–37
30. Dennis DT, Gage KL. 2003. Plague. In *Infectious Diseases*, ed. J Cohen, WG Powderly, pp. 1641–48. London: Mosby
31. Dennis DT, Mead PS. 2010. *Yersinia* species, including plague. In *Mandell: Mandell, Douglas, and Bennett's Principles and Practice of Infectious Diseases, 17th edition*, ed. GL Mandell, JE Bennett, R Dolin, pp. 2943–49. Philadelphia: Elsevier
32. Douglas JR, Wheeler CM. 1943. Sylvatic plague studies. II. The fate of *Pasteurella pestis* in the flea. *J. Infect. Dis.* 72:18–30
33. Drancourt M, Houhamdi L, Raoult D. 2006. *Yersinia pestis* as a telluric, human ectoparasite-borne organism. *Lancet Infect. Dis.* 6:234–41
34. Du Y, Rosqvist R, Forsberg A. 2002. Role of fraction 1 antigen of *Yersinia pestis* in inhibition of phagocytosis. *Infect. Immun.* 70:1453–60
35. Dumler JS, Taylor JP, Walker DH. 1991. Clinical and laboratory features of murine typhus in south Texas, 1980 through 1987. *JAMA* 266:1365–70
36. Echenberg MJ. 2007. *Plague Ports: The Global Human Impact of Bubonic Plague 1894–1901*. New York: N.Y. Univ. Press
37. Eisen L, Eisen RJ. 2011. Using geographic information systems and decision support systems for the prediction, prevention, and control of vector-borne diseases. *Annu. Rev. Entomol.* 56:41–61
38. **Eisen RJ, Bearden SW, Wilder AP, Montenieri JA, Antolin MF, Gage KL. 2006. Early-phase transmission of *Yersinia pestis* by unblocked fleas as a mechanism explaining rapidly spreading plague epizootics. *Proc. Natl. Acad. Sci. USA* 103:15380–85**

38. First to describe early-phase transmission of *Y. pestis* by unblocked fleas, noting its importance in explaining the rapid rate of spread observed during plague epizootics.

39. Eisen RJ, Borchert JN, Holmes JL, Amatre G, Van Wyk K, et al. 2008. Early-phase transmission of *Yersinia pestis* by cat fleas (*Ctenocephalides felis*) and their potential roles as vectors in a plague endemic region of Uganda. *Am. J. Trop. Med. Hyg.* 78:949–56
40. Eisen RJ, Eisen L, Gage KL. 2009. Studies of vector competency and efficiency of North American fleas for *Yersinia pestis*: state of the field and future research needs. *J. Med. Entomol.* 46:737–44
41. Eisen RJ, Enscore RE, Biggerstaff BJ, Reynolds PJ, Ettestad P, et al. 2007. Human plague in the southwestern United States, 1957–2004: spatial models of elevated risk of human exposure to *Yersinia pestis*. *J. Med. Entomol.* 44:530–37

42. Eisen RJ, Gage KL. 2009. Adaptive strategies of *Yersinia pestis* to persist during inter-epizootic and epizootic periods. *Vet. Res.* 40:1

43. Eisen RJ, Glass GE, Eisen L, Cheek J, Enscore RE, et al. 2007. A spatial model of shared risk for plague and hantavirus pulmonary syndrome in the southwestern United States. *Am. J. Trop. Med. Hyg.* 77:999–1004

44. Eisen RJ, Griffith KS, Borchert JN, MacMillan K, Apangu T, et al. 2010. Assessing human risk of exposure to plague bacteria in northwestern Uganda based on remotely sensed predictors. *Am. J. Trop. Med. Hyg.* 82:904–11

45. Eisen RJ, Holmes JL, Schotthoefer AM, Vetter SM, Montenieri JA, Gage KL. 2008. Demonstration of early-phase transmission of *Yersinia pestis* by the mouse flea, *Aetheca wagneri*, and implications for the role of deer mice as enzootic reservoirs. *J. Med. Entomol.* 45:1160–64

46. Eisen RJ, Reynolds PJ, Ettestad P, Brown T, Enscore RE, et al. 2007. Residence-linked human plague in New Mexico: a habitat-suitability model. *Am. J. Trop. Med. Hyg.* 77:121–25

47. Eisen RJ, Wilder AP, Bearden SW, Montenieri JA, Gage KL. 2007. Early-phase transmission of *Yersinia pestis* by unblocked *Xenopsylla cheopis* (Siphonaptera: Pulicidae) is as efficient as transmission by blocked fleas. *J. Med. Entomol.* 44:678–82

48. Engelthaler DM, Hinnebusch BJ, Rittner CM, Gage KL. 2000. Quantitative competitive PCR as a technique for exploring flea-*Yersinia pestis* dynamics. *Am. J. Trop. Med. Hyg.* 62:552–60

49. Enscore RE, Biggerstaff BJ, Brown TL, Fulgham RE, Reynolds PJ, et al. 2002. Modeling relationships between climate and the frequency of human plague cases in the southwestern United States, 1960–1997. *Am. J. Trop. Med. Hyg.* 66:186–96

50. Eskey CR, Haas VH. 1940. Plague in the western part of the United States. *Public Health Bull.* 254:1–83

51. Fahrang-Azad A, Traub R. 1985. Transmission of murine typhus rickettsiae by *Xenopsylla cheopis*, with notes on experimental infection and effects of temperature. *Am. J. Trop. Med. Hyg.* 34:555–63

52. Fahrang-Azad A, Traub R, Baqar S. 1985. Transovarial transmission of murine typhus rickettsiae in *Xenopsylla cheopis* fleas. *Science* 227(4686):543–45

53. Finkelstein JL, Brown TP, O'Reilly KL, Wedincamp J Jr, Foil LD. 2002. Studies on the growth of *Bartonella henselae* in the cat flea (Siphonaptera: Pulicidae). *J. Med. Entomol.* 39:915–19

54. Foil L, Andress E, Freeland RL, Roy AF, Rutledge R, et al. 1998. Experimental infection of domestic cats with *Bartonella henselae* by inoculation of *Ctenocephalides felis* (Siphonaptera: Pulicidae) feces. *J. Med. Entomol.* 35:625–28

55. Gage KL, Burkot TR, Eisen RJ, Hayes EB. 2008. Climate and vectorborne diseases. *Am. J. Prev. Med.* 35:436–50

56. Gage KL, Kosoy MY. 2005. Natural history of plague: perspectives from more than a century of research. *Annu. Rev. Entomol.* 50:505–28

57. Gillespie JJ, Williams K, Shukla M, Snyder EE, Nordberg EK, et al. 2008. Rickettsia phylogenomics: unwinding the intricacies of obligate intracellular life. *PLoS One* 3:e2018

58. Gratz N. 1999. Rodent reservoirs and flea vectors of natural foci of plague. In *Plague Manual: Epidemiology, Distribution, Surveillance and Control*, pp. 63–96. Geneva: World Health Org.

59. Guinet F, Ave P, Jones L, Huerre M, Carniel E. 2008. Defective innate cell response and lymph node infiltration specify *Yersinia pestis* infection. *PLoS One* 3:e1688

60. Hayes EB, Piesman J. 2003. How can we prevent Lyme disease? *N. Engl. J. Med.* 348:2424–30

61. Hinnebusch BJ. 2005. The evolution of flea-borne transmission in *Yersinia pestis*. *Curr. Issues Mol. Biol.* 7:197–212

62. Hinnebusch BJ, Perry RD, Schwan TG. 1996. Role of the *Yersinia pestis* hemin storage (hms) locus in the transmission of plague by fleas. *Science* 273:367–70

63. Hirst LF. 1953. *The Conquest of Plague*. Oxford: Clarendon. 478 pp.

64. Holdenried R. 1952. Sylvatic plague studies: VII. Plague transmission potentials for the fleas *Diamanus montanus* and *Polygnis gwyni* compared with *Xenopsylla cheopis*. *J. Infect. Dis.* 90:131–40

65. Holt AC, Salkeld DJ, Fritz CL, Tucker JR, Gong P. 2009. Spatial analysis of plague in California: niche modeling predictions of the current distribution and potential response to climate change. *Int. J. Health Geogr.* 8:38

42. Compares competing hypotheses of how *Y. pestis* is maintained during interepizootic periods and transmitted during epizootic periods.

50. Compilation of initial studies conducted during the early twentieth century while *Y. pestis* spread across the western United States.

56. Summarizes plague ecology and evolution, *Y. pestis* transmission dynamics, and molecular biology.

61. Summarizes flea anatomy and physiology and key *Y. pestis* genes that are important for flea-borne transmission.

66. Hoogland JL, Davis S, Benson-Amram S, Labruna D, Goossens B, Hoogland MA. 2004. Pyraperm kills fleas and halts plague among Utah prairie dogs. *Southwest. Nat.* 49:376–83
67. Hopla CE. 1974. The ecology of tularemia. *Adv. Vet. Sci. Comp. Med.* 18:25–53
68. Hopla CE. 1977. *Fleas as vectors of tularemia in Alaska*. Presented at Fleas Proc. Int. Conf. Fleas, Ashton Wold, Peterborough, UK
69. Hubbard CA. 1947. *Fleas of Western North America: Their Relation to Public Health*. Ames: Iowa State Coll. Press. 533 pp.
70. Jones RT, McCormick KF, Martin AP. 2008. Bacterial communities of *Bartonella*-positive fleas: diversity and community assembly patterns. *Appl. Environ. Microbiol.* 74:1667–70
71. Kartman L, Prince FM. 1956. Studies on *Pasteurella pestis* in fleas. V. The experimental plague-vector efficiency of wild rodent fleas compared with *Xenopsylla cheopis*, together with observations on the influence of temperature. *Am. J. Trop. Med. Hyg.* 5:1058–70
72. Kartman L, Prince FM, Quan SF. 1958. Studies on *Pasteurella pestis* in fleas. VII. The plague-vector efficiency of Hystrichopsylla linsdalei compared with *Xenopsylla cheopis* under experimental conditions. *Am. J. Trop. Med. Hyg.* 7:317–22
73. Kartman L, Prince FM, Quan SF, Stark HE. 1958. New knowledge on the ecology of sylvatic plague. *Ann. N.Y. Acad. Sci.* 70:668–711
74. Kartman L, Quan SF, McManus AG. 1956. Studies on *Pasteurella pestis* in Fleas. IV. Experimental blocking of *Xenopsylla vexabilis hawaiiensis* and *Xenopsylla cheopis* with an avirulent strain. *Exp. Parasitol.* 5:435–40
75. Kosoy M, Bai Y, Lynch T, Kuzmin IV, Niezgoda M, et al. 2010. *Bartonella* spp. in bats, Kenya. *Emerg. Infect. Dis.* 16:1875–81
76. Kosoy M, Morway C, Sheff KW, Bai Y, Colborn J, et al. 2008. *Bartonella tamiae* sp. nov., a newly recognized pathogen isolated from three human patients from Thailand. *J. Clin. Microbiol.* 46:772–75
77. Krasnov BR, Shenbrot GI, Mouillot D, Khokhlova IS, Poulin R. 2006. Ecological characteristics of flea species relate to their suitability as plague vectors. *Oecologia* 149:474–81
78. Lahteenmaki K, Kukkonen M, Jaatinen S, Suomalainen M, Soranummi H, et al. 2003. *Yersinia pestis* Pla has multiple virulence-associated functions. *Adv. Exp. Med. Biol.* 529:141–45
79. Laudisoit A, Leirs H, Makundi RH, Van Dongen S, Davis S, et al. 2007. Plague and the human flea, Tanzania. *Emerg. Infect. Dis.* 13:687–93
80. Levy CE, Gage KL. 1999. Plague in the United States, 1995–1997. *Infect. Med.* 16:54–64
81. Lien-Teh W. 1926. *A Treatise on Pneumonic Plague*. Geneva: Leag. Nations
82. Link VB. 1955. A history of plague in the United States. *Public Health Monogr. 26*, Dep. Health Educ. Welf., Washington, DC
83. Lorange EA, Race BL, Sebbane F, Hinnebusch BJ. 2005. Poor vector competence of fleas and the evolution of hypervirulence in *Yersinia pestis*. *J. Infect. Dis.* 191:1907–12
84. MacMillan K, Enscore RE, Ogen-Odoi A, Borchert JN, Babi N, et al. 2011. Landscape and residential variables associated with plague-endemic villages in the West Nile region of Uganda. *Am. J. Trop. Med. Hyg.* 84:435–42
85. Manea SJ, Sasaki DM, Ikeda JK, Bruno PP. 2001. Clinical and epidemiological observations regarding the 1998 Kauai murine typhus outbreak. *Hawaii Med. J.* 60:7–11
86. McCoy GW. 1910. A note on squirrel fleas as plague carriers. *Publ. Health. Rep.* 25:465
87. McElroy KM, Blagburn BL, Breitschwerdt EB, Mead PS, McQuiston JH. 2010. Flea-associated zoonotic diseases of cats in the USA: bartonellosis, flea-borne rickettsioses, and plague. *Trends Parasitol.* 26:197–204
88. Mogollon-Pasapera E, Otvos L Jr, Giordano A, Cassone M. 2009. *Bartonella*: emerging pathogen or emerging awareness? *Int. J. Infect. Dis.* 13:3–8
89. Morelli G, Song YJ, Mazzoni CJ, Eppinger M, Roumagnac P, et al. 2010. *Yersinia pestis* genome sequencing identifies patterns of global phylogenetic diversity. *Nat. Genet.* 42:1140–51
90. Nakazawa Y, Williams R, Peterson AT, Mead P, Staples E, Gage KL. 2007. Climate change effects on plague and tularemia in the United States. *Vector-Borne Zoonotic Dis.* 7:529–40
91. Neerinckx S, Bertherat E, Leirs H. 2009. Human plague occurrences in Africa: an overview from 1877 to 2008. *Trans. R. Soc. Trop. Med. Hyg.* 104:97–103

92. Neerinckx S, Peterson AT, Gulinck H, Deckers J, Kimaro D, Leirs H. 2010. Predicting potential risk areas of human plague for the Western Usambara Mountains, Lushoto District, Tanzania. *Am. J. Trop. Med. Hyg.* 82:492–500
93. Neerinckx SB, Peterson AT, Gulinck H, Deckers J, Leirs H. 2008. Geographic distribution and ecological niche of plague in sub-Saharan Africa. *Int. J. Health Geogr.* 7:54
94. Oyston PC, Isherwood KE. 2005. The many and varied niches occupied by *Yersinia pestis* as an arthropod-vectored zoonotic pathogen. *Antonie Van Leeuwenhoek* 87:171–77
95. Parmenter RR, Yadav EP, Parmenter CA, Ettestad P, Gage KL. 1999. Incidence of plague associated with increased winter-spring precipitation in New Mexico. *Am. J. Trop. Med. Hyg.* 61:814–21
96. Parola P, Raoult D. 2006. Tropical rickettsioses. *Clin. Dermatol.* 24:191–200
97. Perez-Osorio CE, Zavala-Velazquez JE, Arias Leon JJ, Zavala-Castro JE. 2008. *Rickettsia felis* as emergent global threat for humans. *Emerg. Infect. Dis.* 14:1019–23
98. Piesman J, Eisen L. 2008. Prevention of tick-borne diseases. *Annu. Rev. Entomol.* 53:323–43
99. Poland JD, Barnes AM. 1979. Plague. In *CRC Handbook Series in Zoonoses. Section A: Bacterial, Rickettsial and Mycotic Diseases*, ed. JH Steele, 1:515–59. Boca Raton, FL: CRC Press
100. Pollitzer R. 1954. Plague. *WHO Monogr. Ser. 22*, World Health Org., Geneva, Switz. 698 pp.
101. Prince FM. 1943. Report on the fleas *Opisocrostis bruneri* (Baker) and *Thrassis bacchi* (Roths.) as vectors of plague. *Public Health Rep.* 58:1013–16
102. Quan SF, Burroughs AL, Holdenried R, Meyer KF. 1953. Studies on the prevention of experimental plague epizootics instituted among mice by infected fleas. *Estratto VI Congr. Int. Microbiol.* 5:1–4
103. Reif KE, Macaluso KR. 2009. Ecology of *Rickettsia felis*: a review. *J. Med. Entomol.* 46:723–36

103. Reviews the ecology of *R. felis*; its potential modes of transmission, development, and distribution within fleas; and its geographic distribution and possible medical significance.

104. Reisen WK. 2010. Landscape epidemiology of vector-borne diseases. *Annu. Rev. Entomol.* 55:461–83
105. Schriefer ME, Sacci JB Jr, Dumler JS, Bullen MG, Azad AF. 1994. Identification of a novel rickettsial infection in a patient diagnosed with murine typhus. *J. Clin. Microbiol.* 32:949–54
106. Sebbane F, Gardner D, Long D, Gowen BB, Hinnebusch BJ. 2005. Kinetics of disease progression and host response in a rat model of bubonic plague. *Am. J. Pathol.* 166:1427–39
107. Deleted in proof
108. Seery DB, Biggins DE, Montenieri JA, Enscore RE, Tanda DT, Gage KL. 2003. Treatment of black-tailed prairie dog burrows with deltamethrin to control fleas (Insecta: Siphonaptera) and plague. *J. Med. Entomol.* 40:718–22
109. Snall T, O'Hara RB, Ray C, Collinge SK. 2008. Climate-driven spatial dynamics of plague among prairie dog colonies. *Am. Nat.* 171:238–48
110. Stapp P, Antolin MF, Ball M. 2004. Patterns of extinction in prairie dog metapopulations: Plague outbreaks follow El Niño events. *Front. Ecol. Environ.* 2:235–40
111. Stark H, Hudson BW, Pittman MS. 1966. Plague epidemiology. Atlanta, GA: US Dep. Health Educ. Welf. 117 pp.
112. Stenseth NC, Samia NI, Viljugrein H, Kausrud KL, Begon M, et al. 2006. Plague dynamics are driven by climate variation. *Proc. Natl. Acad. Sci. USA* 103:13110–15
113. Stevenson HL, Bai Y, Kosoy MY, Montenieri JA, Lowell JL, et al. 2003. Detection of novel *Bartonella* strains and *Yersinia pestis* in prairie dogs and their fleas (Siphonaptera: Ceratophyllidae and Pulicidae) using multiplex polymerase chain reaction. *J. Med. Entomol.* 40:329–37
114. Tikhomirov E. 1999. Epidemiology and distribution of plague. In *Plague Manual: Epidemiology, Distribution, Surveillance and Control*, ed. DT Dennis, KL Gage, N Gratz, JD Poland, E Tikhomirov, pp. 11–37. Geneva: World Health Org.
115. Titball RW, Hill J, Lawton DG, Brown KA. 2003. *Yersinia pestis* and plague. *Biochem. Soc. Trans.* 31:104–7
116. Traub R, Wisseman CL. 1978. The ecology of murine typhus—a critical review. *Trop. Dis. Bull.* 75:237–317
117. Verjbitski DT. 1908. The part played by insects in the epidemiology of plague. *J. Hyg.* 8:162–208
118. Vetter SM, Eisen RJ, Schotthoefer AM, Montenieri JA, Holmes JL, et al. 2010. Biofilm formation is not required for early-phase transmission of *Yersinia pestis*. *Microbiology* 156:2216–25
119. Walker DH, Ismail N. 2008. Emerging and re-emerging rickettsioses: endothelial cell infection and early disease events. *Nat. Rev. Microbiol.* 6:375–86

120. Webb CT, Brooks CP, Gage KL, Antolin MF. 2006. Classic flea-borne transmission does not drive plague epizootics in prairie dogs. *Proc. Natl. Acad. Sci. USA* 103:6236–41
121. Wedincamp J Jr, Foil LD. 2002. Vertical transmission of *Rickettsia felis* in the cat flea (*Ctenocephalides felis* Bouché). *J. Vector Ecol.* 27:96–101
122. Welkos SL, Friedlander AM, Davis KJ. 1997. Studies on the role of plasminogen activator in systemic infection by virulent *Yersinia pestis* strain C092. *Microb. Pathog.* 23:211–23
123. Wheeler CM, Douglas JR. 1941. Transmission studies of sylvatic plague. *Proc. Soc. Exp. Biol. Med.* 47:65–66
124. Deleted in proof
125. Wheeler CM, Douglas JR. 1945. Sylvatic plague studies. V. The determination of vector efficiency. *J. Infect. Dis.* 77:1–12
126. World Health Org. 2003. Human plague in 2000 and 2001. *Wkly. Epidemiol. Rec.* 16:130–35
127. Wilder AP, Eisen RJ, Bearden SW, Montenieri JA, Gage KL, Antolin MF. 2008. *Oropsylla hirsuta* (Siphonaptera: Ceratophyllidae) can support plague epizootics in black-tailed prairie dogs (*Cynomys ludovicianus*) by early-phase transmission of *Yersinia pestis*. *Vector-Borne Zoonotic Dis.* 8:359–67
128. Wilder AP, Eisen RJ, Bearden SW, Montenieri JA, Tripp DT, et al. 2008. Transmission efficiency of two flea species (*Oropsylla tuberculata cynomuris* and *Oropsylla hirsuta*) involved in plague epizootics among prairie dogs. *EcoHealth* 5:205–12
129. Williams SG, Sacci JB Jr, Schriefer ME, Andersen EM, Foujioka KK, et al. 1992. Typhus and typhuslike rickettsiae associated with opossums and their fleas in Los Angeles County, California. *J. Clin. Microbiol.* 30:1758–62
130. Winters AM, Staples JE, Ogen-Odoi A, Mead PS, Griffith K, et al. 2009. Spatial risk models for human plague in the West Nile region of Uganda. *Am. J. Trop. Med. Hyg.* 80:1014–22

RELATED RESOURCES

Chomel BB, Boulouis HJ, Breithschwerdt EB, Kasten RW, Vayssier-Taussat M, et al. 2010. Ecological fitness strategies of adaptation of *Bartonella* species to their hosts and vectors. *Vet. Res.* 40:29

Insect Nuclear Receptors

Susan E. Fahrbach,[1,*] Guy Smagghe,[2] and Rodrigo A. Velarde[1]

[1]Department of Biology, Wake Forest University, Winston-Salem, North Carolina 27109; email: fahrbach@wfu.edu; velardra@wfu.edu

[2]Laboratory of Agrozoology, Department of Crop Protection, Ghent University, B-9000 Ghent, Belgium; email: guy.smagghe@ugent.be

Annu. Rev. Entomol. 2012. 57:83–106

First published online as a Review in Advance on October 10, 2011

The *Annual Review of Entomology* is online at ento.annualreviews.org

This article's doi: 10.1146/annurev-ento-120710-100607

0066-4170/12/0107-0083$20.00

*Corresponding author

Keywords

ecdysteroids, diacylhydrazines, gene switch, genome project, isoform, transcription factor

Abstract

The nuclear receptors (NRs) of metazoans are an ancient family of transcription factors defined by conserved DNA- and ligand-binding domains (DBDs and LBDs, respectively). The *Drosophila melanogaster* genome project revealed 18 canonical NRs (with DBDs and LBDs both present) and 3 receptors with the DBD only. Annotation of subsequently sequenced insect genomes revealed only minor deviations from this pattern. A renewed focus on functional analysis of the isoforms of insect NRs is therefore required to understand the diverse roles of these transcription factors in embryogenesis, metamorphosis, reproduction, and homeostasis. One insect NR, ecdysone receptor (EcR), functions as a receptor for the ecdysteroid molting hormones of insects. Researchers have developed nonsteroidal ecdysteroid agonists for EcR that disrupt molting and can be used as safe pesticides. An exciting new technology allows EcR to be used in chimeric, ligand-inducible gene-switch systems with applications in pest management and medicine.

INTRODUCTION

Puffs: swollen regions visible in changing patterns on polytene chromosomes; believed to represent regions of intense transcription

Polytene chromosomes: endoreplicated chromosomes that remain in precise alignment resulting in giant chromosomes; well studied in salivary gland cells of larval flies

***EcR*, EcR:** the gene and the protein encoded by that gene that, when dimerized with the product of the *ultraspiracle* gene, forms the functional ecdysteroid receptor

NR: nuclear receptor

Ligand: any signaling molecule that binds to a site on a target protein

DNA-binding domain (DBD): highly conserved region of nuclear receptor proteins with two zinc fingers that binds to a hormone-response element in DNA

Ligand-binding domain (LBD): moderately conserved region of nuclear receptor proteins that binds an activating ligand, usually a small lipophilic compound

The sequence of the *Drosophila melanogaster E75* gene was reported in 1990 (124). *E75* was cloned as part of an effort to characterize ecdysone-inducible gene products associated with puffs visible on the polytene chromosomes of salivary glands in late third-instar larvae. The *E75* gene contained overlapping transcription units encoding two proteins, both of which, in the words of the authors, "surprisingly" contained "sequences homologous to the DNA-binding and hormone-binding domains of proteins in the steroid receptor superfamily." The surprise likely lessened as the list of vertebrate steroid receptor-like genes in *D. melanogaster* grew to include *tailless*, *seven-up*, *ultraspiracle*, *DHR3*, and *FTZ-F1* (66, 75, 90, 99, 109). The identification in 1991 of a gene encoding ecdysone receptor (EcR), a nuclear receptor (NR) that binds insect-molting hormones, initiated the modern era of molecular studies of metamorphosis (67). Subsequent investigations established that the product of the *EcR* gene in *D. melanogaster* functions as a ligand-activated transcription factor by forming a heterodimer with USP, the product of the *ultraspiracle* gene (161). The primary molting hormone of insects is 20-hydroxyecdysone (20E). 20E is often referred to informally as ecdysone, although this term is also used as the trivial name for a different specific ecdysteroid, the secretion of the prothoracic glands (47).

Quests for *EcR* orthologs in other insects were successful because of the conserved DNA- and ligand-binding domains (DBDs and LBDs, respectively) of NRs. Examples include the orthologs of *D. melanogaster EcR* in spruce budworm (*Choristoneura fumiferana*), cotton boll weevil (*Anthonomus grandis*), and the yellow fever mosquito (*Aedes aegypti*) (31, 68, 149). As even this brief list suggests, many researchers were inspired by the prospect of developing ecdysteroid-based pest-control strategies. This led to a focus on *EcR* and *USP* during the pioneering gene-by-gene era of NR studies in insects.

The focus widened and pace of discovery increased with the dawning of the era of genome projects, as it then became possible to list all (or almost all, given unavoidable errors in sequence data and genome assembly) NRs of a species. To date, the following genome projects (listed in order of publication) have contributed to our knowledge of insect NRs: *D. melanogaster*, *Anopheles gambiae*, *Drosophila pseudoobscura*, *Apis mellifera*, *Ae. aegypti*, *Tribolium castaneum*, *Bombyx mori*, *Nasonia* spp., and *Acyrthosiphon pisum* (1, 50, 51, 54, 55, 96, 114, 115, 151). Other insect genomes are being annotated or have been published so recently that analysis of their NR complements is incomplete. This group includes the mosquitoes *Culex pipiens* and *Cx. quinquefasciatus*; several species of ant; the bumble bee *Bombus terrestris*; and the human body louse, *Pediculus humanus humanus* (3, 65, 130, 131, 157). Even with modern bioinformatics tools, it can be a daunting task to face raw sequence data with the goal of extracting a full list of NRs. Focused companion papers to the main genome publications therefore provide invaluable guides to would-be annotators of insect NR genes (13, 24, 25, 27, 64, 147).

In the first decade of the twenty-first century, evolution of sequencing technology led to a shift from massive, carefully annotated genome projects to next-generation (pyrosequencing-based) transcriptome analyses (e.g., 106, 123). It is exciting that ever-accumulating sequence data continue to provide raw sequences to be mined for insect NRs. Even more exciting, the development of robust RNA interference (RNAi) techniques now permits effective experimental regulation of gene expression in species other than *D. melanogaster* (8). RNAi is an essential tool for establishing the function of NRs.

The goal of this review is to assess current knowledge of insect NRs and to guide investigators interested in identification of NRs in their own species of interest. Because NR signaling in *D. melanogaster* and scenarios for the evolution of the entire superfamily have received attention in excellent reviews, we focus here on studies of NRs in insects other than *D. melanogaster* (64, 86, 87).

It is, however, impossible to present this subject without referring extensively to the framework provided by research on *D. melanogaster*.

WHAT IS A NUCLEAR RECEPTOR?

NRs constitute a superfamily of metazoan proteins that includes the steroid receptors of vertebrates. NR proteins have modular functional domains designated (from the NH_2-terminal end) as A/B, C, D, E, and F (2, 37). The C domain is also referred to as the DBD; it is the most conserved region of NRs and is characterized by invariant cysteine residues that stabilize two zinc fingers essential for DNA binding. The E domain contains the LBD, which permits NRs to function as ligand-dependent regulators of transcription: it is characterized by a COOH-terminal motif (AF-2) that drives ligand-dependent transcription upon binding of the receptor (sometimes as a monomer, but typically in the form of either a homodimer or a heterodimer with another member of the NR superfamily) to enhancers referred to as hormone response elements (typically a purine followed by GGTCA, although mutations, extensions, and repeats have generated receptor-specific enhancers) in nuclear DNA. The E domain also mediates dimerization and interactions with other categories of proteins, including heat-shock proteins. It is the second-most conserved region of superfamily members. The A/B domain is variable and in many NR proteins contains a motif (AF-1) that can drive ligand-independent transcription. The D domain is also variable; it is sometimes referred to as the hinge, as it connects the DBD (C domain) and the LBD (E domain). The D domain, however, is much more than a simple connector, as it provides the critical function of nuclear localization and modulates transcription through interactions with other nuclear proteins. Known ligands of NRs include steroids, thyroid hormones, retinoids, vitamin D, mammalian bile acids, farnesoids, fatty acids, phospholipids, and even diatomic gases (112). Despite the length of this list, many NRs, including those of insects, remain orphan receptors in search of endogenous or xenobiotic ligands (122). An active area of current research investigates interactions of the insect juvenile hormones (JH) with USP (47).

Genome project: research aimed at determining the sequence of chemical base pairs composing the DNA of a species and then identifying the associated genes

Pyrosequencing: a DNA-sequencing method based on detection of released pyrophosphate during DNA synthesis

Metazoan: a major group of multicellular, eukaryotic organisms of the kingdom Animalia

Orphan receptor: a nuclear receptor for which an endogenous ligand has not yet been conclusively identified

NRs have been identified using polymerase chain reaction (PCR)-based approaches in many metazoans, including taxa as atypical as cnidarians, ctenophores, and sponges (45, 113, 154). In 1999, phylogenetic analysis of the 65 NR genes then sequenced prompted a proposal for a formal system of nomenclature, which has since been widely adopted (98). Six NR subfamilies (NR1–NR6) were initially identified; added since then is a seventh (NR7) that comprises unusual receptors to date found only in genomes of the cephalochordate amphioxus and the sea urchin, an echinoderm (9, 121). A small NR0 subfamily includes NR-related proteins with a DBD but no LBD. Representatives of all six major subfamilies are present in humans and other vertebrates, but the chordates are not exceptional in this regard, as numerous comparative studies have revealed that all NR subfamilies were present prior to ancient splits in the metazoan lineage (10, 37).

Initial phylogenetic analyses suggested that the earliest NRs were orphan receptors that acted as constitutive transcription factors, with ligand-binding capacity acquired later in evolution and expressed most profligately in the steroid hormone-binding NRs of vertebrates (10, 37). An alternative scenario proposes that the ancestral NRs were ligand sensors (e.g., lipid sensors) that bound ligands with low affinity. Under this scenario, it is envisioned that high-affinity binding to specific compounds was acquired later by some receptors while others lost their ligand-sensing abilities (15, 86). The implication of this new thinking is that interactions of ligands and receptors may need to be redefined as a network shared across different NR types, instead of being viewed from a one ligand–one receptor perspective.

Cloning of NRs on the basis of the conserved DBD and LBD regions is a powerful tool for discovery of receptors, but contemporary analyses draw heavily on genome projects. The first

(1998) and second (1999) animals for which the entire set of NRs was analyzed were the nematode *Caenorhabditis elegans* and the fruit fly *D. melanogaster* (1, 18). The results from *C. elegans* were surprising in that more than 250 NRs were identified (126). The genus *Caenorhabditis* still holds the record for number of NRs, as far fewer have been found to date in all other groups studied, including other nematode genera (141). By contrast, the *D. melanogaster* genome encodes only 18 NRs with both a DBD and LBD (64). Mammalian genome projects subsequently revealed that insects have slightly fewer than half the NRs (50, 52) typically present in vertebrates (87).

With one insect genome published, it became a pleasant diversion for biologists interested in the origins of insect diversity to speculate that yet-to-be-discovered differences in the number and type of NRs may account for some of this diversity. As shown in **Figure 1**, results from completed insect genome projects do not support this view. Instead, insect life appears to be regulated by a conserved core set of NRs. But **Figure 1** also highlights the spectacular gaps in our knowledge. The first gap is obvious in that a focus on model organisms, insect vectors of disease, and pest management has resulted in poor coverage of the breadth of insect diversity from the perspective of NRs. The second gap is invisible but equally important. The identification and functional analysis of NRs is substantially complicated by the existence of multiple receptor isoforms (61).

NUCLEAR RECEPTOR ISOFORMS

The term protein isoform is used to refer to all the different forms of a single protein. Isoforms can be generated in many ways, including post-translational modification of proteins or as a result of minor allelic variation. Here we focus on isoforms arising by transcriptional mechanisms. Related genes may produce different forms of a protein, transcription of a gene may be driven by alternative promoters, or a single gene may give rise to isoforms by means of post-transcriptional modifications referred to as alternative splicing (150). Alternative promoters and alternative splicing can significantly expand the protein repertoire of a particular genome. For example, it has been estimated that more than half of all human genes contain at least one alternatively spliced exon and, famously, that the single *D. melanogaster* gene encoding the DSCAM protein can potentially produce more than 38,000 different proteins via alternative splicing (150, 163).

The complexity of the process is evident in the numerous forms of alternative splicing. A partial list includes exon skipping, alternative 5′ splice-site usage, alternative initial exons, and alternative terminal exons. Splice sites present in introns (5′ splice site, 3′ splice site, and branch-point sequence) constitute the core splicing signals that interact with exonic and intronic *cis*-regulatory elements to determine the final mRNA that will be translated. Definition of an integrated splicing code is an active area of research, but it is not yet possible to predict with certainty the isoforms individual genes will produce even when a sequenced genome is available.

Before the availability of sequences from genome projects, the primary methods for detection of isoforms were mapping of exons through analysis of clones in genomic phage libraries and screening of cDNA libraries with exon-specific probes. That the different predicted protein

Figure 1

Distribution of insect nuclear receptors (NRs), organized by NR subfamily (NR1–NR6) and order. Bolded names indicate orders containing at least one species with a completed genome project for which NRs have been annotated. The name of the species is given to the right of the order name. Solid bars indicate the presence of a particular NR in the annotated genome. Asterisks indicate the existence of published NRs from species in orders without a completed genome project. Phylogenetic relationships among the insect orders are not intended to be definitive but rather to organize known NRs. The interordinal relationships depicted are based on an analysis by Ishiwata et al. (58).

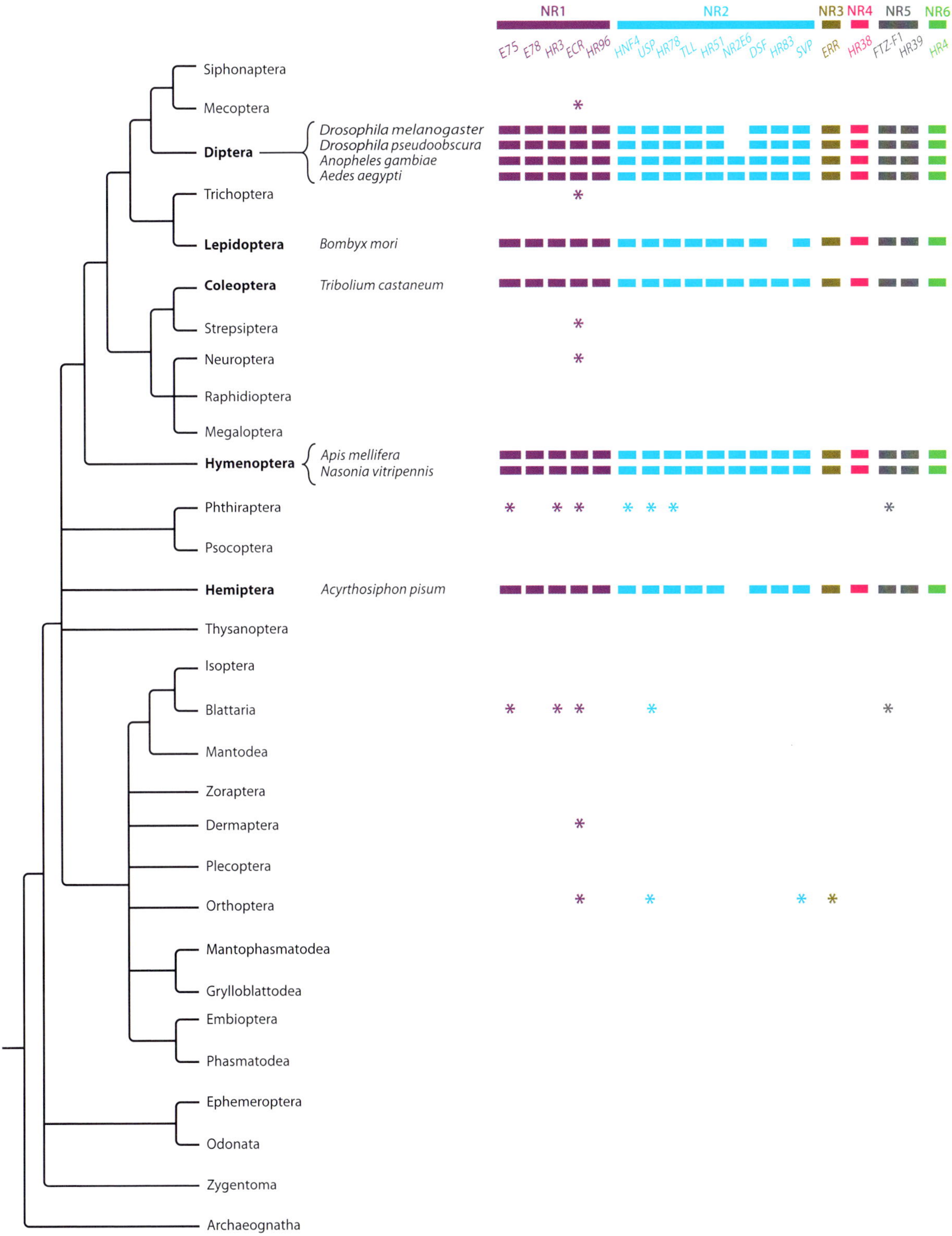

NR1
NR2
NR3
NR4
NR5
NR6
E75
E78
HR3
ECR
HR96
HNF4
USP
HR78
TLL
HR51
NR2E6
DSF
HR83
SVP
ERR
HR38
FTZ-F1
HR39
HR4
Siphonaptera
Mecoptera
Diptera
Drosophila melanogaster
Drosophila pseudoobscura
Anopheles gambiae
Aedes aegypti
Trichoptera
Lepidoptera
Bombyx mori
Coleoptera
Tribolium castaneum
Strepsiptera
Neuroptera
Raphidioptera
Megaloptera
Hymenoptera
Apis mellifera
Nasonia vitripennis
Phthiraptera
Psocoptera
Hemiptera
Acyrthosiphon pisum
Thysanoptera
Isoptera
Blattaria
Mantodea
Zoraptera
Dermaptera
Plecoptera
Orthoptera
Mantophasmatodea
Grylloblattodea
Embioptera
Phasmatodea
Ephemeroptera
Odonata
Zygentoma
Archaeognatha

isoforms were expressed was confirmed by use of isoform-specific antibodies. Now, in silico methods can be used to search for potential isoforms via exon mapping and identification of the location of splice-junction sequences.

In silico: performed on a computer, as opposed to being performed in a laboratory

Conventional sequencing and profiling methods led to underestimation of alternative splicing in insect genomes because of cost constraints on sequencing and reliance on splicing-insensitive methods (microarrays and qRT-PCR) for study of gene expression. The development of high-throughput next-generation sequencing methods makes it possible to analyze extremely large sets of short cDNA reads (e.g., mRNA-Seq data) with the goal of estimating prevalence (and relative abundances) of isoforms in individual species and in individual tissues (105). The development of high-throughput proteomics methods (e.g., tandem mass spectrometry) that can be paired with new bioinformatics approaches (e.g., analysis-driven experimentation) now makes attainable the goal of completing a catalog of isoforms for key model species such as *D. melanogaster* (17).

Because NR isoforms vary in dimerization properties, ligand binding, DNA binding, and interactions with coactivators and corepressors, it is likely that the isoforms are functionally significant. All the vertebrate NRs have multiple isoforms (61). Vertebrate-like complexity was evident in insect NRs from the initial studies of the *E75* gene in *D. melanogaster*: *E75* transcripts encode two distinct proteins termed E75A and E75B. E75A is a canonical member of the NR superfamily, but E75B has an altered DBD with only a single zinc finger (124). Many questions related to the function of NR isoforms remain unanswered even in the intensively studied *D. melanogaster* model. We believe that one of the major challenges facing researchers in this field is assignment of function to specific NR isoforms. To accomplish this goal, researchers must identify cross-species correspondences of receptor isoforms. At times this may seem like just one more burden to be shouldered by weary researchers already lagging far behind a torrent of sequence data in terms of their ability to perform detailed gene expression profiles and meaningful developmental and physiological analyses! Yet, it is just such labor-intensive, tissue- and organ-system-based analyses, carried out with isoform sensitivity, species by species, that will lead to a meaningful understanding of NR function in the lives of insects.

METHODS FOR CHARACTERIZATION OF INSECT NUCLEAR RECEPTORS

Two eras in the characterization of insect NRs can be recognized: an era during which genome projects were expensive and rare and an era, currently in full swing, in which genome projects are affordable and unglamorous. In addition, it is possible to envision sequencing the genomes of 5,000 arthropods during the next five years (117). Note that, following convention, insect NR genes and proteins that are here referred are designated by the name of the orthologous gene or gene product in *D. melanogaster*, preceded by a two-letter prefix indicating the species from which the sequence was obtained.

Pregenome Studies of Insect Nuclear Receptors

Studies through the mid-2000s typically focused on EcR and its usual heterodimeric partner, USP. Projects were motivated by the desire to define the diversity of insect NRs and with the goal of exploiting this diversity to develop taxon-specific insecticides. Two of the many studies published during this era exemplify common approaches. In 1997, Mouillet et al. (93) reported the identification of two isoforms of EcR in the coleopteran *Tenebrio molitor*. This was accomplished by low-stringency screening of a *T. molitor* genomic library using an EcoR1-KpnI 637–base pair (bp) fragment of *D. melanogaster* cDNA that included the DBD of *DmEcR*. A genomic fragment identified in this screen with high similarity to the *D. melanogaster* DBD was used to screen a

T. molitor cDNA library prepared from pupal stage epidermal RNA. The two isoforms of *TmEcR* identified by screening the cDNA library were used for isoform-specific Northern blot analysis of the temporal profile of *TmEcR* mRNAs in the epidermis during metamorphosis. The results illustrate the conservation of the EcR DBD across species (the *T. molitor* genomic fragment was 89% identical to the DBD of DmEcR) and the difficulty of cross-species-matching NR isoforms: The authors were confident in their identification of a *T. molitor* homolog of the B1 isoform of DmEcR, but they noted that a second isoform tentatively designated TmEcR-A showed "little similarity" to previously cloned EcR-A proteins from either *D. melanogaster* or *Manduca sexta*. No further functional characterization, including a demonstration that either isoform can bind a ligand, was attempted. In 1998, Saleh et al. (119) used PCR with primers based on the DBDs of known NR family members to identify putative EcRs in *Locusta migratoria*, the first such study in a hemimetabolous insect. The resulting PCR products were sequenced, and one of the fragments was used to screen a cDNA library prepared from the fat body of adult females. The translated 2.4-kb sequence obtained predicted a protein similar to the published *T. molitor* (74% identity) and dipteran (53–54% identity) EcR proteins and was, therefore, designated *LmEcR*. A developmental Northern blot analysis revealed tissue-specific expression profiles and, in some cases, a doublet transcript pattern that suggested the presence of multiple isoforms. These important studies, and many others like them, set the stage for species-based analysis of EcR expression, but they were limited by a lack of specification of ligand binding. The results hint at the challenges and opportunities arising from the existence of NR isoforms with distinct spatial and temporal expression profiles. The challenges are to distinguish isoforms and establish their nonredundant functions; the opportunities include the tantalizing prospect of explaining the evolution of species and lineage differences on the basis of NR isoform diversity.

Genome Projects and Beyond

The successful *D. melanogaster* genome project was a landmark event in insect biology that established a paradigm of research community cooperation for manual gene identification (4, 21). Here we offer a perspective on how NRs were annotated in subsequent insect genome projects. This basic method remains useful as the backlog of sequenced insect genomes lengthens.

The conserved modular organization of NRs facilitates BLAST-based, in silico detection of NR sequences (116). In most cases, the 18 canonical NR proteins from *D. melanogaster* and the 3 members of the NR0 subfamily plus any newly annotated orthologs available from subsequent genomes are used to query the novel genome sequence data set to find putative NR sequences. The resulting protein or nucleotide BLAST hits provide a link to a genome browser (GBrowse) that contains a map of different gene predictions resulting from multiple gene-prediction algorithms (14). The genome browser displays the gene predictions in a format from which the annotator can retrieve and then compare gene predictions for a particular genomic region using sequence-alignment and -editing tools (33). Recent insect genome projects have also integrated APOLLO into the annotation process (77). APOLLO software provides a genome map with the gene predictions and orthologs in a visual interface similar to that of GBrowse, but it permits manual editing of automatic annotations in the same interface. Sequences curated in APOLLO can be uploaded to a common annotation database, making the annotation process more centralized and thereby avoiding redundant annotations by different researchers (79).

After finding a region encoding a candidate NR, two approaches are followed to determine if the predictions are correct, and, if necessary, create a corrected model RNA. First, the predictions are aligned with all previously annotated insect members and selected vertebrate members of the particular NR subfamily (sequences obtained from NURSA or NCBI) using a sequence-alignment program. Then, major alignment discrepancies are used as feedback information to spur a return to the sequence to check manually for missing exons, erroneous splice-site predictions, truncations, frameshifts, and erroneous stop codons. The results from this manual editing, as well as the alignment information, are used to construct a corrected RNA model or models that can be checked in ORFinder (NCBI) as encoding a putative NR with a complete DBD and LBD. Additional checks for proper identification are performed by aligning the corresponding DNA sequence with existing ESTs (expressed sequence tags) or full-length cDNAs, if available from previously published data.

TBLASTN with predicted mRNA sequences of the genome being annotated can be used to identify putative NR sequences not included in the combined prediction data set or hidden in the unassembled sequences. The putative NR protein sequences are then sequentially blasted (BLASTP) back against the genomes for preliminary ortholog/homolog identification. If the putative NRs are present in unassembled regions or if the constructed model RNAs have erroneous exon predictions (identified by comparing the model sequence with their orthologs), then the predictions must be validated using RT-PCR or RACE-PCR. At the end of this process, all putative NRs must be analyzed for consistency in their phylogenetic positioning among known NRs using standard methods for phylogenetic analysis. Sequences representing the diversity of NR proteins are aligned with the sequences identified in the new genome being annotated, and phylogenetic tree reconstruction is performed using neighbor-joining methods.

The efficiency of annotation for insect genomes has been enhanced by the development of centralized bioinformatic resources for the specific genome or genomes being annotated (36). AphidBase, the Hymenoptera Genome Database (HGD), and VectorBase are three examples of resource environments created for individual insect genomes (*Ac. pisum*, *Ap. mellifera*, and *An. gambiae*) that can grow to include newly sequenced genomes in the same taxon or focal group (76, 77, 94). For example, the origins of HGD are in BeeBase, a resource created for the *Ap. mellifera* genome project. HGD now includes the sequenced *Nasonia* spp. and new ant genome data sets. The HGD provides a GBrowse environment and access to manually curated data as well as data to support annotations including ESTs/cDNAs, small RNAs, and guanine-cytosine composition domains. Continued maintenance of these resources permits the annotation and curation process to continue beyond the initial community efforts that led to the publication of global genome papers. In the case of NRs, as the focus shifts from individual genomes to multiple sets of genomes from related species, the annotation process will be the necessary first step in the comparative analysis of NRs. The functional annotation of the specific isoforms encoded by the annotated genes will be facilitated by integration of RNA-Seq data with the sequenced genomes (46).

Lessons from the Genome Projects

What have we learned from annotation of complete sets of NRs in the sequenced insect genomes? First, orthologs for all canonical (with LBD and DBD both present) and two out of the three NR0 *D. melanogaster* NRs are present in all published insect genomes (**Figure 1**). This nearly one-to-one conservation across approximately 300 million years indicates that a core set of approximately 20 NRs for Insecta can already be defined. Few surprises in terms of major expansions or losses are expected from any further sequenced genomes. In particular, there appears to be no obvious divide between holometabolous and hemimetabolous NR complements.

The subfamilies of NRs for which sequenced genomes have uncovered minor differences in the number of genes are restricted to NR1, NR2, and the atypical NR0 group. At least one ortholog for the two genes in the NR0 group is present in other sequenced insect genomes. Given the presence of orthologs of both genes in all lineages, a gene-duplication event early in insect evolution may be the origin of the pair *knirps-like* and *eagle*. *knirps* may have appeared later as a paralog or divergent *knirps-like* in the brachyceran flies (134). There are NR0 duplications (of *eagle* and *knirps-like*) unique to the *Ap. mellifera* and *Ac. pisum* genomes (25, 147).

The *Ac. pisum* genome lacks a member of the NR1 group, *HR96* (NR1J1). This loss is unexpected because the NR1 group includes the major insect ecdysteroid-responsive genes: *EcR*, *E75*, *Hr3*, and *E78*. HR96 and the EcR-USP heterodimer share DNA-binding targets in *D. melanogaster* (40). If this is also the case in the pea aphid, the result may be a degree of redundancy for *HR96* that allows aphids to develop without HR96 activity (25).

The *Ap. mellifera* genome project uncovered a new member of the NR2E group. This gene was initially termed *PNR-like* and is proposed as the sixth member of the NR2E group: NR2E6. NR2E6 has apparently been lost from the drosophilid lineage, but it has been identified in two other dipteran genomes (*An. gambiae* and *Ae. aegypti*) and in the other sequenced holometabolous genomes. Notably, this gene is not present in the genome of *Ac. pisum*. It is tempting to propose, on the basis of this limited evidence, that the loss of this gene in *D. melanogaster* and *Ac. pisum* is secondary. We predict that NR2E6 will be recovered from subsequently sequenced hemimetabolous genomes.

Future functional analyses should strive to be isoform sensitive. This will be facilitated by the significant decrease in the cost of sequencing, which permits deep coverage and extensive RNA-Seq of insect genomes. Given the extraordinary availability of sequences, the major challenge for those interested in insect NRs may be the difficulty of engaging the necessary communities of scientists for manual curation of the newly sequenced genomes. The challenge arises because such efforts are typically unfunded, voluntary efforts by self-identified interested individuals.

Functional Studies of Insect Nuclear Receptors

Studies in vertebrates have demonstrated key roles for NRs in development, reproduction, and homeostatic regulation of metabolism. On the basis of sparse data, a similarly broad range of roles is attributable to insect NRs. An unusual aspect of NR function in insects without a clear parallel in vertebrates is a conserved cascade of NR gene expression triggered by the liganded EcR-USP complex. This cascade represents the initial cellular response to ecdysteroids, and it includes other insect NRs expressed in an ecdysteroid-induced sequence first described in the context of the larval-pupal transition in *D. melanogaster*. This sequence is essentially independent of cell type, so that the diverging late responses of different hormone target cells are coupled to a fixed early sequence. Most of what is known about postembryonic functions of insect NRs is related to this specific cascade.

EcR, *USP*, *HR3*, *HR4*, *HR78*, *E75*, *E78*, and *FTZ-F1* function as early genes in the metamorphosis cascade in *D. melanogaster* (136). The steroid hormone 20E triggers this cascade of gene expression through the EcR/USP receptor heterodimer (80). Low 20E concentrations induce expression of *EcR*; higher 20E concentrations both repress *EcR* expression and induce other members of the set of NR early genes. *E75* induction in this cascade is coincident with the 20E pulses and independent of protein synthesis, whereas *Hr3*, *E78*, and *Hr4* require a period of de novo protein synthesis triggered by 20E to reach maximum expression (53, 73, 124). *E75* mRNA levels, therefore, increase prior to those of *Hr3*, *E78* and *Hr39*. These interactions between *E75* and *Hr3* protein products coordinate expression of *Ftz-f1*. *Ftz-f1* mRNA levels decrease in response to high 20E levels and increase only in mid-prepupal stage larvae when 20E levels are low (6). *Hr3* activates the expression of *Ftz-f1* dependent on the absence of *E75* protein products (152). In turn, *Ftz-f1* acts as a competence factor that determines the nature of responses to a second 20E pulse (16). This expression cascade can be summarized in a simplified form as a sequence of *E75*, *Hr3*, and *Ftz-f1* expression common to all preimaginal 20E pulses of *D. melanogaster* development.

A similar cascade was defined for metamorphosis in the yellowfever mosquito, *Ae. aegypti* (85), and in the tobacco hornworm, *Manduca sexta* (49).

Prior to completion of the aphid genome project, the only hemimetabolous insect in which this cascade had been studied was the German cockroach, *Blattella germanica*. The response to ecdysteroid pulses in *B. germanica* reveals a high degree of conservation (26). *B. germanica* exposed to systemic RNAi for EcR, USP, E75, Hr3, and FTZ-F1 in early metamorphosis displayed stage-specific arrest of development plus morphology consistent with previously described roles of each of these NRs in *D. melanogaster*, with one striking exception: In *B. germanica*, *Ftz-f1* appears not to play the role of a competence factor because the sequence of gene expression was not altered when *Ftz-f1* expression was downregulated by RNAi, although the timing of the cascade was precocious. The *B. germanica* studies are notable for the use of isoform-specific RNAi, and they provide a model for future studies. Functional studies of *Ftz-f1* in the pea aphid or other hemimetabolous insects are now required to ask if the function of *Ftz-f1* as a competence factor is restricted to holometabolous insects. The 20E cascade is also conserved in *T. castaneum* and has been characterized using isoform-specific RNAi as a direct result of the availability of the full set of NRs streaming from this genome project (139).

The same NRs assigned roles at metamorphosis also regulate vitellogenesis. In *Ae. aegypti* adult females, a blood meal triggers synthesis of 20E and activates transcription of *vitellogenin* (*Vg*), the major yolk-protein precursor gene (29). In previtellogenic-cultured fat bodies, 20E induces transcription of *EcR*, *USP*, *Hr3*, and *E75* with a profile similar to that observed during metamorphosis (108). *Vg* should, therefore, be considered a late gene in this ecdysteroid-induced cascade of gene expression (60). As in *D. melanogaster* metamorphosis, *Ftz-f1* serves as a competence factor for the response of the adult mosquito fat body to the 20E pulse: In cultured fat bodies, a second 20E challenge that emulates the in vivo signal triggers a second vitellogenic period resulting in induction of *E75* and *Vg*, but reduction of mRNA levels of *Ftz-f1* by RNAi in previtellogenic mosquitoes diminished activation of *EcR*, *E74*, and *E75* in response to a blood meal (81, 162).

In *Ap. mellifera*, only one study has shown that interference with the canonical cascade (reduction of *USP* expression using RNAi) delays metamorphosis (5). Prior to the *Ap. mellifera* genome project, however, partial cDNA sequences for *USP*, *Hr3*, *ERR*, *SVP*, *Ftz-f1*, and *Hnf4* were identified in an EST library developed from adult bee brain (153). Possible relevance of the metamorphosis transcriptional cascade to patterns of gene expression in the adult honey bee brain was suggested by localized expression of ecdysteroid responsive genes (*E93*, *E75*, *E74*, *Hr38*, and *EcR*) in the mushroom bodies of the worker (107, 160). It was subsequently shown that expression of the *EcR*, *USP*, *E75*, *Ftz-f1*, and *Hr3* genes in adult honey bee mushroom bodies responds to endogenous ecdysteroid pulses and that treatment with a high dose of 20E induced a cascade similar to the canonical cascade defined for *D. melanogaster* metamorphosis and *Ae. aegypti* vitellogenesis (148).

The functions of NRs during embryonic development have been characterized primarily in *D. melanogaster*. Mutations in *EcR* resulted in embryonic lethality with minor morphological defects; a similar outcome was observed for *USP* mutants (100). These phenotypes contrast with major defects observed with loss of 20E. This discrepancy was interpreted as reflecting the presence of maternal *EcR* expression in the EcR mutant embryos and the specific alleles used in the USP study, which resulted in a hypomorphic rather than a null mutation (48). It was subsequently demonstrated that the EcR complex is first activated in extraembryonic amnioserosa, coincident with the rise in active ecdysteroids in mid-embryogenesis. This observation provides a functional parallel between embryonic and metamorphic functions (69). Expression of *E75*, *Hr3*, and *Ftz-f1* in embryos is necessary for embryonic viability (20). Recently, expression of *E75*, *Hr3*, and *Ftz-f1* in embryos has been shown to mimic the metamorphosis cascade (23). Other ecdysone-responsive nuclear receptors, including E78, Hr4, and Hr39, are not required during embryogenesis (64, 118).

The roles of NRs in early development extend beyond steroid signaling. One member of the NR2 group, *tailless* (NR2E2), has key roles in embryonic development. *D. melanogaster tll* acts early in embryogenesis at the posterior pole as a terminal gene that establishes the domain from which abdominal segments, the telson, and posterior gut develop (109, 110). In late fly embryos, *tll* acts as a gap gene expressed in head and posterior segments, where it patterns the brain and hind gut, respectively (32, 72). *tll* acts primarily as a transcriptional repressor of other patterning genes (92). Embryonic expression patterns of the *tll* ortholog in *An. gambiae*, *N. vitripennis*, *T. castaneum*, and *Ap. mellifera* have confirmed a conserved role as a repressor for *tll* in terminal signaling (e.g., 42, 83, 120).

Members of the NR0 group have demonstrated relevance for embryogenesis in *D. melanogaster* and *T. castaneum*, primarily in head patterning (22, 43), but surprisingly, in situ analysis of expression of these genes in honey bee embryos did not recover *knirps-like* mRNA signal during segmentation (28).

Dynamic changes of *ERR* activation were observed in the *D. melanogaster* embryos using a GAL4 ligand-sensor strategy; a similar pattern of activation was also detected in third-instar larvae (101). It was suggested that ERR was responding to a general but temporally restricted signal. It was later demonstrated that ERR is a key regulator of carbohydrate metabolism genes and acts as a switch for the transition to a coordinated metabolic program that promotes cellular proliferation (144). The mechanisms that regulate the timing and accumulation of activated ERR remain to be determined.

The COUP-TF (chicken-ovalbumin upstream-promoter transcription factors) group of NRs are orphan receptors expressed in specific neuronal cell lineages in all animals studied, including cnidarians (41). The COUP-TF gene in *D. melanogaster* is called *seven-up* (*SVP*) for its role in the specification of photoreceptor cell identity during formation of the fly-compound eye during metamorphosis (90). *SVP* is also expressed during embryonic development in non-neural tissues, such as the Malpighian tubules and the heart (62, 82).

E75 as a Model for Isoform-Based Analyses

E75 is a classic 20E early-response gene. A remarkable feature of E75 is that it contains heme in its ligand-binding pocket: This property allows nitric oxide and carbon monoxide to control E75 activity by affecting interactions with its heterodimer partner Hr3 (112). Four isoforms of E75 have been identified in *D. melanogaster* and *M. sexta*, whereas *B. mori* and *Ae. aegypti* have three and *B. germanica* has at least five E75 isoforms (84).

The three *D. melanogaster* E75 isoforms have distinct N-terminal sequences encoded by different 5′ exons. E75A and E75C 5′ exons splice to the same set of five 3′ exons, whereas E75B shares only the last three 3′ exons with the other forms. E75B lacks one of the two zinc fingers of the DBD, making this isoform unable to bind DNA, although it can dimerize with Hr3 (152). When null mutants for each of the isoforms were compared, distinct phenotypes emerged. E75B mutants are viable and fertile, and E75C mutants die after adult emergence, while some E75A mutant larvae die at a delayed second instar and others fail to molt to the third instar but instead transition directly to the prepupal stage. E75A mutant phenotypes can be rescued by exogenous ecdysteroid treatments, supporting a role for this isoform in the regulation of ecdysteroid levels during larval molts through genes in the ecdysteroidogenic pathway. E75B appears to share redundant roles with another ecdysteroid-responsive NR, E78B. E75C has a similar role as that of E75A but is temporally restricted in its expression to the prepupal-pupal transition, a period when both isoforms are active to specify the appropriate ecdysone levels (11). The proposed functions for E75A and E75C do not preclude other roles. A fourth *D. melanogaster* isoform (E75D) was later identified and shown, together with E75A, to be responsive to JH treatments in cultured *D. melanogaster* S2 cells (35). The same isoform was induced in *M. sexta* CH1 cells in response to 20E as well as to methoprene treatments, leading to the proposition that E75 acts as an integrator of 20E and JH signals (34). However, studies in vivo and in cultured epidermal tissue have failed to find increased expression of E75 isoforms in *M. sexta* in response to JH (63). E75 is upregulated in response to JH treatment in adult brain of worker honey bees, but the isoform diversity of E75 has not been determined in *Ap. mellifera* (147).

The five isoforms of E75 identified in *B. germanica* have been classified on the basis of their similarity to previously identified isoforms in other species. Of these, BgE75B and BgE75D lack one and both zinc fingers of the DBD, respectively. In contrast to the different patterns of E75 isoform expression in *D. melanogaster* larval molts, the five E75 isoforms of *B. germanica* show a sequential expression pattern in response to the ecdysteroids at each nymphal molt cycle. This sequential response may reflect coupling of growth and maturation in Hemimetabola. The roles of E75 isoforms in oogenesis and vitellogenesis have been studied in *D. melanogaster*, *Ae. aegypti*, and *B. mori*. BmE75A is implicated in the early ecdysteroid-dependent processes of previtellogenesis and vitellogenesis, whereas the E75C form is expressed during the transition from vitellogenesis to chorionogenesis (137). In *D. melanogaster* ovaries, E75A and E75B isoforms have opposing roles: E75A inhibits and E75B induces nurse cell apoptosis (145). All three *Ae. aegypti* E75 isoforms are induced in the ovaries in response to the ecdysteroid peak following a blood meal, albeit with different intensity and duration, which may suggest isoform-specific roles in the ovaries (108). In *T. castaneum*, E75 is necessary for metamorphosis and oogenesis, but the roles of specific E75 isoforms have not been determined (158). A recent study in the large milkweed bug, *Oncopeltus fasciatus*, suggested that one E75 isoform of this species (E75A) is expressed in the head, thorax, and abdomen during embryogenesis, with an abdominal pattern of expression similar to that of the well-known *D. melanogaster* pair-rule genes (39). These intriguing but scattered data are insufficient to serve as the basis of a model for the E75-regulatory network, but it is clear that the role of E75 in cell signaling will not be understood without a thorough accounting of isoform diversity.

Nuclear Receptors and Behavioral Plasticity in Adult Insects

A substantial subset of NRs is expressed in the tissues, including the brain, of adult insects. In *Ap. mellifera*, for example, this subset includes EcR and several orphan NRs, including all NR members of the metamorphosis cascade (147, 148). Disruption of signaling via EcR disrupts sleep and learning in adult *D. melanogaster* (56, 57). Even after completion of metamorphosis, adult tissues, including the ovaries and possibly the brain, synthesize ecdysteroids (159). Study of the role of NRs in the regulation of adult insect behavior, especially the NRs other than EcR, will lead to improved understanding of behavioral plasticity. This new knowledge may also lead to novel strategies for insect pest control.

CONTRIBUTIONS OF NUCLEAR RECEPTOR STUDIES TO INSECT PEST MANAGEMENT AND BIOTECHNOLOGY

Use of EcR in Development of Target-Specific Insecticides

The most dramatic deployment of NRs in applied entomology has focused on *EcR* in its role as the master transcription factor for insect steroid hormone signaling. The goal of developing insecticides to target specific groups of insects led directly to attempts to employ ecdysteroid analogs for agricultural pest control. These strategies exploit subtle differences in the ability of nonsteroidal agonists to bind to the LBD of the EcRs of different groups of insects. Thus, specificity can be obtained despite the high degree of cross-taxa sequence and functional homology for insect NRs described in the preceding sections.

Diacylhydrazine (DAH): an example of a molt-accelerating compound

The most significant discovery occurred in the early 1980s, when chemists at Rohm and Haas synthesized 1,2-diacyl-1-substituted hydrazines (DAHs). The structure of the first nonsteroidal ecdysteroid agonist with potent insecticide activity was published in 1988 (155). This compound was termed RH-5849. Because these ecdysteroid agonists are not easily metabolized, they can disrupt the molting process and lead to death. Treatment typically induces a precocious larval molt in susceptible insects. Induction of this premature molt requires binding of the agonist to *EcR* (30, 95, 127).

These compounds are referred to as molt-accelerating compounds. In contrast to conventional insecticides, a narrow spectrum of activity makes these compounds excellent tools for integrated pest-management programs. For example, tebufenozide and methoxyfenozide (**Figure 2**) are effective against many lepidopterans at low dosages, but they have no or only few side effects on natural enemies such as parasitic wasps and predators. They are also safe for pollinators such as honey bees and bumble bees (30, 91, 127, 128, 129). Because of their benign and selective profile, EcR-binding ecdysone agonists can also be used as insect-control agents in urban settings and forestry. At present, five DAH-based agonists (**Figure 2**) are commercially available for control of lepidopteran and coleopteran species (30).

After successful development of DAH-based, EcR-binding insecticides, the search continued for novel chemistries that could control other pests, particularly sucking insects such as mosquitoes, aphids, leaf hoppers, and whiteflies. EcR sequences, first obtained by cloning and then from

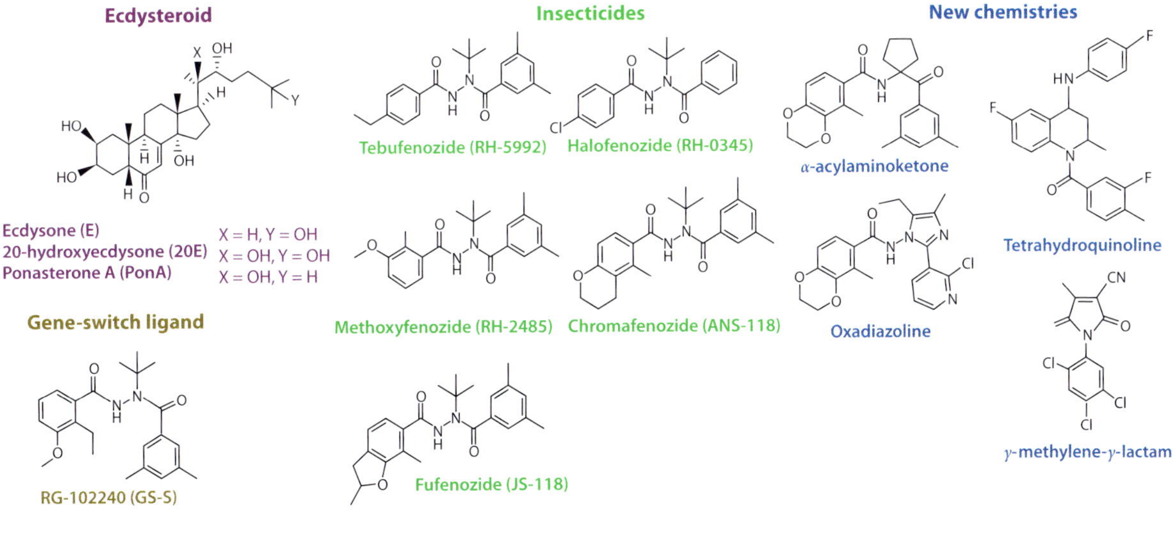

Figure 2

Chemical structures of the steroidal ecdysteroids (ecdysone, 20-hydroxyecdysone, ponasterone A) and stable, nonsteroidal ecdysone-receptor (EcR) ligands used as insecticides in agriculture/forestry and in gene-switch applications together with a series of new chemistries: diacylhydrazine (DAH)-based tebufenozide, methoxyfenozide, and halofenozide (RH-5992, RH-2485, and RH-0345, respectively; all developed by Rohm and Haas, United States); chromafenozide (ANS-118, CM-001; developed jointly by Nippon Kayaku and Sankyo, Japan) and fufenozide (JS-118; developed by Jiangsu Institute, China); tetrahydroquinoline (THQ) (developed by FMC, United States), α-acylaminoketone and oxadiazoline (both developed by Intrexon, United States), and γ-methylene-γ-lactam (developed by CSIRO, Australia).

genome projects, have been used to design assays using high-throughput screening in cell lines and yeast (7, 103, 138). These high-throughput screens, together with conventional lead optimization, resulted in identification of new EcR-binding compounds belonging to the DAH, 3,5-di-tert-butyl-4-hydroxy-*N*-isobutyl-benzamide, tetrahydroquinoline, α-acylaminoketone, and oxadiazoline chemistries (**Figure 2**) (89, 132, 133, 146). Some compounds of the tetrahydroquinoline group have higher potency in mosquitoes than in lepidopterans (102).

QSAR (quantitative structure-activity relationship): development of a mathematical expression by which a chemical structure is quantitatively correlated with a biological response

As more EcRs are identified from additional pest insects and other arthropods, it should become increasingly feasible to identify new EcR-binding ligands that safely and selectively control various pests. For example, Birru et al. (12) recently described synthesis, binding, and selective toxicity of a new group of high-affinity nonsteroidal ligands, the γ-methylene-γ-lactams, targeted to the EcRs from *Bovicola ovis* (Phthiraptera) and *Lucilia cuprina* (Diptera). Another interesting recent contribution is the comprehensive RNAi analysis conducted by Tan & Palli (140) in *T. castaneum*. These investigators showed that 10 out of the 19 canonical NRs (E75, HR3, HR4, EcR, USP, FTZ-F1, HR51, SVP, HR38, HR39) are important for metamorphosis. DsEcR-injected larvae did not feed, remained smaller, and died prior to entering the quiescent stage. The mortality of larvae injected with dsRNA for EcR, E75, HR3, RXR, FTZ-F1, and HR4 was 100%. NRs with lethal phenotypes could be candidates for novel biorational insecticides because the ligands recognized by the insect receptors are likely different from ligands recognized by their human homologs. Recall that, although most of the ligands for these receptors are unknown, the gases nitric oxide and carbon monoxide can activate E75 (47, 112). This raises the possibility of targeting E75 with gaseous substances for control of stored-grain pests.

An important question is how these nonsteroidal ligands bind to the LBD of EcR. The answer to this question could lead to development of new pest-control agents. On the basis of the crystal structure of the EcR of *H. virescens*, it was reported that the phytoecdysteroid ponasterone A and DAH-based ligands (exemplified by BYI106830) show different and only partially overlapping binding cavities (44). The differences between 20E- and BYI106830-bound EcR LBDs occur primarily in the region encompassing helix H6, helix H7, the β-sheet, and the loop between helices H1 and H3. It was demonstrated in 2005 that the LBD-EcR crystal structure of the hemipteran sweetpotato whitefly (*Bemisia tabaci*) is structured differently from that of HvEcR; these data also suggested that these differences may provide a molecular basis for the taxonomic order selectivity of the DAHs (19). A link between LBD structure and selectivity is also supported by classical and advanced QSAR (quantitative structure-activity relationship) modeling in different insects for ecdysteroids and nonsteroidal agonists (52, 111). In parallel, other investigators have used mutational studies of the LBD of the EcR of *C. fumiferana* and tested different ligand chemistries (70, 71). Taken together, current findings have provided a three-dimensional spatial explanation for the differential activity of these ligands in insects.

Use of Nuclear Receptors to Control Gene Expression in Artificial Systems

The first success of gene regulation with an insect transcription factor was with the *D. melanogaster* heat-shock protein 70 promoter (156). Early insect-derived systems supported rapid induction of endogenous genes, but pleiotropic effects resulting from induction using heat shock, hypoxia, and growth regulators limited their use in vivo.

In the past decade, EcR has been regarded favorably as a ligand-controlled transcription factor because ecdysteroids and EcR are found only in insects and related invertebrates, and the ligands are safe and relatively inexpensive. An ecdysteroid-inducible gene-expression system with *Drosophila* DmEcR and human RXR developed in 1996 was functional in mammalian cells and transgenic mice (97). Suhr et al. (135) demonstrated in 1998 that tebufenozide could induce high levels of transactivation of reporter genes in mammalian cells through a construct of *Bombyx*

BmEcR and endogenous RXR. The most successful EcR-based gene switch to date consists of a two-hybrid format in which the GAL4 DBD is fused to the *C. fumiferana* CfEcR DEF domains and the VP16 (the herpes simplex virus regulatory domain) activation domain is fused to the EF domains of mouse RXR (104); success is here defined both in terms of low background levels of reporter gene activity in the absence of a ligand and high levels of reporter gene activity in the presence of a ligand. Other advances have followed (e.g., 70, 142, 143).

Gene switch: an inducible gene-expression system based on a hybrid regulatory protein that binds a nonendogenous ligand that, when present, drives transcription

The first EcR-based gene switch appropriate for field use was developed by the pioneers Martinez et al. (88) using a hybrid transactivator with sequences of the glucocorticoid receptor, the VP16 activation domain, the DBD of the glucocorticoid receptor, and the LBD of the EcR of *H. virescens*. In transgenic tobacco plants expressing this construct, tebufenozide induced the expression of a reporter to approximately 150% of the transactivation of the viral 35S promoter.

Collectively, these projects and the other successful systems that followed confirmed the principle that the EcR gene switch provides one of the best inducible systems for regulation of transgene expression in plants under field conditions. However, a limiting factor for practical use of these pioneering systems was the high doses of ligand (micromolar) required for activation. Recent developments have circumvented this problem. Future use of gene switches in field applications depends on continued development of EcR-based gene switches that respond to systemic nanomolar doses

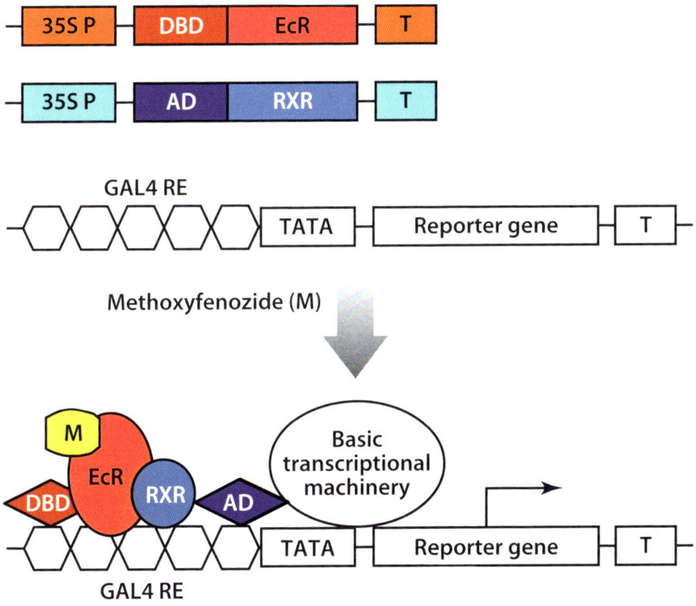

Figure 3

Schematic diagram of an exemplar ecdysone receptor (EcR) two-hybrid gene switch using *Choristoneura fumiferana* EcR and a chimera between helices 1–8 of *Homo sapiens* retinoid X receptor (HsRXR) and helices 9–12 of *Locusta migratoria* RXR (LmRXR), here designated RXR. CfEcR plasmid was constructed by cloning a fusion of the GAL4 DNA-binding domain (DBD) and CfEcR ligand-binding domain (LBD) cloned under the control of the 35S promoter (35S P) in the pKYLX80 vector containing the terminator sequence (T) and represented by the label EcR in the figure. LmRXR plasmid was constructed by cloning the fusion of the VP16 activation domain (AD) and the LmRXR LBD (RXR in the figure) under the control of the 35S P in the pKYLX80 vector. The reporter vector 4635SLuc was constructed by cloning the luciferase reporter under the control of five GAL4 response elements (RE) and a 35S minimal promoter containing −46 to the TATA box. The ligand used in this particular switch is the nonsteroidal EcR ligand, methoxyfenozide (M). Based on Reference 125.

of nonsteroidal EcR ligands, preferably ligands already registered for field use. An example of a switch construct is given in **Figure 3**.

Ligand-inducible gene-expression systems using ecdysteroid-dependent gene switches have also been developed for applications in medicine. In this field, scientists at RheoGene (now Intrexon Ltd.) developed a RheoSwitch system using nonsteroidal ligands for EcR. For example, an EcR-based switch was used to regulate the expression of inwardly rectifying K channels (Kir2.1 channel, AdKir) in rat superior cervical ganglion neurons (59). Lessard et al. (78) established LNCaP human prostate cancer cell lines that constitutively express RheoSwitch transcription factors. This format facilitates production of stable cell lines and will be useful for study of proteins involved in prostate cancer. Ecdysteroid-inducible systems also allow high induction and adjustable control of short-hairpin RNA expression for silencing gene expression in vertebrate cells. For example, Esengil & Chen (38) described an ecdysteroid-based system for conditional transgene expression in zebrafish. Lapenna et al. (74) recently reported on novel semisynthetic ecdysteroids with high potency reflecting their good permeability and metabolic stability.

These efforts constitute valuable progress toward the goal of identifying ecdysteroid-based gene-switch activator molecules suitable for drug development. These studies, inspired by basic research on insect NRs, are likely to come full circle eventually and offer novel compounds and gene switches for continued functional analysis of the NRs in vivo in insects.

SUMMARY POINTS

1. The metazoan family of NR transcription factors is fully represented in insect genomes. The pace of discovery for insect NRs is accelerating as a result of the ambitious application of next-generation sequencing technologies to insect genomes. There are surprisingly few differences in NR complements across insect orders, even when hemimetabolous and holometabolous insects are compared.
2. Functional analyses of NR isoforms (including isoform-sensitive studies of tissue- and stage-specific gene expression) lag behind sequence analysis, but new approaches (RNA-Seq and isoform-specific RNAi) should lead to rapid progress.
3. The functions of NRs in adult insects are largely unknown.
4. Structural studies of EcR have demonstrated that the pocket of the LBD varies across insect groups and is flexible and adaptive within insect groups. This feature of EcR can facilitate development of insect-specific pesticides targeting this receptor.
5. Development of EcR-based gene-switch systems with practical applications in agricultural pest control and medicine is already well under way; these efforts are leading to the development of novel synthetic ecdysteroid agonists that will be useful in basic research.
6. Research based on EcR currently dominates applied research on insect NRs; deorphaning of additional insect NRs will result in new targets for pesticide development.

DISCLOSURE STATEMENT

The authors are not aware of any affiliations, memberships, funding, or financial holdings that might be perceived as affecting the objectivity of this review.

ACKNOWLEDGMENTS

Financial support past and present from the National Science Foundation of the United States, the Special Research Council of Ghent University, and the Fund for Scientific Research (FWO-Vlaanderen, Brussels) is gratefully acknowledged. Warm thanks to Erika Vardeman for assisting with the preparation of figures.

LITERATURE CITED

1. Adams MD, Celniker SE, Holt RA, Evans CA, Gocayne JD, et al. 2000. The genome sequence of *Drosophila melanogaster*. *Science* 287:2185–95
2. Aranda A, Pascual A. 2001. Nuclear hormone receptors and gene expression. *Physiol. Rev.* 81:1269–304
3. Arensburger P, Megy K, Waterhouse RM, Abrudan J, Amedeo P, et al. 2010. Sequencing of *Culex quinquefasciatus* establishes a platform for mosquito comparative genomics. *Science* 330:86–88
4. Ashburner M, Bergman CM. 2005. *Drosophila melanogaster*: a case study of a model genomic sequence and its consequences. *Genome Res.* 15:1661–67
5. Barchuk AR, Figueiredo VLC, Simões ZLP. 2008. Downregulation of *ultraspiracle* gene expression delays pupal development in honeybees. *J. Insect Physiol.* 54:1035–40
6. Beckstead R, Lam G, Thummel C. 2005. The genomic response to 20-hydroxyecdysone at the onset of *Drosophila* metamorphosis. *Genome Biol.* 6:R99
7. Beatty JM, Smagghe G, Ogura T, Nakagawa Y, Spindler-Barth M, Heinrich VC. 2009. Properties of ecdysteroid receptors from diverse insect species in a heterologous cell culture system—a basis for screening novel insecticidal candidates. *FEBS J.* 276:3087–98
8. Bellés X. 2010. Beyond *Drosophila*: RNAi in vivo and functional genomics in insects. *Annu. Rev. Entomol.* 55:111–28
9. Bertrand S, Belgacem MR, Escriva H. 2010. Nuclear hormone receptors in chordates. *Mol. Cell. Endocrinol.* 334:67–75
10. **Bertrand S, Brunet FG, Escriva H, Parmentier G, Laudet V, Robinson-Rechavi M. 2004. Evolutionary genomics of nuclear receptors: from twenty-five ancestral genes to derived endocrine systems. *Mol. Biol. Evol.* 21:1923–37**

10. Significant review of the phylogeny of nuclear receptors.

11. Bialecki M, Shilton A, Fichtenberg C, Segraves WA, Thummel CS. 2002. Loss of the ecdysteroid-inducible E75A orphan nuclear receptor uncouples molting from metamorphosis in *Drosophila*. *Dev. Cell* 3:209–20
12. Birru W, Fernley RT, Graham LD, Grusovin J, Hill RJ, et al. 2010. Synthesis, binding and bioactivity of gamma-methylene gamma-lactam ecdysone receptor ligands: advantages of QSAR models for flexible receptors. *Bioorg. Med. Chem.* 18:5647–60
13. Bonneton F, Chaumot A, Laudet V. 2008. Annotation of *Tribolium* nuclear receptors reveals an increase in evolutionary rate of a network controlling the ecdysone cascade. *Insect Biochem. Mol. Biol.* 38:416–29
14. Brent MR. 2008. Steady progress and recent breakthroughs in the accuracy of automated genome annotation. *Nat. Rev. Genet.* 9:62–73
15. Bridgham JT, Eick GN, Larroux C, Deshpande K, Harms MJ, et al. 2010. Protein evolution by molecular tinkering: diversification of the nuclear receptor superfamily from a ligand-dependent ancestor. *PLoS Biol.* 8:e1000497
16. Broadus J, McCabe JR, Endrizzi B, Thummel CS, Woodard CT. 1999. The *Drosophila* βFTZ-F1 orphan nuclear receptor provides competence for stage-specific responses to the steroid hormone ecdysone. *Mol. Cell* 3:143–49
17. Brunner E, Ahrens CH, Mohanty S, Baetschmann H, Loevenich S, et al. 2007. A high-quality catalog of the *Drosophila melanogaster* proteome. *Nat. Biotechnol.* 25:576–83
18. *C. elegans* Sequencing Consortium. 1998. Genome sequence of the nematode *C. elegans*: a platform for investigating biology. *Science* 282:2012–18
19. Carmichael JA, Lawrence MC, Graham LD, Pilling PA, Epa VC, et al. 2005. The X-ray structure of a hemipteran ecdysone receptor ligand-binding domain: comparison with a lepidopteran ecdysone receptor ligand-binding domain and implications for insecticide design. *J. Biol. Chem.* 280:22258–69

20. Carney GE, Wade AA, Sapra R, Goldstein ES, Bender M. 1997. DHR3, an ecdysone-inducible early-late gene encoding a *Drosophila* nuclear receptor, is required for embryogenesis. *Proc. Natl. Acad. Sci. USA* 94:12024–29
21. Celniker SE, Rubin GM. 2003. The *Drosophila melanogaster* genome. *Annu. Rev. Genomics Hum. Genet.* 4:89–117
22. Cerny AC, Grossmann D, Bucher G, Klingler M. 2008. The *Tribolium* ortholog of *knirps* and *knirps-related* is crucial for head segmentation but plays a minor role during abdominal patterning. *Dev. Biol.* 321:284–94
23. Chavoshi TM, Moussian B, Uv A. 2010. Tissue-autonomous EcR functions are required for concurrent organ morphogenesis in the *Drosophila* embryo. *Mech. Dev.* 127:308–19
24. Cheng D, Xia Q, Duan J, Wei L, Huang C, et al. 2008. Nuclear receptors in *Bombyx mori*: insights into genomic structure and developmental expression. *Insect Biochem. Mol. Biol.* 38:1130–37
25. Christiaens O, Iga M, Velarde RA, Rougé P, Smagghe G. 2010. Halloween genes and nuclear receptors in ecdysteroid biosynthesis and signalling in the pea aphid. *Insect Mol. Biol.* 19(Suppl. 2):187–200
26. Cruz J, Nieva C, Mané-Padrós D, Martín D, Bellés X. 2008. Nuclear receptor BgFTZ-F1 regulates molting and the timing of ecdysteroid production during nymphal development in the hemimetabolous insect *Blattella germanica*. *Dev. Dyn.* 237:3179–91
27. Cruz J, Sieglaff DH, Arensburger P, Atkinson PW, Raikhel AS. 2009. Nuclear receptors in the mosquito *Aedes aegypti*: annotation, hormonal regulation and expression profiling. *FEBS J.* 276:1233–54
28. Dearden PK, Wilson MJ, Sablan L, Osborne PW, Havler M, et al. 2006. Patterns of conservation and change in honeybee developmental genes. *Genome Res.* 16:1376–84
29. Deitsch KW, Chen JS, Raikhel AS. 1995. Indirect control of yolk protein genes by 20-hydroxyecdysone in fat body of the mosquito, *Aedes aegypti*. *Insect Biochem. Mol. Biol.* 25:449–54
30. Dhadialla TS, Carlson GR, Le DP. 1998. New insecticides with ecdysteroidal and juvenile hormone activity. *Annu. Rev. Entomol.* 43:545–69
31. Dhadialla TS, Tzertzinis G. 1997. Characterization and partial cloning of ecdysteroid receptor from a cotton boll weevil embryonic cell line. *Arch. Insect Biochem. Physiol.* 35:45–57
32. Diaz RJ, Harbecke R, Singer JB, Pignoni F, Janning W, Lengyel JA. 1996. Graded effect of *tailless* on posterior gut development: molecular basis of an allelic series of a nuclear receptor gene. *Mech. Dev.* 54:119–30
33. Donlin MJ. 2009. Using the generic genome browser (GBrowse). *Curr. Protoc. Bioinform.* 28:9.9.1–25
34. Dubrovskaya VA, Berger EM, Dubrovsky EB. 2004. Juvenile hormone regulation of the E75 nuclear receptor is conserved in Diptera and Lepidoptera. *Gene* 340:171–77
35. Dubrovsky EB, Dubrovskaya VA, Berger EM. 2004. Hormonal regulation and functional role of *Drosophila* E75A orphan nuclear receptor in the juvenile hormone signaling pathway. *Dev. Biol.* 268:258–70
36. Elsik CG, Worley KC, Zhang L, Milshina NV, Jiang H, et al. 2006. Community annotation: procedures, protocols, and supporting tools. *Genome Res.* 16:1329–33
37. Escriva H, Bertrand S, Laudet V. 2004. The evolution of the nuclear receptor superfamily. *Essays Biochem.* 40:11–26
38. Esengil H, Chen JK. 2008. Gene regulation technologies in zebrafish. *Mol. Biosyst.* 4:300–8
39. Erezyilmaz DF, Kelstrup HC, Riddiford LM. 2009. The nuclear receptor E75A has a novel pair-rule-like function in patterning the milkweed bug, *Oncopeltus fasciatus*. *Dev. Biol.* 334:300–10
40. Fisk GJ, Thummel CS. 1995. Isolation, regulation, and DNA-binding properties of three *Drosophila* nuclear hormone receptor superfamily members. *Proc. Natl. Acad. Sci. USA* 92:10604–8
41. Gauchat D, Escriva H, Miljkovic-Licina M, Chera S, Langlois M-C, et al. 2004. The orphan COUP-TF nuclear receptors are markers for neurogenesis from cnidarians to vertebrates. *Dev. Biol.* 275:104–23
42. Goltsev Y, Hsiong W, Lanzaro G, Levine M. 2004. Different combinations of gap repressors for common stripes in *Anopheles* and *Drosophila* embryos. *Dev. Biol.* 275:435–46
43. González-Gaitán M, Rothe M, Wimmer EA, Taubert H, Jäckle H. 1994. Redundant functions of the genes *knirps* and *knirps-related* for the establishment of anterior *Drosophila* head structures. *Proc. Natl. Acad. Sci. USA* 91:8567–71

44. Graham LD, Moras D, Hill RJ, Billas ILM, Browing C, Lawrence MC. 2009. The structure and function of ecdysone receptors. In *Ecdysone: Structures and Functions*, ed. G Smagghe, pp. 335–60. Dordrecht: Springer-Verlag
45. Grasso LC, Hayward DC, Trueman JW, Hardie KM, Janssens PA, Ball EE. 2001. The evolution of nuclear receptors: evidence from the coral *Acropora*. *Mol. Phylogenet. Evol.* 21:93–102
46. Hawkins T, Chitale M, Kihara D. 2010. Functional enrichment analyses and construction of functional similarity networks with high confidence function prediction by PFP. *BMC Bioinform.* 11:265
47. Henrich VC, Beatty JM. 2009. Nuclear receptors in *Drosophila melanogaster*. In *Handbook of Cell Signaling*, pp. 2027–37. Oxford, UK: Academic
48. Henrich VC, Szekely AA, Kim SJ, Brown NE, Antoniewski C, et al. 1994. Expression and function of the *ultraspiracle* (*usp*) gene during development of *Drosophila melanogaster*. *Dev. Biol.* 165:38–52
49. Hiruma K, Riddiford LM. 2010. Developmental regulation of mRNAs for epidermal and fat body proteins and hormonally regulated transcription factors in the tobacco hornworm, *Manduca sexta*. *J. Insect Physiol.* 56:1390–95
50. Holt RA, Subramanian GM, Halpern A, Sutton GG, Charlab R, et al. 2002. The genome sequence of the malaria mosquito *Anopheles gambiae*. *Science* 298:129–49
51. Honeybee Genome Sequencing Consortium. 2006. Insights into social insects from the genome of the honeybee *Apis mellifera*. *Nature* 443:931–49
52. Hormann RE, Dinan L, Whiting P. 2003. Superimposition evaluation of ecdysteroid agonist chemotypes through multidimensional QSAR. *J. Comput. Aided Mol. Design* 17:135–53
53. Horner MA, Chen T, Thummel CS. 1995. Ecdysteroid regulation and DNA-binding properties of *Drosophila* nuclear hormone receptor superfamily members. *Dev. Biol.* 168:490–502
54. International Aphid Genomics Consortium. 2010. Genome sequence of the pea aphid *Acyrthosiphon pisum*. *PLoS Biol.* 8:e1000313
55. International Silkworm Genome Consortium. 2008. The genome of a lepidopteran model insect, the silkworm *Bombyx mori*. *Insect Biochem. Mol. Biol.* 38:1036–45
56. Ishimoto H, Kitamoto T. 2010. The steroid molting hormone ecdysone regulates sleep in adult *Drosophila melanogaster*. *Genetics* 185:269–81
57. Ishimoto H, Sakai T, Kitamoto T. 2009. Ecdysone signaling regulates the formation of long-term courtship memory in adult *Drosophila melanogaster*. *Proc. Natl. Acad. Sci. USA* 106:6381–86
58. Ishiwata K, Sasaki G, Ogawa J, Miyata T, Su Z-H. 2011. Phylogenetic relationships among insect orders based on three nuclear protein-coding gene sequences. *Mol. Phylogenet. Evol.* 58:169–80
59. Johns DC, Marx R, Mains RE, O'Rourke B, Marbán E. 1999. Inducible genetic suppression of neuronal excitability. *J. Neurosci.* 19:1691–97
60. Kapitskaya MZ, Li C, Miura K, Segraves W, Raikhel AS. 2000. Expression of the early-late gene encoding the nuclear receptor Hr3 suggests its involvement in regulating the vitellogenic response to ecdysone in the adult mosquito. *Mol. Cell. Endocrinol.* 160:25–37
61. Keightley MC. 1998. Steroid receptor isoforms: exception or rule? *Mol. Cell. Endocrinol.* 137:1–5
62. Kerber B, Fellert S, Hoch M. 1998. *Seven-up*, the *Drosophila* homolog of the COUP-TF orphan receptors, controls cell proliferation in the insect kidney. *Genes Dev.* 12:1781–86
63. Keshan B, Hiruma K, Riddiford LM. 2006. Developmental expression and hormonal regulation of different isoforms of the transcription factor E75 in the tobacco hornworm *Manduca sexta*. *Dev. Biol.* 295:623–32
64. King-Jones K, Thummel CS. 2005. Nuclear receptors: a perspective from *Drosophila*. *Nat. Rev. Genet.* 6:311–23
65. Kirkness EF, Haas BJ, Sun W, Braig HR, Perotti MA, et al. 2010. Genome sequences of the human body louse and its primary endosymbiont provide insights into the permanent parasitic lifestyle. *Proc. Natl. Acad. Sci. USA* 107:12168–73
66. Koelle MR, Segraves WA, Hogness DS. 1992. DHR3: a *Drosophila* steroid receptor homolog. *Proc. Natl. Acad. Sci. USA* 89:6167–71
67. **Koelle MR, Talbot WS, Segraves WA, Bender MT, Cherbas P, Hogness DS. 1991. The *Drosophila EcR* gene encodes an ecdysone receptor, a new member of the steroid receptor superfamily. *Cell* 67:59–77**

67. Provides the first description of EcR in any insect.

68. Kothapalli R, Palli SR, Ladd TR, Sohi SS, Cress D, et al. 1995. Cloning and developmental expression of the ecdysone receptor gene from the spruce budworm, *Choristoneura fumiferana*. *Dev. Genet.* 17:319–30
69. Kozlova T, Thummel CS. 2003. Essential roles for ecdysone signaling during *Drosophila* mid-embryonic development. *Science* 301:1911–14
70. Kumar MB, Fujimoto T, Potter DW, Deng Q, Palli SR. 2002. A single point mutation in ecdysone receptor leads to increased ligand specificity: implications for gene switch applications. *Proc. Natl. Acad. Sci. USA* 99:14710–15
71. Kumar MB, Potter DW, Hormann RE, Edwards A, Tice CM, et al. 2004. Highly flexible ligand binding pocket of ecdysone receptor: a single amino acid change leads to discrimination between two groups of nonsteroidal ecdysone agonists. *J. Biol. Chem.* 279:27211–18
72. Kurusu M, Maruyama Y, Adachi Y, Okabe M, Suzuki E, Furukubo-Tokunaga K. 2009. A conserved nuclear receptor, Tailless, is required for efficient proliferation and prolonged maintenance of mushroom body progenitors in the *Drosophila* brain. *Dev. Biol.* 326:224–36
73. Lam G, Hall BL, Bender M, Thummel CS. 1999. *DHR3* is required for the prepupal-pupal transition and differentiation of adult structures during *Drosophila* metamorphosis. *Dev. Biol.* 212:204–16
74. Lapenna S, Dinan L, Friz J, Hopfinger AJ, Liu J, Hormann RE. 2009. Semi-synthetic ecdysteroids as gene-switch actuators: synthesis, structure-activity relationships, and prospective ADME properties. *ChemMedChem* 4:55–68
75. Lavorgna G, Ueda H, Clos J, Wu C. 1991. FTZ-F1, a steroid hormone receptor-like protein implicated in the activation of *Fushi tarazu*. *Science* 252:848–51
76. Lawson D, Arensburger P, Atkinson P, Besansky NJ, Bruggner RV, et al. 2009. VectorBase: a data resource for invertebrate vector genomics. *Nucleic Acids Res.* 37:D583–87
77. Legeai F, Shigenobu S, Gauthier J-P, Colbourne J, Rispe C, et al. 2010. AphidBase: a centralized bioinformatic resource for annotation of the pea aphid genome. *Insect Mol. Biol.* 19(Suppl. 2):5–12
78. Lessard J, Aicha SB, Fournier A, Calvo E, Lavergne E, et al. 2007. Characterization of the RSL1-dependent conditional expression system in LNCaP prostate cancer cells and development of a single vector format. *Prostate* 67:808–19
79. Lewis SE, Searle SMJ, Harris N, Gibson M, Lyer V, et al. 2002. Apollo: a sequence annotation editor. *Genome Biol.* 3:research0082–0082.14
80. Lezzi M, Bergman T, Henrich VC, Vögtli M, Frömel C, et al. 2002. Ligand-induced heterodimerization between the ligand binding domains of the *Drosophila* ecdysteroid receptor and ultraspiracle. *Eur. J. Biochem.* 269:3237–45
81. Li C, Kapitskaya MZ, Zhu J, Miura K, Segraves W, Raikhel AS. 2000. Conserved molecular mechanism for the stage specificity of the mosquito vitellogenic response to ecdysone. *Dev. Biol.* 224:96–110
82. Lo PC, Frasch M. 2001. A role for the COUP-TF-related gene *seven-up* in the diversification of cardioblast identities in the dorsal vessel of *Drosophila*. *Mech. Dev.* 104:49–60
83. Lynch JA, Olesnicky EC, Desplan C. 2006. Regulation and function of *tailless* in the long germ wasp *Nasonia vitripennis*. *Dev. Genes Evol.* 216:493–98
84. Mané-Padrós D, Cruz J, Vilaplana L, Pascual N, Bellés X, Martín D. 2008. The nuclear hormone receptor BgE75 links molting and developmental progression in the direct-developing insect *Blattella germanica*. *Dev. Biol.* 315:147–60
85. Margam VM, Gelman DB, Palli SR. 2006. Ecdysteroid titers and developmental expression of ecdysteroid-related genes during metamorphosis of the yellow fever mosquito, *Aedes aegypti* (Diptera: Culicidae). *J. Insect Physiol.* 52:558–68
86. **Markov GV, Laudet V. 2011. Origin and evolution of the ligand-binding ability of nuclear receptors. *Mol. Cell. Endocrinol.* 334:21–30**

86. New hypothesis for the origin of NR ligand binding.

87. Markov G, Bonneton F, Laudet V. 2010. What does evolution teach us about nuclear receptors? In *Nuclear Receptors: Current Concepts and Future Challenges*, ed. CM Bunce, MJ Campbell, 8:15–29. New York: Springer
88. Martinez A, Sparks C, Drayton P, Thompson J, Greenland A, Jepson I. 1999. Creation of ecdysone receptor chimeras in plants for controlled regulation of gene expression. *Mol. Gen. Genet.* 261:546–52

89. Mikitani K. 1996. A new nonsteroidal chemical class of ligand for the ecdysteroid receptor 3, 5-di-tert-butyl-4-hydroxy-*N*-isobutyl-benzamide shows apparent insect molting hormone activities at molecular and cellular levels. *Biochem. Biophys. Res. Commun.* 227:427–32
90. Mlodzik M, Hiromi Y, Weber U, Goodman CS, Rubin GM. 1990. The *Drosophila seven-up* gene, a member of the steroid receptor gene superfamily, controls photoreceptor cell fates. *Cell* 60:211–24
91. Mommaerts V, Sterk G, Smagghe G. 2006. Bumblebees can be used in combination with juvenile hormone analogues and ecdysone agonists. *Ecotoxicology* 15:513–21
92. Morán E, Jiménez G. 2006. The *tailless* nuclear receptor acts as a dedicated repressor in the early *Drosophila* embryo. *Mol. Cell. Biol.* 26:3446–54
93. Mouillet JF, Delbecque JP, Quennedey B, Delachambre J. 1997. Cloning of two putative ecdysteroid receptor isoforms from *Tenebrio molitor* and their developmental expression in the epidermis during metamorphosis. *Eur. J. Biochem.* 248:856–63
94. Munoz-Torres MC, Reese JT, Childers CP, Bennett AK, Sundaram JP, et al. 2011. Hymenoptera Genome Database: integrated community resources for insect species of the order Hymenoptera. *Nucleic Acids Res.* 39:D658–62
95. Nakagawa Y. 2005. Nonsteroidal ecdysone agonists. *Vitam. Horm.* 73:131–73
96. Nene V, Wortman JR, Lawson D, Haas B, Kodira C, et al. 2007. Genome sequence of *Aedes aegypti*, a major arbovirus vector. *Science* 316:1718–23
97. No D, Yao TP, Evans RM. 1996. Ecdysone-inducible gene expression in mammalian cells and transgenic mice. *Proc. Natl. Acad. Sci. USA* 93:3346–51
98. **Nuclear Receptor Nomenclature Consortium. 1999. A unified nomenclature system for the nuclear receptor superfamily. *Cell* 97:161–63**

98. Establishes conceptual framework organizing nuclear receptors by phylogenetic analysis.

99. Oro AE, McKeown M, Evans RM. 1990. Relationship between the product of the *Drosophila ultraspiracle* locus and the vertebrate retinoid X receptor. *Nature* 347:298–301
100. Oro AE, McKeown M, Evans RM. 1992. The *Drosophila* nuclear receptors: new insight into the actions of nuclear receptors in development. *Curr. Opin. Genet. Dev.* 2:269–74
101. Palanker L, Necakov AS, Sampson HM, Ni R, Hu C, et al. 2006. Dynamic regulation of *Drosophila* nuclear receptor activity in vivo. *Development* 133:3549–62
102. Palli SR, Tice CM, Margam VM, Clark AM. 2005. Biochemical mode of action and differential activity of new ecdysone agonists against mosquitoes and moths. *Arch. Insect Biochem. Physiol.* 58:234–42
103. Palli SR, Hormann RE, Schlattner U, Lezzi M. 2005. Ecdysteroid receptors and their applications in agriculture and medicine. *Vitam. Horm.* 73:59–100
104. Palli SR, Kapitskaya MZ, Kumar MB, Cress DE. 2003. Improved ecdysone receptor–based inducible gene regulation system. *Eur. J. Biochem.* 270:1308–15
105. Pan Q, Shai O, Lee LJ, Frey BJ, Blencowe BJ. 2008. Deep surveying of alternative splicing complexity in the human transcriptome by high-throughput sequencing. *Nat. Genet.* 40:1413–15
106. Papanicolaou A, Stierli R, ffrench-Constant RH, Heckel DG. 2009. Next generation transcriptomes for next generation genomes using *est2assembly*. *BMC Bioinform.* 10:447
107. Paul RK, Takeuchi H, Kubo T. 2006. Expression of two ecdysteroid-regulated genes, *Broad-Complex* and *E75*, in the brain and ovary of the honeybee (*Apis mellifera* L.). *Zool. Sci.* 23:1085–92
108. **Pierceall WE, Li C, Biran A, Miura K, Raikhel AS, Segraves WA. 1999. E75 expression in mosquito ovary and fat body suggests reiterative use of ecdysone-regulated hierarchies in development and reproduction. *Mol. Cell. Endocrinol.* 150:73–89**

108. Links ecdysteroid-triggered metamorphosis gene cascade to reproduction.

109. Pignoni F, Baldarelli RM, Steingrímsson E, Diaz RJ, Patapoutian A, et al. 1990. The *Drosophila* gene *tailless* is expressed at the embryonic termini and is a member of the steroid receptor superfamily. *Cell* 62:151–63
110. Pignoni F, Steingrímsson E, Lengyel JA. 1992. *bicoid* and the terminal system activate *tailless* expression in the early *Drosophila* embryo. *Development* 115:239–51
111. Ravi M, Hopfinger AJ, Hormann RE, Dinan L. 2001. 4D-QSAR analysis of a set of ecdysteroids and a comparison to CoMFA modeling. *J. Chem. Inf. Comput. Sci.* 41:1587–604
112. Reinking J, Lam MMS, Pardee K, Sampson HM, Liu S, et al. 2005. The *Drosophila* nuclear receptor E75 contains heme and is gas responsive. *Cell* 122:195–207

113. Reitzel AM, Pang K, Ryan JF, Mullikin JC, Martindale MQ, et al. 2011. Nuclear receptors from the ctenophore *Mnemiopsis leidyi* lack a zinc-finger DNA-binding domain: lineage-specific loss or ancestral condition in the emergence of the nuclear receptor superfamily? *EvoDevo* 2:3
114. Richards S, Gibbs RA, Weinstock GM, Brown SJ, Denell R, et al. 2008. The genome of the model beetle and pest *Tribolium castaneum*. *Nature* 452:949–55
115. Richards S, Liu Y, Bettencourt BR, Hradecky P, Letovsky S, et al. 2005. Comparative genome sequencing of *Drosophila pseudoobscura*: chromosomal, gene, and *cis*-element evolution. *Genome Res.* 15:1–18
116. Robinson-Rechavi M, Laudet V. 2003. Bioinformatics of nuclear receptors. *Methods Enzymol.* 364:95–118

116. Describes the tools for annotation of nuclear receptors in sequenced genomes.

117. Robinson GE, Hackett KJ, Purcell-Miramontes M, Brown SJ, Evans JD, et al. 2011. Creating a buzz about insect genomes. *Science* 331:1386
118. Russell SR, Heimbeck G, Goddard CM, Carpenter AT, Ashburner M. 1996. The *Drosophila Eip78C* gene is not vital but has a role in regulating chromosome puffs. *Genetics* 144:159–70
119. Saleh DS, Zhang J, Wyatt GR, Walker VK. 1998. Cloning and characterization of an ecdysone receptor cDNA from *Locusta migratoria*. *Mol. Cell. Endocrinol.* 143:91–99
120. Schroder R, Eckert C, Wolff C, Tautz D. 2000. Conserved and divergent aspects of terminal patterning in the beetle *Tribolium castaneum*. *Proc. Natl. Acad. Sci. USA* 97:6591–96
121. Schubert M, Brunet F, Paris M, Bertrand S, Benoit G, Laudet V. 2008. Nuclear hormone receptor signaling in amphioxus. *Dev. Genes Evol.* 218:651–65
122. Schupp M, Lazar MA. 2010. Endogenous ligands for nuclear receptors: digging deeper. *J. Biol. Chem.* 285:40409–15
123. Schwarz D, Robertson HM, Feder JL, Varala K, Hudson ME, et al. 2009. Sympatric ecological speciation meets pyrosequencing: sampling the transcriptome of the apple maggot *Rhagoletis pomonella*. *BMC Genomics* 10:633
124. Segraves WA, Hogness DS. 1990. The *E75* ecdysone-inducible gene responsible for the 75B early puff in *Drosophila* encodes two new members of the steroid receptor superfamily. *Genes Dev.* 4:204–19

124. First to describe an insect nuclear receptor.

125. Singh AK, Tavva VS, Collins GB, Palli SR. 2010. Improvement of ecdysone receptor gene switch for applications in plants: *Locusta migratoria* retinoid X receptor (LmRXR) mutagenesis and optimization of translation start site. *FEBS J.* 277:4640–50
126. Sluder AE, Mathews SW, Hough D, Yin VP, Maina CV. 1999. The nuclear receptor superfamily has undergone extensive proliferation and diversification in nematodes. *Genome Res.* 9:103–20
127. Smagghe G, Degheele D. 1994. Action of a novel nonsteroidal ecdysteroid mimic, tebufenozide (RH-5992), on insects of different orders. *Pesticide Sci.* 42:85–92
128. Smagghe G, Degheele D. 1995. Biological activity and receptor-binding of ecdysteroids and the ecdysteroid agonists RH-5849 and RH-5992 in imaginal wing discs of *Spodoptera exigua* (Lepidoptera: Noctuidae). *Eur. J. Entomol.* 92:333–40
129. Smagghe G, Degheele D. 1995. Selectivity of nonsteroidal agonists RH 5849 and RH 5992 to nymphs and adults of the predatory soldier bugs, *Podisus nigrispinus* and *P. maculiventris* (Hemiptera: Pentatomidae). *J. Econ. Entomol.* 88:40–45
130. Smith CD, Zimin A, Holt C, Abouheif E, Benton R, et al. 2011. Draft genome of the globally widespread and invasive Argentine ant (*Linepithema humile*). *Proc. Natl. Acad. Sci. USA* 108:5673–78
131. Smith CR, Smith CD, Robertson HM, Helmkampf M, Zimin A, et al. 2011. Draft genome of the red harvester ant *Pogonomyrmex barbatus*. *Proc. Natl. Acad. Sci. USA* 108:5667–72
132. Soin T, Iga M, Swevers L, Rougé P, Janssen CR, Smagghe G. 2009. Towards Coleoptera-specific high-throughput screening systems for compounds with ecdysone activity: development of EcR reporter assays using weevil (*Anthonomus grandis*)-derived cell lines and *in silico* analysis of ligand binding to *A. grandis* EcR ligand-binding pocket. *Insect Biochem. Mol. Biol.* 39:523–34
133. Soin T, Swevers L, Kotzia G, Iatrou K, Janssen CR, et al. 2010. Comparison of the activity of non-steroidal ecdysone agonists between dipteran and lepidopteran insects, using cell-based EcR reporter assays. *Pest Manag. Sci.* 66:1215–29
134. Sommer R, Tautz D. 1991. Segmentation gene expression in the housefly *Musca domestica*. *Development* 113:419–30

135. Suhr ST, Gil EB, Senut MC, Gage FH. 1998. High level transactivation by a modified *Bombyx* ecdysone receptor in mammalian cells without exogenous retinoid X receptor. *Proc. Natl. Acad. Sci. USA* 95:7999–8004

135. Pioneering gene-switch study.

136. Sullivan AA, Thummel CS. 2003. Temporal profiles of nuclear receptor gene expression reveal coordinate transcriptional responses during *Drosophila* development. *Mol. Endocrinol.* 17:2125–37
137. Swevers L, Eystathioy T, Iatrou K. 2002. The orphan nuclear receptors BmE75A and BmE75C of the silkmoth *Bombyx mori*: hormonal control and ovarian expression. *Insect Biochem. Mol. Biol.* 32:1643–52
138. Swevers L, Kravariti L, Ciolfi S, Xenou-Kokoletsi M, Ragoussis N, et al. 2004. A cell-based high-throughput screening system for detecting ecdysteroid agonists and antagonists in plant extracts and libraries of synthetic compounds. *FASEB J.* 18:134–36
139. Tan A, Palli SR. 2008. Ecdysone receptor isoforms play distinct roles in controlling molting and metamorphosis in the red flour beetle, *Tribolium castaneum*. *Mol. Cell. Endocrinol.* 291:42–49
140. Tan A, Palli SR. 2008. Identification and characterization of nuclear receptors from the red flour beetle, *Tribolium castaneum*. *Insect Biochem. Mol. Biol.* 38:430–39
141. Taubert S, Ward JD, Yamamoto KR. 2011. Nuclear hormone receptors in nematodes: evolution and function. *Mol. Cell. Endocrinol.* 334:49–55
142. Tavva VS, Dinkins RD, Palli SR, Collins GB. 2007. Development of a tightly regulated and highly inducible receptor gene switch for plants through the use of retinoid X receptor chimeras. *Transgenic Res.* 16:599–61
143. Tavva VS, Palli SR, Dinkins RD, Collins GB. 2008. Improvement of a monopartite ecdysone receptor gene switch and demonstration of its utility in regulation of transgene expression in plants. *FEBS J.* 275:2161–76
144. Tennessen JM, Baker KD, Lam G, Evans J, Thummel CS. 2011. The *Drosophila* estrogen-related receptor directs a metabolic switch that supports developmental growth. *Cell Metab.* 13:139–48
145. Terashima J, Bownes M. 2006. *E75A* and *E75B* have opposite effects on the apoptosis/development choice of the *Drosophila* egg chamber. *Cell Death Differ.* 13:454–64
146. Tice CM, Hormann RE, Thompson CS, Friz JL, Cavanaugh CK, Saggers JA. 2003. Optimization of alpha-acylaminoketone ecdysone agonists for control of gene expression. *Bioorg. Med. Chem. Lett.* 13:1883–86
147. Velarde RA, Robinson GE, Fahrbach SE. 2006. Nuclear receptors of the honey bee: annotation and expression in the adult brain. *Insect Mol. Biol.* 15:583–95
148. Velarde RA, Robinson GE, Fahrbach SE. 2009. Coordinated responses to developmental hormones in the Kenyon cells of the adult worker honey bee brain (*Apis mellifera* L.). *J. Insect Physiol.* 55:59–69
149. Wang SF, Miura K, Miksicek RJ, Segraves WA, Raikhel AS. 1998. DNA binding and transactivation characteristics of the mosquito ecdysone receptor-*Ultraspiracle* complex. *J. Biol. Chem.* 273:27531–40
150. Wang Z, Burge CB. 2008. Splicing regulation: from a parts list of regulatory elements to an integrated splicing code. *RNA* 14:802–13
151. Werren JH, Richards S, Desjardins CA, Niehuis O, Gadau J, et al. 2010. Functional and evolutionary insights from the genomes of three parasitoid *Nasonia* species. *Science* 327:343–48

152. White KP, Hurban P, Watanabe R, Hogness DS. 1997. Coordination of *Drosophila* metamorphosis by two ecdysone-induced nuclear receptors. *Science* 276:114–17

152. Establishes the dynamics of key nuclear-receptor members of the metamorphosis cascade.

153. Whitfield CW, Band MR, Bonaldo MF, Kumar CG, Liu L, et al. 2002. Annotated expressed sequence tags and cDNA microarrays for studies of brain and behavior in the honey bee. *Genome Res.* 12:555–66
154. Wiens M, Batel R, Korzhev M, Müller WEG. 2003. Retinoid X receptor and retinoic acid response in the marine sponge *Suberites domuncula*. *J. Exp. Biol.* 206:3261–71

155. Wing KD. 1988. RH 5849, a nonsteroidal ecdysone agonist: effects on a *Drosophila* cell line. *Science* 241:467–69

155. Provides the first description of RH 5849.

156. Wurm FM, Gwinn KA, Kingston RE. 1986. Inducible overproduction of the mouse c-myc protein in mammalian cells. *Proc. Natl. Acad. Sci. USA* 83:5414–18
157. Wurm Y, Wang J, Riba-Grognuz O, Corona M, Nygaard S, et al. 2011. The genome of the fire ant *Solenopsis invicta*. *Proc. Natl. Acad. Sci. USA* 108:5679–84
158. Xu J, Tan A, Palli SR. 2010. The function of nuclear receptors in regulation of female reproduction and embryogenesis in the red flour beetle, *Tribolium castaneum*. *J. Insect Physiol.* 56:1471–80

159. Yamazaki Y, Kiuchi M, Takeuchi H, Kubo T. 2011. Ecdysteroid biosynthesis in workers of the European honeybee *Apis mellifera* L. *Insect Biochem. Mol. Biol.* 41:283–93
160. Yamazaki Y, Shirai K, Paul RK, Fijiyuki T, Wakamoto A, et al. 2006. Differential expression of *Hr38* in the mushroom bodies of the honeybee brain depends on the caste and division of labor. *FEBS Lett.* 580:2667–70
161. Yao TP, Forman BM, Jiang Z, Cherbas L, Chen JD, et al. 1993. Functional ecdysone receptor is the product of *EcR* and *Ultraspiracle* genes. *Nature* 366:476–79
162. Zhu J, Chen L, Raikhel AS. 2003. Posttranscriptional control of the competence factor βFTZ-F1 by juvenile hormone in the mosquito *Aedes aegypti*. *Proc. Natl. Acad. Sci. USA* 100:13338–43
163. Zipursky SL, Wojtowicz WM, Hattori D. 2006. Got diversity? Wiring the fly brain with Dscam. *Trends Biochem. Sci.* 31:581–88

RELATED RESOURCES

AphidBase: **http://www.aphidbase.com/aphidbase/**
Apollo Genome Annotation Curation Tool: **http://apollo.berkeleybop.org/current/**
ArthropodBase wiki: **http://arthropodgenomes.org/wiki/**
BeetleBase: **http://beetlebase.org/**
FlyBase: **http://flybase.org/**
Hymenoptera Genome Database: **http://hymenopteragenome.org/**
NCBI (National Center for Biotechnology Information): **http://www.ncbi.nlm.nih.gov/**
NURSA (Nuclear Receptor Signaling Atlas): **http://www.nursa.org/**
VectorBase: **http://www.vectorbase.org/**

Plasmodium knowlesi: A Malaria Parasite of Monkeys and Humans*

William E. Collins

Division of Parasitic Diseases and Malaria, Center for Global Health, Centers for Disease Control and Prevention, Atlanta, Georgia 30333; email: wec1@cdc.gov

Annu. Rev. Entomol. 2012. 57:107–21

The *Annual Review of Entomology* is online at ento.annualreviews.org

This article's doi:
10.1146/annurev-ento-121510-133540

0066-4170/12/0107-0107$20.00

Keywords

human malaria, mosquitoes, *Anopheles leucosphyrus*, Southeast Asia, Borneo

Abstract

Plasmodium knowlesi is a malaria parasite of monkeys of Southeast Asia that is transmitted by mosquitoes of the *Anopheles leucosphyrus* group. Humans are frequently infected with this parasite and misdiagnosed as being infected with *Plasmodium malariae*. The parasite was a major monkey animal model for developing antimalarial vaccines and investigations of the biology of parasite invasion. *P. knowlesi* is the first monkey malaria parasite genome to be sequenced and annotated.

INTRODUCTION

Plasmodium knowlesi is found primarily in monkeys on peninsular Malaysia. It was probably first seen by Franchini (31) in the blood of *Macaca fascicularis* monkeys. Later, Napier & Campbell (58) investigated the tendency of the parasite to produce hemoglobinuria in *M. fascicularis* and *M. mulatta* monkeys. The original animal was given to Dr. Das Gupta, who maintained the parasite by subpassage (49). Knowles & Das Gupta (50) described the blood stages and transmitted the parasite to humans. Sinton & Mulligan (80) noted the distinctive stippling of the red cells, the presence of an accessory dot, and the 24-h schizogonic cycle, which convinced them that the parasite represented a new species. They named it *Plasmodium knowlesi* in honor of Dr. R. Knowles, who was the first to infect humans with the parasite. Until recently, *P. knowlesi* was known only as a parasite of monkeys and was extensively studied, primarily in macaques, for basic immunological, chemotherapeutic, and biological relationships between malaria parasites and their primate hosts. This parasite was used because of its high rate of infectivity and high mortality in rhesus monkeys (*Macaca mulatta*). In drug and vaccine studies, efficacy could be readily measured by the high rate of death of the host.

The recent finding that many humans were infected with this organism in Sabah and Sarawak, Malaysia, and subsequently elsewhere throughout southeastern Asia has led people to consider *P. knowlesi* to be the fifth human malaria parasite (90). The resemblance of the late blood-stage forms of *P. knowlesi* to those of *P. malariae* made it difficult to differentiate these two species by blood film examination. Separation was accurately made only by the recent application of PCR technology. Distribution of the parasite in the natural monkey hosts and transmission to humans appear to be restricted to mosquito vectors of the *Anopheles leucosphyrus* group confined to Southeast Asia. Because it is a human pathogen, *P. knowlesi* was the first monkey malaria parasite genome to be sequenced (61).

PARASITE

Life History

The developmental cycle in the erythrocyte lasts approximately 24 h (**Figure 1**); this is the only malaria parasite of primates with this quotidian erythrocytic cycle. All other species have cycles of approximately 48 or 72 h (19). Following ingestion of the microgametocytes and

CLASSIFICATION

Plasmodium knowlesi:
Domain: Eukaryota
Kingdom: Chromalveolata
Superphylum: Alveolata
Phylum: Apicomplexa
Class: Aconoidasida
Order: Haemosporida
Family: Plasmodiidae
Genus: *Plasmodium*
Species: *knowlesi* Sinton and Mulligan 1932
The clade with the most closely related species consists of *P. coatneyi* and *P. knowlesi*.

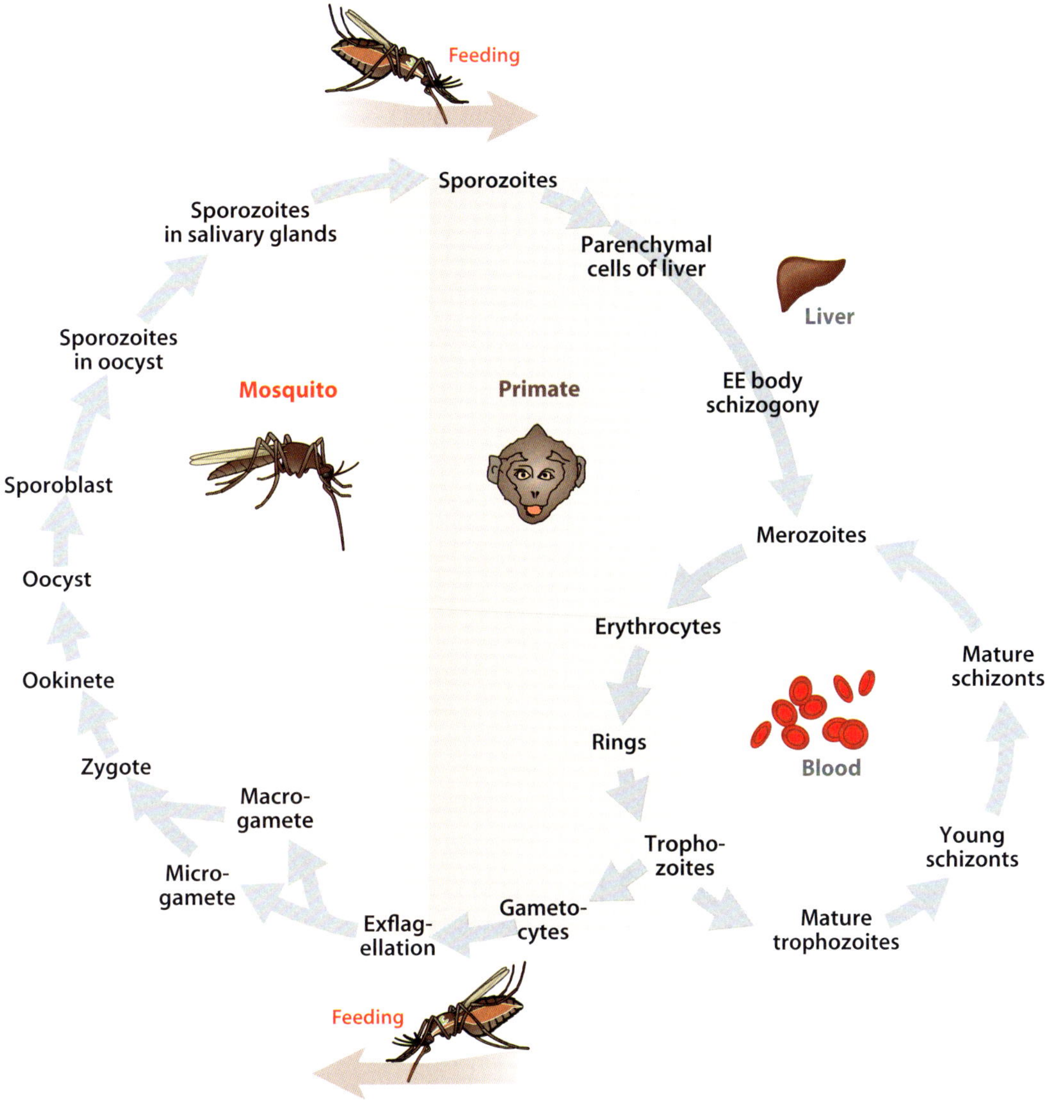

Figure 1

Life cycle of the malaria parasite. Sporozoites are injected into the primate by a mosquito bite. This is followed by the development of the exoerythrocytic (EE) body, the production of merozoites that invade the erythrocytes, the production of gametocytes that are taken into the gut of the mosquito during feeding, and the sporogonic cycle in the mosquito that results in the production of sporozoites that are now injected into the primate to complete the cycle.

macrogametocytes by the mosquito during feeding, the fusion of the gametes takes place in the gut of the vector to produce the ookinete that migrates to the wall of the mosquito's gut, where it develops into the oocyst. This sporogonic development on the gut of the mosquito requires approximately 9 to 10 days at 25°C (19). At this time, thousands of sporozoites are released from each oocyst and are then pumped by the heart to the salivary glands. Sporozoites are concentrated in the acinar cells of the salivary glands. During feeding, up to 100 sporozoites are injected into the primate host. The sporozoites are transported by the circulatory system to the liver, where they bind tightly to the sinusoidal cell layer, cross the Kupffer cells, and finally invade liver parenchymal cells. Within these cells, the exoerythrocytic (EE) stages develop. This stage requires approximately 5 days to reach maturity. Thousands of merozoites are released from each EE stage and invade the erythrocytes of the primate host. Gametocytes are subsequently produced to complete the life cycle of the parasite.

Erythrocytic Stage

The parasites, as they appear in the erythrocytes, are illustrated in drawings prepared by G.H. Nicholson (**Figure 2**, panels 1–25) from Reference 19. Photomicrographs of the blood stages as seen in Giemsa-stained blood films are shown in **Figure 3**. The young rings are similar to those of *P. falciparum*. The nucleus is spherical and many times seen lying inside the ring. When full grown, the nonamoeboid ring may occupy half or more of the host erythrocyte. Band forms (panel 11) appear similar to those of *P. malariae*. With the loss of the vacuole, the parasite shrinks and becomes compact, and pigment appears in the form of dark grains. The nucleus increases in size. With Giemsa stain, the cytoplasm stains a deep blue and the nucleus a deep red. The erythrocyte shows a faint stippling (panels 13–19). With the advent of schizogony, the nucleus divides, producing as many as 16 merozoites (10 on average). These merozoites then fill the host cell. The pigment then collects into one or more yellowish-black masses and eventually into a single mass in the mature schizont. The asexual cycle in the blood lasts only 24 hours and is known as a quotidian cycle.

The sexual forms grow more slowly, taking approximately 48 h to complete their development. The mature macrogametocyte (panel 24) is generally spherical and fills the host cell. The cytoplasm stains a distinctive blue and the nucleus takes a deep pink stain. Black pigment granules are scattered throughout the cytoplasm. The microgametocyte (panel 25) is sometimes smaller. The cytoplasm stains a medium pink, and the nucleus is a darker shade of pink. Pigment is jet black and is also scattered in the cytoplasm.

Tissue Stage

Sporozoites injected into the bloodstream of the host enter the liver either by the hepatic artery or the portal vein. They bind to the sinusoidal cell layer, presumably mediated by proteoglycans protruding from the space of Disse (or perisinusoidal space). The sporozoites position themselves and pass through a Kupffer cell and the space of Disse to enter the liver parenchyma. Sporozoites eventually settle into individual parenchymal cells for development into the EE stage (EE body). The tissue forms of *P. knowlesi* were first described by Garnham et al. (33). The earliest forms seen were those taken at biopsy 92 h postinfection. In a subsequent study, Held et al. (40) injected infected salivary glands from *Anopheles dirus* mosquitoes directly into the liver of rhesus monkeys. Beginning 48 h postinjection, liver biopsies were taken at 8-h intervals through 120 h. At that time, young ring forms were present in the circulating blood of the animals. At the same time, nearly mature exoerythrocytic forms (EE bodies) were demonstrable in the liver sections, indicating a delay in the maturation of some of the EE forms. The greatest rate of growth of these EE bodies appeared to take place between 72 and 96 h after sporozoite injection (24).

Subsequently, tissue stages were demonstrated in different species of New World monkeys. **Figure 4** shows maturing and fully mature EE bodies developing in the parenchymal cells of squirrel monkeys.

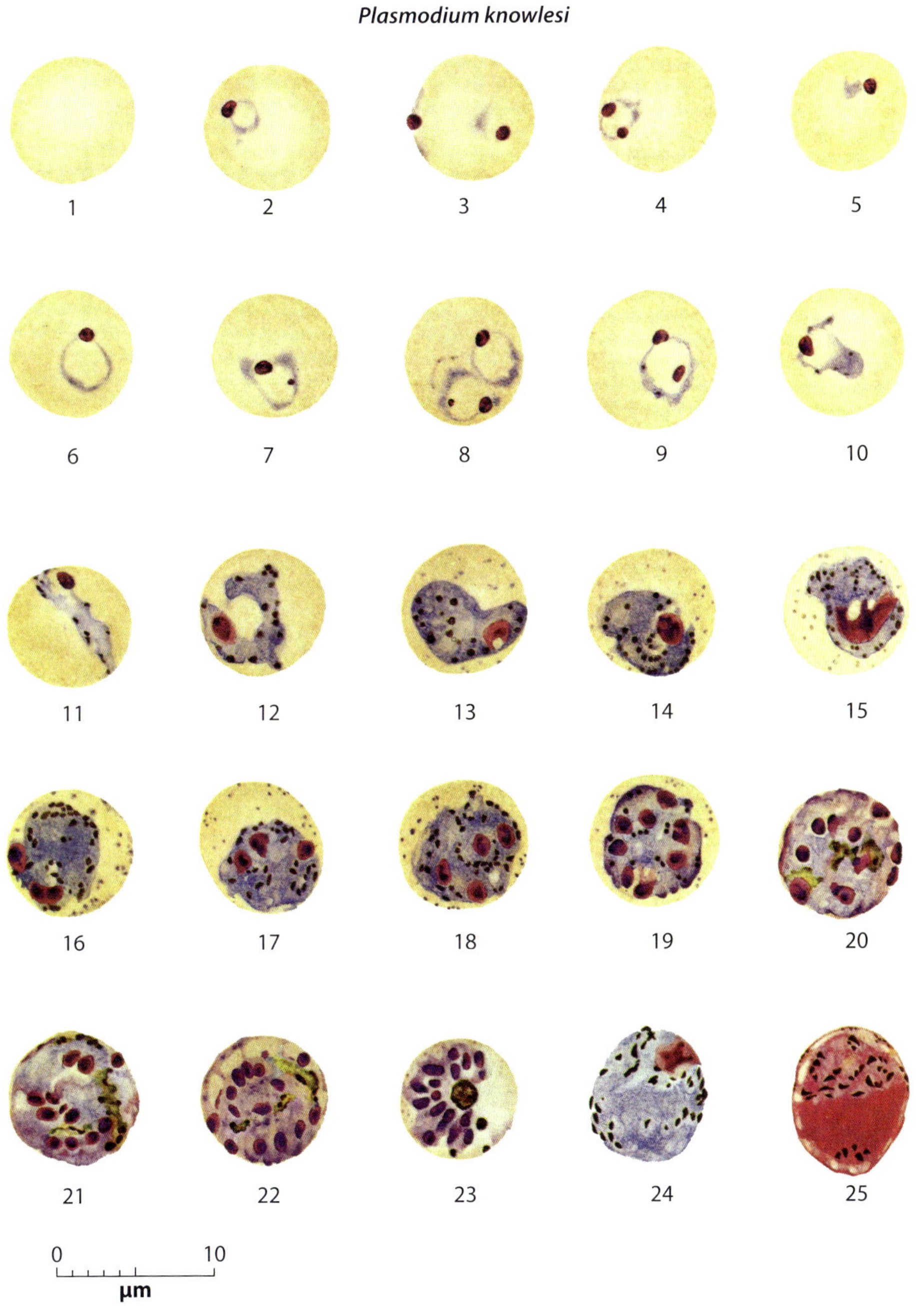

Figure 2

Erythrocytic stages of *Plasmodium knowlesi*. Drawings prepared by G.H. Nicholson.

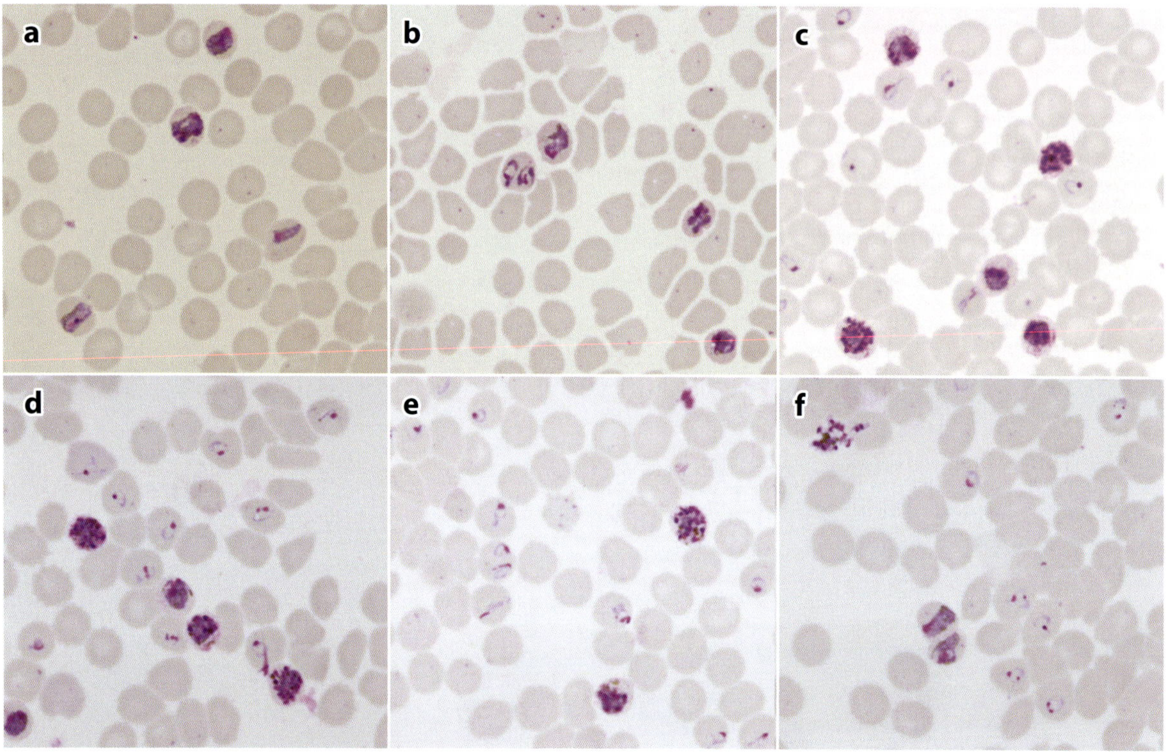

Figure 3

Photomicrographs of erythrocytes of a rhesus monkey infected with *Plasmodium knowlesi*. Panels *a*, *b*, and *f* show band forms similar to some trophozoite forms of *Plasmodium malariae*. Panels *d–f* show young ring forms typical of *P. malariae* and *P. falciparum*. Panels *c–e* show mature schizonts. The number of merozoites in the mature forms are usually greater than that observed in *P. malariae*.

INFECTION OF HUMANS

Experimental Infections

The first experimental infection of humans was that performed by Knowles & Das Gupta (50). This was followed by numerous reports of humans treated for neurosyphilis by infection with *P. knowlesi* (15, 16, 18, 43, 44, 54, 55, 60, 85). In these studies, most authors characterized the disease in humans as mild with a tendency toward spontaneous self-recovery. However, Ciuca et al. (17) reported in 1955 that after 170 transfers, the infection became virulent and had to be terminated with drugs. Following the natural infection of a person in Malaysia in 1965, 20 volunteers were infected with the H strain of *P. knowlesi*, 8 via the bites of *A. dirus* mosquitoes, and 12 by blood passage (13, 19). Parasite counts as high as 1,200 per microliter were encountered as late as the twenty-eighth day of patent parasitemia. Most patients cleared their detectable parasitemia by day 16. Infections were transmitted from human to human and from human to rhesus monkey by mosquito bite.

Natural Infections

The first reported natural transmission of *P. knowlesi* to humans was the case of a 37-year-old American who had spent 5 days in the bush in Malaysia in 1965 (12). However, the close

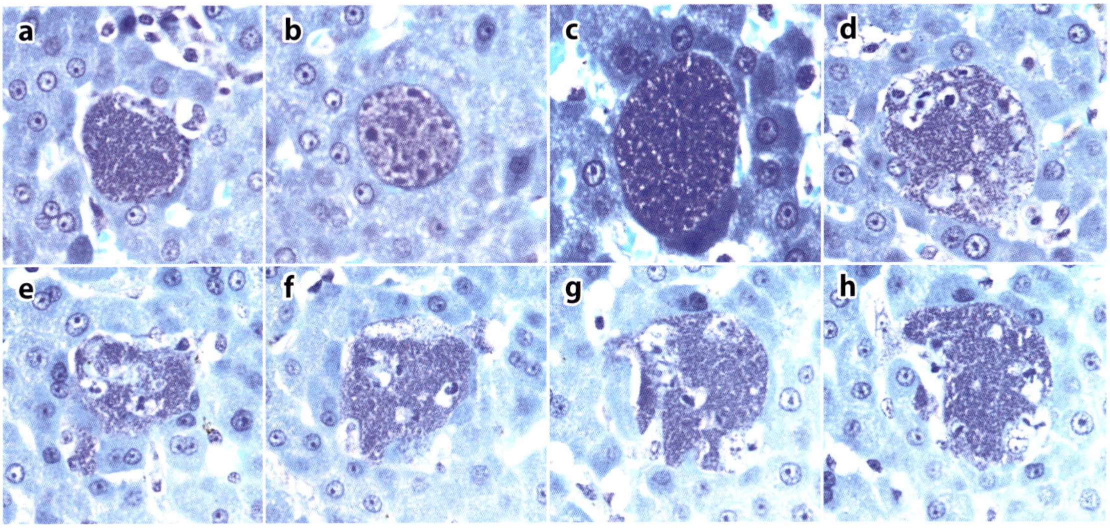

Figure 4

Exoerythrocytic (EE) stages of *Plasmodium knowlesi* in 5-μm sections of the liver of *Saimiri boliviensis* monkeys. Panels *a* and *b*: 96-h EE bodies; panels *c* and *d*: 120-h EE bodies; and panels *e–h*: serial sections of an individual 120-h EE body.

resemblance of the blood stages of this parasite to that of *P. malariae* suggested that detection of other human cases would be readily missed or misdiagnosed. Singh et al. (78) clarified the situation through the use of PCR techniques. In a retroactive study in Malaysian Borneo, 58% of blood samples from people that had been diagnosed with malaria actually contained the monkey malaria parasite *P. knowlesi*. Microscopic examination had indicated the presence of *P. malariae*, yet this parasite was not detected by PCR. There had been four fatal human infections due to *P. knowlesi* (27). *M. fascicularis* monkeys infected with *P. knowlesi* apparently had served as the continued source of infection, and *Anopheles latens* (a member of the *Leucosphyrus* group of mosquitoes) served as the vector (87).

Since the initial indirect studies in Borneo, human infections have been reported from additional areas of Southeast Asia including peninsular Malaysia (86), Singapore (59), the Philippines (52), and Thailand (45, 69). The distribution of this parasite is apparently confined to Southeast Asia because mosquitoes of the *Anopheles* (*Cellia*) *leucosphyrus* Donitz group are the only mosquitoes shown to be capable of transmitting this parasite.

NONHUMAN INFECTIONS

The natural hosts for *P. knowlesi* in Malaysia are the crab-eating macaque (*M. fascicularis*), the pig-tailed macaque (*M. nemestrina*), and the langur (*Presbytis melalophos*). Experimentally, almost all primates, including humans, are susceptible to infection. Both Old and New World monkeys are used in biological, chemotherapeutic, and immunological studies with *P. knowlesi* (21). Removal of the spleen greatly increases the parasite counts in animals that could normally tolerate infections. The most commonly used experimental host monkey has been the rhesus monkey (*M. mulatta*). Infection is usually fatal if the monkeys are inoculated with parasitized erythrocytes. Following infection via sporozoites, approximately 70% of the animals die with overwhelming parasitemia (22, 25). The remaining animals control their infections and infect susceptible mosquitoes, often over a period of many days. The endpoint for studies for early vaccine trials in this host was often death; therefore, interpretation of the effectiveness of such studies was straightforward. Those who performed immunization trials with rhesus monkeys (6, 7, 23, 29, 36, 46, 70, 73, 77) might have been better served had they used the natural host, *M. fascicularis*. The disadvantage of using *M. fascicularis* is that many of the wild-caught animals that are imported have already been naturally infected. Nonetheless, much information has been obtained from these studies on *P. knowlesi* in rhesus monkeys.

IMMUNOLOGIC AND ANTIGENIC STUDIES

P. knowlesi has been one of the major models in the search for a vaccine for malaria because (*a*) it can be grown in culture, (*b*) antigens similar to those of human malaria parasites are produced by *P. knowlesi*, and (*c*) in trials, the animals can be challenged via parasitized erythrocytes or via sporozoites with predictable outcomes for the controls.

In Vitro Culture

Soon after the in vitro culture of *P. falciparum* was developed by Trager & Jensen (84), the culture of *P. knowlesi* was established (34, 62–64, 91). This made the parasite available to those investigators lacking the facilities to work with primates. In addition, both the erythrocyte and sporozoite stage parasites could be maintained in the frozen state and then used to initiate infections in animals after many years of storage. Normally, parasites are preserved using Glycerolyte® (20, 26); successful preservation with DMSO (dimethyl sulfoxide) has also been reported (5).

Antigen Isolation and Characterization

Many of the major antigens studied for the development of human vaccines have also been isolated from *P. knowlesi* for study in monkeys or culture. Aikawa et al. (1) localized the protective 143-/140-kDa antigens by using antibodies and ultramicrotomy. Barnwell et al. (3, 4) studied the expression of the variant antigen on the erythrocyte membrane of cloned *P. knowlesi*. Chitnis & Miller (14) identified the erythrocyte-binding protein domains involved in erythrocyte invasion. The Duffy gene, which is involved with cellular receptors, was also a center of investigation. Chaudhuri et al. (11) purified and characterized the Duffy blood group antigens. Fried et al. (32) identified two cysteine-rich, lipophilic proteins on the surface of ookinetes (Pks20 and Pks24). Howard & Barnwell (41) analyzed the surface membrane antigens on erythrocytes infected with *P. knowlesi*. Hudson et al. (42) examined a merozoite surface protein of the parasite with a molecular weight of 14,000. Klotz et al. (48) examined vaccination-induced variation in the 140-kDa merozoite surface antigen. The *P. knowlesi* schizont-infected cell agglutination (SICA) antigen gene family and its variation, compared to *P. falciparum*, were described by al-Khedery et al. (2). Korir & Galinski (51) demonstrated the relationship between *P. knowlesi* SICA variant antigens and *P. falciparum* EMP1. Schmidt-Ullrich et al. (74, 75) studied the 65,000-Mr glycoprotein at the surface of infected erythrocytes and the protective 74,000-Mr antigen in membranes of schizont-infected rhesus erythrocytes. Ellis et al. (30) cloned and expressed the malarial sporozoite surface antigen in *E. coli*. Ruiz et al. (72) reported the organization and expression of the *P. knowlesi* circumsporozoite antigen, and Sharma et al. (76) reported the immunogenicity of the nonrepetitive regions of the circumsporozoite protein.

Vaccine Trials

Rhesus monkeys have been the primary host for trials using candidate experimental *P. knowlesi* vaccines and Freund's adjuvant. Brown & Hills (6) and Brown & Tanaka (7) immunized rhesus monkeys using formalin-inactivated whole parasites and Freund's adjuvant. Butcher et al. (8) determined the antibody-mediated mechanisms that were induced by vaccination with *P. knowlesi* merozoites. Cabrera et al. (9, 10) immunized rhesus monkeys with a parasite preparation that had been put through a French pressure cell press. Animals were protected 4 years after immunization against a heterologous strain of the parasite. Collins et al. (23) immunized rhesus monkeys by using heat-stable, serum-soluble antigens. David et al. (28) immunized monkeys with a 140-kDa merozoite surface protein and Deans et al. (29) conducted vaccine trials in rhesus monkeys with a minor, invariant 66-kDa merozoite antigen. Gwadz & Green (36) and Gwadz et al. (35) reported the vaccination of rhesus monkeys with irradiated sporozoites of *P. knowlesi.* Gwadz & Koontz (37) also reported the development of transmission-blocking immunity in monkeys immunized with gamete antigens. Kaushik et al. (46) protected rhesus monkeys with a merozoite vaccine, and Khanna et al. (47) vaccinated rhesus monkeys using whole antigen and an aqueous suspension of muramyl dipeptide as an adjuvant. Mitchell et al. (56, 57) also used a merozoite vaccine to effectively immunize rhesus monkeys. Rieckmann et al. (70) immunized rhesus monkeys with blood-stage antigens of *P. knowlesi*. Schenkel et al. (73) vaccinated rhesus monkeys by the use of nonviable antigen and Simpson et al. (77) vaccinated rhesus against malaria by use of sucrose density gradient fractions of blood-stage antigens. Targett & Fulton (83) were among the first researchers to successfully use rhesus monkeys and *P. knowlesi* for the study of malarial vaccines.

VECTORS

Natural Vectors

The first mosquito species to be incriminated as a vector was *Anopheles hackeri*, collected in peninsular Malaysia (89). Sporozoites were dissected from this mosquito and then injected into a rhesus monkey that subsequently developed *P. knowlesi* malaria. *A. latens* is the vector in Sarawak (82, 87). Using nested PCR, Vythilingam et al. (86) detected *P. knowlesi* in *A. cracens* mosquitoes collected in peninsular Malaysia. *P. knowlesi* has not been found in monkeys outside the range of mosquitoes of the *A. leucosphyrus* group. The parasite is so lethal to rhesus monkeys that the geographic range of this primate is limited by the range of the vector mosquitoes for *P. knowlesi*. According to Manguin et al. (53), the *Leucosphyrus* group consists of the *Dirus* Complex, which includes seven species, and the *Leucosphyrus* Complex, which includes four species. These are forest mosquitoes but are occasionally present in the open areas on the forest fringes.

Experimental Vectors

Sporozoite-positive salivary glands have been reported in *A. stephensi* (33, 38, 39, 79), *A. annularis* (79, 80), *A. aztecus* (33), *A. atroparvus* (39, 88), *A. freeborni* (22), and *A. dirus* (22, 25). In only the last species were sporozoites found in abundance. *A. stephensi* was first used to transmit the parasite from monkey to monkey (38, 39). However, the sporozoite counts in the salivary glands were low. Chin et al. (13) experimentally transmitted *P. knowlesi* to human volunteers and monkeys using laboratory-reared *A. dirus* mosquitoes. Collins et al. (22, 25) repeatedly transmitted the H strain of the parasite to rhesus monkeys using *A. dirus*; Sullivan et al. (81) transmitted three different strains of *P. knowlesi* to New World monkeys using the same vector. Rosenberg (71) determined that *A. freeborni* mosquitoes could not transmit the infection because sporozoites are unable to invade the salivary glands. Sporozoites develop within the oocysts normally. Other mosquitoes that support normal development of the oocysts only are *A. maculatus*, *A. quadrimaculatus*, and *A. atroparvus* (19).

TREATMENT

Treatment with schizonticidal drugs is sufficient to prevent or control infections. Because *P. knowlesi* does not relapse from residual forms in the liver, treatment with primaquine is not needed. Chloroquine is most commonly used to treat monkeys infected with this parasite (300 mg for an adult rhesus or *M. fascicularis* given over 3 days) (W.E. Collins, unpublished observations). There are no reports of resistant strains. The standard treatment with chloroquine for humans would be 1500 mg for a 60-kg adult. Prasad et al. (65–68) studied the kinetic effects of chloroquine as well as its effect on complement levels, cellular immune responses, and the phagocytic function of monocytes by using *P. knowlesi*–infected rhesus monkeys. In addition, infections in monkeys have been treated successfully with quinine, sulfonamides, mefloquine, and the newer artemisinin drugs (W.E. Collins, unpublished observations).

DIAGNOSIS

Currently, diagnosis is made by nested PCR using different primers (45, 78). On blood films from monkeys, infected erythrocytes are not enlarged and any stippling is faint and restricted to more mature trophozoites. The additional presence of trophozoite band forms would indicate *P. knowlesi* in monkeys or either *P. malariae* or *P. knowlesi* in humans as a tentative diagnosis. The definitive diagnosis is the 24-h developmental cycle of the erythrocytic stage. Mosquitoes are infected by subpassage to rhesus monkeys (89), and sporozoites and oocysts in captured mosquitoes are identified by using nested PCR (82, 86).

Future studies should determine the different members of the *Leucosphyrus* group of mosquitoes that are transmitting *P. knowlesi* in Southeast Asia. Moreover, humans with malaria acquired in the vicinity of monkey habitat should be tested by PCR for infection with *P. knowlesi* in addition to the other human parasites.

SUMMARY POINTS

1. *Plasmodium knowlesi* is the primary parasite of monkeys of Southeast Asia and it occasionally infects humans.
2. The parasite morphologically resembles *P. malariae*; specific diagnosis of human infection is determined by nested PCR.
3. Infection may occur anyplace within the distribution range of members of the *A. leucosphyrus* complex of mosquitoes if infected monkeys, such as *M. fascicularis*, *M. nemestrina*, and *Presbytis melalophos*, are present.
4. In most instances, the vectors of this parasite are forest-dwelling, canopy-feeding mosquitoes such as *A. latens* and *A. cracens*.
5. Workers or travelers who enter this environment are at risk of being fed upon by infected mosquitoes and of developing infection and disease.
6. This parasite has been widely used in the development of different types of experimental antimalarial vaccines.
7. The primary hosts for immunologic studies are *M. mulatta* monkeys, although other primates such as New World *Aotus* spp. and *Saimiri* spp. have been infected.
8. The parasite has been grown in culture and successfully stored in the frozen state.

FUTURE ISSUES

1. How extensive is the infection of humans with *P. knowlesi* in Southeast Asia?
2. Are other species of *Plasmodium* (*P. inui*, *P. cynomolgi*) being transmitted to humans?
3. Are infections of *P. knowlesi* transmitted from human to human?
4. Are vectors other than *A. latens* and *A. cracens* responsible for the transmission of *P. knowlesi* to monkeys and humans?

DISCLOSURE STATEMENT

The author is not aware of any affiliations, memberships, funding, or financial holdings that might be perceived as affecting the objectivity of this review.

LITERATURE CITED

1. Aikawa M, David P, Fine E, Hudson D, Klotz F, et al. 1986. Localization of protective 143/140 kDa antigens of *Plasmodium knowlesi* by the use of antibodies and ultramicrotomy. *Eur. J. Cell Biol.* 41:207–13
2. al-Khedery B, Barnwell JW, Galinski MR. 1999. Antigenic variation in malaria: a 3′ genomic alteration associated with the expression of a *P. knowlesi* variant antigen. *Mol. Cell* 3:131–41
3. Barnwell JW, Howard RJ, Coon HG, Miller LH. 1983. Splenic requirement for antigenic variation and expression of the variant antigen on the erythrocyte membrane of cloned *Plasmodium knowlesi* malaria. *Infect. Immun.* 40:985–94
4. Barnwell JW, Howard RJ, Miller LH. 1982. Altered expression of *Plasmodium knowlesi* variant antigen on the erythrocyte membrane in splenectomized rhesus monkeys. *J. Immunol.* 128:224–26
5. Booden T, Geiman QM. 1973. *Plasmodium falciparum* and *P. knowlesi*: low temperature preservation using dimethylsulfoxide. *Exp. Parasitol.* 33:495–98
6. Brown KN, Hills LA. 1972. Immunization against *Plasmodium knowlesi* malaria. *Trans. R. Soc. Trop. Med. Hyg.* 66:668–69
7. Brown KN, Tanaka A. 1975. Vaccination against *Plasmodium knowlesi* malaria. *Trans. R. Soc. Trop. Med. Hyg.* 69:350–53
8. Butcher GA, Mitchell GH, Cohen S. 1978. Antibody mediated mechanisms of immunity to malaria induced by vaccination with *Plasmodium knowlesi* merozoites. *Immunology* 34:77–86
9. Cabrera EJ, Barr ML, Silverman PH. 1977. Long-term studies on rhesus monkeys (*Macaca mulatta*) immunized against *Plasmodium knowlesi*. *Infect. Immun.* 15:461–65
10. Cabrera EJ, Speer CA, Schenkel RH, Barr ML, Silverman PH. 1976. Delayed dermal hypersensitivity in rhesus monkeys (*Macaca mulatta*) immunized against *Plasmodium knowlesi*. *Z. Parasitenkd.* 50:31–42
11. Chaudhuri A, Zbrzezna V, Johnson C, Nichols M, Rubinstein P, et al. 1989. Purification and characterization of an erythrocyte membrane protein complex carrying Duffy blood group antigenicity. Possible receptor for *Plasmodium vivax* and *Plasmodium knowlesi* malaria parasite. *J. Biol. Chem.* 264:13770–74
12. Chin W, Contacos PG, Coatney GR, Kimbal HR. 1965. A naturally acquired quotidian-type malaria in man transferable to monkeys. *Science* 149:865
13. Chin W, Contacos PG, Collins WE, Jeter MH, Alpert E. 1968. Experimental mosquito-transmission of *Plasmodium knowlesi* to man and monkey. *Am. J. Trop. Med. Hyg.* 17:355–58
14. Chitnis CE, Miller LH. 1994. Identification of the erythrocyte binding domains of *Plasmodium vivax* and *Plasmodium knowlesi* proteins involved in erythrocyte invasion. *J. Exp. Med.* 180:497–506
15. Chopra RN, Das Gupta BM. 1936. A preliminary note on the treatment of neuro-syphilis with monkey malaria. *Indian Med. Gaz.* 77:187–88

16. Ciuca M, Ballif L, Chelarescu M, Lavrinenko M, Zotta E. 1937. Contributions á l'étude de l'action pathogéne de *Pl. knowlesi* pour l'homme (considerations sur l'immunité naturelle et l'immunité acquise contre cette especé de parasite). *Bull. Soc. Path. Exot. Fil. Ouest-Afr.* 30:305–15
17. Ciuca M, Chelarescu M, Sofletea A, Constantinescu P, Teriteanu E, et al. 1955. Contribution expérimentale á l'étude de l'immunité dans le paludisme. *Ed. Acad. Rep. Pop. Roum.* pp. 1–108
18. Ciuca M, Tomescu P, Badescu G, Badenski A, Ionescu P, Teriteanu M. 1937. Contribution á l'étude de la virulence du *Pl. knowlesi* chez l'homme. Caractéres de la maladie et biologie du parasite. *Arch. Roum. Pathol. Exp. Microbiol.* 10:5–28
19. Coatney GR, Collins WE, Warren M, Contacos PG. 1971. The primate malarias. *US Govt. Print. Off.*, Washington, DC, pp. 1–366
20. Collins WE. 2008. Animal models. I. Infection of monkeys with *Plasmodium* spp. II. Infection of mosquitoes with *Plasmodium* spp. in monkeys. In *Methods in Malaria Research*, ed. MK Ljungstrom, H Perlman, A Scherf, M Wahlgren, pp. 141–46. Manassas, VA: MR4/ATCC. 5th ed.
21. Collins WE, Contacos PG, Chin W. 1978. Infection of the squirrel monkey *Saimiri sciureus*, with *Plasmodium knowlesi*. *Trans. R. Soc. Trop. Med. Hyg.* 72:662–63
22. Collins WE, Contacos PG, Guinn EG. 1967. Studies on the transmission of simian malarias. II. Transmission of the H strain of *Plasmodium knowlesi* by *Anopheles balabacensis balabacensis*. *J. Parasitol.* 53:841–44
23. Collins WE, Contacos PG, Harrison AJ, Stanfill PS, Skinner JC. 1977. Attempts to immunize monkeys against *Plasmodium knowlesi* by using heat-stable, serum-soluble antigens. *Am. J. Trop. Med. Hyg.* 26:373–76
24. Collins WE, Contacos PG, Jumper JR, Smith CS, Skinner JC. 1973. Studies on the exoerythrocytic stages of simian malaria. VIII. *Plasmodium knowlesi*. *J. Parasitol.* 59:344–52
25. Collins WE, Contacos PG, Skinner JC, Guinn EG. 1971. Studies on the transmission of simian malaria. IV. Further studies on the transmission of *Plasmodium knowlesi* by *Anopheles balabacensis balabacensis* mosquitoes. *J. Parasitol.* 57:961–66
26. Collins WE, Sullivan JS, Nace D, Williams T, Williams A, et al. 2004. Additional observations on the sporozoite transmission of *Plasmodium knowlesi* to monkeys. *J. Parasitol.* 90:866–67
27. Cox-Singh J, Davis TM, Lee KS, Shamsul SS, Matusop A, et al. 2008. *Plasmodium knowlesi* malaria in humans is widely distributed and potentially life threatening. *Clin. Infect. Dis.* 46:165–71
28. David PH, Hudson DE, Hadley TJ, Klotz FW, Miller LH. 1985. Immunization of monkeys with a 140 kilodalton merozoite surface protein of *Plasmodium knowlesi* malaria: appearance of alternate forms of this protein. *J. Immunol.* 134:4146–52
29. Deans JA, Knight AM, Jean WC, Waters AP, Cohen S, Mitchell GH. 1988. Vaccination trials in rhesus monkeys with a minor, invariant, *Plasmodium knowlesi* 66 kD merozoite antigen. *Parasite Immunol.* 10:535–52
30. Ellis J, Ozaki LS, Gwadz RW, Cochrane AH, Nussenzweig V, et al. 1983. Cloning and expression in *E. coli* of the malarial sporozoite surface antigen of *Plasmodium knowlesi*. *Nature* 302:536–38
31. Franchini G. 1927. Su di un plasmodio pigmentato di una scimmia. *Arch. Ital. Sci. Med. Colon. Parassitol.* 8:187–90
32. Fried M, Gwadz RW, Kaslow DC. 1994. Identification of two cysteine-rich, lypophilic proteins on the surface of *Plasmodium knowlesi* ookinetes: Pks20 and Pks24. *Exp. Parasitol.* 78:326–30
33. Garnham PC, Lainson R, Cooper W. 1957. The tissue stages and sporogony of *Plasmodium knowlesi*. *Trans. R. Soc. Trop. Med. Hyg.* 51:384–96
34. Geiman QM, Siddiqui WA, Schnell JV. 1966. Plasma replacement for in vitro culture of *Plasmodium knowlesi*. *Science* 153:1129–30
35. Gwadz RW, Cochrane AH, Nussenzweig V, Nussenzweig RS. 1979. Preliminary studies on vaccination of rhesus monkeys with irradiated sporozoites of *Plasmodium knowlesi* and characterization of surface antigens of these parasites. *Bull. WHO* 57(Suppl. 1):165–73
36. Gwadz RW, Green I. 1978. Malaria immunization in rhesus monkeys. A vaccine effective against both the sexual and asexual stages of *Plasmodium knowlesi*. *J. Exp. Med.* 148:1311–23
37. Gwadz RW, Koontz LC. 1984. *Plasmodium knowlesi*: persistence of transmission blocking immunity in monkeys immunized with gamete antigens. *Infect. Immun.* 44:137–40

38. Hawking F, Mellanby H. 1953. Transmission of *Plasmodium knowlesi* through *Anopheles stephensi*. *Trans. R. Soc. Trop. Med. Hyg.* 47:438–39
39. Hawking F, Mellanby H, Terry RJ, Webber WA. 1957. Transmission of *Plasmodium knowlesi* by *Anopheles stephensi*. *Trans. R. Soc. Trop. Med. Hyg.* 51:397–402
40. Held JR, Contacos PG, Jumper JR, Smith CS. 1966. Direct hepatic inoculation of sporozoites for the study of exoerythrocytic stages of simian malarias. *J. Parasitol.* 53:656–57
41. Howard RJ, Barnwell JW. 1985. Immunochemical analysis of surface membrane antigens on erythrocytes infected with non-cloned SICA[+] or cloned SICA[–] *Plasmodium knowlesi*. *Parasitology* 91:245–61
42. Hudson DE, Miller LH, Richards RL, David PH, Alving CR, et al. 1983. The malaria merozoite surface: a 140,000 m.w. protein antigenically unrelated to other surface components of *Plasmodium knowlesi* merozoites. *J. Immunol.* 130:2886–90
43. Ionesco-Mihaiesti C, Zotta G, Radacovici E, Badenski. 1934. Transmission expérimentale a l'homme du paludisme proper des singes. *C. R. Séan. Soc. Biol. Fil. Assoc.* 115:1311–14
44. Jolly AMD, Lavergne, Tanguy Y. 1937. Etude expérimentale du *Plasmodium knowlesi* chez le singe et chez l'homme. *Ann. Inst. Pasteur* 58:297–325
45. Jongwutiwes S, Putaporntip C, Iwasaki T, Sata T, Kanbara H. 2004. Naturally acquired *Plasmodium knowlesi* malaria in human, Thailand. *Emerg. Infect. Dis.* 10:2211–13
46. Kaushik NK, Ananthanarayanan M, Subrahmanyam D, Sehgal S. 1986. Protection of rhesus monkeys against *Plasmodium knowlesi* infection with merozoite vaccine. *Indian J. Med. Res.* 83:471–79
47. Khanna R, Ahmad S, Khan HM, Kumar H, Mahdi AA. 1991. Vaccination of rhesus monkeys against *Plasmodium knowlesi* with aqueous suspension of MDP as an adjuvant. *Indian J. Malariol.* 28:99–104
48. Klotz FW, Hudson DE, Coon HG, Miller LH. 1987. Vaccination-induced variation in the 140 kD merozoite surface antigen of *Plasmodium knowlesi* malaria. *J. Exp. Med.* 165:359–67
49. Knowles R. 1935. Monkey malaria. *Br. Med. J.* 11:1020
50. Knowles R, Das Gupta BM. 1932. A study of monkey-malaria and its experimental transmission to man. *Indian Med. Gaz.* 67:301–20
51. Korir CC, Galinski MR. 2006. Proteomic studies of *Plasmodium knowlesi* SICA variant antigens demonstrate their relationship with *P. falciparum* EMP1. *Infect. Genet. Evol.* 6:75–79
52. Luxhavez J, Espino F, Curameng P, Espina R, Bell D, et al. 2008. Human infections with *Plasmodium knowlesi*, the Philippines. *Emerg. Infect. Dis.* 14:811–13
53. Manguin S, Garros C, Dusfour I, Harbach RE, Coosemans M. 2008. Bionomic, taxonomy, and distributions of the major malaria vector taxa of *Anopheles* subgenus *Cellia* in Southeast Asia: an updated review. *Infect. Genet. Evol.* 8:489–503
54. Milam DF, Coggshall LT. 1938. Duration of *Plasmodium knowlesi* infections in man. *Am. J. Trop. Med.* 18:331–38
55. Milam DF, Kusch E. 1938. Observations on *Plasmodium knowlesi* malaria in general paresis. *South. Med. J.* 31:947–49
56. Mitchell GH, Butcher GA, Cohen S. 1974. A merozoite vaccine effective against *Plasmodium knowlesi* malaria. *Nature* 252:311–13
57. Mitchell GH, Butcher GA, Cohen S. 1975. Merozoite vaccination against *Plasmodium knowlesi* malaria. *Immunology* 29:397–407
58. Napier LE, Campbell HGM. 1932. Observations on a *Plasmodium* infection which causes haemoglobinuria in certain species of monkey. *Indian Med. Gaz.* 67:151–60
59. Ng OT, Ooi EE, Lee CC, Lee PJ, Ng LC, et al. 2008. Naturally acquired human *Plasmodium knowlesi* infection, Singapore. *Emerg. Infect. Dis.* 14:814–16
60. Nicol WD. 1935. Monkey malaria in G.P.I. *Br. Med. J.* 2:760
61. Pain A, Bohme U, Berry AE, Mungalle K, Finn RO, et al. 2008. The genome of a simian and human malaria parasite *Plasmodium knowlesi*. *Nature* 455:799–803
62. Polet H. 1966. In vitro cultivation of erythrocytic forms of *Plasmodium knowlesi* and *Plasmodium berghei*. *Mil. Med.* 131:1026–31
63. Polet H, Conrad ME. 1969. In vitro studies on the amino acid metabolism of *Plasmodium knowlesi* and the antiplasmodial effect of the isoleucine antagonists. *Mil. Med.* 134:939–44

64. Polet H, Conrad ME. 1969. The influence of three analogs of isoleucine on in vitro growth and protein synthesis of erythrocytic forms of *Plasmodium knowlesi*. *Proc. Soc. Exp. Biol. Med.* 130:581–86
65. Prasad RN, Ganguly NK, Mahajan RC. 1986. Phagocytic function of monocytes of rhesus monkeys during *Plasmodium knowlesi* infection and the effect of treatment with chloroquine. *Trans. R. Soc. Trop. Med. Hyg.* 80:886–88
66. Prasad RN, Ganguly NK, Mahajan RC, Garg SK. 1984. Effect of chloroquine treatment on complement levels in *Plasmodium knowlesi* infected rhesus monkeys. *Indian J. Malariol.* 21:17–20
67. Prasad RN, Garg SK, Mahajan RC, Ganguly NK. 1985. Chloroquine kinetics in normal and *P. knowlesi*-infected rhesus monkeys. *Int. J. Clin. Pharmacol. Ther. Tox.* 23:302–4
68. Prasad RN, Mahajan RC, Ganguly NK. 1987. Effect of chloroquine on cellular immune responses of normal and *P. knowlesi*–infected rhesus monkeys. *Immunol. Cell Biol.* 65:211–16
69. Putaporntip C, Hongsrimuang T, Seethamchai S, Kobasa T, Limkittikul K, et al. 2009. Differential prevalence of *Plasmodium* infections and cryptic *Plasmodium knowlesi* malaria in humans in Thailand. *J. Infect. Dis.* 199:1143–50
70. Rieckmann KH, Cabrera EJ, Campbell GH, Jost RC, Miranda R, et al. 1979. Immunization of rhesus monkeys with blood-stage antigens of *Plasmodium knowlesi*. *Bull. WHO* 57(Suppl. 1):139–51
71. Rosenberg R. 1985. Inability of *Plasmodium knowlesi* sporozoites to invade *Anopheles freeborni* salivary glands. *Am. J. Trop. Med. Hyg.* 34:687–91
72. Ruiz I, Altaba A, Ozaki LS, Gwadz RW, Godson GN. 1987. Organization and expression of the *Plasmodium knowlesi* circumsporozoite antigen gene. *Mol. Biochem. Parasitol.* 23:233–45
73. Schenkel RH, Simpson GL, Silverman PH. 1973. Vaccination of rhesus monkeys (*Macaca mulatta*) against *Plasmodium knowlesi* by the use of nonviable antigen. *Bull. WHO* 48:597–604
74. Schmidt-Ullrich R, Miller LH, Wallach DF, Lightholder J, Powers KG, et al. 1981. Rhesus monkeys protected against *Plasmodium knowlesi* malaria produce antibodies against a 65,000-Mr *P. knowlesi* glycoprotein at the surface of infected erythrocytes. *Infect. Immun.* 34:519–25
75. Schmidt-Ullrich R, Lightholder J, Monroe MT. 1983. Protective *Plasmodium knowlesi* Mr 74,000 antigen in membranes of schizont-infected rhesus erythrocytes. *J. Exp. Med.* 158:146–58
76. Sharma S, Gosami A, Singh NJ, Kabilan L, Deodhar SS. 1996. Immunogenicity of the nonrepetitive regions of the circumsporozoite protein of *Plasmodium knowlesi*. *Am. J. Trop. Med. Hyg.* 55:635–41
77. Simpson GL, Schenkel RH, Silverman PH. 1974. Vaccination of rhesus monkeys against malaria by use of sucrose density gradient fractions of *Plasmodium knowlesi* antigens. *Nature* 247:304–5
78. Singh B, Kim Sung L, Matusop A, Radhakrishnann A, Shamsul SS, et al. 2004. A large focus of naturally acquired *Plasmodium knowlesi* infections in human beings. *Lancet* 363:1017–24
79. Singh J, Ray AP, Nair CP. 1949. Transmission experiments with *Plasmodium knowlesi*. *Indian J. Malariol.* 3:145–50
80. Sinton JA, Mulligan HW. 1932–1933. A critical review of the literature relating to the identification of the malaria parasites recorded from monkeys of the families Cercopithecidae and Colobidae. *Rec. Malaria Surv. India* III:357–443
81. Sullivan JS, Morris CL, Richardson BB, Galland GG, Sullivan JJ, et al. 1996. Sporozoite transmission of three strains of *Plasmodium knowlesi* to *Aotus* and *Saimiri* monkeys. *J. Parasitol.* 82:268–71
82. Tan CH, Vythilingam I, Matusop A, Chan ST, Singh B. 2008. Bionomics of *Anopheles latens* in Kapit, Sarawak, Malaysian Borneo in relation to the transmission of zoonotic simian malaria parasite *Plasmodium knowlesi*. *Malaria J.* 7:52
83. Targett GA, Fulton JD. 1965. Immunization of rhesus monkeys against *Plasmodium knowlesi* malaria. *Exp. Parasitol.* 17:180–93
84. Trager W, Jensen JB. 1976. Human malaria parasites in continuous culture. *Science* 193:673–75
85. Van Rooyen CE, Pile GR. 1935. Observations on infection by *Plasmodium knowlesi* (ape malaria) in the treatment of general paralysis of the insane. *Br. Med. J.* 2:662–66
86. Vythilingam I, Noorazian M, Huat TC, Jiram AI, Yusri M, et al. 2008. *Plasmodium knowlesi* in humans, macaques and mosquitoes in peninsular Malaysia. *Parasit. Vectors* 1:26
87. Vythilingam I, Tan CH, Asmad M, Chan ST, Lee KS, et al. 2008. Natural transmission of *Plasmodium knowlesi* to humans by *Anopheles latens* in Sarawak, Malaysia. *Trans. R. Soc. Trop. Med. Hyg.* 100:1087–88

88. Weyer F. 1937. Versuche zur Übertragung der affenmalaria durch stechmücken. *Arch. Schiffs Trop. Hyg. Pathol. Ther. Exot. Krankeiten* 41:167–72
89. Wharton RH, Eyles DE. 1961. *Anopheles hackeri*, a vector of *Plasmodium knowlesi* in Malaysia. *Science* 134:279–80
90. White NJ. 2008. *Plasmodium knowlesi*: the fifth human malaria parasite. *Clin. Infect. Dis.* 46:172–73
91. Wickham JM, Dennis ED, Mitchell GH. 1980. Long-term cultivation of a simian malaria parasite (*Plasmodium knowlesi*) in a semi-automated apparatus. *Trans. R. Soc. Trop. Med. Hyg.* 74:789–92

Group Size and Its Effects on Collective Organization

Anna Dornhaus,* Scott Powell, and Sarah Bengston

Department of Ecology and Evolutionary Biology, University of Arizona, Tucson, Arizona 85721; email: dornhaus@email.arizona.edu, scottpowell@mac.com, bengston@email.arizona.edu

Annu. Rev. Entomol. 2012. 57:123–41

First published online as a Review in Advance on September 2, 2011

The *Annual Review of Entomology* is online at ento.annualreviews.org

This article's doi:
10.1146/annurev-ento-120710-100604

0066-4170/12/0107-0123$20.00

*Corresponding author

Keywords

colony size, communication, division of labor, self-organization, scaling, caste

Abstract

Many insects and arthropods live in colonies or aggregations of varying size. Group size may affect collective organization either because the same individual behavior has different consequences when displayed in a larger group or because larger groups are subject to different constraints and selection pressures than smaller groups. In eusocial colonies, group size may have similar effects on colony traits as body size has on organismal traits. Social insects may, therefore, be useful to test theories about general principles of scaling, as they constitute a distinct level of organization. However, there is a surprising lack of data on group sizes in social insects and other group-living arthropods, and multiple confounding factors have to be controlled to detect effects of group size. If such rigorous studies are performed, group size may become as important to understanding collective organization as is body size in explaining behavior and life history of individual organisms.

INTRODUCTION

Division of labor: different tasks in the colony, such as foraging or defense, are performed by statistically distinct sets of workers

Unitary organism: an individual organism that is not composed of independent subunits, as opposed to a superorganism

Group-living insects dominate terrestrial ecosystems, in terms of both their biomass and their ecological impact. Social insects, i.e., ants, termites, social bees, and social wasps, have been estimated to make up more than 75% of the biomass in the Amazon rain forest and possibly elsewhere (53). Bees are the dominant pollinators for most plants (49, 74). Termites and ants are major decomposers, especially in tropical ecosystems, and often major herbivores (e.g., leaf-cutting ants), predators (e.g., army ants), or granivores (e.g., harvester ants) (53). Other group-living insects, for example, migrating locusts and crickets, also play major ecological roles (6, 111).

The importance of these animals lies not only in the extraordinarily high local densities that they can achieve (e.g., 1500/m^2 in juvenile aggregations of the beetle *Bledius spectabilis*; 136), but also in their ability to display coordinated and complex collective behaviors. For both ecological importance and complex collective organization, group size is thought to be a crucial factor. For example, the density of locusts in an area has to reach a certain level before these insects change their behavior and physiology in ways that make the group appear as a coordinated swarm of migrating locusts (6). Similarly, larger groups may display more effective collective foraging strategies, more structured division of labor, and more regulated interaction networks (1), possibly leading to a much bigger impact on their habitat: For example, army ants, considered major predators of invertebrates in tropical ecosystems, reach group sizes of several million individuals; similarly, leaf-cutting ant colonies, major herbivores in the tropics, may contain over one million individuals (53). In spite of this, data on colony sizes and careful studies relating it to collective organization or ecology are rare. Here, we explore a variety of hypotheses about group-size effects on collective organization. We focus on the eusocial insects, particularly ants, because these have been most intensively studied, but we give examples from other groups where appropriate. We also present a large-scale survey of what is known about colony size in group-living arthropods.

Why might we expect group organization to be affected by colony size? For unitary organisms, there has been a consensus in studies of ecology and organismal biology that body size may be the most important factor determining life-history traits as well as ecological and physiological traits (15–17, 33, 36). Metabolic rate, life span, territory size, temperature tolerances, abundance, cellular differentiation, and many other variables are thought to be predicted by body size for unitary organisms (reviewed in 15, 17, 33). If colonies of eusocial insects evolve as "superorganisms" (54), i.e., are under selection for high colony fitness (114), we may expect, in an analogous way, that the body size of these superorganisms, namely colony size, should predict their life-history and other traits, including many aspects of collective organization (44).

The argument above states that we may expect larger colonies to have evolved different traits, just as larger organisms tend to differ from smaller organisms in particular ways, because they likely face different constraints and selection pressures (1, 18, 79, 89). There are also mechanistic reasons to expect collective organization to be dependent on group size, which may, therefore, also apply in groups that are not under colony-level selection. Insect groups are usually thought to be self-organized, i.e., their collective behavior emerges from the interactions of many individuals without central control. In such systems, even if the behavioral rules that individuals employ stay the same, the resulting collective behavior may go through major transitions as colony size increases (9, 43, 66, 68).

We believe that colony size has the potential to explain a large amount of variation in social insect behavior and phenotype, both inter- and intraspecifically, for the reasons stated above. However, we find that data on colony sizes are lacking, and methods, even definitions, vary between studies to such a degree that rigorous comparisons are difficult. We also argue that, to uncover any general colony-size-dependent patterns, there is a need for careful studies that control for species phylogeny in interspecific comparisons as well as colony age, genetic background, and environment in intraspecific studies. If such data-driven, rigorous studies are done, we think not only that the field of social insect research will be significantly advanced, but that its results may also become major components of a general theory of biological scaling across levels of organization.

A SURVEY OF ARTHROPOD COLONY SIZES

There is a lack both of group-size information and of agreement on how to measure it. Surprisingly, this is true even for relatively well-studied species. For example, approximately 12,000 species of ants have been described (85), but we found good colony-size information for only 437 ant species (see method details below). Of these, 74 were from single-colony measurements, and 115 reported only mean colony size, which can be misleading if immature colonies are included. We found records for only 267 species where the size of least 2 mature colonies was measured and the median sample size in this data set is still only 3 colonies per species, usually from a single location. Even for the best-studied social insect of all, the honey bee, *Apis mellifera*, we found only eight records of wild colonies (105, 107), only four of which are from their native distribution (105). Obviously, this makes the detection of general patterns in colony size across species very difficult.

We collected colony-size information from the literature by executing a search on Google Scholar using the terms "colony size or aggregation," "insect or arthropod," and "not ant" to find nonant colony sizes and checking the first 200 references. For ant data, we executed a Google Scholar search for "ant" and "collected" and at least one of the terms "colony size," "colony collection," or "worker number." Dates were set to 1990–2011, and the search was limited to Biology, Life Sciences, and Environmental Science. We examined approximately 900 papers for colony-size information in this way (we stopped when 50 results in sequence yielded no colony-size data). When duplicate studies existed for certain species, we preferred the one that recorded maximum or mature colony sizes and higher replication, in that order. We used Google Scholar because it catalogs the full text of papers. Colony-size data is typically not the focus of papers and, thus, is buried in one or two lines of the methods or results sections. It is, therefore, less likely to be recovered by literature databases that contain only keywords, titles, and abstracts. We also added information from several books (28, 53, 59, 82, 99).

We found records for a total of 731 species, most of which are ants. For ants, we then excluded all records of single colonies per species, of supercolonies, and where mature colony size could not be determined. This survey suggests that most group-living insects, including noneusocial ones, live in groups of 100 to 1,000 individuals (**Table 1**). An exception is termites, a large proportion of which have very large colonies (**Figure 1**). The migrating locust from Africa, *Melanoplus spretus*, is the species with, by far, the largest aggregations recorded; at the other extreme, many social bee species in our survey had very small colony sizes (fewer than 10 individuals). We also investigated how colony sizes were distributed across ant subfamilies (**Figure 2**) (**Table 2**). This data set is almost certainly affected by study biases. Some larger colonies are more easily noticed and more often

Table 1 Colony sizes from our literature survey on social insects and arthropods

Mature colony sizes	Median	Minimum (species)	Maximum (species)
Termites (Termitoidae)	40,000	100 (*Cryptotermes piceatus*)	7,000,000 (*Mastotermes darwiniensis*)
Bees (Apoidea)	135	2 (*Exoneurella lawsoni*)	180,000 (*Trigona spinipes*)
Ants (Formicidae)	375	9 (*Thaumatomyrmex atrox*)	22,000,000 (*Dorylus wilverthi*)
Wasps (Vespidae)	295	3 (*Ropalidia taiwana koshuensis*)	1,000,000 (*Stelopolybia vicina*)
Other arthropods	175	25 (*Thasus acutangulus*)	3,500,000,000,000 (*Melanoplus spretus*)

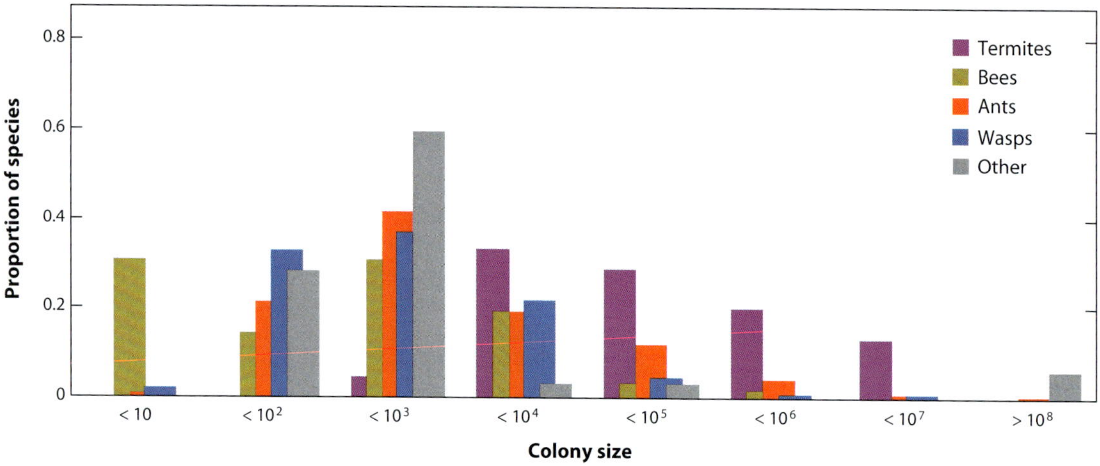

Figure 1

The frequency of different colony sizes in social insects and arthropods, according to the literature. See text for details on data collection.

Hymenoptera: insect order containing the most-studied social insect species, i.e., wasps, bees, and ants

Colony ontogeny: a colony's development over time, from founding to colony death

studied. However, large-colony species may be under-represented in the quantitative estimates that we found, with researchers typically using rough guesses instead of quantitative approaches such as mark-recapture or subsampling. By contrast, many small-colony species, certainly in terms of ants, are probably undescribed. Another problem with such comparisons is the heterogeneous definitions of colony size. Generally for hymenopteran social insects, only adult workers are counted, but in other group-living insects, immatures or eggs may be included in group-size estimates. Furthermore, studies differ in whether they report only the maximum colony size found or the average of a set of observed colonies and whether only mature colonies are included. Given that many species vary in colony size across colony ontogeny, often starting from a single founding individual, colony age is likely to have a major influence on colony size, and immature colonies may not be representative of the species-typical colony size (53). Finally, the boundaries of a colony

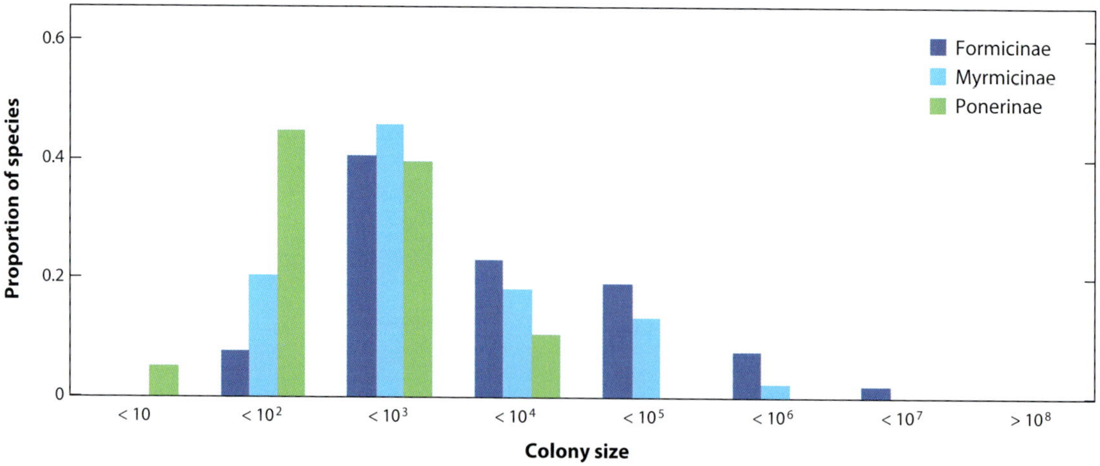

Figure 2

The frequency of different mature colony sizes in the three biggest ant subfamilies. See text for details on data collection.

Table 2 Colony-size distributions in ant subfamilies according to our literature survey (see text for details)

Ant subfamilies	Median	Minimum	Maximum	Percentage of subfamily included
Aenictinae	110,000	110,000	110,000	0.8%
Amblyoponinae	396	35	1,603	5.6%
Cerapachyinae	600	600	600	0.4%
Dolichoderinae	1,000	1,000	2,912,000	1.2%
Dorylinae	22,000,000	22,000,000	22,000,000	1.7%
Ecitoninae	85,000	30,000	700,000	3.8%
Ectatomminae	329	104	1,000	3.5%
Formicinae	1,258	70	1,000,000	1.7%
Leptanillinae	200	200	200	1.9%
Myrmeciinae	862	79	1,859	5.3%
Myrmicinae	300	15	300,000	2.0%
Paraponerinae	1,355	1,355	1,355	50.0%
Ponerinae	109	9	2,444	3.6%
Proceratiinae	25	21	60	2.2%
Pseudomyrmecinae	93	30	1,104	2.5%

or group are not always easy to define, making colony-size measurements difficult to obtain, especially in noneusocial species. In these cases, density per area may be more relevant than total group size. Similarly, in ants, so-called supercolonies may extend across whole continents, and in polydomous species (in which one colony inhabits multiple nests), finding all nests that belong to the same colony may be extremely difficult (30).

Even with these limitations, we see that basically all broader taxonomic groups vary in colony size by six orders of magnitude (**Figure 1**); even within ant subfamilies, variation of several orders of magnitude is common (**Table 2**). In addition, within genera, colony size is also extremely variable: Including only ant genera for which we had at least two species, the colony size of the largest-colony species is, on average, 400 times larger than the smallest-colony species in the same genus (**Figure 3**). This demonstrates that one species cannot be assumed to be representative for its group with regard to colony size, even at the genus level. In summary, colony-size information must be collected more consistently in the future, and for more species, to allow progress in understanding its role in the collective organization and ecology of social insects.

COLLECTIVE BEHAVIOR

Foraging and Recruitment

Social insects show some of their most interesting and intricate collective behaviors when collecting resources from outside the nest. By directly or indirectly exchanging information about the environment, members of a colony coordinate their actions to find and exploit effectively the most valuable resources (53, 106). The number of individuals participating in this process, which is a function of colony size, has been predicted via modeling studies to affect foraging efficiency positively (9, 89; but see 35), and indeed, this has been demonstrated empirically in some cases (9, 79, 103, 113; but see 8, 31). Why would foraging efficiency depend on colony size? First,

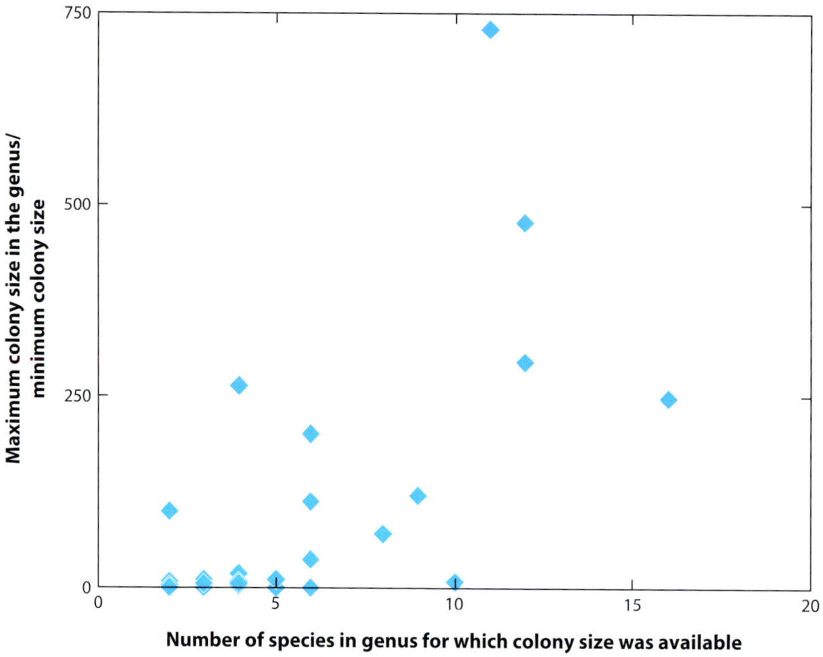

Figure 3

The range of colony sizes in different ant genera, depending on how many species from a genus were included in the analysis. In many genera, particularly those for which more than a few species were available, the largest-colony species have colony sizes that are orders of magnitude larger than the smallest-colony species. This graph, for visibility purposes, excludes the three genera with the largest maximum/minimum colony-size ratio, *Polyrhachis* (1,000,000/89 = 11,236; 9 species), *Pristomyrmex* (300,000/200 = 1,500; 2 species), and *Solenopsis* (150,000/50 = 3,000; 10 species).

foraging by larger groups can inherently be subject to different constraints than that by smaller colonies. For example, if colonies forage from a central place, foragers in larger colonies have to travel further to collect food, because smaller colonies need only a smaller area to satisfy their needs (8, 66, 125). However, each resource within a certain distance is more likely to be found in a shorter amount of time by a larger group of foragers. If others can be recruited there, then larger colonies will spend less effort on discovering and more on exploiting resources than smaller colonies will (32, 79). Second, stochastic effects are likely to be dampened at the colony level in larger groups, leading to less variation in resource intake (35, 68). This may lead to reduced risk aversion in larger colonies (51, 125). In unitary organisms, larger body size also necessitates larger foraging ranges (15, 65) and reduces susceptibility to risk (67). Third, if information is collected at the nest, then workers in a larger colony have potentially more information available to them about the foraging environment. However, this is the case only if all information brought to the colony is available to every individual, which may not be the case if communication signals have limited range (see below). Individuals in larger groups are also likely to interact with nestmates more frequently, possibly leading to higher rates of information flow (22, 47, 68). This is particularly relevant in cases of task partitioning, where resources or tasks are passed along a chain of workers, such as honey bee foragers giving nectar to receiver bees or wasp foragers passing wood pulp to nest-building workers (2). In these cases, queuing delays are shorter and more consistent when group size is larger, enabling the system to work more efficiently and workers to use the

Task partitioning: tasks may consist of several sequential steps that are performed by distinct worker groups

Queuing delay: in partitioned tasks, workers of one group may have to wait to receive jobs from workers performing the preceding step in the sequence delays as cues for which tasks are currently most needed (2, 61). However, task partitioning is rare in social insects, and even where it exists, its relevance to colony fitness is not always clear (68).

All the above are effects that will emerge with larger colony size even if individual behavior stays constant. However, several authors have proposed that individuals in larger colonies behave differently, in particular, that different mechanisms of communication are used in larger colonies (1, 7). Mass recruitment, i.e., recruitment of nestmates by pheromone trails, is thought to be confined to the largest colonies, whereas group recruitment, tandem running, and individual foraging (without communication between foragers) are common in successively smaller colonies. This information was interpreted to mean that larger colonies needed, and had evolved, more complex communication systems (7). The problems with this analysis are that it was not phylogenetically corrected and that it is not clear how complexity was measured here. Also, some authors (7, 66) have proposed that larger colonies need better communication systems to compensate for their disadvantages, whereas others proposed that better communication enables larger colonies to have higher fitness (1) (also see Colony Productivity, below). However, different recruitment mechanisms may have evolved because such mechanisms react differently to group-size changes. Crucially, larger colonies may be under selection for communication mechanisms that reach more recruits per recruiter (33); only such mechanisms allow the colony to take full advantage of a large potential recruit pool as well as the larger amount of information accumulating at the nest. For example, ant pheromone trails, which are effective at recruiting a large number of recruits per recruiter and are easier to maintain in large groups (9), are mostly found in large-colony species (7). However, in other groups, for example, bees, this is not apparent: The honey bee waggle dance is a communication mechanism that reaches an extremely small audience (reviewed in 35) in spite of the large colonies in which it occurs. Indeed, the benefits of this communication system are probably not affected by colony size (8, 35).

Castes: sets of individuals in a colony that differ morphologically, often primarily in body size, with allometric scaling of body parts

Response thresholds: individuals may differ in the level that a task-specific stimulus must reach before they respond by performing the task

Division of Labor

Division of labor can be found in many complex systems, particularly in cellular societies (of which multicellular animals may be considered an extremely well-integrated version), engineered systems, and human societies (14, 17). In these cases, it is generally thought that larger systems will develop a more sophisticated and strict division of labor: For example, larger multicellular animals are thought to have more cell types, most of which are unable to redifferentiate into other types (17), and human societies are thought to have developed a more sophisticated division of labor as they became larger (14).

If self-organized systems follow general rules, one may expect that social insects would also show more division of labor in larger colonies, i.e., individuals in larger colonies may differentiate into more types and be less flexible to switch between types. For example, Oster & Wilson (89) predicted more morphological castes, i.e., an inflexible mechanism for division of labor, in larger colonies. However, their prediction has not been supported in a phylogenetically controlled study (37; see Group Size and the Individual in the Group, below). Division of labor may also be achieved in a response-threshold system, where each individual is, in principle, available to do each task but individuals differ in their responsiveness to stimuli that indicate that a task is needed (10). Such a system can produce division of labor without further coordination among individuals; indeed, models predict that the resulting division of labor is maintained more strictly if colony size is larger (43). Because this is an argument not about optimality, but about emergence of differences with group size, it is likely to apply particularly within species (64, 116). Finally, models of task partitioning predict that this type of dividing labor emerges only in larger colonies (see Foraging and Recruitment, above), and there is support for this in nest building in wasps (61, 68).

Overall, empirical evidence for increased division of labor in larger colonies is mixed [e.g., support (116); no support (33)]. Besides the number of specialist types and their flexibility to switch tasks, colony size likely also affects selection for the mechanism by which division of labor is achieved. For example, Murakami et al. (86) found that, across attine ant species, the smaller-colony species were more likely to employ age polyethism, whereas larger-colony species more often had morphologically differentiated castes; however, colony size was also correlated with different ecology and mating frequency across species. Other interesting aspects of division of labor may also be affected by colony size. For example, social insect colonies generally contain many workers who appear to be mostly inactive. Larger colonies have been hypothesized to be able to afford more inactive workers, but, again, empirical evidence is mixed (reviewed in 34).

COLONY PRODUCTIVITY

It is tempting to think that larger is always better, and studies sometimes seem to bear this out in terms of fitness, both for unitary organisms (112) and for colonies (25, 63, 128). However, if that were always the case, larger species should eventually outcompete smaller ones (117). An alternative view is that the mature body size or the mature colony size of each species is an adaptation to its particular niche (73) and thus that fitness declines on either size of this optimum within species (5, 15, 20, 117). If this is the case, one would expect no consistent relationship between colony size and reproductive efficiency, usually measured as per capita brood or sexual production in social insects, across species. In the most frequently cited paper on the topic, Michener (81) measured how reproductive output correlated with colony size across hymenopteran species. He found that total colony-level productivity increased with colony size but that reproductive efficiency, i.e., offspring produced per individual in the colony, decreased. Michener's methods have been criticized for combining species across genera and for not controlling for colony age or developmental period (19, 63). However, other studies have found a similar pattern of fewer broods per worker, implying lower reproductive efficiency, in larger colonies [wasps (58, 68, 75), ants (25, 40, 125), across several groups (55)].

By contrast, there is also evidence in other species for an increase in reproductive efficiency as colony size increases [ants (70), wasps (63, 119), halictid bees (115), gregarious moth larvae (98)]. Yet other studies have found no clear relationship between colony size and reproductive output. Bouwma et al. (19) tested Michener's hypothesis in the swarm-founding wasp *Parachartergus fraternus*, but unlike in Michener's study, colony stage and development were controlled for. They found that reproductive efficiency was neither increased nor decreased; instead, there was increased variability in productivity in the small colonies. This was also seen in an earlier study by Cole (26) using the ant *Leptothorax allardycei*. Variability was higher in small colonies, but as colony size increased, there was a linear increase in the number of brood items, meaning there was no effect of colony size on per-individual productivity.

What are the mechanisms by which colony size affects production of brood or sexuals? If larger colonies are more efficient at foraging or division of labor, as discussed above, this should affect their ability to reproduce. In addition, group size often affects the survival of individuals, the queen, or the colony as a whole, thereby likely also affecting reproductive success (5, 55, 73, 95, 98, 119). By contrast, larger colonies can be more conspicuous to predators or suffer from increased parasitism rates (5, 115).

Colony size has also been proposed to correlate with worker reproduction or ovary development. This is generally more common in small colonies (18), but in other species it can occur more frequently in large colonies (115). Worker ovary development is usually considered a cost to the colony: Because reproductive workers are assumed to be not "working" (27), there is a need for policing (126) and increased conflict within the colony can arise (42, 129). However, such may not always be the case. There may be indirect fitness benefits associated with having workers reproduce, and a certain amount of worker ovarian development can act as an insurance strategy against the death of the queen. Workers with some degree of ovarian development will be able to ascend more rapidly to egg-laying status (115).

Finally, the hypothesis that colony size affects productivity may be an artifact of the method of measurement (e.g., 68). For example, many ants cannibalize brood items during times of starvation (102), which means brood items can work as a type of insurance against environmental variation. Being subject to higher costs from environmental fluctuations (73), small colonies, in particular, may therefore appear to have higher productivity despite not producing more adults (68, 102). Similarly, excess worker production may be an insurance against environmental variability if production of sexuals (new colony-founding units) is limited by other factors.

A related problem is that different types of colony growth show very different results depending on sampling method and point of development. For example, there are likely trade-offs between the size and the number of reproductives produced, which is not always measured. Shik (109) focused on reproductively mature colonies and used phylogenetical controls on a relatively large comparative data set. Of the ant species he analyzed, species with larger colony sizes produced fewer, but larger, winged reproductives, suggesting such a trade-off at play.

In their seminal paper, Macevicz & Oster (78) on the one hand predicted that annual insect colonies should have an exponential growth phase followed by a reproductive phase. Poitrineau et al. (93) on the other hand showed that given certain conditions (e.g., high worker mortality or decreasing efficiency with larger colony size) there should be a shift to a more graded reproductive effort between workers and sexuals. Depending on which strategy a colony is using, production of sexuals may have to be measured over a whole year to give an accurate estimate of reproductive success (125). Kaspari et al. (72) compared reproductive phenologies across 81 ant species. They found differing strategies may not be tied to resource availability, but instead are conserved within genera and subfamilies. Because of these challenges, studies showing higher productivity or higher fitness in groups of particular sizes must be examined carefully.

GROUP SIZE AND THE INDIVIDUAL IN THE GROUP

Individual Morphology

Larger body size in unitary organisms often correlates with both larger and more morphologically differentiated cells (4, 17). However, how selection for larger body size affects individual cell size is still a matter of debate (4). On the other hand, colony size in social insects has long been thought to affect worker morphology and the number of different morphotypes within a colony, called castes (e.g., 53, 89, 132). In particular, it has been hypothesized that (*a*) larger colony size is associated with the origin of distinct reproductive (queen) and worker morphotypes and their subsequent divergence (e.g., 18, 92); (*b*) larger colony size is associated with worker polymorphism (18, 89); and (*c*) larger colony size may be associated with smaller mean worker size (18, 68) (**Figure 4**). To date, empirical evidence has consisted mostly of informal comparisons (e.g., Reference 89, ch. 4; Reference 68, figure 2; Reference 18, tables 1 and 2; Reference 1, table 3). However, this approach is inherently subject to biased taxon selection, with counter-examples to the proposed patterns often overlooked. More importantly, shared ancestry among selected taxa may confound such analyses (but see 68). The scarcity of phylogenetically corrected studies of colony size and caste evolution may be explained by the relative newness of the methodologies, the lack of phylogenies

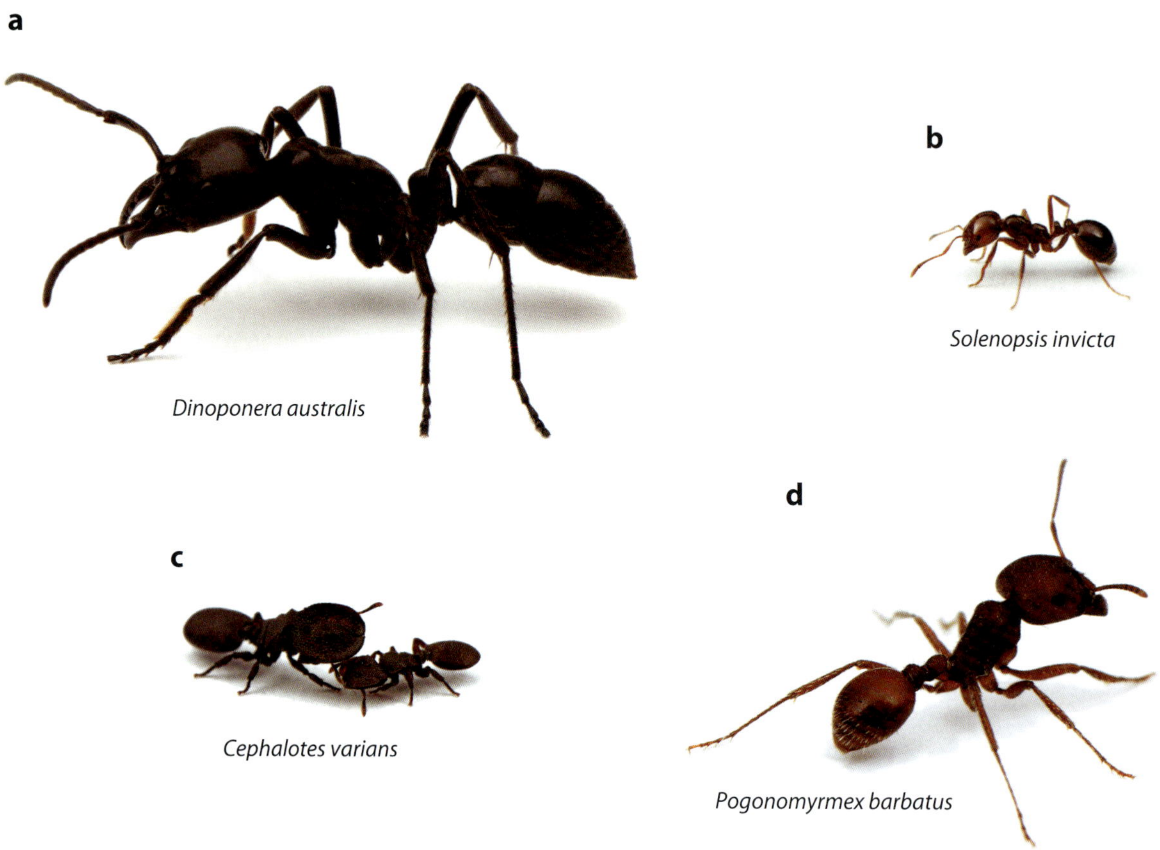

Figure 4

Ant species with extreme contrasts in colony size and worker size (worker sizes to scale). (*a*) *Dinoponera australis* has small colonies (19 ants) (83) and the largest workers of any ants. (*b*) *Solenopsis invicta* has large maximum colony size (250,000 ants) (120) and polymorphic workers with small mean size. (*c*) *Cephalotes varians* has extreme caste diversification, has small mean worker size, and lives in small colonies (100–200 ants) (133; S. Powell, unpublished data). This is contrary to the patterns thought to be common in small-colony species. (*d*) Similarly, *Pogonomyrmex barbatus* has relatively large workers and large colonies (maximum of approximately 12,000 ants) (46). Image copyrights by Alexander Wild, reproduced with permission.

(although increasingly available and easier to produce) (84), and the lack of colony-size and worker-morphology data (but see 37).

Why should colony size affect caste evolution? One potentially powerful constraint in smaller colonies is the higher and more common incidence of reproductive-worker conflict over reproduction (18). Such individual-level conflict may counter colony-level selection for morphologically distinct reproductives and workers. Moreover, the degree of reproductive-worker differentiation may act as a developmental constraint on the evolution of worker polymorphism (86, 130). The influential theory of Oster & Wilson (89) also proposed that the production and maintenance costs of more morphologically specialized and inflexible castes are ergonomically possible only in large colonies; however, this assumes that larger colonies are more ergonomically efficient (but see Colony Productivity, above). Recent evidence also suggests that the higher genetic diversity achieved through multiple mating (polyandry) may provide the necessary genetic diversity for the evolution of worker polymorphism (e.g., 29, 57, 60), a mating strategy that seems limited to derived, larger-colony species (56, 86).

Fjerdingstad & Crozier (37) provide a particularly valuable test of the macroevolutionary relationships between worker polymorphism and a number of putative constraints, including colony size. This phylogenetically corrected study showed that, whereas the degree of queen-worker differentiation was significantly correlated with worker polymorphism (as predicted in Reference 130), colony size was not (contradicting the prediction in Reference 89). In addition, the study suggested that mating frequency is positively correlated with worker polymorphism (see also 29, 86). Generally, then, this study provided evidence that colony size does not directly constrain or promote the evolution of worker polymorphism, once the influence of phylogeny and other life-history traits is removed from the analysis. Not only does this study highlight the crucial importance of phylogenetic correction in comparative studies, it also shows the importance of considering other factors in the same analysis.

Sociogenesis: changes in the worker-size distribution, and thus the makeup of a colony, across its ontogeny

In general, castes enable superior performance of key colony-related tasks (e.g., 13, 38, 50, 94, 96, 118). Nevertheless, this empirical evidence does not necessarily support a central assumption of the ergonomic theory of caste, i.e., that castes are inherently adaptive and thus proliferate when constraints, such as colony size, are relaxed (89). The alternative is that castes are adaptive only under certain types of ecological scenarios (94). If this is the case, no general relationship with colony size across a broad range of taxa should be expected.

Colony Ontogeny and Individual Phenotype

In addition to differing in colony and individual traits, insect colonies can also vary in their ontogenetic trajectory (e.g., 50, 123, 134). Colony size in particular may vary seasonally (39, 106) or as the colony ages (53). Thus, even when the traits of mature organisms are similar, they may differ across various life-history stages. The idea that this developmental process, sociogenesis, is adaptive was formulated in detail by Oster & Wilson (89; see also 135). This "adaptive-demography" theory provided a number of detailed predictions of how worker-size distributions should match resource distributions as colonies grow. Tests of this theory have yielded mixed support (reviewed in 104; see also 11, 12, 50, 137). Generally, they suggest that, although some aspects of sociogenesis are adaptive, many of the more specific predictions of adaptive-demography theory are not met.

One possibility is that sociogenesis is nonadaptive and simply an epiphenomenon of other processes that are under selection (104, 130). An alternative middle ground is that only gross aspects of sociogenesis are adaptive (104). For example, one detailed prediction of adaptive-demography theory is that worker-size distributions (i.e., proportional representation of workers of different sizes or castes) optimally match and adjust to prevailing ecological conditions. Support for this prediction has been particularly mixed (e.g., 11, 12, 23, 50, 127, 137). However, environmental pressures (e.g., predation, competition, weather) may change worker-size distributions too frequently and/or unpredictably for the production capabilities of a colony to compensate for them. In addition, behavioral flexibility can in some cases be enough to compensate for these changes in caste structure (104), reducing selection for constant adjustment of caste proportions. Sociogenesis could then have adaptive components (e.g., colony size at first soldier production) and epiphenomenological components (e.g., precise proportion of soldiers).

In ants, we know that the proportions of different worker-size classes are typically stable after maturity (reviewed in 53; but see 12). Large-size classes are often added late, with the largest added just before colony maturity (e.g., 122, 134). It also seems that this schedule of production is tied directly to colony size, not age (134). This is often seen as typical sociogenesis in polymorphic ant species, but there are at least two other distinct patterns. One is immediate production of highly specialized castes in newly founded colonies (e.g., *Camponotus nipponicus*, 50). The other is the maintenance of all worker sizes and castes and a large minimum colony size via reproduction by colony fission (e.g., *Eciton burchellii*, 39). These broad differences in the timing of first production of certain worker sizes and castes may be examples of coarse-scale adaptive sociogenesis.

Initial investment primarily in small workers has been interpreted as the result of constraints that make larger individuals too costly within small colony sizes (89). Alternatively, it could be the result of selection for strength in numbers in early life stages. For instance, territory disputes in *Atta* leaf-cutting ants are faced early in colony life and involve large numbers of small ants (131), consistent with the advantages of this type of fighting force in an open combat arena (41). Conversely, *Atta* soldiers, added later in sociogenesis, are perhaps adaptive only at the largest colony sizes. *Atta* soldiers are critical in colony defense against predation by the massive colonies of the army ant *Nomamyrmex esenbeckii* (95). From a combat standpoint, an *Atta* colony may have to pass a critical large size to stand a chance of defending itself against army ants, and only then is adding soldiers adaptive. Indeed, only large *Atta* colonies with soldiers fight back against *N. esenbeckii* attacks. *Camponotus* (*Colobopsis*) *nipponicus* soldiers, by contrast, defend the entrances of arboreal cavity nests, and colonies use the same kind of cavities regardless of colony size (50). Thus, selection for soldiers is likely constant across colony sizes, and concordantly soldiers are produced in the first brood. Similarly, the broad range of worker sizes and discrete castes in the army ant *Eciton burchellii* are involved in critical colony functions that are present in all colonies both before and after fission (39, 96).

Whereas the relative timing of caste production may be similar among colonies and populations, relative proportions may not be. But, is this adaptive or largely an epiphenomenon resulting from the interaction of various factors? Production levels for specific size classes are typically stable in ants from one brood cohort to the next after first production (reviewed in 53). The exact level of this stable production may be a coarse adaptation to the average environmental conditions (89) and, in part, limited by the developmental constraints of each taxon (130). After catastrophic loss of particular size classes, colonies typically recover via steady accumulation through normal production and not via elevated production levels (reviewed in 104). However, in at least one species, soldier production increases with increased intraspecific competition (91). Proportional representation may also increase or decrease as colonies increase in size (e.g., 120, 123, 134), but it is unclear if this is due either to differences in caste-specific mortality rates or to active and adaptive shifts in production levels over time. A number of environmental pressures can also alter proportional representation of worker sizes. For instance, resource availability can change caste production (80). In addition, rates of army ant raids can be surprisingly high in Neotropical forests (71, 88), and this may have significant effects on the colony size of prey ant species (69) and specific castes that play a dominant role in colony defense (95).

In contrast to ants, termites seem to have significantly more flexible and diverse caste-development pathways that are coupled with more tightly regulated caste production (97). This may allow for adaptive adjustment of caste production or, at least, active restoration of caste proportions after environmental impacts on the caste structure. Differences in caste ratios among termite colonies may also be partly under genetic control (77). In eusocial aphids, soldier proportions seem to increase with colony size (108, 139). This pattern could be adaptive to a higher predation threat in larger colonies (108), or it could simply result from passive soldier accumulation under steady production rates and environmental conditions (3). Nevertheless, one aphid species is known to increase soldier production when its members are no longer defended by attending ants (110). In arguably the most unusual social insects, parasitoid polyembryonic wasps in the family Encyrtidae, soldier production at different stages of colony growth seems to be an adaptation to different competitive threats within the host (45).

CONCLUSION

Theory, intraspecific empirical studies, and interspecific comparative studies suggest that group size can affect group organization in multiple, sometimes conflicting, ways. Collective behaviors can change as a consequence of adaptive changes in individual behavior with colony size or as nonadaptive consequences of the number of individuals in a group. Larger colonies have to forage longer distances, but they are less susceptible to variation, such as in food intake, caused by individual errors, stochastic discovery of resources, predation on individuals, or environmental variability. This may lead to reduced selection for individual reliability in larger colonies (51). It is also possible that high quality of individual performance, such as that achieved through individual learning, plays a smaller role in larger colonies (32, 125). Larger colonies allow higher rates of information exchange and may evolve communication signals that support this (9, 48). Another hallmark of collective organization, division of labor, is often more pronounced in larger colonies. Other collective strategies not discussed here, such as colony defense (76, 95, 100) or nest building and architecture (21, 62, 138), can also be affected by colony size.

Differences in group-level organization and behavior are often, although not always, the results of changes in behavior, morphology, or physiology of individuals associated with colony size. Such differences, if they occur between species, may be explained by genetic differences. However, if these differences occur intraspecifically, i.e., if colonies change their organization with colony size across colony ontogeny, then either workers may measure their own colony size and adapt accordingly or they may use their own or the colony's age as a proxy (62). Even the metabolic rate of individuals may depend on the size of the colony they are in (44, 128), although this effect was not found to be statistically significant across species (55). Differences in metabolic rate may be due to differences in activity level (given that all individuals are not usually at rest when a whole group is being measured), and there is some evidence that activity level may be affected by group size (34). For example, individuals in larger colonies invest less in defense (76), and they can display higher tempo in larger colonies (52, 79). Such differences likely affect life-history traits of individuals, such as life span, which was found to be both longer (87) and shorter (101) in larger colonies.

Why do so many studies find contradictory effects of colony size, particularly when we compare intraspecific studies of different species? This finding would suggest that some putative group-size effects are not necessary consequences of group size. In many cases, the relationships found may not be directly causal. For example, individual density often, though not necessarily, correlates with group size; it could also be independently regulated by the insects (47, 90) or limited by outside factors such as nest size. Density effects on collective organization (24, 90) may then be mistaken for group-size effects. Similarly, if field-collected colonies are compared, small colonies may have low-quality genetic background, come from low-quality microhabitats, or be younger—all traits that affect individual and collective traits independently of colony size. Intraspecific studies should, therefore, control for such effects, ideally by artificially manipulating colony size, although it can be difficult to do this without changing relatedness structure in the colony (32, 73).

SUMMARY POINTS

1. Body size may be the most important single factor explaining variation in behavior, life history, physiology, and ecology of organisms. Group size is therefore likely to also be an important determinant of collective behavior, colony development, social physiology, and other traits.

2. Larger group or colony size can cause evolution of distinct behavior, morphology, or other traits of individuals because of differing constraints and selection pressures. Besides actual selection for different traits, larger colonies sometimes also display different behaviors as an emergent consequence of group size, if selection pressures do not prevent this. Future studies should carefully characterize whether proposed colony-size effects are the consequence of selection and individual differences or if they are emergent effects with no difference in individual behaviors.
3. Social insect colonies constitute a distinct level of organization, sometimes called superorganisms. They therefore have the potential to be an independent test case for general principles that are thought to apply to all biological systems. In particular, general "laws" about scaling relationships and the mechanisms causing them may be tested in social insects. This makes social insect research relevant to a much broader audience.
4. However, this promise can be fulfilled only if much more comprehensive and rigorous colony-size data are collected. Other authors have demanded this for decades (7, 121, 124). Students of social insects need to realize that this is not tedious and unnecessary natural-history detail, but vital information for rigorous testing of hypotheses on group-size effects. Modern comparative approaches should be used; even with small data sets, coarse relationships between colony size and organization, morphology, and sociogenesis can be investigated, which can guide further detailed empirical studies.
5. There has been an increase in studies of colony-size effects using larger data sets and employing phylogenetic controls. Intraspecific studies can, likewise, be made more rigorous by controlling for colony age, environment, and genetic background. Only such well-controlled studies can separate group-size effects from effects of shared ancestry, differences in colony quality, and differences in experience or nutrition of individuals in larger colonies.

DISCLOSURE STATEMENT

The authors are not aware of any affiliations, memberships, funding, or financial holdings that might be perceived as affecting the objectivity of this review.

ACKNOWLEDGMENTS

We thank the National Science Foundation (grant numbers IOS-0921280, IOS-0841756, and DEB 0842144) for funding, and Eric Porter for sharing his unpublished termite colony size data.

LITERATURE CITED

1. Anderson C, McShea DW. 2001. Individual versus social complexity, with particular reference to ant colonies. *Biol. Rev.* 76:211–37
2. Anderson C, Ratnieks FLW. 1999. Task partitioning in insect societies. I. Effect of colony size on queueing delay and colony ergonomic efficiency. *Am. Nat.* 354:521–35
3. Aoki S, Imai M. 2005. Factors affecting the proportion of sterile soldiers in growing aphid colonies. *Popul. Ecol.* 47:127–36
4. Arendt J. 2007. Ecological correlates of body size in relation to cell size and cell number: patterns in flies, fish, fruits and foliage. *Biol. Rev.* 82:241–56

5. Aviles L, Tufino P. 1998. Colony size and individual fitness in the social spider *Anelosimus eximius*. *Am. Nat.* 152:404–18
6. Bazazi S, Buhl J, Hale JJ, Anstey ML, Sword GA, et al. 2008. Collective motion and cannibalism in locust migratory bands. *Curr. Biol.* 18:735–39
7. Beckers R, Goss S, Deneubourg JL, Pasteels JM. 1989. Colony size, communication and ant foraging strategy. *Psyche* 96:239–56
8. Beekman. 2004. Comparing foraging behaviour of small and large honey-bee colonies by decoding waggle dances made by foragers. *Funct. Ecol.* 18:829–35
9. Beekman M, Sumpter D, Ratnieks F. 2001. Phase transition between disordered and ordered foraging in Pharaoh's ants. *Proc. Natl. Acad. Sci. USA* 98:9703–4
10. Beshers S, Fewell JH. 2001. Models of division of labor in social insects. *Annu. Rev. Entomol.* 46:413–40
11. Beshers SN, Traniello JFA. 1994. The adaptiveness of worker demography in the attine ant *Trachymyrmex septentrionalis*. *Ecology* 75:763–75
12. Billick I. 2002. The relationship between the distribution of worker sizes and new worker production in the ant *Formica neorufibarbis*. *Oecologia* 132:244–49
13. Billick I, Carter C. 2007. Testing the importance of the distribution of worker sizes to colony performance in the ant species *Formica obscuripes* Forel. *Insectes Soc.* 54:113–17
14. Bird D, O'Connell J. 2006. Human behavioral ecology and archaeology. *J. Archaeol. Res.* 14:143–88
15. Blanckenhorn WU. 2000. The evolution of body size: What keeps organisms small? *Q. Rev. Biol.* 75:385–407
16. Blueweiss L, Fox H, Kudzma V, Nakashima D, Peters R, Sams S. 1978. Relationships between body size and some life history parameters. *Oecologia* 37:257–72
17. Bonner JT. 2006. *Why Size Matters: From Bacteria to Blue Whales*. Princeton, NJ: Princeton Univ. Press

17. Reviews the effects of body size with many examples.

18. Bourke AFG. 1999. Colony size, social complexity and reproductive conflict in social insects. *J. Evol. Biol.* 12:245–57

18. Reviews the role of colony size in intracolony reproductive competition.

19. Bouwma AM, Nordheim EV, Jeanne RL. 2006. Per-capita productivity in a social wasp: no evidence for a negative effect of colony size. *Insectes Soc.* 53:412–19
20. Brown JH, Marquet PA, Taper ML. 1993. Evolution of body-size: consequences of an energetic definition of fitness. *Am. Nat.* 142:573–84
21. Buhl J, Gautrais J, Deneubourg J-L, Theraulaz G. 2004. Nest excavation in ants: group size effects on the size and structure of tunneling networks. *Naturwissenschaften* 91:602–6
22. Burkhardt. 1998. Individual flexibility and tempo in the ant, *Pheidole dentata*, and the influence of group size. *J. Insect Behav.* 11:493–503
23. Calabi P, Traniello JFA. 1989. Social-organization in the ant *Pheidole dentata*: Physical and temporal caste ratios lack ecological correlates. *Behav. Ecol. Sociobiol.* 24:69–78
24. Cao TT, Dornhaus A. 2008. Ants under crowded conditions consume more energy. *Biol. Lett.* 4:613–15
25. Cassill D. 2002. Yoyo-bang: a risk-aversion investment strategy by a perennial insect society. *Oecologia* 132:150–58
26. Cole B. 1984. Colony efficiency and the reproductivity effect in *Leptothorax allardycei* (Mann). *Insectes Soc.* 31:403–7
27. Cole B. 1986. The social behavior of *Leptothorax allardycei* (Hymenoptera, Formicidae): time budgets and the evolution of worker reproduction. *Behav. Ecol. Sociobiol.* 18:165–73
28. Costa JT. 2006. *The Other Insect Societies*. Cambridge, MA: Belknap
29. Crozier RH, Page RE. 1985. On being the right size: male contributions and multiple mating in social Hymenoptera. *Behav. Ecol. Sociobiol.* 18:105–15
30. Debout G, Schatz B, Elias M, McKey D. 2007. Polydomy in ants: What we know, what we think we know, and what remains to be done. *Biol. J. Linn. Soc.* 90:319–48
31. Dornhaus A. 2008. Specialization does not predict individual performance in an ant. *PLoS Biol.* 6:e285
32. Dornhaus A, Franks NR. 2006. Colony size affects collective decision-making in the ant *Temnothorax albipennis*. *Insectes Soc.* 53:420–27

32. Provides an empirical study of collective decision making revealing the pitfalls of using natural colony-size variation.

33. Dornhaus A, Holley J-A, Franks NR. 2009. Larger colonies do not have more specialized workers in the ant *Temnothorax albipennis*. *Behav. Ecol.* 20:922–29

34. Dornhaus A, Holley J-A, Pook VG, Worswick G, Franks NR. 2008. Why don't all workers work? Colony size and workload during emigrations in the ant *Temnothorax albipennis*. *Behav. Ecol. Sociobiol.* 63:43–51
35. Dornhaus A, Klügl F, Oechslein C, Puppe F, Chittka L. 2006. Benefits of recruitment in honey bees: effects of ecology and colony size in an individual-based model. *Behav. Ecol.* 17:336–44
36. Enquist B, Economo E, Huxman T, Allen A, Ignace D, Gillooly J. 2003. Scaling metabolism from organisms to ecosystems. *Nature* 423:639–42
37. **Fjerdingstad EJ, Crozier RH. 2006. The evolution of worker caste diversity in social insects. *Am. Nat.* 167:390–400**

37. Conducts a phylogenetically controlled analysis of the effect of colony size on morphological worker castes across ant species.

38. Foster WA. 1990. Experimental evidence for effective and altruistic colony defence against natural predators by soldiers of the gall-forming aphid *Pemphigus spyrothecae* (Hemiptera: Pemphigidae). *Behav. Ecol. Sociobiol.* 27:421–30
39. Franks NR. 1985. Reproduction, foraging efficiency and worker polymorphism in army ants. In *Experimental Behavioral Ecology and Sociobiology: In Memoriam Karl von Frisch, 1886–1982*, ed. B Hölldobler, M Lindauer, 31:91–107. Sunderland, MA: Sinauer Assoc.
40. Franks NR, Dornhaus A, Best CS, Jones EL. 2006. Decision-making by small and large house-hunting ant colonies: One size fits all. *Anim. Behav.* 53:611–16
41. Franks NR, Partridge LW. 1993. Lanchester battles and the evolution of combat in ants. *Anim. Behav.* 45:197–99
42. Franks NR, Scovell E. 1983. Dominance and reproductive success among slave-making worker ants. *Nature* 304:724–25
43. Gautrais J, Theraulaz G, Deneubourg JL, Anderson C. 2002. Emergent polyethism as a consequence of increased colony size in insect societies. *J. Theor. Biol.* 215:363–73
44. Gillooly J, Hou C, Kaspari M. 2010. Eusocial insects as superorganisms: insights from metabolic theory. *Commun. Integr. Biol.* 3:360–62
45. Giron D, Ross KG, Strand MR. 2007. Presence of soldier larvae determines the outcome of competition in a polyembryonic wasp. *J. Evol. Biol.* 20:165–72
46. Gordon DM. 1995. The development of an ant colony's foraging range. *Anim. Behav.* 49:649–59
47. Gordon DM, Mehdiabadi NJ. 1999. Encounter rate and task allocation in harvester ants. *Behav. Ecol. Sociobiol.* 45:370–77
48. Greene MJ, Gordon DM. 2007. Interaction rate informs harvester ant task decisions. *Behav. Ecol.* 18:451–55
49. Greenleaf SS, Williams NM, Winfree R, Kremen C. 2007. Bee foraging ranges and their relationship to body size. *Oecologia* 153:589–96
50. Hasegawa E. 1993. Nest defense and early production of the major workers in the dimorphic ant *Colobopsis nipponicus* (Wheeler) (Hymenoptera, Formicidae). *Behav. Ecol. Sociobiol.* 33:73–77
51. Herbers JM. 1981. Reliability theory and foraging by ants. *J. Theor. Biol.* 89:175–89
52. Herbers JM, Choiniere E. 1996. Foraging behaviour and colony structure in ants. *Anim. Behav.* 51:141–53
53. Hölldobler B, Wilson EO. 1990. *The Ants*. Cambridge, MA: Harvard Univ. Press
54. Hölldobler B, Wilson EO. 2008. *The Superorganism: The Beauty, Elegance, and Strangeness of Insect Societies*. New York: W.W. Norton & Co.
55. Hou C, Kaspari M, Zanden H, Gillooly J. 2010. Energetic basis of colonial living in social insects. *Proc. Natl. Acad. Sci. USA* 107:3634–38
56. Hughes WOH, Oldroyd BP, Beekman M, Ratnieks FLW. 2008. Ancestral monogamy shows kin selection is key to the evolution of eusociality. *Science* 320:1213–16
57. Hughes WOH, Sumner S, Van Borm S, Boomsma JJ. 2003. Worker caste polymorphism has a genetic basis in *Acromyrmex* leaf-cutting ants. *Proc. Natl. Acad. Sci. USA* 100:9394–97
58. Ito Y. 1985. Colony development and social structure in a subtropical paper wasp, *Ropalidia fasciata* (F.) (Hymenoptera: Vespidae). *Res. Popul. Ecol.* 27:333–49
59. Ito Y. 1993. *Behavior and Social Evolution of Wasps*. New York: Oxford Univ. Press
60. Jaffe R, Kronauer DJC, Kraus FB, Boomsma JJ, Moritz RFA. 2007. Worker caste determination in the army ant *Eciton burchellii*. *Biol. Lett.* 3:513–16

61. Jeanne RL. 1986. The organization of work in *Polybia occidentalis*: costs and benefits of specialization in a social wasp. *Behav. Ecol. Sociobiol.* 19:333–41
62. Jeanne RL, Bouwma AM. 2002. Scaling in nests of a social wasp: a property of the social group. *Biol. Bull.* 202:289–95
63. Jeanne RL, Nordheim EV. 1996. Productivity in a social wasp: per capita output increases with swarm size. *Behav. Ecol.* 7:43–48
64. Jeanson R, Fewell JH, Gorelick R, Bertram SM. 2007. Emergence of increased division of labor as a function of group size. *Behav. Ecol. Sociobiol.* 62:289–98
65. Jetz W, Carbone C, Fulford J, Brown J. 2004. The scaling of animal space use. *Science* 306:266–68
66. Jun J, Pepper JW. 2003. Allometric scaling of ant foraging trail networks. *Evol. Ecol. Res.* 5:297–303
67. Kamilar JM, Bribiescas RG, Bradley BJ. 2010. Is group size related to longevity in mammals? *Biol. Lett.* 6:736–39
68. Karsai IN, Wenzel JW. 1998. Productivity, individual-level and colony-level flexibility, and organization of work as consequences of colony size. *Proc. Natl. Acad. Sci. USA* 95:8665–69

68. Uses comparative study on wasps to describe caveats of measuring per-capita reproductive output of colonies.

69. Kaspari M. 2005. Global energy gradients and size in colonial organisms: worker mass and worker number in ant colonies. *Proc. Natl. Acad. Sci. USA* 102:5079–83
70. Kaspari M, Byrne MM. 1995. Caste allocation in litter *Pheidole*: lessons from plant defense theory. *Behav. Ecol. Sociobiol.* 37:255–63
71. Kaspari M, O'Donnell S. 2003. High rates of army ant raids in the Neotropics and implications for ant colony and community structure. *Evol. Ecol. Res.* 5:933–39
72. Kaspari M, Pickering J, Longino J, Windsor D. 2001. The phenology of a Neotropical ant assemblage: evidence for continuous and overlapping reproduction. *Behav. Ecol. Sociobiol.* 50:382–90
73. Kaspari M, Vargo E. 1995. Colony size as a buffer against seasonality: Bergmann's rule in social insects. *Am. Nat.* 145:610–32

73. Shows how buffering larger colonies against environmental variation leads to latitudinal gradients.

74. Kremen C, Ostfeld RS. 2005. A call to ecologists: measuring, analyzing, and managing ecosystem services. *Front. Ecol. Environ.* 3:540–48
75. Litte M. 1977. Behavioral ecology of the social wasp, *Mischocyttarus mexicanus*. *Behav. Ecol. Sociobiol.* 2:229–46
76. London KB, Jeanne RL. 2003. Effects of colony size and stage of development on defense response by the swarm-founding wasp *Polybia occidentalis*. *Behav. Ecol. Sociobiol.* 54:539–46
77. Long CE, Thorne BL, Breisch NL. 2003. Termite colony ontogeny: a long-term assessment of reproductive lifespan, caste ratios and colony size in *Reticulitermes flavipes* (Isoptera: Rhinotermitidae). *Bull. Entomol. Res.* 93:439–45
78. Macevicz S, Oster G. 1976. Modeling social insect populations II. Optimal reproductive strategies in annual eusocial insect colonies. *Behav. Ecol. Sociobiol.* 1:265–82
79. Mailleux A-C, Deneubourg J-L, Detrain C. 2003. How does colony growth influence communication in ants? *Insectes Soc.* 50:24–31
80. McGlynn TP, Owen JP. 2002. Food supplementation alters caste allocation in a natural population of *Pheidole flavens*, a dimorphic leaf-litter dwelling ant. *Insectes Soc.* 49:8–14
81. Michener C. 1964. Reproductive efficiency in relation to colony size in hymenopterous societies. *Insectes Soc.* 11:317–41
82. Michener C. 1974. *The Social Behavior of the Bees: A Comparative Study*. Cambridge, MA: Belknap
83. Monnin T, Ratnieks FLW, Brandão C. 2003. Reproductive conflict in animal societies: Hierarchy length increases with colony size in queenless ponerine ants. *Behav. Ecol. Sociobiol.* 54:103–15
84. Moreau CS. 2009. Inferring ant evolution in the age of molecular data (Hymenoptera: Formicidae). *Myrmecol. News* 12:201–10
85. Moreau CS, Bell CD, Vila R, Archibald B, Pierce NE. 2006. Phylogeny of the ants: diversification in the age of angiosperms. *Science* 312:101–4
86. Murakami T, Higashi S, Windsor D. 2000. Mating frequency, colony size, polyethism and sex ratio in fungus-growing ants (Attini). *Behav. Ecol. Sociobiol.* 48:276–84

86. Across leaf-cutting ants, this study finds relationships between mating frequency, colony size, and division of labor.

87. O'Donnell S, Jeanne RL. 1992. Lifelong patterns of forager behavior in a tropical swarm-founding wasp: effects of specialization and activity level on longevity. *Anim. Behav.* 44:1021–27

88. O'Donnell S, Lattke J, Powell S, Kaspari M. 2007. Army ants in four forests: geographic variation in raid rates and species composition. *J. Anim. Ecol.* 76:580–89
89. Oster GF, Wilson EO. 1978. *Caste and Ecology in the Social Insects*. Princeton, NJ: Princeton Univ. Press
90. Pacala SW, Gordon DM, Godfray HCJ. 1996. Effects of social group size on information transfer and task allocation. *Evol. Ecol.* 10:127–65
91. Passera L, Roncin E, Kaufmann B, Keller L. 1996. Increased soldier production in ant colonies exposed to intraspecific competition. *Nature* 379:630–31
92. Peeters C. 1997. Morphologically "primitive" ants: comparative review of social characters, and the importance of queen-worker dimorphism. In *Social Behavior in Insects and Arachnids*, ed. JC Choe, BJ Crespi, pp. 372–91. Cambridge, UK: Cambridge Univ. Press
93. Poitrineau K, Mitesser O, Poethke HJ. 2009. Workers, sexuals, or both? Optimal allocation of resources to reproduction and growth in annual insect colonies. *Insectes Soc.* 56:119–29
94. Powell S. 2009. How ecology shapes caste evolution: linking resource use, morphology, performance and fitness in a superorganism. *J. Evol. Biol.* 22:1004–13
95. Powell S, Clark E. 2004. Combat between large derived societies: a subterranean army ant established as a predator of mature leaf-cutting ant colonies. *Insectes Soc.* 51:342–51
96. Powell S, Franks NR. 2005. Caste evolution and ecology: a special worker for novel prey. *Proc. R. Soc. Lond. Ser. B* 272:2173–80
97. Roisin Y. 2000. Diversity and evolution of caste patterns. In *Termites: Evolution, Sociality, Symbioses, Ecology*, ed. T Abe, DE Bignell, M Higashi, pp. 95–119. New York: Springer
98. Ronnas C, Larsson S, Pitacco A, Battisti A. 2010. Effects of colony size on larval performance in a processionary moth. *Ecol. Entomol.* 35:436–45
99. Ross K, Matthews R. 1991. *The Social Biology of Wasps*. Ithaca, NY: Cornell Univ. Press
100. Roubik DW. 1989. *Ecology and Natural History of Tropical Bees*. New York: Cambridge Univ. Press
101. Rueppell O, Kaftanouglu O, Page RE. 2009. Honey bee (*Apis mellifera*) workers live longer in small than in large colonies. *Exp. Gerontol.* 44:447–52
102. Rueppell O, Kirkman RW. 2005. Extraordinary starvation resistance in *Temnothorax rugatulus* (Hymenoptera, Formicidae) colonies: demography and adaptive behavior. *Insectes Soc.* 52:282–90
103. Rypstra AL. 1979. Foraging flocks of spiders. *Behav. Ecol. Sociobiol.* 5:291–300
104. Schmid-Hempel P. 1992. Worker castes and adaptive demography. *J. Evol. Biol.* 5:1–12
105. Schneider S. 1990. Nest characteristics and recruitment behavior of absconding colonies of the African honey bee, *Apis mellifera scutellata*, in Africa. *J. Insect Behav.* 3:225–40
106. Seeley TD. 1995. *The Wisdom of the Hive: The Social Physiology of Honey Bee Colonies*. Cambridge, MA: Harvard Univ. Press
107. Seeley TD, Morse RA. 1976. The nest of the honey bee (*Apis mellifera* L.). *Insectes Soc.* 23:495–512
108. Shibao H. 1998. Social structure and the defensive role of soldiers in a eusocial bamboo aphid, *Pseudoregma bambucicola* (Homoptera: Aphididae): a test of the defence-optimization hypothesis. *Res. Popul. Ecol.* 40:325–33
109. **Shik JZ. 2008. Ant colony size and the scaling of reproductive effort. *Funct. Ecol.* 22:674–81**

109. Phylogenetically controlled study of reproduction across ant species reveals a trade-off between queen size and number.

110. Shingleton AW, Foster WA. 2000. Ant tending influences soldier production in a social aphid. *Proc. R. Soc. Lond. Ser. B* 267:1863–68
111. Simpson SJ, Sword GA, Lorch PD, Couzin ID. 2006. Cannibal crickets on a forced march for protein and salt. *Proc. Natl. Acad. Sci. USA* 103:4152–56
112. Sokolovska N, Rowe L, Johansson F. 2000. Fitness and body size in mature odonates. *Ecol. Entomol.* 25:239–48
113. Sorvari J, Hakkarainen H. 2007. The role of food and colony size in sexual offspring production in a social insect: an experiment. *Ecol. Entomol.* 32:11–14
114. Strassmann JE, Queller DC. 2010. The social organism: congresses, parties, and committees. *Evolution* 64:605–16
115. Strohm E, Bordon-Hauser A. 2003. Advantages and disadvantages of large colony size in a halictid bee: the queen's perspective. *Behav. Ecol.* 14:546–53
116. Thomas M, Elgar M. 2003. Colony size affects division of labour in the ponerine ant *Rhytidoponera metallica*. *Naturwissenschaften* 90:88–92

117. Thompson DJ, Fincke OM. 2002. Body size and fitness in Odonata, stabilising selection and a meta-analysis too far? *Ecol. Entomol.* 27:378–84
118. Thorne BL, Breisch NL, Muscedere ML. 2003. Evolution of eusociality and the soldier caste in termites: influence of intraspecific competition and accelerated inheritance. *Proc. Natl. Acad. Sci. USA* 100:12808–13
119. Tibbetts E, Reeve HK. 2003. Benefits of foundress associations in the paper wasp *Polistes dominulus*: increased productivity and survival, but no assurance of fitness returns. *Behav. Ecol.* 14:510–14
120. Tschinkel WR. 1988. Colony growth and the ontogeny of worker polymorphism in the fire ant, *Solenopsis invicta*. *Behav. Ecol. Sociobiol.* 22:103–15
121. Tschinkel WR. 1991. Insect sociometry, a field in search of data. *Insectes Soc.* 38:77–82
122. Tschinkel WR. 1993. Sociometry and sociogenesis of colonies of the fire ant *Solenopsis invicta* during one annual cycle. *Ecol. Monogr.* 63:425–57
123. Tschinkel WR. 1998. Sociometry and sociogenesis of colonies of the harvester ant, *Pogonomyrmex badius*: worker characteristics in relation to colony size and season. *Insectes Soc.* 45:385–410
124. Tschinkel WR. 2011. Back to basics: sociometry and sociogenesis of ant societies (Hymenoptera: Formicidae). *Myrmecol. News* 14:49–54

124. Calls for old-fashioned ant counting (as do we in this paper).

125. Tschinkel WR. 2011. The organization of foraging in the fire ant, *Solenopsis invicta*. *J. Insect Sci.* 11:26
126. Visscher P. 1996. Reproductive conflict in honey bees: a stalemate of worker egg-laying and policing. *Behav. Ecol. Sociobiol.* 39:237–44
127. Walker J, Stamps J. 1986. A test of optimal caste ratio theory using the ant *Camponotus* (*Colobopsis*) *impressus*. *Ecology* 67:1052–62
128. Waters JS, Holbrook CT, Fewell JH, Harrison JF. 2010. Allometric scaling of metabolism, growth, and activity in whole colonies of the seed-harvester ant *Pogonomyrmex californicus*. *Am. Nat.* 176:501–10

128. *Pogonomyrmex* ant colonies of different sizes but similar ages show different mass-specific metabolic rates.

129. Wenseleers T, Helanterä H, Hart A, Ratneiks FLW. 2004. Worker reproduction and policing in insect societies: an ESS analysis. *J. Evol. Biol.* 17:1035–47
130. Wheeler DE. 1986. Developmental and physiological determinants of caste in social Hymenoptera: evolutionary implications. *Am. Nat.* 128:13–34
131. Whitehouse MEA, Jaffe K. 1996. Ant wars: combat strategies, territory and nest defence in the leaf-cutting ant *Atta laevigata*. *Anim. Behav.* 51:1207–17
132. Wilson EO. 1971. *The Insect Societies*. Cambridge, MA: Belknap. 548 pp.
133. Wilson EO. 1976. Behavioral discretization and the number of castes in an ant species. *Behav. Ecol. Sociobiol.* 1:141–54
134. Wilson EO. 1983. Caste and division of labor in leaf-cutter ants (Hymenoptera: Formicidae: Atta) IV. Colony ontogeny of *A. cephalotes*. *Behav. Ecol. Sociobiol.* 14:55–60
135. Wilson EO. 1985. The sociogenesis of insect colonies. *Science* 228:1489–95
136. Wyatt T. 1986. How a subsocial intertidal beetle, *Bledius spectabilis*, prevents flooding and anoxia in its burrow. *Behav. Ecol. Sociobiol.* 19:323–31
137. Yang A, Martin C, Nijhout H. 2004. Geographic variation of caste structure among ant populations. *Curr. Biol.* 14:514–19
138. Yip EC, Powers KS, Aviles L. 2008. Cooperative capture of large prey solves scaling challenge faced by spider societies. *Proc. Natl. Acad. Sci. USA* 105:11818–22
139. Yukawa J, Tsuji K, Tanaka S, Ito Y. 1995. Factors affecting the proportion of soldiers in eusocial bamboo aphid, *Pseudoregma bambucicola*, colonies. *Ethol. Ecol. Evol.* 7:335–45

Mosquito Genomics: Progress and Challenges

David W. Severson* and Susanta K. Behura

Eck Institute for Global Health, Department of Biological Sciences, University of Notre Dame, Notre Dame, Indiana 46556; email: severson.1@nd.edu, sbehura@nd.edu

Annu. Rev. Entomol. 2012. 57:143–66

First published online as a Review in Advance on September 19, 2011

The *Annual Review of Entomology* is online at ento.annualreviews.org

This article's doi: 10.1146/annurev-ento-120710-100651

0066-4170/12/0107-0143$20.00

*Corresponding author

Keywords

Culicidae, transcriptome, proteome, comparative genomics, population biology, vector biology

Abstract

The whole-genome sequencing of mosquitoes has facilitated our understanding of fundamental biological processes at their basic molecular levels and holds potential for application to mosquito control and prevention of mosquito-borne disease transmission. Draft genome sequences are available for *Anopheles gambiae*, *Aedes aegypti*, and *Culex quinquefasciatus*. Collectively, these represent the major vectors of African malaria, dengue fever and yellow fever viruses, and lymphatic filariasis, respectively. Rapid advances in genome technologies have revealed detailed information on genome architecture as well as phenotype-specific transcriptomics and proteomics. These resources allow for detailed comparative analyses within and across populations as well as species. Next-generation sequencing technologies will likely promote a proliferation of genome sequences for additional mosquito species as well as for individual insects. Here we review the current status of genome research in mosquitoes and identify potential areas for further investigations.

INTRODUCTION

A key to our eventual understanding of the complex biology of mosquitoes lies in their genomes. In particular, the how, where, and why of interspecific and intraspecific characters are defined in both the short- and long-term evolutionary context. The Culicidae are remarkably adaptive, with >3,500 extant species and a strong likelihood that many other, likely cryptic, species remain to be discovered. Understanding fundamental biological processes at the genome level among and between mosquito species is of intrinsic interest and also holds potential for application to mosquito control and prevention of mosquito-borne disease transmission. In addition, how genomes shape the transformation to ecotypes and eventual speciation is of emerging interest.

Classical studies have provided useful insights regarding mosquito genome-size variability and complexity, and these studies still find utility in guiding genome-sequencing efforts as they pertain to estimating sequence coverage and potential influence of endogenous repetitive elements. Genome sizes vary enormously among mosquitoes, with estimated sizes ranging from ~0.23 to 1.9 pg as discussed in several previous reviews (95, 149, 162), with the largest genome reported for *Aedes zoosophus* at 1.9 pg (151). In general, species within the Anophelinae are at the low end of the genome-size range, whereas species within the Culicinae range from moderate (e.g., Culicini) to very large (e.g., Aedini). Furthermore, tantalizing evidence exists for fluidity in genome size within individual mosquito species such as *Aedes albopictus* (94, 151), suggesting that selection may drive a demand for smaller or greater genome size, dependent on the prevailing environmental constraints.

Over the past decade, opportunities and technologies for whole-genome sequencing efforts in complex organisms have matured considerably. Advances in mosquito genomics reflect this trend, as evidenced from comparisons of previous reviews on the status of mosquito genomics, genetics, and mapping (124, 137, 162, 163, 176), and the material we discuss in this review. In February 2011, the journal *Science* reflected on the 10-year anniversary of the publication of the human genome (82, 186) with a series of short essays and comments: The consensus was that the importance of the human genome to human health has emerged from guarded speculation on its utility to driving the research agenda today with practical applications emerging as well. Individual-human genome sequences for ~$1,000 are anticipated in the near term; thus, low-cost, individual-mosquito genome sequences will become available as well, and research on many, if not all, mosquito species will eventually benefit from genome sequencing. Today, with rapid advances in sequencing technology, the real challenge at hand is converting the massive amounts of raw genome-sequence information obtained at lower cost and in shorter time frames into a useful biological context. Although the mosquito-research community is much smaller than that associated with human concerns, here we review evidence indicating that the availability of several genome sequences, with more in progress or planned, is driving the direction for much of the ongoing mosquito research.

OVERVIEW OF SEQUENCED MOSQUITO GENOMES

Sanger Sequencing of the "Big Three"

The pioneering mosquito genome-sequencing efforts for *Anopheles gambiae*, *Aedes aegypti*, and *Culex quinquefasciatus* have utilized classical Sanger-sequencing technology, as has also been applied to the human, *Drosophila*, and other eukaryote genomes. This entails end-sequencing of cloned genome sequences from libraries prepared from various-length, random-genome fragments followed by computational assembly of overlapping reads into contigs and scaffolds that

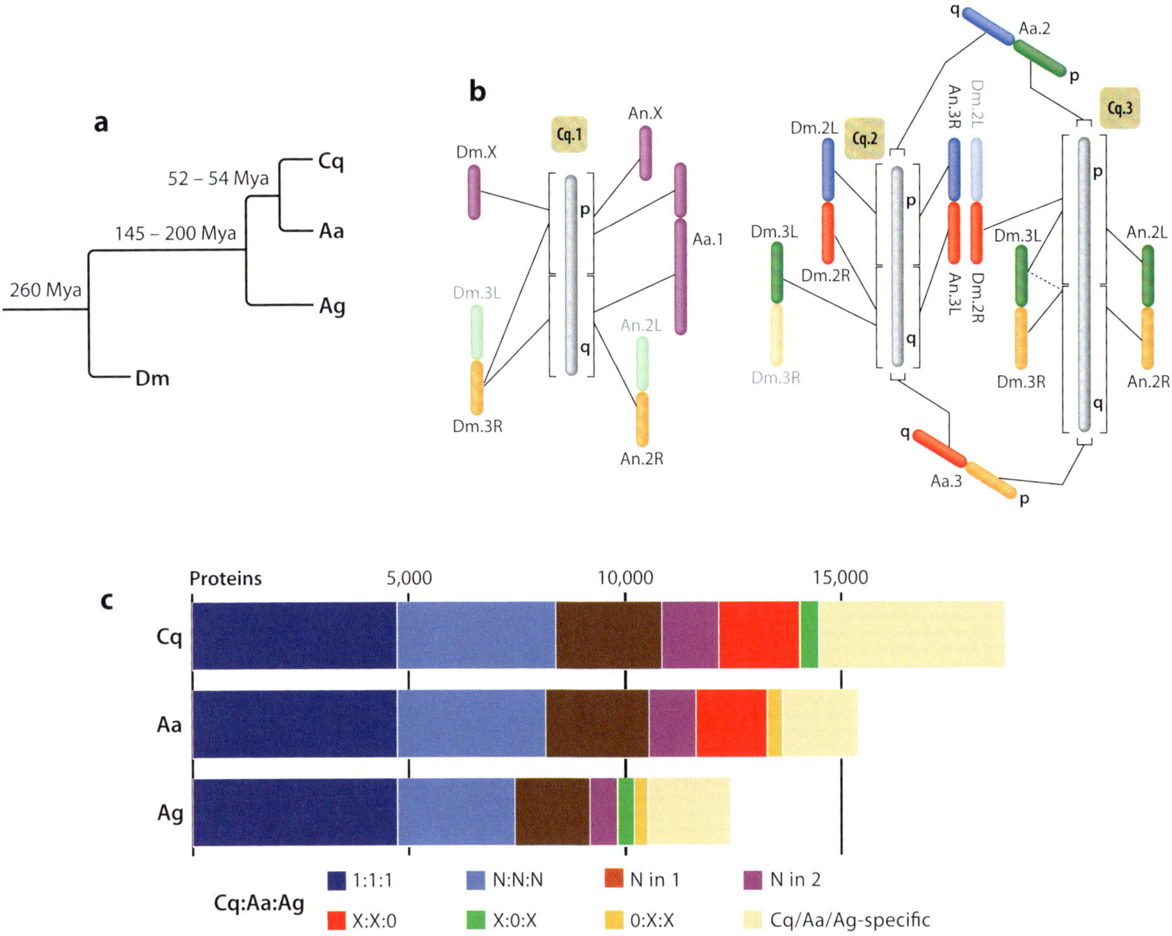

Figure 1

(*a*) Codon-based phylogeny estimates for *Culex quinquefasciatus* (Cq), *Aedes aegypti* (Aa), *Anopheles gambiae* (Ag), and *Drosophila melanogaster* (Dm). (*b*) Chromosomal synteny between mosquitoes and *D. melanogaster*. Colors indicate syntenic chromosome arms with solid lines identifying primary orthologies. (*c*) Orthology comparisons among protein-coding genes for mosquitoes. Categories include single-copy orthologs in each species (1:1:1) and multicopy orthologs in all three (N:N:N), one (N in 1), or two (N in 2) species. Remaining orthologous groups include single or multicopy groups with genes in only two species (X:X:0, X:0:X, 0:X:X). The remaining fractions represent genes with no orthology in the other two mosquitoes. Adapted from Reference 6. Reprinted with permission from AAAS.

represent the majority of the genome sequence. *An. gambiae*, *Ae. aegypti*, and *Cx. quinquefasciatus* represent the "big three," in that they are likely the most important species defining the major nodes for mosquito phylogeny (**Figure 1*a***) (152). They are also the primary vectors of *Plasmodium falciparum*, yellow fever and dengue fever viruses, and lymphatic filariasis, respectively.

The *An. gambiae* (PEST strain) genome was reported in 2002 (77), *Ae. aegypti* (Liverpool-IB12 strain) in 2007 (131), and *Cx. quinquefasciatus* (Johanesburg strain) in 2010 (6). Of these, the *An. gambiae* assembly is the most complete and is linked to physical positions on polytene chromosomes. Assembly quality is better for *Ae. aegypti* than it is for *Cx. quinquefaciatus*, yet supercontig assignments to chromosome position are fairly minimal for both species for several

Table 1 Summary of genome statistics[a]

	Gene characteristics					
Species	**Genome size (Mb)**	**Total number of genes**	**Total number of transcripts (bp)[b]**	**Mean gene size (bp)**	**Exon[b]**	**Intron[b]**
Culex quinquefasciatus	579	18,883	18,883	5,673	356	1,043
Aedes aegypti	1,380	15,419	16,789	15,488	405	3,793
Anopheles gambiae	278	12,457	13,133	5,145	378	875

[a] Data extracted from Reference 6.
[b] Mean size (bp).

reasons including the overall poor utility of polytene chromosomes for physical mapping in both species. For *An. gambiae*, the ~10.2-fold coverage assembly included 8,684 scaffolds comprising ~278 Mb; yet 303 large scaffolds accounted for 91% of the genome. For *Ae. aegypti*, the ~7.6-fold coverage assembly included 4,758 scaffolds comprising ~1,380 Mb, with 1,257 large scaffolds accounting for 98% of the genome. For *Cx. quinquefasciatus*, the ~6.1-fold coverage assembly included 3,171 scaffolds comprising ~579 Mb. The extreme differences in genome size among the three species is largely the result of transposable element (TE) content, with TEs accounting for nearly 50% of the *Ae. aegypti* genome (131). Annotated gene content and average exon sizes are, in general, fairly similar among the three species (**Table 1**) with the greatest number identified in *Cx. quinquefasciatus* and smallest in *An. gambiae*. Average gene sizes are considerably larger in *Ae. aegypti* as a result of its much larger average intron size, again reflecting increased repetitive sequence content.

Genomics of Ecological Speciation

As indicated by laboratory and field studies, ecological speciation, as discussed in another review (157), is a process wherein barriers to gene flow evolve between populations in response to ecologically based divergent selection. Strong support for ongoing ecological speciation among *An. gambiae* populations in west Africa is evident among the sympatric ecotypes referred to as M and S forms and reviewed elsewhere (45, 104). These forms are morphologically indistinguishable, and although no evidence exists for postmating isolation mechanisms, strong assortive mating is evident among sympatric field populations. A growing body of evidence does, however, support ecological niche partitioning as, for example, the forms show preferences in oviposition site selection wherein the S form prefers the more typical, small, ephemeral pools and puddles and the M form prefers larger, more permanent sites (39, 45, 55, 167), which has implications regarding the dynamics of malaria transmission.

TE: transposable element

Speciation islands: relatively small genome blocks that show ecotype- or form-specific diversity suggestive of reduced gene flow associated with reproductive isolation

Single-nucleotide polymorphism (SNP): defined single points in genomes that show polymorphism among individuals and across populations

Efforts to map divergence among M and S forms at a quasi whole-genome level initially took advantage of the existing Affymetrix *Plasmodium/Anopheles* GeneChip array containing ~166,000 unique 25-base probes representing an early *An. gambiae* gene build and random unique sequences across the genome (183, 194). Using variability in signal intensities of individual probes to identify form-specific polymorphisms, these studies identified three small genome regions, termed speciation islands, in the pericentric regions on the X chromosome and the 2L and 3L chromosome arms that show significant divergence between the M and S forms. Maintenance of near-perfect linkage disequilibrium of form-specific single-nucleotide polymorphisms (SNPs) across all three regions indicated limited influence of interform gene flow, suggesting these regions contain genes responsible for reproductive isolation.

Application of Sanger sequencing to the M and S forms at ~sixfold coverage (97) for each provides the opportunity to implement a "reverse-ecology" approach to tease out the actual genetic mechanisms driving speciation. The M- and S-form genome comparisons suggest that the previously identified speciation islands define only a small portion of the polymorphism associated with divergent selection. Indeed, >150,000 fixed SNP differences were identified between M and S forms, and these are distributed across the genome with the highest proportion residing on the X chromosome followed by chromosomes 2 and 3, respectively. Assessment of gene ontologies for genes in genome regions of highest divergence revealed the overrepresentation of genes with functions related to neurohormone signaling, which, in insects, control development, feeding, reproduction, and some complex behaviors. Another region of interest was located around the *resistance to dieldrin* (*Rdl*) gene, which appears to show evidence of selective sweeps where strong positive natural selection favored increases in form-specific resistance mutations and close association with a cluster of odorant receptor genes that could play a role in assortive behavior. Although unclear in mosquitoes, related receptor genes in *Drosophila melanogaster* have been shown to influence social aggregation and female sexual receptivity (120).

Next-generation sequencing (NGS): advanced sequencing technologies that provide high-throughput, low-cost sequence data with higher error rates and shorter sequence reads than conventional Sanger sequencing

Next-Generation Sequencing

Application of next-generation sequencing (NGS) to de novo genome sequencing and assembly of mosquitoes has not been attempted to date, but it is undoubtedly on the horizon, given changes in cost restraints and anticipated advances in sequencing technology. For example, the giant-panda genome based completely on Illumina NGS technology was recently reported (106). However, some caution is warranted as to the expected quality of current NGS-only de novo genome assemblies: As Alkan et al. (2) indicate, de novo genome assemblies of individual humans using only NGS data were ~16% shorter than the reference human genome owing largely to exclusion of common repeats and regions reflecting segmental duplication. They suggest that emerging third-generation sequencing technologies with longer sequence reads and library insert sizes may solve these problems. In the near term, combinations of classical sequencing and NGS technologies are likely to be the most efficient and accurate approaches for de novo genome sequencing. This is already evident in genome sequences reported for the cucumber, *Cucumis sativus* (79), and the domestic turkey, *Meleagris gallopavo* (41).

VectorBase

Generation of complete genome information for mosquitoes provides tremendous opportunities, yet it would be of limited utility without the availability of databases and computing tools to access and mine the data for specific application to field and lab studies. All genome and genome-related data for the big three (other mosquito species will be added as they are sequenced) are accessible in a user-friendly Web-based format through VectorBase (**http://www.vectorbase.org/**), the Bioinformatic Resource Center funded by the National Institute of Allergy and Infectious Diseases and dedicated to invertebrate vectors of human pathogens (98, 99). Genome and gene information is available for download, and access to expression, population, and insecticide-resistance information is also provided. VectorBase is linked to several public databases including nucleotide and protein databases. It provides a genome browser for visualizing genome annotations and gene alignments as well as direct comparative genome analyses. VectorBase has developed controlled vocabularies for mosquito anatomy (180) and insecticide resistance (46). Future plans include the development of additional ontologies and expansion to other arthropod disease vectors (181). Of note, VectorBase has developed a Community Annotation Pipeline that provides the format and tools for manual annotations to be submitted directly by the research community. Thus, community participation is not only welcomed, but also critical to individual-genome advancement efforts.

Transcriptome: total complement of RNA transcripts, both coding and noncoding, in an organism or tissue under specific conditions

DNA microarray: glass slides or silicon thin-film cells containing oligonucleotides that can represent an entire or a fraction of a genome

TRANSITION FROM GENOMES TO BIOLOGY

Genome-Wide Transcriptomics

The opportunity for large-scale transcription profiling is a significant outcome of mosquito genome-sequencing efforts. Access to the annotated gene sets allows for whole-transcriptome microarray studies and also provides the framework for mapping next-generation short-sequence reads to the associated gene and genome positions. Transcriptomics has transitioned from being an exploratory effort to recognition as a highly informative experimental-based application, and in many ways has become an important driver for fundamental biological investigations, particularly for *Ae. aegypti* and *An. gambiae* as the annotations have been available long enough for results to emerge in publications.

Microarrays. DNA microarray technology has matured from early efforts that employed "home-spotted" select collections of cDNAs to a variety of platforms capable of supporting the interrogation of an entire transcriptome with great efficiency. Much of the early microarray work on mosquitoes was reviewed previously (161). More recently, whole as well as some boutique transcriptome assays have targeted a variety of phenotypes.

Two commercial platforms presently account for the published whole-transcriptome microarray efforts in mosquitoes, the Affymetrix *Plasmodium/Anopheles* GeneChip array and Agilent Technologies (**http://www.genomics.agilent.com/**) custom arrays designed for both *Ae. aegypti* and *An. gambiae*. The Affymetrix chips have expanded our knowledge of *An. gambiae* biology by uncovering details on larval gut and salivary gland physiology (128, 129), drought tolerance during embryogenesis (65), postmating changes in adult females (155), and senescence-associated changes in gene expression among adult females (189). In addition, for *An. gambiae*, the custom Agilent chips have been used to characterize the dynamic changes evident in salivary glands in response to blood feeding (43), common and species-specific effects of *P. falciparum* and *Plasmodium berghei* infections on midgut responses (52), and the compartmentalization of midgut gene expression in adult males versus females (190). For *Ae. aegypti*, the custom Agilent chips have been used to demonstrate that the Toll immune signaling pathway is activated in adult females following a dengue-infected blood meal (199), and a similar study looking at response to infection by the filarial nematode *Brugia malayi* identified upregulation of a number of putative immunity-related genes but no apparent role for the Toll pathway (58). Other studies employed Agilent chips to uncover a role for multiple aquaporin genes in regulating diuresis in *Ae. aegypti* females following a blood meal (54); to identify a cluster of genes showing age-specific expression to facilitate development of a predictive model for estimating age among field-collected mosquitoes (34); and to document circadian rhythms associated with the activity of adult females among several molecular pathways important for growth, development, innate immunity, and resistance to insecticides and xenobiotics (148).

Boutique arrays have been used effectively to investigate several traits in mosquitoes. Most notable are the "detox chips" developed for and applied to multiple insecticide- and/or xenobiotic-resistance studies in *Ae. aegypti* (113, 145, 153) and *An. gambiae* (8, 23, 51). These contain a select set of ~200 and ~300 gene probes for *An. gambiae* and *Ae. aegypti*, respectively, that target genes and gene families associated with known detoxification mechanisms that drive resistance to insecticides and various xenobiotics. These are useful research tools for uncovering multiple resistance mechanisms among mosquito populations as well as practical tools for monitoring insecticide-resistance levels to guide vector-control programs. Of further note, the *An. gambiae* detox chip was employed in studies that revealed that *P. berghei* infection altered detoxification gene expression, suggesting that detoxification enzymes are upregulated in midgut and fat-body tissues in response to infection (60). Pyrethroid resistance has recently been examined in *Cx. quinquefasciatus* using a similar detox-chip approach (91).

Proteome: total complement of proteins expressed in an organism or tissue under specific conditions

Next-generation transcriptome sequencing. Technological advances in NGS are rapidly shifting approaches to whole-transcriptome RNA-sequencing (RNA-Seq) analysis, and as costs decrease, they will likely replace large-scale microarray approaches (for reviews, see 115, 168, 197). Limitations associated with the relatively short sequence reads, ~35–400 nucleotides depending on the sequencing platform, are minimized for organisms with reference genome assemblies. NGS is preferable to microarrays, as one can perform similar quantitative expression assays and identify (*a*) SNP and insertion/deletion (indel) mutations that may affect gene function, (*b*) alternate splice forms for individual genes, and (*c*) novel genes not included in a genome annotation. Various computational tools and approaches for expression scoring and quantification of RNA-Seq data have been developed (for a review, see 197).

At present, NGS transcriptome sequencing applications to mosquitoes are fairly limited, but they are expanding. A proof-of-concept examination of Illumina RNA-Seq data from *Ae. aegypti* and *An. gambiae* clearly demonstrated its utility for functional and evolutionary genomics (63). RNA-Seq data have been used to investigate *Ae. aegypti* larval responses to insecticides and several xenobiotics (44) and to compare sugar-fed versus blood-fed females (27). Of note, efforts to optimize de novo transcriptome assembly of NGS data leveraged available data for *Ae. aegypti* downloadable at VectorBase to demonstrate the accuracy of the approach (175). RNA-Seq data for whole, sugar-fed female *Anopheles funestus*, for which a reference genome does not currently exist, were assembled and successfully mapped to the *An. gambiae* sequence data, resulting in the identification of 5,434 1:1 orthologs between the two species (40). On a broader evolutionary scale, RNA-Seq data have been highly informative to making robust phylogenetic inferences among mosquitoes, wherein nine *Anopheles* spp. were compared with *Ae. aegypti* (75). Finally, the utility of RNA-Seq data for evaluating mitochondrial genome expression was demonstrated for *Ae. aegypti*, *An. gambiae*, and *Anopheles quadrimaculatus* (130).

Genome-Wide Proteomics

Proteomics represents a logical extension to interpreting and leveraging genome information for mosquitoes. Although presently most challenging to researchers, proteomics will undoubtedly emerge as a significant tool in driving biological research. Advances in mass spectrometry have transformed the ability to perform global protein profiling, including quantitative expression profiling (for a review, see 112). To date, efforts applied to mosquitoes largely reflect "discovery proteomics," wherein proteins isolated from complex tissues are characterized en masse. In addition to providing information on basic biology, characterization of mosquito proteins has the potential to identify useful candidate antigens for developing transmission-blocking vaccines against pathogens (49, 100).

Anopheles. One of the earliest proteomic efforts in mosquitoes examined both the transcriptome and proteome of salivary glands from *Anopheles stephensi* (184) and, although limited in scope, did show close agreement between the transcript and protein complements of salivary glands. For *An. gambiae*, additional proteomic efforts have included protein identification in hemolymph extracts of adult females in conjunction with an immune challenge (139), determination of differential head protein profiles among uninfected versus *P. berghei*–infected females (103), characterization of protein components of the peritrophic matrix that forms around the blood bolus in adult females (50), comparison of antenna protein profiles between males and females (42), and determination of salivary gland protein profiles of blood-fed females (84, 85) and young versus older females relative to *P. berghei* infection status (36). In a similar vein, midgut protein profiles were compared among *Anopheles albimanus* females following naive versus *P. berghei*–infected blood meals (160).

Aedes. For *Ae. aegypti*, an early proteomic effort identified proteins associated with the egg chorion (202). Additional proteomic efforts have included comparison of cytosolic proteins from isolated Malpighian tubules of females both with and without stimulation by a diuretic peptide (22) as well as identification of proteins extracted from larval midgut brush border membranes (144), including proteins that bind with *Bacillus thuringiensis israelensis* toxin Cry4Ba (12). A comparative proteomic investigation of midgut response to infection by dengue virus and chikungunya virus identified virus-specific as well as common protein modulations at seven days postinfection (177). A comprehensive peptidomic analysis of male and female brain and midgut tissues, in concert with a homology-based search of the *Ae. aegypti* genome, identified a nearly complete list of mature neuropeptides (146). Finally, identification of proteins from *Ae. aegypti* male accessory glands and ejaculatory ducts (169) represents one of the few genomics efforts specifically targeting male mosquitoes.

GENOME APPLICATIONS TO SPECIES AND POPULATIONS

Comparative Genomics

A wealth of information on organismal biology can be drawn from systematic comparative analyses of collections of species at the level of their individual genomes. With the availability of the *An. gambiae* genome (77) following soon after the *D. melanogaster* genome (1), the outstanding potential for comparative genomics among insects, particularly among mosquitoes, was immediately recognized (87). The more recent genome projects for *Ae. aegypti* (131) and *Cx. quinquefasciatus* (5) provided additional useful evolutionary insights on gene and genome structure in mosquitoes. Detailed comparisons of gene families between *Ae. aegypti* and *An. gambiae* were reviewed elsewhere (192). Although these projects are providing incredible new insights on mosquito biology, much information is yet to be gained through genome projects directed at additional mosquito species.

One of the striking results from comparative gene analyses among the big three is the level to which different gene families tend to expand or contract among mosquito genomes, thus demonstrating the evolutionary dynamics of crucial functions such as innate immunity, pheromone binding, xenobiotic degradation, and cuticular development (11, 191). For example, expansions of gene families for proteins containing zinc fingers, insect pheromone binding, cytochrome P450, and insect cuticle domains are evident among mosquitoes. In insects, because of the lack of cellular immunity, innate immunity plays the major role in defense mechanisms. Immune responses begin with molecular recognition of microbial patterns; responsive signals are then modulated and/or transduced before activating effector cascades. Individual cascades are characterized by different evolutionary dynamics among mosquito species, as a result of which the innate immune system shows significant intrinsic plasticity that enables species-specific adaptation to evolving biotic stress. Large-scale investigation of SNPs in *An. gambiae* to determine if mutation patterns were more different among immune genes than those observed among genes not related to immunity identified strong purifying selection among both categories, but no significant differences in the nucleotide diversity between the two categories were found (38). Comparisons of the known odorant-binding proteins of *D. melanogaster* with the whole-genome sequences and expressed sequence tag (EST) sequences of *Ae. aegypti* and *An. gambiae* (207) and subsequent comparisons with *Cx. quinquefasciatus* (6) facilitated the identification of a large number of putative odorant-binding proteins in mosquitoes, with expansion of these genes most evident in *Cx. quinquefasciatus*, which has the largest number reported ($n = 180$) for any dipteran to date. Analysis of developmental genes in mosquitoes and *D. melanogaster* (15) further suggests that, although most fruit fly developmental genes are conserved in mosquitoes, expansions as well as the loss of several genes have occurred in mosquitoes, including among those involved in segmentation, germline development, apoptosis, salivary gland development, and head development.

EST: expressed sequence tag

Synteny: colocalization of two or more genetic loci to the same chromosome regions among species

Macrosynteny and microsynteny. As previous reviews have indicated (116, 162), macrosynteny among mosquitoes, and perhaps among the Diptera, largely reflects whole-chromosome-arm translocations accompanied by extensive within-arm rearrangement. This was clearly evidenced from the detailed comparative analysis of 1:1 orthologs across the *Ae. aegypti*, *An. gambiae*, and *Cx. quinquefasciatus* genomes, which also included *D. melanogaster* (6) (**Figure 1*b***). The three mosquitoes share conservation of 4,744 1:1:1 orthologs. Some other genes show only individual species-pair 1:1 orthologies, and *Cx. quinquefasciatus* contains the largest number of unique genes (**Figure 1*c***).

Microsynteny can be defined as maintenance of the local genome neighborhood for two or more 1:1 orthologs between species. Microsynteny comparisons among the big three identified from ~6,800 (*Anopheles*: *Aedes*) to ~8,000 (*Aedes*: *Culex*) 1:1 orthologs (6, 131). Of interest, among each of the pair-wise species comparisons, ~20% of the 1:1 orthologs were maintained in local microsynteny blocks. However, average microsynteny block sizes are relatively modest, with an average of approxmately three genes per block with *Culex* to *Aedes*/*Anopheles* comparisons (based on minimum block size of $n = 2$ genes) (6) and an average of approximately eight genes per block with *Aedes* to *Anopheles* comparisons (based on minimum block size of $n = 3$ genes) (131).

Regulatory elements. Comparative genomics analyses have been useful in the discovery of *cis*-regulatory elements in mosquitoes (166). The 5′-end flanking regions of orthologous genes among the big three were compared to identify *cis*-regulatory elements that are generally 7 to 9 nucleotides in length, many of which are also conserved in *D. melanogaster*. Regulatory roles for several of these motifs were evident from significant associations between specific motifs and observed gene-expression profiles in mosquitoes. Application of genomic tools to investigate EST sequences between cockroaches and mosquitoes yielded an array of putative genes that could have common functional roles in juvenile hormone biosynthesis in these phylogenetically distinct insects (133).

Codon usage and tRNA genes. Codon usage bias is an evolutionary process in which specific synonymous codons are used more frequently than others while highly expressed genes are being translated. Although codon bias patterns in specific individual mosquito genes were investigated earlier (7, 20, 123), the genome sequences have allowed for the identification of genome-wide patterns in codon usage bias in mosquitoes (17) and revealed a significant positive correlation between codon bias and gene-expression levels in *Ae. aegypti* and *An. gambiae*, thus supporting a hypothesis for higher codon bias among highly expressed genes. Furthermore, the relative abundance of transfer RNA (tRNA) isoacceptor genes is correlated with preferred (or optimal) and nonpreferred (or rare) codons for genes related to translation, energy metabolism, and carbohydrate metabolism pathways, suggesting that these genes and the related pathways may be under translational selection.

Noncoding RNA: genes that are transcribed, but not translated into proteins, but instead act as functional RNA molecules

Comparative analysis of the *Ae. aegypti* and *An. gambiae* genomes (17) also suggested that gene sequences of tRNAs evolve in three distinct groups: (*a*) The Trp, His, Cys, Phe, and Asp tRNAs are highly conserved; (*b*) the Ser, Ala, Met, and Thr tRNAs are weakly conserved; and (*c*) the remaining tRNAs are moderately conserved between them. The tRNA genes are distributed in 61 small physical clusters (2 to 13 tRNAs per cluster) in the *Ae. aegypti* genome and 39 clusters (2 to 37 tRNAs per cluster) in the *An. gambiae* genome. Many tRNA genes are also embedded within protein-coding genes in mosquitoes (S.K. Behura & D.W. Severson, unpublished observations). Interestingly, an unusually large number of tRNA genes ($n = 486$) are embedded within protein-coding genes in *Cx. quinquefasciatus* in comparison to only 41 such embedded tRNAs in *Ae. aegypti* and 31 in *An. gambiae*. Several Ala, Glu, Gly, and Val tRNAs are commonly found as embedded tRNAs among the three species.

MicroRNAs. MicroRNAs (miRNAs) are short noncoding RNAs comprised of ~22 bases that regulate gene expression at the post-transcriptional level by binding to the 3′-untranslated regions of target gene mRNAs. The first report suggesting a role for miRNAs in *An. gambiae* response to *Plasmodium* invasion showed that knocking down *Dicer1* and *Ago1* mRNAs led to an increased sensitivity to infection (196) and revealed that the expression patterns of four miRNAs were modulated during invasion. NGS Roche 454 sequencing of small RNA libraries (107) identified 98 pre-miRNAs that represented 86 distinct miRNAs in *Ae. aegypti* and revealed that several miRNAs were associated with stage-specific expression patterns. By contrast, other miRNAs showed higher expression levels in midguts of blood-fed females compared with sugar-fed females. Expression analysis of miRNAs in *Ae. albopictus* and *Cx. quinquefasciatus* suggested that of the 65 common miRNAs identified, the majority of which were conserved in other insects including *D. melanogaster* and *An. gambiae*, miR-184 was the most highly expressed miRNA in both mosquito species. Furthermore, miR-92 and miR-989 showed significant changes in expression levels in *Cx. quinquefasciatus* following West Nile virus infection. MicroRNA precursor sequences were identified in *Anopheles darlingi* by large-scale sequencing, followed by bioinformatic identification of additional pre-miRNAs on the basis of the stem-loop structure in the genome (121). In addition, miR-275 is indispensable for blood digestion and egg development in *Ae. aegypti* (31), as its depletion results in severe defects in blood digestion, fluid excretion, and egg development in females. Furthermore, miR-275 exhibited an expression profile that suggests it is regulated by the steroid hormone 20-hydroxyecdysone.

Within genomes, specific miRNA genes tend to be localized within small clusters that are generally transcribed as a single primary transcript and then processed to generate the individual precursors (102). Cluster patterns of miRNA genes in mosquitoes show some characteristic structural differences compared with those of *Drosophila* (14). For example, the *miR*-13 gene is clustered with *miR*-2 genes in mosquito genomes but not in *D. melanogaster*. The miR-306 is clustered with *miR*-9c/79 in *Drosophila* but not in mosquitoes. In addition, miRNAs located within introns show positional relocations among species (S.K. Behura & D.W. Severson, unpublished observations). Of all the intronic miRNAs identified in mosquitoes, only three *miR* genes do not show such variation. MicroRNAs *miR*-9b, *miR*-7, and *miR*-283 are all localized within the same orthologous protein-coding gene in each of the big three. *miR*-9b and *miR*-7 are particularly interesting as they are always located in the same gene in other insect species (14). Intronic miRNA genes are often cotranscribed along with their host genes (18). In *D. melanogaster*, miRNAs regulate a variety of developmental processes such as apoptosis, cell division, germline stem cell differentiation, oogenesis, and neural development (14).

Mitochondrial genomes and nuclear insertions. The observed complexity in mosquito genome structure is driven in part by the transfer of gene fragments from the mitochondrial genome to the nuclear genome. In addition, several parameters including mutation rate, intensity of intracellular competition, mtDNA leakage, and effective population size are responsible for the differential rates of mtDNA transfer among species (5, 110, 200). Determination of the complete sequences for the mtDNA genomes for *Ae. aegypti* and *Cx. quinquefasciatus* (16) and comparative analyses of mtDNA-like sequences inserted in the nuclear genomes (commonly known as NUMTs) (16, 26, 76) revealed that NUMT sequences occupy ~0.008% of the *Ae. aegypti* genome, whereas they are less abundant (~0.001%) in the *Cx. quinquefasciatus* genome. It is interesting to note that no NUMTs are detectable in the genome of *An. gambiae* (154).

Phylogenomics

Application of genomic data in inferring phylogenies of species is an emerging area of modern genomics studies and is regarded as a powerful approach for investigating phylogenetic relationships among species. In mosquito research, detailed large-scale phylogenomics studies have not been performed, although some attempts have been made in this direction. Historically, taxonomic groupings in mosquitoes have relied on comparisons of morphological and life-history differences (56). However, for example, the *Aedes* subgenus *Ochlerotatus* includes several taxonomic groups that are difficult to identify by classical morphology (72). With the advent of different molecular marker systems suitable for ecological and evolutionary studies, application of DNA markers has been extensively adopted in molecular systematic and phylogenetic analyses of mosquitoes (96, 126).

ESTs have proven useful as genomic resources for studying transcriptome profiling to understand functional genetics and genomics. ESTs are also reliable molecular marker systems for ecological genomic and phylogenomic studies of insects (13). More than 45 million ESTs from over 1,400 different species of eukaryotes are now available. EST resources provide a reliable avenue for incorporating results of EST sequence and cluster analyses into a phylogenetic framework for studying eukaryotic and animal evolution. A comprehensive study on eukaryote evolution (141) suggested that this approach is fairly reliable when large amounts of sequence information are available from a broad taxonomic range. In insects, several phylogenomic analyses have also been performed using EST sequence information (80, 178). In mosquitoes, although large numbers of ESTs have been generated from the genome-sequencing projects, use of these resources in large-scale phylogenomics studies has not been performed. Some attempts have been made to identify EST clusters in *Ae. aegypti* and *Armigeres subalbatus* using BLAST with other annotated genome sequences, including the *An. gambiae* and *D. melanogaster* genomes (10, 118). Although EST data sets have shown huge promise in phylogenetic analysis (138), these approaches have some shortcomings. More inconsistent results are found in EST-based phylogenies than in phylogenies based on morphological convergences; thus, they may not accurately reflect the actual speciation events and life histories of individual species (4).

A phylogenomic analysis of 185 nuclear genes of *An. gambiae* with orthologous genes of other sequenced major model insects suggested that bees and wasps represent the basal position in the phylogeny of homometabolous insects (158). Consistent phylogenetic groupings were also evident when the extent of observed sequence divergence among insect genomes, including *Ae. aegypti* and *An. gambiae*, was compared (206). In addition, utilization of multigene data sets has proven useful in many studies aimed at resolving deeper ancestral phylogenetic relationships (73, 74, 95, 164, 195). A combined data set of six nuclear protein-coding genes (*arginine kinase*, *CAD*, *catalase*, *enolase*, *hunchback*, and *white*) and an array of morphological characters ($n = 80$) were used (152) to better understand phylogenetic radiation among mosquitoes representing 25 genera. These analyses provided renewed evidence for a basal position and monophyly of Anophelinae as well as Aedini and Sabethini within Culicinae.

SYSTEMS BIOLOGY

Systems biology is an emerging interdisciplinary field that focuses on complex interactions in biological systems, particularly, on understanding how these interactions give rise to the function and behavior of a particular system or mechanism. Prediction of gene networks is a major focus in systems biology of genomes. Gene networks responsive to dengue virus infection have recently been studied in *Ae. aegypti* and humans (53). The study revealed more than 4,000 interactions between dengue virus and humans, but only 176 interactions between dengue virus and *Ae. aegypti*, and suggested that specific interactions involved with interferon signaling, transcriptional regulation, and stress are major components of the global gene network. Protein network analyses have also been performed on *Ae. aegypti* in response to dengue infection (70); the predicted network included 4,214 *Ae. aegypti* proteins with 10,209 interactions, of which 3,500 proteins were interconnected in a scale-free network.

Several studies have also been performed in mosquitoes to better understand the mechanistic steps associated with fundamental cellular processes, such as basic metabolic pathways and signaling pathways (187, 199). The glucose metabolism pathway was investigated in *Ae. aegypti* (187) and revealed that glucose metabolism changes along with developmental stages. The Toll signaling pathway was demonstrated as a major contributing pathway in *Ae. aegypti* to control dengue virus infection (199), including across diverse *Ae. aegypti* strains and against multiple dengue virus serotypes (150). In addition, the JAK-STAT immune signaling pathway also plays a role in anti-dengue defense in *Ae. aegypti* (173) and may act independently of the Toll pathway and the RNAi-mediated antiviral defenses. The pathways of *Ae. aegypti*, *An. gambiae*, and *Cx. quinquefasciatus* have been identified on the basis of gene-expression and protein-interaction data. The global biochemical and signaling pathways for these three species have also been predicted within the Kyoto Encyclopedia of Genes and Genomes database (**http://www.genome.jp/kegg/**), which identifies conserved orthologous mosquito genes, compares them with other reference organisms, and represents important resources for experimental studies in mosquitoes.

GAPS IN KNOWLEDGE

Despite significant progress in many areas, some research areas are obvious candidates for additional attention if we are to utilize fully the potential of the genome sequence. We highlight several examples here, although other areas undoubtedly fit this category as well. Given the impact of such studies in other organisms, it seems clear that the knowledge gained from detailed research in these areas can help bridge the gaps in our understanding of fundamental aspects of mosquito biology.

Genome Plasticity

Genome plasticity generally refers to the changes in the sequences, structures, or state (chemical modification) of the genomic DNA of a species. Identification of genome-wide SNPs and availability of many high-throughput genotyping technologies such as bead array (69), tag array (59), and MassCode (90) genotyping technologies have revolutionized the way genome-wide mutations can now be assessed within and among populations of a species. Application of these technologies to genome analyses in insects has begun only recently (13). Although sequence polymorphisms and SNPs are well-known forms of genome variation, here we focus on two less well-known, but important, aspects of genomic variation patterns: copy-number variation (CNV) and epigenetic variation of genes.

CNV: copy-number variation

Structural variation. Structural variation (SV) generally refers to DNA sequences ~1 kb and larger in size (62) with variation in the genome. SV includes deletions, duplications, and large-scale CNVs. CNVs often overlap with segmental duplications, regions of DNA >1 kb that are present more than once in the genome, copies of which are >90% identical (165). If present at >1% in a population, a CNV may be referred to as a copy-number polymorphism. Within SV analyses, most of the information, including the identification of copy-number polymorphisms (for a review, see 3) as well as genome-wide association of SVs with disease, comes mainly from investigations of human genomics. Rapidly accumulating evidence indicates that structural variants can comprise millions of nucleotides of heterogeneity within every genome, and they are likely to make an important contribution to human diversity and disease susceptibility. Array comparative genomic hybridization (aCGH) is a widely used approach to investigate the CNVs of genes (64, 71, 101, 109, 198). BAC libraries can also be used to detect CNVs. This is achieved by fabricating an array of BAC clones that are then hybridized with test and reference samples similar to an oligonucleotide aCGH method. The BAC-based method has been successful in identifying large numbers of CNVs from various studies (47, 81, 172). Another promising approach to identify SVs is the paired-end-mapping method (92), wherein a genomic library of known insert size is end sequenced. The paired-end sequences are then aligned to the reference genomic assembly to identify indels or inversions. New approaches and high-throughput technologies have been used to discover CNVs and other SVs, but they have not been applied to mosquitoes.

Epigenetics. Epigenetics broadly encompasses the study of heritable differences of gene activities, in terms of expression and regulation, where there is no change in the DNA sequence. These changes are stably maintained in time and space. Genes subject to epigenetic control may become reprogrammed at precise points during development or in response to environmental factors (132, 147, 156). Two major routes to achieve epigenetic regulation of genes are (*a*) methylation of cytosine residues at specific DNA positions (21, 24) and (*b*) chemical modification of histones that can cause structural changes in chromatin (93). The mechanisms of DNA methylating enzymes and stable replication of methylated DNAs are well studied (68, 135). Different chemical modification mechanisms (acetylation, methylation, sumoylation, and ubiquitylation) of histones are also known (93). Noncoding RNAs have also been reported to contribute to epigenetic machinery by interacting with DNA or RNA, by functioning as a specific chromatin modifier (117, 205), or by transcriptional inactivation of large genomic regions (37, 201). In *Drosophila*, the Polycomb system has also been known to play a role in regulating epigenetic programming (111), and the Polycomb binding regions as well as the highly conserved noncoding elements show striking syntenic correspondence between *Drosophila* and mosquitoes (57). Whether mosquitoes might have retained ancestral epigenetic regulators is not known. Another conserved component of *Drosophila* epigenetic machinery in mosquitoes is the *Dnmt2* gene (a DNA methylation enzyme), which suggests that Dnmt2-mediated DNA methylation may be conserved in dipteran insects (114).

Population Genomics and Genome-Wide Association Studies

Advances in NGS and the availability of large-scale "SNP-chips" provide opportunities to perform fine-scale whole-genome scans at the population level. Already possible is large-scale SNP identification in individual insects: Researchers can efficiently obtain partial, full-genome sequences to conduct population studies or genome-wide association studies (9), and technological advancements are likely to facilitate such efforts further. We expect that considerable research effort on mosquitoes will be performed in the near term; some recent studies clearly demonstrate this potential.

The *An. gambiae* M- and S-form genomes, which already provide insight on incipient speciation, can now serve as reference scaffolds for the application of NGS technologies to efficiently perform detailed investigations of genomic divergence at the population level. Likewise, high-density custom microarrays targeting genome-wide SNPs can be employed for population-level studies. Indeed, investigations on ~400,000 SNPs identified in the M- and S-form genomes using custom arrays confirmed high levels of differentiation in pericentromeric regions as well as multiple smaller regions across the genomes of individual and pooled field-collected mosquitoes representing the two forms. These investigations also confirmed the Bamako form and the sibling species *Anopheles arabiensis* (127). Gene ontologies among some regions showing evidence for recent selective sweeps indicated functional enrichment for genes associated with multicellular organismal development and serine-type endopeptidase activity. Also provided was evidence of the enrichment for genes that likely impact several phenotypes of interest.

The potential power as well as challenges of genome-wide association studies for mosquitoes was shown in a study of insecticide resistance in *An. gambiae* collected in Ghana and Cameroon (193). Using a 1,536-SNP array enriched for candidate insecticide-resistance gene SNPs to genotype ~1,500 field-collected mosquitoes, investigators determined that, although evidence for linkage disequilibrium was relatively low across most of the genome, some local high levels of linkage disequilibrium likely reflect a recent selective sweep.

Expression Quantitative Trait Loci Analysis

Expression quantitative trait loci (eQTL) mapping identifies the genetic basis of gene-expression variation for a given phenotype in a genome-wide manner (78, 105). The genotype associated with the observed gene-expression level is identified by statistical correlation of the polymorphism patterns within a gene's coding region or within predicted regulatory sequences localized outside the coding sequence (29, 125, 140). Advancements in high-throughput genotyping and gene-expression platforms have resulted in eQTL analysis of many organisms (32, 66, 83, 174, 204). To date, no eQTL study has been performed in a mosquito species.

Noncoding RNAs

Although several categories of noncoding RNA genes have been annotated from the genome sequences of the big three mosquitoes (**http://www.vectorbase.org/**), the functional roles of these RNAs are not properly understood in any mosquito species. In this section, we describe important classes of noncoding RNAs on which further research is likely to be emphasized in the coming years.

Small nuclear RNAs. The snRNAs are a class of small RNA molecules that are transcribed by RNA polymerase II or RNA polymerase III and function mostly within the nucleus of eukaryotic cells. They bind with specific proteins to form small nuclear ribonucleoproteins (snRNPs) that are involved in a variety of molecular processes such as RNA splicing, regulation of transcription factors, and telomere maintenance. Small nucleolar RNAs (snoRNAs) compose a large group of snRNAs that play an essential role in RNA biogenesis and guide chemical modifications of rRNAs, tRNAs, and other snRNAs (48). Several snRNAs/snoRNAs have been identified from the genome annotation of the big three, including 66 snRNAs and 9 snoRNA in *Ae. aegypti*, 44 snRNAs and 4 snoRNAs in *Cx. quinquefasciatus*, and 28 snRNA and 6 snoRNAs in *An. gambiae* (**http://www.vectorbase.org/**). However, their functions have not been determined.

PIWI-interacting RNA. Another class of small RNA molecules that bind with PIWI proteins is composed of so-called PIWI-interacting RNAs (piRNAs). Primarily during spermatogenesis, the bound complexes act in transcriptional gene silencing of retrotransposons and other genetic elements in germline cells (159). The genes encoding piRNAs are generally found in large clusters in genomes and can vary in size from 1 to 100 kb. The majority of piRNAs are antisense to transposon sequences. Research on *Drosophila* oogenesis has provided critical insights into piRNA biogenesis and transposon silencing (88). PIWI proteins are critical during germline development and gametogenesis in many metazoan species, including germline determination as well as germline stem-cell maintenance, meiosis, spermiogenesis, and transposon silencing (179). In mosquitoes, the Argonaute/PIWI subfamily genes show contrasting patterns of evolution among species (33). *Ae. aegypti* and *Cx. quinquefasciatus* show significant expansion of the Argonaute/PIWI subfamily genes, and these genes are evolving faster than those of *An. gambiae* and *D. melanogaster*.

Long noncoding RNA. In addition to the different classes of small noncoding RNAs described above, long noncoding RNAs (lncRNAs) have also been of significant research interest in functional genomics. Generally, lncRNAs are longer than 200 nucleotides. The genome-wide identification and characterization of abundance and structural patterns of lncRNAs have been mostly limited to the human genome or model mammalian genomes including mouse and rat genomes (25, 35, 86). The lncRNAs have regulatory functions in a wide range of molecular processes, including regulation of gene transcription (67), splicing (19), translational repression (188), epigenetic regulation of genes (89, 122), and chromosome imprinting and inactivation (28, 61, 134). Few lncRNAs have been identified from the genome assemblies of *Ae. aegypti* ($n = 4$), *An. gambiae* ($n = 4$), and *Cx. quinquefasciatus* ($n = 7$) (**http://www.vectorbase.org/**). However, they have not been characterized for function.

Role of transposable elements in genome diversity. TEs are ubiquitous elements of eukaryote genomes (136). In mosquitoes, a large number of different families of TEs, both DNA-mediated and RNA-mediated, have been identified in the genomes of the big three and are available for specific searches or download at TEfam (**http://tefam.biochem.vt.edu/tefam/**). The majority of studies on TEs in mosquitoes have been directed toward identification, classification, and sequence diversity, with very little progress made in understanding the possible functional roles of TEs (182). Numerous studies in other organisms have identified a variety of ways in which TEs have been implicated in several crucial functions in the host genome, including gene silencing by methylation (203), chromosome imprinting (120), and epigenetic regulation (108). Other studies have associated the activity of TEs with the regulatory function of noncoding RNAs such as siRNAs, miRNAs, and rasiRNAs (30, 142, 143, 170, 171, 185).

SUMMARY POINTS

1. Generation of draft genome sequences for the three major mosquito vectors and analyses to date of these clearly demonstrate their utility for understanding mosquito biology and represent a glimpse of what the future holds for basic and translational research.
2. The literature reflects a strong impact of genome-sequence availability not only on mosquito research, but also on comparative genomic and evolutionary studies across diverse phyla.
3. Anticipated advances in sequencing technology are expected to promote a proliferation of genome-sequencing efforts for many additional mosquito species as well as for single individuals.
4. Challenges remain to understand fully the information uncovered with each new mosquito genome.

DISCLOSURE STATEMENT

The authors are not aware of any affiliations, memberships, funding, or financial holdings that might be perceived as affecting the objectivity of this review.

ACKNOWLEDGMENTS

We dedicate this review to the memory of our colleague and friend Dr. Dennis L. Knudson. Our efforts in preparing this review were funded in part by grants RO1-AI059342, RO1-AI079125-A1, RO1-AI081795, R21-AI088335, and R21-AI088035 from the National Institute for Allergy and Infectious Diseases, National Institutes of Health.

LITERATURE CITED

1. Adams MD, Celniker SE, Holt RA, Evans CA, Gocayne JD, et al. 2000. The genome sequence of *Drosophila melanogaster*. *Science* 287:2185–95
2. Alkan C, Sajjadian S, Eichler EE. 2011. Limitations of next-generation genome sequence assembly. *Nat. Methods* 8:61–65
3. Alkan C, Coe BP, Eichler EE. 2011. Genome structural variation discovery and genotyping. *Nat. Rev. Genet.* 12:363–76
4. Andrew DR. 2011. A new view of insect-crustacean relationships II. Inferences from expressed sequence tags and comparisons with neural cladistics. *Arthropod Struct. Dev.* 40:289–302
5. Arctander P. 1995. Comparison of a mitochondrial gene and a corresponding nuclear pseudogene. *Proc. R. Soc. Lond. Ser. B* 262:13–29
6. **Arensburger P, Megy K, Waterhouse RM, Abrudan J, Amedeo P, et al. 2010. Sequencing of *Culex quinquefaciatus* establishes a platform for mosquito comparative genomics. *Science* 330:86–88**
7. Argentine JA, James AA. 1993. Codon preference of *Aedes aegypti* and *Aedes albopictus*. *Insect Mol. Biol.* 1:189–94
8. Awolola TS, Oduola OA, Stode C, Koekemoer KK, Brooke B, et al. 2009. Evidence of multiple pyrethroid resistance mechanisms in the malaria vector *Anopheles gambiae* sensu stricto from Nigeria. *Trans. R. Soc. Trop. Med. Hyg.* 103:1139–45
9. Baird NA, Etter PD, Atwood TS, Currey MC, Shiver AL, et al. 2008. Rapid SNP discovery and genetic mapping using sequenced RAD markers. *PLoS ONE* 3:e3376

6. Describes the genome sequence of *Cx. quinquefasciatus* and compares it with *Ae. aegypti* and *An. gambiae*.

10. Bartholomay LC, Cho WL, Rocheleau TA, Boyle JP, Beck ET, et al. 2004. Description of the transcriptomes of immune response-activated hemocytes from the mosquito vectors *Aedes aegypti* and *Armigeres subalbatus*. *Infect. Immun.* 72:4114–26
11. Bartholomay LC, Waterhouse RM, Mayhew GF, Campbell CL, Michel K, et al. 2010. Pathogenomics of *Culex quinquefasciatus* and meta-analysis of infection responses to diverse pathogens. *Science* 330:88–90
12. Bayyareddy K, Andacht TM, Abdullah MA, Adang MJ. 2009. Proteomic identification of *Bacillus thuringiensis* subsp. *israelensis* toxin Cry4Ba binding proteins in midgut membranes from *Aedes* (*Stegomyia*) *aegypti* Linnaeus (Diptera, Culicidae) larvae. *Insect Biochem. Mol. Biol.* 39:279–86
13. Behura SK. 2006. Molecular marker systems in insects: current trends and future avenues. *Mol. Ecol.* 15:3087–113
14. Behura SK. 2007. Insect microRNAs: structure, function and evolution. *Insect Biochem. Mol. Biol.* 37:3–9
15. Behura SK, Haugen M, Flannery E, Sarro J, Tessier CR, et al. 2011. Comparative genomic analysis of *Drosophila melanogaster* and vector mosquito developmental genes. *PLoS ONE* 6:e21504
16. Behura SK, Lobo NF, Haas B, deBruyn D, Lovin DD, et al. 2011. Complete sequences of mitochondria genomes of *Aedes aegypti* and *Culex quinquefasciatus* and comparative analysis of mitochondrial DNA fragments inserted in the nuclear genomes. *Insect Biochem. Mol. Biol.* 41:770–77
17. Behura SK, Severson DW. 2011. Coadaptation of isoacceptor tRNA genes and codon usage bias for translation efficiency in *Aedes aegypti* and *Anopheles gambiae*. *Insect Mol. Biol.* 20:177–87
18. Behura SK, Whitfield CW. 2010. Correlated expression patterns of microRNA genes with age-dependent behavioural changes in honeybee. *Insect Mol. Biol.* 19:431–39
19. Beltran M, Puig I, Peña C, García JM, Alvarez AB, et al. 2008. A natural antisense transcript regulates Zeb2/Sip1 gene expression during Snail1-induced epithelial-mesenchymal transition. *Genes Dev.* 22:756–69
20. Besansky NJ. 1993. Codon usage patterns in chromosomal and retrotransposon genes of the mosquito *Anopheles gambiae*. *Insect Mol. Biol.* 1:171–78
21. Bestor TH. 2000. The DNA methyltransferases of mammals. *Hum. Mol. Genet.* 9:2395–402
22. Beyenbach KW, Baumgart S, Lau K, Piermarini PM, Zhang S, et al. 2009. Signaling to the apical membrane and to the paracellular pathway: changes in the cytosolic proteome of *Aedes* Malpighian tubules. *J. Exp. Biol.* 212:329–40
23. Bingham G, Strode C, Tran L, Khoa PT, Jamet HP. 2011. Can piperonyl butoxide enhance the efficacy of pyrethroids against pyrethroid-resistant *Aedes aegypti*? *Trop. Med. Int. Health* 16:492–500
24. Bird A. 2002. DNA methylation patterns and epigenetic memory. *Genes Dev.* 16:6–21
25. Birney E, Stamatoyannopoulos JA, Dutta A, Guigó R, Gingeras TR, et al. 2007. Identification and analysis of functional elements in 1% of the human genome by the ENCODE pilot project. *Nature* 447:799–816
26. Black IV WC, Bernhardt SA. 2009. Abundant nuclear copies of mitochondrial origin (NUMTs) in the *Aedes aegypti* genome. *Insect Mol. Biol.* 18:705–13
27. Bonizzoni M, Augstine Dunn W, Campbell CL, Olson KE, Dimon MT, et al. 2011. RNA-seq analyses of blood-induced changes in gene expression in the mosquito vector species, *Aedes aegypti*. *BMC Genomics* 12:82
28. Braidotti G, Baubec T, Pauler F, Seidl C, Smrzka O, et al. 2004. The Air noncoding RNA: an imprinted *cis*-silencing transcript. *Cold Spring Harb. Symp. Quant. Biol.* 69:55–66
29. Brem RB, Kruglyak L. 2005. The landscape of genetic complexity across 5,700 gene expression traits in yeast. *Proc. Natl. Acad. Sci. USA* 102:1572–77
30. Brennecke J, Aravin AA, Stark A, Dus M, Kellis M, et al. 2007. Discrete small RNA-generating loci as master regulators of transposon activity in *Drosophila*. *Cell* 128:1089–103
31. **Bryant B, Macdonald W, Raikhel AS. 2010. microRNA miR-275 is indispensable for blood digestion and egg development in the mosquito *Aedes aegypti*. *Proc. Natl. Acad. Sci. USA* 107:22391–98**
32. Bystrykh L, Weersing E, Dontje B, Sutton S, Pletcher MT, et al. 2005. Uncovering regulatory pathways that affect hematopoietic stem cell function using "genetical genomics." *Nat. Genet.* 37:225–32
33. Campbell CL, Black WC IV, Hess AM, Foy BD. 2008. Comparative genomics of small RNA regulatory pathway components in vector mosquitoes. *BMC Genomics* 9:425

31. Details the importance of microRNA gene activity in controlling physiological events following a blood meal in mosquitoes.

34. Caragata EP, Poinsignon A, Moreira LA, Johnson PH, Leong YS, et al. 2011. Improved accuracy of the transcriptional profiling method of age grading in *Aedes aegypti* mosquitoes under laboratory and semi-field cage conditions and in the presence of *Wolbachia* infection. *Insect Mol. Biol.* 20:215–24
35. Carninci P, Kasukawa T, Katayama S, Gough J, Frith MC, et al. 2005. The transcriptional landscape of the mammalian genome. *Science* 309:1559–63
36. **Choumet V, Carmi-Leroy A, Laurent C, Lenormand P, Rousselle J-C, et al. 2007. The salivary glands and saliva of *Anopheles gambiae* as an essential step in the *Plasmodium* life cycle: a global proteomic study. *Proteomics* 7:3384–94**

36. Characterizes the salivary gland transcriptome in *An. gambiae*.

37. Clark SJ. 2007. Action at a distance: epigenetic silencing of large chromosomal regions in carcinogenesis. *Hum. Mol. Genet.* 16:R88–95
38. Cohuet A, Krishnakumar S, Simard F, Morlais I, Koutsos A, et al. 2008. SNP discovery and molecular evolution in *Anopheles gambiae*, with special emphasis on innate immune system. *BMC Genomics* 9:227
39. Costantini C, Ayala D, Guelbeogo WM, Pombi M, Some CY, et al. 2009. Living on the edge: biogeographic patterns of habitat segregation conform to speciation by niche expansion in *Anopheles gambiae*. *BMC Ecol.* 9:16
40. Crawford JE, Guelbeogo WM, Sanou A, Traoré A, Vernick KD, et al. 2010. De novo transcriptome sequencing in *Anopheles funestus* using Illumina RNA-Seq technology. *PLoS ONE* 5:e14202
41. Dalloul RA, Long JA, Zimin AV, Aslam L, Beal K, et al. 2010. Multi-platform next-generation sequencing of the domestic turkey (*Meleagris gallopavo*): genome assembly and analysis. *PLoS Biol.* 8:e1000475
42. Dani FR, Francese S, Mastrobuoni G, Felicioli A, Caputo B, et al. 2008. Exploring proteins in *Anopheles gambiae* male and female antennae through MALDI mass spectrometry profiling. *PLoS ONE* 3:e2822
43. Das S, Radtke A, Choi Y-J, Mendes AM, Valenzuela JG, et al. 2010. Transcriptomic and functional analysis of the *Anopheles gambiae* salivary gland in relation to blood feeding. *BMC Genomics* 11:566
44. David J-P, Coissac E, Melodelima C, Poupardin R, Asam Riaz M, et al. 2010. Transcriptome response to pollutants and insecticides in the dengue vector *Aedes aegypti* using next-generation sequencing technology. *BMC Genomics* 11:216
45. della Torre A, Tu Z, Petrarca V. 2005. On the distribution and genetic differentiation of *Anopheles gambiae* s.s. molecular forms. *Insect Biochem. Mol. Biol.* 35:755–69
46. Dialynas E, Topalis P, Vontas J, Louis C. 2009. MIRO and IRbase: IT tools for the epidemiological monitoring of insecticide resistance in mosquito disease vectors. *PLoS Negl. Trop. Dis.* 3:e465
47. Díaz de Ståhl T, Sandgren J, Piotrowski A, Nord H, Andersson R, et al. 2008. Profiling of copy number variations (CNVs) in healthy individuals from three ethnic groups using a human genome 32 K BAC-clone-based array. *Hum. Mutat.* 29:398–408
48. Dieci G, Preti M, Montanini B. 2009. Eukaryotic snoRNAs: a paradigm for gene expression flexibility. *Genomics* 94:83–88
49. Dinglasan RR, Jacobs-Lorena M. 2008. Flipping the paradigm on malaria transmission-blocking vaccines. *Trends Parasitol.* 24:364–70
50. Dinglasan RR, Devenport M, Florens L, Johnson JR, McHugh CA, et al. 2009. The *Anopheles gambiae* adult midgut peritrophic matrix proteome. *Insect Biochem. Mol. Biol.* 39:125–34
51. Djouaka RF, Bakare AA, Coulibaly ON, Akogbeto MC, Ranson H, et al. 2008. Expression of the cytochrome P450s, *CYP6P3* and *CYP6M2*, are significantly elevated in multiple pyrethroid-resistant populations of *Anopheles gambiae* s.s. from southern Benin and Nigeria. *BMC Genomics* 9:538
52. Dong Y, Aguilar R, Xi Z, Warr E, Mongin E, et al. 2006. *Anopheles gambiae* immune responses to human and rodent *Plasmodium* parasite species. *PLoS Pathol.* 2:e52
53. Doolittle JM, Gomez SM. 2011. Mapping protein interactions between dengue virus and its human and insect hosts. *PLoS Negl. Trop. Dis.* 5:e954
54. Drake LL, Boudko DY, Marinotti O, Carpenter VK, Dawe AL, et al. 2011. The aquaporin gene family of the yellow fever mosquito, *Aedes aegypti*. *PLoS ONE* 5:e15578
55. Edillo FE, Toure YT, Lanzaro GC, Dolo G, Taylor CE. 2002. Spatial and habitat distribution of *Anopheles gambiae* and *Anopheles arabiensis* (Diptera: Culicidae) in Banambani village, Mali. *J. Med. Entomol.* 39:70–77
56. Edwards JW. 1932. *Genera Insectorum Diptera, Fam. Culicidae. Fascile 194.* Brussels, Belgium: Desmet-Verteneuil

57. Engström PG, Ho Sui SJ, Drivenes O, Becker TS, Lenhard B. 2007. Genomic regulatory blocks underlie extensive microsynteny conservation in insects. *Genome Res.* 17:1898–908
58. Erickson SM, Xi Z, Mayhew GF, Ramirez JL, Aliota MT, et al. 2009. Mosquito infection responses to developing filarial worms. *PLoS Negl. Trop. Dis.* 3:e529
59. Fan JB, Chen X, Halushka MK, Berno A, Huang X. 2000. Parallel genotyping of human SNPs using generic high-density oligonucleotide tag arrays. *Genome Res.* 10:853–60
60. Félix RC, Muller P, Ribeiro V, Ranson H, Silveira H. 2010. *Plasmodium* infection alters *Anopheles gambiae* detoxification gene expression. *BMC Genomics* 11:312
61. Fournier C, Goto Y, Ballestar E, Delaval K, Hever AM, et al. 2002. Allele-specific histone lysine methylation marks regulatory regions at imprinted mouse genes. *EMBO J.* 21:6560–70
62. Freeman JL, Perry GH, Feuk L, Redon R, McCarroll SA, et al. 2006. Copy number variation: new insights in genome diversity. *Genome Res.* 16:949–61
63. Gibbons JG, Janson EM, Hittinger CT, Johnston M, Abbot P, et al. 2009. Benchmarking next-generation transcriptome sequencing for functional and evolutionary genomics. *Mol. Biol. Evol.* 26:2731–44
64. Goidts V, Armengol L, Schempp W, Conroy J, Nowak N, et al. 2006. Identification of large-scale human-specific copy number differences by inter-species array comparative genomic hybridization. *Hum. Genet.* 119:185–98
65. Goltsev Y, Rezende GL, Vranizan K, Lanzaro G, Valle D, et al. 2009. Developmental and evolutionary basis for drought tolerance of the *Anopheles gambiae* embryo. *Dev. Biol.* 330:462–70
66. Gonzales JM, Patel JJ, Ponmee N, Jiang L, Tan A, et al. 2008. Regulatory hot spots in the malaria parasite genome dictate transcriptional variation. *PLoS Biol.* 6:e238
67. Goodrich JA, Kugel JF. 2006. Non-coding-RNA regulators of RNA polymerase II transcription. *Nat. Rev. Mol. Cell Biol.* 7:612–16
68. Groth A, Rocha W, Verreault A, Almouzni G. 2007. Chromatin challenges during DNA replication and repair. *Cell* 128:721–33
69. Gunderson KL, Steemers FJ, Lee G, Mendoza LG, Chee MS. 2005. A genome-wide scalable SNP genotyping assay using microarray technology. *Nat. Genet.* 37:549–54
70. **Guo X, Xu Y, Bian G, Pike AD, Xie Y, et al. 2010. Response of the mosquito protein interaction network to dengue infection. *BMC Genomics* 11:380**

70. Uses a systems-biology approach to construct signaling and regulatory networks for a mosquito response to dengue-virus infection.

71. Guryev V, Saar K, Adamovic T, Verheul M, van Heesch SA, et al. 2008. Distribution and functional impact of DNA copy number variation in the rat. *Nat. Genet.* 40:538–45
72. Harbach RE, Kitching IJ. 1998. Phylogeny and classification of the Culicidae (Diptera). *Syst. Entomol.* 23:327–70
73. Higdon JW, Bininda-Emonds OR, Beck RM, Ferguson SH. 2008. Phylogeny and divergence of the pinnipeds (Carnivora: Mammalia) assessed using a multigene dataset. *BMC Evol. Biol.* 7:216
74. Hines HM, Hunt JH, O'Connor TK, Gillespie JJ, Cameron SA. 2007. Multigene phylogeny reveals eusociality evolved twice in vespid wasps. *Proc. Natl. Acad. Sci. USA* 104:3295–99
75. Hittinger CT, Johnston M, Tossberg JT, Rokas A. 2010. Leveraging skewed transcript abundance by RNA-Seq to increase the genomic depth of the tree of life. *Proc. Natl. Acad. Sci. USA* 107:1476–81
76. Hlaing T, Tun-Lin W, Somboon P, Socheat D, Setha T, et al. 2009. Mitochondrial pseudogenes in the nuclear genome of *Aedes aegypti* mosquitoes: implications for past and future population genetic studies. *BMC Genet.* 10:11
77. **Holt RA, Subramanian GM, Halpern A, Sutton GG, Charlab R, et al. 2002. The genome sequence of the malaria mosquito *Anopheles gambiae*. *Science* 298:129–49**

77. Describes the genome sequence of *An. gambiae*.

78. Houle D, Govindaraju DR, Omholt S. 2010. Phenomics: the next challenge. *Nat. Rev. Genet.* 11:855–66
79. Huang S, Li R, Zhang Z, Li L, Gu X, et al. 2009. The genome of the cucumber, *Cucumis sativus* L. *Nat. Genet.* 41:1275–83
80. Hughes J, Longhorn SJ, Papadopoulou A, Theodorides K, de Riva A, et al. 2006. Dense taxonomic EST sampling and its applications for molecular systematics of the Coleoptera (beetles). *Mol. Biol. Evol.* 23:268–78
81. Iafrate AJ, Feuk L, Rivera MN, Listewnik ML, Donahoe PK, 2004. Detection of large-scale variation in the human genome. *Nat. Genet.* 36:949–51

82. International Human Genome Sequencing Consortium. 2001. Initial sequencing and analysis of the human genome. *Nature* 409:860–921
83. Jansen RC, Nap JP. 2001. Genetical genomics: the added value from segregation. *Trends Genet.* 17:388–91
84. Kalume DE, Okulate M, Zhong J, Reddy R, Suresh S, et al. 2005. A proteomic analysis of salivary glands of female *Anopheles gambiae* mosquito. *Proteomics* 5:3765–77
85. Kalume DE, Peri S, Reddy R, Zhong J, Okulate M, et al. 2005. Genome annotation of *Anopheles gambiae* using mass spectrometry–derived data. *BMC Genomics* 6:128
86. Kapranov P, Cheng J, Dike S, Nix DA, Duttagupta R, et al. 2007. RNA maps reveal new RNA classes and a possible function for pervasive transcription. *Science* 316:1484–88
87. Kaufman TC, Severson DW, Robinson GE. 2002. The *Anopheles* genome and comparative insect genomics. *Science* 298:97–98
88. Khurana JS, Theurkauf W. 2010. piRNAs, transposon silencing, and *Drosophila* germline development. *J. Cell Biol.* 191:905–13
89. Kiefer JC. 2007. Epigenetics in development. *Dev. Dyn.* 236:1144–56
90. Kokoris M, Dix K, Moynihan K, Mathis J, Erwin B, et al. 2000. High-throughput SNP genotyping with the Masscode system. *Mol. Diagn.* 5:329–40
91. Komagata O, Kasai S, Tomita T. 2010. Overexpression of cytochrome P450 genes in pyrethroid-resistant *Culex quinquefasciatus*. *Insect Biochem. Mol. Biol.* 40:146–52
92. Korbel JO, Urban AE, Affourtit JP, Godwin B, Grubert F, et al. 2007. Paired-end mapping reveals extensive structural variation in the human genome. *Science* 318:420–26
93. Kouzarides T. 2007. Chromatin modifications and their function. *Cell* 128:693–705
94. Kumar A, Rai KS. 1990. Intraspecific variation in nuclear DNA content among world populations of a mosquito, *Aedes albopictus* (Skuse). *Theor. Appl. Genet.* 79:748–52
95. Kumar A, Rai KS. 1993. Molecular organization and evolution of mosquito genomes. *Comp. Biochem. Physiol. B* 106:495–504
96. Krzywinski J, Wilkerson RC, Besansky NJ. 2001. Evolution of mitochondrial and ribosomal gene sequences in anophelinae (Diptera: Culicidae): implications for phylogeny reconstruction. *Mol. Phylogenet. Evol.* 18:479–87
97. Lawniczak MKN, Emrich SJ, Holloway AK, Regier AP, Olson M, et al. 2010. Widespread divergence between incipient *Anopheles gambiae* species revealed by whole genome sequences. *Science* 330:512–15
98. Lawson D, Arensburger P, Atkinson P, Besansky NJ, Bruggner RV, et al. 2007. VectorBase: a home for invertebrate vectors of human pathogens. *Nucleic Acids Res.* 35:D503–5
99. Lawson D, Arensburger P, Atkinson P, Besansky NJ, Bruggner RV, et al. 2009. VectorBase: a data resource for invertebrate vector genomics. *Nucleic Acids Res.* 37:D583–87
100. Lavazec C, Bourgouin C. 2008. Mosquito-based transmission blocking vaccines for interrupting *Plasmodium* development. *Microbes Infect.* 10:845–49
101. Lee AS, Gutiérrez-Arcelus M, Perry GH, Vallender EJ, Johnson WE, et al. 2008. Analysis of copy number variation in the rhesus macaque genome identifies candidate loci for evolutionary and human disease studies. *Hum. Mol. Genet.* 17:1127–36
102. Lee Y, Jeon K, Lee JT, Kim S, Kim VN. 2002. MicroRNA maturation: stepwise processing and subcellular localization. *EMBO J.* 21:4663–70
103. Lefevre T, Thomas F, Schwartz A, Levashina E, Blandin S, et al. 2007. Malaria *Plasmodium* agent induces alteration in the head proteome of their *Anopheles* mosquito host. *Proteomics* 7:1908–15
104. Lehmann T, Diabaté A. 2008. The molecular forms of *Anopheles gambiae*: a phenotypic perspective. *Infect. Genet. Evol.* 8:337–40
105. Li J, Burmeister M. 2005. Genetical genomics: combining genetics with gene expression analysis. *Hum. Mol. Genet.* 14:R163–69
106. Li R, Fan W, Tian G, Zhu H, He L, et al. 2010. The sequence and de novo assembly of the giant panda genome. *Nature* 463:311–17
107. Li S, Mead EA, Liang S, Tu Z. 2009. Direct sequencing and expression analysis of a large number of miRNAs in *Aedes aegypti* and a multi-species survey of novel mosquito miRNAs. *BMC Genomics* 10:581

108. Lippman Z, Gendrel AV, Black M, Vaughn MW, Dedhia N, et al. 2004. Role of transposable elements in heterochromatin and epigenetic control. *Nature* 430:471–76
109. Locke DP, Segraves R, Carbone L, Archidiacono N, Albertson DG, et al. 2003. Large-scale variation among human and great ape genomes determined by array comparative genomic hybridization. *Genome Res.* 13:347–57
110. Lopez JV, Yuhki N, Masuda R, Modi W, O'Brien SJ. 1994. Numt, a recent transfer and tandem amplification of mitochondrial DNA to the nuclear genome of the domestic cat. *J. Mol. Evol.* 39:174–90
111. Lyko F, Beisel C, Marhold J, Paro R. 2006. Epigenetic regulation in *Drosophila*. *Curr. Top. Microbiol. Immunol.* 310:23–44
112. Mallick P, Kuster B. 2010. Proteomics: a pragmatic perspective. *Nat. Biotechnol.* 28:695–708
113. Marcombe S, Poupardin R, Darriet F, Reynaud S, Bonnet J, et al. 2009. Exploring the molecular basis of insecticide resistance in the dengue vector *Aedes aegypti*: a case study in Martinique Island (French West Indies). *BMC Genomics* 10:494
114. Marhold J, Rothe N, Pauli A, Mund C, Kuehle K, et al. 2004. Conservation of DNA methylation in dipteran insects. *Insect Mol. Biol.* 13:117–23
115. Marioni JC, Mason CE, Mane SM, Stephens M, Gilad Y. 2008. RNA-Seq: an assessment of technical reproducibility and comparison with gene expression arrays. *Genome Res.* 18:1509–17
116. Matthews TC, Munstermann LE. 1994. Chromosomal repatterning and linkage group conservation in mosquito karyotypic evolution. *Evolution* 48:146–54
117. Mattick JS, Amaral PP, Dinger ME, Mercer TR, Mehler MF. 2009. RNA regulation of epigenetic processes. *Bioessays* 31:51–59
118. Mayhew GF, Bartholomay LC, Kou HY, Rocheleau TA, Fuchs JF, et al. 2007. Construction and characterization of an expressed sequenced tag library for the mosquito vector *Armigeres subalbatus*. *BMC Genomics* 8:462
119. McDonald JF, Matzke MA, Matzke AJ. 2005. Host defenses to transposable elements and the evolution of genomic imprinting. *Cytogenet. Genome Res.* 110:242–49
120. Mehren JE. 2007. Mate recognition: Should fly stay or should fly go? *Curr. Biol.* 17:R240
121. Mendes ND, Freitas AT, Vasconcelos AT, Sagot MF. 2010. Combination of measures distinguishes pre-miRNAs from other stem-loops in the genome of the newly sequenced *Anopheles darlingi*. *BMC Genomics* 11:529
122. Mikkelsen TS, Ku M, Jaffe DB, Issac B, Lieberman E, et al. 2007. Genome-wide maps of chromatin state in pluripotent and lineage-committed cells. *Nature* 448:553–60
123. Morlais I, Severson DW. 2003. Intraspecific DNA variation in nuclear genes of the mosquito *Aedes aegypti*. *Insect Mol. Biol.* 12:631–39
124. Mongin E, Louis C, Holt RA, Birney E, Collins FH. 2004. The *Anopheles gambiae* genome: an update. *Trends Parasitol.* 20:49–52
125. Monks SA, Leonardson A, Zhu H, Cundiff P, Pietrusiak P, et al. 2004. Genetic inheritance of gene expression in human cell lines. *Am. J. Hum. Genet.* 75:1094–105
126. Munstermann LE, Conn JE. 1997. Systematics of mosquito disease vectors (Diptera, Culicidae): impact of molecular biology and cladistic analysis. *Annu. Rev. Entomol.* 42:351–69
127. Neafsey DE, Lawniczak MKN, Park DJ, Redmond SN, Coulibaly MB, et al. 2010. SNP genotyping defines complex gene-flow boundaries among African malaria vector mosquitoes. *Science* 330:514–17

127. Uses high-density, genome-wide SNP mapping to characterize population divergence among *An. gambiae* ecotypes.

128. Neira Oviedo M, VanEkeris, Corena-Mcleod MDP, Linser PJ. 2008. A microarray-based analysis of transcriptional compartmentalization in the alimentary canal of *Anopheles gambiae* (Diptera: Culicidae) larvae. *Insect Mol. Biol.* 17:61–72
129. Neira Oviedo M, Ribeiro JMC, Heyland A, VanEkeris L, Moroz T, et al. 2009. The salivary transcriptome of *Anopheles gambiae* (Diptera: Culicidae) larvae: a microarray-based analysis. *Insect Biochem. Mol. Biol.* 39:382–94
130. Neira-Oviedo M, Tsyganov-Bodounov A, Lycett GJ, Kokoza V, Raikhel AS, et al. 2011. The RNA-Seq approach to studying the expression of mosquito mitochondrial genes. *Insect Mol. Biol.* 20:141–52
131. Nene V, Wortman JR, Lawson D, Haas B, Kodira C, et al. 2007. Genome sequence of *Aedes aegypti*, a major arbovirus vector. *Science* 316:1718–23

131. Describes the genome sequence for *Ae. aegypti*.

132. Ng RK, Gurdon JB. 2008. Epigenetic inheritance of cell differentiation status. *Cell Cycle* 7:1173–77
133. Noriega FG, Ribeiro JM, Koener JF, Valenzuela JG, Hernandez-Martinez S, et al. 2006. Comparative genomics of insect juvenile hormone biosynthesis. *Insect Biochem. Mol. Biol.* 36:366–74
134. Ogawa Y, Sun BK, Lee JT. 2008. Intersection of the RNA interference and X-inactivation pathways. *Science* 320:1336–41
135. Okano M, Bell DW, Haber DA, Li E. 1999. DNA methyltransferases Dnmt3a and Dnmt3b are essential for de novo methylation and mammalian development. *Cell* 99:247–57
136. Orgel LE, Crick FH. 1980. Selfish DNA: the ultimate parasite. *Nature* 284:604–7
137. Osta A, Christophides GK, Vlachou D, Kafatos FC. 2004. Innate immunity in the malaria vector *Anopheles gambiae*: comparative and functional genomics. *J. Exp. Biol.* 207:2551–63
138. Parkinson J, Blaxter M. 2009. Expressed sequence tags: an overview. *Methods Mol. Biol.* 533:1–12
139. Paskewitz SM, Shi L. 2005. The hemolymph proteome of *Anopheles gambiae*. *Insect Biochem. Mol. Biol.* 35:815–24
140. Petretto E, Mangion J, Dickens NJ, Cook SA, Kumaran MK, et al. 2006. Heritability and tissue specificity of expression quantitative trait loci. *PLoS Genet.* 2:e172
141. Philippe H, Snell EA, Bapteste E, Lopez P, Holland PW, et al. 2004. Phylogenomics of eukaryotes: impact of missing data on large alignments. *Mol. Biol. Evol.* 21:1740–52
142. Piriyapongsa J, Jordan IK. 2007. A family of human microRNA genes from miniature inverted-repeat transposable elements. *PLoS ONE* 2:e203
143. Piriyapongsa J, Mariño-Ramírez L, Jordan IK. 2007. Origin and evolution of human microRNAs from transposable elements. *Genetics* 176:1323–37
144. Popova-Butler A, Dean DH. 2009. Proteomic analysis of the mosquito *Aedes aegypti* midgut brush border membrane vesicles. *J. Insect Physiol.* 55:264–72
145. Poupardin R, Reynaud S, Strode C, Ranson H, Vontas J, et al. 2008. Cross-induction of detoxification genes by environmental xenobiotics and insecticides in the mosquito *Aedes aegypti*: impact on larval tolerance to chemical insecticides. *Insect Biochem. Mol. Biol.* 38:540–51
146. Predel R, Neupert S, Garczynski SF, Crim JW, Brown MR, et al. 2010. Neuropeptidomics of the mosquito *Aedes aegypti*. *J. Proteome Res.* 9:2006–15
147. Probst AV, Dunleavy E, Almouzni G. 2009. Epigenetic inheritance during the cell cycle. *Nat. Rev. Mol. Cell Biol.* 10:192–206
148. Ptitsyn AA, Reyes-Solis G, Saavedra-Rodriguez K, Betz J, Suchman EL, et al. 2011. Rhythms and synchronization patterns in gene expression in the *Aedes aegypti* mosquito. *BMC Genomics* 12:153
149. Rai KS, Black WC IV. 1999. Mosquito genomes: structure, organization, and evolution. *Adv. Genet.* 41:1–33
150. Ramirez JL, Dimopoulos G. 2010. The Toll immune signaling pathway control conserved anti-dengue defenses across diverse *Ae. aegypti* strains and against multiple dengue virus serotypes. *Dev. Comp. Immunol.* 34:625–29
151. Rao PN, Rai KS. 1987. Inter- and intraspecific variation in nuclear DNA content in *Aedes* mosquitoes. *Heredity* 59:253–58
152. Reidenbach KR, Cook S, Bertone MA, Harbach RE, Wiegmann BM, Besansky NJ. 2009. Phylogenetic analysis and temporal diversification of mosquitoes (Diptera: Culicidae) based on nuclear genes and morphology. *BMC Evol. Biol.* 9:298
153. Riaz MA, Poupardin R, Reynaud S, Strode C, Ranson H, et al. 2009. Impact of glyphosate and benzo[a]pyrene on the tolerance of mosquito larvae to chemical insecticides. Role of detoxification genes in response to xenobiotics. *Aquat. Toxicol.* 93:61–69
154. Richly E, Leister D. 2004. NUMTs in sequenced eukaryotic genomes. *Mol. Biol. Evol.* 21:1081–84
155. Rogers, DW, Whitten MMA, Thailayil J, Soichot J, Levashina EA, et al. 2008. Molecular and cellular components of the mating machinery in *Anopheles gambiae* females. *Proc. Natl. Acad. Sci. USA* 105:19390–95
156. Roloff TC, Nuber UA. 2005. Chromatin, epigenetics and stem cells. *Eur. J. Cell Biol.* 84:123–35
157. Rundle HD, Nosil P. 2005. Ecological speciation. *Ecol. Lett.* 8:336–52

158. Savard J, Tautz D, Richards S, Weinstock GM, Gibbs RA, et al. 2006. Phylogenomic analysis reveals bees and wasps (Hymenoptera) at the base of the radiation of Holometabolous insects. *Genome Res.* 16:1334–38
159. Senti KA, Brennecke J. 2010. The piRNA pathway: a fly's perspective on the guardian of the genome. *Trends Genet.* 26:499–509
160. Serrano-Pinto V, Acosta-Pérez M, Luviano-Bazan D, Hurtado-Sil G, Batista CVF, et al. 2010. Differential expression of proteins in the midgut of *Anopheles albimanus* infected with *Plasmodium berghei*. *Insect Biochem. Mol. Biol.* 40:752–58
161. Severson DW. 2008. Mosquitoes. In *Genome Mapping in Animals: Insects*, ed. C Kole, WB Hunter, 5:69–91. Heidelberg/Berlin: Springer
162. Severson DW, Brown SE, Knudson DL. 2001. Genetic and physical mapping in mosquitoes: molecular approaches. *Annu. Rev. Entomol.* 46:183–219
163. Severson DW, Knudson DL, Soares MB, Loftus BJ. 2004. *Aedes aegypti* genomics. *Insect Biochem. Mol. Biol.* 34:715–21
164. Shalchian-Tabrizi K, Minge MA, Espelund M, Orr R, Ruden T, et al. 2008. Multigene phylogeny of choanozoa and the origin of animals. *PLoS ONE* 3:e2098
165. Sharp AJ, Locke DP, McGrath SD, Cheng Z, Bailey JA, et al. 2005. Segmental duplications and copy-number variation in the human genome. *Am. J. Hum. Genet.* 77:78–88
166. Sieglaff DH, Dunn WA, Xie XS, Megy K, Marinotti O, et al. 2009. Comparative genomics allows the discovery of *cis*-regulatory elements in mosquitoes. *Proc. Natl. Acad. Sci. USA* 106:3053–58
167. Simard F, Ayala D, Kamdem GC, Pombi M, Etouna J, et al. 2009. Ecological niche partitioning between the M and S molecular forms of *Anopheles gambiae* in Cameroon: the ecological side of speciation. *BMC Ecol.* 9:17
168. Simon SA, Zhai J, Sekhar Nandety R, McCormick KP, Zeng J, et al. 2009. Short-read sequencing technologies for transcriptional analysis. *Annu. Rev. Plant Biol.* 60:305–66
169. Sirot LK, Poulson RL, McKenna MC, Girnary H, Wolfner MF, et al. 2008. Identity and transfer of male reproductive gland proteins of the dengue vector mosquito, *Aedes aegypti*: potential tools for control of female feeding and reproduction. *Insect Biochem. Mol. Biol.* 38:176–89
170. Slotkin RK, Freeling M, Lisch D. 2005. Heritable transposon silencing initiated by a naturally occurring transposon inverted duplication. *Nat. Genet.* 37:641–44
171. Smalheiser NR, Torvik VI. 2005. Mammalian microRNAs derived from genomic repeats. *Trends Genet.* 21:322–26
172. Snijders AM, Nowak NJ, Huey B, Fridlyand J, Law S, et al. 2005. Mapping segmental and sequence variations among laboratory mice using BAC array CGH. *Genome Res.* 15:302–11
173. Souza-Neto JA, Sim S, Dimopoulos G. 2009. An evolutionary conserved function of the JAK-STAT pathway in anti-dengue defense. *Proc. Natl. Acad. Sci. USA* 106:17841–46

173. Demonstrates the role of the JAK-STAT immune-signaling pathway in the mosquito response to dengue-virus infection.

174. Stranger BE, Forrest MS, Clark AG, Minichiello MJ, Deutsch S, et al. 2005. Genome-wide associations of gene expression variation in humans. *PLoS Genet.* 1:e78
175. Surget-Groba Y, Montoya-Burgos JI. 2010. Optimization of de novo transcriptome assembly from next-generation sequencing data. *Genome Res.* 20:1432–40
176. Tabachnick WJ. 2003. Reflections on the *Anopheles gambiae* genome sequence, transgenic mosquitoes and the prospect for controlling malaria and other vector-borne diseases. *J. Med. Entomol.* 40:597–606
177. Tchankouo-Nguetcheu S, Khun H, Pincet L, Roux P, Bahut M, et al. 2010. Differential protein modulation in midguts of *Aedes aegypti* infected with chikungunya and dengue 2 viruses. *PLoS ONE* 5:e13149
178. Theodorides K, De Riva A, Gómez-Zurita J, Foster PG, Vogler AP. 2002. Comparison of EST libraries from seven beetle species: towards a framework for phylogenomics of the Coleoptera. *Insect Mol. Biol.* 11:467–75
179. Thomson T, Lin H. 2009. The biogenesis and function of PIWI proteins and piRNAs: progress and prospect. *Annu. Rev. Cell Dev. Biol.* 25:355–76
180. Topalis P, Tzavlaki C, Vestaki K, Dialynas E, Sonenshine DE, et al. 2008. Anatomical ontologies of mosquitoes and ticks, and their web browsers at VectorBase. *Insect Mol. Biol.* 17:87–89
181. Topalis P, Dialynas E, Mitraka E, Deligianni E, Siden-Kiamos E, et al. 2011. A set of ontologies to drive tools for the control of vector-borne diseases. *J. Biomed. Inform.* 44:42–47

182. Tu Z, Li S. 2009. Mobile genetic elements of malaria vectors and other mosquitoes. In *Mobile Genetic Elements in Metazoan Parasites*, ed. PJ Brindley, pp. 17–34. Austin, TX: Landes Biosci.
183. Turner TL, Hahn MW, Nuzhdin SV. 2005. Genomic islands of speciation in *Anopheles gambiae*. *PLoS Biol.* 3:e285
184. Valenzuela JG, Francischetti IMB, My Pham V, Garfield MK, Ribeiro JMC. 2003. Exploring the salivary gland transcriptome and proteome of the *Anopheles stephensi* mosquito. *Insect Biochem. Mol. Biol.* 33:717–32
185. Vastenhouw NL, Plasterk RH. 2004. RNAi protects the *Caenorhabditis elegans* germline against transposition. *Trends Genet.* 20:314–19
186. Venter JC, Adams MD, Myers EW, Li PW, Mural RJ, et al. 2001. The sequence of the human genome. *Science* 291:1304–51
187. Vital W, Rezende GL, Abreu L, Moraes J, Lemos FJ, et al. 2010. Germ band retraction as a landmark in glucose metabolism during *Aedes aegypti* embryogenesis. *BMC Dev. Biol.* 10:25
188. Wang H, Iacoangeli A, Lin D, Williams K, Denman RB, et al. 2005. Dendritic BC1 RNA in translational control mechanisms. *J. Cell Biol.* 171:811–21
189. Wang M-H, Marinotti O, James AA, Walker E, Githure, et al. 2010. Genome-wide patterns of gene expression during aging in the African malaria vector *Anopheles gambiae*. *PLoS ONE* 5:e13359
190. Warr E, Aguilar R, Dong Y, Mahairaki V, Dimopoulos G. 2007. Spatial and sex-specific dissection of the *Anopheles gambiae* midgut transcriptiome. *BMC Genomics* 8:37
191. Waterhouse RM, Kriventseva EV, Meister S, Xi Z, Alvarez KS, et al. 2007 Evolutionary dynamics of immune-related genes and pathways in disease-vector mosquitoes. *Science* 316:1738–43
192. Waterhouse RM, Wyder S, Zdobnov EM. 2008 The *Aedes aegypti* genome: a comparative perspective. *Insect Mol. Biol.* 17:1–8
193. Weetman D, Wilding CS, Steen K, Morgan JC, Simard F, et al. 2010. Association mapping of insecticide resistance in wild *Anopheles gambiae* populations: major variants identified in a low-linkage disequilibrium genome. *PLoS ONE* 5:e13140
194. White BJ, Cheng C, Simard F, Costantini C, Besansky NJ. 2010. Genetic association of physically unlinked islands of genomic divergence in incipient species of *Anopheles gambiae*. *Mol. Ecol.* 19:925–39
195. Wiegmann BM, Trautwein MD, Winkler IS, Barr NB, Kim JW, et al. 2011. Episodic radiations in the fly tree of life. *Proc. Natl. Acad. Sci. USA.* 108:5690–95
196. Winter F, Edaye S, Hüttenhofer A, Brunel C. 2007. *Anopheles gambiae* miRNAs as actors of defence reaction against *Plasmodium* invasion. *Nucleic Acids Res.* 35:6953–62
197. Wilhelm BT, Landry J-R. 2009. RNA-Seq: quantitative measurement of expression through massively parallel RNA-sequencing. *Methods* 48:249–57
198. Wilson GM, Flibotte S, Missirlis PI, Marra MA, Jones S, 2006. Identification by full-coverage array CGH of human DNA copy number increases relative to chimpanzee and gorilla. *Genome Res.* 16:173–81
199. Xi Z, Ramirez JL, Dimopoulos G. 2008. The *Aedes aegypti* toll pathway controls dengue virus infection. *PLoS Pathog.* 4:e1000098
200. Yamauchi A. 2005. Rate of gene transfer from mitochondria to nucleus: effects of cytoplasmic inheritance system and intensity of intracellular competition. *Genetics* 171:1387–96
201. Yang PK, Kuroda MI. 2007. Noncoding RNAs and intranuclear positioning in monoallelic gene expression. *Cell* 128:777–86
202. Yao R, Li J. 2003. Towards global analysis of mosquito chorion proteins through sequential extraction, two-dimentional electrophoresis and mass spectrometry. *Proteomics* 3:2036–43
203. Yoder JA, Walsh CP, Bestor TH. 1997. Cytosine methylation and the ecology of intragenomic parasites. *Trends Genet.* 13:335–40
204. Yvert G, Brem RB, Whittle J, Akey JM, Foss E, et al. 2003. *Trans*-acting regulatory variation in *Saccharomyces cerevisiae* and the role of transcription factors. *Nat. Genet.* 35:57–64
205. Zaratiegui M, Irvine DV, Martienssen RA. 2007. Noncoding RNAs and gene silencing. *Cell* 128:763–76
206. Zdobnov EM, Bork P. 2007. Quantification of insect genome divergence. *Trends Genet.* 23:16–20
207. Zhou JJ, He XL, Pickett JA, Field LM. 2008. Identification of odorant-binding proteins of the yellow fever mosquito *Aedes aegypti*: genome annotation and comparative analyses. *Insect Mol. Biol.* 17:147–63

191. Provides comparative phylogenomic analysis of mosquito and fruit fly innate immune systems.

Reevaluating the Arthropod Tree of Life

Gonzalo Giribet[1,*] and Gregory D. Edgecombe[2]

[1]Museum of Comparative Zoology, Department of Organismic and Evolutionary Biology, Harvard University, Cambridge, Massachusetts 02138; email: ggiribet@oeb.harvard.edu

[2]Department of Palaeontology, The Natural History Museum, London SW7 5BD, United Kingdom; email: g.edgecombe@nhm.ac.uk

Annu. Rev. Entomol. 2012. 57:167–86

First published online as a Review in Advance on September 9, 2011

The *Annual Review of Entomology* is online at ento.annualreviews.org

This article's doi:
10.1146/annurev-ento-120710-100659

0066-4170/12/0107-0167$20.00

*Corresponding author

Keywords

arthropod phylogeny, anatomy, fossils, molecular data, phylogenomics

Abstract

Arthropods are the most diverse group of animals and have been so since the Cambrian radiation. They belong to the protostome clade Ecdysozoa, with Onychophora (velvet worms) as their most likely sister group and tardigrades (water bears) the next closest relative. The arthropod tree of life can be interpreted as a five-taxon network, containing Pycnogonida, Euchelicerata, Myriapoda, Crustacea, and Hexapoda, the last two forming the clade Tetraconata or Pancrustacea. The unrooted relationship of Tetraconata to the three other lineages is well established, but of three possible rooting positions the Mandibulata hypothesis receives the most support. Novel approaches to studying anatomy with noninvasive three-dimensional reconstruction techniques, the application of these techniques to new and old fossils, and the so-called next-generation sequencing techniques are at the forefront of understanding arthropod relationships. Cambrian fossils assigned to the arthropod stem group inform on the origin of arthropod characters from a lobopodian ancestry. Monophyly of Pycnogonida, Euchelicerata, Myriapoda, Tetraconata, and Hexapoda is well supported, but the interrelationships of arachnid orders and the details of crustacean paraphyly with respect to Hexapoda remain the major unsolved phylogenetic problems.

INTRODUCTION

Tagmosis: type of body organization where batches of segments acquire a specific function and delimit different body regions

Arthropods, with nearly 85% of the described extant animal species and the richest fossil record of any animal group (22), are by far the most successful metazoan phylum. Mites, for example, can be found in any ecosystem on earth, from the deepest seafloor to the highest mountain peak, and spiders have even been collected ballooning through the stratosphere. Insects thrive in almost every terrestrial environment and were the first true conquerors of the air. A study of arthropod abundance in a Bornean lowland tropical rainforest shows that arthropod biomass in the aboveground regions was 23.6 kg ha^{-1}, that abundance was 23.9 million individuals ha^{-1}, and that density on leaf surfaces was 280 individuals m^{-2} leaf area (17). Likewise, copepods and krill constitute a sizeable fraction of the marine biomass and sustain a large part of the ocean's food chain. Arthropods are the most important ecosystem builders on land and are fundamental for breaking down and recycling organic matter in the soil. They are also of tremendous importance to humans as a food source, as pollinators, as producers of material goods (e.g., wax, honey, silk), and for biomedical studies, but they are also pests, vectors of disease, and the direct source of stings, bites, and envenomation, most prominently in the case of spiders, scorpions, and centipedes.

The contemporary importance of arthropods in terms of diversity and ecosystem function is the outcome of a geological history that spans at least 525 million years, since the main burst of the Cambrian radiation (11). Arthropod body fossils date to the early Cambrian and are preceded by trace fossils indicative of arthropods for at least 5 million years in the earliest Cambrian. Trilobites, which appear nearly as early as any other arthropods, are the most diverse animal clade in the Cambrian Period, and when unmineralized diversity is considered alongside the more typically preserved "shelly" fossil record—as in sites of exceptional preservation such as the Burgess Shale and Chengjiang—arthropods are both the most abundant and the most species-rich Cambrian animal group (44). The fossil record provides a chronology for the conquest of land by arachnids and myriapods by at least the Silurian Period (94). The evolution of land plants has been tightly connected to the evolution of insects in a series of mutualistic interactions, with insects acting mostly as probable pollinators of gymnosperms since the mid-Mesozoic (80) and most prominently nectar-feeding flies, butterflies, and beetles pollinating angiosperms diversified in concert with plants during the Cretaceous (80).

Morphologically, arthropods are characterized by a special body plan formed by numerous segments, grouped into functional units or tagmata (**Figure 1**). Segmentation and tagmosis are most certainly responsible for the diversity of the group, allowing arthropods to adapt to different environmental conditions. Most arthropods concentrate the sensorial functions in an anterior tagma or head, the locomotory function (walking or swimming legs and wings) in an intermediate tagma (thorax in insects), and the reproductive functions in a posterior tagma or abdomen. These tagmata fuse or are otherwise modified in many groups; myriapods have the body divided into head and trunk (**Figure 1*d***), arachnids fuse the head and thorax into a prosoma and the abdomen is called opisthosoma (**Figure 1*c***), and crustaceans vary their body plan enormously. Remipedes, for example, have a basic division between head and trunk (**Figure 1*f***), whereas most malacostracans structure their body into a cephalon, pereion, and pleon (**Figure 1*e***). In the arthropod groundpattern, each segment bears a pair of appendages that can be modified for specific functions, and the homology of the head appendages has been debated for a long time (see **Figure 2** for current interpretations). The appendages of the head are transformed into mouthparts (mandibles, maxillae), grasping appendages (chelicerae, so-called frontal appendages of many Cambrian arthropods), and sensorial organs (antennae, antennulae, pedipalps). The trunk appendages can deviate from a locomotory role by acquiring a function in reproduction (e.g., gonopods of millipedes) or respiration (e.g., limbs of many crustaceans). The enormous possibilities for adaptation of the appendages

Figure 1

Arthropod body plans. (*a*) *Mesoperipatus tholloni* (Onychophora, Peripatidae) from Gabon. (*b*) *Anoplodactylus evansi* (Pycnogonida) from New South Wales, Australia, photographed by M. Harris. (*c*) *Euscorpius* sp. (Chelicerata, Arachnida, Scorpiones) from Sicily, Italy. (*d*) *Scolopendra laeta* (Myriapoda, Chilopoda) from Western Australia. (*e*) *Quadrimaera* sp. (Crustacea, Malacostraca, Amphipoda) from British Virgin Islands, photographed by A.J. Baldinger and E.A. Lazo-Wasem. (*f*) *Speleonectes tulumensis* (Crustacea, Remipedia) from Mexico, photographed by J. Pakes. (*g*) Japygoidea sp. (Hexapoda, Diplura) from New Zealand. All photos, except where specified, by the authors.

and the regional specialization of a modular body plan have been interpreted as responsible for the success of the arthropods (9). The developmental genetic basis for the differentiation of appendicular structures along the body axis, e.g., chelicerae, pedipalps, walking legs, book lungs, or spinnerets, in the case of spiders, is being elucidated (71).

Taxonomically the phylum Arthropoda includes several major lineages that traditionally have received the ranks of subphylum, class, or subclass, and their interrelationships are the crux of ongoing debate over arthropod phylogeny. For the sake of consistency and convenience, we use the following names in this review: Pycnogonida, Euchelicerata, Myriapoda, Crustacea, and Hexapoda. For some authors Chelicerata includes pycnogonids, and we follow this practice and

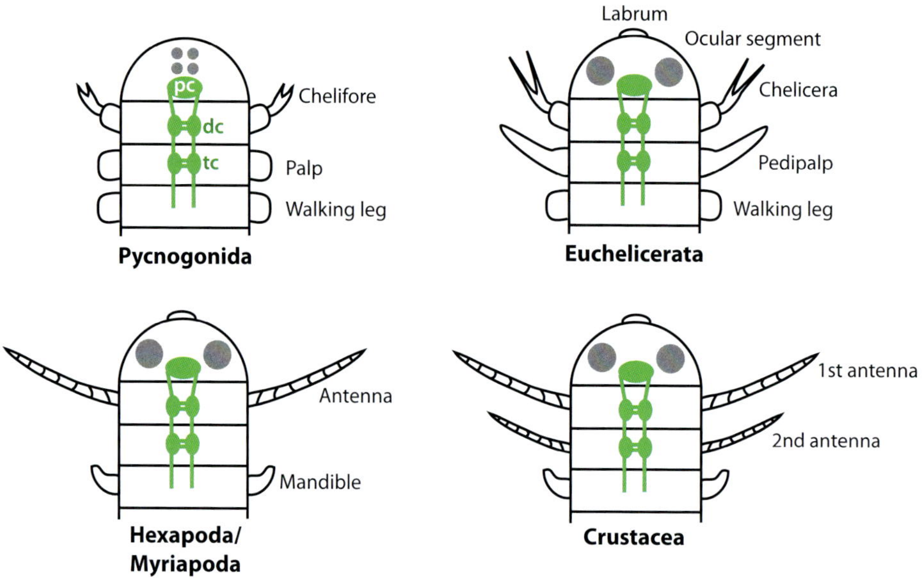

Figure 2

Alignment of head segments and homology of appendicular structures in the major arthropod lineages. Abbreviations: dc, deutocerebrum; pc, protocerebrum; tc tritocerebrum.

use the term Euchelicerata to refer to the nonpycnogonid chelicerates (36). The pycnogonid body plan differs markedly from that of other chelicerates, and maintaining the two groups makes the phylogenetic alternatives easier to discuss. Crustacea and Hexapoda form a clade named Tetraconata or Pancrustacea (81), although Crustacea is most likely paraphyletic with respect to a monophyletic Hexapoda.

THE PHYLOGENETIC POSITION OF ARTHROPODS

Arthropods are protostome animals and as such have an apical dorsal brain with a ventral longitudinal nerve chord and a mouth that typically originates from the embryonic blastopore. They have been traditionally considered to have a primary body cavity, or coelom, that has been restricted to the pericardium, gonoducts, and nephridial structures (coxal glands, antennal/maxillary glands). The true coelomic nature of arthropods is however questionable (4). Similarly, although many authors at one time considered arthropods to have a modified spiral cleavage—as found in annelids, mollusks, nemerteans, and platyhelminthes—this idea is now rejected (91). Their lateral jointed appendages have been homologized with the lobopods of onychophorans (**Figure 1*a***), a view strengthened by similar genetic patterning of the proximo-distal axes (51), as well as with the limbs of tardigrades (90). Earlier they were also considered possible homologs of the annelid parapodia, a homology that is generally rejected by systematists today (apart from a broad correspondence as lateral outgrowths of the body).

The position of arthropods among animals has changed radically in the past two decades as a result of refinements in cladistic analysis and especially by the introduction of molecular data. Traditionally, arthropods (and their allies, onychophorans and tardigrades) were grouped with annelids in a clade named Articulata by Cuvier in the early nineteenth century, in reference to the segmental body plan in both phyla (92). The competing Ecdysozoa hypothesis (32, 89), allying arthropods, onychophorans, and tardigrades with a group of mostly pseudocoelomate animal phyla (**Figure 3**) that share a cuticle that is molted at least once during their life cycle, was proposed originally on the basis of 18S rRNA sequence data (1) but is now broadly accepted because of support from diverse kinds of molecular information (22, 104). The exact sister group relationship of arthropods is, however, still debated. Alternative hypotheses suggest either Onychophora, Tardigrada, or a clade composed of them both as the candidate sister group of arthropods, with phylogenomic data decanting toward the first option (2, 21, 42, 85). Whether tardigrades are related to Onychophora + Arthropoda or to Nematoda remains more contentious, as both alternatives are resolved for the same EST (expressed sequence tag) (21) or mitogenomic (87) datasets under different analytical conditions. In the latter case, conditions intended to counter certain kinds of systematic error strengthen the support for tardigrades grouping with arthropods and onychophorans rather than with nematodes. The alliance of Tardigrada with Onychophora and Arthropoda is consistent with a single origin of paired, segmental ventrolateral appendages in a unique common ancestor, and the name Panarthropoda is usually applied to this group.

EST: expressed sequence tag

Arthrodial membrane: the unsclerotized part of the arthropod exoskeleton, for example, between joints

Arthropod monophyly [including the parasitic Pentastomida (68) as ingroup crustaceans] is now nearly universally accepted based on morphological, developmental, and molecular evidence (see review in Reference 23). Advocacy for arthropod polyphyly in the 1960s and 1970s (62) was not based on characters that supported alternative sister group hypotheses and was abandoned on unsound logical grounds. Evidence for arthropod monophyly comes from the shared presence of a sclerotized exoskeleton, legs composed of sclerotized podomeres separated by arthrodial membranes, muscles that attach at intersegmental tendons, compound eyes in which new eye elements are added in a proliferation zone at the sides of the developing eye field (40), and the presence of two optic neuropils. Segmentation gene characters (30) and a stereotypical pattern of how neural precursors segregate (25) can also be identified as autapomorphies for Arthropoda compared with Onychophora and Tardigrada.

THE RELATIONSHIPS AMONG THE MAJOR ARTHROPOD LINEAGES

Relationships among major arthropod lineages have been debated for centuries, and for a long time the only nearly universally accepted result was the monophyly of Atelocerata—a group that included hexapods and myriapods. However, the addition of molecular and novel anatomical and developmental data has helped us reinterpret arthropod relationships, such that hexapods are associated with crustaceans instead of with myriapods in a clade named Tetraconata (= Pancrustacea) in reference to the shared presence of four crystalline cone cells in the compound eye ommatidia in both groups (81). We are still far from having a perfectly resolved arthropod tree of life, but several patterns, including a basic unrooted topology, are congruent among all new sources of data. Today, nearly all authors interpret the arthropod phylogeny problem as a rooting problem of five taxa (13, 37). Three alternative roots (of seven possible positions) are consistently recovered in different analyses, with support falling mostly on one hypothesis—the monophyly of all arthropods with a mandible, or Mandibulata—as the sister clade to Chelicerata. Alternative rootings support pycnogonids as sister to all other arthropods (= Cormogonida) (34, 117), or a clade named Paradoxopoda (= Myriochelata) that joins myriapods with the chelicerate groups (61, 75).

In this section we focus on developments in three key areas, comparative anatomy, the fossil record, and novel molecular approaches, each of which has advanced greatly since the publication of the first arthropod phylogenies combining morphology and multiple molecular markers (34, 109). Since then, the amount of molecular data devoted to this problem has increased exponentially with recent genomic approaches. The techniques used to analyze fossil information as well as developmental and anatomical data have improved considerably, especially with the increased usage of confocal laser scanning microscopy, but also with the appearance of new techniques such as X-ray microtomography (31), serial grinding with computer reconstruction of virtual fossils (97), and synchrotron X-ray tomographic microscopy (29, 56, 98).

Contributions from Anatomy

Nervous system characters, including the ultrastructure of the eyes and configurations of the optic neuropils, played an important role in arthropod phylogenetics in the early twentieth century, with major contributions by N. Holmgren and B. Hanström in particular. One of the major insights of this early neuroanatomical research, the putative ancestry of hexapods from crustaceans rather than from myriapods, was revitalized in the past 20 years by neuroanatomists using new staining/immunoreactivity and imaging techniques and cladistic methods, an approach called neurophylogeny (82).

Current datasets based on neural characters (39, 101, 102) reinforce a closer relationship between Malacostraca and Hexapoda than either shares with Branchiopoda or Maxillopoda, as evidenced by such shared features as optic neuropils with a nesting of the lamina, medulla, lobula, and lobula plates and their connections by chiasmata. Branchiopod brains could be secondarily simplified from a more malacostracan or remipede-like ancestor (102), although character polarities are dependent on the exact pattern of relationships between these crustacean groups and Hexapoda.

For centuries the internal anatomy of arthropods has been studied by dissection and/or serial sectioning of small species and subsequent examination by light or electron microscopy. Traditional comparative morphological analyses and subsequent three-dimensional reconstructions suffer from a number of drawbacks. This is evident particularly in the case of soft tissue studies that are technically demanding, time consuming, and often prone to producing artifacts (116). Some of these problems have been overcome by employing noninvasive, nondestructive imaging techniques, initially confocal laser microscopy and then more recently microcomputed tomography or magnetic resonance imaging (29, 43). Micro-computer tomography techniques and three-dimensional reconstruction have also been applied to the study of the circulatory system of several arthropods using corrosion casting (111), and these have clarified important phylogenetic questions, e.g., within crustaceans (112). Rapid and relatively inexpensive imaging techniques will be required if morphology is to continue playing a role in formulating phylogenetic hypotheses in a world ever more inundated by molecular data.

Contributions from the Fossil Record

A contribution of fossils to understanding arthropod evolution is in providing snapshots of extinct diversity, morphology, and inferred ecology. Fossils are our only record of gigantism in lineages such as stem-group arachnids (i.e., eurypterids), an extinct clade of millipedes with possible affinities to the minute extant order Penicillata (arthropleurids in Carboniferous coal swamp

Figure 3

Hypothesis of the protostome tree of life, placing Arthropoda within the ecdysozoan phyla. This tree is a summary of diverse sources, with emphasis on groups recognized in phylogenomic analyses.

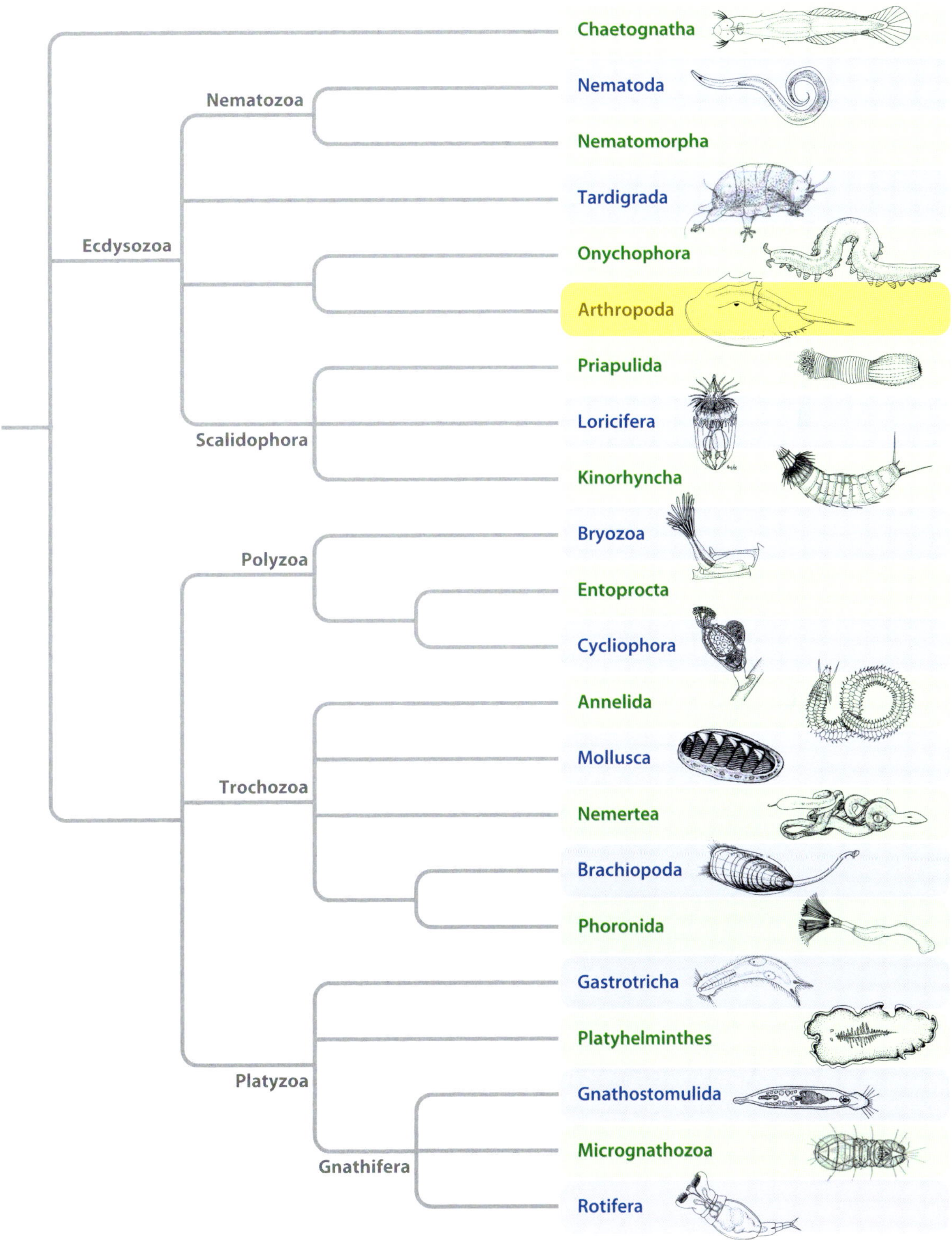

Chaetognatha
Nematozoa
Nematoda
Nematomorpha
Tardigrada
Ecdysozoa
Onychophora
Arthropoda
Priapulida
Loricifera
Scalidophora
Kinorhyncha
Bryozoa
Polyzoa
Entoprocta
Cycliophora
Annelida
Mollusca
Trochozoa
Nemertea
Brachiopoda
Phoronida
Gastrotricha
Platyhelminthes
Platyzoa
Gnathostomulida
Micrognathozoa
Gnathifera
Rotifera

forests), and insects with wingspans on the order of 71 cm (Permian griffinflies of the extinct order Protodonata). Inclusion of fossils may influence estimates of the interrelationships of extant taxa, as exemplified by cladograms for the basal lineages of beetles (5) and the interordinal relationships of arachnids (35, 96).

Stem group: a paraphyletic assemblage of fossil taxa that diverged basal to a crown group but is more closely related to it than are its closest extant relatives

Crown group: a clade composed of the most recent common ancestor of the extant members of a taxon and all of its descendants

A particularly significant forum for fossils in arthropod phylogenetics concerns Cambrian taxa recognized as constituting stem-group Arthropoda (23). Most information about these fossils comes from sites with soft-part preservation, so-called Burgess Shale-type localities, approximately 40 of which are known from the Cambrian worldwide. The most important of these localities are the Burgess Shale of western Canada (Stage 5 in the contemporary 10-stage Cambrian timescale), the Chengjiang biota of south China (Cambrian Stage 3), and Sirius Passet in north Greenland (Cambrian Stage 3).

Broad consensus has been reached that anomalocaridids (including such animals as *Anomalocaris* and *Hurdia*) and *Opabinia* are stem-group arthropods that branched from the stem lineage after the acquisition of stalked, compound eyes but before the evolution of a sclerotized tergal exoskeleton (11, 23). Whether anomalocaridids and other large-bodied, lobopod-bearing Cambrian animals with which they share spinose frontal appendages, such as *Kerygmachela* and *Pambdelurion*, unite as a clade named Dinocaridida (59) or comprise a paraphyletic series in the arthropod stem group (16) is debated. A Devonian taxon with a radial mouthpart and anomalocaridid-like frontal appendages, *Schinderhannes* (55), may be positioned even more crownward than anomalocaridids in the arthropod stem group because it appears to share additional derived characters with the arthropod crown group (notably an articulated tergal exoskeleton).

Another emerging point of agreement is that a growing sample of taxa (mostly from Chengjiang) with lobopodial trunk limbs collectively known as Cambrian lobopodians represent a grade of panarthropods that includes stem-group Onychophora and stem-group Arthropoda and possibly stem-group Tardigrada or stem-group Panarthropoda. The most recent phylogenetic analyses of these taxa resolve "armored" lobopodians with paired, segmentally arranged dorsal spines such as *Hallucigenia* and *Luolishania* either on the arthropod stem lineage (59), though branching stemward of the dinocaridids, or on the onychophoran stem lineage (58).

Another style of fossil preservation has figured prominently in research on the early history of some major crown-group euarthropod clades, especially the crustaceans. Orsten refers to secondarily phosphatized fossils, known from numerous localities that span the Early Cambrian to Early Ordovician window. This phosphate replacement permits exquisitely preserved, uncompacted fossils smaller than 2 mm to be extracted from limestones and examined by scanning electron microscopy, providing unique insights into larval development and highly detailed information on appendage morphology. Orsten arthropods have recently been revealed from the early Cambrian, from rocks as old as the Chengjiang fauna, demonstrating that crown-group Arthropoda and, more precisely, crown-group "crustaceans" have a fossil record as early as Cambrian Stage 3. These fossils include *Yicaris* (114), an entomostracan crustacean, and a metanauplius named *Wujicaris* (115), which is convincingly identified as a maxillopodan crustacean. Late Cambrian Orsten of Sweden has contributed a series of species that have been resolved as stem-lineage crustaceans (41). Character analysis to date has interpreted these fossils in the context of crustacean monophyly, but alternative placements with Crustacea as a grade within Tetraconata remain an open question.

Although molecular techniques now allow essentially precise dating of old arthropod lineages (70, 88), paleontology contributes most of the data on the age of modern lineages, and minimum ages from fossils calibrate molecular estimates for divergencies. Most molecular estimates of the splits between the deep arthropod clades such as Chelicerata versus Mandibulata (or Myriochelata versus Tetraconata) date these events to the Ediacaran Period (635–542 My) or even earlier, to the Cryogenian (74). These "long fuse" time trees suggest a considerable duration that lacks any credible fossils. Body plan conservatism is exceptional in some groups of arthropods, notably in Silurian pycnogonids (97) and scorpions, and in Devonian Opiliones (19).

PCR: polymerase chain reaction

cDNA: complementary DNA

mRNA: messenger RNA

Transcriptome: the fraction of the genome that encompasses all transcribed genes

Contributions from Novel Molecular Approaches

Molecular data have revolutionized our understanding of arthropod relationships since the early 1990s. For nearly two decades, molecular phylogenies relied on direct sequencing of a few selected genes amplified with specific primers—called a target-gene approach. Systematists constructing arthropod phylogenies often used nuclear ribosomal genes (36, 60, 108), nuclear protein-encoding genes (78), or a combination of these with mitochondrial genes (37), or they focused on mitogenomics (87)—the analysis of complete mitochondrial genomes, either their sequences, gene order information (57), or both. However, mitogenomic data seem to present strong biases and partly conflict with other sources of information, either from morphology or from the nuclear genome (64, 87).

Some of the earliest papers from the 1990s presented contradictory and sometimes morphologically anomalous results, but many of these problems were a result of deficient taxon sampling, too few molecular data, systematic error, or combinations of these defects. Initially controversial issues, such as the monophyly of Hexapoda (contradicted in several mitogenomic studies) and Myriapoda, have stabilized in the most recent and more taxonomically complete studies. The phylogenetic signal in support for Euchelicerata, Tetraconata, and paraphyly of Crustacea with respect to hexapods has been strong since the beginning. However, the monophyly and internal relationships of Arachnida, and the crustacean sister group of Hexapoda, remain the most pressing unresolved issues in arthropod phylogenetics.

Modern target-gene approaches using large numbers of markers, as many as 62 nuclear protein-encoding genes (77), and as many as 75 taxa (79), add support to Mandibulata and suggest a sister group relationship of hexapods to remipedes + cephalocarids but do not resolve the exact position of pycnogonids (a sister group relationship to Euchelicerata is recovered but without strong support). Although the use of large numbers of markers obtained through standard PCR (polymerase chain reaction) approaches has been an important advance, this method is time-consuming and it is difficult to consistently amplify large numbers of genes for many taxa.

Developments in sequencing technology and shotgun approaches following the sequencing of the first complete eukaryotic genomes changed our views on how to produce DNA sequence data. For a fraction of the effort and cost required to amplify multiple markers, random sequencing strategies allow automated processes to be applied to collecting hundreds or thousands of genes from complementary DNA (cDNA) libraries obtained from messenger RNA (mRNA). Although this requires specimens specially preserved for RNA extraction (live or frozen specimens, or animals preserved in special solutions such as RNA*later*®), thus limiting the usability of recent collections for molecular work of specimens preserved in high-degree ethanol, it opened the doors to true phylogenomic analyses based on a sizeable fraction of the transcriptome of an organism (69). The random sequencing of clones from a cDNA library generates large numbers of ESTs, and soon studies combined the data from full genomes with ESTs for a diverse sampling of protostomes (21, 42) or arthropods in particular (2, 67, 84, 86). Whereas some EST-based studies supported the Myriochelata hypothesis (21, 42, 67, 84), more recent studies support the monophyly of Chelicerata as the sister group of Mandibulata (86), in line with the anatomical evidence for jawed arthropods as a natural group. New characters from rare genomic changes add more support to Mandibulata; myriapods share two putatively novel microRNAs (noncoding regulatory genes) with crustaceans and hexapods that are not shared with chelicerates (86).

PHYLOGENOMICS: TARGET-GENE APPROACHES VERSUS RANDOM SEQUENCING

Phylogenomics often refers to the use of genome-level data in phylogenetic studies. Such data can be obtained from the comparison of complete genomes or from approaches based on random sequencing of genes (ESTs if the sequenced genes are expressed genes; the transcriptome). Although some authors apply the term phylogenomics to the use of multiple genes obtained from direct sequencing of candidate genes (normally via PCR sequencing), we restrict it to those studies based on genome-level data. The use of whole genomes or fractions of the transcriptome poses analytical challenges that do not apply to target-gene approaches, in particular the problem of homology assessment. Some authors identify sets of preselected genes for analysis, but approaches that use automated and explicit methods for assigning homology based on reproducible criteria (21) should be preferred to approaches based on manual curation of genomes, which do not scale well. To date, the largest analysis of animal phylogeny includes 1,487 genes selected using these methods (42).

Most of the earliest EST libraries were obtained using standard Sanger capillary sequencers. High-throughput sequencing with next-generation sequence technologies such as Roche *454* (63) and Solexa *illumina* (45) can produce hundreds of thousands or millions of sequences per sample, respectively, at a fraction of the cost of the earlier Sanger technology sequencing. Currently the cost for library construction and 150-bp paired-end Illumina sequencing is approximately US$2,500, producing up to 50 million reads. Transcriptomes for arthropods are now being produced in these ways (28, 84), and dozens or hundreds of such libraries will become available in the next few years (e.g., the authors have already generated *illumina* data for several arachnids and myriapods). The first analyses of complete genomes of multiple species of insects are already available (15).

STANDING ISSUES WITHIN THE MAJOR ARTHROPOD LINEAGES

The technological breakthroughs discussed above have already contributed toward resolving and stabilizing many relationships among the arthropod taxa, but, still, several areas need improvement. The exact position of the root (**Figure 4**), now best supported between Mandibulata and Chelicerata, requires further testing with more genomic data on pycnogonids, arachnids, and myriapods, because taxon sampling in those groups is sparse and the EST libraries are shallow when compared with those of other arthropod groups. A solution to this problem is foreseeable in the near future because several investigators have already generated the data.

Chelicerata

Although Euchelicerata is nearly always identified as monophyletic (but see mitogenomic analyses in Reference 64), molecular datasets to date (35, 64, 72, 79), with a few exceptions, are at odds with morphology (96), often not recovering the dichotomy between Xiphosura (horseshoe crabs) and Arachnida (**Figure 5**). Possible causes for the difficulty in recovering these relationships are the long history of the group, the extinction of key lineages, or intrinsic problems of the molecular data, but identifying the cause requires more densely sampled phylogenomic analyses. Other recurring controversies are the monophyly and phylogenetic affinities of Acari (18, 72) and the precise position of Palpigradi and Ricinulei. Similarly, resolving the exact relationships among the "basal" arachnid orders (Scorpiones, Opiliones, Pseudoscorpiones, and Solifugae) remains challenging. The currently favored morphological hypothesis in which scorpions and harvestmen

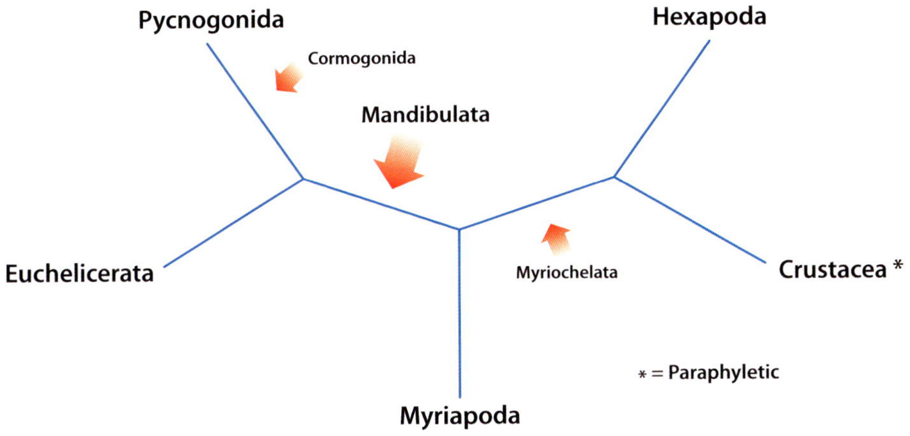

Figure 4

The arthropod five-taxon rooting problem. The left rooting position recognizes the taxon Cormogonida. The mid rooting position is the best supported and divides arthropods into Chelicerata and Mandibulata. The right rooting position is compatible with the Myriochelata hypothesis.

are united as Stomothecata, named for a unique formation of the preoral chamber (96), conflicts with the largest available molecular datasets for arachnids (79).

The sister group relationship between Pycnogonida and Euchelicerata is a long-standing morphological argument (**Figure 4**), though the homology of chelifores and chelicerae remains one of the only clearly documented autapomorphies (20). The segmental alignment of these appendages and their identity as deutocerebral (**Figure 2**) have been corroborated by *Hox* gene expression domains (48) and neuroanatomy (8).

Myriapoda

The long tradition of postulating that Myriapoda is nonmonophyletic stemmed from the Atelocerata hypothesis. In that framework, myriapods were identified as a grade from which hexapods evolved. Although some morphologists continue to advocate Atelocerata as a clade (3, 6), and its members share a unique pattern of expression of the *collier* gene in the limbless intercalary segment of the head (50), others have cautioned that the putative apomorphies of the group are likely convergences due to terrestrial habits (39). The very strong molecular and neuroanatomical support for a hexapod-crustacean clade that excludes Myriapoda means that myriapod paraphyly is untenable (95). Analyses that used large sampling of genes (79) have resolved Myriapoda as monophyletic, with strong support, a finding consistent with the unique structure of the tentorial endoskeleton throughout Myriapoda. Additional molecular evidence for myriapod monophyly comes from a novel microRNA (86) and antisense *Ultrabithorax* expression (49) shared by centipedes and millipedes, although the presence of these characters remains to be confirmed in symphylans and pauropods.

The standard morphological tree for myriapod relationships (Chilopoda as sister group to Progoneata) is retrieved in a 62-gene sampling (79). Within Progoneata, the union of diplopods and pauropods as a clade named Dignatha is regarded as a strong anatomical and developmental argument (95), but sequence-based analyses have instead retrieved a grouping of Pauropoda with Symphyla rather than with Diplopoda. Pauropods and symphylans are observed to attract in anomalous positions (sometimes even outside Arthropoda) in well-sampled analyses of nuclear

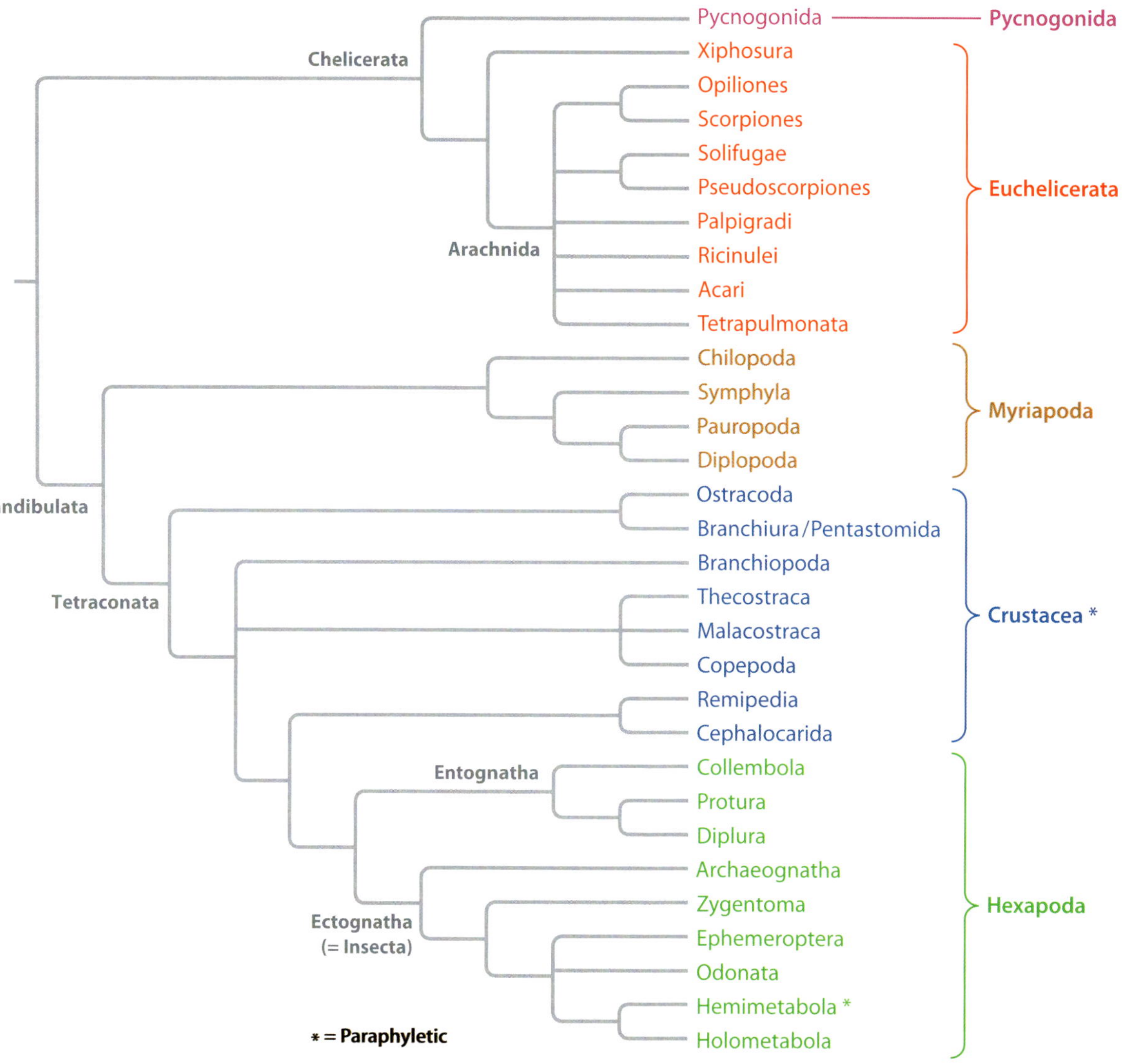

Figure 5

Arthropod tree following the Mandibulata hypothesis. Not all arthropod orders are listed. For Euchelicerata, Tetrapulmonata includes Araneae, Amblypygi, Uropygi, and Schizomida. Crustacean relationships are based mostly on Reference 79.

ribosomal genes (108), so the possibility that their grouping with nuclear coding genes may be a long-branch artifact needs careful investigation.

Tetraconata

Tetraconata has long been recognized as a clade based on molecular data and reinforced by important morphological characters of eye ultrastructure (81), brain and optic lobe anatomy (40, 101, 102), and similarities in neurogenesis (107). The issue of hexapod monophyly, which was disputed in some mitogenomic analyses (12), has been resolved in favor of a single origin using larger molecular datasets (67, 79, 106). At the base of Hexapoda, the status of Entognatha as a clade or a grade remains sensitive to taxon sampling and methods of molecular data analysis. The Nonoculata hypothesis (sister group relationship between Protura and Diplura to the exclusion of Collembola, the traditional sister group of Protura) was originally proposed on the basis of nuclear ribosomal genes (33, 108), but it finds further support in phylogenomic analyses (67) and is consistent with some morphological data (53). The internal phylogeny of insects (Ectognatha) continues to be refined (47), including the discovery and placement of the order Mantophasmatodea (105), the suggested paraphyly of the order Mecoptera (110), and the proposal that Isoptera be dismissed as an order and reclassified as a family of Blattodea (46, 105). However, whether crustaceans are monophyletic or paraphyletic with respect to hexapods (37), and, if the latter, precisely which crustacean lineage constitutes the sister group of hexapods, remains labile (38).

Crustacean relationships have been recently reviewed (83), including summaries of the alternative sister group hypotheses for each major crustacean clade (52). Molecular analyses using large numbers of genes have introduced some new, unanticipated hypotheses based on other data sources. For example, an analysis of 62 markers suggests that a putative clade composed of Cephalocarida + Remipedia (newly named as Xenocarida) is sister to Hexapoda, and that Branchiopoda forms a clade with Malacostraca, Thecostraca, and Copepoda (79). Cladistic analyses based on nervous system characters instead identify Malacostraca as the likely sister group of hexapods (101, 102). In contrast, larger gene samples in phylogenomic analyses repeatedly resolve Branchiopoda as sister to Hexapoda (although Cephalocarida and Remipedia were not sampled in those studies) (67, 84, 86). Denser taxon sampling of key crustacean lineages is still needed in phylogenomic analyses before a definitive solution can be proposed with strong support. The attraction of remipedes and cephalocarids, a union not anticipated by morphology (99) but long detected in molecular datasets (34), requires further evaluation as a potential long-branch artifact.

Among the potential crustacean sister groups of Hexapoda, Remipedia currently receives the most focus (108). Recent studies have documented the larvae and postembryonic development of remipedes, and some similarities to Malacostraca have been singled out (54). Brain anatomy of a remipede provided evidence for affinities to Malacostraca and Hexapoda (39), and hexapod-type hemocyanins have been discovered in remipedes (27). The largest available molecular datasets for these inhabitants of anchialine caves are, as noted (79), similarly in favor of a close affinity to Hexapoda.

ARTHROPODS AS MODELS IN DEVELOPMENTAL BIOLOGY

Arthropods in general, and the fruit fly, *Drosophila melanogaster*, in particular, have traditionally served as models in developmental biology for understanding morphology or for biomedical reasons. However, more recently, researchers have been studying development in other arthropods by using modern molecular techniques such as immunoreactivity and cell labeling, among others, often with the aim of testing specific phylogenetic hypotheses. The number of these studies has grown substantially in the past decade, and we focus on a few examples of special relevance to some of the hypotheses addressed here. In addition, the reliable sequencing of transcriptomes is opening new doors to studying many arthropods at levels comparable to those of previous model organisms (28).

Although the mandible and eye ultrastructure have been foci of morphological studies (76, 81) that have supported the Mandibulata hypothesis, neurogenesis has also played an important role in the Myriochelata versus Mandibulata debate. The neurogenesis pattern observed in selected myriapods and chelicerates, in which neural precursors migrate as postmitotic clusters of cells rather than as single cells as in the neuroblasts of hexapods and crustaceans, is considered to be homologous (14, 73, 100). In addition, myriapods and chelicerates share segmental invaginations of the neuroectoderm of each hemisegment from which the ventral organs are derived. The absence of these specific patterns in onychophoran outgroups suggests that they may be autapomorphies for Myriochelata (65). However, these putative apomorphies conflict with molecular phylogenetic analyses using dense arthropod sampling (79, 86), which instead defend Mandibulata rather than Myriochelata, and neural gene expression has alternatively been viewed as compatible with Mandibulata (25).

The composition of the arthropod brain is one of the most contentious issues in animal evolution (10, 93). In particular, controversy surrounds the innervation of segmental cephalic appendages by the brain and therefore the homology of such appendages (see **Figure 2**). For the major arthropod groups, *Hox* expression data have aided in aligning head segments (48, 93); these data are also available for onychophorans (24). In the case of onychophorans, the major brain neuropils arise from only the anterior-most body segment and only two pairs of segmental appendages (the antenna and jaw) are innervated by the brain (66). This set of traits is taken as an indication that the region of the central nervous system corresponding to the arthropod tritocerebrum is not differentiated as part of the onychophoran brain (contradicting other recent investigations; 26, 103) but instead belongs to the ventral nerve cords. If the last common ancestor of Onychophora and Arthropoda possessed a brain consisting of a protocerebrum and deutocerebrum but lacked the tritocerebrum, the latter would be a novel character of arthropods (66).

Whether the primitive arthropod appendage is uniramous or biramous and the specific homologies between different rami (e.g., exopods, epipods, exites) in branched appendages have been debated for centuries (7). A study (113) using a comparative cell lineage analysis of uniramous and biramous limbs in an amphipod crustacean via single-cell labeling suggested that "biramy" in crustaceans results from the splitting of a single limb axis and may not correspond to the state described as biramy in many fossil arthropods, such as trilobites, in which the putative exopod more closely resembles another axis. If correct, biramy as observed in crown-group Tetraconata may be a relatively novel character rather than a plesiomorphy retained from the arthropod stem group as conventionally hypothesized.

The possibilities for testing these and other evolutionary hypotheses with comparative developmental biology studies have no limits. As whole genomes of more arthropods become available and more functional assays are applied to these questions, we should be able to provide more explicit hypotheses of homology that will continue to be tested phylogenetically.

CONCLUSIONS

Arthropods have dominated animal diversity throughout their evolutionary history. Here we have discussed key issues for evaluating the arthropod tree of life, focusing on novel aspects contributed by anatomy, the early Paleozoic fossil record, and molecular approaches, the last increasingly being phylogenomic in scope. We conclude that this knowledge and the field of developmental biology, which is now incorporating data from nonmodel organisms, will contribute toward resolving standing issues on homology and phylogenetic relationships.

SUMMARY POINTS

1. Arthropods are the most diverse group of animals in the extant biota and have been so since the early Cambrian.
2. The position of arthropods among the protostome animals has been elucidated by the Ecdysozoa hypothesis. Onychophora (velvet worms) is the most likely sister group of arthropods.

3. The arthropod tree of life can be divided into five major branches: Pycnogonida, Euchelicerata, Myriapoda, Crustacea, and Hexapoda. The monophyly of each branch is well supported apart from Crustacea, which is likely paraphyletic with respect to Hexapoda in a clade named Tetraconata or Pancrustacea.
4. Three competing hypotheses describe the relationships of these major lineages, but Chelicerata is most probably sister group to Mandibulata, which includes the three groups of arthropods with mandibles as mouthparts: myriapods, crustaceans, and hexapods.
5. Noninvasive three-dimensional reconstruction techniques for studying anatomy, the application of such techniques to fossils, and next-generation sequencing techniques are promising sources of new character data for arthropod phylogenetics.
6. The arthropod stem group includes lobopodians and anomalocaridids, the anatomy of which is becoming increasingly understood from exceptionally preserved Cambrian fossils.
7. Remaining standing issues are the internal relationships of Arachnida and the relationships of the major lineages of Crustacea, including the identity of the sister group of hexapods. Various lines of evidence point to remipedes as a strong candidate for the hexapod sister group.

DISCLOSURE STATEMENT

The authors are not aware of any affiliations, memberships, funding, or financial holdings that might be perceived as affecting the objectivity of this review.

ACKNOWLEDGMENTS

We are indebted to the Editorial Committee of the *Annual Review of Entomology* for the invitation to write this review. M. Harris, C. Arango, and J. Pakes kindly assisted with photographs. A. Schmidt-Rhaesa kindly provided the original illustrations modified for **Figure 2**.

LITERATURE CITED

1. Aguinaldo AMA, Turbeville JM, Lindford LS, Rivera MC, Garey JR, et al. 1997. Evidence for a clade of nematodes, arthropods and other moulting animals. *Nature* 387:489–93
2. Andrew DR. 2011. A new view of insect-crustacean relationships II. Inferences from expressed sequence tags and comparisons with neural cladistics. *Arthropod Struct. Dev.* 40:289–302
3. Bäcker H, Fanenbruck M, Wägele JW. 2008. A forgotten homology supporting the monophyly of Tracheata: the subcoxa of insects and myriapods re-visited. *Zool. Anz.* 247:185–207
4. Bartolomaeus T, Quast B, Koch M. 2009. Nephridial development and body cavity formation in *Artemia salina* (Crustacea: Branchiopoda): no evidence for any transitory coelom. *Zoomorphology* 128:247–62
5. Beutel RG, Ge S-Q, Hörnschemeyer T. 2008. On the head morphology of *Tetraphalerus*, the phylogeny of Archostemata and the basal branching events in Coleoptera. *Cladistics* 24:270–98
6. Bitsch C, Bitsch J. 2004. Phylogenetic relationships of basal hexapods among the mandibulate arthropods: a cladistic analysis based on comparative morphological characters. *Zool. Scr.* 33:511–50
7. **Boxshall GA. 2004. The evolution of arthropod limbs. *Biol. Rev.* 79:253–300**
8. Brenneis G, Ungerer P, Scholtz G. 2008. The chelifores of sea spiders (Arthropoda, Pycnogonida) are the appendages of the deutocerebral segment. *Evol. Dev.* 10:717–24
9. Brusca RC, Brusca GJ. 2003. *Invertebrates*. Sunderland, MA: Sinauer. 936 pp. 2nd ed.

7. Synthesizes homologies of rami and podomeres of limbs of different body segments across Arthropoda, drawing on musculature, paleontology, and gene expression.

10. Budd GE. 2002. A palaeontological solution to the arthropod head problem. *Nature* 417:271–75
11. Budd GE, Telford MJ. 2009. The origin and evolution of arthropods. *Nature* 457:812–17
12. Carapelli A, Lió P, Nardi F, van der Wath E, Frati F. 2007. Phylogenetic analysis of mitochondrial protein coding genes confirms the reciprocal paraphyly of Hexapoda and Crustacea. *BMC Evol. Biol.* 7(Suppl. 2):S8
13. Caravas J, Friedrich M. 2010. Of mites and millipedes: recent progress in resolving the base of the arthropod tree. *Bioessays* 32:488–95
14. Chipman AD, Stollewerk A. 2006. Specification of neural precursor identity in the geophilomorph centipede *Strigamia maritima*. *Dev. Biol.* 290:337–50
15. Clark AG, Eisen MB, Smith DR, Bergman CM, Oliver B, et al. 2007. Evolution of genes and genomes on the *Drosophila* phylogeny. *Nature* 450:203–18
16. Daley AC, Budd GE, Caron JB, Edgecombe GD, Collins D. 2009. The Burgess shale anomalocaridid *Hurdia* and its significance for early euarthropod evolution. *Science* 323:1597–600
17. Dial RJ, Ellwood MDF, Turner EC, Foster WA. 2006. Arthropod abundance, canopy structure, and microclimate in a Bornean lowland tropical rain forest. *Biotropica* 38:643–52
18. Dunlop JA, Alberti G. 2008. The affinities of mites and ticks: a review. *J. Zool. Syst. Evol. Res.* 46:1–18
19. Dunlop JA, Anderson LI, Kerp H, Hass H. 2003. Preserved organs of Devonian harvestmen. *Nature* 425:916
20. Dunlop JA, Arango CP. 2005. Pycnogonid affinities: a review. *J. Zool. Syst. Evol. Res.* 43:8–21
21. Dunn CW, Hejnol A, Matus DQ, Pang K, Browne WE, et al. 2008. Broad taxon sampling improves resolution of the Animal Tree of Life. *Nature* 452:745–49
22. Edgecombe GD. 2009. Palaeontological and molecular evidence linking arthropods, onychophorans, and other Ecdysozoa. *Evol. Educ. Outreach* 2:178–90
23. Edgecombe GD. 2010. Arthropod phylogeny: an overview from the perspectives of morphology, molecular data and the fossil record. *Arthropod Struct. Dev.* 39:74–87
24. Eriksson BJ, Tait NN, Budd GE, Janssen R, Akam M. 2010. Head patterning and Hox gene expression in an onychophoran and its implications for the arthropod head problem. *Dev. Genes Evol.* 220:117–22
25. Eriksson J, Stollewerk A. 2010. Expression patterns of neural genes in *Euperipatoides kanangrensis* suggest divergent evolution of onychophoran and euarthropod neurogenesis. *Proc. Natl. Acad. Sci. USA* 107:22576–81
26. Eriksson J, Stollewerk A. 2010. The morphological and molecular processes of onychophoran brain development show unique features that are neither comparable to insects nor to chelicerates. *Arthropod Struct. Dev.* 39:478–90
27. Ertas B, von Reumont BM, Wägele JW, Misof B, Burmester T. 2009. Hemocyanin suggests a close relationship of Remipedia and Hexapoda. *Mol. Biol. Evol.* 26:2711–18
28. Ewen-Campen B, Shaner N, Panfilio KA, Suzuki Y, Roth S, Extavour CG. 2011. The maternal and early embryonic transcriptome of the milkweed bug *Oncopeltus fasciatus*. *BMC Genomics* 12:61
29. Friedrich F, Beutel RG. 2010. Goodbye Halteria? The thoracic morphology of Endopterygota (Insecta) and its phylogenetic implications. *Cladistics* 26:579–612
30. Gabriel WN, Goldstein B. 2007. Segmental expression of Pax3/7 and Engrailed homologs in tardigrade development. *Dev. Genes Evol.* 217:421–33
31. Garwood R, Dunlop JA, Sutton MD. 2009. High-fidelity X-ray micro-tomography reconstruction of siderite-hosted Carboniferous arachnids. *Biol. Letters* 5:841–44
32. Giribet G. 2003. Molecules, development and fossils in the study of metazoan evolution; Articulata versus Ecdysozoa revisited. *Zoology* 106:303–26
33. Giribet G, Edgecombe GD, Carpenter JM, D'Haese CA, Wheeler WC. 2004. Is Ellipura monophyletic? A combined analysis of basal hexapod relationships with emphasis on the origin of insects. *Org. Divers. Evol.* 4:319–40
34. Giribet G, Edgecombe GD, Wheeler WC. 2001. Arthropod phylogeny based on eight molecular loci and morphology. *Nature* 413:157–61
35. Giribet G, Edgecombe GD, Wheeler WC, Babbitt C. 2002. Phylogeny and systematic position of Opiliones: a combined analysis of chelicerate relationships using morphological and molecular data. *Cladistics* 18:5–70

36. Giribet G, Ribera C. 2000. A review of arthropod phylogeny: new data based on ribosomal DNA sequences and direct character optimization. *Cladistics* 16:204–31

37. Giribet G, Richter S, Edgecombe GD, Wheeler WC. 2005. The position of crustaceans within the Arthropoda—evidence from nine molecular loci and morphology. In *Crustacean Issues 16: Crustacea and Arthropod Relationships. Festschrift for Frederick R. Schram*, ed. S Koenemann, RA Jenner, pp. 307–52. Boca Raton, FL: Taylor & Francis

37. A combined analysis of morphology and molecules for extant arthropods using a target-gene approach, focusing on the status of Crustacea.

38. Grimaldi DA. 2010. 400 million years on six legs: on the origin and early evolution of Hexapoda. *Arthropod Struct. Dev.* 39:191–203

39. Harzsch S. 2006. Neurophylogeny: architecture of the nervous system and a fresh view on arthropod phyologeny. *Integr. Comp. Biol.* 46:162–94

40. Harzsch S, Hafner G. 2006. Evolution of eye development in arthropods: phylogenetic aspects. *Arthropod Struct. Dev.* 35:319–40

41. Haug JT, Waloszek D, Haug C, Maas A. 2010. High-level phylogenetic analysis using developmental sequences: the Cambrian *Martinssonia elongata*, *Musacaris gerdgeyeri* gen. et sp. nov. and their position in early crustacean evolution. *Arthropod Struct. Dev.* 39:154–73

42. Hejnol A, Obst M, Stamatakis A, Ott M, Rouse GW, et al. 2009. Assessing the root of bilaterian animals with scalable phylogenomic methods. *Proc. R. Soc. B* 276:4261–70

43. Hörnschemeyer T, Beutel RG, Pasop F. 2002. Head structures of *Priacma serrata* Leconte (Coleoptera, Archostemata) inferred from X-ray tomography. *J. Morphol.* 252:298–314

44. Hou X-G, Aldridge RJ, Bergström J, Siveter DJ, Siveter DJ, Feng X-H. 2004. *The Cambrian Fossils of Chengjiang, China. The Flowering of Early Animal Life*. Malden, MA: Blackwell. 233 pp.

45. Illumina_Inc. 2007. DNA sequencing with Solexa® technology. **http://www.plantsciences.ucdavis.edu/bit150/2006/JD_Lecture/Lecture%201%20Databases/Solexa_DNAsequencing.pdf**

46. Inward D, Beccaloni G, Eggleton P. 2007. Death of an order: a comprehensive molecular phylogenetic study confirms that termites are eusocial cockroaches. *Biol. Lett.* 3:331–35

47. Ishiwata K, Sasaki G, Ogawa J, Miyata T, Su Z-H. 2011. Phylogenetic relationships among insect orders based on three nuclear protein-coding gene sequences. *Mol. Phylogenet. Evol.* 58:169–80

48. Jager M, Murienne J, Clabaut C, Deutsch J, Le Guyader H, Manuel M. 2006. Homology of arthropod anterior appendages revealed by Hox gene expression in a sea spider. *Nature* 441:506–8

49. Janssen R, Budd GE. 2010. Gene expression suggests conserved aspects of *Hox* gene regulation in arthropods and provides additional support for monophyletic Myriapoda. *EvoDevo* 1:4

50. Janssen R, Damen WGM, Budd GE. 2011. Expression of *collier* in the premandibular segment of myriapods: support for the traditional Atelocerata concept or a case of convergence? *BMC Evol. Biol.* 11:50

51. Janssen R, Eriksson JB, Budd GE, Akam M, Prpic N-M. 2010. Gene expression patterns in onychophorans reveal that regionalization predates limb segmentation in pan-arthropods. *Evol. Dev.* 12:363–72

52. Jenner RA. 2010. Higher-level crustacean phylogeny: consensus and conflicting hypotheses. *Arthropod Struct. Dev.* 39:143–53

53. Koch M. 2009. Protura. In *Encyclopedia of Insects*, ed. VH Resh, R Cardé, pp. 855–58. San Diego, CA: Academic Press/Elsevier Science. 2nd ed.

54. Koenemann S, Olesen J, Alwes F, Iliffe TM, Hoenemann M, et al. 2009. The post-embryonic development of Remipedia (Crustacea)—additional results and new insights. *Dev. Genes Evol.* 219:131–45

55. Kühl G, Briggs DEG, Rust J. 2009. A great-appendage arthropod with a radial mouth from the Lower Devonian Hunsrück Slate, Germany. *Science* 323:771–73

56. Lak M, Néraudeau D, Nel A, Cloetens P, Perrichot V, Tafforeau P. 2008. Phase contrast X-ray synchrotron imaging: opening access to fossil inclusions in opaque amber. *Microsc. Microanal.* 14:251–59

57. Lavrov DV, Brown WM, Boore JL. 2004. Phylogenetic position of the Pentastomida and (pan)crustacean relationships. *Proc. R. Soc. B* 271:537–44

58. Liu J, Steiner M, Dunlop JA, Keupp H, Shu D, et al. 2011. An armoured Cambrian lobopodian from China with arthropod-like appendages. *Nature* 470:526–30

59. Ma X, Hou X, Bergström J. 2009. Morphology of *Luolishania longicruris* (Lower Cambrian, Chengjiang Lagerstätte, SW China) and the phylogenetic relationships within lobopodians. *Arthropod Struct. Dev.* 38:271–91

60. Mallatt J, Giribet G. 2006. Further use of nearly complete 28S and 18S rRNA genes to classify Ecdysozoa: 37 more arthropods and a kinorhynch. *Mol. Phylogenet. Evol.* 40:772–94
61. Mallatt JM, Garey JR, Shultz JW. 2004. Ecdysozoan phylogeny and Bayesian inference: first use of nearly complete 28S and 18S rRNA gene sequences to classify the arthropods and their kin. *Mol. Phylogenet. Evol.* 31:178–91
62. Manton SM. 1977. *The Arthropoda: Habits, Functional Morphology, and Evolution*. Oxford: Clarendon Press. 527 pp.
63. Margulies M, Egholm M, Altman WE, Attiya S, Bader JS, et al. 2005. Genome sequencing in microfabricated high-density picolitre reactors. *Nature* 437:376–80
64. Masta SE, Longhorn SJ, Boore JL. 2009. Arachnid relationships based on mitochondrial genomes: asymmetric nucleotide and amino acid bias affects phylogenetic analyses. *Mol. Phylogenet. Evol.* 50:117–28
65. Mayer G, Whitington PM. 2009. Velvet worm development links myriapods with chelicerates. *Proc. R. Soc. B* 276:3571–79
66. Mayer G, Whitington PM, Sunnucks P, Pflüger H-J. 2010. A revision of brain composition in Onychophora (velvet worms) suggests that the tritocerebrum evolved in arthropods. *BMC Evol. Biol.* 10:255
67. **Meusemann K, von Reumont BM, Simon S, Roeding F, Strauss S, et al. 2010. A phylogenomic approach to resolve the arthropod tree of life. *Mol. Biol. Evol.* 27:2451–64**

67. The broadest taxon/gene coverage yet undertaken for an EST-based analysis of arthropod phylogeny.

68. Møller OS, Olesen J, Avenant-Oldewage A, Thomsen PF, Glenner H. 2008. First maxillae suction discs in Branchiura (Crustacea): development and evolution in light of the first molecular phylogeny of Branchiura, Pentastomida, and other "Maxillopoda". *Arthropod Struct. Dev.* 37:333–46
69. Morozova O, Hirst M, Marra MA. 2009. Applications of new sequencing technologies for transcriptome analysis. *Annu. Rev. Genom. Human Gen.* 10:135–51
70. Murienne J, Edgecombe GD, Giribet G. 2010. Including secondary structure, fossils and molecular dating in the centipede tree of life. *Mol. Phylogenet. Evol.* 57:301–13
71. Pechmann M, Khadjeh S, Sprenger F, Prpic NM. 2010. Patterning mechanisms and morphological diversity of spider appendages and their importance for spider evolution. *Arthropod Struct. Dev.* 39:453–67
72. Pepato AR, Rocha CE, Dunlop JA. 2010. Phylogenetic position of the acariform mites: sensitivity to homology assessment under total evidence. *BMC Evol. Biol.* 10:235
73. Pioro HL, Stollewerk A. 2006. The expression pattern of genes involved in early neurogenesis suggests distinct and conserved functions in the diplopod *Glomeris marginata*. *Dev. Genes Evol.* 216:417–30
74. Pisani D. 2009. Arthropods. In *The Timetree of Life*, ed. SB Hedges, S Kumas, pp. 251–54. Oxford: Oxford Univ. Press
75. Pisani D, Poling LL, Lyons-Weiler M, Hedges SB. 2004. The colonization of land by animals: molecular phylogeny and divergence times among arthropods. *BMC Biol.* 2:1–10
76. Popadic A, Panganiban G, Rusch D, Shear WA, Kaufman TC. 1998. Molecular evidence for the gnathobasic derivation of arthropod mandibles and for the appendicular origin of the labrum and other structures. *Dev. Genes Evol.* 208:142–50
77. Regier JC, Shultz JW, Ganley AR, Hussey A, Shi D, et al. 2008. Resolving arthropod phylogeny: exploring phylogenetic signal within 41 kb of protein-coding nuclear gene sequence. *Syst. Biol.* 57:920–38
78. Regier JC, Shultz JW, Kambic RE. 2005. Pancrustacean phylogeny: Hexapods are terrestrial crustaceans and maxillopods are not monophyletic. *Proc. R. Soc. B* 272:395–401
79. **Regier JC, Shultz JW, Zwick A, Hussey A, Ball B, et al. 2010. Arthropod relationships revealed by phylogenomic analysis of nuclear protein-coding sequences. *Nature* 463:1079–83**

79. Provides the largest gene set for arthropods produced by the target-gene approach, with several new systematic proposals for crustaceans.

80. Ren D, Labandeira CC, Santiago-Blay JA, Rasnitsyn A, Shih C, et al. 2009. A probable pollination mode before angiosperms: Eurasian, long-proboscid scorpionflies. *Science* 326:840–47
81. Richter S. 2002. The Tetraconata concept: hexapod-crustacean relationships and the phylogeny of Crustacea. *Org. Divers. Evol.* 2:217–37
82. Richter S, Loesel R, Purschke G, Schmidt-Rhaesa A, Scholtz G, et al. 2010. Invertebrate neurophylogeny: suggested terms and definitions for a neuroanatomical glossary. *Front. Zool.* 7:29

83. Richter S, Møller OS, Wirkner CS. 2009. Advances in crustacean phylogenetics. *Arthropod Syst. Phylogenet.* 67:275–86
84. Roeding F, Borner J, Kube M, Klages S, Reinhardt R, Burmester T. 2009. A 454 sequencing approach for large scale phylogenomic analysis of the common emperor scorpion (*Pandinus imperator*). *Mol. Phylogenet. Evol.* 53:826–34
85. Roeding F, Hagner-Holler S, Ruhberg H, Ebersberger I, von Haeseler A, et al. 2007. EST sequencing of Onychophora and phylogenomic analysis of Metazoa. *Mol. Phylogenet. Evol.* 45:942–51
86. Rota-Stabelli O, Campbell L, Brinkmann H, Edgecombe GD, Longhorn SJ, et al. 2011. A congruent solution to arthropod phylogeny: phylogenomics, microRNAs and morphology support monophyletic Mandibulata. *Proc. R. Soc. B* 278:298–306
87. Rota-Stabelli O, Kayal E, Gleeson D, Daub J, Boore JL, et al. 2010. Ecdysozoan mitogenomics: evidence for a common origin of the legged invertebrates, the Panarthropoda. *Genome Biol. Evol.* 2:425–40
88. Sanders KL, Lee MS. 2010. Arthropod molecular divergence times and the Cambrian origin of pentastomids. *Syst. Biodivers.* 8:63–74

88. Up-to-date relaxed clock methods use paleontological calibration to date deep divergencies in Arthropoda.

89. Schmidt-Rhaesa A, Bartolomaeus T, Lemburg C, Ehlers U, Garey JR. 1998. The position of the Arthropoda in the phylogenetic system. *J. Morphol.* 238:263–85
90. Schmidt-Rhaesa A, Kulessa J. 2007. Muscular architecture of *Milnesium tardigradum* and *Hypsibius* sp. (Eutardigrada, Tardigrada) with some data on *Ramazotius oberhaeuseri*. *Zoomorphology* 126:265–81
91. Scholtz G. 1998. Cleavage, germ band formation and head segmentation: the ground pattern of the Euarthropoda. In *Arthropod Relationships*, ed. RA Fortey, RH Thomas, pp. 317–32. London: Chapman & Hall
92. Scholtz G. 2002. The Articulata hypothesis—or what is a segment? *Org. Divers. Evol.* 2:197–215
93. Scholtz G, Edgecombe GD. 2006. The evolution of arthropod heads: reconciling morphological, developmental and palaeontological evidence. *Dev. Genes Evol.* 216:395–415

93. Reviews the main controversies in aligning head segments between different arthropod groups, including the segmental affinities of the labrum.

94. Shear WA. 1991. The early development of terrestrial ecosystems. *Nature* 351:283–89
95. Shear WA, Edgecombe GD. 2010. The geological record and phylogeny of Myriapoda. *Arthropod Struct. Dev.* 39:174–90
96. Shultz JW. 2007. A phylogenetic analysis of the arachnid orders based on morphological characters. *Zool. J. Linn. Soc.* 150:221–65
97. Siveter DJ, Sutton MD, Briggs DEG, Siveter DJ. 2004. A Silurian sea spider. *Nature* 431:978–80
98. Socha JJ, Westneat MW, Harrison JF, Waters JS, Lee W-K. 2007. Real-time phase-contrast X-ray imaging: a new technique for the study of animal form and function. *BMC Biol.* 5:6
99. Stegner MEJ, Richter S. 2011. Morphology of the brain in *Hutchinsoniella macracantha* (Cephalocarida, Crustacea). *Arthropod Struct. Dev.* 40:221–43
100. Stollewerk A, Tautz D, Weller M. 2003. Neurogenesis in the spider: new insights from comparative analysis of morphological processes and gene expression patterns. *Arthropod Struct. Dev.* 32:5–16
101. Strausfeld NJ. 2009. Brain organization and the origin of insects: an assessment. *Proc. R. Soc. B* 276:1929–37
102. Strausfeld NJ, Andrew DR. 2011. A new view of insect-crustacean relationships I. Inferences from neural cladistics and comparative neuroanatomy. *Arthropod Struct. Dev.* 40:276–88

102. Provides a recent cladistic treatment of nervous system characters with a focus on crustacean ancestry of insects.

103. Strausfeld NJ, Strausfeld CM, Loesel R, Rowell D, Stowe S. 2006. Arthropod phylogeny: onychophoran brain organization suggests an archaic relationship with a chelicerate stem lineage. *Proc. R. Soc. B* 273:1857–66
104. Telford MJ, Bourlat S, Economou A, Papillon D, Rota-Stabelli O. 2009. The origins and evolution of the Ecdysozoa. In *Animal Evolution. Genomes, Fossils, and Trees*, ed. MJ Telford, DTJ Littlewood, pp. 71–79. Oxford: Oxford Univ. Press
105. Terry MD, Whiting MF. 2005. Mantophasmatodea and phylogeny of the lower neopterous insects. *Cladistics* 21:240–57
106. Timmermans MJTN, Roelofs D, Mariën J, van Straalen NM. 2008. Revealing pancrustacean relationships: Phylogenetic analysis of ribosomal protein genes places Collembola (springtails) in a monophyletic Hexapoda and reinforces the discrepancy between mitochondrial and nuclear DNA markers. *BMC Evol. Biol.* 8:83

107. Ungerer P, Scholtz G. 2008. Filling the gap between identified neuroblasts and neurons in crustaceans adds new support for Tetraconata. *Proc. R. Soc. B* 275:369–76
108. von Reumont BM, Meusemann K, Szucsich NU, Dell'Ampio E, Gowri-Shankar V, et al. 2009. Can comprehensive background knowledge be incorporated into substitution models to improve phylogenetic analyses? A case study on major arthropod relationships. *BMC Evol. Biol.* 9:1–19

108. Provides a large taxonomic sample using nuclear ribosomal genes and probabilistic tree reconstruction approaches.

109. Wheeler WC, Cartwright P, Hayashi CY. 1993. Arthropod phylogeny: a combined approach. *Cladistics* 9:1–39
110. Whiting MF. 2002. Mecoptera is paraphyletic: multiple genes and phylogeny of Mecoptera and Siphonaptera. *Zool. Scr.* 31:93–104
111. Wirkner CS, Prendini L. 2007. Comparative morphology of the hemolymph vascular system in scorpions—a survey using corrosion casting, microCT, and 3D-reconstruction. *J. Morphol.* 268:401–13
112. Wirkner CS, Richter S. 2007. The circulatory system in Mysidacea—implications for the phylogenetic position of Lophogastrida and Mysida (Malacostraca, Crustacea). *J. Morphol.* 268:311–28
113. Wolff C, Scholtz G. 2008. The clonal composition of biramous and uniramous arthropod limbs. *Proc. R. Soc. B* 275:1023–28
114. Zhang X-G, Siveter DJ, Waloszek D, Maas A. 2007. An epipodite-bearing crown-group crustacean from the Lower Cambrian. *Nature* 449:595–98
115. Zhang XG, Maas A, Haug JT, Siveter DJ, Waloszek D. 2010. A eucrustacean metanauplius from the Lower Cambrian. *Curr. Biol.* 20:1075–79
116. Ziegler A, Faber C, Mueller S, Bartolomaeus T. 2008. Systematic comparison and reconstruction of sea urchin (Echinoidea) internal anatomy: a novel approach using magnetic resonance imaging. *BMC Biol.* 6:33
117. Zrzavý J, Hypša V, Vlášková M. 1998. Arthropod phylogeny: taxonomic congruence, total evidence and conditional combination approaches to morphological and molecular data sets. In *Arthropod Relationships*, ed. RA Fortey, RH Thomas, pp. 97–107. London: Chapman & Hall

RELATED RESOURCES

Edgecombe GD, Giribet G. 2007. Evolutionary biology of centipedes (Myriapoda: Chilopoda). *Annu. Rev. Entomol.* 52:151–70
Sierwald P, Bond JE. 2007. Current status of the myriapod class Diplopoda (millipedes): taxonomic diversity and phylogeny. *Annu. Rev. Entomol.* 52:401–20
Trautwein MD, Wiegmann BM, Beutel RG, Kjer KM, Yeates DK. 2012. Advances in insect phylogeny. *Annu. Rev. Entomol.* 57:449–68
Whitfield JB, Kjer KM. 2008. Ancient rapid radiations of insects: challenges for phylogenetic analysis. *Annu. Rev. Entomol.* 53:449–72

Morphology and Diversity of Exocrine Glands in Lepidopteran Larvae

Francesca Vegliante[1,*] and Ivar Hasenfuss[2]

[1]Senckenberg Naturhistorische Sammlungen Dresden, Museum für Tierkunde, D-01109 Dresden, Germany; email: napoliacoppe@tiscali.it

[2]Retired, Department of Biology, University of Erlangen-Nürnberg, D-91058 Erlangen, Germany; email: IHasenfuss@t-online.de

Annu. Rev. Entomol. 2012. 57:187–204

First published online as a Review in Advance on September 9, 2011

The *Annual Review of Entomology* is online at ento.annualreviews.org

This article's doi:
10.1146/annurev-ento-120710-100646

0066-4170/12/0107-0187$20.00

*Corresponding author

Keywords

caterpillars, anatomy, histology, ultrastructure, secretion, chemistry

Abstract

The morphology of 21 exocrine glands and 13 supposedly exocrine structures recorded for lepidopteran larvae is reviewed. The epitracheal glands, for which a double role (exocrine and endocrine) has been demonstrated, are examined as well. Function is well known for at least 8 glands but completely unknown for 6 glands, for 10 putative glandular structures, and for the exocrine component of the epitracheal glands. Functional studies on the remaining structures are insufficient; in some cases (mandibular gland and adenosma) homologous glands may play a different role depending on the species, and only a few taxa have been examined. The secretions of 13 glandular types have been analyzed chemically. The histology of 11 glands is known at the ultrastructural level, whereas that of 6 glands and 7 putative glandular structures is completely unknown. Comparative anatomical studies of the osmeterium, adenosma, and Verson's glands may yield useful information for phylogenetic reconstructions.

INTRODUCTION

Most glands of lepidopteran larvae can be classified as exocrine or endocrine. Exocrine glands release their secretion to the exterior, whereas endocrine glands secrete hormones into the larva's hemolymph or into target tissues. Hormones are substances that act at very low concentrations, influencing the physiology of target tissues in the same organism that produced them (50). The epitracheal glands are the only glands that fulfill both exocrine and endocrine functions in lepidopteran larvae. Most exocrine glands of caterpillars consist exclusively of class I gland cells sensu Noirot & Quennedey (90); class III cells are present in the epitracheal and Verson's glands; and the Newcomer's organ cannot be classified according to these criteria.

Here we provide a complete summary of all exocrine glands described in caterpillars, some of which have not been included in previous reviews (e.g., 11, 51). We define glands as structures that include more than one secretory cell; hence, glandular setae and most of their derivatives, such as lenticles (79), pore cupola organs (80), and the spraying glands of some Saturniidae (51), are excluded from this review. Because of space limitations, we provide figures only of structures thus far illustrated insufficiently in the literature. The morphology of a typical lepidopteran larva is shown in **Supplemental Figure 1** (follow the **Supplemental Material link** from the Annual Reviews home page at **http://www.annualreviews.org**), the terms indicating the orientation of histological sections are explained in **Supplemental Figure 2**, and the position of the different structures in the caterpillar's body are schematically illustrated in **Supplemental Figures 3** (glands) and **4** (putative glands). Serial sections and scanning electron microscopy micrographs were obtained as described in Reference 111. We follow Kristensen et al. (75) for lepidopteran classification and Hasenfuss & Kristensen (54) for setal nomenclature.

MANDIBULAR GLANDS

Most lepidopteran larvae have one pair of tubular glands opening into the lumen of the apodeme of the cranial adductor muscle of the mandible (11, 111, 124). The apodeme in turn opens to the exterior mesally at the base of the mandible; hence, the glands never open lateral to the mandible (60, 111). These richly tracheated glands (60) usually reach posterior to the thorax (**Supplemental Figure 3*a***); more rarely they end in the head (49) or extend far into the abdomen (31). They receive one nerve from the subesophageal ganglion (60) and one nerve from the retrocerebral endocrine glands (5). In all examined Cossidae, except for *Zeuzera pyrina*, a reservoir is interposed between the duct and the secretory region of the gland (e.g., 21, 85). The cuticular intima is continuous over the entire lumen, and the cells do not divide but grow by polyploidization during the larval stage (60, 68). Ultrastructural data are available for two species, in which the glands appear to secrete saliva (1, 68). A digestive function of the mandibular glands (82) is demonstrated in some species, whereas in others the secretion is defensive against ants and pathogenic fungi (96) or it acts as a pheromone to regulate population density (4). In some Notodontidae, the mandibular glands are modified into endocrine glands of unknown function (59, 60). On the basis of their presence in a micropterigid embryo (73), the mandibular glands are ascribed to the lepidopteran ground plan.

ACCESSORY MANDIBULAR GLANDS

One pair of trilobate glands (**Figure 1**), which open through numerous small pores on the mesal surface of the mandibles, is recorded from representatives of the Incurvarioidea, Zygaenoidea, Yponomeutoidea, Pyraloidea, Geometroidea, and Papilionoidea (112, 124). Morphologically

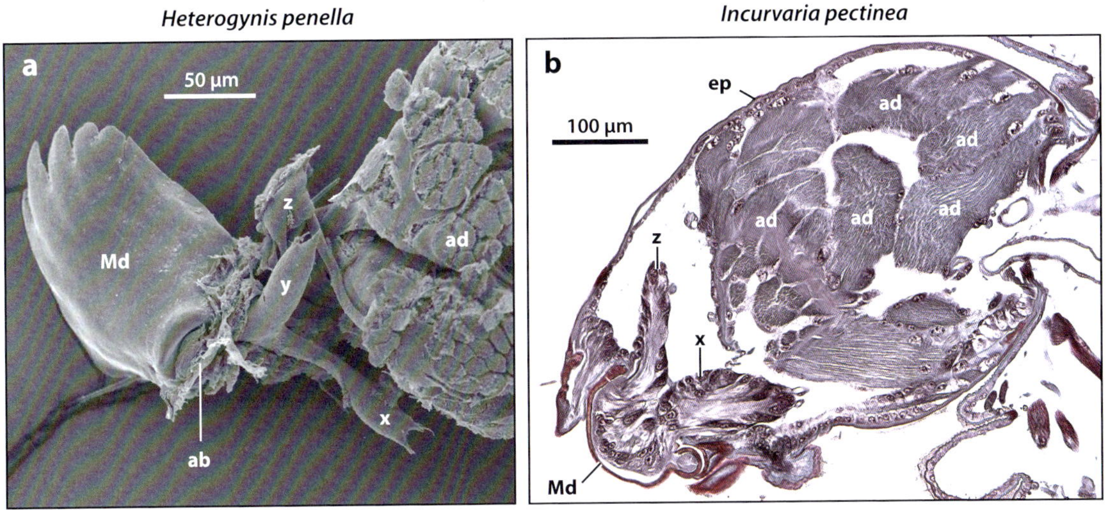

Figure 1

Accessory mandibular glands. (*a*) A scanning electron microscopy (SEM) micrograph of the mandible (Md) of *Heterogynis penella* (Zygaenoidea: Heterogynidae), dissected out of the head together with its cranial adductor muscle (ad) and with the accessory mandibular gland (x, y, z), in lateral view. The apodeme of the abductor muscle (ab) has been cut short. (*b*) Parasagittal section of the head of *Incurvaria pectinea* (Incurvariidae) showing two lobes (x, z) of the accessory mandibular gland. Abbreviation: ep, epicranium.

similar structures have been described in a cossid, but their homology to the accessory mandibular glands needs confirmation based on a reexamination of their position relative to the mandibles (111). The function of the accessory mandibular glands is unknown.

LABIAL GLANDS, OR SILK GLANDS

All caterpillars have one pair of tubular labial glands, or silk glands, the ducts of which are fused at their outermost portion and open on the premento-hypopharyngeal lobe. The presence of a spinneret, or fusulus (**Figure 2**) (figures 19 and 20 in Reference 52), bearing the unpaired orifice of these glands is an autapomorphy of the Glossata (54). The region of the common duct passing through the premento-hypopharyngeal lobe, incorrectly called the silk press (54, p. 143), has a thickened cuticle (**Figure 2**) and it bears the insertion of muscles from the hypopharynx (1–10 pairs) and from the prementum (1–2 pairs) (106, 111). A spinning larva attaches the silk to the substrate and then moves its head away, pulling the silk out of the gland (54). The shearing stress thus applied to the silk, adjusted by the abovementioned muscles, causes the liquid silk to solidify (74). The paired ducts of the labial glands, located ventral to the gut (21), may be histologically uniform (most species) or differentiated into two regions (115). The more or less convoluted and richly tracheated secretory portions lie lateral and/or dorsal to the gut, terminating into the abdomen (3, 21, 106) (**Supplemental Figure 3*b***). The cuticular intima of the secretory portions is very thin and porous; in some species it does not extend up to the posterior end of the gland (3, 106) and in others it is missing (18). The secretory portion may be histologically subdivided into two (most species) or more (121) regions. In the Bombycoidea, provided with two regions, the posterior region secretes the fibroin core of the silk, and the anterior region secretes an outer layer of sericin, which allows the silk filaments of both glands to adhere to each other and to the substrate (3, 106, 121). The labial gland cells do not divide; they grow by polyploidization during the larval stage (3).

Premento-hypopharyngeal lobe: conical structure deriving from the fusion of the prementum (ventral part) with the hypopharynx (dorsal part)

Spinneret: tubular, partially sclerotized prolongation of the premento-hypopharyngeal lobe, bearing the silk gland orifice

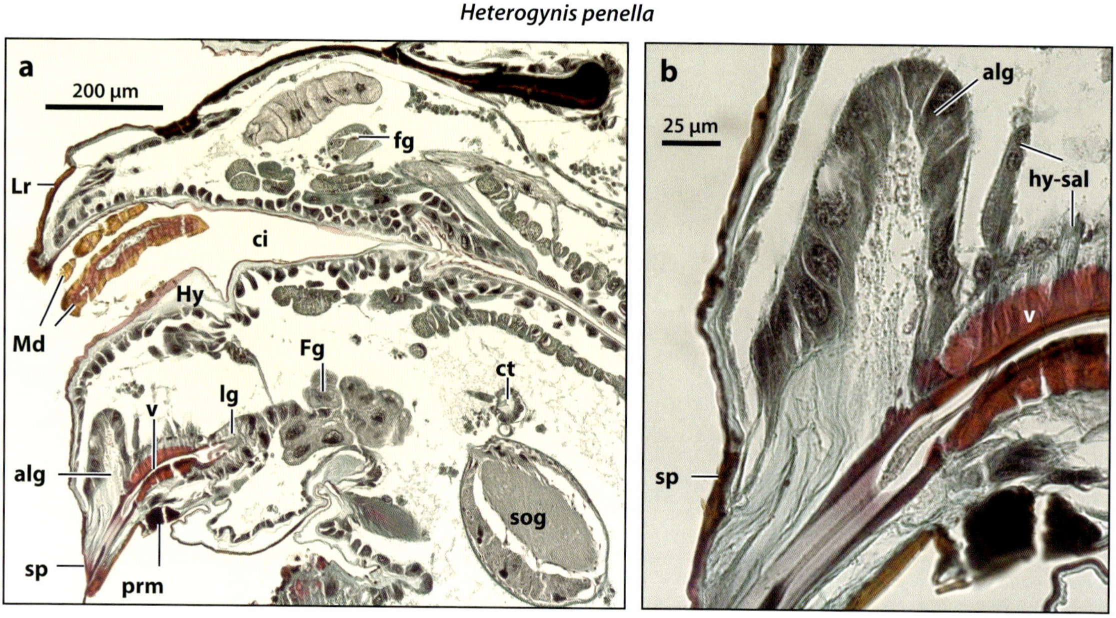

Figure 2

Heterogynis penella. (*a*) Sagittal section of the head, showing the labial gland (lg), Filippi's gland (Fg), and second accessory labial gland (alg). In *H. penella*, the brain is displaced into the thorax (111), and it is therefore not visible in this section. (*b*) Close-up of panel *a* showing the second accessory labial gland; note insertions of the dorsal muscles (hy-sal) on the wall of the "silk press" (v). Abbreviations: ci, cibarium; ct, corporotentorium; fg, frontal ganglion; Hy, hypopharynx; Lr, labrum; Md, mandible; prm, prementum; sog, subesophageal ganglion; sp, spinneret.

Cervical nerve: paired nerve arising from the subesophageal ganglion posterior to the mandibular, maxillary, and labial nerves

Esophageal nerve: nerve arising posteriorly from the hypocerebral ganglion, which in turn marks the posterior end of the recurrent nerve

Trail pheromone: pheromone used to mark paths, which are recognized by conspecific larvae

There is little agreement on the innervation of the labial glands; no innervation is explicitly recorded for the secretory region. The duct, or the labial gland in general, is reportedly innervated by the labial nerve (also innervating the silk press muscles; 65), the cervical nerve (109), and the esophageal nerve (107). An innervation by the labral nerve or by the corpus allatum (108) requires confirmation.

In addition to silk proteins, the labial glands of some species secrete digestive (82) and/or antimicrobial (77) enzymes. The antimicrobial glucose oxidase also influences the host plant's defenses against herbivory (37, 77). The labial glands of some gregarious species secrete trail pheromones soluble in polar solvents, helping the larvae to follow their nestmates (51, 99).

FILIPPI'S GLANDS, OR LYONET'S GLANDS

In many Neolepidoptera (75), a Filippi's gland opens in the paired duct of each labial gland (64, 111). In some Obtectomera, an evagination of the labial gland duct forms the Filippi's gland duct, which bears a tuft of unicellular lobes (absent in the Pieridae) at its blind end (111). Ductless Filippi's glands, the cells of which directly face the cuticle of the labial gland duct, occur in nonobtectomeran Neolepidoptera (64) and in some obtectomerans as well; the glands have been lost several times independently (111). Apart from the absence of glandular lobes at the blind end of the duct in the two examined species of *Pieris* (56), which may be an autapomorphy of this genus or of the family Pieridae, the presence and type of Filippi's glands do not seem to reflect phylogenetic relationships within the Obtectomera; however, the monophyly and phylogeny of the Obtectomera are still debated. Innervation, possibly including neurosecretory axons (116), comes from the labial nerve (65). In *Bombyx mori*, Filippi's glands undergo cycles of activity in correspondence to molts (114). Their function is unknown and probably not correlated with silk production (111). Ultrastructure suggests a role in exchanging small molecules (e.g., water, ions) between the hemolymph and the labial gland rather than synthesis of their own secretion (116).

SECOND ACCESSORY LABIAL GLAND

Sorensen et al. (106) first described an unpaired gland opening in the common duct of the labial glands. The main body of this second accessory labial gland is located on the dorsal wall of the duct, anterior to the muscular insertions; paired posterior lobes lie on the laterodorsal wall of the duct, between the insertions of the dorsal and ventral muscles (106). The gland cells are part of the epidermal layer of the labial gland duct (**Figure 2**); their ultrastructure is poorly known (106). This gland coexists with Filippi's glands in at least three species (112) (**Figure 2*a***) and its function is unknown.

VERSON'S GLANDS

Most caterpillars have 15 pairs of Verson's glands: one opening anterodorsal to the spiracle (or in the corresponding position) in T1-A8, one opening lateral to the base of the legs in T1-T3, and one opening lateroventrally in A8 (11) (**Supplemental Figure 3*c***) or A9 (70). Some species lack one or more pairs (70). Each gland consists of an outermost canal (or duct) cell, an intercalary (or saccule) cell, and a basal cell (also called the secretory cell, although it is not the only secretory cell of the gland) (see figure 1 in Reference 76). A duct traversing the canal cell ends in the intercalary cell with a terminal swelling (saccule; 76). The canal cell only synthesizes duct cuticle, whereas the intercalary cell produces the discontinuous saccule cuticle and, together with the basal cell, the gland's secretion (76). During intermolts, the basal cell gradually fills up with secretory vacuoles, greatly increasing in volume; it establishes a connection to the saccule just before releasing the secretion (76). The secretion flows over the newly formed cuticle during (118) or after ecdysis (6), and it is believed to form the cement layer, which in other insects is secreted on the cuticle by the dermal glands (118). Secretion chemistry depends on the stage (larva or pupa) following ecdysis and on the segmental location of the glands (63). The Verson's glands are not innervated (76) and they are under hormonal control (63, 110).

In the Lymantriinae, the Verson's glands of A1–A7 are displaced toward the dorsal midline, and two or more of them open into small, usually brightly colored protrusions of the body wall, called funnel warts (70). An unpaired, volcano-like middorsal funnel wart is present on A7 (family synapomorphy) and often on A6; paired, volcano-, or horn-like funnel warts may be present on A1–A4 (24, 70, 97) (**Supplemental Figure 3*d***). The crater-like depression of each unpaired funnel wart is eversible by increases in hemolymph pressure; it bears anteriorly the openings of two Verson's glands and posteriorly the insertions of one to two pairs of retractor muscles originating posterodorsally in the same segment (24, 70). Each paired funnel wart lacks muscles and it bears the opening of a single Verson's gland (24, 70). The glands opening into funnel warts remain active during intermolts; they release their secretion spontaneously or in response to disturbance (11, 70). The secretion deters feeding by ants (23), and some species smear it periodically over the body (11).

The grooming gland(s), opening dorsally on A1 in the Morphinae (Nymphalidae), might be modified Verson's glands as well (**Supplemental Figure 3*e***). In *Antirrhea weymeri*, they open through a pair of slightly eversible pores (see figure 3b in Reference 57) similar to paired funnel

Neolepidoptera: lepidopteran monophylum characterized by the presence of musculated, crochet-bearing larval prolegs

Obtectomera: lepidopteran group characterized by the immobility of A1–A4 in the pupa and by specialized pulvilli in the adult

T1, T2, T3: the three thoracic segments

Cement layer: a layer of polar substances embedded in the surface lipids coating the cuticle

A1–A10: abdominal segments 1–10

warts. Within an hour after molting, each gland releases a drop of secretion, which the caterpillar gathers with its head and smears over its trunk for unknown purposes (30, 57).

ADENOSMA, OR JUGULAR GLAND

In some Yponomeutidae, Noctuoidea, Hesperiidae, and Papilionoidea, a tubular to sacciform, usually unpaired jugular gland (or adenosma) opens ventrally on T1, anterior to the legs and antero-mesal to the microsetae MV2 and MV3 (e.g., 46, 88) (**Figure 4*d*, Supplemental Figure 3*f***). The scattered systematic distribution of this gland and the coexistence of two glands (one anterior, unpaired, and one posterior, paired) in a nymphalid (22) suggest that not all described adenosmas may be homologous. In the Yponomeutidae, the gland is not eversible; it opens on a movable conical protrusion of the body wall (98), with a pair of muscles inserting close to the orifice (102). In the other families, an invagination of the body wall around the orifice forms a vestibule, which can be everted by an increase in hemolymph pressure and retracted by several pairs of muscles originating on the head and/or on T1 (26, 84). In some Noctuoidea and Nymphalidae, extrinsic muscles insert on the glandular part of the adenosma (72, 84), which can be actively everted by some nymphalids (e.g., 35). Innervation from the T1 ganglion and tracheation from the T1 spiracle are recorded in the Notodontidae (26, 59). In most Notodontidae, in Nymphalidae, and possibly in the Noctuidae (84), the adenosma is used for defense; the secretion is sprayed against the enemy (Notodontidae: e.g., 26) or evaporates, diffusing volatiles repellant to ants and in many cases unpleasant to the human nose (Nymphalidae: e.g., 30, 92, 93). Larvae of *Cerura vinula* (Notodontidae) also add the jugular gland secretion to the silk of their cocoons (11). A riodinid uses its adenosma for communication with symbiotic ants (28). The adenosma of yponomeutids does not secrete trail pheromones (99); its function is unknown. Depending on the species, the secretion is dominated by formic acid (most notodontids and a noctuid; 84, 88), other carboxylic acids (nymphalids; 92), straight-chain hydrocarbons and terpenes (a noctuid; 105), or alcohols and esters (a notodontid; 51).

OSMETERIUM

An exclusive autapomorphy of the Papilionidae is the presence, in the larvae, of an eversible, often brightly colored organ (osmeterium) that is composed of a pair of blind-ending tubular arms sharing a common base, and opens middorsally on T1 (11) (**Supplemental Figure 3*g***). In most species the osmeterium is Y-shaped, with a conspicuous brownish patch of variable morphology (ellipsoid gland) on the posterior side of each arm (103) (**Figure 3*a***). When retracted, the Y-shaped osmeterium lies immediately ventral to the dorsal longitudinal muscles; several oblique muscles cross each osmeterial arm, and the tips of the retracted organ lie in the anterior third of A1 (see figure 10 in Reference 72). A retractor muscle from A1, which in some species crosses the contralateral muscle, inserts at the tip of each arm, and several retractor muscles from T1 insert on the stem of the organ (72, 103). A more complex type of osmeterium exists in *Zerynthia* (**Figure 3*b***). Here, each arm of the organ is bifurcated, and a glandular tubule, homologous to the ellipsoid gland, opens on the tip of the mesal branch (119). The lateral branch of each osmeterial arm is permanently invaginated, sharing a common basal membrane with the epidermis of the glandular tubule (119). The three pairs of retractor muscles have not been traced to their origins (119). The specialized and richly tracheated epithelium of the ellipsoid gland (17, 103, 119) may be the only source of secretion in *Zerynthia* (119), whereas in other genera histology and ultrastructure suggest a secretory role for all epidermal cells of the organ (17, 103). Papilionid larvae evert their osmeterium in response to mechanical disturbance or spontaneously (103); the secretion repels

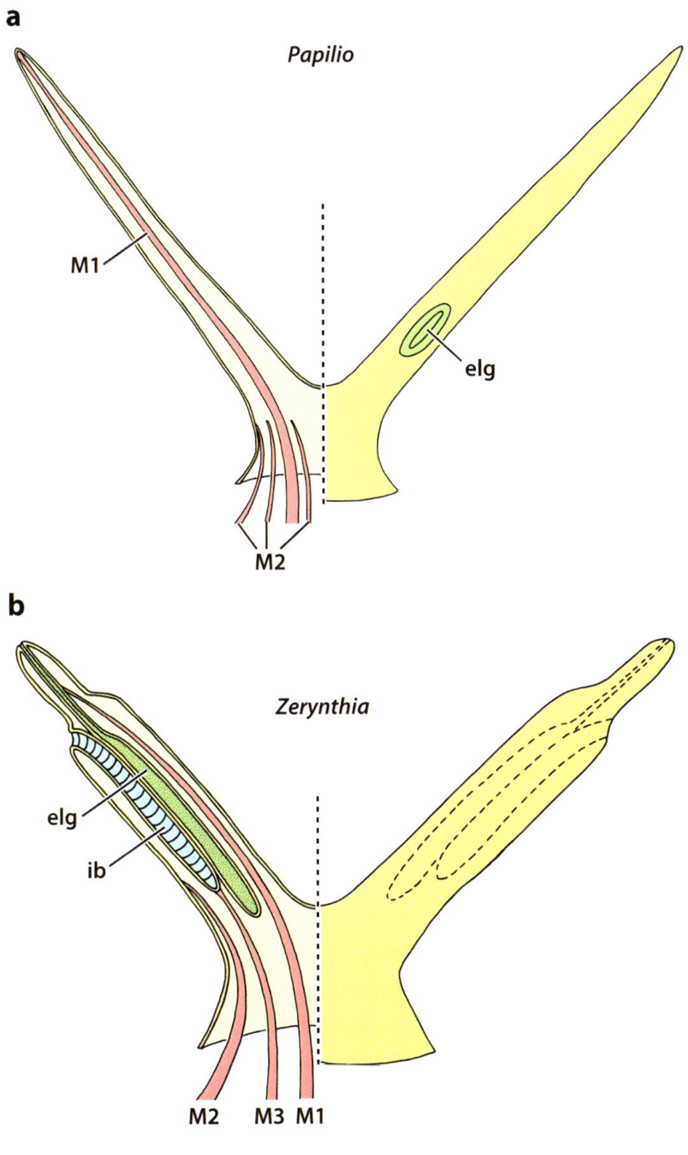

Figure 3

Scheme of the osmeterium in (*a*) *Papilio* (based on the description in Reference 103) and (*b*) *Zerynthia* (based on the description in Reference 119). Left: cross-sectional view; right: posterior view. Homologies according to Wegener (119). Abbreviations: elg, ellipsoid gland; ib, permanently invaginated branch; M1, M2, M3, retractor muscles.

ants (62), but no effect on vertebrates has been convincingly demonstrated. All major volatile components of the secretion (terpenoids, or aliphatic acids and their esters, depending on the species and instar) are synthesized by the larva, but small amounts of toxic compounds from the food plants may be present as well (91).

MYRMECOPHILIC ORGANS

L1: first larval instar

Apocrine: secretion process in which the gland cell releases its apical cytoplasm together with the secretion in membrane-bound vesicles

Merocrine: secretion process in which no portion of the cell is released together with the secretion

TNO: tentacle nectary organ

ATO: anterior tentacle organ

TO: tentacular organ

Larvae of the sister-group families Lycaenidae and Riodinidae show a number of adaptations against predation by ants. Myrmecophilous species have glandular organs that secrete nutritious fluids, which are eagerly consumed by ants (38). At least one myrmecophilous species is protected by the ants against predators and parasitoids (39).

The Newcomer's organ (or dorsal nectary organ), autapomorphic for the subfamily Lycaeninae, appears in a different instar (never in L1) depending on the species (38). At rest, it is externally visible as an unpaired, middorsal transverse slit on A7 (**Supplemental Figure 3*b***). This slit is the opening of an integumental invagination, the bottom of which bears centrally the orifices of two (earlier instars) or four (later instars) glands (80) and laterally the insertions of a pair of muscles (figure 2 in Reference 81); the muscles originate ventrolaterally on the body wall (89). Each gland consists of two cells, one of which (Halszelle) is muff-shaped and surrounds the apical part of the other cell (Drüsenzelle) (figure 11 in Reference 80). The apical plasmalemma of the Drüsenzelle is invaginated, forming a large extracellular cavity (80). The cuticle above this cavity is shaped like a flaccid seta, the tip of which may break off at the first wave of secretion (33, 80). Owing likely to apocrine (not merocrine) secretion, both cells gradually degenerate during intermolts, and they are replaced by another two cells at each molt (80). The redifferentiation of the gland from two epidermal cells closely recalls the development of setae, suggesting that each gland derives from a modified seta (80). Upon antennation by ants, the organ becomes more or less everted by an increase in hemolymph pressure, and a drop of secretion appears on its opening (38, 80). It is unclear whether the muscles serve as retractors, or whether they flatten the sac and release the fluid (80). Larvae of some species also offer drops of secretion when they feel threatened, in order to call the attention of attending ants; some obligate myrmecophiles (which cannot survive in nature if not attended by ants) release the secretion periodically even in the apparent absence of external stimuli (39). Depending on the species, the secretion contains different percentages of amino acids and sugars (38).

The dew patches (or dish organs) are unpaired, mediodorsal, dish-like depressions found on A2–A5 in larvae of some Aphnaeini (Lycaeninae); absent in L1, they appear successively, starting from the second molt (14) (**Supplemental Figure 3*b***). Their histology is unknown; dew patches continuously release a fluid that, if not removed by ants, becomes moldy, and the fungal infection kills the caterpillar (14).

The tentacle nectary organs (TNOs), present in some tribes of the Riodininae (38), are a pair of partially eversible, tubular invaginations of the integument and are found posterodorsal to the spiracles on A8 (**Supplemental Figure 3*i***). In the only species examined in detail, only the outermost half of each tube, which has a flat epidermis, is eversible; the duct of a gland opens in the innermost half of the tube, which has a columnar epidermis (100). A muscle originating on the "suprapedal lobe" of A8 inserts at the blind end of the organ (100). Upon antennation by ants, the TNOs can be everted independently from each other, each yielding a drop of secretion (27). Drops not utilized are reabsorbed when the TNOs are retracted by their muscles (27). The secretion, analyzed in a single species, is poor in sugars and rich in amino acids (27).

The metathoracic anterior tentacle organs (ATOs) (**Supplemental Figure 3*i***) of the Lemoniadini and Nymphidiini (Riodininae) and the tentacular organs (TOs) (**Supplemental Figure 3*b***) found on A8 in scattered lycaenid species do not produce nutritious secretions, but their eversion alters the behavior of attending ants (38). ATOs and TOs are anatomically similar: Both are a pair of eversible, tubular invaginations of the laterodorsal body wall, with plumose setae arranged around a muscular insertion at their tip (80, 100). Each organ is provided with a single retractor muscle, which originates from the ventral body wall of the same segment and inserts at the tip of the organ (80, 100). The organs of both sides are everted spontaneously, independent from each other, by an increase in hemolymph pressure (27, 80). The ATOs bear glandular "nipples" (probably modified setae) among the plumose setae (100). Ethological and biochemical investigations suggest a secretory role of the TOs (38, 39); Ehrhardt (33) but not Malicky (80) regarded their plumose setae as glandular. A (serial) homology of TNOs, TOs, and ATOs (e.g., 80) is unlikely in view of their systematic distribution (38).

MIDVENTRAL ABDOMINAL TRACHEAL GLANDS

An unpaired gland, deriving from the modified epidermis of the midventral tracheal node in each segment from A3 to A6 (**Supplemental Figure 3*k***), is recorded from some Noctuoidea, Saturniidae, and Papilionidae, particularly (but not only) in species distasteful to predators (12, 58). The midventral tracheal nodes, which are a common feature of the tracheal system in lepidopteran larvae, arise during embryogenesis by the fusion in the sagittal plane of the ventral tracheae, which originate directly from the spiracles and serve the ventral ganglionic chain (12, 58, 117). The midventral abdominal tracheal glands, deriving from the specialization of these nodes, are best developed in the Arctiinae, in which they have been studied in detail. Each glandular node, located just posteroventral to the ganglion, has an enlarged lumen lined by a thin cuticle; its epithelium consists of a few very large, possibly polyploid, glandular cells (12, 58, 117). The glands, which lack muscles and innervation, receive tracheoles from the ventral tracheae (12, 117). Histochemical and ultrastructural data suggest that the gland cells take up substances from the hemolymph to incorporate them in a lipoid secretion of unknown function (12, 58).

WAX GLANDS

Glands secreting wax-like substances [e.g., paraffin (83) or long-chain saturated alcohols (66)] have evolved several times independently in caterpillars (7, 8, 25, 66, 83; 104, p. 296). In the few species examined in detail, wax glands are specialized areas of the integument, where secretion of wax(-like) tubules occurs around glandular setae (Lasiocampidae: 7) or around repeated microsculptural elements of the epicuticle (Hesperiidae: 78; Epipyropidae: 83). In both species examined ultrastructurally, the procuticle lacks pore canals; wax canals are present in the epicuticle (78, 83). In the Hesperiidae, the wax glands, located ventrally on A7 and A8 (**Supplemental Figure 3*j***), are active only in the last larval instar; wax protects the pupa from drowning (25). Ventral abdominal wax glands are present on different segments in some Lasiocampidae, depending on the species (7, 67). Some Saturniidae produce wax-like substances with their abdominal scoli (66), whereas in the Epipyropidae early instars produce paraffin from the ventral surface of the body and later instars produce it from the dorsal surface (83).

TRAIL PHEROMONE GLANDS

Gregarious larvae of some Thaumetopoeinae, Lasiocampidae, Saturniidae, and Pieridae lay down a trail pheromone, soluble in apolar solvents, by brushing the ventral surface of the last abdominal segment (**Supplemental Figure 3*l***) against the substrate (41, 42). Scanning electron microscopy and gross dissection of the last abdominal segment failed to reveal any glands or glandular openings, which suggests that the secretion may be produced by specialized areas of the integument (41, 44) or, less probably, by glandular setae (43). The pheromone of different *Malacosoma* spp. consists of 5β-cholestane-3,24-dione and/or 5β-cholestane-3-one (41).

CYANOGENIC GLANDS

A pair of protuberances, the spinulose apex of which can be wetted with a defensive secretion, is present just ventral to the A1 spiracles in two species of Thyrididae (19, 20). The larvae apply the tip of these protuberances to attacking enemies (ants) or sources of disturbance (forceps); one species invaginates the protuberances at rest (19). In *Calindoea trifascialis*, one pair of sacciform glands, so far only superficially described, opens on A1 just behind the base of the protuberances (**Supplemental Figure 3*m***) (19, 20). Their secretion, which is effective against ants (19, 20), is a mixture of aromatic compounds, sesquiterpenes, and aliphatic esters dominated by benzaldehyde and mandelonitrile (20).

Cuticular cavities: endocuticular spaces full of cyanogenic defensive secretion, probably synthesized by the fat bodies and epidermis

SER: smooth endoplasmic reticulum

SUBDORSAL ABDOMINAL GLANDS

One pair of eversible, hemispherical, wrinkled protuberances, each bearing three glandular openings, is present on A2 between setae D1 and SD1 in some ennomine Geometridae (55) (**Supplemental Figure 3*n***). Each protuberance bears the insertions of five circular and two longitudinal muscles; the gland is served by a trachea from the A2 spiracle (55). The function of this gland is unknown. Eversible vesicles dorsal to setae SD are also recorded on A2–A7 of *Selepa* spp. (Noctuoidea; 69).

EPICRANIAL GLAND

Larvae of some *Morpho* species, if disturbed, emit a drop of fluid from a pore located on the epicranium (**Supplemental Figure 3*o***) and then comb it onto the subdorsal setae of the trunk using two sclerotized spikes located near the pore (16). The secretion repels ants, parasitic wasps, and water (16). The gland has not been described.

MEDIODORSAL GLANDS OF ZYGAENIDAE

Larvae of *Neurosymploca* bear a conspicuously colored, posteriorly bent, unpaired protuberance mediodorsally on T2 (**Supplemental Figure 3*p***); some species have serially homologous organs on one or more segments from T3 to A8 (10). The cuticle of the protuberance is thinner than the surrounding body cuticle and it lacks the cuticular cavities (45, 87, 123) typical of the family (10). The epidermis of the body wall in the immediate surroundings of the protuberance is columnar; the epidermis of the protuberance is flatter but still taller than that of the rest of the body wall (10). No secretion has been observed; the presence of numerous peroxisomes and an axial tubule of smooth endoplasmic reticulum (SER) in each microvillus of the protuberance cells suggests production of lipids or waxes, although SER is scarce (10). The ultrastructure of the columnar epidermis surrounding the protuberance is unknown (10).

VENOMOUS SCOLI

In most urticating caterpillars (including the Megalopygidae) the venom is secreted by modified glandular setae, which may or may not be arranged on nonglandular scoli; each seta is provided with a single gland cell (47). The presence in saturniids of venomous scoli with a glandular epidermis consisting of two cell types (113) requires confirmation.

EPITRACHEAL GLANDS

Nine pairs of epitracheal glands have been detected in pyraloid, noctuoid, and bombycoid larvae (2, 71, 125); homologous glands occur in tortricoids (101), but they have never been looked for in lower lepidopterans. Each gland is attached to the branching point of the tracheae from the very short common trunk coming from a spiracle, or to the ventral trachea near the branching point (2, 71, 126; 110, unnumbered figure) (**Supplemental Figure 3*q***). In the best-investigated species, each epitracheal gland consists of four cells, one of which (the Inka cell) is a large endocrine cell responsible for the induction of the ecdysis motor pattern (71, 126). One of the other three cells apparently lacks a connection to the exterior, and one is a class III (sensu Noirot & Quennedey; 90) exocrine cell associated with a canal cell (71, 126). Each epitracheal gland hangs in the hemocele suspended by its canal cell, and it is enveloped by the basal membrane of the trachea (71). Reports of bi- or tricellular epitracheal glands including an Inka cell (e.g., 2) are probably erroneous. Only the Inka cell, which occasionally lies separate from the others, survives at metamorphosis (126). The exocrine cell apparently releases its secretion in the tracheal lumen during and just after ecdysis (71, 126). The three smaller cells, taken together, may represent a tracheal analog of the Verson's glands. Verson's glands degenerate in the pupa as well (126).

Blown specimen: a caterpillar that has been eviscerated and then blown with air and dried on a heat source, for dry preservation

STRUCTURES OF PUTATIVE GLANDULAR NATURE

A short, tubular pharyngeal gland opening in the hypopharynx or "pharynx" is recorded from *Yponomeuta*, *Zeuzera*, and *Sesia* (as *Trochilium*) (8, p. 730; 21, p. 233, figure 12*i*). Berlese's (8, figure 577) "sagittal section" of *Yponomeuta* is evidently a reconstruction from a series of sections; the pharyngeal glands of yponomeutids are paired cuticular thickenings of the laterodorsal wall of the hypopharynx (**Figure 4*a*,*b***). What appears to be a lumen (**Figure 4*a***) at low magnification is actually spongy endocuticle (**Figure 4*b***), and no orifice is visible in histological sections (112). The epidermis is equally thick in the entire hypopharynx, including the glands. A study of the better-developed, probably homologous Schlunddrüsen (pharyngeal glands) of cossids and sesiids (21) may clarify their possible glandular nature. The superficially described "maxillary glands" of a gelechioid (49) (**Supplemental Figure 4*a***) might actually be accessory mandibular glands or, less probably, Filippi's or pharyngeal glands.

Stemapods are the modified, nonambulatory anal prolegs of some Notodontidae (**Supplemental Figure 4*b***). Their eversible, often brightly colored distal portion (lash; 86), possibly homologous to the planta, is invaginated at rest by the contraction of a muscle, and it becomes everted by an increase in hemolymph pressure upon disturbance (61). In *Cerura* spp., the eversion of the lashes may be accompanied by the emission of a strong odor or by the appearance of clouds of condensate on neighboring plastic walls (61, 120). Cuticle microsculpture suggests an adaptation for the release of volatiles (61, 120), but no volatile acids were found in lash extracts (13). The lashes have a flat epidermis with irregular nuclei (61). Stemapods probably evolved independently many times in the Notodontidae (86), and not all of them may be glandular.

The supracoxal vesicles (**Figure 4*c***), recorded only for the Drepanini, are a pair of possibly glandular sacs opening laterally on T1, just dorsal to the base of the legs (104). Their spontaneous eversion has never been observed, but they can be everted when a living larva is compressed between two fingers (9). Everted supracoxal vesicles are sometimes seen in blown specimens (**Figure 4*c***) (see Reference 15, p. 228, for this preservation technique). The similarly located and shaped prothoracic subventral tubes of some Zygaenidae, provided with one or more retractor muscles, are probably not glandular (36, 122).

Some Nolinae (Noctuoidea) have an unpaired, medioventral bulge, likely to be a gland, just behind the legs on T2 and T3 (**Figure 4*d***) and, more rarely, on T1 (94). Different authors (8, 9, 122) erroneously regarded the medioventral glands of the Nolinae, the supracoxal vesicles, and the prothoracic subventral tubes as (serial) homologs of the adenosma.

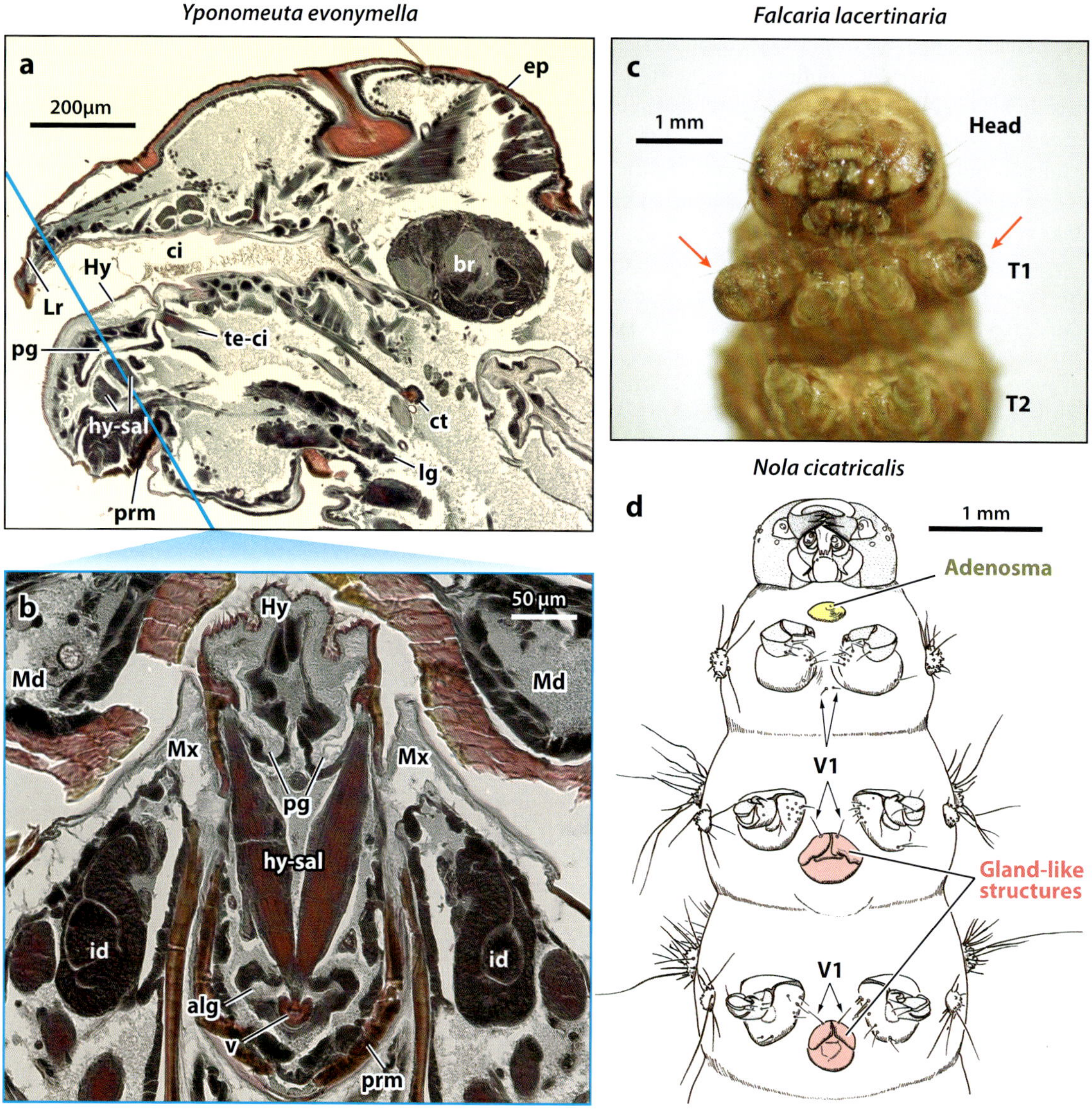

Figure 4

Putative glands. (*a,b*) Paired pharyngeal gland (pg) of *Yponomeuta evonymella* (L., 1758) (Yponomeutidae) as seen (*a*) in a parasagittal section of the head and (*b*) in a transverse section of the maxillolabium-hypopharynx along the blue line in panel *a*. Abbreviations: alg, second accessory labial gland; br, brain; ci, cibarium; ct, corporotentorium; ep, epicranium; Hy, hypopharynx; hy-sal, dorsal muscles of the silk press; id, imaginal disc; lg, labial gland; Lr, labrum; Md, mandible; Mx, maxilla; prm, prementum; te-ci, ventral cibarial dilator muscle; v, silk press. (*c,d*) Appearance of putative thoracic glands in blown larvae, ventral view (specimens from the collection of the Museum für Tierkunde Dresden). (*c*) Supracoxal vesicles (*arrows*) of *Falcaria lacertinaria* (Drepanidae). (*d*) Medioventral glands (*pink*) of *Nola cicatricalis* (Nolinae); camera lucida drawing. Serial homology of these glands to the partially everted adenosma can be excluded on the basis of their position relative to the legs and to the setae V1.

Hemileucine Saturniidae have a small, possibly glandular pocket, provided with a retractor muscle, just ventral to the A1 and A7 spiracles (**Supplemental Figure 4*c***); vestiges of such structures are recorded on A2–A6 and A8 in a single species (94; 97, figure L54E). These lateral abdominal glands are everted upon disturbance, but no secretion is evident (94). Similarly located, partially eversible protuberances are present on A2 and more rarely on A7 in some Zygaenidae (32) (**Supplemental Figure 4*d***). A permanently everted postspiracular lobe, usually hidden under the larva's dense cover of setae, lies anteroventral (T1) or posteroventral (A1–A8) to each spiracle in the Megalopygidae (34, 95) (**Supplemental Figure 4*e***). Epstein (34, p. 75) regarded these lobes as sensilla, but their histology (95) suggests a glandular nature.

Curetis spp. (Lycaenidae) have a pair of perforated chambers on the T1 shield and one laterally on A7 (**Supplemental Figure 4*f***). These organs, originally described as possibly glandular chambers opening through several orifices (29), may simply be clusters of modified pore cupola organs (40). Some Notodontidae have modified integumental areas in the labium and tarsi (86, p. 135, p. 146) (**Supplemental Figure 4*g***). The tarsal ones, adhesive in function, are probably not glandular (53). Secretion of a sticky substance from the horn on A8 of early-instar Sphingidae (48) (**Supplemental Figure 4*h***) needs confirmation.

CONCLUSION

Of more than 900 publications providing information on exocrine glands of caterpillars and their secretions, most deal with the labial gland, adenosma, and myrmecophilic organs; many other glands have been only superficially mentioned in a few papers. Much work is still needed to uncover the function of several (putative) glands, some of which could be of practical importance. Among these, the Filippi's, second accessory labial, mandibular, accessory mandibular, and pharyngeal glands, possibly together with the adenosma (37), may play a role in inducing or suppressing host plant defenses. As demonstrated for the mandibular gland (4), they may provide olfactory cues to ovipositing parasitoids. The second accessory labial gland might play a role in silk spinning. Investigations on the homology, musculature, and systematic distribution of the adenosma; on the comparative anatomy of the osmeterium (shape and position of the ellipsoid gland, musculature); and on the diversity in number, development, and modifications of the Verson's glands are likely to improve our understanding of lepidopteran phylogeny, particularly below the family level for the last two cases.

DISCLOSURE STATEMENT

The authors are not aware of any affiliations, memberships, funding, or financial holdings that might be perceived as affecting the objectivity of this review.

ACKNOWLEDGMENTS

This review began in occasion of the 2008 Annual Meeting of the Entomological Society of America, when F. Vegliante was invited by Dr. D.R. Davis, Prof. Dr. S.J. Weller, and Prof. Dr. C. Mitter to give a talk on caterpillar anatomy. Prof. M.P. Zalucki proposed its publication in this journal. Prof. Dr. R.L. Brown, Dr. A. Zilli, Dr. H. Yoshitake, and Dr. C. Schmidt provided us with interesting literature. Dr. Yoshitake and Dr. Schmidt also helped with translations. U. Kallweit photographed the larva in **Figure 4*c***. Prof. Dr. N.P. Kristensen and two anonymous reviewers provided helpful comments on the manuscript. To all of them we give our sincere gratitude.

LITERATURE CITED

1. Akai H. 1976. *Ultrastructural Morphology of Insects*. Tokyo: Jpn. Sci. Soc. Press
2. Akai H. 1992. Ultrastructure of epitracheal gland during larval-pupal molt of *Bombyx mori*. *Cytologia* 57:195–201
3. Akai H. 1998. Silk glands. In *Microscopic Anatomy of Invertebrates*, ed. FW Harrison, 11A:219–53. New York: Wiley-Liss
4. Anderson P, Lofqvist J. 1996. Asymmetric oviposition behaviour and the influence of larval competition in the two pyralid moths *Ephestia kuehniella* and *Plodia interpunctella*. *Oikos* 76:47–56
5. Audsley N, Duve H, Thorpe A, Weaver RJ. 2000. Morphological and physiological comparisons of two types of allatostatin in the brain and retrocerebral complex of the tomato moth, *Lacanobia oleracea* (Lepidoptera: Noctuidae). *J. Comp. Neurol.* 424:37–46
6. Barbier R. 1982. Activités cellulaires et évolution d'un appareil ciliaire lors de l'organogenèse et de l'ontogenèse de la glande de Verson de *Galleria mellonella* L. (Lepidoptera, Pyralidae). *Bull. Soc. Zool. Fr.* 107(1):111–25
7. Barth R. 1953. Estudos sôbre as placas das glândulas de cêra da lagarta de *Tolype serralta* (Lepidoptera, Lasiocampidae). *Mem. Inst. Oswaldo Cruz* 51:263–75
8. Berlese A. 1909. *Gli Insetti*, 1. Milan, Italy: Soc. Ed. Libr.
9. Blair KG. 1934. On the prothoracic glands of the larvae of the Drepanidae and Notodontidae (Lep.). *Proc. Trans. South Lond. Entomol. Nat. Hist. Soc.* 1933–34:116–17
10. Bode W, Naumann CM. 1987. Structure of a newly discovered glandular organ in *Neurosymploca* larvae (Lepidoptera, Zygaenidae). *Zool. Jahrb. Anat.* 114(3):319–29
11. Bourgogne J. 1951. Ordre des Lépidoptères. In *Traité de Zoologie: Anatomie, Systématique, Biologie*, ed. PP Grassé, 10(1):174–448. Paris: Masson et Cie Éditeurs
12. Byers JR, Hinks CF. 1976. Fine structure of the midventral abdominal tracheal glands in banded wolly bear caterpillars (Arctiidae: Lepidoptera). *Can. J. Zool.* 54:1824–39
13. Chow YS, Tsai RS. 1989. Protective chemicals in caterpillar survival. *Experientia* 45:390–92
14. Clark GC, Dickson CGC. 1956. The honey gland and tubercles of larvae of the Lycaenidae. *Lepidopt. News* 10:37–43
15. Colas G. 1988. *Guide de l'entomologiste*. Paris: Éditions N. Boubée et Cie
16. Constantino LM. 1997. Natural history, immature stages and hostplants of *Morpho amathonte* from western Colombia (Lepidoptera: Nymphalidae: Morphinae). *Trop. Lepidopt.* 8(2):75–80
17. Crossley AC, Waterhouse DF. 1969. The ultrastructure of the osmeterium and the nature of its secretion in *Papilio* larvae (Lepidoptera). *Tissue Cell* 1:525–54
18. Da Cruz-Landim C. 1973 Ultraestrutura da glândula salivar larval de *Amalo helops megapyrha* (Lepidoptera-Arctiidae). *Anais da Academia Brasileira de Ciências* 45(3-4):565–584
19. Darling DC. 2003. Morphology and behaviour of the larva of *Calindoea trifascialis* (Lepidoptera: Thyrididae), a chemically-defended retreat-building caterpillar from Vietnam. *Zootaxa* 225:1–16
20. Darling DC, Schroeder FC, Meinwald J, Eisner M, Eisner T. 2001. Production of a cyanogenic secretion by a thyridid caterpillar (*Calindoea trifascialis*, Thyrididae, Lepidoptera). *Naturwissenschaften* 88:306–9
21. Dauberschmidt K. 1934. Vergleichende Morphologie des Lepidopterendarmes und seiner Anhänge. *Z. Angew. Entomol.* 20:204–67
22. de Oliveira Borges E, Faccioni-Heuser MC, Moreira GRP. 2010. Morphology of the prosternal glands of *Heliconius erato* (Lepidoptera: Nymphalidae). *Psyche* 2010:1–8
23. Deml R. 2001. Mechanismen chemischer Verteidigung bei larvalen Lymantriiden (Lepidoptera). *Mitt. Dtsch. Ges. Allg. Angew. Entomol.* 13:385–88
24. Deml R, Dettner K. 2001. Comparative morphology and evolution of the funnel warts of larval Lymantriidae (Lepidoptera). *Arthropod Struct. Dev.* 30:15–26
25. Dethier VG. 1942. Abdominal glands of Hesperiinae. *J. N. Y. Entomol. Soc.* 50:203–6
26. Detwiler JD. 1922. The ventral prothoracic gland of the red-humped apple caterpillar (*Schizura concinna* Smith & Abbot). *Can. Entomol.* 54:175–91
27. DeVries PJ. 1988. The larval ant-organs of *Thisbe irenea* (Lepidoptera: Riodinidae) and their effects upon attending ants. *Zool. J. Linn. Soc.* 94:379–93

28. DeVries PJ, Cabral BC, Penz CM. 2004. The early stages of *Apodemia paucipuncta* (Riodinidae): myrmecophily, a new caterpillar ant-organ and consequences for classification. *Milwaukee Public Mus. Contrib. Biol. Geol.* 102:1–13
29. DeVries PJ, Harvey DJ, Kitching IJ. 1986. The ant-associated epidermal organs on the larva of the lycaenid butterfly *Curetis regula* Evans. *J. Nat. Hist.* 20:621–33
30. DeVries PJ, Martinez GE 1993. The morphology, natural history, and behavior of the early stages of *Morpho cypris* (Nymphalidae: Morphinae)—140 years after formal recognition of the butterfly. *J. N. Y. Entomol. Soc.* 101:515–30
31. Drecktrah HG, Knight KL, Brindley TA. 1966. Morphological investigations of the internal anatomy of the fifth larval instar of the European corn borer. *Iowa State J. Sci.* 40(3):257–86
32. Efetov KA, Tarmann GM. 2004. The presence of lateral abdominal 'glands' in some species of Zygaenidae (Insecta, Lepidoptera). *Denisia* 13:301–3
33. Ehrhardt R. 1914. Über die Biologie und Histologie der myrmekophilen Organen von *Lycaena orion*. *Ber. Naturforschenden Ges. Freibg. Breisgau* 20:XC–XCVIII
34. Epstein ME. 1996. Revision and phylogeny of the limacodid-group families, with evolutionary studies on slug caterpillars (Lepidoptera: Zygaenoidea). *Smithson. Contrib. Zool. Nr.* 582:1–102
35. Fanfani A, Valcurone Dazzini M. 1989. The jugular gland of *Inachis io* L. larva (Lepidoptera, Nymphalidae). *Pubbl. Ist. Entomol. Univ. Pavia* 38:1–8
36. Fänger H, Naumann CM. 2001. The morphology of the last instar larva of *Aglaope infausta* (Lepidoptera: Zygaenidae: Chalcosiinae). *Eur. J. Entomol.* 98:201–18
37. Felton GW. 2008. Caterpillar secretions and induced plant responses. In *Induced Plant Resistance to Herbivory*, ed. A Schaller, pp. 369–87. Berlin: Springer
38. Fiedler K. 1991. Systematic, evolutionary and ecological implications of myrmecophily within the Lycaenidae (Insecta: Lepidoptera: Papilionoidea). *Bonn. Zool. Monogr.* 31:1–210
39. Fiedler K, Hölldobler B, Seufert P. 1996. Butterflies and ants: the communicative domain. *Experientia* 52:14–24
40. Fiedler K, Seufert P, Maschwitz U, Azarae HJ. 1995. Notes on larval biology and pupal morphology of Malaysian *Curetis* butterflies (Lepidoptera: Lycaenidae). *Tyô to Ga* 45(4):287–99
41. Fitzgerald TD. 1995. *The Tent Caterpillars*. Ithaca, NY: Cornell Univ. Press
42. Fitzgerald TD. 2003. Role of trail pheromone in foraging and processionary behavior of pine processionary caterpillars *Thaumetopoea pityocampa*. *J. Chem. Ecol.* 29:513–32
43. Fitzgerald TD, Pescador-Rubio A. 2002. The role of tactile and chemical stimuli in the formation and maintenance of the processions of the social caterpillar *Hylesia lineata* (Lepidoptera: Saturniidae). *J. Insect Behav.* 15:659–74
44. Fitzgerald TD, Underwood DLA. 1998. Trail marking by the larva of the madrone butterfly *Eucheira socialis* and the role of the trail pheromone in communal foraging behavior. *J. Insect Behav.* 11:247–63
45. Franzl S. 1992. Synthesis, transport, and storage of cyanogenic glucosides in larvae of *Zygaena trifolii* (Esper, 1783) (Lepidoptera: Zygaenidae). *Theses Zool.* 19:21–37
46. García-Barros E. 1987. Morphology and chaetotaxy of the first instar larve of six species of the *Satyrus* (s. l.) series (Lepidoptera: Nymphalidae). *Syst. Entomol.* 12:335–44
47. Gilmer PM. 1925. A comparative study of the poison apparatus of certain lepidopterous larvae. *Ann. Entomol. Soc. Am.* 18:203–39
48. Goossens T. 1869. M. Goossens communique verbalement diverses remarques q'il a faites sur des particularités que lui ont présentées plusieurs chenilles. *Ann. Soc. Entomol. Fr.* 9(4):LX–LXII
49. Gray J. 1931. The post-embryological development of the digestive system in *Homaledra sabalella* Chambers. *Ann. Entomol. Soc. Am.* 24:45–107
50. Gullan PJ, Cranston PS. 1994. *The Insects: An Outline of Entomology*. London: Chapman & Hall
51. Hallberg E, Poppy G. 2003. Exocrine glands: chemical communication and chemical defense. In *Handbuch der Zoologie*, 4(36): *Lepidoptera, Moths and Butterflies, Part 2*, ed. NP Kristensen, pp. 361–75. Berlin: De Gruyter
52. Hasenfuss I. 1980. Die Präimaginalstadien von *Thyris fenestrella* Scopoli (Thyrididae, Lepidoptera). *Bonn. Zool. Beitr.* 31:168–190

53. Hasenfuss I. 1999. The adhesive devices in larvae of the Lepidoptera (Insecta, Pterygota). *Zoomorphology* 119:143–62
54. Hasenfuss I, Kristensen NP. 2003. Skeleton and muscles: immatures. In *Handbuch der Zoologie*, 4(36): *Lepidoptera, Moths and Butterflies, Part 2*, ed. NP Kristensen, pp. 132–64. Berlin: De Gruyter
55. Heitzman RL. 1982. Descriptions of the mature larva and pupa of *Hypomecis umbrosaria* (Hübner) (Lepidoptera: Geometridae). *Proc. Entomol. Soc. Wash.* 84:111–16
56. Helm FE. 1876. Ueber die Spinndrüsen der Lepidopteren. *Zeitschr. Wiss. Zool.* 26:434–69
57. Heredia MD, Alvarez-Lopez H. 2004. Larval morphology and behavior of *Antirrhea weymeri* Salazar, Constantino & López, 1998 (Nymphalidae: Morphinae) in Colombia. *J. Lepidopt. Soc.* 58:88–93
58. Hinks CF, Byers JR. 1975. A new glandular organ in some toxic caterpillars. *Experientia* 31:965–67
59. Hintze C. 1969. Morphologische Untersuchungen an zwei Drüsentypen (Thoraxdrüse, Mandibeldrüse) von Lepidopterenraupen. *Z. Morphol. Tiere* 64:9–20
60. Hintze-Podufal C. 1972. Zur phylogenetischen Umwandlung einer exokrinen in eine endokrine Drüse: vergleichende Untersuchungen an den Mandibulardrüsen der Notodontidenraupen. *Zool. Beitr., N. F.* 18:167–97
61. Hintze-Podufal C. 1990. Zur Embryonalentwicklung und Funktionsmorphologie der Schwanzgabel von *Cerura vinula* L. (Lepidoptera). *Mitt. Dtsch. Ges. Allg. Angew. Entomol.* 7:470–74
62. Honda K. 1983. Defensive potential of components of the larval osmeterial secretion of papilionid butterflies against ants. *Physiol. Entomol.* 8:173–79
63. Howarth KL, Riddiford LM. 1991. Cellular differentiation of specialised epidermal cells: the dermal glands. In *Physiology of the Insect Epidermis*, ed. K Binnington, A Retnakaran, pp. 185–94. East Melbourne: CSIRO Publ.
64. **Ishimori N. 1927. Note on the silk-gland of *Phassus signifer* Walker. *Proc. Imp. Acad.* 3:614–15**

64. The most basal record of Filippi's glands on the lepidopteran phylogenetic tree (in a hepialid).

65. Ivanova TS. 1953. Innervation of the silk emitting gland and the anatomical structure of its single emitting duct in the oak silk-worm *Anteraea* [sic] *pernyi* Guér. *Entomol. Obozr.* 33:198–200
66. Jones CG, Young AM, Jones TH, Blum MS. 1982. Chemistry and possible roles of cuticular alcohols of the larval atlas moth. *Comp. Biochem. Physiol.* 73B:797–801
67. Jörg ME. 1951. Anatomia microscopica de glandulas cericigenas en orugas de *Artace obumbrata* Köhler. *Rev. Soc. Entomol. Argent.* 15(1–3):173–76
68. Kimura M, Oota Y. 1986. Morphological studies on the salivary gland of the larval monshirocho, *Pieris rapae crucivora* (Lepidoptera). *Rep. Fac. Sci. Shizuoka Univ.* 20:27–37
69. Kitching IJ, Rawlins J. 1998. The Noctuoidea. In *Handbuch der Zoologie*, 4 (35): *Lepidoptera, Moths and Butterflies, Part 1*, ed. NP Kristensen, pp. 355–401. Berlin: De Gruyter
70. **Klatt B. 1909. Die Trichterwarzen der Liparidenlarven. *Zool. Jahrb. Anat.* 27:135–70**

70. Provides a comprehensive anatomical and histological study of the modifications of the Verson's glands in lymantriid larvae.

71. Klein C, Kallenborn HG, Radlicki C. 1999. The "Inka cell" and its associated cells: ultrastructure of the epitracheal glands in the gypsy moth, *Lymantria dispar*. *J. Insect Physiol.* 45:65–73
72. Klemensiewicz S. 1883. Zur näheren Kenntniss der Hautdrüsen bei den Raupen und bei *Malachius*. Verh. *Zool. Bot. Ges. Wien* 32(1882):459–74
73. Kobayashi Y, Ando H. 1983. Embryonic development of the alimentary canal and ectodermal derivatives in the primitive moth, *Neomicropteryx nipponensis* Issiki (Lepidoptera, Micropterygidae [sic]). *J. Morphol.* 176:289–314
74. Komatsu K. 1996. Silk (its formation, structure, character, and utilization). In *Polymeric Materials Encyclopedia*, ed. JC Salomone, 10:7711–21. New York: CRC Press
75. Kristensen NP, Scoble MJ, Karsholt O. 2007. Lepidoptera phylogeny and systematics: the state of inventoring moth and butterfly diversity. *Zootaxa* 1668:699–747
76. Lai-Fook J. 1973. The fine structure of Verson's glands in molting larvae of *Calpodes ethlius* (Hesperiidae, Lepidoptera). *Can. J. Zool.* 51:1201–10
77. Liu F, Cui L, Cox-Foster D, Felton GW. 2004. Characterization of a salivary lysozyme in larval *Helicoverpa zea*. *J. Chem. Ecol.* 30:2439–57
78. Locke M. 1960. The cuticle and wax secretion in *Calpodes ethlius* (Lepidoptera, Hesperiidae). *Q. J. Microsc. Sci.* 101:333–38
79. Locke M. 1998. Lenticles. In *Microscopic Anatomy of Invertebrates*, ed. FW Harrison, 11A: 209–17. New York: Wiley-Liss

80. Malicky H. 1969. Versuch einer Analyse der ökologischen Beziehungen zwischen Lycaeniden (Lepidoptera) und Formiciden (Hymenoptera). *Tijdschr. Entomol.* 112(7):213–98

81. Malicky H. 1970. New aspects on the association between lycaenid larvae (Lycaenidae) and ants (Formicidae, Hymenoptera). *J. Lepidopt. Soc.* 24:190–202
82. Mall SB, Singh AR, Dixit A. 1978. Digestive enzymes of mature larva of *Atteva fabriciella* (Swed.) (Lepidoptera: Yponomeutidae). *J. Anim. Morphol. Physiol.* 25(1–2):86–92
83. Marshall AT, Lewis CT, Parry G. 1974. Paraffin tubules secreted by the cuticle of an insect *Epipyrops anomala* (Epipyropidae: Lepidoptera). *J. Ultrastruct. Res.* 47:41–60
84. Marti OG, Rogers CE. 1988. Anatomy of the ventral eversible gland of fall armyworm, *Spodoptera frugiperda* (Lepidoptera: Noctuidae), larvae. *Ann. Entomol. Soc. Am.* 81:308–17
85. Meyer AJ. 1966. A histological study of the alimentary canal and associated structures in the larva of *Coryphodema tristis* Drury. (Lepidoptera.). *Ann. Univ. Stellenbosch Ser. A* 41:271–96
86. Miller JS. 1991. Cladistics and classification of the Notodontidae (Lepidoptera: Noctuoidea) based on larval and adult morphology. *Bull. Am. Mus. Nat. Hist.* 204:1–230
87. Nahrstedt A. 1994. Cyanogenesis in the Zygaenidae (Lepidoptera): a review of the state of the art. *Theses Zool.* 30:17–29
88. Nakamura M. 1998. The eversible cervical gland and the chemical component of its secretion in noctuid larvae. *Tyô to Ga* 49(2):85–92
89. Newcomer EJ. 1912. Some observations on the relations of ants and lycaenid caterpillars, and a description of the relational organs of the latter. *J. N. Y. Entomol. Soc.* 20:31–36
90. Noirot C, Quennedey A. 1991. Glands, gland cells, glandular units: some comments on terminology and classification. *Ann. Soc. Entomol. Fr.* 27(2):123–28
91. Ômura H, Honda K, Feeny P. 2006. From terpenoids to aliphatic acids: further evidence for late-instar switch in osmeterial defense as a characteristic trait of swallowtail butterflies in the tribe Papilionini. *J. Chem. Ecol.* 32:1999–2012
92. Osborn F, Jaffé K. 1998. Chemical ecology of the defense of two nymphalid butterfly larvae against ants. *J. Chem. Ecol.* 24:1173–86
93. Osborn F, Sánchez S, Jaffe K. 1999. Ultrastructure of the spines and neck gland of *Abananote hylonome* Doubleday, 1844 (Lepidoptera: Nymphalidae). *Int. J. Insect Morphol. Embryol.* 28:321–30
94. Packard AS. 1892. Notes on some points in external structure and phylogeny of lepidopterous larvae. *Proc. Boston Soc. Nat. Hist.* 25:82–114
95. Packard AS. 1893. A study of the transformations and anatomy of *Lagoa crispata*, a bombycine moth. *Proc. Am. Philos. Soc.* 32:275–92
96. Pavan M, Valcurone Dazzini M. 1976. Sostanze di difesa dei Lepidotteri. *Pubbl. Ist. Entomol. Agrar. Univ. Pavia* 3:1–23
97. Peterson A. 1962. *Larvae of Insects: An Introduction to Nearctic Species. Part I: Lepidoptera and Plant Infesting Hymenoptera.* Ann Arbor, MI: Edwards Brothers
98. Povel GDE, Beckers MML. 1982. The prothoracic "defensive" gland of *Yponomeuta*-larvae (Lepidoptera, Yponomeutidae). *Proc. K. Ned. Akad. Wet. Ser. C* 85(3):393–98
99. Roessingh P. 1990. Chemical marker from silk of *Yponomeuta cagnagellus*. *J. Chem. Ecol.* 16:2203–16
100. Ross GN. 1964. Life history studies on Mexican butterflies. II. Early stages of *Anatole rossi*, a new myrmecophilous metalmark. *J. Res. Lepidopt.* 3(2):81–94
101. Sakurai M. 1928. Sur la glande trachéale de quelques insectes. *C. R. Seances Acad. Sci.* 187:614–15
102. Schäffer C. 1889. Beiträge zur Histologie der Insekten. *Zool. Jahrb. Anat.* 3(1888–1889):611–52
103. Schulze P. 1911. Die Nackengabel der Papilionidenraupen. *Zool. Jahrb. Anat.* 32:181–244
104. Scoble MJ. 1992. *The Lepidoptera: Form, Function and Diversity*. Oxford: Oxford Univ. Press
105. Severson RF, Rogers CE, Marti OG, Gueldner RC, Arrendale RF. 1991. Ventral eversible gland volatiles from larvae of the fall armyworm, *Spodoptera frugiperda* (J. E. Smith) (Lepidoptera: Noctuidae). *Agric. Biol. Chem.* 55:2527–30
106. Sorensen GS, Cribb BW, Merritt D, Johnson ML, Zalucki MP. 2006. Structure and ultrastructure of the silk glands and spinneret of *Helicoverpa armigera* (Hübner) (Lepidoptera: Noctuidae). *Arthropod Struct. Dev.* 35:3–13

80. An unsurpassed anatomical and histological study of the Newcomer's organ, tentacular organs, and pore cupola organs.

107. Sorour J, Larink O, Ramadan A, Shalaby AS, Osman S. 1990. Anatomical, histological and electron microscopical studies on the salivary glands of larvae of *Spodoptera littoralis* Boisd. (Lep., Noctuidae). II. The conducting gland and the diverticulum. *Zool. Jahrb. Anat.* 120:273–87
108. Srivastava BBL. 1967. Head nerves of the larva of *Prodenia litura* Fabr. (Lepidoptera, Noctuidae). *Zool. Pol.* 17(4):345–55
109. Swaine JM. 1920. The nervous system of the larva of *Sthenopis thule* Strecker. *Can. Entomol.* 52:275–83
110. Truman JW. 1996. Ecdysis control sheds another layer. *Science* 271:40–41
111. **Vegliante F. 2005. Larval head anatomy of *Heterogynis penella* (Zygaenoidea, Heterogynidae), and a general discussion of caterpillar head structure (Insecta, Lepidoptera). *Acta Zool.* 86:167–94**

111. Reviews caterpillar head anatomy, including the cephalic exocrine and endocrine glands.

112. Vegliante F, Hasenfuss I. 2011. *Little known glands of lepidopteran larvae*. Presented at Eur. Congr. Lepidopterol. 17th, Luxembourg
113. Veiga ABG, Blochtein B, Guimarães JA. 2001. Structures involved in production, secretion and injection of the venom produced by the caterpillar *Lonomia obliqua* (Lepidoptera, Saturniidae). *Toxicon* 39:1343–51
114. Verson E. 1911. Le appendici ghiandolari del seritterio bombicino e il significato di esse nei processi esuviali. *Annu. R. Stn. Bacol. Padova* 38:21–31
115. Victoriano E, Gregório EA. 2002. Ultrastructure of the excretory duct in the silk gland of the sugarcane borer *Diatraea saccharalis* (Lepidoptera: Pyralidae). *Arthropod Struct. Dev.* 31:15–21
116. Victoriano E, Gregório EA. 2004. Ultrastructure of the Lyonet's glands in larvae of *Diatraea saccharalis* Fabricius (Lepidoptera: Pyralidae). *Biocell* 28(2):165–69
117. Vieweger T. 1912. Les cellules trachéales chez *Hypocrita jacobeae* Linn. *Arch. Biol.* 27:1–33
118. **Way MJ. 1950. The structure and development of the larval cuticle of *Diataraxia oleracea* (Lepidoptera). *Q. J. Microsc. Sci.* 91:145–82**

118. Provides convincing evidence that the Verson's glands secrete the cement layer on the cuticle.

119. Wegener M. 1926. Die Nackengabel von *Zerynthia* (*Thais*) *polyxena* Schiff. und die Phylogenese des Osmateriums. *Z. Morphol. Ökol. Tiere* 5:155–206
120. White TR, Weaver JS III, Agee HR. 1983. Response of *Cerura borealis* (Lepidoptera: Notodontidae) larvae to low-frequency sound. *Ann. Entomol. Soc. Am.* 76:1–5
121. **Wiley M, Lai-Fook J. 1974. Studies on the silk glands of *Calpodes ethlius* Stoll (Lepidoptera, Hesperiidae). *J. Morphol.* 144:297–322**

121. Describes silk glands composed of more than three histologically differentiated regions, illustrating their ultrastructure.

122. Yen SH, Robinson GS, Quicke DLJ. 2005. The phylogenetic relationships of Chalcosiinae (Lepidoptera, Zygaenoidea, Zygaenidae). *Zool. J. Linn. Soc.* 143:161–341
123. Zagrobelny M, Bak S, Olsen CE, Møller BL. 2007. Intimate roles for cyanogenic glucosides in the life cycle of *Zygaena filipendulae* (Lepidoptera, Zygaenidae). *Insect Biochem. Mol. Biol.* 37:1189–97
124. Zaka-ur-Rab M. 1978. Morphology of the head of the mature larva of the lemon butter-fly [sic], *Papilio demoleus* L. (Lepidoptera: Papilionidae) with special reference to skeleto-muscular mechanism. *Zool. Anz.* 201(3–4):260–72
125. Žitňan D, Kingan TG, Hermesman JL, Adams ME. 1996. Identification of ecdysis-triggering hormone from an epitracheal endocrine system. *Science* 271:88–91
126. Žitňanová I, Adams ME, Žitňan D. 2001. Dual ecdysteroid action on the epitracheal glands and central nervous system preceding ecdysis of *Manduca sexta*. *J. Exp. Biol.* 204:3483–95

Insects as Weapons of War, Terror, and Torture

Jeffrey A. Lockwood

Department of Philosophy and MFA Program in Creative Writing, University of Wyoming, Laramie, Wyoming 82071; email: lockwood@uwyo.edu

Annu. Rev. Entomol. 2012. 57:205–27

First published online as a Review in Advance on September 9, 2011

The *Annual Review of Entomology* is online at ento.annualreviews.org

This article's doi:
10.1146/annurev-ento-120710-100618

0066-4170/12/0107-0205$20.00

Keywords

crop destruction, arthropod-borne disease, asymmetrical warfare

Abstract

For thousands of years insects have been incorporated into human conflict, with the goals of inflicting pain, destroying food, and transmitting pathogens. Early methods used insects as "found" weapons, functioning as tactical arms (e.g., hurled nests) or in strategic habitats (e.g., mosquito-infested swamps). In the twentieth century the relationship between insects and disease was exploited; vectors were mass-produced to efficiently deliver pathogens to an enemy. The two most sophisticated programs were those of the Japanese in World War II with plague-infected fleas and cholera-coated flies and of the Americans during the Cold War with yellow fever–infected mosquitoes. With continued advances, defenses in the form of insecticides and vaccines meant that insects were no longer considered as battlefield weapons. However, in recent times sociopolitical changes have put insects back into the realm of human conflict through asymmetrical conflicts pitting combatants from nonindustrialized regions against forces from militarily and economically superior nations.

INTRODUCTION

The use of insects as weapons of war, tools of terrorism, and instruments of torture extends from the opportunism of prehistorical assaults to the calculated tactics of modern, asymmetric conflicts. Although an enormous range of insects has been used, including no fewer than 12 orders (59), the objectives of humans who have co-opted these animals fall into three categories.

The earliest uses involve the infliction of pain, for which the Hymenoptera were particularly effective (76). In some instances, insect-derived toxins were weaponized (68), and most recently, insects have been used to induce psychological suffering (7, 14, 39, 49). The second tactic exploited the capacity of insects to cause direct damage to agriculture. Introducing pests of crops and livestock became a focus of military interest in the twentieth century (21, 25, 82), and agricultural bioterrorism represents a contemporary risk (75). The third tactic is the use of insects as vectors of disease-causing microbes—either by releasing infected vectors or by forcing an enemy into an adverse habitat (59). Insect-borne pathogens of livestock and crops also constitute a serious risk of bioterrorism.

The objective of this review is to reveal the breadth of ways in which insects have been used and to explore a selection of cases in some depth, using a historical approach spanning several thousand years but focusing on the past century. For detailed coverage, including the use of insects for defensive purposes such as detecting mines and poison gas, see Reference 59.

Extracting the truth from accounts of warfare, terror, and torture is extremely difficult. Governments suppress information because of legal and moral prohibitions regarding biological warfare. Moreover, entomological warfare is a target for propagandists spreading false information. I have attempted to make clear the evidence pertaining to cases in this review, but there remains considerable debate as to the veracity of various accounts.

PREHISTORICAL TACTICS

The earliest use of insects was in the Upper Paleolithic period. By 100,000 years ago, humans had made extensive use of projectiles, so throwing living weapons is not surprising. According to Neufeld (76), "It may be assumed with reasonable confidence that man has perceived the value of certain insects as instruments of warfare long before recorded history . . . It is almost a logical certainty that insect weaponry belonged to early man's 'natural' objects like those made from wood, bone, or stone."

During the Paleolithic, humans occupied caves and rock shelters, which were highly defensible, particularly when further protected with thorny shrubs or other barriers. Assaulting such an enemy would have been difficult, as thrown objects were unlikely to hit their target. However, tossing a nest of bees, hornets, wasps, or ants over a stockade may well have inflicted damage and driven an opponent into the open (76).

For assailants to protect themselves from the insects, they probably gathered nests during dark or cool times, and by the early Neolithic, humans had likely discovered that smoke could be used to calm bees (59). Scholars of Mesopotamian history infer that people used sacks, baskets, or perhaps pottery to deliver nests to the intended target (76).

Various African peoples probably used insects as weapons well before recorded history, although dates of origin are uncertain. The Tiv people used large, specially crafted horns filled with bees (5). The mouth of the horn was aimed so as to direct the insects toward an enemy. The San bushmen extracted a potent poison from the larvae and pupae of chrysomelid beetles (*Diamphidia nigroornata* and *D. vittatipennis*) found in the soil beneath corkwood trees (68, 90). Evidently an ancient technology, poisoned arrows were developed to kill game animals, but at least some African tribes evidently used these weapons against human enemies (59).

ANCIENT HISTORY: INFLICTING SUFFERING

Using Insects to Inflict Pain

Biblical accounts make clear that ancient people were aware that insects could be used as weapons to cause suffering in an enemy. Hornets were evidently used to dislodge entrenched opponents (Deuteronomy 7:20, Exodus 23:28, Joshua 24:12) (76). The plagues of Egypt described in Exodus have been interpreted as including biting midges (Ceratopogonidae) and stable flies (*Stomoxys calcitrans*) (108, 114, 116), and locust-induced famine inflicted great suffering on the Egyptians.

According to Mayan texts, bees were concealed in the heads of manikins that the enemy smashed open, thereby unwittingly releasing the stinging insects (76). In addition, the Mayans along with various Middle Eastern cultures apparently used pottery hives as "bee grenades." These specially molded containers were set outdoors to be colonized by bees, plugged with grass for transportation to the battlefield, and then thrown at an enemy (76). As early as 332 BCE, earthen hives were thrown onto the decks of enemy ships, and beehives were standard naval armaments throughout the Greco-Roman and Syro-Palestinian worlds (12, 89).

The ancient Greeks were cognizant of how insects and their products could be weaponized. In the fourth century BCE, Aeneas advised "besieged people to release wasps and bees into the tunnels being dug under their walls, in order to plague the attackers" (68). The Greek physician Ctesias described a potent poison from India (29, 68). Although he did not know the source of the poison (the Romans believed it came from the droppings of a bird), we now know that it was pederin—a toxin secreted by *Paederus* beetles (Staphylinidae) (85), which continues to be of interest to the Indian Defense Ministry (68).

Torture in the ancient world involved dipterans (93). The Persian practice of scaphism entailed force-feeding a prisoner milk and honey to induce diarrhea, after which the victim was lashed to a skiff and set adrift. Flies breeding in the accumulating feces laid eggs in the person's anus and gangrenous flesh until the individual succumbed to myiasis and septic shock.

Siberian tribes used flies for torture and execution without such elaborate preparation. A prisoner was tied to a tree, and biting flies (mosquitoes, black flies, biting midges, and deer flies) were allowed to feed on the victim. Death from blood loss may have taken only a few hours in these habitats (59).

Using Insects to Inflict Disease

Exodus (ch. 7–12) recounts a series of divinely ordained plagues. Entomologists have proposed an ecological succession to explain how such events could have occurred, including vectors transmitting pathogens to livestock and humans (bluetongue and African horse sickness via biting gnats, cutaneous anthrax and glanders via stable flies or tabanids, and bubonic plague via fleas) (108). Bubonic plague has been proposed as the disease that decimated the Philistines after they captured the Ark of the Covenant (I Samuel 5:9). Mayor (68) speculated that the chest held "an insect vector that infected the rodents in Philistine territory." Fleas can survive for hundreds of days between blood meals, so they could have functioned as an entomological booby trap. The Israelites would not have known that the fleas were responsible, but they may have armed the chest with a plague victim's clothing, given that contagion was understood by this time (59, 68).

Other ancient people demonstrated their capacity to make use of insects as vectors without explicit entomological knowledge. In the fifth century BCE, the Athenian army was decimated by malaria when Sicilian commanders maneuvered their defensive line to force the invaders to establish summer camps in the marshes or perhaps drew the enemy into the wetlands through the ruse of negotiating surrender (68). A similar fate struck the Carthaginian army a century later (59).

In 306 BCE, a despotic ruler named Clearchus seized control of Heraclea on the Black Sea (68). When the locals opposed his brutal practices, he drafted an army of the troublesome citizens for a campaign against Astrachus in western Turkey. The invasion was a sham, as Clearchus's plan was to encamp his conscripts in the marshy areas outside of the city walls, where they were wiped out by "fevers" while their commander and his personal guard spent the summer in the malaria-free highlands. In this way Clearchus masked his political victory with a military defeat.

THE ROMAN EMPIRE

Weaponization of Stinging Arthropods

At the end of the second century, the Roman emperor Septimus Severus sought to dominate Mesopotamia. The city of Hatra was a vital target controlling the major trading routes in present-day Iraq. The Hatrians prepared for the Roman assault by crafting earthenware vessels loaded with stinging arthropods (68).

Most historians contend that the containers held scorpions (1, 68). However, Herodian's account of the battle referred to "poisonous flying insects." Some scholars speculate that the Hatrians used assassin bugs (Reduviidae) or perhaps a combination of arthropods. The creatures that rained down on Severus's troops inflicted terrible pain. After being held at bay for 20 days, the Romans finally conceded defeat.

For their part, the Romans made extensive use of bees as catapult payloads in other sieges. Indeed, the decline in the number of hives during the late Roman period was probably a result of this military application (4).

Bees and Honey

In the first century, the king of Pontus, Mithridates Eupator VI, became a thorn in the side of the Roman Empire. In 66 BCE, the Romans cornered the Pontic army and laid siege, but the Romans were routed when they tried to bore beneath the city walls and Mithridates' troops released bees into the tunnels. In the next campaign, Pompey the Great vanquished the Pontic forces, but Mithridates escaped. The Romans tracked him to Colchis, in present-day Turkey. Mithridates allied himself with the local people, who set a trap in the form of jars of honey in what appeared to be a hastily abandoned cache along the Romans' route. The legionnaires took the bait, which had come from bees foraging on rhododendron—a poisonous plant. The locals slaughtered 1,000 of the nauseated and disoriented Romans, and Mithridates escaped (91).

MIDDLE AGES AND EARLY MODERN ERA

Bees in Sieges and Battlefields

For centuries, besieged Europeans conscripted bees to repulse invaders. In 908, the Danes and Norwegians assailed Chester, England. When the Scandinavians began to tunnel under the city walls, the English hurled beehives into the subterranean passage and ended the incursion (31). The inhabitants of Güssing, Hungary, defended their city in 1289 against an Austrian force by dumping bees on the enemy (4). Around the same time, castle dwellers on the Aegean island of Astypalaia fended off pirates by dropping beehives from the parapets (68). Indeed, bee boles (recesses in castle walls to hold hives) evidently provided a ready source of entomological weaponry in Great Britain (12, 59).

In the early sixteenth century, the Turks were on the verge of taking Stuhlweissenburg when the Hungarians plugged the breach in the city wall with beehives, effectively blocking the invasion. At this time, the Moors used bees to repulse Portuguese troops (10). During the Thirty Years' War in the 1600s, the Swedes besieged Kissingen (4). The city dwellers threw beehives at their invaders, who were protected by heavy clothing and armor. However, the Swedes' horses were not protected, and the assault collapsed into a melee of frenzied cavalry mounts (4). In the seventeenth century, Wuppertal changed its name to Beyenburg ("bee-town") after nuns toppled beehives to drive marauders from the town gates. Bees were part of city defenses into the eighteenth century, when the people of Belgrade built an impenetrable barrier of beehives to resist the Turks (10).

Beehives were used as catapult payloads between 1000 and 1300. In the eleventh century, Henry I of England turned the tide of battle with the Duke of Lorraine by launching "nest bombs" into the enemy's ranks (10). This tactic was repeated 100 years later by King Richard in the Third Crusade and again in thirteenth-century Spain (10). The technological high point in launching bees came in the fourteenth century with a windmill-like device for propelling straw hives from the ends of rapidly rotating arms (10). Beehives were common in naval arsenals into the Middle Ages, until cannon balls became the preferred projectiles. However, as late as the 1600s a crew of privateers fought off a 500-man galley by heaving earthen hives onto the larger vessel (12).

Fleas and Collateral Casualties

The tactic of launching biological materials into a besieged city is rooted in the fourteenth century, when the French catapulted rotting livestock into the castle at Thun l'Évêque (37). The most devastating act of biological warfare on record relied on launching insect-infested payloads into a besieged city. In 1343, Mongol forces under the command of Janibeg attacked the Genoese seaport of Kaffa on the Crimean peninsula (21, 35, 68, 89). The siege lasted for three years, until the Mongol camp was devastated by bubonic plague. But before abandoning his assault, the Mongol khan catapulted corpses into the city (35).

There is no doubt that plague ravaged the citizenry of Kaffa, but there is debate as to the role of insects in this outbreak (21, 59). Some scholars maintain that fleas were exchanged among the rats moving between the Mongol camp and the city. However, the gap between the two sides was probably much further than the home range of the rodents. It is possible that the corpses were a source of direct transmission of bacteria to the Genoese, as the pathogen can be acquired by contact with infected tissue. However, this would have been an inefficient means of transmission and was probably not sufficient to spark an epidemic. Most probably, enough infected fleas remained within the clothing of the dead Mongols to spread the bacteria among the city's rats, dogs, cats, and humans (59).

In a desperate attempt to escape the outbreak, the people of Kaffa headed to sea (along with stowaway rats), spreading the disease throughout the Mediterranean region. By 1350, the resulting pandemic stretched across Europe, killing 25 million people—more than one-quarter of the continent's population. Thus, it appears that the collateral casualties from this act of unwitting entomological warfare (Janibeg could not have known that the fleas were involved) represents the greatest loss of life from a single military operation in human history.

THE NINETEENTH CENTURY

Insect-Borne Disease in the Napoleonic Wars

In 1799, the Ottoman Empire declared war on France, prompting Napoleon Bonaparte to invade Syria with 13,000 troops (83). When the campaign reached Jaffa, the French soldiers contracted bubonic plague. As Napoleon's flea-infested troops laid siege at Acre, the disease increased in prevalence. Worried that the Turks would overrun his declining army, Napoleon retreated to the safety of Cairo and accepted defeat after having lost some 2,000 men to plague.

In 1801, François L'Ouverture declared himself the governor-general of Haiti in defiance of France (83). Napoleon sent 20,000 troops to reclaim the island, but they were soon afflicted with yellow fever. When the spring rains arrived and *Aedes aegypti* flourished, the French began losing 40 men per day, and by October, 80% of the initial force was dead. Napoleon sent reinforcements, but another 20,000 men succumbed to yellow fever within a year. The French were forced to capitulate and returned to Europe with just 3,000 survivors.

In June of 1812, Napoleon amassed 450,000 soldiers for the invasion of Russia with the ultimate objective of taking India (83). While passing through Poland, the Grand Armée became infested with lice—and infected with typhus. One month into the campaign, the French had lost 80,000 soldiers to disease. Upon reaching Moscow in September, Napoleon had lost two-thirds of his troops and the survivors could no longer continue. Napoleon returned home having lost more than 200,000 men to disease (primarily typhus, although dysentery took a toll).

Insect-Borne Disease in the U.S. Civil War

Of the 488,000 soldiers who perished in the Civil War, two-thirds died of disease—and the two primary causes were enteric pathogens (often carried by flies) and malaria (transmitted by mosquitoes) (72, 99). Many major battles were shaped by malaria (99), and both sides took advantage of this disease. General Winfield Scott timed the Union campaign to capture Vicksburg to avoid the height of the malarial season (99)—a lesson that he learned after losing thousands of men to yellow fever during the Mexican-American War (105).

On the Confederate side, General Joseph Johnston exploited malaria as a tactical weapon (99). In April of 1862, Union troops advanced toward Richmond, Virginia—the capital of the Confederacy—as Johnston continuously withdrew his smaller force. A few miles from the city, the Confederate general applied just enough resistance to pin down the enemy along the sluggish Chickahominy River, where he knew malaria was prevalent. When criticized for not counterattacking, Johnston retorted, "I *am* fighting, sir, every day! Is it nothing that I compel the enemy to inhabit the swamps, like frogs, and lessen their strength every hour, without firing a shot?" (99). By early July, more than half of the original force of nearly 20,000 had been hospitalized or was too sick to fight (99). Union leaders finally realized what Johnston was up to (99), but it was too late and the invading force was withdrawn in August.

The Civil War also saw more direct forms of entomological warfare. The Confederacy alleged that the Union had introduced the harlequin bug (*Murgantia histrionica*) from Mexico to destroy the South's crops (58). On the other side, a Confederate surgeon attempted to smuggle clothing from yellow fever victims into the North (22, 89). Had he known of the role played by insect vectors, he may well have succeeded in transporting infected mosquitoes.

Insects as Instruments of Torture

In the 1800s, Apache Indians used ants to inflict lingering, painful death (7, 88, 109). Victims had honey smeared on their eyes and lips or had their mouths held open with skewers before being staked over anthills. Acceptance into an order of Zuñi priests required the initiate to be stripped and placed for hours on an anthill (39).

Insects were used in torture during the mid-1800s by Nasrullah Bahadur-Khan, the emir of Bukhara in present-day Uzbekistan. The well-documented case of two British captives (2, 13, 46,

64, 70, 112) revealed a torture chamber consisting of a 7-m-deep pit covered with an iron grill and stocked with assassin bugs (Reduviidae) and sheep ticks (probably *Dermacentor marginatus*). According to the emir's jailer, "masses of flesh had been gnawed off [the prisoners'] bones" after two months in the pit (64).

POW: prisoner of war

THE WORLD WARS

World War I

Scientific understanding of the role of insects as vectors of pathogenic microbes turned the battlefields of the First World War into a continent-scale experiment. Beginning in 1914, the Eastern Front became a worst-case scenario for typhus (45). Following the assassination of Archduke Ferdinand, Austria invaded Serbia. The summer offensive destroyed an already tenuous medical infrastructure. By November, louse-borne typhus began to spread among the refugees and the Serbian army. A month later, the Serbs counterattacked and captured 40,000 prisoners. An epidemic irrupted from the filthy prisoner of war (POW) camps, ravaging villages and war-torn cities. By April, 1915, there were 10,000 new cases a day, and eventually more than 200,000 Serbs and half of all POWs died (104).

Paradoxically, typhus protected Serbia, which was helpless against another attack. The Central Powers avoided the disease-ravaged country. As such, the Allied Powers did not have to contend with the enemy sweeping through Serbia and establishing a Russian front—a strategy that may have substantially altered the course of the war. Russia, however, was not spared from the epidemic. From 1917 to 1922, there were at least 20 million cases leaving 3 to 10 million dead (104).

The nations battling on the Western Front had learned from the Crimean War that disease was deadlier than bombs or bullets, with three-quarters of the casualties resulting from typhus. Once the fighting of World War I bogged down into trench warfare, louse infestation rates soared to 90% (59). Military commanders responded with a strategic quarantine by limiting the exchange of troops with the Eastern Front, where typhus was raging. Both sides mobilized programs of prevention and intervention (81, 95). The British Sanitary Units adopted dry-cleaning methods to destroy lice and employed entomologists to advise the soldiers on hygiene. Although typhus was kept under control, trench fever (a previously unknown louse-borne rickettsial disease) emerged in France and Belgium, afflicting 800,000 men with few fatalities (16, 104).

Military commanders understood that if lice won in the trenches, their soldiers would likely lose on the battlefield (59). This form of "passive" entomological warfare was used throughout the twentieth century, with militaries protecting their own troops and allowing the destruction of war to foster insect-borne disease among the enemy. As Zinsser (117) noted, many of the famed battles of early modern warfare "are only the terminal operations engaged in by those remnants of the armies which have survived the camp epidemics."

World War II: The Japanese

The leading figure in the Japanese program of biological and entomological warfare was Shiro Ishii, who was trained as a medical doctor, microbiologist, and military officer (9, 38, 42, 86). In the early 1930s, he convinced the Japanese War Ministry that other nations were developing biological weapons and thereby gained support for his research on weaponizing pathogens. Early successes with animal models at the Tokyo Army Medical College allowed him to expand his operations to the city of Harbin in Manchuria, where the risk of an accidental release would not be borne by the Japanese people. Seeking greater secrecy, in 1932, Ishii oversaw the construction of Zhong Ma Prison Camp outside the city. There, he began studies on human subjects (42). After some prisoners escaped and revealed the nature of the facility (42), the Japanese razed the camp. The military was faced with either terminating the biological warfare project or relocating the operation. When Russian infiltrators were caught with vials of pathogenic bacteria, the decision was made not only to continue, but to expand the program (43).

In 1939, the Japanese completed the facility at Pingfan—a walled compound complete with laboratories and housing for 3,000 scientists, along with a prison for human subjects and a crematorium (9, 38, 42, 43, 65, 87). The newly designated Unit 731 studied yellow fever and other diseases (9, 42, 43), and cholera and plague were deemed to have the greatest potential as weapons. A biological attack on Soviet troops at Nomonhan using pathogenic bacteria dumped into the river and dispersed from shells was a failure (9, 42). The Japanese realized that unprotected microbes survive poorly in the environment and often fail to come into contact with potential hosts. These limitations led Unit 731 to turn to the use of insects as vectors.

Early systems involved dropping flea-infested rats behind enemy lines (19), but it became evident that the rodents were extraneous. Unit 731 developed the Uji bomb (9, 42)—a ceramic shell casing with a small explosive charge that released its 10-liter payload over a target. Fleas were initially reared on prisoners (9, 42), but mass production involved thousands of incubators stocked with rodents. Unit 731 soon had the capacity to produce 45 kg of fleas every 3 to 4 months, with the potential for more than 500 million fleas per year (59, 71).

Ishii's work was presented to the military leadership (9, 42) and became an "open secret" within the Japanese scientific community (9, 42, 59). The success of his experiments on humans—including American and allied POWs—led to an expansion of the effort (9, 42). The program grew to 15,000 scientists working at Pingfan as well as Anda Station (a proving ground to field-test delivery methods on human targets) (71), Detachment 100 (an operation near Changchun devoted to crop and livestock destruction, including the potential of tick-borne piroplasmosis against horses) (9, 42), Unit Ei 1644 (a Nanking-based unit for mass-producing fleas and typhus-infested lice) (9, 42), and Unit 673 (a facility in Songo dedicated to epidemic hemorrhagic fever, which is caused by a tick-borne virus) (9, 42).

The first use of entomological warfare apparently involved dropping Uji bombs on Xinjing in the summer of 1940, but details are lacking (38). Shortly after this attack, the Japanese discovered that fleas could be released directly from low-flying aircraft using specialized sprayers. This method was used with limited success at Chuhsien, where 21 people died of plague (87). The raid on Quzhou in the fall of 1940 was far more successful (9, 42). The outbreak killed 50,000 people over the course of six years—people were still dying in the city after Japan had lost the war. The attack on Hangzhou involved releasing 15 million fleas (38), and more than 100 million fleas were sprayed over Changteh (89, 100). The best-documented raid occurred at Ningbo, where an American missionary witnessed the aerial release and the extraordinary efforts of the Chinese to contain the resulting outbreak of plague by evacuating and burning the city center (9, 42). Over the next two years, Unit 731 conducted entomological warfare against more than a dozen population centers, causing at least 100,000 casualties (59). Not only Chinese were targeted. Unit 731 planned to release 150 million fleas against American and Philippine troops on Bataan, but the assault was called off when victory was achieved with conventional weapons (9).

During this time, the Japanese continued efforts to contaminate Chinese water supplies with cholera but had little success (9). The challenge for Unit 731 was to deliver the bacteria in sufficient quantities to trigger an initial infection, which could then spread on its own. In 1942, the Japanese solved the problem at Baoshan—a city in the center of a region that hosted an Allied supply line into China. The tactic involved dropping conventional ordnance to decimate the infrastructure, followed by Yagi bombs. The latter device was divided in a section packed with a slurry of bacteria and a compartment loaded with house flies, *Musca domestica*. On impact, the casing burst to splatter the insects with bacteria, and the contaminated vectors spread among the populace. Subsequent bombing runs drove the infected people into the countryside, thereby creating an epidemic that effectively denied the region to the Allies. Approximately 60,000 of the city's refugees died of cholera, and villages were infected as far as 200 km from Baoshan (9). The final tally reached 200,000 victims across an area equal to Pennsylvania in size. This same tactic was repeated in August 1943, in the northern province of Shandong (after occupying Japanese troops were vaccinated), killing 210,000 people.

As Japanese losses mounted, Unit 731 intensified its efforts. Ishii drew up plans to cultivate hundreds of thousands of rats to produce more than 5 billion infected fleas (71) and began using Chinese prisoners as human incubators of plague bacteria (38). In 1944, the Japanese planned to release fleas on Saipan (9), but the commando team was lost when their ship was torpedoed. A similar plan was developed for an attack on Okinawa, but it was never completed for unknown reasons (38). In the waning days of the war, the Japanese were poised to drop fleas on San Diego, California, using special planes carried by submarines (9), but the attack was called off when a general worried that U.S. retaliation could trigger a pandemic.

When Russian troops approached Pingfan, Unit 731's infected rats were released into the countryside, and the ensuing epidemic killed more than 20,000 people (115). After the war, Ishii provided the Americans with documents revealing the nature of the Japanese entomological warfare program in exchange for avoiding war-crime prosecution (9, 42), and others in Unit 731 made a similar deal with the Soviets (9, 42).

World War II: European Developments

The idea of using insects as weapons in modern warfare was broached by Haldane in 1938, when he speculated that, "It would not be surprising, for example, if insects pests, such as the potato beetle, were not introduced into this country by hostile aeroplanes in the course of a future war" (41). The French were the first to attempt to weaponize insects, including mass rearing and release systems for the Colorado potato beetle, *Leptinotarsa decemlineata*—a pest that had been accidentally introduced into Europe in the course of food shipments during the First World War (8, 33, 40). When the Nazis invaded France in 1940, they found records of the French entomological warfare program (33, 36).

Since the 1930s, the Germans had been worried about their enemies introducing crop pests. In response, they initiated an insecticide development program that led to the discovery of the organophosphate-based nerve gases (19, 100). The Germans also developed an extensive pest-monitoring system. The transition from a defensive to an offensive approach was catalyzed by a misinterpretation of a spy's report (33, 36). German espionage revealed that the Americans had delivered thousands of Colorado potato beetles to the British (along with an unspecified number of "Texas ticks"—probably *Amblyomma* spp.). The Germans took this as evidence of an Allied entomological warfare program—and of the need to develop the capacity to retaliate in kind. In fact, the beetles were part of a British research program to defend their fields from a German assault with crop pests (33). Some of the British concern may have been fueled by fantastical stories that the Germans had created a voracious grasshopper strain that would starve England into surrender (84).

Adolf Hitler opposed the development of biological weapons, so the director of Germany's Potato Beetle Defense Service framed his unit's work as an effort to understand what the enemy was plotting. With this political deception, the Potato Beetle Research Institute (33, 36) was converted into facilities for weaponizing insects. Between 1941 and 1944, at least 15 species of aphids, beetles, bugs, flies, and moths were evaluated for their capacity to decimate a range of food crops, forage grasses, and forest trees (36). The Colorado potato beetle emerged as the most viable species for waging entomological warfare.

Around this time, an Institute of Entomology was established at the SS military Medical Academy and focused on vector-borne diseases. Scientists attempted to weaponize typhus-infested lice using concentration-camp prisoners, considered the possibility of triggering plague outbreaks in enemy ports, and analyzed whether it would be possible "to spread malaria artificially by means of mosquitoes" (36). It appears that none of these ventures resulted in an operational weapon system, although louse-ridden corpses were reportedly used to spread typhus during the siege of Stalingrad (21).

The Germans determined that 20 to 40 million beetles were needed to inflict serious damage on England's potato crop. A massive release over the agricultural region in eastern England was predicted to reduce the food calories of the nation by 6%—a substantial deprivation to a people who were already stretched to the limits of endurance.

A mass-production system was devised, which made use of an extensive system of fields and greenhouses to provide a year-round supply of potato leaves. Various dissemination tactics were tested and refined. Two of the early release trials involved a total of 54,000 beetles, of which only 154 were recovered—a result that the Germans interpreted to mean that the insects were dispersing widely (33, 36). When test drops over their own farmlands apparently triggered a major outbreak, Hermann Göring accused the Allies of waging entomological attacks (36, 58). So as not to diminish their stockpile of insects—and perhaps to avoid further infesting their own crops—later trials were conducted with as many as 100,000 wooden models.

In June of 1944, the German High Command was informed that the necessary stockpile of beetles was ready for deployment (33). German records do not provide clear evidence that the entomological weapon system was used. However, a British naturalist recounted that cardboard box-bombs filled with 50 to 100 beetles were dropped on the Isle of Wight (47). There are no substantiating reports, although two years earlier a secret report from the British biological warfare program noted an infestation with "abnormal features in at least one instance suggesting that the occurrence was not due to natural causes" (33).

Accusations that Colorado potato beetles were used by the Americans to destroy crops in Eastern Europe persisted into the years following World War II (59), a possibility explored in a 1969 United Nations report (106). And as recently as 1999, a Russian military commander insinuated that an outbreak of these insects was the consequence of sabotage (34, 57).

World War II: Soviet Developments

The Soviets began weaponizing typhus in 1928 (21). Russian saboteurs planted typhus-infected lice among German troops early in World War II, debilitating 2,800 soldiers (11). However, the Soviet biological warfare program focused on plague, cholera, and anthrax. Although details are scant, in the summer of 1941, human experiments with plague went awry when a prisoner escaped from a laboratory in Mongolia and triggered an epidemic (11). There is also circumstantial evidence that the Soviets used tularemia (which is commonly transmitted from infected tabanids and ticks) to sicken thousands of German troops outside of Stalingrad (67).

World War II: The United States, Great Britain, and Canada

In terms of entomological warfare, the Allies lagged behind the Axis. The American program was impeded in the early 1930s by the view that biological weapons presented insurmountable difficulties (87). This position was weakened when the Army Surgeon General's office concluded that the nation was vulnerable to biological attack, including the release of yellow fever–infected mosquitoes. Of particular concern was an attempt by a Japanese scientist (one of Ishii's agents) to acquire under false pretenses a virus from the Rockefeller Foundation's Yellow Fever Laboratory (9, 42). The American concern aligned with warnings issued by the British that the Germans would be prepared to "introduce an epidemic of [yellow fever] if they wanted to paralyze the Indian Army" (41).

OSS: Office of Strategic Services (precursor of the Central Intelligence Agency, CIA)

In 1939, the Chemical Warfare Service released a report signaling a shift in policy. This document identified nine diseases to which the populace was vulnerable; six were associated with insect vectors (42). Around this time, the Americans learned of the Japanese attack with fleas at Changteh (42). A series of scientific committees were charged with assessing the potential of biological warfare (42, 87). The War Bureau consultants concluded that "the best defense for the United States is to be fully prepared to start a wholesale offensive whenever it becomes necessary to retaliate," and they further recommended that "studies be made to determine whether mosquitoes can be infected with several diseases simultaneously with a view to using these insects as an offensive weapon" (87).

For their part, the Canadians were pursuing the possibilities of spreading yellow fever using infected *Aedes aegypti* along with other pathogen-vector systems (59). Meanwhile, the British conducted preliminary work on the use of house flies to vector *Salmonella* and focused on weaponizing anthrax (17, 87). The British lacked industrial capacity, so the Americans planned to produce millions of anthrax-filled bombs (65). The reality of germ warfare catalyzed the conversion of Camp (later Fort) Detrick, Maryland, into one of the world's foremost biological warfare research and development facilities (87).

After initial work with microbial aerosols, American scientists came to similar conclusions as those drawn by the Japanese: Insects effectively protected and delivered pathogens, and in some cases, the microbe could be amplified within the vector (59). These findings were reinforced by the Canadians' work on mass-producing and disseminating flies (6, 59). In the early 1940s, they collaborated with U.S. scientists in testing insects on Horn Island, Mississippi (87). Prospective agents included fruit flies (probably *Drosophila melanogaster*) as mechanical vectors, wool maggots (calliphorid flies to inflict damage to livestock), and screwworm flies (*Cochliomyia hominivorax*). The trials had limited success, and critics complained that development of biological weapons was being hindered by testing "unconventional modes of dissemination such as the use of insects" (6).

The most elaborate entomological warfare project emerged in response to amassing troops by the Germans in Morocco in preparation for cutting off the Allied supply line to Algiers (60). The U.S. Office of Strategic Services (OSS) collaborated with Canadian entomological warfare experts to dislodge the Nazi forces. Project Capricious was to use house flies to disseminate a mixture of enteric pathogens among the enemy. The logistical challenges of mass-producing, contaminating, and releasing flies were overcome in two ways. First, rather than culture and transport the vectors, the scientists decided to make use of the abundant local flies. Second, contamination of the flies was to be accomplished by coating goat dung with pathogens. However, collecting sufficient dung became a problem, so the OSS developed a synthetic version with a chemical attractant to draw the insects to bacterially coated bait disguised as goat droppings. The plan was to drop loads of the contaminated bait over towns where the Germans were garrisoned, so that the local flies would pick up and spread the microbes. However, just before the attack, Hitler withdrew his troops from Morocco to bolster the German forces in the siege of Stalingrad (60).

"Passive" entomological warfare was also vital to the U.S. invasion of Italy and the war in the Pacific. When typhus threatened to decimate American troops after they landed in Naples, a massive lice-control program was initiated (59, 98, 110). Within a few months, the U.S. army dusted more than 3 million people with 127 tons of DDT and suppressed the incipient epidemic. As for the Pacific theater, in May 1943, General Douglas MacArthur declared, "This will be a long war, if for every division I have fighting the enemy, I must count on a second division in the hospital with malaria and a third division convalescing from this debilitating disease" (95). By the next year, the U.S. military had established a formidable medical infrastructure with more than 100 vector-control programs that reduced the malaria rate among allied troops by 40-fold (95).

THE COLD WAR

Research and Development

Camp Detrick developed an array of pathogens and vectors including mosquitoes infected with yellow fever, malaria, and dengue; flies carrying dysentery, cholera, and anthrax; fleas harboring plague; and ticks infected with tularemia, relapsing fever, and Colorado fever. The American entomological warfare effort peaked in the 1950s, when laboratory studies generated secret field tests (59).

Operation Big Itch involved the release of fleas from specially designed munitions that expelled the insects as the device fell from a low-flying aircraft (44). The fleas survived and infested caged guinea pigs, although the vectors sought hosts for only 24 h, which was a disappointing result. A facility was planned to produce 50 million fleas per week, until microbiologists proved unable to culture enough plague bacteria.

Yellow fever became the mainstay of the Camp Detrick's entomological program, when it was discovered that mosquito larvae would uptake the virus from an aqueous medium, allowing the mass production of infected adults without the need for blood feeding (43, 44). The U.S. military then conducted an extensive series of simulated attacks using uninfected mosquitoes.

In 1955, Operation Big Buzz involved the production and storage of more than one million *A. aegypti*. The test in rural Georgia was considered successful when the mosquitoes reached human volunteers and guinea pigs 1 km from the release site (44, 58, 92). Subsequent trials (Operations Drop Kick and Gridiron) (44) were sufficiently promising that the U.S. military conducted a simulated attack on an American city. From April to November of 1956, the people of Savannah, Georgia, served as uninformed targets. In Operation May Day, mosquitoes were released as if dispersed from bombs and warheads (92). This trial was followed by the Avon Park Experiment in which 200,000 mosquitoes were released over Florida using a new "bagged-agent dispenser" with a 320-kg payload consisting of 2,090 paper bags loaded with insects.

The Bellwether tests in 1959 were conducted to refine the American understanding of entomological warfare (44). Bellwether One involved field experiments designed to assess the role of environmental factors on the capacity of mosquitoes to find and feed on hosts. In Bellwether Two, researchers monitored the biting frequency of mosquitoes and found that a single release would infest an area of approximately 1 hectare. Detailed observations revealed that humans moving erratically and near buildings were bitten most frequently, which boded well for an attack on an urban setting. The details of Bellwether Three remain classified, but Bellwether Four consisted of testing strains of mosquitoes that had been bred for aggressive host seeking and biting. Researchers also produced insect strains resistant to insecticides as these "represent a potentially more effective vehicle for the offensive use of BW [biological warfare] of insect borne pathogens" (27).

In 1960, the U.S. Army Chemical Corps issued an "Entomological Warfare Target Analysis" to identify vulnerable sites for an attack (44, 74). China and the Soviet Union had many cities that met the criteria, and in the judgment of the analysts, it "would be impossible for a nation such as the USSR to quickly undertake a mass-immunization program to protect millions of people"

(74). In the same year, plans were drawn up for a facility at Pine Bluff, Arkansas, with the capacity to produce 130 million infected mosquitoes per month (43, 65).

Although Camp Detrick was the centerpiece of entomological warfare, the U.S. Army's 406 Medical General Laboratory in Japan flourished in the late 1940s (27). Originally tasked with providing health services, the laboratory expanded its work on insect-borne diseases into offensive research. Communist infiltrators reported that the Americans were working on mass cultivation of insects for infection with a wide range of pathogens (27), and Unit 406's entomology department was clearly interested in the potential of using biting flies as vectors (27).

ISC: International Scientific Commission for Investigating the Facts Concerning Bacteriological Warfare in Korea in China

By this time, Canada's Defense Research Laboratory had devised a simple entomological weapon system that combined elements of Japan's Yagi bomb and the OSS's Project Capricious (27). The Canadian scientists had developed a 500-lb bomb capable of delivering a payload of pathogen-contaminated salmon along with 200,000 flies, but stockpiling so many insects became an operational obstacle. They soon realized that simply dropping baits enhanced with attractants and laced with pathogens would effectively exploit the naturally occurring house flies in most habitats.

The Korean War

The Korean War began on June 25, 1950, and within six months, the conflict was at a stalemate (45). The following year, the North Koreans accused the U.S. forces of spreading smallpox virus (21), and records indicate that the Americans were actively considering both nuclear and biological weapons to break the deadlock (27, 59).

In February 1952, North Korea officially alleged to the United Nations that the U.S. military had been "systematically scattering large quantities of bacteria-carrying insects by aircraft in order to disseminate infectious diseases" (21). The People's Republic of China expanded the accusations, claiming that during a one-week period there had been 68 airdrops of contaminated insects on northeast China (27). The commander of the United Nations forces in Korea flatly denied the charges, asserting that the disease outbreaks reflected the public health ineptitude of the enemy (54). But with ongoing reports of American planes "dropping flies, mosquitoes, spiders, ants, bed bugs, fleas ... in a wide area" (27), the Chinese initiated a massive epidemic-prevention program in North Korea.

In the spring of 1952, an investigation by the left-leaning International Association of Democratic Lawyers concluded that the Americans had waged biological warfare (59). At this time, a Chinese newspaper printed stories of entomological attacks along with photographs of the agents. A *New York Times* front-page story derided this evidence, which included images of a marsh springtail (*Isotomurus palustris*), stoneflies, and an unaccountably wingless mosquito (77). An investigation by the International Committee of the Red Cross was fruitless, as they were denied access to records and witnesses (21, 27).

The most extensive inquiry was conducted by the International Scientific Commission for Investigating the Facts Concerning Bacteriological Warfare in Korea in China (ISC)—a group of six scientists assembled by the Soviet-funded World Peace Council (21). After a two-month investigation, the ISC issued a massive report documenting the use of 14 different arthropods, infected with at least eight different pathogens (48). The ISC drew connections between these attacks and those of Unit 731 during World War II, noting that the Americans had sheltered the Japanese war criminals in exchange for their scientific secrets.

The insects (and pathogens) used in the raids included various flies: *Musca vicina* (anthrax), *Muscina stabulans* (typhoid and plant pathogens), *Hylemya* sp. (anthrax, cholera, dysentery, paratyphoid, typhoid, and plant pathogens), *Lucilia sericata*, *Helomyza modesta* (paratyphoid), *Orthocladius* sp. (typhoid), *Culex pipiens* var. *pallens*, *Aedes koreicus*, and *Trichocera maculipennis* (neurotropic virus). Not unexpectedly, the list also included the human flea, *Pulex irritans* (bubonic plague). The more unusual insects in the report included spider beetles, *Ptinus fur* (anthrax); several orthopterans such as *Acrydium* sp., *Locusta migratoria*, and *Gryllus testaceus*; the springtail *Isotoma negishina* (dysentery); and nemourid stoneflies. Finally, two spiders were also listed: *Tarentula* sp. (anthrax and fowl cholera) and *Lycosa* sp. (anthrax and fowl cholera). Other insects noted in the earlier report by the International Association of Democratic Lawyers were confirmed by the North Korean Minister of Health but not included in the ISC list: ants (Formicidae), bed bugs (Cimicidae), mealworm beetles (*Tenebrio molitor*), and nycteribiid flies (48).

Several lines of evidence were presented to establish that entomological warfare had been waged. Eyewitnesses reported insects falling from American planes (48). In other cases, ecological anomalies provided circumstantial evidence, e.g., large numbers of springtails in a cement stadium (48). In addition, there were many incidents in which species were found at unusual times, e.g., migratory locusts in mid-March (48). The ISC presumed that releases of insects during the winter reflected the Americans' capacity to breed selectively for cold tolerance (48).

Unnaturally dense aggregations were reported, and these were sometimes associated with bomb casings, e.g., tens of thousands of anthomyiid flies and field crickets (48). Other unnatural phenomena included bizarre biological associations of insects, e.g., dense assemblages of springtails and fleas as well as spider beetles contaminated with anthrax (48). However, the centerpiece of the ISC report included accounts of plague-infected *P. irritans* in North Korean villages—and sometimes on bare hillsides—after American planes passed overhead (48). The final line of evidence consisted of rambling confessions of entomological attacks handwritten by downed American pilots (20, 48).

The charges of entomological warfare were rebutted by the Americans (87). They noted that the chair of the ISC was an avowed Marxist and that the delegates uncritically accepted all Chinese and North Korean accounts (54). As such, the report was taken to be political propaganda. The Americans noted that the purported confessions by POWs were filled with communist rhetoric, undermining the claim that the writings were uncoerced (48). However, the U.S. case was harmed by the Attorney General's threats to charge returning POWs with treason if they failed to retract "false confessions" (27), thereby coercing their recantations.

Officials also claimed that the U.S. military "had never investigated the potential of using arthropods for BW [biological warfare]"—an odd assertion given that it was made by the chief of the Entomological Division at Fort Detrick (27). Other rebuttals were more compelling, particularly the argument that no competent entomologist would consider using spider beetles, springtails, stoneflies, and spiders to carry pathogens or grouse locusts and crickets to attack crops (59). The communists' discovery of "new" species, it was contended, simply reflected a poor understanding of their countries' insect fauna (100), and the various aggregations, emergences, and associations were simply natural events. Thus, if the communists did not know their own insects, then they could not know about normal behavior or development rates. Canadian scientists echoed these rebuttals, providing ecological explanations for the various accounts in the ISC's report (59).

Pentagon officials further noted that the bomb casings described by the ISC were merely those of leaflet bombs that were used to warn civilians of an impending attack and allow them to evacuate (27). This seems plausible, but some operation orders specify that leaflet bombs were dropped *after* conventional ordnance—such timing would be contrary to a warning and consistent with a biological payload (20, 27).

The World Health Organization also repudiated the ISC's charges, noting that, had the Americans made hundreds of airdrops of infected or contaminated insects, the result would have been widespread epidemics, but no such events occurred (59). The ISC claimed to have such evidence but withheld it to keep the United States from obtaining vital data for assessing their tactics (95).

Military scholars and historians remain divided as to whether the United States waged entomological warfare (27, 54, 59, 74, 84, 100). Even the discovery in 1998 of documents from the Russian Presidential Archives showing that the Soviet and Chinese governments conspired to generate false accusations (54) may not fully exonerate the Americans. Although it is clear that the communists faked evidence in 1953, the documents do not mention earlier time frames, including the years in which the majority of entomological attacks supposedly occurred (59).

USDA: United States Department of Agriculture

The Vietnam War

The three major entomological warfare tactics were used during the Vietnam War. First, insect-borne disease was pursued through both active and passive approaches. Operation Magic Sword assessed the capacity of yellow fever mosquitoes to make landfall after being released from a ship anchored off the warm, humid shores of the United States to approximate the tropical conditions of southeast Asia (44). In terms of passive tactics, the Americans used a campaign of vaccination and hygiene to protect their troops from plague, while rats and fleas thrived in areas controlled by the Vietcong. Whereas only one province was afflicted with plague in 1961, 22 of the 29 provinces north of Saigon had reported cases in 1966.

Second, the North Vietnamese accused the Americans of releasing insects to destroy rice and fruit trees (20). These infestations were probably due to local pests, but the use of chemical defoliants by the U.S. military to deny cover to the enemy caused large-scale deforestation (106). Although unplanned, herbicidal warfare catalyzed outbreaks of arthropod-borne disease. The secondary forests and grasslands were ideal habitats for rats and the mites, which transmit scrub typhus (59).

Third, both sides sought to use stinging insects. Within the tunnels of Cu Chi, the Vietcong set booby traps of scorpions (66). Their simplest aboveground tactic involved lobbing wasp and hornet nests into U.S. positions (101). In a more elaborate approach, the Vietcong relocated colonies of the giant honey bee, *Apis dorsata*, along trails. When an enemy patrol passed within range, a small charge was detonated near the bees to trigger an attack. There were also reports of the North Vietnamese training bees to attack anyone wearing an American uniform. For their part, the Americans considered using pheromones to "mark target individuals and then release bees to attack them" (4, 107).

The U.S.-Cuban Conflict

During the Cuban Missile Crisis in 1962, President Kennedy's advisors contemplated a range of retaliatory scenarios including entomological warfare (84). The Army Corps of Engineers had been cooperating with the U.S. Department of Agriculture (USDA) in weaponizing planthoppers (58). The primary target was to be Cuba's sugarcane crop, and the primary agent was the sugarcane leafhopper, *Perkinsiella vitiensis*, which transmits the virus that causes Fiji disease. The American arsenal may also have included the rice hoja blanca virus, a planthopper-borne pathogen studied at Fort Detrick (111).

Although Fidel Castro accused the United States of waging entomological warfare in the decades that followed, credible evidence was lacking until 1981. A five-month epidemic of dengue fever, a mosquito-borne disease, resulted in 344,203 cases and 158 deaths (52). Epidemiological and ecological anomalies led some to conclude that the outbreak had an anthropogenic origin (86, 94). The outbreak was Cuba's first occurrence of dengue in nearly four decades and the first large-scale irruption of hemorrhagic cases in the Caribbean since the turn of the century. Furthermore, the disease emerged contemporaneously in three widely separated cities. Cuban officials claimed that in the month prior to the outbreak only a dozen people had entered the country from regions where dengue was endemic, and these individuals were free of the disease. Moreover, around this time, the Afghan and Soviet governments also accused the United States of waging biological warfare with mosquito-borne diseases in Pakistan (94).

The United States had been pursuing the development of entomological weapons and had the capacity to mass-produce *A. aegypti* (59). Moreover, in 1981, the U.S. Army issued "An Evaluation of Entomological Warfare as a Potential Danger to the United States and European NATO Nations" (92). Declassified portions of the report included detailed logistical and economic analyses for attacking cities with yellow fever–infected mosquitoes. Although framed in terms of defense, the report could have served as a blueprint for offensive uses of insects.

Despite the entomological warfare capacity of the U.S. military, medical entomologists argued that an unusual pattern of disease did not necessitate human agency. The Americans noted that Cuba had extensive military operations in Africa, a continent with hot spots of type-2 dengue. A garrison of returning soldiers could well have triggered the outbreak (59).

In the years following the dissolution of the USSR, the Cubans issued a series of statements accusing the United States of waging entomological warfare with brown citrus aphid, *Toxoptera citricida* (to transmit tristeza de citrico) (79); citrus leafminer, *Phyllocnistis citrella* (23); coffee berry borer, *Hypothenemus hampei* (23); panicle rice mite, *Steneotarsonemus spinki* (3); honey bee tracheal mite, *Acarapis woodi* (24); and the bee mite *Varroa jacobsoni* (78). In all cases, the Cubans relied on circumstantial evidence to support their assertions. For example, the panicle rice mite appeared in a crucial center for the production of seeds at precisely the same time as widespread rice production was being promoted: The pest must have been introduced from Asia, as it was not found in the Americas, and Cuba imported only seeds that did not harbor the mite (3).

In 1996, a U.S. State Department plane flew over Cuba and released a gray mist (21, 25, 82). The Americans explained that the pilot had observed a Cuban plane and released a smoke signal to ensure visual contact and avoid a collision (82). The Cuban government claimed that the "smoke" was a cloud of *Thrips palmi*, which seeded a pest outbreak. The Cubans initially took their case to the United Nations (25, 82) and then prevailed upon the Russian government to file charges under the Biological and Toxin Weapons Convention (55).

A Formal Consultative Meeting was convened to hear the case, which came down to three pieces of evidence. First, a substance—either smoke or insects—was released from an American plane while flying over the Giron corridor (the flight path taken by the U.S. pilot). Second, in the two months following the flyover, a thrips outbreak decimated potato fields in the Giron corridor. The Cubans argued that a natural invasion from one of the islands to their east would not have skipped 650 km of vulnerable farms to infest fields in the flight path of the American plane (82). Third, the Cubans maintained that *T. palmi* was an ideal agent for waging biological warfare (82, 111); eight months before the alleged attack, the Federation of American Scientists had listed this species among the organisms of concern to signatories of the Convention (111). The rebuttal by the Americans was that erratic patterns of pest outbreaks were common, the thrips could have arrived via agricultural trade, and not every ecological coincidence constituted evidence of biological warfare (59).

The Formal Consultative Meeting failed to render a decision favoring either nation, citing the complexity of the case and the passage of time (111). Some believe that this equivocation opened the door for other charges (56). In 1999, the Russian Defense Ministry insinuated that a locust outbreak in the Saratovskaya region had been the work of American saboteurs (57). In the same year, Saddam Hussein accused a United Nations worker of planting locust eggs in Iraq to trigger an outbreak (61, 73). The Cubans continued to levy charges against the United States, filing suits in 1999 and 2000 that sought damages for attacks with plant-feeding insects and insect-borne diseases (32, 102). For their part, the American government suggested that various animal and plant diseases in the United States could be the result of Cuban biological warfare experiments (30).

MODERN, ASYMMETRICAL WARFARE

Contemporary Torture

In the first half of the twentieth century, Soviet jailers used bed bugs, *Cimex lectularius*, as instruments of torture in the gulags (97). Prisoners were placed in a closet with thousands of bed bugs, until the victims were psychologically traumatized and physically debilitated. In modern China, practitioners of the banned religious sect Falun Gong reportedly have been stripped and handcuffed to poles during the summer at dusk or dawn in areas with high densities of mosquitoes (28). In addition, U.S. interrogators at Guantanamo Bay detention camp used insects as a form of psychological torture on an entomophobic captive (14, 15, 62).

Contemporary Terrorism

Agricultural terrorism has been a concern since the early 1960s, when the USDA warned of the nation's vulnerability to the Mediterranean fruit fly (*Ceratitis capitata*), khapra beetle (*Trogoderma granarium*), Asiatic rice borer (*Chilo suppressalis*), silver "Y" moth (*Autographa gamma*), Sunn pest (*Eurygaster integriceps*), dura stem borer (*Sesamia cretica*), and several species of potato weevils (19). The American citrus industry remains highly vulnerable to several insect-borne diseases (59). A report issued by the Air War College (51) included a scenario in which saboteurs released grape phylloxera (*Phylloxera vitifoliae*) to inflict one billion dollars' worth of damage. The report also described how insects could be used to attack Pakistan's cotton crop and thereby destabilize the economy and politics of a strategically vital region. It was further suggested that the 1991 arrival of the sweetpotato whitefly (*Bemisia tabaci*), which caused $300 million in damage to California agriculture, had biological and ecological features consistent with a clandestine attack.

The livestock industry is also a viable target according to a 2003 report of the National Research Council (75). In one scenario, screwworm fly outbreaks from Florida to California were seeded by a single terrorist who obtained fertile pupae from a foreign, mass-production facility for sterile male flies. The cost of responding to this attack was estimated in the tens of millions of dollars. Ironically, the eradication of pests such as screwworm fly and cotton boll weevil (*Anthonomus grandis*) to protect agriculture creates targets of opportunity for terrorists (59).

The National Research Council report also included the possibility of insect-borne diseases as terrorist weapons. The introduction of the virus that causes Rift Valley fever was viewed as a serious risk given the occurrence of competent vectors; the likelihood of the virus establishing in a wildlife reservoir; and an inadequate infrastructure for surveillance, diagnosis, and response (75). The director of the U.S. National Center for Biodefense recently argued that introducing infected mosquito eggs would be a simple and effective tactic (59). As with West Nile virus, the country would be unable to contain the spread of Rift Valley fever (59), although the latter disease would be far more damaging to the economy and human health (69, 96). Other arthropod-borne diseases, such as tick-borne Crimean-Congo hemorrhagic fever, also warrant concern (59). Yellow fever remains viable, given the interest of North Korea in this agent (103), the spread of *A. aegypti* across the southern United States, and the state of the American health-care system (113).

ARE WE READY?

"The easiest [method to introduce Rift Valley fever] by far—and there's no way authorities would ever detect it—is to simply go to an endemic area during an outbreak, collect floodwater *Aedes* from prime habitats, let them feed on a viremic animal, collect the eggs, put them on filter paper, let them dry, put them in your shirt pocket, come into the country, go to a suitable habitat, drop the filter paper into the water, and walk away."

—Charles Bailey, director of the U.S. National Center for Biodefense (59)

"How you define the problem is how you will find solutions . . . If you believe that others will inflict chronic harm on our nation, then you develop a strategy for a war of attrition—and we haven't defined the problem or our responses in that way. We've thought about car bombs and nuclear materials, but we haven't thought about weapons that are in the terrorists' domain and endemic to where they are living. Quite frankly, vectors are underappreciated."

—Robert Kadlec, former director for the U.S. Senate Subcommittee on Bioterrorism and Public Health (59)

Entomological terrorism using genetically modified vectors or insect-borne pathogens is a possible tactic. Research at Fort Detrick pursued the development of insect strains with insecticide resistance (27) and with enhanced biting activity (44). Recently, a USDA medical entomologist maintained that mosquitoes could be genetically engineered to transmit HIV (59). And a particularly innovative scenario described how a whitefly-transmitted plant virus could be genetically modified to produce botulinum toxin so that vast areas of corn would be rendered deadly (63).

The best-documented case of entomological terrorism took place in 1989. Opposed to insecticides (59) and calling themselves "The Breeders," a group of domestic ecoterrorists revealed that they had been breeding and releasing medflies in Los Angeles and Orange counties and would expand their campaign into California's San Joaquin Valley unless state and federal agencies terminated their malathion-based eradication program (18, 59).

Some officials considered the threat to be a hoax, but the USDA relied on four lines of evidence to argue otherwise (59). First, the fruit flies were persisting well after normal population buildups. Second, the erratic distribution of flies as well as the occurrence of adults without larval infestations were unusual. Third, the Mediterranean fruit fly and the oriental fruit fly (*Bactrocera dorsalis*) inexplicably co-occurred. Finally, in a rare sequence of events, mated females were trapped before males (50).

Despite the circumstantial evidence of an anthropogenic role in the outbreak, entomologists were divided as to human agency (18). Whereas some argued that the tactic was self-defeating, others pointed out that the approach was successful. Not only was the public increasingly upset with the health, environmental, and economic costs of the program, but pest managers were forced to second-guess their operations (26, 59). Law enforcement agencies were unable to make any arrests despite intensive investigations (26, 59), and the case remains unsolved (53, 59, 80) (see sidebar, Are We Ready?).

CONCLUSION

The limitations of space preclude putting the history of entomological warfare into a social and political context. How such factors as nationalism, racism, and economics served to justify the use of insects as weapons is important to understanding the morally darkest days in the science of entomology (59). However, even without a cultural analysis, the arc of history may suggest the future of entomological armaments.

For millennia, insects were used as "found" weapons either as tactical arms (e.g., hurled nests) or strategic allies (e.g., mosquito-infested swamps). In the early twentieth century the relationship between insects and disease was exploited, and vectors were mass-produced as microguided missiles loaded with pathogens. With further scientific advances, defenses in the form of insecticides and vaccines meant that insects were no longer considered as battlefield weapons. However, in recent times sociopolitical changes have put insects back into the realm of human conflict through asymmetrical conflicts pitting combatants from nonindustrialized regions against forces from militarily and economically superior nations. In a sense, history has come full circle with insects having the potential to become the "six-legged box-cutters" (59) of primitively armed terrorists waging a war of attrition against modern societies.

SUMMARY POINTS

1. Insects were first used to inflict pain on human enemies, a practice that continued into the twentieth century.
2. Insects were strategically used as vectors of pathogens in 300 BCE, long before people understood the underlying biology.
3. When the mechanisms of insect-borne diseases were discovered, entomological warfare flourished as a means of attacking both soldiers and noncombatants.
4. Insects have considerable potential to destroy crops and livestock, although the damage is primarily economic.
5. Eradication of agricultural and other pests can create opportunities for bioterrorists to reintroduce damaging insects.
6. In modern, asymmetrical warfare, insects may be tempting weapons for terrorists to inflict human suffering or to cause serious economic losses.

FUTURE ISSUES

1. Continued archeological research may provide clearer evidence of the early uses of insects as weapons.
2. The full nature and extent of the Japanese biological warfare program of World War II have yet to be revealed, although continued investigations may provide substantially greater information (e.g., **http://search.japantimes.co.jp/cgi-bin/nn20110221x1.html**).
3. The secrecy surrounding entomological weapons by the United States and other nations in the 1950s and 1960s makes it difficult to assemble a complete picture of research and development programs, although as documents are declassified and otherwise become available, researchers should be able to improve our understanding.
4. The complexity of the politics and history during the Cold War makes it difficult to know the extent of entomological warfare conducted by the United States and other nations, but further research may prove enlightening in this regard.
5. There is considerable controversy as to whether the United States and other nations are adequately prepared for acts of entomological terrorism, and continued discussion of the most effective tactics and efficient strategies is in order.

DISCLOSURE STATEMENT

I receive royalties from *Six-Legged Soldiers: Using Insects as Weapons of War* (Oxford University Press, 2009), and it is conceivable that this review will encourage readers to purchase this book.

LITERATURE CITED

1. Aelian. 1959. *On the Characteristics of Animals*, Vol. 1–3. Cambridge, MA: Harvard Univ. Press (Loeb Class. Library). 1296 pp.
2. Allworth EA. 1990. *The Modern Uzbeks: From the Fourteenth Century to the Present, A Cultural History*. Stanford, CA: Hoover Inst. Press. 410 pp.
3. Alonso R, Ovies J. 2002. *Transcript of Cuban television interview*. **http://cuba.cu/gobierno/documentos/2002/ing/m240502i.html**
4. Ambrose J. 1974. Insects in warfare. *Army* Dec.:33–38
5. Aouade JAA. 1979. *Traditional Beekeeping in Nigeria: Editorial Summary from 'Beekeeping Among the Tiv'*. London: Commonw. Secr. Int. Bee Res. Assoc. 23 pp.
6. Avery D. 1999. Canadian biological and toxin warfare research, development and planning, 1925–45. See Ref. 37, pp. 190–214
7. Baldwin GC. 1965. *A Story of the Chiricahua and Western Apache*. Tucson, AZ: Dale Stuart King. 144 pp.
8. Ban J. 2000. *Agricultural Biological Warfare: An Overview*. Washington, DC: Chem. Biol. Arms Control Inst. 8 pp.
9. Barenblatt D. 2004. *A Plague Upon Humanity: The Secret Genocide of Axis Japan's Germ Warfare Operation*. New York: HarperCollins
10. Bérubé C. 2008. *War and bees: military applications of apiculture*. **http://beekeeping.com/articles/us/war_bees.htm**
11. Bojtzov V, Geissler E. 1999. Military biology in the USSR, 1920–45. See Ref. 37, pp. 153–67
12. Burgett M. 2008. *Plagues, pests and politics*. **http://ent.orst.edu/burgettm/ent300_lecture14.htm**
13. Burnes A. 1973. *Travels into Bokhara*. London: Oxford Univ. Press. 502 pp.
14. Bybee J. 2009. *Memo from Chief of Justice Department's Office of Legal Counsel*. **http://dspace.wrlc.org/doc/bitstream/2041/70967/00355_020801_004display.pdf**
15. Byrne J. 2009. *Bush memos parallel claim 9/11 mastermind's children were tortured with insects*. **http://forum.prisonplanet.com/index.php?topic = 99987.0;wap2**
16. Carson-DeWitt RS. 2008. *Trench fever*. Encyclopedia of Medicine. **http://findarticles.com/p/articles/mi_g2601/is_0013/ai_2601001395**
17. Carter GB, Pearson GS. 1999. British biological warfare and biological defence, 1925–45. See Ref. 37, pp. 168–89
18. Chavez S, Simon R. 1988. Mystery letter puts a strange twist on latest Medfly crisis. *Los Angel. Times* (Orange County Edition), Dec. 3:B1
19. Clarke R. 1968. *The Silent Weapons*. New York: David McKay. 270 pp.
20. Cookson J, Nottingham J. 1969. *A Survey of Chemical and Biological Warfare*. New York: Mon. Rev. 424 pp.
21. Croddy E. 2002. *Chemical and Biological Warfare: A Comprehensive Survey for the Concerned Citizen*. New York: Springer. 352 pp.
22. Crosby MC. 2006. *The American Plague: The Untold Story of Yellow Fever, the Epidemic that Shaped Our History*. New York: Berkley. 384 pp.
23. Cuban Government. 2000. *Action brought by the people of Cuba against the government of the United States of America for economic damages caused to Cuba*. Work. Pap., Ad Hoc Group States Parties Conv. Prohib. Dev. Prod. Stockpiling Bacteriol. (Biol.) Toxin Weapons Destr., 20th Sess., Geneva. **http://opbw.org/ahg/docs/20th%20session/wp417.pdf**
24. Cuba Portal. 2011. *The People of Cuba vs. The Government of the United States of America for Human Damages to be Submitted to the Civil and Administrative Court of Law at the Provincial People's Court in Havana City*. **http://cuba.cu/gobierno/documentos/1999/ing/d310599i.html**
25. Dinger J. 1997. *Cuba: no use of biological weapons*. Press Statement, US Dep. State, May 6

26. Dunn A. 1990. Officials advertise to contact group claiming Medfly releases. *Los Angel. Times*, Feb. 10:A13
27. Endicott S, Hagerman E. 1998. *The United States and Biological Warfare: Secrets from the Early Cold War and Korea*. Bloomington: Indiana Univ. Press. 304 pp.
28. Falun Dafa. 2004. *Illustrations of torture methods used to persecute Falun Gong practitioners*. **http://clearwisdom.net/emh/articles/2004/6/11/49032.html**
29. Frank JH, Kanamitsu K. 1987. *Paederus*, sensu lato (Coleoptera: Staphylinidae): natural history and medical importance. *J. Med. Entomol.* 24:155–91
30. Frazier TW. 1999. Natural and bioterrorist/biocriminal threats to food and agriculture. *Ann. N.Y. Acad. Sci.* 894:1–8
31. Free JB. 1982. *Bees and Mankind*. London: George Allen & Unwin. 154 pp.
32. Fujii E, Zilinskas R. 2009. *Cuba profile: biological overview. Nuclear Threat Initiative*. **http://www.nti.org/e_research/profiles/Cuba/Biological/index.html**
33. Garrett BC. 1996. The Colorado potato beetle goes to war. *Chem. Weapons Conv. Bull.* 33:2–3
34. Garrett BC. 2000. A plague of locusts. *Nonprolif. Demilitarization Arms Control* 6:11–12
35. Geissler E, ed. 1986. *Biological and Toxin Weapons Today*. New York: Oxford Univ. Press. 172 pp.
36. Geissler E. 1999. Biological warfare activities in Germany, 1923–45. See Ref. 37, pp. 91–126
37. Geissler E, van Courtland Moon JE, eds. 1999. *Biological and Toxin Weapons: Research, Development and Use from the Middle Ages to 1945. SIPRI Biological and Chemical Warfare Studies*. New York: Oxford Univ. Press. 296 pp.
38. Gold H. 1996. *Unit 731 Testimony*. Singapore: Yen Books. 256 pp.
39. Green J, ed. 1979. *Zuni: Selected Writings of Frank Hamilton Cushing*. Lincoln: Univ. Neb. Press. 449 pp.
40. Grubinger V. 2008. *Colorado potato beetle*. **http://www.uvm.edu/vtvegandberry/factsheets/potatobeetle.html**
41. Haldane JBS. 1938. Science and future warfare. *Chem. Warf. Bull.* 24:7–17
42. Harris SH. 2002. *Factories of Death: Japanese Biological Warfare, 1932–1945, and the American Cover-Up*. New York: Routledge. 352 pp.
43. Harris R, Paxman J. 1983. *A Higher Form of Killing*. New York: Random House. 336 pp.
44. Hay A. 1999. A magic sword or a big itch: an historical look at the United States biological weapons programme. *Med. Confl. Surviv.* 15:215–34
45. Holmes R, ed. 2001. *The Oxford Companion to Military History*. New York: Oxford Univ. Press. 1072 pp.
46. Hopkirk P. 1992. *The Great Game: The Struggle for Empire in Central Asia*. New York: Kodansha. 564 pp.
47. *International Herald Tribune*. 1970. When the Nazis tried to starve out Britain by beetle-bombing crops. Feb. 25:5
48. International Scientific Commission. 1952. *Report of the International Scientific Commission for the Investigation of the Facts Concerning Bacterial Warfare in Korea and China*. Peking. 660 pp.
49. Isikoff M, Thomas E. 2009. The lawyer and the caterpillar. *Newsweek* Apr. 18. **http://www.newsweek.com/2009/04/17/the-lawyer-and-the-caterpillar.html**
50. Johnson J. 1990. Female medfly found in Sun Valley close to area targeted earlier. *Los Angel. Times*, Jan. 4:B3
51. Kadlec RP. 1995. Biological weapons for waging economic warfare. In *Battlefield of the Future*, ed. BR Schneider, LE Grinter, ch. 10. Maxwell Air Force Base, AL: Air War Coll. Stud. Natl. Security
52. Kourí G, Guzmán MG, Bravo J. 1986. Hemorrhagic dengue in Cuba: history of an epidemic. *Pan Am. Health Organ. Bull.* 20:24–30
53. Lapidus F. 2003. Could insects be used as instruments of biological warfare? *Voice Am.*, Jan. 29. **http://worldnewssite.com/News/2003/January/2003-01-29-38-Could.html**
54. Leitenberg M. 1998. The Korean War biological warfare allegations resolved. *Cent. Pac. Asia Stud. Stockh. Univ. Occas. Pap.* 36:1–40
55. Leitenberg M. 2008. *Biological weapons in the 20th century: a review and analysis*. Prepared for Int. Symp. Prot. Chem. Biol. Warf., 7th, Stockholm. **http://www.fas.org/bwc/papers/bw20th.htm**
56. Leitenberg M. 2008. Undermining the international regime: false allegations of BW use. See Ref. 55; **http://www.fas.org/bwc/papers/review/under.htm**

57. Litovkin D. 1999. Valentin Yevstigneyev on issues, relating to Russian biological weapons. *Yaderny Kontrol Dig.* 11:43–51
58. Lockwood JA. 1987. Entomological warfare: history of the use of insects as weapons of war. *Bull. Entomol. Soc. Am.* 33:76–82
59. Lockwood JA. 2009. *Six-Legged Soldiers: Using Insects as Weapons of War*. New York: Oxford. 377 pp.
60. Lovell SP. 1963. *Of Spies & Stratagems*. Englewood Cliffs, NJ: Prentice-Hall. 229 pp.
61. Lynch C. 1999. U.N. employee planned locust plague, Iraq says. *Wash. Post*, July 7:2
62. MacAskill E. 2009. Bush officials defend physical abuse described in memos released by Obama. *Guardian*, Apr. 17. **http://www.guardian.co.uk/world/2009/apr/17/bush-torture-memos-obama-mukasey**
63. MacKenzie D. 1999. Run, radish, run. *New Sci.* Dec.:36–39
64. Maclean F. 1959. *Back to Bokhara*. Oxford: Alden. 125 pp.
65. Mangold T, Goldberg J. 1999. *Plague Wars: The Terrifying Reality of Biological Warfare*. New York: St. Martin's Griffin. 496 pp.
66. Mangold T, Penycate J. 1986. *The Tunnels of Cu Chi*. New York: Berkley. 290 pp.
67. Mauroni A. 2003. *Chemical and Biological Warfare: A Reference Handbook*. Denver, CO: ABC-CLIO
68. Mayor A. 2003. *Greek Fire, Poison Arrows and Scorpion Bombs: Biological and Chemical Warfare in the Ancient World*. New York: Overlook Duckworth. 319 pp.
69. McGinnis D. 2004. Looking for loopholes. *BEEF Mag.*, July 1. **http://beefmagazine.com/mag/beef_looking_loopholes/**
70. Meyer KE, Brysac SB. 1999. *Tournament of Shadows: The Great Game and the Race for Empire in Central Asia*. Washington, DC: Counterpoint. 704 pp.
71. Military Tribunal of the Primorye Military Area. 1950. *Materials on the Trial of Former Servicemen of the Japanese Army Charged with Manufacturing and Employing Bacteriological Weapons*. Transcripts of the Khabarovsk Trial. Moscow: Foreign Lang. Publ. House. 535 pp.
72. Miller GL. 1997. Historical natural history: insects and the Civil War. *Am. Entomol.* 43:227–45
73. Miller J. 1999. U.N. backs mine expert expelled by Iraq. *N.Y. Times*, July 9
74. Murphy S, Hay A, Rose S. 1984. *No Fire, No Thunder: The Threat of Chemical and Biological Weapons*. New York: Mon. Rev. 145 pp.
75. National Research Council. 2003. *Countering Agricultural Bioterrorism*. Washington, DC: Natl. Acad. Press. 192 pp.
76. Neufeld E. 1980. Insects as warfare agents in the Ancient Near East. *Orientalia* 49:30–57
77. *New York Times*. 1952. Red photographs exposed as fakes. Apr. 3:1
78. Pages R. 2001. Biological warfare against Cuba: Bee-eating insect causes losses of two million dollars. *Granma Int.*, Aug. 3. **http://blythe.org/nytransfer-subs/2001-Caribbean-Vol-3/BIOLOGICAL_WARFARE_AGAINST_CUBA**
79. Pages R. 2003. Cuba: Washington's objective is to "cause hunger, desperation, and overthrow the government." *Green Left Wkly.*, Nov. 12
80. Pate J, Cameron G. 2001. *Covert biological weapons attacks against agricultural targets: assessing the impact against US agriculture*. Discuss. Pap. 2001–9, Belfer Cent. Sci. Int. Aff. 30 pp.
81. Payne D. 2008. *The other British war on the western front in the great war: the hygiene war*. **http://www.westernfrontassociation.com/great-war-on-land/78-cas-med/246-hyg-war.html**
82. Permanent Mission of Cuba to the United Nations. 1997. *Note verbale, addressed to the Secretary-General, as Item 80 of the preliminary list of the 52nd session of UN General Assembly*. **http://afrocubaweb.com/biowar.htm**
83. Peterson RKD. 1995. Insects, disease, and military history. *Am. Entomol.* 41:147–60
84. Peterson RKD. 2008. *The role of insects as biological weapons*. **http://entomology.montana.edu/historybug/insects_as_bioweapons.htm**
85. Piel J, Höfer I, Hui D. 2004. Evidence for a symbiosis island involved in horizontal acquisition of pederin biosynthetic capabilities by the bacterial symbiont of *Paederus fuscipes* beetles. *J. Bacteriol.* 186:1280–86
86. Ray E, Schaap WH. 2003. *Bioterror: Manufacturing Wars the American Way*. New York: Ocean Press. 80 pp.
87. Regis E. 1999. *The Biology of Doom: The History of America's Secret Germ Warfare Project*. New York: Henry Holt. 272 pp.

88. Roberts D. 1993. *Once They Moved Like the Wind: Cochise, Geronimo, and the Apache Wars*. New York: Simon & Schuster. 368 pp.
89. Robertson AG. 1995. From asps to allegations: biological warfare in history. *Military Med.* 160:369–73
90. Robertson H. 2008. *San people's use of poisonous beetles*. **http://biodiversityexplorer.org/beetles/chrysomelidae/alticinae/arrows.htm**
91. Root-Bernstein RS. 1991. Infectious terrorism. *Atlantic* May:44–50
92. Rose WH. 1981. *An Evaluation of Entomological Warfare as a Potential Danger to the United States and European NATO Nations*. US Army Dugway Proving Ground, UT: US Army Test Eval. Command. **http://www.thesmokinggun.com/archive/mosquito1.html**
93. Sair R. 1944. *The Book of Torture and Executions*. Toronto: Golden Books. 191 pp.
94. Schapp W. 1982. US biological warfare: the 1981 Cuba dengue epidemic. *Covert Action Inform. Bull.* 17:28–31
95. Schultz HA. 1992. 100 years of entomology in the Department of Defense. In *Insect Potpourri: Adventures in Entomology*, ed. J Adams, pp. 61–72. Gainesville, FL: Sandhill Crane
96. Selim J. 2005. Virus code red. *Discov. Mag.* 26:14
97. Solzhenitsyn A. 1974. *The Gulag Archipelago 1918–1956: An Experiment in Literary Investigation*. New York: Harper & Row. 660 pp.
98. Soper FL, Davis WA, Markham FS, Riehl LA. 1947. Typhus fever in Italy, 1943–1945, and its control with louse powder. *Am. J. Hygiene* 45:305–34
99. Steiner PE. 1968. *Disease in the Civil War: Natural Biological Warfare in 1861–1865*. Springfield, IL: Charles C. Thomas. 243 pp.
100. Stockholm International Peace Research Institute. 1975. *The Problem of Chemical and Biological Warfare: A Study of the Historical, Technical, Military, Legal and Political Aspects of CBW, and Possible Disarmament Measures. Vol. I: The Rise of CB Weapons*. New York: Humanities. 395 pp.
101. Sutherland R. 2003. *The importance of bees in war time*. **http://www.honeyflowfarm.com/newsletters/2003/november/novhoney.htm**
102. Tamayo JO, Laughlin M. 1999. Cuba files $181 billion claim against US. *Miami Herald*, June 2
103. Treble A. 2008. *Chemical and biological weapons: possession and programs past and present*. Monterey Inst. Int. Stud. James Martin Cent. Nonproliferation Stud. **http://cns.miis.edu/cbw/possess.htm**
104. Tschanz DW. 2008. *Typhus fever on the Eastern Front in World War I*. **http://entomology.montana.edu/historybug/WWI/TEF.htm**
105. Tschanz DW. 2008. *Yellow fever and the strategy of the Mexican-American War*. **http://entomology.montana.edu/historybug/mexwar/mexwar.htm**
106. United Nations. 1969. *Chemical and Bacteriological (Biological) Weapons and the Effects of Their Possible Use*. New York: Ballantine
107. United States Air Force. 2003. When killing just won't do. From "Nonlethal Weapons: Terms and References," a report published by the United States Air Force Institute for National Security Studies. *Harper's Mag.* Feb:16. **http://harpers.org/archive/2003/02/0079475**
108. University of Saskatchewan. 2008. *Climate change between 5000 and 4000 years ago*. **http://geochemistry.usask.ca/bill/Courses/Climate/Disturbance%20&%20Decline%20prt.pdf**
109. Wellman PI. 1935. *Death in the Desert: The Fifty Years' War for the Great Southwest*. New York: Macmillan. 318 pp.
110. Wheeler CM. 1946. Control of typhus in Italy 1943–1944 by use of DDT. *Am. J. Public Health* 36:119–29
111. Whitby SM. 2002. *Biological Warfare Against Crops*. New York: Palgrave. 288 pp.
112. Wolff J. 2008. *Ameer of Bokhara Nasir Ullah, report of Josef Wolff 1843–1845*. **http://www.oocities.org/athens/5246/amir.html**
113. Woodall J. 2006. Why mosquitoes trump birds. *Scientist* Jan.:61
114. Wotton RS. 2007. *The ten plagues of Egypt, Opticon 1826*. **http://www.ucl.ac.uk/opticon1826/archive/issue3/RfP_Art_LIFE_Wotton_Plagues.pdf**
115. Wu T. 2008. *A preliminary review of studies of Japanese biological warfare Unit 731 in the United States*. **http://www.freerepublic.com/focus/f-news/530696/posts**
116. Xyroth Enterprises. 2008. *The ten plagues of Egypt*. **http://xyroth-enterprises.co.uk/10plague.htm**
117. Zinsser H. 2007. *Rats, Lice and History*. Edison, NJ: Transaction Publ. 332 pp.

Mites (Acari) as a Factor in Greenhouse Management

Uri Gerson[1] and Phyllis G. Weintraub[2,*]

[1]Department of Entomology, Faculty of Agricultural, Food and Environmental Quality Sciences, The Hebrew University, Rehovot 76100, Israel; email: gerson@agri.huji.ac.il

[2]Department of Entomology, Agricultural Research Organization, Gilat Research Center, Israel, 85280; email: phyllisw@volcani.agri.gov.il

Annu. Rev. Entomol. 2012. 57:229–47

First published online as a Review in Advance on September 9, 2011

The *Annual Review of Entomology* is online at ento.annualreviews.org

This article's doi:
10.1146/annurev-ento-120710-100639

0066-4170/12/0107-0229$20.00

*Corresponding author

Keywords

biological control, integrated pest management

Abstract

This review discusses the economically important pest mites (Acari) of greenhouses, aspects of their biology, and the acarine predators that attack them as well as various insect pests. Greenhouse factors affect pest mites as well as their natural enemy populations and their interactions. Conversely, pest mites affect greenhouse management in terms of the chemical and biological methods required to control their populations. Structure affects heating, cooling, and light, which can be manipulated with suitable screens. Crops often select for pests and their mite enemies. Both groups may be affected in greenhouses by adding pollen and by a CO_2-enriched atmosphere. These factors impact pest mite populations, the damage they cause, and the methods used to control them. The possibility of incipient evolution occurring in greenhouses, along with the benefits and consequences for pest control, is discussed.

INTRODUCTION

Until the early 1900s, pest mites were usually controlled with plant extracts or inorganic compounds such as sulfur, but after World War II, synthetic pesticides were employed. Over-reliance on synthetic acaricides led quickly to the development of resistance in many pest mite species (48). As a result of this and of a growing awareness of the environment, a more integrated approach to pest management has taken place. These tactics include physical, biological, and chemical control measures. Whereas greenhouses were initially built to protect plants from harsh weather, various forms of screenhouses were developed solely as a means of physical control. However, in both cases, the continuous cropping systems now employed by most growers have allowed these structures to become unique incubators for acarine and insect pest populations. It was not until the early 1960s that the first trials were performed with a newly discovered spider mite predator, *Phytoseiulus persimilis* (7), a Mediterranean species (100). Massive commerce of produce and flowers in recent decades has brought about the undetected movement of species from distant lands all over the world so that the number of pest mites in temperate and subtropical areas is ever increasing (73). Here, we examine acarine predators and pests and how the greenhouse/screenhouse environment is influencing and can be manipulated to affect these and other arthropod populations. Although the majority of covered crops are found in China, there is virtually no information in English language journals. Whether this dearth is due to lack of research or lack of publication is unknown. The vast majority of the information in this review is from research conducted in Europe and North America.

Arrenotoky: also termed arrhenotokous parthenogenesis; a type of parthenogenic reproduction in which unfertilized eggs develop into haploid males

Twospotted spider mite (TSSM): *Tetranychus urticae*

Webbing: a protective silk covering produced by spider mites and some insects

ECONOMICALLY IMPORTANT PEST MITES AND THEIR ACARINE BIOCONTROL AGENTS

Mites are arachnid arthropods, of which more than 50,000 species have been identified to date (43). Most are approximately 0.2 to 0.6 mm in length with fused bodies that bear four pairs of legs as nymphs and adults (except the eriophyoids, which have only two pairs). Mites occur in all major habitats, including jungles, deserts, polar regions, and the oceans. They display a vast variety of nutritional habits, feeding on other animals (whether as predators or as endo- or ectoparasites of vertebrates and invertebrates), plants, and dead organic matter.

The higher classification of the Acari has recently been stabilized by Lindquist et al. (64) and is used to accommodate the species occurring in greenhouses. These mites belong to three orders: Trombidiformes, Sarcoptiformes, and Mesostigmata. Members of the first two include pests of greenhouse crops, whereas the Mesostigmata contribute predatory species, which feed on pest mites and several insect species. Three Trombidiformes families (Tetranychidae, Tarsonemidae, and Eriophyidae) include greenhouse pests, most of which have worldwide distribution (see 40 for a table of commercially available Acari and their uses). Most members of these families reproduce by arrenotoky.

Trombidiformes

The most important tetranychid greenhouse pest is the twospotted spider mite (TSSM), *Tetranychus urticae*. A red form of this species, formerly known as *Tetranychus cinnabarinus* (carmine spider mite), is a synonym of the green-form TSSM (5), so that data published about the former are applicable to the latter. A female TSSM completes a generation in 2 to 3 weeks, lays (on suitable plants and under benign conditions) more than 100 eggs, and produces copious amounts of webbing, within which the TSSM lives its entire life. Because the mites can quickly overexploit their environment, dispersal is essential for survival (32). Dispersal in open fields is accomplished by being wind-borne on web strands or by walking; in greenhouses, dispersal occurs primarily by walking or by being passively carried on or by human activities.

The TSSM, which attacks many diverse greenhouse plants, initially forms colonies on the underside of leaves and feeds on cell chloroplasts just under the leaf epidermis, causing yellowish stippled spots. As feeding continues and intensifies, the leaf may appear brownish; it eventually desiccates and falls, ultimately leading to plant death. The TSSM thrives best in warm, dry temperatures and has developed resistance to most commonly used acaricides. Its webbing hinders many generalist insect and acarine predators but attracts specialist natural enemies (37), of which the best known is *Phytoseiulus persimilis* (Mesostigmata: Phytoseiidae). *P. persimilis* is a fast-moving, proactive predator that feeds only on web-producing spider mites; its long legs allow it to move easily within the webbing. Being a voracious feeder, this predator may overexploit its prey and then disappear. Owing to the ability of *P. persimilis* to control spider mites, it is being mass produced and sold under various commercial labels. Multiple other predators are increasingly being employed to control spider mites. The more prevalent of these predators is *Neoseiulus californicus*, a generalist that can survive on pollen during periods of low prey density. Generation time varies widely (5–10 days) with food source, and adult females can live up to 60 days, producing approximately 30 eggs. Owing to its polyphagous nature and tolerance to a wide range of temperatures and humidities, *N. californicus* is now also mass reared for use against spider mites. Another phytoseiid predator, *Amblyseius swirskii*, although not particularly effective in terms of absolute control owing to its inability to contend with the webbing created by the spider mites, feeds on isolated protonymphs and deutonymphs (124). Although only middling numbers of spider mites are consumed, this suffices to affect positively the predator's ability to control other pests (thrips and whiteflies) found on the plants (74).

Deutonymph: the third active developmental instar in the Acari

Protonymph: the second active developmental instar in the Acari (after the larva)

Pharate: the penultimate developmental stage in arthropods before their emergence as adults

Functional response: an ecological term describing the rate at which a predator consumes prey; there are four recognized types of functional responses

The broad mite, *Polyphagotarsonemus latus* (Tarsonemidae), is a polyphagous pest that infests approximately 60 plant families (38). It is essentially a cosmopolitan pest of ornamentals and vegetables under protected cultivation in temperate zones, attacking these and many perennial crops in warmer parts of the world. The mite may complete a generation in one week at 25°C to 30°C, and it is most active in warm and wet seasons. It does not undergo a diapause. The sex ratio is strongly female biased (4:1) but may be lower under arid conditions. In the field, perennial crops as well as weeds serve as reservoirs for this pest. The quality of heavily attacked, susceptible plants deteriorates rapidly. Dispersal is by various means: On infested plants, pharate females are transported upward by the males. Mites can arrive at feeding sites by walking, borne on winds, or with various whiteflies, especially the sweetpotato whitefly, *Bemisia tabaci* (85), another greenhouse pest.

Several phytoseiid mites have been assayed against the broad mite. Weintraub et al. (117) released *Neoseiulus cucumeris* on sweet peppers, which was as efficacious as were pesticides in controlling broad mites. Yields obtained when four *Neoseiulus californicus* per plant were released on greenhouse-grown peppers were not significantly different from those of an uninfested control treatment (55). Tal et al. (101) were first to show that *A. swirskii* eats approximately 40 broad mites per 24-h period and has a type II functional response. Using *A. swirskii*, van Maanen et al. (109) subsequently obtained promising results in controlling broad mites on peppers.

The cyclamen mite, *Phytonemus pallidus*, is a widely distributed pest of many ornamentals in greenhouses. Its feeding causes leaf stunting and crinkling, resulting in compact leaf masses within plants as well as flower withering and (in strawberries) poor fruit production (54, 98). Heavy infestations kill African violets and cyclamens by dwarfing the leaves at the crown, and some leaves fail to open. The mite, which avoids light, requires a warm, humid environment, and under such conditions, it may raise a generation in 2 to 3 weeks. In temperate regions, it overwinters at the adult stage. Females may lay approximately 90 eggs, most of which develop into females.

Tomato russet mite (TRM): *Aculops lycopersici*

Easterbrook et al. (30) assayed two phytoseiids against the cyclamen mite infesting strawberry in England. They reported that *N. californicus* and *N. cucumeris* reduced pest mites by 70% to 80%, compared with nonrelease plants. A ratio of one *N. cucumeris* to ten *P. pallidus* provided satisfactory control if the predators were released at an early stage of infestation. Tuovinen & Lindqvist (106) later found that *Anthoseius rhenanus* and *N. cucumeris* were the most promising preventive predators against *P. pallidus* in Finland.

Tomato russet mite (TRM), *Aculops lycopersici*, is the only member of the Eriophyidae that is a pest in greenhouses. It affects mainly tomatoes, but eggplants, petunias, peppers, and potatoes may also be damaged. Infestations on tomato usually begin in the lower stems and leaves, which lose their color, wilt, and drop (90). The mite is a warm-weather leaf vagrant that has no dormancy and dies if exposed to low temperatures. Development is also retarded under high-humidity conditions at high temperatures, above 30°C (45). In temperate regions, the pest survives winters only within greenhouses, but under warmer conditions, TRM lives out of season on other host plants (90), which serve as sources for subsequent infestations. The mites disperse with winds, on insects, or by clinging to farming implements and personnel. An entire life cycle can be completed in approximately one week, with each female producing 30 to 50 progeny.

Representatives of several mite families were assayed against the TRM, showing various degrees of control. *Homeopronematus anconai* (Tydeidae) provided uneven rates of control (8, 56). Osman & Zaki (84) tried the stigmaeid *Agistemus exsertus* against the pest, and most work was conducted with several phytoseiids. Brodeur et al. (8) reported that *N. cucumeris* attacked all TRM stages and appeared to have the biological attributes required to control the pest. Two strains of *N. californicus* were offered TRM, and they killed a mean of 24 active prey per day (15). Several authors found *A. swirskii* suitable for TRM control. The predator may consume >100 individual pests per day and completed its development in approximately 5 days on that diet (86). Momen & Abdel-Khaleka (76) reported that *A. swirskii* feeding on the TRM had approximately 35 progeny. Other phytoseiids assayed against the TRM include *Euseius concordis* (25) and *Amblyseius andersoni* (34). Notwithstanding this array of natural enemies, at this time, no predator provides adequate TRM control.

Sarcoptiformes

The bulb mite, *Rhizoglyphus robini*, is another major pest in greenhouses. It injures the bulbs, tubers, and corms of many plants in storage; potato tubers are sometimes damaged by mites burrowing into their buds (the "eyes"). Gladioli corms in storage may be partially consumed and fail to produce commercial flowers, with approximately 50% or more damage (27). In other cases, young flower leaves shrivel and flower production is faulty. Phytopathogenic fungi, such as *Fusarium*, add to the damage after gaining entrance to corms and bulbs through mite-inflicted wounds. In turn, they promote the pest's development, thereby aggravating overall damage (44). The mite completes a generation in a fortnight at 25°C, producing 400 to 700 eggs during six weeks. The mites are sensitive to low humidities, and they form hypopodes (heteromorphic second-stage nymphs) when their substrate dries up. The hypopodes, which may be disseminated by soil-borne insects, molt to third-instar nymphs upon returning to high humidities (39).

A search for natural enemies of the bulb mite in various parts of the world found several acarine predators, of which *Gaeolaelaps aculeifer* (Laelapidae) was the most effective (61). *G. aculeifer* reduces the numbers of *R. robini* that infest lily scales in greenhouse experiments on intact lily bulbs in pots boxes and in small plots with peat soil when released in a ratio of one predator to two or five prey. In doing so, it suppressed bulb mite populations to fewer than 10 individuals per bulb within six weeks. Complete elimination of bulb mites was observed only when the predator-to-prey ratio at release was equal to 3:1 (62).

ECONOMICALLY IMPORTANT INSECT PESTS, THEIR ACARINE BIOCONTROL AGENTS, AND INTRAGUILD PREDATION BETWEEN INSECT AND ACARINE PREDATORS

Representatives of several pest insect groups such as thrips (Thysanoptera: Thripidae), whiteflies (Hemiptera: Aleyrodidae), true bugs (Hemiptera: Anthocoridae), and various small flies (Diptera) interact with and may be affected by mites. These relationships are generally more complex than the mite-mite interactions because insect predators or parasitoids are often simultaneously released for pest control. In these cases, there is the potential for intraguild predation or other complex tritrophic interactions. There is currently much debate about whether these interactions will enhance or deter target pest suppression (12, 75, 91).

Western flower thrips (WFT): *Frankliniella occidentalis*

Thigmotaxis: a description of behavior in which an organism seeks a tight physical place where it is in proximal contact, e.g., a gall, calyx, and fruit

Trichome: a fine outgrowth or hair on the surface of a plant

Thripidae

Only a few thrips species damage greenhouse crops. The more prominent include the western flower thrips (WFT), *Frankliniella occidentalis*; the onion thrips, *Thrips tabaci*; the common blossom thrips, *Frankliniella schultzei*; and the melon thrips, *Thrips palmi*, all of which transmit plant viruses (63). Herein we are concerned only with the first two, which are often found in flowers and damage many crops.

The life cycle of WFT, which infests more than 500 host plants, may require 3 to 8 weeks for development to adult. A WTF female lays 40 to 100 eggs in plant tissues, often in the flowers, but also in the fruit or foliage. The plant is injured by feeding, which produces holes and areas of silvery discoloration as a result of air entering into the damaged cells. The pest is the major vector of *Tomato spotted wilt virus*. In addition, WTF is resistant to several groups of insecticides (57, 103, 127).

The life cycle of the onion thrips may require several weeks, and a female produces more than 250 eggs (102). It is a cosmopolitan, polyphagous species that may complete its life cycle on leaves or in flowers. This species, formerly a major pest of ornamentals in greenhouses, was partially replaced by *F. occidentalis*, possibly owing to its habit of pupating in the soil (e.g., not on foliage exposed to chemicals and to natural enemies) and its reduced susceptibility to some chemicals (35, 66, 71).

As more insecticides fail to control these two important thrips species, alternative biological control methods become increasingly important. Because of the cryptic and thigmotactic nature of thrips, their control by insecticides and by biological control agents has not been wholly satisfactory. A number of phytoseiid species feed on thrips, primarily on the first instar and to a lesser extent on the second. One of the first mites to be marketed as a predator of both WFT and onion thrips was *N. cucumeris* (117 and references therein). Not only is it an effective predator, but it is also compatible with plant-growth regulators and some insecticides (117). *N. cucumeris* generally exhibits a type II functional response to onion thrips, but crops with dense trichomes (e.g., eggplant) reduce the efficacy of this predator (68). In laboratory trials, *N. californicus* consumed WFT and completed its life cycle, but the first significant reduction in field populations was only fortuitously observed in pepper plants (118). Although primarily used to control spider mites, this mite also contributes to the control of thrips.

A. swirskii, the most recent of the commercialized thrips predators, is an effective WFT and onion thrips predator (122). However, *A. swirskii* had high mortality rates when juvenile mites fed on these thrips, and it has an intrinsic rate of growth of less than one predator egg per day in adult females. In a laboratory study in which spider mite protonymphs and deutonymphs were offered in addition to first-instar WFT, thrips were consumed at approximately twice the rate as spider mites (124).

Laboratory tests showed that the simultaneous release of two acarine thrips predators may lead to a negative interaction between them, thus resulting in less efficacious thrips control (10). Both *A. swirskii* and *N. cucumeris* exhibited intraguild predation; however, *A. swirskii* preferred *N. cucumeris* juveniles to WFT. Unless these two predators exhibit some sort of resource partitioning on the crop, there is the potential for control failure. Another predatory mite (*Protogamasellopsis posnaniensis*), originally described from Poland but found in Brazil and not yet commercially available, was tested for efficacy against WFT larvae in the soil and was found to kill between four and five thrips per day and to have long-term survival of 98% (16). This mite also feeds on other soil organisms and may be a new biological control agent, provided it can be mass reared.

Furthermore, since Trichilo & Leigh (104) first demonstrated that thrips can bite back and feed on TSSM eggs, a number of other studies have shown that thrips are also facultative consumers of other predatory mites, including *Iphiseius degenerans* (33) and *P. persimilis* (52).

Aleyrodidae

Whiteflies, especially the sweetpotato whitefly, *B. tabaci*, and the greenhouse whitefly, *Trialeurodes vaporariorum*, are major pests in greenhouses. They are small (2–3 mm long) insects whose wings are covered with whitish mealy flakes (hence the vernacular name). Their stalked eggs are inserted into the tissues of host plants, and the emerging crawlers can move up to a few centimeters away. They then settle, begin to feed, and remain stationary until becoming adults. The common pest species, which are polyphagous, raise a generation in 3 to 4 weeks, producing 100 to 200 eggs per female; reproduction is usually by arrenotoky (36). The harm they inflict is a result of (*a*) directly damaging leaves, thereby causing withering and premature drop; (*b*) contaminating the host plant surfaces with their honeydew, which serves as substrate for dark sooty mold fungi that hinder photosynthesis and reduce the quantity and quality of the product; (*c*) transmitting various plant viruses, especially Potyviridae and Geminiviridae (9); and (*d*) serving as vectors for another greenhouse pest, the broad mite (85). These polyphagous pests also attack weeds, which serve as alternate hosts when commercial crops are unavailable (78). Strains of *B. tabaci* (11, 41) as well as *T. vaporariorum* (6, 126) have shown resistance to a number of insecticides.

A. swirskii, first shown to be a whitefly predator back in the 1960s (99), has only recently been rediscovered. In a series of laboratory and semifield studies, Nomikou et al. (80, 81) demonstrated the ability of *A. swirskii* to control *B. tabaci* populations in laboratory trials. Calvo et al. (13) also examined the ability of *A. swirskii* to control *B. tabaci* on sweet pepper when in the presence of another predator (the hemipterous *Nesidiocoris tenuis*) and/or a parasitoid (*Eretmocerus mundus*). They found that *A. swirskii* improved whitefly control regardless of whether the predator or parasitoid was present, but best control of *B. tabaci* was achieved when the mite was coupled with the parasitoid. This is probably due to resource partitioning: The predatory mite feeds primarily on eggs and crawler stages, whereas the parasitoid lays eggs primarily inside the second- and third-instar nymphs.

Even in the presence of thrips, *A. swirskii* is a voracious whitefly predator (75). Most importantly, this study showed that the presence of a less-preferred host did not reduce predation pressure on the preferred host. In fact, there was a 15-fold increase in predator numbers in the presence of both host species, and when spider mites and thrips were present, there was an even stronger numerical response (up to 50-fold). In the latter case, control of whiteflies was improved while damage induced by spider mites was reduced (74).

Anthocoridae

Orius species are predatory hemipterans often released in greenhouses to control thrips. Under some conditions, *O. albidipennis* may be the intraguild prey upon which *N. cucumeris* feeds (67). Under most conditions, *Orius* feeds on the smaller predatory mite species. In fact, Urbaneja et al. (107) concluded that the presence of *N. cucumeris* enhances the establishment of *O. laevigatus* in pepper greenhouses. Recently, Chow et al. (20) showed that, on greenhouse roses, *O. insidiosus* always feeds on the most abundant prey, either the WFT or *A. swirskii*. They showed a similar relationship between *O. insidiosus* and another thrips predator, *I. degenerans* (19). The role of pollen, either supplemental or as it naturally occurs on the plant, can alter the relationships between the mite predators and *Orius* (94, 95). The relationships between *Orius* spp. and predatory mite species are complex and need to be examined on an individual basis.

Diptera

The larvae of shore flies (Sciaridae) live in moist soil and leaf litter. Adult shore flies cause aesthetic damage to plants, whereas their larvae burrow into roots, promoting plant diseases (110). Sciarids are usually mycophagous. However, *Bradysia* also feed on roots of ornamentals and may transmit plant pathogens (17), and *Scatella* spp. transmit fungal pathogens (97). *Stratiolaelaps* (= *Hypoaspis*) *scimitus* (Laelapidae) (formerly called *Hypoaspis miles*), a soil mite, has been assayed to control several *Bradysia* spp. (17). The predator completed a generation at 25°C when reared on a diet of *Bradysia* spp. and produced approximately 60 eggs per female (125). The habitats of predator and young sciarid larvae overlap because the pests deposit most of their eggs in the top 1 cm of the substrate where the mites aggregate (123). Populations of *S. scimitus* survived without food for several weeks. When subsequently fed, the adults oviposited and lived for more than four months, a trait that suggests *S. scimitus* could be utilized as a prophylactic, or predator-in-first, biological control agent (17).

Bradysia difformis causes direct damage to poinsettia seedlings (53). Researchers found that almost 100% control of the sciarid may be obtained when 10 to 20 of the commercially available *Gaeololaelaps aculeifer* were released per seedling at 7 days posttransplantation; when released at 14 days posttransplantation, only 76% to 84% control was achieved. Another predatory mite, *P. posnaniensis*, was tested against *Bradysia matogrossensis* (16). This mite fed on approximately two fly larvae per day, and long-term survival was 98%. It is considered a potential new biological control agent. Control of *Scatella tenuicosta* in mint was achieved by releasing 36 *G. aculeifer* mites per 0.3-liters peat pot (112).

THE GREENHOUSE AS A HABITAT FOR MITES

Modern-day greenhouses are a marvel of computerized technology: They can maintain suitable temperatures, remotely open and close shade curtains, turn irrigation systems on and off at the moment infrared beams detect slight declines in leaf turgor, and occupy an increasing role in vegetable (and sometimes ornamental) production in temperate and subtropical climates. However, these same conditions are also highly benign for diverse pests, of which the mites are an important, sometimes major, component.

The worldwide area of greenhouses is difficult to estimate for several reasons: (*a*) Government records of greenhouse structures are not kept, and when they are, greenhouse use or disuse from year to year is hard to ascertain. (*b*) Records are usually kept of the acreage of different crops, but there is no uniformity in reporting. For example, if there are two crops in one year in the same greenhouse structure, the total acreage recorded may be double the actual greenhouse area. (*c*) Because of the aforementioned problems, another estimate of greenhouse acreage is provided by biological control suppliers, but this may suffer drawbacks similar to that associated with the lack of record-keeping uniformity. A decade ago, van Lenteren (108) estimated the total greenhouse area to be 400,000 hectares worldwide. More recently, Zheng et al. (128) reported that China has more than 2,000,000 hectares of greenhouses—five times the previous worldwide estimate. Combining these two outdated sources, the (under-)estimated vegetable production includes 2,280,000 hectares and ornamental production occupies 120,000 hectares.

Structure

The first structures built to regulate climate to produce fruits and vegetables out of season were described from the first century of the Common Era (51 and references therein). These specularia were covered with sheets and mica and built on wheels to be easily moved into the sun and back indoors before the cold of night. Modern greenhouse structures and cladding vary according to prevailing climatic conditions, with the goal of optimizing temperature, humidity, and photosynthetically active radiation to achieve maximum plant yield. Although they offer physical protection against arthropod pests, they are not built with this goal in mind.

In the humid tropics, the major problem in greenhouse construction is heat reduction; this is exacerbated by poor economic conditions in which technologically advanced methods cannot be employed. In an extensive review of greenhouse design, orientation, cladding, and ventilation, Kuman et al. (59) concluded that there is a real and present need to develop cheap and effective technology to reduce temperatures inside these structures. Greenhouses with 15% to 30% ventilation, clad with material that reflected near-infrared radiation, and with insect-proof nets (20–40 mesh) were best suited to the tropics. However, mesh sizes of 20 to 40 do not offer protection against most arthropod pests: Aphids, leafminer flies, thrips, whiteflies, and mites can enter and are present year-round in these environments. In another study by Harmanto et al. (46), mesh sizes of 40 to 78 were evaluated in tomato greenhouses. These authors concluded that 52 mesh was a good compromise between air exchange and protection against arthropods in humid tropics.

In temperate and subpolar regions, greenhouses need to be constructed of solid material that can retain heat during prolonged cold temperatures. These greenhouses are often clad with glass (traditional), double-layered polyethylene, or polycarbonate (65). Ventilation during warm weather is usually through roof vents. The best protection against arthropod invasion is provided when openings are covered with insect-proof screening (50 mesh or more), doors are doubled, and there is positive pressure in the greenhouse, reducing the chance of pest entry. Greenhouses in these climates have the possibility of being completely free of all pest species if the structures are fallowed and allowed to remain crop free during the coldest months. Because most pest species are similarly unable to develop in the areas surrounding the greenhouses, invasion will be slow and the greenhouse can subsequently remain pest free for months.

In subtropical, i.e., Mediterranean, climates, most greenhouses are not heated during mild winters, but they need adequate heat exchange during the relatively hot summer months. These structures are often covered with a single layer of polyethylene (65) or knitted or woven insect-proof screening (114) that provides protection from larger arthropod pests year-round; mites, thrips, and whiteflies can penetrate even well-sealed 50-mesh greenhouse structures. Cooling greenhouses to mid-20°C in warm climates achieves better fruit quality and yield (88) and improves ornamentals (87, 121). This temperature can be maintained through a number of means: fan-ventilation with or without an evaporative cooling pad (120), fogging (89), shade screens, or a combination of these factors.

New Technologies and Manipulations

The effects of different technologies on pest and beneficial populations are usually addressed only after the equipment has been installed. Only in the case of insect screening are different screen types and colors tested primarily for their effects on arthropods and then made available for growers. Insect-exclusion screens are made of plastic and inherently have certain properties of ultraviolet (UV) absorption. Through the addition of certain materials, the UV properties can be altered (31), which can affect vegetable pigments (105), produce larger fruit (58), and affect pest (26, 119) and beneficial (18) populations including mites (60). In a comparison of seven nets with different optical properties and no application of acaricides or biological control agents, Legarrea et al. (60) showed that nets that transmitted less than 40% of UV radiation had significantly lower broad mite populations than did nets allowing 40% to 50% UV transmission. In addition, the significantly highest populations occurred with greater than 75% UV transmission.

Recently, acaricide-treated nets were shown to be effective against *P. latus* and *Tetranychus* spp. in eggplant crops (72). Although these nets were applied to field-grown crops, the principle of significant protection against phytophagous mites was demonstrated and could be applied to greenhouse situations.

Manipulation of the greenhouse environment (light, humidity, and temperature) can also have consequences on acarine predators and pests. Decades of study have showed that the TSSM prefers warm, dry temperatures, whereas *P. persimilis* requires higher humidity to be efficacious. Tomato greenhouses were manipulated with whitewash and an automatic humidifying system to maintain ≥70% relative humidity, and Nihoul (79) found that increased greenhouse light intensity and temperatures altered the morphology of tomato glandular trichomes, causing the predator to be frequently entrapped by the exudates and thus not as efficacious against spider mites as was anticipated. This accentuates the necessity of evaluating tritrophic relationships, not just predator-pest interactions. Working with cucumbers, Duso et al. (29) found that fogging adversely affected TSSM populations. However, this was probably due to direct contact of the TSSM with the mist rather than the increased humidity, as nighttime humidity was regularly 90%.

Whereas the conditions that promote the development of spider mite populations are fairly well known, the ability to detect nascent populations has lagged behind until recently. Techniques of remote sensing and precision agriculture, which had heretofore been applied only in open fields, are being adapted for greenhouses. Because spider mites destroy chloroplast-containing cells during feeding, this damage can be spectrally detected in the reflectance of visible and near-infrared regions. A recent study (49) demonstrated the ability to distinguish feeding damage by TSSM at very low levels. With this information, either predators could be released or chemical interventions could be applied to the precise locations of infestations, thereby treating the pest population in its nascent stage and with reduced effort, costs, and side effects.

One of the best natural forms of pest control in northern climes is the very cold winters, which, given the absence of heating and natural light, cause all pest populations to fall to zero. At the beginning of each season, pest populations start at zero and can remain nil if the greenhouse is properly closed and maintained. In northern temperate regions, light intensity and day length are

ABA: acarine biocontrol agent

severely reduced in the winter, which may be a factor in the poor establishment and reproductive rate of *N. cucumeris* (129). To compensate for inadequate light in winter, most growers in temperate regions (and further north) rely on supplemental lighting, the dominant form being high-pressure sodium lamps (113). In Scandinavian countries, as of five years ago, approximately 30% of cucumber, 17% of tomato, and 92% of rose growers were using assimilation lighting (photosynthesis enhancing) (111). These growers were usually using 20 or more hours of artificial lighting per day. With this extended lighting, pest species tended to be enhanced more than their arthropod natural enemies (113). The authors observed several greenhouses in Finland where growers had installed high-intensity sodium lighting. Aside from the fact that the crops were now being grown year-round, thus maintaining ever-larger pest populations, another observed consequence on tomatoes and peppers was the abundance of spider mites on upper plant parts. The *Bombus* sp. pollinators were so disoriented that hives had to be replaced weekly instead of once every six weeks, and some predatory mites tended to avoid light (83, 115). The ultimate consequences of this new innovation are the promotion of pest populations and the deterrence of many forms of beneficial arthropods.

Flowering/pollen-providing plants are beneficial to generalist acarine biocontrol agents (ABAs); however, the predators must move from these resource plants to the crop to control the pests effectively. Because crops grown in greenhouses are protected from wind, the pollen from these resource plants cannot be blown onto the crop plants. Artificially applied pollen supplements, although beneficial to ABAs, have not been extensively used because work on a commercial application unit did not begin until recently (116). In that study, the effects of pollen on improving the efficacy of the general predator, *A. swirskii*, were clearly demonstrated. Its increased efficacy when pollen was added is due to a numerical response (82): The use of pollen can allow general predator populations to develop and establish on plants before the first pests appear. Three general predators (*Anthoseius rhenanus*, *Euseius finlandicus*, and *N. cucumeris*) were successfully established from a single release on greenhouse-grown strawberries before the pest *Phytonemus pallidus*, which was successfully controlled for three months, appeared (106).

The enrichment of greenhouses with CO_2 to increase crop yield has been practiced for many years (77), resulting in elevated photosynthetic levels and increased flower and nectar production (reviewed in 23). Such atmospheric changes may have various effects on greenhouse mites. The elevated-CO_2 environment increases the number of TSSM (47), possibly indirectly via the host plants, but increases in available nectar and pollen would also encourage the population growth of predatory mites. More recently, Ballhorn et al. (3 and references therein) demonstrated changes in plant-leaf chemistry (in cyanide, phenol, and protein levels) as a result of elevated CO_2 levels that led to a redistribution of herbivores on the plant and higher damage levels on young leaves. Changes included redistribution of proteins, sugars, and plant phenolics. Although mites have not yet been used as models in these systems, it is reasonable to assume that they would be affected by changes in plant chemistry. Any effect on pest mites will lead to changes in predatory mites as well, but these remain to be evaluated.

Horticultural Manipulations

More than 300 species of potted ornamentals and more than 100 species of cut flowers are grown under protected conditions in Europe (108). Such variety greatly contributes to mite presence and abundance in greenhouses: by providing specialist phytophagous species with their specific hosts and by enabling polyphagous mites to move between hosts. The most prominent vegetable crops are cucumber, pepper, and tomato, and among the ornamentals, the most common are roses, gerbera, and chrysanthemum. All six crops are attacked by the polyphagous TSSM and *P. latus*, thus affording these pests season- (or year-) long, continuous, host plants.

The nature of the crop and its growing cycle affect pest mites. Tolerance of mite damage is usually zero for ornamentals that are marketed for aesthetic purposes, especially if intended for export (73), whereas edible plants, whose nutritional factors are dominant, can carry a certain number of pest mites before the commercial product suffers; they are thus more amenable to the use of nonspecific biocides (22), including biological control (73). This difference necessitates different management strategies: Ornamentals (especially annuals) depend more heavily on chemical pesticides, often making them unsuitable for biocontrol. However, mites infesting long-term ornamentals (e.g., roses), especially if grown as hedges within plastic-covered tunnels, may successfully be controlled by predatory mites (42). The practice of arching rose stems, which form natural bridges between plants, also provides an environment beneficial to predators. This structure has facilitated the movement of *P. persimilis* between plants and resulted in lower numbers of the TSSM (14). Such a practice may be used as a model for other crops.

Some crops (e.g., tomatoes) possess defense mechanisms against mites, but these defense mechanisms affect pests as well as predatory mites. One example is the trichomes of tomatoes, which carry sticky exudates that repel or entrap mites and are a major cause of tomato resistance to spider mites (96). These trichomes hinder the free movement and predation of *P. persimilis* on leaves (28). The amount of exudates per trichome was affected by greenhouse conditions, as more and larger trichome heads were produced when the plants were grown at 18°C in light than when tomatoes were kept in shade at 23°C. In consequence, the efficacy of the predator was reduced under the cooler conditions.

Arancon et al. (2) tested a vermicompost (produced from food waste) for its abilities to suppress populations of TSSM as well as other pests of beans and eggplants and to decrease the damage by these populations in greenhouses. Plants supplied with vermicompost had significantly less TSSM damage when compared with controls, but the vermicompost had the least effect on mite reproduction. This effect (reminiscent of the effect of elevated CO_2 levels noted above) was postulated to be due to added nitrogen and phenols to the plants, making them less attractive and palatable to the mites.

INCIPIENT MITE EVOLUTION (OR LACK THEREOF) IN GREENHOUSES

Does evolution take place in the greenhouse? Here we must distinguish between annual and perennial greenhouses. Within the time frame during which the former are used for growing crops (e.g., only for a single season), there are probably insufficient mite generations for selective pressures to exert their effects. However, Agrawal (1) recorded one exception: After five generations (approximately eight weeks), the adaptation of mites to cucumber was higher (threefold) in the host plant than it was in control lines. However, even if a mite population is selected for any beneficial trait (e.g., resistance to pesticides), the short life of the annual greenhouse would tend to kill all mites and thus negate any selective benefits accrued. In perennial greenhouses, by contrast, wherein the same crops may be grown for several years (e.g., roses), thereby reinforcing the selective factors, environmental pressures may change critical mite traits. Belliure et al. (4) provided several examples of such selection, also noting that populations stemming from several host plants harbor higher genetic variation (the potential for more evolution) than do populations collected from a single host plant. Whether such incipient evolution leads to host-race formation (69) in greenhouses is still unclear. Using selection pressure by pesticides, Markwick (70) and Sato et al. (93) obtained a resistant phytoseiid after six (approximately 10 weeks) and seven (approximately

12 weeks) generations, respectively, thus indicating that genetic change may also occur in predatory mites used in greenhouses. In perennial greenhouses, when selection pressure is maintained (e.g., by novel host plants or by pesticide applications), the relevant mite population could form host or resistant races. Such resistance could be reinforced if mite individuals that are already resistant arrived in the greenhouse and established and mated with members of the local population. Whether the formation of host races leads to speciation is still an open question (e.g., 69); perennial greenhouses could be suitable venues for relevant studies.

Species evolution, incipient species, and the claim that *Bemisia tabaci* is actually composed of 24 morphologically indistinguishable (cryptic) species (24) all point to the irrefutable role and importance of proper taxonomic identification of both pests and biological control agents. In his seminal paper, Rosen (92) enumerated a number of biological control failures due to lack of adequate taxonomic identification. Certainly our awareness of cryptic species has increased in recent years, and the question of how we apply our current level of science to improve the chances for successful introduction of natural enemies (50) is being discussed among researchers in the field.

Development of artificial rearing methods has allowed the commercial production of some predatory acarine species and, in light of the information presented in the above paragraph, may allow biological control companies to enhance the efficacy of existing acarine predators through manipulation of environmental parameters in the rearing of their predators. Despite the potential to "evolve" more efficacious predators, increasing the range of prey species is probably beyond the realm of possibility. As new pests arrive from foreign lands through commerce, new predatory species need to be found and developed for pest management. Limiting the discovery of new predators is a consequence of the Convention on Biological Diversity. Under the Convention, countries have sovereign rights over the germplasm of all species found on their lands: Even though this applies primarily to the highly lucrative enterprises pertaining to the development of drugs, chemical pesticides, and crop cultivars, it equally applies to the discovery of new biological control agents (21). Thus, the commercial development of new acarine predators is very slow and limited; yet, numbers of pest species manage to move quite freely.

Even when researchers have identified an effective new ABA, development to a commercial product is not a foregone conclusion. The development of new ABAs is a result of a cost-benefit analysis by companies. Questions that must be addressed include the following: Will mass rearing be achieved within a reasonable time frame and budget? Will the market be large enough to warrant the monetary output for the development? Will the new product fill a void in the market or will it duplicate another predator(s)?

SUMMARY POINTS

1. Acarine and insect pests managed by ABAs are here reviewed. The efficacy of ABAs varies among horticultural plants but can be manipulated by changing agrotechnical conditions.
2. Development of new agrotechnological methods is aimed at increasing production in terms of either year-round crops or yield improvement. Often, these new innovations have negative consequences on biological control agents and increase pest populations and/or damage levels.
3. A limited number of ABAs are being developed for a number of reasons, e.g., limited access to new predators in developing countries and profit-driven biological control suppliers.

FUTURE ISSUES

1. To date, the development of genetically modified organisms for pest control has focused on the insertion of genome sequences from the delta endotoxin of *Bacillus thuringiensis* and on limited work with lectins, neither of which affects pest mites. Future efforts should focus on control mechanisms for spider mites, which already have resistance to a broad range of pesticides and a limited number of effective predators.
2. Taxonomic issues are a constant concern, especially as delays and mistakes in the identification of pests and their natural enemies have led to costly errors.

DISCLOSURE STATEMENT

The authors are not aware of any affiliations, memberships, funding, or financial holdings that might be perceived as affecting the objectivity of this review.

LITERATURE CITED

1. Agrawal AA. 2000. Host-range evolution: adaptation and trade-offs in fitness of mites on alternative hosts. *Ecology* 81:500–8
2. Arancon NQ, Edwards CA, Yardim EN, Oliver TJ, Bryne RJ, et al. 2007. Suppression of two-spotted spider mite (*Tetranychus urticae*), mealy bug (*Pseudococcus* sp.) and aphid (*Myzus persicae*) populations and damage by vermicomposts. *Crop Prot*. 26:29–39
3. Ballhorn DJ, Schmitt I, Fankhauser JD, Katagiri F, Pfanz H. 2011. CO_2-mediated changes of plant traits and their effects on herbivores are determined by leaf age. *Ecol. Entomol.* 36:1–13
4. **Belliure B, Montserrat M, Magalhaes S. 2010. Mites as models for experimental evolution studies. *Acarologia* 50:513–29**
5. Ben-David T, Gerson U, Morin S. 2009. Asymmetric reproductive interference between two closely related spider mites: *Tetranychus urticae* and *T. turkestani* (Acari: Tetranychidae). *Exp. Appl. Acarol.* 48:213–27
6. Bi JK, Toscani NC. 2007. Current status of the greenhouse whitefly, *Trialeurodes vaporariorum*, susceptibility to neonicotinoid and conventional insecticides on strawberries in southern California. *Pest Manag. Sci.* 63:747–52
7. Bravenboer L, Dosse G. 1962. *Phytoseiulus riegeli* Dosse als Pradator einiger Schadmilben aus der *Tetranychus urticae*-gruppe. *Entomol. Exp. Appl.* 5:291–304
8. Brodeur J, Bouchard A, Turcotte G. 1997. Potential of four species of predatory mites as biological control agents of the tomato russet mite, *Aculops lycopersici* (Massee) (Eriophyidae). *Can. Entomol.* 129:1–6
9. Brown JK, Bird J, Frohlich D, Rosell RC, Bedford ID, Markham PG. 1996. The relevance of variability within the *Bemisia tabaci* species complex to epidemics caused by subgroup III geminiviruses. *IOBC-WPRS Bull.* 28(1):77–89
10. Buitenhuis R, Shipp L, Scott-Dupree C. 2010. Intra-guild versus extra-guild prey: effect on predator fitness and preference of *Amblyseius swirskii* (Athias-Henriot) and *Neoseiulus cucumeris* (Oudemans) (Acari: Phytoseiidae). *Bull. Entomol. Res.* 100:167–73
11. Byrne FJ, Gorman KJ, Cahill M, Denholm I, Devonshire AL. 2000. The role of B-type esterases in conferring insecticide resistance in the tobacco whitefly, *Bemisia tabaci* (Genn.). *Pest Manag. Sci.* 56:867–74
12. Cakmak I, Janssen A, Sabelis MW, Baspinar H. 2009. Biological control of an acarine pest by single and multiple natural enemies. *Biol. Control* 50:60–65

4. Reviews studies using mites as models to explore evolution of host plant selection, pesticide resistance, behavior, and sex-related traits.

13. Calvo FJ, Blockmans K, Belda JE. 2009. Development of a biological control–based integrated pest management method for *Bemisia tabaci* for protected sweet pepper crops. *Exp. Appl. Entomol.* 133: 9–18
14. Casey C, Parrella M. 2002. Distribution, thresholds, and biological control of the two-spotted spider mite (Acari: Tetranychidae) on bent cane cut roses in California. *IOBC/WPRS Bull.* 25(1):41–44
15. Castagnoli M, Sauro S, Liguori M. 2003. Evaluation of *Neoseiulus californicus* (McGregor) (Acari Phytoseiidae) as a candidate for the control of *Aculops lycopersici* (Tryon) (Acari Eriophyoidea): a preliminary study. *Redia* 86:97–100
16. Castilho RC, de Moraes GJ, Silva ES, Silva LO. 2009. Predation potential and biology of *Protogamasellopsis posnaniensis* Wisniewski & Hirshmann (Acari: Rhodacaridae). *Biol. Control* 48:164–67
17. Chambers RJ, Wright EM, Lind RJ. 1993. Biological control of glasshouse sciarid flies (*Bradysia* spp.) with the predatory mite, *Hypoaspis miles*, on cyclamen and poinsettia. *Biocontrol Sci. Technol.* 3:285–93
18. Chiel E, Messika Y, Steinberg S, Antignus Y. 2006. The effect of UV-absorbing plastic sheet on the attraction and host location ability of three parasitoids: *Aphidius colemani*, *Diglyphus isaea* and *Eretmocerus mundus*. *BioControl* 51:65–78
19. Chow A, Chau A, Heinz KM. 2008. Compatibility of *Orius insidiosus* (Hemiptera: Anthocoridae) with *Amblyseius (Iphiseius) degenerans* (Acari: Phytoseiidae) for control of *Frankliniella occidentalis* (Thysanoptera: Thripidae) on greenhouse roses. *Biol. Control* 44:259–70
20. Chow A, Chau A, Heinz KM. 2010. Compatibility of *Amblyseius (Typhlodromips) swirskii* (Athias-Henriot) (Acari: Phytoseiidae) and *Orius insidiosus* (Hemiptera: Anthocoridae) for biological control of *Frankliniella occidentalis* (Thysanoptera: Thripidae) on roses. *Biol. Control* 53:188–96
21. Cock MJW, van Lenteren JC, Brodeur J, Barratt BIP, Bigler F, et al. 2009. Do new access and benefit sharing procedures under the convention on biological diversity threaten the future of biological control? *BioControl* 55:199–18
22. **Copping LG. 2009. *The Manual of Biocontrol Agents*. Alton/Hampshire, UK: BCPC. 851 pp.**

22. A manual listing all available biological control agents.

23. Dag A. 2008. Bee pollination of crop plants under environmental conditions unique to enclosures. *Bee World* 47:164–68
24. De Barro PJ, Liu S-S, Boykin LM, Dinsdale AB. 2011. *Bemisia tabaci*: a statement of species status. *Annu. Rev. Entomol.* 56:1–19
25. De Moraes GJ, Lima HC. 1983. Biology of *Euseius concordis* (Chant) (Acarina, Phytoseiidae): a predator of the tomato russet mite. *Acarologia* 24:251–55
26. Diaz BM, Fereres A. 2007. Ultraviolet-blocking materials as a physical barrier to control insect pests and pathogens in protected crops. *Pest Technol.* 1:85–95
27. Diaz A, Okabe K, Eckenrode CJ, Villani MG, OConnor BM. 2000. Biology, ecology, and management of the bulb mites of the genus *Rhizoglyphus* (Acari: Acaridae). *Exp. Appl. Acarol.* 24:85–113
28. Drukker B, Janssen A, Ravensberg W, Sabeli MW. 1997. Improved control capacity of the mite predator *Phytoseiulus persimilis* (Acari: Phytoseiidae) on tomato. *Exp. Appl. Acarol.* 21:507–18
29. Duso C, Chiarini F, Conte L, Bonora V, Dalla Monta L, et al. 2004. Fogging can control *Tetranychus urticae* on greenhouse cucumbers. *J. Pest Sci.* 77:105–11
30. Easterbrook MA, Fitzgerald JD, Solomon MG. 2001. Biological control of strawberry tarsonemid mite *Phytonemus pallidus* and two-spotted spider mite *Tetranychus urticae*, on strawberry in the UK using species of *Neoseiulus* (*Amblyseius*) (Acari: Phytoseiidae). *Exp. Appl. Acarol.* 25:25–36
31. Edser C. 2002. Light manipulation additives extend opportunities for agricultural plastic films. *Plast. Addit. Compd.* 4:20–24
32. Ellner S, McCauley E, Kendall BE, Briggs CJ, Hosseini PR, et al. 2001. Habitat structure and population persistence in an experimental community. *Nature* 412:538–43
33. Faraji F, Janssen A, Sabelis MW. 2001. Predatory mites avoid ovipositing near counterattacking prey. *Exp. Appl. Acarol.* 25:613–23
34. Fischer S, Kloetzli F, Falquet L, Celle O. 2005. An investigation on biological control of the tomato russet mite *Aculops lycopersici* (Massee) with *Amblyseius andersoni* (Chant). *IOBC-WPRS Bull.* 28(1):99–102
35. Foster SP, Gorman K, Denholm I. 2010. English field samples of *Thrips tabaci* show strong and ubiquitous resistance to deltamethrin. *Pest Manag. Sci.* 66:861–64

36. Gerling D, Mayer RT. 1996. *Bemisia: 1995. Taxonomy, Biology, Damage, Control and Management.* Andover, UK: Intercept
37. Gerson U. 1985. Webbing. In *Spider Mites, Their Biology, Natural Enemies and Control*, ed. W Helle, MW Sabelis, 1A:223–32. Amsterdam: Elsevier. 405 pp.
38. Gerson U. 1992. Biology and control of the broad mite, *Polyphagotarsonemus latus* (Banks) (Acari: Tarsonemidae). *Exp. Appl. Acarol.* 13:163–78
39. Gerson U, Capua S, Thorens D. 1983. Life history and life tables of *Rhizoglyphus robini* Claparède (Acari: Astigmata: Acaridae). *Acarologia* 24:439–48
40. Gerson U, Weintraub PG. 2007. Review: mites for the control of pests in protected cultivation. *Pest Manag. Sci.* 63:658–76
41. Gorman K, Slater R, Blande JD, Clarke A, Wren J, et al. 2010. Cross-resistance relationships between neonicoitinoides and pymetrozine in *Bemisia tabaci* (Hemiptera: Aleyrodidae). *Pest Manag. Sci.* 66:1186–90
42. Gough N. 1991. Long-term stability in the interaction between *Tetranychus urticae* and *Phytoseiulus persimilis* producing successful integrated control on roses in southeast Queensland. *Exp. Appl. Acarol.* 12:83–101
43. Halliday RB, O'Connor BM, Baker AS. 1999. Global diversity of mites. In *Nature and Human Society*, ed. PH Raven, T Williams, pp. 192–203. Washington, DC: Natl. Acad. Press
44. Hanuny T, Inbar M, Tsror L, Palevsky E. 2008. Complex interactions between *Rhizoglyphus robini* and *Fusarium oxysporum*: implications on onion pest management. *IOBC/WPRS Bull.* 32:71–74
45. Haque MM, Kawai A. 2003. Effect of temperature on development and reproduction of the tomato russet mite, *Aculops lycopersici* (Massee) (Acari). *Appl. Entomol. Zool.* 38:97–101
46. Haramanto, Tantau HJ, Salokhe VM. 2006. Microclimate and air exchange rates in greenhouses covered with different nets in the humid tropics. *Biosyst. Eng.* 94:239–53
47. Heagle AS, Brandenburg RL, Bums JC, Miller JE. 1994. Ozone and carbon dioxide effects on spider mites in white clover and peanut. *J. Environ. Qual.* 23:1168–76
48. Helle W. 1965. Resistance in the Acarina: mites. In *Advances in Acarology*, ed. JA Naegele, 2:71–93. Ithaca, NY: Comstock
49. Herrmann I, Bernstein M, Sade A, Karnieli A, Bonfil DJ, et al. 2011. Spectral monitoring of two-spotted spider mite damage to pepper leaves. *Remote Sens. Lett.* 3:277–83
50. Hoelmer KA, Kirk AA. 2005. Selecting arthropod biological control agents against arthropod pests: Can the science be improved to decrease the risk of releasing ineffective agents? *Biol. Control* 34:255–64
51. Janick J, Paris H, Parrish DC. 2007. The cucurbits of Mediterranean antiquity: identification of taxa from ancient images and descriptions. *Ann. Bot.* 100:1441–57
52. Janssen A, Pallini A, Venzon M, Sabelis MW. 1998. Review: behavior and indirect interactions in food webs of plant-inhabiting arthropods. *Exp. Appl. Acarol.* 22:497–521
53. Jeon HY, Kim HH, Jung JA, Kang TJ, Yang CY. 2007. Damage status of poinsettia by the fungus gnat (*Bradysia difformis*) and US control with predatory mite (*Hypoaspis aculeifer*). *Kor. J. Hortic. Sci. Technol.* 25:468–73
54. Jeppson LR, Keifer HH, Baker EW. 1975. *Mites Injurious to Economic Plants.* Berkeley, CA: Univ. Calif. Press. 613 pp.
55. Jovicich E, Cantliffe DJ, Stoffella PJ, Osborne LS. 2008. Predatory mites released on transplants can protect from early broad mite infestations. *Acta Hortic.* 782:229–33
56. Kawai A, Haque MM. 2004. Population dynamics of tomato russet mite, *Aculops lycopersici* (Massee), and its natural enemy, *Homeopronematus anconai* (Baker). *Jpn. Agric. Res. Q.* 38:161–66
57. Kay IR, Herron GA. 2010. Evaluation of existing and new insecticides including spirotetramat and pyridalyl to control *Frankliniella occidentalis* (Pergande) (Thysanoptera: Thripidae) on peppers in Queensland. *Aust. J. Entomol.* 49:175–81
58. Kittas C, Tchamitchian M, Kasoulas N, Kariskou P, Papaioannou CH. 2006. Effect of two UV-absorbing greenhouse-covering films on growth and yield of an eggplant soilless crop. *Sci. Hortic.* 110:30–37
59. Kuman KS, Tiwari KN, Madan KJ. 2009. Design and technology for greenhouse cooling in tropical and subtropical regions: a review. *Energy Build.* 41:1269–72

60. Legarrea S, Karnieli A, Fereres A, Weintraub PG. 2010. Comparison of UV-absorbing nets in pepper crops: spectral properties, effects on plants and pest control. *Photochem. Photobiol.* 86:324–30
61. Lesna I, Sabelis MW, Bolland HR, Conijn CGM. 1995. Candidate natural enemies for control of *Rhizoglyphus robini* Claparède (Acari: Astigmata) in lily bulbs: exploration in the field and pre-selection in the laboratory. *Exp. Appl. Acarol.* 19:655–69
62. Lesna I, Conijn CGM, Sabelis MW, van Straalen NM. 2000. Biological control of the bulb mite, *Rhizoglyphus robini*, by the predatory mite, *Hypoaspis aculeifer*, on lilies: predator-prey dynamics in the soil, under greenhouse and field conditions. *Biocontrol Sci. Technol.* 10:179–93
63. Lewis T, ed. 1997. *Thrips as Crop Pests*. Wallingford, UK: CAB Int. 740 pp.
64. Lindquist EE, Krantz GW, Walter DE. 2009. Classification. In *A Manual of Acarology*, ed. GW Krantz, SE Walter, pp. 97–103. Lubbock: Texas Tech Univ. Press. 807 pp.
65. Lindquist RK, Short TL. 2004. Effects of greenhouse structure and function on biological control. In *Biocontrol in Protected Culture*, ed. KM Heinz, RG Driesche van, MP Parrella, pp. 37–53. West Chicago, IL: Ball. 552 pp.
66. MacIntyre AJK, Scott-Dupree CD, Tolman JH, Harris CR. 2005. Resistance of *Thrips tabaci* to pyrethroid and organophosphorus insecticides in Ontario, Canada. *Pest Manag. Sci.* 61:809–15
67. Madadi H, Enkegaard A, Brodsgaard HF, Kharrazi-Pakdel A, Ashouri A, et al. 2008. *Orius albidipennis* (Heteroptera: Anthocoridae): intraguild predation of and prey preference for *Neoseiulus cucumeris* (Acari: Phytoseiidae) on different host plants. *Entomol. Fenn.* 19:1–9
68. Madadi H, Enkegaard A, Brodsgaard HF, Kharrazi-Pakdel A, Mohaghegh J, et al. 2007. Host plant effects on the functional response of *Neoseiulus cucumeris* to onion thrips larvae. *J. Appl. Entomol.* 131:728–33
69. Magalhães S, Forbes MR, Skoracka A, Osakabe M, Chevillon C, et al. 2007. Host race formation in the Acari. *Exp. Appl. Acarol.* 42:225–38
70. Markwick NP. 1986. Detecting variability and selecting for pesticide resistance in two species of phytoseiid mites. *Entomophaga* 31:225–36
71. Martin NA, Workman PJ, Butler RC. 2003. Insecticide resistance in onion thrips (*Thrips tabaci*) (Thysanoptera: Thripidae). *N.Z. J. Crop Hortic. Sci.* 31:99–106
72. Martin T, Assogba-Komlan F, Sidick I, Ahle V, Chandre F. 2010. An acaricide-treated net to control phytophagous mites. *Crop Prot.* 29:470–75
73. Marsh TL, Gallardo K. 2009. Adopting biological control for ornamental crops in greenhouses. *Biocontrol News Inform.* 30:1–9
74. Messelink G, van Maanen R, van Holstein-Saj R, Sabelis MW, Janssen A. 2010. Pest species diversity enhances control of spider mites and whiteflies by a generalist phytoseiid predator. *BioControl* 55: 387–98
75. Messelink G, van Maanen R, van Steenpaal SEF, Janssen A. 2008. Biological control of thrips and whiteflies by a shared predator: Two pests are better than one. *Biol. Control* 44:372–79
76. Momen FM, Abdel-Khaleka A. 2008. Effect of the tomato rust mite *Aculops lycopersici* (Acari: Eriophyidae) on the development and reproduction of three predatory phytoseiid mites. *Int. J. Trop. Insect Sci.* 28:53–57
77. Mortensen LM. 1987. Review: CO_2 enrichment in greenhouses. Crop responses. *Sci. Hortic.* 33:1–25
78. Naranjo SE, Butler GD Jr, Henneberry TJ. 2002. Complete bibliography of *Bemisia tabaci* and *Bemisia argentifolii*. In *Silverleaf Whitefly: National Research, Action and Technology Transfer Plan, 1997–2001. Fourth Annual Review of the Second 5-Year Plan and Final Report for 1992–2002*, pp. 227–415. Beltsville, MA: USDA-ARS
79. **Nihoul P. 1993. Controlling glasshouse climate influences the interaction between tomato glandular trichomes, spider mite and predatory mites. *Crop Prot.* 12:443–47**
80. Nomikou M, Janssen A, Schraag R, Sabelis MW. 2001. Phytoseiid predators as potential biological control agents for *Bemisia tabaci*. *Exp. Appl. Acarol.* 25:271–91
81. Nomikou M, Janssen A, Schraag R, Sabelis MW. 2004. Vulnerability of *Bemisia tabaci* immatures to phytoseiid predators: consequences for oviposition and influence of alternative food. *Entomol. Exp. Appl.* 110:95–102
82. Nomikou M, Sabelis MW, Janssen A. 2010. Pollen subsidies promote whitefly control through the numerical response of predatory mites. *BioControl* 55:253–60

79. Describes the effects of changes in the greenhouse environment, especially humidity, on the efficacy of a predator feeding on spider mites infesting tomatoes.

83. Onzo A, Hanna R, Negloh KM, Sabellis MW, Yaninek JS. 2003. Dynamics of refuge use: diurnal, vertical migration by predatory and herbivorous mites within cassava plants. *Oikos* 101:59–69
84. Osman AA, Zaki AM. 1986. Studies on the predation efficiency of *Agistemus exsertus* Gonzalez (Acarina, Stigmaeidae) on the eriophyid mite *Aculops lycopersici* (Massee). *Anz. Schädlingskunde* 59:135–36
85. Palevsky E, Soroker V, Weintraub P, Mansour F, Abu-Moach F, et al. 2001. How species-specific is the phoretic relationship between the broad mite, *Polyphagotarsonemus latus* (Acari: Tarsonemidae), and its insect hosts? *Exp. Appl. Acarol.* 25:217–24
86. Park H-H, Shipp L, Buitenhuis R. 2010. Predation, development, and oviposition by the predatory mite *Amblyseius swirkii* (Acari: Phytoseiidae) on tomato russet mite (Acari: Eriophyidae). *J. Econ. Entomol.* 103:563–69
87. Pearson S, Hadley P, Wheldon AE. 1993. A reanalysis of the effects of temperature and irradiance on time to flowering in chrysanthemum (*Dendranthema grandiflora*). *J. Hortic. Sci.* 68:89–97
88. Peet MM, Willits DH, Gardner R. 1997. Response of ovule development and post-pollen production processes in male-sterile tomatoes to chronic, subacute high temperature stress. *J. Exp. Bot.* 48:101–11
89. Perdigones A, Garcia JL, Romero A, Rodriguez A, Luna L, et al. 2008. Cooling strategies for greenhouses in summer: control of fogging by pulse width modulation. *Biosyst. Eng.* 99:573–86
90. Perring TM, Farrar CA. 1986. Historical perspective and current world status of the tomato russet mite (Acari: Eriophyidae). *Entomol. Soc. Am. Misc. Publ.* 63:1–19
91. Rahman T, Spafford H, Broughton S. 2011. Single versus multiple releases of predatory mites combined with spinosad for the management of western flower thrips in strawberry. *Crop Prot.* 30:468–75
92. Rosen D. 1986. The role of taxonomy in effective biological control programs. *Agric. Ecosyst. Environ.* 15:121–29
93. Sato ME, Tanaka T, Miyata T. 2006. Monooxygenase activity in methidathion resistant and susceptible populations of *Amblyseius womersleyi* (Acari: Phytoseiidae). *Exp. Appl. Acarol.* 39:13–24
94. Shakya S, Coll M, Weintraub PG. 2010. Incorporation of intraguild predation into a pest management decision-making tool: the case of thrips and two pollen-feeding predators in strawberry. *J. Econ. Entomol.* 103:1086–93
95. Shakya S, Weintraub PG, Coll M. 2009. Effect of pollen supplement on intraguild predatory interactions between two omnivores: the importance of spatial dynamics. *Biol. Control* 50:281–87
96. Snyder JC, Carter CD. 1984. Leaf trichomes and resistance of *Lycopersicon hirsutum* and *L. esculentum* to spider mites. *J. Am. Soc. Hortic. Sci.* 109:837–43
97. Stanghellini ME, Rasmussen SL, Kim DH. 1999. Aerial transmission of *Thielaviopsis basicola*, a pathogen of corn-salad, by adult shore flies. *Phytopathology* 89:476–79
98. Stenseth C, Nordby A. 1976. Damage and control of the strawberry mite, *Steneotarsonemus pallidus* (Acarina: Tarsonemidae), on strawberry. *J. Hortic. Sci.* 51:49–54
99. Swirski E, Amitai S, Dorzia N. 1967. Laboratory studies on the feeding, development and reproduction of the predaceous mites *Amblyseius rubini* Swirski and Amitai and *Amblyseius swirskii* Athias-Henriot (Acarina: Phytoseiidae) on various kinds of food substances. *Isr. J. Agric. Res.* 17:101–18
100. Takahashi F, Chant DA. 1993. Phylogenetic relationships in the genus *Phytoseiulus Evans* (Acari: Phytoseiidae). I. Geographic distribution. *Int. J. Acarol.* 19:15–22
101. Tal C, Coll M, Weintraub PG. 2007. Biological control of *Polyphagotarsonemus latus* (Acari: Tarsonemidae) by the predaceous mite *Amblyseius swirskii* (Acari: Phytoseiidae). *IOBC/WPRS Bull.* 30(5):111–15
102. Tamotsu M. 2000. Effect of temperature on development and reproduction of the onion thrips, *Thrips tabaci* Lindeman (Thysanoptera: Thripidae), on pollen and honey solution. *Appl. Entomol. Zool.* 35:499–504
103. Thalavaisundaram S, Herron GA, Clift AD, Rose H. 2008. Pyrethroid resistance in *Frankliniella occidentalis* (Pergande) (Thysanoptera: Thripidae) and implications for its management in Australia. *Aust. J. Entomol.* 47:64–69
104. Trichilo P, Leigh TF. 1986. Predation on spider mite eggs by the western flower thrips, *Frankliniella occidentalis* (Thysanoptera: Thripidae), an opportunist in a cotton agroecosystem. *Environ. Entomol.* 15:821–25

105. Tsormpatsidis E, Henbest RGC, Davis FJ, Battey NH, Hadley P, et al. 2008. UV irradiance as a major influence on growth, development and secondary products of commercial importance in Lollo Rosso lettuce "Revolution" grown under polyethylene films. *Environ. Exp. Bot.* 63:232–39
106. Tuovinen T, Lindqvist I. 2010. Maintenance of predatory phytoseiid mites for preventative control of strawberry tarsonemid mite *Phytonemus pallidus* in strawberry plant propagation. *Biol. Control* 54: 119–25
107. Urbaneja A, Leon FJ, Gimenez A, Aran E, van der Blom J. 2003. Interaccion de *Neoseiulus* (*Amblyseius*) *cucumeris* (Oudemans) (Aca.: Phytoseiidae) en la instalacion de *Orius laevigatus* (Fieber) (Hem.: Anthocoridae) en invernaderos de pimiento. *Bol. Sanid. Veg. Plagas* 29:1–12
108. van Lenteren JC. 2000. A greenhouse without pesticides: fact or fantasy? *Crop Prot.* 19:375–84
109. van Maanen R, Vila E, Sabelis SW, Janssen A. 2010. Biological control of broad mite (*Polyphagotarsonemus latus*) with the generalist predator *Amblyseius swirskii*. *Exp. Appl. Acarol.* 52:29–34
110. Vänninen I. 2001. Biology of the shore fly *Scatella stagnalis* in rockwood under greenhouse conditions. *Entomol. Exp. Appl.* 98:317–28
111. Vänninen I, Johansen NS. 2005. Artificial lighting (AL) and IPM in greenhouses. *IOBC/WPRS Bull.* 28(1):295–304
112. Vänninen I, Koskula H. 2003. Biocontrol of the shore fly *Scatella tenuicosta* with *Hypoaspis miles* and *H. aculeifer* in peat pots. *BioControl* 49:137–52
113. Vänninen I, Pinto DM, Nissinen AI, Johansen NS, Shipp L. 2010. In the light of new greenhouse technologies: 1. Plant-mediated effects of artificial lighting on arthropods and tritrophic interactions. *Ann. Appl. Biol.* 157:393–414
114. Weintraub PG, Berlinger M. 2004. Physical control in greenhouses and field crops. In *Novel Approaches to Insect Pest Management*, ed. AR Horowitz, I Ishaaya, pp. 301–18. Berlin: Springer
115. Weintraub PG, Kleitman S, Alchanatis V, Palevsky E. 2007. Factors affecting the distribution of a predatory mite on greenhouse sweet pepper. *Exp. Appl. Acarol.* 42:23–35
116. Weintraub PG, Kleitman S, Mori R, Gan-Mor S, Ganot L, et al. 2009. Novel application of pollen to augment the predator *Amblyseius swirskii* on greenhouse sweet pepper. *IOBC/WPRS Bull.* 50:119–24
117. Weintraub PG, Kleitman S, Mori R, Shapira N, Palevsky E. 2003. Control of broad mites (*Polyphagotarsonemus latus* (Banks)) on organic greenhouse sweet peppers (*Capsicum annuum* L.) with the predatory mite, *Neoseiulus cucumeris* (Oudemans). *Biol. Control* 27:300–9
118. Weintraub PG, Palevsky E. 2008. Evaluation of the predatory mite, *Neoseiulus californicus*, for spider mite control on greenhouse sweet pepper under hot arid field conditions. *Exp. Appl. Acarol.* 45:29–37
119. Weintraub PG, Pivonia S, Gera A. 2008. Physical control of leafhoppers. *J. Econ. Entomol.* 101:1337–40
120. Willits DH. 2003. Cooling fan-ventilated greenhouses: a modeling study. *Biosyst. Eng.* 84:315–29
121. Willits DH, Bailey DA. 2000. The effect of night temperature on chrysanthemum flowering: heat-tolerant versus heat-sensitive cultivars. *Sci. Hortic.* 83:325–30
122. Wimmer D, Hoffmann D, Schausberger P. 2008. Prey suitability of western flower thrips, *Frankliniella occidentalis*, and onion thrips, *Thrips tabaci*, for the predatory mite *Amblyseius swirskii*. *Biocontrol Sci. Technol.* 18:541–50
123. Wright EM, Chambers RJ. 1994. The biology of the predatory mite *Hypoaspis miles* (Acari: Laelapidae), a potential biological control agent of *Bradysia paupera* (Dipt.: Sciaridae). *Entomophaga* 39:225–35
124. Xu X, Enkegaard A. 2010. Prey preference of the predatory mite, *Amblyseius swirskii* between first instar western flower thrips *Frankliniella occidentalis* and nymphs of the two-spotted spider mite *Tetranychus urticae*. *J. Insect Sci.* 10:149
125. Ydergaard S, Enkegaard A, Brødsgaard HF. 1997. The predatory mite *Hypoaspis miles*: temperature dependent life table characteristics on a diet of sciarid larvae, *Bradysia paupera* and *B. tritici*. *Entomol. Exp. Appl.* 85:177–87
126. Zanic K, Goreta S, Perica S, Sutic J. 2008. Effects of alternative pesticides on greenhouse whitefly in protected cultivation. *J. Pest Sci.* 81:161–66
127. Zhao G, Liu W, Brown JM, Knowles CO. 1995. Insecticide resistance in field and laboratory strains of western flower thrips (Thysanoptera: Thripidae). *J. Econ. Entomol.* 88:1164–70

128. Zheng L, Zhou Y, Song K. 2005. Augmentative biological control in greenhouses: experiences from China. *Proc. Int. Symp. Biol. Control Arthropods, 12–16 Sept., Davos, Switzerland*, pp. 538–45. Washington, DC: USDA For. Serv. For. Health Technol. Enterp. Team
129. Zilahi-Balogh GMG, Shipp JL, Cloutier C, Brodeur J. 2007. Predation by *Neoseiulus cucumeris* on western flower thrips, and its oviposition on greenhouse cucumber under winter versus summer conditions in a temperate climate. *Biol. Control* 40:160–67

RELATED RESOURCES

Gerson U, Smiley RL, Ochoa R. 2003. *Mites (Acari) for Pest Control*. Oxford, UK: Blackwell. 539 pp.

Zhang Z-Q. 2003. *Mites of Greenhouses, Identification, Biology and Control*. Wallingford, UK: CABI Publ. 244 pp.

Evolutionary Ecology of Odonata: A Complex Life Cycle Perspective

Robby Stoks[1,*] and Alex Córdoba-Aguilar[2]

[1]Laboratory of Aquatic Ecology and Evolutionary Biology, University of Leuven, B-3000 Leuven, Belgium; email: robby.stoks@bio.kuleuven.be

[2]Departamento de Ecología Evolutiva, Instituto de Ecología, Universidad Nacional Autónoma de México, 04510 DF, Mexico; email: acordoba@ecologia.unam.mx

Annu. Rev. Entomol. 2012. 57:249–65

First published online as a Review in Advance on September 9, 2011

The *Annual Review of Entomology* is online at ento.annualreviews.org

This article's doi: 10.1146/annurev-ento-120710-100557

0066-4170/12/0107-0249$20.00

*Corresponding author

Keywords

carry-over effects, complex life cycle, decoupling mechanisms, maternal effects, fitness components, sublethal stress effects

Abstract

Most insects have a complex life cycle with ecologically different larval and adult stages. We present an ontogenetic perspective to analyze and summarize the complex life cycle of Odonata within an evolutionary ecology framework. Morphological, physiological, and behavioral pathways that generate carry-over effects across the aquatic egg and larval stages and the terrestrial adult stage are identified. We also highlight several mechanisms that can decouple life stages including compensatory mechanisms at the larval and adult stages, stressful and stochastic events during metamorphosis, and stressful environmental conditions at the adult stage that may overrule effects of environmental conditions in the preceding stage. We consider the implications of these findings for the evolution, selection, and fitness of odonates; underline the role of the identified numerical and carry-over effects in shaping population and metapopulation dynamics and the community structure across habitat boundaries; and discuss implications for applied conservation issues.

INTRODUCTION

Complex life cycle (CLC): a life cycle that includes an abrupt ontogenetic change in ecology and morphology, often between larval and adult stages

Hemimetabolous: describes a life cycle in which larvae resemble adults except for their small size and lack of wings and genitalia

More than 80% of animals, including most insects, have a so-called complex life cycle (CLC) with discrete larval and adult stages (112). This is in contrast to animals with a simple life cycle, such as birds and mammals, that gradually turn into adults. The general adaptive explanation for the existence of CLCs, i.e., the adaptive decoupling hypothesis, states that CLCs and the associated evolutionary origin of metamorphosis reflect selection for decoupling traits across life stages (66). It is still unclear to what extent life stages are decoupled, and it has even been argued that metamorphosis is not a new beginning (73) and that the prominence of CLCs may reflect difficulties in losing larvae from life cycles more than selection for their retention (72). The latter studies were based on reviews of the literature on marine invertebrates; so far no overview has been done in an insect order.

In hemimetabolous insects a major transition occurs at metamorphosis, where a larval stage specialized for growth is followed by a metamorphosis to an adult stage specialized for dispersal and reproduction (113). These specialized functions together with the associated differences in habitat use, lifestyle, and appearance cause most entomologists to study only one stage where a specific function of interest occurs or is more easy to study. This focus on a single life stage may be misleading because it assumes that both stages may respond to challenges imposed on one stage independently from what happens in the other stage. Increasing evidence suggests that life stages are not independent and may affect each other across metamorphosis (28, 73). Responses to stressful environmental conditions at the larval stage may carry over and shape fitness at the adult stage, and similarly, responses at the adult stage may be propagated and shape fitness at the larval stage of the next generation. This effect of the environment of previous or successive life stages can substantially alter the inferences that can be drawn from studies that end or start at metamorphosis. An integrated life cycle approach to studies of the fitness consequences of environmental conditions is thus necessary.

Insects of the order Odonata (dragonflies), like most insects, have a CLC. We have exceptionally well-documented knowledge on odonate natural histories and ecologies (21), and they are increasingly used as model organisms, shaping both ecological and evolutionary theories (22). In this review we use an ontogenetic perspective to analyze and summarize the CLC of these animals within an evolutionary ecology framework. We pay special attention to integrating information on the different stages of the life history to understand how environmental conditions in one life stage have fitness consequences in other life stages. By doing so, we elucidate the (de)coupling of both stages and the evolution of CLCs, topics that surpass this insect order (66).

THE COMPLEX LIFE CYCLE OF ODONATA

Odonata are hemimetabolous insects showing a striking habitat shift during their CLC. Here we describe the CLC of a typical odonate (21). The egg stage is short (a few weeks), and eggs are deposited in aquatic plant tissue or in the water. The larval stage is the longest (months but sometimes years) and is aquatic. During this stage considerable growth, both in size and mass, occurs. Odonate larvae are important intermediate predators in aquatic food webs, feeding on a wide array of small animals including other odonates and conspecifics, and are themselves food of predators such as fish. Larvae undergo about 10 molts, and the final molt is the metamorphosis to the terrestrial, flying adult stage. Once the exoskeleton has hardened, the size and shape of the adult are fixed. Freshly emerged adults disperse away from their breeding site. During the next period of days to weeks, the maturation period, adults forage away from the water, further increase body mass, and develop sexual characters; females begin to develop eggs. Once sexually mature, adults return to water bodies for reproduction. The reproductive period takes 1 to 3 weeks and dispersal to other water bodies may occur. In most species males scramble to obtain females, whereas in other species males are territorial.

In the following sections, we give for each life stage short overviews of environmental conditions that cause mortality and thereby directly contribute to densities in the next stage, i.e., numerical effects. The main focus, however, is on the sublethal effects of these environmental conditions and how these effects may generate trait-mediated carry-over effects across stages.

Carry-over effect: effect in which an environmental condition in one life stage changes fitness-related traits in the next life stage

Time constraints: constraints on the timing of metamorphosis

EGG STAGE

The egg is the least studied life stage in odonates. Egg mortality in the field can be high, up to 25% in *Pyrrhosoma nymphula* (11). Several environmental conditions may increase mortality, including extreme temperatures, desiccation, pollutants, parasitoids, and occasionally predators (reviewed in 21). Environmental conditions may also shape two key egg traits that are carried over to the larval stage. First, the embryonic development time, and hence the timing of egg hatching, is increased at low temperatures (for overview, see 37, 111) and decreased under time constraints (93). Second, hatchling size decreases with decreasing temperature (111). Both traits may have fitness implications for the larval stage. Smaller eggs give rise to smaller hatchlings (45). Larvae that hatch later and at a smaller size may, for example, suffer more predation by other odonates (71, 104). Intriguingly, egg traits may even bridge adult metamorphosis; for example, survival to reproductive maturity increased with later egg hatching dates in male *Lestes viridis* (29).

LARVAL STAGE

Several environmental conditions at the larval stage may cause numerical effects at the adult stage by increasing larval mortality rates. This has been documented for food shortage (3, 13, 84, 95, 109), consumptive and nonconsumptive predation (59, 60, 95), pollutant exposure (41), time constraints (27, 28, 46), and high larval densities (3, 65). Whereas most studies looked at effects of these larval environmental conditions on larval traits, a considerable number considered carry-over effects at the adult stage. Given that mostly the same traits are affected in both stages and given the focus of this review, we summarize only the latter (**Supplemental Table 1**, follow the **Supplemental Material link** from the Annual Reviews home page at **http://www.annualreviews.org**).

Larval Carry-Over Effects to Adult Fitness

Larvae with higher values for a given trait likely metamorphose into adults with higher values for the same trait. This has been explicitly confirmed only for a small number of traits by correlating individual trait values across both stages. Evidence is available for size and mass (e.g., 43, 64) and for behavioral traits such as activity levels (15). We lack direct information for physiological traits; yet indirect evidence comes from studies showing that physiological differences among treatment groups can be similar across stages (30, 32).

Given the evidence for some degree of coupling of larval and adult traits, larval environmental conditions have the potential to shape adult fitness components. Two of the three studies that directly looked for effects of larval environmental conditions on adult fitness components found these carry-over effects. *Enallagma boreale* larvae reared in field enclosures at high density or low food level emerged later and with a lower mass (3). Subsequent monitoring under natural field conditions indicated that the effects of the larval conditions on adult fitness components, survival to reproductive maturity and lifetime number of matings, were well correlated with these two traits at emergence (5). *L. viridis* larvae reared under time constraints and low food in the laboratory emerged earlier and later, respectively, and at a lower mass under both conditions (29). The effects of the larval environmental conditions negatively affected lifetime mating success under seminatural conditions, yet only partly through their effects on mass and date of emergence, indicating a role for other unmeasured pathways (29). In contrast, in a third study, independent manipulation of food shortage in the larval and adult stages of *Ischnura verticalis* under more artificial laboratory conditions demonstrated no carry-over effects of larval food shortage on fecundity. Instead, 75% of the variance in fecundity could be explained by the adult food level (81). This finding indicates that environmental conditions at the adult stage can overrule effects of stressful larval environmental conditions (see below).

Flight performance: a combination of maneuverability, speed, and endurance

Water mites: ectoparasites that crawl from the larva onto the adult and insert their mouthparts and suck hemolymph; of the subclass Acari

Behavioral syndrome: a suite of correlated behaviors reflecting among-individual consistency in behavior across multiple situations

In addition to these studies, there is much indirect evidence for larval environmental conditions influencing adult traits that have fitness consequences. One obvious pathway is mediated by body mass and energy reserves at emergence and influences survival during the maturation period. Several larval conditions (e.g., food shortage, time constraints, high temperatures, and predation risk) reduce body mass and energy storage at emergence (**Supplemental Table 1**), which has been associated with reduced survival during the maturation period (14, 50, 56). Smaller or less well-provisioned animals may be less able to survive periods of suboptimal weather conditions that do not allow enough foraging. Fat content measured in freshly emerged adults can indeed be near starvation levels (54). Additionally, adults may compensate for low mass at emergence by foraging more, which increases their chances of being killed by predators (7, 96). Lower energy stores may also negatively affect adult survival through a reduced investment in costly defense mechanisms. Several larval environmental conditions (e.g., food shortage, time constraints, pesticide exposure, and predation risk) reduce immune function at emergence (**Supplemental Table 1**). Furthermore, high larvae-rearing temperatures in *L. viridis* resulted at emergence in lower levels of a stress protein associated with a reduced cold resistance (97).

Flight performance is another major pathway by which larval environmental conditions may shape adult fitness components (52). In adult odonates, flight performance is important for foraging, evading predators, and reproducing. Therefore, any effects of larval conditions on flight performance are likely to shape survival and reproductive success. The few studies dealing with this pathway considered proxies of flight performance such as flight muscle mass and wing symmetry. Food shortage at the larval stage resulted in adults with a lower size-corrected flight muscle mass, and food shortage, pesticide exposure, and parasitism by water mites can all result in less symmetric wings (**Supplemental Table 1**). Furthermore, food shortage, time constraints, and predation risk can reduce fat content (**Supplemental Table 1**), the metabolic fuel consumed during periods of prolonged flying such as when defending territories (52). The effects of larval environmental conditions on other important correlates of flight performance such as muscle ultrastructure, physiology, and protein composition in odonates remain unstudied. Yet, such effects are likely. In the fall armyworm, *Spodoptera frugiperda*, food shortage at the larval stage altered the composition of flight muscle proteins, resulting in reduced muscle performance (53).

Behavioral syndromes (89) have been identified across metamorphosis in damselflies (15) and may mediate another potential pathway coupling larval conditions to adult fitness. Direct empirical evidence is lacking. It has been suggested, for example, that territoriality at the larval stage of *P. nymphula* enhances food intake, resulting in larger adults that will benefit in territorial interactions, hence mating success, at the adult stage (43, but see 40). Environmental factors such as predators can shape the magnitude of behavioral syndromes as documented in three-spined sticklebacks, *Gasterosteus aculeatus* (9). Furthermore, in other taxa, behavioral syndromes are under sexual selection (87).

Decoupling Mechanisms

Stressful environmental conditions at the larval stage do not always detectably affect adult traits at emergence (**Supplemental Table 1**). This may be the case even when clear sublethal effects are present at the larval stage. To some extent this may be an artifact as only specific subsets of all traits are included in empirical studies, and therefore effects on unmeasured traits may have been missed. Yet effects on specific traits may also disappear during three periods: the larval stage, metamorphosis, and the adult stage.

Compensatory mechanisms may already occur at the larval stage. This is well documented after transient low food conditions. Low food-intake rates can cause lowered larval body mass, immune function, and energy reserves; however, full compensation often occurs when food becomes plentiful again (30, 32, 99). Intriguingly, even after a full compensation for transient food shortage at the larval stage, negative effects on the same traits may become apparent again after emergence. This has been observed after full compensation of body mass (30, 99) and of physiological traits linked to immune function (32) and energy storage (99). One reason for this may be that larvae showing compensation have an increased metabolic rate (31, 99), which is costly to maintain and may persist across metamorphosis. Moreover, in the time preceding metamorphosis animals do not eat for several days, which may magnify costs of increased metabolism.

Decoupling may also occur during metamorphosis, which is a stressful event and as such may overrule effects of stressful environmental conditions experienced at the larval stage. Whereas food shortage and pesticide exposure decreased leg symmetry in *Coenagrion puella* larvae, these effects were offset after metamorphosis, during which symmetry levels in the control treatments also strongly decreased (16). Further, stressful stochastic events, such as bad weather conditions and parasitism by water mites, during metamorphosis may interfere with the expansion of wings (12) and thereby decouple the link between larval environmental conditions and adult wing size and shape. Bad weather conditions may also prompt larvae to delay emergence (82), thereby potentially overruling effects of stressful environmental conditions on development time.

After metamorphosis, compensatory mechanisms can make carry-over effects transient. Given that the odonate exoskeleton is fixed after emergence, any carry-over effects on size and shape (including symmetry) will persist throughout the adult life. Other affected traits at emergence, however, may be compensated for throughout the adult stage. During the maturation period, when mass increase is often considerable, adults emerging at a lower mass may compensate for this effect (5, 7, 74, 96). This may explain why *I. verticalis* females that experienced food shortage as larvae did not have a lower fecundity (81). Much of the body mass increase during the maturation period is due to development of the flight muscles (51), suggesting that this trait might also show compensatory growth. Effects may also be magnified after metamorphosis. In *Libellula pulchella*, 67% of the animals lost mass after emergence, and animals with lower initial body mass were more likely to lose mass (56). In addition, negative effects on energetically costly traits such as energy storage and immune function may be compensated for through intense feeding during the maturation period. Freshly emerged *L. pulchella*, however, frequently has low fat reserves from which it does not recover (54). Other correlates of flight performance such as muscle ultrastructure, physiology, and protein composition also change considerably throughout maturation (54, 55). This suggests the potential for the operation of compensatory mechanisms, but direct evidence for these mechanism is lacking. Finally, unpredictable bad weather conditions at the adult stage may decouple the association between traits such as size and fitness, potentially promoting associations with other traits such as the ability to endure bad weather conditions (75, 106).

ADULT STAGE

Gregarines: gut parasites that position themselves in the intestinal tract where they drain resources; of the group Protozoa

Several environmental conditions at the adult stage, including parasites, predators, adverse weather conditions, food shortage, and harassment of females by males, cause mortality and therefore generate numerical carry-over effects to the next generation (21) (**Supplemental Table 2**). Most studies of environmental conditions in adults have been done in the field and focused on fitness components at the adult stage; carry-over effects on offspring fitness were considered only rarely. This is partially explained by the logistic problems in manipulating adults under controlled conditions. Therefore, and given that reproduction occurs at the adult stage, we summarize studies reporting effects of environmental conditions at the adult stage.

Effects of Environmental Conditions at the Adult Stage

Parasites, mainly water mites and gregarine parasites, are the dominant environmental condition studied in adults (**Supplemental Table 2**). Both parasites drain energy from their hosts by extracting resources (including fat), by damaging host tissue that must be repaired, and by boosting a costly immune response in the host (e.g., 18, 91). In addition, parasites may reduce the energy intake of the host because of two types of mechanical costs that have not been investigated in detail. First, as an internal parasite, gregarines may obstruct the gut and interfere with food processing and limit space for egg production. Second, as an external parasite, water mites may impair flight performance (68, 79) and therefore potentially reduce foraging rates. The resulting lowered energy content may also cause a resource allocation conflict between immune defense and fat storage. This finding is supported by a study in calopterygid damselflies in which experimental manipulation of juvenile hormone levels caused a reallocation of energy between immune defense and fat storage (19, 20). In addition, both water mites and gregarines have been shown to reduce fat content (**Supplemental Table 2**).

These energetic and mechanical costs may explain the negative effects of parasites on fitness components such as life span, mating success, and fecundity (**Supplemental Table 2**). Tests of a direct causal link between these costs and fitness effects are lacking, however, partly because most studies did not manipulate parasite load (but see, e.g., 14). Reduced energetic content may have direct negative effects on life span through starvation and, together with the mechanical costs, cause a reduced ability to escape from predators such as birds (77). Effects on lifetime mating success may be explained indirectly by the shortened life span (2, 24) but also by the increased need to allocate time to foraging (14) and by the lowered ability to pay the energetic costs of searching for females and fighting (18, 36). In one experimental study, however, artificially infected males, despite suffering from reduced muscle mass, were as successful in defending their territory as controls were (38). Reduced fat content in females is expected to translate to reduced egg production (**Supplemental Table 2**).

Despite the often high predation on adults (reviewed in 78), nonconsumptive predator effects are poorly studied in adult odonates. One study reported that under a manipulated high predation risk, damselflies increased their mass less during the maturation period (96). Studies showed that consumptive predation may shift phenotypic distributions of several traits, including immune traits (76) and sexually selected traits such as body size and wing spot size (105). This indicates that both nonconsumptive and consumptive predation changes the adult phenotype and therefore is expected to indirectly shape fitness components such as life span, mating success, and fecundity.

Adverse weather conditions can have a large impact on lifetime reproductive success in these flying ectotherms (**Supplemental Table 2**). Low temperatures reduce flight performance (14), which can make animals more vulnerable to predators and reduce foraging success (21). The latter reduces body condition including the buildup of fat storage (38), thereby reducing the ability to deal with parasites (14) and delaying the formation of new egg clutches (8, 102). Similarly, several studies reported negative effects of low temperature on life span, mating success, and fecundity (**Supplemental Table 2**).

Although the effect of food has been little explored, some field studies suggest adults can be food limited (6, 81). Food shortage generates negative effects on all adult fitness components. Food shortage reduces fat storage (74) and immune function (38). The few studies that manipulated food availability and quantified fitness components reported reduced survival during the maturation period (81, 108) and reduced fecundity (81). Direct effects on mating success have not been examined, but lower feeding rates can reduce wing pigmentation, a sexually selected trait, which suggests that food shortage can lead to reduced mating success (44).

Harassment of females by males is another stressful environmental condition. High harassment levels are associated with reduced thoracic fat levels probably because animals are forced to engage more in costly flights (23) and have reduced foraging activity (90). As a result, high harassment levels translate to reduced female survival, mating success, and fecundity (**Supplemental Table 2**).

Maternal effect: when the mother's phenotype or the environment she provides causes phenotypic effects in her offspring independent of the offspring genes

Adult Carry-Over Effects to Larval Fitness

Several of the above-discussed environmental conditions reduce life span and fecundity and thereby lifetime egg production, which causes direct numerical effects at the egg and larval stages. In contrast, trait-mediated carry-over effects from the adult stage to offspring traits and fitness, i.e., maternal effects (67), are poorly documented in odonates. Studies that looked specifically at maternal effects on larval growth and development using a breeding design suggested them to be weak (103) or absent (88). However, parasite-mediated maternal effects have been demonstrated. *C. puella* females with manipulated higher water mite loads produced fewer but larger larvae that also had a higher growth rate (83). Other environmental conditions that could potentially affect offspring traits through maternal effects have not been examined. *Libellula saturata* females that dispersed more and as a result oviposited in more isolated tubs produced larvae with a higher foraging rate (57). Although clearly a coupling of adult and larval traits, it is not clear whether this coupling was driven by a maternal effect or by genetic differences among the mothers. In both cases the offspring fitness was likely positively influenced, as larger larvae that forage and grow more benefit in terms of competition and avoiding cannibalism.

A special group of maternal effects are mediated by parental care (67). Although in the strict sense odonates do not directly provide parental care, there is some proof for paternal care sensu lato. One mechanism is through the choice of optimal oviposition patches within a given site. *Calopteryx splendens* eggs oviposited into faster-flowing water developed faster and had lower mortality than eggs placed in slowly flowing water because encrusting algae were less likely to overgrow the eggs in faster water (92). Because only a subset of males can defend territories at these good patches, any stressful environmental condition at the adult stage likely reduces the ability of males to provide optimal oviposition patches, hence growth conditions, for the males' offspring. A second suggested mechanism of maternal care is through the overproduction of eggs, thereby providing extra food for the larvae through cannibalism. In *Megaloprepus coerulatus*, providing excess eggs indeed resulted in larger offspring at emergence in small artificial tree holes. The increase in larval competition, however, offsets this effect in large artificial tree holes (34). Any environmental condition that reduces fecundity (**Supplemental Table 2**) also reduces the ability of females to rely on this strategy to improve their offspring fitness.

Decoupling Mechanisms

The effects of stressful environmental conditions on adult fitness components do not always detectably affect larval fitness components. Studies on this topic are scarce. A recent study showed that fecundity (clutch size) in *Enallagma cyathigerum* is well correlated with offspring number early in larval life, but this relation is reduced in later developmental stages (13). In specific breeding systems such as that of *M. coerulatus*, which breeds in tree holes, there may no longer be a correlation between the number of eggs laid by a female or fertilized by a male and the number of offspring that survive to emerge (35). This is mainly because of severe cannibalism in this study system, with few to sometimes one animal emerging from a given tree hole. As a result, although body size was correlated with female clutch size and male mating success, larger parents did not realize greater fitness than smaller parents did (35). Also, maternal effects may weaken throughout larval ontogeny especially in the presence of stressful environmental conditions. For example, larger *Sympetrum striolatum* eggs result in larger larvae, but the larvae do not maintain their size benefit under food shortage (45).

EMERGING INSIGHTS AND PERSPECTIVES

Evolution, Selection, and Fitness in the Complex Life Cycle

In support of the adaptive decoupling hypothesis, we found ample direct and indirect evidence for decoupling mechanisms between the larval and adult stages in odonates. Our review, however, also identified several trait-mediated carry-over pathways that couple the larval and adult stages for both sexes and confirm the view that metamorphosis is not a new beginning (73). This would imply that larval and adult traits cannot completely evolve independently. A needed piece of information is the identification of genetic correlations across life stages that, under the adaptive decoupling hypothesis, should be less strong than genetic correlations between traits of the same stage (66). Another approach that would add mechanistic insight is the identification and comparison of gene expression profiles in both life stages. Such studies are still rare in general and limited mostly to *Drosophila*. For example, a recent study in *D. melanogaster* reported genetic correlations between larval and adult immunities: A gene encoding a defensive antimicrobial peptide was controlled by the same genetic factors in larvae and adults (33). In the genus *Enallagma*, strong parallel evolution of the larval ecomorphology and of adult traits involved in mate recognition occurred across the Holarctic (101). Both stages do not share the same selective environment, which may suggest a phylogenetic correlation across life stages. Unraveling the molecular basis of these traits will clarify whether the observed parallel changes in both stages are a factor of chance combined with a limited number of evolutionary outcomes, or whether the same genes drive the evolution of both stages.

An important emerging insight is that the coupling of traits across metamorphosis may not necessarily negatively affect an individual's fitness. Individuals with more (or less) optimal larval values for a given trait under a tight coupling will not automatically benefit (or suffer) from more (or less) optimal adult values. This depends on the consistency of direction of the selection pressure on that trait across metamorphosis. We lack direct information on this in odonates, but it is known that at the adult stage sexual selection may change direction depending on the environment (39, 49). Changes in the direction of selection may as well be expected across metamorphosis for traits such as size, timing of emergence, and activity level. For example, larger larvae are more susceptible to predation (e.g., 110), whereas larger adults may have an advantage in terms of mating success and fecundity (94; but see 107). Emerging early may reduce cumulative predation risk at the larval stage, but emerging too early will lead, for example, to unfavorable weather conditions at the adult stage (106). Also, in fish lakes, larvae with a lower activity will survive best (102), but low activity may not optimize reproductive success at the adult stage. To resolve this issue, we need studies across metamorphosis that estimate selection on these traits in both life stages. What holds for baseline trait coupling (i.e., not affected by stressful environmental conditions) also holds for carry-over of any induced suboptimal trait changes. Stressful environmental conditions at the larval stage do not necessarily decrease adult fitness components; they may increase them. For example, at high density and at low food level, *Enallagma boreale* larvae emerged later, which in one of the two years of study increased the probability to survive to reproductive maturity. Further, both of these stressful environmental conditions reduced size at emergence, which in one year increased the male's mating probability (3, 5). If these patterns are general, this would indicate most traits are under stabilizing selection in which across the life cycle intermediate trait values have highest fitness. This finding illustrates that a CLC perspective may be crucial to understanding the total selection on fitness-related traits and that fitness from the resulting compromise may be maximized across life cycle stages.

What our review also highlights is that stressful environmental conditions at the larval stage do not necessarily carry over to adult fitness through the traditionally measured end points, mass, size, and age at emergence. This may as well happen independently through effects on physiology, behavior, and proxies of flight performance (**Supplemental Table 1**). Failure to take account of these less considered carry-over effects may have two consequences. First, it may generate hidden carry-over effects from larval conditions to adult fitness that become apparent only when they translate to measurable fitness components (29). Second, ignoring the environmental conditions experienced at the larval stage may result in unexplained variation at the adult stage in selection studies that typically try to link body size to fitness components.

Population and Metapopulation Dynamics

Identifying key environmental conditions that shape local population abundances in animals with a CLC remains challenging for investigators. Consumptive effects of predation at the larval stage in odonates appear to be the dominant factor limiting abundances (59, 61, 63). However, non-consumptive effects of predation at the larval stage caused by behavioral and physiological stress responses on growth rate (60, 62, 98, 100, 101) and food shortage can also be important drivers of abundances (61) (**Supplemental Table 1**). Drivers of population abundances such as predation at the larval stage may reduce adult numbers not only by reducing larval numbers but also by negatively affecting adult traits of surviving animals (such as decreased energy storage; **Supplemental Table 1**) in such a way that their survival as adults is impaired. Furthermore, the negatively affected adult traits of surviving animals may also reduce fecundity. As a result, environmental conditions such as predation at the larval stage may drive abundances at the larval and adult stages and, to some extent, independently through carry-over effects. The ecological processes limiting abundances are less studied at the adult stage, but parasites likely play an important role given their negative effects on survival and fecundity (61) (**Supplemental Table 2**). This is true especially in the presence of carry-over effects from the many larval environmental conditions that impair adult immune function (**Supplemental Table 1**). Also at the adult stage, ecological processes limit the numbers in the next stage not only by reducing the number of adults and the fecundity of the survivors, but likely also through mediating carry-over effects on the fitness of eggs and larvae. For example, under predation risk, animals may avoid ovipositing at high-quality places, thereby lowering egg survival and larval growth rates (as shown in mosquitoes; 47).

So far, we cannot determine directly the relative contribution of carry-over effects to population dynamics because studies spanning the entire life cycle (from egg numbers to egg numbers) are missing. More general, no studies have considered how odonate abundances at the larval and adult stages fluctuate through time. We may advance our insights in the short term by using a modeling approach. A logical starting point would be the demographic model of McPeek & Peckarsky (63), which combines numerical effects and carry-over effects of environmental conditions.

By examining the CLC and the associated coupling of the aquatic larval stage and terrestrial adult stage, investigators may discover unexpected effects of environmental conditions on population dynamics. A recent model indicated that the effects of food levels in the aquatic or terrestrial habitat of animals with food-dependent life-history traits (as clearly present in odonates, **Supplemental Table 1**) can lead to surprisingly complex long-term dynamics (86). For example, owing to the coupling between both stages, higher food levels at the larval stage can unexpectedly decrease the survival and abundance of larvae but increase the abundance of the adult stage. Although a strong modeling framework has been developed for the coupling of terrestrial and aquatic ecosystems for animals with a CLC, we lack the demographic parameters, especially at the adult stage, to gauge the strength of the effects generated (58, 61).

Carry-over effects between the environmental conditions experienced at the larval stage and dispersal performance at the adult stage may not be limited to the local population; it may also shape metapopulation dynamics (10). This link between larval local environmental conditions and adult dispersal has been identified in *E. boreale*, where larvae reared at high density or at low food emerged with a lower mass and were less likely to disperse away from their natal pond (37). There is also indirect support for this link. Several larval environmental conditions have been shown to affect proxies of flight performance (see **Supplemental Table 1**). Therefore, there is large potential for such carry-over effects on dispersal performance in a metapopulation network. For example, several larval environmental conditions reduce adult size (**Supplemental Table 1**), and larger males may show a higher tendency to disperse to other ponds (e.g., 4, 17). A special case of coupling is mediated by water mites, which climb onto larvae when emerging and then engorge the adult odonate. Adult males parasitized by water mites are more likely to disperse than nonparasitized males (1, 17).

Link to Community Structure Across Habitat Boundaries

Ecologists have only recently examined how organisms with a CLC can couple aquatic and terrestrial ecosystems (e.g., 48, 58, 86). These studies demonstrated how ecological processes, such as predation, at the aquatic stage generate numerical effects that affect processes in the terrestrial ecosystem. Odonates play an important mediatory role. Fish indirectly facilitate terrestrial plant reproduction by limiting the number of *Erythemis simplicicollis* larvae, thereby reducing the number of adults, and hence terrestrial predation, on insect plant pollinators (48). As a result, plants near fish ponds are less pollen-limited than plants near fish-free ponds. No study across ecosystems has considered carry-over effects in which changed traits at metamorphosis differentially affect the terrestrial ecosystem, even though such effects are likely. For example, predation risk at the larval stage can reduce size and mass at emergence (**Supplemental Table 1**), which may negatively affect fecundity and lead to lower population numbers in the next generation (63), which also contributes to less predation on terrestrial prey.

Relevance for Applied Issues

The above-mentioned carry-over effects and decoupling pathways in the CLC hold for anthropogenic stressors. Therefore, a life cycle approach may prove rewarding in risk assessment and management strategies. Risk assessment is typically done on one life stage. For pollutants, the focus is almost uniquely on the larval stage (**Supplemental Table 1**). Adults, however, also may suffer from pollutants both through direct exposure and through carry-over effects from the larval stage. Moreover, life stages may be differentially sensitive to anthropogenic stressors (see, e.g., 40). Taking into account the CLC also widens the spatial scale needed to assess the impact of aquatic pollutants, even if it is a point source of pollution. A pollutant in the aquatic habitat generates carry-over effects to the terrestrial stage, but when it bioaccumulates it may also be transported to the terrestrial stage and away from the pollution source (25). This has been demonstrated, for example, for cadmium in odonates (26). For global warming, risk assessment seems to focus mainly on the adult stage (70). Nevertheless, larvae may suffer and these effects may carry over to the adult stage. For example, higher temperatures and shorter hydroperiods may result in smaller body size and mass at emergence (**Supplemental Table 1**), which may translate to lowered survival and fecundity at the adult stage and potentially to lowered flight and dispersal ability. Furthermore, the degree of coupling between the larval and adult stages and between adult traits and fitness may also change with changing frequencies of periods of bad weather.

The management of odonate populations and communities typically focuses on a single life stage, usually the adult (69). Improving conditions experienced by both life stages is important. For example, a recent monitoring study indicated that the odonate diversity in north-temperate lakes of the United States increased not only when there are more aquatic macrophytes but when there is more terrestrial herbaceous vegetation (80). Understanding interactions across ecosystems may enable investigators to better gauge the effects of anthropogenic environmental change (48, 86). For example, both the increase (e.g. due to deliberate fish introductions) and the decrease (e.g., due to eutrophication) of fish numbers may change not only densities but also traits of adult odonates and thereby their impact on terrestrial communities. This factor, among others, may affect butterfly biodiversity (85). This implies that it is necessary to think across ecosystem boundaries when making management decisions affecting animals with a CLC (86).

SUMMARY POINTS

1. The hemimetabolic Odonata have a CLC consisting of aquatic egg and larval stages separated from the terrestrial adult stage by metamorphosis. Environmental conditions in each stage impose mortality in that stage, thereby generating strong numerical effects across stages.
2. Environmental conditions at the egg stage may have fitness implications at the larval stage such as delayed embryonic development time and reduced hatchling size. Intriguingly, egg-hatching traits may even bridge adult metamorphosis and shape adult fitness components.
3. Larval environmental conditions may influence adult fitness components through carry-over effects on adult size, energy storage, flight performance, and behavior. Decoupling mechanisms exist in the form of compensatory mechanisms at the larval and adult stages, stressful and stochastic events during metamorphosis, and stressful environmental conditions at the adult stage that may overrule preceding larval conditions.
4. Adult environmental conditions can reduce life span and fecundity, thereby reducing lifetime egg production and leading to numerical effects at the egg and larval stages. Carry-over effects from the adult stage to offspring fitness (maternal effects) are poorly documented, and may take the form of egg size manipulation, oviposition patch selection, and excess production of eggs as food. Decoupling of these effects happens to some extent because throughout the larval stage egg numbers and size are decreasingly correlated with larval numbers and size.

5. In support of the adaptive decoupling hypothesis, there is ample direct and indirect evidence for decoupling mechanisms between the larval and adult stages. However, we identify several carry-over pathways of environmental conditions that couple the larval and adult stages for both sexes and indicate that metamorphosis is not a new beginning. Therefore, fitness may be maximized as a compromise across life cycle stages.
6. In addition to numerical effects, carry-over effects may shape population and metapopulation dynamics and community structure across habitat boundaries. This asks for a CLC perspective when dealing with applied issues.

FUTURE ISSUES

1. The egg is the least-studied life stage. To what extent and how do environmental conditions imposed at the egg stage shape larval and adult fitness components?
2. We have reasonable knowledge on how larval environmental conditions affect adult morphology and physiology, whereas other aspects remain unknown. What role do behavioral syndromes play in coupling the larval and adult stages? To what extent do larval environmental conditions affect adult flight performance and thereby shape dispersal and metapopulation dynamics?
3. How are the larval and adult stages coupled genetically? Are the same genes active in both stages? Does this constrain independent evolution of adaptation in both life stages?
4. Carry-over effects from the adult stage to the egg and larval stages need more attention. How important are maternal effects and which environmental conditions modulate maternal effects?
5. The largest challenges remain in understanding the consequences of the CLC and carry-over effects at the population and community levels. Which environmental factors at which stage are the main drivers of odonate population dynamics? What are the relative contributions of numerical and carry-over effects in determining (meta-)population dynamics and community structure across habitat boundaries?

DISCLOSURE STATEMENT

The authors are not aware of any affiliations, memberships, funding, or financial holdings that might be perceived as affecting the objectivity of this review.

ACKNOWLEDGMENTS

We want to dedicate this review to the late Philip Corbet who inspired so many of us. We thank Marjan De Block, Frank Johansson, Mark McPeek, Jean Richardson, Martín A. Serrano-Meneses and Lieven Therry for valuable comments and discussions. Ola Fincke, Frank Suhling, Dave Thompson and Josh Van Buskirk helped us with literature. We acknowledge that the work of many of our colleagues could not be included because of space restrictions. While preparing this review we were supported by funds from the K.U.Leuven and the Research-Fund Flanders (FWO) to R.S. and PAPIIT IN204610-2 to A.C.-A. Raúl I. Martínez-Becerril provided logistic support to A.C.-A.

LITERATURE CITED

1. Allen KA, Thompson DJ. 2010. Movement characteristics of the scarce blue-tailed damselfly, *Ischnura pumilio*. *Insect Conserv. Div.* 3:5–14
2. Andrés JA, Cordero A. 1998. Effects of water mites of the damselfly *Ceriagrion tenellum* (Odonata: Coenagrionidae). *Ecol. Entomol.* 23:103–9
3. Anholt BR. 1990. An experimental separation of interference and exploitative competition in a larval damselfly. *Ecology* 71:1483–93
4. Anholt BR. 1990. Size-biased dispersal prior to breeding in a damselfly. *Oecologia* 83:385–87
5. **Anholt BR. 1991. Measuring selection on a population of damselflies with a manipulated phenotype. *Evolution* 45:1091–106**
6. Anholt BR. 1992. Sex and habitat differences in feeding by an adult damselfly. *Oikos* 65:428–32
7. Anholt BR, Marden JH, Jenkins DM. 1991. Patterns of mass gain and sexual dimorphism in adult dragonflies (Insecta, Odonata). *Can. J. Zool.* 69:1156–63
8. Banks MJ, Thompson DJ. 1987. Lifetime reproductive success of females of the damselfly *Coenagrion puella*. *J. Anim. Ecol.* 56:815–32
9. Bell AM, Sih A. 2007. Exposure to predation generates personality in threespined sticklebacks (*Gasterosteus aculeatus*). *Ecol. Lett.* 10:828–34
10. **Benard MF, McCauley SJ. 2008. Integrating across life-history stages: consequences of natal habitat effects on dispersal. *Am. Nat.* 171:553–67**
11. Bennett S, Mill PJ. 1995. Lifetime egg production and egg mortality in the damselfly *Pyrrhosoma nymphula* (Sulzer) (Zygoptera, Coenagrionidae). *Hydrobiologia* 310:71–78
12. Bonn A, Gasse M, Rolff J, Martens A. 1996. Increased fluctuating asymmetry in the damselfly *Coenagrion puella* is correlated with ectoparasitic water mites: implications for fluctuating asymmetry theory. *Oecologia* 108:596–98
13. Bots J, Van Dongen S, De Bruyn L, Van Houtte N, Van Gossum H. 2010. Clutch size and reproductive success in a female polymorphic insect. *Evol. Ecol.* 24:1239–53
14. Braune P, Rolff J. 2001. Parasitism and survival in a damselfly: Does host sex matter? *Proc. R. Soc. Lond. B* 268:1133–37
15. Brodin T. 2009. Behavioral syndrome over the boundaries of life - carryovers from larvae to adult damselfly. *Behav. Ecol.* 20:30–37
16. Campero M, De Block M, Ollevier F, Stoks R. 2008. Metamorphosis offsets the link between larval stress, adult asymmetry and individual quality. *Funct. Ecol.* 22:271–77
17. Conrad KF, Willson KH, Whitfield K, Harvey IF, Thomas CJ, Sherratt TN. 2002. Characteristics of dispersing *Ischnura elegans* and *Coenagrion puella* (Odonata): age, sex, size, morph and ectoparasitism. *Ecography* 25:439–45
18. Contreras-Garduño J, Canales-Lazcano J, Córdoba-Aguilar A. 2006. Wing pigmentation, immune ability and fat reserves in males of the rubyspot damselfly, *Hetaerina americana*. *J. Ethol.* 24:165–73
19. Contreras-Garduño J, Córdoba-Aguilar A, Azpilicueta-Amorín M, Cordero Rivera A. 2011. Juvenile hormone favors sexually-selected traits in males and females but impairs fat reserves and abdomen mass. *Evol. Ecol.* 25:845–56
20. Contreras-Garduño J, Córdoba-Aguilar A, Lanz-Mendoza H, Cordero Rivera A. 2009. Territorial behaviour and immunity are mediated by juvenile hormone: the physiological basis of honest signaling? *Funct. Ecol.* 23:157–63
21. **Corbet PS. 1999. *Dragonflies: Behavior and Ecology of Odonata*. Ithaca, NY: Cornell Univ. Press. 829 pp.**
22. **Córdoba-Aguilar A. 2008. *Dragonflies and Damselflies: Model Organisms for Ecological and Evolutionary Research*. Oxford, UK: Oxford Univ. Press. 290 pp.**

5. Presents the first evidence of carry-over effects from larval conditions to adult fitness in odonates.

10. Conceptual framework for exploring the link between local environmental conditions, phenotype at metamorphosis, and dispersal.

21. Provides a detailed, extensive overview of natural history, ecology, and behavior of odonates.

22. Reviews topics per life stage of how odonate studies advanced general ecological and evolutionary theory.

23. Córdoba-Aguilar A, González-Tokman D. 2011. Male harassment and female energetics in the territorial damselfly *Hetaerina americana* (Fabricius) (Zygoptera: Calopterygidae). *Odonatologica* 40:1–15
24. Córdoba-Aguilar A, Salamanca-Ocaña JC, Lopezaraiza M. 2003. Female reproductive decisions and parasite burden in a calopterygid damselfly (Insecta: Odonata). *Anim. Behav.* 66:81–87
25. Cristol DA, Brasso RL, Condon AM, Fovargue RE, Friedman SL, et al. 2008. The movement of aquatic mercury through terrestrial food webs. *Science* 320:335–35
26. Currie RS, Fairchild WL, Muir DCG. 1997. Remobilization and export of cadmium from lake sediments by emerging insects. *Environ. Toxicol. Chem.* 16:2333–38
27. De Block M, Stoks R. 2004. Cannibalism-mediated life history plasticity to combined time and food stress. *Oikos* 106:587–97
28. De Block M, Stoks R. 2004. Life-history variation in relation to time constraints in a damselfly. *Oecologia* 140:68–75
29. **De Block M, Stoks R. 2005. Fitness effects from egg to reproduction: bridging the life history transition. *Ecology* 86:185–97**
30. De Block M, Stoks R. 2008. Compensatory growth and oxidative stress in a damselfly. *Proc. R. Soc. Lond. B* 275:781–85
31. De Block M, Slos S, Johansson F, Stoks R. 2008. Integrating life history and physiology to understand latitudinal size variation in a damselfly. *Ecography* 31:115–23
32. De Block M, Stoks R. 2008. Short-term larval food stress and associated compensatory growth reduce adult immune function in a damselfly. *Ecol. Entomol.* 33:796–801
33. Fellous S, Lazzaro BP. 2011. Potential for evolutionary coupling and decoupling of larval and adult immune gene expression. *Mol. Ecol.* 20:1558–67
34. Fincke OM. 2011. Excess offspring as a maternal strategy: constraints in the shared nursery of a giant damselfly. *Behav. Ecol.* 22:543–51
35. Fincke OM, Hadrys H. 2001. Unpredictable offspring survivorship in the damselfly *Megaloprepus coerulatus* shapes parental behavior, constrains sexual selection, and challenges traditional fitness estimates. *Evolution* 55:762–72
36. Forbes MRL. 1991. Ectoparasites and mating success of male *Enallagma ebrium* damselflies (Odonata, Coenagrionidae). *Oikos* 60:336–42
37. Gillooly JF, Dodson SI. 2000. The relationship of egg size and incubation temperature to embryonic development time in univoltine and multivoltine aquatic insects. *Freshw. Biol.* 44:595–604
38. González-Tokman DM, Córdoba-Aguilar A, González-Santoyo I, Lanz-Mendoza H. 2011. Infection effects on feeding and territorial behaviour in a predatory insect in the wild. *Anim. Behav.* 81:1185–94
39. Gosden TP, Svensson EI. 2008. Spatial and temporal dynamics in a sexual selection mosaic. *Evolution* 62:845–56
40. Gribbin SD, Thompson DJ. 1991. The effects of size and residency on territorial disputes and short-term mating success in the damselfly *Pyrrhosoma nymphula* (Sulzer) (Zygoptera, Coenagrionidae). *Anim. Behav.* 41:689–95
41. Hardersen S, Frampton CM. 1999. Effects of short term pollution on the level of fluctuating asymmetry - a case study using damselflies. *Entomol. Exp. Appl.* 92:1–7
42. Hardersen S, Wratten SD. 2000. Sensitivity of aquatic life stages of *Xanthocnemis zealandica* (Odonata: Zygoptera) to azinphos-methyl and carbaryl. *N. Z. J. Mar. Freshw. Sci.* 34:117–23
43. Harvey IF, Corbet PS. 1985. Territorial behavior of larvae enhances mating success of male dragonflies. *Anim. Behav.* 33:561–65
44. Hooper RE, Tsubaki Y, Siva-Jothy M. 1999. Expression of a costly, plastic secondary sexual trait is correlated with age and condition in a damselfly with two male morphs. *Physiol. Entomol.* 24:364–69
45. Hottenbacher N, Koch K. 2006. Influence of egg size on egg and larval development of *Sympetrum striolatum* at different prey availability (Odonata: Libellulidae). *Int. J. Odonatol.* 9:165–74
46. Johansson F, Rowe L. 1999. Life history and behavioral responses to time constraints in a damselfly. *Ecology* 80:1242–52

29. In-depth study of carry-over effects from larval environmental conditions to adult fitness.

47. Kiflawi M, Blaustein L, Mangel M. 2003. Predation-dependent oviposition habitat selection by the mosquito *Culiseta longiareolata*: a test of competing hypotheses. *Ecol. Lett.* 6:35–40
48. Knight TM, McCoy MW, Chase JM, McCoy KA, Holt RD. 2005. Trophic cascades across ecosystems. *Nature* 437:880–83
49. Koenig WD. 2008. Lifetime reproductive success and sexual selection theory. See Ref. 22, pp. 153–66
50. Leung B, Forbes MR. 1997. Fluctuating asymmetry in relation to indices of quality and fitness in the damselfly *Enallagma ebrium* (Hagen). *Oecologia* 110:472–77
51. Marden JH. 1989. Bodybuilding dragonflies - costs and benefits of maximizing flight-muscle. *Physiol. Zool.* 62:505–21
52. Marden JH. 2008. Dragonfly flight performance: a model system for biomechanics, physiology and animal competitive behaviour. See Ref. 22, pp. 249–59
53. Marden JH, Fescemyer HW, Saastamoinen M, MacFarland SP, Vera JC, et al. 2008. Weight and nutrition affect pre-mRNA splicing of a muscle gene associated with performance, energetics and life history. *J. Exp. Biol.* 211:3653–60
54. Marden JH, Fitzhugh GH, Wolf MR. 1998. From molecules to mating success: integrative biology of muscle maturation in a dragonfly. *Am. Zool.* 38:528–44
55. Marden JH, Fitzhugh GH, Wolf MR, Arnold KD, Rowan B. 1999. Alternative splicing, muscle calcium sensitivity, and the modulation of dragonfly flight performance. *Proc. Natl. Acad. Sci. USA* 96:15304–9
56. Marden JH, Rowan B. 2000. Growth, differential survival, and shifting sex ratio of free-living *Libellula pulchella* (Odonata: Libellulidae) dragonflies during adult maturation. *Ann. Entomol. Soc. Am.* 93:452–58
57. McCauley SJ, Brodin T, Hammond J. 2010. Foraging rates of larval dragonfly colonists are positively related to habitat isolation: results from a landscape-level experiment. *Am. Nat.* 175:E66–73
58. McCoy MW, Barfield M, Holt RD. 2009. Predator shadows: complex life histories as generators of spatially patterned indirect interactions across ecosystems. *Oikos* 118:87–100
59. McPeek MA. 1998. The consequences of changing the top predator in a food web: a comparative experimental approach. *Ecol. Monogr.* 68:1–23
60. McPeek MA. 2004. The growth/predation risk trade-off: So what is the mechanism? *Am. Nat.* 163:E88–111
61. McPeek MA. 2008. Ecological factors limiting the distribution and abundances of Odonata. See Ref. 22, pp. 51–62
62. McPeek MA, Grace M, Richardson JML. 2001. Physiological and behavioral responses to predators shape the growth/predation risk trade-off in damselflies. *Ecology* 82:1535–45
63. McPeek MA, Peckarsky BL. 1998. Life histories and the strengths of species interactions: combining mortality, growth, and fecundity effects. *Ecology* 79:867–79
64. Mikolajewski DJ, Joop G, Wohlfahrt B. 2007. Coping with predators and food limitation: testing life history theory for sex-specific larval development. *Oikos* 116:642–49
65. Mikolajewski DJ, Stoks R, Rolff J, Joop G. 2008. Predators and cannibals modulate sex-specific plasticity in life-history and immune traits. *Funct. Ecol.* 22:114–20
66. Moran NA. 1994. Adaptation and constraint in the complex life cycles of animals. *Annu. Rev. Ecol. Syst.* 25:573–600
67. Mousseau TA, Fox CW. 1998. *Maternal Effects as Adaptations*. Oxford, UK: Oxford Univ. Press. 375 pp.
68. Nagel L, Zanuttig M, Forbes MR. 2010. Selection on mite engorgement size affects mite spacing, host damselfly flight, and host resistance. *Evol. Ecol. Res.* 12:653–65
69. Oertli B. 2008. The use of dragonflies in the assessment and monitoring of aquatic habitats. See Ref. 22, pp. 79–95
70. Ott J. 2010. *Monitoring Climate Change with Dragonflies*. Sofia, Bulgaria: Pensoft Publ. 286 pp.
71. Padeffke T, Suhling F. 2003. Temporal priority and intra-guild predation in temporary waters: an experimental study using Namibian desert dragonflies. *Ecol. Entomol.* 28:340–47
72. Pechenik JA. 1999. On the advantages and disadvantages of larval stages in benthic marine invertebrate life cycles. *Mar. Ecol. Prog. Ser.* 177:269–97
73. Pechenik JA. 2006. Larval experience and latent effects - metamorphosis is not a new beginning. *Integr. Comp. Biol.* 46:323–33

48. First evidence of how animals with a complex life cycle may couple processes in aquatic and terrestrial ecosystems.

66. Review on the roles of adaptation and constraints in the macroevolution of complex life cycles.

74. Plaistow SJ, Tsubaki Y. 2000. A selective trade-off for territoriality and non-territoriality in the polymorphic damselfly *Mnais costalis*. *Proc. R. Soc. Lond. B* 267:969–75
75. Purse BV, Thompson DJ. 2005. Lifetime mating success in a marginal population of a damselfly, *Coenagrion mercuriale*. *Anim. Behav.* 69:1303–15
76. Rantala MJ, Honkavaara J, Dunn D, Suhonen J. 2011. Predation selects for increased immune function in male damselflies, *Calopteryx splendens*. *Proc. R. Soc. Lond. B* 278:1231–38
77. Rantala MJ, Honkavaara J, Suhonen J. 2010. Immune system activation interacts with territory-holding potential and increases predation of the damselfly *Calopteryx splendens* by birds. *Oecologia* 163:825–32
78. Rehfeldt G. 1995. *Parasiten und Fortpflanzen Von Libellen*. Braunschweig, Ger.: Wolfram Schmidt. 173 pp.
79. Reinhardt K. 1996. Negative effects of *Arrenurus* water mites on the flight distances of the damselfly *Nehalennia speciosa* (Odonata: Coenagrionidae). *Aquat. Insects* 18:233–40
80. Remsburg AJ, Turner MG. 2009. Aquatic and terrestrial drivers of dragonfly (Odonata) assemblages within and among north-temperate lakes. *J. N. Am. Benthol. Soc.* 28:44–56
81. Richardson JML, Baker RL. 1997. Effect of body size and fitness on fecundity in the damselfly *Ischnura verticalis*. *Oikos* 79:477–83
82. Richter O, Suhling F, Mueller O, Kern D. 2008. A model for predicting the emergence of dragonflies in a changing climate. *Freshw. Biol.* 53:1868–80
83. Rolff J. 1999. Parasitism increases offspring size in a damselfly: experimental evidence for parasite-mediated maternal effects. *Anim. Behav.* 58:1105–8
84. Rolff J, Van de Meutter F, Stoks R. 2004. Time constraints decouple age and size at maturity and physiological traits. *Am. Nat.* 164:559–65
85. Sang A, Teder T. 2011. Dragonflies cause spatial and temporal heterogeneity in habitat quality for butterflies. *Insect Conserv. Div.* 4:257–64
86. Schreiber S, Rudolf VHW. 2008. Crossing habitat boundaries: coupling dynamics of ecosystems through complex life cycles. *Ecol. Lett.* 11:576–87
87. Schuett W, Tregenza T, Dall SRX. 2010. Sexual selection and animal personality. *Biol. Rev.* 85:217–46
88. Shama LNS, Campero-Paz M, Wegner KM, De Block M, Stoks R. 2011. Latitudinal and voltinism compensation shape thermal reaction norms for growth rate. *Mol. Ecol.* 20:2929–41
89. Sih A, Bell A, Chadwick J. 2004. Behavioral syndromes: an ecological and evolutionary overview. *Trends Ecol. Evol.* 19:372–78
90. Sirot LK, Brockmann HJ. 2001. Costs of sexual interactions to females in Rambur's forktail damselfly, *Ischnura ramburi* (Zygoptera: Coenagrionidae). *Anim. Behav.* 61:415–24
91. Siva-Jothy MT. 2000. A mechanistic link between parasite resistance and expression of a sexually selected trait in a damselfly. *Proc. R. Soc. Lond. B* 267:2523–27
92. Siva-Jothy MT, Gibbons DW, Pain D. 1995. Female oviposition site preference and egg hatching success in the damselfly *Calopteryx splendens xanthostoma*. *Behav. Ecol. Sociobiol.* 37:39–44
93. Sniegula S, Johansson F. 2010. Photoperiod affects compensating developmental rate across latitudes in the damselfly *Lestes sponsa*. *Ecol. Entomol.* 35:149–57
94. Sokolovska N, Rowe L, Johansson F. 2000. Fitness and body size in mature odonates. *Ecol. Entomol.* 25:239–48
95. Stoks R. 2001. Food stress and predator-induced stress shape developmental performance in a damselfly. *Oecologia* 127:222–29
96. Stoks R. 2001. What causes male-biased sex ratios in mature damselfly populations? *Ecol. Entomol.* 26:188–97
97. Stoks R, De Block M. 2011. Rapid growth reduces cold resistance: evidence from latitudinal patterns in growth rate, cold resistance and stress proteins. *PLoS ONE* 6:e16935
98. Stoks R, De Block M, McPeek MA. 2005. Alternative growth and energy storage responses to mortality threats in damselflies. *Ecol. Lett.* 8:1307–16
99. Stoks R, De Block M, McPeek MA. 2006. Physiological costs of compensatory growth in a damselfly. *Ecology* 87:1566–74
100. Stoks R, De Block M, Van de Meutter F, Johansson F. 2005. Predation cost of rapid growth: behavioural coupling and physiological decoupling. *J. Anim. Ecol.* 74:708–15

101. Stoks R, Nystrom JL, May ML, McPeek MA. 2005. Parallel evolution in ecological and reproductive traits to produce cryptic damselfly species across the Holarctic. *Evolution* 59:1976–88
102. Strobbe F, McPeek MA, De Block M, Stoks R. 2011. Fish predation selects for reduced foraging activity. *Behav. Ecol. Sociobiol.* 65:241–47
103. Strobbe F, Stoks R. 2004. Life history reaction norms to time constraints in a damselfly: differential effects on size and mass. *Biol. J. Linn. Soc.* 83:187–96
104. Suhling F, Lepkojus S. 2001. Differences in growth and behaviour influence asymmetric predation among early-instar dragonfly larvae. *Can. J. Zool.* 79:854–60
105. Svensson EI, Friberg M. 2007. Selective predation on wing morphology in sympatric damselflies. *Am. Nat.* 170:101–12
106. Thompson DJ. 1990. The effects of survival and weather on lifetime egg production in a model damselfly. *Ecol. Entomol.* 15:455–62
107. Thompson DJ, Fincke OM. 2002. Body size and fitness in Odonata, stabilising selection and a meta-analysis too far? *Ecol. Entomol.* 27:378–84
108. Tsubaki Y, Hooper R. 2004. Effects of eugregarine parasites on adult longevity in the polymorphic damselfly *Mnais costalis* Selys. *Ecol. Entomol.* 29:361–66
109. Van Buskirk J. 1987. Influence of size and date of emergence on male survival and mating success in a dragonfly *Sympetrum rubicundulum*. *Am. Midl. Nat.* 118:169–76
110. Van de Meutter F, De Meester L, Stoks R. 2005. Water turbidity affects predator-prey interactions in a fish-damselfly system. *Oecologia* 144:327–36
111. Van Doorslaer W, Stoks R. 2005. Thermal reaction norms in two *Coenagrion* damselfly species: contrasting embryonic and larval life-history traits. *Freshw. Biol.* 50:1982–90
112. Werner EE. 1988. Size, scaling, and the evolution of complex life cycles. In *Size-Structured Populations*, ed. B Ebenman, L Persson, pp. 60–81. Berlin: Springer-Verlag
113. Wilbur HM. 1980. Complex life cycles. *Annu. Rev. Ecol. Syst.* 11:67–93

Insect Transgenesis: Current Applications and Future Prospects

Malcolm J. Fraser, Jr.

Eck Institute for Global Health, Department of Biological Sciences, University of Notre Dame, Notre Dame, Indiana 46556-0369; email: Fraser.1@nd.edu

Annu. Rev. Entomol. 2012. 57:267–89

The *Annual Review of Entomology* is online at ento.annualreviews.org

This article's doi:
10.1146/annurev.ento.54.110807.090545

0066-4170/12/0107-0267$20.00

Keywords

transposon, zinc finger, nuclease, homing, endonuclease, integrase

Abstract

The ability to manipulate the genomes of many insects has become a practical reality over the past 15 years. This has been led by the identification of several useful transposon vector systems that have allowed the identification and development of generalized, species-specific, and tissue-specific promoter systems for controlled expression of gene products upon introduction into insect genomes. Armed with these capabilities, researchers have made significant strides in both fundamental and applied transgenics in key model systems such as *Bombyx mori*, *Tribolium casteneum*, *Aedes aegypti*, and *Anopheles stephensi*. Limitations of transposon systems were identified, and alternative tools were developed, thus significantly increasing the potential for applied transgenics for control of both agricultural and medical insect pests. The next 10 years promise to be an exciting time of transitioning from the laboratory to the field, from basic research to applied control, during which the full potential of gene manipulation in insect systems will ultimately be realized.

INTRODUCTION

Transgenesis: the transfer of cloned genetic material from one species to another

Transposon: a mobile DNA sequence with terminal inverted repeats that encodes a transposase, which catalyzes excision and random insertion within chromosomes

Recombinase: an enzyme that catalyzes the exchange of short of homologous regions of DNA between two DNA strands

Research on transgenesis of invertebrates has progressed past the identification and development of transgene vectors and analysis of their mobility in a given species to establishing practical applications for these capabilities. Multiple gene vectors are available for purposes of transgene insertion and expression in virtually any insect species, genetic analyses of model insect species, and applied insect and vectored disease-control strategies. Nonetheless, even though significant advancements are facilitated with existing technologies, there remains a need to develop newer approaches. In part, this results from concerns over the relative inefficiency of current transgenic manipulations in important target species as well as the loss and variability of transgene activity from some established transgenic lines. Of particular concern for practical transgenesis applications are the difficulties in defining and standardizing the long-term effectiveness of transgenic manipulations.

The intention of this review is to highlight important observations that have resulted from the use of various transgene vectors over the past 10 years and to point out promising prospects for new approaches, analyses, and techniques aimed at maximizing the utility of transgenic manipulations in insects. For complementary background reviews on the development of many of these transgene vectors and the confirmation of their utility in various insect species, including a more complete analysis of the early development of the field, the reader is referred to previous review articles (6, 105).

TRANSPOSABLE ELEMENTS

Transposons have received wide attention and have demonstrated significant success as a means for integrating genes within insect and other invertebrate genomes. These mobile DNAs have the general properties of practical frequencies of successful transgenesis, relative randomness of integration, and, in some cases, controlled remobilization. They are useful for inducing genetic mutations, analyzing gene expression, and transforming target species to express genes that may produce advantageous phenotypes.

At present, there are four transposon vector systems that have been studied relatively extensively for the transformation of nondrosophilid invertebrate species. These include the *mariner* family elements *Mos1* and *Minos*, the *hAT*-related element *Hermes*, and the relatively distinct transposable element *piggyBac*. Although each of these transposon-based systems is effective in generating transgenics in various species, their utility as a means for analyzing some important invertebrate genomes has proven to be limited.

Tc1- and *mariner*-Related Transposons

Tc1 and *mariner* elements are monophyletic in origin, sharing 18% to 25% amino acid identity, and are distantly related to the IS family of bacterial mobile elements, retrotransposons and retroviruses (26). *mariner* family elements are remarkably widespread in the animal kingdom, having been identified in a diversity of species from flatworms to insects and humans. Likewise, the *Tc1* family is widespread and diverse; it is found in nematodes, insects, vertebrates, and fungi (104). Both possess the DD(35)E catalytic core common to integrases, recombinases, and other DNA-cutting and -splicing enzymes. In the *Tc1* family, this motif takes the form of DD(34)E, whereas DD(34)D is the signature of *mariner*-like elements (99). The members of this superfamily most widely used for insect manipulation are *Mos1* and *Minos*.

Mos1. The original *mariner* element was identified as an unstable insertion in the *white eye* locus causing the w^{peach} phenotype in *Drosophila mauritiana* (52). Although this original element was not autonomously mobile, spontaneous mobile representatives called *mosaic* (*Mos*) elements were subsequently identified. The *Mos1* transposon is fully mobile, and its transposase catalyzes the excision of the original w^{peach} *mariner* element (for a review, see 52).

ITR: inverted terminal repeat

Mos1 is 1,286 base pairs (bp) long, terminating in 28-bp imperfect inverted terminal repeats (ITRs), and contains a single open reading frame coding for the transposase. The first 119 amino acids of the *Mos1* transposase contain a helix-turn-helix motif that is implicated in the ITR binding step of transposition. The C terminus of *Mos1* contains the catalytic center of the transposase, including the DD(34)D motif (7).

mariner element activity can be effectively manipulated. Random mutagenesis of the transposase gene of a reconstructed *mariner* from *Haematobia irritans*, termed *Himar1*, generates a hyperactive element (71), and when the identified amino acid mutations are applied to analogous positions in *Mos1*, there is a dramatic increase in the frequency of transposition in both *Escherichia coli* and *Aedes aegypti*, with a concomitant increase in the number of precisely integrated transpositions in *Ae. aegypti* embryos (100). Other manipulations, such as replacing the imperfect terminal repeat structure with dual flanking 3′ ITRs, result in increased transposition frequencies in *E. coli*, but not *Ae. aegypti*, embryos (101). Simply coinjecting purified transposase protein instead of expressing the protein from a traditional helper plasmid also increases the rate of transposition (20). *Mos1* has demonstrated transformation capabilities for a wide variety of insect species but has its greatest impact as a means for introducing genes into *Ae. aegypti* (20, 21, 82, 138).

Minos. *Minos* is a *mariner*-related element first identified from a genomic library scan in *Drosophila hydei* as a repetitive element situated between the 18S and 28S rRNA coding units (35). Homologous sequences are present in 27 species of *Drosophila* across both the *replete* and *saltans* groups. Comparative sequence analyses of these related transposons are incongruent with the phylogenic distribution of the *Drosophila* species, suggesting recent and multiple occurrences of horizontal transfers (24).

This 1,775-bp-long element terminates in perfect inverted repeats of 255 nucleotides. The terminal repeats contain direct repeat sequences, with the 5′-ITR inner direct repeat overlapping putative transcription initiation sequences (97). *Minos* transposase also functions as an autoregulatory mechanism to prevent unregulated amplification and spread of the transposon within the genome of a host (76).

Minos generates a TA dinucleotide duplication at the insertion site, and excision is typically either precise, restoring the original sequence of the insertion site, or predictably imprecise, leaving behind a 6-bp footprint composed of four *Minos* nucleotides with the duplicated TA sequence (4), reflecting the involvement of DNA repair in the movement of this cut-and-paste element. Analysis of excision sites following remobilization of *Minos* reveals occasional imprecise excisions, including one instance in which 800 bp of flanking sequence were deleted (85). *Minos* has been used to transform a wide variety of invertebrate species (6, 67, 96). Despite the demonstrated ability of *Minos* to remobilize in the germ line of some species, germ-line remobilization is not observed in the mosquito *Anopheles stephensi* (114) and may not be efficient in other mosquito species.

hAT-Related Transposons

The mobile elements of the *hAT* superfamily all share common structural features and functional characteristics, including the generation of 8-bp target-site duplications upon integration that share the general consensus sequence of 5′-GTNNNNAC-3′ (109). The archetype for this superfamily in insects is the *hobo* transposon of *Drosophila melanogaster*. Two of these *hAT*-related elements with potential for wide utility in insect transformations are *Hermes* and *Herves*.

Hermes. Observation of nonautonomous *hobo* excision in *Musca domestica* in the absence of a coinjected transposase helper implicated an endogenous, cross-mobilizing *hAT* family element that was isolated using degenerate PCR primers and designated *Hermes* (6, 128). *Hermes* is 2,749 bp long with 17-bp terminal inverted repeats flanking a 1,839-bp transposase coding domain that encodes a predicted protein of 70.2 kDa. The presence of a functional DDE motif in *Hermes* is confirmed by loss-of-function mutations, and the mechanism of excision is similar to that of the V(D)J recombinase RAG (152).

Hermes is a versatile mobile element for the germ-line transformation of a diversity of insects (6, 80). However, movement properties are not always predictable in a given species. Analysis of *Hermes* integration sites in transformed lines of *Ae. aegypti* (58) reveals an atypical mechanism of movement in that there was no 8-bp target-site duplication, and segments of the donor plasmid were also integrated into the target genome (58, 125). These unexpected results contrast with the interplasmid transposition assays performed in *Ae. aegypti* embryos that reflected precise cut-and-paste transposition (113). This irregular integration in *Ae. aegypti* may be useful in designing postintegrative stabilization vectors that employ site-specific recombinases, if plasmid sequences could be effectively removed in the process.

Herves. The more recently identified insect *hAT* element, *Herves*, is 3,708 bp long, including the flanking 11-bp imperfect ITRs and the 603-amino-acid open reading frame encoding the transposase, and is flanked by the consensus 8-bp target-site duplication of 5′-GTNNNNAC-3′. *Herves* was identified in the PEST strain of *Anopheles gambiae* and was isolated from the RSP strain. Differences in insertion sites between the strains provided evidence of recent movement of *Herves* in this species. The presence and distribution of *Herves* among African mosquito populations support the conclusion that *Herves* is an ancient transposable element introduced into an ancestor mosquito lineage before its divergence into the different *Anopheles* species (94).

Interplasmid transposition assays performed in S2 cells indicate that both the PEST and the RSP strain transposases catalyze cut-and-paste transposition of the *Herves* element. Transposition assays in injected *Drosophila* embryos using the PEST strain transposase yielded 27 perfect insertion events and 13 imperfect insertion events. Analysis of insertion points demonstrates a markedly different site preference of *Herves* when compared with *Hermes* and *hobo*. *Herves* also catalyzes the germ-line transformation of *D. melanogaster*, with an average insertion frequency of 30.1%. As yet, there are no published reports of the use of this promising transposon in nondrosophilid insects.

The *piggyBac* Transposon

piggyBac is a distinct class II mobile element and the archetype for the so-called TTAA-specific family of transposable elements (36). Although *piggyBac*-related sequences are widespread in insects and other eukaryotic genomes (112), a functional representative of this family of transposons may have remained undiscovered had it not been for a peculiar plaque morphology mutation of baculoviruses propagated in the TN-368 cell line. Genetic characterization of these mutants identified *Trichoplusia ni* mobile elements inserting within the FP25K baculovirus gene (36). The original baculovirus-derived *piggyBac* element is the best-characterized, fully autonomous transposon from this family, making it capable of being used as a transgene vector. Interestingly, a putatively active *piggyBac*-related transposon has been recovered in another mutant baculovirus (15).

The structure and mobility of *piggyBac* are unusual among mobile elements. The 2,472-bp-long element is structured with two sets of inverted repeats at both ends bounding a 1,785-bp transposase-encoding open reading frame expressing a protein with a demonstrated mass of nearly

68 kDa. The 13-bp terminal inverted repeats terminate in 5′ CCC...GGG 3′, whereas the 19-bp internal, or subterminal, repeats are asymmetrically separated from these terminal repeats (17). The internal domain contains sequences essential for efficient chromosomal mobility as well as a functional transcriptional enhancer (122).

Sequence analysis reveals a putative promoter for the transposase, which has a Kozak consensus start codon that has apparent transcriptional activity as measured in transposition assays (37) and in insect transformation (37, 51). However, when the native promoter is replaced with the *hsp70* promoter, transformation efficiency is increased more than eightfold (50). *piggyBac* may not have much similarity to other known recombinases with respect to primary sequence, but amino acid substitutions and analyses of the mechanism of transposition confirm its relatedness to the DDE/DDD family of recombinases (61, 87, 112).

piggyBac is presently the most widely used transposon vector and has been successfully employed for transgenic engineering in many eukaryotic systems including monocellular parasites (9), a diversity of insects (see 47), and vertebrates. The *piggyBac* transposon facilitated the extension of enhancer trapping strategies, enabling identification and functional analysis of genes in two of the most important model insect systems, *Bombyx mori* and *Tribolium casteneum*. Jumpstarter strains created using the *Minos* transposon expressing the *piggyBac* transposase are crossed with mutator transgenics harboring *piggyBac* integrations of Gal4 expression cassettes. Remobilization of the mutator *piggyBac* to active sites of transcription affects expression of Gal4, and altered expression patterns are detected when mated to a *piggyBac* upstream activating sequence (UAS)-linked reporter transgenic as tissue- or developmental-specific expression of a fluorescent gene. This approach is particularly fruitful in identifying many genes that are linked with tissue- or developmental-stage expression (117, 137, 140).

Unfortunately, *piggyBac* does not function in every species, perhaps as a result of interference from resident homologous elements. For example, divergent remnants of nonautonomous *piggyBac*-like elements bearing 78.5% nucleotide identity were identified in the *Spodoptera frugiperda* genome by degenerate PCR, and attempts to transform this species have proven unfruitful (153). This suggests the activity of a self-inhibitory mechanism for *piggyBac* movement in this species, which suppresses movement, possibly as a result of abundant expression of defective transposase.

The unusual properties of *piggyBac* nonreplicative cut-and-paste mobilization (75, 87) include characteristically precise integration and excision, targeting and duplication of TTAA tetranucleotide sequences during integration (37), and restoration of a single copy of this TTAA target site upon excision (28). The 5′- and 3′-terminal repeat configurations are not interchangeable, and when used in a configuration with one 5′ ITR and two 3′ ITRs, *piggyBac* demonstrates no particular preference for the proximal or distal 3′ ITR relative to the 5′ ITR, thus suggesting an independent location of terminal repeat configurations by the transposase (29). Similar results are obtained using duplicate 5′ ITRs and a single 3′ ITR (51). This characteristic provides some interesting possibilities for designing transgene vectors that can be immobilized following genomic insertion (86, 115).

Recent experiments demonstrate that the transpositional specificity of *piggyBac* for TTAA target sites can be directed to a degree. Fusing a Gal4 DNA binding domain (DBD) to the N terminus of the *piggyBac* transposase produces a chimeric transposase that targets TTAA sites adjacent to the UAS recognized by the Gal4 DBD. In addition to directing transposase activity to a particular insertion site, a drastic (6-fold) increase in transpositional activity is observed (79), suggesting the possibility of creating chimeric transposases with greater gene-targeting capabilities. This approach would provide a relatively simple way to use transposons to effect gene-specific disruption or targeted integration of transgenes into reliably stable and optimally active chromosomal locations while taking advantage of their properties for remobilization.

Limitations of Transposon Vectors

Even though several transposons are available for transgenic manipulations of insect genomes, there remains room for improvement and development of additional tools for insects. Transposons remain limited in their utility, primarily as a result of four factors: randomness of integration, relatively low transforming frequency, possible instability of integrated sequences, and limited carrying capacity. Random integration leads to frequent problems with transgene expression owing to variations in local genome environments. Given inequalities in local environments within a genome, not all transgenic insects will express the transgene equally, a phenomenon known as the position effect. This necessitates the generation and evaluation of multiple transgenic strains, and these position effects may take several generations to become evident. One recent example of the relative importance of this problem involves the loss of activity of a dengue virus suppressive gene in transgenic *Ae. aegypti* mosquitoes after 17 generations (34). Although transposons allow the insertion of transgenes in a variety of mosquito species with an experimentally effective frequency, the process remains relatively laborious and time consuming. Frequencies on the order of 0.1% to 10% are achievable, with higher frequencies less probable than lower ones. Obviously, the utility of transgenesis both as an experimental tool and for development of control measures is improved with increasing transformation frequencies. Mutagenesis of the transposase may lead to greater activity (e.g., *Himar1*). A simpler and more reliable way is to increase the amount of active transposase in infected embryos by providing the transposase as coinjected in vitro in transcribed mRNA. This significantly improves the recovery of transformed insects for most transposons and has become a preferred method for supplying transposase function in embryo injections.

Physical stability of the integrated transgene, although addressable in some transposon/insect combinations, remains problematic in others. Postintegrative stabilization of transposon vectored transgenes is possible with *piggyBac* by taking advantage of the unique properties of the noninterchangeable 5′ and 3′ ITRs as well as the lack of transposase preference for either one of two duplicated termini in a transposing unit (29, 51, 86, 115). Two approaches have been devised to stabilize transgenes postintegration (23, 51). Both rely on positioning the desired transgene within one or another dual transposon configurations that first integrate as an entire unit containing the transgene and markers and then allow postintegrative remobilization of a smaller transposing unit that does not contain the transgene of interest from the original integrated sequence. In the process, the transgene is left without flanking complementary ITRs and is incapable of further movement in the genome. This approach relies on the ability to remobilize the transposon sequences following integration, something that may not be possible in a given species.

One alternative that has been explored for insuring stability of the transgene is to use transposons from prokaryotic sources. The prokaryotic transposon Tn*5* can be used in an active intermediate configuration as a preassembled synaptic complex with purified transposase to improve efficiency of mobilization (44). Because no eukaryotic source for the transposase is evident, this could also effectively eliminate the possibility of remobilization following integration in insect genomes. Although Tn*5*-transformed insects are recovered at an acceptable frequency, efficiency is not significantly better than the more commonly employed insect transposons. In addition, integration using the presynaptic complex seems to generate a significant number of complex arrangements of multiple elements, most likely because preassembled synaptic complexes are immediately activated upon injection and integrated into the most abundantly available DNA, i.e., the vector (108). Although manipulation of concentrations of injected presynaptic complexes may reduce this occurrence, it would also result in a reduced efficiency of transformation.

Many of the most important target species for transgenic manipulation do not appear to support germ-line remobilization of transposons. In these species, the apparent stability of integrated transposon sequences is viewed as a potential advantage, and some suggest it may be possible to rely on the lack of apparent remobilization of a given transposon to insure stability. For example, *Mos1* has extremely low remobilization capacity in *Ae. aegypti* (146), whereas none was detected for *piggyBac* (121) and *Minos* is apparently unable to remobilize in *An. gambiae* (114). However, lack of detectable remobilization in a laboratory setting does not rule out the possibility that remobilization could occur during mass rearing or field release, and it would be much better to have a reliable means of insuring the transgene is incapable of further movement.

Finally, even though some transposons appear to have carrying capacities as high as 14 to 15 kb, alternative approaches can permit transformations with much larger sequences. For many functional genomics analyses, the ability to manipulate and introduce BAC-sized sequences into the genome would yield decided advantages.

SITE-SPECIFIC RECOMBINASES

Site-specific recombinases provide many advantageous properties for transgenic engineering that are lacking with transposons. The ability to allow reproducible insertion into genetically active loci can be useful in defining and utilizing chromosomal sites that have low silencing potential. Some recombinases exhibit significantly greater integration frequencies than do transposons. Integration can be unidirectional, avoiding the potential loss of the transgene as a result of remobilization by homologous elements. The carrying capacity for integrases is often far greater than it is for transposons, permitting movement of BAC-sized clones into genomes. Site-specific recombinases have been utilized as effective tools for the functional analysis of genes in a few, select model genetic organisms, most notably the mouse and *D. melanogaster* (106, 132).

Although several site-specific integrases have been developed as effective targeted integration systems, they have one drawback: Naturally occurring integrase sites are extremely rare. Occasionally, there may be functional pseudointegration sites, but these sites are generally not ideal and cannot be targeted by the integrases with the frequency of native recombination sites. This requires the prior positioning of a canonical site within the genome using transposon-mediated transgenesis and, if necessary, postintegrative immobilization of the vectored sequence.

Tyrosine-Catalyzed Integrases

The tyrosine-catalyzed integrase family contains hundreds of members that mediate functionally diverse processes such as integration, excision, and conjugative transposition. Members of this family are characterized by having four conserved active-site residues including a tyrosine nucleophile that covalently bonds the DNA upon cleavage of the phosphodiester backbone (31, 129). The best-characterized tyrosine-catalyzed integrases for genomic manipulations are the *Cre* and *FLP* recombinases.

The baceriophage P1 *Cre* recombinase has demonstrated capabilities for mediating effective site-specific recombination in a variety of animal systems, including insects (57). The *Cre* recombinase recombines DNA at 34-bp *loxP* sites that are not normally present within an animal genome. The *FLP* recombinase from the yeast *Saccharomyces cerevisiae* 2-μ circle targets a similarly organized recombination site called *FRT* that differs in sequence from the *loxP* site (120). Both of these recombinases mediate site-specific recombination either intramolecularly, leading to inversions or deletions of intervening sequences between recombination sites, or intermolecularly, leading to integration of circular DNA or reciprocal translocation of linear DNA (142). *FLP* is more commonly utilized in *Drosophila* genetics and has been successfully employed for the mediation of site-specific gene targeting in this system (54, 106), whereas *Cre* is commonly utilized in mammalian transgenesis (65).

The procedure of site-specific recombination as applied in mammalian systems, termed recombinase-mediated cassette exchange, employs the random integration of *loxP* or *FRT* sites within the genome that then serve as recombination points for subsequent plasmid-vectored gene cassettes flanked by the same recombination site (8, 72). Efficiencies can be problematic, largely owing to the reversibility of the recombination reaction (72). A modification of the approach utilizes paired *loxP* and *FRT* recombination sites in the genome to effect recombinase-mediated cassette exchange of a *loxP/FRT*-flanked gene cassette, an approach termed Froxing (72). This allows for unidirectional site-specific recombination with higher frequency, up to 14%, than used in recombination with a single site alone. Recombination at single *loxP* or *FRT* sites is a reversible process, allowing one to easily remove the inserted gene for confirmation of phenotypic effect. Recombination between multiple *loxP* or *FRT* sites positioned in a genome makes it possible to manipulate the genetics of the organism on a chromosomal scale, allowing induction of inversions, deletions, and transversions (65, 142).

There have been attempts to explore the utility of *Cre* and *FLP* in mosquito systems (57, 90). Initial interplasmid recombination assays demonstrated the effectiveness of the *FLP* recombinase (90), but an elegant follow-up study using transgenic mosquitoes with integrated *FRT* sites was unsuccessful in validating the utility of *FLP/FRT* in *Ae. aegypti* (57). The apparent incongruity between the plasmid-based assay and the integrated *FRT* assay is not easily explained, especially in light of the fact that the *FLP/FRT* system works with relative efficiency in *D. melanogaster* as well as vertebrate systems. A possible factor is the relative thermolability of the *FLP* recombinase (12). Under the heat-shock conditions that were used to induce *FLP* expression, the activity could have been severely limited. Alternative means for obtaining efficient expression, or the use of thermostable *FLP*, may lead to better results.

In contrast, the same report (57) successfully demonstrated the *Cre*-mediated excision of a sequence bounded by *loxP* sites from the mosquito genome. In a separate attempt to exploit the *loxP/Cre* recombination system for generating transgenic mosquitoes, *loxP* sites were integrated into the genome of *Ae. aegypti* using the *piggyBac* transposon and examined for their ability to support integration of *loxP* plasmids (93). In this case, no transgenics were recovered, suggesting that, at least in this species, the utility of the *Cre/loxP* system is limited to localized recombinations leading to excision. Although the *Cre/loxP* and *FLP/FRT* recombination systems do not appear to allow construction of "docking" strains carrying useful site-specific recombination sites for consistent and possibly more efficient recombination and transformation, they may still have utility in strategies for posttransformation stabilization of transgenes (115).

Serine-Catalyzed Integrases

The serine-catalyzed family of site-specific integrases includes the Tn*3* and $\gamma\delta$ resolvases, the Gin and Hin invertases, and a number of bacteriophage integrases (124). These types of integrases require no host accessory factors to mediate site-specific recombination, and they act in a unidirectional manner, precluding recombinase-mediated excision. In addition, they are capable of mediating recombination events between phage-sized DNA molecules of approximately 41 kb and the bacterial genome, which suggests their carrying capacity for effective insertion of DNA is of a similar size, if not larger. The ability of these serine-catalyzed integrases to insert sequences at pseudo *attP* sites in native genomes, coupled with the ability to evolve increased specificity for a given pseudo *attP* site, is a powerful capability for insect transgenesis.

The best-studied bacteriophage serine integrase is ϕC31, which is associated with *Streptomyces*. ϕC31 integrase *attB* and *attP* recognition sites have been defined as 34-bp and 39-bp sequences, respectively, surrounding a core cleavage and ligation sequence of TTG. ϕC31 integrase mediates recombination between its *attB* sequence and an *attP* recognition site without requiring cofactors, and it operates efficiently in a diversity of eukaryotic genomes including the insect genome (45, 70, 93).

Sequences having partial identity to the bacteriophage *attP* sequence, termed pseudo *attP* sites, occur randomly in the genome of eukaryotic cells and can also serve as effective integration sites (134). One such functional site has been identified in the *Ae. aegypti* genome (19). However, the recombination frequency toward previously integrated genuine *attP* sites demonstrates a decided preference for the native *attP* site in recognition and recombination. Similar results have been demonstrated with the related *Streptomyces* phage R4 *sre* integrase (95), and many of the other as-yet-uncharacterized members of this family of integrases will likely exhibit the same properties.

Endonuclease: an enzyme that catalyzes hydrolysis of phosphodiester bonds between nucleic acids

HEG: homing endonuclease

Application of ϕC31 integrase in *Drosophila* (10, 45) validated the significant potential of this integrase for transgenesis of insects, providing a 50% transformation frequency targeting a P-element-integrated *attP* site. Subsequent reports demonstrate the utility of this integrase system in both *Ae. aegypti* and *An. gambiae* as well as in the Mediterranean fruit fly, *Ceratitis capitata*, and the silkworm, *B. mori* (3, 39, 84, 91, 93, 116). In all cases, the *attP* integrase site is first randomly integrated into the insect genome using a transposon vector to generate "docking" strains. This results in relatively random integrations of the *attP* docking site, and in some cases, transformed lines exhibit fitness costs (e.g., 3), illustrating the importance of generating multiple *attP* docking strains for analysis before settling on a preferred strain for routine targeted integration of transgenes. Ideally, this procedure allows more routine, reliable, and stable integration and expression of transgenes in the species of concern, eliminating instabilities that can result from random integrations.

Homing Endonucleases

Homing endonucleases (HEGs) are site-specific DNA endonucleases that promote their own movement from their position on one chromatid to the identical, unoccupied position on a homologous chromatid by inducing double-strand breaks and homologous DNA repair, a process called gene conversion (127). These double-strand break points are within or near specific target sites that are between 15 and 40 bp in length and that are typically unique within genomes. HEGs can also be engineered to recognize and cleave a DNA sequence of choice (107).

In their native form, HEGs recognize a specific sequence that flanks the HEG, but only when the sequence is not interrupted by the HEG itself (13). If an HEG is introduced into the target sequence of one chromosome of a diploid organism, the endonuclease will cut only the homologous copy of the chromosome that lacks the HEG. When this occurs during meiosis, DNA-repair mechanisms can use the chromosome carrying the HEG as a template for repair of the cleaved homologous allele, duplicating the HEG within the cleaved chromosome. If this process occurs in the germ line, the proportion of gametes containing the HEG will be greater than 0.5 and in some cases may be more than 0.9 (13). HEGs are generally spliced out when the gene in which they reside is expressed, because they are part of a self-splicing intron or intein (13). Thus, gene function is typically maintained, and there is no cost to the host organism for maintenance of the HEG.

Naturally occurring HEGs are reported only in fungi, plants, bacteria, and bacteriophages (14). For HEGs to be useful in insects, the insect genomes would likely need substantial modification unless a cleavage site is fortuitously positioned within a highly conserved gene. In fact, sequences with demonstrated HEG cleavage susceptibility are present in *An. gambiae* and *Ae. aegypti* genomes (139, 147). Alternatively, HEGs can be manipulated to recognize novel DNA targets (5), facilitating the targeting of particular genes for manipulation within insect genomes.

SIT: sterile insect technique

Because of their self-maintaining properties, HEGs provide a real possibility to exploit gene-drive strategies (25). Alternatively, their site-specific cleavage functions can be useful for several other purposes. Particular applications that are envisioned for HEGs in insect transgenesis include use in homologous recombination for site-directed mutagenesis or disruption of genes that support vectored pathogen maintenance or transmission (13) as well as introduction and spread of genes that induce refractoriness to a pathogen (46). They may also be used as a means of inducing sex-ratio bias (13). In principle, an HEG can be developed to vector an antipathogen gene into any highly conserved target gene in an insect genome; it should then be able to invade the population from a very low starting frequency. Because they will remain in one genomic location and are self-sustaining, HEGs are expected to be more genetically stable than transposable elements. Furthermore, because no more than two copies of an HEG will exist per genome, gene silencing is not expected to be a problem (123). Alternatively, targeting of the X chromosome at male meiosis for attack by HEGs should lead to sex-ratio distortion (25).

All HEGs tested in either *An. gambiae* or *Ae. aegypti* retain activity and recognition capabilities in both cells and embryos, and they mediate recombinations leading to deletions or insertions in the absence of templates for homologous repair (139, 147). When homologous plasmid templates are supplied, homologous repair is also evident (147) and found at levels comparable to those in other animal systems. Among the most significant observations is that the HEG I-PpoI cleaves within the sequence encoding the peptidyl transferase domain of the 28S rRNA, a sequence that is one of the most highly conserved sequences in eukaryotes and that is located as repeated units on the X chromosome of *An. gambiae*. Attack on this sequence effectively shreds the X chromosome and would be expected to lead to sterility in males.

This X-chromosome-linked HEG site was effectively employed to induce Y chromosome transmission distortion during spermatogenesis in *An. gambiae* (148). Mosquitoes transformed with a *piggyBac* vector that expresses an EGFP::I-PPOII fusion protein under the control of the β-tubulin promoter (*βPpo*) exclusively express the fusion protein in the testes of male larvae with no loss of viable sperm production. The ribosomal DNA of these transformed males is cleaved at the X-linked I-PpoI site, yet they still yield fertilization-competent and viable sperm. Crosses with *βPpo* transgenic males and wild-type (WT) females yield inviable eggs arrested very early in development, whereas complementary crosses with *βPpo* females and WT males do not show anomalies in fertility, number of eggs laid, hatching rate, pupal development, or adult sex ratio. Cage experiments mating identical numbers of WT and *βPpo* males with WT females indicate no loss of mating competitiveness for transgenic males (148). This particular approach has several desirable features of an optimal transgenic sterile insect technique (SIT) including a visible marker, eGFP, for monitoring dispersal and competitiveness, a sexing system that could be automated, and, perhaps most importantly, complete and dominant genetic male sterility. Because the I-PpoI site is located within a sequence that is highly conserved among all eukaryotes, this approach should be applicable to other species as well (148).

Zinc-Finger Nucleases

Genome editing is the process of precise addition or deletion of genetic information via the introduction of double-strand breaks in targeted genome sequences followed by introduction of the desired modification through subsequent DNA repair. Genome-editing approaches can be useful for directed gene-replacement strategies that allow direct examination of gene function in the appropriate chromosomal context or targeted delivery of genes to chromosomal locations without the necessity of first introducing a landing site. This can be accomplished using zinc-finger nucleases (ZFNs) customized to cleave a specified DNA target.

Zinc-finger nuclease (ZFN): an artificial endonuclease generated by fusing a zinc-finger DNA-binding domain to a DNA-cleavage domain

Zinc-finger DBDs are found in the DBDs of the most abundant family of transcription factors in eukaryotic genomes (62). Each finger is composed of a 30-amino-acid sequence that coordinates one Zn^+ atom using two cysteine and two histidine residues to contact a 3-bp sequence of DNA. Because each finger can bind its 3-bp recognition sequence independently, it can be linked tandemly in a linear fashion to recognize DNA, or RNA, sequences of varying lengths. These nucleic acid recognition helices can be modified to achieve chemically distinct behavior through variations in the number and type of amino acid residues that constitute the finger structure.

Given our current understanding of the conserved structure of zinc fingers and the particular amino acid motifs that interact with a given triplet nucleotide sequence, it is possible to customize these DNA-interacting domains in combinations that permit site-specific targeting to virtually any DNA sequence. These interacting domains may be associated with active domains taken from other DNA-interacting proteins including endonucleases and transcription factors to create unique capabilities (for recent reviews, see 63, 141).

ZFNs are effectively chimeric restriction endonucleases that take advantage of a non-sequence-specific cleavage domain of the FokI type II restriction endonuclease and fuse the zinc-finger DBDs to this cleavage domain (for a review, see 102). By combining zinc fingers with different triplet targets, the binding specificity of the ZFN can be changed, effectively altering the specificity of the FokI endonuclease domain for a selected DNA sequence. Archives of defined zinc-finger sequences and their target sites are available, and researchers have developed methods that allow assembly of combinations of active zinc fingers in configurations that potentially target any gene sequence, or at least a sequence within any gene. These customized ZFNs can operate similarly to HEGs to induce double-strand breaks that may then be repaired with or without plasmids containing homologous sequences, leading to effective targeted-gene disruption or replacement.

Although ZFNs have seen limited use in insect transgenesis, they have recently received much attention as viable alternatives to standard transgenesis methods largely because of their capabilities to target specific gene sequences and mediate irreversible insertion of genes. Among other potential uses, coupling these ZFNs with site-specific integrase docking sequences should provide a powerful means for creating ideal docking strains destined for field releases. A simplified protocol employing direct injection of mRNAs encoding the ZFN has proven effective in a number of hosts (11, 130). The effectiveness of this approach for targeted mutagenesis in insects is demonstrated by disruption of the genes for epidermal color in the silkworm, *B. mori*. Mutations in the *BmBLOS2* gene results in mutant larvae displaying a translucent skin phenotype called oily (40). Direct microinjection of embryos with mRNAs encoding ZFNs that target these genes induces germ-line mutations that reflect DNA repair, generating a range of deletions and insertions within the target gene (130) and thus establishing this method as a viable technique for gene knockouts in this model organism. Presumably, the provision of plasmids carrying homologous sequences flanking transgenes for integration should work equally well in this system.

An interesting combination of site-specific DNA-binding capabilities with transposases suggests that it may be possible to utilize the best attributes of both transposases and ZFNs to generate efficient and targeted gene integration without the need for homologous recombination. The combining of the DBD of Gal4 with the transposases of either *Mos1* or *piggyBac* significantly increased the efficiency of integration near UASs of target plasmids in interplasmid transposition assays in *Ae. aegypti* embryos (79). A similar strategy was undertaken using Gal4-*piggyBac* transposase fusion in *B. mori* and *D. melanogaster* cell cultures with similar results (143). Although several studies have evaluated ZFN-transposase fusions with *Tc1/mariner* elements using interplasmid transposition assays in human cells (32, 150), at the time of this writing, there are no reports of successful site-directed transposon integration into genomic DNA of any insect species.

NOTABLE RECENT APPLICATIONS OF INSECT TRANSGENESIS

Numerous published research reports have documented the successful transformation of a new species by a new method, and several transgenic platforms have been successful enough to allow development of more advanced applications of the technologies. These platforms include *B. mori*, *Ae. aegypti*, and *An. stephensi.* The successes of these systems result from both their importance as model insects and their relative tractability to transgenetic manipulation

Transgenic Silkworms as Protein Bioreactors

By far the most published application of nondrosophilid insect transgenesis has been the transformation using *piggyBac* of the silkworm, *B. mori*. This economically important insect has served as an effective protein bioreactor for more than 5,000 years for the production of silk. The first successful transformation of *B. mori* was accomplished using the *piggyBac* vector system with a *B. mori* Actin 3 (*BmA3*) promoter driving both the transposase helper and the enhanced green fluorescent protein (EGFP)-tagged *piggyBac* vector (131). This transformation yielded whole-body fluorescent transgenic larvae. Subsequent studies have exploited the *3XP3* eye-specific promoter (133) and the silk-gland-specific fibroin light chain promoter (136) to drive expression of the marker fluorescent protein genes. Additional promoters that express genes exclusively in the silk gland have been developed for expression of any number of gene products, creating a viable transgenic insect platform to produce proteins (for recent reviews, see 60, 135).

One of the most sought-after applications of transformation in the *B. mori* system is the expression of novel silk proteins, in particular, spider silks. Spider silks have a number of potential biomedical and industrial applications (reviewed in 64, 77). The major ampulate spidroin-1 and spidroin-2 as well as the flagelliform silk proteins of *Nephila clavipes* and other spider species have been cloned and sequenced, and their structural properties have been analyzed (73). Although numerous efforts to produce recombinant spider silk proteins in heterologous systems from *E. coli* to goats have been successful, none of these hosts are naturally equipped to spin silk fibers. Current efficient and reliable postproduction spinning technologies fall short of practical production-scale capabilities.

Transgenic silkworms have the potential of providing commercial-scale production of this important biomaterial. *Bombyx* silk and spider dragline silk are very similar in composition, leading many to speculate that expression of the major ampulate proteins of spider dragline silk in silkworms could yield fibers with the desired properties of strength and flexibility found in native spider silks. Expression of the MaSp1 protein from *Nephila clavata* using the *B. mori* silk gland active *Ser1* promoter yielded cocoons containing the MaSp1 protein, but analysis of the mechanical properties of the silk fiber did not show significant alteration in fiber strength or flexibility (145). However, this study did not establish whether the MaSp1 component of the cocoons was physically incorporated into the structure of the fiber or was simply adhered to the native silk fiber. This is an important distinction because other reports have demonstrated that *Ser1*-produced proteins can affix themselves to the extruding silk fiber in transgenic silkworms (reviewed in 135). An alternative strategy that has proven effective is to fuse silkworm protein genes with gene-coding sequences of choice to express chimeric proteins that can become part of the silk fiber (53, 69).

Transgenic Strategies for Inducing Pathogen Refractoriness in Vectors

A number of methods are currently being developed to introduce pathogen refractoriness in mosquitoes by transgenic means. The most advanced of these methods include ribozymes and small interfering RNA (siRNA) strategies that target the dengue virus genome in *Ae. aegypti* (16, 33, 92, 138) and antiparasite antibodies and peptides that target the malaria protozoan in *Anopheles* species (41, 59, 144).

Attendant with the development of antipathogen effectors is the identification and analyses of suitable promoters for appropriate expression of these effectors in vector tissues. Among the most studied are salivary-gland-, gut-, and fat-body-specific promoters (66, 82, 83, 88, 151). Owing to the availability of these demonstrably effective tissue-specific promoters, researchers are able to establish transgenics that effectively incorporate a fail-safe backup of multiple layers of inhibition in the mosquito pathway for transmission. They can also apply multiple suppressive genes.

The anti-dengue siRNA strategy has developed to the point of generating transgenic mosquitoes that exhibit significant suppression of dengue virus infection and transmission. Using the carboxypeptidase promoter, antiviral siRNAs targeting the premembrane region of the dengue virus genome can be effectively expressed in midgut cells following a blood meal (27, 88). When applied in a transgenic mosquito, the analysis of suppression of both virus infection and transmission yields promising results (33). However, analyses of suppression over several generations reveals a sudden loss of expression of the effector gene for undefined reasons (34). The data clearly show that there is no loss of the transgene from the mosquito genome; however, the gene appears to be silenced. This could be related to a position effect, though one may expect such an effect to be evident much earlier. Although there is considerable importance in understanding why this particular transgene expression ceased, a global solution may be to introduce landing sites for consistent and reliable integration and long-term expression of any gene. Alternatively, insulators may be useful to insure that local effects on integrated genes are minimized (68, 111). Nonetheless, this analysis is highly significant, as it points to the unexpected problems that may be encountered when transgenes are not targeted to better-defined locations within the genome.

Whereas mosquito salivary gland expression using the *Maltase-like I* or *Apyrase* promoters produces discouraging results (21, 77), the anopheline antiplatelet protein gene promoter is capable of high yield (83, 151) and is useful for expression of secreted proteins from the salivary gland. A similar salivary-gland-specific bidirectional promoter from *Ae. aegypti* that encodes antiplatelet proteins 30Ka and 30Kb is useful for constructing a single transgene that can express two proteins with equal effectiveness. Transgenic mosquitoes expressing both a selectable marker, EGFP, and a dengue-suppressing effector antisense RNA gene, *Mnp*, exhibit reduced transmission of virus (82).

There are reported successes using the carboxypeptidae promoter for antimalarial transgene approaches as well (see 56 for review). The 12-amino-acid SM1 peptide, identified from a phage-display library (42), binds to both salivary gland and midgut epithelial surfaces, interfering with *Plasmodium* parasite invasion of these cells. By expressing this peptide under control of the carboxypeptidase promoter in transgenic *An. stephensi*, vectorial capacity of mosquitoes for *Plasmodium berghei* is reduced by as much as 100% in the model (55). Subsequent analyses of transgenic mosquito lines expressing this SM1 peptide show no evidence of a fitness cost to the transgenics, whereas expression of a second transgene, PLA2, does induce a fitness cost and would not be suitable for introduction into natural populations (89). Furthermore, an apparent fitness advantage is conferred to transgenic mosquitoes compared with WT when they are fed on *P. berghei*–infected mice (81), and this advantage is significant enough that it could favor transgenics in field releases. These results emphasize the fact that transgenic manipulation of pathogen vectorial capacity does not necessarily impose a fitness cost, but it could benefit the fitness of transgenic vectors.

Favorable results were also obtained when *An. gambiae* were transgenically modified to express cecropin A (*cecA*) under control of the *Ae. aegypti* carboxypeptidase promoter, which alters the spatial pattern of expression of *cecA* so that expression is localized in the posterior midgut, where ookinete invasion occurs (62). The resulting suppression of oocyst formation using the *P. berghei* model is significant (approximately 61%). Although fitness analyses were not performed on these insects, on the basis of the advantages conferred on transgenic mosquitoes that have a reduced burden of midgut oocysts, one would expect this strategy could also improve the fitness of transgenics relative to WT mosquitoes with infected blood meals.

Alternative expression of the SM1 peptide using the vitellogenin promoter is possible, although the first attempt suffered from an apparent associated fitness cost apparently unrelated to the expression of the transgene (74). An explanation for this fitness-cost effect that seems supported by the data is the presence of lethal recessive genes in the vicinity of the transgene. WT mosquitoes quickly replaced homozygous transgenics, whereas heterozygous transgenics seemed capable of persistence, supporting the interpretation that detrimental recessive traits are linked to the transgenes. This analysis points to the necessity of careful screening of multiple transgenics and selection of those for which homozygous fitness costs are minimal or absent (74).

APPLIED TRANSGENICS FOR EFFECTIVE PEST CONTROL

A major application envisioned for insect transgenesis is in the development of transgenic insects for biological control of both agriculturally and medically important pests (52, 105). Safe and reliable transgenic manipulation is of paramount concern for any planned field releases. In these cases, the implementation of effective transgene manipulations must consider not only the efficiency of transgenesis and optimal expression of the transgene, but also the stability of the transgene and the natural competitiveness of the transgenic insect. There are significant advances that now make this approach a practical reality for several important insect pests.

Long-term stability of integrated transgenes is a potential concern in the absence of continued controlled selection for an associated marker phenotype. This is particularly important when considering large-scale rearing of transgenic insects for field release as well as maintenance of the transgene following release. With respect to transposon-integrated transgenes, the possibility of remobilization at some future point can be evaluated in a variety of ways, but it cannot be absolutely ruled out, even in the cases in which no apparent remobilization appears possible under laboratory manipulations. Postintegrative disabling of transposon vectored sequences, where possible to employ, provides a decided advantage.

The *piggyBac* transposon has demonstrated capabilities for postintegrative stabilization because of the unique properties of its termini as well as its capacity for remobilization in many insects. Experiments defining the necessity of the TTAA target site for *piggyBac* mobilization identified another unique attribute of *piggyBac* movement: When presented with multiple transposon termini, the *piggyBac* transposase utilizes alternative combinations of transposon ends with similar frequencies as long as the mobilized unit is bounded by 5′- and 3′-terminal sequences in the correct relative orientations. Supplying duplicate 5′ or 3′ termini with a single complementary terminus creates two transposing units, one utilizing the proximal and the other the distal repeated termini (29). If different selectable marker genes are positioned between the duplicated termini, selection for integration of the larger transposing unit containing the duplicated terminus is possible. Remobilization of the smaller unit bounded by the unique terminus and the proximal duplicated terminus eliminates the unique terminus and leaves behind the duplicated terminus and transgene without a complementing terminus, effectively immobilizing the transgene within the genome (51).

An effective corollary to this approach is to position the gene of interest inside a large transposing unit consisting of two minitransposons flanking the desired transgene (23). In this configuration, the movement of the composite transposon is favored through the use of less optimal terminal sequences at the 3′ and 5′ ends of the left and right minitransposon sequences, respectively. Removal of each minitransposon flanking the transgene is accomplished through postintegrative remobilization, leaving the integrated transgene without flanking transposon sequences and, therefore, unable to remobilize.

RIDL: release of insects carrying a dominant lethal gene

Alternative methods utilizing site-specific recombinases *FLP* and *Cre* have also been proposed (115), but these seem problematic because they involve multiple transformations and more complicated mating and can result in potentially damaging recombinations such as inversions and deletions of genomic sequences. These methods could find their best utility in creating well-defined transgenic lines having landing sites positioned at optimal locations within the genome so that the effort required to generate and screen for optimal stability, fitness, and expression need not be repeated each time a new gene is inserted.

Transgenic approaches have great potential for improving upon the established SIT (2). Transgenic insects may be used to improve SIT programs by providing capabilities for sexing, sterilization, and monitoring (118, 119). In the simplest case, transgenic insects expressing marker genes can be used to monitor the success of releases. This was one of the rationales for exploring the fitness of transgenic fluorescently marked New World screwworms (48). Alternatively, because male-only releases are much more effective in SIT control (103), marking sperm of released males by expressing the marker with a β2-tubulin promoter can be used to sort sterile males for release as well as determine the success of sterile male mating upon field release (18, 48, 126, 148). Y-linked transgenics can also be useful in sorting males for release employing automated sorting devices (22, 48).

Sex-specific lethality is more challenging but no less practical given current technologies. Traditional SIT programs utilize irradiation to sterilize males for release, which can lead to reduced fitness for competition in mating with females. Introduction of sex-lethal genes could be used as a partial or complete replacement for irradiation methods, which could, in turn, increase the effectiveness of SIT programs by reducing fitness costs for released sterile males (1, 110).

A promising derivative of the SIT approach is the release of insects carrying a dominant lethal gene (termed the RIDL approach) (1). The RIDL approach has been implemented in *C. capitata* (43) and in aedine mosquitoes (39, 98). Taking advantage of the repressible properties of the *tetO* promoter and the lethal characteristics of highly expressed *rTAV* gene in insects, researchers developed a dominant lethal scheme in *C. capitata* (43) to allow maintenance of the insects by repression using diet supplemented with doxycycline. In these insects, larval and pupal death occurs in the absence of the antibiotic. Of significance was the absence of appreciable adult toxicity of the system, thus ensuring released adults would be competitive. This approach may be extended to other insect species (98) and has been modified for sex-specific lethality by incorporating an intron from the *C. capitata transformer* gene (*Cctra*), which is spliced in a female-specific fashion so that only males are capable of surviving in the absence of the doxycycline repressor (38).

Perhaps the most exciting application of the RIDL approach is in the development of a flightless female mosquito strain (39), which takes advantage of the identified differences of both abundance and splicing in female and male expression of the *Ae. aegypti* Actin-4 gene (*AeAct-4*) in indirect flight muscles. Coupling the female-specific expression and splicing of the *AeAct-4* gene with the *rTAV* gene led to a transgenic mosquito, OX3604C, which has a repressible female flightless phenotype. This mosquito strain has demonstrated effectiveness in eliminating mosquitoes in cage studies within an epidemiologically relevant time frame (149). In a controversial field release, these insects seem to have performed as expected, though at the time of this writing the published results were not available (30). This is an important advance for applied insect transgenics, and this or similar female-specific flightless strategies will almost certainly find favorable application in other insect pests.

SUMMARY

This is an exciting period for invertebrate transgenics, as the basic science of understanding the utility of transposons and other genetic recombination systems transitions to improvements in both functional genetics and pest management. The results are exceptionally encouraging and justify continued exploration of this technology in other important pest and nonpest species.

The available transposon-based transgenesis methods have allowed effective analysis and identification of antipathogen suppression strategies with significant potential, but they have also pointed out the difficulties inherent in generating transgenics that have optimal properties for potential field application. Although we are close to realizing the potential of these approaches, newer strategies still need to be explored to make this approach a practical reality, especially for control of disease transmission.

Of key importance is the relative stability of expression of transgenes, a factor that will require rigorous analysis. Even if transgene expression cannot be maintained indefinitely, knowing the duration of expression afforded by a specific integration site with a specific gene could allow for the optimization of protocols for the application of transgenics in the field. This is particularly crucial for transgenics constructed in insects that cannot be stored as embryos until needed, where simple maintenance and amplification will result in reaching the end point generation of transgene activity in a relatively short time. With the array of technologies developed thus far, many insects should now be amenable to genetic manipulation. In large measure, the only limitations are desire and imagination of researchers in finding fruitful applications of these technologies.

SUMMARY POINTS

1. Transposons have facilitated the advancement of genetic engineering in a host of important insect species.
2. Genetic engineering has developed novel approaches to pest control.
3. Genetic engineering has developed novel approaches to disease control through modification of insect vectors for disease refractoriness.
4. Alternative means for modifying genomes are needed for continued development of applied genetic engineering in insects.
5. Successful applications of genetic engineering to pest control are already being realized.

DISCLOSURE STATEMENT

The author is not aware of any affiliations, memberships, funding, or financial holdings that might be perceived as affecting the objectivity of this review.

LITERATURE CITED

1. Alphey L. 2002. Re-engineering the sterile insect technique. *Insect Biochem. Mol. Biol.* 32:1243–47
2. Alphey L, Benedict M, Bellini R, Clark GG, Dame DA, et al. 2010. Sterile-insect methods for control of mosquito-borne diseases: an analysis. *Vector-Borne Zoonotic Dis.* 10:295–311

3. Amenya DA, Bonizzoni M, Isaacs AT, Jasinskiene N, Chen H, et al. 2010. Comparative fitness assessment of *Anopheles stephensi* transgenic lines receptive to site-specific integration. *Insect Mol. Biol.* 19:263–69
4. Arca B, Zabalou S, Loukeris TG, Savakis C. 1997. Mobilization of a *Minos* transposon in *Drosophila melanogaster* chromosomes and chromatid repair by heteroduplex formation. *Genetics* 145:267–79
5. Arnould S, Chames P, Perez C, Lacroix E, Duclert A, et al. 2006. Engineering of large numbers of highly specific homing endonucleases that induce recombination on novel DNA targets. *J. Mol. Biol.* 355:443–58
6. Atkinson PW, Pinkerton AC, O'Brochta DA. 2001. Genetic transformation systems in insects. *Annu. Rev. Entomol.* 46:317–46
7. Auge-Gouillou C, Brillet B, Germon S, Hamelin MH, Bigot Y. 2005. *mariner Mos1* transposase dimerizes prior to ITR binding. *J. Mol. Biol.* 351:117–30
8. Baer A, Bode J. 2001. Coping with kinetic and thermodynamic barriers: RMCE, an efficient strategy for the targeted integration of transgenes. *Curr. Opin. Biotechnol.* 12:473–80
9. Balu B, Shoue DA, Fraser MJ Jr, Adams JH. 2005. High-efficiency transformation of *Plasmodium falciparum* by the lepidopteran transposable element *piggyBac*. *Proc. Natl. Acad. Sci. USA* 102:16391–96
10. Bateman JR, Lee AM, Wu CT. 2006. Site-specific transformation of *Drosophila* via phiC31 integrase-mediated cassette exchange. *Genetics* 173:769–77
11. Beumer KJ, Trautman JK, Bozas A, Liu JL, Rutter J, et al. 2008. Efficient gene targeting in *Drosophila* by direct embryo injection with zinc-finger nucleases. *Proc. Natl. Acad. Sci. USA* 105:19821–26
12. Buchholz F, Ringrose L, Angrand PO, Rossi F, Stewart AF. 1996. Different thermostabilities of *FLP* and *Cre* recombinases: implications for applied site-specific recombination. *Nucleic Acids Res.* 24:4256–62
13. Burt A. 2003. Site-specific selfish genes as tools for the control and genetic engineering of natural populations. *Proc. R. Soc. Lond. Ser. B* 270:921–28
14. Burt A, Koufopanou V. 2004. Homing endonuclease genes: the rise and fall and rise again of a selfish element. *Curr. Opin. Genet. Dev.* 14:609–15
15. Carpes MP, Nunes JF, Sampaio TL, Castro ME, Zanotto PM, Ribeiro BM. 2009. Molecular analysis of a mutant *Anticarsia gemmatalis* multiple nucleopolyhedrovirus (AgMNPV) shows an interruption of an inhibitor of apoptosis gene (*iap-3*) by a new class-II *piggyBac*-related insect transposon. *Insect Mol. Biol.* 18:747–57
16. Carter JR, Keith JH, Barde PV, Fraser TS, Fraser MJ Jr. 2010. Targeting of highly conserved dengue virus sequences with anti-dengue virus trans-splicing group I introns. *BMC Mol. Biol.* 11:84
17. Cary LC, Goebel M, Corsaro BG, Wang HG, Rosen E, Fraser MJ. 1989. Transposon mutagenesis of baculoviruses: analysis of *Trichoplusia ni* transposon IFP2 insertions within the FP-locus of nuclear polyhedrosis viruses. *Virology* 172:156–69
18. Catteruccia F, Benton JP, Crisanti A. 2005. An *Anopheles* transgenic sexing strain for vector control. *Nat. Biotechnol.* 23:1414–17
19. Chompoosri J, Fraser T, Rongsriyam Y, Komalamisra N, Siriyasatien P, et al. 2009. Intramolecular integration assay validates integrase phi C31 and R4 potential in a variety of insect cells. *Southeast Asian J. Trop. Med. Public Health* 40:1235–53
20. Coates CJ, Jasinskiene N, Morgan D, Tosi LR, Beverley SM, James AA. 2000. Purified *mariner* (*Mos1*) transposase catalyzes the integration of marked elements into the germ-line of the yellow fever mosquito, *Aedes aegypti*. *Insect Biochem. Mol. Biol.* 30:1003–8
21. Coates CJ, Jasinskiene N, Pott GB, James AA. 1999. Promoter-directed expression of recombinant fire-fly luciferase in the salivary glands of *Hermes*-transformed *Aedes aegypti*. *Gene* 226:317–25
22. Condon KC, Condon GC, Dafa'alla TH, Fu G, Phillips CE, et al. 2007. Genetic sexing through the use of Y-linked transgenes. *Insect Biochem. Mol. Biol.* 37:1168–76
23. Dafa'alla TH, Condon GC, Condon KC, Phillips CE, Morrison NI, et al. 2006. Transposon-free insertions for insect genetic engineering. *Nat. Biotechnol.* 24:820–21
24. de Almeida LM, Carareto CM. 2005. Multiple events of horizontal transfer of the *Minos* transposable element between *Drosophila* species. *Mol. Phylogenet. Evol.* 35:583–94
25. Deredec A, Burt A, Godfray HC. 2008. The population genetics of using homing endonuclease genes in vector and pest management. *Genetics* 179:2013–26

26. Doak TG, Doerder FP, Jahn CL, Herrick G. 1994. A proposed superfamily of transposase genes: transposon-like elements in ciliated protozoa and a common "D35E" motif. *Proc. Natl. Acad. Sci. USA* 91:942–46
27. Edwards MJ, Lemos FJ, Donnelly-Doman M, Jacobs-Lorena M. 1997. Rapid induction by a blood meal of a carboxypeptidase gene in the gut of the mosquito *Anopheles gambiae*. *Insect Biochem. Mol. Biol.* 27:1063–72
28. Elick TA, Bauser CA, Fraser MJ. 1996. Excision of the *piggyBac* transposable element in vitro is a precise event that is enhanced by the expression of its encoded transposase. *Genetica* 98:33–41
29. Elick TA, Lobo N, Fraser MJ Jr. 1997. Analysis of the *cis*-acting DNA elements required for *piggyBac* transposable element excision. *Mol. Gen. Genet.* 255:605–10
30. Enserink M. 2010. Science and society. GM mosquito trial alarms opponents, strains ties in Gates-funded project. *Science* 330:1030–31
31. Esposito D, Scocca JJ. 1997. The integrase family of tyrosine recombinases: evolution of a conserved active site domain. *Nucleic Acids Res.* 25:3605–14
32. Feng X, Bednarz AL, Colloms SD. 2010. Precise targeted integration by a chimaeric transposase zinc-finger fusion protein. *Nucleic Acids Res.* 38:1204–16
33. Franz AW, Sanchez-Vargas I, Adelman ZN, Blair CD, Beaty BJ, et al. 2006. Engineering RNA interference-based resistance to dengue virus type 2 in genetically modified *Aedes aegypti*. *Proc. Natl. Acad. Sci. USA* 103:4198–203
34. Franz AW, Sanchez-Vargas I, Piper J, Smith MR, Khoo CC, et al. 2009. Stability and loss of a virus resistance phenotype over time in transgenic mosquitoes harbouring an antiviral effector gene. *Insect Mol. Biol.* 18:661–72
35. Franz G, Savakis C. 1991. *Minos*, a new transposable element from *Drosophila hydei*, is a member of the *Tc1*-like family of transposons. *Nucleic Acids Res.* 19:6646
36. Fraser M. 2000. The TTAA-specific family of transposable elements: identification, functional characterization, and utility for transformation of insects. In *Insect Transgenesis: Methods and Applications*, ed. AM Handler, AA James, pp. 249–68. Boca Raton, FL: CRC Press
37. Fraser MJ, Cary L, Boonvisudhi K, Wang HG. 1995. Assay for movement of lepidopteran transposon IFP2 in insect cells using a baculovirus genome as a target DNA. *Virology* 211:397–407
38. Fu G, Condon KC, Epton MJ, Gong P, Jin L, et al. 2007. Female-specific insect lethality engineered using alternative splicing. *Nat. Biotechnol.* 25:353–57
39. Fu G, Lees RS, Nimmo D, Aw D, Jin L, et al. 2010. Female-specific flightless phenotype for mosquito control. *Proc. Natl. Acad. Sci. USA* 107:4550–54
40. Fujii T, Abe H, Katsuma S, Mita K, Shimada T. 2008. Mapping of sex-linked genes onto the genome sequence using various aberrations of the Z chromosome in *Bombyx mori*. *Insect Biochem. Mol. Biol.* 38:1072–79
41. Ghosh AK, Moreira LA, Jacobs-Lorena M. 2002. *Plasmodium*-mosquito interactions, phage display libraries and transgenic mosquitoes impaired for malaria transmission. *Insect Biochem. Mol. Biol.* 32:1325–31
42. Ghosh AK, Ribolla PE, Jacobs-Lorena M. 2001. Targeting *Plasmodium* ligands on mosquito salivary glands and midgut with a phage display peptide library. *Proc. Natl. Acad. Sci. USA* 98:13278–81
43. Gong P, Epton MJ, Fu G, Scaife S, Hiscox A, et al. 2005. A dominant lethal genetic system for autocidal control of the Mediterranean fruitfly. *Nat. Biotechnol.* 23:453–56
44. Goryshin IY, Jendrisak J, Hoffman LM, Meis R, Reznikoff WS. 2000. Insertional transposon mutagenesis by electroporation of released Tn*5* transposition complexes. *Nat. Biotechnol.* 18:97–100
45. Groth AC, Fish M, Nusse R, Calos MP. 2004. Construction of transgenic *Drosophila* by using the site-specific integrase from phage phiC31. *Genetics* 166:1775–82
46. Hahn MW, Nuzhdin SV. 2004. The fixation of malaria refractoriness in mosquitoes. *Curr. Biol.* 14:R264–65
47. Handler AM. 2002. Use of the *piggyBac* transposon for germ-line transformation of insects. *Insect Biochem. Mol. Biol.* 32:1211–20
48. Handler AM, Allen ML, Skoda SR. 2009. Development and utilization of transgenic New World screwworm, *Cochliomyia hominivorax*. *Med. Vet. Entomol.* 23(Suppl. 1):98–105

49. Handler AM, Harrell RA 2nd. 1999. Germline transformation of *Drosophila melanogaster* with the *piggyBac* transposon vector. *Insect Mol. Biol.* 8:449–57
50. Handler AM, McCombs SD, Fraser MJ, Saul SH. 1998. The lepidopteran transposon vector, *piggyBac*, mediates germ-line transformation in the Mediterranean fruit fly. *Proc. Natl. Acad. Sci. USA* 95:7520–25
51. Handler AM, Zimowska GJ, Horn C. 2004. Post-integration stabilization of a transposon vector by terminal sequence deletion in *Drosophila melanogaster*. *Nat. Biotechnol.* 22:1150–54
52. Hartl D. 2001. Discovery of the transposable element *mariner*. *Genetics* 157:471–76
53. Hino R, Tomita M, Yoshizato K. 2006. The generation of germline transgenic silkworms for the production of biologically active recombinant fusion proteins of fibroin and human basic fibroblast growth factor. *Biomaterials* 27:5715–24
54. Horn C, Handler AM. 2005. Site-specific genomic targeting in *Drosophila*. *Proc. Natl. Acad. Sci. USA* 102:12483–88
55. Ito J, Ghosh A, Moreira LA, Wimmer EA, Jacobs-Lorena M. 2002. Transgenic anopheline mosquitoes impaired in transmission of a malaria parasite. *Nature* 417:452–55
56. Jacobs-Lorena M. 2003. Interrupting malaria transmission by genetic manipulation of anopheline mosquitoes. *J. Vect. Borne Dis.* 40:73–77
57. Jasinskiene N, Coates CJ, Ashikyan A, James AA. 2003. High efficiency, site-specific excision of a marker gene by the phage P1 *Cre-loxP* system in the yellow fever mosquito, *Aedes aegypti*. *Nucleic Acids Res.* 31:e147
58. Jasinskiene N, Coates CJ, James AA. 2000. Structure of *Hermes* integrations in the germline of the yellow fever mosquito, *Aedes aegypti*. *Insect Mol. Biol.* 9:11–18
59. Jasinskiene N, Coleman J, Ashikyan A, Salampessy M, Marinotti O, James AA. 2007. Genetic control of malaria parasite transmission: threshold levels for infection in an avian model system. *Am. J. Trop. Med. Hyg.* 76:1072–78
60. Kato T, Kajikawa M, Maenaka K, Park EY. 2010. Silkworm expression system as a platform technology in life science. *Appl. Microbiol. Biotechnol.* 85:459–70
61. Keith JH, Schaeper CA, Fraser TS, Fraser MJ Jr. 2008. Mutational analysis of highly conserved aspartate residues essential to the catalytic core of the *piggyBac* transposase. *BMC Mol. Biol.* 9:73
62. Kim W, Koo H, Richman AM, Seeley D, Vizioli J, et al. 2004. Ectopic expression of a cecropin transgene in the human malaria vector mosquito *Anopheles gambiae* (Diptera: Culicidae): effects on susceptibility to *Plasmodium*. *J. Med. Entomol.* 41:447–55
63. Klug A. 2010. The discovery of zinc fingers and their applications in gene regulation and genome manipulation. *Annu. Rev. Biochem.* 79:213–31
64. Kluge JA, Rabotyagova O, Leisk GG, Kaplan DL. 2008. Spider silks and their applications. *Trends Biotechnol.* 26:244–51
65. Klysik J, Dinh C, Bradley A. 2004. Two new mouse chromosome 11 balancers. *Genomics* 83:303–10
66. Kokoza V, Ahmed A, Cho WL, Jasinskiene N, James AA, Raikhel A. 2000. Engineering blood meal–activated systemic immunity in the yellow fever mosquito, *Aedes aegypti*. *Proc. Natl. Acad. Sci. USA* 97:9144–49
67. Koukidou M, Klinakis A, Reboulakis C, Zagoraiou L, Tavernarakis N, et al. 2006. Germ line transformation of the olive fly *Bactrocera oleae* using a versatile transgenesis marker. *Insect Mol. Biol.* 15:95–103
68. Kuhn EJ, Geyer PK. 2003. Genomic insulators: connecting properties to mechanism. *Curr. Opin. Cell Biol.* 15:259–65
69. Kurihara H, Sezutsu H, Tamura T, Yamada K. 2007. Production of an active feline interferon in the cocoon of transgenic silkworms using the fibroin H-chain expression system. *Biochem. Biophys. Res. Commun.* 355:976–80
70. Labbe GM, Nimmo DD, Alphey L. 2010. *piggybac*- and PhiC31-mediated genetic transformation of the Asian tiger mosquito, *Aedes albopictus* (Skuse). *PLoS Negl. Trop. Dis.* 4:e788
71. Lampe DJ, Akerley BJ, Rubin EJ, Mekalanos JJ, Robertson HM. 1999. Hyperactive transposase mutants of the *Himar1 mariner* transposon. *Proc. Natl. Acad. Sci. USA* 96:11428–33
72. Lauth M, Spreafico F, Dethleffsen K, Meyer M. 2002. Stable and efficient cassette exchange under non-selectable conditions by combined use of two site-specific recombinases. *Nucleic Acids Res.* 30:e115

73. Lewis RV. 2006. Spider silk: ancient ideas for new biomaterials. *Chem. Rev.* 106:3762–74
74. Li C, Marrelli MT, Yan G, Jacobs-Lorena M. 2008. Fitness of transgenic *Anopheles stephensi* mosquitoes expressing the SM1 peptide under the control of a vitellogenin promoter. *J. Heredity* 99:275–82
75. Lobo N, Li X, Hua-Van A, Fraser MJ Jr. 2001. Mobility of the *piggyBac* transposon in embryos of the vectors of dengue fever (*Aedes albopictus*) and La Crosse encephalitis (*Ae. triseriatus*). *Mol. Genet. Genomics* 265:66–71
76. Lohe AR, Hartl DL. 1996. Autoregulation of *mariner* transposase activity by overproduction and dominant-negative complementation. *Mol. Biol. Evol.* 13:549–55
77. Lombardo F, Nolan T, Lycett G, Lanfrancotti A, Stich N, et al. 2005. An *Anopheles gambiae* salivary gland promoter analysis in *Drosophila melanogaster* and *Anopheles stephensi*. *Insect Mol. Biol.* 14:207–16
78. MacIntosh AC, Kearns VR, Crawford A, Hatton PV. 2008. Skeletal tissue engineering using silk biomaterials. *J. Tissue Eng. Regen. Med.* 2:71–80
79. Maragathavally KJ, Kaminski JM, Coates CJ. 2006. Chimeric *Mos1* and *piggyBac* transposases result in site-directed integration. *FASEB J.* 20:1880–82
80. Marcus JM, Ramos DM, Monteiro A. 2004. Germline transformation of the butterfly *Bicyclus anynana*. *Proc. R. Soc. Lond. Ser. B* 271(Suppl. 5):S263–65
81. Marrelli MT, Li C, Rasgon JL, Jacobs-Lorena M. 2007. Transgenic malaria-resistant mosquitoes have a fitness advantage when feeding on *Plasmodium*-infected blood. *Proc. Natl. Acad. Sci. USA* 104:5580–83
82. Mathur G, Sanchez-Vargas I, Alvarez D, Olson KE, Marinotti O, James AA. 2010. Transgene-mediated suppression of dengue viruses in the salivary glands of the yellow fever mosquito, *Aedes aegypti*. *Insect Mol. Biol.* 19:753–63
83. Matsuoka H, Ikezawa T, Hirai M. 2010. Production of a transgenic mosquito expressing circumsporozoite protein, a malarial protein, in the salivary gland of *Anopheles stephensi* (Diptera: Culicidae). *Acta Med. Okayama* 64:233–41
84. Meredith JM, Basu S, Nimmo DD, Larget-Thiery I, Warr EL, et al. 2011. Site-specific integration and expression of an anti-malarial gene in transgenic *Anopheles gambiae* significantly reduces *Plasmodium* infections. *PLoS One* 6:e14587
85. Metaxakis A, Oehler S, Klinakis A, Savakis C. 2005. *Minos* as a genetic and genomic tool in *Drosophila melanogaster*. *Genetics* 171:571–81
86. Meza JS, Nirmala X, Zimowska GJ, Zepeda-Cisneros CS, Handler AM. 2011. Development of transgenic strains for the biological control of the Mexican fruit fly, *Anastrepha ludens*. *Genetica* 139:53–62
87. Mitra R, Fain-Thornton J, Craig NL. 2008. *piggyBac* can bypass DNA synthesis during cut and paste transposition. *EMBO J.* 27:1097–109
88. Moreira LA, Edwards MJ, Adhami F, Jasinskiene N, James AA, Jacobs-Lorena M. 2000. Robust gut-specific gene expression in transgenic *Aedes aegypti* mosquitoes. *Proc. Natl. Acad. Sci. USA* 97:10895–98
89. Moreira LA, Wang J, Collins FH, Jacobs-Lorena M. 2004. Fitness of anopheline mosquitoes expressing transgenes that inhibit *Plasmodium* development. *Genetics* 166:1337–41
90. Morris AC, Schaub TL, James AA. 1991. *FLP*-mediated recombination in the vector mosquito, *Aedes aegypti*. *Nucleic Acids Res.* 19:5895–900
91. Nakayama G, Kawaguchi Y, Koga K, Kusakabe T. 2006. Site-specific gene integration in cultured silkworm cells mediated by phiC31 integrase. *Mol. Genet. Genomics* 275:1–8
92. Nawtaisong P, Keith J, Fraser T, Balaraman V, Kolokoltsov A, et al. 2009. Effective suppression of dengue fever virus in mosquito cell cultures using retroviral transduction of hammerhead ribozymes targeting the viral genome. *Virol. J.* 6:73
93. Nimmo DD, Alphey L, Meredith JM, Eggleston P. 2006. High-efficiency site-specific genetic engineering of the mosquito genome. *Insect Mol. Biol.* 15:129–36
94. O'Brochta DA, Subramanian RA, Orsetti J, Peckham E, Nolan N, et al. 2006. *hAT* element population genetics in *Anopheles gambiae* s.l. in Mozambique. *Genetica* 127:185–98
95. Olivares EC, Hollis RP, Calos MP. 2001. Phage R4 integrase mediates site-specific integration in human cells. *Gene* 278:167–76
96. Pavlopoulos A, Berghammer AJ, Averof M, Klingler M. 2004. Efficient transformation of the beetle *Tribolium castaneum* using the *Minos* transposable element: quantitative and qualitative analysis of genomic integration events. *Genetics* 167:737–46

97. Pavlopoulos A, Oehler S, Kapetanaki MG, Savakis C. 2007. The DNA transposon *Minos* as a tool for transgenesis and functional genomic analysis in vertebrates and invertebrates. *Genome Biol.* 8(Suppl. 1):S2
98. Phuc HK, Andreasen MH, Burton RS, Vass C, Epton MJ, et al. 2007. Late-acting dominant lethal genetic systems and mosquito control. *BMC Biol.* 5:11
99. Plasterk RH, Izsvak Z, Ivics Z. 1999. Resident aliens: the *Tc1/mariner* superfamily of transposable elements. *Trends Genet.* 15:326–32
100. Pledger DW, Coates CJ. 2005. Mutant *Mos1 mariner* transposons are hyperactive in *Aedes aegypti. Insect Biochem. Mol. Biol.* 35:1199–207
101. Pledger DW, Fu YQ, Coates CJ. 2004. Analyses of *cis*-acting elements that affect the transposition of *Mos1 mariner* transposons in vivo. *Mol. Genet. Genomics* 272:67–75
102. Porteus MH, Carroll D. 2005. Gene targeting using zinc finger nucleases. *Nat. Biotechnol.* 23:967–73
103. Rendon P, McInnis D, Lance D, Stewart J. 2004. Medfly (Diptera: Tephritidae) genetic sexing: large-scale field comparison of males-only and bisexual sterile fly releases in Guatemala. *J. Econ. Entomol.* 97:1547–53
104. Robertson HM. 1995. The *Tc1-mariner* superfamily of transposons in animals. *J. Insect Physiol.* 41:99–105
105. Robinson AS, Franz G, Atkinson PW. 2004. Insect transgenesis and its potential role in agriculture and human health. *Insect Biochem. Mol. Biol.* 34:113–20
106. Rong YS, Titen SW, Xie HB, Golic MM, Bastiani M, et al. 2002. Targeted mutagenesis by homologous recombination in *D. melanogaster*. *Genes Dev.* 16:1568–81
107. Rosen LE, Morrison HA, Masri S, Brown MJ, Springstubb B, et al. 2006. Homing endonuclease I-CreI derivatives with novel DNA target specificities. *Nucleic Acids Res.* 34:4791–800
108. Rowan KH, Orsetti J, Atkinson PW, O'Brochta DA. 2004. Tn*5* as an insect gene vector. *Insect Biochem. Mol. Biol.* 34:695–705
109. Rubin E, Lithwick G, Levy AA. 2001. Structure and evolution of the *hAT* transposon superfamily. *Genetics* 158:949–57
110. Rull J, Brunel O, Mendez ME. 2005. Mass rearing history negatively affects mating success of male *Anastrepha ludens* (Diptera: Tephritidae) reared for sterile insect technique programs. *J. Econ. Entomol.* 98:1510–16
111. Sarkar A, Atapattu A, Belikoff EJ, Heinrich JC, Li X, et al. 2006. Insulated *piggyBac* vectors for insect transgenesis. *BMC Biotechnol.* 6:27
112. Sarkar A, Sim C, Hong YS, Hogan JR, Fraser MJ, et al. 2003. Molecular evolutionary analysis of the widespread *piggyBac* transposon family and related "domesticated" sequences. *Mol. Genet. Genomics* 270:173–80
113. Sarkar A, Yardley K, Atkinson PW, James AA, O'Brochta DA. 1997. Transposition of the *Hermes* element in embryos of the vector mosquito, *Aedes aegypti. Insect Biochem. Mol. Biol.* 27:359–63
114. Scali C, Nolan T, Sharakhov I, Sharakhova M, Crisanti A, Catteruccia F. 2007. Post-integration behavior of a *Minos* transposon in the malaria mosquito *Anopheles stephensi. Mol. Genet. Genomics* 278:575–84
115. Schetelig MF, Gotschel F, Viktorinova I, Handler AM, Wimmer EA. 2011. Recombination technologies for enhanced transgene stability in bioengineered insects. *Genetica* 139:71–78
116. Schetelig MF, Scolari F, Handler AM, Kittelmann S, Gasperi G, Wimmer EA. 2009. Site-specific recombination for the modification of transgenic strains of the Mediterranean fruit fly *Ceratitis capitata. Proc. Natl. Acad. Sci. USA* 106:18171–76
117. Schinko JB, Weber M, Viktorinova I, Kiupakis A, Averof M, et al. 2010. Functionality of the GAL4/UAS system in *Tribolium* requires the use of endogenous core promoters. *BMC Dev. Biol.* 10:53
118. Scolari F, Schetelig MF, Bertin S, Malacrida AR, Gasperi G, Wimmer EA. 2008. Fluorescent sperm marking to improve the fight against the pest insect *Ceratitis capitata* (Wiedemann; Diptera: Tephritidae). *Nat. Biotechnol.* 25:76–84
119. Scolari F, Siciliano P, Gabrieli P, Gomulski LM, Bonomi A, et al. 2011. Safe and fit genetically modified insects for pest control: from lab to field applications. *Genetica* 139:41–52
120. Senecoff JF, Bruckner RC, Cox MM. 1985. The *FLP* recombinase of the yeast 2-micron plasmid: characterization of its recombination site. *Proc. Natl. Acad. Sci. USA* 82:7270–74
121. Sethuraman N, Fraser MJ Jr, Eggleston P, O'Brochta DA. 2007. Post-integration stability of *piggyBac* in *Aedes aegypti. Insect Biochem. Mol. Biol.* 37:941–51

122. Shi X, Harrison RL, Hollister JR, Mohammed A, Fraser MJ Jr, Jarvis DL. 2007. Construction and characterization of new *piggyBac* vectors for constitutive or inducible expression of heterologous gene pairs and the identification of a previously unrecognized activator sequence in *piggyBac*. *BMC Biotechnol.* 7:5
123. Sinkins SP, Gould F. 2006. Gene drive systems for insect disease vectors. *Nat. Rev. Genet.* 7:427–35
124. Smith MC, Thorpe HM. 2002. Diversity in the serine recombinases. *Mol. Microbiol.* 44:299–307
125. Smith RC, Atkinson PW. 2011. Mobility properties of the *Hermes* transposable element in transgenic lines of *Aedes aegypti*. *Genetica* 139:7–22
126. Smith RC, Walter MF, Hice RH, O'Brochta DA, Atkinson PW. 2007. Testis-specific expression of the beta2 tubulin promoter of *Aedes aegypti* and its application as a genetic sex-separation marker. *Insect Mol. Biol.* 16:61–71
127. Stoddard BL. 2005. Homing endonuclease structure and function. *Q. Rev. Biophys.* 38:49–95
128. Sundararajan P, Atkinson PW, O'Brochta DA. 1999. Transposable element interactions in insects: cross-mobilization of *hobo* and *Hermes*. *Insect Mol. Biol.* 8:359–68
129. Swalla BM, Gumport RI, Gardner JF. 2003. Conservation of structure and function among tyrosine recombinases: homology-based modeling of the lambda integrase core-binding domain. *Nucleic Acids Res.* 31:805–18
130. Takasu Y, Kobayashi I, Beumer K, Uchino K, Sezutsu H, et al. 2010. Targeted mutagenesis in the silkworm *Bombyx mori* using zinc finger nuclease mRNA injection. *Insect Biochem. Mol. Biol.* 40:759–65
131. Tamura T, Thibert C, Royer C, Kanda T, Abraham E, et al. 2000. Germline transformation of the silkworm *Bombyx mori* L. using a *piggyBac* transposon-derived vector. *Nat. Biotechnol.* 18:81–84
132. Testa G, Zhang Y, Vintersten K, Benes V, Pijnappel WW, et al. 2003. Engineering the mouse genome with bacterial artificial chromosomes to create multipurpose alleles. *Nat. Biotechnol.* 21:443–47
133. Thomas JL, Da Rocha M, Besse A, Mauchamp B, Chavancy G. 2002. 3xP3-EGFP marker facilitates screening for transgenic silkworm *Bombyx mori* L. from the embryonic stage onwards. *Insect Biochem. Mol. Biol.* 32:247–53
134. Thyagarajan B, Guimaraes MJ, Groth AC, Calos MP. 2000. Mammalian genomes contain active recombinase recognition sites. *Gene* 244:47–54
135. Tomita M. 2011. Transgenic silkworms that weave recombinant proteins into silk cocoons. *Biotechnol. Lett.* 33:645–54
136. Tomita M, Munetsuna H, Sato T, Adachi T, Hino R, et al. 2003. Transgenic silkworms produce recombinant human type III procollagen in cocoons. *Nat. Biotechnol.* 21:52–56
137. Trauner J, Schinko J, Lorenzen MD, Shippy TD, Wimmer EA, et al. 2009. Large-scale insertional mutagenesis of a coleopteran stored grain pest, the red flour beetle *Tribolium castaneum*, identifies embryonic lethal mutations and enhancer traps. *BMC Biol.* 7:73
138. Travanty EA, Adelman ZN, Franz AW, Keene KM, Beaty BJ, et al. 2004. Using RNA interference to develop dengue virus resistance in genetically modified *Aedes aegypti*. *Insect Biochem. Mol. Biol.* 34:607–13
139. Traver BE, Anderson MA, Adelman ZN. 2009. Homing endonucleases catalyze double-stranded DNA breaks and somatic transgene excision in *Aedes aegypti*. *Insect Mol. Biol.* 18:623–33
140. Uchino K, Sezutsu H, Imamura M, Kobayashi I, Tatematsu K, et al. 2008. Construction of a *piggyBac*-based enhancer trap system for the analysis of gene function in silkworm *Bombyx mori*. *Insect Biochem. Mol. Biol.* 38:1165–73
141. Urnov FD, Rebar EJ, Holmes MC, Zhang HS, Gregory PD. 2010. Genome editing with engineered zinc finger nucleases. *Nat. Rev. Genet.* 11:636–46
142. Van Duyne GD. 2001. A structural view of Cre-*loxP* site-specific recombination. *Annu. Rev. Biophys. Biomol. Struct.* 30:87–104
143. Wang N, Jiang CY, Jiang MX, Zhang CX, Cheng JA. 2010. Using chimeric *piggyBac* transposase to achieve directed interplasmid transposition in silkworm *Bombyx mori* and fruit fly *Drosophila* cells. *J. Zhejiang Univ. Sci. B* 11:728–34
144. Warburg A, Touray M, Krettli AU, Miller LH. 1992. *Plasmodium gallinaceum*: Antibodies to circumsporozoite protein prevent sporozoites from invading the salivary glands of *Aedes aegypti*. *Exp. Parasitol.* 75:303–7

145. Wen H, Lan X, Zhang Y, Zhao T, Wang Y, et al. 2010. Transgenic silkworms (*Bombyx mori*) produce recombinant spider dragline silk in cocoons. *Mol. Biol. Rep.* 37:1815–21
146. Wilson R, Orsetti J, Klocko AD, Aluvihare C, Peckham E, et al. 2003. Post-integration behavior of a *Mos1 mariner* gene vector in *Aedes aegypti*. *Insect Biochem. Mol. Biol.* 33:853–63
147. Windbichler N, Papathanos PA, Catteruccia F, Ranson H, Burt A, Crisanti A. 2007. Homing endonuclease mediated gene targeting in *Anopheles gambiae* cells and embryos. *Nucleic Acids Res.* 35:5922–33
148. Windbichler N, Papathanos PA, Crisanti A. 2008. Targeting the X chromosome during spermatogenesis induces Y chromosome transmission ratio distortion and early dominant embryo lethality in *Anopheles gambiae*. *PLoS Genet.* 4:e1000291
149. Wise de Valdez MR, Nimmo D, Betz J, Gong HF, James AA, et al. 2011. Genetic elimination of dengue vector mosquitoes. *Proc. Natl. Acad. Sci. USA* 108:4772–75
150. Yant SR, Huang Y, Akache B, Kay MA. 2007. Site-directed transposon integration in human cells. *Nucleic Acids Res.* 35:e50
151. Yoshida S, Watanabe H. 2006. Robust salivary gland-specific transgene expression in *Anopheles stephensi* mosquito. *Insect Mol. Biol.* 15:403–10
152. Zhou L, Mitra R, Atkinson PW, Hickman AB, Dyda F, Craig NL. 2004. Transposition of *hAT* elements links transposable elements and V(D)J recombination. *Nature* 432:995–1001
153. Zimowska GJ, Handler AM. 2006. Highly conserved *piggyBac* elements in noctuid species of Lepidoptera. *Insect Biochem. Mol. Biol.* 36:421–28

The Ecology of Nest Movement in Social Insects

Terrence P. McGlynn

Department of Biology, California State University Dominguez Hills, Carson, California 90747; email: terry.mcglynn@gmail.com

Annu. Rev. Entomol. 2012. 57:291–308

First published online as a Review in Advance on September 9, 2011

The *Annual Review of Entomology* is online at ento.annualreviews.org

This article's doi:
10.1146/annurev-ento-120710-100708

0066-4170/12/0107-0291$20.00

Keywords

absconding, ant, emigration, migration, nomadism, relocation

Abstract

Social insect colonies are typically mobile entities, moving nests from one location to another throughout the life of a colony. The majority of social insect species—ants, bees, wasps, and termites—have likely adopted the habit of relocating nests periodically. The syndromes of nest relocation include legionary nomadism, unstable nesting, intrinsic nest relocation, and adventitious nest relocation. The emergence of nest movement is a functional response to a broad range of potential selective forces, including colony growth, competition, foraging efficiency, microclimate, nest deterioration, nest quality, parasitism, predation, and seasonality. Considering the great taxonomic and geographic distribution of nest movements, assumptions regarding the nesting biology of social insects should be reevaluated, including our understanding of population genetics, life-history evolution, and the role of competition in structuring communities.

INTRODUCTION

Nest: the physical structure inhabited by a colony

Legionary nomadism: a condition in predatory ants in which colonies do not inhabit established nest structures and move at a high frequency to gain access to prey

It is a popular misconception that social insect colonies are sessile entities. The bulk of social insects do not spend their lives anchored to a single nest location. Social insects are itinerantly unsettled critters like much of their animal brethren, in which individuals may occupy a variety of domiciles throughout their lifetimes. In 1990, Hölldobler & Wilson (32) argued in their field-defining tome on ant biology that the prevalence of nest movements of ant colonies was underestimated. Since that time, investigators have accidentally and by design learned much about the systematic movements of colonies of ants and other social insects.

Making a nest is hard work. Both time and energy are invested into the construction or excavation of a nest. Why would an ant colony emigrate from a good hole or a honey bee colony abscond from a fine comb? Although the investment into nest structures is a disincentive for movement, even species that utilize expensive nests move on a regular basis. Investigators often have made the perfectly reasonable assumption that colonies depart from intact nests because there is a problem with the nest itself or the location of that particular nest, that moving from one nest site to another serves the function of fixing a particular deficiency. Sometimes colonies move because things have gone wrong at home. It is now clear, however, that most nest relocations do not occur because a nest is spoiled.

The preponderance of data and observations shows that periodic nest movements are built into the life histories of many social insect species, probably the vast majority of all described species. This conclusion is drawn from numerous discoveries over the past few decades in which researchers have observed the spontaneous disappearance of known colonies. Historically, nest movements have been considered to be anomalous or uncommon events (79). The phenomenon is gaining recognition and is best described in ants perhaps because of the frequency of observations of many species and the relative ease of tracking movements.

Although the ecology of nest movements remains enigmatic, the behavioral patterns of colony organization in the process of nest movement have been well characterized in model systems such as acorn ants, *Temnothorax* spp., and honey bees, *Apis mellifera* (95). Because the behavioral processes associated with nest movements in model systems have been well summarized (25, 70, 95), the present review addresses the distribution and ecology of nest movement among social insects.

NEST MOVEMENT SYNDROMES

Many social insect colonies are not bound to their nests throughout their lifetime, and the spatial and temporal aspects of nest movement are highly variable. The patterns of nest movement may be categorized into four discrete syndromes that range along a continuum indicating the frequency and relative role in the biology of the colony. The four stages in this continuum, described below, are legionary nomads, unstable nesters, intrinsic relocators, and adventitious nest relocators.

Legionary Nomadism

Army ants are a monophyletic group of legionary predators inhabiting temporary nests called bivouacs, characterized by a biphasic nest movement pattern (42). In the nomadic phase, colonies move from one temporary nest to another nest each night. The statary phase is of equal duration to the nomadic phase, and the same bivouac is occupied continuously while the colony conducts hunting raids from this central nesting site. As the ecology of nest movements in the doryline clade of army ants is particularly well described (9, 42), the review focuses on the remaining and more enigmatic nest movement patterns.

Table 1 A partial list of species whose nest movement behavior has been studied in the field

Species	Taxon	Syndrome	Reference(s)
Aphaenogaster araneoides	Ant	Intrinsic nest relocation: serial monodomy	54, 56, 57, 59
Aphaenogaster rudis	Ant	Intrinsic nest relocation: itinerant relocation	82–84
Aphaenogaster senilis	Ant	Intrinsic nest relocation: serial monodomy	5
Apis mellifera	Bee	Intrinsic nest relocation: seasonal migration	48, 81
Apis dorsata	Bee	Intrinsic nest relocation: seasonal migration	21, 41, 66
Cataglyphis iberica	Ant	Intrinsic nest relocation	15
Cubitermes fungifaber	Termite	Intrinsic nest relocation: itinerant relocation	65
Euprenolepis procera	Ant	Legionary nomadism	98
Linepithema humile	Ant	Unstable nesting	28, 29
Messor andrei	Ant	Intrinsic nest relocation: itinerant relocation	11
Myrmica punctiventris	Ant	Intrinsic nest relocation: itinerant relocation	85
Pachycondyla analis	Ant	Legionary nomadism	50
Pheidole desertorum	Ant	Intrinsic nest relocation: serial monodomy	18–20
Pogonomyrmex badius	Ant	Intrinsic nest relocation: itinerant relocation	14
Pogonomyrmex barbatus	Ant	Adventitious nest relocation	27
Pogonomyrmex californicus	Ant	Intrinsic nest relocation: itinerant relocation	16
Pogonomyrmex mayri	Ant	Intrinsic nest relocation: itinerant relocation	43
Polistes bistrata	Wasp	Adventitious nest relocation	17
Polistes instabilis	Wasp	Intrinsic nest relocation: seasonal migration	36
Polyrhachis ammon	Ant	Intrinsic nest relocation: itinerant relocation	26
Pristomyrmex pungens	Ant	Intrinsic nest relocation: serial monodomy	92

A selected number of other ant species have evolved legionary nomadism in a pattern reminiscent of army ants. These species are specialized predators and often move their nests to new locations, finding prey en route. However, unlike army ants, the nest movements of other legionary nomads do not follow the temporally consistent phases of army ants that track brood development. The nonarmy ant legionary nomads are typified by ants such as *Pachycondyla apicalis* and *P. marginata*, which periodically move nests presumably to track access to termite prey (46, 50). Similar legionary and predatory nest movements are found in other lineages (**Table 1**), such as *Leptogenys* spp. (97). While the prey acquisition strategy of the group-hunting ants *Pheidologeton diversus* and *P. silenus* is reminiscent of army ants, these ants lack the nomadic habit; colony movements occur in most if not all mature colonies and may be as infrequent as once a year (62). In a unique find, Witte & Maschwitz (98) have recently discovered that the ant *Euprenolepis procera* demonstrates characteristic traits of other legionary nomads, except for the fact that its prey are fungi.

Unstable Nesting

Many species of ants are perennially located in ephemeral nesting environments and do not require long-term physical stability of nests for colonies to thrive. For example, the ant *Wasmannia auropunctata* opportunistically nests in open areas that experience high rates of local disturbance, such as the undersides and bases of leaves in plantations and orchards (87). Some litter-dwelling species of ants, such as *Nylanderia steinheili*, nest opportunistically in dried leaves and in other relatively exposed surfaces that are ephemeral (55).

Many invasive ant species exhibit unstable nesting patterns and are capable of rapidly occupying and departing temporary nests (93). This unstable nesting habit may predispose these animals to more frequent human-mediated jump-dispersal events, rapid colonization of new areas, and enhanced acclimation to microclimates that facilitate ecological success. Although some species of unstable nesters may occupy low-cost and low-quality nest sites because other nests are not available as a result of competition (55), unstable nesting may also be an adaptive approach to tracking and maintaining access to ephemeral resources.

Emigration: a term used for the nest relocations of social insects

Absconding: describes nest relocations in which bees and wasps fly away from their nest to a new nest location

Serial monodomy: a nest movement pattern in which a single colony occupies one nest at a time but maintains multiple nests for its exclusive use

Seasonal polydomy: a pattern of nest movement in which colonies converge during the winter and spread among multiple nests in warmer periods, potentially as a thermoregulatory mechanism

Polydomy: a condition in which a single colony occupies multiple nests

Seasonal migration: a nest movement pattern in which colonies move nest locations, tracking changes in the seasons

Intrinsic Nest Relocation

Intrinsic nest relocation occurs in species with colonies that occupy a discrete nesting environment and periodically depart for another similar nesting environment as a part of their life history. This pattern of nest movement is more widespread than commonly recognized among observers of social insects. Nest relocation events have often been described as "emigration" in ants or "absconding" in bees and wasps, but this review avoids these terms as their use implies that such relocation events are uncommon or elicited by circumstances external to the colony. Owing to page limitations, and to nest movement behaviors that remain undocumented, a complete list of intrinsic relocating species is not possible; several are listed in **Table 1**.

Intrinsic nest relocation may be subdivided into four mutually exclusive categories. Serial monodomy is a pattern of nest movement in which a colony occupies a single nest at a time but maintains multiple nests for the colony's exclusive use (56, 88). Serial monodomy is described in a number of ant species from a broad variety of biomes. This habit is likely to serve an adaptive function for the colony, although the benefits vary from species to species. A number of ant species practice serial monodomy, including *Aphaenogaster araneoides* (56), *Pheidole desertorum* (19), *Pristomyrmex pungens* (92), and *Stenamma expolitum* (51); this pattern is not known to occur outside of ants.

Seasonal polydomy is likely to be practiced by many ant species in the temperate zone, in which colonies converge during the winter and spread among multiple nests in warmer periods, potentially as a thermoregulatory mechanism (6, 45, 85). Several widespread human commensal ant species with unicolonial habit and unstable nests, such as the Argentine ant, *Linepithema humile*, practice seasonal polydomy (12, 29), if not for thermoregulation then perhaps for foraging efficiency. Some seasonally polydomous ants, such as mound-building *Formica* spp. (22), however, maintain their nests in the same locations for many years.

Seasonal migration, often along elevational gradients, is practiced by many tropical bee species as well as a number of tropical wasp species. Seasonal migration may be more common in the tropics than across equivalent distances in temperate regions because seasonal shifts in elevation produce a greater relative change in temperature. In a seasonally migratory species, not all colonies migrate every year. Among the tropical honey bees, *Apis* spp., colony life history is coupled with seasonal migration, and the nutritional and brood status of the colony influences whether seasonal migration occurs (21, 80).

Itinerant relocation occurs when colonies periodically move their nests from one location to another and do not demonstrate fidelity to prior nesting sites. This mode of nest relocation prevails in ephemeral environments, such as continuously decomposing leaf litter and fine woody debris occupied by ants and termites on the floor of forests (13, 55). Itinerant relocation is distinguished from nomadism by the frequency of relocation, as truly nomadic species do not remain in a single nest for extended periods, and nomads are predators that move to track the access to prey. The termite *Cubitermes fungifaber* demonstrates itinerant relocation in Africa (65). Colonies of the harvester ant *Messor andrei* are itinerant relocators. In this species, single relocation events do not result in a shift in foraging area, but the cumulative result of several relocation events results in a shift in the use of space. In the course of one year, one-third of colonies under observation had moved their nests outside of a fixed observation area (11).

Swarming: a collective behavior synonymous with budding in bees and wasps

Adventitious Nest Relocation

It is likely that nearly all species have the capability of moving their nests in the event of some kind of traumatic event or destruction of the nest site. A few species are particularly known for their fidelity to nest sites, in which colonies can be observed and reobserved in the same nest for well over a decade. Such species, however, have the capacity to move nests on occasion, as observed in the leafcutting ants *Atta colombica* (72) and *Atta cephalotes* (T.P. McGlynn, personal observation). The wasp *Polybia occidentalis* apparently has a consistent behavioral repertoire for moving nests in response to damage (from weather or predation), but nest movements are not a regular part of its life history (86). In other species that tend to establish long-term nests, such as *Pogonomyrmex barbatus*, a fraction of colonies may be relatively mobile whereas most colonies stay put (27).

THE TAXONOMIC AND GEOGRAPHIC DISTRIBUTION OF NEST MOVEMENTS

Ants

In ants, nest relocation occurs throughout the phylogeny, and its occurrence appears to be independent of evolutionary history, aside from the evolution of legionary nomadic life history. Because many species are likely to demonstrate nest movement behaviors that remain undocumented, it is not yet possible to develop a robust phylogenetic test of the origins of nest movement behavior.

Nest relocations in ants occur in many kinds of environments: deserts, tropical rain forests, temperate deciduous forests, and the urban matrix. Researchers have surmised the function of nest relocation only in some circumstances, and there does not appear to be a tight association between biome and functionality. The author surmises, based on cumulative prior findings, that ants in temperate areas do not appear more or less likely to relocate for favorable microhabitats than ants in tropical environments are, and the effect of army ant predators on nest relocation may operate in the desert as well as in the rain forest.

Although the mode of nest relocation may be inferred for many terrestrial species, arboreal ants move their colonies quite readily, even though the underlying patterns remain unclear. Experimental work in forest and plantation canopies with supplemental nests indicates that mature colonies from many taxa of ants readily take up residence in artificial cavities (68). An increase in the diversity of cavity types increases the diversity of ants inhabiting these cavities, although the mechanism driving this pattern is not known (3). In arboreal *Cephalotes* of the Brazilian cerrado, species are differentiated by the characteristics of preferred nests (69).

Unlike ants, all adult residents of bee and wasp colonies have wings; therefore, tracking nest movements presents a greater challenge. Nevertheless, experimental and observational work has led to some understanding of nest movements in winged social insects.

Bees

The biology of nest movements in honey bees has been comprehensively reviewed by Hepburn (30). Nest movements in bees are typically described as absconding. Swarming is different than absconding as swarms result in nest reproduction by the budding of a new colony, whereas an absconding colony merely flies away from its nest to a new nest location. Among bees, the long-term nesting patterns are best described in honey bees, *Apis* spp. Tropical honey bees apparently perform seasonal migration; this behavior does not occur with regularity in nontropical climates (30). Honey bee colonies demonstrate close fidelity to migratory nest sites, a remarkable feat considering that each migratory event is performed by separate generational cohorts of worker bees (64).

Budding: a form of colony reproduction in which a fraction of workers depart their natal nest to create a new colony at a new nest

Honey bees use dancing behaviors in different contexts to direct colonies to both food and new nesting sites. When nest relocations occur, the preceding dance bears some characteristics to the classic food "waggle dance" of foragers. However, the pattern of dancing prior to seasonal migration has a distinct manifestation, and directionality is communicated more clearly than distance (21, 41). In *Apis dorsata* colonies, nest relocation events are organized differently than reproductive swarming events are (81). However, in temperate *A. mellifera mellifera*, Lewis & Schneider (48) found the reproductive swarming dance and nest relocation dance to be equivalent and suggested calling this behavior the "relocation dance," as it is performed prior to all relocation events, including seasonal migration and swarming.

Bees with annual life cycles, such as bumble bees, are not likely to demonstrate nest relocation behaviors. Little is known about the long-term establishment of nest sites in stingless bees; however, absconding events have been observed (39, 75). Because a number of colonies in a variety of species maintain nests in the same location for long durations, if nest relocations occur among stingless bees, then adventitious nest relocation may be the prevailing syndrome.

Wasps

Nest relocations in social wasps are not well characterized, although the incidence is documented in a number of lineages. The Neotropical polistine wasp *Apoica pallens* apparently conducts seasonal nest movements tied to seasonal dry periods in the llanos of Venezuela (37); however, it is not clear if seasonal nest relocations occur throughout its broad range throughout the Neotropics. The Costa Rican wasp *Polistes instabilis* seasonally migrates from tropical dry forests to cooler, high-elevation dormancy sites (36). Nest relocation events have been observed in other tropical wasps, such as *Rhopalidia fasciata* (40), *Provespa anomala* (53), and several species of *Vespa* (63). Substantial circumstantial evidence suggests seasonal migration in a number of tropical wasp species (38). Seasonal migration may be the prevailing mode of nesting behavior of social wasps in tropical localities with suitable heterogeneity to afford the benefits of seasonal movement, such as an increase in prey availability or a reduction in metabolic rate. However, even in temperate regions, nest relocations occur in 25% to 88% of *Vespa simillima* and *V. crabro flavofasciata* wasp colonies to allow for nest expansion (74).

Termites

Relative to our understanding of other social insects, the ecology of termites is enigmatic. Whereas other social insects forage for resources typically outside their nests, foraging behaviors of termites are constrained usually to locations that are not readily observed (76). Nevertheless, observations and experiments have been conducted on nest movements of a few termite species. Termite colonies are not sessile and shift locations even in the absence of significant changes in environmental conditions. Work on structure-infesting termites indicates that colonies may move their nests from one structure to another, effectively abandoning the old nest location for a new one. This pattern has also been documented in some species in the field outside of infested structures (65). Areas once occupied by a colony may become vacant as that colony grows and expands. In carton-nesting termites, *Nasutitermes* spp., nest sites change with colony ontogeny (90). Colonies of termites move their nests to track seasonal changes (61).

HYPOTHESES FOR THE EVOLUTION AND MAINTENANCE OF NEST MOVEMENT

Many functions are served by the movements of nests, which vary with the natural history of each species. Many selection forces may have worked to favor nest movement and have been evaluated with observational or manipulative approaches. Many of these hypotheses were posited and evaluated by Smallwood & Culver (84) and Smallwood (82). Not all these hypotheses apply to all systems, but it is likely that multiple factors, with varying temporal importance, may be assessed by nest-relocating species to influence nest relocation behavior (26).

Colony Growth

Colonies, especially those that live in preformed cavities that do not have the potential for expansion, may outgrow their nesting space. This pattern of nest movements occurs in *Nasutitermes* termites, which initially grow in wood but then shift the bulk of the colony to carton structures as the colony grows (90). Colony growth may trigger adventitious nest movements in temperate honey bees and potentially in twig-dwelling ants. Colony growth is thought to influence the movement of vespid wasps from enclosed sites to more open areas to allow for expansion (63). Although this is a feasible hypothesis, there are no explicit tests to evaluate whether this is a cause for intrinsic nest relocation in any species. Colony growth does influence the pattern of nest movements in the serially monodomous Central American gypsy ant, *Aphaenogaster araneoides*, as colonies with higher growth rates maintain a greater number of unoccupied nests than slower growing colonies do; however, relocation rates in this species are governed by colony size (57).

Distance from Competition

There is little evidence that nest movements occur in response to interactions with conspecific competitors. Even though distance from neighbors does not predict nest relocation events, once nest movements occur, there may be increases in conspecific nearest-neighbor distances (11, 16, 57). Encounter rates while foraging, and distance to neighboring nests, have not been found to be predictive of movements (11, 57). However, in the polydomous nesting ant *Cataglyphis iberica*, relocation events from nests are triggered by heterospecific attacks by the behaviorally dominant ant *Camponotus foreli*, suggesting that the occurrence of polydomy may exist to reduce the costs of harassment by *C. foreli* (15).

Foraging Efficiency and Local Food Depletion

Legionary nomads may continue to move nests to increase the probability of encountering specialized prey (46). It is unlikely that intrinsic nest relocation occurs to enhance access to resources, as in most cases the distances moved by species are not adequate to have such an effect, and a number of experiments with a variety of species have found that food availability has little effect on relocation behavior (57, 58). However, Aron et al. (4) found that in the laboratory the ant *Temnothorax unifasciatus* increases foraging effort after completing a nest relocation. Similarly, *A. araneoides* colonies closest to neighbors prior to relocation were more likely to forage over a larger home range after relocation (59). Whereas the removal or supplementation of food did not result in nest movements in other ant species, the removal of resources from the serially monodomous ant *Pristomyrmex pungens* in the field resulted in nest movements (92).

Ant colonies, especially polydomous species, may move nests to localities that are closer to food resources with the result of increased foraging efficiency (33). There is less evidence to suggest that monodomous species relocate nests to improve foraging efficiency, because the other hypotheses listed more often apply to monodomous species.

Microclimate

Nest relocation events have often been correlated with shifts toward more favorable microclimates. When *Aphaenogaster rudis* ant colonies move nests, the new nest locations are found in areas that afford greater insolation (83). The Neotropical ant *Ectatomma ruidum* frequently moves nests preferentially under experimental shade apparatuses from nests in adjacent sunny areas, with no effect of food supplementation on nest movement behaviors (58). Rates of nest relocation for the Florida harvester ant, *Pogonomyrmex badius*, increase greatly when shading treatments are applied (14). Unstable nesting species such as urban pest ants (e.g., *Linepithema humile*) move in response to changes in weather (28).

Nest Deterioration

When nest structures are destroyed by an external trauma, colonies often move to a suitable environment or create a new nesting space. For example, the termite *Nasutitermes princeps* often creates nests in tree branches; if a nest-containing branch falls to the ground and the reproductives survive the trauma, a new nest will be created in the canopy (73).

Many species of ants typically nest in inexpensively constructed cavities, in ephemeral environments such as the fine woody debris, and in seed pods in the leaf litter of forests; other species construct inadequate nests that may be subject to decay from flooding and other environmental hazards. Nearly all litter-nesting ant species demonstrate intrinsic nest relocation (13, 31, 55). Laboratory experiments on the social organization of nest movements typically initiate relocation events by damaging the nest structure, such as removing the cover of a laboratory colony (24).

Nest Quality

It is difficult to measure how social insects value the quality of one nesting space over another. During nest movements and swarming events, honey bees may communicate their own perception of nest quality as a component of the waggle dance as a part of the collective decision-making process (48). Once a nest is occupied, however, it is not clear whether nest movements occur for the selective advantage of higher-quality nesting sites as opposed to other incentives for relocation. Field colonies of the ant *Proformica longiseta* nest under rocks and will relocate to larger rocks if available (91). Likewise, in the ant *Polyrhachis ammon*, smaller nests are more subject to emigration than larger nests are (26). In *Temnothorax* ants, laboratory experiments indicate that colonies prefer certain nest characteristics, such as a small-sized opening to the nest and adequately large space for a mature colony (24). Preferential nest characteristics vary among taxa, as soil-nesting *A. araneoides* colonies will reoccupy nests with large-sized entrances more quickly compared with nests with small-sized entrances (54).

Parasitic Load and Disease

Social insect nests house a wealth of concentrated resources and are prone to attract agents of top-down population regulation. Parasites and disease may not be subject to localized control. Although some ants support mutualists (e.g., actinomycetes) that work against the spread of parasites in nests, disease and parasites are often not readily controlled. Some colonies may adventitiously emigrate from nests that have been spoiled by disease or parasites to start anew at a new location, as is the case for the wasp *Mischocyttarus labiatus* (49). In other cases, a persistent load of parasites may keep colonies in a constant state of emigration. Many social parasites are adapted to the itinerant lifestyle of social insect colonies. This has been documented most extensively in the army ant *Eciton burchellii* (71).

An alternative explanation for the movement away from parasitized nests is host manipulation by parasites. Hughes et al. suggest that the aggregations of workers of the wasp *Polistes dominula* away from their natal nest may serve to complete the life cycle of strepsipterans that are infecting the workers (35). Whereas for *P. dominula* these aggregations do not result in the creation of a new colony, it is quite possible that for other species frequent nest relocations may occur due to a parasite manipulating a colony into moving its nest. This could explain the pattern of relocation in the red harvester ant, *Pogonomyrmex barbatus*, in which rates of relocation vary among colonies, with a small fraction of colonies relocating much more often than others. Because this pattern is not explained by competition and is not tied to any life-history variable that was measured, it is suggested that these colonies may have sought to escape an infestation or infection in their nests that was transferred during the move (27). As an alternative explanation, differences in the genetic diversity of the workforce may account for differential responses to nest movement decisions, as has been found for foraging decisions in another *Pogonomyrmex* species (96).

Predation

Predatory attacks may be the cause for adventitious nest relocation, as occurred in the wasp *Polistes bellicosus*, in which nest relocation events were precipitated by predatory attacks (89). Predation pressure produces an adaptive benefit to maintaining empty nests should they be needed in the event of an attack. For example, the serially monodomous desert ant *Pheidole desertorum* evacuates from the nest at the moment the colony is attacked underground by army ants (*Neivamyrmex* spp.), and the colony flees to unoccupied nests maintained by the colony (19). Army ants are also implicated in nest relocations by the serially monodomous rainforest ant *A. araneoides*, although upon attack by army ants, colonies evacuate to low-lying vegetation rather than occupy one of the empty nests maintained by the colony. Experiments on nest-bound odors suggest that army ants are attracted to colony odor buildup resulting from continuous nest occupation (54, 56).

In more temperate environments lacking army ants, it is possible that slave-making ants have an effect functionally similar to that of army ants. Slave-making ants attack relocating colonies (82). Intrinsic nest-relocating species are typically subject to attacks by slave-making ants; I suggest that these species relocate nests possibly to avoid the attraction of slave-makers, as continuous occupation of a nest is more likely to provide location cues to slave-making ants.

Seasonality

Tropical honey bees and wasps perform seasonal nest movements (21). In the giant honey bee, *Apis dorsata*, high rates of swarming and absconding tied to seasonal events result effectively in seasonal migration (21). A similar pattern is found in *A. mellifera* in more tropical climates (80). The tropical wasp *Polistes bistriata* experiences high mortality associated with heavy seasonal rainfall events, and surviving colonies move their nests to microsites that receive less trauma from rainfall (17). Less work has been conducted on termites, but multiple species in northern Australia migrate seasonally to track weather conditions (61).

MEASUREMENT OF NEST MOVEMENT

Nest relocation rates can be measured by marking nests and tracking the persistence of nest occupation over time. A comprehensive approach to fieldwork is required to track colonies as they move from one site to the other. To follow an individual colony, occupants of a nest should be marked; when the colony has departed the nest, the presence of marked individuals will distinguish the focal colony in its new abode.

In a system with short relocation distances and the possibility of locating all colonies in a prescribed area, an alternative tactic for monitoring nest movements is possible. Nests may be marked and monitored at high frequency. As one nest becomes empty and a newly occupied nest is found in the vicinity, the identity of the relocated colony may be inferred (11, 57). This method is reliable insofar as adjacent colonies do not move in the same time interval between observations.

Nest relocation rates have been evaluated by three measures. In all these approaches, marked and occupied nests are checked regularly for occupancy until the colony has departed the focal nest. The most common measure of nest relocation rate is the mean nest occupancy time, also called occupation duration or nest longevity (57). Nest occupancy time is simply calculated by the mean duration that colonies continuously occupy a single nest (11, 29, 57). This is most appropriately calculated by observing a nest regularly from the time it is initially occupied by a colony to the time the colony departs.

The second measure of nest relocation rate is relocation frequency, which ranges from 0 to 1 (57). Relocation frequency is calculated as follows:

$$\text{relocation frequency} = \frac{\text{the number of relocation events per observed unit time}}{\text{the number of occupied nests observed per unit time}}.$$

The time unit for relocation frequency is the time interval between consecutive observation events. For example, if a researcher checks for nest occupancy every day, then relocation frequency would be measured as relocations per day. Unlike mean nest occupancy time, relocation frequency may be used to evaluate the rate of relocation without having to observe the initial occupation of a nest. To avoid bias, however, once a colony departs a nest, it should continue to be tracked in its new nest. The reciprocal of relocation frequency, without tracking individual colonies from initial occupation to emigration, has been called residence time (82).

A third measure of nest relocation rate is nest half-life (82). This measure uses the same information required for mean nest occupancy. Half-life is calculated as follows:

$$\text{half-life} = (\text{mean occupancy time}) \ln 2.$$

Caution is recommended in the calculation and evaluation of relocation frequency or residence time estimates. Noncomprehensive sampling (in space or time) may result in bias (82). This is most obvious in seasonally migratory species. However, even the rates of nest movements in adventitious and intrinsic nest-relocating species vary with environmental conditions. For example, colonies of *A. araneoides* are more likely to move nests during peaks in temperature and associated declines in humidity (57). Colonies in seasonally flooded forests move from the litter into low-lying vegetation during periods of high rainfall (60).

CONSEQUENCES AND SIGNIFICANCE OF NEST MOVEMENTS

Ecologists have a predilection to draw parallels between social insects and plants mostly because both are rooted to a fixed location and demonstrate modular growth (1, 52). Because nest movements may be the norm rather than the exception, conclusions that assume the sessile nature of social insect colonies should be reconsidered. In particular, because social insect colonies move, caution must be used when applying spatially explicit models of foraging behavior and competition to the interpretation of hypotheses regarding the evolution and community ecology of social insects.

Population Genetics

Gene flow is increased in seasonally migrating social insects. In *Apis dorsata*, colonies both migrate and aggregate together in large groups, and as may be expected, there is appreciable relatedness among colonies within aggregation sites. Nevertheless, migrations provide gene flow that minimizes genetic differentiation among sites (66).

The genetic origins of unicoloniality (in which colony boundaries dissolve at the local or regional scale) in nonclonal species remain unclear. In some species, such as the unstable nesting Argentine ant, *Linepithema humile*, it has been argued that unicoloniality emerged from the loss of diversity in nestmate recognition cues caused by a genetic bottleneck and exacerbated by increased aggression against colonies with higher genetic diversity (94). In the seasonally polydomous species *Formica truncorum*, it has been suggested that nest movements have facilitated the evolution of unicoloniality through the mixing of genotypes (22). Because *F. truncorum* also went through a genetic bottleneck, the hypothesis regarding *L. humile* may also apply. Nest movements might homogenize the existing genetic variance that might further reduce colony-level differences in recognition cues. However, not all species are unicolonial as a result of nest movements and genetic bottlenecks; in the case of the unstable nesting *Wasmannia auropunctata*, for example, genetic similarity may emerge as a result of clonality in reproductives, even though workers are produced sexually (23).

Life Histories

Colonies that move nests on a regular basis may be predisposed to colony reproduction by budding (8). Legionary predators reproduce mostly by budding (42), and a number of intrinsic nest-relocating species also are facultative or obligate budders (67). Boulay et al. (8) suggested a mechanistic association between intrinsic nest relocation and reproduction by budding. The queen pheromone of the ant *Aphaenogaster senilis* suppresses the production of sexuals, so there is a selective advantage for and a functionally possible option for workers to leave their mother during nest relocation to raise sexuals in the absence of a queen.

Competition

Even before Hölldobler & Wilson (32) pronounced competition as the "hallmark of ant ecology," ant biologists had followed a tradition of invoking competition as a driving force behind behavioral phenomena in social insects. Nevertheless, there is little indication that competition is the cause of nest relocation in social insects. Experiments in a variety of systems have consistently convinced investigators that competition is not the cause of nest relocation, as demonstrated above. The spatial distribution of nests is one of the major lines of evidence supporting the primacy of competition in the organization of ant communities. Even if fine-scale nest distributions are caused by competition, then this does not necessarily indicate that colony establishment, survival, or growth is contingent on competition.

A classic marker of competition in ants, both intraspecifically and interspecifically, is overdispersion, in which nests are spaced more evenly from one another than expected by chance alone (44). The scientific dialogue among myrmecologists regarding the spatial distribution of ant colonies, however, often overlooks the fact that colonies might move their nests throughout their life history.

A well-cited example of intraspecific overdispersion is the work of Ryti & Case (77, 78) on the harvester ants *Pogonomyrmex californicus* and *Messor pergandei*. Their analyses explicitly "ignore nest relocation, since nest relocation may or may not be related to the local competitive environment" (78). Nest movements in harvester ants may be directed away from the closest conspecific neighbor (16), and this may or may not affect nearest-neighbor distance (16, 27). The causes of relocation in harvester ants are unknown, although Gordon (27) suggested that the function of relocation may not be connected to the factors considered in the selection of a new nest site and that parasitism may likely be a cause for nest movements in *P. barbatus*.

After evaluating competing mechanisms to account for overdispersion, Ryti & Case (78) argued that resource competition and queen predation are responsible for spatial structuring of the community as a consequence of differential survival of young colonies. However, it has since become clear that nest relocation occurs in this system and may explain the pattern of overdispersion. Although competition among neighbors may cause this spatial pattern, it is probably not the result of differential survival among colonies and is not informative about the relationship between competition and community structure.

Interspecific and intraspecific overdispersion in Panama was documented in a classic study by Levings & Franks (47). Many of the colonies in this system nest in leaf litter and hence perform intrinsic nest relocation, and at least some of the common soil-nesting species also perform nest relocation (58). Because ants nesting in this environment may move their nests on a weekly to monthly basis (13, 55), the overdispersed pattern must be generated by the decisions to place nests away from competitors. A parsimonious explanation for overdispersion is that interspecific interactions are a factor in nest choice but not necessarily predictive of levels of competition, density, or species richness.

I offer an analogy to explain how overdispersion is not evidence that competition structures communities. A family is seeking to buy or a build a new house in the woods. A real estate agent is hired, and the family evaluates several sites to build a new house. All these plots of land are near one another, though they differ in a variety of ways. After evaluating all the potential sites, the family chooses a plot of land that is far away from loud neighbors, on a large lot, close to the spouses' work, near the children' school, and has a great view. Clearly, living some distance from loud neighbors factored into this decision. However, why did this family need to buy or build a new house in the first place? They could have had many reasons. Their old house might have burnt down, or the family was growing and needed more space, or perhaps they were purchasing a vacation house. However, it is unlikely that the family moved away from their old home because of loud neighbors. Is it fair to compare neighborhood competition in ants with loud neighbors in this analogy? The comparison may be apt, but to know for sure one would require experiments demonstrating that the introduction of new neighbors triggers nest relocation events. As described above, in most systems there is no evidence to suggest that neighborhood competition triggers nest relocation.

Consider that ant colonies moving their nests are house-hunting on a regular basis. Colonies integrate many kinds of information to choose the best possible site (25). Colonies may reap many benefits from moving. However, a colony would preferentially choose a site distant from competitors. This fact does not necessarily indicate that competition is one of the more important variables in the decision-making process, as competitive exclusion may not prevail even in environments with behaviorally dominant species (2).

Overdispersion among trees might indicate competition for light, because most trees cannot walk (7). However, because ant colonies can walk, overdispersion may merely reflect a preference for colonies to separate themselves from one another, and this preference may have no bearing on the composition or assembly of communities.

In other social insects, there is even less evidence to suggest that competition might result in changes in spatial distributions that are caused by nest movements. Stingless bee colonies in Costa Rica maintain territories, though the mechanism by which colonies avoid inhabiting the territories of competitors is not known (10, 34). It is reasonable to suggest that colonies are spaced evenly as a cumulative effect of founding decisions, differential survival, and nest relocation, although more work is needed to determine the frequency and breadth of nest movements in stingless bees. On the other hand, as beekeepers can attest, honey bee colonies may happily coexist next door to one another and it is unlikely that relocation events in any *Apis* species reflect competition. Our limited knowledge of nest relocation events in wasps suggests that seasonal migration and predation are the principal causes of nest relocation.

DIRECTIONS FOR FUTURE WORK

Our current understanding of the ecology of nest movements lacks depth. The bulk of research that has documented nest movements in social insects has been the product of serendipity: Field biologists investigating marked colonies are surprised to discover that the colonies they have marked refused to stay still. Most systems are not given further consideration after being subjected to a few tests of hypotheses to attempt to explain the function of nest movements. The majority of experiments have found correlates of movement events, but for the most part the natural triggers for relocation behavior remain mysterious.

To understand how environmental conditions mechanistically cause nest movements, detailed field experimentation on model systems is prescribed. A few potential systems that are understood better than most others include honey bees (*Apis* spp.), acorn ants (*Temnothorax* spp.), and gypsy ants (*Aphaenogaster* spp.). Functional tests of hypotheses may be conducted by developing field manipulations to observe the initiation and outcomes of nest relocation events. Iterative experiments to build on prior results are required to create a comprehensive understanding. Whereas scientific research (stereo)typically follows the course of building on prior results to construct a larger understanding of a phenomenon, this pattern has not emerged among field ecologists studying nest movements in social insects. Fieldwork on a particular species often ends when nest relocation has been discovered in the field. In most species, nest relocation in the field has been addressed only by a single publication before an investigator apparently moves on to a new research topic.

In addition to the prescription for experimental work on model systems, little work has been done to evaluate large-scale taxonomic or geographic patterns in nest movements. Working interspecifically within genera that demonstrate variation in nest movements, some lineages are likely to present patterns that may be predicted by phylogeography or large-scale climatic factors.

Continued experimentation in the field will inevitably reveal new examples of nest movements in social insects. This review has shown that there is no shortage of examples of species that exhibit this behavior, but what remains to be discovered are the overarching patterns that provide a more uniform theory for the evolution and maintenance of the phenomenon. Because social insect nest movements serve many functions and are presumably organized through a multitude of behavioral processes, the most fruitful avenues of research will synthesize colony organizational processes with ecological predictors and outcomes.

SUMMARY POINTS

1. Nest movements commonly occur among social insects.
2. Many social insects relocate their nests on a regular basis as a part of their life history.
3. The behavioral processes of finding new nest sites are better described than the ecological causes and effects of nest movements are.
4. Nest relocations occur broadly across taxa and are more reflective of the ecology of a particular species than of a phylogenetic constraint.
5. Ants perform nest relocations in many biomes, whereas regular nest movements in bees and wasps predominate in the tropics.
6. Many selective forces may drive nest relocation, and the selective forces at work are different for each species, reflecting differences in life history and natural history. In most cases nest relocations are triggered by abiotic conditions and there is little evidence that nest relocations occur in response to biotic factors.
7. Although competition does not cause nest relocations, the positions of nests in ant communities reflect that colonies choose locations distant from competitors.

DISCLOSURE STATEMENT

The author is not aware of any affiliations, memberships, funding, or financial holdings that might be perceived as affecting the objectivity of this review.

ACKNOWLEDGMENTS

The preparation of this manuscript occurred under the support of NSF (OISE-0854259). The author thanks Michael Breed, Amelia Chapman, Rob Dunn, Jim Hunt, Jennifer Jandt, Sean O'Donnell, and David Roubik for helpful comments and conversations.

LITERATURE CITED

1. Andersen AN. 1991. Parallels between ants and plants: implications for community ecology. In *Ant-Plant Interactions*, ed. CR Huxley, DF Cutler, pp. 539–53. Oxford: Oxford Univ. Press
2. Andersen AN. 2008. Not enough niches: non-equilibrial processes promoting species coexistence in diverse ant communities. *Austral Ecol.* 33:211–20
3. Armbrecht I, Perfecto I, Vandermeer J. 2004. Enigmatic biodiversity correlations: Ant diversity responds to diverse resources. *Science* 304:284–86
4. Aron S, Pasteels JM, Deneubourg JL, Boevé JL. 1986. Foraging recruitment in *Leptothorax unifasciatus*: the influence of foraging area familiarity and the age of the nest-site. *Insectes Soc.* 33:338–51
5. Avargues-Weber A, Monnin T. 2009. Dynamics of colony emigration in the ant *Aphaenogaster senilis*. *Insectes Soc.* 56:177–83
6. Banschbach VS, Levit N, Herbers JM. 1997. Nest temperatures and thermal preferences of a forest ant species: Is seasonal polydomy a thermoregulatory mechanism? *Insectes Soc.* 44:109–22
7. Bodley J, Benson F. 1980. Stilt-root walking by an iriarteoid palm in the Peruvian Amazon. *Biotropica* 12:67–71
8. Boulay R, Hefetz A, Cerdá X, Devers S, Francke W, et al. 2007. Production of sexuals in a fission-performing ant: dual effects of queen pheromones and colony size. *Behav. Ecol. Sociobiol.* 61:1531–41

9. Brady SG. 2003. Evolution of the army ant syndrome: the origin and long-term evolutionary stasis of a complex of behavioral and reproductive adaptations. *Proc. Natl. Acad. Sci. USA* 100:6575–79
10. Breed MD, McGlynn TP, Sanctuary MD, Stocker EM, Cruz R. 1999. Distribution and abundance of colonies of selected meliponine species in a Costa Rican tropical wet forest. *J. Trop. Ecol.* 15:765–77
11. Brown MJF. 1999. Nest relocation and encounters between colonies of the seed-harvesting ant *Messor andrei*. *Insectes Soc.* 46:66–70
12. Buczkowski G, Bennett G. 2008. Seasonal polydomy in a polygynous supercolony of the odorous house ant, *Tapinoma sessile*. *Ecol. Entomol.* 33:780–88
13. Byrne MM. 1994. Ecology of twig-dwelling ants in a wet lowland tropical forest. *Biotropica* 26:61–72

13. Demonstrates that nest movements prevail in a litter-nesting ant community and that relocation is frequent.

14. Carlson DM, Gentry JB. 1973. Effects of shading on the migratory behavior of the Florida harvester ant, *Pogonomyrmex badius*. *Ecology* 54:452–53
15. Dahbi A, Retana J, Lenoir A, Cerdá X. 2008. Nest-moving by the polydomous ant *Cataglyphis iberica*. *J. Ethol.* 26:119–26
16. De Vita J. 1979. Mechanisms of interference and foraging among colonies of the harvester ant *Pogonomyrmex californicus* in the Mojave Desert. *Ecology* 60:729–37
17. Dejean A, Carpenter JM, Gibernau M, Leponce M, Corbara B. 2010. Nest relocation and high mortality rate in a Neotropical social wasp: impact of an exceptionally rainy La Niña year. *C. R. Biol.* 333:35–40
18. Droual R. 1983. The organization of nest evacuation in *Pheidole desertorum* Wheeler and *P. hyatti* Emery (Hymenoptera: Formicidae). *Behav. Ecol. Sociobiol.* 12:203–8
19. Droual R. 1984. Anti-predator behaviour in the ant *Pheidole desertorum*: the importance of multiple nests. *Anim. Behav.* 32:1054–58

19. Uses manipulative experiments to show that serially monodomous ants use empty nests as refuges when under attack by army ants.

20. Droual R, Topoff H. 1981. The emigration behavior of two species of the genus *Pheidole* (Formicidae: Myrmicinae). *Psyche* 88:135–50
21. Dyer FC, Seeley TD. 1994. Colony migration in the tropical honey bee *Apis dorsata* (Hymenoptera: Apidae). *Insectes Soc.* 41:129–40
22. Elias M, Rosengren R, Sundström L. 2005. Seasonal polydomy and unicoloniality in a polygynous population of the red wood ant *Formica truncorum*. *Behav. Ecol. Sociobiol.* 57:339–49
23. Fournier D, Estoup A, Orivel J, Fourcaud J, Jourdan H, et al. 2005. Clonal reproduction by males and females in the little fire ant. *Nature* 435:1230–34
24. Franks NR, Dornhaus A, Best CS, Jones EL. 2006. Decision making by small and large house-hunting ant colonies: One size fits all. *Anim. Behav.* 72:611–16
25. Franks NR, Hooper JW, Gumn M, Bridger TH, Marshall JAR, et al. 2007. Moving targets: collective decisions and flexible choices in house-hunting ants. *Swarm Intell.* 1:81–94
26. Gibb H, Hochuli DF. 2003. Nest relocation in the golden spiny ant, *Polyrhachis ammon*: environmental cues and temporal castes. *Insectes Soc.* 50:323–29
27. Gordon DM. 1992. Nest relocation in harvester ants. *Ann. Entomol. Soc. Am.* 85:44–47
28. Gordon DM, Moses L, Falkovitz-Halpern M, Wong EH. 2001. Effect of weather on infestation of buildings by the invasive Argentine ant, *Linepithema humile* (Hymenoptera: Formicidae). *Am. Midl. Nat.* 146:321–28
29. Heller NE, Gordon DM. 2006. Seasonal spatial dynamics and causes of nest movement in colonies of the invasive Argentine ant (*Linepithema humile*). *Ecol. Entomol.* 31:499–510
30. Hepburn HR. 2011. Absconding, migration and swarming. In *Honeybees of Asia*, ed. HR Hepburn, SE Radloff, pp. 133–58. Berlin: Springer
31. Herbers JM. 1985. Seasonal structuring of a north temperate ant community. *Insectes Soc.* 32:224–40
32. Hölldobler B, Wilson EO. 1990. *The Ants*. Cambridge, MA: Harvard Univ. Press. 732 pp.
33. Holway D, Case T. 2000. Mechanisms of dispersed central-place foraging in polydomous colonies of the Argentine ant. *Anim. Behav.* 59:433–41
34. Hubbell SP, Johnson LK. 1977. Competition and nest spacing in a tropical stingless bee community. *Ecology* 58:950–63
35. Hughes DP, Kathirithamby J, Turillazzi S, Beani L. 2004. Social wasps desert the colony and aggregate outside if parasitized: parasite manipulation? *Behav. Ecol.* 15:1037–43

36. Hunt JH, Brodie RJ, Carithers TP, Goldstein PZ, Janzen DH. 1999. Dry season migration by Costa Rican lowland paper wasps to high elevation cold dormancy sites. *Biotropica* 31:192–96
37. Hunt JH, Jeanne RL, Keeping MG. 1995. Observations on *Apoica pallens*, a nocturnal Neotropical social wasp (Hymenoptera: Vespidae, Polistinae, Epiponini). *Insectes Soc.* 42:223–36
38. Hunt JH, O'Donnell S, Chernoff N, Brownie C. 2001. Observations on two Neotropical swarm-founding wasps, *Agelaia yepocapa* and *A. panamaensis* (Hymenoptera: Vespidae). *Ann. Entomol. Soc. Am.* 94:555–62
39. Inoue T, Sakagami S, Salmah S, Nukmal N. 1984. Discovery of successful absconding in the stingless bee *Trigona (Tetragonula) laeviceps*. *J. Apic. Res.* 23:136–42
40. Itô Y. 1992. Relocation of nests by swarms and nest reconstruction in late autumn in the primitively eusocial wasp, *Ropalidia fasciata*, with discussions on the role of swarming. *J. Ethol.* 10:109–17
41. Koeniger N, Koeniger G. 1980. Observations and experiments on migration and dance communication of *Apis dorsata* in Sri Lanka. *J. Apicult. Res.* 19:21–34
42. Kronauer DJC. 2009. Recent advances in army ant biology (Hymenoptera: Formicidae). *Myrmecol. News* 12:51–65
43. Kugler C, Hincapié MdC. 1983. Ecology of the ant *Pogonomyrmex mayri*: distribution, abundance, nest structure, and diet. *Biotropica* 15:190–98
44. Lach L, Parr C, Abbott K. 2010. *Ant Ecology*. Oxford: Oxford Univ. Press
45. Laskis KO, Tschinkel WR. 2009. The seasonal natural history of the ant, *Dolichoderus mariae*, in northern Florida. *J. Insect Sci.* 9:2
46. Leal IR, Oliveira PS. 1995. Behavioral ecology of the Neotropical termite-hunting ant *Pachycondyla* (=*Termitopone*) *marginata*: colony founding, group-raiding and migratory patterns. *Behav. Ecol. Sociobiol.* 37:373–83
47. **Levings SC, Franks NR. 1982. Patterns of nest dispersion in a tropical ground ant community. *Ecology* 63:338–44**

47. Examines a finely detailed spatially explicit search in an itinerant ant community, showing that colonies space themselves apart from one another.

48. Lewis LA, Schneider SS. 2008. "Migration dances" in swarming colonies of the honey bee, *Apis mellifera*. *Apidologie* 39:354–61
49. Litte M. 1981. Social biology of the polistine wasp *Mischocyttarus labiatus*: survival in a Colombian rain forest. *Smiths. Contrib. Zool.* 327:1–27
50. Longhurst C, Howse PE. 1979. Foraging, recruitment and emigration in *Megaponera foetens* (Fab.) (Hymenoptera: Formicidae) from the Nigerian Guinea savanna. *Insectes Soc.* 26:204–15
51. Longino JT. 2005. Complex nesting behavior by two Neotropical species of the ant genus *Stenamma* (Hymenoptera: Formicidae). *Biotropica* 37:670–75
52. López F, Serrano JM, Acosta FJ. 1994. Parallels between the foraging strategies of ants and plants. *Trends Ecol. Evol.* 9:150–53
53. Matsuura M. 1999. Size and composition of swarming colonies in *Provespa anomala* (Hymenoptera, Vespidae), a nocturnal social wasp. *Insectes Soc.* 46:219–23
54. McGlynn T. 2010. Serial monodomy in the gypsy ant, *Aphaenogaster araneoides*: Does nest odor reduction influence colony relocation? *J. Insect Sci.* 10:1–7
55. McGlynn TP. 2006. Ants on the move: resource limitation of a litter-nesting ant community in Costa Rica. *Biotropica* 38:419–27
56. McGlynn TP. 2007. Serial monodomy in ants: an antipredator strategy? *Ecol. Entomol.* 32:621–26
57. McGlynn TP, Carr RA, Carson JH, Buma J. 2004. Frequent nest relocation in the ant *Aphaenogaster araneoides*: resources, competition, and natural enemies. *Oikos* 106:611–21
58. McGlynn TP, Dunn T, Wayman E, Romero A. 2010. A thermophile in the shade: light-directed nest relocation in the Costa Rican ant *Ectatomma ruidum*. *J. Trop. Ecol.* 26:559–62
59. McGlynn TP, Shotell MD, Kelly MS. 2003. Responding to a variable environment: home range, foraging behavior, and nest relocation in the Costa Rican rainforest ant *Aphaenogaster araneoides*. *J. Insect Behav.* 16:687–701
60. Mertl AL, Wilkie KTR, Traniello JFA. 2009. Impact of flooding on the species richness, density and composition of amazonian litter-nesting ants. *Biotropica* 41:633–41
61. Miller LR. 1994. Nests and queen migration in *Schedorhinotermes actuosus* (Hill), *Schedorhinotermes breinli* (Hill) and *Coptotermes acinaciformis* (Froggatt) (Isoptera: Rhinotermitidae). *Aust. J. Entomol.* 33:317–18

62. Moffett MW. 1988. Nesting, emigrations, and colony foundation in two group-hunting myrmicine ants (Hymenoptera: Formicidae: Pheidologeton). In *Advances in Myrmecology*, ed. JC Trager, pp. 355–70. Leiden: Brill
63. Nakamura M, Sonthichai S. 2004. Nesting habits of some hornet species (Hymenoptera, Vespidae) in northern Thailand. *Kasetsart J.* 38:196–206
64. Neumann P, Koeniger N, Koeniger G, Tingek S, Kryger P, Moritz RFA. 2000. Entomology: home-site fidelity in migratory honeybees. *Nature* 406:474–75
65. Noirot C, Noirot-Timothée C, Han S. 1986. Migration and nest building in *Cubitermes fungifaber* (Isoptera, Termitidae). *Insectes Soc.* 33:361–74
66. Paar J, Oldroyd BP, Huettinger E, Kastberger G. 2004. Genetic structure of an *Apis dorsata* population: the significance of migration and colony aggregation. *J. Hered.* 95:119–26
67. Peeters C, Ito F. 2001. Colony dispersal and the evolution of queen morphology in social Hymenoptera. *Annu. Rev. Entomol.* 46:601–30
68. Philpott SM, Foster PF. 2005. Nest-site limitation in coffee agroecosystems: Artificial nests maintain diversity of arboreal ants. *Ecol. Appl.* 15:1478–85
69. Powell S. 2008. Ecological specialization and the evolution of a specialized caste in *Cephalotes* ants. *Funct. Ecol.* 22:902–11
70. Pratt SC. 2008. Efficiency and regulation of recruitment during colony emigration by the ant *Temnothorax curvispinosus*. *Behav. Ecol. Sociobiol.* 62:1369–76
71. Rettenmeyer C, Rettenmeyer M, Joseph J, Berghoff S. 2011. The largest animal association centered on one species: the army ant *Eciton burchellii* and its more than 300 associates. *Insectes Soc.* 58:281–293

71. The culmination of a career dedicated to the study of army ant parasites and other associates.

72. Rockwood LL. 1973. Distribution, density and dispersion of two species of *Atta* (Hymenoptera: Formicidae) in Guanacaste Province, Costa Rica. *J. Anim. Ecol.* 42:803–17
73. Roisin Y, Pasteels JM. 1986. Replacement of reproductives in *Nasutitermes princeps* (Desneux) (Isoptera: Termitidae). *Behav. Ecol. Sociobiol.* 18:437–42
74. Ross KG, Matthews RW. 1991. *The Social Biology of Wasps*. Ithaca, NY: Cornell Univ. Press
75. Roubik DW. 2006. Stingless bee nesting biology. *Apidologie* 37:124–43
76. Rupf T, Roisin Y. 2008. Coming out of the woods: Do termites need a specialized worker caste to search for new food sources? *Naturwissenschaften* 95:811–19
77. Ryti RT, Case TJ. 1986. Overdispersion of ant colonies: a test of hypotheses. *Oecologia* 69:446–53
78. Ryti RT, Case TJ. 1992. The role of neighborhood competition in the spacing and diversity of ant communities. *Am. Nat.* 139:355–74
79. Sallee RM, King RL. 1947. An ant colony which moved over two hundred feet. *Proc. Iowa Acad. Sci.* 54:349–52
80. Schneider SS, McNally LC. 1992. Factors influencing seasonal absconding in colonies of the African honey bee *Apis mellifera scutellata*. *Insectes Soc.* 39:403–23
81. Schneider SS, McNally LC. 1994. Waggle dance behavior associated with seasonal absconding in colonies of the African honey bee, *Apis mellifera scutellata*. *Insectes Soc.* 41:115–27
82. Smallwood J. 1982. Nest relocations in ants. *Insectes Soc.* 29:138–47

82. An early field effort to systematically study the pattern of nest relocations.

83. Smallwood J. 1982. The effect of shade and competition of emigration rate in the ant *Aphaenogaster rudis*. *Ecology* 63:124–34
84. Smallwood J, Culver DC. 1979. Colony movements of some North American ants. *J. Anim. Ecol.* 48:373–82
85. Snyder LE, Herbers JM. 1991. Polydomy and sexual allocation ratios in the ant *Myrmica punctiventris*. *Behav. Ecol. Sociobiol.* 28:409–15

85. A detailed description of seasonal polydomy in a single ant community.

86. Sonnentag PJ, Jeanne RL. 2009. Initiation of absconding-swarm emigration in the social wasp *Polybia occidentalis*. *J. Insect Sci.* 9:1–11
87. Spencer H. 1941. The small fire ant *Wasmannia* in citrus groves: a preliminary report. *Fla. Entomol.* 24:6–14
88. Steiner FM, Crozier RH, Schlick-Steiner BC. 2010. Colony structure. In *Ant Ecology*, ed. L Lach, CL Parr, KL Abbott, pp. 177–94. Oxford, UK: Oxford Univ. Press

89. Strassmann JE, Queller DC, Hughes CR. 1988. Predation and the evolution of sociality in the paper wasp *Polistes bellicosus*. *Ecology* 69:1497–505
90. Thorne BL, Haverty MI. 2000. Nest growth and survivorship in three species of Neotropical *Nasutitermes* (Isoptera: Termitidae). *Environ. Entomol.* 29:256–64
91. Tinaut A, Fernández Escudero I, Ruano F, Cerdá X. 1999. The relationship of nest rock dimensions to reproductive success and nest permanence in a high mountain ant, *Proformica longiseta* (Hymenoptera: Formicidae). *Sociobiology* 34:99–117
92. Tsuji K. 1988. Nest relocations in the Japanese queenless ant *Pristomyrmex pungens* Mayr. (Hymenoptera: Formicidae). *Insectes Soc.* 35:321–40
93. Tsutsui ND, Suarez AV. 2003. The colony structure and population biology of invasive ants. *Conserv. Biol.* 17:48–58
94. Tsutsui ND, Suarez AV, Grosberg RK. 2003. Genetic diversity, asymmetrical aggression, and recognition in a widespread invasive species. *Proc. Natl. Acad. Sci. USA* 100:1078–83
95. Visscher PK. 2007. Group decision making in nest-site selection among social insects. *Annu. Rev. Entomol.* 52:255–75
96. Wiernasz DC, Hines J, Parker DG, Cole BJ. 2008. Mating for variety increases foraging activity in the harvester ant, *Pogonomyrmex occidentalis*. *Mol. Ecol.* 17:1137–44
97. Witte V, Maschwitz U. 2000. Raiding and emigration dynamics in the ponerine army ant *Leptogenys distinguenda* (Hymenoptera, Formicidae). *Insectes Soc.* 47:76–83
98. Witte V, Maschwitz U. 2008. Mushroom harvesting ants in the tropical rainforest. *Naturwissenschaften* 95:1049–54

Molecular Bases of Plant Resistance to Arthropods

C. Michael Smith[1,*] and Stephen L. Clement[2]

[1]Department of Entomology, Kansas State University, Manhattan, Kansas 66506; email: cmsmith@ksu.edu

[2]Retired, USDA ARS Plant Germplasm Introduction and Testing Research Unit, Washington State University, Pullman, Washington 99164-6402

Annu. Rev. Entomol. 2012. 57:309–28

First published online as a Review in Advance on September 9, 2011

The *Annual Review of Entomology* is online at ento.annualreviews.org

This article's doi:
10.1146/annurev-ento-120710-100642

0066-4170/12/0107-0309$20.00

*Corresponding author

Keywords

antixenosis, antibiosis, QTL, marker-assisted selection, tolerance, virulence

Abstract

Arthropod-resistant crops provide significant ecological and economic benefits to global agriculture. Incompatible interactions involving resistant plants and avirulent pest arthropods are mediated by constitutively produced and arthropod-induced plant proteins and defense allelochemicals synthesized by resistance gene products. Cloning and molecular mapping have identified the *Mi-1.2* and *Vat* arthropod resistance genes as CC-NBS-LRR (coiled coil–nucleotide binding site–leucine rich repeat) subfamily NBS-LRR resistance proteins, as well as several resistance gene analogs. Genetic linkage mapping has identified more than 100 plant resistance gene loci and linked molecular markers used in cultivar development. Rice and sorghum arthropod-resistant cultivars and, to a lesser extent, raspberry and wheat cultivars are components of integrated pest management (IPM) programs in Asia, Australia, Europe, and North America. Nevertheless, arthropod resistance in most food and fiber crops has not been integrated due primarily to the application of synthetic insecticides. Plant and arthropod genomics provide many opportunities to more efficiently develop arthropod-resistant plants, but integration of resistant cultivars into IPM programs will succeed only through interdisciplinary collaboration.

INTRODUCTION

Host plant resistance (HPR): the sum of the genetically inherited qualities that results in a plant of one cultivar or species being less damaged by a pest arthropod than a susceptible plant lacking these qualities

Antibiosis: the adverse effects of a resistant plant on the survival, development, or fecundity of an arthropod

The evolutionary history of terrestrial plants and their arthropod associates is inextricably linked. This coevolutionary relationship, widely accepted by biologists and ecologists, is based on an inherent feature of life on earth in which land plants and herbivores have continually adapted to changing environments and biotic pressures to survive (43, 51). Following the evolution of the earliest land plants from their aquatic ancestors in the Mid-Ordovician (~450 Ma), vascular plants began to evolve (4), followed by large-scale arthropod speciation (38). During arthropod speciation, herbivory began to impose natural selection on vascular plants, leading to plant expression of direct and indirect defensive adaptations (42, 90). In conforming with the reciprocal adaptation of interacting species (coevolutionary hypothesis), phytophagous arthropods then evolved ways to overcome plant defenses (42, 43).

Although the coevolutionary nature of arthropod–host plant associations is not universally accepted by scientists (see 42), vascular plant evolution has yielded vast genetic diversity, enabling plants to surmount biotic pressures (including arthropods) and abiotic stresses over several millennia. *Homo sapiens* inherited this plant biodiversity, recognized it, and began to use portions of it to form agrarian societies about 10,000 years ago. These first efforts at farming involved the cultivation of wild crop relatives in small gardens and fields, a far cry from today's practice of cropping high-yielding, genetically uniform cultivars on large tracks of land (51). As significant as plant genetic diversity was for early agriculture, so it is for the future of world agricultural production. Such diversity is widely recognized and highly sought by plant breeders and entomologists engaged in the development of pest-arthropod-resistant crops through the use of conventional and molecular genetic tools to characterize arthropod-plant relationships (30, 115, 125, 144).

In modern agriculture, host plant resistance (HPR) is an integral component, if not the foundation, of arthropod pest regulation in integrated pest management (IPM) programs (90, 115, 125). The ecological benefits associated with the deployment of resistance are reduced or eliminated insecticide applications and residues, cleaner streams and lakes, and reduced mortality of beneficial arthropod populations. Arthropod-resistant cultivars are economically advantageous for producers because arthropod control is included in the cost of the seed alone (115). The annual value of arthropod resistance genes currently deployed in global agriculture is greater than US$2 billion (115). A detriment to the use of resistant cultivars is yield drag or other plant fitness costs related to the use of resistance genes from wild relatives of crop species and other unadapted plant germplasm. In a few instances, the level of antibiosis resistance in a cultivar from such relatives may be incompatible with some biological control agents (47). Moreover, antibiosis resistance (see below) controlled by single genes inherited as dominant traits may be transitory, which could promote the development of populations of virulent individuals that are unaffected by plant resistance genes (42, 115, 125, 138).

This review is an in-depth examination of molecular genetic tools and approaches for HPR to arthropod pests, with specific attention given to advances in using these tools and approaches to develop a wide diversity of resistant germplasm and crop cultivars over the past decade. Thus, we update and complement previous literature on the subject (88, 104, 115, 118, 138, 144). We briefly cover the history, basic concepts (resistance categories and mechanisms), factors affecting the expression of plant resistance, and transgenic plant resistance to arthropods because previous reviews have comprehensively addressed these subjects. We conclude this review by describing the current state of affairs regarding the integration and deployment of arthropod resistance genes into IPM programs, and in so doing, we attempt to determine the extent molecular genetic and genomic innovations have benefited producers and consumers through the delivery of arthropod-resistant crops.

PLANT RESISTANCE TO ARTHROPOD PESTS: VIGNETTES

History

Farmers engaged in the early practice of agriculture in the Fertile Crescent and other regions of the world several thousand years ago likely recognized that the plants they selected for agricultural purposes varied in susceptibility to pests (51, 90). Insect-resistant cultivars were cultivated much later, during the onset of applied entomology in the eighteenth and nineteenth centuries. Such cultivars included *Mayetiola destructor*–resistant wheat (cv. Underhill) in the 1780s in New York and *Eriosoma lanigerum*–resistant apple cultivars (cv. Winter Majetin) in the United Kingdom. Additionally, the grafting of European grapevines onto rootstocks of native American grapes resistant to *Daktulosphaira vitifoliae* restored the profitability of the French wine industry (90, 113).

The breeding of arthropod-resistant plants was formalized after the rediscovery of Mendel's law of heredity in 1900 and blossomed as a field of research in the first half of the twentieth century with the work of Painter (88). Over the past 60 years, breeding crops for pest resistance has accelerated through the efforts of public- and private-sector plant breeders and entomologists in several countries, including active involvement of researchers at Consultative Group for International Agricultural Research (CGIAR) agricultural research centers. These efforts led to spectacular successes in developing arthropod-resistant crops during the Green Revolution in Southeast Asia during the 1960s. A classic example is the development of the rice cultivar IR36, which is resistant to multiple insect pests. This cultivar, developed at the International Rice Research Institute in the 1970s and cropped on 11 million ha by the early 1980s, provided an annual income increase of approximately $1 billion to Asian rice farmers (90, 115).

By the mid-1970s, over 500 arthropod-resistant cultivars and parent and germplasm lines of food and fiber crops had been developed and registered in the United States (113). Moreover, twentieth-century researchers recorded resistance to several arthropod pest species in crop cultivars not intentionally selected for resistance (58). With the advent and use of molecular tools over the past 30 years, the field of plant resistance to arthropods has been transformed into a new era, offering enormous opportunities for continued development of new crop cultivars with genes for durable arthropod resistance (85, 115, 144).

Tolerance: a polygenic trait enabling a plant to withstand or recover from arthropod damage without adversely affecting the growth or survival of the attacking arthropod

Antixenosis: the nonpreference reaction of an arthropod to a resistant plant that occurs when biophysical or allelochemical factors adversely affect arthropod behavior, leading to delayed acceptance and possible outright rejection of a plant as a host

Resistance Categories

Plant tolerance is a complex set of genetic traits that enable a plant to withstand or recover from arthropod damage. This plant characteristic, which does not adversely affect the growth and survival of attacking arthropods, exists in crop cultivars across a wide taxonomic range (90, 115). Antixenosis describes the nonpreference reaction of arthropods to a resistant plant. Antixenosis occurs when plant morphological or chemical factors adversely affect arthropod behavior, leading to delayed acceptance and possible outright rejection of a plant as a host. By contrast, the antibiosis category of plant resistance occurs when a resistant plant adversely affects the life-history traits (survival, development, fecundity) of an arthropod attempting to use that plant as a host (**Figure 1**). **Table 1** presents the category(s) of resistance identified for more than 40 arthropod resistance genes presently characterized by molecular mapping. Antibiosis resistance alone or in combination with other categories has been identified in more than 90% of the cases in **Table 1**. Conversely, plant tolerance has been identified in less than 10% of the cases. Several excellent reviews on resistance categories in a wide diversity of crop cultivars and germplasm lines have been published (30, 90, 115).

Table 1 Crop-plant arthropod resistance genes, number of resistance loci, gene products (where known), inheritance of resistance, and phenotypic resistance categories

Plant	Arthropod pest(s)	Order	Gene(s)[a]	Category(ies)	Reference(s)[b]
Apple	*Dysaphis devecta*	Hemiptera	*Sd-* (3); QTL	Ab	25, 123
	Dysaphis plantaginea	Hemiptera	*Sm-h*; QTL	Ab	2, 123
	Eriosoma lanigerum	Hemiptera	*Er* (3)	Ab, Ax	18, 106
Barley	*Diuraphis noxia*	Hemiptera	*Rdn* (2); QTL unnamed; QTL	Ab, Tol	27, 82, 83
	Rhopalosiphum padi	Hemiptera			
	Schizaphis graminum	Hemiptera	*Rsg* (2)	Ab, Tol	94
Barrel medic	*Acyrthosiphon kondoi*	Hemiptera	*AKR, AIN RAP1 TTR*	Ab, Ax, Tol	63, 122
	Acyrthosiphon pisum,	Hemiptera		Ab, Ax, Tol	
	Therioaphis maculata	Hemiptera		Ab, Ax, Tol	
Common bean	*Apion godmani*	Coleoptera	*Arc1* (2) (arcelin) *Agm, Agr*	Ab	8, 9, 87
	Zabrotes subfasciatus	Coleoptera		Ab	
	Thrips palmi	Thysanoptera	Unnamed; QTL	Tol	41
Cowpea	*Aphis craccivora*	Hemiptera	*Rac* (2)	Ab	84
Lettuce	*Nasonovia ribisnigri*	Hemiptera	*Nr*	Ab	76
	Pemphigus bursarius	Hemiptera	*Ra* or *Lra*	Ab	141
Maize	*Ostrinia nubilalis*	Lepidoptera	*bx* (7) DIMBOA), leaf cell wall factors; QTL	Ab	19, 20
	Diatraea grandiosella	Lepidoptera	*Glossy15* (1) (leaf structure); QTL	Ab	12, 17
	Diatraea saccharalis	Lepidoptera			
	Spodoptera frugiperda	Lepidoptera	*Mir* (4) (cysteine proteinase)	Ab	92
	Helicoverpa zea	Lepidoptera	*p1* (1) (maysin); QTL	Ab	48, 148
	Rhopalosiphum maidis	Hemiptera	*aph* (2)	Ab	21
Melon	*Aphis gossypii*	Hemiptera	*Vat* (1) (CC-NBS-LRR); QTL	Ab, Ax	13, 33
Mungbean	*Callosobruchus* spp	Coleoptera	*Br* (1)	Ab	70
	Zabrotes subfasciatus	Coleoptera			
	Riptortus clavatus	Coleoptera			
Pea	*Bruchus pisorum*	Coleoptera	*Np*	Ab	34
Peach	*Myzus persicae*	Hemiptera	*Rm1*	Ab, Ax	91
Peanut	*Aphis craccivora*	Hemiptera	Unnamed	Ab	49
Pear	*Dysaphis pyri*	Hemiptera	*Dp-1*	Ab	39
Perennial ryegrass	*Listronotus bonariensis*	Coleoptera	*perA* (peramine-endophyte alkaloid)	Ax	129
Potato	*Leptinotarsa decemlineata*	Coleoptera	*Lep, AL* (2) (leptine alkaloids); QTL	Ab, Ax	105
Raspberry	*Amphorophora idaei*	Hemiptera	*A* (12), *dw*	Ab, Ax	7, 107
Rice	*Nilaparvata lugens*	Hemiptera	*Bph* (≥23); *Qbp* (2); QTL	Ab, Ax, Tol	98, 99, 102
	Sogatella furcifera	Hemiptera	*Wbph* (6), *wbph* (1)	Unknown	128
	Laodelphax striatellus	Hemiptera	Unnamed; QTL	Ab, Ax, Tol	35
Sorghum	*Schizaphis graminum*	Hemiptera	*Ssg* (9); QTL	Ab, Tol	143
	Stenodiplosis sorghicola	Diptera	Unnamed; >1; QTL	Ab, Ax	130, 131
	Atherigona soccata	Diptera	*Trit*; QTL	Ax	108
Soybean	*Aphis glycines*	Hemiptera	*Rag* (3), *rag* (2); QTL	Ab, Ax	50, 78, 147
	Helicoverpa zea	Lepidoptera	Unnamed; QTL	Ab, Ax	101

(*Continued*)

Table 1 (*Continued*)

Plant	Arthropod pest(s)	Order	Gene(s)[a]	Category(ies)	Reference(s)[b]
Tall fescue	*Rhopalosiphum padi*	Hemiptera	*LOL* (2); (loline-endophyte alkaloid)	Ab, Ax	89, 109, 121
	Spodoptera frugiperda	Lepidoptera			
	Schizaphis graminum	Hemiptera			
Tomato	*Macrosiphum euphorbiae*	Hemiptera	*Mi-1.2* (CC-NBS-LRR)	Ab, Ax	22, 86, 103
	Bemisia argentifolii	Hemiptera			
	Bemisia tabaci	Hemiptera			
	Bactericerca cockerelli	Hemiptera			
Wheat	*Mayetiola destructor*	Diptera	*H* (>33)	Ab	6
	Diuraphis noxia	Hemiptera	*Dn* (10); QTL	Ab, Ax, Tol	68, 72
	Schizaphis graminum	Hemiptera	*Gb* (>10); QTL	Ab, Ax, Tol	150
	Sitodiplosis mosellana	Diptera	*Sm* (1); QTL	Ab, Ax	46, 134
	Cephus cinctus	Hymenoptera	*Qssmsub* (2); QTL	Ab, Ax, Tol	66, 112
	Aceria tosichella	Acari	*Cmc* (4)	Ab	74

[a]Gene symbol (lowercase denotes recessive inheritance); number of resistance loci; resistance factor(s) if known; QTL indicate multiple resistance loci mapped.
[b]See **Supplemental References** for additional references on each plant-arthropod combination.
Abbreviations: Ab, antibiosis; Ax, antixenosis; QTL, quantitative trait loci; Tol, tolerance.

Resistance Mechanisms

Here we use the term mechanism "to describe the underlying chemical or morphological plant processes that, where known, are responsible for the negative reactions of arthropods to resistant plants (115). Over time, plants evolved traits for direct and indirect defense mechanisms to counteract arthropod attacks. Direct defenses include structural barriers such as tissue toughness, plant pubescence, and glandular and nonglandular trichomes. Direct defenses also include allelochemicals in plant tissues exhibiting antifeedant, toxic, or repellent effects on attacking arthropods, such as cyanogenic glycosides, digestive enzyme inhibitors, lectins, glucosinolates, alkaloids, and terpenoids (104, 116). Constitutive and induced morphological and chemical plant defenses mediating antixenosis and antibiosis have been extensively reviewed (26, 90, 115, 124) (**Figure 1**). Indirect defenses consist of volatile organic compounds released by pest-arthropod-damaged plants that attract arthropod predators and parasitoids or that repel oviposition of pest arthropods (59). Herbivore-associated molecular patterns (HAMPs) represent specific plant indirect defense responses to specific herbivore-derived elicitors in oral or ovipositor secretions that facilitate indirect defenses against herbivores (81). The most-studied HAMPs are insect fatty acid–plant amino acid conjugates from lepidopterous larvae (59, 110) (**Figure 1**).

Resistance mechanisms: directly and indirectly expressed allelochemical or biophysical plant factors responsible for incompatible interactions between an arthropod and a resistant plant

Transgenic Resistance

Transgenes from *Bacillus thuringiensis* (*Bt*), which encode insecticidal crystalline proteins and other genes for proteins exhibiting toxicity to or growth inhibition of arthropods (proteinase inhibitors, α-amylase inhibitors, lectins, chitinases), have been expressed effectively in the genomes of many crop plants during the past 30 years. Transgenic *Bt* cotton, maize, and rice cultivars that express resistance to several lepidopteran pests are now major components of agriculture (97). Both *Bt* and non*Bt* transgenic plants are often referred to as insecticidal plants and express, in plant resistance

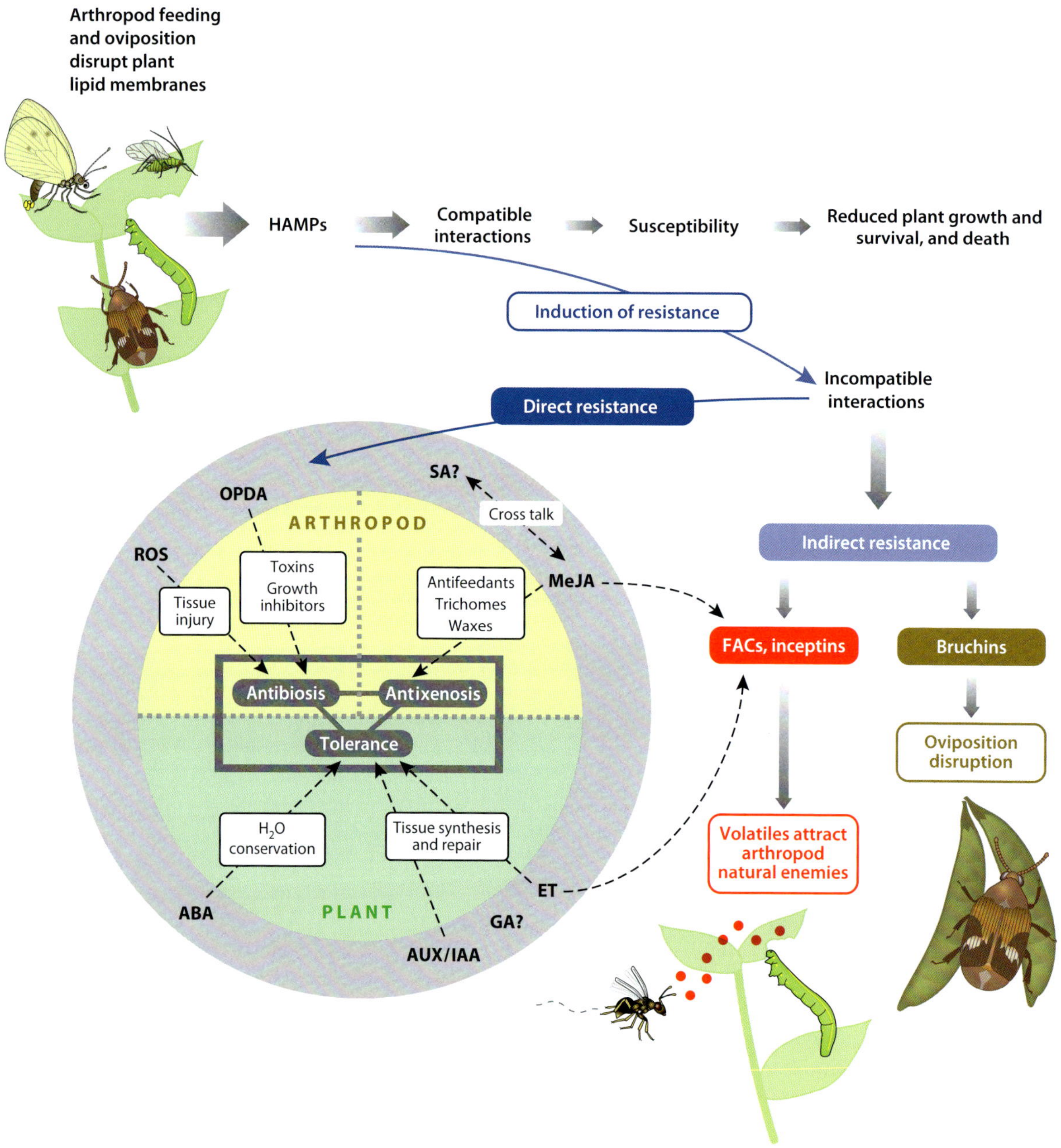

Figure 1

Representative steps in the activation of plant defense responses to HAMPs resulting in compatible plant-arthropod interactions (plant susceptibility) or incompatible interactions (plant resistance) after induction of phytohormone-based signaling pathways that activate direct or indirect resistance responses. Direct resistance may result from induction of MeJA, OPDA, ROS, or SA, which produce anti-arthropod factors expressed as antibiosis or antixenosis, or from induction of ABA, ET, GA, or IAA, which produce plant metabolic components that contribute to expression of tolerance. Arthropod or plant factors contributing to antibiosis, antixenosis, or tolerance may result from either induced or constitutive resistance gene expression. Abbreviations: ABA, abscisic acid; AUX, auxin; ET, ethylene; FAC, fatty acid–plant amino acid conjugate; GA, gibberellic acid; HAMP, herbivore-associated molecular pattern; IAA, indole-3-acetic acid; MeJA, methyl jasmonate; OPDA, 12-oxo-phytodienoic acid; ROS, reactive oxygen species; SA, salicylic acid.

terms, an extreme degree of antibiosis. Insect virulence (the ability to overcome *Bt*) to *Bt* toxins is well documented in the laboratory (127). In the field, the longevity of *Bt* transgenes is successfully extended through the use of insect resistance management programs centered on nontransgene refuge areas that allow survival of individual arthropods homozygous for susceptibility to the *Bt* toxin (44). *Bt* cotton and maize production have substantial economic benefit to producers of non*Bt* crops (54, 142). RNAi technology for insect pest management has also been developed (5) and is becoming available commercially. A thorough discussion of transgenic resistance based on nonplant sources is well beyond the scope of this review, given numerous reviews on the subject (45, 111).

Transgenic resistance: the movement of an arthropod resistance gene from a crop plant, an inaccessible gene pool, or an unrelated organism into a crop plant

Compatible arthropod-plant interactions: successful manipulations of a host plant by an arthropod that renders the plant susceptible

Incompatible arthropod-plant interactions: unsuccessful manipulations of a host plant by an arthropod resulting in survival of a resistant plant

***Mi-1.2*:** a CC-NBS-LRR subfamily gene from tomato conferring resistance to *Meloidogyne incognita* and multiple insect species

***Vat*:** a CC-NBS-LRR subfamily gene from melon conferring resistance to virus transmission by *Aphis gossypii*

Factors Affecting Expression of Plant Resistance

Numerous examples illustrate how variables such as the age and density of insects and plants, along with environmental variables (light duration and quantity, temperature, and soil micronutrients), influence expression of plant resistance (90, 115). In addition, fungal endophytes and their secondary metabolites affect the expression of HPR to insects (93).

CONSTITUTIVE AND INDUCED RESISTANCE GENES

Selection of a host-plant tissue substrate by an arthropod depends on a suite of well-coordinated interactions between an evolutionarily conserved protein(s) encoded by the attacking arthropod and the responding host plant. Compatible arthropod-plant interactions result in successful manipulations of the host plant by the arthropod, whereas incompatible arthropod-plant interactions prove unsuccessful for the arthropod and ensure that attacked plants survive (56) (**Figure 1**). In both interactions, plant and fungal endophyte genes expressed either constitutively or through an induced defense response following herbivory are involved in arthropod resistance (126, 135). Limited research to date indicates that effects controlled by constitutive genes more fully explain resistance under field conditions than do effects due to induced gene expression (53, 136). Plant- and plant-endophyte-derived constitutive genes controlling production of defense allelochemicals associated with resistance are shown in **Table 1**.

In response to arthropod herbivory plants generate reactive oxygen species and signal cascades involving jasmonic acid (JA), salicylic acid (SA), ethylene, abscisic acid, and gibberellic acid that result in downstream production of direct and indirect defense proteins (32, 61, 69, 71) (**Figure 1**). Defense signals may also be products of aphid bacterial endosymbionts (57).

Initial reviews indicated that plant tissue damage from arthropods with chewing mouthparts elicits JA-based transcriptomes, whereas JA-SA-based transcriptomes are induced by arthropods with piercing-sucking mouthparts (59). However, JA-SA signaling induced by both types of herbivory, as well as JA-SA cross-talk, has recently been demonstrated (56, 117, 119, 137). JA, 12-oxo-phytodienoic acid, and jasmonoyl-amino acid conjugates (governed by zinc finger protein expressed in inflorescence meristem) repressor proteins control the expression of many plant genes produced in the initial responses to arthropod herbivory (52). Defense response gene upregulation via JA and other pathways results in the production of many defense allelochemicals (26) (**Figure 1**). Less is known about arthropod-induced expression of plant metabolism genes, but sparse evidence indicates that some of these genes are downregulated in the initial hours after the onset of arthropod herbivory and subsequently upregulated during ensuing days. (117, 149, and **Supplemental References**, follow the **Supplemental Material link** from the Annual Reviews home page at **http://www.annualreviews.org**).

Only two arthropod resistance genes have been sequenced, *Mi-1.2* from tomato and *Vat* from melon. *Mi-1.2* is a CC-NBS-LRR (coiled coil–nucleotide binding site–leucine rich repeat) gene conferring resistance to multiple species of insects and nematodes (22, 86, 103, and **Supplemental References**). *Vat*, also a CC-NBS-LRR gene, confers resistance to *Aphis gossypii* (33). The LRR region of *Mi-1.2* signals programmed cell death, and one model proposes a gene-for-gene interaction between *Mi-1.2* and aphid elicitors that is similar to plant-pathogen interactions (55). Other studies suggest NBS-LRR involvement in aphid resistance in other crops (14, 16, 119, 141). Arthropod pest elicitors of resistance genes have yet to be identified, but an undefined *Diuraphis noxia* elicitor protein is recognized by wheat plant receptors, and plant-signaling gene products recognize *D. noxia* feeding in incompatible interactions (67).

Quantitative trait loci (QTL): stretches of DNA containing groups of loci linked to multiple genes affecting arthropod resistance

PLANT RESISTANCE GENES FOR ARTHROPOD PEST MANAGEMENT

The preceding sections in this review and a large body of literature on HPR to arthropods demonstrate the considerable success of plant breeders and entomologists in using conventional plant-breeding methods to develop resistant crop cultivars over the past 50 to 60 years, as well as discovering resistant cultivars not intentionally bred for arthropod resistance. For many of these cultivars, resistance genes have not been named and the mechanistic bases of resistance remain largely unknown, although many are used in cropping systems worldwide to reduce insect and mite damage (90). By contrast, many genes have been identified, named, and correlated with categories of arthropod resistance in cultivars by using classical genetic approaches. Indeed, the vast majority of arthropod resistance genes for cereal, food and forage legumes, fruit, and vegetable cultivars (**Table 1**) have been identified through classical genetic analyses and introgressed into breeding lines and cultivars by using traditional breeding techniques. Many pertinent examples exist for major food crops (6, 7, 18, 29).

MOLECULAR MARKERS FOR ARTHROPOD RESISTANCE GENES IN CROP PEST MANAGEMENT

The emergence and continuing development of molecular tools increase the potential for more rapid breeding of resistant cultivars through the selection of genes directly linked to optimal expression of arthropod resistance (114, 115). Entomologists, breeders, and molecular biologists have used DNA markers to develop genetic linkage maps of resistance genes in apple (to *Eriosoma lanigerum*), barrel medic (to *Acyrthosiphon kondoi*, *Therioaphis maculata*), raspberry (to *Amphorophora idaei*), and wheat (to *Mayetiola destructor*, *Diuraphis noxia*, and *Schizaphis graminum*) (**Table 1**). These approaches have also provided a way to identify new resistance genes to counter damage from virulent populations of *Nilaparvata lugens* on rice (102).

Genetic mapping of quantitative trait loci (QTL) offers a highly efficient molecular approach for working with quantitative traits (115, 144). Several arthropod crop resistance QTL have been identified since Yencho et al. (144) included QTL in six crop genera for resistance to 10 arthropod species from the orders Coleoptera, Hemiptera, and Lepidoptera. **Table 1** summarizes much of the QTL literature since the early 1990s and includes QTL from four additional crop genera mapped for resistance to 11 additional arthropod species, including representatives from Diptera and Thysanoptera.

Over the past decade, QTL mapping has been used to characterize antixenotic, antibiotic resistance, and, to a lesser extent, plant tolerance, thereby increasing the possibility to develop arthropod-resistant germplasm with which to examine the individual effects of specific QTL. Such knowledge about specific QTL provides the potential to broaden the genetic bases of arthropod plant defense and to develop more durable resistance. Examples and references in **Table 1** reveal the extent to which this information has been generated for specific crop–arthropod pest associations. For example, QTL are related to both antixenotic and antibiotic resistance to at least six insects, including *D. noxia*, *Schizaphis graminum* (23, 24), *Stenodiplosis sorghicola* (130), *Laodelphax striatella* (35), *Helicoverpa zea* (101), and *Aphis gossypii* (13). QTL also exist for antixenosis in wheat resistance to *Cephus cinctus* and *Sitodiplosis mosellana* (10, 112) and for antibiosis in apple resistance to *Dysaphis plantaginea* (123). Two antibiotic allelochemicals in maize have long been linked to insect resistance: DIMBOA [2,4-dihydroxy-7-methoxy-2H-1,4-benzoxazin-3 (4H)-one], the main hydroxamic acid in maize, is linked to *Ostrinia nubilalis* resistance (3), and the C-glycosyl flavone maysin in corn silks inhibits *H. zea* larval growth (139). Molecular genetic approaches have successfully elucidated QTL linked with the majority of the DIMBOA metabolic pathway *bx* genes (19), and QTL mapping has identified the *p1* locus as a key to maysin biosynthesis (148) (**Table 1**).

Molecular approaches have also significantly advanced the development and use of insect resistance in perennial ryegrass and tall fescue. Endowing cultivars of these forage grasses with strong anti-insect properties involves infecting host grasses with *Epichloë* and *Neotyphodium* fungal endophyte strains that produce minimal or no amounts of alkaloids [ergot alkaloids (including ergovaline) and indole-diterpenes (including lolitrems)] toxic to grazing livestock yet produce the necessary metabolites (peramine, pyrrolizidine lolines) for insect resistance (36, 93). Endophyte strains producing only peramine or loline alkaloids are called novel strains. In New Zealand, peramine-producing strains, when coupled with perennial ryegrass cultivars, protect plants from attack by *Listronotus bonariensis*. Infecting tall fescue cultivars with strains producing lolines provides strong plant resistance against many pest species of Coleoptera, Hemiptera, and Lepidoptera (**Table 1**) that significantly affect productivity and persistence of Australian tall fescue pastures (93). Given the biological and commercial importance of endophyte secondary metabolites (15), characterizing genes encoding endophyte alkaloid biosynthesis will expedite the development of endophyte-infected cultivars with the required bioprotective features to resist insect herbivory (93). In this regard, there has been progress in indentifying the loline biosynthesis gene clusters (*LOL-1*, *LOL-2*) (65, 121, 146), a peramine gene (*perA*) (129) (**Table 1**), the locus required for the biosynthesis of lolitrem (10 *ltm* genes) (145), and ergot biosynthesis genes (*dmaW*, *1psA*) (89). Cloning these metabolite genes and inactivating them by gene knockout generate direct genetic evidence of the contribution of specific endophyte metabolites to insect resistance, as recently revealed by the elimination of ergot alkaloids in perennial ryegrass by endophyte gene knockout with *Agrotis ipsilon* resistance retained in the infected host (96). This molecular approach has the potential to expedite screening of diverse endophyte strains for the presence and distribution of endophyte genes that produce desirable metabolites for agricultural applications in which insect-resistant grass cultivars are required.

To what extent have breeding programs purposefully bred cultivars with named arthropod resistance genes (**Table 1**) for production agriculture? Genes have been introgressed into wheat for resistance to *D. noxia*, *M. destructor*, and *S. mosellana* (6); sorghum resistance to *S. graminum* and *S. sorghicola* (130); rice resistance to *N. lugens* (99); and mungbean resistance to *Callosobruchus chinensis* and *Riptortus clavatus* (**Supplemental References**). In addition, lettuce cultivars containing the *Nr* gene for resistance to *Nasonovia ribis* have been bred in Europe, and similar conventional breeding efforts are underway in the United States (76). For more than 30 years single major genes or polygenic minor genes have successfully protected European red raspberry cultivars from *A. idaei*, the most important vector of four raspberry viruses (7). Although apple cultivars have long been known to exhibit variable susceptibility to different species of pest aphids, resistance genes were not conclusively identified until molecular results provided answers to this question (18, 123). The initial use of maize QTL in molecular marker-assisted selection (MAS) of resistance to multiple species of stem-boring Lepidoptera was problematic due to epistatic gene interactions, with

DIMBOA: 2,4-dihydroxy-7-methoxy-2H-1,4-benzoxazin-3-one

***bx*:** a maize biosynthesis gene controlling production of the hydroxamic acid DIMBOA that inhibits larval feeding of several species of pest Lepidoptera

***p1*:** a gene controlling production of the C-glycosyl flavone maysin in maize silk that inhibits larval growth of *Helicoverpa zea*

***LOL*:** a loline alkaloid biosynthesis gene in fungal endophytes in tall fescue that imparts resistance to pest species of Coleoptera, Hemiptera, and Lepidoptera

***perA*:** a peramine alkaloid gene in fungal endophytes in perennial ryegrass that imparts resistance to *Listronotus bonariensis*

MAS: marker-assisted selection

QTL offering no advantage over phenotypic selection (140). However, utilizing recently identified QTL for maize allelochemicals (see above) to allow accurate and efficient MAS breeding for arthropod resistance looks promising.

Np: a gene in pea genotypes that promotes formation of neoplastic callus on pods at the oviposition sites of *Bruchus pisorum*

In addition, resistance in many cultivars has not been linked to a specific gene(s) (90, 125). This is illustrated by the incorporation of the pubescence trait into commercial soybean cultivars for resistance to *Empoasca fabae*, which has "virtually relegated this insect to nonpest status on soybean in the U.S." (11). Conversely, there are instances in which the genetic bases of resistance have been characterized in unadapted germplasm and even in advanced breeding lines, but the utility of these resistance genes in agriculture has not been realized. A look at cool-season food legumes (chickpea, faba bean, lentil, pea) reveals little global progress in transferring resistance genes from unadapted germplasm to regionally adapted and agronomically acceptable cultivars for pest management (29, 37).

Given the large increase in global soybean production over the past 40 years, and the large number of pestiferous insects associated with this important crop, it is somewhat surprising that arthropod-resistant cultivars are not yet available to producers. Although breeding programs have developed resistant cultivars, they are not popular among soybean producers, presumably because of yield limitations (11). The arrival of *Aphis glycines* in North America in 2000 resulted in the discovery of multiple sources of aphid resistance and the naming and mapping of resistance genes (**Table 1**) (50, 147). Soybean breeding programs are benefiting from molecular-generated information, but the appearance of new soybean aphid biotypes has complicated the breeding, release, and acceptance of resistant cultivars (62). At the time of this writing, aphid-resistant cultivars were not commercially available in North America (50). Similarly, Latin American bean growers are not growing insect-resistant cultivars, although researchers have discovered dominant genes and tightly linked diagnostic molecular markers for resistance to Mexican bean weevil and bean pod weevil in common bean (**Table 1**) and have developed an improved understanding of the genetic and mechanistic bases of resistance to these pests (79 and **Supplemental References**). Finally, the *Np* gene in pea genotypes that provides resistance to *Bruchus pisorum* has not been deployed in cultivars (29, 34).

INTEGRATION OF ARTHROPOD RESISTANCE GENES INTO IPM PROGRAMS

Although hundreds of insect resistance genes have been deployed in improved cultivars globally (115), the literature offers few examples in which these cultivars have been actually combined with other methods to form IPM programs at the farm level (125, 133). An IPM approach harmoniously combines available pest management methods or tactics (HPR, biological control, cultural control, chemical control, and other methods) to suppress pest densities to below crop-damaging levels (73). Notably, plant resistance is one of multiple management methods, along with biological control and insecticides, comprising highly successful rice IPM programs in Asia (75). Single *N. lugens* resistance genes, gene pyramids, and seasonal rotations have been successfully deployed in Asian rice cultivars (1 and **Supplemental References**).

Australian sorghum production is centered on growing commercial hybrids with antibiosis resistance to *Stenodiplosis sorghicola*, and this resistance has been successfully combined with other management methods such as flexible planting times, synthetic insecticides, and biological control (40). Widespread use of *S. sorghicola*–resistant hybrids by Australian growers has reduced the number of insecticide applications and has allowed significant increases in the survival of parasitoids that reduce *S. sorghicola* populations. North American sorghum growers' use of plant resistance and chemical control to manage *Schizaphis graminum* has reduced insecticide use since 1977, when

S. graminum–resistant commercial hybrids became available (132). Useful multiline resistance also exists in sorghum but has yet to be deployed (131).

Much of the arthropod crop pest management literature shows that HPR is used in conjunction with other management methods. In wheat, examples include the deployment of *H* genes for *M. destructor* resistance in North American production areas where cultural practices such as puparia and volunteer wheat destruction, delayed planting, and crop rotation could be used (100). Several of the same cultural practices and biological control via conservation of parasitoid wasps could be used to augment the value of cultivars resistant to *C. cinctus* (64). A Canadian program for management of *Sitodiplosis mosellana* could potentially incorporate an interspersed refuge of susceptible plants among a resistant wheat crop to help sustain resistance conferred by *Sm1* and biocontrol of the midge by parasitoids (120). In Europe, concerns about *Amphorophora idaei* resistance-breaking biotypes on resistant raspberry cultivars requires additional management tactics to control aphid populations and virus transmission. Biological control and semiochemical technologies are in development, because the few certified insecticides are largely ineffective at controlling aphids in time to prevent virus transmission (77, 80).

Finally, despite repeated justifications in the literature for alternative pest management options such as the cultivation of arthropod-resistant cultivars, early twenty-first century control strategies for most crop pests involve synthetic insecticides. A case in point is sugarcane production in Louisiana, where producers rely heavily on insecticides to control *Diatraea saccharalis* on a widely grown susceptible variety, even though multiple control tactics (plant resistance, chemical control, arthropod predation) effectively reduce infestations (95). The obstacles to increased use of host plant resistance and other economical and environmentally friendly methods in an IPM framework have been reviewed elsewhere (31, 125).

***Mir*:** a gene in maize encoding cysteine proteinases that inhibits larval growth of *Spodoptera frugiperda*

Arcelin α-amylase inhibitor (*Arc1*): a gene in common bean encoding arcelin, an α-amylase inhibitor inhibiting larval growth of *Zabrotes subfasciatus*

***Lep* (leptinidine) and *AL* (acetyl-leptinidine):** genes encoding nonglycosylated steroidal alkaloids from foliage of wild potato, *Solanum chacoense*, that inhibit feeding of *Leptinotarsa decemlineata*

MOLECULAR GENETICS IN ARTHROPOD-RESISTANT CROPS: PROGRESS, BENEFITS, AND CHALLENGES

Steady progress has been made in the past five decades to advance the science of HPR to arthropods and, more importantly, to deploy arthropod-resistant crop plant cultivars as foundations of cropping systems. Major advances have been made in understanding resistance categories and mechanisms mediating resistance, as well as the biotic and abiotic variables affecting resistance. To bridge gaps with plant pathogen resistance research, plant-arthropod relationships are now being described as compatible (susceptible plant) and incompatible (resistant plant) interactions, similar to plant-pathogen interactions (56).

Perhaps the most dramatic shift in research has been the progress made in understanding constitutively expressed arthropod resistance gene products. For example, knowledge of the phenotypic inheritance of Lepidoptera resistance in maize has been greatly improved by a completely new understanding of genes involved in synthesis of DIMBOA (*bx*), maysin (*p1*), and cysteine proteinases (*Mir*). The same is true for genes controlling production of other allelochemicals, including the arcelin α-amylase inhibitor (*Arc1*) in common bean, endophyte-produced alkaloids (*LOL*, *perA*) in grasses, and the steroidal alkaloids acetyl-leptinidine (*AL*) and leptinidine (*Lep*) in potato. Advances in the past decade alone indicate the involvement of numerous plant signaling pathways, primarily the jasmonate pathway, in the production of induced arthropod resistance proteins. Although the balance of interaction between induced and constitutive genes remains unclear, the results of gene silencing experiments reveal essential functions of both (60, 137, 141). Finally, knowledge gained from cloning *Mi-1.2* and *Vat*, both members of the CC-NBS-LRR subfamily of NBS-LRR resistance proteins, has yielded information to facilitate the cloning of other arthropod resistance genes using resistance gene analog (RGA) approaches. For example, the *AIN*, *AKR*, and *TRR* aphid resistance genes in barrel medic are located in RGA clusters that are highly similar to the CC-NBS-LRR subfamily (63 and **Supplemental References**), strongly suggesting that these genes are also NBS-LRR resistance proteins. Comparative analyses of these aphid resistance genes will greatly expand the genomic understanding of what constitutes an arthropod resistance gene.

Arthropod virulence: a mutation of an arthropod avirulence gene(s) that results in a plant's loss of ability to recognize the presence of the arthropod

Given these significant genetic and genomic advances, to what extent have molecular genetic and genomic innovations benefited producers and consumers through the delivery of arthropod-resistant crops? Field integration of rice, sorghum, and wheat arthropod resistance genes into IPM in Asia, Australia, and North America, and to a limited extent Europe, has increased steadily for the past 50 years. Aside from these three major cereal food crops, however, the actual integration of arthropod-resistant cultivars, biological control agents, and cultural control practices has not occurred at the farm level, mainly because of continued but often unnecessary use of synthetic insecticides. The use of VOCs to recruit pest-arthropod natural enemies and synergize field resistance could be developed as an IPM tool to alleviate this dilemma.

Molecular markers are facilitating and improving our ability to develop and deliver arthropod-resistant crops. This is clearly demonstrated by more than 100 arthropod resistance loci and linked markers that have been identified and used to generate numerous crop-plant genetic linkage maps. Many of these markers are used to track arthropod resistance via MAS in breeding lines for deployment in cultivars. This is especially true at CGIAR centers (ICARDA, ICRISAT, and IRRI), where MAS has been used to breed arthropod-resistant crop cultivars and continues to be used to identify different genes in new sources of resistance. Importantly, several markers in **Table 1** have been linked to specific resistance categories and in several cases to allelochemical or biophysical traits. This knowledge offers HPR researchers the capability of deploying resistant cultivars with broader, more durable resistance that reduces the occurrence of arthropod virulence.

Although these data reflect steady progress, QTL must be used more broadly to identify plant arthropod resistance genes, especially to identify and deploy arthropod-resistant cultivars of cool-season food legumes (chickpea, faba bean, lentil, pea) in the semitropical areas of the world currently undergoing rapid population growth. The challenges of developing cultivars with arthropod resistance from wild species remain (28), but transgenic technology has decreased these difficulties. An improved understanding of constitutive and induced gene expression, and the use of plant and arthropod genomic tools associated with gene manipulation, now provide many opportunities to more efficiently develop arthropod-resistant plants. Therefore, the outlook for confronting future challenges of HPR is bright. Nevertheless, the development of durable, higher-yielding arthropod-resistant crop cultivars for global agriculture and their integration into IPM programs will succeed only through interdisciplinary collaborations among entomologists, plant breeders, and molecular biologists.

SUMMARY POINTS

1. Plant genetic diversity resulting from selective pressures due in part to arthropod herbivory provided humans cultivatable food crops with which to form agrarian societies about 10,000 years ago. Conventional plant breeding has since been used to develop hundreds of arthropod-resistant crop cultivars that currently provide major ecological and economic benefits to global agriculture.
2. Arthropod-resistant plants function by producing allelochemical and biophysical plant traits that adversely affect arthropod behavior and survival or that allow plants to tolerate arthropod damage.

3. Incompatible interactions between resistant plants and arthropods are mediated by both constitutively produced resistance proteins and proteins produced via jasmonate- and other signaling pathways following induction by arthropod herbivory.
4. Two arthropod resistance genes have been cloned and are members of the CC-NBS-LRR subfamily of NBS-LRR resistance proteins. *Mi-1.2* (wild tomato) exhibits multispecies insect and nematode resistance, and *Vat* (melon) expresses aphid resistance. Aphid resistance genes in barrel medic are located in RGA clusters that are highly similar to the CC-NBS-LRR subfamily.
5. More than 100 monogenic and polygenic arthropod plant resistance gene loci and their linked markers have been characterized by molecular mapping, and several are in use to track resistance via MAS in breeding lines for deployment in cultivars.
6. Arthropod-resistant cultivars of rice and sorghum are major components of IPM programs in Asia, Australia, and North America, and resistant raspberry and wheat cultivars are near integration in Europe and North America, respectively. For the majority of food and fiber crops, however, arthropod-resistant cultivars have not been integrated into other IPM methods.
7. Numerous opportunities exist to use advances in molecular technology to more efficiently identify, track, and manipulate arthropod resistance genes in arthropod-resistant cultivars. Integration of such cultivars into IPM programs with biological, chemical, and cultural control tactics will succeed only through interdisciplinary collaborations.

DISCLOSURE STATEMENT

The authors are not aware of any affiliations, memberships, funding, or financial holdings that might be perceived as affecting the objectivity of this review.

LITERATURE CITED

1. Alam SN, Cohen MB. 1998. Detection and analysis of QTLs for resistance to the brown planthopper, *Nilaparvata lugens*, in a double-haploid rice population. *Theor. Appl. Genet.* 97:1370–79
2. Alston FH, Phillips KL, Evans KM. 2000. A *Malus* gene list. *Acta Hortic.* 538:561–70
3. Barry D, Alfaro D, Darrah LL. 1994. Relation of European corn borer (Lepidoptera: Pyralidae) leaf-feeding resistance and DIMBOA content in maize. *Environ. Entomol.* 23:177–82
4. Bateman RM, Crane PR, DiMichele WA, Kenrick PR, Rowe NP, et al. 1998. Early evolution of land plants: phylogeny, physiology, and ecology of the primary terrestrial radiation. *Annu. Rev. Ecol. Syst.* 29:263–92
5. Baum JA, Bogaert T, Clinton W, Heck GR, Feldmann P, et al. 2007. Control of coleopteran insect pests through RNA interference. *Nat. Biotechnol.* 25:1322–26
6. Berzonsky WA, Ding H, Haley SD, Harris MO, Lamb RJ, et al. 2010. Breeding wheat for resistance to insects. *Plant Breed. Rev.* Vol. 22. doi: 10.1002/9780470650202.ch5
7. Birch ANE, Jones AT, Fenton B, Malloch G, Geoghegan I, et al. 2002. Resistance-breaking raspberry aphid biotypes: constraints to sustainable control through plant breeding. *Acta Hortic.* 585:315–17
8. Blair MW, Muñoz C, Buendía HF, Flower J, Bueno JM, Cardona C. 2010. Genetic mapping of microsatellite markers around the arcelin bruchid resistance locus in common bean. *Theor. Appl. Genet.* 121:393–402

9. Blair MW, Muñoz C, Garza R, Cardona C. 2006. Molecular mapping of genes for resistance to the bean pod weevil (*Apion godmani* Wagner) in common bean. *Theor. Appl. Genet.* 114:913–23
10. Blake NK, Stougaard RN, Weaver DK, Sherman JD, Lanning SP, et al. 2010. Identification of a quantitative trait locus for resistance to *Sitodiplosis mosellana* (Géhin), the orange wheat blossom midge, in spring wheat. *Plant Breed.* 130:245–30
11. Boethel DJ. 1999. Assessment of soybean germplasm for multiple insect resistance. See Ref. 30, pp. 101–30
12. Bohn M, Groh S, Khairallah MM, Hoisington DA, Utz HF, Melchinger AE. 2001. Re-evaluation of the prospects of marker-assisted selection for improving insect resistance against *Diatraea* spp. in tropical maize by cross validation and independent validation. *Theor. Appl. Genet.* 103:1059–67
13. Boissot N, Thomas S, Sauvion N, Marchal C, Pavis C, Dogimont C. 2010. Mapping and validation of QTLs for resistance to aphids and whiteflies in melon. *Theor. Appl. Genet.* 121:9–20
14. Botha A-M, Lacock L, van Niekerk C, Matsioloko MT, du Preez FB, et al. 2006. Is photosynthetic transcriptional regulation in *Triticum aestivum* L. cv. 'TugelaDN' a contributing factor for tolerance to *Diuraphis noxia* (Homoptera: Aphididae)? *Plant Cell Rep.* 25:41–54
15. Bouton J. 2009. Deployment of novel endophytes in the tall fescue commercial seed trade. In *Tall Fescue for the Twenty-First Century*, ed. HA Fribourg, DB Hannaway, CP West, pp. 367–75. Madison: Am. Soc. Agron., Crop Sci. Soc. Am., Soil Sci. Soc. Am. 540 pp.
16. Boyko EV, Smith CM, Thara VK, Bruno JM, Deng Y, et al. 2006. Molecular basis of plant gene expression during aphid invasion: Wheat *Pto*- and *Pti*-like sequences are involved in interactions between wheat and Russian wheat aphid (Homoptera: Aphididae). *J. Econ. Entomol.* 99:1430–45
17. Brooks TD, Bushman BS, Williams WP, McMullen MD, Buckley PM. 2007. Genetic basis of resistance to fall armyworm (Lepidoptera: Noctuidae) and southwestern corn borer (Lepidoptera: Crambidae) leaf-feeding damage in maize. *J. Econ. Entomol.* 100:1470–75
18. Bus VGM, Chagné D, Bassett HCM, Bowatte D, Calenge F, et al. 2008. Genome mapping of three major resistance genes to woolly apple aphid (*Eriosoma lanigerum* Hausm.) *Tree Genet. Genomes* 4: 233–36
19. **Butrón A, Chen YC, Rottinghaus GE, McMullen MD. 2010. Genetic variation at *bx1* controls DIMBOA content in maize. *Theor. Appl. Genet.* 120:721–34**

19. Association mapping used to determine a QTL that colocalizes with most structural *bx* genes of the DIMBOA pathway.

20. Cardinal AJ, Lee M. 2005. Genetic relationships between resistance to stalk-tunneling by the European corn borer and cell-wall components in maize population B73xB52. *Theor. Appl. Genet.* 111:1–7
21. Carena MJ, Glogoza P. 2004. Resistance of maize to the corn leaf aphid: a review. *Maydica* 49:241–54
22. Casteel CL, Walling LL, Paine TD. 2006. Behavior and biology of the tomato psyllid, *Bactericerca cockerelli*, in response to the *MI-1.2* gene. *Entomol. Exp. Appl.* 121:67–72
23. Castro AM, Vasicek A, Manifiesto M, Giménez DO, Tacaliti MS, et al. 2005. Mapping antixenosis genes on chromosome 6A of wheat to greenbug and to a new biotype of Russian wheat aphid. *Plant Breed.* 124:229–33
24. Castro AM, Worland AJ, Vasicek A, Ellerbrook C, Giménez DO, et al. 2004. Mapping quantitative trait loci for resistance against greenbug and Russian wheat aphid. *Plant Breed.* 121:361–66
25. Cevik V, King GJ. 2002. Resolving the aphid resistance locus *Sd*-1 on a BAC contig within a sub-telomeric region of *Malus* linkage group 7. *Genome* 45:939–45
26. Chen M-S. 2008. Inducible direct plant defense against insect herbivores: a review. *Insect Sci.* 15:101–14
27. Cheung WY, Di Giorgio L, Ahman I. 2010. Mapping resistance to the bird cherry-oat aphid (*Rhopalosiphum padi*) in barley. *Plant Breed.* 129:637–46
28. Clement SL. 2002. Insect resistance in the wild relatives of food legumes and wheat. In *Proc. Australas. Plant Breed. Conf., 12th, Perth, Sept. 15–20*, ed. JA McComb, pp. 287–93. Perth: Australas. Plant Breed. Assoc.
29. Clement SL, Cristofaro M, Cowgill SE, Weigand S. 1999. Germplasm resources, insect resistance, and grain legume improvement. See Ref. 30, pp. 131–48
30. Clement SL, Quisenberry SS, eds. 1999. *Global Plant Genetic Resources for Insect-Resistant Crops*. Boca Raton, FL: CRC Press. 295 pp.

31. Clement SL, Wightman JA, Hardie DC, Bailey P, Baker G, McDonald G. 2000. Opportunities for integrated management of insect pests of grain legumes. In *Linking Research and Marketing Opportunities for Pulses in the 21st Century, Proc. Third Int. Food Legumes Res. Conf.*, ed. R Knight, pp. 467–80. Dordrecht, The Netherlands: Kluwer. 711 pp.
32. Couldridge C, Newbury HJ, Ford-Lloyd B, Bale J, Pritchard J. 2007. Exploring plant responses to aphid feeding using a full *Arabidopsis* microarray reveals a small number of genes with significantly altered expression. *Bull. Entomol. Res.* 97:523–32
33. Dogimont C, Chovelon V, Tual S, Boissot N, Rittener V, et al. 2008. Molecular diversity at the *Vat/PM-W* resistance locus in melon. In *Proc. EUCARPIA Genet. Breed. Cucurbitaceae, IXth*, ed. M Pitrat, pp. 219–28. Avignon: INRA
34. Doss RP, Oliver JE, Proebsting WM, Potter SW, Kuy S-R, et al. 2000. Bruchins: insect-derived plant regulators that stimulate neoplasm formation. *Proc. Natl. Acad. Sci. USA* 97:6218–23
35. Duan CX, Su N, Cheng ZJ, Lei CL, Wang JL, et al. 2010. QTL analysis for the resistance to small brown planthopper (*Laodelphax striatellus* Fallén) in rice using backcross inbred lines. *Plant Breed.* 129:63–67
36. Easton S, Tapper B. 2005. *Neotyphodium* research and application in New Zealand. In *Neotyphodium in Cool-Season Grasses*, ed. CA Roberts, CP West, DE Spiers, pp. 35–42. Oxford: Blackwell. 379 pp.
37. Edwards O, Singh KB. 2006. Resistance to insect pests: What do legumes have to offer? *Euphytica* 147:273–85
38. Ehrlich PR, Raven PH. 1964. Butterflies and plants: a study in coevolution. *Evolution* 18:586–608
39. Evans KM, Govan CL, Fernández-Fernández F. 2008. A new gene for resistance to *Dysaphis pyri* in pear and identification of flanking microsatellite markers. *Genome* 51:1026–31
40. Franzmann BA, Hardy AT, Murray DAH, Henzell RG. 2008. Host-plant resistance and biopesticides: ingredients for successful integrated pest management (IPM) in Australian sorghum production. *Aust. J. Exp. Agric.* 48:1594–600
41. Frei A, Blair MW, Cardona C, Beebe SF, Gu H, Dorn S. 2005. QTL mapping of resistance to *Thrips palmi* Karny in common bean. *Crop Sci.* 45:379–87
42. Fritz RS, Simms EL, eds. 1992. *Plant Resistance to Herbivores and Pathogens: Ecology, Evolution, and Genetics*. Chicago: Univ. Chicago Press. 590 pp.
43. Futuyma DJ, Agrawal AA. 2009. Macroevolution and the biology diversity of plants and herbivores. *Proc. Natl. Acad. Sci. USA* 106:18054–61
44. Gassmann AJ, Carrière Y, Tabashnik BE. 2009. Fitness costs of insect resistance to *Bacillus thuringiensis*. *Annu. Rev. Entomol.* 54:147–63
45. Gatehouse JA. 2008. Biotechnological prospects for engineering insect-resistant plants. *Plant Physiol.* 146:881–87
46. Gharalari AH, Fox SL, Smith MAH, Lamb RJ. 2009. Oviposition deterrence in spring wheat, *Triticum aestivum*, against orange wheat blossom midge, *Sitodiplosis mosellana*: implications for inheritance of deterrence. *Entomol. Exp. Appl.* 133:74–83
47. Groot AT, Dicke M. 2002. Insect transgenic plants in a multi-trophic context. *Plant J.* 31:387–406
48. Guo B, Butrón A, Scully BT. 2010. Maize silk antibiotic polyphenol compounds and molecular genetic improvement of resistance to corn earworm (*Helicoverpa zea* Boddie) in *sh2* sweet corn. *Int. J. Plant Biol.* 1:13–18
49. Herselman L, Thwaites R, Kimmins FM, Courtois B, van der Merwe PJA, Seal SE. 2004. Identification and mapping of AFLP markers linked to peanut (*Arachis hypogaea* L.) resistance to the aphid vector of groundnut rosette disease. *Theor. Appl. Genet.* 109:1426–33
50. Hill CB, Kim K-S, Crull L, Diers BW, Hartman GL. 2009. Inheritance of resistance to the soybean aphid in soybean PI200538. *Crop Sci.* 49:1193–200
51. Holden J, Peacock J, Williams T. 1993. *Genes, Crops and the Environment*. Cambridge/New York: Cambridge Univ. Press. 162 pp.
52. Howe GA, Jander G. 2008. Plant immunity to insect herbivores. *Annu. Rev. Plant Biol.* 59:41–66
53. Huang J, McAuslane HJ, Nuessly GS. 2003. Resistance in lettuce to *Diabrotica balteata* (Coleoptera: Chrysomelidae): the roles of latex and inducible defense. *Environ. Entomol.* 32:9–16
54. Hutchison WD, Burkness EC, Mitchell PD, Moon RD, Leslie TW, et al. 2010. Areawide suppression of European corn borer with *Bt* maize reaps savings to non-*Bt* maize growers. *Science* 330:222–25

52. Describes the roles of jasmonate signaling in coordinating direct and indirect plant responses to herbivory.

55. Hwang CF, Bhakta AV, Truesdell GM, Pudlo WM, Williamson VM. 2000. Evidence for a role of the N terminus and leucine-rich repeat region of the *Mi* gene product in regulation of localized cell death. *Plant Cell* 12:1319–29

56. Kaloshian I. 2004. Gene-for-gene disease resistance: bridging insect pest and pathogen defense. *J. Chem. Ecol.* 30:2419–38

56. First in-depth analysis of gene-for-gene plant resistance to piercing-sucking insects.

57. Kaloshian I, Walling L. 2005. Hemipterans as pathogens. *Annu. Rev. Phytopathol.* 43:491–521

58. Kennedy GG, Barbour JD. 1992. Resistance variation in natural and managed systems. See Ref. 42, pp. 13–41

59. Kessler A, Baldwin IT. 2002. Plant responses to insect herbivory: the emerging molecular analysis. *Annu. Rev. Plant Biol.* 53:299–328

59. Integrated review of transcriptional changes in plants exhibiting constitutive and induced arthropod resistance.

60. Kessler A, Halitschke R, Baldwin IT. 2004. Silencing the jasmonate cascade: induced plant defenses and insect populations. *Science* 305:665–68

61. Kielkiewicz M. 2002. Influence of carmine spider mite *Tetranychus cinnabarinus* Boisd. (Acarida: Tetranychidae) feeding on ethylene production and the activity of oxidative enzymes in damaged tomato plants. In *Acarid Phylogeny and Evolution: Adaptation in Mites and Ticks—Proc. IV Symp. Eur. Assoc. Acarol.*, ed. F Bernini, R Nannelli, G Nuzzaci, E de Lillo, pp. 389–92. Dordrecht, The Netherlands: Kluwer. 452 pp.

62. Kim K-S, Hill CB, Hartman GL, Mian MAR, Diers BW. 2008. Discovery of soybean aphid biotypes. *Crop Sci.* 48:923–28

63. Klingler JP, Nair RM, Edwards OR, Singh KB. 2009. A single gene, *AIN*, in *Medicago truncatula* mediates a hypersensitive response to both bluegreen aphid and pea aphid, but confers resistance only to bluegreen aphid. *J. Exp. Bot.* 60:4115–27

63. Aphid resistance genes in barrel medic occur in clusters very similar to the CC-NBS-LRR subfamily of NBS-LRR resistance proteins that includes *Mi-1.2* and *Vat*.

64. Knodel J, Shanower T, Beauzay P. 2010. Integrated pest management of wheat stem sawfly in North Dakota. *N. D. Ext. Serv. Bull.* E-1479. 8 pp.

65. Kutil BL, Greenwald C, Liu G, Spiering MJ, Schardl CL, Wilkinson HH. 2007. Comparison of loline alkaloid gene clusters across fungal endophytes: predicting the co-regulatory sequence motifs and the evolutionary history. *Fungal Genet. Biol.* 44:1002–10

66. Lanning SP, Fox P, Elser J, Martin JM, Blake NK, Talbert LE. 2006. Microsatellite markers associated with a secondary stem solidness locus in wheat. *Crop Sci.* 46:1701–93

67. Lapitan NLV, Li YC, Peng JH, Botha AM. 2007. Fractionated extracts of Russian wheat aphid eliciting defense responses in wheat. *J. Econ. Entomol.* 100:990–99

68. Lapitan NLV, Peng J, Sharma V. 2007. A high-density map and PCR markers for Russian wheat aphid resistance gene *Dn7* on chromosome 1RS/1BL. *Crop Sci.* 47:811–20

69. Li Y, Zou J, Li M, Bilgin DD, Vodkin LO, et al. 2008. Soybean defense responses to the soybean aphid. *New Phytol.* 179:185–95

70. Lin C, Chen C-S, Horng S-B. 2005. Characterization of resistance to *Callosobruchus maculatus* (Coleoptera: Bruchidae) in mungbean variety VC6089A and its resistance-associated protein VrD1. *J. Econ. Entomol.* 98:1369–73

71. Liu X, Bai J, Huang L, Zhu L, Liu X, et al. 2007. Gene expression of different wheat genotypes during attack by virulent and avirulent Hessian fly (*Mayetiola destructor*) larvae. *J. Chem. Ecol.* 33:2171–94

72. Liu XM, Smith CM, Gill BS, Tolmay V. 2001. Microsatellite markers linked to six Russian wheat aphid resistance genes in wheat. *Theor. Appl. Genet.* 102:504–10

73. Luckmann WH, Metcalf RL, eds. 1994. *Introduction to Insect Pest Management.* New York: Wiley. 650 pp. 3rd ed.

74. Malik R, Brown-Guedira GL, Smith CM, Harvey TL, Gill BS. 2003. Genetic mapping of wheat curl mite resistance genes *Cmc3* and *Cmc4* in common wheat. *Crop Sci.* 43:644–50

75. Matteson PC. 2000. Insect pest management in tropical Asian irrigated rice. *Annu. Rev. Entomol.* 45:549–74

76. McCreight JD. 2008. Potential sources of genetic resistance in *Lactuca* spp. to the lettuce aphid, *Nasanovia ribisnigri* (Mosely) (Homoptera: Aphididae). *HortScience* 43:1355–58

77. McMenemy LS, Mitchell C, Johnson SN. 2009. Biology of the European large raspberry aphid (*Amphorophora idaei*): its role in virus transmission and resistance breakdown in red raspberry. *Agric. For. Entomol.* 11:61–71

78. Mian MAR, Kang S-T, Beil SE, Hammond RB. 2008. Genetic linkage mapping of the soybean aphid resistance gene in PI 243540. *Theor. Appl. Genet.* 117:955–62
79. Miklas PN, Kelly JD, Beebe SE, Blair MW. 2006. Common bean breeding for resistance against biotic and abiotic stresses: from classical to MAS breeding. *Euphytica* 147:105–31
80. Mitchell C, Johnson SN, Gordon SC, Birch ANE, Hubbard SF. 2010. Combining plant resistance and a natural enemy to control *Amphorophora idaei*. *BioControl* 55:321–27
81. Mithöfer A, Boland W. 2008. Recognition of herbivory-associated molecular patterns. *Plant Physiol.* 146:825–31
82. Mittal S, Dahleen LS, Mornhinweg D. 2008. Locations of quantitative trait loci conferring Russian wheat aphid resistance in barley germplasm STARS-9301B. *Crop Sci.* 48:1452–58
83. Mornhinweg DW, Bregitzer PP, Porter DR, Peairs FB, Baltensperger DD, et al. 2009. Registration of 'Sidney' spring feed barley resistant to Russian wheat aphid. *J. Plant Reg.* 3:214–18
84. Myers GO, Fatokun CA, Young ND. 1996. RFLP mapping of an aphid resistance gene in cowpea (*Vigna unguiculata* L. Walp). *Euphytica* 91:181–87
85. Ni X, Li X, Chen Y, Guo F, Feng J, Zhao H. 2010. Metamorphosis of cisgenic insect resistance research in the transgenic crop era. In *Recent Advances in Entomological Research: From Molecular Biology to Pest Management*, ed. T-X Liu, L Kang, pp. 157–69. Beijing: High. Educ. Press. 500 pp.
86. Nombela G, Williamson VM, Muñiz M. 2003. The root-knot nematode resistance gene *MI-1.2* of tomato is responsible for resistance against the whitefly *Bemisia tabaci*. *Mol. Plant-Microbe Interact.* 16:645–49
87. Osborn TC, Blake T, Gepts P, Bliss FA. 1986. Bean arcelin 2. Genetic variation, inheritance and linkage relationships of a novel seed protein of *Phaseolus vulgaris* L. *Theor. Appl. Genet.* 71:847–55
88. Painter RH. 1951. *Insect Resistance in Crop Plants*. Lawrence: Univ. Kans. Press. 520 pp.
89. Panaccione DG, Johnson RD, Wang J, Young CA, Damrongkool P, et al. 2001. Elimination of ergovaline from a grass–*Neotyphodium* endophyte symbiosis by genetic modification of the endophyte. *Proc. Natl. Acad. Sci. USA* 98:12820–25
90. Panda N, Khush GS. 1995. *Host Plant Resistance to Insects*. Wallingford, UK: CABI/IRRI. 431 pp.
91. Pascal T, Pfeiffer F, Kervella J, Lacroze P, Sauge MH. 2002. Inheritance of green peach aphid resistance in the peach cultivar 'Rubira'. *Plant Breed.* 121:459–61
92. Pechan T, Jiang B. Steckler D, Ye L, Lin L. 1999. Characterization of three distinct cDNA clones encoding cysteine proteinases from maize (*Zea mays* L.) callus. *Plant Mol. Biol.* 40:111–19
93. Popay AJ. 2009. Insect pests. In *Tall Fescue for the Twenty-First Century*, Agron. Monogr. 53, ed. HA Fribourg, DB Hannaway, CP West, pp. 129–49. Madison: ASA, CSSA, SSSA. 540 pp.
94. Porter DR, Burd JD, Mornhinweg DW. 2007. Differentiating greenbug resistance genes in barley. *Euphytica* 153:11–14
95. Posey FR, White WH, Reay-Jones FPF, Gravois K, Salassi ME, et al. 2006. Sugarcane borer (Lepidoptera: Crambidae) management threshold assessment on four sugarcane cultivars. *J. Econ. Entomol.* 99:966–71
96. Potter DA, Stokes JT, Redmond CT, Schardl CL, Panaccione DG. 2008. Contribution of ergot alkaloids to suppression of a grass-feeding caterpillar assessed with gene knockout endophytes in perennial ryegrass. *Entomol. Exp. Appl.* 126:138–47
97. Qaim M, Zilberman D. 2003. Yield effects of genetically modified crops in developing countries. *Science* 299:900–2
98. Qiu Y, Guo J, Jing S, Zhu L, He G. 2010. High resolution mapping of the brown planthopper resistance gene *Bph6* in rice and characterizing its resistance in the 9311 and Nipponbare near isogenic backgrounds. *Theor. Appl. Genet.* 121:1601–11
99. Rahman ML, Jiang W, Chu SH, Quiao Y, Ham T-H, et al. 2009. High-resolution mapping of two rice brown planthopper resistance genes, *Bph20(t)* and *Bph21(t)*, originating from *Oryza minuta*. *Theor. Appl. Genet.* 119:1237–46
100. Ratcliffe RH, Cambron SE, Flanders KL, Bosque-Perez NA, Clement SL, Ohm HW. 2000. Biotype composition of Hessian fly (Diptera: Cecidomyiidae) populations from the southeastern, midwestern, and northwestern United States and virulence to resistance genes in wheat. *J. Econ. Entomol.* 93:1319–28
101. Rector BG, All JN, Parrott WA, Boerma HR. 2000. Quantitative trait loci for antibiosis resistance to corn earworm in soybean. *Crop Sci.* 40:233–38

81. Reviews herbivore-derived signaling compounds eliciting plant HAMPs and ensuing defensive responses.

96. First use of an endophyte gene knockout approach to link a specific endophyte alkaloid with arthropod resistance.

102. Renganayaki K, Fritz AK, Sadasivum S, Pammi S, Harrington SE, et al. 2002. Mapping and progress toward map-based cloning of brown planthopper biotype-4 resistance gene introgressed from *Oryza officinalis* into cultivated rice, *O. sativa*. *Crop Sci.* 42:2114–17

103. Reports cloning of the first plant insect resistance gene (*Mi-1.2*).

103. Rossi M, Goggin FL, Milligan SB, Klaoshian I, Ullman DE, Williamson VM. 1998. The nematode resistance gene *Mi* of tomato confers resistance against the potato aphid. *Proc. Natl. Acad. Sci. USA* 95:9750–54

104. Sadasivam S, Thayumanavan B. 2003. *Molecular Host Plant Resistance to Pests*. New York: Marcel Dekker. 479 pp.

105. Sagredo B, Balbyshev N, Lafta A, Casper H, Lorenzen J. 2009. A QTL that confers resistance to Colorado potato beetle (*Leptinotarsa decemlineata* [Say]) in tetraploid potato populations segregating for leptine. *Theor. Appl. Genet.* 119:1171–81

106. Sandanayaka WRM, Bus VGM, Connolly P. 2005. Mechanisms of woolly aphid [*Eriosoma lanigerum* (Hausm.)] resistance in apple. *J. Appl. Entomol.* 129:534–41

107. Sargent DJ, Fernández-Fernández F, Rys A, Knight VH, Simpson DW, Tobutt KR. 2007. Mapping of A_1 conferring resistance to the aphid *Amphorophora idaei* and *dw* (dwarfing habit) in red raspberry (*Rubus idaeus* L.) using AFLP and microsatellite markers. *BMC Plant Biol.* 7:15

108. Satish K, Srinivas G, Madhusudhana R, Padmaja PG, Nagaraja Reddy R, et al. 2009. Identification of quantitative trait loci for resistance to shoot fly in sorghum [*Sorghum bicolor* (L.) Moench]. *Theor. Appl. Genet.* 119:1425–39

109. Schardl CL, Grossman RB, Nagabhyru P, Faulkner JR, Mallik UP. 2007. Loline alkaloids: currencies of mutualism. *Phytochemistry* 68:980–96

110. Schmelz EA, Engelberth J, Alborn HT, Tumlinson JH, Teal PEA. 2009. Phytohormone-based activity mapping of insect herbivore-produced elicitors. *Proc. Natl. Acad. Sci. USA* 106:653–57

111. Sharma HC. 2009. *Biotechnological Approaches for Pest Management and Ecological Sustainability*. Boca Raton, FL: CRC Press. 526 pp.

112. Sherman JD, Weaver DK, Hofland ML, Sing SE, Buteler M, et al. 2010. Identification of novel QTL for sawfly resistance in wheat. *Crop Sci.* 50:73–86

113. Smith CM. 1989. *Plant Resistance to Insects: A Fundamental Approach*. New York: Wiley. 286 pp.

114. Smith CM. 2004. Plant resistance against pests: issues and strategies. In *Integrated Pest Management: Potential, Constraints and Challenges*, ed. O Koul, GS Dhaliwal, GW Cuperus, pp. 147–67. Wallingford/Cambridge, UK: CABI. 329 pp.

115. Smith CM. 2005. *Plant Resistance to Arthropods: Molecular and Conventional Approaches*. Dordrecht, The Netherlands: Springer. 423 pp.

116. Smith CM. 2010. Biochemical plant defenses against herbivores: from poisons to spices. In *All Flesh is Grass, Plant-Animal Interrelationships Series: Cellular Origins, Life in Extreme Habitats and Astrobiology*, ed. Z Dubinsky, J Seckbach, pp. 1–20. Berlin: Springer. 485 pp.

117. Smith CM, Boyko EV. 2007. The molecular bases of plant resistance and defense responses to aphid feeding: current status. *Entomol. Exp. Appl.* 122:1–16

118. Smith CM, Khan ZR, Pathak MD. 1994. *Techniques for Evaluating Insect Resistance in Crop Plants*. Boca Raton, FL: CRC Press. 320 pp.

119. Smith CM, Liu XM, Wang LJ, Liu X, Chen M-S, et al. 2010. Aphid feeding activates expression of a transcriptome of oxylipin-based defense signals in wheat involved in resistance to herbivory. *J. Chem. Ecol.* 36:260–76

120. Smith MAH, Lamb RJ, Wise IL, Olfert OO. 2004. An interspersed refuge for *Sitodiplosis mosellana* (Diptera: Cecidomyiidae) and a biocontrol agent *Macroglenes penetrans* (Hymenoptera: Pteromalidae) to manage crop resistance in wheat. *Bull. Entomol. Res.* 94:179–88

121. Spiering MJ, Moon CD, Wilkinson HH, Schardl CL. 2005. Gene clusters for insecticidal loline alkaloids in the grass-endophytic fungus *Neotyphodium uncinatum*. *Genetics* 169:1403–14

122. Stewart SA, Hodge S, Ismail N, Mansfield JW, Feys BJ, et al. 2009. The *rap 1* gene confers effective, race-specific resistance to the pea aphid in *Medicago truncatula* independent of the hypersensitive reaction. *Mol. Plant-Microbe Interact.* 22:1645–55

123. Stoeckli S, Mody K, Gessler C, Patocchi A, Jermini M, Dorn S. 2008. QTL analysis for aphid resistance and growth traits in apple. *Tree Genet. Genomes* 4:833–47

124. Stout M, Davis J. 2009. Keys to the increased use of host-plant resistance in integrated pest management. In *Integrated Pest Management: Innovation-Development Process*, ed. R Peshin, AK Dhawan, pp. 163–81. New York/Heidelberg: Springer Science + Business Media. 690 pp.

124. Discusses use of conventional and molecular tools to better integrate arthropod-resistant crops into IPM programs.

125. Stout MJ. 2007. Types and mechanisms of rapidly induced plant resistance to herbivorous arthropods. In *Induced Resistance for Plant Defence*, ed. D Walters, A Newton, G Lyon, pp. 89–107. Oxford: Blackwell. 271 pp.

126. Sullivan TJ, Rodstrom J, Vandop J, Librizzi J, Graham C, et al. 2007. Symbiont-mediated changes in *Lolium arundinaceum* inducible defenses: evidence from changes in gene expression and leaf composition. *New Phytol.* 176:673–79

127. Tabashnik BE, Carrière Y, Dennehy TJ, Morin S, Sisterson MS, et al. 2003. Insect resistance to transgenic *Bt* crops: lessons from the laboratory and field. *J. Econ. Entomol.* 96:1031–38

128. Tan GX, Weng QM, Ren X, Huang Z, Zhu LL, He GC. 2004. Two whitebacked planthopper resistance genes in rice share the same loci with those for brown planthopper resistance. *Heredity* 92:212–17

129. Tanaka A, Tapper BA, Popay A, Parker EJ, Scott B. 2005. A symbiosis expressed non-ribosomal peptide synthetase from a mutualistic fungal endophyte of perennial ryegrass confers protection to the symbiotum from insect herbivory. *Mol. Microbiol.* 57:1036–50

130. Tao YZ, Hardy A, Drenth J, Henzell RG, Franzmann BA, et al. 2003. Identifications of two different mechanisms for sorghum midge resistance through QTL mapping. *Theor. Appl. Genet.* 107:116–22

131. Teetes GL, Anderson RM, Peterson GC. 1994. Exploitation of sorghum midge nonpreference resistance in sorghum midge (Diptera: Cecidomyiidae) using mixed plantings of resistant and susceptible sorghum hybrids. *J. Econ. Entomol.* 87:826–31

132. Teetes GL, Peterson GC, Nwanze KF, Pendleton BB. 1999. Genetic diversity of sorghum: a source of insect-resistant germplasm. In *Global Plant Genetic Resources for Insect-Resistant Crops*, ed. SL Clement, SS Quisenberry, pp. 63–82. Boca Raton, FL: CRC Press. 295 pp.

133. Thomas J, Fineberg N, Penner G, McCartney C, Aung T, et al. 2005. Chromosome location and markers of *Sm1*: a gene of wheat that conditions antibiotic resistance to orange wheat blossom midge. *Mol. Breed.* 15:183–92

134. Thomas MB. 1999. Ecological approaches and the development of "truly integrated" pest management. *Proc. Natl. Acad. Sci. USA* 96:5944–51

135. Underwood N, Rausher M. 2002. Comparing the consequences of induced and constitutive plant resistance for herbivore population dynamics. *Am. Nat.* 160:20–30

136. Underwood NC, Rausher M, Cook W. 2002. Bioassay versus chemical assay: measuring the impact of induced and constitutive resistance on herbivores in the field. *Oecologia* 131:211–19

137. van Eck L, Schultz T, Leach JE, Scofield SR, Peairs FB, et al. 2010. Virus-induced gene silencing of *WRKY53* and an inducible *phenylalanine ammonia-lyase* in wheat reduces aphid resistance. *Plant Biotechnol. J.* 8:1023–32

137. Silencing a wheat WRKY transcription factor mediating JA-SA cross-talk, or an inducible phenylalanine ammonia-lyase, reduces aphid resistance.

138. van Emden HF. 2007. Host-plant resistance. In *Aphids as Crop Pests*, ed. HF van Emden, R Harrington, pp. 447–68. Wallingford, UK: CABI. 717 pp.

139. Waiss AC, Chan BG, Elliger CA, Wiseman BR, McMillian WW, et al. 1979. Maysin, a flavone glycoside from corn silks with antibiotic activity toward corn earworm. *J. Econ. Entomol.* 72:256–58

140. Willcox MC, Khairallah MM, Bergvinson D, Crossa J, Deutsch JA, et al. 2002. Selection for resistance to southwestern corn borer using marker-assisted selection and conventional backcrossing. *Crop Sci.* 42:1516–28

141. Wroblewski T, Piskurewicz U, Tomczak A, Ochoa O, Michelmore RW. 2007. Silencing of the major family of NBS–LRR-encoding genes in lettuce results in the loss of multiple resistance specificities. *Plant J.* 51:803–18

142. Wu K-M, Lu Y-H, Feng H-Q, Jiang Y-Y, Zhao J-Z. 2008. Suppression of cotton bollworm in multiple crops in China in areas with *Bt* toxin-containing cotton. *Science* 321:1676–78

143. Wu Y, Huang Y. 2008. Molecular mapping of QTLs for resistance to the greenbug *Schizaphis graminum* (Rondani) in *Sorghum bicolor* (Moench). *Theor. Appl. Genet.* 117:117–24

144. Yencho GC, Cohen MB, Byrne PF. 2000. Applications of tagging and mapping insect resistance loci in plants. *Annu. Rev. Entomol.* 45:393–422

145. Young CA, Tapper BA, May K, Moon CD, Schardl CL, Scott B. 2009. Indole-diterpene biosynthetic capability of *Epichloë* endophytes as predicted by *ltm* gene analysis. *Appl. Environ. Microbiol.* 75:2200–11
146. Zhang D-X, Stromberg AJ, Spiering MJ, Schardl CL. 2009. Coregulated expression of loline alkaloid-biosynthesis genes in *Neotyphodium uncinatum* cultures. *Fungal Genet. Biol.* 46:517–30
147. Zhang G, Gu C, Wang D. 2010. A novel locus for soybean aphid resistance. *Theor. Appl. Genet.* 120:1183–91
148. Zhang P, Wang Y, Zhang J, Maddock S, Snook M, Peterson T. 2003. A maize QTL for silk maysin levels contains duplicated Myb-homologous genes which jointly regulate flavone biosynthesis. *Plant Mol. Biol.* 52:1–15
149. Zhu L, Liu X, Liu XM, Jeannotte R, Reese J, et al. 2008. Hessian fly (*Mayetiola destructor*) attack causes a dramatic shift in carbon and nitrogen metabolism in wheat. *Mol. Plant-Microbe Interact.* 21:70–78
150. Zhu LC, Smith CM, Fritz A, Boyko EV, Voothuluru P, Gill BS. 2005. Inheritance and molecular mapping of new greenbug resistance genes in wheat germplasms derived from *Aegilops tauschii*. *Theor. Appl. Genet.* 111:831–37

RELATED RESOURCES

Núñez-Farfán J, Fornoni J, Valverde PL. 2007. The evolution of resistance and tolerance to herbivores. *Annu. Rev. Ecol. Evol. Syst.* 38:541–66

Orians CM, Ward D. 2010. Evolution of plant defenses in nonindigenous environments. *Annu. Rev. Entomol.* 55:439–59

St. Clair DA. 2010. Quantitative disease resistance and quantitative resistance loci in breeding. *Annu. Rev. Phytopathol.* 48:247–68

Prospects for Managing Turfgrass Pests with Reduced Chemical Inputs

David W. Held[1,*] and Daniel A. Potter[2]

[1]Department of Entomology and Plant Pathology, Auburn University, Auburn, Alabama 36849-5413; email: david.held@auburn.edu

[2]Department of Entomology, University of Kentucky, Lexington, Kentucky 40546-0091; email: dapotter@uky.edu

Annu. Rev. Entomol. 2012. 57:329–54

First published online as a Review in Advance on September 9, 2011

The *Annual Review of Entomology* is online at ento.annualreviews.org

This article's doi:
10.1146/annurev-ento-120710-100542

0066-4170/12/0107-0329$20.00

*Corresponding author

Keywords

urban entomology, integrated pest management, biological control, microbial control, insecticides, landscape ecology

Abstract

Turfgrass culture, a multibillion dollar industry in the United States, poses unique challenges for integrated pest management. Why insect control on lawns, golf courses, and sport fields remains insecticide-driven, and how entomological research and extension can best support nascent initiatives in environmental golf and sustainable lawn care are explored. High standards for aesthetics and playability, prevailing business models, risk management–driven control decisions, and difficulty in predicting pest outbreaks fuel present reliance on preventive insecticides. New insights into pest biology, sampling methodology, microbial insecticides, plant resistance, and conservation biological control are reviewed. Those gains, and innovations in reduced-risk insecticides, should make it possible to begin constructing holistic management plans for key turfgrass pests. Nurturing the public's interest in wildlife habitat preservation, including beneficial insects, may be one means to change aesthetic perceptions and gain leeway for implementing integrated pest management practices that lend stability to turfgrass settings.

INTRODUCTION

Integrated pest management (IPM): an approach to managing pests by combining biological, cultural, physical, and chemical tools in a way that minimizes economic, health, and environmental risks

Thatch: a tightly intermingled layer of living and dead roots, crowns, stolons, and organic debris that accumulates between the zone of green vegetation and the soil surface

Humans have used turfgrasses to enhance their environment for more than 1,000 years (7). The turfgrass industry has grown rapidly since the 1970s when large tracts of land were developed to accommodate an expanding suburban population. Turfgrasses provide recreational health benefits; enhanced property values; a draw for golf tourism; and important ecosystem services including heat dissipation, soil carbon sequestration, soil erosion control, dust stabilization, and reduced noise, glare, and water runoff, compared with impervious surfaces (7). There are concerns, however, about the impacts of turfgrass culture on consumption of limited water resources, surface and groundwater quality, and nontarget terrestrial and aquatic organisms (99, 117). Turf managers everywhere are facing a perfect storm of financial pressures, expectations for high-quality lawns and playing surfaces, and concerns about energy and water conservation and carbon footprint reduction, as well as chemical inputs. In this system, millions of pest control decisions are made by persons ranging from skilled professional grounds managers to homeowners, posing unique challenges for integrated pest management (IPM).

University assignments with responsibility for turfgrass entomology and resulting research publications have proliferated since the first *Annual Review of Entomology* article on the subject was published (109). This review highlights selected studies that have advanced our understanding of turfgrass insects since 1990, as well as the problems and prospects for managing insect pests of lawns, golf courses, and sport fields with reduced chemical inputs. Most recent IPM-oriented research publications on turfgrass insects are from the United States and Canada, but similar pests and issues exist wherever turfgrass is grown. Although our focus is on the North American literature, citations to selected studies that significantly expanded knowledge of turfgrass insects and IPM in other regions of the world also are included.

INTEGRATED PEST MANAGEMENT: CHALLENGES

Turfgrass is frequently maintained as a low-cut monoculture with pulsed inputs of water, fertilizers, and pesticides. In many communities, a lush evenly mowed lawn of a single grass species without weeds or irregularities has become a symbol of pride in the appearance of one's property and the landowner's responsibility for keeping one's neighborhood looking attractive. American golfers historically prefer dense, green fairways and smooth, fast putting surfaces. Such conditions can favor plant-feeding arthropods by influencing bottom-up effects on nutritional quality and chemical defenses of their hosts (22, 36, 134) and by reducing harborage and alternative resources for natural enemies (18, 45). Furthermore, some management practices create favorable microhabitats for pests, and certain pesticides can disrupt ecosystem services, leading to soil compaction, excessive thatch accumulation, pest resurgence, or secondary pest outbreaks (e.g., 87, 104, 107, 129, 142, 155).

TURF AND TURFGRASSES

Turf is a covering of mowed vegetation, usually a turfgrass, that grows intimately with an upper soil stratum of intermingled roots and stems. Turfgrass refers to a species or cultivar of grass, usually of spreading habit, that is maintained as a mowed turf. Cool-season turfgrasses are cold-tolerant species best adapted to temperate regions and growth during cool, moist periods of the year. Warm-season turfgrasses are heat-tolerant species best adapted to warmer regions and growth during warmer periods; the latter are usually dormant during cold weather or may be killed by it.

IMPORTANCE OF TURF

Turfgrasses now cover about 164,000 km^2 of the continental United States, an area three times larger than any irrigated crop (99). More than 75% of that area comprises tens of millions of residential, commercial, and institutional lawns, with the rest subdivided into some 16,000 golf facilities, 700,000 sport fields, and countless playgrounds, parks, cemeteries, grassy roadsides, and other sites (108). The U.S. turfgrass industry generated revenue yields exceeding $62 billion in 2005 dollars while sustaining about 825,000 jobs (56).

University-supported pilot programs exploring ways in which commercial lawn or tree care providers might offer customers a holistic, yet profitable, alternative to calendar-based preventive sprays have found that IPM precepts developed for field crops often do not readily translate to turf, a disaggregated perennial system in which millions of individual pest control decisions are driven more by aesthetics and consumer culture than by traditional metrics, e.g., yield loss (108, 109). Still, the IPM approach—scouting or sampling to assess the need for treatment, setting reasonable action thresholds, and integrating cultural and biological controls into the management plan—is a sensible approach. Why, then, is turf insect management in the United States still largely insecticide driven?

Lawn and garden products accounted for 16% of conventional insecticides used in the United States in 2001 (68). Insecticides account for a higher percentage of annual chemical expenditures for lawn care companies than for golf courses, 31% versus 19%, respectively (117). Most modern turfgrass insecticides have low intrinsic toxicity to vertebrates and low use rates. All modern classes of soil insecticides have several months' residual activity, so they are preventively applied. Such treatments provide insurance against damage, but they also tend to be nonselective because the treatment decision is made before the extent of infestation is known. Additional statistics and citations concerning chemical usage, sources of pest control information, and other industry trends are summarized by Potter (108).

Constraints on Particular Industry Sectors

Apprehension due to a lack of knowledge of pest biology or potential for injury often drives consumers and some professionals to use insecticides as insurance against damage (**Figure 1**). The various providers and consumers of turfgrass services and products differ in the extent of their technical knowledge, as well as priorities when making pest control decisions. Perspective on those variables can help researchers and extension specialists focus their efforts on those components of IPM technology that have the greatest likelihood of being adopted by end users.

High-volume lawn service industry. Most lawn care providers offer calendar-based treatments that include fertilizer and insect and weed controls generally sold as programs. This is a volume-driven, service industry in which local, regional, and national companies compete for a relatively small (about 12%) sector of homeowners that hire professional lawn and landscape services (108). Work is seasonal, turnover is high, and new applicators may receive only cursory training in pest identification and diagnosis primarily through state pesticide applicator training programs. Pretreatment sampling and cultural control tactics are rarely implemented because lawn care technicians spend about 20 min per average (0.1 ha) lawn and have little control over turf culture. Insect control must be reliable because renovation of a damaged lawn is expensive and bad for business. Insecticides, therefore, provide the reliability and ease of application for a minimally

Preventive: a specific timing of an application of insecticide, typically a soil insecticide, before the damaging pest life stage is present

Figure 1

Examples of insect damage in different turf settings. (*a*) Turfgrass ant, *Lasius neoniger*, mounds on a putting green. (*b*) Indirect damage from vertebrate animals foraging for European chafer, *Rhizotrogus majalis*, grubs in a cemetery. (*c*) European crane fly, *Tipula paludosa*, damage to a home lawn in upstate New York. (*d*) Newly laid sod on football field defoliated by fall armyworm, *Spodoptera frugiperda*. Photo credit: panels *a* and *b*, D. Potter; panel *c*, D. Peck; and panel *d*, C. Reynolds.

trained work force. Lawn and landscape consultants may be used by high-end clients, but for IPM to "sell," customers must perceive they are receiving value even when the diagnosis calls for no treatment, or else they may cancel a service then perceived as unnecessary (108).

Golf courses, institutional grounds, and athletic fields. Most golf course superintendents have a turf management degree and years of experience and belong to professional organizations (e.g., Golf Course Superintendents Association of America). Experienced grounds or sport field managers have similar profiles. These persons have a longer history with managed turf, which also results in more familiarity with seasonal and geographical differences in pest populations. They have the experience to implement certain IPM tactics (e.g., mapping, use of resistant grasses, conservation biological control). Risk management—avoiding damage that could compromise aesthetics or playability—drives pest control decisions. The immediate cost for renovating an insect-damaged putting green, fairway, or sport field is measurable, but factors such as inconvenience to club members, lost revenue, and questions about the turf manager's competence may have longer-lasting consequences.

Sod producers. Sod farms supply a product used by other industry sectors. State laws vary, but most discourage or prohibit shipment or sale of insect-infested sod. Preventive control is usually too expensive given the large acreages that are grown. For federally regulated pests (e.g., red imported fire ant, *Solenopsis invicta*), shipment of sod from quarantined areas may be prohibited or else sod inspection and certification of sod as pest free will be required. For compliance, sod farmers may need to treat sod before the order is cut, inspected, and shipped.

Homeowners. Some 82 million households in the United States participated in lawn care or gardening activities in 2007, expending more than $35 billion on chemicals and other products (108). Many homeowners lack the knowledge to diagnose pest problems, evaluate different IPM practices, or even follow pesticide label directions. Pest control by consumers is mainly reactive, relying on lawn and garden product labels on the shelf, or salespersons at retail outlets, for pest control information. Local county extension offices, however, are among the least-used sources for homeowner information. Surveys indicate that homeowners do tend to be concerned about the environment and are receptive to nonchemical controls so long as they are convenient and inexpensive (95).

In summary, IPM technology for turfgrass must be cost effective, be easy to implement, and fit the abilities, requirements, and motivations of the particular industry sectors for which it is intended. Reliability of pest control tactics is especially important to professional turf care providers charged with maintaining attractive lawns and high-quality playing surfaces.

NEW INSIGHTS INTO PEST BIOLOGY

Textbooks and reviews summarizing information about turfgrass insects in the United States and Canada are listed as additional resources. This section briefly highlights key studies published since 1990 that focus on the life history of selected turfgrass insect pests, and surveys documenting invertebrate pests affecting golf courses in Korea (30) and Great Britain (93).

Black Cutworm

Behavioral studies of the black cutworm, *Agrotis ipsilon*, on golf courses revealed aspects of its biology that make it vulnerable to cultural control. Oviposition occurs on the tips of grass blades of low-cut turf of putting greens, where that pest is of highest concern. Daily mowing removes more than 80% of the eggs, but many survive on grass clippings (151). Late instars crawl onto putting surfaces from higher-cut surrounds and occupy holes left by core cultivation (the use of a machine with hollow tines to remove many small plugs of thatch and soil), but they are repelled somewhat by sand topdressing (150). Kentucky bluegrass, *Poa pratensis*, is the only cool-season turfgrass commonly used on golf courses that is resistant to *A. ipsilon* (152). These findings support the recommendation that bagging and disposal of clippings, establishing *P. pratensis* or focusing insecticide applications around the periphery of greens, and manipulating the timing of certain greens-keeping practices have value in an IPM plan. Adult captures in traps, however, were not a good predictor of subsequent larval activity (64). The migratory ecology of *A. ipsilon* in North America was clarified, which will allow better prediction of its annual appearance and disappearance on golf courses at different latitudes (136).

Crane Flies and March Flies

Two species of invasive crane flies, *Tipula* spp., are emerging pests of cool-season turfgrasses in North America (105). Presently established along the West Coast from British Columbia to northern California and in the Great Lakes regions of Canada and the United States, they are predicted to spread as far south as the mid-Atlantic states. Seasonal biology of the two invasive species and morphological features by which they can be distinguished and differentiated from native and noninjurious crane flies have been reported (105). A native crane fly, *Tipula umbrosa*, and larval March flies (*Plecia* sp.; Bibionidae) were collected from beneath centipede grass, *Eremochloa ophiuroides*, sod in Mississippi, the first report of either species damaging turf (57).

White Grubs

Root-feeding scarab larvae (white grubs) cause extensive injury to turfgrasses almost everywhere that they are grown. Recent studies have clarified the spatial ecology of familiar pest species (35, 43, 139), as well as species complexes and life histories in regions of the United States (23, 42, 78, 128) and Korea (30, 31, 84–86) where white grubs damaging to turfgrasses had not been well known (23, 42, 78, 128). Geographical differences, e.g., certain typically univoltine species possibly being bivoltine in Florida (23), challenge traditional guidelines for timing of control measures.

Weevils and Billbugs

The annual bluegrass weevil, *Listronotus maculicollis*, is a burgeoning pest of low-cut *Poa annua* on golf courses in the northeastern United States and eastern Canada (39, 40, 97, 137). Recent work on its overwintering habits, spatial distribution, movement, and population dynamics indicated that adults, which overwinter in high-cut grass or tree litter bordering fairways, crawl and enter putting greens, tees, and fairways from the edges and oviposit over several weeks in spring (39, 40, 96, 97). A sampling plan relating adult counts in suction samples to subsequent larval densities accurately predicted the spatial distribution and risk of damage (96, 97). Behavioral and electrophysiological responses of adults to *P. annua* volatiles suggest applications for such compounds in monitoring (98).

At least 10 species of billbugs (*Sphenophorus* spp.) inhabit turfgrasses in the United States, but relatively little was known about the southern pest species until a recent study clarified their abundance and seasonal activity on Florida golf courses (65). The hunting billbug, *Sphenophorus venatus vestitus*, was the most abundant species found. Unlike the more northern parts of its range, where it is univoltine or bivoltine, *S. venatus vestitus* has as many as six generations per year in Florida (65). Its biology was also clarified in Japan (55). The aforementioned studies on turf-infesting weevils and billbugs also helped refine sampling methodology for those pests.

Mole Crickets

Use of radiography, tunnel castings, photosensors, and other novel methods provided new insights into mole cricket, *Scapteriscus* spp., biology including the unique tunnel architecture of each species (147) and behavioral responses when encountering moisture gradients, pathogens, and pesticide residues in the soil environment (62, 145, 147). Regional differences in the seasonal biology of *Scapteriscus* and *Gryllotalpa* spp. were clarified in the southeastern United States (16) and South Africa (38), respectively, and turf damage by the northern mole cricket, *Neocurtilla hexadactyla*, was documented (126). Advances in classical biological control (44), microbial control, and other tactics for managing mole crickets are discussed in other sections of this review.

Sap-Feeding Pests

Ground pearls (Hemiptera: Sternorrhyncha: Margarodidae) are primitive scale insects that derive their common name from the pearl-like cyst stage. Two univoltine species that suck sap from the roots of warm-season turfgrasses occur in the southern United States, causing irregular dead patches, but the details of their biology are poorly known (63). Populations can be assessed by extracting cysts from a soil sample, but there is no established relationship between cyst counts and damage (63).

Buffalograss, *Bouteloua dactyloides*, is an indigenous, low-maintenance, drought-tolerant grass that has gained popularity as an alternative turfgrass for the North American Great Plains. The western chinch bug, *Blissus occiduus*, and two species of grass-feeding mealybugs (Pseudococcidae) have emerged as important pests of buffalograss (5, 6). Recent studies have clarified their seasonal biology, damage symptoms, reproductive hosts, natural enemies, and responses to management practices (5, 6, 26, 60). Interactions between buffalograss and *B. occiduus* have served as a model system for understanding induced defense responses of grasses to insect feeding (53). Similar work with *Blissus insularis*, an important pest of St. Augustinegrass (*Stenotaphrum secundatum*), investigated responses to cultural practices (22, 146) and mechanisms of grass resistance to its feeding (120, 121).

Mound-Building Nuisance Ants

Lasius neoniger is an important golf course pest because its mounds smother low-cut grass, dull mower blades, and disrupt the smoothness and uniformity of playing surfaces (89). The problem appears to have increased since older, broad-spectrum soil insecticides (e.g., diazinon) were withdrawn. The ant's seasonal biology and spatial distribution on golf courses and its response to management practices were clarified (89, 90). Main nests are located in natural soil around sand-based putting greens, not in the greens themselves, explaining the pattern of mounding and why ant control for greens should focus on perimeter treatment. The importance of *L. neoniger* and various *Solenopsis* spp. in biological control of other turf pests has been documented (87, 100, 155).

SUSTAINABLE PEST MANAGEMENT: PROSPECTS

Monitoring and Risk Assessment

Predicting when and where damaging pest infestations occur is among the greatest hurdles to reducing insecticide usage on turf. Preventive applications, in particular, require the turf manager to make an educated guess about need on the basis of early warning signs, e.g., adult activity, history of infestation, or, more often, the potential repercussions should a decision not to treat be followed by unacceptable levels of damage. Site-specific scouting for pests is practiced daily by golf superintendents but is impractical for lawn care providers servicing hundreds of accounts. Complicated, time-consuming sampling schemes (34, 92, 102) are not used by any industry sector. Degree-day models or plant-flowering dates can predict the appearance of some turf pests (13, 101). Precise timing, however, is less critical with effective, residual preventive insecticides.

Portable acoustic systems have been tested for nondestructively assessing soil insect populations, but they are time-consuming and may not distinguish insects from background noise

A PEST MANAGEMENT EXAMPLE

D.A. Potter visited a Thai golf superintendent who monitored mole crickets with illuminated electric grids on poles over the golf course ponds, with floating baskets tethered below. She graphed cricket flight peaks and used them to time nematode applications for biological control. Electrocuted crickets missing the baskets were fed upon by fish, which were harvested and eaten by the grounds crew.

(20, 157). Remote sensing, also tested for detecting previsible symptoms of grub damage, produced mixed results (54). Neither method detects early instars, the stage targeted with preventive insecticides.

Pheromone lures are available for some turf pests (2, 64, 128). Acoustic traps lure mole crickets with recordings of mating calls (44). Traps can provide useful information for consultants or extension specialists who provide area-wide recommendations, but few turf managers have the expertise or time to deploy them or to extrapolate the information they provide to control decisions.

Only a few studies have examined relationships between adult trap captures and subsequent densities of larvae or nymphs. Captures of adult *L. maculicollis* during peaks in emergence and cumulative counts across the emergence period were a good predictor of larval damage (96). The numbers of male masked chafers (*Cyclocephala* spp.) caught in traps baited with female extracts were weakly correlated with subsequent grub densities on golf courses (110). Such forecasting has more potential for pests that mate and oviposit on the same site (e.g., weevils, billbugs, masked chafers) than for pests that disperse long distances from their natal sites before ovipositing.

Density/damage relationships and action thresholds vary depending on turfgrass species and vigor (33, 96, 146), pest species and life stage, and site requirements. In practice, control decisions for turf pests are usually based on experience and on risk management considerations as opposed to specific action thresholds. Other studies profile the characteristics of turf sites at high risk from insect injury (e.g., 31, 35, 96, 102). Such associations, however, may not translate to different soil types, grass species, or regional climatic differences. For example, the amount of thatch in home lawns was positively correlated with hairy chinch bug, *Blissus leucopterus hirtus*, infestations in Michigan (37) but not in Quebec, Canada (91). Scarab pests can thrive and cause damage across a range of soil types, textures, and pH levels (124).

Cultural Control

Cultural control is more amenable to lawns and recreational fields than to playing surfaces on golf courses or sport fields. Golf superintendents do, however, regularly manipulate mowing, irrigation, dew removal, and other practices, within limits, to suppress turfgrass diseases. Such practices also affect insects but less predictably than for pathogens.

A low cutting height always stresses turfgrass, whereas maintaining the highest practical height of cut promotes a deep, extensive, and fibrous root system that enhances tolerance of injury and may inhibit feeding or oviposition by subsurface pests (113, 153). Frequent low cutting decreases alkaloid levels, and presumably insect resistance, in endophytic turfgrasses (134). Low-cut turf encourages mounding by nuisance ants (89), and it often supports fewer natural enemies, particularly predators (66, 132, 133, 139). On putting greens, mowing and catching the clippings physically remove black cutworm eggs attached to grass blades (151).

Irrigation: the process of adding supplemental water when rainfall is insufficient to meet the needs of the turfgrass

Withholding irrigation during adult flight periods may discourage oviposition by scarabs, mole crickets, and crane flies, whose early life stages are sensitive to dry soils (62, 105, 113). Once the damaging life stages are present, however, irrigation may help turf to tolerate or recover from insect injury (33). Southern chinch bugs seem to be equally damaging to St. Augustinegrass regardless of irrigation regime (146).

Nitrogen fertilization can enhance the food quality of grasses for foliage-feeding insects, promoting faster development and higher populations (22, 36). Subsurface pests seem less affected by application of inorganic nitrogen or urea (113), although autumn fertilization can boost recovery of cool season grasses from grub injury (33). Organic fertilizers made from stabilized sewage sludge, animal waste, or even grass clippings may attract adults of *Ataenius spretulus*, *Cotinis nitida*, or other scarabs whose larvae feed on decaying organic matter (19, 111, 113). Silicon fertilization, which may toughen grass blades and stems, nevertheless seems to provide little or no increased resistance to insect pests (77, 123). Manipulating soil pH within the range suitable for turfgrass vigor seems to have little impact on white grubs (113).

Other cultural practices may discourage infestation by particular pests. Topdressing putting greens with angular sand reduced colonization by black cutworms (150), whereas core cultivation produced holes that cutworms occupy as burrows (150). Core cultivation just before beetle flight did not discourage egg laying by adult scarabs (113). Outdoor floodlights attract night-flying adult scarabs, mole crickets, and cutworms, but manipulating lighting may not be practical for outdoor golf driving ranges and sport complexes operating at night.

Biological Control with Indigenous Natural Enemies

Numerous articles since 1990 document the rich fauna of indigenous predatory arthropods that inhabit lawns and golf courses (e.g., 17, 18, 58, 59, 67, 81, 87, 107, 132, 133, 142). The predominant groups including ants, rove beetles, ground and tiger beetles, predatory bugs, vespid wasps, and spiders are mostly generalists. None of them are commercially available, nor have there been any studies to determine whether there would be any benefit from augmentative release. Their services, however, have been confirmed by placing sentinel prey into turf and either directly observing predation or comparing predation between untreated plots and plots from which predators are suppressed by insecticides (87, 142, 155). Plots where ants were killed with fipronil and baits had much lower predation on cutworm eggs, and significantly higher grub populations, compared with plots where ants were not treated (87).

Much less research has been done on indigenous parasitoids of turfgrass pests. White grubs are parasitized by wasps in the families Tiphiidae and Scoliidae (129–131). Several species of egg and larval parasitoids in the families Encyrtidae, Tachinidae, and Braconidae attack various caterpillars (11, 15). Rhodesgrass mealybug, *Antonina graminis*, is parasitized by a native encyrtid wasp (27).

Classical, augmentative, and conservation biocontrol. For about 10 years, beginning in the mid- to late 1980s, three natural enemies of *Scapteriscus* spp. mole crickets, the tachinid fly *Ormia depleta*, the sphecid wasp *Larra bicolor*, and the nematode *Steinernema scapterisci*, were imported from South America and released into Florida for classical biological control (44). The nematode has been mass-produced and marketed, and *L. bicolor* has expanded its range in Florida and adjacent states (44). The program has contributed to substantial reduction in mole cricket trap captures near Gainesville (44). Registration and subsequent wide usage of neonicotinoid and phenylpyrazole soil insecticides during the same period likely also played a part in area-wide declines in mole cricket populations.

Research on *Tiphia vernalis*, a wasp introduced into the eastern United States from 1925 to 1933 for biological control of Japanese beetle, *Popillia japonica*, clarified its behavior, ecology, and impact on grub populations (129–131). Parasitism rates greater than 50% were found at some sites in Kentucky (130), suggesting that the wasp has become widely established. In contrast, biological control of Rhodesgrass mealybug (*Antonina graminis*) by an introduced encyrtid wasp seems to be breaking down, possibly because of trophic interference by red imported fire ants (27).

Endophyte: species of symbiotic fungi (*Neotyphodium*) that exist intracellularly in certain genera of grasses

Incorporating certain nectar-producing plants into turf habitats can attract and sustain *T. vernalis* (131), *L. bicolor* (1, 45), and predatory arthropods (45) and increase their impact on pests in nearby grass. Wildflower plots augmented populations of some, but not all, taxa of natural enemies in the floral plantings themselves but generally did not boost the already-high predation on pests in nearby turf (18). Diversification to conserve and augment natural enemies is compatible with trends in increased use of naturalized areas on golf courses (46, 88, 133, 141), and with landscaping in residential areas. Some classes of turfgrass insecticides have low impact on natural enemies, making them compatible with conservation biological control (see Advances in Insecticide Chemistry, below).

Host Plant Resistance

Professional turfgrass managers choose a particular turfgrass for site establishment or renovation usually on the basis of its agronomic characteristics, playability, and disease resistance (108). Contractors or homeowners may simply choose the cheapest grass seed available. Insect resistance rarely is a deciding factor nor has it been a focus for grass breeders or the National Turfgrass Evaluation Program. Dozens of studies document differences in insect preference or performance among turfgrass species, cultivars, or accessions (125). The most tangible benefit of such work has been the release and widespread use of several St. Augustinegrass cultivars resistant to southern chinch bug, a major lawn pest in the southern United States (125). Little resistance has been found against white grubs (33, 112) or mole crickets (44, 125), and even relatively grub-tolerant grasses may be severely damaged by vertebrate predators when the insects are present. Although screening for cultivars that are somewhat less preferred or less suitable for one or two sporadic insect pests is unlikely to have much impact, breeding turfgrasses that combine broad pest resistance with good agronomic characteristics would be useful. *Zoysia matrella* 'Cavalier,' which is resistant to several key pests, is an example of such a grass (125).

Most studies of turfgrass resistance to insects have characterized differences within the traditional triad of antibiosis, antixenosis, and tolerance without addressing underlying mechanisms (125). Some work, however, has started to decipher why certain grasses are resistant. Several mechanisms—including compensatory photosynthesis; thick-walled sclerenchyma cells, which reduce stylet penetration to vascular tissues; and induction of oxidative enzymes involved in plant signaling, synthesis of defensive compounds, and oxidative stress tolerance—may be involved in grass resistance to chinch bugs (61, 120, 121). Identifying genes that encode those enzymes could provide useful markers for screening germplasm and breeding new resistant varieties to keep one step ahead of pests such as *Blissus insularis*, which can overcome host resistance (125).

Certain fescue (*Festuca* spp.) and ryegrass (*Lolium* spp.) cultivars benefit from alkaloids produced by endophytic fungi that then convey resistance to many leaf- and stem-feeding insects. A number of endophytic (E+) grass cultivars have been released to the market. Endophytes seem to have little effect on subsurface pests (71, 72) probably because the alkaloids are concentrated in aboveground tissues. New endophyte-grass combinations can be produced through maternal line breeding or direct fungal inoculation, allowing E+ cultivars with elevated alkaloid levels and enhanced insect resistance to be created (114). Endophytes have not been found in Kentucky bluegrass, creeping bentgrass, or warm-season grasses, but advances in molecular genetics of grass-endophyte associations, including identification of the genes that control alkaloid synthesis, may provide additional E+ turfgrasses for use in IPM.

Replacing or renovating a turfgrass stand with a more pest-resistant grass is time-consuming, is expensive, and may cause temporary revenue loss for sport complexes and golf courses. To overcome this hurdle, overseeding existing stands with E+ perennial ryegrass may convey protection against endophyte-sensitive pests. Indeed, only partial stand replacement was needed to reduce population densities and damage from chinch bugs, sod webworms, and billbug larvae, and benefits improved as the proportion of E+ grass increased (127). Grasses that slow the developmental rate of pests can amplify suppression by predators that focus on early instars (67).

Microbial control. Microbial insecticides constitute a miniscule fraction (less than 0.1%) of the United States turfgrass insecticide market (52). Professionals tend not to use them because they are more costly, awkward to use, and often less reliable than chemical insecticides (50, 108). Pathogenic microbes are sensitive to varying degrees to desiccation, UV degradation, pesticides, and biotic factors that can compromise their performance (4, 41, 50, 52, 143), and their relatively narrow activity spectrum, short residual activity, and limited shelf life further discourage adoption (50, 52). Inability to mass-produce baculoviruses and milky disease bacteria in vitro remains a hurdle. Development of microbial turf insecticides waned in the 1990s when companies realized they could not compete with neonicotinoids and other reduced-risk chemistries.

There are, however, niche markets for microbial insecticides for organic lawn care, school grounds and other sensitive sites, and municipalities that strictly regulate pesticide use (8, 52, 108). The products presently marketed in North America include two types of bacterial derivatives, spinosad, and delta endotoxins produced by *B. thuringiensis* var. *kurstaki*; entomopathogenic nematodes (*Steinernema carpocapsae*, *S. scapterisci*, and *Heterorhabditis bacteriophora*); dust and granular products with milky disease bacteria; and a few fungal formulations (52, 108).

Nematodes

Nematodes provide good control of certain turfgrass pests under favorable conditions (50). They pose no environmental hazard, have low impact on beneficial invertebrates (but see 103), and are exempt from federal regulation. Since 1990, numerous studies have evaluated new nematode species and strains, explored large-scale production technology, and furthered our understanding of how nematodes interact with soil conditions, agrichemicals, endophytic grasses, and other biocontrol agents (50, 71, 74, 75). With continued genetic improvement and advances in culture and formulation technology, nematodes will likely be utilized more broadly in turf IPM.

Most nematodes have a limited host range; e.g., *S. scapterisci* infects only mole crickets. Both *S. scapterisci* and *S. riobravis* provide curative control, but because the former species also reproduces

ENTOMOPATHOGENIC NEMATODES

Nematode species differ in host-finding behavior and activity against different pest guilds. Species having a sedentary ambush strategy (e.g., *S. carpocapsae*, *S. scapterisci*) are best suited for controlling mobile insects (e.g., cutworms, mole crickets), whereas more active "cruiser" nematodes (e.g., *H. bacteriophora*) are more effective against relatively sedentary soil-dwelling pests, e.g., white grubs (50). Failure to take those differences into account is a common cause of poor control (50). Nematode susceptibility may change as hosts develop through successive instars (115). Preapplication mowing and aeration sometimes increase nematode efficacy against soil-dwelling pests (83).

within adult crickets and larger nymphs, it is better suited for classical biological control (44). Different nematodes vary in infectivity against particular white grubs; e.g., *H. bacteriophora* can provide good curative control of *P. japonica*, whereas consistent control of some other destructive species has been achieved only with *Steinernema scarabaei*, a nematode that, thus far, has not been possible to mass-produce (76). *Steinernema carpocapsae* and *Steinernema feltiae* control grass-feeding caterpillars and European crane fly, *Tipula paludosa* larvae, respectively (21, 138). Released nematodes, in most cases, do not persist in soil and thatch at densities high enough to reliably control successive pest generations (21, 24).

Chemical or biological agents that weaken a pest can increase its susceptibility to nematode infection. The most practical synergists may be soil insecticides that are already registered for turf. Sublethal exposure to neonicotinoids, for example, disrupts the normal defensive behaviors of late-instar scarab larvae against nematode attack (71, 75). Chlorantraniliprole, an anthranilic diamide, has similar effects, at least for *H. bacteriophora* and *P. japonica* (73). Neither chemical class seems to compromise nematode reproduction in infected grubs or viability in tank mixes (4, 74). Combining nematodes with the scarab-specific Buibui strain of *B. thuringiensis* or the fungus *Metarhizium anisopliae* resulted in additive or synergistic activity against white grubs, but the bacteria or fungi needed to be applied several weeks before the nematode application (3, 74).

Endophytic turfgrasses may synergize or interfere with nematode efficacy in biological control. For cutworms or fall armyworms, both of which are relatively tolerant of endophytes, feeding on such grasses renders them less susceptible to *S. carpocapsae* evidently because endophyte-produced alkaloids are toxic to the nematodes' symbiotic bacterium (80). Interactions between endophytic grasses and *H. bacteriophora* for white grub control are weak and variable (72).

Bacteria

Species-specific strains of *Paenibacillus* and *Serratia* spp. naturally infect white grubs in the field (25, 122). Dusts and granules containing in vivo–produced *Paenibacillus* spores are marketed for suppression of *P. japonica*, but it is questionable whether they induce enough milky disease for site-specific control (122). Inability of *Paenibacillus* spores to grow on artificial media, specificity of strains to particular scarab species, high cost, and poor field performance have discouraged commercial development of milky disease bacteria. No *Serratia* formulations have been marketed for use on turf. Both *Paenibacillus* and *Serratia* are relatively weak pathogens and are unlikely to meet industry needs for fast, consistent control.

Fungi

Virulent isolates of *Beauveria* and *Metarhizium* spp. will infect and kill various pests under controlled conditions (51, 144). Inundative applications of *Beauveria brongniartii*, or of a particularly virulent isolate of *M. anisopliae*, suppressed white grubs on golf courses and sport fields, particularly when applied in combination with the nematode *H. bacteriophora* (3, 29). More often, though, mycoinsecticides have failed to provide consistent control in turf settings (106, 119, 154). Entomopathogenic fungi are sensitive to soil moisture, humidity, temperature, UV degradation, fungistatic effects of other soil microbes, and some pesticides, especially fungicides. They are costly to mass-produce, and different strains vary in virulence to particular pest species. Presently in the United States only a few mycoinsecticides are labeled for turf. They are not widely available, are of questionable efficacy, and are rarely used (52).

Grubs and mole crickets actively avoid soils containing entomopathogenic fungi (145, 148), which may help explain the erratic field performance of fungal insecticides. This does suggest that biologically active compounds may be cultured from fungi for use as feeding deterrents or to repel pests from treated turf areas. It may be possible to prolong conidial viability using UV protectants (144) or to synergize fungi by applying them with neonicotinoids or other agents (143).

Baculoviruses

Agrotis ipsilon multicapsid nucleopolyhedrovirus (AgipMNPV), which naturally infects black cutworms on golf courses, has been evaluated as a microbial insecticide. One-week-old spray residues of in vivo–produced virus lethally infected 75% to 90% of early instars in golf course settings (11, 116). Activity, however, waned after a few weeks and was not extended by adjuvants intended to shield the virus from UV degradation (11). Golf courses are a severe environment for a baculovirus because mowing, irrigation, and exposure to sunlight remove inoculum from the system more rapidly than infective occlusion bodies are replenished by horizontal transmission (11). Smaller cutworms succumb quickly, but larger ones feed for several days after infection, so AgipMNPV seems better suited for targeting early instars than for curative control once damage appears. AgipMNPV is neither synergized nor deactivated by the alkaloids in E+ perennial ryegrass and thus is compatible for use with such grasses (10). The addition of a chitin synthesis-inhibiting fungicide that disrupts peritrophic membrane function failed to synergize AgipMNPV infectivity to cutworms in the field (12).

Other pathogens. *Ovavesicula popilliae*, a microsporidian that naturally infects the Malpighian tubules of *P. japonica*, may be present in 40% or more of the larval population at some sites, reducing fecundity in adults and overwintering survival of larvae (140). The eugregarine *Stictospora villani* reduces survival of postoverwintered third-instar *P. japonica* to adulthood (124). *Thelohania solenopsae*, a microsporidian that weakens and may kill whole colonies of the red imported fire ant (*Solenopsis invicta*), is horizontally transmitted to uninfected colonies (149). Both *O. popilliae* and *T. solenopsae* have potential as agents for classical biological control of their respective hosts (140, 149).

Microbial derivatives. *B. thuringiensis* var. *kurstaki* (*Btk*) is labeled against turfgrass caterpillars but is rarely used because of its rapid degradation in sunlight, narrow activity spectrum, slow action, and weak activity against late instars. Even against susceptible species, success with *Btk* requires monitoring for presence of early instars. Black cutworm, a logical target because of its pest status on putting greens, is resistant to most lepidopteran-active *Bt* Cry proteins. It is, however, susceptible to some genetically modified hybrid *Bt* crystal proteins, suggesting a means by which usefulness of *Bt* toxins for turfgrass IPM might be enhanced (107). An isolate of *B. thuringiensis*, serovar *japonensis* strain Buibui (*Btj*), has varying degrees of activity against different white grub species and instars (9). Combining it with certain naturally occurring bacteria could enhance its activity more than if *Btj* were used alone (94). *Btj* is not commercially available, but it could find a market for curative grub control if problems of formulation and how to deliver it to the root zone could be resolved. Another *Bt* strain, *Bt* var. *israeliensis*, is active against crane fly larvae (106). It is not yet labeled for the U.S. turf market.

Spinosad, which contains macrocyclic lactones produced during fermentation by the soil bacterium *Saccharopolyspora spinosa*, selectively targets the nicotinic acetylcholine receptors of insect nerves (117). Spinosad products are labeled for turf and are effective against grass-feeding caterpillars (51) and fire ants (149). They also are active against annual bluegrass weevil but not against sucking pests, white grubs, or mole crickets (117). Spinosad has a relatively short residual period (about the same as that of pyrethroids), low use rates, and low toxicity to noninsect organisms.

Pheromones and Other Attractants

Synthetic sex pheromones are available for monitoring flights of several lepidopteran and scarabaeid pests (2, 64, 108, 128, 156). Traps can be used in surveys to track the regional spread of invasive pests (2, 31), and in regulatory control efforts to eradicate or slow the spread of infestations in recently invaded areas. Optimization of semiochemicals requires effective synthetic lures and an understanding of the relationship between volatile load and recruitment distances. Volatile loads would likely be lower for semiochemicals used for lures than for ones used for mass-trapping, monitoring, or mating disruption (43). Female *L. maculicollis*, which crawls from overwintering sites to closely mowed playing surfaces, responds to odors emitted from its preferred host grass (98). Because adult captures in pitfall traps are a good indicator of larval damage (96), volatiles could be useful in monitoring systems (98). Response of other turf pests or their natural enemies to volatile semiochemicals is an unexplored area that could yield additional tools for IPM.

Pheromones may find applications for autodissemination of insect pathogens. Japanese beetles captured in live traps containing fungi or nematodes were contaminated with the agents when flying off (69). Whether such adults carry enough inoculum to establish diseases in larval habitats has not yet been shown.

Mating disruption, too, has potential for suppressing pests with localized mating flights and limited dispersal. The concept was tested for Oriental beetle and had promising results (70). An unforeseen nuisance was that shoes of persons who walked through grass sprayed with the pheromone were contaminated and attracted aroused male beetles for several days! Less dislodgeable formulations are being developed.

Botanical Pesticides and Feeding Deterrents

Several azadirachtin-based products are labeled for turf but they are relatively expensive and rarely used. Azadirachtin is active against young caterpillars, but it is too slow acting to be an effective control for late instars, e.g., large cutworms damaging putting greens (49). It is active against mole cricket nymphs and first-instar white grubs in lab assays (14, 49), but application at label rate, followed by watering, failed to control larger grubs in the field (49). Extract of black pepper, *Piper nigrum*, seeds controlled European chafer grubs at levels comparable to those of diazinon (135), suggesting that it may have promise for spot treatment. Botanicals are not necessarily environmentally benign; e.g., *Piper* extract also suppressed earthworms (135).

Advances in Insecticide Chemistry

Since 1993, new classes of turf insecticides with novel target sites and modes of action, low use rates, useful but not excessive residual activity, and favorable toxicological profiles have been labeled (**Table 1**). Many of the products are root-systemic, controlling subsurface and leaf- and stem-feeders from one application, but their selectivity limits the range of pests each product will control. Neonicotinoids, for example, are more active against white grubs than against caterpillars (48), whereas the opposite is true for pyrethroids and indoxacarb. Halofenozide, an ecdysone agonist, controls some scarab species but not others (32).

Most modern soil insecticides (e.g., neonicotinoids, anthranilic diamides, fipronil) provide residual activity and are much more active against neonates of pests than against later instars (48, 79). These factors have driven an industry-wide shift from curative to preventive control of white grubs, mole crickets, and other key pests (108). Professionals favor the latter approach because of the flexibility and insurance against damage it provides. Most turf pests are patchily distributed (35, 102), so preventive control is imprecise because the treatment is made before the extent of

Table 1 Representative insecticides labeled for turfgrass usage in the United States in 1990 and 2011, showing greater diversity of chemistry and generally more favorable toxicology of today's products[a]

Year	Chemical	Chemical class[b]	Rate (kg AI/ha)	Oral LD_{50} (mg/kg)[c]		LC_{50} (ppm)[c]
				Rat	Mallard duck	Rainbow trout
			Insecticides targeting subsurface pests			
1990	Diazinon	OP	3.4–4.5	300–400	1.5–3.0	3
	Ethoprop	OP	5.6	30	4–61	2
	Isofenphos	OP	0.9–2.2	28–38	34	2–4
	Carbaryl[d]	C	9.0	250–850	>2,179	2
2011	Imidacloprid	N	0.34–0.45	424	>4,797	>8,300
	Halofenozide	GR	2.2	>5,000	>5,000	8.6
	Chlorantraniliprole	AD	0.03–0.23	>5,000	>5,620	13.8
	Fipronil	PP	1.4	97	>5,000	246
			Insecticides targeting surface-feeding pests			
1990	Chlorpyrifos	OP	1.7–4.5	97	136–203	8
	Trichlorfon[d]	OP	9.0	400	>5,000	430
	Bendiocarb	C	2.4–4.5	34–156	3	0.4–1.8
2011	Bifenthrin	Py	0.3–2.2	54–70	2,150	0.00015
	Indoxacarb	Ox	0.04–0.25	268–1,730	>5,620	650
	Spinosad	S	0.5	>5,000	>2,000	30

[a]Toxicological data from Etoxnet (2007) or MSDS sheets, based on active ingredient (AI).
[b]Chemical classes: OP, organophosphate; C, carbamate; N, neonicotinoid; GR, growth regulator; AD, anthranilic diamide; PP, phenyl pyrazole; Py, pyrethroid; Ox, oxadiazine; S, spinosyns.
[c]Rat LD_{50}: >5,000, practically nontoxic (PNT); 500–5,000, slightly toxic (ST); 50–500, moderately toxic (MT); 1–50, highly toxic (HT); <1, very highly toxic (VHT). Avian LD_{50}: >2,000, PNT; 501–200, ST; 51–500, MT; 10–50, HT; <10, VHT. Fish LC_{50}: >100, PNT; 10–100, ST; 1–10, MT; 0.1–1, HT; <0.01, VHT (U.S. EPA ratings).
[d]Still labeled for some uses in 2011.

infestation is known. Record keeping would focus such treatments, but many professionals find it less risky to treat all areas where damage would be unacceptable. By developing reduced-risk soil insecticides that quickly control late-instar white grubs at the onset of damage symptoms, investigators would fill a key gap in the present insecticide portfolio and provide a safety net enabling more selective curative control. Trichlorfon and carbaryl, current mainstays for curative grub control in the United States, are old chemistry and likely to be withdrawn.

Pyrethroid resistance in *L. maculicollis* on golf courses has been documented (118), and some populations of *B. insularis* have become resistant to both pyrethroids and nicotinoids (28). Fipronil and nicotinoids have been mainstays for mole cricket and white grub control, respectively, for 15 to 20 years, and although resistance has not yet been documented, it is likely to occur. Development of newer chemistries should facilitate resistance management; e.g., indoxacarb or spinosad could be substituted for pyrethroids to forestall resistance in *L. maculicollis*, and indoxacarb baits or chlorantraniliprole could be rotated with older products for mole cricket or white grub control.

Another trend is to combine two active ingredients, typically a neonicotinoid and pyrethroid, for a broader spectrum of preventive control. Such products may work faster, or at lower rates, owing to synergy between chemistries (79). There is debate whether the purported benefits outweigh the risks of hastening insecticide resistance or affecting beneficial species by applying two chemicals where, in most cases, one or the other would provide sufficient control.

All classes of turf insecticides registered since 1993 have relatively low mammalian and avian toxicity, although pyrethroids are highly toxic to fish (**Table 1**). Neonicotinoids, pyrethroids, and certain other classes can nonetheless kill nontarget arthropods including predators (81, 82, 87), parasitoids (129), and pollinators (47), as well as earthworms and other decomposers (104, 107). Other novel chemistries (e.g., indoxacarb and chlorantraniliprole) seem to have relatively less impact on nontarget species.

TOWARD INTEGRATED PEST MANAGEMENT

Turfgrass managers know that increased environmental stewardship is necessary for their industry to thrive. For example, their trade magazines now routinely address such issues as carbon footprint reduction for golf courses and business plans for eco-friendly lawn service. How can entomological research and extension better support the industry's initiatives toward more sustainable pest management?

About 30% of 18-hole golf facilities in the United States currently participate in voluntary environmental stewardship initiatives, e.g., the Audubon Cooperative Sanctuary certification program, which promotes management practices that improve the quality of golf courses for wildlife (88, 141). Such golf courses usually increase the acreage of naturalized areas (88) that promote biodiversity and can enhance biological control (1, 44, 45). The National Wildlife Federation has a program through which residential landscapes can qualify to become Certified Wildlife Habitats™ (**http://www.nwf.org/Get-Outside/Outdoor-Activities/Garden-for-Wildlife.aspx**). Entomologists and ecologists can help golf course architects, greenskeepers, and grounds managers to plan or redesign courses or landscapes to maximize their conservation potential for native pollinators, butterflies, amphibians, and birds, including rare species, and as stepping-stones for such species' movement between larger natural areas (46). The United States Golf Association has funded a wide variety of ecological projects under its Wildlife Links program, including collaborating with the Xerces Society to protect wildlife through conservation of invertebrates and their habitat (**http://www.usga.org/Content.aspx?id=26127**).

Golf superintendents who communicate with club members to foster a sense of pride and collective responsibility for environmental initiatives can gain their greater tolerance for insect damage that does not compromise play. In Europe, some clubs have engaged members in wildlife (e.g., butterfly) surveys that provide information on the species inhabiting the course. The United States Golf Association's selection of a dune-swept, sustainably managed Scottish-links-style course in Pierce County, Washington, to host the 2015 United States Open Golf Championships will showcase that a golf course need not be uniformly lush and dark green to be attractive, challenging, and playable.

Entomologists can advance IPM for lawns by nurturing the sociocultural shift toward ecological aesthetics, i.e., the perception that what is desirable is that which has fewer environmental consequences. Issues such as honey bee Colony Collapse Disorder can be a teaching point for encouraging garden clubs, school groups, or property owners to plant refuges for pollinators and other beneficial insects and to reduce indiscriminate use of lawn pesticides. Numerous municipalities in Canada and the United States have enacted bylaws banning or restricting chemical pesticide use on lawns (8, 108, 117). If more U.S. municipalities follow suit or require that certain pesticides be used by prescription only, markets for bioinsecticides that now occupy only niche markets will be created. Entomological leadership will be needed to develop better use protocols for bioinsecticides and, in some cases, to defend the freedom of choice to use synthetic insecticides whose toxicological profiles pose no health or environmental hazard.

We could do more to educate clientele that raising the mower blade, returning clippings, deep-watering, proper fertilization, and sowing a few handfuls of grass seed over insect-damaged spots may be less costly and more sustainable than contracting for whole-yard chemical applications. Progressive lawn care providers have begun to offer holistic turfgrass management, versus calendar-based spray programs, creating opportunities to integrate control tactics and reduce pesticide usage.

The reliance of the U.S. turfgrass industry on insecticides has made insecticide resistance an emerging problem (28, 118). We need simple tools, e.g., molecular markers, for early detection, as well as more research on resistance mechanisms and mitigation strategies. Diversification of insecticidal chemistry will help (**Table 1**). A longer-term objective should be to reduce dependency on broad preventive treatments through better understanding host biology, population dynamics, and risk assessment. There are still only a few pests (e.g., annual bluegrass weevil) for which most of components are present to put into place a research-based IPM protocol.

Habitat management, an integral part of conservation biological control in other agroecosystems, has been applied only sparingly to turfgrass systems (45, 46). To what extent can turf management practices be manipulated, or lawn, landscape, and golf course design be altered, to promote greater stability? For example, in a mark-release-recapture experiment involving several thousand predatory ground beetles, no beetle was ever found to cross a fairway (46). Such information could be useful to golf course architects or landscape architects seeking to maximize the benefits from naturalized habitat patches. Residential landscapes, in particular, offer the greatest prospects for exploring designs to promote stability.

Host plant resistance research should be redirected from mass-screening of cultivars against individual pests to probing the molecular and physiological bases for grass resistance and ways to incorporate resistance traits into agronomically desirable grasses by means other than traditional breeding. In a perennial system, tolerance or induced resistance may be more sustainable than antibiosis or antixenosis. Host plant resistance may also interact with efficacy of microbial insecticides, or with diversity, abundance, and effectiveness of endemic natural enemies, so a tiered approach combining lab and field studies would provide greater insight than isolated, out-of-context studies would. Potential applications of RNA interference, molecular genetics of endophyte transfer, transgenic grasses, or inducers such as methyl jasmonates or plant-growth-promoting rhizobacteria that upregulate plant defenses or attract natural enemies are as yet unexplored for turfgrass IPM.

Precision agriculture, a farm management concept based on observing and responding to intrafield variations using satellite imaging, geographical information systems, and information technology, could have useful applications to turfgrass IPM. Wireless handheld devices and cell phones enable practitioners anywhere to access data at any time, facilitating such tasks as record-keeping and accessing degree-day information. Use of this ubiquitous yet practical technology to map pest densities or damage, pesticide use, or incidence of resistance on golf courses and sod farms (94), or the locations of high-risk lawns within neighborhoods, could be valuable in helping turf care providers to better focus their scouting and control actions.

SUMMARY POINTS

1. Turfgrass maintained as a low-cut watered and fertilized monoculture is especially vulnerable to insect outbreaks. Despite continued high standards for aesthetics and play, the turfgrass industry faces pressures to reduce water consumption and chemical inputs and is receptive to more sustainable approaches to insect control so long as they are effective.

2. Research since 1990 on traditional turf pests, such as white grubs, mole crickets, and cutworms, and on emerging pests, such as annual bluegrass weevil, invasive crane flies, hunting billbug, western chinch bug, and nuisance ants, has provided new insights into their life histories and population dynamics and a stronger foundation for IPM.
3. Microbial insecticides have gained only a minuscule market share, but advances in our understanding of factors that limit or enhance the efficacy of pathogens, especially nematodes, should support their wider use against turfgrass pests.
4. Host plant resistance research should focus more on the underlying mechanisms and on using biotechnological approaches to incorporate constitutive or inducible resistance factors into agronomically desirable cultivars.
5. New classes of reduced-risk synthetic insecticides with favorable toxicology characteristics have been developed since 1990. The absence of fast-acting, reduced-risk soil insecticides for remedial control of scarab grubs remains a key gap in the turf insecticide portfolio.
6. Extension and outreach efforts focused on increasing public awareness of beneficial insects, and collective responsibility for conservation of honey bees and native pollinators, can nurture the sociocultural shift toward ecological aesthetics and provide leeway for adoption of sustainable pest control approaches for lawns, golf courses, and sports fields.

DISCLOSURE STATEMENT

The authors are not aware of any affiliations, memberships, funding, or financial holdings that might be perceived as affecting the objectivity of this review.

ACKNOWLEDGMENTS

This is paper no. 11-08-030 of the Kentucky Agricultural Experiment Station. We thank S.K. Braman, S.C. Hong, A.M. Koppenhöfer, and C.T. Redmond for helpful comments on an earlier draft of this manuscript.

LITERATURE CITED

1. Abraham CM, Held DW, Wheeler C. 2010. Seasonal and diurnal activity of *Larra bicolor* (Hymenoptera: Crabronidae) and potential ornamental plants as nectar sources. *Appl. Turfgrass Sci.* doi:10.1094/ATS-2010-0312-01-RS
2. Alm SR, Villani MG, Roelofs W. 1999. Oriental beetles (Coleoptera: Scarabaeidae): current distribution in the United States and optimization of monitoring traps. *J. Econ. Entomol.* 92:931–35
3. Ansari MA, Shah FA, Tirry L, Moens M. 2006. Field trials against *Hoplia philanthus* (Coleoptera: Scarabaeidae) with a combination of an entomopathogenic nematode and the fungus *Metarhizium anisopliae* CLO 53. *Biol. Control* 39:453–59
4. Barbara KA, Buss EA. 2005. Integration of insect parasitic nematodes (Nematoda: Steinernematidae) with insecticides for control of pest mole crickets (Orthoptera: Gryllotalpidae: *Scapteriscus* spp.). *J. Econ. Entomol.* 98:689–93
5. Baxendale FP, Heng-Moss TM, Riordan TP. 1999. *Blissus occiduus* (Hemiptera: Lygaeidae): a chinch bug pest new to buffalograss turf. *J. Econ. Entomol.* 92:1172–76

6. Baxendale FP, Johnson-Cicalese JM, Riordan TP. 1994. *Tridiscus sporoboli* and *Trionymus* sp. (Homoptera: Pseudococcidae): potential new mealybug pests of buffalograss turf. *J. Kans. Entomol. Soc.* 67:169–72
7. Beard JB, Green RL. 1994. The role of turfgrasses in environmental protection and their benefits to humans. *J. Environ. Qual.* 23:452–60
8. Bélair G, Koppenhöfer AM, Dionne J, Simard L. 2010. Current and potential use of pathogens in the management of turfgrass insects as affected by new pesticide regulations in North America. *Int. J. Pest Manag.* 56:51–60
9. Bixby A, Alm SR, Power K, Grewal P. 2007. Susceptibility of four species of turfgrass-infesting scarabs (Coleoptera: Scarabaeidae) to *Bacillus thuringiensis* serovar *japonensis* strain Buibui. *J. Econ. Entomol.* 100:1604–10
10. Bixby AJ, Potter DA. 2010. Influence of endophyte (*Neotyphodium lolii*) infection of perennial ryegrass on susceptibility of the black cutworm (Lepidoptera: Noctuidae) to a baculovirus. *Biol. Control* 54:141–46
11. Bixby-Brosi AJ, Potter DA. 2010. Evaluating a naturally-occurring baculovirus for extended biological control of the black cutworm (Lepidoptera: Noctuidae) in golf course habitats. *J. Econ. Entomol.* 103:1555–63
12. Bixby-Brosi AJ, Potter DA. 2011. Can a chitin synthesis-inhibiting turfgrass fungicide enhance black cutworm susceptibility to a baculovirus? *Pest Manag. Sci.* doi: 10.1002/ps.2252
13. Blanco CA, Hernández G. 2006. Prediction of masked chafer, *Cyclocephala pasadenae*, capture in light traps using a degree-day model. *J. Insect Sci.* 6:1–6
14. Braman SK. 1993. Azadirachtin affects growth and survival of immature tawny mole crickets (Orthoptera: Gryllotalpidae). *Fla. Entomol.* 76:526–30
15. Braman SK, Duncan RR, Hanna WW, Engleke MC. 2004. Turfgrass species and cultivar influences on survival and parasitism of fall armyworm. *J. Econ. Entomol.* 97:1993–98
16. Braman SK, Hudson WG. 1993. Patterns of flight activity of pest mole crickets in Georgia. *Int. Turfgrass Soc. Res. J.* 7:157–59
17. Braman SK, Pendley AF. 1993. Relative and seasonal abundance of beneficial arthropods in centipede grass as influenced by management practices. *J. Econ. Entomol.* 86:494–504
18. **Braman SK, Pendley AF, Corley W. 2002. Influences of commercially available wildflower mixes on beneficial arthropod abundance and predation in turfgrass. *Environ. Entomol.* 31:564–72**

18. Demonstrates the positive effects of lawn diversification on natural enemy abundance.

19. Brandhorst-Hubbard JL, Flanders KL, Appel AG. 2001. Oviposition site and food preference of the green June beetle (Coleoptera: Scarabaeidae). *J. Econ. Entomol.* 94:628–33
20. Brandhorst-Hubbard JL, Flanders KL, Mankin RW, Guertal EA, Crocker RL. 2001. Mapping of soil insect infestations sampled by excavation and acoustic methods. *J. Econ. Entomol.* 94:1452–58
21. Buhler WT, Gibb TJ. 1994. Persistence of *Steinernema carpocapsae* and *S. glaseri* (Rhabditida: Steinernematidae) as measured by their control of black cutworm (Lepidoptera: Noctuidae) larvae in bentgrass. *J. Econ. Entomol.* 87:638–42
22. Busey P, Snyder GH. 1993. Population outbreak of the southern chinch bug is regulated by fertilization. *Int. Turfgrass Soc. Res. J.* 7:353–57
23. Buss EA. 2006. Flight activity and relative abundance of phytophagous scarabs (Coleoptera: Scarabaeidae) in Florida. *Fla. Entomol.* 89:32–40
24. Campbell JF, Lewis E, Yoder F, Gaugler R. 1995. Entomopathogenic nematode (Heterorhabditidae and Steinernematidae) seasonal population dynamics and impact on insect populations in turfgrass. *Biol. Control* 5:598–606
25. Cappaert DL, Smitley DR. 2002. Parasitoids and pathogens of Japanese beetle (Coleoptera: Scarabaeidae) in Southern Michigan. *Environ. Entomol.* 31:573–80
26. Carstens J, Heng-Moss T, Baxendale F, Gaussoin R, Frank K, Young L. 2007. Influence of buffalograss management practices on western chinch bug and its beneficial arthropods. *J. Econ. Entomol.* 100:136–47
27. Chantos JM, Vinson SB, Helms KR. 2009. Distribution and abundance of parasites of the rhodesgrass mealybug, *Antonina graminis*: reassessment of a classic example of biological control in the southeastern United States. *J. Insect Sci.* 9:48
28. Cherry R, Nagata R. 2007. Resistance to two classes of insecticides in southern chinch bugs (Hemiptera: Lygaeidae). *Fla. Entomol.* 90:431–34

29. Choo HY, Kaya HK, Huh J, Lee DW, Kim HH, et al. 2002. Entomopathogenic nematodes (*Steinernema* spp. and *Heterorhabditis bacteriophora*) and a fungus, *Beauveria brongniartii*, for biological control of the white grubs, *Ectinohoplia rufipes* and *Exomala orientalis*, in Korean golf courses. *Biocontrol* 47:177–92
30. Choo HY, Lee DW, Lee SM, Lee TW, Choi WG, et al. 2000. Turfgrass insect pests and natural enemies in golf courses. *Kor. J. Appl. Entomol.* 39:171–79
31. Choo HY, Lee DW, Park JW, Kaya HK, Smitley DR, Choo YM. 2002. Life history and spatial distribution of Oriental beetle (Coleoptera: Scarabaeidae) in golf courses in Korea. *J. Econ. Entomol.* 95:72–80
32. **Cowles R, Alm SR, Villani MG. 1999. Selective toxicity of halofenozide to exotic white grubs (Coleoptera: Scarabaeidae). *J. Econ. Entomol.* 92:427–34**

32. Illustrates the potential trade-offs between selectivity and versatility of reduced-risk insecticides.

33. Crutchfield BA, Potter DA, Powell AJ. 1995. Irrigation and fertilization effects on white grubs feeding injury to tall fescue turf. *Crop Sci.* 35:1122–26
34. Dalthorp D, Nyrop J, Villani MG. 1999. Estimation of local mean population densities of Japanese beetle grubs (Scarabaeidae: Coleoptera). *Environ. Entomol.* 28:255–65
35. Dalthorp D, Nyrop J, Villani MG. 2000. Spatial ecology of the Japanese beetle, *Popillia japonica*. *Entomol. Exp. Appl.* 96:129–39
36. Davidson AW, Potter DA. 1995. Response of plant-feeding, predatory, and soil-inhabiting invertebrates to *Acremonium* endophyte and nitrogen fertilization in tall fescue turf. *J. Econ. Entomol.* 88:367–79
37. Davis MGK, Smitley DR. 1990. Association of thatch with populations of hairy chinch bug (Hemiptera: Lygaeidae) in turf. *J. Econ. Entomol.* 83:2370–74
38. De Graaf J, Schoeman AS, Brandenburg RL. 2004. Flight patterns of *Gryllotalpa africana* on turfgrass in South Africa. *Environ. Entomol.* 33:1431–35
39. Diaz MDC, Peck DC. 2007. Overwintering of annual bluegrass weevils, *Listronotus maculicollis*, in the golf course landscape. *Entomol. Exp. Appl.* 125:259–68
40. Diaz MDC, Seto M, Peck DC. 2008. Patterns of variation in the seasonal dynamics of *Listronotus maculicollis* (Coleoptera: Cucurlionidae) on golf course turf. *Environ. Entomol.* 37:1438–50
41. Dingman DW. 1994. Inhibitory effects of turf pesticides on *Bacillus popilliae* and the prevalence of milky disease. *Appl. Environ. Microbiol.* 60:2343–49
42. Doskocil JP, Walker NR, Bell GE, Marek SM, Reinert JA, Royer TA. 2008. Species composition and seasonal occurrence of *Phyllophaga* (Coleoptera: Scarabaeidae) infesting intensely managed bermudagrass in Oklahoma. *J. Econ. Entomol.* 101:1624–32
43. Facundo HT, Villani MG, Linn CE Jr, Roelofs WL. 1999. Temporal and spatial distribution of the Oriental beetle (Coleoptera: Scarabaeidae) in a golf course environment. *Environ. Entomol.* 28:14–21
44. Frank JH, Walker TJ. 2006. Permanent control of pest mole crickets (Orthoptera: Gryllotalpidae: *Scapteriscus*) in Florida. *Am. Entomol.* 52:138–44
45. Frank SD, Shrewsbury PM. 2004. Effect of conservation strips on the abundance and distribution of natural enemies and predation of *Agrotis ipsilon* (Lepidoptera: Noctuidae) on golf course fairways. *Environ. Entomol.* 33:1662–72
46. Gange AC, Linsay DE, Schofield JM. 2003. The ecology of golf courses. *Biologist* 50:63–68
47. Gels JA, Held DW, Potter DA. 2002. Hazards of insecticides to the bumble bees *Bombus impatiens* (Hymenoptera: Apidae) foraging on flowering white clover in turf. *J. Econ. Entomol.* 95:722–28
48. George J, Redmond CT, Royalty RN, Potter DA. 2007. Residual effects of imidacloprid on Japanese beetle (Coleoptera: Scarabaeidae) oviposition, egg hatch, and larval viability in turfgrass. *J. Econ. Entomol.* 100:431–39
49. George JP, Potter DA. 2008. Potential of azadirachtin for managing black cutworms and Japanese beetle grubs in turf. *Acta Hortic.* 83:499–505
50. Georgis R, Koppenhöfer AM, Lacey LA, Belair G, Duncan LW, et al. 2006. Successes and failures of entomopathogenic nematodes. *Biol. Control* 38:103–23
51. Gosselin ME, Bélair G, Simard L, Brodeur J. 2009. Toxicity of spinosad and *Beauveria bassiana* to the black cutworm, and the additivity of sublethal doses. *Biocontrol. Sci. Technol.* 19:201–17
52. Grewal PS. 1999. Factors in the success and failure of microbial control in turfgrass. *Integr. Pest Manag. Rev.* 4:287–94

53. Gulsen O, Eickhoff T, Heng-Moss T, Shearman R, Baxendale F, et al. 2010. Characterization of peroxidase changes in resistant and susceptible warm-season turfgrasses challenged by *Blissus occiduus*. *Arthropod-Plant Interact.* 4:45–55
54. Hamilton RM, Foster RE, Gibb TJ, Johannsen CJ, Santini JB. 2009. Pre-visible detection of grub feeding in turfgrass using remote sensing. *Photogramm. Eng. Remote Sens.* 75:179–92
55. Hatsukade M. 1997. Biology and control of the hunting billbug, *Sphenophorus venatus vestitus* Chittenden, on golf courses in Japan. *Int. Turfgrass Soc. Res. J.* 9:769–73
56. Haydu JJ, Hodges AW, Hall CR. 2005. Economic impacts of the turfgrass and lawncare industry in the United States. *Fla. Coop. Ext. Serv.* FE 632, Gainesville: Univ. Fla.
57. Held DW, Gelhaus J. 2006. Damage in centipede sod associated with crane and March fly larvae (Diptera: Tupulidae, Bibionidae) in Mississippi. *Fla. Entomol.* 89:89–90
58. Held DW, Wheeler C, Abraham C, Pickett K. 2008. Paper wasps (*Polistes* spp.) attacking fall armyworm larvae (*Spodoptera frugiperda*) in turfgrass. *Appl. Turfgrass Sci.* doi:10.1094/ATS-2008-0806-01-RS
59. Heng-Moss T, Bexendale F, Riordan T. 1998. Beneficial arthropods associated with buffalograss. *J. Econ. Entomol.* 91:1167–72
60. Heng-Moss T, Baxendale F, Riordan T. 2001. Interactions between the parasitoid *Rhopus nigroclavatus* (Ashmead) (Hymenoptera: Encyrtidae) and its mealybug hosts *Tridiscus sporoboli* (Cockerell) and *Trionymus* sp. (Homoptera: Pseudococcidae). *Biol. Control* 22:201–6
61. Heng-Moss T, Macedo T, Franzen L, Baxendale F, Higley L, Sarath G. 2006. Physiological responses of resistant and susceptible buffalograss to *Blissus occiduus* (Hemiptera: Blissidae) feeding. *J. Econ. Entomol.* 99:222–28
62. Hertl PT, Brandenburg RL, Barbercheck ME. 2001. Effect of soil moisture on ovipositional behavior in the southern mole cricket (Orthoptera: Gryllotalpidae). *Environ. Entomol.* 30:466–73
63. Hoffman E, Smith RL. 1991. Emergence and dispersal of *Margarodes meridionalis* (Homoptera: Coccoidea) in hybrid bermudagrass. *J. Econ. Entomol.* 84:1668–71
64. Hong SC, Williamson RC. 2004. Comparison of sticky wing and cone pheromone traps for monitoring seasonal abundance of black cutworm adults and larvae on golf courses. *J. Econ. Entomol.* 97:1666–70
65. Huang TI, Buss EA. 2009. Billbug (Coleoptera: Curculionidae) species composition, abundance, seasonal activity, and development time in Florida. *J. Econ. Entomol.* 102:309–14
66. Joseph SV, Braman SK. 2009. Influence of plant parameters on occurrence and abundance of arthropods in residential turfgrass. *J. Econ. Entomol.* 102:1116–22
67. Joseph SV, Braman SK. 2009. Predatory potential of *Geocoris* spp. and *Orius insidiosus* on fall armyworm in resistant and susceptible turf. *J. Econ. Entomol.* 102:1151–56
68. Kiely T, Donaldson D, Grube A. 2004. *Pesticide Industry Sales and Usage. 2000 and 2001 Market Estimates.* Washington, DC: US Environ. Prot. Agency. 33 pp.
69. Klein MG, Lacey LA. 1999. An attractant trap for autodissemination of entomopathogenic fungi into populations of the Japanese beetle, *Popillia japonica* (Coleoptera: Scarabaeidae). *Biocontrol Sci. Technol.* 9:151–58
70. Koppenhöfer AM, Behle RW, Dunlap CA, Fisher J, Laird C, Vittum PJ. 2008. Pellet formulations of sex pheromone components for mating disruption of Oriental beetle (Coleoptera: Scarabaeidae) in turfgrass. *Environ. Entomol.* 37:1126–35

70. One in a series describing the first evaluation of mating disruption targeting a turf pest.

71. Koppenhöfer AM, Cowles RS, Fuzy EM. 2003. Effects of turfgrass endophytes (Clavipitaceae: Ascomycetes) on white grub (Coleoptera: Scarabaeidae) larval development and field populations. *Environ. Entomol.* 32:895–906
72. Koppenhöfer AM, Fuzy EM. 2003. Effects of turfgrass endophytes (Clavicipitaceae: Ascomycetes) on white grub (Coleoptera: Scarabaeidae) control by the entomopathogenic nematode *Heterorhabditis bacteriophora* (Rhabditida: Heterorhabditidae). *Environ. Entomol.* 32:392–96

72. Highlights the potential for exploiting synergisms between reduced-risk tactics for improved control of pests.

73. Koppenhöfer AM, Fuzy EM. 2008. Effect of the anthranilic diamide insecticide, chlorantraniliprole, on *Heterorhabditis bacteriophora* (Rhabditida: Heterorhabditidae) efficacy against white grubs (Coleoptera: Scarabaeidae). *Biol. Control* 45:93–102

74. Koppenhöfer AM, Grewal PS. 2005. Interactions and compatibility of entomopathogenic nematodes with other control agents. In *Nematodes as Biocontrol Agents*, ed. PS Grewal, R Ehlers, DI Shapiro-Ilan, pp. 363–81. Wallingford, UK: CABI
75. Koppenhöfer AM, Grewal PS, Kaya HK. 2000. Synergism of imidacloprid and entomopathogenic nematodes against white grubs: the mechanism. *Entomol. Exp. Appl.* 94:283–93
76. Koppenhöfer AM, Grewal PS, Fuzy EM. 2006. Virulence of the entomopathogenic nematodes *Heterorhabditis bacteriophora*, *Heterorhabditis zealandica*, and *Steinernema scarabaei* against five white grub species (Coleoptera: Scarabaeidae) of economic importance in turfgrass in North America. *Biol. Control* 38:397–404
77. Korndorfer AP, Cherry R, Nagata R. 2004. Effect of calcium silicate on feeding and development of tropical sod webworms (Lepidoptera: Pyralidae). *Fla. Entomol.* 87:393–95
78. Kostromytska OS, Buss EA. 2008. Seasonal phenology and management of *Tomarus subtropicus* (Coleoptera: Scarabaeidae) in St. Augustinegrass. *J. Econ. Entomol.* 101:1847–55
79. Kostromytska OS, Buss EA, Scharf ME. 2011. Toxicity and neurophysiological effects of selected insecticides on the mole cricket, *Scapteriscus vicinus* (Orthoptera: Gryllotalpidae). *Pestic. Biochem. Physiol.* 100:27–34
80. Kunkel BA, Grewal PS, Quigley MF. 2004. A mechanism of acquired resistance against an entomopathogenic nematode by *Agrotis ipsilon* feeding on perennial ryegrass harboring a fungal endophyte. *Biol. Control* 29:100–8
81. Kunkel BA, Held DW, Potter DA. 1999. Impact of halofenozide, imidacloprid, and bendiocarb on beneficial invertebrates and predatory activity in turfgrass. *J. Econ. Entomol.* 92:922–30
82. Kunkel BA, Held DW, Potter DA. 2001. Lethal and sublethal effects of bendiocarb, halofenozide, and imidacloprid on *Harpalus pennsylvanicus* (Coleoptera: Carabidae) following different modes of exposure in turfgrass. *J. Econ. Entomol.* 94:60–67
83. Lee DW, Choi WG, Lee SM, Choo HY, Kweon TW. 2006. Effect of turfgrass height and aeration on pathogenicity of entomopathogenic nematodes to white grubs in golf courses. *Kor. J. Appl. Entomol.* 45:67–74
84. Lee DW, Choo HY, Lee TW, Park JW, Kweon TW. 1999. Spatial and temporal distribution of chestnut brown chafer, *Adoretus tenuimaculatus* (Coleoptera: Scarabaeidae), in golf courses. *Kor. J. Turfgrass Sci.* 13:113–24
85. Lee DW, Choo HY, Smitley DR, Lee SM, Shin HK, et al. 2007. Distribution and adult activity of *Popillia quadriguttata* (Coleoptera: Scarabaeidae) on golf courses in Korea. *J. Econ. Entomol.* 100:103–9
86. Lee DW, Kim J-H, Shin J-C, Yeom J-R, Jeon J-C, et al. 2008. Seasonal and regional occurrence of Oriental beetle (*Blitopertha orientalis*) in Korean golf courses. *Kor. J. Turfgrass Sci.* 22:35–48
87. López R, Potter DA. 2000. Ant predation on eggs and larvae of the black cutworm and Japanese beetle in turfgrass. *Environ. Entomol.* 29:116–25

87. Documents the importance of predators and secondary pest outbreaks when ecosystem services are disrupted.

88. Lyman GT, Throssell CS, Johnson ME, Brown CD. 2007. Golf course profile describes turfgrass, landscape, and environmental features. *Appl. Turfgrass Sci.* doi:1094/ATS-2007-1107-01-RS
89. Maier RM, Potter DA. 2005. Factors affecting distribution of the mound-building ant *Lasius neoniger* (Hymenoptera: Formicidae) and implications for management on golf course putting greens. *J. Econ. Entomol.* 98:891–97
90. Maier RM, Potter DA. 2005. Seasonal mounding, colony development, and control of nuptial queens of the ant *Lasius neoniger* in turfgrass. *Appl. Turfgrass Sci.* doi:10.1094/ATS-20050502-01-RS
91. Majeau GJ, Brodeur J, Carrière Y. 2000. Lawn parameters influencing abundance and distribution of the hairy chinch bug (Hemiptera: Lygaeidae). *J. Econ. Entomol.* 93:368–73
92. Majeau GJ, Brodeur J, Carrière Y. 2000. Sequential sampling plans for the hairy chinch bug (Hemiptera: Lygaeidae). *J. Econ. Entomol.* 93:834–39
93. Mann RL, Newell AJ. 2005. A survey to determine the incidence and severity of pests and diseases on golf course putting greens in England, Ireland, Scotland, and Wales. *Int. Turfgrass Soc. Res. J.* 10:224–29

94. Mashtoly TA, Abolmaaty A, Thompson N, El-Zemaity ME, Hussien MI, Alm SR. 2010. Enhanced toxicity of *Bacillus thuringiensis japonensis* strain Buibui toxin to Oriental beetle and northern masked chafer (Coleoptera: Scarabaeidae) larvae with *Bacillus* sp. NFD. *J. Econ. Entomol.* 103:1547–54
95. Matheny AL, Traunfeld J, Raupp MJ, Brown AE. 2009. Gardeners and gardening trends in the United States. *Outlooks Pest Manag.* 20:51–56
96. McGraw BA, Koppenhöfer AM. 2009. Development of binomial sequential sampling plans for forecasting *Listronotus maculicollis* (Coleoptera: Curculionidae) larvae based on the relationship to adult counts and turfgrass damage. *J. Econ. Entomol.* 102:1325–35
97. **McGraw BA, Koppenhöfer AM. 2010. Spatial distribution of colonizing *Listronotus maculicollis* populations: implications for targeted management and host preference. *Ann. Appl. Biol.* 134:275–84**
98. McGraw BA, Rodriguez-Saona C, Holdcraft R, Szendrei Z, Koppenhöfer AM. 2011. Behavioral and electrophysiological responses of *Listronotus maculicollis* (Coleoptera: Curculionidae) to volatiles from intact and mechanically damaged annual bluegrass. *Environ. Entomol.* 40:412–19
99. Milesi C, Running SW, Elvidge CD, Dietz JB, Tuttle BT, Nemani RR. 2005. Mapping and modeling the biochemical cycling of turf grasses in the United States. *Environ. Manag.* 36:426–38
100. Nachappa P, Guillebeau PR, Braman SK, All JN. 2006. Susceptibility of twolined spittlebug (Hemiptera: Cercopidae) life stages to entomophagous arthropods in turfgrass. *J. Econ. Entomol.* 99:1711–16
101. Niemczyk HD, Taylor RAJ, Tolley MP, Power KT. 1992. Physiological time-driven model for predicting first generation of the hairy chinch bug (Hemiptera: Lygaeidae) on turfgrass in Ohio. *J. Econ. Entomol.* 85:821–29
102. Nyrop JP, Villani MG, Grant JA. 1995. Control decision rule for European chafer (Coleoptera: Scarabaeidae) larvae infesting turfgrass. *Environ. Entomol.* 24:521–28
103. Parkman JP, Frank JH. 2002. Interaction between *Ormia depleta* (Diptera: Tachinidae) and *Steinernema scapterisci* (Nematoda: Steinernematidae), natural enemies of pest mole crickets (Orthoptera: Gryllotalpidae). *Environ. Entomol.* 31:1226–30
104. Peck DC. 2009. Comparative impacts of white grub (Coleoptera: Scarabaeidae) control products on the abundance of non-target soil-active arthropods in turfgrass. *Pedobiologia* 52:287–99
105. Peck DC, Hoebeke ER, Klass C. 2006. Detection and establishment of the European crane flies *Tipula paludosa* Meigen and *Tipula oleracea* L. (Diptera: Tipulidae) in New York: a review of their distribution, invasion history, biology, and recognition. *Proc. Entomol. Soc. Wash.* 108:985–94
106. Peck DC, Olmstead D, Morales A. 2008. Application timing and efficacy of alternatives for the insecticidal control of *Tipula paludosa* Meigen (Diptera: Tipulidae), a new invasive pest of turf in the northeastern United States. *Pest Manag. Sci.* 64:989–1000
107. Potter DA. 1993. Pesticide and fertilizer effects on beneficial invertebrates and consequences for thatch degradation and pest outbreaks in turfgrass. In *Pesticides in Urban Environments: Fate and Significance*, ed. KD Racke, AR Leslie, pp. 331–43. ACS Symp. Ser. 522. Washington, DC: Am. Chem. Soc.
108. Potter DA. 2005. Prospects for managing destructive turfgrass insects without protective chemicals. *Int. Turfgrass Soc. Res. J.* 10:42–54
109. Potter DA, Braman SK. 1991. Ecology and management of turfgrass insects. *Annu. Rev. Entomol.* 36:383–406
110. Potter DA, Haynes KF. 1993. Field testing pheromone traps for predicting masked chafer grub density in golf course turf and home lawns. *J. Entomol. Sci.* 28:205–12
111. Potter DA, Held DW, Rogers ME. 2005. Natural organic fertilizers as a risk factor for *Ataenius spretulus* infestation on golf courses. *Int. Turfgrass Soc. Res. J.* 10:753–60
112. Potter DA, Patterson CG, Redmond CT. 1992. Influence of turfgrass species and tall fescue endophyte on feeding ecology of southern masked chafer and Japanese beetle grubs (Coleoptera: Scarabaeidae). *J. Econ. Entomol.* 85:900–9
113. Potter DA, Powell AJ, Spicer PG, Williams DW. 1996. Cultural practices affect root-feeding white grubs (Coleoptera: Scarabaeidae) in turfgrass. *J. Econ. Entomol.* 89:156–64

97. Application of spatiotemporal analyses to population dynamics of annual bluegrass weevil with implications for management.

114. Potter DA, Stokes JT, Redmond CT, et al. 2008. Contribution of ergot alkaloids to suppression of a grass-feeding caterpillar assessed with gene-knockout endophytes in perennial ryegrass. *Entomol. Exp. Appl.* 126:138–47

115. Power KT, An R, Grewal PS. 2009. Effectiveness of *Heterorhabditis bacteriophora* strain GPS11 applications targeted against different instars of the Japanese beetle *Popillia japonica*. *Biol. Control* 48:232–36

116. First report of naturally occurring viral epizootic and evaluation of this virus for microbial control.

116. Prater CA, Redmond CT, Barney W, Bonning B, Potter DA. 2006. Microbial control of the black cutworm (Lepidoptera: Noctuidae) in turfgrass using *Agrotis ipsilon* multiple nucleopolyhedrovirus. *J. Econ. Entomol.* 99:1129–37

117. Racke K. 2000. Pesticides for turfgrass pest management: uses and environmental issues. In *Fate and Management of Turfgrass Chemicals* (ACS Symp. Ser. 743), ed. JM Clark, MP Kenna, pp. 45–64. Washington, DC: Am. Chem. Soc.

118. Case study for investigating insecticide resistance and resistance mechanisms in populations of turf pests.

118. Ramoutar D, Alm SR, Cowles RS. 2009. Pyrethroid resistance in populations of *Listronotus maculicollis* Kirby (Coleoptera: Curculionidae) from southern New England golf courses. *J. Econ. Entomol.* 102:388–92

119. Ramoutar D, Legrand AI, Alm SR. 2010. Field performance of *Metarhizium anisopliae* against *Popillia japonica* (Coleoptera: Scarabaeidae) and *Listronotus maculicollis* (Coleoptera: Curculionidae) larvae in turfgrass. *J. Entomol. Sci.* 45:1–7

120. Rangasamy M, Rathinasabapathi B, McAuslane HJ, Cherry RH, Nagata RT. 2009. Oxidative responses of St. Augustinegrasses challenged by southern chinch bug, *Blissus insularis* Barber (Hemiptera: Blissidae). *J. Chem. Ecol.* 35:796–805

121. Rangasamy M, Rathinasabapathi B, McAuslane HJ, Cherry RH, Nagata RT. 2009. Role of leaf sheath lignification and anatomy in southern chinch bug, *Blissus insularis* Barber (Hemiptera: Blissidae), resistance in St. Augustinegrass lines. *J. Econ. Entomol.* 102:432–39

122. Challenges dogma about a microbial insecticide marketed to homeowners for white grub control.

122. Redmond CT, Potter DA. 1995. Lack of efficacy of in vivo- and putatively in vitro-produced *Bacillus popilliae* against field populations of Japanese beetle (Coleoptera: Scarabaeidae) grubs in Kentucky. *J. Econ. Entomol.* 88:846–54

123. Redmond CT, Potter DA. 2006. Silicon fertilization does not enhance creeping bentgrass resistance to black cutworms or white grubs. *Appl. Turfgrass Sci.* doi:10.1094/ATS-2006-1110-01-RS

124. Redmond CT, Potter DA. 2010. Incidence of turf-damaging white grubs (Coleoptera: Scarabaeidae) and associated pathogens and parasitoids on Kentucky golf courses. *Environ. Entomol.* 39:1838–47

125. Reinert JA, Engelke MC, Read JC. 2004. Host resistance to insects and mites, a review: a major IPM strategy in turfgrass culture. *Acta Hortic.* 661:463–86

126. Rethwisch MD, Baxendale FP, Dollison DR. 2009. First report of northern mole cricket damage on a Nebraska golf course (Orthoptera: Gryllotalpidae). *J. Kans. Entomol. Soc.* 82:103–5

127. Richmond DS, Niemczyk HD, Shetlar DJ. 2000. Overseeding endophytic perennial ryegrass into stands of Kentucky bluegrass to manage bluegrass billbug (Coleoptera: Curculionidae). *J. Econ. Entomol.* 93:1662–68

128. Robbins PS, Alm SR, Armstrong AL, Averill AL, Baker TC, et al. 2009. Trapping *Phyllophaga* spp. (Coleoptera: Scarabaeidae: Melolonthinae) in the United States and Canada using sex attractants. *J. Insect Sci.* 6:39

129. Rogers ME, Potter DA. 2003. Effects of spring imidacloprid application for white grub control on parasitism of Japanese beetle (Coleoptera: Scarabaeidae) by *Tiphia vernalis* (Hymenoptera: Tiphiidae). *J. Econ. Entomol.* 96:1412–19

130. Rogers ME, Potter DA. 2004. Biology of *Tiphia pygidialis*, parasitoid of masked chafer grubs, with notes on the seasonal occurrence of *T. vernalis* in Kentucky. *Environ. Entomol.* 33:520–27

131. Rogers ME, Potter DA. 2004. Potential for sugar sprays and flowering plants to increase parasitism of white grubs by tiphiid wasps (Hymenoptera: Tiphiidae). *Environ. Entomol.* 33:619–26

132. Rothwell NL, Smitley DR. 1999. Impact of golf course mowing practices on *Ataenius spretulus* (Coleoptera: Scarabaeidae) and its natural enemies. *Environ. Entomol.* 28:358–66

133. Saarikivi J, Idstrom L, Venn S, Niemala J, Kotze DJ. 2010. Carabid beetle assemblages associated with urban golf courses in the greater Helsinki area. *Eur. J. Entomol.* 107:553–61

134. Salminen SO, Grewal PS, Quigley MF. 2003. Does mowing height influence alkaloid production in endophytic tall fescue and perennial ryegrass? *J. Chem. Ecol.* 29:1319–28
135. Scott IM, Gagnon N, Lesage L, Philogène BJR, Arnason JT. 2005. Efficacy of botanical insecticides from *Piper* species (Piperaceae) extracts for control of European chafer (Coleoptera: Scarabaeidae). *J. Econ. Entomol.* 98:845–55
136. Showers WB. 1997. Migratory ecology of the black cutworm. *Annu. Rev. Entomol.* 42:392–425
137. Simard L, Brodeur J, Dionne J. 2007. Distribution, abundance and seasonal ecology of *Listronotus maculicollis* (Coleoptera: Curculionidae) on golf courses in Quebec, Canada. *J. Econ. Entomol.* 100:1344–52
138. Simard LBG, Gosselin ME, Dionne J. 2006. Virulence of entomopathogenic nematodes (Rhabditida: Steinernematidae, Heterorhabditidae) against *Tipula paludosa* (Diptera: Tipulidae), a turfgrass pest on golf courses. *Biocontrol Sci. Technol.* 16:789–801
139. Smitley DR, Davis TW, Rothwell NL. 1998. Spatial distribution of *Ataenius spretulus*, *Aphodius granarius* (Coleoptera: Scarabaeidae), and predaceous insects across golf course fairways and roughs. *Environ. Entomol.* 27:1336–49
140. Smitley DR, Jo Y, Hudson I. 2011. Association of *Ovavesicula popilliae* (*Dissociodi haplophasida*: Ovavesiculidae), a microsporidial pathogen, with winter mortality of larvae and reduced fecundity of female Japanese beetles (Coleoptera: Scarabaeidae). *Environ. Entomol.* 40:589–96
141. Terman MR. 1997. Natural links: naturalistic golf courses as wildlife habitat. *Landsc. Urban Plan.* 38:183–97
142. Terry LA, Potter DA, Spicer PG. 1993. Insecticides affect predatory arthropods and predation on Japanese beetle (Coleoptera: Scarabaeidae) eggs and fall armyworm (Lepidoptera: Noctuidae) pupae in turfgrass. *J. Econ. Entomol.* 86:871–78
143. Thompson SR, Brandenburg RL. 2006. Effect of combining imidacloprid and diatomaceous earth with *Beauveria bassiana* on mole cricket (Orthoptera: Gryllotalpidae) mortality. *J. Econ. Entomol.* 99:1948–54
144. Thompson SR, Brandenburg RL, Arends LL. 2006. Impact of moisture and UV degradation on *Beauveria bassiana* (Balsamo) Vuillemin conidial viability in turfgrass. *Biol. Control* 39:401–7
145. Thompson SR, Brandenburg RL, Roberson GT. 2007. Entomopathogenic fungi detection and avoidance by mole crickets (Orthoptera: Gryllotalpidae). *Environ. Entomol.* 36:165–72
146. Vázquez JC, Buss EA. 2006. Southern chinch bug feeding impact on St. Augustinegrass grown under different irrigation regimes. *Appl. Turfgrass Sci.* doi:10.1094/ATS-2006-0711-01-RS
147. Villani MG, Allee LL, Preston-Wilsey L, Consolie N, Xia Y, Brandenburg RL. 2002. Use of radiography and tunnel castings for observing mole cricket (Orthoptera: Gryllotalpidae) behavior in soil. *Am. Entomol.* 48:42–50

147. Innovative methodology facilitates study of subsurface pests' behavioral responses to edaphic factors and control tactics.

148. Villani MG, Krueger SR, Schroeder PC, Consolie F, Consolie NH, et al. 1994. Soil application effects of *Metarhizium anisopliae* on Japanese beetle (Coleoptera: Scarabaeidae) behavior and survival in turfgrass microcosms. *Environ. Entomol.* 23:502–13
149. Williams DF, Collins HL, Oi DH. 2001. The red imported fire ant (Hymenoptera: Formicidae): an historical perspective of treatment programs and the development of chemical baits for control. *Am. Entomol.* 47:146–59
150. Williamson RC, Potter DA. 1997. Nocturnal activity and movement of black cutworm (Lepidoptera: Noctuidae) and response to cultural manipulations on golf course putting greens. *J. Econ. Entomol.* 90:1283–89
151. Williamson RC, Potter DA. 1997. Oviposition of black cutworm (Lepidoptera: Noctuidae) on creeping bentgrass putting greens and removal of eggs by mowing. *J. Econ. Entomol.* 90:590–94
152. Williamson RC, Potter DA. 1997. Turfgrass species and endophyte effects on survival, development, and feeding preference of black cutworms (Lepidoptera: Noctuidae). *J. Econ. Entomol.* 90:1290–99
153. Wood TN, Richardson M, Potter DA, Johnson DT, Wiedenmann RN, Steinkraus DC. 2009. Ovipositional preference of the Japanese beetle (Coleoptera: Scarabaeidae) among warm- and cool-season turfgrass species. *J. Econ. Entomol.* 102:2192–97
154. Xia Y, Hertl PT, Brandenburg RL. 2000. Surface and subsurface application of *Beauveria bassiana* for controlling mole crickets (Orthoptera: Gryllotalpidae) in golf courses. *J. Agric. Urban Entomol.* 17:177–89
155. Zenger JT, Gibb TJ. 2001. Identification and impact of egg predators of *Cyclocephala lurida* and *Popillia japonica* (Coleoptera: Scarabaeidae) in turfgrass. *Environ. Entomol.* 30:425–30

156. Zhang A, Facundo HT, Robbins PS, Linn CE, Hanula JL, et al. 1994. Identification and synthesis of sex pheromone of Oriental beetle, *Anomala orientalis* (Coleoptera: Scarabaeidae). *J. Chem. Ecol.* 20:2415–27
157. Zhang M, Crocker RL, Mankin RW, Flanders KL. 2003. Acoustic estimation of infestations and population densities of white grubs (Coleoptera: Scarabaeidae) in turfgrass. *J. Econ. Entomol.* 96:1770–79

RELATED RESOURCES

Clark JM, Kenna M, eds. 2000. *Fate and Management of Turfgrass Chemicals*. ACS Symp. Ser. 522. Washington, DC: Am. Chem. Soc.

Koppenhöfer AM. 2007. Integrated pest management of white grubs. In *Handbook of Turfgrass Management and Physiology*, ed. M Pessarakli, pp. 315–34. Boca Raton, FL: CRC Press

Potter DA. 1998. *Destructive Turfgrass Insects: Biology, Diagnosis, and Control.* New York: Wiley. 344 pp.

Vittum PJ, Villani MG, Tashiro H. 1999. *Turfgrass Insects of the United States and Canada.* Ithaca, NY: Cornell Univ. Press. 422 pp. 2nd ed.

Williamson RC, Held DW, Brandenburg R, Baxendale F. 2011. Turfgrass insect pests. In *Turfgrass Monograph*, ed. B Horgan. Madison, WI: Crop Science Soc. Am. In press

Managing Social Insects of Urban Importance

Michael K. Rust[1,*] and Nan-Yao Su[2]

[1]Department of Entomology, University of California Riverside, Riverside, California 92521-0314; email: michael.rust@ucr.edu

[2]Department of Entomology and Nematology, Ft. Lauderdale Research and Education Center, University of Florida, Davie, Florida 33314; email: nysu@ufl.edu

Annu. Rev. Entomol. 2012. 57:355–75

First published online as a Review in Advance on September 13, 2011

The *Annual Review of Entomology* is online at ento.annualreviews.org

This article's doi: 10.1146/annurev-ento-120710-100634

0066-4170/12/0107-0355$20.00

*Corresponding author

Keywords

ants, termites, yellowjackets, pest management, baits

Abstract

Social insects have a tremendous economic and social impact on urban communities. The rapid urbanization of the world has dramatically increased the incidence of urban pests. Human commerce has resulted in the spread of urban invasive species worldwide such that various species are now common to many major urban centers. We aim to highlight those social behaviors that can be exploited to control these pests with the minimal use of pesticides. Their cryptic behavior often prohibits the direct treatment of colonies. However, foraging and recruitment are essential aspects of their social behavior and expose workers to traps, baits, and pesticide applications. The advent of new chemistries has revolutionized the pest management strategies used to control them. In recent years, there has been an increased environmental awareness, especially in the urban community. Advances in molecular and microbial agents promise additional tools in developing integrated pest management programs against social insects.

INTRODUCTION

Subterranean termite pests: termites (Rhinotermitidae and some non-kalotermitids) that form large colonies with an extensive underground gallery in soil

Drywood termite pests: termites (Kalotermitidae) that usually form small colonies in a piece of wood

Social insects, especially ants, termites, and yellowjackets, are serious pests of the urban environment. They are responsible for extensively damaging structures, mechanically vectoring disease organisms, stinging and biting humans and their pets, and altering urban ecosystems. With increased urbanization and human commerce, some invasive species have spread to urban centers worldwide. This review focuses on their social behavior and efforts to exploit it to control them.

TERMITES

Although the taxonomic status of Isoptera remains uncertain owing to findings of phylogenetic analyses (27, 49, 71), most termitologists agree that termites are social cockroaches and that the wood-feeding genus *Cryptocercus* is the sister group. Specialization in wood-feeding is considered the primary cause for the evolution of sociality in termites (45). Wood fibers are made mostly of stable polymers such as cellulose and are the most abundant products of photosynthesis (64), but only a few organisms are capable of digesting them. With the aid of cellulase-producing symbiotic protozoans, early termites acquired the ability to digest cellulose. These symbionts are lost through molting, and one factor in the origin of termite sociality may be the need to stay together to resupply the symbionts through proctodeal feeding. All termites are eusocial, and a group of conspecific individuals typically lives in an enclosed space to form a colony. Colony members may or may not descend from the same parents, but they cooperatively engage in caring for the young and maintaining the nest. Reproductive castes and overlapping generations are also universal for termite colonies.

Pest Species and Their Economic Importance

Termites are chief decomposers of dead plant materials, and they contribute significantly to the nutrient turnover of soil (47). Some termite species become pests when they feed on structural lumber or any plant materials used by humans. Of the some 3,000 termite species in the world, 183 species (6.1%) are recorded as "pests" by Edwards & Mill (26), and 83 species (2.8%) cause severe damage to wooden structures or furniture. On the basis of the changes in taxonomic and pest status, 80 termite species are currently considered serious pests (**Table 1**).

Subterranean termite pests account for 38 of the serious pests, with the genus *Coptotermes* containing the largest number of species (18 spp.) followed by *Reticulitermes* and *Odontotermes* (**Table 1**). Two *Coptotermes* spp., *Co. formosanus* Shiraki and *Co. gestroi* Wasmann (formerly *Co. havilandi*, *Co. heimi*, and *Co. vastator*; now junior synonyms of *Co. gestroi*), stand out as the most economically important termite pests because of their widespread distribution (**Figure 1**). *Co. formosanus* is found primarily in subtropical and temperate regions, and *Co. gestroi* is found mostly in many areas of the tropics. The majority of drywood termite pests (Kalotermitidae) belong to the genus *Cryptotermes* (eight species are considered serious pests), followed by *Incisitermes* spp. (**Table 1**). Small colonies of drywood termites are confined in a piece of wood and can be easily transported. Thus, many drywood termite pests are found in multiple regions, but the most widely distributed (and the most economically important) species is *Cryptotermes brevis* (Walker) (**Figure 1**).

Based on the insecticide sales figures of 1999, the worldwide annual control and repair cost was estimated at $22 billion (117). A similar estimate with 2010 data showed that the global economic impact of termite pests has increased to $40 billion. Subterranean termites accounted for ≈80% of the costs.

Table 1 Termite species recognized as pests of significant economic importance, and their distribution[a]

Family	Species	Distribution
Rhinotermitidae	*Coptotermes formosanus* Shiraki	Far East, Indian subcontinent, Pacific Islands, North America
	Coptotermes gestroi Wasmann	Southeast Asia, Indian subcontinent, North America, South America, Caribbean, Indian Ocean
	Coptotermes ceylonicus Holmgren	Indian subcontinent
	Coptotermes exiguous (Holmgren)	Indian subcontinent
	Coptotermes premrasmii Ahmad	Southeast Asia
	Coptotermes travians (Havilandi)	Southeast Asia
	Coptotermes grandiceps Snyder	Pacific Islands
	Coptotermes pamuae Snyder	Pacific Islands
	Coptotermes acinaciformis (Froggatt)	Australia
	Coptotermes michaelseni Silvestri	Australia
	Coptotermes lacteus (Froggatt)	Australia
	Coptotermes frenchi Hill	Australia
	Coptotermes crassus Snyder	Central America
	Coptotermes niger Snyder	Central America, Caribbean
	Coptotermes testaceus (Linnaeus)	South America
	Coptotermes amanii (Sjöstedt)	Africa
	Coptotermes sjoestedti Holmgren	Africa
	Coptotermes truncates (Wasmann)	Indian Ocean
	Reticulitermes chinensis Snyder	Far East
	Reticulitermes flaviceps (Oshima)	Far East
	Reticulitermes fukiensis Light	Far East
	Reticulitermes speratus (Kolbe)	Far East
	Reticulitermes flavipes (Kollar)	North America, Europe
	Reticulitermes virginicus (Banks)	North America
	Reticulitermes hesperus Banks	North America
	Reticulitermes hageni Banks	North America
	Reticulitermes tibialis Banks	North America
	Reticulitermes lucifugus (Rossi)	Europe, Middle East
	Heterotermes ceylonicus (Holmgren)	Indian subcontinent
	Heterotermes gertrudae Roonwal	Indian subcontinent
	Heterotermes indicola (Wasmann)	Indian subcontinent
	Heterotermes aureus (Snyder)	North America
	Heterotermes convexinotatus Snyder	Central America, Caribbean, South America
	Heterotermes tenuis (Hagen)	Central America, Caribbean, South America
	Heterotermes philippinensis Light	Indian Ocean
	Heterotermes perfidus Silvestri	Atlantic Ocean
	Globitermes sulphureus (Haviland)	Southeast Asia
	Psammotermes hybostoma Desneux	Africa
Termitidae	*Odontotermes ceylonicus* (Wasmann)	Indian subcontinent
	Odontotermes feae (Wasmann)	Indian subcontinent
	Odontotermes obesus (Rambur)	Indian subcontinent
	Odontotermes obscuriceps (Wasmann)	Indian subcontinent
	Odontotermes redemanni (Wasmann)	Indian subcontinent
	Odontotermes formosanus (Shiraki)	Far East, Southeast Asia

(Continued)

Table 1 (*Continued*)

Family	Species	Distribution
	Odontotermes badius (Haviland)	Africa
	Odontotermes pauperans (Silvestri)	Africa
	Odontotermes latericus (Haviland)	Africa
	Odontotermes transvalensis (Sjöstedt)	Africa
	Nasutitermes ceylonicus (Holmgren)	Indian subcontinent
	Nasutitermes exitiosus (Hill)	Australia
	Nasutitermes corniger (Motschulsky)	Central America
	Nasutitermes costalis (Holmgren)	Central America, Caribbean
	Nasutitermes ephratae (Holmgren)	Central America, Caribbean
	Nasutitermes globiceps (Holmgren)	South America
	Nasutitermes voeltzkowi (Wasmann)	Indian Ocean
	Macrotermes bellicosus (Smeathman)	Africa
	Macrotermes natalensis (Haviland)	Africa
	Macrotermes subhyalinus (Rambur)	Africa
	Microcerotermes diversus Silvestri	Middle East
	Microcerotermes fuscotibialis Sjöstedt	Africa
	Amitermes vilis (Hagen)	Middle East
	Microhodotermes viator (Latreille)	Africa
Hodotermitidae	*Anacanthotermes ochraceus* (Burmeister)	Africa, Middle East
	Anacanthotermes vagans (Hagan)	Middle East
	Anacanthotermes septentrionalis (Jacobson)	Middle East
Mastotermitidae	*Mastotermes darwiniensis* Froggatt	Australia
Kalotermitidae	*Cryptotermes brevis* (Walker)	Australia, Pacific Islands, North America, Central America, Caribbean, South America, Atlantic Ocean, Africa
	Cryptotermes bengalensis Snyder	Indian subcontinent
	Cryptotermes cynocephalus Light	Indian subcontinent, Southeast Asia, Pacific Islands
	Cryptotermes dudleyi Banks	Indian subcontinent, Far East, Southeast Asia, Central America, Caribbean, South America, Africa
	Cryptotermes domesticus (Haviland)	Far East, Southeast Asia, Pacific Islands, Central America
	Cryptotermes rospigliosi Snyder	South America
	Cryptotermes havilandi (Sjöstedt)	Africa
	Cryptotermes pallidus (Rambur)	Indian Ocean
	Incisitermes minor (Hagen)	Far East, North America
	Incisitermes marginipennis (Latreille)	Central America
	Incisitermes snyderi	North America, Central America, Caribbean
	Glyptotermes brevicaudatus (Haviland)	Southeast Asia
	Marginitermes hubbardi (Banks)	North America

[a] Kalotermitids are drywood termites, and others are subterranean termites. Update of the list by Edwards & Mill (26) based on the changes in taxonomic and pest status.

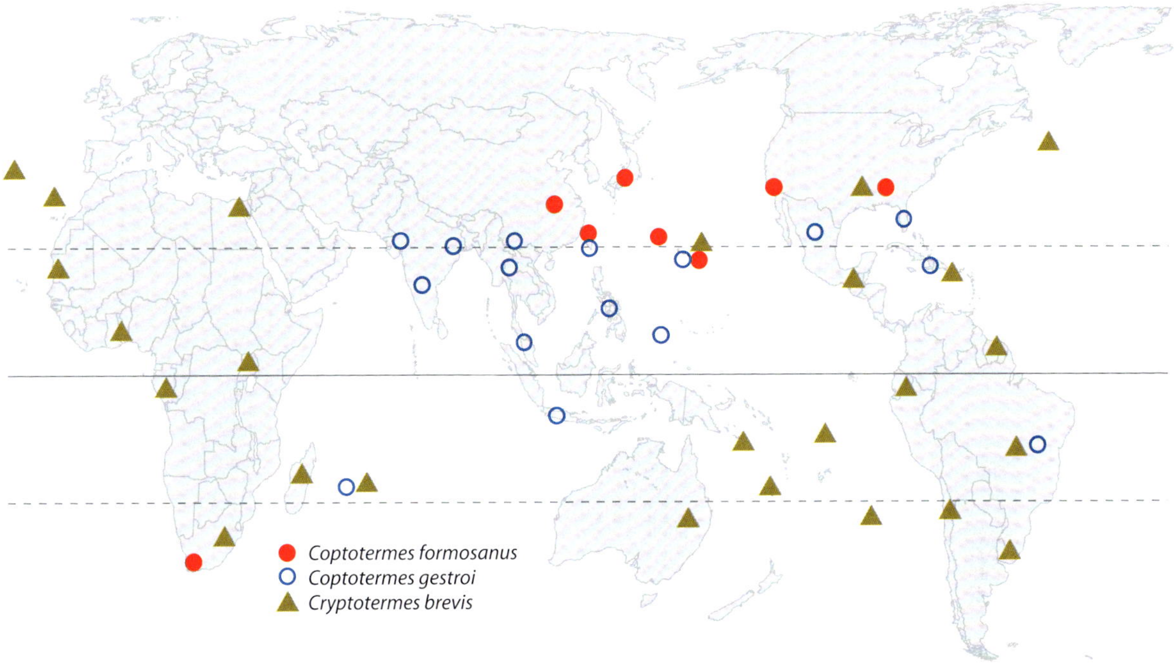

Figure 1

Distributions of the three most economically important and widely distributed termite pest species: *Coptotermes formosanus*, *Coptotermes gestroi*, and *Cryptotermes brevis*. Formerly known as *Coptotermes haviland* in Southeast Asia, *Coptotermes heimi* in India, and *Coptotermes vastator* in the Philippines, these names are now junior synonyms of *Co. gestroi*.

Colony Structure

A termite colony contains three castes, reproductive, soldier, and worker, and undifferentiated individuals of less than third instar are referred to as larvae. For kalotermitids (drywood termites), larvae may molt into the soldier caste or pseudogates (false workers). Pseudogates function as workers but eventually molt into alates before leaving the colony. For some rhinotermitids and all termitids, the worker caste is permanent and does not reach sexual maturity. Colonies of drywood termites inhabit a piece of wood, and a colony may contain as many as a few thousand individuals. Subterranean termites, however, forage in soil in search of food, and for some species, a colony may contain 100,000 to millions of individuals and foraging galleries extending up to 100 m (125).

Foraging Behavior of Subterranean Termites

Early excavation studies showed the extensive underground tunnel system of field colonies of subterranean termites such as *Co. formosanus* (54). Results of laboratory studies with planar foraging arenas indicated that the tunnel distribution of *Reticulitermes flavipes* (Kollar) was optimized for food-searching efficiency (96), but the presence of sound wood did not alter tunneling direction of *Co. formosanus* (15, 91). Instead, a positive moisture gradient increased tunneling activities (124), and tunnels were oriented toward decayed wood extracts carried by water in the sand at a distance of 12–18 cm (119). Living in high-moisture soil also subjects subterranean termites to occasional flooding, but they are apparently well adapted to survival under extended inundation. Recent

Alates: winged adult termites that may become primary reproductives of a new colony following dispersal flight and successful mating studies showed that following Hurricane Katrina, many *Co. formosanus* colonies survived after being submerged in floodwater for more than 2 weeks (19, 82).

Global away vector: the most direct away path that joins the tunnel origin and excavation site of a termite tunnel

Termite tunnels are constructed by a group of workers removing soil particles at tunnel tips (10), yet the emergent tunnel pattern is remarkably consistent (131). The overall geometry of the tunnel systems could be defined by a set of components (e.g., number of primary tunnels, linear segment length, turn angle, branching angle, and probability) used to construct simulated tunnels (131). Arena studies also showed that termite tunnels tend to radiate away from the origin and that the direction was governed by a global away vector (10, 131). Contrary to a previous assumption of stigmergy with pheromone labeling to explain the mechanisms of nest and gallery construction of some termite species (35, 51), observations from an arena study showed that tunnel propagation was the result of tactile interactions between termites and driven by the density and flow rate of individuals through tunnels (11).

One apparent function of termite tunnels is food acquisition, but the role of attractants is unknown because of their limited movement in soil (119). Results of a computer simulation with a gas lattice model suggested that termite tunnel geometry was more efficient in encountering food particles with clumped than nonclumped (random and uniform) distribution (66). Because termite movements are confined within their gallery systems and because termites have to travel back to their nests using the same tunnels after encountering foods, tunnel patterns at the time of initial construction have to be optimized for both search and transport efficiency. Simulation results showed that length distribution of branch tunnels was optimized for foraging efficiency, defined as the "ratio of energy gain for obtained food to loss for transporting food" through termite tunnel systems (67).

Current Control Measures

For practical considerations in termite control, termite pest species are divided into two major groups, drywood and subterranean species. Another group of termite pests is arboreal termites such as *Nasutitermes* spp. (**Table 1**), which build foraging tubes on tree and soil surfaces that connect their tree nests to houses. Control methods for arboreal termites are similar to those for subterranean termites.

Drywood termites. New infestations of drywood termites are initiated exclusively by alate pairs flying from mature colonies nearby. Drywood termites are capable of living in a piece of wood without the need for high wood moisture or free water, and they produce dry fecal pellets that are usually expelled from the galleries through "kickout" holes. The presence of piles of fecal pellets is one sign of drywood termite infestation.

Measures used to eliminate existing drywood termite infestations can be categorized as either whole-structure or localized treatments. When multiple colonies of drywood termites are suspected in a structure and detection of all infestations is unlikely, a whole-structure treatment with fumigants or heat is the best option. If done properly, fumigation with sulfuryl fluoride eradicates all termites, including the hidden ones, in a structure (69). For heat treatments, the structure is also sealed before it is heated to the desired wood temperature for a certain period.

If a drywood infestation is found only in a limited area of relatively small buildings such that all active infestations can be detected, local (or spot) treatments may offer a less costly option. A colony of drywood termites excavates interconnected galleries in wood, and the injection of insecticides (pyrethroids, imidacloprid, disodium octaborate tetrahydrate), as liquid, dust, or foam, into this void can effectively kill all individuals. There are nonchemical options such as localized heat treatments, cold treatment with liquid nitrogen to freeze termites inside wood, or the use of high-voltage electricity to electrocute termites inside wood (69).

Bait: a food or food-like substance containing a toxicant used to lure or entice a pest insect

Dose-independent lethal time: a fixed time span before the onset of death regardless of the amount of toxicant ingested by a termite

Subterranean termites. With the exception of aerial colonies that are founded by alate pairs on high rises, subterranean termites enter a house from soil through expansion joints, through cracks and utility conduits in slabs, or by building shelter tubes on foundation walls.

Soil termiticide barriers as exclusion devices. The primary method used by the industry to control subterranean termites is the application of liquid insecticides in subslab soil. A 2002 survey of the termite control industry in the United States (1) showed that 77% of termite control firms used liquid termiticides and 38% used termite bait products. As of 2009, liquid termiticides probably accounted for more than 80% of the market share for subterranean termite control. The objective of soil termiticide application is to place an insecticide barrier between termites and the structure to be protected. Currently available termiticides include permethrin, cypermethrin, bifenthrin, imidacloprid, fipronil, chlorfenapyr, and chlorantraniliprole. Pyrethroids (permethrin, cypermethrin, and bifenthrin) repel termites from treated barriers, whereas other termiticides prevent termite invasion by lethal contact (128).

Population management using baits. Applications of any control measures are restricted to a small portion of the tunnel system that may contain several million termites inhabiting a colony tunnel network extending up to 100 m. In order to affect a colony, control agents have to be transferred from exposed termites to the nestmates. Early on, it was suggested that, for a control agent to be distributed throughout a colony to cause colony collapse, the control agent has to be both slow-acting and nonrepellent (130). Although several metabolic inhibitors met these requirements (126, 127, 130), none successfully eliminated field colonies of subterranean termites (87, 95, 121, 132). These field results suggest that the inability of metabolic inhibitors to eliminate target colonies may be due to their dose-dependent lethal time; i.e., individuals that ingested higher doses were killed too quickly to transfer lethal doses to nestmates (123, 129, 132).

Unlike that of metabolic inhibitors, the lethal time of chitin synthesis inhibitors (CSIs) is relatively dose independent because CSIs affect termites mainly by disrupting their molting process, and regardless of doses, termites are not affected until they molt. Numerous field studies have demonstrated the elimination of all detectable subterranean termite activity by CSI (hexaflumuron or noviflumuron) baits at a variety of locations with a variety of different termite species (118). In addition to being slow-acting and nonrepellent, the lethal time of a control agent has to be dose independent if it is to eliminate the vast colony of subterranean termites.

Most bait products are used in a monitoring-baiting program to control subterranean termites. Currently, CSIs used in bait products in the United States include noviflumuron, diflubenzuron, and hexaflumuron, but chlorfluazuron, bistrifluron, and triflumuron are also used in termite baits in other countries. One metabolic inhibitor (sulfluramid) is used in bait products that are intended to be applied in conjunction with soil termiticides, without claims to eliminate termite colonies.

The monitoring-baiting procedure depends on termites to intercept the stations before the active-ingredient-containing baits are applied (133). To increase the station interception rate, there have been studies of trail-following substances (17), and arrestants or feeding stimulants (16, 92, 93, 98), but few field data are available to confirm the activity of these semiochemicals. Cornelius & Lax (20) reported that the commercial product Summon™ Preferred Food Source (FMC, Philadelphia) significantly increased the infestation rate of monitoring stations by *Co. formosanus*. The active ingredient(s) of Summon, however, has not been disclosed.

A recent development in bait technology is the active-ingredient-containing weather-resistant durable bait (120), which is placed in the stations at the onset of installation to bypass the monitoring phase. These baits can remain in soil for at least 12 months without significant degradation. A durable bait that contains noviflumuron was recently registered; it requires a single on-site inspection annually, thereby reducing the labor cost.

Integrated Pest Management for Termite Control

The economic injury level (EIL), defined by Stern et al. (115) as "...the lowest population density that will cause economic damage...," is the unifying principle of integrated pest management (IPM) (88). The EIL has been used for formulating IPM programs for agricultural crops, but its application to noncrop pests such as termites has been challenging. Instead of EIL, Su & Scheffrahn (129) suggest that termite IPM should focus on the fundamental principle of applying control measures "...only when the density of the pest at which the loss through damage exceeds the cost of control..." (78). IPM should be regarded as a cost-benefit issue, and EIL is a tool to help investigators arrive at a cost-effective decision in managing termite problems (129). By analyzing the cost-benefit structure of termite control practices, they identified termite damage potential and health and environmental risk of control measures as the most important variables to consider in termite IPM. Although the monetary values of these two variables are nearly impossible to estimate, Su & Scheffrahn (129) argue that, for termite IPM, termite damage potential has to be reduced by eliminating termite colonies near structures and that this has to be accomplished by using less toxic and less persistent control agents in smaller quantities.

Termite IPM project. One termite IPM project in China that has been ongoing is the GEF (Global Environmental Facility) project entitled "Demonstration of Alternatives to Chlordane and Mirex in Termite Control" (33). As one of the POP (persistent organic pollutant) projects under the Stockholm Convention, this project was initiated in 2001 to eliminate two POPs, chlordane and mirex, that have been used extensively in China for termite control. Instead of replacing these two POPs with other termiticides, Chinese termite experts agreed to use this opportunity to implement IPM programs for termite control in China. Published in 2007 (2), the *IPM Operation and Training Manual* identified the baiting system as the core technology because of its low toxicity and its ability to control termite populations through colony elimination. Workshops were held in the participating provinces (Hunan, Jiangsu, and Anhui) to educate technicians on the topics of IPM concept and management tools. By 2009, approximately 400,000 bait stations were applied, resulting in a reduction of approximately 102 metric tons of termiticide used (based on replacement with 0.5% permethrin). Moreover, factories that produced chlordane and mirex in China were closed, thus eliminating these two POPs from China. It remains to be seen whether the IPM practice can sustain itself in China after the project is terminated at the end of 2011.

Area-wide project. The business model for the termite control industry has been to protect the structures under contract with individual homeowners, and most companies use soil termiticides for treatments. When applied properly, termiticide barriers can protect a home from soil-borne termites, but their inability to eliminate a subterranean termite colony allows surviving populations to continue to infest nearby structures; e.g., invasive species such as *Co. formosanus* and *Co. gestroi* spread to other areas (118). Instead of treating individual homes, investigators have attempted area-wide management of subterranean termite populations (39, 111, 122).

Under the federally funded Operation Full Stop, an area-wide project was initiated in 1998 to suppress *Co. formosanus* populations in the French Quarter of New Orleans (39). From 1998 to 2007, participating pest control firms applied baits and nonrepellent termiticides (through several phases at various zones), and the overall alate catch declined 76%, but there remained lingering infestations in some properties. Site inspection revealed numerous isolated infestations in shared walls or common properties that were overlooked by pest control firms whose responsibility was to treat only the structures under the contract. These problems have since been addressed, and it is expected that the overall activity of *Co. formosanus* can be further reduced (39).

One of the most successful area-wide projects was reported from a low-income community in Santiago, Chile (111). Baits were first applied in 2001 in three of the six town blocks severely infested by *R. flavipes*, and by 2002, most of the termite activity in the baited town blocks was eliminated. Following the initial success, more baits were applied in the test site in 2003–2004, and since 2005, *R. flavipes* has not been detected in the area. One major factor for the success of this project was the simple operation structure of using a single pest control firm that was entirely responsible for the outcome. Unlike the area-wide project in the French Quarter, there was a clear objective of eliminating all *R. flavipes* activities within the test area; thus, any sign of termite activity was used as a baiting opportunity. For future area-wide projects with larger areas, it was suggested that the area be divided into reasonably sized portions and that each portion be assigned to a single pest control firm with the condition of eliminating all termite populations in its assigned area (111).

Tramp ants: species characterized by multiple queens and nests, reproduction by budding, and the ability to utilize human-disturbed habitats

ANTS

The broad diversity of ants and the ability of so-called tramp ant species to exploit disturbed human habitats make them serious urban pests. Of the 14,122 described species, approximately 40 to 50 species have attained an urban pest status (9, 25, 44, 57). In the northwestern United States, the odorous house ant, *Tapinoma sessile* (Say), and *Lasius pallitarsis* (Provancher) are the major indoor pest species (46, 57). *Solenopsis xyloni* McCook and *Forelius pruinosus* (Roger) are the most common native ant pests in Arizona (28). However, two invasive tramp ant species, the Argentine ant, *Linepithema humile* (Mayr), and the Pharaoh ant, *Monomorium pharaonis* (L.), are found in urban centers worldwide (44, 57, 80). Other urban species that share some characteristics of tramp ants include the crazy ant, *Paratrechina longicornis* (Latreille), the longlegged ant, *Anoplolepis gracilipes* (Fr. Smith), and the ghost ant, *Tapinoma melanocephalum* (F.) (86).

Urbanization changes microhabitat characteristics, resulting in the simplification of ant communities and groups of competitively dominant species, including tramp ants (68, 107, 137). Suburban forests support a greater variety of ant species, including *T. sessile* (137). This may explain in part the increased incidence of *T. sessile* in urban communities. The vast majority of ants (95%) are collected in residential areas and 90% are collected outdoors (28). Increased urbanization above 30%–40% of the landscape leads to a decline of ant diversity (107). Human activities and not biological invasion may be the primary factor affecting native ant communities. Ants such as the red imported fire ant, *Solenopsis invicta* Buren, may be more appropriately referred to as disturbance specialists (55).

The number of invasive species reported in urban centers has dramatically increased in recent years. Some species go unnoticed for years. For example, *Myrmica rubra* (L.) was first reported in Maine in 1908, but it did not become a serious urban pest until 1993–2003 (38). Similar histories apply to *Pachycondyla chinensis* (Emery) and *Brachymyrmex patagonicus* Mayr (73, 79).

Economic and Medical Importance

Ants affect urban residents by destroying structural materials, stinging and biting humans and pets, contaminating foods, mechanically vectoring disease agents, and tending hemipterans on ornamental plants (25, 42, 44, 57, 80). In Washington and Oregon, *Camponotus* and *Liometopum* represent about 66% of the structural treatments by pest management professionals (PMPs) (42). In Norway, approximately $1.5 million was spent on controlling carpenter ants in 2007 (83). In southern California, approximately 20% of homeowners report hiring a PMP to control their ants, spending between $300 and $424 annually (60). Estimates of the annual losses caused by *S. invicta* range from $87 to $150 per household in the United States (80). In New Zealand, the costs of controlling *L. humile* are estimated at $1 million for 2009–2010 (141).

Anaphylaxis: a rapidly progressing allergic reaction or hypersensitivity that can be life threatening

Perimeter treatments: mode of application in which insecticides are applied to areas likely to harbor pests away from the structure

Monomorium pharaonis has been implicated as a mechanical vector of pathogenic bacteria (25, 70, 80). In Brazilian hospitals, *T. melanocephalum*, *P. longicornis*, and *M. pharaonis* carried 21 species of bacteria including *Staphylococcus*, *Streptococcus*, and *Klebsiella pneumoniae pneumoniae*; many strains were resistant to antimicrobial drugs (76, 97). Five ant species collected from households and industrial kitchens were contaminated with fungi including an alflatoxigenic strain of *Aspergillus flavus* (146). Seventy-five percent of ants collected from hospitals carried airborne fungi and *Candida* yeast (85), and 85% were contaminated by the fungus *Aspergillus* (108).

Stings from various species of fire ants are prevalent where infestations occur, especially in elder care facilities (79, 100). Eighty percent of *P. chinensis* sting victims had local reactions and 8% reported recurring pain and symptoms lasting 3 to 14 days (79). Ants are not typically associated with anaphylaxis, but the number of species reported to cause medical emergencies is increasing (58, 59). Stings from several species of *Pachycondyla* are reported to cause anaphylactic shock (7, 65, 75).

Ants are a source of aeroallergens. Pharaoh ant antigens were found in 32.1% of Korean homes, and 11.5% of the residents were positive for Pharaoh-ant-specific IgE (52). The Pharaoh ant is also an important source of aeroallergens causing bronchial asthma (53).

Control Strategies

Ant control in urban settings has typically evolved around the use of baits and perimeter treatments (25, 44, 56, 74).

Baits. Baits are an ideal approach to ant control because they exploit their foraging behavior and social interactions (25, 44, 57, 74, 143). A seminal paper on ant baits (116) lists four important properties of an active ingredient: (*a*) It exhibits delayed toxicity, (*b*) it is effective over at least a 10-fold range of concentrations, (*c*) it is not repellent, and (*d*) it can be formulated with foods and carriers. Ideally, it should be attractive only to the target pest ant. Delayed toxicity was defined as <15% mortality after 24-h exposure and >89% mortality at the end of the test. This early definition needs revision to accommodate newer, faster-acting baits such as indoxacarb, metaflumizone, spinosad, and thiamethoxam (81, 103). However, the fundamental premise that toxic baits should act slowly enough as not to impair or inhibit social behaviors is common to all the definitions.

Baits formulated with soybean oils are widely accepted by many pestiferous ants belonging to the subfamily Myrmicinae and avoided by species belonging to the subfamily Dolichoderinae (56, 57). Bait formulations with soybean oil and indoxacarb controlled *M. pharaonis* for 3 weeks and *S. invicta* and *Pogonomyrmex barbatus* (F. Smith) for 7 weeks (31). Defatted corncob grits with soybean oil containing indoxacarb and metaflumizone provided significantly faster reductions of active mounds of *S. invicta* than did hydramethylnon alone (48). However, some of these scattered baits affected nontarget ant species (139).

Many of the dolichoderine and some of the formicine ants prefer carbohydrates and readily forage on liquid baits (8, 25, 56, 57). Sucrose solutions containing fipronil, indoxacarb, and boric acid provided reductions of *A. gracilipes* greater than 90% (18).

One challenge with baits is developing cost-effective treatment strategies. Whether they are used in routine pest management service depends on the pest species targeted. Baiting with liquid sucrose formulations of 0.001% thiamethoxam provided control of *L. humile* comparable to that of fipronil sprays but increased costs by approximately 40% (61). Two liquid baits controlled arboreal white-footed ants, *Technomyrmex difficilis* (Bolton), but their application was extremely labor intensive (142).

Perimeter treatments. Perimeter sprays and barriers applied around structures have evolved over the past 60 years because of regulatory changes and new chemistries (25, 44, 56, 57, 74). Perimeter treatments were considered as barriers to prevent access to structures by either killing ants, repelling ants, or both (63, 101). However, research suggests that fast-acting insecticides such as pyrethroids prevent ants from establishing trails across treated barriers (89, 112, 144, 145). The application of fast-acting barriers can result in ants trapped within barriers and structures (56, 57) or colony budding (14, 44, 80).

Certain toxicants with delayed toxicity act slow enough to allow horizontal transfer of toxicant to nestmates by contact and necrophoresis. Fipronil provided excellent reductions of a number of species for 4 weeks or longer (60–62, 109). Their effectiveness is attributable to fipronil's slow-acting toxicity and its horizontal transfer to nestmates (14, 112, 113). Exposed workers continue foraging and interacting with nestmates for several hours after exposure. When the worker dies, nestmates remove them to graveyards and in the process acquire a lethal dose of insecticide. Lethal doses of bifenthrin, fipronil, and thiamethoxam are transferred to *S. invicta* nestmates by topically treated ants (145). Even a brief exposure (1 min) to residual deposits of fipronil provides horizontal transfer to nestmates (41, 112, 113).

Applications of granular insecticides around structures provide marginal control (102) but prevent *S. invicta* from crossing barriers for up to 15 weeks (89). In conjunction with perimeter sprays, granules are effective (60, 62, 102). Use of fipronil granules reduced *S. invicta* populations by 97% on golf course fairways for at least 9 months (36). Avoid applying granules near driveways, sidewalks, and street curbs where irrigation or rain might wash them into storm drains (37).

There has been an increasing awareness that perimeter ant treatments contribute to pesticide runoff into urban waterways (37). Reduced volumes of spray and pin-stream applications restricted to the foundation provide significant reductions in *L. humile* and reduce the risk of pesticide runoff (37, 61). Conventional applications of bifenthrin produce detectable amounts of bifenthrin in runoff water (37). The impact of ant perimeter treatments and potential pesticide runoff in urban waterways will become a major issue over the next decade.

Alternative strategies. Numerous recommendations concerning modifying ant control in the urban habitat have been made (25, 42, 44, 56, 57). Although most of them are reasonable, few studies actually demonstrate their efficacy.

High concentrations of the synthetic trail pheromone (Z)-9-hexadecenal disrupted trail following behavior in *L. humile* (134, 136), and point sources of Z,E-α-farnesene disrupted *S. invicta* (135). When (Z)-9-hexadecenal formulated into microencapsulated product was sprayed onto field sites, it disrupted trail following for at least 14 days (134). The density of ants was not affected.

Foliar sprays or systemic insecticides to reduce hemipteran sources of honeydew have been proposed as a means of controlling ants around structures. Quantifying the impact of such treatments has been difficult (102). Denying *L. humile* access to hemipterans producing honeydew in trees did not result in increased bait consumption or ant control (12). Tree-injected dicrotophos afforded some control of scale vegetation and reductions of *L. humile* density (13). Foliar sprays are helpful in reducing numbers of *Technomyrmex difficilis* (142).

Biological control. The potential use of biological control in urban settings has focused primarily on the control of *S. invicta* (56, 57, 80). Two potentially interesting biological control agents are being evaluated against *S. invicta*: exotic *Pseudacteon* ant-decapitating flies and the microsporidian *Kneallhazia solenopsae*. The latter is a chronic disease that debilitates the queen and causes a slow death of the colony. *S. invicta* colonies infected with *K. solenopsae* were 2.4-fold more susceptible to hydramethylnon bait and declined much faster (138). In another area-wide demonstration study, the release of *Pseudacteon tricuspis* and *K. solenopsae* reduced *S. invicta* density by 85%–99% compared with untreated sites (139).

Williams et al. (143) summarize the potential of *K. solenopsae* to be a tactic for systems in areas where fire ant control is not available. It may help reduce reliance on pesticides, encourage the establishment of native ants and other arthropods, and increase the susceptibility of *S. invicta* to other pathogens, natural enemies, and pesticides.

IPM. Four basic steps readily adaptable to almost any urban ant pest problem are (*a*) inspection and identification, (*b*) monitoring, (*c*) prescription treatment, and (*d*) follow-up monitoring (29, 42, 56, 57). A slightly different but valid approach also includes finding where the ant is living, directing control measures at the harborage sites, and correcting contributing conditions (44). A detailed inspection and questionnaire for the homeowner help the PMP focus on conducive conditions and noninsecticidal solutions (44). Educational materials for tenants, property owners, and the public are important, especially when trying to enlist their cooperation.

Some invasive species such as *L. humile* or *S. invicta* may require an area-wide approach to control them (110, 141, 143). Area-wide approaches are hampered by problems of inspecting and treating private property. An area-wide baiting effort to eradicate *L. humile* from Tiritiri Matangi Island, New Zealand, has dramatically reduced, but not eliminated, ant populations (141). For area-wide efforts to be successful, there must be a cooperative effort between homeowners, PMPs, and governmental agencies.

YELLOWJACKETS, HORNETS, AND PAPER WASPS

The family Vespidae contains approximately 4,250 described species, but only a few are a threat to urban residents (4, 5, 25, 114). Adult vespids feed on carbohydrates such as nectar, plant sap, and sweet liquids from fruits and honeydew. They are general predators of live insects and are considered beneficial (4, 6, 114). A few members of the *Vespula vulgaris* species group, a few species of *Vespa*, and *Vespula squamosa* (Drury) scavenge animal carcasses and human foods (5, 25, 114). They forage around dumpsters, schools, parks, recreation areas, and zoos, posing a serious public health problem.

Vespula germanica (F.), *V. pensylvanica* (Saussure), and *V. vulgaris* (L.) are invasive, with ranges spreading in step with human activities. *V. germanica* is native to Europe, northern Africa, and temperate Asia (114) but has spread to North America, Chile, New Zealand, Australia, and Tasmania (72). *V. pensylvanica* is native to most of the western United States but is now established in the Hawaiian Islands (6). *V. vulgaris* is found throughout the British Isles and northeastern United States and across Canada to the western United States (25); it has colonized Australia and New Zealand (6). *V. germanica* and *V. vulgaris* owe their success as invasive species likely to their ability to recruit workers to food sources with odors (84).

Economic and Medical Importance

Extensive reviews of the economic impact of yellowjackets and wasps on agricultural and natural settings are available (5, 6, 105). One of the greatest urban impacts is their presence around theme parks, recreational areas, and schools. It is not uncommon for parks to close camping sites, refreshment stands, and eating areas at peak yellowjacket periods (4, 25). In 2006, even though 42,367 yellowjackets were successfully trapped at a health spa, 91 stings were still reported (M.K. Rust, unpublished data).

Humans vary in their sensitivity to hymenopteran stings. Golden (34) reports that about 1% of children and 3% of adults are allergic to Hymenoptera stings. About 0.8%–5% of the general population has systemic reactions to Hymenoptera venom, with 19% having severe local reactions. Of 703 patients evaluated, wasps, hornets, or yellowjackets were implicated in 60% of the cases (30). Although stings from *Vespa crabro* L., *Dolichovespula* wasps, bumble bees, and ants are rare in Europe (90), hymenopteran stings, especially from wasps, are the most common cause of anaphylaxis in adults (34). From 1990 to 2006, the German Federal Office of Statistics reported 335 deaths after stings by bees, wasps, or hornets (90). At least 50 fatal insect stings are reported annually in the United States (34).

Insect Pest Management Control Strategies

The pest management of yellowjackets presents a challenge because nests are often considerable distances from the site of human interaction. Workers of *V. pensylvanica* and *V. germanica* forage up to 400 m and 250 m, respectively (6).

Foraging activity. Workers forage for plant fibers, water, protein, and carbohydrates, and individuals may tend to specialize on specific types of resources (94). Workers begin as pulp collectors, change to carbohydrates, and finally collect prey. Long-lived foragers often finish by foraging on fluids (24). Unlike other social insects, recruitment of workers is not well developed (22, 94). Foragers utilize visual, olfactory, and tactile cues, alone or in combination, to locate food sources. Olfaction is important when foraging for less active items (50, 84), whereas visual cues are important to orient others to protein (77). Naïve *V. germanica* and *V. vulgaris* workers learn odors from arriving foragers (59). Dead workers at a dish of honey attract *V. germanica* foragers (21). *V. germanica* and *V. maculifrons* are attracted to baits with conspecifics, a form of social enhancement (90). The use of landmarks as aids in short-ranged navigation is suggested by the fact that *V. germanica* refound feeding locations more often in closed habitats than in open habitats (23).

Vespine species vary in their responses to olfactory cues, with some food-borne volatiles either stimulating or inhibiting certain species (24). Two general groups of odor cues exist: (*a*) heptyl butyrate and acetic acid with isobutanol and (*b*) hexenal/monoterpenol.

Nest treatments. Some species such as *Vespa crabro*, *V. germanica*, *V. pensylvanica*, *Polistes dominula* (Christ), and *Polistes fuscatus aurifer* Saussure may nest within or near human structures and can become a hazard if disturbed (5, 25). If nests are located, they can be treated effectively with pyrethrin or pyrethroid dusts at night with protective clothing (5, 25). The access hole should not be plugged until the cavity containing the nest is properly eliminated (72). Pyrethroid dusts and sprays effectively kill workers in or on nests. Thiamethoxam sprays and foams applied directly to workers and nests killed 100% of *P. dominula* without agitating the workers (99). Resmethrin sprays provide fast knockdown but do not always penetrate the nest envelope (72). Unfortunately, few efficacy data exist for the new active ingredients registered for use.

Baiting strategies. A minimum of five traps set about 25 m apart are recommended for monitoring. A minimum of five yellowjackets per trap per day are recommended before baiting (32). Best results are obtained when *V. pensylvanica* foragers exceed 10 wasps per trap per day (104).

Interceptive trapping: a strategy in which traps are placed along peripheral areas to intercept foraging ants and wasps

Onslaught™ (microencapsulated esfenvalerate), the only registered bait in the United States, was not effective in a protein bait against *V. pensylvanica* (104). Baits with 30% sugar syrup and 0.1% fipronil provided a 99.7% reduction in colony activity (43). Baits with minced beef and 0.1% fipronil provided complete kill of 46 nests at two 6-ha sites with 89% reduction of workers (106). Minced white chicken with 0.0025%–0.025% fipronil provided reductions of *V. pensylvanica* greater than 90% for 4 weeks (105). Chlorfenapyr, chlorantraniliprole, indoxacarb, and spinosad mixed in chicken or fish were ineffective against *V. pensylvanica* (104). Hydramethylnon (2%), permethrin (0.3%), and chlorpyrifos (0.25%) mixed into protein baits did not control *V. germanica* (105).

Alternative strategies. Intensive trapping with heptyl butyrate attractant reduces yellowjacket numbers, but trapping alone does not provide area-wide control. Placement of 80 traps with heptyl butyrate around a 20-ha water park failed to control *V. pensylvanica* (40). In northern California, a picnic area encircled with 24 heptyl butyrate traps captured 30 to 70 yellowjackets per trap per day, whereas 4 traps at the picnic tables had less than 10 yellowjackets per trap per day. Placing rings of traps around picnic areas (interceptive trapping) reduced the number of stings reported by park users (104).

Vespid workers foraging for water at swimming pools can be drowned or repelled by applying the algaecide n-alkyl dimethyl benzyl ammonium chloride (140). Wasp visits declined from 253 to approximately 4 wasps per hour with this application.

CONCLUSIONS

The termite control business model has been to treat and protect individual homes under contract from termites, and more than 80% of subterranean termite treatments rely on soil termiticides that have been used since the early 1900s. With the availability of bait products capable of eliminating termite colonies, there have been attempts to introduce IPM and several area-wide projects have been carried out. Whether these approaches can be incorporated into future termite control business, however, remains to be seen.

PMPs have relied on perimeter applications of sprays and granules for ant control. Baits have been incorporated, but the cost of baits and their applications have been prohibitive. For some invasive species, area-wide control programs may be the only logical way of providing control.

Improved attractants would help increase the performance of both traps and baits against yellowjackets. Lower concentrations of slow-acting toxicants are also needed to help maximize bait performance. The most pressing need is for the registration of formulated baits to control yellowjackets.

SUMMARY POINTS

1. Of the approximately 3,000 termite species in the world, 80 species are considered serious pests with an economic impact of more than US$40 billion annually, and subterranean termites account for 80% of the damage.
2. The two most important variables in termite IPM are termite damage potential and health and environmental risks of control measures.
3. Termite baits with CSIs are ideal for area-wide projects because of their ability to eliminate individual termite colonies with minimum insecticide use, but one challenge is the labor costs associated with bait applications.

4. Of the 14,122 described ant species, approximately 40 to 50 species have attained an urban pest status.
5. Baits are an ideal approach to ant control because they exploit their foraging behavior and social interaction, but one challenge with baits is developing cost-effective treatment strategies.
6. *V. germanica* and *V. vulgaris* owe their success as invasive species likely to their ability to recruit workers to food sources with odors.
7. The pest management of yellowjackets presents a challenge because nests are often considerable distances from the site of human interaction.
8. Intensive trapping with attractants reduces yellowjacket numbers, but trapping alone does not provide area-wide control.

DISCLOSURE STATEMENT

N.-Y. Su is the inventor of one bait product that uses hexaflumuron (in some countries) or noviflumuron (in the United States) as the active ingredient. The intellectual property rights of this invention belongs to his employer, the University of Florida, but he receives part of the royalties from this invention. The name of the product was not mentioned in this review.

LITERATURE CITED

1. 2002. State of the industry. *Pest Control* 70:S1–S18
2. 2007. *IPM operation and training manual.* Chinese Termite Control Expert Committee, Beijing: Stockholm Conv. Implement. Off., Minist. Environ. Prot. 188 pp.
3. Deleted in proof
4. Akre RD. 1995. Our stinging friends? The ambivalent yellowjackets. *Am. Entomol.* 41:21–29
5. Akre RD, Greene A, MacDonald JF, Landolt PJ, Davis HG. 1981. *Yellowjackets of America North of Mexico.* USDA Agric. Handb. No. 552. 102 pp.
6. Akre RD, MacDonald JF. 1986. Biology, economic importance and control of yellow jackets. In *Economic Impact and Control of Social Insects*, ed. SB Vincent, pp. 353–412. New York: Praeger. 421 pp.
7. AlAnazi M, AlAshahrani M, AlSalamah M. 2009. Black ant stings caused by *Pachycondyla sennaarensis*: a significant health hazard. *Ann. Saudi Med.* 29:207–11
8. Alder P, Silverman J. 2005. Effects of interspecific competition between two urban ant species, *Linepithema humile* and *Monomorium minimum*, on toxic bait performance. *J. Econ. Entomol.* 98:493–501
9. **AntWeb. 2011. *Ants of the World.* http://www.antweb.org/**
10. **Bardunias P, Su N-Y. 2009. Dead reckoning in the tunnel propagation of the Formosan subterranean termite (Isoptera: Rhinotermitidae). *Ann. Entomol. Soc. Am.* 102:158–65**
11. Bardunias P, Su N-Y. 2010. Queue size determines the width of tunnels in the Formosan subterranean termite (Isoptera: Rhinotermitidae). *J. Insect Behav.* 23:189–204
12. Brightwell RJ, Bambara SB, Silvermen J. 2010. Combined effect of hemipteran control and liquid bait on Argentine ant populations. *J. Econ. Entomol.* 103:1790–96
13. Brightwell RJ, Silverman J. 2009. Effects of honeydew-producing hemipteran denial on local Argentine ant distribution and boric acid bait performance. *J. Econ. Entomol.* 102:1170–74
14. Buczkowski G, Scharf ME, Ratliff CR, Bennett GW. 2005. Efficacy of simulated barrier treatments against laboratory colonies of Pharaoh ant. *J. Econ. Entomol.* 98:485–92
15. Campora CE, Grace JK. 2001. Tunnel orientation and search pattern sequence of the Formosan subterranean termite (Isoptera: Rhinotermitidae). *J. Econ. Entomol.* 94:1193–99
16. Chen J, Henderson G. 1996. Determination of feeding preference of Formosan subterranean termite (*Coptotermes formosanus* Shiraki) for some amino acid additives. *J. Chem. Ecol.* 22:2359–69

9. Provides an outstanding source of information, references, and species lists of ants of the world.

10. Demonstrates that termite tunnel direction was governed by a global away vector, not by stigmergy.

17. Chen J, Henderson G, Laine RA. 1998. Isolation and identification of a 2-phenoxyethanol from a ballpoint pen ink as a trail-following substance of *Coptotermes formosanus* Shiraki and *Reticulitermes* sp. *J. Entomol. Sci.* 33:97–105
18. Chong K-F, Lee C-Y. 2009. Evaluation of liquid baits against filed populations of the longlegged ant (Hymenoptera: Formicidae). *J. Econ. Entomol.* 102:1586–90
19. Cornelius ML, Duplessis ML, Osbrink WL. 2007. The impact of Hurricane Katrina on the distribution of subterranean termite colonies (Isoptera: Rhinotermitidae) in City Park, New Orleans, Louisiana. *Sociobiology* 50:311–35
20. **Cornelius ML, Lax A. 2005. Effect of Summon Preferred Food Source on feeding, tunneling, and bait station discovery by the Formosan subterranean termite (Isoptera: Rhinotermitidae). *J. Econ. Entomol.* 98:502–8**

20. Shows that one commercial product significantly increased the infestation rate of monitoring stations by termites.

21. D'Adamo P, Corley JC, Lozada M. 2001. Attraction of *Vespula germanica* (Hymenoptera: Vespidae) foragers by conspecific heads. *J. Econ. Entomol.* 94:850–52
22. D'Adamo P, Corley JC, Sackmann P, Lozada M. 2000. Local enhancement in the wasp *Vespula germanica.* Are visual cues all that matter? *Insectes Soc.* 47:289–91
23. D'Adamo P, Lozada M. 2007. Foraging behavior related to habitat characteristics in the invasive wasp *Vespula germanica*. *Insect Sci.* 14:383–88
24. Day SE, Jeanne RJ. 2001. Food volatiles as attractants for yellowjackets (Hymenoptera: Vespidae). *Environ. Entomol.* 30:157–65
25. Ebeling W. 1978. *Urban Entomology*. Berkeley, CA: Div. Agric. Sci. Univ. Calif. 695 pp.
26. Edwards R, Mill AE. 1986. *Termites in Buildings. Their Biology and Control.* East Grinstead, England: Rentokil Ltd. 261 pp.
27. Eggleton P, Beccaloni G, Inward D. 2007. Response to Lo, et al. *Biol. Lett.* 3:564–65
28. Field HC, Evans WE Jr, Hartley R, Hansen LD, Klotz JH. 2007. A survey of structural ant pests of the southwestern U.S.A. (Hymenoptera: Formicidae). *Sociobiology* 49:1–14
29. Forschler BT. 1997. A prescription for ant control success. *Pest Control* 65:34–38
30. Freeman T. 1997. Hymenoptera hypersensitivity in an imported fire ant endemic area. *Ann. Allergy Asthma Immunol.* 78:369–72
31. Furman BD, Gold RE. 2006. The effectiveness of label-rate broadcast treatment with Advion™ at controlling multiple ant species (Hymenoptera: Formicidae). *Sociobiology* 48:559–70
32. Gambino P, Loope L. 1992. Yellowjacket (*Vespula pensylvanica*) Biology and Abatement in the National Parks of Hawaii. *Tech. Rep. 86*, Univ. Hawaii, Monoa. **http://www.botany.hawaii.edu/faculty/duffy/techr/086.pdf**
33. Global Environment Facility. 2005. *China - Demonstration of alternatives to chlordane and mirex in termite control.* **http://www.gefonline.org/projectDetails.cfm?projID = 2359**
34. Golden DBK. 2003. Stinging insect allergies. *Am. Fam. Phys.* 67:2541–46
35. Grasse PP. 1959. La reconstruction du nid et les coordinations inter-individuelles chez *Bellicositermes natalensis* et *Cubitermes* sp. La theore de la stigmergie: essai d'interpretation du comportment des termites constructeurs. *Insectes Soc.* 6:41–81
36. Greenberg L, Reierson DA, Rust MK. 2003. Fipronil trials in California against the red imported fire ant, *Solenopsis invicta* Buren, using sugar water consumption and mound counts as measures of ant abundance. *J. Agric. Urban Entomol.* 20:221–33
37. **Greenberg L, Rust MK, Klotz JH, Haver D, Kabashima JN, et al. 2010. Impact of ant control technologies on insecticide runoff and efficacy. *Pest Manag. Sci.* 66:980–87**

37. Discusses ant treatments that result in insecticide runoff in urban waterways and their importance.

38. Groden E, Drummond FA, Garnas J, Franceour A. 2005. Distribution of an invasive ant, *Myrmica rubra* (Hymenoptera: Formicidae) in Maine. *J. Econ. Entomol.* 98:1774–84
39. Guillot FS, Ring DR, Lax AR, Morgan A, Brown K, Riegel C, Boykin D. 2010. Area-wide management of the Formosan subterranean termite, *Coptotermes formosanus* Shiraki (Isoptera: Rhinotermitidae), in the New Orleans French Quarter. *Sociobiology* 55:311–38
40. Gulmahamad H. 2002. Current traps and baits may not handle large-scale infestations. *Pest Control* 70(7):34–40
41. Hannum CD, Miller DM. 2008. Intercolony variation in the black carpenter ant (*Camponotus pennsylvanicus*) (Hymenoptera: Formicidae) response to fipronil (0.06%) residues. *Sociobiology* 52(3):729–50

42. Hansen LD, Klotz JH. 2005. *Carpenter Ants of the United States and Canada*. Ithaca, NY: Comstock. 204 pp.
43. Harris RJ, Etheridge ND. 2001. Comparison of baits containing fipronil and sulfluramid for the control of *Vespula* wasps. *N. Z. J. Zool.* 28:39–48
44. Hedges SA. 2010. *Field Guide for the Management of Structure-Infesting Ants*. Richfield, OH: GIE Media, Inc. 325 pp.
45. Higashi M, Yamamura M, Abe T. 2000. Theories on the sociality of termites. In *Termites: Evolution, Sociality, Symbioses, Ecology*, ed. T Abe, ED Bignell, M Higashi, pp. 169–87. Dordrecht: Kluwer Academic Publ.
46. Hoey-Chamberlain RV, Hansen LD, Klotz JH, McNeeley C. 2010. A survey of the ants of Washington and surrounding areas of Idaho and Oregon focusing on disturbed sites (Hymenoptera: Formicidae). *Sociobiology* 56(1):195–207
47. Holt JA, Lepage M. 2000. Termites and soil properties. In *Termites: Evolution, Sociality, Symbioses, Ecology*, ed. T Abe, ED Bignell, M Higashi, pp. 389–407. Dordrecht: Kluwer Academic Publ.
48. Hu XP, Song D. 2007. Field evaluation of label-rate broadcast treatment with baits for controlling the red imported fire ant, *Solenopsis invicta* (Hymenoptera: Formicidae). *Sociobiology* 50:1107–16
49. Inward D, Beccaloni G, Eggleton P. 2007. Death of an order: A comprehensive molecular phylogenetic study confirms that termites are eusocial cockroaches. *Biol. Lett.* 3:331–35
50. Jeanne RL, Taylor BJ. 2009. Individual and social foraging in social wasps. In *Food Exploitation by Social Insects: Ecological, Behavioral and Theoretical Approaches*, ed. S Jarau, M Hrncir, pp. 53–79. Boca Raton, FL: CRC Press. 331 pp.
51. Jones RJ. 1979. Expansion of the nest of *Nasutitermes costalis*. *Insectes Soc.* 26:322–42
52. Kim CW, Kim DI, Choi SY, Park JW, Hong CS. 2005. Pharaoh ant (*Monomorium pharaonis*): newly identified important inhalant allergens in bronchial asthma. *J. Kor. Med. Sci.* 20:390–96
53. Kim CW, Song JS, Choi SY, Park JW, Hong CS. 2007. Detection and quantification of Pharaoh ant antigens in household dust samples as newly identified aeroallergens. *Int. Arch. Allergy Immunol.* 144:247–53
54. King EG, Spink WT. 1969. Foraging galleries of the Formosan termite, *Coptotermes formosanus*, in Louisiana. *Ann. Entomol. Soc. Am.* 62:537–42
55. King JR, Tschinkel WR. 2008. Experimental evidence that human impacts drive fire ant invasions and ecological change. *Proc. Natl. Acad. Sci.* 105:20339–43
56. Klotz J, Hansen L, Field H, Rust M, Oi D, Kupfer K. 2010. *Urban Pest Management of Ants in California*. Richmond: Univ. Calif. Agric. Nat. Resour. 72 pp.
57. **Klotz JH, Hansen L, Pospischil R, Rust M. 2008. *Urban Ants of North America and Europe Identification, Biology and Management*. Ithaca, NY: Cornell Univ. Press. 196 pp.**
58. Klotz JH, Klotz SA, Pinnas JL. 2009. Animal bites and stings with anaphylactic potential. *J. Emerg. Med.* 36:148–56
59. Klotz JH, Pinnas JL, Klotz SA, Schmidt JO. 2009. Anaphylactic reactions to arthropod bites and stings. *Am. Entomol.* 55:134–39
60. Klotz JH, Rust MK, Field HC, Greenberg L, Kupfer K. 2008. Controlling Argentine ants in residential settings (Hymenoptera: Formicidae). *Sociobiology* 51:579–88
61. Klotz JH, Rust MK, Field HC, Greenberg L, Kupfer K. 2009. Low impact directed sprays and liquid baits to control Argentine ants (Hymenoptera: Formicidae). *Sociobiology* 54:1–9
62. Klotz JH, Rust MK, Greenberg L, Field HC, Kupfer K. 2007. An evaluation of several urban pest management strategies to control Argentine ants (Hymenoptera: Formicidae). *Sociobiology* 50:391–98
63. Knight RL, Rust MK. 1990. Repellency and efficacy of insecticides against foraging workers of laboratory colonies of Argentine ants (Hymenoptera: Formicidae). *J. Econ. Entomol.* 83:1402–8
64. La Fage JP, Nutting WL. 1978. Nutrient dynamics of termites. In *Production Ecology of Ants and Termites*, ed. Brian MV, pp. 165–232. Cambridge, UK: Cambridge Univ. Press
65. Lee EK, Jeong KY, Lyu D-P, Lee Y-W, Sohn J-H, et al. 2009. Characterization of the major allergens of *Pachycondyla chinensis* in ant sting anaphylaxis patients. *Clin. Exp. Allergy* 39:602–7
66. Lee SH, Bardunias P, Su N-Y. 2006. Food encounter rates of simulated termite tunnels with variable food size/distribution pattern and tunnel branch length. *J. Theor. Biol.* 243:493–500

57. Provides a single source for identifying ants of urban importance and pest management strategies.

67. Lee SH, Bardunias P, Su N-Y. 2007. Optimal length distribution of termite tunnel branches for efficient food search and resource transportation. *BioSystems* 90:802–7
68. Lessard J-P, Buddle CM. 2005. The effects of urbanization on ant assemblages (Hymenoptera: Formicidae) associated with the Molson Nature Reserve, Quebec. *Can. Entomol.* 137:215–25
69. Lewis VR, Haverty MI. 1996. Evaluation of six techniques for control of the western drywood termite (Isoptera: Kalotermitidae) in structures. *J. Econ. Entomol.* 89:922–34
70. Lise F, Garcia FRM, Lutinski JA. 2006. Association of ants (Hymenoptera: Formicidae) with bacteria in hospitals in the State of Santa Catarina. *Rev. Soc. Bras. Med. Trop.* 39:523–26
71. Lo N, Engel MS, Cameron S, Nalepa CA, Tokuda G, et al. 2007. Save Isoptera: a comment on Inward et al. *Biol. Lett.* 3:562–63
72. MacDonald JF, Akre RD, Keyel RE. 1980. The German yellowjacket (*Vespula germanica*) problem in the United States (Hymenoptera: Vespidae). *Entomol. Soc. Am. Bull.* 26:436–42
73. MacGown JA, Hill JG, Deyrup MA. 2007. *Brachymyrmex patagonicus* (Hymenoptera: Formicidae), an emerging pest species in the southeastern United States. *Fla. Entomol.* 90:457–64
74. Mallis A. 1969. *Handbook of Pest Control*. New York: MacNair-Dorland Co. 5th ed.
75. Manso EC, Croce M, Pinto JRAS, Santos KS, Santos LD, et al. 2010. Anaphylaxis due to *Pachycondyla goeldii* ant: a case report. *J. Investig. Allergol. Clin. Immunol.* 20:352–63
76. Moreira DDO, Morais V, Viera-da-Motta O, Campos-Farinhia AEC, Tonhasca A Jr. 2005. Ants as carriers of antibiotic resistant bacteria in hospitals. *Neotrop. Entomol.* 34:999–1006
77. Moreyra S, D'Adamo P, Lozada M. 2006. Odour and visual cues utilized by German yellowjackets (*Vespula germanica*) while relocating protein or carbohydrate resources. *Aust. J. Zool.* 54:393–97
78. Mumford JD, Norton GA. 1984. Economics of decision making in pest management. *Annu. Rev. Entomol.* 29:157–74
79. Nelder MP, Paysen ES, Zungoli PA, Benson EP. 2006. Emergence of the introduced ant *Pachycondyla chinensis* (Formicidae: Ponerinae) as a public health threat in the southeastern United States. *J. Med. Entomol.* 43:1094–98
80. Oi DH. 2008. Pharaoh ants and fire ants. In *Public Health Significance of Urban Pests*, ed. X Bonnefay, H Kampen, K Sweeney, pp. 175–208. Copenhagen: WHO. 569 pp.
81. Oi DH, Oi FM. 2006. Speed of efficacy and delayed toxicity characteristics of fast-acting fire ant (Hymenoptera: Formicidae) baits. *J. Econ. Entomol.* 99:1739–48
82. Osbrink WL, Cornelius ML, Lax A. 2008. Effects of flooding on field populations of Formosan subterranean termites (Isoptera: Rhinotermitidae) in New Orleans, Louisiana. *J. Econ. Entomol.* 101:1367–72
83. Ottesen PS, Birkemoe T, Aak A. 2009. Tracing carpenter ants (*Camponotus* sp.) in buildings with radioactive iodine ^{131}I. *Int. J. Pest Manag.* 55:45–49
84. Overmyer SL, Jeanne RL. 1998. Recruitment to food by the German yellowjacket, *Vespula germanica*. *Behav. Ecol. Sociobiol.* 42:17–21
85. Pantoja LDM, Filho REM, Brito EHS, Aragao TB, Brilhante RSN, et al. 2009. Ants (Hymenoptera: Formicidae) as carriers of fungi in hospital environments: an emphasis on the genera *Tapinoma* and *Pheidole*. *J. Med. Entomol.* 46:895–99
86. Passera L. 1994. Characteristics of tramp species. In *Exotic Ants: Biology, Impact, and Control of Introduced Species*, ed. DF Williams, pp. 23–43. Boulder, CO: Westview. 196 pp.
87. Pawson BM, Gold RE. 1996. Evaluation of baits for termites (Isoptera: Rhinotermitidae) in Texas. *Sociobiology* 28:485–510
88. Pedigo LP, Higley LG. 1992. The economic injury level concept and environmental quality. *Am. Entomol.* 38:12–21
89. Pranschke AM, Hooper-Bui LM, Moser B. 2003. Efficacy of bifenthrin treatment zones against red imported fire ant. *J. Econ. Entomol.* 96:98–105
90. Przybilla B, Ruëff F. 2010. Hymenoptera venom allergy. *J. Ger. Soc. Dermatol.* 8:114–29
91. Puche H, Su N-Y. 2001. Tunneling formation by *Reticulitermes flavipes* and *Coptotermes formosanus* (Isoptera: Rhinotermitidae) in response to wood in sand. *J. Econ. Entomol.* 94:1398–404
92. Reinhard J, Lacey MJ, Ibarra F, Schroeder FC, Kaib M, Lenz M. 2002. Hydroquinone: a general phagostimulating pheromone in termites. *J. Chem. Ecol.* 28:1–14

93. Reinhard J, Lacey MJ, Lenz M. 2002. Application of the natural phagostimulant hydroquinone in bait systems for termite management (Isoptera). *Sociobiology* 39:213–29
94. Richter MR. 2000. Social wasp (Hymenoptera: Vespidae) foraging behavior. *Annu. Rev. Entomol.* 45:121–50
95. Ripa R, Luppicini P, Su N-Y, Rust MK. 2007. Field evaluation of potential area-wide control strategies against the invasive eastern subterranean termite (Isoptera: Rhinotermitidae) in Chile. *J. Econ. Entomol.* 100:1391–99
96. Robson SK, Lesniak MG, Kothandapani RV, Traniello JFA, Thorne BL, Fourcassié V. 1995. Nonrandom search geometry in subterranean termites. *Naturwissenschaften* 82:526–28
97. Rodovalho CM, Santos AL, Marcolino MT, Bonetti AM, Brandeburgo MAM. 2007. Urban ants and transportation of nosocomial bacteria. *Neotrop. Entomol.* 36:454–58
98. Rojas MG, Morales-Ramos JA. 2001. Bait matrix for delivery of chitin synthesis inhibitors to the Formosan subterranean termite (Isoptera: Rhinotermitidae). *J. Econ. Entomol.* 94:506–10
99. Roper EM. 2010. Thiamethoxam for control of European paper wasps. *Proc. 2010 NCUE*, Portland, OR, May 16–19, pp. 182–83
100. Rupp MR, deShazo RD. 2006. Indoor fire ant sting attacks: a risk for frail elders. *Am. J. Med. Sci.* 331:134–43
101. Rust MK, Haagsma K, Reierson DA. 1996. Barrier sprays to control Argentine ants (Hymenoptera: Formicidae). *J. Econ. Entomol.* 89:134–37
102. Rust MK, Reierson DA, Klotz JH. 2003. Pest management of Argentine ants (Hymenoptera: Formicidae). *J. Entomol. Sci.* 38:159–69
103. Rust MK, Reierson DA, Klotz JH. 2004. Delayed toxicity as a critical factor in the efficacy of aqueous baits for controlling Argentine ants (Hymenoptera: Formicidae). *J. Econ. Entomol.* 97:1017–24

103. Discusses the importance of delayed toxicity of active ingredients in aqueous baits against ants.

104. Rust MK, Reierson DA, Vetter R. 2009. *Developing baits for the control of yellow jackets in California.* **http://www.pestboard.ca.gov/howdoi/research/2009_yellowjacket.pdf**
105. Sackmann P, Corley JC. 2007. Control of *Vespula germanica* (Hym. Vespidae) populations using toxic baits: bait attractiveness and pesticide efficacy. *J. Appl. Entomol.* 131(9–10):630–36
106. Sackmann P, Rabinovich M, Corley JC. 2001. Successful removal of German yellowjackets (Hymenoptera: Vespidae) by toxic baiting. *J. Econ. Entomol.* 94:811–16
107. Sanford MP, Manley PN, Murphy DD. 2008. Effects of urban development on ant communities: implications for ecosystem services and management. *Conserv. Biol.* 23:131–41
108. Santos VS, Santos LC Jr, Soares SA, Loureiro ES, Antonialli WF Jr. 2011. Evaluation of methods of baiting ants and record of associated fungi occurring in hospitals in Mato Grosso do Sul, Brazil. *Sociobiology* 57:143–52
109. Scharf ME, Ratliff CR, Bennett GW. 2004. Impacts of residual insecticide barriers on perimeter-invading ants, with particular reference to odorous house ant, *Tapinoma sessile*. *J. Econ. Entomol.* 97:601–5
110. Silverman J, Brightwell RJ. 2008. The Argentine ant: challenges in managing an invasive unicolonial pest. *Annu. Rev. Entomol.* 53:231–52
111. Smith J, Su N-Y, Escobar RN. 2006. An area-wide population management project for the invasive eastern subterranean termite (Isoptera: Rhinotermitidae) in a low-income community in Santiago, Chile. *Am. Entomol.* 52:253–60

111. Reports one of the most successful area-wide projects for subterranean termites by using baits to eliminate all detectable colonies.

112. Soeprono AM, Rust MK. 2004. The effect of delayed toxicity of chemical barriers to control Argentine ants (Hymenoptera: Formicidae). *J. Econ. Entomol.* 97:2021–28

112. Discusses the importance of delayed toxicity and horizontal transfer of insecticides from barrier treatments to kill ants.

113. Soeprono AM, Rust MK. 2004. The effect of horizontal transfer of barrier insecticides to control Argentine ants (Hymenoptera: Formicidae). *J. Econ. Entomol.* 97:1675–81
114. Spradbery JP. 1973. *Wasps: An Account of the Biology and Natural History of Solitary and Social Wasps.* Seattle: Univ. Wash. Press. 408 pp.
115. Stern VM, Smith RF, Bosch R, Hagen KS. 1959. The integrated control concept. *Hilgardia* 29:81–108
116. Stringer CE Jr, Lofgren CS, Bartlett FJ. 1964. Imported fire ant toxic bait studies: evaluation of toxicants. *J. Econ. Entomol.* 57:941–45

116. A seminal publication discussing the factors essential for effective ant baits.

117. Su N-Y. 2002. Novel technologies for subterranean termite control. *Sociobiology* 40:95–101

118. Su N-Y. 2003. Baits as a tool for population control of the Formosan subterranean termite. *Sociobiology* 41:177–92
119. Su N-Y. 2005. Directional change in tunneling of subterranean termites (Isoptera: Rhinotermitidae) in response to decayed wood attractants. *J. Econ. Entomol.* 98:471–75
120. Su N-Y. 2007. Hermetically sealed baits for subterranean termites (Isoptera: Rhinotermitidae). *J. Econ. Entomol.* 100:475–82
121. Su N-Y, Ban PM, Scheffrahn RH. 1991. Suppression of foraging populations of the Formosan subterranean termite (Isoptera: Rhinotermitidae) by field applications of a slow-acting toxicant bait. *J. Econ. Entomol.* 84:1525–31
122. Su N-Y, Ban PM, Scheffrahn RH. 2004. Use of a bait impact index to assess the effects of bait application against populations of the Formosan subterranean termite (Isoptera: Rhinotermitidae) in a large area. *J. Econ. Entomol.* 97:2029–34
123. Su N-Y, Lees M. 2009. Biological activities of a bait toxicant for population management of subterranean termites. In *Household, Structural and Residential Pest Management*, ed. C Peterson, D Stout, pp. 87–96. New York: Oxford Univ. Press
124. Su N-Y, Puche H. 2003. Tunneling activity of subterranean termites (Isoptera: Rhinotermitidae) in sand with moisture gradients. *J. Econ. Entomol.* 96:88–93
125. Su N-Y, Scheffrahn RH. 1988. Foraging population and territory of the Formosan subterranean termite (Isoptera: Rhinotermitidae) in an urban environment. *Sociobiology* 14:353–59
126. Su N-Y, Scheffrahn RH. 1988. Toxicity and feeding deterrency of a dihaloalkyl arylsulfone biocide, A-9248 against the Formosan subterranean termite (Isoptera: Rhinotermitidae). *J. Econ. Entomol.* 81:850–54
127. Su N-Y, Scheffrahn RH. 1988. Toxicity and lethal time of *N*-ethyl perfluorooctane sulfonamide against two subterranean termite species (Isoptera: Rhinotermitidae). *Fla. Entomol.* 71:73–78
128. Su NY, Scheffrahn RH. 1990. Comparison of eleven soil termiticides against the Formosan and eastern subterranean termites (Isoptera: Rhinotermitidae). *J. Econ. Entomol.* 83:1918–24
129. Su N-Y, Scheffrahn RH. 1998. A review of subterranean termite control practices and prospects for integrated pest management programs. *Integr. Pest Manage. Rev.* 3:1–13

129. Establishes a conceptual framework for termite IPM and identifies the two most important variables, termite damage potential and health and environmental risk of control measures, that need to be considered.

130. Su N-Y, Scheffrahn RH, Ban PM. 1995. Effects of sulfluramid-treated bait blocks on field colonies of the Formosan subterranean termite (Isoptera: Rhinotermitidae). *J. Econ. Entomol.* 88:1343–48
131. Su N-Y, Stith BM, Puche H, Bardunias P. 2004. Characterization of tunneling geometry of subterranean termites (Isoptera: Rhinotermitidae) by computer simulation. *Sociobiology* 44:471–83
132. Su N-Y, Tamashiro M, Yates JR, Haverty MI. 1982. Effects of behavior on the evaluation of insecticides for prevention of or remedial control of the Formosan subterranean termite. *J. Econ. Entomol.* 75:188–89
133. Su N-Y, Thoms EM, Ban PM, Scheffrahn RH. 1995. A monitoring/baiting station to detect and eliminate foraging populations of subterranean termites (Isoptera: Rhinotermitidae) near structures. *J. Econ. Entomol.* 88:932–36
134. Suckling DM, Peck RW, Stringer LD, Snook K, Banko PC. 2010. Trail pheromone disruption of Argentine ant trail formation and foraging. *J. Chem. Ecol.* 36:122–28
135. Suckling DM, Stringer LD, Bunn B, El-Sayed AM, Vander Meer RK. 2010. Trail pheromone disruption of red imported fire ant. *J. Chem. Ecol.* 36:744–50
136. Tanaka Y, Nishisue K, Sunamura E, Suzuki S, Sakamoto H, et al. 2009. Trail-following disruption in the invasive Argentine ant with synthetic trail pheromone component (Z)-9-hexadecenal. *Sociobiology* 54:139–52
137. Thompson B, McLachlan. 2007. The effects of urbanization on ant communities and myrmecochory in Manitoba, Canada. *Urban Ecosyst.* 10:43–52
138. Valles SM, Pereirs RM. 2003. Hydramethylnon potentiation in *Solenopsis invicta* by infection with the microsporidium *Thelohania solenopsae*. *Biol. Control* 27:95–99
139. Vander Meer RK, Pereira RK, Porter SD, Valles SM, Oi DH. 2007. Areawide suppression of invasive fire ant *Solenopsis* spp. populations. In *Area-Wide Control of Insect Pests from Research to Implementation*, ed. MJB Vreysenm, AS Robinson, J Hendrichs, pp. 487–96. Dordrecht, Netherlands: Springer. 789 pp.
140. Wagner RE. 1980. Using an algaecide to manage wasps around swimming pools, 1979. *Insect. Acar. Tests* 5:419

141. Ward DF, Green C, Harris RJ, Hartley S, Lester PJ, et al. 2010. Twenty years of Argentine ants in New Zealand: past research and future priorities for applied management. *N. Z. Entomol.* 33:68–78
142. Warner J, Scheffrahn RH, Yang R-L. 2010. Arboreal bioassay for toxicity of residual and liquid bait insecticides against white-footed ants, *Technomyrmex difficilis* (Hymenoptera: Formicidae). *Sociobiology* 55:847–59
143. Williams DF, Collins HL, Oi DH. 2001. The red imported fire ant (Hymenoptera: Formicidae): an historical perspective of treatment programs and the development of chemical baits for control. *Am. Entomol.* 47:146–59
144. Wiltz BA, Sutter DR, Gardner WA. 2009. Activity of bifenthrin, chlorfenapyr, fipronil, and thiamethoxam against Argentine ants (Hymenoptera: Formicidae). *J. Econ. Entomol.* 102:2279–88
145. Wiltz BA, Sutter DR, Gardner WA. 2010. Activity of bifenthrin, chlorfenapyr, fipronil, and thiamethoxam against red imported fire ants (Hymenoptera: Formicidae). *J. Econ. Entomol.* 103:754–61
146. Zarzuela MFM, Campos-Farinha AEC, Russomanno OMR, Kruppa PC, Gonqalez E. 2007. Evaluation of urban ants (Hymenoptera: Formicidae) as vectors of microorganisms in residential and industrial environments: II. Fungi. *Sociobiology* 50:653–58

Systematics, Biodiversity, Biogeography, and Host Associations of the Miridae (Insecta: Hemiptera: Heteroptera: Cimicomorpha)

G. Cassis[1,*] and R.T. Schuh[2]

[1]Evolution & Ecology Research Center, School of Biological, Earth, and Environmental Sciences, University of New South Wales, Sydney, NSW 2052, Australia; email: gcassis@unsw.edu.au

[2]Division of Invertebrate Zoology, American Museum of Natural History, New York, New York 10024-5192; email: schuh@amnh.org

Annu. Rev. Entomol. 2012. 57:377–404

The *Annual Review of Entomology* is online at ento.annualreviews.org

This article's doi:
10.1146/annurev-ento-121510-133533

0066-4170/12/0107-0377$20.00

*Corresponding author

Keywords

classification, morphology, cybertaxonomy, species richness, host specificity

Abstract

The Miridae, a hyperdiverse family containing more than 11,020 valid described species, are discussed and the pertinent literature is reviewed. Diagnoses for the family and subfamilies are given. Color habitus photos are presented for representatives of most of the 35 currently recognized tribes. Key morphological character systems are discussed and illustrated, including pretarsal structures, femoral trichobothria, external efferent system of the metathoracic glands, male and female genitalia, and molecular markers. A historical comparison of tribal classifications and the most up-to-date classification are presented in tabular form. A brief history of the classification of each of the eight recognized subfamilies is presented. Distributional patterns and relative generic diversity across biogeographic regions are discussed; generic diversity by biogeographic region is presented in tabular form. Taxonomic accumulation graphs are presented by biogeographic region, indicating an ongoing need for taxonomic work in the Southern Hemisphere, and most particularly in Australia. Host plant associations are evaluated graphically, showing high specificity for many taxa and a preference among phytophagous taxa for the Asteridae and Rosidae.

INTRODUCTION

The Miridae (Hemiptera: Heteroptera: Cimicomorpha), or plant bugs, are one of the most species-rich families of insects, with approximately 11,020 described species (5, 9–13, 25, 56, 94, 101). The Miridae are one of the 20 most diverse families of insects and, along with the hemipteran family Cicadellidae, are one of only two hyperdiverse (>10,000 species) exopterygote families (32). Plant bugs are found in all major biogeographic regions of the world (94, 101), and are diverse particularly in tropical and Mediterranean ecosystems (32, 107). As with many hyperdiverse groups, the taxonomic impediment for plant bugs is significant, as evidenced by recent species discovery in the Southern Hemisphere and taxonomic accumulation curves (32). In the past five years a profusion of descriptive works for the mirid subfamilies Orthotylinae and Phylinae have addressed said impediments through the application of cybertaxonomic methods (32). Plant bugs exhibit a wide range of food preferences and behaviors, including phytophagy, carnivory, and omnivory (146). Their success is attributable mainly to close association with seed plants, with which they have putatively evolved in concert, with multiple examples of phylogenetic restrictedness in host usage (24, 109, 111). Some mirid species exhibit significant economic impacts; some are pests of food and fiber crops (144, 146), whereas others are beneficial species (145, 146) used as biological control agents (85, 145). Plant bugs are noteworthy for repeated evolution of putative Batesian ant mimics within most subfamilies (31, 54, 73, 88, 91, 93, 147) and for exaggerated genitalic evolution (60, 123), including traumatic insemination and sexual antagonistic coevolution (130, 131, 133). Despite their economic and evolutionary importance, mirids are little recognized outside of heteropterological circles, although they are gaining recognition as a model group for evolutionary and ecological studies.

Plant bugs: the common name for true bug species belonging to the cimicomorphan family Miridae

Biogeographic region: a geographic area defined by its organisms

Taxonomic impediment: a shortfall in taxonomic knowledge and capacity, primarily at the species level

Taxonomic accumulation curve: absolute number of species described over time

Cybertaxonomic methods: applications of the Internet and computer software and databases to expedite the taxonomic process

Seed plants: seed-bearing land plants that comprise angiosperms (Magnoliophyta), conifers (Pinophyta), cycads (Cycadophyta), gingko (Gingkophyta), and Gnetophyta

Phylogenetic restrictedness: host associations of related plant bugs restricted to related plant taxa

FAMILY DIAGNOSIS AND KEY CHARACTER SYSTEMS

Family Diagnosis

Plant bugs range in size from 1 to 15 mm; most species are between 3 and 6 mm. They are elongate to ovoid in shape (**Figures 1** and **2**). The head is triangular and prognathous but it can be hypognathous. The eyes are usually large and ocelli are rarely present. The antennae and labium have four segments. Most species are fully winged (macroptery); the forewings cover the abdomen and are commonly deflexed at the costal fracture. Wing shortening is widespread (submacroptery, brachyptery, microptery, coleoptery), as is sexually dimorphic and intraspecific wing polymorphism. The forewings are distinctive, with the corium divided distally into a triangular cuneus and a distal membrane housing one or two closed cells. Trochanters of all legs are divided. The middle and hind femora possess 2 to 10 trichobothria on the ventral and lateral surfaces. The tarsi are most often three-segmented, although they are occasionally two-segmented. The pretarsi have either setiform or fleshy parempodia, commonly have fleshy pulvilli attached to the vental or medial surface of the claw, and sometimes possess pseudopulvilli which arise from the base of the claw. The metathoracic glands are paired and the external efferent system is usually well developed. The evaporatorium occupies less than half of the metepisternum, with an ostiolar peritreme variously configured and oriented. The metathoracic spiracle is either exposed and teardrop shaped or recessed. The male genitalia are universally asymmetrical, inclusive of the genital opening of the pygophore, parameres, and aedeagus. The endosoma is at least partially membranous and inflatable and is bounded by a distally sclerotized phallotheca. The female ovipositor is laciniate; the sperm storage organ is a large saclike structure (5, 6, 35, 60, 89, 90, 107, 116, 146).

Figure 1

Images of species representing the subfamilies and tribes of the family Miridae (Part 1). (*a*) *Corticoris signatus* (Heidemann) (Isometopinae: Isometopini). (*b*) *Cylapus citus* Bergroth (Cylapinae: Cylapini). (*c*) *Psallops* Usinger sp. (Psallopinae). (*d*) *Monalocoris filicis* (Linnaeus) (Bryocorinae: Bryocorini). (*e*) *Macrolophus brevicornis* Knight (Bryocorinae: Dicyphini: Dicyphina). (*f*) *Neella bicolor* Hsiao (Bryocorinae: Eccritotarsini: Eccritotarsina). (*g*) *Clivinema regalis* Knight (Deraeocorinae: Clivinemini). (*h*) *Deraeocapsus fraternus* (Van Duzee) (Deraeocorinae: Deraeocorini). (*i*) *Nicostratus diversus* Distant (Deraeocorinae: Surinamellini). (*j*) *Imogen* Kirkaldy sp. (Deraeocorinae: Saturniomirini). (*k*) *Termatophylum insigne* Reuter (Deraeocorinae: Termatophylini). (*l*) Undetermined Herdoniini species from South Africa (Mirinae).

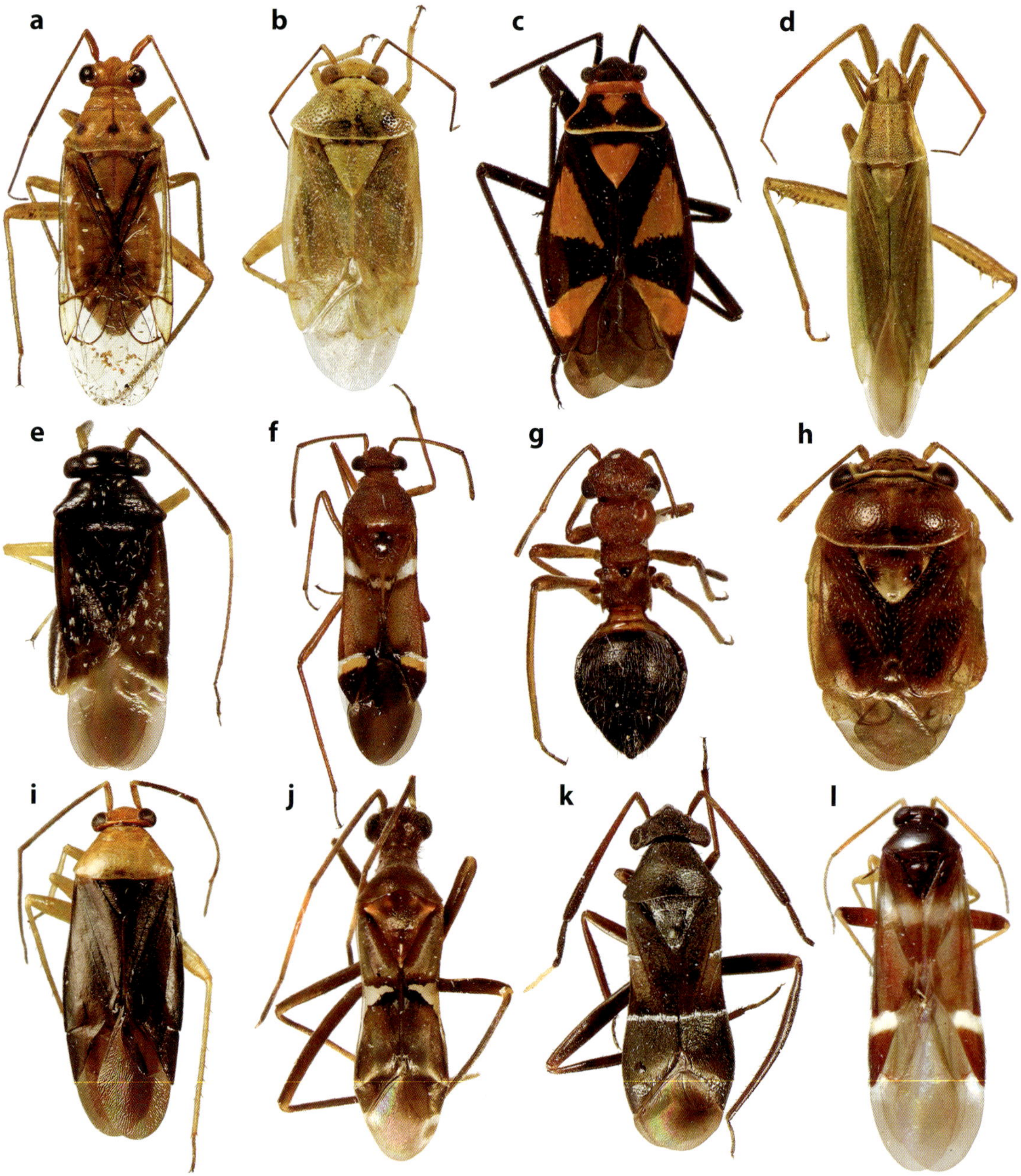

Figure 2

Images of species representing the subfamilies and tribes of the family Miridae (Part 2). (*a*) *Hyalopeplinus malayensis* Carvalho and Gross (Mirinae: Hyalopeplini). (*b*) *Lygus elisus* Van Duzee (Mirinae: Mirini). (*c*) *Eurylomata speciosa* (Signoret) (Mirinae: Resthenini). (*d*) *Stenodema trispinosa* Reuter (Mirinae: Stenodemini). (*e*) *Halticus bractatus* (Say) (Orthotylinae: Halticini). (*f*) *Nichomachus* Distant sp., male. (*g*) *Nichomachus* sp., female (Orthotylinae: Nichomachini). (*h*) *Coridromius* Signoret sp. (Orthotylini: Coridromiini). (*i*) *Jornandes genetivus* (Distant) sp. (Orthotylinae: Orthotylini). (*j*) *Formicopsella regneri* Poppius (Phylinae: Hallodapini). (*k*) *Pilophorus tibialis* Van Duzee (Phylinae: Pilophorini). (*l*) *Tuxedo elongatus* Schuh (Phylinae: Phylini).

Key Character Systems

Plant bugs are routinely differentiated by size, structure, coloration, surface texture, and vestiture (**Figures 1** and **2**). Structures of the pretarsus (**Figure 3**) serve as the most important character system defining the higher classification of the family, supported by characters of the pterothoracic pleuron (metathoracic glands and spiracle; **Figure 4**), genitalia, and femoral trichobothria (**Figures 3** and **5**). The male genitalia are the sine qua non of species differentiation for plant bugs. Herein we document the key morphological systems that have been examined comparatively across subfamilies and that have current traction in the classification of the Miridae.

Pretarsus. Morphology of the pretarsus is central to the suprageneric classification of the Miridae (5, 6, 82, 83, 90, 107) (**Figure 3**). Mirids have paired claws that can be basally unadorned (Cylapinae: Cyalpini, Phylinae, Orthotylinae; **Figure 3*a***) or dentate (Deraeocorinae, Bryocorinae: Dicyphina partim; **Figure 3*e***), with subapical teeth (Isometopinae, Cylapinae, and Psallopinae; **Figure 3*a***) or apically smooth (most Miridae; **Figure 3*b***), and rarely with pulvillar combs (Bryocorinae: Eccritotarsina; **Figure 3*i***). The unguitractor plate houses paired parempodia that are either setiform (**Figure 3*a,g,h***) or lamellate (**Figure 3*b–d***). Lamellate parempodia are either convergent (Orthotylinae, Phylinae: Pilophorini) (**Figure 3*b,c***), divergent (Mirinae, **Figure 3*d***), or parallel-sided (Cylapinae: Vaniini, Termatophylini partim). All Bryocorinae aside from the Eccritotarsini possess parempodia-like pads, which are referred to as accessory parempodia or pseudopulvilli (**Figure 3*f–i***); in the nominotypical tribe Bryocorini the setiform parempodia are absent (**Figure 3*f***). Some taxa have flap-like pulvilli of varying size attached to the ventral or medial surface of the claws (Phylinae, Orthotylinae, Mirinae; **Figure 3*b–d***).

Femoral trichobothria. Schuh (89) first recognized the unique occurrence of femoral trichobothria in the Miridae and found that their arrangement and number were informative. Trichobothria (**Figure 3*j,k***) are always found on ventral and lateral surfaces of the meso- and metafemora (**Figure 5*b***). They are taxonomically significant for taxa within the Phylinae (91), Isometopinae (1), Termatophylini (23), and Mirinae (113).

Metathoracic glands and spiracle. The external efferent system of the metathoracic glands has classificatory significance in the Miridae (**Figure 4**). This system is situated on the metepisternum of the metapleuron and comprises an opening (= ostiole) positioned between the meso- and metacoxae, a usually depressed channel from which the peritreme, a tongue-like structure that has a smooth surface covered with microtrichae, emanates. These structures are bounded by mushroom-shaped cuticular structures called evaporative bodies, which collectively are referred to as the evaporative area(s) or evaporatorium. Cassis (23) recognized suprageneric differences for the evaporatorium and the position of the peritreme, as well as the condition of the metathoracic spiracle. The position of the peritreme is distinctive for suprageneric groups and is placed anteriorly on the metepisternum (Isometopinae partim, Cylapinae: Cylapini; **Figure 4*a,b***), posteriorly (Cylapinae: Fulviini, Bryocorinae: Eccritotarsina; **Figure 4*d,f***), or medially on the segment (most Miridae; **Figure 4*c,e,g,h***). The evaporative areas can be extensive in distribution (Bryocorinae: *Dicyphus* Fieber, Phylinae: Auricillocorini; **Figure 4*c***), greatly reduced (Bryocorinae: Eccritotarsina; **Figure 4*f***), or absent (Bryocorinae: Monaloniini, Odoneillini). The opening of the metathoracic spiracle is positioned at the intersegmental membrane of the mesepimeron and metepisternum, and suprageneric taxa can be recognized by the presence of an evident oval opening bounded by evaporative bodies (most Bryocorinae: Dicyphina, Orthotylinae,

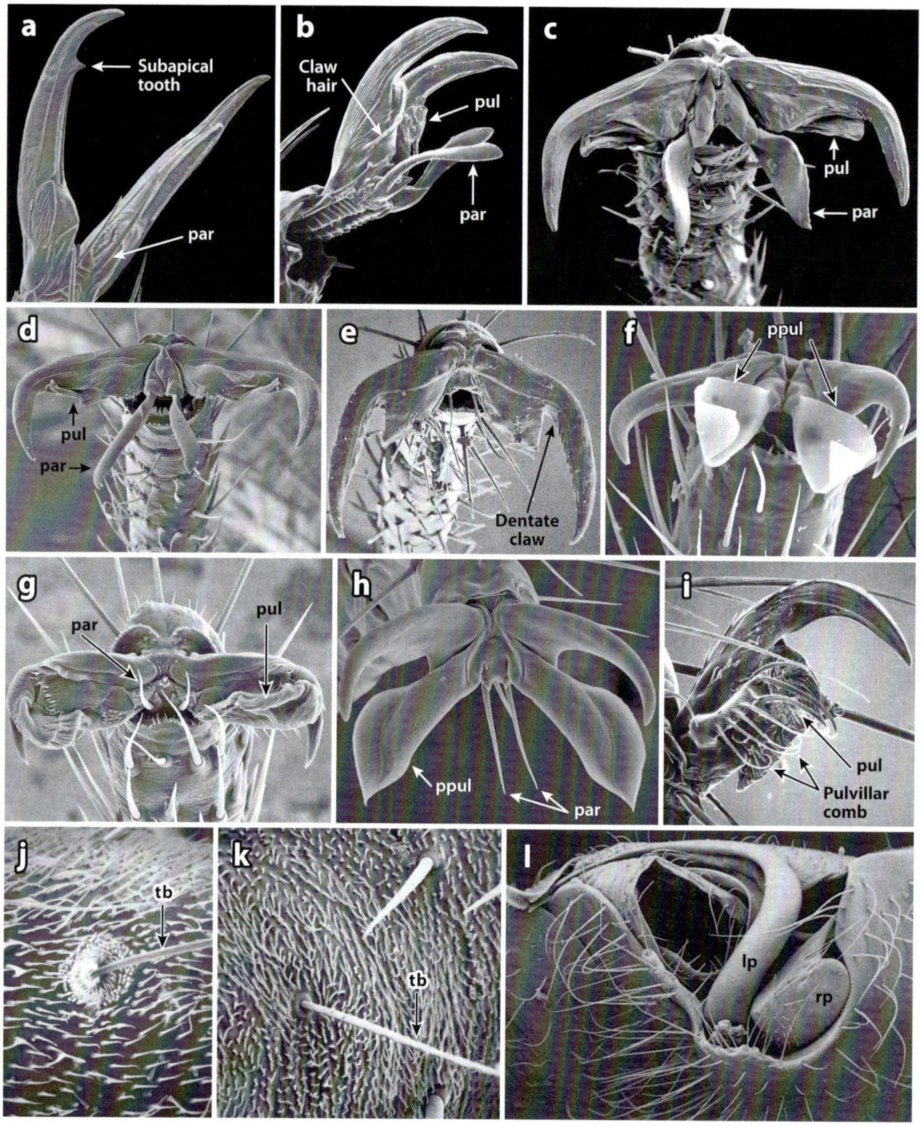

Figure 3

Pretarsi, femoral trichobothria, and male genitalia. (*a–i*) Pretarsal structures. (*a*) *Cylapus* Say sp. (Cylapinae: Cylapini). (*b*) *Moissonia obscuricornis* (Poppius) (Phylinae: Phylini). (*c*) *Slaterocoris stygicus* (Say) (Orthotylinae: Orthotylini) (from Reference 114, with permission). (*d*) *Orientocapsus zhangi* (Lu and Zheng) (Mirinae: Mirini). (*e*) *Nicostratus diversus* Distant (Deraeocorinae: Surinamellini). (*f*) *Bryocoris* Fallén sp. (Bryocorinae: Bryocorini). (*g*) *Campyloneura virgula* (Herrich-Schaeffer) (Bryocorinae: Dicyphini: Dicyphina). (*h*) *Setocoris* China and Carvalho sp. (Bryocorinae: Dicyphini: Dicyphina). (*i*) *Pycnoderes* Guérin-Méneville sp. (Bryocorinae: Eccritotarsini: Eccritotarsina). (*j–k*) Femoral trichobothria. (*j*) *Halticus* Hahn sp. (Orthotylinae: Halticini). (*k*) *Prepops* sp. (Mirini: Resthenini). (*l*) Genital capsule, *Coridromius chinensis* Liu and Zhao (from Reference 130, with permission). Abbreviations: lp, left paramere; par, parempodium; ppul, pseudopulvillus(i); pul, pulvillus; rp, right paramere; tb, trichobothrium.

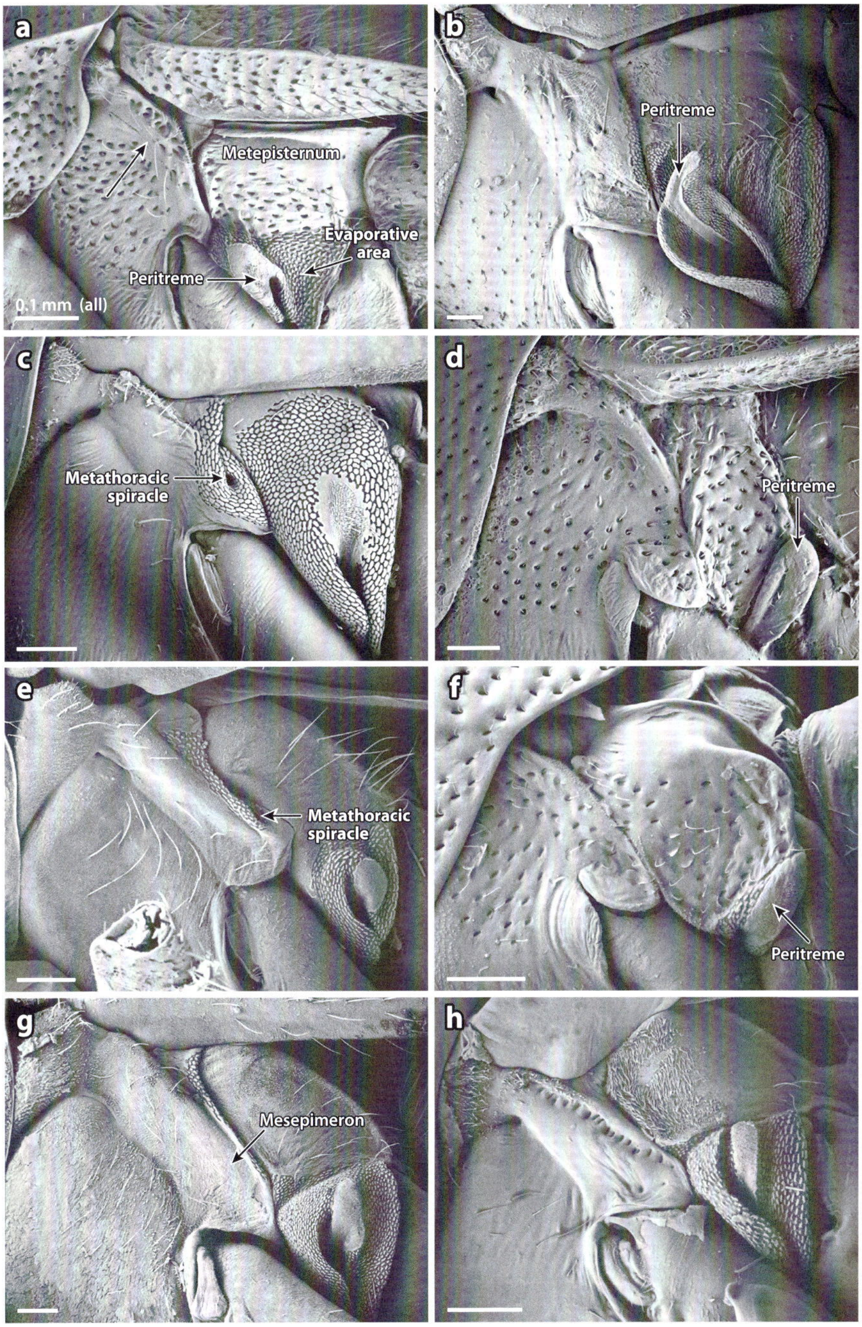

Figure 4

Pterothoracic pleura, metathoracic glands and spiracle. (*a*) Undetermined Isometopinae sp. (from Reference 23 with permission). (*b*) *Cylapus citus* Bergroth (Cylapinae: Cylapini) (from Reference 23 with permission). (*c*) *Dicyphus globulifer* Fallén (Bryocorinae: Dicyphina). (*d*) *Bothrophorella nigra* (Stål) (Bryocorinae: Eccritotarsina). (*e*) *Compsidolon salicellum* (Herrich-Schaeffer) (Phylinae: Phylini). (*f*) *Sulamita* Kirkaldy sp. (Orthotylinae: Orthotylini). (*g*) *Apolygus spinolae* (Meyer-Dür) (Mirinae: Mirini). (*h*) *Hyaliodes* Reuter sp. (Deraeocorinae: Deraeocorini).

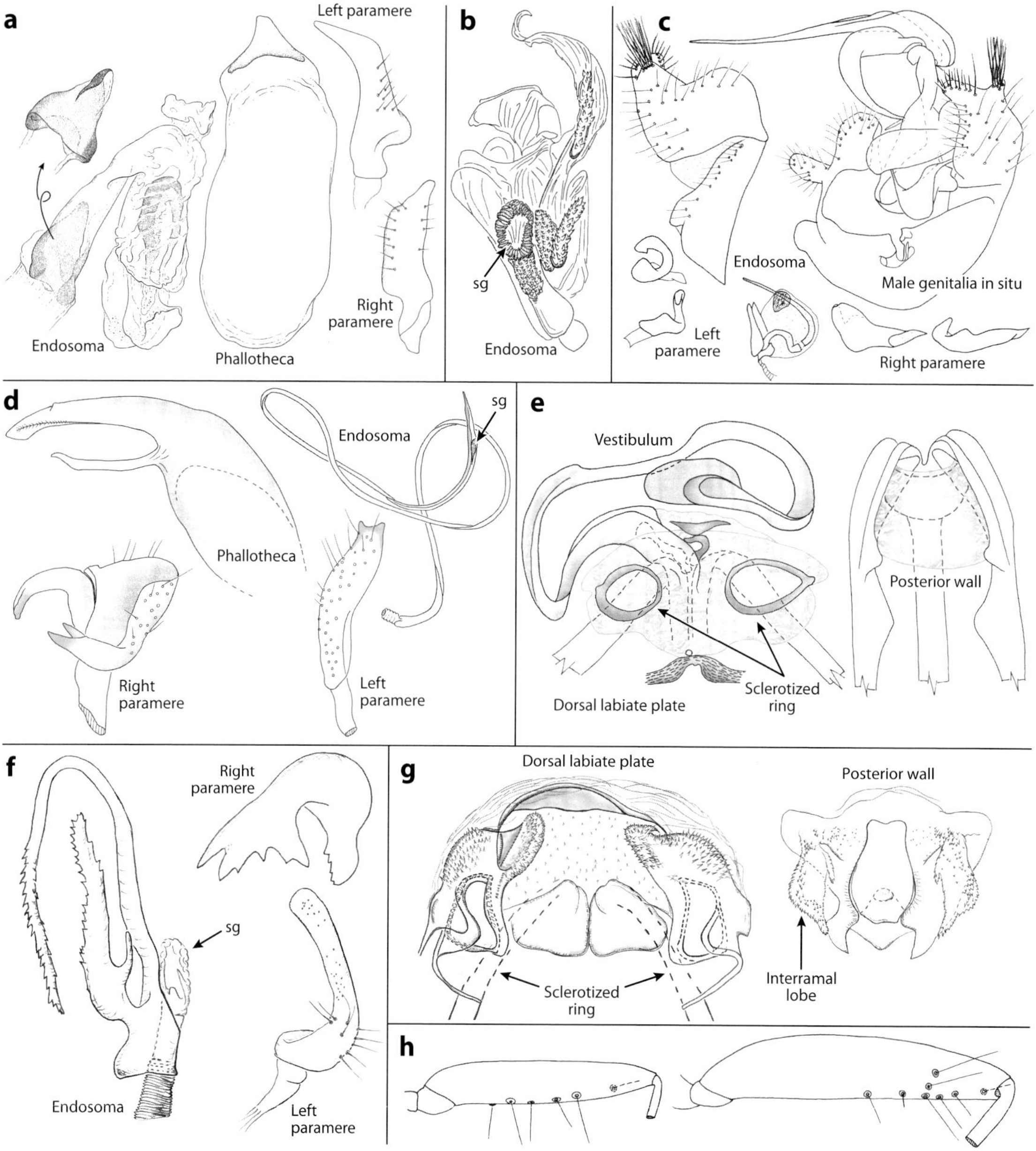

Figure 5

Male and female genitalia and femoral trichobothria. (*a*) Male genitalia, *Caravalhoma malcolmae* Slater (Cylapinae: Fulviini) (from Reference 104, with permission). (*b*) Endosoma, *Collaria occulata* (Reuter) (Mirinae: Stenodemini) (M.D. Schwartz, personal communication). (*c*) Male genitalia, *Mertila malayensis* Distant (Bryocorinae: Eccritotarsini: Eccritotarsina) (from Reference 123, with permission). (*d*) Male genitalia, *Bisulcopsallus polhemorum* Schuh (Phylinae: Phylini) (from Reference 100, with permission). (*e*) Female genitalia, *Bisulcopsallus fuscopunctatus* (Knight) (Phylinae: Phylini) (from Reference 100, with permission). (*f*) Male genitalia, *Slaterocoris atritibialis* (Knight) (Orthotylinae: Orthotylini) (from Reference 114, with permission). (*g*) Female genitalia, *Josephinus reinhardi* (Carvalho and Schaffner) (Orthotylinae: Orthotylini) (from Reference 114, with permission). (*h*) Mesofemoral and metafemoral trichobothrial patterns, *Fulvius* Stål sp. (Cylapinae: Fulviini) (from Reference 89, with permission). Abbreviation: sg, secondary gonophore.

Phylinae; **Figure 4*c,e***), or the spiracle is recessed with no obvious opening (Mirinae: Mirini, most Deraeocorinae; **Figure 4*g,h***).

Male genitalia. The opening of the male genital capsule (=pygophore) and the shape of the parameres and aedeagus (= intromittent organ) are strongly asymmetrical in mirids (60, 107, 110) (**Figure 5**). Homologies are based on the classic comparative works of Singh-Pruthi (119), Kullenberg (67), and Kelton (60), although disagreement remains concerning the terminology and homology of the aedeagus structure. Kelton (60) universally referred to the outer tubule of the aedeagus as the vesica. In contrast, Kerzhner & Konstantinov (62) and Konstantinov (64) identified two aedeagal types: an undifferentiated endosoma and a differentiated endosoma that is divided into a basal conjunctiva and distal vesica, which they argued can be seen upon inflation. Cassis (24) critiqued the latter system, rejecting the application of the term vesica because it represents nonhomologous structures in the Miridae. Lin & Yang (68) proposed a composite origin and concomitant homology for the aedeagus on the basis of original work by Yang & Chang (148). This theory was dismissed by Konstantinov (65), who argued for a singular origin of the aedeagus. Agreement on genital structure terminology and homology is impeded by groundplan and functional approaches. Mirid male genitalia are commonly exaggerated in structure (Orthotylinae, Mirinae, Bryocorinae: Eccritotarsina; **Figure 5*c***) and offer considerable promise for testing competing theories of genitalic evolution. The aedeagus is relatively simple in most basal Miridae, with the endosoma often composed of a saclike membrane (Cylapinae; **Figure 5*a***). Numerous characters of the male genitalia are distinctive for suprageneric groups, such as the strap-like aedeagus and detached phallotheca of Phylinae (**Figure 5*d***), the saw-like spicules of many Orthotylinae (**Figure 5*f***), and the ringlike secondary gonopore of Mirinae (**Figure 5*b***). In the traumatically inseminating genus *Coridromius* Signoret, the aedeagus is greatly reduced and is coupled with a scythe-like left paramere, which is used to pierce the female abdomen (**Figure 3*l***).

Female genitalia. Female genitalia are becoming more widely used in mirid systematics. Kullenberg (67) documented from a functional perspective the female genital tract of a small sample of European species. Slater (120) studied sclerotized structures from the point of view of systematic significance and identified differences in the genital chamber across a broader sampling of Miridae. Davis (35) studied the fine detail of the female reproductive tract and recognized a unique sperm storage organ (=seminal depository) for mirids. The posterior wall of the bursa copulatrix displays the greatest morphological diversification and ranges from undifferentiated (e.g., Bryocorinae: Dicyphini, most Phylinae) to having lateral outgrowths [=interramal lobes or the K-structures of Slater (120); e.g., Orthotylinae: Orthotylini, Mirinae; **Figure 5*g***]. Exaggerated structures are found in the female genitalia of some species, such as the greatly elongate tubelike process of the vestibulum in genera such as *Bisulcopsallus* Schuh (**Figure 5*e***) and *Phymatopsallus* Knight (Phylinae: Phylini) and in the Phylinae: Hallodapini (78, 100). The paired sclerotized ring glands are also distinctive in shape and orientation (**Figure 5*e***). In *Coridromius* Signoret (Orthotylinae: Coridromiini) females, there is a remarkable independent evolution of complex paragenitalia to mitigate against the costs of traumatic insemination (130, 131, 133), which are located on the right-hand side of the pregenital abdomen.

Molecular Markers

The application of DNA sequence data to mirid systematics has had minimal impact to date. A study of cimicomorphan relationships includes mitochondrial and nuclear sequence data (16S, 18S, and 28s rDNA, mitochondrial cytochrome *c* oxidase subunit I) for 44 species of mirids (110).

Total evidence analysis of the above DNA data and morphological data resulted in contentious outcomes, such as the nonmonophyly of the Bryocorinae, Cylapinae, Orthotylinae, and the loss of the Orthotylinae+Phylinae sister-group relationship. The use of DNA sequence data in species-level studies has been near negligible (73, 84, 103), and broader application has been hampered by the lack of adequately preserved collections.

PHYLOGENETIC POSITION IN THE HETEROPTERA

The land bug infraorder Cimicomorpha comprise 17 families, inclusive of primarily predaceous and phytophagous clades (108, 110, 128). The largely phytophagous superfamily Miroidea includes the lace bug family Tingidae and the Miridae, whose sister-group relationship has been found with morphological data (108) and a combination of morphological and molecular data (110). In contrast, Tian et al. (134), using approximately 3,000 base pairs of nuclear DNA, recovered a paraphyletic Miroidea, with Miridae sister to the predaceous clades.

SYSTEMATICS OF SUPRAGENERIC TAXA

Multiple suprageneric classifications for the Miridae have been proposed, with pivotal schemes given in **Table 1**. Fieber (41, 42) established genera that served as a foundation for future work on the higher classification of the Miridae. Douglas & Scott (36) erected a large number of families but without explicit diagnoses. Reuter (82, 83) proposed a classification system of global scope that has served as a baseline for all subsequent work on plant bug classification. Van Duzee (135, 136) revised Reuter's system, drawing a close relationship between the Mirinae and the Deraeocorinae as well as a more subdivided Orthotylinae. Carvalho (5–13) proposed a refinement of these previous arrangements, with extended tribal categorization, particularly for the Deraeocorinae and Mirinae, as well as the transfer of Dicyphini sensu stricto to the Phylinae; he later described the Surinamellini (Deraeocorinae) (20), Austromirini (Orthotylinae) (15), and Palaucorinae (8, 17). Subsequent to the publication of the Carvalho catalog, the suprageneric classification was relatively stable, although European miridologists differed on the position of the Halticini and Dicyphini, referring them to subfamilial rank (137–139).

Schuh (88, 90, 91, 94) revolutionized our conception of suprageneric groups within the Miridae with the application of cladistic methods and codification of character systems such as the pretarsus and male genitalia. His classification resulted in a revised Bryocorinae. The Orthotylinae and Phylinae were reconstituted by the transfer of the Pilophorini from the former to the latter. Schuh (94) did not follow published tribal classifications for the basal subfamilies Isometopinae and Cylapinae. Herein, we propose a suprageneric classification for the Miridae (**Table 1**) that, among other additions, incorporates modern treatments of the subfamilies Isometopinae and Cylapinae (1, 47, 59), a review of tribal groups within the Mirinae (112, 113), and acceptance of the previously described orthotyline tribes Austromirini (24) and Ceratocapsini (54, 55).

The suprageneric phylogeny of Schuh (90), inclusive of later amendments (91, 94, 101), serves as a baseline for mirid relationships in the contemporaneous literature. The following subfamilial discussion follows his sister-group relationships for the Miridae: (Isometopinae (Cylapinae (Psallopinae (Orthotylinae+Phylinae) (Bryocorinae (Mirinae+Deraeocorinae)))))).

Isometopinae

The subfamily Isometopinae (**Figure 1*a***) are defined by the presence of ocelli (unique within the Miridae), two-segmented tarsi, a hypognathous and often flattened head, reduced femoral

Table 1 Alternative suprageneric classifications of the Miridae

Douglas & Scott (1865) (36)	Reuter (1905, 1910) (82, 83)	Van Duzee (1917) (136)	Carvalho (1952–1960) (5, 6, 9–13)	Schuh (1995) (94)	Cassis & Schuh, this work
Halticoridae	Mirina	Mirinae	Mirinae	Isometopinae	Isometopinae
Stiphrosomidae	Capsaria	Mirini	Herdoniini	Isometopini	Diphlebini
Litosomidae	Dionoconotaria	Hortisini	Hyalopeplini	Cylapinae	Gigantometopini
Globocepidae	Miraria	Capsini	Mecistoscelini	Cylapini	Isometopini
Phylidae	Mecistoscelaria	Capsaria	Mirini	Psallopinae	Myiommini
Oncotylidae	Restheniaria	Deraeocoraria	Pithanini	Orthotylinae	Cylapinae
Psallidae	Bothynotina	Dichrooscytaria	Resthenini	Halticini	Bothriomirini
Harpoceridae	Bothynotaria	Myrmecoraria	Stenodemini	Nichomachini	Cylapini
Eroticoridae	Dashymeniaria	Pithaniaria	Orthotylinae	Orthotylini	Fulviini
Camaronotidae	Ambraciina	Phytocoraria	Austromirini	Phylinae	Rhinomirini
Pilophoridae	Ambraciaria	Bryocorinae	Halticini	Auricillocorini	Vaniini
Idolocoridae	Cylapina	Bryocorini	Orthotylini	Hallodapini	Psallopinae
Deraeocoridae	Cylaparia	Eccritotarsini	Pilophorini	Leucophoropterini	Orthotylinae
Bothynotidae	Fulviaria	Pycnoderini	Phylinae	Phylini	Austromirini
	Fulvidiaria	Clivineminae	Dicyphini	Pilophorini	Ceratocapsini
	Bryocorina	Cylapinae	Hallodapini	Bryocorinae	Coridromiini
	Macrolophina	Cylapini	Phylini	Bryocorini	Halticini
	Cremnocephalaria	Fulviini	Bryocorinae	Dicyphini	Nichomachini
	Macrolopharia	Dicyphinae	Bryocorini	Dicyphina	Orthotylini
	Oamerideria	Hallodapini	Monaloniini	Monaloniina	Phylinae
	Heterotomaria	Dicyphini	Odoniellini	Odoniellina	Auricillocorini
	Halticaria	Orthotylinae	Deraeocorinae	Eccritotarsini	Hallodapini
	Heterotomaria	Orthotylini	Clivinemini	Eccritotarsina	Leucophoropterini
	Phylina	Ceratocapsaria	Deraeocorini	Palaucorina	Phylini
	Boopidocoraria	Halticaria	Hyaliodini	Deraeocorinae	Pilophorini
	Phylaria	Laboparia	Saturniomirini	Clivinemini	Pronotocrepini
	Lygaeoscitina	Lopidearia	Surinamellini	Deraeocorini	Bryocorinae
		Orthotylaria	Termatophylini	Hyaliodini	Bryocorini
		Pilophoraria	Cylapinae	Saturniomirini	Dicyphini
		Phylinae	Bothriomirini	Surinamellini	Dicyphina
		Phylini	Cylapini	Termatophylini	Monaloniina
		Oncotylaria	Fulviini	Mirinae	Odoniellina
		Phylaria	Palaucorinae	Herdoniini	Eccritotarsini
		Termatophylidae		Hyalopeplini	Eccritotarsina
				Mecistoscelini	Palaucorina
				Mirini	Deraeocorinae
				Resthenini	Clivinemini
				Stenodemini	Deraeocorini
					Hyaliodini
					Saturniomirini
					Surinamellini
					Termatophylini
					Mirinae
					Herdoniini
					Hyalopeplini
					Mecistoscelini
					Mirini
					Resthenini
					Stenodemini

trichobothrial number [except in *Gigantometopus* (117)], simple phallotheca, a membranous endosoma with an undifferentiated secondary gonopore, and pretarsal claws often with a subapical tooth (1, 59, 90, 107). Isometopines were originally ranked as a separate family (41, 42), and their possession of ocelli has led some authors to maintain that family ranking (5, 6, 137). They are now routinely placed within the Miridae on the basis of the presence of femoral trichobothria and genitalic morphology (90, 107).

McAtee & Malloch (70, 71) recognized two tribes, with the nominotypical tribe subdivided into two subtribes (Isometopini: Isometoparia and Myiommaria; Diphlebini). Herczek (59) established a tribal classification for the Isometopinae on the basis of a phylogenetic analysis of the group. He recognized two extant tribes each having three subtribes (Isometopini: Gigantometopina, Isometopina, and Nesocryphina, and Myiommini: Myiommina, Plaumanocorina, and Tottina), as well as a new fossil tribe with two subtribes from Baltic amber (Electromyiommini: Clavimyiomma and Electromyiomma), and removed the Diphlebini from the Isometopinae. In the most detailed morphological examination of the subfamily, Akingbohungbe (1), presumably unaware of Herzcek's work, maintained the Diphlebini within isometopines and also recognized the uniqueness of *Nesocrypha* Kirkaldy. On the basis of male genitalic characters, Konstantinov (64) supported exclusion of *Diphleps* Bergroth from the Isometopinae and provided implicit support for retaining Isometopini and Myiommini (as Myiommatini) as tribes.

Phylogenetic analysis has resulted in equivocal positions for the Isometopinae: as sister to the remainder of the Miridae on the basis of primarily the pretarsus and the absence of ocelli in other Miridae (90), with the Psallopinae and Cylapinae as sisters to the rest of the Miridae (68) and a novel position sister to Cylapinae partim removed from the basal position within the family on the basis of combined molecular and morphological data (110). The Isometopinae are in need of a globally based classification to integrate the largely Old and New World classifications (1, 50, 51, 53) and to test alternative theories of the infrasubfamilial classification (1, 59). We maintain the Diphlebini in the Isometopinae, pending further study of their morphology, including their idiosyncratic forewing and genitalic morphology.

Cylapinae

Members of the Cylapinae (**Figure 1*b***) have long and slender pretarsal claws often with a subapical tooth, setiform parempodia, and no pulvilli. At the subfamilial level there are no additional unifying features, although a great diversity of body forms is represented. Gorczyca (48) is the primary investigator of this group and provides a phylogenetic tribal reclassification as follows: Bothriomirini, Cylapini, Fulviini, Rhinomirini, and Vaniini (**Table 1**). The Fulviini are the most speciose tribe and, among other genera, are represented by the putatively monophyletic and cosmopolitan *Fulvius* Stål and *Peritropis* Uhler, which have received significant taxonomic attention (18, 47, 74). They are most readily recognized by a prognathous head, elongate labium, and often posteriorly positioned ostiolar peritreme (5, 6, 47). The Rhinomirini are an Old World taxon comprising large species with elongate antennae (47, 49). The Cylapini and Vaniini possess a hypognathous head but can be distinguished from each other by the presence of a short labium, claws that are often toothed, and flattened parempodia in vaniines (46), as well as an auriculate evaporatorium in members of the nominotypical tribe (23). Cassis et al. (29) and Cassis & Monteith (27) provided a phylogenetic reclassification of vaniine genera. The Bothriomirini are distinct within the subfamily, possessing a robust and densely punctate body and a polished metathoracic peritreme (5, 6). Regional works of significance for the Cylapinae include those for the Western Hemisphere (18), Afrotropical region (47), and Japan (151).

Psallopinae

The Psallopinae (**Figure 1*c***) are a small subfamily comprising three genera and 12 species from the tropical regions of the Old and New Worlds (94, 101), as well as a number of fossil taxa (81). They are allied to the Isometopinae and Cylapinae by the presence of subapical teeth on the pretarsal claws (90, 104). They have two-segmented tarsi; a single membrane cell; a fine, upturned, pronotal collar; and a membranous endosoma with numerous elongate spicules (64). Representatives from Eocene Baltic amber have been assigned to the subfamily, but those specimens have three-segmented tarsi (80). New species have recently been described from the Oriental region (149, 152). The identity and relationships of the group are still poorly understood, and their subfamilial status may be compromised by a more comprehensive phylogenetic assessment of the Isometopinae and Cyalpinae.

Orthotylinae

The Orthotylinae (**Figure 2*e–i***) are a cosmopolitan group defined by the presence of convergent lamellate parempodia and male genitalia that are commonly greatly exaggerated in structure (24, 60, 62, 114, 127). Unlike the Phylinae: Pilophorini, which possess the same parempodial type, members of the Orthotylinae do not possess a strap-like aedeagus. The Orthotylinae comprise five recognizable tribes; the definition of the nominotypical tribe Orthotylini is uncertain because it is made paraphyletic by the recognition of the tribes Austromirini and Ceratocapsini. Many taxa within the Orthotylini (**Figure 2*i***) possess greatly enlarged male parameres, and exaggerated endosomal spicules (**Figure 5*f***), which are serrate and elongate and whose bases are bound to the secondary gonopore (2–4, 28, 30, 43, 127, 150), a condition that also occurs in the Austromirini (24).

Schuh (88) postulated that a number of putatively natural groups, which he typified as the *Orthotylus*, *Falconia*, *Zanchius*, and *Sericophanes* groups, were recognizable in the Orthotylini. The *Falconia* and *Zanchius* groups are likely to be elevated to tribal status; members of the *Zanchius* group have a distinctive head and a membranous endosoma with simple spicules (88, 150). Forero (45) proposed placement of Neotropical taxa, such as *Carvalhomiris*, in the *Zanchius* group on the basis of genitalic and pretarsal characters. The *Falconia* group has a heavily punctate body and a posteriorly oriented peritreme (**Figure 4*f***), and the metathoracic spiracle is not visible. The Ceratocapsini are equivalent to the *Sericophanes* group of Schuh and were first erected as a suprageneric group by Van Duzee (135, 136); of late this tribe has been upheld as a valid group (52, 54, 55). The tribe Austromirini were erected by Carvalho (15) for a group of Australian taxa that are elongate and have a sulcate vertex. This group is extremely diverse in Australia, is recognized by a tumescent peritreme of the metathoracic glands, and includes both myrmecomorphic and nonmyrmecomorphic clades (24, 28, 31). All of the above tribes possess interramal lobes on the posterior wall of bursa copulatrix. In contrast, the remaining tribes of the Orthotylinae lack interramal lobes on the posterior wall of the female bursa copulatrix. Among these tribes, the Nichomachini (**Figure 2*f,g***) are a small group of three ant-mimetic Afrotropical genera that have unique male genitalia (88).

The Halticini (**Figure 2*e***) are a well-studied group (138) that has recently received considerable taxonomic attention (128, 132). Tatarnic & Cassis (132) provided a generic conspectus of the group, redescribed the tribe, analyzed their phylogenetic relationships, and maintained their position within the Orthotylinae. Wagner (138) regarded halticines as a separate subfamily on the basis of what he considered distinctive male genitalia and divided them into two tribes, the Halticini and the Chorosomellini, on the basis of head and first antennomere characters. This classification is supported by other European investigators (63). Tatarnic & Cassis (132) erected a new tribe for the genus *Coridromius* (**Figure 2*b***), the Coridromiini, which they posited as having a sister-group relationship with the Nichomachini.

Phylinae

The Phylinae (**Figure 2*j–l***) are also cosmopolitan but show their greatest diversity in temperate regions; they are least well represented in the Neotropics. Phylinae are defined by a weakly upturned pronotal collar (flattened in Hallodapini), setiform parempodia (except Pilophorini), fleshy pulvilli, claws not toothed basally or apically, a phallotheca attached to the pygophore, a boat-shaped left paramere, a rigid and strap-like (usually S-shaped) endosoma, and a simple posterior wall in females (except in some Australian taxa) (103).

The subfamily comprises six tribes (**Table 1**) and has received considerable taxonomic attention over the past 35 years. Schuh and colleagues (37, 88, 91–95, 97, 98, 103, 124) have published monographs on mirids of southern Africa, North America, and the Indo-Pacific, and numerous, additional revisions have been recently published (see Plant Bug Inventory Project, below). The nominotypical tribe Phylini (**Figure 2*l***) comprise over 50% of all phyline species but are not likely to be a monophyletic group. Schuh (91) erected two strongly myrmecomorphic tribes: the Oriental tribe Auricillocorini, which are defined by an enlarged external efferent system of the metathoracic glands and the weak, fleshy parempodia; and the Leucophoropterini, which are defined by contrasting transverse hemelytral fascia, small male genitalia, setiform parempodia, with the base of the claws thickened with a series of denticles (see revised diagnosis in Reference 73). The Hallodapini (**Figure 2*j***) are defined by head structure, flattened pronotal collar, hemelytral maculae, and male genitalic structure (88, 91).

Wyniger (147) redefined the hallodapines, removing a group of genera on the basis of pretarsal and male genital characters, to a resurrected Pronotocrepini. The Pilophorini (**Figure 2*k***) are a largely myrmecomorphic tribe defined by the convergent lamellate parempodia and male genitalic characters. Schuh (91) provided a phylogenetic analysis of the Indo-Pacific phylines, recognizing the Pilophorini as basal to a polytomy for the remaining phyline tribes. Pilophorines have been revised in the New World (105); a recent taxonomic treatment (102) includes the first recognition of the mistletoe-inhabiting genus *Hypseloecus* Reuter in Australia.

Bryocorinae

The Bryocorinae (**Figure 1*d–f***) are a heterogeneous subfamily comprising four tribes. Schuh (90) revised the definition of the group on the basis of the swollen tarsus, but their monophyly is debatable. The nominotypical tribe Bryocorini (**Figure 1*d***) are best recognized by pseudopulvilli and no parempodia (90, 107). Schuh (90) also redefined the Dicyphini sensu lato to include the Monaloniini + Odoneillini based on the near universal possession of pseudopulvilli, except for the Dicyphina genus *Campyloneura* (**Figure 3*g***), which, like the Eccritotarsini, appears to possess true pulvilli, albeit arising from the medial surface of the claw. In so doing, he downgraded the three dicyphine suprageneric groups to subtribes (**Table 1**). Cassis (22) provided a generic reclassification of the Dicyphina (**Figure 1*e***), recognizing them in part on the basis of the rounded pronotal collar, exposed metathoracic spiracle, greatly asymmetrical parameres, and an undifferentiated secondary gonopore of the aedeagus. The subtribes Monaloniina and Odoniellina have received scant taxonomic attention. Many of the species are either elongate and highly polished (Monaloniina) or are robust and have a dull appearance (Odoniellina); they lack an evaporatorium and sometimes have exaggerated processes on the scutellum (77, 87, 125). The Eccritotarsini are an insufficiently studied group with a significant taxonomic impediment. Schuh (90) transferred the Palaucorina to the Eccritotarsini and erected two subtribes: Palaucorina and Eccritotarsina (**Figure 1*f***). The Eccritotarsina have received recent attention in the Old World (123) but are in need of modern revisionary work in the Neotropics (14). Carvalho (7, 16) described many bryocorines from Micronesia and Papua New Guinea.

Deraeocorinae

The Deraeocorinae (**Figure 1*g–i***) are recognized as a monophyletic subfamily by the presence of a rounded pronotal collar, basally dentate claws, setiform parempodia, and the absence of pulvilli (5, 6, 90, 107, 126). The tribal classification of Carvalho (5, 6) included six tribes (**Table 1**). Cassis (23) provided a phylogenetic reclassification of the tribe Termatophylini (**Figure 1*k***), recognizing it as a monophyletic group on the basis of a short first labial segment and a pair of erect anterolateral pronotal setae. In addition, he questioned the validity of the other deraeocorine tribes, in particular suggesting that the nominotypical tribe may not be monophyletic (**Figure 1*h***). Members of the Clivinemini (38–40) have a robust and punctate body (**Figure 1*g***). Ferreira (38) recognized them as a monophyletic group on the basis of male genitalic characters. The Hyaliodini, ant-mimetic Surinamellini (**Figure 1*i***), and aposematic Saturniomirini (**Figure 1*j***) have received little taxonomic attention.

Mirinae

The Mirinae (**Figures 1*l*** and **2*a–d***) are the most speciose subfamily (>4,000 species) of plant bugs. In a seminal study of the subfamily, Schwartz (113) reviewed the key character systems and infrasubfamilial classifications, including a generic reclassification of the Stenodemini. Mirines are defined by pretarsal and genitalic characters: The endosoma is membranous with sclerotized spicules and a ringlike secondary gonopore (60, 112, 113), the posterior wall of the bursa copulatrix possesses a median process (= sigmoid process; 112, 113), and the pretarsus has divergent lamellate parempodia. In an unpublished thesis, Schwartz (112) recognized six tribes and assessed their sister-group relationships (**Table 1**); we follow his classification in this work. The nominotypical Mirini (**Figure 2*b***) are an unwieldy cosmopolitan group whose generic relationships have been assessed phylogenetically in an unpublished thesis by Chérot (34). There have been numerous significant revisions over the past 30 years (33, 57, 111, 115, 116, 122). The primarily Neotropical Herdoniini (**Figure 1*l***) are a myrmecomorphic tribe manifesting a broad range of morphological modifications. The Hyalopeplini (**Figure 2*a***) often have transparent wings and resemble wasps (107); Carvalho & Gross (19) revised the world fauna. The Resthenini (**Figure 2*c***) are a New World tribe of aposematically colored bugs that often have reduced metathoracic glands (107). The Stenodemini (**Figure 2*d***) are a cosmopolitan group recognized by an elongate body, elongate first metatarsal segment, a narrow ductus seminis, and female bursa copulatrix without lateral lobes (112, 113). Carvalho & Wagner (21) monographed the genus *Trigonotylus* Fieber.

BIODIVERSITY AND BIOGEOGRAPHY

Taxonomic Activity and Catalogs

Miridology commences with the *Systema Naturae*. Linnaeus (69) described the European species *Cimex striatus* Linnaeus, now attributed to the type genus for the family; *Miris* Fabricius; and 16 other species. About two-thirds of all plant bug species have been described by seven miridologists. They include the Finn Odo Reuter (publication period: 1870–1912), Robert Poppius (1909–1921), and Rauno Linnavuori (1951–present); the Englishman William Distant (1879–1920); the German Eduard Wagner (1938–1978); the American Harry Knight (1916–1974); and the remarkable Brazilian José Carvalho (1944–1993), who described more than 2,000 species (94). Much of the early work was regional in scope, resulting in genus-group classifications that were cursory, and often included monotypic taxa with unknown affinities. In addition, a number of convenience groups (e.g., *Orthotylus* Fieber) that had inadequate definition were maintained.

Species richness: absolute number of species per region or community

From 1758 onward, phases of descriptive activity for the Miridae have been stimulated by the seminal world catalogs of Carvalho (5, 9–13) and Schuh (94, 101); regional catalogs for North America (58), the Palearctic (61), and Australia (25); and a catalog of the Cylapinae (48). There has been a large increase in taxonomic activity for plant bugs over the past 15 years, the rate of description having doubled compared with the previous 50 years (32, 94).

Global Species Richness

The Miridae are one of the most diverse insect families, with over 11,020 described species (101). Mirids comprise about 25% of all described species of Heteroptera (25, 26, 56, 107). However, the taxonomic impediment in absolute numbers is greater for the Miridae, compared with all other true bug families. Estimates of total species richness for the Miridae are lacking, but in all likelihood less than 50% of species are currently described, based on recent discoveries and escalating rates of species description over the past 50 years (**Figure 6**). For the best-known biogeographic regions, the Palearctic and Nearctic, the asymptote is being approached (**Figure 6**), but there has been significant taxonomic activity for the Orthotylinae and Phylinae in the Western Hemisphere since the publication of the Schuh world catalog. For regions such as Australia, the taxonomic accumulation curve suggests that the mirids are poorly represented. However, this

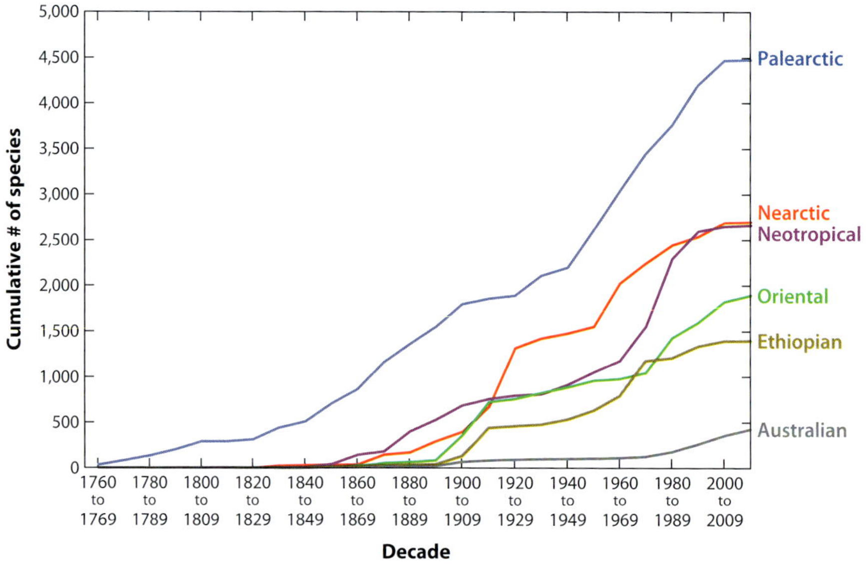

Figure 6

Taxonomic accumulation curve for the Miridae by biogeographic region. Data from Reference 101, updated August 2011.

is due to inadequate sampling, with recent collecting and taxonomic effort indicating a highly species-rich plant bug fauna in Australia, as evidenced by the recent rise in the rate of species description as a result of the Plant Bug Inventory project (32).

Plant Bug Inventory Project

The Plant Bug Inventory project (funded by the U.S. National Science Foundation) addressed the taxonomic impediment of the mirid subfamilies Orthotylinae and Phylinae (32) in regions such as Australia, South Africa, New Caledonia, and western North America. The cybertaxonomic methods utilized in this project incorporate information technology and team-based research (32). As a result, major monographic and revisionary works have been produced for the Orthotylini (24, 30, 31, 43–45, 79, 80, 86, 114, 140), Coridromiini (130), Halticini (75, 129, 132), Leucophoropterini (73), and Phylini (66, 99, 100, 103, 106, 109, 141–143), as well as the reinstated status of the phyline tribe Pronotocrepini (147).

Distribution Patterns of Suprageneric Groups and Key Genera

The Miridae are a cosmopolitan family found broadly across all biogeographic regions, with areas of high richness and endemicity in the Old and New World tropics, as well as in Mediterranean-type ecosystems (32, 94, 101). All eight subfamilies are found in the Palearctic, Oriental, Australian, and Neotropical regions (**Table 2**); the Psallopinae are not known from the Nearctic and Afrotropical regions. Sixteen of the 35 tribes have a cosmopolitan distribution, although the doubtful monophyly of the Phylini (Phylinae), Orthothylini sensu stricto (Orthotylinae), Deraeocorini, and Surinamellini (Deraeocorinae) affects this assessment. Each biogeographic region has between 27 and 31 tribes, with the Palearctic having all but 3 of the recognized tribes (**Table 2**). In the Eastern Hemisphere, only the Diphlebini (Isometopinae), Clivinemini (Deraeocorinae), and Ceratocapsini (Orthotylinae) are unrepresented. In comparison, the Gigantometopini, Isometopini (Isometopinae), Bothriomirini, Rhinomirini (Cylapinae), Austromirini (Orthotylinae), Nichomachini (Orthotylinae), Auricillocorini, Leucophoropterini (Phylinae), Odoniellina, Palaucorina (Bryocorinae), Saturniomirini (Deraeocorinae), Hyalopeplini, and Mecistoscelini (Mirinae) have not been recorded from the Americas.

Endemism becomes evident at the tribe level and below. For example, mirines of the tribe Rethenini are restricted to the New World, with most of their diversity confined to the Neotropics, as are the Ceratocapsini and nearly all Herdoniini. The Hallodapini sensu stricto have an Indo-Pacific distribution with some taxa in the Palearctic and a single genus in North America. Whereas at one time the genus *Lygus* Hahn appeared to be cosmopolitan, numerous recent revisionary works have restricted the conception of that genus and have shown it to have a Holarctic distribution.

BIOLOGY AND HOST ASSOCIATIONS

Biology

Wheeler (146) surveyed the biology of plant bugs in his encyclopedic treatise of the family. Mirids have economic impacts as natural enemies (85, 144–146), and numerous species are major pests of food and fiber crops (115, 116, 144, 146). The life cycle of mirids comprises an egg, five nymphal instars, and adults. Eggs are laid interstitially within stems and petioles of plants. Mirids are noteworthy for specialized behaviors, including a range of defensive strategies such as cryptic

Table 2 Distribution of suprageneric groups of Miridae with numbers of genera (including fossil groups) by biogeographic region

Subfamily	Tribe/subtribe	AF	PA	OR	AU	NE	NT
Isometopinae	Diphlebini	–	–	–	–	1	–
	Gigantometopini	–	1	1	–	–	–
	Isometopini	7	4	7	1	–	–
	Myiommini	3	3	6	–	5	9
Cylapinae	Bothriomirini	1	–	5	–	–	–
	Cylapini	2	12	7	1	1	12
	Fulviini	10	6	24	10	3	15
	Rhinomirini	1	–	4	–	–	–
	Vaniini	1	–	3	2	–	1
Psallopinae	Psallopini	–	3	1	–	–	1
Orthotylinae	Austromirini	–	–	–	3	–	–
	Ceratocapsini	–	–	–	–	4	6
	Coridromiini	1	1	1	1	–	–
	Halticini	7	18	4	3	5	2
	Nichomachini	4	1	–	–	–	–
	Orthotylini	20	37	34	16	57	95
Phylinae	Auricillocorini	–	–	5	–	–	–
	Hallodapini	31	20	9	2	1	1
	Leucophoropterini	–	1	12	5	–	–
	Phylini	63	136	27	20	101	35
	Pilophorini	8	7	7	1	2	2
	Pronotocrepini	–	1	–	–	3	–
Bryocorinae	Bryocorini	1	3	3	–	1	1
	Dicyphini						
	Dicyphina	9	8	7	2	7	8
	Monaloniina	8	3	11	5	1	1
	Odoniellina	13	2	5	1	–	–
	Eccritotarsini						
	Eccritotarsina	7	5	34	1	19	70
	Palaucorina	–	–	1	–	–	–
Deraeocorinae	Clivinemini	–	1	–	–	10	17
	Deraeocorini	8	9	18	8	14	28
	Hyaliodini	3	1	3	–	6	20
	Saturniomirini	–	–	4	2	–	–
	Surinamellini	2	2	3	–	1	5
	Termatophylini	1	3	2	4	2	4
Mirinae	Herdoniini	3	1	–	–	9	24
	Hyalopeplini	3	2	13	4	–	–
	Mecistoscelini	–	3	1	–	–	–
	Mirini	54	110	76	37	56	86
	Resthenini	–	–	–	–	9	27
	Stenodemini	6	12	8	4	15	13

Abbreviations: AF, Afrotropical; PA, Palearctic; OR, Oriental; AU, Australian; NE, Nearctic; NT, Neotropical.

coloration, Batesian ant-mimicry (72), and association with plants with antiherbivore strategies, such as sticky trichomes in *Drosera* (22).

Research on the biology of mirids focuses typically on their food preferences and host and habitat affiliations (146). Mirids are phytophagous (Bryocorinae, Orthotylinae, Phylinae, and Deraeocorinae), mycetophagous (Cylapinae), carnivorous (Isometopinae and Deraeocorinae), and zoophytophagous (Bryocorinae: Dicyphina), but the details of their life history could still stand significant further investigation. For example, predaceous genera such as *Phytocoris* Fallén show very strong associations with given plant species, but whether this occurs because they require some plant matter for completion of development or because they feed exclusively on herbivores associated with the plant is known for very few species.

Host Plant Associations

The majority of mirids live on seed plants; their development is often synchronous with meristematic growth and reproductive development of their host plants (146). For those species with host plant records (94, 101), 60% of mirid species are host plant specific, and less than 20% of species are known to occur on more than two hosts (**Figure 7**). Host restrictedness suggests that mirids and seed plant interactions have resulted in coevolution or, at least, that seed plants have provided a biotic resource upon which mirids have radiated. However, there are no demonstrated cases of strict cospeciation, although degrees of phylogenetic restrictedness of hosts utilized are known. For example, there are cases in which mirid genera are associated primarily with species of a plant genus (e.g., the austromirine genus *Metopocoris* Cassis and the she-oak genus *Allocasuarina* L. Johnson; 24) or species of a mirid clade are found mainly on a suprageneric group of plants (e.g., oak-inhabiting phyline species; 141).

In **Figure 8**, we have graphed the host associations of mirid tribes and plant orders (based on the Angiosperm Phylogeny Group classification; 121). As in a previous study for pentatomomorphan bugs (32), a pattern emerges in which most mirids exploit rosid and asterid eudicot clades and there is greatest frequency of association with the rosid orders Caryophyllales, Fabales,

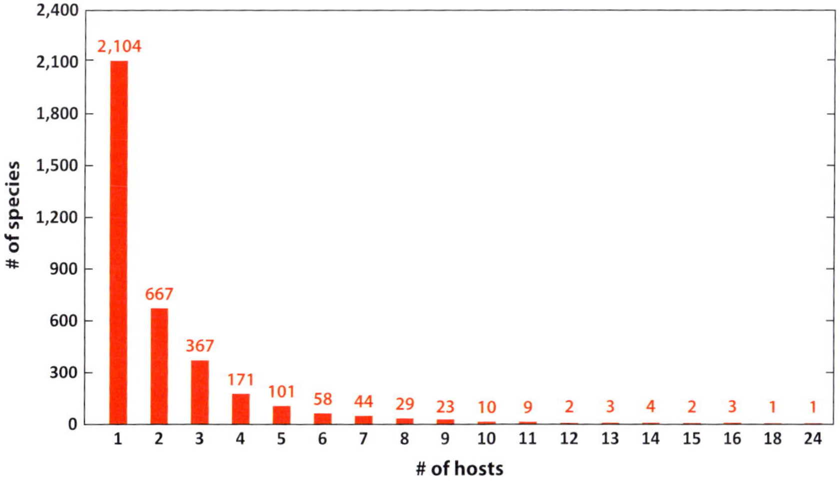

Figure 7

Histogram of the host plant specificity of the Miridae. Data from Reference 101, updated August 2011.

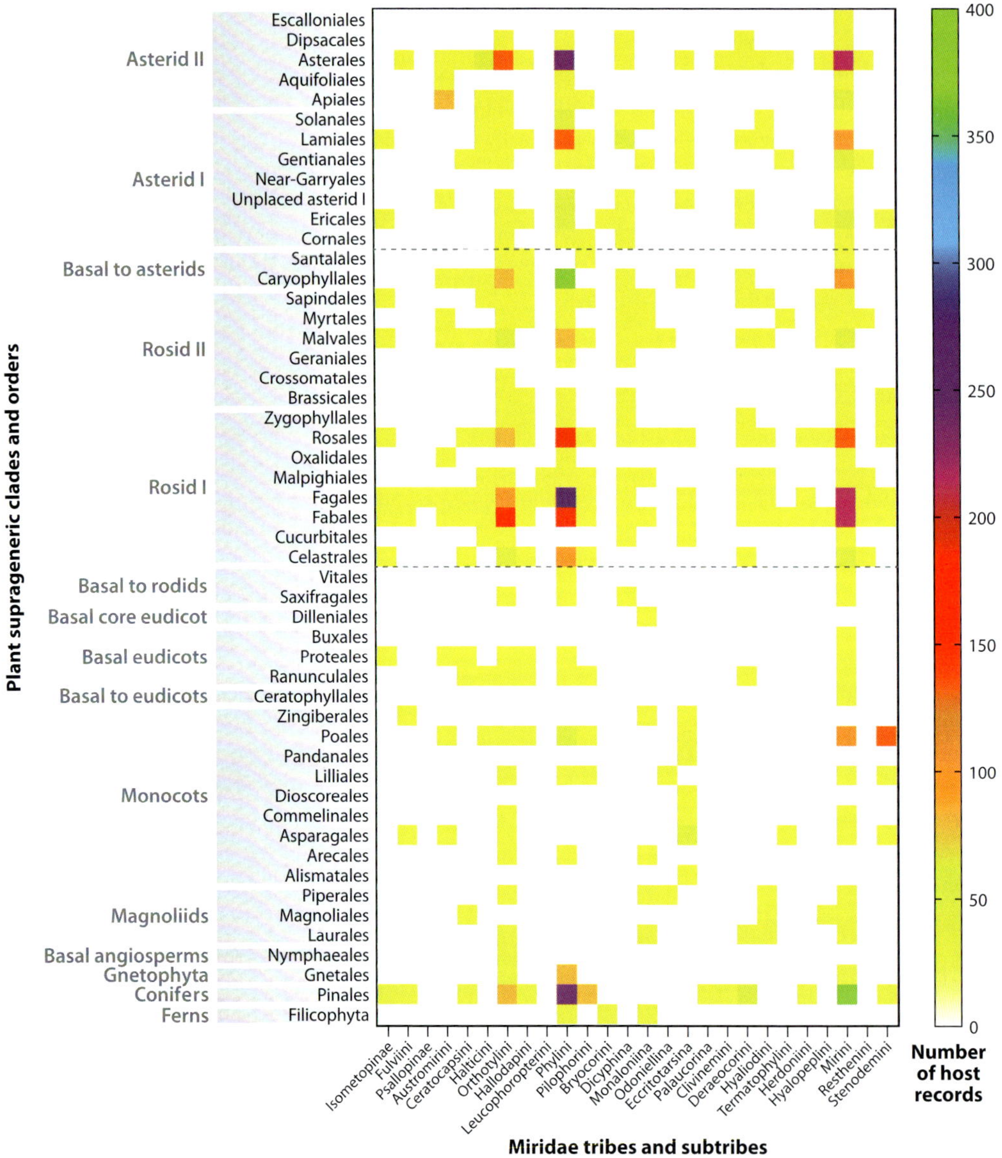

Figure 8

Level plot of the frequency of association of Miridae tribes and subtribes by plant order. Plant classification is based on Reference Coridromiini host records included in Halticini.

Fagales, and Rosales, and the asterid orders Lamiales and Asterales. These peak frequencies are repeated for the three most speciose phytophagous tribes, the Orthotylini, Phylini, and Mirini, an observation congruent with the fact that asterid and rosid angiosperms increased in abundance and diversity through the Cenozoic (76). A few mirid taxa show specializations that are not widespread across the family, including monocot feeding, for example, grass associations for the mirine tribes Mecistoscelini and Stenodemini, the genus *Irbisia* (Mirini; 111), and some members of the Halticini (132) and Phylini (94), and association of Eccritotarsina with plants belonging to the families Musaceae, Orchidaceae, and Araceae. There are few records of mirid associations with basal angiosperms, such as the Nymphaeales or the magnoliid clade, although substantial numbers of taxa use Australian Proteales as hosts. Mirids are also found on the nonangiosperm seed plant orders Ephedrales, Gnetales, and Pinales. A substantial number of phyline (118) and mirine taxa are found on the genus *Pinus* Linnaeus in the Northern Hemisphere; lesser numbers of mirid taxa are found on other genera of Pinales. The Bryocorini and the monaloniine genus *Felisacus* Distant are associated primarily with ferns.

The above discussion emphasizes the variable nature of information on host associations within the Miridae. Clarification of these issues lies partly in an improved knowledge of insect biology, such as better knowledge of the feeding habits of large well-collected groups such as *Phytocoris* and of obscure taxa such as the Palaucorina. In conjunction with continued host documentation, additional revisionary studies and phylogenetic analyses will be necessary to better understand the patterns of host association in plant bugs. For example, within the phyline genus *Plagiognathus*, there appear to be multiple independent colonizations of conifers from angiosperms (97), but details of the pattern will require a phylogenetic analysis of this large Holarctic genus. At the opposite end of the classification spectrum, the phylogenetic relationships of those groups that do show substantial host fidelity, such as the monocot-feeding Stenodemini, the fern-feeding Bryocorini and *Felisacus*, and the Protales-feeding Phylinae from Australia, will also be clarified only through rigorous cladistic analyses.

CONCLUSIONS

Future studies of the Miridae are predicted to continue to address the significant taxonomic impediment, particularly in the tropics and the Southern Hemisphere. The Plant Bug Inventory project revealed that many hundreds of species had not been collected until the past 10 years. Although the greatest taxonomic impediment is probably in Australia and Melanesia, many areas of the Afrotropical and Oriental regions also require increased sampling and description. In the process, we envisage that the supraspecific classifications will be less strongly influenced by regional work, with likely synonymy at the generic level. Unlike many other insect groups, the application of molecular techniques to mirid systematics is near negligible, but with additional collections more DNA sequencing will provide a basis for testing current taxon theories of relationships within the family. The Plant Bug Inventory project addressed the importance of collection and accurate identification of host plant data. These extrinsic data provide supporting evidence of species theories and allow for analysis of host associations, which have potentially significant impacts on the fields of coevolution and coextinction, as well as bionomic applications. Plant bugs are a remarkable group of exopterygote insects that have potential as model groups in ecology and evolutionary biology, and we are now well placed to see a major enhancement of knowledge of the group.

SUMMARY POINTS

1. The hyperdiverse family Miridae are one of the 20 most species-rich families of insects, with over 11,000 described species.
2. Taxonomic accumulation curves indicate that for the Miridae there is a significant taxonomic impediment, with greatest taxonomic effort still being required in the tropics and the Southern Hemisphere.

3. The Miridae are a monophyletic taxon recognized by the presence of one or two closed cells in the forewing membrane, femoral trichobothria, divided trochanters, female seminal depository, and highly asymmetrical male genitalia.
4. The family Miridae comprise eight subfamilies; the most diverse are the Mirinae, Orthotylinae, and Phylinae.
5. A suprageneric classification of the Miridae, based primarily on characters of the pretarsus, metathoracic glands, femoral trichobothria, and genitalia, is proposed.
6. All mirid subfamilies except the Psallopinae are found in all major zoogeographic regions of the world, with centers of diversity in tropical and Mediterranean-type habitats. Many tribe- and genus-level taxa show restricted patterns of endemism.
7. Available evidence indicates that plant bugs exhibit a high degree of host plant specificity, with the majority of species found on a single plant species.
8. Plant bugs show highest frequency of association with asterid and rosid clades of angiosperms, and also high levels of association with conifers and grasses.

DISCLOSURE STATEMENT

The authors are not aware of any affiliations, memberships, funding, or financial holdings that might be perceived as affecting the objectivity of this review.

ACKNOWLEDGMENTS

This work was supported by the Australian Biological Resources Study and the U.S. National Science Foundation (DEB-0316495). Ryan Choi, Ruth Salas, Celia Symonds, Rossana Silveira, Nik Tatarnic, Steve Thurston, and Alex Brown are thanked for the assistance with the preparation of figures. Michael Schwartz is thanked for reading and commenting on the manuscript. We also thank the Entomological Society of Washington for the use of **Figure 4*a,b***.

LITERATURE CITED

1. Akingbohungbe AE. 1996. *The Isometopinae (Heteroptera: Miridae) of Africa, Europe, and the Middle East.* Ibadan, Nigeria: Delar Tertiary Publ. 170 pp.
2. Asquith A. 1991. Revision of the genus *Lopidea* in America north of Mexico (Heteroptera: Miridae: Orthotylinae). *Theses Zool.* 16:1–280
3. Asquith A. 1993. Patterns of speciation in the genus *Lopidea* (Heteroptera: Miridae: Orthotylinae). *Syst. Entomol.* 18:169–80
4. Asquith A. 1994. Revision of the endemic Hawaiian genus *Sarona* Kirkaldy (Heteroptera: Miridae: Orthotylinae). *Bishop Mus. Occas. Pap.* 40:1–81
5. **Carvalho JCM. 1952. On the major classification of the Miridae (Hemiptera). (With keys to subfamilies and tribes and a catalogue of the world genera.) *An. Acad. Brasil. Cien.* 24:31–110**

5. First global and modern synthesis of plant bug classification.

6. Carvalho JCM. 1955. Keys to the genera of Miridae of the world (Hemiptera). *Bol. Mus. Paran. Em. Goel. Zool.* 11:1–151
7. Carvalho JCM. 1956. Insects of Micronesia: Miridae. Bishop Museum, Honolulu. *Insects Micrones.* 7:1–100
8. Carvalho JCM. 1956. Neotropical Miridae, LXXVIII: a peculiar new genus of Orthotylinae (Hemiptera). *Rev. Brasil. Biol.* 16:235–37

9. Carvalho JCM. 1957. A catalogue of the Miridae of the world. Part I. *Arq. Mus. Nac., Rio de Janeiro* 44:1–158
10. Carvalho JCM. 1958. A catalogue of the Miridae of the world. Part II. *Arq. Mus. Nac., Rio de Janeiro* 45:1–216
11. Carvalho JCM. 1958. A catalogue of the Miridae of the world. Part III. *Arq. Mus. Nac., Rio de Janeiro* 47:1–161
12. Carvalho JCM. 1959. A catalogue of the Miridae of the world. Part IV. *Arq. Mus. Nac., Rio de Janeiro* 48:1–384
13. Carvalho JCM. 1960. A catalogue of the Miridae of the world. Part V. *Arq. Mus. Nac., Rio de Janeiro* 51:1–194
14. Carvalho JCM. 1960. Mirideos neotropicais, LXXXVIII: dois novos generos do complexo *Neela* Reuter-*Neoneella* Costa Lima (Hemiptera, Heteroptera). *Arq. Mus. Nac., Rio de Janeiro* 50:47–60
15. Carvalho JCM. 1976. Analecta Miridologica: concerning changes of taxonomic positions of some genera and species (Hemiptera). *Rev. Brasil. Biol.* 36:49–59
16. Carvalho JCM. 1981. The Bryocorinae of Papua New Guinea (Hemiptera, Miridae). *Arq. Mus. Nac. Rio Jan.* 56:35–89
17. Carvalho JCM. 1984. On the subfamily Palaucorinae Carvalho (Hemiptera, Miridae). *Rev. Brasil. Biol.* 44:81–86
18. Carvalho JCM, Costa LAA. 1994. The genus *Fulvius* from the Americas (Hemiptera: Miridae). *Ann. Inst. Biol. Univ. Nac. Aut. Mex. Zool.* 65:63–135
19. Carvalho JCM, Gross GF. 1979. The tribe Hyalopeplini of the world (Hemiptera: Miridae). *Rec. S. Aust. Mus.* 17:429–531
20. Carvalho JCM, Rosas AF. 1962. Mirideos neotropicais, XCI: uma tribo e dois generos novos (Hemiptera). *Rev. Brasil. Biol.* 22:427–32
21. Carvalho JCM, Wagner E. 1957. A world revision of the genus *Trigonotylus* Fieber (Hemiptera-Heteroptera, Miridae). *Arq. Mus. Nac. Rio Jan.* 43:121–55
22. Cassis G. 1986. *A systematic study of the subfamily Dicyphinae (Heteroptera: Miridae)*. PhD Diss. Oregon State Univ., Corvallis. 390 pp.
23. Cassis G. 1995. A reclassification and phylogeny of the Termatophylini (Heteroptera: Miridae: Deraeocorinae), with a taxonomic revision of the Australian species, and a review of the tribal classification of the Deraeocorinae. *Proc. Entomol. Soc. Wash.* 97:258–330
24. Cassis G. 2008. The *Lattinova* complex of austromirine plant bugs (Hemiptera: Heteroptera: Orthotylinae). *Proc. Entomol. Soc. Wash.* 110(4):845–939
25. Cassis G, Gross GF. 1995. *Zoological Catalogue of Australia. Heteroptera*, Vol. 27.3B: *Coleorrhyncha to Cimicomorpha*. Melbourne: CSIRO. 506 pp.
26. Cassis G, Gross GF. 2002. *Zoological Catalogue of Australia. Heteroptera*, Vol. 27.3B: *Pentatomomorpha*. Melbourne: CSIRO. 732 pp.
27. Cassis G, Monteith GB. 2006. A new genus and species of Cylapinae (Insecta: Heteroptera: Miridae: Cylapinae) from New Caledonia, with re-analysis of the genera. *Mem. Qld. Mus.* 52:13–26
28. Cassis G, Moulds T. 2002. A systematic revision of the plantbug genus *Kirkaldyella* Poppius (Heteroptera: Miridae: Orthotylinae: Austromirini). *Insect Syst. Evol.* 33:53–90
29. Cassis G, Schwartz MD, Moulds T. 2003. Systematics and new taxa of the *Vannius* complex (Hemiptera: Miridae: Cylapinae) from the Australian region. *Mem. Qld. Mus.* 49:125–43
30. Cassis G, Symonds C, Tatarnic N. 2010. A remarkable new species of stone-dwelling Orthotylini (Heteroptera: Miridae: Orthotylinae) from Australia. *Zootaxa* 2485:58–68
31. Cassis G, Wall MA. 2010. Systematics and phylogeny of the hatchet-head plant bug genus *Myrmecoroides* Gross (Insecta: Heteroptera: Miridae: Orthotylinae). *Entomol. Am.* 116(3/4):29–49
32. **Cassis G, Wall M, Schuh R. 2007. Insect biodiversity and industrializing the taxonomic process: a case study with the Miridae (Heteroptera). In *Towards the Tree of Life: Taxonomy and Systematics of Large and Species Rich Clades*, ed. T Hodkinson, J Parnell, pp. 193–212. Boca Raton, FL: CRC Press**

32. Application of cybertaxonomy methods to plant bugs.

33. Chérot F. 1997. Revision du genre *Horistus* Fieber, 1861 (Heteroptera: Miridae). *Bull. Ann. Soc. R. Belg. Entomol.* 133:113–96

34. Chérot F. 2001. Eléments de classification générique et de phylogenée des Mirini (Insecta: Heteroptera: Miridae) avec un discussion préliminaire de la relativité des concepts, de l'importance de la notion de classes et de l'interdépendance des ecoles en taxonomie. PhD Diss. Univ. Libre Bruxelles. 787 pp.
35. Davis NT. 1955. Morphology of the female organs of reproduction in the Miridae (Hemiptera). *Ann. Entomol. Soc. Am.* 48:132–50
36. Douglas JW, Scott J. 1865. *The British-Hemiptera. Vol. 1. Hemiptera-Heteroptera.* London: The Ray Soc. 627 pp.
37. Eyles AC, Schuh RT. 2003. Revision of New Zealand Bryocorinae and Phylinae (Insecta: Hemiptera: Miridae). *N. Z. Zool.* 30:263–325
38. Ferreira PSF. 1998. The tribe Clivinematini: cladistic analysis, geographic distribution and biological considerations (Heteroptera, Miridae). *Rev. Brasil. Entomol.* 42:53–57
39. Ferreira PSF. 2000. A taxonomic review of the tribe Clivinematini, with a key to world genera (Heteroptera: Miridae). *Stud. Neot. Faun. Env.* 35:38–43
40. Ferreira PSF. 2001. Diagnoses and description of the world genera of the tribe Clivinematini (Heteroptera: Miridae). *Stud. Neot. Faun. Env.* 36:227–40
41. Fieber FX. 1860. Die europäischen Hemipteren. Halbflügler (Rhynchota Heteroptera). Vienna: Gerold's Sohn. 112 pp.
42. Fieber FX. 1861. Die europäischen Hemipteren. Halbflügler (Rhynchota Heteroptera). Vienna: Gerold's Sohn. 113–444 pp.
43. Forero D. 2008. Revision and phylogenetic analysis of the *Hadronema* group (Miridae: Orthotylinae: Orthotylini) with descriptions of new genera and new species, and comments on the Neotropical genus *Tupimiris*. *Bull. Am. Mus. Nat. Hist.* 312:1–172
44. Forero D. 2009. Description of one new species of *Chileria* and three new species of *Orthotylus*, with nomenclatural and distributional notes on Neotropical Orthotylinae (Heteroptera: Miridae: Orthotylini). *Am. Mus. Novit.* 3642:1–50
45. Forero D. 2009. Revision of the genus *Carvalhomiris* (Hemiptera: Miridae: Orthotylinae). *Entomol. Am.* 115(2):115–42
46. Gorczyca J. 1997. Revision of the *Vannius* complex and its subfamily placement (Hemiptera: Heteroptera: Miridae). *Genus* 8:517–53
47. Gorczyca J. 2000. *A Systematic Study on Cylapinae with a Revision of the Afrotropical Region (Heteroptera, Miridae)*. Katowice, Poland: Wydawnictwo Uniw. Slask. 176 pp.
48. Gorczyca J. 2006. The catalogue of the subfamily Cylapinae Kirkaldy, 1903, of the world: (Hemiptera, Heteroptera, Miridae). *Mon. Upp. Siles. Mus.* 5:1–100
49. Gorczyca J, Chérot F. 1998. A revision of the *Rhinomiris* complex (Heteroptera: Miridae: Cylapinae). *Polsk. Pis. Entomol.* 67:23–64
50. Henry TJ. 1977. *Teratodia* Bergroth, new synonym of *Diphleps* Bergroth with descriptions of two new species (Heteroptera: Miridae: Isometopinae). *Fla. Entomol.* 60:201–10
51. Henry TJ. 1980. Review of *Lidopus* Gibson and *Wetmorea* McAtee and Malloch, descriptions of three new genera and two new species, and key to New World genera (Hemiptera: Miridae: Isometopinae). *Proc. Entomol. Soc. Wash.* 82:178–94
52. Henry TJ. 1983. [Description of new species] In: Carvalho, JCM, Fontes, AV, Henry, TJ. Taxonomy of South American species of *Ceratocapsus*, with description of 45 new species (Hemiptera: Miridae). *US Dept. Agric. Tech. Bull.* 1676
53. Henry TJ. 1984. New species of Isometopinae (Hemiptera: Miridae) from Mexico, with new records for previously described North American species. *Proc. Entomol. Soc. Wash.* 82:337–45
54. Henry TJ. 1994. Revision of the myrmecomorphic plant bug genus *Schaffneria* Knight (Heteroptera: Miridae: Orthotylinae). *Proc. Entomol. Soc. Wash.* 96(4):701–12
55. Henry TJ. 2006. *Izycapsus* (Heteroptera: Miridae: Orthotylinae), a new ceratocapsine plant bug genus established to accommodate two new species from Mexico. *Russ. Entomol. J.* 15:163–70
56. Henry TJ. 2009. Biodiversity of Heteroptera. In *Insect Biodiversity: Science and Society*, ed. G Foottit, PH Adler, pp. 223–63. London: Blackwell Publ.
57. Henry TJ, Kim KC. 1984. Genus *Neurocolpus* Reuter (Heteroptera: Miridae): taxonomy, economic implications, hosts and phylogenetic review. *Trans. Am. Entomol. Soc.* 110:1–75

58. Henry TJ, Wheeler AJ Jr. 1988. Miridae. In *Catalog of the Heteroptera, or True Bugs, of Canada and the Continental United States*, ed. TJ Henry, RC Froeschner, pp. 251–507. Leiden: E.J. Brill
59. Herczek A. 1993. Systematic position of Isometopinae Fieb. (Miridae, Heteroptera) and their interrelationships. *Prace Nauk. Uniw. Slask.* 1357:1–86
60. Kelton LA. 1959. Male genitalia as taxonomic characters in the Miridae (Hemiptera). *Can. Entomol. Suppl.* 11:1–72

60. Provides a critical comparative study of male genitalia and classificatory significance.

61. Kerzhner IM, Josifov M. 1999. *Catalogue of the Heteroptera of the Palearctic Region, Volume 3. Cimicomorpha II*, ed. B Aukema, C Rieger. Amsterdam: Neth. Entomol. Soc. 577 pp.
62. Kerzhner IM, Konstantinov FV. 1999. Structure of the aedeagus in Miridae (Heteroptera) and its bearing to suprageneric classification. *Acta Soc. Zool. Boh.* 63:117–37
63. Kiyak S. 1995. Replacement name for the genus *Halticidea* Reuter, 1901, and the subfamily Halticinae Kirkaldy, 1902 of Miridae (Insecta, Hemiptera). *Beitr. Entomol.* 45:215–16
64. Konstantinov FV. 2003. Male genitalia in Miridae (Heteroptera) and their significance for suprageneric classification of the family. Part I: general review, Isometopinae and Psallopinae. *Belg. J. Entomol.* 5:3–36
65. Konstantinov FV. 2007. Male genitalia in Miridae: structure, terminology and application to phylogenetic inference. Critical comments on Cheng-Shing Lin & Chung-Tu Yang's ideas. *Zoosyst. Ross.* 16(2):235–38
66. Konstantinov FV. 2008. Review of *Solenoxyphus* Reuter, 1875 (Heteroptera: Miridae: Phylinae). *Am. Mus. Novit.* 3607:1–42
67. Kullenberg B. 1947. Über Morphologie und Funktion der Kopulations-apparates der Capsiden und Nabiden. *Zool. Bid. Fr. Upps.* 24:218–418
68. Lin C-S, Yang CT. 2005. External male genitalia of the Miridae (Hemiptera: Heteroptera). *Spec. Publ. Nat. Mus. Nat. Hist. Taiwan* 9:1–174
69. Linnaeus C. 1758. *Systema Naturae. L. Salvii, Holmiae. Vol. 1.* 10th ed. 10. 823 pp.
70. McAtee WL, Malloch JR. 1924. Some annectant bugs of the superfamily Cimicoideae (Heteroptera). *Bull. Brool. Entomol. Soc.* 19:69–82
71. McAtee WL, Malloch JR. 1932. Notes on the genera of Isometopinae (Heteroptera). *Stylops* 1:62–70
72. McIver JD, Stonedahl GM. 1993. Myrmecomorphy: morphological and behavioral mimicry of ants. *Annu. Rev. Entomol.* 38:351–79
73. Menard KL, Schuh RT. 2011. Revision of Leucophoropterini: key to genera, redescription of the Australian fauna, and descriptions of additional new genera and species. *Bull. Am. Mus. Nat. Hist.* In press
74. Moulds T, Cassis G. 2006. Review of Australian species of *Peritropis* (Insecta: Heteroptera: Miridae: Cylapinae). *Mem. Qld. Mus.* 52:171–90
75. Namyatova AA, Konstantinov FV. 2009. Revision of the genus *Orthocephalus* Fieber, 1858 (Hemiptera: Heteroptera: Miridae: Orthotylinae). *Zootaxa* 2316:1–118
76. Niklas KJ, Tiffney BH, Knoll AH. 1983. Patterns in vascular plant diversification. *Nature* 303:614
77. Odhiambo TR. 1962. Review of some genera of the subfamily Bryocorinae (Hemiptera: Miridae). *Bull. Br. Mus. Nat. Hist. Entomol.* 2(6):245–331
78. Pluot-Sigwalt D, Matocq A. 2006. On some particular sclerotized structures associated with the vulvar area and the vestibulum in the Orthotylinae and Phylinae (Heteroptera, Miridae). *Denisia* 19:557–70
79. Polhemus DA. 2002. An initial review of *Orthotylus* in the Hawaiian Islands, with descriptions of twenty-one new species (Heteroptera: Miridae). *J. N.Y. Entomol. Soc.* 110:270–340
80. Polhemus DA. 2004. Further studies on the genus *Orthotylus* (Heteroptera: Miridae) in the Hawaiian Islands, with descriptions of thirty-four new species. *J. NY Entomol. Soc.* 112(4):227–333
81. Popov YA, Herczek A. 2006. *Cylapopsallops kerzhneri* gen. et sp. n.—a new peculiar mirid from Baltic amber (Heteroptera: Miridae: Psallopinae). *Russ. Entomol. J.* 15(2):187–88
82. Reuter OM. 1905. Hemipterlogische Spekulationen, I. Die Klassifikation der Capsiden. In: Festschr. f. Palmén. II. Helsingfors, 1905, pp. 4–58, 1 Stammbaumstabel; Hemipterologische Spekulation. II. Die Gesetzmässigkeit im Abändern der Zeichnung bei Hemipter Festschrift fur Palmen. II. Helsingfors, 105:3–30
83. Reuter OM. 1910. Neue Beiträge zur Phylogenie und Systematik der Miriden nebst einleitenden Bemerkungen über die Phylogenie der Heteropteren-Familien. Mit einer Stammbaumstafel. *Acta Soc. Sci. Fenn.* 37(3):1–167

83. First establishment of plant bug classification on a global basis and on character information.

84. Sadowska-Woda I, Chérot F, Malm T. 2008. A preliminary phylogenetic analysis of the genus *Fulvius* Stål (Hemiptera: Miridae: Cylapinae) based on molecular data. *Insect Syst. Evol.* 39(4):407–417
85. Sanchez JA, Gillespie DR, Gillespie RR. 2004. Plant preference in relation to life history traits in the zoophytophagous predator *Dicyphus hesperus*. *Entomol. Exp. Appl.* 112:7–19
86. Schafner J, Schwartz MD. 2008. Revision of the Mexican genera *Ficinus* Distant and *Jornandes* Distant with the description of 21 new species (Heteroptera: Miridae: Orthotylinae: Orthotylini). *Bull. Am. Mus. Nat. Hist.* 309:1–87
87. Schmitz G. 1968. Monographie des especes africaines du genre *Helopeltis* Signoret (Heteroptera, Miridae). *Ann. Mus. R. Afr. Cent. Ser. 8 Zool.* 168:1–247
88. Schuh RT. 1974. The Orthotylinae and Phylinae (Hemiptera: Miridae) of South Africa with a phylogenetic analysis of the ant-mimetic tribes of the two subfamilies for the world. *Entomol. Am.* 47:1–332
89. Schuh RT. 1975. The structure, distribution, and taxonomic importance of trichobothria in the Miridae (Hemiptera). *Am. Mus. Novit.* 2585:1–26
90. Schuh RT. 1976. Pretarsal structure in the Miridae (Hemiptera) with a cladistic analysis of relationships within the family. *Am. Mus. Novit.* 2601:391–39
91. **Schuh RT. 1984. Revision of the Phylinae (Hemiptera, Miridae) of the Indo-Pacific. *Bull. Am. Mus. Nat. Hist.* 177(1):1–476**

91. Seminal monograph of a plant bug subfamily.

92. Schuh RT. 1989. Old World Pilophorini: descriptions of nine new species with additional synonymic and taxonomic changes (Heteroptera: Miridae: Phylinae). *Am. Mus. Novit.* 2945:1–16
93. Schuh RT. 1991. A phylogenetic host and biogeographic analysis of the Pilophorini (Heteroptera: Miridae: Phylinae). *Cladistics* 7:157–89
94. **Schuh RT. 1995. *Plant Bugs of the World (Insecta: Heteroptera: Miridae). Systematic Catalog, Distributions, Host List, and Bibliography.* New York: New York Entomol. Soc. 1329 pp.**

94. Universally accepted modern classification and catalog of plant bugs.

95. Schuh RT. 2000. Revision of *Oligotylus* Van Duzee with descriptions of ten new species from western North America and comments on *Lepidargyrus* in the Nearctic (Heteroptera: Miridae: Phylinae: Phylini). *Am. Mus. Novit.* 3300:1–44
96. Schuh RT. 2000. Revision of the North American plant bug genus *Megalopsallus* Knight, with the description of eight new species from the West (Heteroptera: Miridae: Phylinae). *Am. Mus. Novit.* 3305:1–69
97. Schuh RT. 2001. Revision of New World *Plagiognathus* Fieber, with comments on the Palearctic fauna and the description of a new genus (Heteroptera: Miridae: Phylinae). *Bull. Am. Mus. Nat. Hist.* 266:1–267
98. Schuh RT. 2004. Revision of *Europiella* in North America, with the description of a new genus (Heteroptera: Miridae: Phylinae). *Am. Mus. Novit.* 3463:1–58
99. Schuh RT. 2004. Revision of *Tuxedo* Schuh (Heteroptera: Miridae). *Am. Mus. Novit.* 3435:1–26
100. Schuh RT. 2006. Revision, phylogenetic, biogeographic, and host analysis of the endemic western North American *Phymatopsallus* group, with the description of 9 new genera and 15 new species (Insecta: Hemiptera: Miridae: Phylinae). *Am. Mus. Novit.* 301:1–115
101. Schuh RT. 2008. *On-line systematic catalog of plant bugs (Insecta: Heteroptera: Miridae).* **http://research.amnh.org/pbi/catalog/**
102. Schuh RT, Menard K. 2011. Santalalean-feeding plant bugs: 10 new species in the genus *Hypseloecus* Reuter from Australia and South Africa (Heteroptera: Miridae: Phylinae): their hosts and placement in the Pilophorini. *Aust. J. Entomol.* In press
103. Schuh RT, Pedraza P. 2010. *Wallabicoris*, new genus (Hemiptera: Miridae: Phylinae: Phylini) from Australia, with the description of 37 new species and an analysis of host associations. *Bull. Am. Mus. Nat. Hist.* 338:1–118
104. Schuh RT, Schwartz MD. 1984. *Carvalhoma* (Hemiptera: Miridae): new subfamily placement. *J. N. Y. Entomol. Soc.* 92:48–52
105. Schuh RT, Schwartz MD. 1988. A revision of the New World Pilophorini (Heteroptera: Miridae: Phylinae). *Bull. Am. Mus. Nat. Hist.* 187:101–201
106. Schuh RT, Schwartz MD. 2005. Review of North American *Chlamydatus* Curtis species, with new synonymy and the description of two new species (Heteroptera: Miridae: Phylinae). *Am. Mus. Novit.* 3471:1–55
107. Schuh RT, Slater JA. 1995. *True Bugs of the World (Hemiptera: Heteroptera). Classification and Natural History.* Ithaca, NY: Cornell Univ. Press. 336 pp.

108. Schuh RT, Štys P. 1991. Phylogenetic analysis of cimicomorphan family relationships (Heteroptera). *J. N.Y. Entomol. Soc.* 99:298–350

109. Schuh RT, Weirauch C. 2010. Myrtaceae-feeding Phylinae (Hemiptera: Miridae) from Australia: description and analysis of phylogenetic and host relationships for a monophyletic assemblage of three genera. *Bull. Am. Mus. Nat. Hist.* 344:1–95

110. Schuh RT, Weirauch C, Wheeler WC. 2009. Phylogenetic relationships within the Cimicomorpha (Hemiptera: Heteroptera): a total-evidence analysis. *Syst. Entomol.* 34:15–48

111. Schwartz MD. 1984. A revision of the black grass bug genus *Irbisia* Reuter (Heteroptera: Miridae). *J. N. Y. Entomol. Soc.* 92:193–306

112. Schwartz MD. 1987. *Phylogenetic revision of the Stenodemini with a review of the Mirinae (Heteroptera: Miridae)*. PhD diss. City University of New York. 383 pp.

113. Schwartz MD. 2008. Revision of the Stenodemini with a review of the included genera (Hemiptera: Heteroptera: Miridae: Mirinae). *Proc. Entomol. Soc. Wash.* 110:1111–201

113. Provides a phylogenetically based reclassification of a plant bug tribe and subfamilial commentary.

114. Schwartz MD. 2011. Revision and phylogenetic analysis of the North American genus *Slaterocoris* Wagner with new synonymy, the description of five new species and a new genus from Mexico, and a review of the genus *Scalponotatus* Kelton (Heteroptera: Miridae: Orthotylinae). *Bull. Am. Mus. Nat. Hist.* 354:1–290

115. Schwartz MD, Foottit RG. 1992. *Lygus* bugs of the prairies. Biology, systematics, and distribution. *Agric. Can. Tech. Bull.* 1992:1–44

116. Schwartz MD, Foottit RG. 1998. Revision of the Nearctic species of *Lygus* Hahn, with a review of the Palearctic species (Heteroptera: Miridae). *Mem. Entomol. Inst.* 10:1–428

117. Schwartz MD, Schuh RT. 1990. The world's largest isometopine, *Gigantometopus rossi* new genus and new species (Heteroptera: Miridae). *J. N. Y. Entomol. Soc.* 98:9–13

118. Schwartz MD, Schuh RT. 1999. New genera and species of conifer-inhabiting phylinae plant bugs from North America (Heteroptera: Miridae). *J. N. Y. Entomol. Soc.* 107:204–37

119. Singh-Pruthi H. 1925. The morphology of the male genitalia of the Rhynchota. *Trans. Entomol. Soc. Lond.* 1925:127–254

120. Slater JA. 1950. An investigation of the female genitalia as taxonomic characters in the Miridae (Hemiptera). *Iowa St. Coll. J. Sci.* 25:1–81

120. A critical comparative study of female genitalia and classificatory significance.

121. Stevens PF. 2008. *Angiosperm Phylogeny Website*. Version 9. **http://www.mobot.org/MOBOT/research/APweb/**

122. Stonedahl GM. 1988. Revision of the mirine genus *Phytocoris* Fallén (Heteroptera: Miridae) for western North America. *Bull. Am. Mus. Nat. Hist.* 188:1–257

122. Groundbreaking review of the most diverse plant bug genus.

123. Stonedahl GM. 1988. Revisions of *Dioclerus*, *Harpedona*, *Mertila*, *Myiocapsus*, *Prodromus* and *Thaumastomiris* (Heteroptera: Miridae, Bryocorinae: Eccritotarsini). *Bull. Am. Mus. Nat. Hist.* 187:1–99

124. Stonedahl GM. 1990. Revision and cladistic analysis of the Holarctic genus *Atractotomus* Fieber (Heteroptera: Miridae: Phylinae). *Bull. Am. Mus. Nat. Hist.* 198:1–88

125. Stonedahl GM. 1991. The Oriental species of *Helopeltis* (Heteroptera: Miridae): a review of economic literature and guide to identification. *Bull. Entomol. Res.* 81:465–90

126. Stonedahl GM, Cassis G. 1991. Revision and cladistic analysis of the plant bug genus *Fingulus* Distant (Heteroptera: Miridae: Deraeocorinae). *Am. Mus. Novit.* 3028:1–55

127. Stonedahl GM, Schwartz MD. 1986. Revision of the plant bug genus *Pseudopsallus* Van Duzee (Heteroptera: Miridae). *Am. Mus. Novit.* 2842:1–58

128. Štys P, Kerzhner I. 1975. The rank and nomenclature of higher taxa in recent Heteroptera. *Acta Entomol. Bohem.* 72:65–79

129. Tatarnic NJ. 2009. *Dampierella* and *Goodeniaphila*: two new genera and three new species of Halticini from Australia, with a species key to the Halticini of Australia (Hemiptera: Heteroptera: Miridae: Orthotylinae). *Zootaxa* 2105:43–60

130. Tatarnic NJ, Cassis G. 2008. Revision of the plant bug genus *Coridromius* Signoret (Insecta: Heteroptera: Miridae). *Bull. Am. Mus. Nat. Hist.* 315:1–95

131. Tatarnic NJ, Cassis G. 2010. Sexual coevolution in the traumatically inseminating plant bug genus *Coridromius*. *J. Evol. Biol.* 23:1321–26

132. Tatarnic NJ, Cassis G. 2011. The Halticini of the world (Insecta: Heteroptera: Miridae: Orthotylinae): generic reclassification, phylogeny and host plant associations. *Zool. J. Linn. Soc.* In press

133. Tatarnic NJ, Cassis G, Hochuli DF. 2005. Traumatic insemination in the plant bug genus *Coridromius* Signoret (Heteroptera: Miridae). *Biol. Lett.* 2:58–61

134. Tian Y, Zhu W, Li M, Xie Q, Bu W. 2008. Influence of data conflict and molecular phylogeny of major clades in cimicomorphan true bugs (Insecta: Hemiptera: Heteroptera). *Mol. Phylogenet. Evol.* 47:581–97

135. Van Duzee EP. 1916. *Check List of the Hemiptera (Excepting Aphididae, Aleurodidae, Coccidae) of America North of Mexico*. New York: New York Entomol. Soc. 111 pp.

136. Van Duzee EP. 1917. Catalogue of the Hemiptera of America north of Mexico (excepting the Aphididae, Coccidae, and Aleurodidae). *Univ. Calif. Publ. Entomol., Tech. Bull.* 2. 902 pp.

137. Wagner E. 1974. Die Miridae Hahn, 1831, des Mittelmeerraumes und der Makaronesischen Inseln (Hemiptera, Heteroptera). Teil. 1. *Entomol. Abhandl.* Suppl. 37. 484 pp.

138. Wagner E. 1974. Die Miridae Hahn, 1831, des Mittelmeerraumes und der Makaronesischen Inseln (Hemiptera, Heteroptera). Teil 2. *Entomol. Abhandl.* Suppl. 39. 421 pp.

139. Wagner E. 1975. Die Miridae Hahn, 183l, des Mittelmeerraumes und der Makaronesischen Inseln (Hemiptera, Heteroptera). Teil 3. *Entomol. Abhandl.* Suppl. 40. 483 pp.

140. Wall M. 2007. A new genus and new species of Austro-Papuan Orthotylinae (Heteroptera: Miridae). *Am. Mus. Novit.* 3358:1–30

141. Weirauch C. 2006. New genera and species of oak-associated Phylini (Heteroptera: Miridae: Phylinae) from western North America. *Am. Mus. Novit.* 3522:1–54

142. Weirauch C. 2007. Revision and cladistic analysis of the *Polyozus* group of Australian Phylini (Heteroptera: Miridae: Phylinae). *Am. Mus. Novit.* 3590:1–60

143. Weirauch C, Schuh RT. 2011. Southern hemisphere distributional patterns in plants bugs (Hemiptera: Miridae: Phylinae): *Xiphoidellus*, gen. nov. from Australia, and *Ampimpacoris*, gen. nov. from Argentina, show transantarctic relationships. *Invertebr. Syst.* 24:473–508

144. Wheeler AG Jr. 2000. Plant bugs (Miridae) as plant pests. In *Heteroptera of Economic Importance*, ed. CW Schaefer, AR Panizzi, pp. 37–83. Boca Raton, FL: CRC Press

145. Wheeler AG Jr. 2000. Predacious plant bugs (Miridae). In *Heteroptera of Economic Importance*, ed. CW Schaefer, AR Panizzi, pp. 657–93. Boca Raton, FL: CRC Press

146. A seminal review of plant bug biology.

146. Wheeler AG Jr. 2001. *Biology of the Plant Bugs (Hemiptera: Miridae). Pests, Predators, Opportunists.* Ithaca, NY: Cornell Univ. Press. 507 pp.

147. Wyniger D. 2010. Resurrection of the Pronotocrepini, with revisions of the Nearctic genera *Orectoderus* Uhler, *Pronotocrepis* Knight, and *Teleorhinus* Uler, and comments on the Palearctic *Ethelastia* Reuter (Heteroptera: Miridae: Phylinae). *Am. Mus. Novit.* 3703:1–67

148. Yang C-T, Chang T-Y. 2000. *The External Male Genitalia of Hemiptera (Homoptera-Heteroptera)*. Taichung, Taiwan: Shih Way Publ. 746 pp.

149. Yasunaga T. 1999. First record of the plant bug subfamily Psallopinae (Heteroptera: Miridae) from Japan, with descriptions of three new species of the genus *Psallops* Usinger. *Proc. Entomol. Soc. Wash.* 101:737–41

150. Yasunaga T. 1999. The plant bug tribe Orthotylini in Japan (Heteroptera: Miridae: Orthotylinae). *Tidjschr. Entomol.* 142:143–83

151. Yasunaga T. 2000. The mirid subfamily Cylapinae (Heteroptera: Miridae) or fungal inhabiting plant bugs in Japan. *Tidjschr. Entomol.* 143:183–209

152. Yasunaga T, Yamada, Artchawakom KT. 2010. First record of the plant bug subfamily Psallopinae (Heteroptera: Miridae) from Thailand, with descriptions of new species and immature forms. *Tijdschr. Entomol.* 151(1):91–98

Essential Oils in Insect Control: Low-Risk Products in a High-Stakes World

Catherine Regnault-Roger,[1] Charles Vincent,[2,*] and John Thor Arnason[3]

[1]UMR CNRS UPPA 5254 IPREM-EEM, Université de Pau et des Pays de l'Adour, F64000 Pau, France; email: catherine.regnault-roger@univ-pau.fr

[2]Centre de Recherche et de Développement en Horticulture, Agriculture et Agroalimentaire Canada, Saint-Jean-sur-Richelieu, Quebec J3B 3E6, Canada; email: charles.vincent@agr.gc.ca

[3]Faculty of Science, University of Ottawa, Ottawa, Ontario K1N 6N5, Canada; email: John.Arnason@uOttawa.ca

Annu. Rev. Entomol. 2012. 57:405–24

First published online as a Review in Advance on September 19, 2011

The *Annual Review of Entomology* is online at ento.annualreviews.org

This article's doi:
10.1146/annurev-ento-120710-100554

0066-4170/12/0107-0405$20.00

*Corresponding author

Keywords

biopesticide, botanical, terpenes, phenolics, repellent, fumigant

Abstract

In recent years, the use of essential oils (EOs) derived from aromatic plants as low-risk insecticides has increased considerably owing to their popularity with organic growers and environmentally conscious consumers. EOs are easily produced by steam distillation of plant material and contain many volatile, low-molecular-weight terpenes and phenolics. The major plant families from which EOs are extracted include Myrtaceae, Lauraceae, Lamiaceae, and Asteraceae. EOs have repellent, insecticidal, and growth-reducing effects on a variety of insects. They have been used effectively to control preharvest and postharvest phytophagous insects and as insect repellents for biting flies and for home and garden insects. The compounds exert their activities on insects through neurotoxic effects involving several mechanisms, notably through GABA, octopamine synapses, and the inhibition of acetylcholinesterase. With a few exceptions, their mammalian toxicity is low and environmental persistence is short. Registration has been the main bottleneck in putting new products on the market, but more EOs have been approved for use in the United States than elsewhere owing to reduced-risk processes for these materials.

INTRODUCTION

Repellent: a compound applied to skin, clothing, or other substrates that decreases normal contact time of arthropods with the treated surface

Steam distillation: a type of distillation in which water is added to the distillation mixture, to allow volatile aromatic compounds to be distilled with water vapor at temperatures that avoid degradation

Risks associated with the use of synthetic insecticides have led to the growth of an environmental movement seeking sustainable alternatives in pest control. Evidence of this includes the growth of organic agriculture products that are now found in mainstream supermarkets and the banning of ornamental use of synthetic pesticides in many local jurisdictions (22). Among the alternatives for pest control, biopesticides had a global market value of approximately US$1 billion in 2010. This market is expected to grow to US$3.3 billion in 2014 (63). Biopesticides encompass a large number of technologies, from microbials to botanicals. Among the botanicals, essential oils (EOs) are a major category that began to develop with research in the 1980s (90). They are derived from aromatic plants that, in the course of evolution, developed myriad constitutive and induced chemical defenses against herbivorous insects (117). The EO market has had the strongest growth of all the botanical pesticide markets in recent years. Safety and regulatory issues have played a role in this growth. Their widespread use as herbal medicines in Europe, Japan, and North America has increased confidence in their safety. However, EOs, like many natural products, are not always subject to rigorous testing or formal registration (113).

EOs have many industrial applications: perfumery, cosmetics, detergents, pharmacology, fine chemistry, and food production products. As a result, overlapping markets sometimes add important scientific information but also complicate their interpretation for the biopesticide area. Although EOs have a promising future within the biopesticide market, progress on registration must be achieved before EOs occupy a significant market share of global pesticide markets.

Among key reviews on EOs, some are general (26, 61), whereas others focus on microorganisms (17, 29, 52), cellular biological activities (7), or insects (5, 46, 48, 50, 51, 90, 92). We provide a critical treatment of EOs as insecticides. After defining them and discussing their main chemical components and properties, we focus on their bioactivities relevant to insect management in medical and agricultural contexts from a sustainable development perspective. Registration considerations in both North America and Europe, which enforce the largest and most rigorous legislation about plant protection products, are addressed because they are a key constraint on marketing EOs as insecticides or repellents.

PHYTOCHEMISTRY OF ESSENTIAL OILS

Plant EOs have been used since antiquity, but the first written description of distillation dates from the thirteenth century by Ibn al-Baitar in Andalusia, Spain (9), after which they were included in the pharmacopeias of European countries (17). EOs are defined as the products obtained from hydrodistillation, steam distillation, dry distillation, or mechanical cold pressing of plants (35). The classical preparation method is based on the Clevenger steam distillation apparatus developed in 1928. Today this method has been adapted and scaled up for industrial production. Steam distillation requires large containers because of the low (generally <1%) yield from biomass and is costly because of high temperatures needed for distillation. Citrus peel is an exception because large quantities of oils can be obtained cheaply by cold pressing and conventional distillation. Modern methods of extraction include microwave-assisted process and supercritical fluid extraction (18, 100), which may have great advantages such as lower oxidation of compounds, a feature especially useful for flower fragrances. However, these methods require some cleanup by fractionation because higher-molecular-weight lipids are also extracted. The advantage of the original steam distillation process is that it separates a relatively clean secondary metabolite fraction from plants, including mainly low-molecular-weight volatile phytochemicals, chiefly of terpene and phenolic origin, while excluding most primary metabolites and high-molecular-weight secondary compounds, which have highly variable structures and modes of action. Chiasson et al. (18) compared three EO extraction methods, microwave-assisted process, supercritical fluid extraction, and steam distillation, on two aromatic plants and found that the three methods did not produce the same products.

EOs are produced in 17,500 aromatic species of higher plants belonging mostly to a few families, including the Myrtaceae, Lauraceae, Lamiaceae, and Asteraceae. The synthesis and accumulation of EOs are associated with the presence of complex secretory structures such as glandular trichomes (Lamiaceae), secretory cavities (Myrtaceae, Rutaceae), and resin ducts (Asteraceae, Apiaceae) (101). Depending on the species considered, EOs are stored in various plant organs, e.g., flowers (bergamot orange, *Citrus bergamia*), leaves (lemon grass, *Citronella* spp.; eucalyptus, *Eucalyptus* spp.), wood (sandalwood, *Santalum* spp.), roots (vetiver grass, *Chrysopogon zizanioides*), rhizomes (ginger, *Zingiber officinale*; turmeric, *Curcuma longa*), fruits (anise, *Pimpinella anisum*), and seeds (nutmeg, *Myristica fragrans*).

EO constituents belong mainly to two phytochemical groups: terpenoids (monoterpenes and sesquiterpenes of low molecular weight) and, to a lesser extent, phenylpropanoids. Terpenoids are major constituents of EOs. Monoterpenes are biosynthesized via the methyl erythritol phosphate pathway in plastids, which yields the 5-carbon precursors isopentenyl pyrophosphate and dimethylallyl pyrophosphate, which condense via geranyl pyrophosphate synthase to give the monoterpenes (10-carbon) (13). Although isopentenyl pyrophosphate can transfer between compartments, the monoterpenes and diterpenes tend to be formed in the plastid, where unique cyclases yield the fenchane, bornane, camphane, thujone, and pinane ring structures (13). The sesquiterpenes (15-carbon) are formed via the mevalonate pathway in the cytosol. Monoterpenes present in EOs may contain terpenes that are hydrocarbons (α-pinene), alcohols (menthol, geraniol, linalool, terpinen-4-ol, *p*-menthane-3,8-diol), aldehydes (cinnamaldehyde, cuminaldehyde), ketones (thujone), ethers [1,8-cineole (=eucalyptol)], and lactones (nepetalactone) (**Figure 1**). Sesquiterpenes have a wide variety of structures, more than 100 skeletons, as the elongation of the chain to 15 carbons increases the number of possible cyclizations.

Aromatic compounds are less common and are derived mainly from the shikimate pathway, for example, the phenylpropanoid dillapiole (**Figure 1**), but a few phenols, such as carvacrol and cuminaldehyde (**Figure 1**), are a rare group derived from terpene biosynthesis by desaturation. Products of nonvolatile compounds, e.g., compounds derived from fatty acids (jasmonic acid) or glycosides of volatiles (e.g., linalool glucoside), are also identified in EOs (15).

EO composition is highly diverse across different plant species (92). For example, 1,8-cineole is the major constituent of the EO of eucalyptus (*Eucalyptus globulus*), whereas linalool is abundant in coriander (*Coriandrum sativum*). Within the same plant species, chemotypes are very common. For example, thyme (*Thymus vulgaris*) has numerous chemotypes named according to the major compound, e.g., thymol, carvacrol, terpineol, and linalool. A typical EO may contain 20 to 80 phytochemicals.

Physiological expression of secondary metabolism of the plant may be different at all stages of its development. The proportions of monoterpenes depend on temperature and circadian rhythm (42, 88) and vary according to plant stage (23). For example, Gershenzon et al. (39) showed that limonene and menthone are the major monoterpenes present in the youngest leaves of peppermint, but limonene content declines rapidly with development, whereas menthone increases and then declines at later stages as menthol becomes the dominant constituent. Soil acidity and climate (heat, photoperiod, humidity) directly affect the secondary metabolism of the plant (71) and EO composition.

Production of a standardized product, which is important for regulatory and marketing purposes, is a challenge. For example, rosemary oil extracted from plants harvested in two different

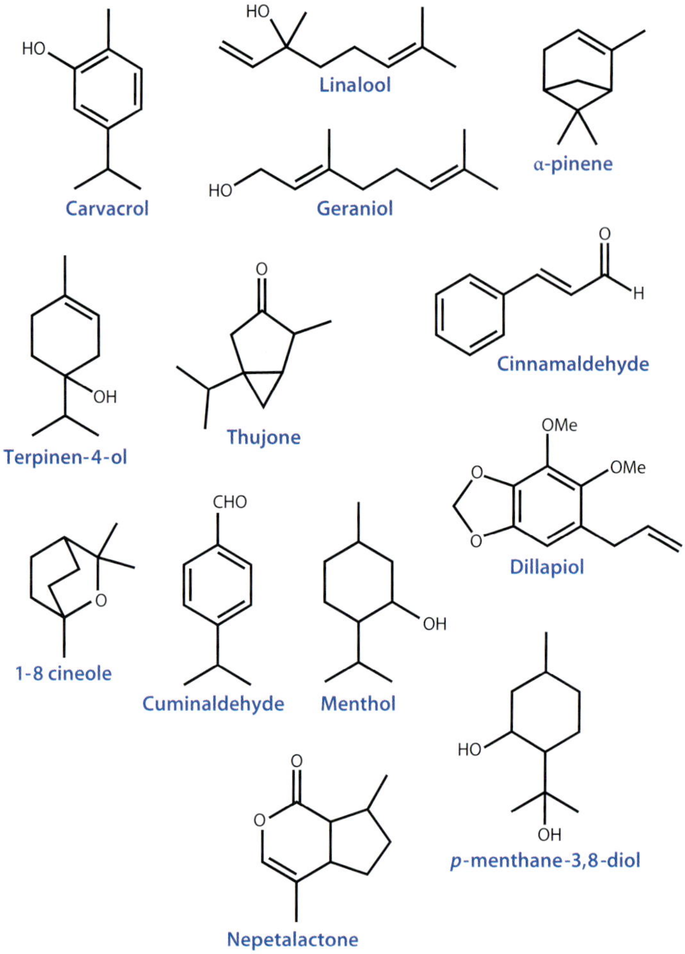

Figure 1

Representative constituents of essential oils. Stereochemistry not presented.

areas of Italy contained 1,8-cineole concentrations ranging from 7% to 55% and α-pinene concentrations ranging from 11% to 36% (51). This variability has important consequences on the biological activity of this EO. Regnault-Roger et al. (96) noted that EOs extracted from different chemotypes of *T. vulgaris* did not have the same toxicity against the bruchid *Acanthoscelides obtectus*. Industrial exploitation of an EO must establish a number of parameters related to good agriculture practices for the cultivation of the plants (e.g., genotypes, selection and orientation of plots and practices, harvest time, conditions and technical parameters, and extraction) in order to minimize the heterogeneity of EOs. After harvest, good manufacturing processes are required to ensure a consistent and ethical product. Good agriculture practices and good manufacturing processes have been achieved for a number of EO crops.

Analysis of EO products is a fairly well-established procedure, but some recent innovations have been introduced (103). Typically, analysis can be achieved by capillary gas chromatography (GC) (**Figure 2**) on a carbowax column with a combination of flame ionization or mass spectrometry (MS) detection. Compounds are identified by the Kovats retention index, analysis of

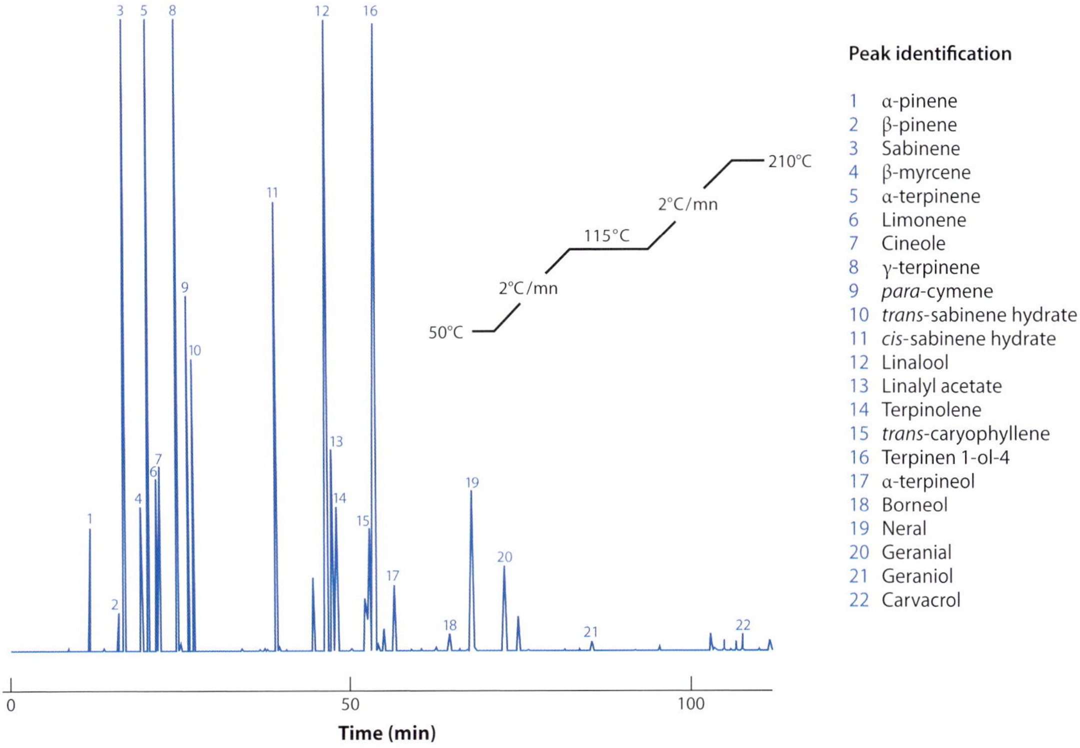

Figure 2

Gas liquid chromatography analysis of *Origanum majorana* essential oil. Reproduced from Reference 96, with kind permission from Springer Science+Business Media B.V.

MS spectra, or comparisons to standards. Today, fast-GC can improve run time to 10 min, and quadruple MS or time-of-flight MS can record reliable spectra rapidly and facilitate identification of constituents. Enantiomer-selective GC has been made possible by a second dimension in separation on cyclodextrin derivatives and can provide separation of isomers such as *R*(−) and *S*(+) 10:linalool in lavender. Advanced statistical software available with modern analytical instruments allows EO chemotypes to be classified by principal components or discriminant analysis and rapid assignment of new samples to proper chemotype (103).

MAIN USES

Target Arthropods

A literature search encompassing the past 40 years with the keywords EOs and insects yielded no less than 2,000 scientific papers. Representative lists of EOs have been published by Bakkali et al. (7) and Sosa & Tonn (110). Most papers document the immediate effects (acute toxicity or repellency) of given EOs on a number of arthropod taxa, frequently on the basis of assays lasting less than 48 h. Papers with similar approaches demonstrated effects across a wide range of taxa or species.

EOs and their constituents exert insecticidal effects or reduce and disrupt insect growth at several life stages (58, 93, 118). Phytochemical profiles of 22 EOs were determined, and the bioactivity of each of their major constituents was studied on different insects (96). Eugenol, abundant in cloves (*Eugenia caryophyllata*), or cinnamaldehyde, abundant in cinnamon (*Cinnamomum verum*), exerts ovicidal, larvicidal, and adulticidal toxicity on the bean weevil, *A. obtectus*, and inhibits its reproduction. Toxicity levels of EOs to the Mediterranean fruit fly, *Ceratitis capitata*, and the cereal aphids *Rhopalosiphum padi* and *Metopolophium dirrhodum* have been determined (41, 95).

The efficacy of EOs and their constituents varies according to the phytochemical profile of the plant extract and the entomological target. The bruchid *A. obtectus* is more sensitive to phenolic monoterpenes and the aphid *R. padi* to methoxylated monoterpenes, whereas *C. capitata* flies respond to both types of compounds (91). EOs such as oil of thyme, rosemary (*Rosmarinus officinalis*), and eucalyptus have antifeedant (94) or repellent activity (111). The oil of citronella (*Cymbopogon nardus*) repels mosquitoes and flies, and garlic (*Allium sativum*) oil is a deterrent to many insect herbivores (90). These are currently marketed to horticulturists, greenhouses, and home gardens in the United States and the United Kingdom (24).

EOs have several characteristics that improve their efficacy as insecticides. They are both phytochemically diverse (containing many biosynthetically different compounds) and redundant (containing many analogs of one class). Phytochemical analogs of pure piperamides from extracted pepper oils increased in toxicity to house flies and mosquito larvae as they were evaluated singly and in binary, ternary, and quaternary mixtures while holding the total concentration the same (70, 105). Mixtures of plant compounds reduce the evolution of tolerance to natural insecticides, compared to a single compound, as exemplified with the green peach aphid, *Myzus persicae* (37).

EOs from aromatic plants have been assayed to address several crop protection problems in pre- and postharvest situations, as seen in the following early studies. For the protection of stored products, the toxicity of EOs of patchouli (*Pogostemon* spp.) and of sweet basil (*Ocimum basilicum*) to the coleopterans *Sitophilus oryzae* (rice weevil), *Stegobium paniceum* (drugstore beetle), *Tribolium castaneum* (red flour beetle), and *Bruchus chinensis* (pulse beetle) (27, 28) and EOs of *Eucalyptus* or thyme to the lesser grain borer (*Rhyzopertha dominica* (60, 112) were determined. A wide range of flying insects, e.g., *S. oryzae*, *Musca domestica* (house fly) (3), *M. persicae*, *Trialeurodes vaporariorum* (greenhouse whitefly), and *Stephanitis pyri* (pear bug) (67), are affected by *Gaultheria* spp. or *Eucalyptus* spp. EOs.

Recent papers further demonstrate the wide range of insect taxa that are affected by EOs. In screening assays for fumigant activity of EOs and compounds extracted from 21 plant species from 12 plant families against the sciarid fly *Lycoriella ingenua*, Park et al. (79) found that good larvicidal activity was achieved with EOs of *Acorus gramineus*, *Schizonepeta tenuifolia*, and *Zanthoxylum piperitum* at 25 $\mu g\ ml^{-1}$ air. GC-MS of *S. tenuifolia* oil revealed the presence of three major compounds, pulegone, menthone, and limonene, which had LC_{50} values of 1.21, 6.03, and 15.42 $\mu g\ ml^{-1}$, respectively. As a comparison, the LC_{50} value of dichlorvos was 8.13 $\mu g\ ml^{-1}$. In an another study, Park et al. (78) performed fumigant bioassays of an additional 40 plant species to determine their larvicidal activity against *L. ingenua.* The best fumigant activities were obtained with EOs of horseradish (*Armorica rusticana*), anise (*P. anisum*), and garlic oils. Papachristos et al. (77) corroborated the EOs toxicity already observed on *C. capitata.* They experimented with EOs of citrus peel, in which limonene is the most abundant ingredient, and larvae were administered diets in which the LC_{50} values of limonene ranged from 7 to 11 $ml\ g^{-1}$. Liu et al. (65) extended the work of Shaaya et al. (108) on the toxicity of EOs to four major stored-product insects: *T. castaneum*, *Sitophilus zeamais* (maize weevil), *R. dominica*, and *Oryzaephilus surinamensis* (sawtoothed grain beetle). They found that EOs of *Ostericum sieboldii* flowers possess strong insecticidal activity against *T. castaneum* and *S. zeamais*, with LC_{50} values of 27.4 and 20.9 mg liter^{-1} air, respectively. In that case, EOs of *O. sieboldii* flowers were myristicin (30.3%), α-terpineol (9.9%), α-cadinol (7.3%), β-farnesene (6.3%), and linalool (5.9%).

Deterrent and fumigant activities of EOs extracted from the leaf and bark of *Laurelia sempervirens* and *Drimys winteri* were assessed on the pea aphid, *Acyrthosiphon pisum* (120). Applied as a fumigant, *L. sempervirens* EOs exerted a strong and rapid impairment of the insect's settling behavior, whereas *D. winteri* EO did not. This property, as well as the aphicidal activity of *L. sempervirens* EO, is promising not only to manage aphid populations, but also to reduce the spread of plant viruses in enclosed spaces such as greenhouses or plastic tunnels. As a complement to previous studies conducted with patchouli oil, Zhu et al. (122) conducted a series of experiments to assess the repellency and toxicity of patchouli oil and its main constituent, patchouli alcohol, against the Formosan subterranean termite, *Coptotermes formosanus*. They demonstrated repellency and that paper filters treated with patchouli oil were less consumed by worker termites.

The effects of EOs on many other arthropods are poorly documented; however, a notable exception is the acaricidal activity of *Chenopodium ambrosioides* var. *ambrosioides* against adult mites *Tetranychus urticae* and *Panonychus ulmi* (21).

Modes of Action

EOs are good penetrants that increase their own bioavailability and that of coadministered products. A considerable literature on penetrants is derived from the pharmacognosy literature (1). These properties are related to the disruption of lipid bilayers in cells.

Some EOs have specific modes of action that make them good synergists. In particular, a number of compounds are well-established inhibitors of insect P450 cytochromes responsible for phase I metabolism of xenobiotics, including insecticides. These include phytochemicals containing methylene dioxy rings such as dillapiole in dill oil (*Anthema sowa*), piperamides from *Piper* spp. oils, and furanocoumarins from oil of bergamot (*C. bergamia*). Dillapiole and semisynthetic derivatives have a synergism factor of two- to sixfold when combined with botanical insecticides (11), but piperamides have a remarkable synergism factor of 11 when combined with pyrethrin (53) and they have profound effects on the cytochrome P450 transcriptome of treated insects.

Acyclic or monocyclic monoterpenes are small-volatile molecules. They are therefore involved in the transmission of airborne signals from plants to insects. In the sensilla of insects, specialized odorant binding proteins (OBPs) respond to volatile monoterpenes. For example, trichoid sensilla of the female silkworm, *Bombyx mori*, respond to linalool (83).

Detection of bouquets of fragrant and chemosensory-active compounds by insects involves different families of proteins, including OBPs and chemosensory proteins (CSPs). OBPs and CSPs are found on the periphery of the sensory receptors and function in the capture and transport of molecular stimuli (82). In moths, the OBPs include proteins that bind general odorants (GOBPs, general odorant binding proteins) such as volatile compounds from plants. GOBPs have polypeptide chains consisting of 146 and 129 amino acids, including six cysteines in characteristic positions (115, 116). The protein identified in tobacco hornworm, *Manduca sexta*, GOBP2, preferentially interacts with floral aromas and green plant odors such as (Z)-3-hexen-1-ol, geraniol, geranyl acetate, and limonene (36). The different types of GOBPs therefore serve to detect the different categories of odorants released by plants. Two-choice assays showed that both innate and learned behaviors play important roles in attraction to individual volatile components of a floral blend (25). They altered the oviposition of native versus experienced females on nonhost plants (64, 121). The use of volatile plant allelochemicals and EOs in plant protection may be more effective with a better understanding of these mechanisms.

Several monoterpenes contained in EOs are neurotoxic to insects. Huignard et al. (45) describe several different types of receptors, including GABA-gated neurons, that are target sites of the compounds. Thymol binds to GABA receptors associated with chloride channels located on the membrane of postsynaptic neurons and disrupts the functioning of GABA synapses (86). Eugenol acts through the octopaminergic system by activating receptors for octopamine, which is a neuromodulator (32). Low doses of eugenol and octopamine lead to an increase in adenyl cyclase activity of cells in the nervous system of the cockroach *Periplaneta americana*, whereas high doses of eugenol reduce the production of cyclic AMP (cAMP). Increasing the concentration of cAMP induced by octopamine was inhibited in the presence of a mixture of eugenol, α-terpineol, and cinnamic alcohol (31). Further studies on cultured cells of *P. americana* and brains of *Drosophila melanogaster* demonstrated that eugenol mimics the action of octopamine and increases intracellular calcium levels (33). The role of the octopaminergic system in the cytotoxicity of EOs was also demonstrated in cultures of epidermal cells of *Helicoverpa armigera* (59). Tyramine (a precursor of octopamine) receptors are also involved in the recognition of monoterpenes such as thymol, carvacrol, and α-terpineol in *D. melanogaster* (32). These monoterpenes influence the production of cAMP and calcium at the cellular level.

Octopamine: a neurotransmitter analogous to the vertebrate noradrenaline

From electrophysiological experiments, Price & Berry (85) showed that eugenol nearly inhibits neuronal activity, whereas citral and geraniol have a biphasic effect that is dose dependent. At low doses, citral and geraniol induce an increase in spontaneous electrical activity and at high doses cause a decrease. Using the same electrophysiological techniques, Huignard et al. (45) observed that the EO of *O. basilicum* inhibited neuronal electrical activity by decreasing the amplitude of action potentials and reducing both the posthyperpolarization phase and firing frequency of action potentials. This effect, they explained, was the result of the combined action of two major components of the EO of *O. basilicum*, linalool and estragole. The application of pure linalool produces a reduction in the amplitude of action potential and causes a decrease in posthyperpolarization. Estragole specifically induces a reduction of posthyperpolarization.

A number of monoterpenes also act on acetylcholinesterase. Terpinen-4-ol and 1,8-cineole, found in EOs of *E. globulus*, *Laurus nobilis*, and *Origanum majorana* (96), inhibit acetylcholinesterase (68). A comparative in vitro study demonstrated that fenchone, *S*-carvone, and linalool produce the highest inhibition. Several types of inhibition are involved. Fenchone, γ-terpinene, geraniol, and linalool showed a reversible competitive inhibition occupying the hydrophobic site of the enzyme's active site. *S*-carvone, estragole, and camphor produced a mixed inhibition for this enzyme binding either to free enzyme or to the enzyme-substrate complex but linking to a different site from the active site where the substrate binds (66). These studies confirm that the insecticidal activity of monoterpene content in EOs is due to several mechanisms that affect multiple targets, thereby disrupting more effectively cellular activity and biological processes of insects.

Main Uses of Oils as Insecticides or Repellents in Plant Protection and Health

To paraphrase the title of Isman's (49) paper on botanical insecticides, the use of EOs can be divided in two: for richer and for poorer. In developing countries, aromatic plants were widely used for stored-product insects in traditional agricultural systems. Currently, there is a move to replace these plants with the steam-distilled EOs. Unfortunately, few of these products have been rigorously registered owing to lack of resources and weak regulatory systems. The flora of many developing countries is remarkably diverse and can be a rich source of potent and valuable EOs. However, results needed for risk analysis are variable or elusive and are often unsupported by scientific experimentation. As a result, the potential of numerous EOs remains untapped. In developed countries, strict regulations prevail and further tightening of these regulations is likely, providing a good level of risk analysis leading to ethical EO products that have been successfully registered.

Much remains to be done to bridge the gap between unsubstantiated traditional use and experimentally substantiated potential, but some studies have taken this approach. On the basis of reports from ancient China, Jiang et al. (54) assessed the contact toxicity (LD_{50}) of *Litsea pungens* and *L. cubeba* blends and found that both oils have moderate larvicidal activity against *Trichoplusia ni*. In Africa, EOs have traditionally been used by small farmers to protect stored grains from insect pests. Inspired by the traditional practices in Guinea, extracts of four West African plant species, *Tagetes minuta*, *Hyptis suaveolens*, *Ocimum canum*, and *O. basilicum*, were assayed against adults of the bruchid *Callosobruchus maculatus* as protectants for stored cowpeas (56). Among the EOs tested, both *Ocimum* species exerted maximal effects on adults by fumigation and on eggs by contact. Phytochemical analysis of plant material has been completed to ensure reproducibility (57). Further experiments were done with extracts from sweet basil, *O. basilicum*, and African basil, *O. gratissimum*, obtained by steam distillation (55). Kaolin powder aromatized with 65 ml g^{-1} of *O. basilicum* and 116 ml g^{-1} of *O. gratissimum* oils provided 50% adult mortality after 48 h. The extracts also exerted ovicidal effects such that adequate protection was ensured for three months at doses of 400 mg in traditional storage facilities in Guinea. Both *O. basilicum* and *O. gratissimum* are abundant in Guinea and affordable to small farmers. Likewise, steam distillation is affordable to them by means of using a domestic pressure cooker. In both cases, as in several other situations, much more must be done to fully understand the mechanisms involved and to determine optimal parameters of use (e.g., dose, timing, and application technology) and safety of EOs, especially in humans, such that the use of traditional practices can be improved for safety and efficacy in developing countries on the basis of scientific knowledge.

FIFRA Section 25(b): minimum-risk, EPA-approved class of pesticides not subject to U.S. federal registration requirements because their ingredients, both active and inert, are demonstrably safe for their intended use

In developed countries, several EO are used in registered commercial formulations. Among these products, the most frequent are garlic, clove, cedar (*Juniperus virginiana*), peppermint (*Mentha piperita*), and rosemary oils. Several EOs are used in the United States in relatively closed spaces such as houses, as exemplified by the numerous formulations aimed at managing numerous arthropods, including flies, gnats, mosquitoes, moths, wasps, spiders, and centipedes (see **Supplemental Table 1**, follow the **Supplemental Material link** from the Annual Reviews home page at **http://www.annualreviews.org**).These formulations are based mainly on five EOs [rosemary, peppermint, thyme, sesame (*Sesamum indicum*), and cinnamon], which apparently confer optimal properties for given targets when mixed in various proportions (ranging from zero to 5%) with active ingredients from minimum-risk products [as deemed by Section 25(b) of FIFRA (Federal Insecticide, Fungicide, and Rodenticide Act)] such as 2-phenethyl propionate, D-limonene, geraniol, or sodium lauryl sulfate (a soap).

One of the most recently registered EO-based pesticides in the United States is Requiem®. Plants of the genus *Chenopodium*, notably the species *C. quinoa*, *C. album*, and *C. ambrosioides*, have traditionally been used in agriculture as food staples or as natural insecticides (87). From that simple observation, a collaborative project was initiated in 1993 between Codena Inc. and Agriculture and Agri-Food Canada at Saint-Jean-sur-Richelieu, Quebec, to develop and register a botanical insecticide. Extracts of some varieties were assayed and shown to have insecticidal properties against the western flower thrips (*Frankliniella occidentalis*), green peach aphid, and the greenhouse whitefly (*Trialeurodes vaporariorum*) (21), and acaricidal properties against the twospotted spider mite and the European red mite (*P. ulmi*) (19).

Essential Oils for Human Health

EOs offer untapped potential in medical entomology. They have been used experimentally as larvicides for the control of biting insects, especially mosquito larvae vectors of diseases. Despite a large research effort, especially in tropical countries (107), the commercial market for these products has not been developed. This may be due in part to the availability of other effective treatments with low environmental impact such as *Bacillus thuringiensis* var. *israelensis*, to an emphasis on adult control in some suppression programs, and to a general lack of funding for insect control in developing countries. In addition, efficacy is often marginal. Larvicidal concentrations for typical EOs are 49 mg liter^{-1} for *Thymus capitatus* against *Culex pipiens*, and 91.4 mg liter^{-1} for *Cymbopogon flexuosus* against *Anopheles stephensi*, which is well above the World Health Organization guideline of 1 mg liter^{-1} for larvicides. More active oils include *Acorus calamus* EO (larvicidal concentrations of 3.6 mg liter^{-1} against *Culex quinquefasciatus*) and many Neotropical *Piper* spp. with efficacy in the 1 mg liter^{-1} range against *Aedes atropalpus* (12). Development of these products requires extensive field efficacy testing and nontarget organism studies (107).

The major promising entomological uses for EOs in the human health arena are for repelling biting flies and ticks. Concerns over the use of *N,N*-diethyl-3-methylbenzamide (DEET) have led to the formulation of a large number of EO repellent products. By decreasing order of frequency, the most commonly used EOs are citronella, geranium (*Pelargonium* sp.), cedar, peppermint, rosemary, soybean (*Glycine max*), and eucalyptus (5). Oil of lemon eucalyptus (containing *p*-menthane-3,8-diol) has among the highest established efficacy under controlled assays and is recommended by the U.S. Center for Disease Control. A variety of other eucalyptus oils are reported to be very good repellents to mosquitoes (8), but they are attractive to other biting flies (10). However, oil of lemon eucalyptus or *p*-menthane-3,8-diol were listed as active ingredients in only four products of 88 U.S. products examined by Arnason et al. (5). Unfortunately many of these products suffer from a short period of efficacy compared to DEET, because they are volatile or quickly absorbed and are lost from the skin surface. An exception is catnip EO, which contains the highly oxygenated compound nepetalactone, which is heavier than water and has an efficacy up to 4 h against *Aedes* sp., when properly formulated, compared to 6 h for DEET (6). Although catnip oils are attractive to some species of felines, the attraction of domesticated cats has not been a problem so far. However, this product is definitely not recommended in cougar or puma (*Felis concolor*) country (e.g., the Rocky Mountains)!

TOXICOLOGY AND ENVIRONMENTAL IMPACT

Although the biological effects of individual chemical components of EOs are known, the toxicokinetics of their blends is much more difficult to evaluate. However, one of the most attractive features of EOs is that they are, in general, low-risk products. Their mammalian toxicity is low and they are relatively well-studied experimentally and clinically because of their use as medicinal products. The majority of EOs, including chamomile (*Chamaemelum nobile*), citronella, lavender (*Lavandula angustifolia*), clove, eucalyptus, anise, and marjoram (*Majorana hortensis*), have an oral LD_{50} value ranging from 2,000 to 5,000 mg kg^{-1} in rats. Less than a dozen EOs, e.g., basil, tarragon (*Artemisia dracunculus*), hyssop (*Hyssopus officinalis*), oregano (*Origanum vulgare*), savory (*Satureja hortensis*), tea-tree (*Melaleuca alternifolia*), and sassafras (*Sassafras albidum*), have LD_{50} values ranging from 1,000 to 2,000 mg kg^{-1}, but some are moderately toxic to very toxic. For example, EOs of Boldo (*Peumus boldus*), cedar, and Pennyroyal (a mixture of *Mentha pulegium* and *Hedeoma pulegiodes*) have LD_{50} values of 130, 830, and 400 mg kg^{-1}, respectively. In addition, the EO of Boldo can cause convulsions at a dose of 70 mg kg^{-1}.

Isolated constituents of EOs show similar toxicities. Very few constituents have an LD_{50} value less than 2,000 mg kg^{-1}, which suggests very low toxicity. Moderately toxic compounds include thujone (LD_{50} is 134 mg kg^{-1}), pulegone (470 mg kg^{-1}), carvacrol (810 mg kg^{-1}), carvone (1,640 mg kg^{-1}), and thymol (980 mg kg^{-1}) (15, 76), among others. Some constituents of EOs may be protoxins. For example, menthofuran, a component produced by the metabolism of pulegone (a major component of EO of pennyroyal), may cause hepatic and pulmonary toxicity (4).

The toxicity of EO components has been divided into three structural classes based on toxicological potential (72). Class I compounds with little functionality, such as the aliphatic compound limonene, have a low order of oral toxicity. Class II compounds with some functionality are intermediate. Class III compounds have a high potential toxicity owing to reactive functionality. For example, elemicin, which is an allyl-substituted benzene derivative with a reactive benzylic/allylic position, is assigned to Class III. These classes correlate to the NOEL (no observed effect limit) of the compounds. On the basis of this classification and other criteria, a procedure for assessing the safety of EOs has been developed (109).

Dermal toxicity was observed with some EOs or at least with monoterpenes included therein. For example, wintergreen (*Gaultheria procumbens*), eucalyptus, clove, and sage EOs are known for their irritancy (40). D-limonene itself produces further irritating transdermal absorption (75). Bergamot and angelica (*Angelica archangelica*) EOs cause photosensitivity (7). EOs such as tea-tree oil can cause skin allergies (102, 104).

EO compounds can easily pass the blood-brain barrier of the nervous system and there are numerous examples of neurotoxicity. Thujone has neurotoxic effects. It is a well-known constituent of the banned alcoholic drink absinthe, made famous by the painter Van Gogh and the poet Baudelaire, which causes delusions and hallucinations. The EO of rosemary is a convulsant, and pinocamphone, which is abundant in the EO of hyssop, causes seizures. Menthol may lead to bulbar paralysis (16, 119).

Although chronic toxicity of EOs is poorly documented, some examples of adverse effects from long-term animal and human use are mentioned in the literature. EOs are used in veterinary medicine, and some EOs have demonstrated, in cases of repeated use, manifestations of toxicity. Cats and dogs develop disease symptoms when treated with EOs of wintergreen, sassafras, tea-tree oil, or pennyroyal (84). Dermal applications of an insecticide containing 78.2% D-limonene, a compound found in abundance in the EOs of celery (*Apium graveolens*) or lemon (*Citrus limon*) (96), to cats at doses exceeding 15 times the concentration recommended in the instructions for use, resulted in severe symptoms (hypersalivation, ataxia, hypothermia) (44). Adverse reaction reports suggest that EOs are not safe for administration to infants under two years of age. Individuals who have developed chemical sensitivities are often adversely affected by perfumes, scents, and products with odor, making some EOs prime candidates for adverse reactions.

Although most EOs are not particularly toxic, some need to be handled with caution. The toxicities of some EOs do not coincide with that of the plant from which they are extracted and whose safety is generally recognized (97). It must be kept in mind that risk includes both hazard and exposure. In the context of plant protection with an EO, exposure may result from dermal contact or inhalation. EOs are usually delivered by spraying or fogging. Dermal or respiratory exposure resulting from improper equipment or handling of a treated plant before the oil has dried is not negligible and must not be ignored simply because a botanical, i.e., natural product, is used. It is therefore recommended that applicators carefully observe the labeling recommendations given for each situation.

In terms of ecotoxicology, EOs are safe to use but not without potential problems. For example, constituents of EOs are biodegradable, with short half-lives ranging from 30 to 40 h for α-terpineol (69) and about 10 days for *E*-isomers, *Z*-nepetalactone (5.7 to 12.6 days), and *Z,E*-nepetalactone (7.7 to 18.6 days) (contained in the EO of catnip) (81). Thus, most EOs tested have little persistence in the environment, and in contrast to some synthetic insecticides, no bioaccumulation or biomagnification has been reported to date. However, allelopathic and phytotoxic effects and unintended effects on nontarget animal species have been described. Dudai et al. (30)

extracted the EOs of 32 herbs of the Mediterranean basin and observed that several of them, e.g., *Cymbopogon citratus* or *Origanum vulgare*, inhibited the growth of both crops such as wheat (*Triticum aestivum*) and tomatoes (*Lycopersicon esculentum*), and weed species such as amaranth (*Amaranthus palmeri*) and *Euphorbia hirta*. EOs of wild marigold (*Tagetes minuta*) and pepper tree (*Schinus areira*) have allelopathic effect on maize (*Zea mays*) and inhibit roots (106). EOs of oregano and basil act on the weeds barnyardgrass (*Echinochloa crus-galli*) and lambsquarters (*Chenopodium album*) (114).

Very few investigators have documented the effects of EOs on nontarget arthropods. Bostanian et al. (14) assayed a *Chenopodium*-based botanical against the anthocorid *Orius insidiosus* and the braconid *Aphidius colemani*, two biocontrol agents used for the management of thrips in flower and vegetable greenhouses. The botanical showed little contact and residual activities on adults of both species and as well as nymphs of *O. insidiosus*. Huignard et al. (45) have shown that EOs of citronella and basil were toxic to the bruchid *C. maculatus* and to its parasitoid *Dinarmus basalis*, thus compromising its biocontrol.

Strikingly, very few studies have examined the chronic (long-time-exposure) effects of EOs. A notable exception is by Larocque et al. (62), who reared obliquebanded leafroller (*Choristoneura rosaceana*) larvae for 75 days on tansy (*Tanacetum vulgare*) EO mixed into diet and showed significant decrease in larval survival rate. Furthermore, short (24-h) exposures to tansy oil exerted antifeeding activity in larvae and significantly decreased egg laying in adult females. Such information is needed to determine the fit of EOs in existing integrated pest management programs.

MARKET AND REGULATORY ISSUES

The procedure for regulatory approval of plant protection products is expensive. Because the market for botanicals is narrower than that for synthetic organic pesticides, industrial producers of biopesticides need a simplified procedure in place if a reasonable return on investment is to be achieved. Therefore, established government policies seeking low-risk, alternative plant protection products such as EOs must be accompanied by an adaptable regulatory process that takes into account the special situation of these products.

A reduced regulation process for these products has existed in the United States since 1996 and it is particularly relevant to EOs. Biopesticides are subject to special procedures outlined in Title 40, Code of Federal Regulations, of FIFRA. A number of natural substances, such as EOs of mint, thyme, rosemary, and lemon grass, that did not benefit from this simplified procedure, however, were classified as GRAS (generally regarded as safe). They were placed on a list [FIFRA Section 25(b)], exempting them from the registration process (34). This exemption has become a marketing strategy to promote these products, such as the EcoEXEMPT® products (47, 99). Paulizt & Bélanger (80) confirmed that this relaxation of the approval procedure in the United States has led to a large diversity of EO-based products available to users. A review showed at least 88 insect repellent products sold in the U.S. market contain EOs (5). Among them, Requiem, developed by Codena, was registered in the United States in 2008; it was the first botanical to be registered in the United States since 1995 (20). Codena was bought by the California-based company AgraQuest in January 2008. Requiem is now registered in the United States against a number of pests, including green peach aphid, turnip aphid, silverleaf whitefly, western flower thrips, onion thrips, sixspotted mite, Texas citrus mite, citrus rust mite, and melon thrips (2). Typical issues arose throughout the development of Requiem: a developmental time that spanned over more than 10 years, standardization of cultivated genome and extraction methods, selective removal of undesirable constituents, considerations of nontargets organisms (14), and phytotoxicity (21).

Fewer EO products are available in the European Union (EU) and Canada (5), where registration has been stricter than in the United States. In fact, the Pest Management Regulatory Agency (PMRA, Canada) recently conducted a periodic reevaluation of citronella oil based on a classic risk analysis approach. Although an independent committee recommended consideration of safety in historical use information, PMRA decided to effectively deregister citronella products owing to a lack of toxicological data (43).

In the European Union, the procedure for reevaluation of plant protection products ended in 2008. To conduct this reevaluation, four groups of active substances were distinguished: synthetic organic pesticides (82%), pheromones (8%), botanicals (7%), and microorganisms (3%) (89). Natural substances including some EOs were placed on List 4. Some of them were listed in Annex 1 of Directive 91/414/EEC on January 1, 2009, in the context of an "expeditious" procedure. This listing in Annex 1 is required for all plant protection products derived from biological or chemical synthesis before marketing. The expeditious procedure allows inclusion of active substances in Annex 1 without the full scientific assessment that EFSA (European Food Safety Authority) must normally conduct but under the condition that the active substances concerned have no harmful effect(s) on human health, animals, or groundwater, or any unacceptable effect on the environment.

As a result, some of these List 4 active substances were allowed a maximum use period of 10 years (until August 31, 2019), whereas others were banned (e.g., nicotine, rotenone). Some vegetable oils have been authorized for uses that are not insecticidal (73): tea-tree oil for use as a fungicide, citronella oil as a herbicide, clove oil as a fungicide and bactericide, and spearmint oil as a plant growth regulator. The status of EOs extracted from thyme, orange (*Citrus sinensis*), or marigold (*Tagetes* sp.) for insecticide use is pending (under Directive 91/414/EEC) and should be approved soon. Orange oil is now allowed in France for control of sweetpotato whitefly, *Bemisia tabaci*, on field pumpkin (*Cucurbita pepo*) and for control of greenhouse whitefly on tomato (74).

Among the arguments used to seek reduced regulation for biopesticides in Europe is the finding that many active ingredients in these products are used daily in homes and in the production of food. It is therefore tempting to conclude that it would be unreasonable to request the establishment of heavy and costly registration requirements for these products that have no history of adverse effects (113). However, arguments based on using previously safe products in a new context have sometimes led to the reality of unintended and undesirable effects. We must therefore evaluate the benefit-to-risk ratio on a case-by-case basis and according to the permitted-use basis. However, to address this concern, the notion of active substances or plant protection products with low risk has been recently introduced in the European Regulation (EC) No. 1107/2009. Annex II defines active substances of low risk from exclusion criteria. It should not be (*a*) carcinogenic, mutagenic, toxic to reproduction; (*b*) sensitizing; (*c*) toxic or very toxic; (*d*) explosive, corrosive, persistent (half-life in soil is greater than 60 days); (*e*) prone to bioaccumulation [bioconcentration factor (BCF) > 100]; or (*f*) deemed to be an endocrine disruptor or show neurotoxic or immunotoxic effects. Most EOs will meet these criteria.

Today it is vital that EOs, like other pesticides marketed, meet safety requirements for users, consumers, and the environment. Some countries (e.g., Canada) add the notion of efficiency and selectivity. Economically and ethically, the availability and cost of the natural source should be considered. Oregano or rosemary EOs, for example, are abundant and sell for US\$155 kg^{-1} (at the time of this writing) (38). At such prices and required application rates, EOs can be used only for high-value crops or domestic markets.

Another concern is to preserve source biodiversity. Collection of wild plants must be properly managed, and it is preferable to select plant species with rapid turnover in the wild or that can be cultivated.

THE FUTURE OF ESSENTIAL OIL PRODUCTS

The selection of EOs as botanicals for pest control restricts products to extracts containing several hundred well-known compounds with a long history of human use, predictable toxicology, efficacy, and environmental fate. This long history allows one to make an educated choice from the 139,000 known plant secondary metabolites, eliminating the uncertainties inherent in considering the many other classes of botanical insecticides. The development of EOs as plant protection products is especially suited to organic farming as well as to integrated pest management. They are natural in origin and biodegradable, have diverse physiological targets within insects, and, consequently, may delay the evolution of insect resistance. As a result, EOs have been embraced by the public and organic growers as an alternative or complementary approach to synthetic pesticides, but in many developed countries, it has been difficult to meet this demand because of registration requirements. EOs are not large-volume products for large-scale commercial agriculture, and, consequently, few companies have attempted to steer them through the costly conventional insecticide registration process. The U.S. EPA is the only regulatory regime that has considered reduced risk seriously and as a result has registered a significant number of EOs for commercial use. However, the list of products approved by FIFRA 25(b) appears to be somewhat arbitrary and has not been updated. Clearly, if the public wishes to have access to botanical products for home, garden, organic agriculture, or greenhouse use, then governments must be lobbied to consider reduced registration processes more seriously. In addition, most research has focused on lab and greenhouse experiments, and field evaluation deserves more attention.

SUMMARY POINTS

1. EOs are extracted from plants by hydrodistillation, steam distillation, dry distillation, or cold pressing.
2. Used in several trades, i.e., perfumery, cosmetics, detergents, pharmacology, and fine chemistry, EOs have been used in plant protection.
3. EOs are usually a mixture of phytochemicals, whose constituents belong mainly to terpenoids or, to a lesser extent, phenylpropanoids.
4. Because they are volatile, EOs may act upon contact or through inhalation.
5. EOs exert bioactivity toward numerous arthropod taxa. Little has been published on untargeted arthropods, including natural enemies.
6. Several EOs have been registered recently, mainly in the United States, owing to provision of Section 25(b) of FIFRA.

DISCLOSURE STATEMENT

The authors are not aware of any affiliations, memberships, funding, or financial holdings that might be perceived as affecting the objectivity of this review. Mention of commercial products does not constitute an endorsement by Université of Pau et des Pays de l'Adour, University of Ottawa and Agriculture and Agri-Food Canada.

ACKNOWLEDGMENTS

We thank Pierre Lemoyne, Sandra Hindson, and Asim Muhammad for technical input.

LITERATURE CITED

1. Adorjan B, Buchbauer G. 2010. Biological properties of essential oils: an updated review. *Flavour Fragance J.* 25:407–26
2. Agraquest. 2011. Requiem®. **http://www.agraquest.com/docs/labels-msds/ReqEC-Label-LUS0111-001.pdf**
3. Ahmed SM, Eapen M. 1986. Vapour toxicity and repellency of some essential oils to insect pests. *Indian Perfum.* 30:273–78
4. Anderson IB, Mullen WH, Meeker JE, Khojasteh-Bakht SC, Oishi S, et al. 1996. Pennyroyal toxicity: measurement of toxic metabolite levels in two cases and review of the literature. *Ann. Intern. Med.* 124:726–34
5. Arnason JT, Sims SR, Scott IM. 2011. Natural products from plants as insecticides in agriculture and human health. In *Encyclopedia of Life Support Systems* (*EOLSS*), ed. JM Pezzuto, M Kato. Oxford, UK: EOLSS. In press. **http://www.eolss.net/outlinecomponents/Phytochemistry-Pharmacognosy.aspx**
6. Baker JD, Arnason JT, McRae C, Wade JM, Alkemade SJ. 2008. Insect repellent: composition, useful to reduce the incidence of infectious diseases, comprises evening primrose oil and a carrier. *US Patent Application 2008/0213408*
7. **Bakkali F, Averbeck S, Averbeck D, Idaomar M. 2008. Biological effects of essential oils—a review. *Food Chem. Toxicol.* 46:446–75**

7. Provides coverage of biological effects of EOs, notably on animal cells. Also provides extensive lists of references documenting cytotoxic activities.

8. Batish DR, Singh HP, Kohli RK, Kaur S. 2008. Eucalyptus essential oil as a natural pesticide. *For. Ecol. Manag.* 256:2166–74
9. Bauer K, Garbe D, Surburg H, eds. 2001. *Common Fragrance and Flavor Materials: Preparation, Properties and Uses.* Weinheim: Wiley-VCH. 2nd ed.
10. Braverman Y, Chizov-Ginzburg A, Mullens BA. 1999. Mosquito repellent attracts *Culicoides imicola* (Diptera: Ceratopogonidae). *J. Med. Entomol.* 36:113–15
11. Belzile AS, Majerus SL, Podeszfinski C, Guillet G, Durst T, et al. 2000. Dillapiol derivatives as synergists: structure-activity relationship analysis. *Pestic. Biochem. Physiol.* 66:33–40
12. Bernard CB, Krishnamurty HG, Chauret D, Durst T, Philogène BJR, et al. 1995. Insecticidal defenses of Piperaceae from the Neotropics. *J. Chem. Ecol.* 21:801–14
13. Bernards MA. 2010. Plant natural products: a primer. *Can. J. Zool.* 88:601–14
14. Bostanian NJ, Akalach M, Chiasson H. 2005. Effects of a *Chenopodium*-based botanical insecticide/acaricide on *Orius insidiosus* (Hemiptera: Anthocoridae) and *Aphidius colemani* (Hymenoptera : Braconidae). *Pest Manag. Sci.* 61:979–84
15. Bruneton J. 1999. *Pharmacognosie: Phytochimie, Plantes Médicinales.* Paris: Lavoisier Tech & Doc. 3rd ed.
16. Bruneton J. 2001. *Plantes Toxiques.* Paris: Lavoisier Tech & Doc. 2nd ed.
17. Burt S. 2004. Essential oils: their antibacterial properties and potential applications in foods—a review. *Int. J. Food Microbiol.* 94:223–53
18. Chiasson H, Bélanger A, Bostanian NJ, Vincent C, Poliquin A. 2001. Acaricidal properties of *Artemisia absinthium* and *Tanacetum vulgare* (Asteraceae) essential oils obtained by three methods of extraction. *J. Econ. Entomol.* 94:167–71
19. Chiasson H, Bostanian NJ, Vincent C. 2004. Acaricidal properties of a *Chenopodium*-based botanical. *J. Econ. Entomol.* 97:1373–77
20. Chiasson H, Delisle U, Bostanian NJ, Vincent C. 2008. Recherche, développement et commercialisation de FACIN^{MD}, un biopesticide d'origine végétale. Étude d'un cas de réussite en Amérique du Nord. See Ref. 98, pp. 451–63
21. Chiasson H, Vincent C, Bostanian NJ. 2004. Insecticidal properties of a *Chenopodium*-based botanical. *J. Econ. Entomol.* 97:1378–83
22. Christie M. 2010. *Private property pesticide by-laws in Canada.* **http://www.flora.org/healthyottawa/BylawList.pdf**
23. Clark RJ, Menary RC. 1981. Variations in composition of peppermint oil in relation to production areas. *Econ. Bot.* 35:59–69

24. Copping LG, ed. 2009. *The Manual of Biocontrol Agents: A World Compendium*. Alton: Br. Crop Prod. Counc. 4th ed.
25. Cunningham JP, Moore CJ, Zalucki MP, West SA. 2004. Learning, odour preference and flower foraging in moths. *J. Exp. Biol.* 207:87–94
26. **Dayan FE, Cantrell CL, Duke SO. 2009. Natural products in crop protection. *Bioorg. Med. Chem.* 17:4022–34**
27. Deshpande RS, Adhikary PR, Tipnis HP. 1974. Stored grain pest control agents from *Nigella sativa* and *Pogostemon heyneanus*. *Bull. Grain Technol.* 12:232–34
28. Deshpande RS, Tipnis HP. 1977. Insecticidal activity of *Ocimum basilicum* Linn. *Pesticides* 11:11–12
29. Dubey NK, Kumar A, Singh P, Shukla R. 2009. Exploitation of natural compounds in eco-friendly management of plant pests. In *Recent Developments in Management of Plant Diseases*, ed. U Gisi, I Chet, ML Gullino, pp. 181–98. The Netherlands: Springer
30. Dudai N, Poljakoff-Mayber A, Mayer AM, Putievsky E, Lerner HR. 1999. Essential oils as allelochemicals and their potential use as bioherbicides. *J. Chem. Ecol.* 25:1079–89
31. Enan EE. 2001. Insecticidal activity of essential oils: octopaminergic sites of action. *Comp. Biochem. Physiol.* 130:325–27
32. Enan EE. 2005. Molecular response of *Drosophila melanogaster* tyramine receptor cascade to plant essential oils. *Insect Biochem. Mol. Biol.* 35:309–21
33. Enan EE. 2005. Molecular and pharmacological analysis of an octopamine receptor from American cockroach and fruit fly in response to essential oils. *Arch. Insect Biochem. Physiol.* 59:161–71
34. Environ. Prot. Agency (EPA). 2011. *Regulating biopesticides*. **http://www.epa.gov/pesticides/biopesticides/**
35. Eur. Pharmacop. Comm., ed. 2008. *European Pharmacopoeia*. Strasbourg, Fr.: EDQM. 6th ed.
36. Feng L, Prestwich GD. 1997. Expression and characterization of a lepidopteran general odorant binding protein. *Insect Biochem. Mol. Biol.* 27:405–12
37. Feng R, Isman MB. 1995. Selection for resistance in green peach aphid. *Experientia* 51:831–33
38. France Lavande. 2011. *Le groupement de producteurs France Lavande*. **http://www.france-lavande.com**
39. Gershenzon J, McConkey ME, Croteau RB. 2000. Regulation of monoterpene accumulation in leaves of peppermint. *Plant Physiol.* 122:205–13
40. Hammer KA, Carson CF, Riley TV. 1999. Antimicrobial activity of essential oils and other plant extracts. *J. Appl. Microbiol.* 86:985–90
41. Hamraoui A, Regnault-Roger C. 1997. Comparaison des activités insecticides des monoterpènes sur deux espèces d'insectes ravageurs des cultures *Ceratitis capitata* et *Rhopalosiphum padi*. *Acta Bot. Gallica* 144:413–17
42. Hansted L, Jakobsen HB, Olsen CE. 1994. Influence of temperature on the rhythmic emission of volatiles from *Ribes nigrum* flowers in situ. *Plant Cell Environ.* 17:1069–72
43. Health Canada. 2004. Information note: proposed phase-out of citronella-based personal insect repellents. **http://www.hc-sc.gc.ca/cps-spc/alt_formats/pdf/pubs/pest/_fact-fiche/citronella-Information-citronnelle-eng.pdf**
44. Hooser SB, Beasley VR, Everitt JI. 1986. Effects of an insecticidal dip containing D-limonene in the cat. *J. Am. Vet. Med. Assoc.* 189:905–8
45. Huignard J, Lapied B, Dugravot S, Magnin-Robert M, Ketoh GK. 2008. Modes d'action neurotoxiques des dérivés soufrés et de certaines huiles essentielles et risques liés à leur utilisation. See Ref. 98, pp. 219–31
46. **Isman MB. 2000. Plant essential oils for pest and disease management. *Crop Prot.* 19:603–8**
47. Isman MB. 2004. Plant essential oils as green pesticides for pest and diseases management. *ACS Symp. Ser.* 887, pp. 41–51
48. **Isman MB. 2006. Botanical insecticides, deterrents and repellents in modern agriculture and an increasingly regulated world. *Annu. Rev. Entomol.* 50:45–66**
49. Isman MB. 2008. Botanical insecticides: for richer, for poorer. *Pest Manag. Sci.* 64:8–11
50. Isman MB, Machial CM. 2006. Pesticides based on plant essential oils: from traditional practice to commercialization. In *Naturally Occurring Bioactive Compounds*, ed. M Rai, MC Carpinella, pp. 29–44. Amsterdam: Elsevier BV

26. Provides an authoritative treatment of natural products in crop protection.

46. Discusses the role of EOs in plant protection.

48. Provides an authoritative treatment of botanicals in crop protection.

51. Isman MB, Machial CM, Miresmailli S, Bainard LD. 2007. Essential oil-based pesticides: new insights from old chemistry. In *Pesticide Chemistry. Crop Protection, Public Health, Environmental Safety*, ed. H Ohkawa, H Miyagawa, PW Lee, pp. 201–9. Weinheim: Wiley-VCH Verlag GmbH & Co. KGaA
52. Janssen AM, Scheffer JJC, Baerheim SA. 1987. Antimicrobial activity of essential oils: a 1976–1986 literature review. Aspects of the test methods. *Planta Med.* 53:395–98
53. Jensen HR, Scott IM, Sims SR, Trudeau VL, Arnason JT. 2006. The effect of a synergistic concentration of a *Piper nigrum* extract used in conjunction with pyrethrum upon gene expression in *Drosophila melanogaster*. *Insect Mol. Biol.* 15:329–39
54. Jiang Z, Akhtar Y, Bradbury R, Zhang X. 2009. Comparative toxicity of essential oils of *Litsea pungens* and *Litsea cubeba* and blends of their major constituents against the cabbage looper, *Trichoplusia ni*. *J. Agric. Food Chem.* 57:4833–37
55. Keita SM, Vincent C, Schmit JP, Arnason JT, Bélanger A. 2001. Efficacy of essential oil of *Ocimum basilicum* L. and *O. gratissimum* L. applied as an insecticidal fumigant and powder to control *Callosobruchus maculatus* (F.) [Coleoptera: Bruchidae] main pest of cowpea grains in storage. *J. Stored Prod. Res.* 37:339–49
56. Keita SM, Vincent C, Schmit JP, Bélanger A. 2000. Essential oil composition of *Ocimum basilicum* L., *O. gratissimum* L. and *O. suave* L. in the Republic of Guinea. *Flavour Fragance J.* 15:339–41
57. Keita SM, Vincent C, Schmit JP, Ramaswamy S, Bélanger A. 2000. Effects of various oils on *Callosobruchus maculatus* (Fabricius) (Coleoptera: Bruchidae). *J. Stored Prod. Res.* 36:355–64
58. Konstantopoulou I, Vassipoulou L, Mauragani-Tsipidov P, Scouras ZG. 1992. Insecticidal effects of essential oils. A study of the effects of essential oils extracted from eleven Greek aromatic plants on *Drosophila auraria*. *Experientia* 48:616–19
59. Kostyukovsky M, Rafaeli A, Gileadi C, Demchenko N, Shaaya E. 2002. Activation of octopaminergic receptors by essential oil constituents isolated from aromatic plants. *Pest Manag. Sci.* 58:1101–6
60. Kurowska A, Kalemba D, Gora J, Majda T. 1991. Analysis of essential oils: influence on insects. Part IV. Essential oil or garden thyme (*Thymus vulgaris* L.). *Pestycydy* 2:25–29
61. Lahlou M. 2004. Methods to study the phytochemistry and bioactivity of essential oils. *Phytother. Res.* 18:435–48
62. Larocque N, Vincent C, Bélanger A, Bourassa JP. 1999. Effects of tansy oil, *Tanacetum vulgare* L., on the biology of the obliquebanded leafroller, *Choristoneura rosaceana* (Harris) (Lepidoptera:Tortricidae). *J. Chem. Ecol.* 25:1319–30
63. Lehr PS. 2010. *Biopesticides: the global market*, ed. BCC Res, Febr. **http://bccresearch.com/report/biopesticides-market-chm029c.html**
64. Liu S-S, Li Y-H, Liu Y-Q, Zalucki MP. 2005. Experience-induced preference for oviposition repellents derived from a non-host plant by a specialist herbivore. *Ecol. Lett.* 8:722–29
65. Liu ZL, Chu SS, Jiang GH. 2011. Insecticidal activity and composition of essential oil of *Ostericum sieboldii* (Apiaceae) against *Sitophilus zeamais* and *Tribolium castaneum*. *Rec. Nat. Prod.* 5:74–81
66. López MD, Pascual-Villalobosa MJ. 2010. Mode of inhibition of acetylcholinesterase by monoterpenoids and implications for pest control. *Ind. Crops Prod.* 31:284–88
67. Mateeva A, Karov S. 1983. Studies on the insecticidal effect of some essential oils. *Nauchni Trudove–Vissha Selskostop. Inst. 'Vasil Kolarov' Plodiv* 28:129–39
68. Mills C, Cleary BJ, Gilmer JF, Walsh JJ. 2004. Inhibition of acetylcholinesterase by tea tree oil. *J. Pharm. Pharmacol.* 56:375–79
69. Misra G, Pavlostathis SG. 1997. Biodegradation kinetics of monoterpenes in liquid and soil-slurry systems. *Appl. Microbiol. Biotechnol.* 47:572–77
70. Miyakado M, Nakayama I, Yoshioka H. 1980. Insecticidal joint action of pipercide and co-occurring compounds isolated from *Piper nigrum* L. *Agric. Biol. Chem.* 44:1701–3
71. Müller-Riebau FJ, Berger BM, Yegen O, Cakir C. 1997. Seasonal variations in the chemical compositions of essential oils of selected aromatic plants growing wild in Turkey. *J. Agric. Food Chem.* 45:4821–25
72. Munro I, Ford R, Kennepohl E, Sprenger J. 1996. Correlation of structural class with no-observed-effect-levels: a proposal for establishing a threshold of concern. *Food Chem. Toxicol.* 34:829–67
73. Off. J. Eur. Union. (OJEU). 2008. Commission Directive 2008/127/EC of 18 December 2008 amending Council Directive 91/414/EEC to include several active substances. L 344/89. Vol. 51, 20 Dec. 2008

74. Off. J. Eur. Union. (OJEU). 2009. Commission Decision of 8 June 2009 recognising in principle the completeness of the dossier submitted for detailed examination in view of the possible inclusion of orange oil in Annex I to Council Directive 91/414/EEC (*notified under document number C(2009) 4232*). L145/47. Vol. 52, 10 June 2009
75. Okabe H, Obata Y, Takayama K, Nagai T. 1990. Percutaneous absorption enhancing effect and skin irritation of monocyclic monoterpenes. *Drug Des. Deliv.* 6:229–38
76. O' Neil MJ, Smith A, Heckelman PE, Budavari S, eds. 2006. *The Merck Index: An Encyclopedia of Chemicals, Drugs, and Biologicals.* Whitehouse Station, NJ: Merck & Co. 4th ed.
77. Papachristos DP, Kimbaris AC, Papadopoulos NT, Polissiou MG. 2009. Toxicity of citrus essential oils against *Ceratitis capitata* (Diptera: Tephritidae) larvae. *Ann. Appl. Biol.* 155:381–89
78. Park IK, Choi K-S, Kim D-H, Choi I-O, Kim L-S, et al. 2006. Fumigant activity of plant essential oils and components from horseradish (*Armorica rusticana*), anise (*Pimpinella anisum*) and garlic (*Allium sativum*) oils against *Lycoriella ingenua* (Diptera: Sciaridae). *Pest Manag. Sci.* 62:723–28
79. Park IK, Kim L-S, Choi I-O, Lee Y-S, Shin S-C. 2006. Fumigant activity of plant essential oils and components from *Schizonepeta tenuifolia* against *Lycoriella ingenua* (Diptera: Sciaridae). *J. Econ. Entomol.* 99:1717–21
80. Paulitz TC, Bélanger RR. 2001. Biological control in greenhouse systems. *Annu. Rev. Phytopathol.* 39:103–33
81. Peterson CJ, Ems-Wilson J. 2003. Catnip essential oil as a barrier to subterranean termites (Isoptera: Rhinotermitidae) in the laboratory. *J. Econ. Entomol.* 96:1275–82
82. Picimbon JF. 2005. Synthesis of odorant reception-suppressing agents, odorants-binding proteins (OBPs) and chemosensory proteins (CSPs): molecular targets for pest management. In *Biopesticides of Plant Origin*, ed. C Regnault-Roger, BJR Philogène, C Vincent, pp. 383–416. Andover/Paris: Intercept–Lavoisier
83. Picimbon JF, Regnault-Roger C. 2008. Composés sémiochimiques volatils, phytoprotection et olfaction: cibles moléculaires pour la lutte intégrée. See Ref. 98, pp. 383–416
84. Poppenga RH. 2002. Herbal medicine: potential for intoxication and interaction with conventional drugs. *Clin. Tech. Small Anim. Pract.* 17:6–18
85. Price DN, Berry MS. 2006. Comparison of effects of octopamine and insecticidal essential oils on activity in the nerve cord, foregut and dorsal unpaired median neurons of cockroaches. *J. Insect Physiol.* 52:309–19
86. Priestley CM, Williamson EM, Wafford KA, Satelle DB. 2003. Thymol, a constituent of thyme essential oils, is a positive modulator of human GABA and a homo-oligosteric GABA receptor from *Drosophila melanogaster*. *Br. J. Pharmacol.* 140:1363–72
87. Quarles W. 1992. Botanical pesticides from *Chenopodium*? *The IPM Pract.* 14:1–11
88. Raguso RA, Pichersky E. 1999. New perspectives in pollination biology: floral fragrances. A day in the life of a linalool molecule: chemical communication in a plant-pollinator system. Part 1: linalool biosynthesis in flowering plants. *Plant Species Biol.* 14:95–120
89. Redbond M. 2003. Biocontrol 2003. *Pesticide Outlook* 4:168–70
90. Regnault-Roger C. 1997. The potential of botanical essential oils for insect pest control. *Integr. Pest Manag. Rev.* 2:25–34

90. The first review paper on EOs affecting insects.

91. Regnault-Roger C. 2002. De nouveaux phyto-insecticides pour le troisième millénaire? In *Biopesticides d'Origine Végétale*, ed. C Regnault-Roger, BJR Philogène, C Vincent, pp. 19–40. Paris: Lavoisier Tech & Doc
92. Regnault-Roger C. 2008. Recherche de nouveaux biopesticides d'origine végétale à caractère insecticide: démarches méthodologiques et application aux plantes aromatiques méditerranéennes. See Ref. 98, pp. 25–50
93. Regnault-Roger C, Hamraoui A. 1994. Reproductive inhibition of *Acanthoscelides obtectus* Say (Coleoptera), bruchid of kidney bean (*Phaseolus vulgaris* L.) by some aromatic essential oils. *Crop Prot.* 13:624–28
94. Regnault-Roger C, Hamraoui A. 1994. Antifeedant effect of Mediterranean plant essential oils upon *Acanthoscelides obtectus* Say (Coleoptera), bruchid of kidney beans, *Phaseolus vulgaris* L. In *Stored Product Protection*, ed. E Highley, EJ Wright, HJ Banks, BR Champ, 2:837–40. Wallingford, UK: CABI

95. Regnault-Roger C, Hamraoui A. 1995. Fumigant toxic activity and reproductive inhibition induced by monoterpenes upon *Acanthoscelides obtectus* Say (Coleoptera), bruchid of kidney bean (*Phaseolus vulgaris* L.). *J. Stored Prod. Res.* 31:291–99
96. Regnault-Roger C, Hamraoui A, Holeman M, Théron E, Pinel R. 1993. Insecticidal effect of essential oils from Mediterranean plants upon *A. obtectus* Say (Coleoptera, Bruchidae), a pest of kidney bean (*Phaseolus vulgaris* L.). *J. Chem. Ecol.* 19:1231–42
97. Regnault-Roger C, Philogène BJR. 2008. Past and current prospects for the use of botanicals and plant allelochemicals in integrated pest management. *Pharm. Biol.* 46:1–12
98. Regnault-Roger C, Philogène BJR, Vincent C, eds. 2008. *Biopesticides d'Origine Végétale*. Paris: Lavoisier Tech & Doc. 2nd ed.
99. Regnault-Roger C, Silvy C, Alabouvette C. 2005. Biopesticides: réalités et perspectives commerciales. In *Enjeux Phytosanitaires pour l'Agriculture et l'Environnement*, ed. C Regnault-Roger, pp. 849–80. Paris: Lavoisier Tech & Doc
100. Reverchon E. 1997. Supercritical fluid extraction and fractionation of essential oils and related products. *J. Supercrit. Fluids* 10:1–37
101. Rodriguez E, Healey PL, Mehla I. 1984. *Biology and Chemistry of Plant Trichomes*. New York: Plenum
102. Rubel DM, Freeman S, Southwell IA. 1998. Tea tree oil allergy: What is the offending agent? Report of three cases of tea tree oil allergy and review of the literature. *Aust. J. Dermatol.* 39:244–47
103. Rubiolo P, Sgorbini B, Liberto E, Cordero C, Bicchi C. 2010. Essential oils and volatiles: sample preparation and analysis. *Flavour Fragrance J.* 25:282–90
104. Rutherford T, Nixon R, Tam M, Tate B. 2007. Allergy to tea tree oil: retrospective review of 41 cases with positive patch tests over 4.5 years. *Aust. J. Dermatol.* 48:83–77
105. Scott IM, Puniani E, Durst T, Phelps D, Merali S, et al. 2002. Insecticidal activity of *Piper tuberculatum* Jacq. extracts: synergistic interaction of piperamides. *Agric. For. Entomol.* 4:137–44
106. Scrivanti LR, Zunino MP, Zygadlo JA. 2003. *Tagetes minuta* and *Schinus areira* essential oils as allelopathic agents. *Biochem. System Ecol.* 31:563–72
107. Shaalan EAS, Canyon D, Younes MW, Abdel-Wahab H, Manour AH. 2005. A review of phytochemicals with mosquiticidal potential. *Environ. Int.* 31:1149–66
108. Shaaya E, Ravid U, Paster N, Juven B, Lisman U, Pissarev V. 1991. Fumigant toxicity of essential oils against four major stored-product insects. *J. Chem. Ecol.* 7:499–504
109. Smith RL, Cohen SM, Doull J, Feron VJ, Goodman JI, et al. 2005. A procedure for the safety evaluation of natural flavor complexes used as ingredients in food: essential oils. *Food Chem. Toxicol.* 43:345–63
110. Sosa ME, Tonn CE. 2008. Plant secondary metabolites from Argentinean semiarid lands: bioactivity against insects. *Phytochem. Rev.* 7:3–24
111. Tapondjou LA, Adler C, Hamilton B, Fontem DA. 2003. Bioefficacité des poudres et des huiles essentielles de feuilles de *Chenopodium ambrosioides* et *Eucalyptus saligna* à l'égard de la bruche du niébé, *Callosobruchus maculatus* Fab. (Coleoptera, Bruchidae). *Cah. Agric.* 12:401–7
112. Thakur AK, Sankhyan SD. 1992. Studies on the persistent toxicity of some plant oils to storage pests of wheat. *Indian Perfumer* 36:6–16
113. Trumble JT. 2002. Caveat emptor: safety considerations for natural products used in pest control. *Am. Entomol.* 48:7–13
114. Vasilakoglou I, Dhima K, Wogiatzi E, Eleftherohorinos I, Lithourgidis A. 2007. Herbicidal potential of essential oils of oregano or marjoram (*Origanum* spp.) and basil (*Ocimum basilicum*) on *Echinochloa crus-galli* (L.) P. Beauv. and *Chenopodium album* L. weeds. *Allelopathy J.* 20:297–306
115. Vogt RG, Prestwich GD, Lerner MR. 1991. Odorant-binding protein subfamilies associate with distinct classes of olfactory receptor neurons in insects. *J. Neurobiol.* 22:74–84
116. Vogt RG, Rybczynski R, Lerner MR. 1991. Molecular cloning and sequencing of general odorant-binding proteins GOBP1 and GOBP2 from the tobacco hawk moth *Manduca sexta*: comparisons with other insect OBPs and their signal peptides. *J. Neurosci.* 11:2972–84
117. Walling LL. 2000. The myriad plant responses to herbivores. *J. Plant Growth Regul.* 19:195–216
118. Weaver DK, Dubkel FV, Netzububanza L, Jackson LL, Stock DT. 1991. The efficacy of linalool, a major component of freshly milled *Ocimum canum* Sim (Lamiaceae) for protection against post-harvest damage by certain stored Coleoptera. *J. Stored Prod. Res.* 27:213–70

119. Wichtl M, Anton R. 2003. *Plantes Thérapeutiques*. Paris: Lavoisier Tech & Doc. 2nd ed.

120. Zapata N, Lognay G, Smagghe G. 2010. Bioactivity of essential oils from leaves and bark of *Laurelia sempervirens* and *Drimys winteri* against *Acyrthosiphon pisum*. *Pest Manag. Sci.* 66:1324–31

121. Zhang P-J, Liu S-S, Wang H, Zalucki MP. 2007. The influence of early adult experience and larval food restriction on responses toward nonhost plants in moths. *J. Chem. Ecol.* 33:1528–41

122. Zhu BCR, Henderson G, Yu Y, Laine RA. 2003. Toxicity and repellency of patchouli oil and patchouli alcohol against Formosan subterranean termites *Coptotermes formosanus* Shiraki (Isoptera: Rhinotermitidae). *J. Agric. Food Chem.* 51:4585–88

Key Aspects of the Biology of Snail-Killing Sciomyzidae Flies

William L. Murphy,[1,*] Lloyd V. Knutson,[2] Eric G. Chapman,[3] Rory J. Mc Donnell,[4] Christopher D. Williams,[5] Benjamin A. Foote,[6] and Jean-Claude Vala[7]

[1]Research Collaborator, Smithsonian Institution, Fishers, Indiana 46038-2257; email: billmurphy8@sbcglobal.net

[2]Salita degli Albito 29, 04024 Gaeta LT, Italy; email: lvknutson@tiscali.it

[3]Department of Entomology, University of Kentucky, Lexington, Kentucky 40546-0091; email: ericgchapman@gmail.com

[4]Department of Entomology, University of California, Riverside, California 92521-0001; email: rjmcdonnell@gmail.com

[5]Behavioural Ecology and Biocontrol Laboratory, Department of Biology, National University of Ireland, Maynooth, County Kildare, Ireland; email: chris.david.williams@gmail.com

[6]Emeritus Professor of Biological Sciences, Department of Biological Sciences, Kent State University, Kent, Ohio 44242; email: bfoote@kent.edu

[7]Laboratoire des Ligneux et des Grandes Cultures, UPRES EA2107, Université d'Orléans, BP 6749, 45067 Orléans Cedex 2, France; email: jean-claude.vala@univ-orleans.fr

Annu. Rev. Entomol. 2012. 57:425–47

The *Annual Review of Entomology* is online at ento.annualreviews.org

This article's doi:
10.1146/annurev-ento-120710-100702

0066-4170/12/0107-0425$20.00

*Corresponding author

Keywords

Diptera, Mollusca, zoogeography, systematics, phylogenetics, ecology, biocontrol

Abstract

The biology of snail-killing flies (Diptera: Sciomyzidae) has been studied intensively over the past half-century, especially over the past decade. Today, sciomyzids are biologically the best-known group of higher Diptera. The overarching research objectives are evaluation of sciomyzids as biocontrols of disease-carrying or agriculturally important snails and slugs and as a paradigm group for the study of the evolution of diverse feeding and associated behaviors in flies. We present reviews and analyses of some key features of particular scientific and societal interest, including behavioral and phenological groups; laboratory experimental studies on behavior and development; population biology, bioindicators, ecosystem service provision, and conservation; phylogenetics, molecular studies, and evolutionary biology; and biocontrol.

INTRODUCTION

With life cycles known for 240 of 540 species in 41 of 61 genera, and immature stages described for 176 species in 39 genera, the Sciomyzidae are, from those aspects, the most thoroughly studied family of Acalyptratae. We suggest that Sciomyzidae are emerging as a richer knowledge base for broad evolutionary studies, especially of larval feeding behavior and associated adaptations, than are larger but lesser-known families of higher Diptera; some outstanding research needs in this regard are noted herein. (Supplemental figures, a film, tables, and text provide further information relating to sections of this chapter. See **Supplemental Text 1** for a rationale for use of Sciomyzidae as a resource for the study of the evolution of life cycle strategies; follow the **Supplemental Material link** from the Annual Reviews home page at **http://www.annualreviews.org**.)

Sciomyzidae are of particular interest in regard to the feeding behavior and hosts/prey of the larvae and associated behavioral and morphological adaptations throughout the life cycle (**Supplemental Figures 1** and **2**). All known larvae are obligate natural enemies of Mollusca, except for three killers of freshwater Oligochaeta. Larvae range from overt rapacious predators of freshwater snails (**Supplemental Film 1**) to covert, intimately associated, insidious parasitoids of terrestrial snails or aestivating freshwater snails (one larva per snail, one snail per larva). Many species behave variably as predators, parasitoids, or saprophages during their development, depending, for example, on relative sizes of larvae and snails, intraspecific competition, age of larvae, and microhabitat condition.

In 1850 in France, Perris (98) first reared an adult sciomyzid from a larva found in a terrestrial snail; he did not know whether the snail was dead or alive when he collected it. For 100 years, most authors described sciomyzid larvae as general saprophages until, a continent away and a century later, in 1950 in Alaska, Berg (18) first proved the obligate snail-killing behavior of six species in five genera. Berg and 16 graduate students at Cornell University subsequently (1953–1978) pursued life cycle studies and descriptions of immature stages worldwide as well as studies on populations, physiology, natural enemies, and other aspects. Soon after the initial studies (e.g., 21) began, a closely knit international coterie of researchers developed. With the resurgence of interest in Sciomyzidae during the past decade, the current directory of sciomyzid enthusiasts (**http://www.sciomyzidae.info/news.php**) now lists 89 persons in 32 countries.

Basic resources for researchers are a nearly complete, alphabetical, serially numbered bibliography of 3,000+ publications on Sciomyzidae (ScioBiblio), upon which are based the citations in a Cornucopia, a new format for tabulating information—a table of nine key features for each of the known species of Sciomyzidae, with ScioBiblio numbers for publications documenting these features. Both resources are available on the Sciomyzidae Web site (Sciomyzidae.info, **http://www.sciomyzidae.info/news.php**) and are updated from time to time. **Supplemental Table 1** is a summary, by major zoogeographic region, of numbers of genera and species, extent of life cycle knowledge, and availability of descriptions of immature stages.

DISTRIBUTION AND ZOOGEOGRAPHY

A wealth of data on the geographical distribution of sciomyzids, including tables and maps, has been published. Distribution of genera and species by major regions has been presented (101) and updated (67). Species distributions are best known for the Palearctic (by countries, 102) and Nearctic (by state/province, 62), whereas distribution of Oriental species is least known (see **Supplemental Table 2**). Species distributions closely follow classical delimitations of major zoogeographic regions. Except for 28 Holarctic species in six genera, few species are broadly shared with adjacent regions, and few are even slightly adventive from one region into adjacent regions.

Approximately 70% of the 540 species and 82% of the 61 genera occur in the Nearctic and Palearctic (Nearctic: 201 species/23 genera, Palearctic: 176 species/27 genera). The dominant genera, *Pherbellia* (tribe Sciomyzini, 95 species) and *Sepedon* (tribe Tetanocerini, 80 species), occur worldwide except in the Subantarctic (including New Zealand), where all 25 species in four genera are endemic. The third-largest genus, *Dictya*, comprises 42 Nearctic and Neotropical and 1 Palearctic species. No sciomyzid is cosmopolitan.

Malacophagous: killing and feeding on Mollusca, primarily snails or slugs

Zoogeographic research on Sciomyzidae suffers from a lack of cladistic analyses of species within most genera. Such analyses would facilitate vicariant zoogeographic studies. They are available only for the Neotropical genera *Protodictya* (75), *Thecomyia* (78), *Sepedonea* (77), and *Tetanoceroides* (138, phyletic analysis), and for the Nearctic *Tetanocera* (24). The only modern vicariant analysis is that of *Sepedonea* (99). No comparative sciomyzid/mollusc zoogeographic studies have been conducted. Zoogeography is discussed in some taxonomic and biological papers [Neotropical, *Perilimnia* and *Shannonia* (58) and *Tetanoceroides* (138); Nearctic, three *Sepedon* species (39); Palearctic, one *Elgiva* (64) and two *Pherbellia* species (128)] and in some faunistic studies (see Identification and Systematics, below). An overview of descriptive (dispersal) zoogeography focuses primarily on species and genera shared among regions, extent of endemicity, and likely dispersal routes (67).

The distribution of many described genera/species is poorly known, as indicated by recent collections of species well beyond their documented range (e.g., *Dictya disjuncta*, known only from the holotype collected in Mississippi in 1927 and recently rediscovered in Indiana and Arkansas) and genera new to major regions (e.g., the Holarctic *Colobaea* and *Pteromicra* and the Holarctic-Neotropical *Ditaeniella* from sub-Saharan Africa). Several monotypic genera are known only from one or two specimens from the type and nearby localities: Palearctic (*Apteromicra*, *Ellipotaenia*, *Neodictya*, and *Oligolimnia*), Afrotropical (*Tetanoptera* and *Verbekaria*), Neotropical (*Calliscia*), and Oriental (*Steyskalina*).

Many species and some genera remain undescribed. About 100 undescribed species in approximately 20 genera are listed at Sciomyzidae.info (**http://www.sciomyzidae.info/news.php**) by "species near sp.x," locality, date, collector, number-sex, museum/current location, and specialist. This list serves as a request for more specimens, indicates areas for further exploration, and notes the locations of museum collections for further study.

HOSTS/PREY

Sciomyzidae are the only dipteran family whose larvae are almost exclusively obligate killers of molluscs; a few other families include some obligate or opportunistic snail or slug killers. Of the eight families of Sciomyzoidea (sensu McAlpine, 80), all are saprophagous, coprophagous, fungivorous, or microflora grazers except for one dryomyzid that feeds on barnacles and some helosciomyzids that prey on ants.

Of the 240 reared species of the 540 valid species of Sciomyzidae, only 3 species, all Afrotropical, are not strictly malacophagous: *Sepedonella nana* and *Sepedon knutsoni*, which prey on freshwater oligochaetes, and *Sepedon ruficeps*, facultative on snails or oligochaetes. One species of the sister group Phaeomyiidae (subfamily Phaeomyiinae of Sciomyzidae in earlier classifications) is the only fly documented as a parasitoid of millipedes (4, 5).

Most sciomyzids are restricted to nonoperculate (pulmonate) freshwater, semiterrestrial (Succineidae), or terrestrial snails. A few species attack brackish or freshwater operculate (prosobranch) snails, one attacks marine coastal strandline *Littorina*, five attack only slugs, nine are restricted at least during early larval life to eggs of freshwater and semiterrestrial snails, and six species in three genera are the only Insecta proven to be natural enemies of bivalve Mollusca (Sphaeriidae). None is cannibalistic.

Supplemental Table 3 lists 56 natural prey species (field records) in 43 genera of aquatic, terrestrial, and semiterrestrial gastropods representing 21 families. The natural prey of most of the many freshwater predators (all Tetanocerini) are unknown, as these larvae feed only until satiated and then leave the prey to rest before killing additional snails. The natural prey of only 11 such species have been documented (84). The most polyphagous is the Holarctic *Tetanocera ferruginea*, recorded to consume nine snail species in seven genera. Although freshwater predators kill most snails offered to them during laboratory rearings, their natural prey probably are more limited. Terrestrial parasitoids, restricted to one or a few genera of gastropods, are generally more host specific than are predators.

The natural hosts/prey of larvae of many terrestrial or semiterrestrial parasitoids and predators of the tribe Sciomyzini are better known than those of the Tetanocerini because (*a*) many Sciomyzini attack snails exposed in aquatic-terrestrial ecotone (shoreline) situations and thus are more easily collected, (*b*) such larvae remain feeding, often saprophagously, in the snail long after it has died, and (*c*) many Sciomyzini pupariate in the snail shell. Such infested shells are collected more easily than are freshwater snails with larvae feeding in them (**Supplemental Table 4**).

During laboratory rearings, one of the Palearctic Sciomyzini shoreline predator/parasitoid/saprophages, *Pherbellia dorsata*, killed and fed on 28 snail species in 20 genera, more than recorded for any other sciomyzid, although it was found only in the freshwater *Planorbis planorbis* in extensive collections in a well-studied habitat in nature (22). In the laboratory, larvae of some freshwater Tetanocerini, with morphological features such as elongate segment 12, elongate interspiracular processes, and elongate posterior spiracular disk lobes, obviously adapted to an aquatic existence (24, 122), readily kill and feed on terrestrial snails; e.g., the Palearctic *Pherbina coryleti* consumed terrestrial snails of five species in four genera (65).

Sciomyzid life cycle and biocontrol studies are deficient in prey-choice experiments. Most sciomyzid larvae recalcitrant to laboratory rearing generally have not been offered nonmolluscan food. However, the extensively studied (e.g., 92, 93) Nearctic *Sepedon fuscipennis*, a surface predator of nonoperculate freshwater snails in calm waters, was reared from hatching to maturity on a diet consisting solely of limpets (Ancylidae) (93). These cone-shaped gastropods are common in streams (which are not *S. fuscipennis* microhabitats), where they adhere to riffle stones and feed by scraping biofilm. The aggressive larvae squeezed under the adhered shell and "flipped the limpet over for feeding."

Many sciomyzids have been characterized as feeding on freshwater snails stranded on, foraging at, or migrating through shoreline situations. Taxonomic-ecological-behavioral analyses are needed of the snail and fly members of this major complex of hosts/prey of sciomyzid larvae in terms of diel, seasonal, climatic, and other factors. Such information might be useful, especially in selecting biocontrols of fluke-transmitting snails not in open water, i.e., aestivating, migrating, or stranded; such individuals are not susceptible to molluscicides.

The historical lack of joint research by entomologists and malacologists on sciomyzid larvae and their hosts/prey is a deficiency from theoretical and practical viewpoints. A theoretical perspective in regard to biocontrol possibilities from the viewpoint of malacologists has been provided (1, 7). Barker et al. (7) mapped a cladogram of sciomyzid genera onto a cladogram of potential molluscan prey (**Supplemental Figure 3**) and examined the pattern of prey diversification. They concluded that "the considerable number of molluscan clades not utilized as prey indicates the ecological conservatism of Sciomyzidae" and that operculate snails are strongly underrepresented as prey. Major categories of hosts/prey have been mapped above the cladogram of genera of Sciomyzidae (67). These considerations are further discussed below.

LIFE CYCLES, LARVAL FEEDING BEHAVIOR, AND ASSOCIATED ADAPTATIONS

Life cycles, larval feeding behavior, and associated morphological, microhabitat, and phenological adaptations essential to evolutionary and biocontrol aspects continue as focal points of Sciomyzidae research. Over the past 50 years, information on the sciomyzid life cycle has been presented in over 100 publications on 240 species in 41 genera, for all major regions (see "A Cornucopia for Sciomyzidae and Phaeomyiidae" at **http://www.sciomyzidae.info/downloads.php?cat_id=1**). Many ecological equivalents exist among regions, but some of these species show a multitude of special adaptations. Classification of Behavioral Groups, based on hosts/prey, feeding behavior, and microhabitats of larvae, has been used extensively to capture the essence and broad range of sciomyzid behaviors. Earlier reviews (21, 37, 48) recognized 7 or 8 groups on the basis of these descriptors, but Barker et al. (7), who included morphology of immatures as a descriptor, recognized 9 groups, whereas Knutson & Vala (67), who excluded morphology, recognized 15 groups (**Supplemental Text 2** depicts the classification as of 2011, with examples of species and genera). The diverse feeding behavior of Sciomyzidae and the coevolved behavioral and morphological adaptations throughout the life cycles suggest further refinement of behavioral or ecomorphological groups. Considering the many characters and character states, correspondence analyses or some numerical taxonomic or other analytic procedures probably would be useful. Here we take the opposite tack and simplify discussion to examples of the three extremes in feeding behavior: parasitoid, mixed parasitoid/predator/saprophage, and predation.

Uni-, bi-, or multivoltine: one, two, or several generations per year

Sciomyzid life cycles have been elucidated either (*a*) by beginning with a collection of larvae and/or puparia (occasionally in snails) in nature, indicating microhabitats and potential hosts/prey for laboratory rearings, or (*b*) by beginning laboratory rearings with field-collected adults, obtaining eggs, and offering neonates various hosts/prey, the results indicating where to look in nature. The morphology of larvae and puparia often indicates whether the species is aquatic or terrestrial, also helping direct field collections. Rearing methods are described in many life cycle publications and are summarized in Reference 67.

Parasitoid Behavior

The best studied of the highly parasitoid species (all in Sciomyzini) are the Nearctic *Sciomyza varia* and its almost exact ecological equivalent, the Palearctic *Colobaea bifasciella*; the Nearctic *Sciomyza aristalis*; the Nearctic and Palearctic subspecies of *Pherbellia schoenherri*; the Palearctic *Tetanura pallidiventris*; and the Nearctic *Oidematops ferrugineus*. Some Sciomyzini and Tetanocerini with partially similar parasitoid behaviors are placed in three parasitoid groups in the most recent Behavioral Group classification (see **Supplemental Text 2**). The best-studied example is the uncommon, univoltine *S. varia* (11, 19), which Barnes (11) characterized as having "one of the most fully developed suites of specialized habits found in the Sciomyzidae, including parasitoid feeding, host specificity, oviposition on the shell, solitary life in a single host, and completion of larval and pupal life in the host shell." The strategy of this group seems to be one snail per larva and one larva per snail. Although several eggs are sometimes laid on one snail, only one larva survives. Unlike some true parasitoid sciomyzid larvae, in which the first instar penetrates far into the snail between the shell and mantle and is deprived of outside air, first-instar larvae of *S. varia* penetrate until only their posterior spiracles are exposed at the edge of the snail's peristomal collar.

Barnes (11) provided the only thorough analysis of the sequence of snail organ destruction by a sciomyzid, dissecting snails after they had been fed upon by first, second, and third instars of *S. varia*. Host snails died 5–14 days after eggs were laid on them; larvae pupariated 6–14 days after entering snails. Host individuals of an amazingly broad size range were utilized. The shell-free dry weight of tissue available in field-collected snail shells 7.0–19.8 mm long, from which *S. varia* adults were reared, was calculated as 1.6–40.4 mg (11). Small snails produced small flies. Adults ranged in size (body length) from 3.6 to 6.5 mm.

Mixed Parasitoid/Predator/Saprophage Behavior

The widely distributed Nearctic *Atrichomelina pubera* is an abundant, multivoltine, non-host-specific, opportunistic parasitoid/predator/saprophage of exposed semiaquatic and aquatic nonoperculate snails in diverse moist habitats (40). Eggs are laid on the shell or on other substrates. Larvae have been reared from five genera of field-collected snails. In the laboratory they feed on additional snail genera, including terrestrial species. Larvae can also develop on dead bivalves (59). They apparently kill and feed on an ecological assemblage of snail species, not on a particular taxonomic group. Feeding behavior is variable and depends on circumstances. The larvae display parasitoid, predatory, and saprophagous capabilities. Feeding behavior is variable and dependent upon availability of snails, relative sizes of larva and snail, and intraspecific competition. Such labile feeding behavior is typical of many other Sciomyzini and semiterrestrial Tetanocerini, especially during early larval life. Morphologically, the immature stages of *A. pubera* are typical of the Sciomyzini (e.g., reticulate egg chorion, unpigmented larval integument, ventral body spinules, microscopic interspiracular processes, and barrel-shaped puparia), but larvae share with a few *Pherbellia* only slightly elongate posterior spiracular disk lobes, indicating adaptation to wet microhabitats (22). Many saprophagous Diptera (including Ephydridae, Phoridae, Piophilidae, and Sarcophagidae) have been reared from snails also containing *A. pubera*. No other sciomyzid has been reared from snails containing larvae of other families of flies. Such communal feeding might have been typical of ancestral sciomyzids.

Predation

Predatory sciomyzid larvae exhibit a broad range of feeding behaviors, kinds of prey, and associated adaptations.

Freshwater predators. This largest group consists of 74 species in 14 genera, all in Tetanocerini, all in the terminal half of cladograms, occurring in all zoogeographical regions, and all with rather stereotyped larval feeding behavior (see "A Cornucopia for Sciomyzidae and Phaeomyiidae" at **http://www.sciomyzidae.info/downloads.php?cat_id=1**). Although their behavior and associated adaptations differ somewhat, these larvae are the most overtly rapacious Sciomyzidae. Their prey range in the laboratory is broad (but probably narrower in nature). They attack and kill their prey within a few minutes, feed until gorged, and then rest away from the prey. They kill up to 50 snails of various sizes during the three stadia. They are wasteful predators, killing snails even when their gut is full. Whereas aquatic predaceous Tetanocerini probably evolved from shoreline predators early after divergence from a common stock with the Sciomyzini, they then probably acquired aquatic adaptations and became the basic line from which semiterrestrial and terrestrial Tetanocerini evolved (24). This group includes species that have been the main subjects of controlled laboratory experiments [*Ilione albiseta* (46, 47), *Sepedon fuscipennis* (8, 31), *S. sphegea* (44, 50), *S. spinipes* (75, 83, 85, 86), and *Tetanocera ferruginea* (71–74, 124)] (see Laboratory Experimental Studies on Behavior and Development, below).

Terrestrial predators. A few Sciomyzini and 25 Tetanocerini in eight genera are considered terrestrial predators, although their behavioral, phenological, and morphological adaptations and their polyphyletic ancestry likely represent several evolutionary lines (7, 24). Major differences and nuances in behavior are especially striking in this group, ranging from outright predation to aspects of parasitoid behavior (e.g., prey limited to a few species from one or two genera, slow death of the prey, and few prey individuals killed), especially during early larval life. Examples in Tetanocerini include four slug-killing *Tetanocera* species (24), a few *Sepedon* and *Tetanocera* parasitoids and predators of succineid snails, truly terrestrial predators such as *Tetanocera phyllophora* and *Trypetoptera punctulata* (119), and some Sciomyzini in *Pherbellia*, *Pteromicra*, and *Sciomyza* (see "A Cornucopia for Sciomyzidae and Phaeomyiidae" at **http://www.sciomyzidae.info/downloads.php?cat_id=1**).

Plesiotypic: describes a given behavior or habitat preference that is ancestral as opposed to derived

Evaluation of the life cycles of the highly specialized, apomorphic/apotypic fingernail-clam-killing species (in three unrelated genera), the snail-egg-feeding *Anticheta*, and the oligochaete-feeding *Sepedonella* and *Sepedon* species (all in Tetanocerini) in relation to their (unresolved) positions in cladistic analyses is critical to an evolutionary scenario of feeding behavior in Sciomyzidae.

The taxonomic value, phyletic significance, and functional morphology of sciomyzid eggs, larvae, and puparia have been presented (67). We summarize here important morphological adaptations of larvae relative to feeding behavior. Feeding behavior of Sciomyzini larvae, which generally feed in a somewhat insidious manner, differs strongly from that of Tetanocerini larvae, which are generally more overt feeders. All Sciomyzini lack accessory teeth below the mouthhook, indicating a less rapacious behavior than in Tetanocerini, in which accessory teeth are present, even in the derived terrestrial species. The ventral arch and pharyngeal sclerite of predatory Tetanocerini are much more expansive than those of Sciomyzini, providing increased area for muscle attachment. Although many larvae, especially Sciomyzini, feed for long periods in decaying, liquefying tissues of hosts/prey, only *Salticella fasciata* (one of three species of the plesiomorphic Salticellinae) has oral grooves around the mouth opening and ridges in the pharynx floor—adaptations common among saprophagous muscoid larvae for filtering microorganisms from decaying animal or plant tissues (66). Whereas *S. fasciata* is the only sciomyzid reared to pupariation and emergence solely on dead tissues of nonmolluscs (sowbugs and annelids), its first instars feed as parasitoids or saprophagously in terrestrial snails, and older larvae are strictly saprophagous.

Morphological adaptations to microhabitat limit the hosts/prey available to larvae and thus, to some extent, determine the type of feeding behavior (24, 122). Adaptations of many Tetanocerini to a surface or, rarely, subsurface existence (i.e., elongate last segment with upturned posterior spiracular disk having elongate lobes and interspiracular processes, pigmented integument with sensilla hairs) are lacking in Sciomyzini. The latter have a short last segment with a rear-facing posterior spiracular disk, short lobes on the disk, short interspiracular processes, unpigmented integument, and extensive ventral spinule patches that probably enhance mobility across substrates populated by "stranded" snails. Secondarily terrestrial Tetanocerini larvae (assuming a freshwater existence as the plesiotypic condition) have the same cephalopharyngeal skeleton features as do aquatic species but resemble Sciomyzini in having a short last segment with a rear-facing posterior spiracular disk, short lobes on the disk, short interspiracular processes, and colorless integument but no ventral spinule patches.

The 26 behaviorally, morphologically, and phenologically diverse reared species of *Tetanocera* (the fourth largest genus, with 39 species) are among the biologically best-known Sciomyzidae and have been the subjects of many experimental and life cycle studies (see "A Cornucopia for Sciomyzidae and Phaeomyiidae" at **http://www.sciomyzidae.info/downloads.php?cat_id=1**). With a phylogeny (from a cladistic analysis of molecular characters) as a framework, analyses of the morphological features and microhabitats of 17 *Tetanocera* species suggested the freshwater habitat as the ancestral condition for the genus, with at least three parallel transitions to terrestrial habitat and one reversal (24). Hosts/prey, feeding behavior, and phenology were not included in the analyses, but the evolution of microhabitat selection delimited available hosts/prey and associated adaptations in feeding behavior and phenology.

PHENOLOGY

Diverse phenological adaptations are associated with macrohabitats and microhabitats, hosts/prey, and feeding behavior. More species have been analyzed from cool temperate latitudes of North America than from elsewhere; five groups of voltinism and overwintering were proposed, as listed below (20). These groups are summarized and modified, with representative species included, in **Supplemental Text 3**; **Supplemental Figures 4** and **5** are graphic displays.

- Group 1: Multivoltine species overwintering in the puparium as diapausing or quiescent prepupae, pupae, or pharate adults
- Group 2: Multivoltine species overwintering as diapausing adults
- Group 3: Univoltine species overwintering within the egg membranes
- Group 4: Univoltine species overwintering partly or entirely in the larval stage
- Group 5: Univoltine species overwintering in the puparium

No sciomyzid has a life cycle lasting much more than one year, although in a few species, members of a cohort (i.e., larvae developing from eggs laid on the same day during autumn) may include individuals that overwinter either in the puparium or as adults, and some of these overwintering adults possibly live a few months more than a year. The capture, marking, and release of a female *Sepedon fuscipennis* in Ithaca, New York, during August and her recapture in a reproductively active condition the following May (2) indicate a life cycle slightly longer than one year.

Berg et al. (20) summarized that most multivoltine species overwinter in puparia and that some overwinter as adults, whereas univoltine species overwinter as embryonated eggs, partly grown larvae, or in puparia. They concluded that multivoltinism with overwintering in the puparium is the most common and widespread phenology and that some species, especially some in Group 5, are labile and develop seasonally in alternative ways. Puparia of many aquatic and semiaquatic predatory species in cold-winter areas that eventually produce adults are often found at the surface during periods of ice melt during winter. Puparia of most species apparently survive freezing in the ice cover.

Many semiaquatic and terrestrial univoltine and multivoltine Sciomyzini form puparia in the host/prey shell. This behavior, especially in *Pherbellia* that produce a calcareous septum occluding the aperture, might be an adaptation for overwintering as well as for protection, the shell serving perhaps as a cocoon. In regions with cold winters, many species that overwinter as adults, e.g., most *Sepedon* and *Elgiva* and some *Pherbellia* in southern parts of their ranges, are active on warm days during winter. Their apparent "basking" behavior likely raises their metabolic rate.

Stereotyped phenology characterizes aquatic and semiaquatic predators in tropical and warm areas. They appear to be multivoltine, with a variable number of generations (perhaps 4–12) per year that are not discrete but are successive and overlapping. In laboratory rearings they show no indication of diapause, develop promptly, have a short preoviposition period, a long oviposition period, and short egg, larval, and pupal periods. Similarly behaving species from warm areas of the Neotropical, Afrotropical, and Oriental regions have been consigned to a separate group, Group 6 (67). A few temperate-zone New Zealand and Neotropical species also seem to fit into Group 6.

LABORATORY EXPERIMENTAL STUDIES ON BEHAVIOR AND DEVELOPMENT

Many aspects of Sciomyzidae have been studied experimentally, primarily in the laboratory and to a lesser extent in the field, but on relatively few species. We focus on laboratory experiments on key aspects of behavior and development conducted mostly under at least partially controlled conditions. Other aspects studied experimentally include the impacts of molluscicides on larvae (81), natural enemies of sciomyzids (57, 95), use of a salivary gland toxin by larvae to immobilize their prey (116), mass rearing potential (88), thermal constants (137), numerical responses (123), and coefficient of food for larval growth and energy gain (31).

Experimental conditions, especially water depth, varied significantly among studies. Although benchtop life cycle investigations conducted under ambient conditions might be considered experiments, we consider most of the results to be observations only. Such life cycle studies have often included simple short-term experiments resulting in conclusions that should be investigated further with current methods. Results of almost all experimental studies were reviewed recently (67), but the authors did not synthesize most research results to derive possibly new outcomes or to resolve conflicting conclusions. Among aquatic predators, the best studied are the multivoltine *T. ferruginea* (Holarctic), *Sepedon senex* (Oriental), *S. sphegea* and *S. spinipes* (Palearctic), and *S. fuscipennis* (Nearctic); the univoltine *Ilione albiseta* (Palearctic); and among terrestrial parasitoids/predators the multivoltine *Pherbellia schoenherri schoenherri* and the univoltine *Salticella fasciata*, *Euthycera* spp. (all Palearctic), and *Sciomyza varia* (Nearctic), a parasitoid on aestivating *Lymnaea* snails.

Oviposition by several terrestrial and some semiterrestrial species appears to be triggered by various factors including number of available prey (123), size and maturity of suitable hosts (29), and presence of snail feces (28). Stimulatory cues for aquatic and semiaquatic species are unknown but could be worth researching, given the potential for the development of kairomones to attract potential biocontrols into target areas. During mass-rearing studies, addition of protein, e.g., crushed snails (25), reduced the preoviposition period while increasing the number of eggs laid and adult longevity. Sigmoidal oviposition curves have been described for many insects (55), including some Sciomyzidae (14, 47, 83, 119), and are useful indicators of egg production of wild-caught females, e.g., a curve truncated on the left indicates that oviposition had commenced in nature. Using oviposition data, Haab (50) identified 15°C as the oviposition threshold temperature for *S. sphegea* overwintering as nonreproductive adults in France under natural autumn photoperiod (8:16); at 12°C, no females oviposited. Identifying such threshold temperatures will be useful in the future for matching sciomyzids to climates of areas where inoculative biocontrol programs are planned.

Hatching of submerged eggs of *Ilione albiseta* is facilitated by low oxygen levels (45). The thermal reaction norm is useful for determining whether an animal is cold or warm adapted (117). Eggs of the univoltine *I. albiseta* are significantly cold adapted (100). Cryopreservation of sciomyzid eggs for long-term storage or transportation has received little attention (83); there has been some success with other flies (e.g., *Musca domestica*, 129).

Much experimental research on Sciomyzidae has focused on larvae, the active malacophagous stage. The impact of prey species and prey and larval density on the duration of the larval stage has been elucidated for some aquatic species (**Supplemental Figure 6**). The length of time before attacking the first gastropod seems variable for neonate survival (13). Starvation of neonate larvae of *S. sphegea* adversely affected survival of later instars, pupae, and adults (**Supplemental Figures 7** and **8**). Survival doubled at 20°C, 23°C, and 26°C when neonate larvae of *Sepedon spinipes* were fed one snail before starvation (82), an important finding in terms of release of larvae in biocontrol. However, determining which stage of sciomyzids to release remains a question. Prey searching by first instars tends to be random; efficacy depends on crawling speed, prey density and distribution, and water depth (17, 31, 43). Neonates of some freshwater predators actively pursued prey by following fresh snail mucus trails but not trails aged 45 min (86) (**Supplemental Figure 9**). Subsurface foraging is practiced by a few freshwater Tetanocerini (126); *I. albiseta* larvae use dissolved oxygen (47), but the means of uptake remains unknown.

Many studies have examined photoperiod and temperature effects on survival and development time. In general, duration of all stadia decreased with increasing temperature (8, 85, 119, 137), percentage hatch was greater at lower temperatures, photoperiod manipulation caused *T. ferruginea* to bypass diapause (124), and the temperature at which the immature stages were reared influenced the longevity of adults of *S. sphegea* (**Supplemental Table 5**). The above data are crucial for defining optimum conditions for mass-rearing purposes in biocontrol.

The amount of prey consumed by individual larvae depends on their feeding behavior, relative sizes of larvae and prey, and density of prey and larvae (**Supplemental Figure 10**). For strict parasitoids, the larval stage tends to be completed on one host, whatever its size; such larvae rarely forage for additional hosts. For predators attacking aquatic snails, the relationship tends to be size dependent, with neonate larvae killing smaller snails and later instars killing larger snails (42). In terms of prey density, a strong functional response has been reported, ranging from Type I (second- and third-instar *S. senex*; 17) to Type II (second- and third-instar *S. sphegea*; 50) to Type III (third-instar *S. senex*; 17). Water depth appeared to be insignificant in governing functional response, but the addition of vegetation to experimental arenas increased snail biomass consumed (50) when prey density decreased (**Supplemental Figure 11**), apparently because it facilitated snail aggregation at the water surface. Eckblad (31), using equations to predict total number of snails killed per larva in shallow water, found that a simple power function might be more predictive than the predator models of Holling's classic work (53). At high snail densities, many freshwater predators showed high food conversion ratios when they killed many snails but only partially consumed them (120). Such wasteful feeding (56) can be related to optimal foraging theory because it might increase the energy-intake rate of predators by enabling them to consume only the most nutritious parts of their prey. Because more prey are killed in this scenario than otherwise, such behavior would be a useful trait in selection of potential biocontrols.

Many studies have investigated prey preference. The first, in regard to freshwater species (91), showed that larvae of 10 species killed only nonoperculate snails, all hosts of *Schistosoma* and all from outside the geographical range of the sciomyzids studied, thus highlighting their biocontrol potential. Larvae of the freshwater predator *T. ferruginea* displayed labile feeding behavior depending on the combinations of available snail species (73, 74). Those larvae chose prey providing the greatest return per unit of energy expended (72). As with other insects (e.g., Pteromalidae, 26), *T. ferruginea* displayed a "switching" phenomenon sensu Murdoch (89). As a measure of predation, biomass consumed (being independent of snail size and number of snails) has been the preferred index to number and sizes of snails killed. Larvae of *T. ferruginea* consumed more snails but less biomass when offered one prey species but consumed fewer individuals and more biomass when offered multiple prey species; overall they preferred large, sexually mature individuals (71). As a result, this species might have considerable impact on snail populations in the wild. Because *T. ferruginea* is one of the best-studied sciomyzids, it should be a priority for biocontrol in temperate areas. Number and biomass of snails consumed daily by *S. sphegea* also increased with various combinations of temperatures (12°C–30°C) and photoperiods (8:16, 12:12, and 16:8) (44, 50).

Studies have been conducted on intra- and interspecific competition (15, 16), but limitations include mixing of unlikely ecological equivalents (e.g., species partitioned spatially in different microhabitats) and exclusion of other malacophagous taxa (e.g., Lampyridae). As with some Tephritidae (3), intraspecific competition among the parasitoid *P. schoenherri schoenherri* (123) and the aquatic predator *Sepedon sphegea* (44) often resulted in some larvae gaining and maintaining a competitive advantage at the expense of conspecifics (123). Emerging adults ranged widely in size (44) (**Supplemental Figure 12**).

Experimental studies on pupae have focused on sexual dimorphism and overwintering. It is possible to predict the adult sex of *Tetanocera ferruginea* and *Sepedon spinipes* adults prior to eclosion by measuring puparium length (69) and weight (85), respectively; this method could be used to determine differences in hymenopteran parasitoid load between sexes. Its use also would facilitate establishment of cultures for mass rearing because puparia are more easily manipulated than motile adults are and sex ratios of cultures could be set prior to the emergence of adults. Puparia can be dissected to determine the overwintering stage within (i.e., young or old prepupae, pupae, or pharate adults), and temperature can be manipulated to elucidate their physiological state (i.e., quiescence or true diapause) (20). This area, critical for fine-tuning phenologies for selecting biocontrols and for studying the overall evolution of the family, is in need of further research.

Metacommunity: a set of local communities linked by dispersal

Biodiversity indicator: group of taxa or functional group whose diversity reflects diversity of other higher taxa in a habitat or set of habitats

POPULATION BIOLOGY, BIOINDICATORS, ECOSYSTEM SERVICE PROVISION, AND CONSERVATION

Populations of adult Sciomyzidae are found in metacommunities over large areas of similar habitat. Within these macrohabitats are egg, larval, and puparial microhabitats, of which the last two may be sampled by a variety of methods (**Supplemental Text 4**). Adults move infrequently within a macrohabitat and between nearby macrohabitats (**Supplemental Text 5**), but the wide geographical ranges of many sciomyzids suggest broader saltatory movements. Peacock (97) studied the movements of the Nearctic aquatic predator *Sepedon fuscipennis* using mark-recapture techniques and suggested in his unpublished thesis that movements of adults were more extensive in lotic macrohabitats than in lentic macrohabitats. Restricted movement of Sciomyzidae also has been noted in a number of Palearctic studies (109, 121, 133). Four mark-recapture studies on Sciomyzidae, two of which concern *S. fuscipennis*, have been published. Adult populations of approximately 1 (32) and 0.53 (2) flies per m^2 were reported from a backwater habitat and an experimentally flooded area, respectively, in New York, and population estimates of an assemblage of 10 species were as high as 6.08 flies per m^2 in an Irish turlough (temporary karstic lake) (133). Although the latter estimates are 6–12 times higher than the former estimates, they are consistent with a wider study in Irish turloughs (133, 135). In a study of an assemblage of sciomyzids (three *Sepedon* and one *Sepedonella* species), with emphasis on *Sepedon ruficeps* (42), in temporary and permanent freshwater habitats in Bénin, West Africa, the population of *S. ruficeps* in both habitats peaked three months after maximal rainfall, but adults were present continually in the permanently wet habitat. This was one of the few studies, in addition to those by Eckblad & Berg (32) and Arnold (2), in which snail and sciomyzid populations were studied simultaneously.

Substantial information has been published on seasonal variation in population sizes of sciomyzids, especially adults, but more precision and variety are needed in sampling methods throughout the year. Mark-recapture was used to illustrate diel fluctuations in a forest population of *Trypetoptera punctulata* and eight associated species in southern France (118). High temperatures reduced activity during midday. In a turlough in Ireland, sweep-net collecting showed that five species tended to peak between the end of July and mid-August, although some *Tetanocera* peaked earlier (133). In a study on a different turlough, the proportion of individuals of *Ilione albiseta* captured in two vegetation zones on either side of a hillock shifted seasonally (134) (**Supplemental Text 5**). The shift was interpreted as an effect of water depth on the temperature at which each subpopulation developed. A succession of population peaks (May/June, July/August, October) was found for 14 species by sweep-net collecting in a temporarily inundated habitat in southern France (125). The same study showed a peak in species richness in June/July that coincided with a dip in equitability (species evenness), suggesting dominance of one or a few species.

Although scant explicit work has been conducted on Sciomyzidae as biodiversity indicators (94, 103), sciomyzids often appear in a supporting role in studies of wetlands and forests (**Supplemental Text 6**). Sciomyzidae as bioindicators may be considered in a normative framework, i.e., in terms of a set of ideal rules as to their selection, verification, and application (87), and in terms of pragmatic constraints, i.e., ease of collection, ubiquity, taxonomic stability, and availability of literature. The latter factors were considered in a European context, and Sciomyzidae were suggested as an auxiliary group especially suited to wetland habitats (108). Sciomyzidae were listed along with Chloropidae, Ephydridae, Scathophagidae, and Sphaeroceridae as among the most important families of Diptera in freshwater wetlands in North America in terms of population size and species richness (60). Microhabitat selectivity and the significant role played in food webs add to the flies' utility as bioindicators. Populations of the relatively sedentary adults display qualitative and quantitative changes in species composition and relative abundance with habitat type, habitat management (e.g., grazing), and hydrology. Species richness and biomass productivity typically are their highest at medium hydroperiods (130, 135), consistent with the intermediate disturbance hypothesis (132).

Environmental indicator: a species or group of species responding predictably to environmental disturbance or to a change in environmental state

Ecological bioindicators: species representing the response of at least a subset of other organisms to stresses in the environment

Fuzzy-coded databases: means of representing expert knowledge of species habitat/trait associations, coding species 0-3 by strength of association with habitats/traits

Economic externality: a cost or benefit not transmitted through prices

Species lists and faunistic studies can be extremely useful in conservation work, especially in interpreting site history and management factors (110). Fuzzy-coded habitat-association and species-trait databases are ideal means of integrating expert knowledge and powerful multivariate statistical techniques. Such databases have proven useful for different taxa in a number of ecological contexts (**Supplemental Text 7**). A similar database being prepared for the European Sciomyzidae will widen their application as ecological bioindicators. Similar projects on the well-known Nearctic fauna would be useful, but wider sampling and more detailed ecological and basic biological research are needed before such projects can be attempted in Afrotropical, Neotropical, and Oriental regions.

Much interest in ecosystem service provision has resulted from the realization that services provided by nature can no longer be regarded as economic externalities of zero value (30). The value of insects as dung buriers, pollinators, pest controllers, and food for wildlife has been estimated to be US$57 billion per year in the United States alone (68). The snail-killing impact of Sciomyzidae has not been included in published assessments of ecosystem services, yet it is well known that dam construction and concomitant environmental change result in expanded distributions of freshwater snails serving as intermediate hosts of flatworms that cause diseases of humans and livestock.

One of the best-known Sciomyzidae faunas is that of Britain and Ireland. Early collation of these records is continually supplemented, with new records regularly reported for both areas (**Supplemental Text 8**). Even in such relatively small, well-known faunas, baseline data are lacking on which to judge the importance of conservation of Sciomyzidae. Nevertheless, attempts have been made to list species of greatest concern and to attribute causes of decline of populations (36, 107) (**Supplemental Table 6**). With few invertebrates protected through legislation [no Diptera are listed in Annex II of the European Habitats Directive (34)], the most effective means of conserving Sciomyzidae is probably through the coarse filter of habitat protection. A third approach to conservation, between the fine filter provided by species lists—faunistic studies—and the coarse filter, is the so-called mesofilter of critical ecosystem elements (54). Many of these elements are not recorded in standard vegetation surveys but are critical to documenting insect communities. Sensitive management for invertebrates can be attained even in the absence of surveys by gross habitat protection (61, 105). Data on macrohabitat/microhabitat associations and species traits will contribute to adoption of a mesofilter approach to Sciomyzidae conservation and improved use of Sciomyzidae as bioindicators and ecosystem service providers (111).

IDENTIFICATION AND SYSTEMATICS

Adult sciomyzids are readily recognized by porrect, projecting to slightly decumbent or drooping antennae; parallel to slightly divergent postocellar setae; lack of oral vibrissae; unexposed clypeus;

unbroken costal vein without strong setae; vein $A_1 + CuA_2$ (anal vein) usually reaching the wing margin; and one or more tibiae with a dorsal preapical seta but no medial setae. The ease of identifying live adults of many species in the field or in a vial under the microscope—as well as the sedentary behavior, longevity, and tolerance of both adults and larvae—renders the family ideal for field and laboratory studies.

The most complete source of generic keys to sciomyzid adults and larvae (and to Nearctic and Palearctic puparia) by zoogeographic region, for all regions, is by Knutson & Vala (67). Also listed therein and in **Supplemental Texts 9** and **10** are other publications with keys, primarily to adults, for regions or subregions.

Species-level taxonomy for Sciomyzidae is well developed. Molecular studies of several species complexes are needed, e.g., several so-called subspecies, Holarctic species, the Nearctic *Sepedon fuscipennis* complex (70), and many Afrotropical *Sepedon* species. Taxonomic catalogs are available for all regions (**Supplemental Text 11**). The Smithsonian Institution, with 411 species and type specimens of 110 species, holds the most complete, authoritatively identified collection. A world checklist of valid species, with location of type material (in 64 collections in 27 countries), is available (67).

Sciomyzidae seem well placed in the superfamily Sciomyzoidea (which also includes Coelopidae, Dryomyzidae, Helosciomyzidae, Natalimyzidae, Phaeomyiidae, Ropalomeridae, and Sepsidae) (9, 10, 12, 51, 52, 80, 131), although some authors (e.g., 79) disagree as to which families should be included in Sciomyzoidea and whether the superfamily is monophyletic. We follow McAlpine (80) in considering Lauxanioidea as the sister group to Sciomyzoidea. Using maximum likelihood (ML) and Bayesian (BI) methods, Wiegmann et al. (131) analyzed a comprehensive Diptera data set [>200 taxa; 149 of 157 families; 5 nuclear genes: 7 kilobases with 42 taxa having sequences from 14 nuclear genes, complete mitochondrial genomes (approximately 30 kilobases), and 371 morphological characters]. The analyses recovered a clade for Sciomyzoidea containing six families traditionally classified as Sciomyzoidea + Huttoninidae and Conopidae and the recently described family Natalimyzidae (12). Previously, family status was proposed for the generally recognized sciomyzid subfamily Phaeomyiinae (which then included only three Palearctic *Pelidnoptera* species, one of which is an obligate parasitoid of millipedes) (49). That placement generally has been followed, with Phaeomyiidae considered the sister group to Sciomyzidae, but a revision of *Pelidnoptera* that described the new genus *Akebono* (Japan) placed both genera in the Phaeomyiinae without discussion (113). Other segregates, especially the Helosciomyzinae and Huttonininae, have been included in or excluded from the Sciomyzidae by various authors (see **Supplemental Table 7**).

Before recent cladistic analyses of genera within Sciomyzidae and Phaeomyiidae (7, 23, 76) (see next section), major works were published on the suprageneric classification of Sciomyzidae (9, 10, 49, 51, 52, 112, 127). Although Steyskal's (112) and Verbeke's (127) papers were not couched in Hennigian (51) cladistic terminology, those authors were well acquainted with and sometimes used Hennigian principles.

Several genera, especially the species-rich worldwide genus *Pherbellia*, are obviously polyphyletic, and several subgenera in various genera probably should be raised to generic level. Taxonomy of Sciomyzidae lacks rigorous, comparative diagnoses, as pointed out in a major study of Sciomyzidae of the U.S. mid-Atlantic states (L.V. Knutson, W.L. Murphy & W.N. Mathis, unpublished manuscript). Many genera are based on descriptions/figures of only a few key characters. Studies of underutilized character systems are needed, especially of female abdomens.

Morphological studies of immature stages generally support the suprageneric classification based on adults, but systematics research and cladistic analyses of immatures are needed at the generic level. Detailed analyses of character states of features of immature stages are available, with diagnoses at the family, subfamily, and tribe levels (67).

PHYLOGENETICS, MOLECULAR STUDIES, AND EVOLUTIONARY BIOLOGY

Only two family-wide phylogenetic studies of adult Sciomyzidae, and four studies of species within a genus (*Protodictya*, *Sepedonea*, *Tetanocera*, and *Thecomyia*; see below), have been conducted. The first family-level phylogeny used maximum parsimony (MP), analyzing 38 characters (36 adult, 1 larval morphological, and 1 larval behavioral) scored for the type species of 50 of the 61 genera (76). Seven adult morphological characters were added to those data, the larval characters were removed, and they were reanalyzed with MP (7). Both analyses recovered a monophyletic Salticellinae, Sciomyzini, and Tetanocerini. An MP bootstrap analysis of the former data set revealed that whereas relationships among most genera received relatively low support, relationships were well supported among *Sepedon* and five related genera that share derived states of eight characters. Most notably, the *Sepedon* lineage completely lacks a ptilinum (present in all other 42,000 ± Schizophora species) (67). Studies of individual genera using MP included 21 adult morphological characters scored for all 8 *Protodictya* species (75), 21 adult morphological characters analyzed to produce a phylogeny for all 12 *Thecomyia* species (78), and 27 adult morphological characters analyzed for all 13 *Sepedonea* species (77). The only published molecular-based phylogenetic study analyzed a concatenated four-gene data set (*COI*, *COII*, *16S*, *28S*; 3,787 characters) of 31 species among nine genera (54 specimens) focusing on *Tetanocera*, using BI, ML, and MP methods (24).

Five approaches (7, 21, 37, 48, 63) were used to categorize sciomyzids into Behavioral Groups on the basis of commonalities in larval microhabitat (aquatic, damp shoreline, terrestrial), mode of feeding (parasitoid, predator, saprophage), and prey type (freshwater and terrestrial nonoperculate snails, littoral and brackish-water operculate snails, succineid snails, snail eggs, slugs, fingernail clams, oligochaetes) (see Life Cycles, Larval Feeding Behavior, and Associated Adaptations, above). Of these, the ordination analysis by Barker et al. (7) used semistrong, hybrid, multidimensional scaling of 36 egg and larval morphological characters, larval behavior (omitting prey type), and habitat, recognizing nine "Eco-Groups." However, without placement in a phylogenetic context, it cannot be determined whether closely related species in these groupings represent monophyletic lineages or whether feeding behaviors evolved in parallel.

Knutson & Vala (63) mapped their own Behavioral Groups onto the Marinoni & Mathis cladogram (76), numbering their groups in an evolutionary sequence. Utility of this approach was limited because the cladogram was relatively unresolved and did not estimate species-level evolutionary relationships within genera, but we provide some generalizations on the basis of that effort: (*a*) Ancestral sciomyzid habitat undoubtedly was terrestrial because Salticellinae and Sciomyzini (the basal lineages in the cladogram) are terrestrial (although some Sciomyzini occur on moist surfaces along terrestrial-aquatic interfaces)—as are all but the most derived members of other families of Sciomyzoidea. (*b*) Ancestral feeding behavior was likely similar to that of the extant *Atrichomelina pubera* because both are facultative (parasitoids/predators/saprophages depending upon food availability, level of intraspecific competition, etc.) and both attack assemblages of aquatic and semiaquatic snails in diverse moist habitats. (*c*) Aquatic habitats were invaded early during the phylogenesis of Tetanocerini (based upon phylogenetic relationships of aquatic and terrestrial Tetanocerini) and occurred multiple times in parallel, once followed by parallel reinvasions of terrestrial habitats, or both.

ML was used to optimize larval habitat onto a molecular phylogeny of *Tetanocera* (24). Results of this optimization were consistent with the hypothesis that larvae invaded aquatic habitats early during Tetanocerine evolution and that *Tetanocera* invaded terrestrial habitats multiple times from their aquatic ancestry. The latter study is one of the first to use phylogenetic comparative methods to explore morphological adaptations to both aquatic and terrestrial habitats of insects.

Ferrar (37) concluded that sciomyzid "larval morphology is predominantly functional and that larvae show a number of interesting examples of parallel evolution." This hypothesis was examined using the program Discrete® (96) to test for correlated evolution among larval habitat and four larval morphological characters apparently associated with larval habitat (24). (Discrete® uses an ML framework and examines distributions of character states across a phylogeny, testing for potential correlations among two binary characters.) Correlations were significant between transitions in larval habitat (aquatic versus terrestrial) and changes in the states of the four morphological characters. These analyses demonstrated at least three parallel aquatic-to-terrestrial larval habitat transitions in *Tetanocera*. In each transition, larvae of terrestrials lost pigmentation, and float hairs and ventrolateral lobes of posterior spiracular disks and the last segment became shortened, resulting in a rear-facing spiracular disk (upturned in aquatics). These analyses supported Ferrar's (37) hypothesis regarding the functionality and parallel evolution of larval morphology.

Sciomyzid phylogenetic studies have focused primarily on adult and secondarily on larval morphological characters. One study (24) included molecular characters and, in an ecological context, attempted to reconstruct habitat transitions of ancestral species. As of September 2011, DNA sequence data for only 32 of the 540 sciomyzid species were available from GenBank. Researchers currently are developing molecular phylogenies of Sciomyzidae using a combination of mitochondrial and nuclear genes. A molecular phylogeny that included 61 sciomyzid species in 22 genera was presented (115). In his PhD dissertation, Chapman (23) presented a molecular phylogeny with 65 sciomyzid species in 22 genera (123 terminal taxa). He optimized feeding group transitions on the phylogeny and found multiple examples of parallel evolution of feeding behaviors within the family. More extensive phylogenetic work on adult and larval morphological and molecular characters, combined with explicit tests of hypotheses related to evolutionary transitions in ancestral species, will provide a more complete understanding of the family as a paradigm for the evolution of parasitoid/predator/saprophage feeding habits along a terrestrial-aquatic ecological gradient.

Schistosomiasis: an important parasitic disease of humans caused by three *Schistosoma* species; also called bilharzia

Fascioliasis: a disease of humans and certain animals caused by *Fasciola* trematode flatworms in temperate and warm parts of the world

BIOCONTROL

Researchers have evaluated sciomyzids for use as biocontrols of freshwater snails (Hydrobiidae, Lymnaeidae, and Planorbidae) that serve as obligate intermediate hosts of the flatworm parasites *Schistosoma*, which cause schistosomiasis of humans and cattle in tropical and subtropical areas (see **Supplemental Figure 13**), and *Fasciola*, which cause fascioliasis of humans and livestock worldwide. Biocontrol potential has also been studied for two sciomyzids against snail pests of pasture and grain crops in Australia (27). Among reviews of biocontrol of snails and slugs by sciomyzids, that by the malacologist Barker (7) is a particularly valuable analysis of the use of sciomyzids in relation to modern ecological and biocontrol theory.

Advantages of using predatory sciomyzids as biocontrols, by augmentation and/or introduction of exotics, include the following: (*a*) They are obligate natural enemies of gastropods. (*b*) Many species have several generations per year. (*c*) They feed voraciously. (*d*) They live long and have high survival rates. (*e*) Natural enemy pressure on them is apparently low (research is under way). (*f*) Their diverse feeding behaviors and microhabitat preferences enable researchers to select "tailor-made" agents. (*g*) They are broadly distributed both geographically and across macrohabitats, i.e., traits advantageous to selecting agents targeted to diverse recipient environments. (*h*) They are easy to mass rear. Other specific biological advantages are noted throughout this review. The wealth of background information and active research by many cooperators are significant, synergistic advantages.

Aquatic, predaceous sciomyzids were field tested in a preliminary manner as biocontrols, e.g., through inoculative releases on Hawaii and several other Pacific Islands and augmentative trials in Iran. The first, best-documented inoculative release was of *Sepedomerus macropus* from Nicaragua into Hawaii (where there are no native sciomyzids) against a liver-fluke host (25). Only a few pupae were shipped to persons inexperienced with sciomyzids but who reared many adults for release. Larvae subsequently have been found feeding on target snails in nature (67); the species is established (33). This trial showed that sciomyzids could be shipped effectively, reared with local expertise and materials, and released effectively and could establish and disperse. In Iran, a native predator, *Sepedon sphegea*, was mass reared and released as larvae in rice fields against a snail host of *Schistosoma* (114).

A three-year study was conducted at six sites in South Africa to determine, in an augmentative approach managed at the rural community level, the value of the endemic *Sepedon neavei* and *S. scapularis* against host snails of *Schistosoma* (1). The authors considered mainly their laboratory results on aspects of predation, prey specificity, prey range, and competition. They projected the cost of operating a mass-rearing facility to treat several foci of transmission to be about US$700 per year (1992 US$), not including salaries. Their study reached Stage 3 b (controlled field trials—effectiveness under local conditions) of the WHO 1984 Plan for Development of Biological Vector Control Agents (136), the stage of final laboratory tests for indigenous control agents. On the basis of extensive laboratory studies and a brief, preliminary, small-scale field trial (with no evidence that the sciomyzid became established), the authors concluded that *S. neavei* satisfied most criteria proposed by Samways (104) and WHO (136) for an effective, predaceous biocontrol agent. They also concluded that *Sepedon* spp. used in large numbers likely would be effective only in shallow transmission foci and as part of an integrated control program.

Efforts to control snail intermediate hosts of flatworms with molluscicides and habitat management waned recently as emphasis shifted toward use of antihelminthic drugs for the vertebrate-definitive hosts. However, interest in Sciomyzidae and other biocontrols of snail intermediate hosts and conservation of sciomyzids as ecosystem service providers likely will grow because of increasing costs of and resistance to antihelminthics (35). Snail populations are increasing as a result of extensive construction of dams and irrigation systems in many countries. As early as 1972, Bardach (6), reviewing the ecological implications of water resource development projects in the Lower Mekong Valley, noted "there can easily be a sharp rise in schistosomiasis" and at least five other diseases, with snails and mosquitoes being of greatest concern as vectors. In their 2008 analysis of the global burden of schistosomiasis, Finkelstein et al. (38) found the impact of symptoms associated with *Schistosoma japonicum* to be 7–46 times greater than 1996 estimates (90). Schelle et al. (106) focused on environmental impacts of dam construction, especially biodiversity of natural ecosystems; for example, despite the known risks, the World Bank provided US$270 million in 2005 to construct a 38-m-high dam on a Mekong River tributary in Laos (41).

In conclusion, field research is needed on sciomyzids as biocontrols, particularly predation levels in natural populations, natural host/prey preferences, hymenopterous parasitoid pressure, numerical and functional response to predation, integrated control methods, and laboratory studies on cryopreservation, acclimatization, and mass rearing.

SUMMARY POINTS

1. Larvae of Sciomyzidae are obligate natural enemies of freshwater, brackish-water, littoral, semiterrestrial, and terrestrial snails, snail eggs, slugs, and fingernail (sphaeriid) clams; three species feed on freshwater oligochaetes.

2. With life cycles known for 240 of 540 species in 41 of 61 genera, Sciomyzidae are a resource for studying the evolution of feeding behavior, as biocontrol agents of gastropods that are intermediate hosts of flatworms that cause diseases of humans and livestock or are agricultural pests, as ecosystem service providers of snail and slug control, and as bioindicators.
3. Characterizations of 15 Behavioral Groups and 6 Phenological Groups provide templates for evolutionary studies and guidelines for further research on life cycles.
4. Focal points of research are coevolved features of larval microhabitat, parasitoid/predatory/saprophagous feeding behavior, phenology, and morphology of immature stages.
5. Phylogenetic work has focused on adult and larval morphological characters, but some work, notably on *Tetanocera*, has included molecular characters, and studies have included an ecological context in an attempt to reconstruct habitat transitions of ancestral species.
6. Research is needed to determine hosts/prey in nature, many aspects of natural populations, natural enemies, impact of sciomyzids on gastropod populations in the wild, databases on microhabitats and macrohabitats and species characteristics, priority bioindicators for a range of protected habitats, efficacy of potential biocontrol agents under controlled field trials, cladistic analyses of species and genera including molecular and morphological characters, and internal anatomy of larvae and adults.

DISCLOSURE STATEMENT

The authors are not aware of any affiliations, memberships, funding, or financial holdings that might be perceived as affecting the objectivity of this review.

ACKNOWLEDGMENTS

For reviewing the manuscript we thank J. Abercrombie, R. Anderson, J. Badmin, J.K. Barnes, J.B. Coupland, T. Gittings, K.C. Kim, W.N. Mathis, I. McLean, R.E. Orth, T.D. Paine, R. Rozkošný, M.C.D. Speight, and K.R. Valley. For permission to use data in the supplemental materials we thank S.A. Marshall for the photo of mating sciomyzids; M. Schlabach and the Division of Rare and Manuscript Collections, A.R. Mann Library, Cornell University, for including the film by K. Sandved and the late C.O. Berg; M. Ghamizi, C. Haab, and D. Peacock for use of unpublished material from their theses; and authors and copyright holders for reproduction of figures and tables.

LITERATURE CITED

1. Appleton CC, Miller RM, Maharaj R. 1993. Control of schistosomiasis host snails in South Africa—the case for biocontrol by predator augmentation using sciomyzid flies. *J. Med. Appl. Malacol.* 5:107–16
2. Arnold SL. 1978. Sciomyzidae (Diptera) population parameters estimated by the capture-recapture method. *Proc. Entomol. Soc. Ont.* 107(1976):3–9
3. Averill AL, Prokopy RJ. 1987. Intraspecific competition in the tephritid fruit fly, *Rhagoletis pomonella*. *Ecology* 68:878–86
4. Bailey PT. 1989. The millipede parasitoid *Pelidnoptera nigripennis* (F.) (Diptera: Sciomyzidae) for the biological control of the millipede *Ommatoiulus moreleti* (Lucas) (Diplopoda: Julida: Julidae) in Australia. *Bull. Entomol. Res.* 79:381–91

5. Baker GH. 1985. Parasites of the millipede *Ommatoiulus moreletii* (Lucas) (Diplopoda: Julidae) in Portugal, and their potential as biological control agents in Australia. *Aust. J. Zool.* 33:23–32
6. Bardach JE. 1972. Some ecological implications of Mekong River development plans. In *The Careless Technology: Ecology and International Development: The Record of the Conference on the Ecological Aspects of International Development*, ed. MT Farvar, JP Milton, pp. 236–44. Garden City, NY: Nat. Hist. Press. 1030 pp.
7. **Barker GM, Knutson L, Vala J-C, Coupland JB, Barnes JK. 2004. Overview of the biology of marsh flies (Diptera: Sciomyzidae), with special reference to predators and parasitoids of terrestrial gastropods. In *Natural Enemies of Terrestrial Molluscs*, ed. GM Barker, pp. 159–219. Wallingford, UK: CABI. 644 pp.**

7. Reviews the biology of Sciomyzidae, especially predators/parasitoids of terrestrial gastropods and behavior/biocontrol potential in a theoretical framework.

8. Barnes JK. 1976. Effect of temperature on development, survival, oviposition, and diapause in laboratory populations of *Sepedon fuscipennis* (Diptera: Sciomyzidae). *Environ. Entomol.* 5(6):1089–98
9. Barnes JK. 1979. The taxonomic position of the New Zealand genus *Prosochaeta* Malloch (Diptera: Sciomyzidae). *Proc. Entomol. Soc. Wash.* 81(2):285–97
10. Barnes JK. 1981. Revision of the Helosciomyzidae (Diptera). *J. R. Soc. N. Z.* 11(1):45–72
11. **Barnes JK. 1990. Biology and immature stages of *Sciomyza varia* (Diptera: Sciomyzidae), a specialized parasitoid of snails. *Ann. Entomol. Soc. Am.* 83(5):925–38**

11. Life cycle study of an intimately associated parasitoid of snails, incorporating analysis of larval feeding sites.

12. Barraclough DA, McAlpine DK. 2006. Natalimyzidae, a new African family of acalyptrate flies (Diptera: Schizophora: Sciomyzoidea). *Afr. Invertebr.* 47:117–34
13. Beaver O. 1972. Notes on the biology of some British sciomyzid flies (Diptera: Sciomyzidae). II. Tribe Tetanocerini. *Entomologist* 105:284–99
14. Beaver O. 1973. Egg laying studies on some British sciomyzid flies (Diptera: Sciomyzidae). *Hydrobiologia* 43(1–2):1–12
15. Beaver O. 1974. Laboratory studies on competition for food of the larvae of some British sciomyzid flies (Diptera: Sciomyzidae). I. Intra-specific competition. *Hydrobiologia* 44(4):443–62
16. Beaver O. 1974. Laboratory studies on competition for food of the larvae of some British sciomyzid flies (Diptera: Sciomyzidae). II. Interspecific competition. *Hydrobiologia* 45(1):135–53
17. Beaver O. 1989. Study of effect of *Sepedon senex* W. (Sciomyzidae) larvae on snail vectors of medically important trematodes. *J. Sci. Soc. Thail.* 15:171–89
18. Berg CO. 1953. Sciomyzid larvae that feed in snails. *J. Parasitol.* 39(6):630–36
19. Berg CO. 1964. Snail control in trematode diseases: the possible value of sciomyzid larvae, snail-killing Diptera. *Adv. Parasitol.* 2:259–309
20. Berg CO, Foote BA, Knutson L, Barnes JK, Arnold SL, Valley K. 1982. Adaptive differences in phenology in sciomyzid flies. In *Recent Advances in Dipteran Systematics: Commemorative Volume in Honor of Curtis W. Sabrosky*, ed. WN Mathis, FC Thompson, pp. 15–36. *Mem. Entomol. Soc. Wash.* 10. 227 pp.
21. Berg CO, Knutson L. 1978. Biology and systematics of the Sciomyzidae. *Annu. Rev. Entomol.* 23:239–58
22. Bratt AD, Knutson LV, Foote BA, Berg CO. 1969. Biology of *Pherbellia* (Diptera: Sciomyzidae). *N. Y. Agric. Exp. Stn. Ithaca Mem.* 404:1–247
23. Chapman EG. 2008. *Bayesian phylogenetics of snail-killing flies (Diptera: Sciomyzidae) and freshwater mussels (Bivalvia: Unionidae): implications of parallel evolution, feeding group structure and molecular evolution.* PhD diss. Kent State Univ., Kent, Ohio
24. **Chapman EG, Foote BA, Malukiewicz J, Hoeh WR. 2006. Parallel evolution of larval morphology and habitat in the snail-killing fly genus *Tetanocera*. *J. Evol. Biol.* 19(5):1459–74**

24. Shows the parallel evolution of larval morphology and habitat in the snail-killing fly genus *Tetanocera*.

25. Chock QC, Davis CJ, Chong M. 1961. *Sepedon macropus* (Diptera: Sciomyzidae) introduced into Hawaii as a control for the liver fluke snail, *Lymnaea ollula*. *J. Econ. Entomol.* 54(1):1–4
26. Cornell H, Pimentel D. 1978. Switching in the parasitoid *Nasonia vitripennis* and its effects on host competition. *Ecology* 59(2):297–308
27. Coupland JB. 1996. The biological control of helicid snail pests in Australia: surveys, screening and potential agents. In *Slug and Snail Pests in Agriculture: Proceedings of a Symposium Held at the University of Kent, 24-26 September 1996*, ed. IF Henderson, pp. 255–61. Br. Crop Prot. Counc. Symp. Proc. 66. 450 pp.
28. Coupland JB. 1996. Influence of snail faeces and mucus on oviposition and larval behavior of *Pherbellia cinerella* (Diptera: Sciomyzidae). *J. Chem. Ecol.* 22(2):183–89

29. Coupland JB, Espiau A, Baker G. 1994. Seasonality, longevity, host choice, and infection efficiency of *Salticella fasciata* (Diptera: Sciomyzidae), a candidate for the biological control of pest helicid snails. *Biol. Control* 4:32–37
30. Daily GC, Söderqvist T, Aniyar S, Arrow K, Dasgupta P, et al. 2000. The value of nature and the nature of value. *Science* 289(5478):395–96
31. Eckblad JW. 1973. Experimental predation studies of malacophagous larvae of *Sepedon fuscipennis* (Diptera: Sciomyzidae) and aquatic snails. *Exp. Parasitol.* 33(2):331–42
32. Eckblad JW, Berg CO. 1972. Population dynamics of *Sepedon fuscipennis* (Diptera: Sciomyzidae). *Can. Entomol.* 104(11):1735–42
33. Englund RA, Arakaki K, Preston DJ, Evenhuis NL, McShane KK. 2003. Systematic inventory of rare and alien aquatic species in selected O'ahu, Maui, and Hawai'i Island streams. *Contrib. No. 2003–17, Hawaii Biol. Surv.*
34. ECE (Eur. Commission Environ.). 1992. Council Directive 92/43/EEC on the conservation of natural habitats and of wild fauna and flora. *Off. J. L 206*, July 27, 1992. Brussels
35. Fairweather I, Boray JC. 1999. Mechanisms of fasciolicide action and drug resistance in *Fasciola hepatica*. In *Fasciolosis*, ed. JP Dalton, pp. 225–76. Wallingford, UK: CABI. 552 pp.
36. Falk SJ. 1991. A review of the scarce and threatened flies of Great Britain (Part 1). *Res. Surv. Nat. Conserv.* 39. Peterborough, UK: Nat. Conserv. Counc. 194 pp.
37. Ferrar P. 1987. A guide to the breeding habits and immature stages of Diptera. Cyclorrhapha. In *Entomonograph*, ed. L Lyneborg, 8:329–40, 815–27. Leiden/Copenhagen: Brill/Scand. Sci. Press. 907 pp.
38. Finkelstein JL, Schleinitz MD, Carabin H, McGarvey ST. 2008. Decision-model estimation of the age-specific disability weight for *Schistosomiasis japonica*: a systematic review of the literature. *PLoS Negl. Trop. Dis.* 2(3):e158
39. Fisher TW, Orth RE. 1972. Resurrection of *Sepedon pacifica* Cresson and redescription of *Sepedon praemiosa* Giglio–Tos with biological notes (Diptera: Sciomyzidae). *Pan-Pac. Entomol.* 48(1):8–20
40. Foote BA, Neff SE, Berg CO. 1960. Biology and immature stages of *Atrichomelina pubera* (Diptera: Sciomyzidae). *Ann. Entomol. Soc. Am.* 53(2):192–99
41. Fountain H. 2005. Despite worries, push to build big dams is strong. *N. Y. Times*, Le Monde ed., June 11, p. 3
42. Gbedjissi LG, Vala J-C, Knutson L, Dossou C. 2003. Predation by larvae of *Sepedon ruficeps* (Diptera: Sciomyzidae) and population dynamics of the adult flies and their freshwater prey. *Rev. Suisse Zool.* 110(4):817–32
43. Geckler RP. 1971. Laboratory studies of predation of snails by larvae of the marsh fly *Sepedon tenuicornis* (Diptera: Sciomyzidae). *Can. Entomol.* 103(5):638–49
44. **Ghamizi M. 1985. *Predation des mollusques par les larves de* Sepedon sphegea *Fab. (Diptera: Sciomyzidae) aspects de la dynamique proie–predateur.* PhD thesis. Acad. Montpellier, Fr. 180 pp.**

44. Analyzes the influence of intraspecific competition on a wide variety of biotic factors involving *S. sphegea*.

45. Gormally MJ. 1985. The effect of temperature on the duration of the egg stage of certain sciomyzid flies which predate *Lymnaea truncatula*. *J. Therm. Biol.* 10(4):199–203
46. Gormally MJ. 1988. Studies on the oviposition and longevity of *Ilione albiseta* (Diptera: Sciomyzidae)—potential biological control agent of liver fluke. *Entomophaga* 33(4):387–95
47. Gormally MJ. 1988. Temperature and the biology and predation of *Ilione albiseta* (Diptera: Sciomyzidae)—potential biological control agent of liver fluke. *Hydrobiologia* 166:239–46
48. Greathead DJ. 1981. Arthropod natural enemies of bilharzia snails and the possibilities for biological control. *Biocontrol News Inf., CIBC* 2:197–202
49. Griffiths GCD. 1972. *The Phylogenetic Classification of Diptera Cyclorrhapha with Special Reference to the Structure of the Male Postabdomen*. Ser. Entomol. No. 8. The Hague: Junk. 340 pp.
50. Haab C. 1984. *Etude expérimentale de la biologie de* Sepedon sphegea *(Fabricius, 1775) et aspects de sa prédation larvaire (Diptera: Sciomyzidae)*. PhD thesis. Acad. Montpellier, Univ. Sci. Tech. Languedoc, Montpellier, Fr. 136 pp.
51. Hennig W. 1958. Die Familien der Diptera Schizophora und ihre phylogenetischen Verwandtschafts-beziehungen. *Beitr. Entomol.* 8:505–688
52. Hennig W. 1965. Die Acalyptratae des Baltischen Bernsteins und ihre Bedeutung für die Erforschung der phylogenetischen Entwicklung dieser Dipteran–Gruppe. *Stuttg. Beitr. Naturkd.* 145:1–212

53. Holling CS. 1959. Some characteristics of simple types of predation and parasitism. *Can. Entomol.* 91(7):385–98
54. Hunter ML Jr. 2005. A mesofilter conservation strategy to complement fine and coarse filters. *Conserv. Biol.* 19(4):1025–29
55. Jarvis JL, Brindley TA. 1965. Predicting moth flight and oviposition of European corn borer by the use of temperature accumulations. *J. Econ. Entomol.* 58(2):300–3
56. Johnson DM, Akre BG, Crowley PH. 1975. Modelling arthropod predation: wasteful killing by damselfly naiads. *Ecology* 56(5):1081–93
57. Juliano SA. 1982. Influence of host age on host acceptability and suitability for a species of *Trichogramma* (Hymenoptera: Trichogrammatidae) attacking aquatic Diptera. *Can. Entomol.* 114:713–20
58. Kaczynski VW, Zuska J, Berg CO. 1969. Taxonomy, immature stages, and bionomics of the South American genera *Perilimnia* and *Shannonia* (Diptera: Sciomyzidae). *Ann. Entomol. Soc. Am.* 62(3):572–92
59. Keiper JB. 2006. Snail-killing flies (Sciomyzidae). In *Cleveland Museum of Natural History: Research & Collections: Invertebrate Zoology*. **http://www.cmnh.org/site/ResearchandCollections/InvertebrateZoology/Research/Diptera.aspx**
60. Keiper JB, Walton WE, Foote BA. 2002. Biology and ecology of higher Diptera from freshwater wetlands. *Annu. Rev. Entomol.* 47:207–32
61. Kirby P. 1992. *Habitat Management for Invertebrates: A Practical Handbook*. Sandy, Bedfordshire: R. Soc. Prot. Birds. 150 pp.
62. Knutson L, Orth RE, Fisher TW, Murphy WL. 1986. Catalog of Sciomyzidae (Diptera) of America North of Mexico. *Entomography* 4:1–53
63. Knutson L, Vala J-C. 2002. An evolutionary scenario of Sciomyzidae and Phaeomyiidae (Diptera). *Ann. Soc. Entomol. Fr.* 38(1–2):145–62
64. Knutson LV, Berg CO. 1967. Biology and immature stages of malacophagous Diptera of the genus *Knutsonia* Verbeke (Sciomyzidae). *Bull. Inst. R. Sci. Nat. Belg.* 43:1–60
65. Knutson LV, Rozkošný R, Berg CO. 1975. Biology and immature stages of *Pherbina* and *Psacadina* (Diptera: Sciomyzidae). *Acta Sci. Nat. Acad. Sci. Bohem.-Brno* 9(1):1–38
66. Knutson LV, Stephenson JW, Berg CO. 1970. Biosystematic studies of *Salticella fasciata* (Meigen), a snail–killing fly (Diptera: Sciomyzidae). *Trans. R. Entomol. Soc. Lond.* 122(3):81–100
67. **Knutson LV, Vala J-C. 2011. *Biology of Snail-Killing Sciomyzidae Flies*. Cambridge, UK: Cambridge Univ. Press. 584 pp.**

67. The single most comprehensive review of all aspects of the Sciomyzidae worldwide, with keys.

68. Losey JE, Vaughan M. 2006. The economic value of ecological services provided by insects. *BioScience* 56(4):311–23
69. Manguin S. 1989. Sexual dimorphism in size of adults and puparia of *Tetanocera ferruginea* Fallén (Diptera: Sciomyzidae). *Proc. Entomol. Soc. Wash.* 91(4):523–28
70. Manguin S. 1990. Population genetics and biochemical systematics of marsh flies in the *Sepedon fuscipennis* group (Diptera: Sciomyzidae). *Biochem. Syst. Ecol.* 18(6):447–52
71. Manguin S, Vala J-C. 1989. Prey consumption by larvae of *Tetanocera ferruginea* (Diptera: Sciomyzidae) in relation to number of snail prey species available. *Ann. Entomol. Soc. Am.* 82(5):588–92
72. Manguin S, Vala J-C, Reidenbach JM. 1986. Prédation de mollusques dulçaquicoles par les larves malacophages de *Tetanocera ferruginea* Fallén, 1820 (Diptera, Sciomyzidae). *Can. J. Zool.* 64(12):2832–36
73. Manguin S, Vala J-C, Reidenbach JM. 1988. Action prédatrice des larves de *Tetanocera ferruginea* (Diptera: Sciomyzidae) dans des systèmes à plusieurs espèces de mollusques–proies. *Acta Ecol./Ecol. Appl.* 9(3):249–59
74. Manguin S, Vala J-C, Reidenbach JM. 1988. Détermination des préférences alimentaires des larves de *Tetanocera ferruginea* (Diptera: Sciomyzidae), prédateur de mollusques dulçaquicoles. *Acta Ecol./Ecol. Appl.* 9(4):353–70
75. Marinoni L, Barros de Carvalho CJ. 1993. A cladistic analysis of *Protodictya* Malloch (Diptera, Sciomyzidae). *Proc. Entomol. Soc. Wash.* 95(3):412–17
76. Marinoni L, Mathis WN. 2000. A cladistic analysis of Sciomyzidae Fallén (Diptera). *Proc. Biol. Soc. Wash.* 113(1):162–209
77. Marinoni L, Mathis WN. 2006. A cladistic analysis of the Neotropical genus *Sepedonea* Steyskal (Diptera: Sciomyzidae). *Zootaxa* 1236:37–52

78. Marinoni L, Steyskal GC, Knutson L. 2003. Revision and cladistic analysis of the Neotropical genus *Thecomyia* (Diptera: Sciomyzidae). *Zootaxa* 191:1–36
79. McAlpine DK. 1991. Relationships of the genus *Heterocheila* (Diptera: Sciomyzoidea) with description of a new family. *Tijdschr. Entomol.* 134:193–99
80. McAlpine JF. 1989. Phylogeny and classification of the Muscomorpha. In *Manual of Nearctic Diptera*, ed. JF McAlpine, 3:1397–505. Ottawa: Res. Branch, Agric. Can. Monogr. No. 32. vi + 1333–1518
81. McCoy LE, Joy JE. 1977. Tolerance of *Sepedon fuscipennis* and *Dictya* sp. larvae (Diptera: Sciomyzidae) to the molluscicides Bayer 73 and sodium pentachlorophenate. *Environ. Entomol.* 6(2):198–202
82. Mc Donnell RJ. 2004. *The biology and behaviour of selected marsh fly (Diptera: Sciomyzidae) species, potential biological control agents of liver fluke disease in Ireland.* PhD thesis. Natl. Univ. Irel., Galway. 236 pp.
83. Mc Donnell RJ, Gormally MJ. 2007. Thermal effects on the egg stage of four sciomyzids with reference to phenology and biocontrol potential. *J. Appl. Entomol.* 131(2):65–70
84. Mc Donnell RJ, Knutson L, Vala J-C, Abercrombie J, Henry P-Y, Gormally MJ. 2005. Direct evidence of predation by aquatic, predatory Sciomyzidae (Diptera, Acalyptrata) on freshwater snails from natural populations. *Entomol. Mon. Mag.* 141:49–56
85. Mc Donnell RJ, Mulkeen CJ, Gormally MJ. 2005. Sexual dimorphism and the impact of temperature on the pupal and adult stages of *Sepedon spinipes spinipes*, a potential biological control agent of fascioliasis. *Entomol. Exp. Appl.* 115:291–301
86. Mc Donnell RJ, Paine TD, Gormally MJ. 2007. Trail-following behaviour in the malacophagous larvae of the sciomyzid flies *Sepedon spinipes spinipes* and *Dictya montana*. *J. Insect Behav.* 20(3):367–76
87. McGeoch MA. 1998. The selection, testing and application of terrestrial insects as bioindicators. *Biol. Rev. Camb. Philos. Soc.* 73:181–201
88. McLaughlin HE, Dame DA. 1989. Rearing *Dictya floridensis* (Diptera: Sciomyzidae) in a continuously producing colony and evaluation of larval food sources. *J. Med. Entomol.* 26(6):522–27
89. Murdoch WW. 1969. Switching in general predators: experiments on predator specificity and stability of prey populations. *Ecol. Monogr.* 39:335–54
90. Murray CJL, Lopez AD, eds. 1996. *The Global Burden of Disease: A Comprehensive Assessment of Mortality and Disability from Diseases, Injuries and Risk Factors in 1990 and Projected to 2020.* Cambridge, MA: Harvard Univ. Press. 1022 pp.
91. Neff SE. 1964. Snail-killing sciomyzid flies: application in biological control. *Verh. Int. Ver. Limnol.* 15(2):933–39
92. Neff SE, Berg CO. 1966. Biology and immature stages of malacophagous Diptera of the genus *Sepedon* (Sciomyzidae). *Va. Agric. Exp. Stn. Bull.* 566:1–113
93. Nelson M, Keiper JB. 2009. Observations of the snail-killing fly *Sepedon fuscipennis* (Sciomyzidae) consuming limpets in the laboratory. *Fly Times* 43(Oct.):8–10
94. O'Halloran J, Harrison S, Gittings T, O'Callaghan E, O'Mahony L. 2011. Effects of habitat loss and fragmentation on the biodiversity maintenance function of remnant wetland and pond habitats within typical Irish agricultural landscapes. In *Biodiversity and Environmental Change: An Integrated Study Encompassing a Range of Scales, Taxa and Habitats*, ed. L Scally, S Waldre, pp. 9–25. (2005-CD-B2-M1). Techn. Proj. Rep. Wexford: Environ. Prot. Agency
95. O'Neill WL. 1973. Biology of *Trichopria popei* and *T. atrichomelinae* (Hymenoptera: Diapriidae), parasitoids of the Sciomyzidae (Diptera). *Ann. Entomol. Soc. Am.* 66(5):1043–50
96. Pagel M. 1994. Detecting correlated evolution on phylogenies: a general method for the comparative analysis of discrete characters. *Proc. R. Soc. Lond. Ser. B* 255:37–45
97. Peacock DB. 1973. *Ecology of the snail-killing fly*, Sepedon fuscipennis *Loew (Diptera: Sciomyzidae) in lentic and lotic habitats.* MS thesis. Univ. Conn., Storrs. 61 pp.
98. Perris E. 1850. Histoire des métamorphoses de quelques diptères. *Mem. Soc. Sci. Lille* 1850:122–24
99. Pires AC, Marinoni L, Barros de Carvalho CJ. 2008. Track analysis of the Neotropical genus *Sepedonea* Steyskal (Diptera: Sciomyzidae): a proposal based on the phylogenetic analysis of its species. *Zootaxa* 1716:21–34
100. Pritchard G, Harder LD, Mutch RA. 1996. Development of aquatic insect eggs in relation to temperature and strategies for dealing with different thermal environments. *Biol. J. Linn. Soc.* 58:221–44

101. Rozkošný R. 1995. World distribution of Sciomyzidae based on the list of species (Diptera). *Stud. Dipterol.* 2:221–38
102. Rozkošný R, Knutson L. 2005. Sciomyzidae. In *Fauna Europaea: Diptera Brachycera*, ver.1.2. ed. T. Pape. **http://www.faunaeur.org/**
103. Ryder C, Moran J, Mc Donnell RJ, Gormally MJ. 2005. Conservation implications of grazing practices on the plant and dipteran communities of a turlough in Co. Mayo, Ireland. *Biodivers. Conserv.* 14:187–204
104. Samways MJ. 1981. *Biological Control of Pests and Weeds*. London: Edward Arnold. 57 pp.
105. Samways MJ. 2007. Insect conservation: a synthetic management approach. *Annu. Rev. Entomol.* 52:465–87
106. Schelle P, Collier U, Pittock J. 2004. Rivers at risk—dams and the future of freshwater ecosystems. Presented at *7th Int. River Symp., Brisbane, Aust.*
107. Shirt DB, ed. 1987. *British Red Data Books: 2. Insects*. Peterborough, UK: Nat. Conserv. Counc. 402 pp.
108. Speight MCD. 1986. Criteria for the selection of insects to be used as bio-indicators in nature conservation research. In *Proc. 3rd Eur. Congr. Entomol., Amsterdam*, ed. HMW Velthuis, pp. 485–88
109. Speight MCD. 2004. Predicting impacts of changes in farm management on sciomyzids (Diptera, Sciomyzidae): a biodiversity case study from southern Ireland. *Dipter. Dig.* 11:147–66
110. Speight MCD, Castella E. 2001. An approach to interpretation of lists of insects using digitized biological information about the species. *J. Insect Conserv.* 5:131–39
111. Speight MCD, Knutson LV. 2011. Species accounts for Sciomyzidae and Phaeomyiidae (Diptera) known from the Atlantic Zone of Europe. *Dipter. Dig.* 19(1):1–38
112. Steyskal GC. 1965. The subfamilies of Sciomyzidae of the world (Diptera: Acalyptratae). *Ann. Entomol. Soc. Am.* 58(4):593–94
113. Sueyoshi M, Knutson L, Ghorpade KD. 2009. A taxonomic review of *Pelidnoptera* Rondani (Diptera) with discovery of a related new genus and species from Asia. *Insect Syst. Evol.* 40:389–409
114. Tirgari S, Massoud J. 1981. Study on the biology of snail-killing flies and prospect of biological control of aquatic snails *Sepedon sphegea* (Fabricius) (Insecta, Diptera, Sciomyzidae). Sci. Publ. 2051, Sch. Public Health, Inst. Public Health Res. Teheran Univ.
115. Tóthová A, Rozkošný R, Kutty SN, Wiegmann BM, Meier R. 2010. A molecular analysis of Sciomyzidae (Diptera). *Proc. 7th Int. Congr. Dipterol., San Jose, Costa Rica* (Abstr.)
116. Trelka DG, Berg CO. 1977. Behavioral studies of the slug-killing larvae of two species of *Tetanocera* (Diptera: Sciomyzidae). *Proc. Entomol. Soc. Wash.* 79(3):475–86
117. Trudgill DL, Honek A, Li D. 2005. Thermal time—concepts and utility. *Ann. Appl. Biol.* 146(1):1–14
118. Vala J-C. 1984. Phenology of Diptera Sciomyzidae in a Mediterranean forestry biotop. *Entomol. Basiliensia* 9:432–40
119. Vala J-C. 1986. Description des stades larvaires et données sur la biologie et la phénologie de *Trypetoptera punctulata* (Diptera, Sciomyzidae). *Ann. Soc. Entomol. Fr.* 22(1):67–77
120. Vala J-C. 1989. *Diptères Sciomyzidae Euro-méditerranéens. Faune de France. France et Régions Limitrophes.* No. 72. Paris: Féd. Franc. Soc. Sci. Nat., 300 pp.
121. Vala J-C, Brunel C. 1987. Diptères Sciomyzides capturés dans le Département de la Somme. *Bull. Soc. Linn. Lyon* 56(6):187–91
122. Vala J-C, Gasc C. 1990. Ecological adaptations and morphological variation in the posterior disc of larvae of Sciomyzidae (Diptera). *Can. J. Zool.* 68(3):517–21
123. Vala J-C, Ghamizi M. 1992. Aspects de la biologie de *Pherbellia schoenherri* parasitoïde de *Succinea elegans* (Mollusca) (Diptera, Sciomyzidae). *Bull. Soc. Entomol. Fr.* 97(2):145–54
124. Vala J-C, Haab C. 1984. Etude expérimentale du développement larvaire de *Tetanocera ferruginea* Fallén 1820. Influences de la température et de la photopériode, diapause pupale, biomasse alimentaire. *Bull. Ann. Soc. R. Belg. Entomol.* 120(7–8):165–78
125. Vala J-C, Manguin S. 1987. Dynamique et relations Sciomyzidae—Mollusques d'un biotope aquatique asséchable dans le sud de la France (Diptera). *Bull. Ann. Soc. R. Belg. Entomol.* 123(2):153–64
126. Valley KR, Berg CO. 1977. Biology and immature stages of snail-killing Diptera of the genus *Dictya* (Sciomyzidae). *Search Agric. Entomol.* 187(2):1–44
127. Verbeke J. 1950. Sciomyzidae (Diptera Cyclorrhapha). Fasc. 66. In *Exploration Parc Natl. Albert, Miss. G. F. de Witte (1933–35)*. Brussels: Inst. Parcs Nat. Congo Belge. 97 pp.

128. Verbeke J. 1967. Contribution à l'étude des diptères malacophages. IV. L'identité de *Pherbellia obtusa* (Fallén) (1820) et la description d'une espèce paléarctique nouvelle *Pherbellia argyra* sp. n. (Diptera: Sciomyzidae). *Bull. Inst. R. Sci. Nat. Belg.* 43(2):1–9
129. Wang WB, Leopold RA, Nelson DR, Freeman TP. 2000. Cryopreservation of *Musca domestica* (Diptera: Muscidae) embryos. *Cryobiology* 41(2):153–66
130. Whiles MR, Goldowitz BS. 2001. Hydrologic influences on insect emergence production from Central Platte River wetlands. *Ecol. Appl.* 11(6):1829–42
131. Wiegmann BM, Trautwein MD, Winkler IS, Barr NB, Kim J-W, et al. 2011. Episodic radiations in the fly tree of life. *Proc. Natl. Acad. Sci. USA* 108(14):5690–95
132. Wilkinson DM. 1999. The disturbing history of the intermediate disturbance hypothesis. *Oikos* 84(1):145–47
133. Williams CD, Gormally MJ, Knutson LV. 2010. Very high population estimates and limited movement of snail-killing flies (Diptera: Sciomyzidae) on an Irish turlough (temporary lake). *Biol. Environ. Proc. R. Ir. Acad.* 110B:81–94
134. Williams CD, Moran J, Doherty O, Mc Donnell RJ, Gormally MJ, et al. 2009. Factors affecting Sciomyzidae (Diptera) across a transect at Skealoghan Turlough (Co. Mayo, Ireland). *Aquat. Ecol.* 43(1):117–33
135. Williams CD, Sheahan J, Gormally MJ. 2009. Hydrology and management of turloughs (temporary lakes) affect marsh fly (Sciomyzidae: Diptera) communities. *Insect Conserv. Divers.* 2:270–83
136. World Health Organ. (WHO). 1984. Report of an Informal Consultation on Research on the Biological Control of Snail-Intermediate Hosts. Unpubl. *TDR/BCV-SCH/SIH/* 84:13–16. Geneva
137. Yoneda Y. 1981. The effect of temperature on development and predation of marsh fly, *Sepedon aenescens* Wiedemann (Diptera: Sciomyzidae). *Jpn. J. Sanit. Zool.* 32(2):117–23
138. Zuska J, Berg CO. 1974. A revision of the South American genus *Tetanoceroides* (Diptera: Sciomyzidae), with notes on colour variations correlated with mean temperatures. *Trans. R. Entomol. Soc. Lond.* 125(3):329–62

Advances in Insect Phylogeny at the Dawn of the Postgenomic Era

Michelle D. Trautwein,[1] Brian M. Wiegmann,[1,*] Rolf Beutel,[2] Karl M. Kjer,[3] and David K. Yeates[4]

[1]Department of Entomology, North Carolina State University, Raleigh, North Carolina 27695; email: mdtrautw@ncsu.edu; brian_wiegmann@ncsu.edu

[2]Entomology Group, Institut für Spezielle Zoologie und Evolutionsbiologie mit Phyletischem Museum, FSU Jena, 07743 Jena, Germany

[3]Department of Ecology, Evolution, and Natural Resources, Rutgers, the State University of New Jersey, New Brunswick, New Jersey 08901

[4]CSIRO Ecosystem Sciences, P.O. Box 1700, Canberra ACT, Australia

Annu. Rev. Entomol. 2012. 57:449–68

The *Annual Review of Entomology* is online at ento.annualreviews.org

This article's doi:
10.1146/annurev-ento-120710-100538

0066-4170/12/0107-0449$20.00

*Corresponding author

Keywords

Holometabola, Hexapoda, Palaeoptera, Polyneoptera, next-generation sequencing, phylogenomics

Abstract

Most species on Earth are insects and thus, understanding their evolutionary relationships is key to understanding the evolution of life. Insect relationships are increasingly well supported, due largely to technological advances in molecular sequencing and phylogenetic computational analysis. In this postgenomic era, insect systematics will be furthered best by integrative methods aimed at hypothesis corroboration from molecular, morphological, and paleontological evidence. This review of the current consensus of insect relationships provides a foundation for comparative study and offers a framework to evaluate incoming genomic evidence. Notable recent phylogenetic successes include the resolution of Holometabola, including the identification of the enigmatic Strepsiptera as a beetle relative and the early divergence of Hymenoptera; the recognition of hexapods as a crustacean lineage within Pancrustacea; and the elucidation of Dictyoptera orders, with termites placed as social cockroaches. Regions of the tree that require further investigation include the earliest winged insects (Palaeoptera) and Polyneoptera (orthopteroid lineages).

INTRODUCTION

PCR: polymerase chain reaction

micro-CT: microcomputer tomography

Insects account for most of the species-richness of life on Earth. As a result, their phylogenetic history and diversification are central to understanding the evolution of life more generally. Our knowledge of the history and diversification of insects has expanded greatly in the 30 years since a landmark review of the subject was published in the *Annual Review of Entomology* (68). This progress continues to develop through major conceptual and technological advances in the practice of systematic entomology. The most significant change is the rapid acquisition of large amounts of molecular sequence data from high-throughput genomics, providing an ever-expanding evidence base for reexamination of long-standing controversies in insect phylogeny. Parallel advances in computational biology, bioinformatics, and computation speed have spurred analytical achievements in phylogeny reconstruction. Just a decade ago, when insect systematists were relying largely on easy-to-acquire molecular markers such as mitochondrial genes and ribosomal DNA, the annotated genomes of *Drosophila melanogaster* and *Anopheles gambiae* were published (48, 65). As sequenced genomes accumulated, it became easier to develop taxon-specific primers for conserved genes, and an emphasis on the phylogenetic utility of nuclear protein-coding genes emerged (97, 100). We are now at a turning point where large-scale-targeted polymerase chain reaction (PCR) may no longer be a cost-effective alternative to next-generation sequencing methods that can return hundreds of candidate genes per taxon for phylogenetic analysis. Today, complete genome sequences are available only for critical insect model organisms, yet in the very near future, genomic data for a much broader sampling of insects will rapidly accrue.

With this great increase in molecular data comes a new set of challenges; instead of struggling to add another gene to a data set, we will winnow down large harvests of genes to identify single-copy orthologs to recover phylogeny. We will determine whether "more genes" or "less noise" is the superior approach. Another hurdle in analyzing large data sets is systematic error. Unlike the phylogenetic inaccuracy that results from stochastic error in small genetic samples, systematic error masquerades as strongly supported resolution and results from undetected genetic biases and/or errors inherent in model estimation and algorithm design. As the practice of phylogenetics intersects with the world of comparative genomics, it has become evident that molecular data, even complete genome sequences, are not always an independent solution to resolving the tree of life (93, 105). The entomological advances of this postgenomic era will be characterized by an emphasis on the analytical integration of and congruence among multiple sources of phylogenetic evidence. The progression toward more thoroughly integrative systematics that includes rich new evidence from morphological, paleontological, and molecular data (11, 41, 130), along with methods that enable greater synthesis across data types, will dramatically improve our ability to assess the accuracy of our hypotheses of the evolutionary relationships of insects.

The major outlines of insect phylogeny were first recognized by morphology (46, 68), and even today virtually every evolutionary relationship resolved by molecular data has been at some point previously hypothesized by morphologists. Now, in concert with phylogenomic data, morphology offers not only additional data points, but also an independent estimate of phylogeny that permits both the corroboration of relationships and the placement of fossil taxa. Morphological studies have become increasingly sophisticated, now routinely analyzing hundreds of characters quantitatively, either independently or in combination with molecular data sets (36). In the past decade (e.g., 35), new techniques, such as microcomputer tomography (micro-CT) combined with computer-based three-dimensional reconstruction, have revolutionized insect anatomy. An optimized combination of traditional and innovative techniques and a standardized work-flow has made it possible to acquire well-documented, high-quality morphological data at a greatly accelerated rate (e.g., 7).

The need for phylogenetic resolution within the insect tree of life has never been more acute. Accurate, up-to-date, and accessible studies of biodiversity depend on stable, predictive classifications; in a world faced with rapid climate change and extensive global habitat loss, increasingly accurate knowledge of the Earth's biota is critically important (78). In addition, many insects are important model organisms across scientific disciplines, and comparative studies of these organisms rely on a phylogenetic framework to inform us about genetics, development, medicine, and basic science. As large-scale data acquisition and analysis become more routine, we will necessarily rely on the knowledge of a current best estimate of insect relationships to assess incoming genomic evidence.

rDNA: ribosomal DNA

mtDNA: mitochondrial DNA

A REVIEW OF INSECT PHYLOGENY

Mapping the evolutionary relationships of insects, with their stunning diversity, remains a challenge, even in light of new theory and technology (109, 130). Across the tree of all life we are seeing that evolution has taken place in episodic bursts of radiation (108, 130, 135). Whereas the relationships among some lineages are easy to resolve, ancient divergencies and groups that underwent rapid diversification may be difficult, if not impossible, to recover (105). Higher-level insect phylogeny perfectly mirrors this broad evolutionary paradigm of episodic diversification. With the collection of phylogenomic data and the discovery and interpretation of new morphological characters and paleontological data, the relationships among several key orders have been clearly revealed, yet others remain obscured by conflicting evidence.

In recent years, we have seen comparative analyses of complete genomes of insect model organisms (111, 145), analyses of full mitochondrial genomes (16–18), a new understanding of the origin of insects within Arthropoda (85, 97, 110), new evidence for phylogenetic placement of insect orders (55, 111, 131, 134), and phylogenetic arrangements of major insect subgroups (7, 9, 10, 77, 115, 134). These studies add to early molecular work aimed at resolving relationships among insect orders that relied primarily on ribosomal DNA (rDNA) and mitochondrial DNA (mtDNA) (often in combination with morphology). rDNA is a standard, reliable marker, but it can generate results that are highly dependent on character/taxon inclusion and alignment method, whereas mtDNA can be ineffective for deep divergencies. The first broadly sampled study to rely on nuclear protein-coding genes recovered both traditional relationships and controversial hypotheses (56). Here we review the current consensus of higher-level insect phylogeny (largely similar to Reference 66, with new insights and supports) based on a survey of the most recent and modern systematic analyses, with the goal of highlighting notable successes as well as persisting challenges (**Figure 1**).

Holometabola: A Success Story

Holometabola—insects that undergo complete metamorphosis—are what make insects the most diverse lineage of life on Earth. Approximately 80% of their species richness is concentrated in four superradiations: beetles, flies, bees and wasps, and moths and butterflies. After centuries of debate, there is general agreement on the evolutionary relationships among the 11 included holometabolan orders, resolving one of the most substantial branches of the tree of life. The recent widely accepted phylogeny of Holometabola (= Endopterygota) is a primary example of the success and progress resulting from integrative systematics and emphasizes the importance of corroborating results from independent data types. The initial approach to resolving Holometabola was driven by the sudden availability of sequenced genomes from insect model organisms from each major holometabolan lineage: *Apis mellifera* (honey bee), *Tribolium castaneum* (red flour

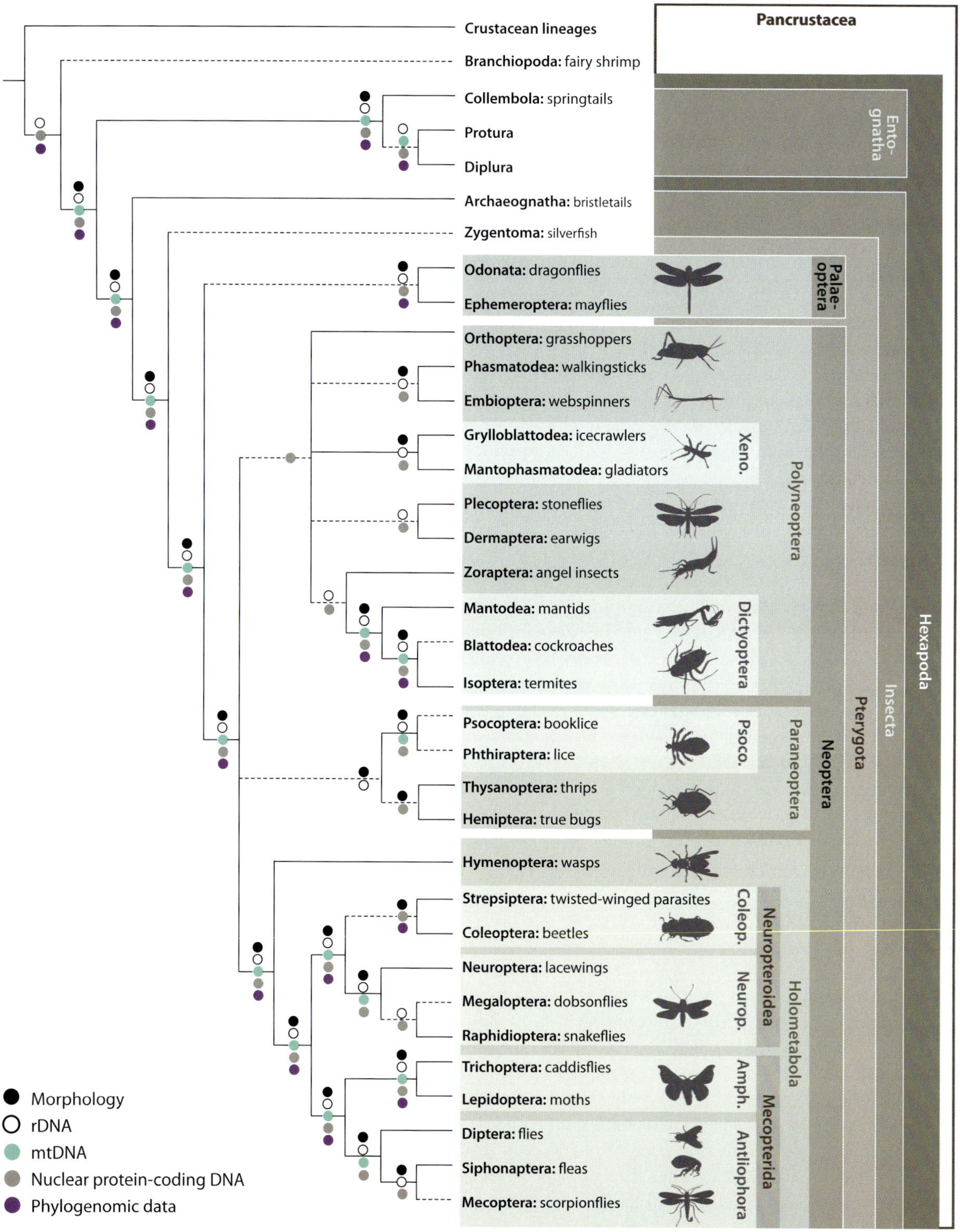
Pancrustacea
Crustacean lineages
Branchiopoda: fairy shrimp
Collembola: springtails
Protura
Diplura
Ento-gnatha
Archaeognatha: bristletails
Zygentoma: silverfish
Odonata: dragonflies
Ephemeroptera: mayflies
Palae-optera
Orthoptera: grasshoppers
Phasmatodea: walkingsticks
Embioptera: webspinners
Grylloblattodea: icecrawlers
Mantophasmatodea: gladiators
Xeno.
Plecoptera: stoneflies
Dermaptera: earwigs
Zoraptera: angel insects
Polyneoptera
Mantodea: mantids
Blattodea: cockroaches
Isoptera: termites
Dictyoptera
Psocoptera: booklice
Phthiraptera: lice
Psoco.
Thysanoptera: thrips
Hemiptera: true bugs
Paraneoptera
Neoptera
Pterygota
Insecta
Hexapoda
Hymenoptera: wasps
Strepsiptera: twisted-winged parasites
Coleoptera: beetles
Coleop.
Neuroptera: lacewings
Megaloptera: dobsonflies
Raphidioptera: snakeflies
Neurop.
Neuropteroidea
Trichoptera: caddisflies
Lepidoptera: moths
Amph.
Diptera: flies
Siphonaptera: fleas
Mecoptera: scorpionflies
Antliophora
Mecopterida
Holometabola
Morphology
rDNA
mtDNA
Nuclear protein-coding DNA
Phylogenomic data

beetle), *Bombyx mori* (silkworm), and *Drosophila melanogaster* (fruit fly) (111, 145). Although initially acquired for their importance to other fields of biology, these model organism genomes have now revealed the evolutionary relationships of these superdiverse lineages, and the resulting phylogenetic framework can facilitate comparative studies across scientific disciplines (145).

One notable success within Holometabola involves the resolution of the controversial Strepsiptera problem. Until just a few years ago, the enigmatic, parasitic Strepsiptera were considered the most phylogenetically ambiguous insect order, with even their placement within Holometabola in question (69). Strepsipterans are fascinating endoparasites of other insects with primarily wingless, legless females that never leave their host (except in the family Menginillidae). Hypotheses regarding the Strepsiptera problem varied from traditional morphology-based classifications that placed the parasites as close relatives to beetles (or as beetles themselves) (9, 10), to a combined molecular/morphological study that placed them as the sister group to flies (Halteria) on the basis of rDNA and putative homology between the hind halteres of flies and the fore halteres of Strepsiptera (132, 133). The latter finding implied that a homeotic mutation, a change in the genes that dictate segment order, was responsible for the divergence of flies and strepsipterans. Halteria instigated intense debate and became the best-known empirical example of long-branch attraction (52) and an important case study for the complexities of ribosomal alignments (60). Amid great controversy, multiple reanalyses and several genetic studies failed to find evidence to unite flies and strepsipterans (14, 45, 107), and the Strepsiptera problem persisted without much additional data or further elucidation.

Now, a close relationship between Strepsiptera and Coleoptera (beetles), joined in the clade Coleopterida, appears well established from both molecular and morphological data and brings a controversial chapter in insect phylogenetics to a close (although the refinement of this relationship remains a pressing issue). A recent phylogenetic analysis across holometabolan orders, based on nuclear protein-coding genes, found strong support for a sister-group relationship between Strepsiptera and Coleoptera (134). This result was confirmed by analyses of an extensive morphological data set (7, 36, 73) and by two subsequent molecular studies (56, 77). Alternative placements of Strepsiptera were also proposed (83) and placed Strepsiptera either as a sister group to Neuropterida (Neuroptera: lacewings, Raphidioptera: snakeflies, and Megaloptera: dobsonflies) or as a subordinate group of polyphagan beetles.

Although each of these aforementioned studies recovers Strepsiptera as a close beetle relative with varying placement within Neuropteroidea (Coleopterida + Neuropterida), they do not all equally sample the four extant beetle suborders; thus leaving open the question, Are strepsipterans an order-level sister group to beetles, or are they actually highly derived beetles that originated from within Coleoptera? Neuropterida-Strepsiptera morphological synapomorphies are lacking (7), however. Although Coleoptera and their included suborders are strongly supported (9, 10), stresipteran placement as a polyphagan subgroup is a possible alternative (24). Some males of the polyphagan family Rhipiphoridae strongly resemble strepsipterans, and both groups possess a highly active triungulin larval instar. In addition, the reversal of features in the highly specialized

Figure 1

This tree represents the best current estimate of insect relationships based on a review of recent literature. Dashed lines indicate tenuously supported relationships or possible nonmonophyly (in the case of terminal branches). The types of data supporting each node are displayed if a node was recovered by a particular line of evidence alone or in a combined analysis. Phylogenomic data refer to a molecular data set of at least 20 kb, to data collected through EST harvests, or to large-scale genome comparison. Abbreviations: EST, expressed sequence tag; mtDNA, mitochondrial DNA; rDNA, ribosomal DNA; Amph., Amphiesmenoptera; Coleop., Coleopterida; Neurop., Neuropterida; Psoco., Psocodea; Xeno., Xenonomia.

parasitic Strepsiptera cannot be fully excluded. Future work to clarify the origin of Strepsiptera must emphasize increased taxon sampling within Neuropteroidea, specifically Coleoptera, to discern whether twisted-winged parasites are truly a unique lineage deserving of order status or whether they are simply highly derived polyphagan beetles.

All these studies support an emerging consensus on the phylogeny of the holometabolan orders, including new evidence for the previously ambiguous phylogenetic placement of Hymenoptera (bees, wasps, and ants). Initially, two phylogenomic projects with limited taxon sampling but large numbers of genes found conflicting placements for Hymenoptera: Mitochondrial genomes supported a sister-group relationship between Hymenoptera and Mecopterida (Lepidoptera, Trichoptera, Diptera, Mecoptera, and Siphonaptera) (22), whereas 185 nuclear genes provided the first convincing evidence for Hymenoptera as the earliest-branching lineage of Holometabola (111). The basal position of Hymenoptera has been confirmed by every molecular study that has since addressed the question (56, 77, 83, 134, 145), including a large phylogenomic study (of arthropod relationships; 177 genes) (85) and a new analysis of mitochondrial genomes (18). Furthermore, recent morphological analyses also unequivocally place Hymenoptera as the sister group to the rest of Holometabola (7). Hymenoptera display a remarkable mixture of unique, highly specialized features along with characters preserved across nonholometabolan insects, a high number of Malphigian tubules, well-developed glossae and paraglossae in adults (including muscles), and a fully developed orthopteroid ovipositor (7).

Holometabola, excluding Hymenoptera, are composed of two main lineages: Neuropteroidea (Neuropterida, Coleoptera, Strepsiptera) and Mecopterida (Amphiesmenoptera and Antliophora). Neuropteroidea require further resolution not only in the exact placement of Strepsiptera, but within the arrangement of the Neuropterida. Neuropteridans, lacewings, snakeflies, and dobsonflies, include three orders of archaic, large-winged predators that exhibit ancient morphologies; the greatest species richness is within the lacewings. Traditional classifications and a recent extensive morphological study (7) place Neuroptera (Neu) as the sister group to the Raphidioptera (Raph) + Megaloptera (Meg) (46). Alternatively, a sister-group relationship between Megaloptera and Neuroptera is purported on the basis of morphology and a shared aquatic larval stage inferred for their most recent common ancestor (3). Molecular work of the past decade, as with morphological data, offers no robust support for any single alternative topology, thus highlighting this area as a current enigma of the insect tree of life. Molecular studies, with limited support, agree with the traditional morphological hypothesis of Neu + (Raph + Meg) (83, 134), as well as recovering (Neu + Raph) + Meg (27, 56) and (Neu + Meg) + Raph (18, 43). Studies that have included morphological characters conflict in their arrangement of the orders but have found Megaloptera to be paraphyletic (7, 136). Expanded taxon sampling, in combination with a broader sample of genes to get beyond the minimal and nonconclusive signal of rDNA and mtDNA, respectively, is the next important step in elucidating these relationships.

Mecopterida, the largest lineage within Holometabola, include the traditionally well-founded Amphiesmenoptera (Lepidoptera: butterflies and moths, and Trichoptera: caddisflies) and Antliophora (Diptera: flies, Mecoptera: scorpionflies, and Siphonaptera: fleas). Both superorders are well supported in recent molecular studies (56, 83, 134), and morphologically, the union of moths and caddisflies is supported by shared features such as setulose wings, similar venation, and larvae with silk-producing mouthparts. Within Antliophora, recent molecular evidence supports a monophyletic Mecoptera with Siphonaptera as its sister group as the closest relatives of Diptera (56, 83, 134). Mecoptera, excluding Siphonaptera, were also retrieved in a morphology-based study (7). This stands in contrast to the widely accepted hypothesis that fleas are actually mecopterans, sister group to the wingless family of snow scorpionflies, Boreidae (60, 61, 131). The expansion of Mecoptera to include Siphonaptera is supported primarily by rDNA and mtDNA, as well as some aspects of morphology such as winglessness and oogenesis (but see 8). Of the aforementioned studies, however, only one (131) has an extensive taxon sample for scorpionflies and fleas, thus emphasizing the need for an additional broadly sampled phylogenetic study focused on Antliophora.

Origin of Hexapods: Achievements of Phylogenomic Data

Another successful and significant paradigm shift within insect systematics has been the emerging discovery that insects are a crustacean lineage, members of the Pancrustacea clade ('Crustacea' + Hexapoda) (39, 60, 61, 82, 85, 97, 99, 110). This new view stands in contrast to longstanding classifications supported by morphology that place Myriapoda (millipedes and centipedes), or one of their members, as the closest relatives of insects (66), together called Tracheata (=Atelocerata, Antennata). However, as molecular evidence grows in unequivocal support of Pancrustacea, reinterpretations of morphological characters contribute support as well (15, 40, 42, 110, 119). The strong support for Pancrustacea implies an evolutionary scenario for the origin of Hexapoda strikingly different from that traditionally hypothesized for Tracheata, including the independently acquired terrestrial habits of both insects and myriapods. In addition, an entire suite of shared characters that were once considered to belong uniquely to Tracheata (insects + myriapods) instead appear to have evolved independently in two disparate lineages (15) in response to the common environmental pressures of a terrestrial life. These include the tracheal system, Malpighian tubules at the midgut-hindgut border, completely fused second maxillae, a movable head with specialized neck musculature, undivided coxae, the loss of the ventral food rim, the loss of exopodites, and other features. However, a critical and formal evaluation of these characters is required.

The new clarity that phylogenomic approaches offer in some lineages can simultaneously reveal uncertainty in other lineages. The same large-scale phylogenomic work on Arthropoda that has supported the monophyly of Pancrustacea has highlighted uncertainty in the arrangement of crustacean lineages, particularly which crustacean is closest to the hexapods. Now, no fewer than four different sister taxa have support on the basis of at least one analysis. Results from both multigene and phylogenomic analyses suggest a close relationship between Branchiopoda and Hexapoda (1, 28, 81, 85, 99), whereas another phylogenomic study inferred Remipedia + Cephalocarida as the sister group to Hexapoda (100). Morphological synapomorphies support Remipedia + Hexapoda (32), Malacostra + Hexapoda (44), and Malacostra + Remipedia + Hexapoda (33), indicating general incongruence between recent molecular and morphological hypotheses.

Early Wingless Lineages of Hexapods and Insects: Molecular Data Provide Clarity and Ambiguity

Ambiguity regarding crustacean relationships extends even to the monophyly of the hexapods. Hexapoda include not only Insecta sensu stricto (ectognaths: exposed jaws) but also three early-diverging lineages of minute, wingless entognaths (enclosed jaws: orders Protura, Diplura, and Collembola). Although hexapods (entognaths + Insecta) have long been considered monophyletic primarily on the basis of their shared body plan features—head, thorax, and abdomen and three pairs of thoracic legs (46, 62)—the relationship between entognaths and insects was called into question by an early comparison of partial mitochondrial genomes that found collembolans to be more closely related to crustaceans (19, 90). Hexapod monophyly is difficult to resolve with morphological characters alone because the early-diverging entognath lineages exhibit many traits of reduction coinciding with their habitation in substrate (85). rDNA (60, 79, 82, 86, 129) in addition to recent phylogenomic (85, 122) analyses recovers a monophyletic Hexapoda and newly converges on the arrangement of Collembola + (Protura + Diplura) (38, 61, 79, 85, 86; but see 19, 98) in contrast to the more traditional Ellipura (Collembola + Protura) (98). Although hexapod monophyly is considered well established, uncertainty remains regarding the relative placement of these early hexapod lineages, leaving the possibility that one alone is the closest relative of Insecta, rendering Entognatha paraphyletic (10, 38, 61, 98). For reviews of hexapod origins and monophyly see References 20 and 42.

Within Insecta, the earliest lineages are the wingless jumping bristletails (Archeognatha: ancient jaws = Microcoryphia) and silverfish (Zygentoma). Members of these two early insect lineages appear largely similar and were previously joined in the order Thysanura, together constituting Apterygota (wingless insects), the sister group to Pterygota (winged insects) (41). Now, the silverfish are found to be closer relatives to winged insects, and together these two groups form Dicondylia (named for the shared trait of mandibles with two points of articulation) (56, 100, 129). The primary unresolved issue that remains for early insect relationships is the placement of the enigmatic silverfish Tricholepidion and thus the monophyly of Zygentoma (9, 30).

INTRACTABLE REGIONS: EARLIEST WINGED INSECTS, OR THE PALAEOPTERA PROBLEM

In contrast to the recent successes in resolving the evolutionary relationships of Holometabola and the origin of Hexapoda, the elucidation of the relationships of the earliest-diverging lineages of winged insects remains a problem for insect phylogenetics despite the application of both phylogenomic and morphological data. Winged insects (Pterygota) are a well-established group. Odonata (dragonflies and damselflies) and Ephemeroptera (mayflies) are the first lineages of winged insects and, in contrast to the great majority of insects, are unable to fold their wings flat over their abdomen and thus have long been grouped together in Palaeoptera (old wings) as sister to all remaining Insecta (Neoptera: new wings). Where the palaeopteran orders fit is a persistently enigmatic phylogenetic question that has been addressed by rDNA, multigene data sets, phylogenomic data (including complete mitochondrial genomes), and morphology, yet palaeopteran relationships have never been murkier. Conflicting evidence from both molecules and morphology has demonstrated support for Palaeoptera (Odonata + Ephemeroptera) as well as hypotheses known as Metapterygota (Odonata + Neoptera) and Chiastomyaria (Ephemeroptera + Neoptera). The three ancient lineages Ephem, Odo, and Neo appear to have diverged rapidly, leaving few characters to discern their relationships (130). Evolutionary rate heterogeneity across clades and the representation of old lineages by recent extant taxa make this one of the most difficult ancient insect radiations to decipher (130).

Molecular studies based primarily on rDNA conflict in their support for relationships among palaeopteran orders. Much of this conflict may be attributable to alternative alignment, sampling, and analysis strategies (50, 60, 86, 91, 125). Multigene data sets (56, 61) have shown robust support for Palaeoptera monophyly. Conversely, phylogenomic data have produced conflicting results. Simon et al. (115) found strong support for mayflies as the closest relatives to Neoptera (Chiastomyaria) based on a sample of 125 genes. This finding was both confirmed (Maximum Likelihood) and contested (Bayesian Inference) by a phylogenomic study of arthropods that included single representatives of Odonata and Ephemeroptera (85). Another phylogenomic study of arthropods, based only on nuclear protein-coding genes and including four paleopteroids, recovered Palaeoptera with modest support (100). On the contrary, mitochondrial genomes and several morphological studies recovered Odonata as the closest relatives to Neoptera (Metapterygota) (10, 17, 117, 146). Adult head structures and features related to the mandible support Metapterygota (e.g., 117), whereas characters of the wing base and wing venation support Palaeoptera (70).

Shortcomings of the presently available morphological evaluations include the lack of reliable anatomical data for Odonata and the narrowness of the analyzed data, i.e., only characters related to the flight apparatus. In addition, the assessment of polarity between early winged insects and their wingless ancestors is difficult because wings had a major effect on transforming insect morphology, and it is impossible to use outgroup comparison for characters that did not exist.

The Palaeoptera problem continues. It is one area of insect phylogeny that has received the most attention and sequence data, yet it remains intractable. Palaeopteran relationships have the potential to be an informative case study for exploring and resolving incongruence in phylogenomic analyses, as multiple large-scale molecular studies have shown support for competing hypotheses. Exploring the cause of systematic bias and continuing the search for critical genetic and morphological synapomorphies are important components of future work on this phylogenetically ambiguous region of the insect tree of life.

Neoptera: Modest Progress amid Impediments

Phylogenetic uncertainty remains across much of the midsection of the insect tree of life owing to an apparent rapid diversification of lineages approximately 300–350 mya (41, 61, 130). Although Neoptera are a widely accepted monophyletic group, two of the three putative lineages nested within it, Polyneoptera and Paraneoptera (=Acercaria), at the exclusion of the well-supported Holometabola, lack robust support, and the evolutionary interrelationships among many included orders are largely unconfirmed. There have been, however, some exciting phylogenetic developments in the past decade, including the description of the new polyneopteran order Mantophasmatodea (64), new evidence placing termites within cockroaches (55, 61, 63, 127), the refinement of the placement of the enigmatic order Zoraptera (31, 56, 142), and the union of the orders of lice (143).

Polyneoptera: An Unresolved Radiation

Polyneoptera, traditionally thought to be the earliest-branching lineage of Neoptera, include the orthopteroid orders Plecoptera (stoneflies), Dermaptera (earwigs), Embioptera (webspinners), Phasmatodea (walking sticks), Mantophasmatodea (gladiators), Grylloblattodea (icecrawlers), Dictyoptera ('Blattodea': roaches, Isoptera: termites, and Mantodea: mantids), Orthoptera (grasshoppers), and possibly Zoraptera (angel insects). Definitive morphological support of relationships among most of these orders is lacking, whereas the vast majority of molecular evidence comes from rDNA (60, 61, 129) and mtDNA (16, 17, 94), which have reached the limits of their phylogenetic utility (130). Major questions regarding the composition and relationships among polyneopteran lineages remain (130), but there is new molecular evidence supporting their monophyly (56).

Among the many outstanding issues of polyneopteran relationships, the relationships of Dictyoptera are a notable success—consensus between morphology and molecules has largely been achieved (27, 55, 63). Dictyoptera have traditionally been considered monophyletic (46), yet the relationships among the termites, cockroaches, and mantids were unclear (27). Shared endosymbionts in the guts of woodroaches (Cryptocercidae) and termites, along with shared morphology, initiated the hypothesis that termites are a roach lineage (75, 76). It is now well established that termites are actually social cockroaches, with the family Cryptocercidae as their closest relative, rendering the Blattodea paraphyletic, and with Mantodea as the sister group to a monophyletic cockroach/termite clade (27, 55–57, 61, 63, 121).

The identification of the new insect order Mantophasmatodea was a recent and exciting find for insect systematists (64). Although new insect species are described regularly, the magnitude of discovering a new order has been described as the equivalent of discovering bats (D. Vane-Wright, published comment). Called gladiators, these rare, wingless carnivores have a limited African distribution, and even though they were known by both fossils in amber and specimens within collections, they had never been previously described. Evidence from nuclear genes and morphology consistently places them as the closest relative of the Grylloblattodea (10, 56, 61, 121). This clade, called Xenonomia (121), or Chimaeraptera (123), has also gained support in a recent detailed study of head structures (137). In contrast, mtDNA recovers a sister-group relationship between Mantophasmatodea and Phasmatodea (16, 94).

Other putative relationships within Polyneoptera that have been recovered by multiple recent studies are a clade joining Phasmatodea and Embioptera (34, 56, 61, 121) and a tentative sister-group relationship between Plecoptera and Dermaptera (56, 60, 61, 121). Support for these hypotheses is limited, and conflicting evidence was reviewed in Reference 10.

The Zoraptera Problem

Zoraptera (angel insects) comprise a single family of tiny, aggregating, primarily wingless scavengers often found under wood bark. The morphological knowledge of Zoraptera has greatly increased in recent years (12, 35, 54, 140). Nevertheless, angel insects remain the most phylogenetically ambiguous order of insects. Zoraptera have been placed in both the Polyneoptera and the Acercaria, with affinity to almost every other included order. Although there is no consensus on the evolutionary relationships of Zoraptera, current morphological and molecular data converge on two competing hypotheses: Molecular data, both rDNA and nuclear protein-coding data, support Zoraptera as a close relative of Dictyoptera (56; 129, discussion tree; 142), whereas recent morphological evidence points toward an affinity to Embioptera (31, 140; but see 10, 12, 35). Additional studies recover relationships between Zoraptera and both Paraneoptera (10, 12, 35) and Dermaptera (57, 121), but these hypotheses have not been independently (Paraneoptera) or robustly (Dermaptera) corroborated by molecular data. The 18S used to place Zoraptera as a close relative of Dermaptera (57, 121, 139) was likely a dermapteran contaminant (141).

Paraneoptera (Acercaria)

Paraneoptera include insects that have primarily sucking mouthparts, such as Hemiptera (true bugs), Thysanoptera (thrips), and Psocodea (Pthiraptera: parasitic lice and Psocoptera: book lice) and have traditionally been considered a monophyly. Although some morphological synapomorphies support the group (e.g., the detachment of the stylet-like lacinia from the stipes), much of the evidence for monophyly relies on the shared loss of external characters (68). rDNA and mtDNA support a primarily monophyletic Paraneoptera (60, 61, 129), yet nuclear protein-coding genes alone recover lice as the closest relative of Holometabola and thrips as the sister group to true bugs (although robust support values are lacking) (56). Morphological data also corroborate a relationship between thrips and true bugs (68, 144). The louse lineage Psocodea are well-established, but molecular and morphological evidence indicates that at least Psocoptera, if not both orders of lice, are paraphyletic (58, 88, 143), with the psocopteran Liposcelidae as the sister group to the phthirapteran Amblycera (58).

Advances Within Orders

In addition to the phylogenetic advances made among insect orders, progress has been made toward resolving higher-level relationships within many of the major insect orders. The past decade has seen an emphasis on multilaboratory collaborations within the systematics community, and modern methods have allowed research teams to tackle larger-scale phylogenetic questions. The National Science Foundation (NSF) Assembling the Tree of Life (AToL) program, as well as the NSF Partnerships for Enhancing Expertise in Taxonomy (PEET) program, has helped catalyze and fund initiatives to revitalize and modernize systematic knowledge and practice. Major new phylogenetic hypotheses have emerged for order-level relationships (e.g., Diptera, 135; Strepsiptera, 95; Coleoptera, 5; Lepidoptera, 89, 101; Hymenoptera, 113, 124; Membracoidea, 25; Trichoptera, 49; Neuroptera, 6, 136; Odonates, 21). Ideally, these large projects, which involve multiple laboratories and data types, have promoted a new systematics paradigm of collaborative data sharing and research coordination to study megadiverse clades. Additional collaborative efforts are critical to address major remaining issues in insect phylogeny as data sets grow in size and complexity.

INTEGRATIVE PHYLOGENETICS FOR THE POSTGENOMIC ERA

Phylogenetic Utility of New Genomic Characters

Genome acquisition, comparative genomic analysis, and the application of these data in phylogenetics have been key to the recent progress in resolving long-standing controversies regarding the insect tree of life. Currently, at least 80 insect genomes have been sequenced or are in progress (Genomes On Line Database, 74), and considering the importance of insects as model organisms, vectors of disease, and pests of agriculture, many more will soon be underway (103). Comparative genomics has provided us with a greater understanding of the evolution of insect genomes and offers guidance at different levels to more efficiently harvest genomic data with increased phylogenetic utility (e.g., primer design, gene selection, orthology determination across divergencies). In addition, genomic data can uncover new phylogenetic characters, such as rare genomic changes, that can potentially provide independent corroboration of more standard data types (106). Synteny and gene order, gene duplications, genome rearrangement, indels, and introns, as well as transposable elements, are alternative genetic characters that have demonstrated utility in recovering evolutionary relationships.

Genomic characters play an important role in phylogenetics of many groups, such as mammals (87), birds (29), and Metazoa (120). The use of alternative genomic characters has trickled into insect systematics as well (14, 45, 85, 107), yet their abundance and utility show some limitations not found in younger, less-speciose lineages. Comparative genomics has revealed that insect genomes have undergone rapid change and are more diverse than vertebrate genomes (145). Zdobnov & Bork (145) provide the example that *Drosophila* and *Apis*, who diverged from each other 320 mya, have only 10% of their shared orthologous genes in synteny, whereas the same comparison for human and puffer fish is approximately 50%, even though they diverged from each other 450 mya. Thus, it is likely that many types of genomic characters that have provided resolution within other groups will be more effective at resolving more recently diverging lineages in insects, such as those within orders. This limitation has been demonstrated in mitochondrial genome arrangements (17) and transposable elements (118). MicroRNAs (110, 126), introns (67, 114, 139), and gene duplications (4) are among the genomic characters that have shown promise for insects and their relatives.

Next-Generation Sequencing

For systematic labs, the use of next-generation sequencing is a bridge to the practice of phylogenomics. Acquisition of genomic data may be less expensive and more time efficient than large-scale targeted PCR methods, as indicated by reviews of new sequencing technology (59, 104). A recent series of studies on mosquitoes demonstrated a successful and relatively affordable approach to use next-generation sequencing to harvest transcriptome data from nonmodel organisms without reliance on an available closely related genome (37, 47). ESTs (expressed sequence tags) have been used successfully for phylogenetic resolution of several insect groups and their relatives (53, 77, 85, 113).

In the postgenomic era, as genomic data accrue from nonmodel organisms, bioinformatics becomes a new, critical tool for effectively managing, filtering, and vetting the extensive influx of sequences. Complicating factors include the management of extensive amounts of data, filtration and identification of appropriate orthologous markers, taxon sampling limitations due to cost, and computational issues; similar problems are encountered when performing large-scale targeted PCR as well. Indirect gene harvesting methods have been advocated over targeted PCR for some time (92; but see 97) even though next-generation sequencing sacrifices the a priori discernment and selection of applicable, single-copy orthologous markers for the rapid acquisition of copious amounts of sequence data. Nevertheless, marker choice and orthology determination remain of primary importance for accurate phylogeny recovery. At present, there is no broad consensus on how either can best be achieved, yet recent phylogenomic studies and reviews on bioinformatic pipelines for orthology determination are useful guides in determining how to proceed (2, 23, 28, 71, 85, 93, 102). Although the cost of sequencing continues to decrease, the near future still dictates an approach that considers feasibility and affordability trade-offs between the scope of the phylogenetic question, the extent of taxon sampling, and the depth of molecular data collection.

The Role of Morphology

Morphological systematics continues to play a vital role in the postgenomic era of insect systematics. In addition to providing an independent data set for a critical evaluation of molecular phylogenies (and vice versa), morphological systematics is the basis for reconstructing complex evolutionary scenarios focused on changes at the phenotypic level. Likewise, ontogenetic studies (e.g., 80, 138) and detailed ultrastructural investigations (e.g., 26) will help elucidate the complex mosaic of hexapod evolution. New visualization techniques such as micro-CT scanning (35) are making the study of many more character systems, most importantly those of the internal skeletal and soft anatomy (e.g., Deuterophlebiidae, 112; Osmylidae, 13), tractable. These studies provide exquisitely detailed accounts of the anatomy of phylogenetically critical taxa. Although broad phylogenetic conclusions are difficult to achieve with suites of modified characters owing to lineage-specific adaptations, these studies are necessary first steps that later lead to comprehensive data sets. Some broader phylogenetic comparisons at this level are already providing evolutionary insights (8, 36). Another breakthrough is the application of micro-CT to amber fossils. Recently, the anatomy including internal soft parts of a 40-mya-old strepsipteran fossil was reconstructed almost completely using micro-CT (96). It is conceivable that this new technique will greatly facilitate the placement of fossil taxa crucial for understanding evolutionary history and for which morphology is the only available source of phylogenetic information. Recent fossil discoveries continue to push back the first appearance of major groups (e.g., 84, 116, 128) and further detail the relationships between insects and plants (51, 72).

FUTURE WORK TOWARD THE INSECT TREE OF LIFE

Although great advances have been made toward resolving the insect tree of life, particularly within Holometabola, phylogenetic ambiguity remains for a substantial number of branches, such as the polyneopteran lineages. As genomic data are brought to bear on these uncertainties, we anticipate further resolution. Yet the case of Palaeoptera makes clear that an increase in sequence data alone is not likely to reveal the relationships among all lineages (93), particularly those that diverged rapidly from one another long ago, leaving little trace of their shared genetic history. Such cases exist at many taxonomic levels and account for several of the most significant evolutionary changes in the insects. Their resolution depends on the use of integrated methods and hypothesis confirmation from congruence among independent data sets. Without corroboration from multiple sources of data, it is often unclear whether a lineage's resistance to resolution is due to rapid ancestral diversification, to inappropriate or insufficient markers (e.g., saturated or noisy), or to systematic bias (e.g., errors in model estimation or analytical methodology). In some cases, we may need to be satisfied with a "bush of life" (105) with multiple plausible histories of particular lineages, but only after the addition and thorough exploration of many new data points and data types. Progress hinges on the selection of orthologous and least-saturated genes, on improved models of sequence evolution to overcome systematic error, and on the continued search for new characters among genomic, morphological, and paleontological data. Ultimately, we look to the combination of robust phylogenetic hypotheses and well-documented morphological transformations at the phenotypic level, along with improved morphological knowledge of fossil taxa, to ultimately guide us to a deeper understanding of insect evolution.

SUMMARY POINTS

1. Advances in molecular sequencing and computational evolutionary theory, as well as new techniques for the discovery of morphological characters, have furthered resolution of the insect tree of life. Progress in insect systematics in the postgenomic era will rely not only on molecular evidence, but also on integrative methods and corroboration among independent lines of evidence from molecular, morphological, and paleontological sources.
2. Notable phylogenetic successes include the discovery that insects are a crustacean lineage and members of a monophyletic Pancrustacea; the resolution of the relationships of Holometabola, including the enigmatic parasitic order Strepsiptera as a beetle relative and an early-diverging Hymenoptera; and the elucidation of dictyopteran relationships, with the recognition of termites as social roaches.
3. Some regions of the insect tree remain unresolved. Despite the application of extensive phylogenomic data and morphological evidence, the arrangement of the palaeopteran orders (dragonflies and mayflies) and their relationship to Neoptera (the rest of the winged insects) are ambiguous. The Polyneoptera (orthopteroid lineages) and Neuropterida (lacewings, snakeflies and dobsonflies) also remain unclear, yet the utility of phylogenomic data for these groups has yet to be explored. In addition, the monophyly of several orders, Zygentoma, Psocoptera and Pthiraptera, Megaloptera, and Mecoptera, remains in question.
4. Complete genome sequences for nonmodel organisms are the future. Until then, the choice to acquire data by targeted PCR or by high-throughput sequencing is a trade-off of feasibility, affordability, taxon sampling, and depth of data collection. Ongoing challenges for phylogenomics are managing data and bioinformatics, filtering large data harvests to find suitable orthologous markers, overcoming the limitations of extensive computation time and power, and avoiding systematic error (often disguised as robustly supported resolution).

5. Comparative genomics can lead to the discovery of new genomic characters for phylogenetics. Genomic characters such as gene order, genome rearrangement, indels, introns, and transposable elements have been useful in other groups but often present challenges in insects because of their variable genome evolution. More genomic characters should be explored for phylogenetic use in insects both within and among orders.
6. Morphology continues to play a primary role in the postgenomic era. New techniques, such as micro-CT scanning, can reveal new internal characters and uncover details of fossil specimens. Morphological data contribute independent estimates of phylogeny for comparison and corroboration with molecular data, as well as providing the means to incorporate paleontological evidence.
7. Standard phylogenetic characters, sequence data, and morphology will likely not resolve all branches of the insect tree, particularly ancient lineages that diverged rapidly. As we move from reliance on primarily rDNA and mtDNA to a greater emphasis on nuclear protein-coding genes and genomic data sets, we will need to prioritize thorough exploration of our data, with the awareness of systematic error. Further advancement of insect systematics will rely on independent confirmation of phylogenetic hypotheses from molecular, morphological, and paleontological evidence in combination with the discovery of and reliance on new character systems.

DISCLOSURE STATEMENT

The authors are not aware of any affiliations, memberships, funding, or financial holdings that might be perceived as affecting the objectivity of this review.

ACKNOWLEDGMENTS

We thank L. Deitz, A. Seago, and two anonymous reviewers for edits on an earlier version of this manuscript. This project was supported by U.S. National Science Foundation grants EF-0334948 and DEB-0731528 to B. Wiegmann and D. Yeates, and NSF DEB 0816865 to K.M. Kjer.

LITERATURE CITED

1. Aleshin VV, Mikhailov KV, Konstantinova AV, Nikitin MA, Rusin LY, et al. 2009. On the phylogenetic position of insects in the Pancrustacea clade. *Mol. Biol.* 43:808–18
2. Altenhoff, Dessimoz C. 2009. Phylogenetic and functional assessment of ortholog inference projects and methods. *PLoS Comput. Biol.* 5:e1000262
3. Aspock U, Plant JD, Nemeschkal HL. 2001. Cladistic analysis of Neuroptera and their systematic position within Neuropterida (Insecta: Holometabola: Neuropterida: Neuroptera). *Syst. Entomol.* 26:73–86
4. Bao R, Friedrich M. 2009. Molecular evolution of the *Drosophila* retinome: exceptional gene gain in higher Diptera. *Mol. Biol. Evol.* 26:1273–87
5. Beutel RG, Friedrich F. 2008. A renaissance of insect morphology—μ-Ct and other innovative techniques. *DGaaE Nachr.* 22:5–8
6. Beutel RG, Friedrich F, Aspöck U. 2010. The larval head of Nevrorthidae and the phylogeny of Neuroptera (Insecta). *Zool. J. Linn. Soc.* 158:533–62
7. **Beutel RG, Friedrich F, Hörnschemeyer T, Pohl H, Hünefeld F, et al. 2010. Morphological and molecular evidence converging upon a robust phylogeny of the megadiverse Holometabola. *Cladistics* 26:1–15**

7. The first morphological study to corroborate the phylogeny of Holometabola based on molecular work.

8. Beutel RG, Friedrich F, Whiting MF. 2008. Head morphology of *Caurinus* (Boreidae, Mecoptera) and its phylogenetic implications. *Arthropod Struct. Dev.* 37:418–33
9. Beutel RG, Gorb S. 2001. Ultrastructure of attachment specializations of hexapods (Arthropoda): evolutionary patterns inferred from a revised ordinal phylogeny. *J. Zool. Syst. Evol. Res.* 39:177–207
10. Beutel RG, Gorb S. 2006. A revised interpretation of the evolution of attachment structures in Hexapoda with special emphasis on Mantophasmatodea. *Arthropod Syst. Phylogeny* 64:3–25
11. Beutel RG, Pohl H. 2006. Endopterygote systematics—Where do we stand and what is the goal (Hexapoda, Arthropoda)? *Syst. Entomol.* 31:202–19
12. Beutel RG, Weide D. 2005. Cephalic anatomy of *Zorotypus hubbardi* (Hexapoda: Zoraptera): new evidence for a relationship with Acercaria. *Zoomorphology* 124:121–36
13. Beutel RG, Zimmermann D, Krauß M, Randolf S, Wipfler B. 2010. Head morphology of *Osmylus fulvicephalus* (Osmylidae, Neuroptera) and its phylogenetic implications. *Org. Divers. Evol.* 10:311–29
14. Bonneton F, Brunet FG, Kathirithamby J, Laudet V. 2006. The rapid divergence of the ecdysone receptor is a synapomorphy for Mecopterida that clarifies the Strepsiptera problem. *Insect. Mol. Biol.* 15:351–62
15. Budd GE, Telford MJ. 2009. The origin and evolution of arthropods. *Nature* 457:812–17
16. Cameron SL, Barker SC, Whiting MF. 2006. Mitochondrial genomics and the new insect order Mantophasmatodea. *Mol. Phylogenet. Evol.* 38:274–79
17. Cameron SL, Beckenbach AT, Dowton MA, Whiting MF. 2006. Evidence from mitochondrial genomics on interordinal relationships in insects. *Arthropod Syst. Phylogeny* 64:27–34
18. Cameron SL, Sullivan J, Song H, Miller KB, Whiting FW. 2009. A mitochondrial genome phylogeny of the Neuropterida (lace-wings, alderflies and snakeflies) and their relationship to the other holometabolous insect orders. *Zool. Scr.* 38:575–90
19. Carapelli A, Liò P, Nardi F, van der Wath E, Frati F. 2007. Phylogenetic analysis of mitochondrial protein coding genes confirms the reciprocal paraphyly of Hexapoda and Crustacea. *BMC Evol. Biol.* 7(Suppl. 2):S8
20. Carapelli A, Nardi F, Dallai R, Frati F. 2006. A review of molecular data for the phylogeny of basal hexapods. *Pedobiologia* 50:191–204
21. Carle FL, Kjer KM, May ML. 2008. Evolution of Odonata, with special reference to Zygoptera. *Arthropod Syst. Phylogeny* 66:37–44
22. Castro LR, Dowton M. 2005. The position of the Hymenoptera within the Holometabola as inferred from the mitochondrial genome of *Perga condei* (Hymenoptera: Symphyta: Pergidae). *Mol. Phylogenet. Evol.* 34:469–79
23. Chen F, Mackey AJ, Vermunt JK, Roos DS. 2007. Assessing performance of orthology detection strategies applied to eukaryotic genomes. *PLoS ONE* 2(4):e383
24. Crowson RA. 1960. The phylogeny of Coleoptera. *Annu. Rev. Entomol.* 5:111–34
25. Cryan J, Svenson GJ. 2010. Family-level relationships of the spittlebugs and froghoppers (Hemiptera: Cicaomorpha: Cercopidea). *Syst. Entomol.* 35:393–415
26. Dallai R. 2009. The contribution of the sperm structure to the reconstruction of the hexapod phylogeny. *Proc. Arthropod Embryol. Soc. Jpn.* 43:23–38
27. Deitz LL, Nalepa C, Klass KD. 2003. Phylogeny of the Dictyoptera re-examined (Insecta). *Entomol. Abh.* 61:69–91
28. Dunn CW, Hejnol A, Matus DQ, Pang K, Browne WE, et al. 2008. Broad phylogenomic sampling improves resolution of the animal tree of life. *Nature* 452:745–49
29. Edwards SV, Jennings BW, Shedlock AM. 2004. Phylogenetics of modern birds in the era of phylogenomics. *Proc. R. Soc. B* 272:979–92
30. Engel MS. 2006. A note on the relic silverfish *Tricholepidion gertschi* (Zygentoma). *Trans. Kans. Acad. Sci.* 109:236–38
31. Engel MS, Grimaldi DA. 2000. A winged *Zorotypus* in Miocene amber from the Dominican Republic (Zoraptera: Zorotypidae), with discussion on relationships of and within the order. *Acta Geol. Hisp.* 35:149–64
32. Ertas B, von Reumont BM, Wägele JW, Misof B, Burmester T. 2009. Hemocyanin suggests a close relationship of Remipedia and Hexapoda. *Mol. Biol. Evol.* 26:2711–18

33. Fanenbruck M, Harzsch S, Wägele W. 2004. The brain of the Remipedia (Crustacea) and an alternative hypothesis on their phylogenetic relationships. *Proc. Natl. Acad. Sci. USA* 101:3868–73
34. Friedemann K, Wipfler B, Bradler S, Beutel RG. 2011. On the head morphology of *Phyllium* and the phylogenetic relationships of Phasmatodea (Insecta). *Acta Zool.* doi: 10.1111/j.1463-6395.2010.00497.x
35. Friedrich F, Beutel RG. 2008. The thorax of *Zorotypus* (Hexapoda, Zoraptera) and a new nomenclature for the musculature of Neoptera. *Arthropod Struct. Dev.* 37:29–54
36. Friedrich F, Beutel RG. 2010. Goodbye Halteria? The thoracic morphology of Endopterygota (Insecta) and its phylogenetic implications. *Cladistics* 26:1–34
37. Gibbons JG, Janson EM, Hittlinger CT, Johnston M, Abbot P, Rokas A. 2009. Benchmarking next generation transcriptome sequencing for functional and evolutionary genomics. *Mol. Biol. Evol.* 26:2731–44
38. Giribet G, Edgecombe GD, Carpenter JM, D'Haese CA, Wheeler WC. 2004. Is Ellipura monophyletic? A combined analysis of basal hexapod relationships with emphasis on the origin of insects. *Org. Divers. Evol.* 4:319–40
39. Giribet G, Edgecombe GD, Wheeler WC. 2001. Arthropod phylogeny based on eight molecular loci and morphology. *Nature* 413:157–61
40. Giribet G, Richter S, Edgecombe GD, Wheeler W. 2005. The position of crustaceans within Arthropoda—evidence from nine molecular loci and morphology. *Crustacean Issues* 16:307–52
41. **Grimaldi D, Engel MS. 2005. *Evolution of the Insects*. Cambridge, UK: Cambridge Univ. Press.**
42. Grimaldi DA. 2010. 400 million years on six legs: on the origin and early evolution of Hexapoda. *Arthropod Struct. Dev.* 39:191–203
43. Haring E, Aspöck U. 2004. Phylogeny of the Neuropterida: a first molecular approach. *Syst. Entomol.* 29:415–30
44. Harzsch S, Hafner G. 2006. Evolution of eye development in arthropods: phylogenetic aspects. *Arthropod Struct. Dev.* 35:319–40
45. Hayward DC, Trueman JWH, Bastiani MJ, Ball EE. 2005. The structure of the USP/PXR of *Xenos pecki* indicates that Strepsiptera are not closely related to Diptera. *Dev. Genes Evol.* 215:213–19
46. Hennig W. 1969. *Die Stammesgeschichte der Insekten*. Frankfurt: Waldemar Kramer. 436 pp.
47. Hittinger CT, Johnston M, Tossberg JT, Rokas A. 2009. Leveraging skewed transcript abundance by RNA-Seq to increase the genomic depth of the tree of life. *Proc. Natl. Acad. Sci. USA* 107:1476–81
48. Holt RA, Subramanian GM, Halpern A, Sutton GG, Charlab R, et al. 2002. The genome sequence of the malaria mosquito *Anopheles gambiae*. *Science* 298:129–49
49. Holzenthal RW, Blahnik RJ, Kjer KM, Prather AL. 2007. An update on the phylogeny of caddisflies (Trichoptera). In *Proc. XIIth Int. Symp. Trichoptera*, ed. J Bueno-Soria, R Barba-Álvarez, B Armitage, pp. 143–53. Columbus, OH: The Caddis Press
50. Hovmöeller R, Pape T, Kallersjö M. 2002. The Palaeoptera problem: basal pterygote phylogeny inferred from 18S and 28S rDNA sequences. *Cladistics* 18:313–23
51. Hu SS, Dilcher DL, Jarzen DM, Taylor DW. 2008. Early steps of angiosperm-pollinator coevolution. *Proc. Natl. Acad. Sci. USA* 105:240–45
52. Huelsenbeck JP. 1998. Systematic bias in phylogenetic analysis: Is the Strepsiptera problem solved? *Syst. Biol.* 47:519–37
53. Hughes J, Longhorn SJ, Papadopoulou A, Theodorides K, de Riva A, et al. 2006. Dense taxonomic EST sampling and its applications for molecular systematics of the Coleoptera (beetles). *Mol. Biol. Evol.* 23:268–78
54. Hünefeld F. 2007. The genital morphology of *Zorotypus hubbardi* Caudell (Hexapoda: Zoraptera: Zorotypidae). *Zoomorphology* 126:135–51
55. Inward D, Beccaloni G, Eggleton P. 2007. Death of an order: A comprehensive molecular phylogenetic study confirms that termites are eusocial cockroaches. *Biol. Lett.* 3:331–35
56. **Ishiwata K, Sasaki G, Ogawa J, Miyata T, Su Z. 2010. Phylogenetic relationships among insect orders based on three nuclear protein coding gene sequences. *Mol. Phylogenet. Evol.* 58:169–80**
57. Jarvis K, Haas F, Whiting M. 2005. Phylogeny of earwigs (Insecta: Dermaptera) based on morphological evidence: reconsidering the classification of Dermaptera. *Syst. Entomol.* 30:442–53

41. Provides a thorough review of insect relationships and natural histories, including a review of fossil evidence

56. The first broadly sampled study evaluating higher-level insect relationships that is based on nuclear genes.

58. Johnson KP, Yoshizawa K, Smith VS. 2004. Multiple origins of parasitism in lice. *Proc. R. Soc. Lond. B* 271:1771–76
59. Kerr Wall P, Leebens-Mack J, Chanderbali AS, Barakat A, Wolcott E, et al. 2009. Comparison of next generation sequencing technologies for transcriptome characterization. *BMC Genomics* 10:347
60. Kjer KM. 2004. Aligned 18S and insect phylogeny. *Syst. Biol.* 53:506–14
61. Kjer KM, Carle FL, Litman J, Ware J. 2006. A molecular phylogeny of Insecta. *Arthropod Syst. Phylogeny* 64:35–44
62. Klass K-D, Kristensen NP. 2001. The ground plan and affinities of hexapods: recent progress and open problems. *Ann. Soc. Entomol. Fr.* 37:265–98
63. Klass K-D, Meier R. 2006. A phylogenetic analysis of Dictyoptera (Insecta) based on morphological characters. *Entomol. Abh.* 63:3–50
64. Klass K-D, Zompro O, Kristensen NP, Adis J. 2002. Mantophasmatodea: a new insect order with extant members in the Afrotropics. *Science* 296:1456–59
65. Kornberg TB, Krasnow MA. 2000. The *Drosophila* genome sequence: implications for biology and medicine. *Science* 287:2281–20
66. Kraus O. 2001. 'Myriapoda' and the ancestry of the Hexapoda. *Ann. Soc. Entomol. Fr.* 37:105–27
67. Krauss V, Pecyna M, Kurz K, Sass H. 2005. Phylogenetic mapping of intron positions: a case study of translation initiation factor eIF2γ. *Mol. Biol. Evol.* 22:74–84
68. Kristensen NP. 1981. Phylogeny of insect orders. *Annu. Rev. Entomol.* 26:135–57
69. Kristensen NP. 1999. Phylogeny of endopterygote insects, the most successful lineage of living organisms. *Eur. J. Entomol.* 96:237–53
70. Kukalová-Peck J, Lawrence JF. 2004. Use of hind wing characters in assessing relationships among coleopteran suborders and major endoneopteran lineages. *Eur. J. Entomol.* 101:95–144
71. Kuzniar A, van Ham RCHJ, Pongor S, Leunissen JAM. 2008. The quest for orthologs: finding the corresponding gene across genomes. *Trends Genet.* 24:539–51
72. Labandeira CC. 2010. The pollination of mid-Mesozoic seed plants and the early history of long-proboscid insects. *Ann. Mo. Bot. Gard.* 97:469–513
73. Lawrence JF, Slipinski A, Seago AE, Thayer MK, Newton AF, Marvaldi AE. 2011. Phylogeny of the Coleoptera based on morphological characters of adults and larvae. *Ann. Zool.* 61:1–217
74. Liolios K, Chen IM, Mavromatis K, Tavernarakis N, Hugenholtz P, et al. 2010. The Genomes On Line Database (GOLD) in 2009: status of genomic and metagenomic projects and their associated metadata. *Nucleic Acids Res.* 38:D346–54
75. Lo N, Bandi C, Watanabe H, Nalepa C, Beninati T. 2003. Evidence for cocladogenesis between diverse dictyopteran lineages and their intracellular endosymbionts. *Mol. Biol. Evol.* 20:907–13
76. Lo N, Tokuda G, Watanabe H, Rose H, Slaytor M, et al. 2000. Evidence from multiple gene sequences indicates that termites evolved from wood-feeding cockroaches. *Curr. Biol.* 10:801–4
77. Longhorn SJ, Pohl HW, Vogler AP. 2010. Ribosomal protein genes of holometabolan insects reject the Halteria, instead revealing a close affinity of Strepsiptera with Coleoptera. *Mol. Phylogenet. Evol.* 55:846–59
78. Lovejoy TE, Hannah L. 2005. *Climate Change and Biodiversity*. New Haven, CT: Yale Univ. Press
79. Luan YX, Mallatt JM, Xie RD, Yang YM, Yin WY. 2005. The phylogenetic positions of three basal-hexapod groups (Protura, Diplura, and Collembola) based on ribosomal RNA gene sequences. *Mol. Biol. Evol.* 22:1579–92
80. Machida R. 2006. Evidence from embryology for reconstructing the relationships of basal hexapod clades. *Arthropod Syst. Phylogeny* 64:95–104
81. Mallatt J, Craig CW, Yoder MJ. 2010. Nearly complete rRNA genes assembled from across the metazoan animals: effects of more taxa, a structure-based alignment, and paired-sites evolutionary models on phylogeny reconstruction. *Mol. Phylogenet. Evol.* 55:1–17
82. Mallatt J, Giribet G. 2006. Further use of nearly complete 28S and 18S rRNA genes to classify Ecdysozoa: 37 more arthropods and a kinorhynch. *Mol. Phylogenet. Evol.* 40:772–94
83. McKenna DD, Farrell BD. 2010. 9-genes reinforce the phylogeny of Holometabola and yield alternate views on the phylogenetic placement of Strepsiptera. *PLoS ONE* 5(7):e11887

60. Stresses the importance of alignment in rDNA analyses and shows how the exclusion of hypervariable regions could rectify artifactual placements.

84. Meller B, Ponomarenko AG, Vasilenko DV, Fischer TC, Aschauer B. 2011. First beetle elytra, abdomen (Coleoptera) and a mine trace from Lunz (Carnian, Late Triassic, Lunz-am-See, Austria) and their taphonomical and evolutionary aspects. *Palaeontology* 54:97–110

85. Meusemann K, von Reumont BM, Simon S, Roeding F, Strauss S, et al. 2010. A phylogenomic approach to resolve the arthropod tree of life. *Mol. Biol. Evol.* 27:2451–64

86. Misof B, Niehuis O, Bischoff I, Rickert A, Erpenbeck D, Staniczek A. 2007. Towards an 18S phylogeny of hexapods: accounting for group-specific character covariance in optimized mixed nucleotide/doublet models. *Zoology* 110:409–29

87. Murphy WJ, Pevzner PA, O'Brien SJ. 2004. Mammalian phylogenomics comes of age. *Trends Genet.* 20:631–39

88. Murrell A, Barker SC. 2005. Multiple origins of parasitism in lice: Phylogenetic analysis of SSU rDNA indicates that the Phthiraptera and Psocoptera are not monophyletic. *Parasitol. Res.* 97:274–80

89. Mutanen M, Wahlberg N, Kaila L. 2010. Comprehensive gene and taxon coverage elucidates radiation patterns in moths and butterflies. *Proc. R. Soc. B.* 277:2839–48

90. Nardi F, Spinsanti G, Boore JL, Carapelli A, Dallai R, Frati F. 2003. Hexapod origins: monophyletic or paraphyletic? *Science* 299:1887–89

91. Ogden TH, Whiting MF. 2003. The problem with the Palaeoptera Problem: sense and sensitivity. *Cladistics* 19:432–42

92. Philippe H, Telford MJ. 2006. Large-scale sequencing and the new animal phylogeny. *Trends Ecol. Evol.* 21:614–20

93. Philippe H, Brinkmann H, Lavrov DV, Littlewood DTJ, Manuel M, et al. 2011. Resolving difficult phylogenetic questions: why more sequences are not enough. *PLoS Biol.* 9:e1000602

94. Plazzi F, Ricci A, Passamonti M. 2011. The mitochondrial genome of *Bacillus* stick insects (Phasmatodea) and the phylogeny of orthopteroid insects. *Mol. Phylogenet. Evol.* 58:274–79

95. Pohl H, Beutel RG. 2005. The phylogeny of Strepsiptera (Hexapoda). *Cladistics* 21:1–47

96. Pohl H, Wipfler B, Grimaldi D, Beckmann F, Beutel RG. 2010. Reconstructing the anatomy of the 42 million-year-old fossil *Mengea tertiara* (Insecta, Strepsiptera). *Naturwissenschaften* 97:855–59

97. Regier JC, Shultz JW, Ganley AR, Hussey A, Shi D, et al. 2008. Resolving arthropod phylogeny: exploring phylogenetic signal within 41 kb of protein-coding nuclear gene sequence. *Syst. Biol.* 57:920–38

98. Regier JC, Shultz JW, Kambic RE. 2004. Phylogeny of basal hexapod lineages and estimates of divergence times. *Ann. Entomol. Soc. Am.* 97:411–19

99. Regier JC, Shultz JW, Kambic RE. 2005. Pancrustacean phylogeny: Hexapods are terrestrial crustaceans and maxillopods are not monophyletic. *Proc. R. Soc. Lond. B* 272:395–401

100. Regier JC, Shultz JW, Zwick A, Hussey A, Ball B, et al. 2010. Arthropod relationships revealed by phylogenomic analysis of nuclear protein coding sequences. *Nature* 463:1079–83

101. Regier JC, Zwick A, Cummings MP, Kawahara AY, Cho S, et al. 2009. Toward reconstructing the evolution of advanced moths and butterflies (Lepidoptera: *Ditrysia*): an initial molecular study. *BMC Evol. Biol.* 9:280

102. Robbertse B, Yoder RJ, Boyd A, Reeves J, Spatafora JW. 2011. Hal: an automated pipeline for phylogenetic analyses of genomic data. *PLoS Curr.* 3:RRN1213

103. Robinson GE, Hackett KJ, Purcell-Miramontes M, Brown SJ, Evans JD, et al. 2011. Creating a buzz about insect genomes. *Science* 331:1386

104. Rokas A, Abbott P. 2009. Harnessing genomics for evolutionary insights. *Trends Ecol. Evol.* 24:192–200

105. Rokas A, Carroll SB. 2006. Bushes in the tree of life. *PLoS Biol.* 4:1899–904

106. Rokas A, Holland PWH. 2000. Rare genomic changes as a tool for phylogenetics. *Trends Ecol. Evol.* 15:454–59

107. Rokas A, Kathirithamby J, Holland PWH. 1999. Intron insertion as a phylogenetic character: The engrailed homeobox of Strepsiptera does not indicate affinity with Diptera. *Insect Mol. Biol.* 8:527–30

108. Rokas A, Krueger D, Carroll SB. 2005. Animal evolution and the molecular signature of radiations compressed in time. *Science* 310:1933–38

85. Provides a large data set and thorough analyses of arthropods, including recovery of many higher-level insect relationships; also presents a novel pipeline for orthology determination and data filtering.

93. Addresses many of the pressing issues for systematists in the postgenomic era.

106. Emphasizes the use of alternate genomic characters for phylogeny resolution, which is of increasing importance in light of systematic error in large data sets.

109. Ronquist F, Deans AR. 2010. Bayesian phylogenetics and its influence on insect systematics. *Annu. Rev. Entomol.* 55:189–206

110. Rota-Stabelli O, Campbell L, Brinkmann H, Edgecombe GD, Longhorn SJ, et al. 2011. A congruent solution to arthropod phylogeny: Phylogenomics, microRNAs and morphology support monophyletic Mandibulata. *Proc. R. Soc. Lond. B* 278:298–306

111. Savard J, Tautz D, Richards S, Weinstock GM, Gibbs RA, et al. 2006. Phylogenomic analysis reveals bees and wasps (Hymenoptera) at the base of the radiation of holometabolous insects. *Genome Res.* 16:1334–38

112. Schneeberg K, Courtney GW, Beutel RG. 2011. Adult head structures of Deuterophlebiidae (Insecta), a highly derived "ancestral" dipteran lineage. *Arthropod Struct. Dev.* 40:93–104

113. Sharanowski BJ, Robbertse B, Walker J, Voss SR, Yoder R, et al. 2010. Expressed sequence tags reveal Proctotrupomorpha (minus Chalcidoidea) as sister to Aculeata (Hymenoptera: Insecta). *Mol. Phylogenet. Evol.* 57:101–12

114. Simon S, Schierwater B, Hadrys H. 2010. On the value of elongation factor-1α for reconstructing pterygote phylogeny. *Mol. Phylogenet. Evol.* 54:651–56

115. Simon S, Strauss S, von Haeseler A, Hadrys H. 2009. A phylogenomic approach to resolve the basal pterygote divergence. *Mol. Biol. Evol.* 26:2719–30

116. Smith DM, Gorman MA, Pardo JD, Small BJ. 2011. First fossil Orthoptera from the Jurassic of North America. *J. Paleontol.* 85:102–5

117. Staniczek A. 2000. The mandible of silverfish (Insecta: Zygentoma) and mayflies (Ephemeroptera): its morphology and phylogenetic significance. *Zool. Anz.* 239:147–78

118. Struchiner CJ, Massad E, Tu Z, Ribeiro JMC. 2009. The tempo and mode of evolution of transposable elements as revealed by molecular phylogenies reconstructed from mosquito genomes. *Evolution* 63:3136–46

119. Szucsich NU, Pass G. 2008. Incongruent phylogenetic hypotheses and character conflicts in morphology: the root and early branches of the hexapodan tree. *Mitt. Dtsch. Ges. Allg. Angew.* 16:415–29

120. Telford MJ, Copely RR. 2011. Improving animal phylogenies with genomic data. *Trends Genet.* 27:186–95

121. Terry MD, Whiting MF. 2005. Mantophasmatodea and phylogeny of the lower neopterous insects. *Cladistics* 21:240–57

122. Timmermans MJ, Roelofs D, Mariën J, van Straalen NM. 2008. Revealing pancrustacean relationships: Phylogenetic analysis of ribosomal protein genes places Collembola (springtails) in a monophyletic Hexapoda and reinforces the discrepancy between mitochondrial and nuclear DNA markers. *BMC Evol. Biol.* 8:83

123. Uchifune T, Machida R. 2005. Embryonic development of *Galloisiana yuasai* Asahina, with special reference to external morphology (Insecta: Grylloblattodea). *J. Morphol.* 266:182–207

124. Vilhelmsen L, Miko I, Krogmann L. 2010. Beyond the wasp-waist: structural diversity and phylogenetic significance of the mesosoma in apocritan wasps (Insecta: Hymenoptera). *Zool. J. Linn. Soc.* 159:22–194

125. von Reumont BM, Meusemann K, Szucsich NU, Dell'Ampio E, Gowri-Shankar V, et al. 2009. Can comprehensive background knowledge be incorporated into substitution models to improve phylogenetic analyses? A case study on major arthropod relationships. *BMC Evol. Biol.* 9:119

126. Wang X, Gu J, Zhang MQ, Li Y. 2008. Identification of phylogenetically conserved microRNA *cis*-regulatory elements across 12 *Drosophila* species. *Bioinformatics* 24:165–71

127. Ware JL, Litman J, Klass KD, Spearman L. 2008. Relationships among the major lineages of Dictyoptera: the effect of outgroup selection on dictyopteran tree topology. *Syst. Entomol.* 33:429–50

128. Wedmann S, Bradler S, Rust J. 2007. The first fossil leaf insect: 47 million years of specialized cryptic morphology and behavior. *Proc. Natl. Acad. Sci. USA* 104:565–69

129. Wheeler WC, Whiting M, Wheeler QD, Carpenter JM. 2001. The phylogeny of the extant hexapod orders. *Cladistics* 17:113–69

130. Whitfield JB, Kjer KM. 2008. Ancient rapid radiations of insects: challenges for phylogenetic analysis. *Annu. Rev. Entomol.* 53:449–72

131. Whiting MF. 2002. Mecoptera is paraphyletic: multiple genes and phylogeny of Mecoptera and Siphonaptera. *Zool. Scr.* 31:93–104

110. A thorough study of arthropods that relies on an integrated approach by seeking corroboration of independent data types for hard-to-recover phylogenetic regions.

132. Whiting MF, Carpenter JM, Wheeler QD, Wheeler WC. 1997. The Strepsiptera problem: phylogeny of the holometabolous insect orders inferred from 18S and 28S ribosomal DNA sequences and morphology. *Syst. Biol.* 46:1–68
133. Whiting MF, Wheeler WC. 1994. Insect homeotic transformation. *Nature* 368:696
134. Wiegmann B, Trautwein M, Kim JW, Cassel B, Bertone M, et al. 2009. Single-copy nuclear genes resolve the phylogeny of the holometabolous insects. *BMC Biol.* 7:34
135. Wiegmann BM, Trautwein M, Winkler I, Barr N, Kim J-W, et al. 2011. Episodic radiations in the fly tree of life. *Proc. Natl. Acad. Sci. USA* 108:5690–95
136. Winterton SL, Hardy NB, Wiegmann BM. 2010. On wings of lace: phylogeny and Bayesian divergence time estimates of Neuropterida (Insecta) based on morphological and molecular data. *Syst. Entomol.* 35:349–78
137. Wipfler B, Machida R, Müller B, Beutel RG. 2011. On the head morphology of Grylloblattodea (Insecta) and the systematic position of the order—with a new nomenclature for the head muscles of Dicondylia. *Syst. Entomol.* 36:241–66
138. Xiaoyun Y, Weber M, Zarin-Kamar N, Posnien N, Friedrich F, et al. 2009. Probing the *Drosophila* retinal determination gene network in *Tribolium* (II): the Pax6 genes *eyeless* and *twin of eyeless*. *Dev. Biol.* 333:215–27
139. Xie Q, Tian X, Qin Y, Bu W. 2009. Phylogenetic comparison of local length plasticity of the small subunit of nuclear rDNA among all Hexapoda orders and the impact of hyper-length-variation on alignment. *Mol. Phylogenet. Evol.* 59:310–16
140. Yoshizawa K. 2007. The Zoraptera problem: evidence for Zoraptera + Embioptera from the wing base. *Syst. Entomol.* 32:197–204
141. Yoshizawa K. 2010. Direct optimization overly optimizes data. *Syst. Entomol.* 35:199–206
142. Yoshizawa K, Johnson K. 2005. Aligned 18S for Zoraptera (Insecta): phylogenetic position and molecular evolution. *Mol. Phylogenet. Evol.* 37:572–80
143. Yoshizawa K, Johnson KP. 2010. How stable is the "Polyphyly of Lice" hypothesis (Insecta: Psocodea)? A comparison of phylogenetic signal in multiple genes. *Mol. Phylogenet. Evol.* 55:939–51
144. Yoshizawa K, Saigusa T. 2001. Phylogenetic analysis of paraneopteran orders (Insecta: Neoptera) based on forewing base structure, with comments on monophyly of Auchenorrhyncha (Hemiptera). *Syst. Entomol.* 26:1–13
145. Zdobnov EM, Bork P. 2006. Quantification of insect genome divergence. *Trends Genet.* 23:16–20
146. Zhang J, Zhou C, Gai Y, Song D, Zhou K. 2008. The complete mitochondrial genome of *Parafronurus youi* (Insecta: Ephemeroptera) and the phylogenetic position of Ephemeroptera. *Gene* 424:18–24

134. First multigene study to readdress the Strepsiptera problem and place the parasites as beetle relatives. Includes thorough exploration for long-branch attraction.

Cumulative Indexes

Contributing Authors, Volumes 48–57

R

S

T

V

W

Y

Z

Chapter Titles, Volumes 48–57

Acarines, Arachnids, and Other Noninsect Arthropods

Agricultural Entomology

Behavior and Neuroscience

Biological Control

Forest Entomology

Genetics and Genomics

Medical and Veterinary Entomology

Miscellaneous

Morphology and Development

Pathology

Systematics, Evolution, and Biogeography

Vectors of Plant Pathogens